ROBERT TIGNOR

JEREMY ADELMAN

STEPHEN ARON

PETER BROWN

BENJAMIN ELMAN

STEPHEN KOTKIN

XINRU LIU

SUZANNE MARCHAND

HOLLY PITTMAN

GYAN PRAKASH

BRENT SHAW

MICHAEL TSIN

Worlds Together, WORLDS APART

A HISTORY OF THE WORLD FROM THE BEGINNINGS OF HUMANKIND TO THE PRESENT

W · W · NORTON & COMPANY
NEW YORK · LONDON

W. W. Norton & Company has been independent since its founding in 1923, when William Warder Norton and Mary D. Herter Norton first published lectures delivered at the People's Institute, the adult education division of New York City's Cooper Union. The Nortons soon expanded their program beyond the Institute, publishing books by celebrated academics from America and abroad. By mid-century, the two major pillars of Norton's publishing program—trade books and college texts—were firmly established. In the 1950s, the Norton family transferred control of the company to its employees, and today—with a staff of four hundred and a comparable number of trade, college, and professional titles published each year—W. W. Norton & Company stands as the largest and oldest publishing house owned wholly by its employees.

Editor: Jon Durbin
Developmental Editors: Sandy Lifland, Alice Falk
Copy Editors: Alice Falk, Ellen Lohman
Project Editor: Rebecca Homiski
Photo Researchers: Stephanie Romeo, Jennie Bright, Julie Tesser
Production Manager: Roy Tedoff
Managing Editor, College: Marian Johnson
Emedia Editor: Steve Hoge
Book Designer: Rubina Yeh
Ancillary Editors: Matthew Arnold, Alexis Hilts
Layout Artist: Brad Walrod
Editorial Assistants: Rob Haber, Alexis Hilts
Cartographer: Carto-Graphics

About the Cover Image: This saltcellar carved in ivory depicts Portuguese soldiers; it originated from Benin in West Africa in the fifteenth and sixteenth centuries. Benin rulers often asked the Portuguese for help with their warring neighbors. Here the African artist has created a blending of cultures, giving the soldiers both European and African features as they support one of the Benin ruler's most precious commodities—salt.

ISBN: 978-0-393-92547-0

W. W. Norton & Company, Inc., 500 Fifth Avenue, New York, NY 10110
wwnorton.com

W. W. Norton & Company Ltd., Castle House, 75/76 Wells Street, London W1T 3QT

1 2 3 4 5 6 7 8 9

Contents in Brief

Contents

CHAPTER 1   BECOMING HUMAN   *3*

CHAPTER 2   RIVERS, CITIES, AND FIRST STATES, 4000–2000 BCE   51

CHAPTER 7   HAN DYNASTY CHINA AND IMPERIAL ROME, 300 BCE–300 CE   275

CHAPTER 8   THE RISE OF UNIVERSAL RELIGIONS, 300–600 CE   321

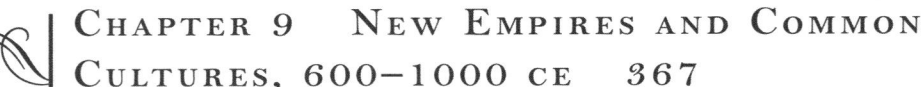

CHAPTER 9   NEW EMPIRES AND COMMON CULTURES, 600–1000 CE   367

CHAPTER 10 BECOMING "THE WORLD," 1000–1300 CE 417

CHAPTER 15   REORDERING THE WORLD, 1750–1850   639

CHAPTER 18 AN UNSETTLED WORLD, 1890–1914 763

Global Connections & Disconnections Features

Primary Source Documents

Maps

Preface

THE MAKING OF *Worlds Together, Worlds Apart*

Most books have a back story, though authors often hesitate to trot out the truly revealing details. In this case, however, some details should be disclosed because they illuminate the shape and substance of the narrative. The story begins nearly twenty years ago, when the Princeton University history department established its first course in world history. Called "The World and the West," the course surveyed the major developments in the history of the modern world from 1500 to the present. Although the importance of the course for students of an increasingly globalized era was immediately recognized, the course placed immense demands on teachers and students. The greatest challenge was how to treat the many regions of the world and the many centuries in an integrated way and in a single semester. The instructors searched in vain for a textbook that would provide both coverage and integrated analysis. Some of the books available at the time were written by a single author; these tended to have a clear narrative framework but to suffer from the limitations that a single individual, no matter how well read, necessarily encountered when dealing with the immensity of world history. Others were written by a team of regional experts and had authoritative treatments of regions but lacked integration and balance.

With the full support of Princeton University, a small group of modern historians in the Princeton history department decided to try our hand at world history, agreeing to meet on a regular basis to plan a text that addressed the weaknesses in the other books. Each of us had a regional specialization as well as an interest in how our regions fitted into larger cross-regional relationships. For an entire year we met to discuss the ways in which we would craft a modern world history and the global themes we wanted to stress. After intensive and sometimes contentious discussions, we decided on an overarching framework, the chapter divisions, and the global themes and regional variations. During these meetings, we also settled on the all-important idea of building each chapter around a turning point or central story in world history, such as the spread of the Black Death or the rise of the nation-state, that would enable us to integrate all the regions of the world into most chapters. Then we began to write. We wrote a lot—and a lot of what we wrote ended up in recycling bins. We all wrote sections in each of the chapters, shared them with one another, and then gave one of our group the assignment of integrating each chapter. All this meant that every one of us wrote something for each of the chapters. Different individuals coordinated the chapters, after which the drafts circulated to everyone once again for additional thoughts and revisions. The general editor then wrote the final draft to ensure that a strong, single voice would emerge and that the level of presentation would be consistent throughout. *Worlds Together, Worlds Apart: A History of the Modern World* (WTWA), the final product, was truly a collaborative work. No section, no matter how seemingly specialized, was the product of just one author.

We were pleased to discover, very soon after publication, that teachers and students liked WTWA. The original text (now Volume Two) was adopted widely in its first year of publication and has gone on to be used at over 200 colleges and universities worldwide and has sold over 40,000 copies. Then, instructors began to ask, Why not apply the WTWA model to the early period of world history? In 2003 we set out to do just that, with Robert Tignor and Jeremy Adelman from the modern volume joining forces with a distinguished group of historians of the earlier periods. In crafting the stories and chapters that would cover the earlier periods of world history, we have used the same highly collaborative writing model that proved so successful with the original volume, and we have built the chapters covering the earlier periods around turning points and central stories in world history, such as the formation of the Silk Road and the rise of universal religions, just as we did the chapters in the original volume. While we were hard at work writing the chapters covering the earlier periods, the authors of the modern chapters set about revising them so that all the chapters would fit seamlessly together. Ten years after we began our work, we are very pleased to offer *Worlds Together, Worlds Apart: A History of the World from the Beginnings of Humankind to the Present.*

Over the ten-year period of work on this book, world history has gained even more prominence in college classrooms and historical studies. Courses in the history of the world now abound, often replacing the standard surveys of European history and western civilization overviews. Graduate history students receive training in world history, and journals routinely publish studies in this field. A new generation of textbooks is needed to help students and instructors make sense of this vast, complex, and rapidly evolving field. WTWA hopes to be the first to plot this new course and to inspire its readers to continue their studies in this increasingly critical field.

OUR GUIDING PRINCIPLES

Five principles inform this book, guiding its framework and the organization of its individual chapters. The first is that **world history is global history**. There are many fine histories of the individual regions of the world, which we have endeavored to make good use of. But unlike the authors of many other so-called world histories, we have chosen not to deal with the great regions and cultures of the world as separate units, reserving individual chapters to East Asia, South Asia,

Southwest Asia, Europe, Africa, and the Americas. Our goal is to place each of these regions in its largest geographical context. It would be misleading to say that the context is the world, because none of these regions, even the most highly developed commercially, enjoyed commercial or cultural contact with peoples all over the globe before Columbus's voyage to the Americas and the sixteenth century. But the peoples living in the Afro-Eurasian landmass, probably the single most important building block for our study, were deeply influenced by one another, as were the more scattered peoples living in the Americas and in Africa below the Sahara. Products, ideas, and persons traveled widely across the large land units of Eurasia, Africa, and the Americas. Indeed, Afro-Eurasia was not divided or thought of as divided into separate landmasses until recent times. It is in this sense that our world history is global.

The second principle informing this work is **the importance of chronology in framing world history**. Rather than telling the story of world history by analyzing separate geographical areas, we have elected to frame the chapters around significant historical turning points or periods that transcended regional and cultural boundaries—moments or periods of meaningful changes in the way that human beings organized their lives. Some of these changes were dramatic and affected many people. Environments changed; the earth became drier and warmer; humans learned to domesticate plants and animals; technological innovations in warfare, political organization, and commercial activities occurred; and the appeal of new religious and cultural beliefs spread far and wide. These changes swept across large landmasses, paying scant heed to preexisting cultural and geographical unity. They affected peoples living in widely dispersed societies. In other cases, changes occurred in only one locality while other places retained their traditions or took alternative routes. Chronology helps us understand the ways in which the world has, and has not, shared a common history. Chapter headings give a clue to the turning points or periods that paid no heed to geography and culture. At the outset of human existence, after *Homo sapiens* populated the world and became truly human (Chapter 1), men and women established the first cities and hierarchical polities and societies in the riverine basins of the Near East and northwest India (4000–2000 BCE; Chapter 2). Several millennia later, nomadic invaders provided a stimulus to re-create powerful territorial polities, employing horse-drawn chariots to undermine the old polities and to fashion new ones (2000–1200 BCE; Chapter 3). During the next millennium, powerful Asian monarchs established the first large-scale kingdoms that even aspired to world domination (1200 BCE–250 CE; Chapters 4 through 6). In more modern times, the spread of the bubonic plague across the Afro-Eurasian landmass brought great loss of life and undermined existing polities, preparing the groundwork for a new set of political organizations that proved to be long-lived (Chapter 11). The discovery of large silver mines in Spanish America in the sixteenth century provided a precious metal that brought the economies of the world into closer contact (Chapter 12). In the nineteenth century, ideas of freedom swept across the world, propelled by the American and French revolutions, only to be superseded by European imperial ambitions (Chapters 16 through 18). Two world wars linked the entire international community on battlefields and in great loss of life (Chapters 19 and 20).

The third principle is **historical and geographical balance**. Ours is not a history focused on the rise of the West. We seek to pay attention to the global histories of all peoples and not to privilege those developments that led directly into European history as if the rest of the history of the world was but a prelude to the rise of western civilization. We deal with peoples living outside Europe on their own terms and try to see world history from their perspective. Even more significantly, while we describe societies that obviously influenced Europe's historical development, we do so in a context very different from that which western historians have stressed. Rather than simply viewing these cultures in terms of their role in western development, we seek to understand them in their own terms and to illuminate the ways they influenced other parts of the world. From our perspective, it is historically inaccurate to annex Mesopotamia and Egypt to western civilization, because these territories lay well outside Europe and had a large influence on Africa, South Asia, and East Asia as well as on Europe. Indeed, our presentation of Europe in the period leading up to and including the founding of the Roman Empire is different from many of the standard treatments. The Europeans we describe are rather rough, wild-living, warring peoples living on the fringes of the settled parts of the world and looked down on by more politically stable communities. They hardly seem to be made of the stuff that will catapult Europeans to world leadership a millennium later—indeed, they were very different people from those who, as the result of myriad intervening and contingent events, founded the nineteenth- and twentieth-century empires whose ruins are still all around us.

Our fourth principle is **an emphasis on connections and what we call disconnections across societal and cultural boundaries**. World history is not the history of separate regions of the world at different periods of time. It is the history of the connections among peoples living often at great distances from one another, and it is also the history of the resistances of peoples living within and outside societies to connections that threatened to put them in subordinate positions or to rob them of their independence.

A stress on connections inevitably foregrounds those elements within societies that promoted long-distance ties. Merchants are important, as are military men and political potentates seeking to expand their polities. So are scholars and religious leaders, particularly those who believed that they had universalistic messages with which to convert others to their visions. Perhaps most important of all in premodern world history, certainly the most understudied, are the nomadic pastoral peoples, who were often the agents for the transmission of products, peoples, and ideas across long and harsh distances. They exploded onto the scene of settled societies at critical junctures, erasing old cultural and geographical barriers and producing new unities, as the Arabs did in the seventh century CE and the Mongols in the thirteenth century. *Worlds Together, Worlds Apart* is not intended to convey the message that the history of the world is a story of increasing integration. What for one ruling group brought benefits in the form of increased workforces, material prosperity, and political stability often meant enslavement, political subordination, and loss of territory for other groups. The historian's task, then, is not only to represent the different experiences of increased connectedness, describing worlds that came together, but also to be attentive to the opposite trends, describing peoples and communities that remained apart.

The fifth and final principle is that **world history is a narrative of big themes and high-level comparisons**. *Worlds Together, Worlds Apart* is not a book of record. Indeed, in a work that covers the whole of the historical record of humankind from the beginnings of history to the present, the notion that no event or individual worthy of attention would be excluded is the height of folly. We have sought to offer clear themes and interpretations in order to synthesize the vast body of data that often overwhelms histories of the world. Our aspiration is to identify the main historical forces that have moved history, to highlight those monumental innovations that have changed the way humans lived, and to describe the creation and evolution of those bedrock institutions, many of which, of course, endure. In this regard, self-conscious cross-cultural comparisons of developments, institutions, and even founding figures receive attention to make students aware that some common institutions, such as slavery, did not have the same features in every society. Or, in the opposite fashion, the seemingly diverse terms that were used, say, to describe learned and religious men in different parts of the world—monks in Europe, ulama in Islam, Brahmans in India, and scholar-gentries in China— often meant much the same thing in very different settings. We have constructed *Worlds Together, Worlds Apart* around big ideas, stories, and themes rather than filling the book with names and dates that encourage students only to memorize rather than understand world history concepts.

OUR MAJOR THEMES

The primary organizing framework of *Worlds Together, Worlds Apart*—one that runs through the chapters and connects the different parts of the volume—is the theme of **interconnection and divergence**. While describing movements that facilitated global connectedness, this book also shows how different regions developed their own ways of handling or resisting connections and change. Throughout history, different regions and different population groups often stood apart from the rest of the world until touched by traders or explorers or missionaries or soldiers. Some of these regions welcomed global connections. Others sought to change the nature of their connections with the outside world, and yet others resisted efforts to bring them into the larger world. All, however, were somehow affected by their experience of connection. Yet, the history of the world is not simply one of increasing globalization, in which all societies eventually join a common path to the present. Rather, it is a history of the ways in which, as people became linked, their experience of these global connections diverged.

Besides the central theme of interconnection and divergence, other themes also stand out in WTWA. First, the book discusses **how the recurring efforts of people to cross religious, political, and cultural borders brought the world together**. Merchants and educated men and women traded goods and ideas. Whole communities, in addition to select groups, moved to safer or more promising environments. **The transregional crossings of ideas, goods, and peoples produced transformations and conflicts**—a second important theme. Finally, the movement of ideas, peoples, products, and germs over long distances upset the balance of power across the world and within individual societies. Such movements changed the relationship of different population groups with other peoples and areas of the world and led over time to dramatic shifts in the ascendancy of regions. **Changes in power arrangements within and between regions explain which parts of the world and regional groups benefited from integration and which resisted it**. These three themes (exchange and migration, conflict and resistance, and alterations in the balance of power) weave themselves through every chapter of this work.

In *Worlds Together, Worlds Apart,* we tell the stories of people caught in these currents of exchange, conflict, and changing power relations. We describe those historical actors, such as Roman legionnaires, early Christian and Muslim proselytizers, Indian Ocean merchants in the sixteenth century, and late-nineteenth-century European imperialists, who sought a more closely integrated world economy and polity. But we also describe those individuals who led movements in defense of cherished historical and cultural heritages. Jewish prophets under Roman rule, the Indian prophet Tenskwatawa in North America, and the religious cleric al-Wahhab on the Arabian Peninsula all urged their people to return to traditional identities. Others, such as Shiite clerics under Umayyad rule in the seventh and eighth centuries CE, Indian rebels in 1857, and advocates of a third way after World War II, sought a less unified world and used their historical and cultural traditions to favor new arrangements of world power.

From the beginnings of humanity to the present, in examining the forces that brought peoples and cultures together and those that kept them apart, this book explores not only the changing power relations between societies but also those within societies. Chief among these have been the divisions between rulers and subjects, between commoners and nobles,

and between men and women. The **gender divide** has been one of the most important factors in shaping the evolution of societies, and this theme receives attention in Volume One and fresh accenting in the revised chapters of Volume Two.

Women and men lived in small-scale, relatively egalitarian societies until about 8,000 years ago, when hierarchical, urbanized, and centralized societies sprang up in three of the major river basins of Afro-Eurasia. One of the primary divides across all societies was the difference between men and women. If there was a world apart, from the time of the early agrarian breakthrough, it was within the family itself, as divisions of labor sharpened between men and women. Not all societies stratified themselves along gender lines in the same way. Indeed, many left open the possibility of women exercising influence and authority. But what underlay so many of the world's first civilizations was the way in which societies defined some traits as virtuous (such as the ability to fight) or created new social roles for rulers but restricted them mainly to men (such as scribes or priests). In this fashion, the social order took on gendered features from the very start. This was a long-term legacy that evolved over the ensuing centuries of human history.

By the same token, over the sweep of the millennia people acquired more and more skills and aptitudes for changing the environment to suit their needs and wants. They went from adapting to nature to controlling it, though this was hardly a linear process. There was plenty of backsliding. As with gender, not all societies related to their environments in the same way. To a very large extent, the differences in habitat were influential. In arid steppe lands, nomads followed their food around, while in large river basins, urban zones and complex, stratified societies emerged because water helped with transportation and settled agriculture. Similarly, societies coped with nature's vagaries in different ways. Some learned from experience, such as when China developed vast hydraulics to control flooding. Others could not cope with shocks, such as when the bubonic plague ravaged Afro-Eurasian populations in the fourteenth century and, most devastatingly, Old World diseases were introduced to the New World after 1492. A recurring theme, however, is **the way in which adaptation to environmental constraints was the source of large-scale unintended consequences that often brought societies face to face with similar plights**. In this sense, environmental history was a force that divided and united world societies.

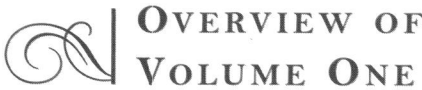

OVERVIEW OF VOLUME ONE

Volume One of *Worlds Together, Worlds Apart* deals with the period from the beginnings of human history through the Mongol invasions of the thirteenth century and the spread of the Black Death across Afro-Eurasia. It is divided into eleven chapters, each of which marks a distinct historical period. Hence, each chapter has an overarching theme or small set of themes that hold otherwise highly diverse material together.

Chapter 1, "Becoming Human," presents biological and cultural perspectives on the way that early hominoids became truly human. World history books now have a nearly mandatory opening chapter on prehistory. We believe that this chapter is important in establishing the global context of world history. We believe too that our chapter is unique in its focus on how humans became humans, so we discuss how early humans became bipedal and how they developed complex cognitive processes such as language and artistic abilities. Recent research indicates that *Homo sapiens* originated in Africa, probably no more than 200,000 years ago. These early men and women walked out of the African landmass sometime between 120,000 and 50,000 years ago, gradually populating all regions of the world. What is significant in this story is that the different population groups around the world, the so-called races of humankind, have only recently broken off from one another. Also in this chapter, we describe the domestication of plants and animals and the founding of the first village settlements around the globe.

In **Chapter 2, "Rivers, Cities, and First States, 4000–2000 BCE,"** we focus on five of the great river basins where extraordinary breakthroughs in human activity occurred. On the flood plains of the Tigris and Euphrates in Mesopotamia, the Nile in Egypt, the Indus valley in modern-day northern India and Pakistan, and the Yellow and Yangzi rivers in China, men and women mastered annual floods and became expert in seeding and cultivating foodstuffs. In these areas, populations became dense. Riverine cultures had much in common. They had highly developed hierarchical political, social, and cultural systems, priestly and bureaucratic classes, and organized religious and cultural systems. But they also differed greatly, and these differences were passed from generation to generation. Compare ancient Egypt, which had a dearth of large cities, with Mesopotamia, which was the heartland of urban development. Consider as well the Chinese ruling elites, who early on displayed a talent for organizing large swaths of territories with heavy population densities and gradually imposing on them a unified culture. The development of these major complex societies certainly is a turning point in world history.

In **Chapter 3, "Nomads, Territorial States, and Microsocieties, 2000–1200 BCE,"** extensive climatic and technological changes serve as major turning points. Drought, environmental degradation, and political instability brought the first riverine societies to a crashing end around 2000 BCE. When aridity forced tribal and nomadic peoples living on the fringes of the settled populations to move closer to settled areas, they brought with them an insurmountable military advantage. They had become adept at yoking horses to war chariots, and hence they were in a position to subjugate or in-

termarry with the peoples in the settled polities in the river basins. Around 2000 BCE these peoples established new territorial kingdoms in Mesopotamia, Egypt, the Indus valley, and China, which gave way a millennium later (1000 BCE) to even larger, militarily and politically more powerful states. In the Americas, the Mediterranean, sub-Saharan Africa, and the Pacific worlds, microsocieties arose as an alternative form of polity in which peoples lived in much smaller-scale societies that showcased their own unique and compelling features.

Chapter 4, "First Empires and Common Cultures in Afro-Eurasia, 1200–350 BCE," describes the different ways in which larger-scale societies grew and became unified. In the case of the world's first empires, the neo-Assyrian and Persian, political power was the main unifying element. Both states established different models that future empires would emulate. The Assyrians used brutal force to intimidate and subjugate different groups within their societies and neighboring states. The Persians followed a pattern that relied less on coercion and more on tributary relationships, while reveling in cultural diversity. The Zhou state in China offered yet a third way of political unity, basing its rule on the doctrine of the mandate of heaven, which legitimated its rulers' succession as long as they were able to maintain stability and order. Vedic society in South Asia offers a dramatically different model in which religion and culture are the main unifying forces. Religion moves to the forefront of the narrative in other ways in this chapter. The birth of monotheism occurred in the Zoroastrian and Hebrew faiths and the beginnings of Buddhism—all three religions endure today.

During the last millennium before the common era, the worlds surrounding these centralized, riverine polities emerged as major players on the historical stage just as these first empires were declining. As **Chapter 5, "Worlds Turned Inside Out, 1000–350 BCE,"** demonstrates, these worlds took advantage of the small-scale and more intimate relationships to create highly individualistic cultures, even in some cases to experiment with a democratic polity. They also developed new strategies for understanding the natural world and humankind. The Greek city-states were the most dynamic of these new cultures, and they spread their Hellenistic culture far and wide. In China, Confucians and Daoists debated how best to create a well-ruled and stable society during the Warring States period. Similar debates occurred in South Asia, where early Buddhists and Brahmin priests in Vedic society strove to provide a more spiritually compelling belief system for their followers. In Greece, Plato, Socrates, and the Sophists discussed nature and humanity. In Africa, the Bantu peoples spread across sub-Saharan Africa, and the Sudanic peoples of Meroe created a society that blended Egyptian and sub-Saharan influences. These were all dynamic hybrid societies building on existing knowledge. Equally dramatic transformations occurred in the Americas, where the Olmec and Chavín peoples were creating hierarchical societies of the like never before seen in their part of the world.

Chapter 6, "Shrinking the Afro-Eurasian World, 350 BCE–250 CE," describes three major forces that simultaneously integrated large segments of the Afro-Eurasian landmass culturally and economically. First, Alexander and his armies changed the political and cultural landscape of North Africa and Southwest and South Asia. Culturally, Alexander spread Hellenism through North Africa and Southwest and central Asia, making it the first cultural system to achieve a transregional scope. Hellenism's appeal to peoples with varying historical and cultural backgrounds was irresistible. Alexander and his men followed existing pathways across Southwest Asia on their way to South Asia, but it was in the post-Alexander world that these commercial roads were stabilized and intensified. For the first time, a trading network, known as the Silk Road, stretching from Palmyra in the West to Central Asia in the East, came into being. Buddhism was the first religion to seize on the Silk Road's more formal existence as its followers moved quickly with the support of the Mauryan Empire to spread their ideas into central Asia. Finally, we witness the growth of a "silk road of the seas" as new technologies and bigger ships allowed for a dramatic expansion in maritime trade from South Asia all the way to Egypt and East Africa.

Chapter 7, "Han Dynasty China and Imperial Rome, 300 BCE–300 CE," describes Han China and the Roman Empire. The world's first empires appeared in Chapter 4, and developments introduced in previous chapters paved the way for the massive Roman and Han empires, which provided two political, economic, and cultural systems that dominated much of the Afro-Eurasian landmass from 200 BCE to 200 CE. Both the Han Dynasty and the Roman Empire ruled effectively in their own way, providing an instructive comparative case study. Both left their imprint on Afro-Eurasia, and rulers for centuries afterward tried to revive these glorious polities and use them as models of greatness. This chapter also discusses the effect of state sponsorship on religion, as Christianity came into existence in the context of the late Roman Empire and Buddhism was introduced to China during the decline of the Han.

Chapter 8, "The Rise of Universal Religions, 300–600 CE," describes how out of the crumbling Roman Empire new polities and a new religion emerged. The Byzantine Empire, claiming to be the successor state to the Roman Empire, embraced Christianity as its state religion. The Tang rulers patronized Buddhism to such a degree that Confucian statesmen feared it had become the state religion. Both Buddhism and Christianity enjoyed spectacular success in the politically fragmented post-Han era in China and in the feudal world of western Europe. These dynamic religions represent a decisive turning point in world history. Christianity enjoyed its eventual successes through state sponsorship via the Roman and Byzantine empires and by providing spiritual comfort and hope during the chaotic years of Rome's decline. Buddhism grew through imperial sponsorship and significant changes to

its fundamental beliefs, when adherents to the faith deified Buddha and created notions of an afterlife. In Africa we see a wide range of significant developments and a myriad of cultural practices, yet we also witness the ongoing development of large common cultures. The Bantu peoples spread throughout the southern half of the landmass, spoke closely related languages, and developed similar political institutions based on the prestige of individuals of high achievement. In the Americas the Olmecs established their own form of the city-state, while the Mayans owed their success to a decentralized common culture built around a strong religious belief system and a series of spiritual centers.

In Chapter 9, "New Empires and Common Cultures, 600–1000 CE," we look at how from a relatively remote corner of the Arabian Peninsula arose another world religion, Islam, which enjoyed unanticipated political, military, cultural, and economic successes. The rise of Islam, clearly another turning point in world history, provides a contrast to the way in which universalizing religions and political empires interacted. Islam and empire arose in a fashion quite different from Christianity and the Roman Empire. Christianity took over an already existing empire—the Roman—after suffering persecution at its hands for several centuries. In contrast, Islam created an empire almost at the moment of its emergence. Toward the end of his life, the Prophet Muhammad was already establishing the rudiments of an empire as he contemplated taking control of the whole Arabian Peninsula and extending his influence to Syria and Iraq. By the time the Abbasid Empire came into being in the middle of the eighth century, Islamic armies, political leaders, and clerics exercised power over much of the Afro-Eurasian landmass from southern Spain, across North Africa, all the way to Central Asia. Islam worked its way into West and East Africa, as Muslim clerics and traders crossed the Sahara and the Indian Ocean. They reached far into the interior of the sub-Saharan region. The Tang Empire in China, however, served as a counterweight to Islam's power both politically and intellectually. Confucianism enjoyed a spectacular recovery in this period. With the Tang rulers, Confucianism slowed the spread of Buddhism and further reinforced China's development along different, more secular pathways. Japan and Korea also enter world history at this time, as tributary states to Tang China and as hybrid cultures that mixed Chinese customs and practices with their own. The Vikings highlight the role that nomadic peoples played in developing trade in Afro-Eurasia. The Christian world split in this period between the western Latin church and the eastern Byzantine church. Both branches of Christianity played a role in unifying societies, especially in western Europe, which lacked strong political rule.

Chapter 10, "Becoming 'The World,' 1000–1300 CE," looks at the increase of prosperity and population across most of Afro-Eurasia and into West and East Africa. Just as importantly, the world in this period divided into regional zones that are recognizable today. And trade grew rapidly.

A look at the major trading cities of this time demonstrates how commerce transformed cultures. Sub-Saharan Africa also underwent intense regional integration via the spread of the Mande-speaking peoples and the Mali Empire. The Americas witness their first empire in the form of the Chimu peoples in the Andes. This chapter ends with the Mongol conquests of the twelfth and thirteenth centuries, which brought massive destruction. The Mongol Empire, however, once in place, promoted long-distance commerce, scholarly exchange, and travel on an unprecedented scale. The Mongols brought Eurasia and North Africa and many parts of sub-Saharan Africa into a new connectedness. The Mongol story also underscores the important role that nomads played throughout the history of the early world.

Finally, **Chapter 11, "Crises and Recovery in Afro-Eurasia, 1300s–1500s,"** brings into relief the turning point of the Black Death, which turned this period into one where many traditional institutions and polities gave way and peoples were compelled to rebuild their cultures. The polities that came into being at this time and the intense religious experimentation that took place effected a sharp break with the past. The bubonic plague wiped out as much as two-thirds of the population in many of the densely settled locations of Afro-Eurasia. Societies were brought to their knees by the Mongols' depredations as well as by biological pathogens. In the face of one of humanity's grimmest periods, peoples and societies demonstrated tremendous resilience as they looked for new ways to rebuild their communities, some turning inward and others seeking inspiration, conquests, and riches elsewhere. Volume One concludes on the eve of the "Columbian Exchange," the moment when "old" worlds discovered "new" ones and a vast series of global interconnections and divergences commenced.

OVERVIEW OF VOLUME TWO

The organizational structure for Volume Two reaffirms the commitment to write a decentered, global history of the world. Christopher Columbus is not the starting point, as he is in so many modern world histories. Rather, we begin in the eleventh and twelfth centuries with two major developments in world history. The first, set forth in **Chapter 10, "Becoming 'The World,' 1000–1300 CE,"** describes a world that was divided for the first time into regions that are recognizable today. This world experienced rapid population growth, as is shown by a simple look at the major trading cities from Asia in the East to the Mediterranean in the West. Yet nomadic peoples remain a force as revealed in the Mongol invasions of Afro-Eurasia. **Chapter 11, "Crises and Recovery in Afro-Eurasia, 1300s–1500s,"** describes how the Mongol warriors, through

their conquests and the integration of the Afro-Eurasian world, spread the bubonic plague, which brought death and depopulation to much of Afro-Eurasia. Both these stories set the stage for the modern world and are clear-cut turning points in world history. The primary agents of world connection described in this chapter were dynasts, soldiers, clerics, merchants, and adventurers who rebuilt the societies that disease and political collapse had destroyed. They joined the two hemispheres, as we describe in **Chapter 12, "Contact, Commerce, and Colonization, 1450s–1600,"** bringing the peoples and products of the Western Hemisphere into contact and conflict with Eurasia and Africa. It is the collision between the Eastern and Western Hemispheres that sets in motion modern world history and marks a distinct divide or turning point between the premodern and the modern. Here, too, disease and increasing trade linkages were vital. Unprepared for the advanced military technology and the disease pool of European and African peoples, the Amerindian population experienced a population decline even more devastating than that caused by the Black Death.

Europeans sailed across the Atlantic Ocean to find a more direct, less encumbered route to Asia and came upon lands, peoples, and products that they had not expected. One item, however, that they had sought in every part of the world and that they found in abundance in the Americas was precious metal. In **Chapter 13, "Worlds Entangled, 1600–1750,"** we discuss how New World silver from Mexico and Peru became the major currency of global commerce, oiling the long-distance trading networks that had been revived after the Black Death. The effect of New World silver on the world economy was so great that it, even more than the Iberian explorations of the New World, brought the hemispheres together and marks the true genesis of modern world history. We also discuss the importance of sugar, which linked the economies and polities of western Europe, Africa, and the Americas in a triangular trade centered on the Atlantic Ocean. Sugar, silver, spices, and other products sparked and expanded commercial exchanges and led to cultural flourishing around the world.

Chapter 14, "Cultures of Splendor and Power, 1500–1780," discusses the Ottoman scientists, Safavid and Mughal artists, and Chinese literati, as well as European thinkers, whose notable achievements were rooted in their own cultures but tempered by awareness of the intellectual activities of others. In this chapter, we look closely at how culture is created as a historical process and describe how the massive growth in wealth during this period, growing out of global trade, led to one of the great periods of cultural flourishing in world history.

Around 1800, transformations reverberated outward from the Atlantic world and altered economic and political relationships in the rest of the world. In **Chapter 15, "Reordering the World, 1750–1850,"** we discuss how political revolutions in the Americas and Europe, new ideas about how to trade and organize labor, and a powerful rhetoric of freedom and universal rights underlay the beginning of "a great divide" between peoples of European descent and those who were not. These forces of laissez-faire capitalism, industrialization, the nation-state, and republicanism not only attracted diverse groups around the world; they also threatened groups that put forth alternative visions. Ideas of freedom, as manifested in trading relations, labor, and political activities, clashed with a traditional world based on inherited rights and statuses and further challenged the way men and women had lived in earlier times. These political, intellectual, and economic reorderings changed the way people around the world saw themselves and thus represent something quite novel in world history. But these new ways of envisioning the world did not go unchallenged, as **Chapter 16, "Alternative Visions of the Nineteenth Century,"** makes clear. Here, intense resistance to evolving modernity reflected the diversity of peoples and their hopes for the future. This chapter looks at Wahabbism in Islam, the strongman movement in Africa, Indian resistance in America and Mexico, socialism and communism in Europe, the Taiping Rebellion in China, and the Indian Mutiny in South Asia. Prophets and leaders had visions that often drew on earlier traditions and that led these individuals to resist rapid change.

Chapter 17, "Nations and Empires, 1850–1914," discusses the political, economic, military, and ideological power that thrust Europe and North America to the fore of global events and led to an era of nationalism and modern imperialism, new forces in world history. Yet this period of seeming European supremacy was to prove short-lived. **Chapter 18, "An Unsettled World, 1890–1914,"** demonstrates that even before World War I shattered Europe's moral certitude, many groups at home (feminists, Marxists, and unfulfilled nationalists) and abroad (anticolonial nationalists) had raised a chorus of complaints about European and North American dominance. As in Chapter 14, we look at the processes by which specific cultural movements arise and reflect the concerns of individual societies. Yet here, too, syncretistic movements emerged in many cultures and reflected the sway of global imperialism, which by then had become a dominant force.

Chapter 19, "Of Masses and Visions of the Modern, 1910–1939," briefly covers World War I and then discusses how, from the end of World War I until World War II, different visions of being modern competed around the world. It is the development of modernism and its effects on multiple cultures that integrate the diverse developments discussed in this chapter. In the decades between the world wars, proponents of liberal democracy struggled to defend their views and often to impose their will on authoritarian rulers and anticolonial nationalists.

Chapter 20, "The Three-World Order, 1940–1975," presents World War II and describes how new adversaries arose after the war. A three-world order came into being— the First World, led by the United States and extolling capitalism, the nation-state, and democratic government; the Second World, led by the Soviet Union and favoring authoritarian polities and economies; and the Third World, made up of former colonies seeking an independent status for themselves in world affairs. The rise of this three-world order dominates the second half of the twentieth century and constitutes another major theme of world history.

In **Chapter 21, "Globalization, 1970–2000,"** we explain that, at the end of the cold war, the modern world, while clearly more unified than before, still had profound cultural differences and political divisions. At the beginning of the twenty-first century, capital, commodities, peoples, and ideas move rapidly over long distances. But cultural tensions and political impasses continue to exist. It is the rise of this form of globalism that represents a vital new element as humankind heads into a new century and millennium. We close with an **Epilogue,** which tracks developments since the turn of the millennium. These last few years have brought profound changes to the world order, yet we hope readers of *Worlds Together, Worlds Apart* will see more clearly how this most recent history is, in fact, entwined with trends of much longer duration that are the chief focus of this book.

The history of the world is not a single, sweeping narrative. On the contrary, the last 5,000 years have produced multiple histories, moving along many paths and trajectories. Sometimes these histories merge, intertwining themselves in substantial ways. Sometimes they disentangle themselves and simply stand apart. Much of the time, however, they are simultaneously together and apart. In place of a single narrative, the usual one being the rise of the West, this book maps the many forks in the road that confronted the world's societies at different times and the surprising turns and unintended consequences that marked the choices that peoples and societies made, including the unanticipated and dramatic rise of the West in the nineteenth century. Formulated in this way, world history is the unfolding of many possible histories, and readers of this book should come away with a reinforced sense of the unpredictability of the past, the instability of the present, and the uncertainty of the future.

Let us begin our story!

PEDAGOGICAL PROGRAM

Worlds Together, Worlds Apart is designed for maximum readability. The crisp, clear narrative, built around stories, themes, and concepts, is accompanied by a highly useful pedagogical program designed to help students study while engaging them in the subject matter. Highlights of this innovative program are described below.

STELLAR MAP PROGRAM WITH ENHANCED CAPTIONS

The book's more than 120 beautiful maps are designed to reinforce the main stories and concepts in each chapter.

Every chapter opens with a two-page map of the world designed to highlight the main story line of the chapter. Within the chapter appear four to five more maps that focus on the regions covered. Enhanced captions encourage more interaction with the map program. Each caption provides contextual information and then asks three types of questions:

- *Factual.* Understanding basic geography
- *Analytical.* Understanding patterns and trends on the map
- *Interpretive.* Thinking beyond the map

Focus-Question System

The focus-question system helps the reader remain alert to key concepts and questions on every page of the text. Focus questions guide students' reading in three ways: (1) a focus-question box at the beginning of the chapter previews the chapter's contents, (2) relevant questions reappear at the start of the section where they are discussed, and (3) running heads on right-hand pages keep these questions in view throughout the chapter.

Primary Source Documents

The authors have selected three to five primary source documents for each chapter. Unlike the primary sources found in other books, which are designed to cover only the greatest hits, our selections reinforce the book's main themes and provide colorful material to augment the chapter's main story line. Perhaps most importantly, many of them challenge students to see world history through the eyes of others and from different perspectives. Each excerpt is accompanied by at least two study questions. Additional primary sources are available on the Digital History Reader, which is part of the Norton StudySpace website.

Global Connections & Disconnections Features

Each chapter contains one thematic feature built around key individuals or phenomena that exemplify the main emphasis of the text. Among the many topics included are how historians use technology to date bones and objects from early history, the use of ritual funeral objects in the contexts of religion and trade, the role of libraries in early world history, the travels of Marco Polo and Ibn Battuta, coffee drinking and coffeehouses in different parts of the world, cartography and maps as expressions of different worldviews, the growth of universities around the world, and Che Guevera as a radical visionary who tried to export revolution throughout the Third World.

New Chapter Chronologies

With the Second Edition come new chronologies that are organized regionally rather than temporally. Each chapter ends with a chronology. The chronologies allow students to track unifying concepts and to see influences across cultures and societies within a given time period.

Study Questions

Following each chapter's conclusion is a series of study questions to help ensure that students have grasped the major concepts and ideas.

Further Readings

Each chapter includes an ample list of suggested further readings, annotated so that students can see what each book or article covers.

ACKNOWLEDGMENTS

Worlds Together, Worlds Apart would never have happened without the full support of Princeton University. In a highly unusual move, and one for which we are truly grateful, the university helped underwrite this project with financial support from its 250th Anniversary Fund for undergraduate teaching and by allowing release time for the authors from campus commitments.

The history department's support of the effort over many years has been exceptional. Two chairs—Daniel Rodgers and Philip Nord—made funds and departmental support available, including the department's incomparable administrative talents. We would be remiss if we did not single out the department manager, Judith Hanson, who provided us with assistance whenever we needed it. We also thank Eileen Kane, who provided help in tracking down references and illustrations and in integrating changes into the manuscript. We also would like to thank Pamela Long, who made all of the complicated arrangements for ensuring that we were able to discuss matters in a leisurely and attractive setting. Sometimes that meant arranging for long-distance conference calls. She went even further and proofread the entire manuscript, finding many errors that we had all overlooked.

We drew shamelessly on the expertise of the departmental faculty, and although it might be wise simply to include a roster of the Princeton history department, that would do an injustice to those of whom we took most advantage. So here they are: Robert Darnton, Sheldon Garon, Anthony Grafton, Molly Greene, David Howell, Harold James, William Jordan, Emmanuel Kreike, Michael Mahoney, Arno Mayer, Kenneth Mills, John Murrin, Susan Naquin, Willard Peterson, Theodore Rabb, Stanley Stein, and Richard Turits. When necessary, we went outside the history department, getting help from L. Carl Brown, Michael Cook, Norman Itzkowitz, Martin Kern, Thomas Leisten, and Heath Lowry. Two departmental colleagues—Natalie Z. Davis and Elizabeth Lunbeck—were part of the original team but had to withdraw because of other commitments. Their contributions were vital, and we want to express our thanks to them. David Gordon, now at the University of Maryland, used portions of the text while teaching an undergraduate course at the University of Durban in South Africa and shared comments with us. Shamil Jeppie, like

David Gordon a graduate of the Princeton history department, now teaching at the University of Cape Town in South Africa, read and commented on various chapters.

Beyond Princeton, we have also benefited from exceptionally gifted and giving colleagues who have assisted this book in many ways. Colleagues at Louisiana State University, the University of Florida, the University of North Carolina, the University of Pennsylvania, and the University of California at Los Angeles, where Suzanne Marchand, Michael Tsin, Holly Pittman, and Stephen Aron, respectively, are now teaching, pitched in whenever we turned to them. Especially helpful have been the contributions of James Gelvin, Naomi Lamoreaux, Gary Nash, and Joyce Appleby at UCLA; Michael Bernstein at the University of California at San Diego; and Maribel Dietz, John Henderson, Christine Kooi, David Lindenfeld, Reza Pirbhai, and Victor Stater at Lousiana State University. It goes without saying that none of these individuals bears any responsibility for factual or interpretive errors that the text may contain. Xinru Liu would like to thank her Indian mentor, Romila Thapar, who changed the way we think about Indian history.

The quality and range of reviews on this project were truly exceptional. The final version of the manuscript was greatly influenced by the thoughts and ideas of numerous instructors. We wish to particularly thank our consulting reviewers, who read multiple versions of the manuscript from start to finish.

First Edition Consultants
Hugh Clark, Ursinus College
Jonathan Lee, San Antonio College
Pamela McVay, Ursuline College
Tom Sanders, United States Naval Academy

Second Edition Consultants
Jonathan Lee, San Antonio College
Pamela McVay, Ursuline College
Steve Rapp, Georgia State University
Cliff Rosenberg, City University of New York

We are also indebted to the many other reviewers from whom we benefited greatly.

First Edition Reviewers
Lauren Benton, New Jersey Institute of Technology
Ida Blom, University of Bergen, Norway
Ricardo Duchesne, University of New Brunswick
Major Bradley T. Gericke, United States Military Academy
John Gillis, Rutgers University
David Kenley, Marshall University
John Kicza, Washington State University
Matthew Levinger, Lewis and Clark College
James Long, Colorado State University
Adam McKeown, Columbia University
Mark McLeod, University of Delaware

John Mears, Southern Methodist University
Michael Murdock, Brigham Young University
David Newberry, University of North Carolina, Chapel Hill
Tom Pearcy, Slippery Rock State University
Oliver B. Pollak, University of Nebraska, Omaha
Ken Pomeranz, University of California, Irvine
Major David L. Ruffley, United States Air Force Academy
William Schell, Murray State University
Major Deborah Schmitt, United States Air Force Academy
Sarah Shields, University of North Carolina, Chapel Hill
Mary Watrous-Schlesinger, Washington State University

Second Edition Reviewers
William Atwell, Hobart and William Smith Colleges
Susan Besse, City University of New York
Tithi Bhattacharya, Purdue University
Mauricio Borrerero, St. John's University
Charlie Briggs, Georgia Southern University
Antoinne Burton, University of Illinois, Urbana-Champaign
Jim Cameron, St. Francis Xavier University
Kathleen Comerford, Georgia Southern University
Duane Corpis, Georgia State University
Denise Davidson, Georgia State University
Ross Doughty, Ursinus College
Alison Fletcher, Kent State University
Phillip Gavitt, Saint Louis University
Brent Geary, Ohio University
Henda Gilli-Elewy, California State Polytechnic University, Pomona
Fritz Gumbach, John Jay College
William Hagen, University of California, Davis
Laura Hilton, Muskingum College
Jeff Johnson, Villanova University
David Kammerling Smith, Eastern Illinois University
Jonathan Lee, San Antonio College
Dorothea Martin, Appalachian State University
Don McGuire, State University of New York, Buffalo
Pamela McVay, Ursuline College
Joel Migdal, University of Washington
Anthony Parent, Wake Forest University
Sandra Peacock, Georgia Southern University
David Pietz, Washington State University
Jared Poley, Georgia State University
John Quist, Shippensburg State University
Steve Rapp, Georgia State University
Paul Rodell, Georgia Southern University
Ariel Salzman, Queen's University
Bill Schell, Murray State University
Claire Schen, State University of New York, Buffalo
Jonathan Skaff, Shippensburg State University
David Smith, California State Polytechnic University, Pomona
Neva Specht, Appalachian State University
Ramya Sreeniva, State University of New York, Buffalo
Charles Stewart, University of Illinois, Urbana-Champaign

Rachel Stocking, Southern Illinois University, Carbondale
Heather Streets, Washington State University
Tim Teeter, Georgia Southern University
Charlie Wheeler, University of California, Irvine
Owen White, University of Delaware
James Wilson, Wake Forest University

We do want to pay special thanks to our most ardent supporter of the *Worlds Together, Worlds Apart* enterprise. Jon Lee, San Antonio College, has played many important roles on this project. He has served as a super reviewer on both editions, reading the draft manuscripts multiple times. He also created many of the original support materials that accompanied the First Edition. With the Second Edition, he was the primary force behind the map and pedagogy program for Volume One. He also has taken on the responsibilities for creating the digital history reader that accompanies the text. We are ever grateful to him for his ongoing support and contributions. We also want to thank Nancy Khalek (Ph.D. Princeton University), who has just taken her first tenure-track job, at Franklin and Marshall College. Nancy was our jack-of-all-trades who helped in any way she could. She attended all the monthly meetings during the development of the early volume. She provided critiques of the manuscript, helped with primary research, worked on the photo program and the Global Connections and Disconnections features, and contributed content to the student website. She was invaluable.

Our association with the publisher of this volume, W. W. Norton & Company, has been everything we could have asked for. Jon Durbin took us under the wing of the Norton firm. He attended all of our monthly meetings spanning the better part of four years across the creation of both volumes. How he put up with some of our interminable discussions will always be a mystery, but his enthusiasm for the endeavor never flagged, even when we seemed to grow weary. Sandy Lifland was the ever-watchful and ever-careful development editor for each volume. She let us know when we were making sense and when we needed to explain ourselves more fully. We also want to thank newcomers to the project Alice Falk and Rebecca Homiski. Alice Falk was our talented and insightful co-developmental editor and copyeditor on Volume One. Between the efforts of Sandy and Alice, we couldn't have asked for more from our manuscript editors. Rebecca Homiski did a fabulous job as our project editor, coordinating the responses of up to twelve authors on both volumes combined and locking down all the details on the project. We also want to thank Ellen Lohman for copyediting the Volume Two manuscript ably and with just the right touch under a very tight schedule and Sarah England for providing comments on our Volume Two revisions in a timely and thoughtful fashion. Stephanie Romeo, Jennifer Bright, and Julie Tesser shared duties in finding wonderful photos for both volumes. Rubina Yeh created a beautiful design. Roy Tedoff guided the manuscripts through the production process under a very tight schedule. On the media front, we want to thank Steve Hoge for creating the Norton StudySpace website, which includes the impressive Norton Digital History Reader. On the print ancillary front, we'd like to thank Matt Arnold for finding an excellent group of authors to create the instructor's manual, test bank, and study guide. We also want to thank Alexis Hilts, the most recent newcomer to the project, for helping to pull together many loose ends during the copyediting and production stages.

Finally, we must recognize that while this project often kept us apart from family members, their support held our personal worlds together.

About the Authors

ROBERT TIGNOR (Ph.D. Yale University) is Professor Emeritus and the Rosengarten Professor of Modern and Contemporary History at Princeton University and the three-time chair of the history department. With Gyan Prakash, he introduced Princeton's first course in world history nearly twenty years ago. Professor Tignor has taught graduate and undergraduate courses in African history and world history and written extensively on the history of twentieth-century Egypt, Nigeria, and Kenya. Besides his many research trips to Africa, Professor Tignor has taught at the University of Ibadan in Nigeria and the University of Nairobi in Kenya.

JEREMY ADELMAN (D.Phil. Oxford University) is currently the chair of the history department at Princeton University and the Walter S. Carpenter III Professor of Spanish Civilization and Culture. He has written and edited five books, including *Republic of Capital: Buenos Aires and the Legal Transformation of the Atlantic World,* which won the best book prize in Atlantic history from the American Historical Association. Professor Adelman is the recent recipient of a Guggenheim Memorial Foundation Fellowship and the Frederick Burkhardt Award from the American Council of Learned Societies.

STEPHEN ARON (Ph.D. University of California, Berkeley) is professor of history at the University of California, Los Angeles, and executive director of the Institute for the Study of the American West, Autry National Center. A specialist in frontier and Western American history, Aron is the author of *How the West Was Lost: The Transformation of Kentucky from Daniel Boone to Henry Clay* and *American Confluence: The Missouri Frontier from Borderland to Border State.* He has also published articles in a variety of books and journals, in-

cluding the *American Historical Review,* the *Pacific Historical Review,* and the *Western Historical Quarterly.*

PETER BROWN (Ph.D. Oxford University) is the Rollins Professor of History at Princeton University. He previously taught at London University and the University of California, Berkeley. He has written on the rise of Christianity and the end of the Roman Empire. His works include *Augustine of Hippo, The World of Late Antiquity, The Cult of the Saints, Body and Society, The Rise of Western Christendom,* and *Poverty and Leadership in the Later Roman Empire.* He is presently working on issues of wealth and poverty in the late Roman and early medieval Christian worlds.

BENJAMIN ELMAN (Ph.D. University of Pennsylvania) is professor of East Asian studies and history at Princeton University. He is currently serving as the director of the Princeton Program in East Asian Studies. He taught at the University of California, Los Angeles, for over fifteen years. His teaching and research fields include Chinese intellectual and cultural history, 1000–1900; the history of science in China, 1600–1930; the history of education in late imperial China; and Sino-Japanese cultural history, 1600–1850. He is the author of five books: *From Philosophy to Philology: Intellectual and Social Aspects of Change in Late Imperial China; Classicism, Politics, and Kinship: The Ch'ang-chou School of New Text Confucianism in Late Imperial China; A Cultural History of Civil Examinations in Late Imperial China; On Their Own Terms: Science in China, 1550–1900;* and *A Cultural History of Modern Science in China.* He is the creator of Classical Historiography for Chinese History at www.princeton.edu/~classbib/, a bibliography and teaching website published since 1996.

STEPHEN KOTKIN (Ph.D. University of California, Berkeley) is professor of history and teaches European and Asian history at Princeton University, where he also serves as director of Russian studies. He is the author of *Armageddon Averted: The Soviet Collapse, 1970–2000* and *Magnetic Mountain: Stalinism as a Civilization* and is a coeditor of *Mongolia in the Twentieth Century: Landlocked Cosmopolitan.* He is currently finishing a book entitled *Lost in Siberia: Dreamworlds of Eurasia,* which is a study of the Ob River valley over the last seven centuries. Professor Kotkin has twice been a visiting professor in Japan.

XINRU LIU (Ph.D. University of Pennsylvania) is assistant professor of early Indian history and world history at the College of New Jersey. She is associated with the Institute of World History and the Chinese Academy of Social Sciences. She is the author of *Ancient India and Ancient China, Trade and Religious Exchanges,* AD *1–600; Silk and Religion, an Exploration of Material Life and the Thought of People,* AD *600–1200; Connections across Eurasia, Transportation, Communication, and Cultural Exchange on the Silk Roads,* co-authored with Lynda Norene Shaffer; and *A Social History of Ancient India* (in Chinese). Professor Liu promotes South Asian studies and world history studies in both the United States and the People's Republic of China.

SUZANNE MARCHAND (Ph.D. University of Chicago) is associate professor of European and intellectual history at Louisiana State University, Baton Rouge. Professor Marchand also spent a number of years teaching at Princeton University. She is the author of *Down from Olympus: Archaeology and Philhellenism in Germany, 1750–1970* and is currently writing a book on German "orientalism."

HOLLY PITTMAN (Ph.D. Columbia University) is professor of art history at the University of Pennsylvania, where she teaches art and archaeology of Mesopotamia and the Iranian Plateau. She also serves as curator in the Near East Section of the University of Pennsylvania Museum of Archaeology and Anthropology. Previously she served as a curator in the Ancient Near Eastern Art Department of the Metropolitan Museum of Art. She has written extensively on the art and culture of the Bronze Age in the Middle East and has participated in excavations in Cyprus, Turkey, Syria, Iraq, and Iran, where she currently works. Her research investigates works of art as media through which patterns of thought, cultural development, and historical interactions of ancient cultures of the Near East are reconstructed.

GYAN PRAKASH (Ph.D. University of Pennsylvania) is professor of modern Indian history at Princeton University and a member of the Subaltern Studies Editorial Collective. He is the author of *Bonded Histories: Genealogies of Labor Servitude in Colonial India* and *Another Reason: Science and the Imagination of Modern India.* Professor Prakash edited *After Colonialism: Imperial Histories and Postcolonial Displacements* and has written a number of articles on colonialism and history writing. He is currently working on a history of the city of Bombay. With Robert Tignor, he introduced the modern world history course at Princeton University.

BRENT SHAW (Ph.D. Cambridge University) is the Andrew Fleming West Professor of Classics at Princeton University, where he is director of the Program in the Ancient World. He was previously at the University of Pennsylvania, where he chaired the Graduate Group in Ancient History. His principal areas of specialization as a Roman historian are Roman family history and demography, sectarian violence and conflict in Late Antiquity, and the regional history of Africa as part of the Roman Empire. He has published *Spartacus and the Slaves Wars;* edited the papers of Sir Moses Finley, *Economy and Society in Ancient Greece;* and published in a variety of books and journals, including the *Journal of Roman Studies,* the *American Historical Review,* the *Journal of Early Christian Studies,* and *Past & Present.*

MICHAEL TSIN (Ph.D. Princeton) is associate professor of history and international studies at the University of North Carolina at Chapel Hill. He previously taught at the University of Illinois at Chicago, Princeton University, Columbia University, and the University of Florida. Professor Tsin's primary interests include the histories of modern China and colonialism. He is the author of *Nation, Governance, and Modernity in China: Canton, 1900–1927.* His current research explores the politics of cultural translation with regard to the refashioning of social and institutional practices in China since the mid-nineteenth century.

NORTH
AMERICA

ATLANTIC
OCEAN

SAHARA

Niger R.

PACIFIC
OCEAN

SOUTH
AMERICA

0   1000   2000 Miles
0   1000   2000 Kilometers

THE GEOGRAPHY OF THE ANCIENT AND MODERN WORLDS

Today, we believe the world to be divided into continents, and most of us think that it was always so. Geographers usually identify six inhabited continents: Africa, North America, South America, Europe, Asia, and Australia. Inside these continents they locate a vast number of subcontinental units, such as East Asia, South Asia, Southeast Asia, the Middle East, North Africa, and sub-Saharan Africa. Yet this geographical understanding would have been completely alien to premodern men and women, who did not think that they inhabited continents bounded by large bodies of water. Lacking a firm command of the seas,

they saw themselves living on contiguous landmasses, and they thought these territorial bodies were the main geographical units of their lives. Hence, in this volume we have chosen to use a set of geographical terms, the main one being *Afro-Eurasia*, that more accurately reflect the world that the premoderns believed that they inhabited.

The most interconnected and populous landmass of premodern times was Afro-Eurasia. The term *Eurasia* is widely used in general histories, but we think it is in its own ways inadequate. The preferred term from our perspective must be *Afro-Eurasia*, for the interconnected landmass of premodern and indeed much of modern times included large parts of Europe and Asia and significant regions in Africa. The major African territories that were regularly joined to Europe and Asia were Egypt, North Africa, and even parts of sub-Saharan Africa.

Only gradually and fitfully did the divisions of the world that we take for granted today take shape. The peoples inhabiting the northwestern part of the Afro-Eurasian landmass did not see themselves as European Christians, and hence as a distinctive cultural entity, until the Middle Ages drew to a close in the twelfth and thirteenth centuries. Islam did not arise and extend its influence throughout the middle zone of the Afro-Eurasian landmass until the eighth and ninth

centuries. And, finally, the peoples living in what we today term the *Indian subcontinent* did not feel a strong sense of their own cultural and political unity until the Delhi Sultanate of the thirteenth and fourteenth centuries and the Mughal Empire, which emerged at the beginning of the sixteenth century, brought political unity to that vast region. As a result, we use the terms *South Asia, Vedic society,* and *India* in place of *Indian subcontinent* for the premodern part of our narrative, and we use *Southwest Asia* and *North Africa* to refer to what today is designated as the *Middle East*. In fact, it is only in the period from 1000 to 1300 that some of the major cultural areas that are familiar to us today truly crystallized.

Worlds Together, WORLDS APART

1

BECOMING HUMAN

In a remote and desolate corner of the Ethiopian highlands, a University of California team of evolutionary biologists came upon a remarkable cache of fossil remains. The task of identifying and reassembling these finds took six years of painstaking work, but the researchers eventually reconstructed one of the most revealing sets of human fossils ever found: a nearly complete skeleton of an adult male and the partial remains of another adult and a juvenile. The bones were lodged in volcanic rock. By dating this rock through analysis of its chemical structure, the team was able to determine that the bones were about 160,000 years old. Although the skeletal remains were not identical to those of modern men and women—who are technically *Homo sapiens sapiens*, a specific biological subspecies that emerged approximately 200,000 years ago and is the only surviving subspecies of *Homo sapiens*—they were close enough to form part of the family of modern humans. In short, the bones represented the oldest record of *Homo sapiens*. The fossil finds confirmed what earlier blood analyses and DNA studies had already suggested: *Homo sapiens*, or modern humans, first emerged in a small region of Africa about 200,000 years ago and migrated out of Africa only about 100,000 years ago. As Tim White, the team leader, proclaimed, "We are all Africans."

Not everyone agrees with the "Out of Africa" thesis, a label that emphasizes the contention that modern human beings are all recent descendants of people from Africa. The doubters have continued to believe that the "races" of the world evolved separately in the different regions of the world for up to one million years after their original but distant exodus out of Africa. They contend that as these early descendants of modern men and women evolved, they took on distinctive physical appearances and diverse personality traits in widely dispersed geographical settings, with the result that they appear today as different "races." In their view, the story of humanity was about deep and fundamental differences. But what is now becoming clear is the opposite: all humans share a common heritage, and humanity's differences are not genetic or crudely physical, but mainly cultural. We are also much newer than was once imagined.

Recent and mounting evidence suggests that humans have a common African heritage and that they spread to the rest of the world a relatively short time ago. This is an important insight: as a consequence of the relatively brief period of time spent living separately from one another, all of the world's "races" have a great deal in common. The characteristics that make us human are in fact quite recent in origin. Most of the common traits of human beings—an ability to make tools, to engage in family life, to use language, and to refine cognitive abilities—evolved over many millennia and crystallized on the eve of the exodus from Africa. Only in the last 100,000 years did modern humans gradually make their way out of Africa and populate the world. Only with the advent of settled agriculture did significant cultural divergences become apparent, as seen in material remains (for example, tools, cooking devices, and storage containers) uncovered by archaeologists. The big differences in humankind's cultures are less than about 15,000 or 20,000 years old.

This chapter lays out the origins of humanity from its common source. It will show how many different earlier hominids (humanlike beings who walked erect) preceded modern humans, and that humans came from only one—very recent—stock of migrants out of Africa. Then, fanning out across the world, our ancestors devised new ways to adapt to environmental constraints and opportunities. They created languages, families, and clan systems, often innovating to defend themselves against predators. One of the biggest breakthroughs was the domestication of animals and plants—the creation of agrarian settlements. With this development, humans could dispense with following food and begin producing it in their own backyards.

PRECURSORS TO MODERN HUMANS

> → *What traits differentiated early hominids from other animal species?*

To understand the origins of modern humans, we must confront what is common to all humans and what divides them from each other. We must also come to terms with time. Though the hominids that finally evolved into modern humans (*Homo sapiens*) lived millions of years ago, we have only recently developed the tools to analyze these precursors to modern humans. What is now known about the origins of human existence and the evolution into modern humans over the millennia would have astonished individuals all around the globe a century ago. Only 350 years ago, learned English clerics claimed on the basis of biblical calculations and early Christian tradition about the earth's origin that the first day of creation was Sunday, October 23, 4004 BCE. One scholar even refined the figures to specify that creation happened at 9:00

Focus Questions BECOMING HUMAN

- → *What traits differentiated early hominids from other animal species?*
- → *How did* Homo sapiens *become the only hominid species?*
- → *How did art and language increase* Homo sapiens' *chances of survival?*
- → *What factors contributed to the domestication of plants and animals?*
- → *What factors contributed to autonomous innovation in agriculture versus early borrowing?*
- → *How did agricultural revolutions foster new communal hierarchies and interaction?*

WWNORTON.COM/STUDYSPACE

→ *What traits differentiated early hominids from other animal species?*

Human Evolution	
Australopithecus anamensis	4.2 million years ago
Australopithecus afarensis (Lucy)	3.4 million years ago
Australopithecus africanus	3.0 million years ago
Homo habilis (Dear Boy)	2.5 million years ago
Homo erectus (Java and Peking Man)	1.8 million years ago
Neanderthals	120,000 years ago
Homo sapiens	200,000 years ago
Homo sapiens sapiens (modern humans)	35,000 years ago

A.M. on the morning of that day. Now we see things differently. The origin of the universe dates back some 15 billion years; and the hominid separation from African pongids, or members of the ape family, began some 6 or 7 million years ago. These discoveries have proved as mind-boggling to Hindus and Muslims as to Christians and Jews, all of whom believe, in their different ways, in a creationist account of humanity's origins.

Modern discoveries about humanity's origins have also challenged other major cultural traditions. The Chinese from East Asia, who did not appear to have an indigenous creation story, and Buddhists believed in an apparently endlessly repeated reappearance of human and animal souls over time. But no cultural tradition ever developed the idea that creatures evolved into new kinds of life, that humans were related to apes, and that all of humanity originated in a remote corner of Africa. Take as an example the creation story of the Yoruba peoples of West Africa, representative of many African creation accounts. The Yorubas believed that in the beginning God descended from the heavens in human form, becoming the godlike king of the Yorubas, Oduduwa, who established the Yoruba kingdom and laid down the tenets by which his subjects were to conduct their lives. Or as another example consider the creation story of the Buddhists, who believed in a cosmos of thousands, even millions of worlds, each of which consisted of a central mountain encircled by four continents, its seas surrounded by a girdle or wall of iron. Or consider the time frame for creation as described in the Brahmanical Vedas and the Upanishads, which date to the seventh or sixth century BCE and are still fundamental to Hindu faith today; they count the age of the world in millions, not billions, of years. Moreover, note that Chinese Han dynasty (202 BCE to 220 CE) astronomers believed that at the beginning of the world, perhaps some 23 million years ago, the planets had been conjoined and were likely to merge again at the end of time. Even the million-year time frames and multiple planetary systems that ancient Asian thinkers endorsed did not prepare them for the idea that humans are

related to apes. In all of the traditional cosmologies, humans came into existence fully formed, at a single moment, as did the other beings that populated the world.

EVOLUTIONARY FINDINGS AND RESEARCH METHODS

In their study of the origins and descent of species, evolutionary biologists and archaeologists have recently transformed humanity's understanding of its own history, a shift comparable to the realization some five centuries ago that the earth rotates around the sun. And so we see that understanding the long sweep of human history, calculated in millions of years, requires a radically new sense of time. Moreover, the findings have important, if often unsettling, implications concerning who we are as human beings. A mere century ago, who would have accepted the fact that the universe came into being 15 billion years ago, that the earth appeared about 4.5 billion years ago, and that the earliest life forms began to exist 3.8 billion years ago? The great cultural traditions would not have even considered the idea that human beings are part of a long evolutionary chain, stretching from microscopic bacteria to cells and algae and finally to African apes who appeared about 23 million years ago. And they would not have countenanced the findings, which are even more at variance with their origin stories, that Africa's great ape population had broken off into three different groups: one becoming present-day gorillas; the second becoming chimpanzees; and the third group, the one that we call

Selection of Stone Tools from Essex, Southeastern England. The tools shown include a pounder, macelike hammers, a knife, and axes (one of flint). They are typical of the range of implements being made by agriculturalists in the period between 2700 and 1800 BCE, when agricultural settlements were beginning to develop in the region. Tools made of bone, wood, and other perishable materials were also part of the tool-kit used by these same peoples.

Primary Source

A HINDU CREATION MYTH

This hymn of Rig-Veda describes the creation of the universe by the gods' sacrifice of a creature— Purusha, *which means "Man." From the body of Purusha come four different kinds of people: the Brahman, the Rajanya, the Vaishyas, and the Shudra. They are ritually the four forefathers of the four castes of India.*

Thousand-headed Purusha, thousand-eyed, thousand-footed—he, having pervaded the earth on all sides, extends ten fingers beyond it.

Purusha alone is all this—whatever has been and whatever is going to be. Further, he is the lord of immortality and also of what grows on account of food.

Such is his greatness; greater, indeed than this is Purusha. All creatures constitute but one-quarter of him, his three-quarters are the immortal in the heaven.

With his three-quarters did Purusha rise up; one-quarter of him again remains here. With it did he variously spread out on all sides over what eats and what eats not.

From him was Viraj born, from Viraj the evolved Purusha. He, being born, projected himself behind the earth as also before it.

When the gods performed the sacrifice with Purusha as the oblation, then the spring was its clarified butter, the summer the sacrificial fuel, and the autumn the oblation.

The sacrificial victim, namely, Purusha born at the very beginning, they sprinkled with sacred water upon the sacrificial grass. With him as oblation, the gods performed the sacrifice, and also the Sādhyas [a class of semidivine beings] and the rishis [ancient seers].

From that wholly offered sacrificial oblation were born the verses [rc] and the sacred chants; from it were born the meters [chandas]; the sacrificial formula was born from it.

From it horses were born and also those animals who have double rows [i.e., upper and lower] of teeth; cows were born from it, from it were born goats and sheep.

When they divided Purusha, in how many different portions did they arrange him? What became of his mouth, what of his two arms? What were his two thighs and his two feet called?

His mouth became the brāhman; his two arms were made into the rājanya; his two thighs the vaishyas; from his two feet the shūdra was born.

The moon was born from the mind, from the eye the sun was born; from the mouth Indra and Agni, from the breath [prāna] the wind [vāyu] was born.

From the navel was the atmosphere created, from the head the heaven issued forth; from two feet was born the earth and the quarters (the cardinal directions) from the ear. Thus did they fashion the worlds.

Seven were the enclosing sticks in this sacrifice, thrice seven were the fire-sticks made when the gods, performing the sacrifice, bound down Purusha, the sacrificial victim.

With this sacrificial oblation did the gods offer the sacrifice. These were the first norms [dharma] of sacrifice. These greatnesses reached to the sky wherein live the ancient Sādhyas and gods.

→ *What makes the Brahman the highest, and Shudra the lowest, caste in the hierarchy? What is the origin of the varnas?*

SOURCE: *Sources of Indian Tradition*, vol. 1, *From the Beginning to 1800*, edited and revised by Ainslie T. Embree, 2nd ed. (New York: Columbia University Press, 1988), pp. 18–19.

hominids, becoming modern-day humans only after following a long and complicated evolutionary process.

At what stage did humanity's earliest ancestors, the first hominids, initially appear? What traits distinguished hominids from other animals? In fact, no single variable separated these early humanlike beings from other creatures; instead, a combination of traits began to set off hominids from other animals as they evolved over several million years. These include lifting the torso and walking on two legs—a trait called *bipedalism*—thereby freeing hands and arms to carry objects and hurl weapons; controlling and then making fire; fashioning and using tools; developing an enlarged brain and therefore the capacity for language; and acquiring a consciousness of one's "self." Taken together, these traits began to differentiate hominids from other animal species and in the long (long!) run provided humans with the capacity to become the dominant species on the globe. Moreover, all of these traits were fully in place 50,000 years ago. Yet this was just a beginning in human development. It was only about 12,000 years ago that modern humans were ready to make another spectacular advance: domesticating plants and animals and living sedentary lives in village communities.

EARLY HOMINIDS AND ADAPTATION

What was it like to be a hominid, an ancestor of modern humans, in the millions of years before the emergence of modern humans? The first clue came from an important discovery made in 1924 at Taung, not far northwest of where the city of Johannesburg, South Africa, is now located. There, a scientist named Raymond Dart happened upon a skull and the bones of various body parts that appeared to be partly human and partly ape. Believing the creature to be "an extinct race of apes intermediate between living anthropoids (apes) and man," Dart labeled the creature the "Southern Ape of Africa," or *Australopithecus africanus*. This *Australopithecus africanus* had a brain capacity of approximately one pint, or a little less than one-third of the brain size of a modern man and about the same size as modern-day African apes. Yet these beings were different from other animals, for—however shakily or wobbly—they walked on two legs. (See Map 1-1.) In the vicinity of Dart's hominid fossils were scattered the bones of animals. Dart mistakenly concluded that our early ancestors were violent and bloodthirsty creatures who carried their prey to slaughtering grounds. In fact, early hominids were only about five feet tall and weighed at most 110 pounds. They were no match for the big, muscular, and swift animal predators: they were the hunted, not the hunters. That they survived at all in such a hostile environment is a bit of a miracle. But they did, and over the first million years of their existence in Africa, the australopithecines managed to develop into more than six distinct species. Yet it must be strongly emphasized that these australopithecines were not humans, but rather had the genetic and biological material out of which modern humans would later emerge.

Australopithecines not only were found in southern Africa but were discovered in the north as well. In 1974, an archaeological team working at a site in present-day Hadar, Ethiopia, unearthed a relatively intact skeleton of a young adult female australopithecine in the valley of the Awash River. The researchers gave the skeleton a nickname, "Lucy," based on the popular Beatles' song "Lucy in the Sky with Diamonds."

Lucy was remarkable. She stood a little over three feet tall, she walked upright, her skull contained a brain within the ape size range, and her jaw and teeth were humanlike. Her arms were long, hanging halfway from her hips to her knees, suggesting that she might not have been bipedal at all times and still often resorted to arms for locomotion, in the fashion of a modern baboon. Above all, Lucy's skeleton was relatively complete and was very, very old. In fact, it was a

solid half million years older than any other complete hominid skeleton found up to that time. Lucy showed us that human precursors were walking around as early as 3 million years ago. Her skeleton provided some big answers. But it also raised some big questions: Was Lucy a precursor to modern-day humans? If so, what kind of a precursor? What species did she represent? Or was she a modern human?

To survive, hominids had to adapt and evolve as their environments altered. During the first millions of years of human existence, these adaptations and changes were slow. They entailed far more physical adaptations to the environment than cultural transformations. Hominids, like the rest of the plant and animal world, had to keep pace with rapidly

Fossil Bones of Lucy. Archaeologist Donald Johanson discovered the fossilized bones of this young female in the Afar region of Ethiopia. They are believed to date from approximately 3.2 million years ago and provide evidence of some of the first hominids to appear in Africa. This find was of great importance because the bones were so fully and completely preserved.

MAP 1-1   EARLY HOMINIDS

The earliest hominid species evolved in Africa millions of years ago. Bipedalism made them distinct from other primates. What advantages did bipedalism give early hominids? How did the changing environment of eastern and southern Africa shape the evolution of these modern human ancestors?

ern Africa had environments that changed radically from lush and heavily forested and watered locales to arid, waterless, desertlike wastelands, and then back again. Survival required constant adaptation, and some of the hominid groups happened to be better at it than others.

In adapting, early hominids began to distinguish themselves from other mammals that were physically similar to themselves. It was not their hunting prowess that made them stand out; plenty of other species chased their prey with skill and dexterity. The single trait that gave early hominids a real advantage for survival was bipedalism: they became "two-footed" creatures who stood upright. At some point, the first hominids were not just able to stand up on two feet, they were able to remain upright and move about, leaving their arms and hands free to perform other useful tasks, like carrying food over longer distances. Once they ventured into open savannas (grassy plains with a few scattered trees), about 1.7 million years ago, hominids had a tremendous advantage. They were the only primates to move consistently on two legs. They could move continuously and could travel great distances, and they were therefore able to migrate out of hostile environments and into newer and more hospitable environments as needed.

The physical design of the body of the earliest hominids represents a fundamental overhaul of the basic body design of tree-living apes. That hominids ever came down out of the trees was also a bit of a miracle. The process took a very long time, and was erratic and unpredictable; but once it took hold, it went beyond the

changing physical environments, for if they did not, they would die out. Many of the early hominid groups did just that. No straight-line genealogical tree exists from the first hominids to modern men and women. The places in which early hominid remains have been found in southern and east-

What we know of our recent and shared origins has been the result of some remarkable scientific breakthroughs. The past four or five decades have been critical for charting humankind's earliest history. Only recently have scholars been able to date fossil remains and to use biological and linguistic research to understand the past relationship of the peoples of the world to each other. The first major advance in the study of prehistory (before there were written historical records) occurred immediately after World War II. It involved the use of radiocarbon dating for determining the age of objects of great antiquity. All living things contain the radiocarbon isotope C^{14}, which plants acquire directly from the atmosphere and animals acquire indirectly when they consume plants or other animals. When these living things die, the C^{14} isotope begins to decay into a stable nonradioactive element, C^{12}. Because the rate of decay is regular and measurable, it is possible to ascertain the date of fossils that leave organic remains for ages of up to 40,000 years.

A second major dating technique, known as the *potassium-argon method*, is based on the changing chemical structure of objects over time. Scientists can calculate the age of nonliving objects by measuring the ratio of potassium to argon in them, since over time potassium decays into argon. This method makes possible the dating of objects up to a million years old, and it enables scientists to date the sediments in which fossils are found—as a gauge of the age of the fossils themselves.

DNA (deoxyribonucleic acid) analysis is a third innovation that provides a crucial tool for unraveling the beginnings of modern humans. DNA analysis makes it possible for researchers to pinpoint human descent from an original African population to populations that lived approximately 100,000 years ago. DNA, which determines biological inheritances, is found in two different places within the cells of all living organisms, including the human body. DNA occurs in the nucleus of every cell, where it is known as *nuclear DNA*. It is also found outside the nucleus of cells, where it serves as their microscopic power packs and is known as *mitochondrial DNA*. Examining mitochondrial DNA enables researchers to measure the genetic variation among living objects, including human beings. By studying the mitochondrial DNA of a broad sample of humans, researchers have concluded that there is remarkable genetic homogeneity among the world's peoples today. Gorilla populations now living in the same African valley display more genetic variation than the most widely dispersed human populations. The genetic similarity of modern humans suggests that the human population from whom all modern men and women descended, *Homo sapiens*, originated in Africa about 200,000 years ago. These humans then moved out of Africa about 100,000 years ago, dispersing eastward into the area of Southwest Asia and then through the rest of Afro-Eurasia. One branch moved across to Australia about 50,000 years ago. Another group moved westward into the area of Europe about 40,000 years ago. When the scientific journal *Nature* published these findings in 1987, it inspired a groundswell of public interest and astonishment—and a scientific debate that remains hotly contested today.

point of return. The hominids became permanent land-dwelling rather than tree-dwelling creatures.

Explaining why and how hominids began to walk on two legs is critical to understanding long-term human origins. The first hominids enjoyed, along with the other primates, the advantages of being long-limbed, tree-loving animals, with good vision and dexterous digits. But why did these primates, in contrast to their closest relatives, gorillas and chimpanzees, leave the shelter of trees and venture out into the open grasslands, where they were vulnerable to attack? The answer is not at all self-evident. Explaining how and why some apes took these first steps also sheds light on why humanity's origins lie in Africa. Fifteen million years ago there were apes all over the world—so why did a small number of them evolve new traits in Africa?

What eastern and southern Africa offered was a climate conducive to the development of a diversified milieu of plant and animal species. At a critical moment, the environment in this region changed dramatically. The world had entered its fourth great Ice Age approximately 40 million years ago, during which the earth's temperatures diminished and its continental ice sheets, polar ice sheets, and mountain glaciers increased. This Ice Age was to last until 10,000 years ago. Like all Ice Ages, it was characterized by warming and cooling phases that usually lasted between 40,000 and 100,000 years. Between 10 and 15 million years ago, the climate in

Africa went through one such cooling and drying cycle. To the east of Africa's Rift Valley, stretching from South Africa north to the Ethiopian highlands, the cooling and drying forced forests to contract and savannas to spread. It was in this region, where the environment changed dramatically, that apes came down from trees, stood up, and learned to walk, run, and to live in savanna lands—thus becoming the precursors to humans, and more and more distinctive as a new species of animal.

Using two feet for locomotion did more than augment the means of survival for creatures whose environments were changing, sometimes quite fundamentally. It increased their options for subsistence and led to the acquisition of a variety of cognitive skills, such as thought, memory, problem-solving, and ultimately language, to obtain food and avoid predators. Cognition itself became the basis for further developments. Thus, as hands were freed from the drudgery of pulling bodies around, they could be used for carrying around other things, and eventually for making the first tools. A free hand could be used for holding a spear or the ever-useful digging stick.

In addition to being bipedal, hominids had another feature that helped them to survive and create and use tools—opposable thumbs. This trait, shared with other primates such as apes and monkeys, gave hominids great physical dexterity, enhancing their ability to explore and to alter materials that they found around them. Manual dexterity and standing upright also enabled them to carry their own young family members if they needed

With larger brains, hominids could do more things and become what we call more "human."

to relocate, or to throw missiles with deadly accuracy to protect themselves or to obtain food. They used their increased powers of observation and memory to gather wild berries and grains and to scavenge the meat and marrow of animals who had died of natural causes or who had been killed by large predators. These are activities at which all primates are good, but at which hominids came to excel.

These early hominids were highly social. They lived in small bands of about twenty-five individuals, trying to survive in hostile environments by hunting small game and by gathering wild plants and their produce. They were not yet a match for large predators, however, and had to find safe havens in which to hide. They were also looking for specialized habitats or ecological niches where a diverse supply of wild grains and fruits and abundant wildlife ensured a secure, even comfortable existence. In such highly diversified environmental niches, small hunting bands of twenty-five could swell through alliances with other bands to as many as 500 individuals. The hominids soon learned to communicate mainly through gestures, but they also may have developed a simple early form of language that facilitated the establish-

ment of distinct cultural codes such as common rules and customs.

The early hominids lived in this manner for as many as 3 million years, changing their way of life very little, except for moving around the African landmass in their never-ending search for more favorable environments. Even so, their survival is somewhat surprising. There were relatively few of them, and they struggled in often hostile environments, surrounded by a huge diversity of very large mammals, some of which were threatening carnivores. As the environment changed over the millennia, these early hominids gradually altered in appearance, with small modifications in their bodies reflecting the effects of their adaptation to the changing environment. Fossils from 3 million years ago reveal that their brains became larger, almost doubling in size; their foreheads became more elongated; their jaws became less massive; and they took on a much more modern look. Similarly, adaptation to changes in the environment also created new skills and aptitudes, which in turn expanded cognitive capacities—the ability to store and to analyze information. With larger brains, hominids could do more things and become what we call more "human." A larger brain gave hominids the capacity to form mental maps of their worlds—to learn, to remember what they learned, and to convey these lessons to their neighbors and offspring. In this fashion, larger groups of hominids created communities with shared understandings of their immediate environments, which enhanced the advantages of those with larger brains as they underwent natural selection—the process whereby offspring inherit traits that improve the probability of survival and reproduction.

We know that hominids are much older than we thought, but it also turns out that there was much more diversity than we thought in this early hominid world. A series of startling finds in Ethiopia and Kenya have recently transformed the understanding of these early stages of hominid development. In the Tugen Hills of southern Kenya, bone remains dating to at least 6 million years ago have been discovered of a chimpanzee-sized hominid, named *Orrorin tugenensis*, who walked upright on two feet, indicating that bipedalism must be millions of years older than previously thought. Moreover, the teeth of these hominids seem to indicate that they were closer to modern humans than to australopithecines. But in their arms and hands, which display the characteristics needed for tree climbing, the *Orrorin* hominids seemed more apelike than the australopithecines. So *Orrorin* hominids were still at least half tied to an environment in the trees. Also, recent discoveries of the bones of five individuals in the Afar depression in Ethiopia (in an area just south of where Lucy was found) have revealed the existence of bipedal ho-

→ *What traits differentiated early hominids from other animal species?*

Searching for Hominid Fossils. Olorgasalie in Kenya has proved to be one of the most important archaeological sites for uncovering evidence of early hominid development. Rick Potts, a leader in the field, is shown here on-site. Among his discoveries were hand axes and indications that hominids in this area had learned to use fire.

minids of a yet different kind that dates to at least 5 million years ago. And still another recent discovery, this time in northern Kenya, has revealed another species of early hominids. The fact that quite different kinds of early hominids were living side by side in the same environment in eastern Africa between 3 and 4 million years ago shows that there was much greater diversity and development among early hominid populations than has been previously imagined. The environment in eastern Africa was generating a fair number of different hominid populations, a few of which would provide our genetic base, but most of which would not survive in the long run. In fact, the survival of any of these hominid lines was no certain thing. The bones of *Orrorin* hominids discovered in Kenya had been chewed and broken by the shearing teeth of a large carnivore. A huge leopardlike cat had torn them to pieces.

THE FIRST HUMANS:
HOMO HABILIS

The fossil record reveals that nearly 1 million years after Lucy, the first examples of human beings, to whom we give the name *homo* or "true human," appeared. They, too, were bipedal, possessing a smooth walk based on true upright posture. They had an even more important advantage over other hominids: they had large brains. They were also the first beings to create and use tools systematically, consistently, and on a large scale in order to exploit the resources in their en-

vironment (and, presumably, to defend themselves) more efficiently. These important traits were identified by Mary and Louis Leakey, who made astonishing fossil discoveries in the 1950s at Olduvai Gorge (part of the Great Rift Valley) in present-day northeastern Tanzania. Theirs are regarded as the most significant discoveries of early humans in Africa— especially one find of a totally intact skull that potassium-argon dating methods indicated was 1.8 million years old.

The Olduvai Gorge is a thirty-mile-long canyon through which a winding stream has exposed many layers of volcanic rock containing abundant fossil remains. Louis S. B. Leakey, the son of Anglican missionary parents who had been living in the central highlands of Kenya since the turn of the twentieth century, was a paleontologist (a scientist studying fossil remains from past geological periods) educated at the University of Cambridge. In 1931, Leakey launched a small research project in Olduvai, along with his wife, Mary Nicol Leakey, who was a trained archaeologist. Together, they defied their Cambridge mentors, who had rejected the notion of humanity's African origins. After decades of frustrating work and financial troubles, Mary Leakey could hardly believe her good fortune when she stumbled upon an almost totally intact skull. The Leakeys nicknamed it "Dear Boy."

Other objects discovered with Dear Boy demonstrated that by this time, early humans had begun to fashion tools and to use them for butchering animals and also, possibly, for hunting and killing smaller animals. The tools were flaked stones with sharpened edges that enabled these early humans to cut apart animal flesh and to scoop out the marrow from

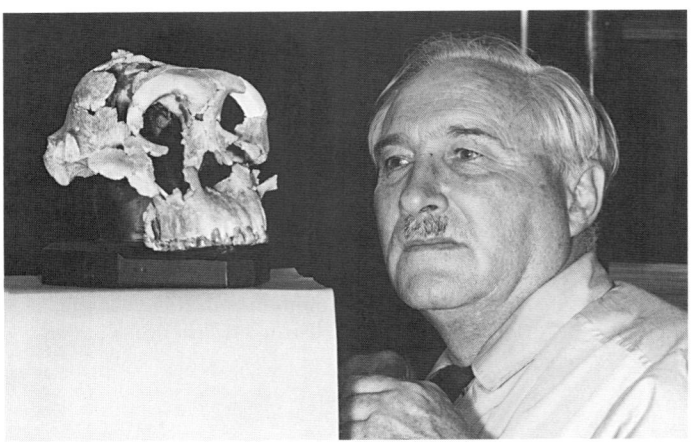

Louis Leakey (1903–1972). The Leakeys (Louis and his wife, Mary) were dedicated archaeologists whose work in East Africa established the area as one of the starting points of human development.

animal bones. To mimic substitutes for the slicing teeth that lions, leopards, and other carnivores used in stripping meat from a carcass, the Oldowans had devised these tools—deliberately crafting them by careful chipping. Mary Leakey found that Dear Boy and his companions had carried usable rocks over long distances to places where they made their implements and had learned to employ special hammer stones, tools to make tools; sometimes they even carried their favorite toolmaking devices around with them. Unlike other tool-using animals (for example, the chimpanzees), early human men and women were now intentionally fashioning implements, not simply finding them when they were needed. Even more important, they were passing on knowledge of these new tools to their offspring, and in the process they were gradually improving the tools. Because these beings were making tools and because the Leakeys believed that making and using them represented a new stage in the evolution of human beings, they gave these creatures a new name, *Homo habilis*, or "Skillful Man." This toolmaking ability truly made them the forerunners, though very distant, of modern men and women.

EARLY HUMANS ON THE MOVE: MIGRATIONS OF *HOMO ERECTUS*

All the different species of hominids flourished together in Africa between 1 and 2.5 million years ago. By 1 million years ago, however, almost all had gradually died out. The one surviving species, which emerged about 1.5 million years ago, had a large brain and walked truly upright; it therefore was named "Standing Man," or *Homo erectus*. But the success of *Homo erectus* was hardly a foregone conclusion, even though this species was better adapted to the challenging environ-

mental changes with which it was confronted than other hominids had been. Only with the hindsight of millions of years can we understand the decisive advantage of having larger brains over having larger teeth. This story was not a predictable triumph. There were many more failures than successes in the gradual changes that led *Homo erectus* to be the one species of hominids that would survive until the arrival of *Homo sapiens*.

One of the traits that contributed to the survival of the *Homo erectus* species was the early development of extended periods of caring for their young, which further distinguished them from other primates. Having a brain more than twice the size of the australopithecines gave these hominids real advantages over the rest of the animal world. But an enlarged brain brought one significant problem in its wake: the pelvises of *Homo erectus* females were only big enough to allow an infant with a cranial capacity that was about a third an adult's size to pass through at birth. As a result, infants required a

Tracking Footprints. Mary Leakey was among the most successful archaeologists studying hominids in Africa. Her finds, including the one in this photograph from Laetoli, Tanzania, highlight the activities of early men and women in Africa. The footprints, believed to be those of an *Australopithecus afarensis*, date from 3.7 to 3 million years ago.

→ *What traits differentiated early hominids from other animal species?*

Olduvai Gorge, Tanzania. Olduvai Gorge is arguably the most famous archaeological site containing hominid finds. Mary and Louis Leakey, convinced that early human beings originated in Africa, discovered the fossil remains of *Homo habilis* ("Skillful Man") in this area between 1960 and 1963. They argued that these findings represent a direct link to *Homo erectus*.

long period during which they would be protected by adults as they matured and their brain size tripled.

This big difference from other species also affected family dynamics. A long process of maturing rendered children dependent on their parents for protection against the dangers of the world, but it also provided the adult members of hunting and gathering bands with the opportunity to train their offspring in those activities. In addition, maturation and brain growth required years of energy transfers from mothers to their infants, via long lactation cycles and the preparation of food for dependent children after weaning. This investment was such a critical part of survival that mothers devised means to disperse the risks of accidents (or attacks) and to share the burden of helping their children's brains grow. Sometimes mothers even had to fend off assaults by predatory fathers and other males. In effect, mothers relied on other women (their own mothers, sisters, and friends) and girls (often their own daughters) to help in the nurturing and protecting, a process known as "allomothering" (literally, "other mothering").

There were two main features of *Homo erectus* that distinguished them from their competitors. Since they were fully bipedal, they were able to move with a smooth rapid gait, which meant they were able to move over large distances quickly. They were the world's first long-distance travelers, forming the first truly mobile human communities. In addition, they began to make rudimentary attempts to control their environment. Not only did these early human ancestors become proficient at making stone tools for hunting and food preparation, they also began to control fire, another significant marker in the development of human culture. It is very hard to tell from the fossil evidence when humans learned to use fire.

The most reliable evidence of fire mastery comes from cave sites, less than 250,000 years old, where it seems that people cooked. By less conservative estimates, fire had become more than an accidental luxury as early as 500,000 years ago. Fire provided heat, protection, a gathering point for small communities, and a way to cook food. It was also symbolically powerful: here was a source of energy that humans could extinguish and revive at will. The uses of fire had enormous long-term effects on human evolution. Because they were able to boil, steam, and fry wild plants, early humans could expand their diets; fire rendered palatable otherwise indigestible foods—especially raw muscle fiber, which human stomachs are ill equipped to handle—and expanded the potential food base, making it possible to exploit food sources that could not be used without fire. Mastery of fire also made it possible for early humans to survive in the colder regions of the world. Without fire, Africans might not have ventured out of their continent.

As scientists gained a clearer sense of when and where the early hominids lived, they also had to figure out how—and, just as important, which—hominids fanned out across the world. What their research indicated was that hominids migrated out of Africa about 1.5 million years ago and gradually spread throughout much of the world. Members of the *Homo erectus* species proved to be the first globe-trotters. Yet despite their tremendous success in moving rapidly to populate most of the globe (except the Americas), these hominids were still not modern humans. They were only the ancestors, or precursors, of modern humans.

The populating of the world by hominids proceeded in waves. Around 1 or 2 million years ago, *Homo erectus* individuals migrated first into the lands of Southwest Asia; then, according to some scholars, they traveled along the Indian Ocean shoreline, moving into South Asia and Southeast Asia and later northward into what is now China. Their movement out of Africa was a response in part to the huge environmental changes that were transforming the world. The Northern Hemisphere was shaken by thirty major cold phases during this period marked by the advance of glaciers (huge sheets of ice) over vast expanses of the northern parts of Eurasia and the Americas. The glaciers had been formed by widespread intense cold that froze much of the water in the world's oceans, lowering them some 325 feet below their present-day levels. So it was possible for the migrants to travel across land bridges into Southeast Asia and from East Asia to Japan, as well as from New Guinea to Australia. The last part of the Afro-Eurasian landmass to be occupied consisted of areas in Europe, at the time one of the most forbidding regions in the world because of its extensive ice cover. The geological record

Zhoukoudian Cave. Located in a cluster of limestone hills twenty-six miles west of Beijing, China, Zhoukoudian is the largest and most important early Stone Age site in China. In addition to the bones of Peking Man, a *Homo erectus* found there, archaeologists discovered two piles of ash residues on a big limestone block, which was used to preserve a fire after kindling. Peking Man's average cranial capacity was approximately 80 percent that of modern man.

indicates that mantles of ice completely blanketed present-day Scotland, Ireland, Wales, Scandinavia, and the whole of northern Europe, including the areas where today's cities of Berlin, Warsaw, Moscow, and Kiev are located. Here, too, however, a lowered ocean level enabled early human predecessors to cross by foot from areas in what we now know as Europe into what is now England.

It is truly astonishing how far these *Homo erectus* hominids traveled. The discoveries of the bone remains of "Java Man" and "Peking Man" (as archaeologists named specific *Homo erectus* hominids, from where their remains were discovered) confirmed early settlements of *Homo erectus* hominids in Southeast and Eastern Asia. The remains of Java Man, found in 1891 on the banks of the Solo River in central Java, were later verified as an early *Homo erectus* that had dispersed into Asia perhaps as early as 2 million years ago. This would mean that the first *Homo erectus* walked out of Africa almost a million years earlier than had been originally believed. In 1969, at Sangiran (also on the island of Java), archaeologists uncovered remains with a fuller cranium, which was very thick, indicating that the individual's brain was about half the size of a modern human's. The most complete discovery from Southeast Asia, it dates from about 800,000 years ago. Accordingly, scientists realized that African hominids were moving north and eastward into Asia at least a million years ago, and more likely 2 million years ago, and had reached Java, which was then connected by land to the rest of the Afro-Eurasian landmass.

Similar finds made in China in the early twentieth century give us a clearer picture of the daily lives of these pioneering hominids, who retained many of the lifeways of their African ancestors. Peking Man was a cave dweller, toolmaker, and hunter and gatherer (surviving by hunting animals and gathering wild fruit such as berries and wild plants), who settled in the warmer climate in northern China perhaps 400,000 years ago. Peking Man's brain was larger than that of his Javan cousins, and there is evidence that he controlled fire and cooked meat, in addition to hunting big animals. He made tools with vein quartz, quartz crystals, flint, and sandstone. The *Homo erectus* hominids proved to be even more adept at making tools than were their predecessors. Their major innovation, dated as far back as 1.7 million years ago, was the double-faced axe, a stone instrument that was whittled down on both sides to make a sharp edge capable of being used as a hand axe, a cleaver, a pick, and probably as a weapon to be hurled against foes or animals. Even so, and in spite of their enlarged brains, these early predecessors still had a long way to go before becoming modern humans.

Rather than seeing human evolution as a single, gradual development, increasingly scientists see our origins as shaped by progressions and retrogressions, as hominids adapted or failed to adapt and went extinct. As the climate changed, especially with the cyclical fluctuations of warming and cooling that were typical of the ice ages, weather conditions altered the course of what is called *speciation* (species formation). Several species could exist simultaneously, but some would be more suited to changing environmental conditions—and thus more likely to survive—than others. Although those in the *Homo habilis* and *Homo erectus* species were some of the world's first humanlike inhabitants, they are unlikely to have been direct ancestors of modern man and woman. The early settlers of Afro-Eurasia from the *Homo erectus* group went extinct, unable to compete against more highly evolved hominids. They were followed by later waves of hominids who walked out of the African landmass just as their predecessors had done. Certainly, by 500,000 years ago, caves in areas of Afro-Eurasia were full of residents who made fire, flaked stones into implements, and formed settlements. Yet we are not their descendants. In effect, the existence of *Homo erectus* hominids may have been a necessary precondition for the evolution into modern humans, or *Homo sapiens*. But it was not, in itself, sufficient.

THE FIRST
MODERN HUMANS

> → *How did* Homo sapiens *become the only hominid species?*

Homo sapiens moved out of Africa and became the sole "human" species on the earth sometime between 120,000 and 50,000 years ago. If we can think of the 5 million years of hominid life as a single hour of our time, then the history of *Homo sapiens* has occurred in slightly less than two minutes. The history that we study has happened in an incredibly short interval within the hominid time frame.

The early hominids did not and could not form large communities, as they had limited communication skills. Although hominids could utter simple commands and communicate with hand signals, complex linguistic expression eluded them. This achievement was one of the last in the evolutionary process of becoming truly human. Developing language apparently did not occur until sometime between 100,000 and 50,000 years ago. Many scholars view it as the most critical ingredient in distinguishing human beings from other animals. It is this skill that ultimately made *Homo sapiens* "sapiens," which is to say "wise" or "intelligent": humans who could create culture. Creating language enabled humans to become modern humans.

HOMO SAPIENS AND
THEIR MIGRATION

About 200,000 years ago, large-scale ecological shifts in climate and environment in Africa put huge pressures on all types of mammals, including hominids. In these new extremely warm and dry environments, the smaller, quicker, and more adaptable mammals survived. All forms of mammalian life, including early humans, began to become smaller. It was no longer large size and brute strength but rather the ability to respond quickly, to have great agility in responding to challenges, and to be able to move with great speed that counted.

Caught up in these environmental transformations, early humans were no different from other mammals. It is therefore no surprise that a bigger-brained, more dexterous, and more agile species of humans appeared in the highlands of eastern Africa. Referred to technically as *Homo sapiens*, these humans differed notably from their precursors. The eclipse of *Homo erectus* by *Homo sapiens* was hardly inevitable. After all, the *Homo erectus* species of humans was

Skulls of Ancestors of *Homo sapiens*. Shown here are seven skulls of ancestors of modern-day men and women, arranged to highlight brain growth over time. The skulls represent (left to right): *Adapis*, a lemur-like animal that lived 50 million years ago; *Proconsul*, a primate that lived about 23 million years ago; *Australopithecus africanus*; *Homo habilis*; *Homo erectus*; *Homo sapiens* from the Qafzeh site in Israel, about 90,000 years old; and Cro-Magnon from France, about 22,000 years old.

The Physical Evolution of Hominids. These three figures show the femur bones of Lucy, *Orronin tugenensis* (one of the earliest of the hominids, who may have existed as much as 6 million years ago), and *Homo sapiens*. *Homo sapiens* has a larger femur bone and was bigger than Lucy—a representative of the hominid species *Australopithecus afarensis*—but has the same bone structure.

already scattered around Africa and Eurasia; in contrast, even as late as 100,000 years ago there were no more than 10,000 *Homo sapiens* adults, and they were still confined to a small part of the African landmass. But when *Homo sapiens* moved out of Africa and the two species did find each other in the same places across the globe, *Homo sapiens* individuals were better suited to survive, certainly in part because of their greater cognitive and language skills compared to members of the *Homo erectus* species.

The *Homo sapiens* newcomers followed the trails blazed earlier by other migrants from Africa. (See Map 1-2.) In many places, they moved into the same ecological areas as their genetic cousins, migrating from Africa by way of the Levant (the area encompassing modern-day Lebanon, Israel, and Syria), moving across the area of Southwest Asia, and from there migrating into central Asia—but not at this time into the area of Europe. They flourished and reproduced. By 30,000 years ago, the population of *Homo sapiens* had grown to about 300,000. Between 50,000 and 12,000 years ago, these modern humans were moving with extraordinary rapidity into areas that were tens of thousands of miles from the Rift Valley and the Ethiopian highlands of Africa—for example, into what is now China, where they were thriving and even creating distinct regional cultures, with differences between those who lived in the north and those who lived in the south. Shandingdong

Man, for example, was a *Homo sapiens* whose fossil remains and relics can be dated to about 18,000 years ago. His physical characteristics were closer to those of modern humans, and he had a similar brain size. His stone tools, which included choppers and scrapers used to prepare food, were similar to the tools of the *Homo erectus* Peking Man. His bone needles, however, were the first stitching tools of their kind found in China, and they indicated that garments were being made. Some of the needles measured a little over an inch in length and had small holes drilled in them. Shandingdong Man also buried his dead. A tomb of grave goods includes ornaments suggesting that these individuals already had developed aesthetic tastes and religious beliefs. The social unit of the Upper Cave Man appeared to be some sort of clan descended from a common ancestor and thus linked by genealogy.

Homo sapiens were also moving into the furthest northeastern fringe of East Asia. In the more frigid climate, they learned to follow the herds of big Siberian grazing animals. Mastodon bones and dung, for instance, made decent fuel and good building material. They pursued their prey ever eastward as the herds looked for pastures in the steppes (treeless grasslands) and marshes. These groups migrated east across the ice to Japan, also following animal herds. A mammoth fossil has been uncovered in the colder north of Japan, for example, and an elephant fossil in the warmer south. Elephants in particular roamed the warmer parts of East Asia that stretched thousands of miles across inner Eurasia from 300,000 years ago until 15,000 years ago. The hunters and gatherers who moved into Japan hunted animals and gathered wild plants for their sustenance. Meat was dried, smoked, or broiled using fire, practices that the migrants refined once the seas separated the islands from Asia and limited the supplies of game and plants.

Several thousand years later, about 18,000 years ago, *Homo sapiens* went further than their predecessors had gone, edging into the weedy landmass that linked Siberia and North America (which had not been populated by hominids). This prehistoric thousand-mile-long land bridge, called "Beringia," must have seemed to the people who crossed over it simply an extension of familiar steppeland terrain. For thousands of years, modern humans poured eastward and south into the uninhabited terrain of North America. The oldest currently known location of human settlement in the Americas is Broken Mammoth, a 14,000-year-old site in central Alaska. A second, and last, migration seems to have taken place about 8,000 years ago and was by boat, since by then the land bridge had disappeared under the waters of the sea.

Once in the Americas, these mobile and expansionist migrants began to fill up the landmasses. They were the first discoverers of America, and they found ample prey in the herds of wooly mammoths, caribou, giant sloths (weighing nearly three tons), and 200-pound beavers. But the explorers could also themselves be prey—for they encountered saber-toothed tigers, long-legged eagles, and giant bears that moved faster than horses. The melting of the glaciers about 8,000 years ago and

Migrations of *Homo sapiens*	
Homo erectus leave Africa	c. 1.5 million years ago
Homo sapiens leave Africa	c. 100,000 mya
Homo sapiens migrate into Asia	c. 60,000 mya
migrate into Europe	c. 50-40,000 mya
migrate into Australia	c. 40,000 mya
migrate into the Americas	c. 16–11,000 mya

the resulting disappearance of the land bridge eventually cut off the first Americans from their Afro-Eurasian origins. Thereafter, the Americas became a world apart.

CRO-MAGNON *HOMO SAPIENS* REPLACE NEANDERTHALS

Homo sapiens spread out and occupied habitats previously inhabited by earlier hominid migrants. Over the millennia between 100,000 and 30,000 years ago, they eventually migrated over the whole globe and gradually eclipsed their earlier precursors. By that date, as DNA reveals, all genetic cousins to the *Homo sapiens* were extinct, leaving only modern humans' ancestors to populate the world. Neanderthals, members of an early wave of hominids from Africa, had settled in the western area of Afro-Eurasia, ranging from present-day Uzbekistan and Iraq to Spain, perhaps 150,000 years ago. They were there well before *Homo sapiens*. Therein lies a tale, for Western scholars have had a long fascination with these hominids.

Many believed that Neanderthals were the precursors to modern-day Europeans. We now know that this is not true. The first knowledge of Neanderthals came with the discovery in 1856 of a skull in the Neander Valley of present-day Germany—hence their name (*thal* or *tal* is the German word for "valley"). Some authorities wondered if the skull represented the so-called missing link between apes and humans. Not only did Neanderthals have big brains, probably slightly larger than those of modern humans, but they also used tools, buried their dead, hunted, and lived in caves. Yet their brains were not as complex in their structure as those of modern humans, and so their cognitive abilities were far more limited than those of *Homo sapiens*, especially in their perception and creation of symbols.

These characteristics prompted some to conclude that the Neanderthals were the ancestors of modern humans, with important implications for how "racial" differences were explained. Carleton Coon, a leading American anthropologist in the 1940s and 1950s, was an admirer of Neanderthal culture. He also firmly believed that the races of the world were not of recent origin (thus rejecting the "Out of Africa" thesis); he instead maintained that they had been evolving separately

from each other for at least a million years (the multiregional thesis). Disputing the prevailing reputation of Neanderthal man at the time "as a squat, slouching, low-browed, stupid, and vicious brute, wooing his women by clubbing them over the head and eating his deceased parents" (Coon, *The Story of Man*, 39), he advanced the radical claim that if a Neanderthal were dressed up in modern garb, wearing a fedora, a shirt, and a tie, he could enter a New York City subway and pass as a modern man. Coon and others were uncomfortable with the idea that modern humans had emerged from common origins in Africa a mere 100,000 years ago and shared the same genetic foundations. They used fossil remains of Neanderthal Man, Java Man, and Peking Man to attempt to prove that modern men and women, *Homo sapiens*, had evolved separately from *Homo erectus* in markedly different geographical settings. Coon and others erroneously believed that these different groups had taken on deep-seated, nearly unbridgeable racial differences based on lengthy genetic distances from the first humans.

Neanderthals turned out not to be the ancestors of modern humans at all. They eventually gave way to a group of *Homo sapiens* known as the Cro-Magnon peoples (named after the 1868 fossil discoveries in Cro-Magnon in France). Although Neanderthal and Cro-Magnon communities overlapped in Europe for thousands of years, the Neanderthals were not nearly as well equipped to survive as the Cro-Magnon *Homo sapiens*. The Neanderthals' short arms and legs and bulky torso probably made them stronger than modern men and women but extremely awkward and clumsy. Assuming that Neanderthals had proficiency in language (an assumption that cannot be made easily), the location of their voice box put them at a great disadvantage in comparison with modern humans. They would have found it impossible

Skulls of a Neanderthal Man (left) and Cro-Magnon (right). These two skulls show that Neanderthals had a large brain capacity and a larger head than modern man. However, Neanderthals lost out to *Homo sapiens* in the struggle to survive as they spread across the globe.

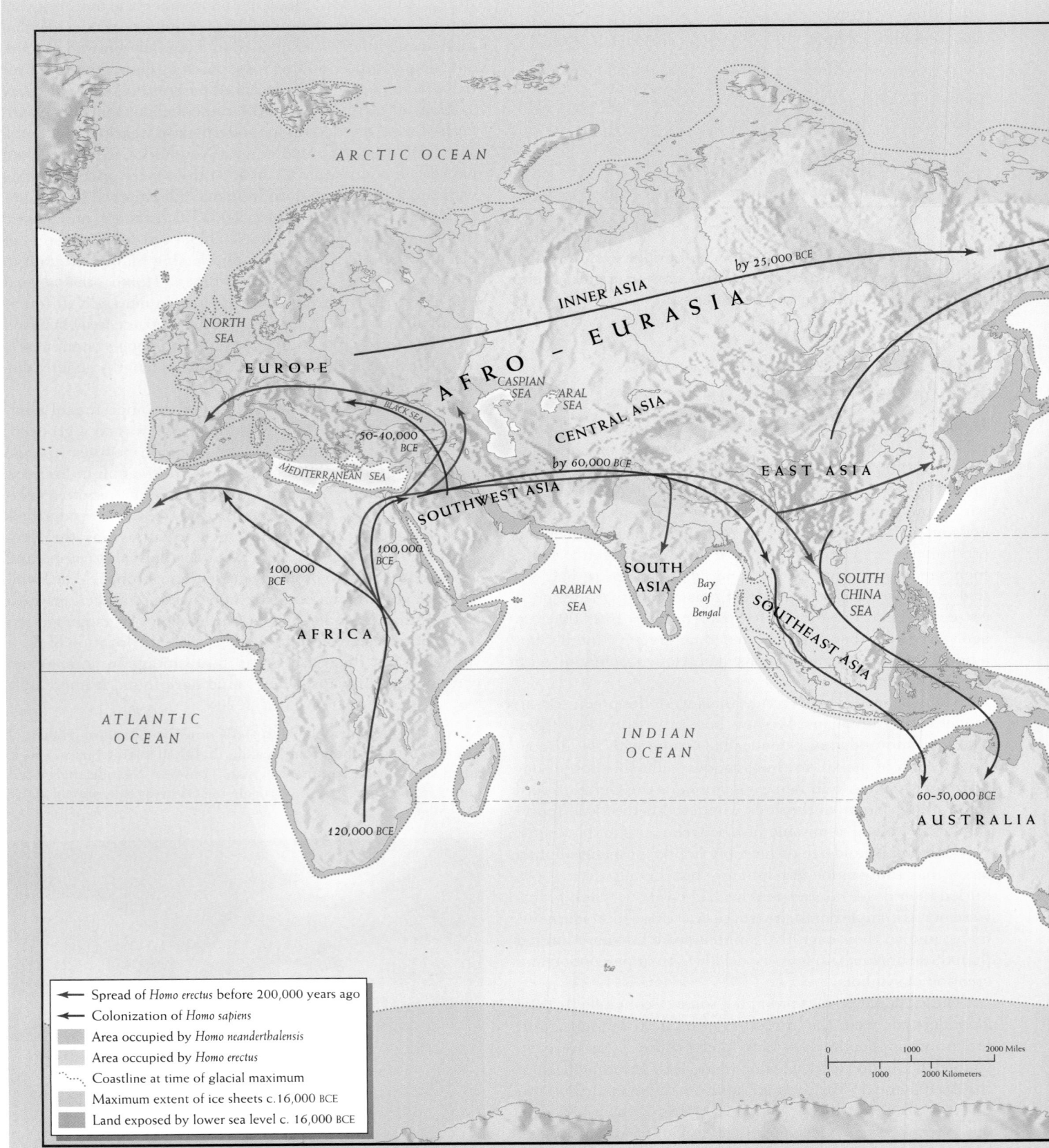

ARCTIC OCEAN

INNER ASIA

by 25,000 BCE

AFRO - EURASIA

NORTH
SEA

EUROPE

CASPIAN
SEA

ARAL
SEA

CENTRAL ASIA

BLACK SEA

50-40,000
BCE

EAST ASIA

by 60,000 BCE

MEDITERRANEAN SEA

SOUTHWEST ASIA

100,000
BCE

SOUTH
ASIA

Bay
of
Bengal

SOUTH
CHINA
SEA

100,000
BCE

ARABIAN
SEA

SOUTHEAST ASIA

AFRICA

ATLANTIC
OCEAN

INDIAN
OCEAN

60-50,000 BCE

AUSTRALIA

120,000 BCE

Spread of *Homo erectus* before 200,000 years ago
Colonization of *Homo sapiens*
Area occupied by *Homo neanderthalensis*
Area occupied by *Homo erectus*
Coastline at time of glacial maximum
Maximum extent of ice sheets c.16,000 BCE
Land exposed by lower sea level c. 16,000 BCE

0   1000   2000 Miles
0   1000   2000 Kilometers

MAP 1-2 EARLY MIGRATIONS: OUT OF AFRICA

Hominid species began migrating out of Africa hundreds of thousands of years ago, but only Homo sapiens migrated to all major inhabitable regions. Why do you think *Homo sapiens* migrated to more distant lands than *Homo erectus*? How did physical geography shape each species' migration patterns? What opportunities did shifts in global climate present each species?

ARCTIC OCEAN

From Asia
16,000 BCE

NORTH
AMERICA

ATLANTIC
OCEAN

Tropic of Cancer

12,000 BCE

PACIFIC
OCEAN

Equator

SOUTH
AMERICA

Tropic of Capricorn

9000 BCE

to make certain vowel sounds—specifically, *i, u,* and *a*—as well as two consonants, *k* and *g.* This physical limitation constrained their repertoire to grunting, calling, and some very simple "words." Whole sets of speech patterns could therefore not evolve.

Neanderthals and other advanced hominids in China and Java represented the culmination of a long evolutionary process that made individuals more and more specialized and better adapted to specific environmental conditions. So, when the environment began to change, and the climate turned warmer and wetter, these earlier descendants from Africa had difficulty coping. They lacked the range and adaptive fluidity that *Homo sapiens* had. In the scramble for food and shelter, *Homo sapiens* had an edge. From their last refuge around Zafarraya in Spain, the Neanderthals vanished without leaving a genetic trace in the gene pool that evolved into modern humanity. Like the *Homo erectus* species in Java and China, this alternative trajectory of hominid development came to a dead end.

EARLY *HOMO SAPIENS* AS HUNTERS AND GATHERERS

Like their hominid predecessors, modern humans were hunters and gatherers, and they subsisted in this way until around 12,000 years ago. They hunted animals, fished, and gathered wild berries, nuts, fruit, and grains by foraging for what they could find in their environment, rather than planting crops or vines or trees. Even today, hunting and gathering societies endure, although now they are found only in the least fertile and most marginal locations of the world, often at the edge of deserts. For example, the present-day San hunting and gathering peoples of southern Africa have attracted researchers who see the San as an isolated, exotic remnant still continuing their traditional modes of life. They believe that the San can reveal to modern scholars how men and women lived hundreds of thousands of years ago. Yet even as late as 1500 CE, as much as 15 percent of the world's population still lived by hunting and gathering.

The fact that hominid men and women lived as hunters and gatherers for millions of years, that early *Homo sapiens* also lived this way, and that people in a few contemporary communities still forage for their food suggests the powerful attractions of this way of life. Hunters and gatherers could find enough food for themselves in about three hours of foraging each day, thus affording themselves time for many other pursuits, which might have included hours of relaxation, interaction, and friendly competitions with other members of their bands. Moreover, scholars believe that these small bands were highly egalitarian. They speculate that men specialized in hunting and women in gathering and child rearing,

The San Hunters and Gatherers of Southern Africa. The San, who live in the Kalahari Desert in present-day Botswana, continue to follow a hunting and gathering existence that has died out in many parts of the world. Hunting and gathering was the way that most humans lived for millennia.

Primary Source

PROBLEMS IN THE STUDY OF HUNTERS AND GATHERERS

One of the main challenges in studying prehistory and the origins of humanity is that the evidence available to us is incomplete. Archaeologists and anthropologists are forced to theorize and speculate on the basis of what they can lay their hands on. In the case of archaeologists, these are fossil records. In the case of anthropologists, their subjects are tribal peoples—such as the San of southern Africa—whose lifeways today are thought to be similar to those of their ancestors, tens of thousands of years ago.

To date, the hunting way of life has been the most successful and persistent adaptation man has ever achieved. Nor does this evaluation exclude the present precarious existence under the threat of nuclear annihilation and the population explosion. It is still an open question whether man will be able to survive the exceedingly complex and unstable ecological conditions he has created for himself. If he fails in this task, interplanetary archeologists of the future will classify our planet as one in which a very long and stable period of small-scale hunting and gathering was followed by an apparently instantaneous efflorescence of technology and society leading rapidly to extinction. "Stratigraphically" the origin of agriculture and thermonuclear destruction will appear as essentially simultaneous.

On the other hand, if we succeed in establishing a sane and workable world order, the long evolution of man as a hunter in the past and the (hopefully) much longer era of technical civilization in the future will bracket an incredibly brief transitional phase of human history—a phase which included the rise of agriculture, animal domestication, tribes, states, cities, empires, nations, and the industrial revolution. These transitional stages are what cultural and social anthropologists have chosen as their particular sphere of study. We devote almost all of our professional attention to organizational forms that have emerged within the last 10,000 years and that are rapidly disappearing in the face of modernization.

It is appropriate that anthropologists take stock of the much older way of life of the hunters. This is not simply a study of biological evolution, since zoologists have come to regard behavior as central to the adaptation and evolution of all species. The emergence of economic, social, and ideological forms are as much a part of human evolution as are the developments in human anatomy and physiology . . .

. . . Ever since the origin of agriculture, Neolithic peoples have been steadily expanding at the expense of the hunters. Today the latter are often found in unattractive environments, in lands which are of no use to their neighbors and which pose difficult and dramatic problems of survival. The more favorable habitats have long ago been appropriated by peoples with stronger, more aggressive social systems.

. . . Taking hunters as they are found, anthropologists have naturally been led to the conclusion that their life (and by implication the life of our ancestors) was a constant struggle for survival.

At the dawn of agriculture 12,000 years ago, hunters covered most of the habitable globe, and appeared to be generally most successful in those areas which later supported the densest populations of agricultural peoples. By 1500 CE the area left to hunters had shrunk drastically and their distribution fell largely at the peripheries of the continents and in the inaccessible interiors. However, even at this late date, hunting peoples occupied all of Australia, most of western and northern North America, and large portions of South America and Africa. This situation rapidly changed with the era of colonial expansion, and by 1900, when serious ethnographic research got under way, much of this way of life had been destroyed. As a result, our notion of unacculturated hunter-gatherer life has been largely drawn from peoples no longer living in the optimum portion of their traditional range.

To mention a few examples, the Netsilik Eskimos, the Arunta, and the Kung Bushmen are now classic cases in ethnography. However, the majority of the precontact Eskimos, Australian aborigines, and Bushmen lived in much better environments. Two-thirds of the Eskimos, according to Laughlin, lived *south* of the Arctic circle, and the populations in the Australian and Kalahari deserts were but a fraction of the populations living in the well-watered regions of southeast Australia and the Cape Province of Africa. Thus, within a given region the "classic cases" may, in fact, be precisely the opposite: namely, the most isolated peoples who managed to avoid contact until the arrival of the ethnographers. In order to understand hunters better it may be more profitable to consider the few hunters in rich environments, since it is likely that these peoples will be more representative of the ecological conditions under which man evolved than are the dramatic and unusual cases that illustrate extreme environmental pressure. Such a perspective may better help us to understand the extraordinary persistence and success of the human adaptation.

→ *Why is it important to study hunting and gathering communities? Why did these societies give way to other ways of life?*

SOURCE: *Man the Hunter*, edited by Richard B. Lee, Irven DeVore, and Jill Nash (Chicago: Aldine Publishing, 1968), pp. 3, 5.

but that men and women alike contributed equally to the bands' welfare. If anything, they believe that women made a larger contribution and enjoyed a higher status because the main items in the diet were cereals and fruits, whose harvesting and preparation were thought to be the responsibility of women.

ART AND LANGUAGE

> → *How did art and language increase* Homo sapiens' *chances of survival?*

Despite the remorselessly nature-bound quality of everyday life for early humans, the first *Homo sapiens* made a noteworthy evolutionary breakthrough. They developed cultural forms that reflected their consciousness of themselves and

Painting of a Bison from the Cave at Altamira, Northern Spain. When descriptions of the Altamira paintings were first published in 1880, they shocked scholars who did not believe that the earliest modern humans in this region of Europe would be capable of such artistic expression. Dating much later than similar cave paintings recently discovered at Chauvet (compare the bison on the opposite page) and rather different from them, the Altamira paintings show that distinctive regional traditions of cave art developed in different parts of Europe.

their quests to survive and to forge indispensable relationships with their environments.

ART

Few of the cultural achievements of early communities of *Homo sapiens* have captured the attention of modern-day observers more completely than their artistic endeavors. These accomplished drawings by early humans were created in areas in Europe, probably in part as a response to the harsher environment there and also in part because of intense competition with the Neanderthals. The ability to draw allowed *Homo sapiens* to understand their environment, to bond tightly among their kingroups, and to establish important mythologies. In times of stress, these behaviors certainly gave these individuals an adaptive advantage to survive in extremely challenging circumstances. The drawings and reliefs (raised wall carvings) that men and women made on the walls of caves are so vivid and realistic that modern scholars at first did not want to attribute them to artists living thousands of years ago. Take, for example, a brilliant set of images of bison, horses, wolves, boars, and deer that was discovered in a cave in northern Spain in the 1870s. The images fairly bristle with life and energy; the color and figure formations have an uncanny quality of realism.

"Look, Daddy, oxen!" That is what Maria, the daughter of Marcelino Sanz de Sauruola, cried to her father as she looked at the ceiling of a deep cave on his property at Altamira in Spain that he was exploring one summer afternoon. As he looked up, Sauruola could not believe what he saw. Arranged across the ceiling of the huge chamber were more than two dozen life-size figures of bison, horses, and wild bulls, all painted in vivid colors of red, black, yellow, and brown. He did not think that anyone would believe that these fabulous images were made tens of thousands of years ago, but he knew in his heart that they were. That was in 1879. Only in 1906 did the world finally accept that the paintings in Altamira, and those in other caves that were later discovered, were in fact the work of early humans. Even today, with more than 50,000 works of art of early humans found in Europe, these paintings compel wonder and awe at the innate artistic abilities unique to humans.

The images on cave walls were painted over a period of 25,000 years, and they changed very little in that time. The subjects are most often large game, animals that would not have been often hunted but would have been considered powerful symbols. These animals were rendered with a striking economy of line. Frequently they were placed so that the natural contours of the cave wall defined a bulging belly or the socket of an eye. Many were drawn more than once, suggesting that they were made on several occasions or by several artists. There are remarkably few images of humans, but those that exist are often male and are usually shown dancing. There are also many handprints that were made by blowing paint

Primary Source

THE ART OF CHAUVET CAVE

A spectacular discovery made at Chauvet Cave in southwestern France in 1994 upset all previously held ideas about the place and development of prehistoric art. Dating to about 35,000 years ago—much older than the 20,000-year-old paintings from Lascaux in southeastern France, discovered in 1940, or the 17,000-year-old paintings from Altamira in northwestern Spain—they are the oldest prehistoric cave paintings known in Europe. The hundreds of representations found at Chauvet Cave are more detailed and more brilliant than the ones at Altamira and Lascaux. There are detailed drawings of mammoths, musk oxen, horses, lions, bears, and even rhinoceroses, as well as human palm prints (together with footprints on the floor of the cave) and striking "Venus" female figures that feature exaggerated depictions of female genitalia—these last obviously connected to a preoccupation with human fertility. These amazing engravings and paintings shocked scholars—they come only a few thousand years after the first appearance of modern humans in Europe.

Almost as soon as their first appearance in western Europe, modern humans seemed to have rapidly developed a sense, ability, and desire to portray other living beings in their environment. This brilliant drawing shows the detail in a depiction of horses' heads.

This image uses a doubling effect—drawing additional hindquarters and legs for the animal—to give the bison the appearance of motion and speed. This ability to portray dynamic movement was once thought to be a skill that humans developed only much later.

→ *Are these drawings evidence of an early impulse to artistic creation? If so, what does that tell us about modern humans during this period? What does their decision to portray certain animals but not others tell us?*

SOURCE: French Ministry of Culture and Communication, Regional Direction for Cultural Affairs—Rhône-Alpes Region—Regional Department of Archaeology.

around a hand placed on the stone wall, or by dipping hands in paint and then pressing them to the wall. Finally, there are abstract symbols such as circles, wavy lines, and checkerboards; these are most likely to appear at places of transition in the caves.

Lacking any writings to indicate what the images meant to ancient humans, we can only speculate about their meaning. At first, decoration seemed to be their purpose—art for art's sake. But that explanation has long been discarded. Why would these peoples have decorated caves deep in the earth that were not their homes and that had no natural light that would allow the images to be seen? Perhaps, as some scholars have proposed, the paintings were ways in which humans defined themselves as separate from other parts of nature. Other more interesting interpretations have also been put forward. Most recently, the cave drawings have been described as the work of powerful shamans, individuals believed to hold special powers to understand and control the tremendous forces of the cosmos. The subjects and the style of the paintings in the caves of Europe are very similar to images engraved or painted on rocks by some hunter and gatherer societies living today, especially the San and the !Kung peoples of southern Africa. In those societies, paintings are used to mark important places of ritual. Often they are made during trances by shamans who intercede with the spirit world on behalf of their community.

Paintings were not the only form of artistic expression for early humans. Small sculptures of animals that were shaped out of bone and stone tools are dated as being even older than the paintings. Most famous are the three-dimensional figurines of enormously fat and pregnant females. Statuettes like the so-called Venus of Willendorf, found in Austria, demonstrate that successful reproduction was a very important theme, requiring special attention. Some of the most exquisite of the sculptures are of animals carved in postures that fit the shape of bone spear-throwers. The ancient artist captured the essence of the animal either in movement or at rest.

While the paintings found in the caves of Europe are the most spectacular examples of prehistoric art, there were other types as well. Sculpture and drawing are the oldest forms of visual expression, which was a fundamental part of the life of early humans; yet very few examples exist that were produced by hominid lines, with the possible exception of the Neanderthals. Only members of *Homo sapiens* exploited and developed this cognitive capacity for symbolic expression by permanently leaving their mark on the landscape.

Did ancient art have an important social function? What can be said is that early ornamental and decorative expressions covering Afro-Eurasian cave rock faces marked the dawn of human culture and of a consciousness of men and women's place in the world. Symbolic activity of this sort helped early humans to make sense of themselves, nature, and the relationships between humanity and nature.

Because dance, music, and other performance activities do not survive the ages, while paintings and drawings do, historians must use the surviving artifacts to probe the psyche of early men and women. Art historians have come to believe that the drawings contained underlying social messages, conveying mood and meaning to those who stood around the fire pit gazing at the walls of the cave, deeply inspired by the magic of the animal depictions as they prepared to hunt creatures whose meat and bones would bring them life-sustaining strength. Yet many of the most frequently employed images were of animals that were rarely hunted or eaten, and this observation has prompted some

Willendorf Venus. This squat limestone statuette—only about six inches in height—was discovered in 1908 near the village of Willendorf, Austria, and dates back about 25,000 years. As one of the earliest representations of a female figure found in Europe, it is one of the most famous icons of prehistoric art. The emphasis on the woman's breasts and reproductive organs—to the exclusion, for example, of her facial features—and the presence of a red ochre dye on her genitalia suggest the maker's concern with the woman's fertility and procreative functions.

Paleolithic Bone Carving. This decorated piece of bone from Germany probably dates to about the same time as the Altamira cave paintings in Spain. Both pieces depict a common subject matter—the capture of wild animals—but this carving is notable for its material and degree of preservation. Prehistoric representations once existed on a wide range of materials like bone and wood, but most of these pieces are now lost.

scholars to suggest that certain animals were simply interesting to observe because they projected maleness (horses) or femaleness (bison).

LANGUAGE

In the final analysis, few things set humans off from the rest of the animal world more starkly than their use of language, whose genesis and evolution are wrapped in heated controversies. (See Map 1-3.) What is generally agreed is that the cognitive abilities involved in language development marked an evolutionary milestone. It is important to make the distinction between vocal-utterance speech, possessed by many precursor hominids (such as the Neanderthals), and natural language (words arranged in particular sequences to convey meaning), which is unique to modern humans. Its development necessitated a large brain and complex cognitive organization to create words that would verbally convey symbolic meanings. Verbal communication thus required an ability to think abstractly and to communicate abstractions. The invention of language was a huge breakthrough, because words could be taught to neighbors and offspring and could be used to integrate communities for human survival. Language expanded the lessons that could be learned and shared with others. It enhanced the ability to communicate and to accumulate bodies of knowledge that could be transmitted across both space and time.

Biological research has demonstrated that humans can make and process many more primary and distinctive sounds,

> *Art, language, learning, and teaching were developed by early humans to increase their chances of survival.*

called *phonemes*, than can other animals. Whereas a human being can utter fifty phonemes, an ape can form only twelve. What is more, humans can mentally process sounds far more quickly than can other primates. With fifty phonemes, it is possible to create more than 100,000 words; and by arranging those words in different sequences and developing syntax in language, individuals can express an almost infinite number of subtle and complex meanings. Recent research suggests that the breakthrough in the use of complex languages occurred about 50,000 years ago and that the nearest approximation to humanity's proto-language (earliest language) existing today belongs to two small click-speaking African peoples, the !Kung of southern Africa and the Hadza of Tanzania. These peoples make a clicking sound by dropping the tongue down from the roof of the mouth and exhaling—a sound similar to that made by vervet monkeys warning one another of impending danger. As humans moved out of Africa and dispersed around the globe, they expanded their original language into nineteen separate and basic language families, from which all of the world's languages then evolved.

Art, language, learning, and teaching were developed by early humans to increase their chances of survival. All of these behaviors accelerated the rate of change and augmented humans' ability to adapt to environmental changes. What is more, their combination gave humans the ability to fundamentally change their relationship to their environment. Though still dependent on the natural world, increasingly humans turned to the challenge of manipulating it to their advantage, a process we first see in the flaking of stones to make tools.

MAP 1-3   ORIGINAL LANGUAGE FAMILY GROUPS
Research suggests that the use of complex language developed 50,000 years ago among *Homo sapiens* living in Africa. Eventually, as humans dispersed throughout the globe, nineteen separate language families evolved from which all modern languages originate. What advantages did complex language give *Homo sapiens* as they migrated throughout the various regions in the world? Why do you think separate languages emerged over time? How do you think the agricultural revolution affected the development of languages?

THE BEGINNINGS OF FOOD PRODUCTION

> → *What factors contributed to the domestication of plants and animals?*

About 12,000 years ago, at a time when the earth's population may have been around a million people, one of the world's most fundamental changes occurred. It involved an extended and huge shift in the way that humans controlled and produced food for themselves—what some have called a revolution in agriculture and ecology. (See Map 1-4.) In this era of major change, humans established a firmer control over nature, especially over plants and animals, resulting in changes in human modes of life. In at least five (and perhaps as many as nine) separate locations and over a period of 5,000 years, men and women engaged in experiments that led to basic changes in food production. This transformation consisted of the cultivation of wild grasses and cereals and the domestication (human control) of wild animals. For the

→ What factors contributed to the domestication of plants and animals?

cause, it was certainly a precipitating element. The population could not have continued to increase if it had had to subsist through hunting and gathering. It is just possible, though difficult to verify, that some regions of the world had reached the saturation point for a hunting and gathering way of existence (exhausting the food supply that could be gathered to feed the larger population with no cultivation of crops or domestication of animals). Without doubt, the agricultural revolution led to a vast population expansion, since men and women could now produce many more calories per unit of land than they had in the past. To be sure, learning to control environments and domesticate resources did not liberate humans from the risks of drought, floods, storms, or other natural "disasters." Indeed, without food storage systems, a sharp drought could wipe out or uproot entire communities.

EARLY DOMESTICATION OF PLANTS AND ANIMALS

Why and how did the domestication of plants and animals come about? To begin with, the changeover from a mobile way of life dependent on hunting and gathering to agriculture, which requires people to stay in one place, unfolded gradually. It was an evolutionary process that depended not on physical changes in nature but on accumulated knowledge of plants and animals. Climatic change, beginning with the ending of the last ice age (10,000 years ago) and culminating in the onset of drought, was a catalyst, causing hunters and gatherers living in a specific part of Southwest Asia—the southern Levant (roughly the area covered in modern times by Israel, Palestine, and Jordan) and its environs—to disperse to neighboring regions. Around 9000 BCE, when the rains returned and temperatures rose, abundant rainfall in the summer and mild winters created optimal conditions in Southwest Asia for settled life. These conditions lasted about 3,000 years, during which time humans experimented with new ways of organizing themselves and thought about the meaning of what it was to be human. The foundations were laid for modern societies as we know them now.

Hunters and gatherers, now able to meet all of their subsistence needs in one diverse ecological niche, could afford to settle in a single location. They did so throughout Southwest Asia, in considerably greater numbers than had ever come together before, learning to exploit mountainous areas covered with forest vegetation and home to wild sheep, wild goats, and aurochs (long-horned wild oxen). Here, in especially attractive locations such as the valleys of the Taurus Mountains in Upper Mesopotamia (present-day Iraq) and the Anatolian plateau (in modern-day Turkey), permanent settlements were established.

The formation of settled communities enabled humans to take advantage of favorable regions and to take risks, thus spurring agricultural innovation. In areas that were full of abundant wild game and edible plants, people began to

first time, nature was essentially, deliberately, and consciously refashioned by human intelligence to meet human needs. The five locations acknowledged to be independent centers of this agricultural revolution were Southwest Asia, East Asia, Southeast Asia, Mesoamerica, and northeastern America. Four other regions may also have been independent regions for this revolution, although the evidence strongly suggests some borrowing. These were East Africa, inland West Africa, southeastern Europe, and South America.

A large number of factors triggered the move to settled agriculture. While population pressure was not a direct

NORTH
AMERICA

Eastern Woodlands
3000 BCE
(Squash)

ATLANTIC
OCEAN

Gulf of Mexico

Tehuacan Valley

Mesoamerica
8000–4000 BCE
(Maize, Squash)

Sahel
2000 BCE
(Millet, Sorghum)

Niger R.

ANDES

SOUTH
AMERICA

Mesotropics
8000–5000 BCE
(Manioc, Squash,
Palms, Yams)

PACIFIC
OCEAN

Central Andes
8000–5000 BCE
(Llamas, Potatoes, Guinea Pigs)

MOUNTAINS

⬭ Origin of food domestication
▨ Present-day agricultural land

0   1000   2000 Miles
0   1000   2000 Kilometers

ARCTIC OCEAN

ASIA

EUROPE

CASPIAN SEA

CAUCASUS MTS

MEDITERRANEAN SEA

Tigris R.

SYRIAN
DESERT

ZAGROS MTS

Euphrates R.

Persian Gulf

AFRICA

Nile R.

RED SEA

Yellow R.

Yangzi R.

Yellow River
6000 BCE (Millet)
Yangzi River
6000 BCE (Rice)

PACIFIC
OCEAN

ETHIOPIAN
HIGHLANDS

Congo R.

Fertile Crescent
8000 BCE
(Barley, Cattle,
Goats, Pigs,
Sheep, Wheat)

INDIAN
OCEAN

AUSTRALIA

MAP 1-4   THE ORIGINS OF FOOD PRODUCTION

Agricultural production emerged in many regions of the world at different times. The variety of patterns reflected the local resources and conditions. Are there any common geographic features among these early food-producing areas? Is there any evidence of agricultural borrowing between various regions? Why do you think agriculture emerged in these areas and not others?

observe and to experiment with the most adaptable plants. For ages, people gathered grains by relying on seeds falling freely from their stalks. At some point, observant collectors perceived that they could obtain larger harvests if grain seeds were pulled directly from plants rather than picked off the ground. The process of domestication of plants probably began when people noticed that certain edible plants retained their nutritious grains longer than others and so collected the seeds of these grains and scattered them across fertile soils. When ripe, these plants produced bigger and more concentrated crops. It took a great deal of time for the overall pattern of these steps to be completed, but by the end, a community that supported this kind of innovation realized that it could sustain a larger population than its neighbors. Plant domestication occurred when the structure of the plant naturally retained its seeds even when ripe. With the domesticated plant, seeds could be easily harvested. Most were used for food but some were saved for planting in the next growing cycle, resulting in a steady food supply. The process of gradual domestication of plants happened first in the southern Levant and spread from there into the rest of Southwest Asia.

The domestication of animals ultimately led to one of the great divides in Afro-Eurasian history: the pastoralists versus the agriculturalists.

At about the same time, the domestication of animals was taking place, probably as an independent development concentrated in the central Zagros Mountains, where wild sheep and wild goats were abundant. In other parts of the world, animal domestication preceded that of plants. It, too, was a gradual process that did not require force or domination. A favored explanation is that hunters returned home with very young wild sheep, which then grew up within the human community. They reproduced, and their offspring never returned to the wild. The animals accepted their state of dependence because the humans fed them. Gradually it became clear that controlling animal reproduction was more reliable than hunting, and so domesticated herds became the primary source of protein. This shift probably happened first and quite quickly with the wild sheep that lived in herds on the mountain slopes. When the number of animals under human control and living close to the settlement outstripped the supply of food needed to feed them, members of the community could move them to grassy steppes for grazing. Later this lifeway, called pastoralism, became an important alternative to settled farming. Pastoralists herded domesticated animals, moving them to new pastures on a seasonal basis. Goats, the other main domesticated animal of Southwest Asia, are smarter than sheep but more difficult to bring under control. Probably goats were gradually introduced into herds of sheep as a way to better control herd movement. While goats were far more widely dispersed than sheep, their natural habitat was mountain slopes, not grassy steppes. Furthermore, they were far more independent and less docile in their wild state. Pigs and cattle, even more important domesticated animals, were also brought under human control at this time.

The domestication of animals ultimately led to one of the great divides in Afro-Eurasian history: the pastoralists versus the agriculturalists, or those from the steppe lands versus those from the arable zones (regions suited for crop cultivation). The northern areas of the Eurasian landmass stretching from what is today the Ukraine across Siberia and Mongolia to the Pacific Ocean became the preserve of pastoral peoples, for this region has not been able to support the extensive agriculture necessary for large settled populations until recent times. From here would come the Turkic-speaking peoples of the eighth century CE, who would migrate into the Islamic empire, and the Mongol peoples of the thirteenth century, who would erupt out of the eastern steppe lands and establish the far-flung Mongol empire. As these examples demonstrate, from time to time the pastoral, often nomadic peoples living in northern Afro-Eurasia descended through the natural gateways that linked northern and southern Afro-Eurasia to impose their authority over settled societies.

Historians know much less about these pastoral peoples than about the agriculturalists. Their numbers were small, and they have left fewer archaeological traces or historical records for scholars to work with. But their role in world history is as important as that of the people in settled societies. In Afro-Eurasia, they domesticated horses and developed weapons and techniques that at certain points in history would enable them to conquer sedentary societies. They also transmitted ideas, products, and people across long distances, maintaining the linkages that connected east and west. The archaeological record indicates that full-fledged pastoralism had crystallized in the steppe lands of northern Eurasia by 3000 BCE. By this time, the peoples living there had learned to yoke and ride animals, to milk them, and to use their hair for clothing, as well as to slaughter them for food. Of all the domesticated animals in the steppe lands, the horse was to prove the most important. Because horses provided decisive advantages in transportation and warfare, they gained more value in people's minds than other equally hardworking and serviceable domesticated animals. Thus, horses soon became the measure of household wealth and prestige. Steppe peoples made good use of their horsemanship repeatedly throughout Afro-Eurasian history, imposing themselves and their ways on the settled communities to the south.

SOUTHWEST ASIA: THE REVOLUTION BEGINS

The world's first agricultural revolution occurred in Southwest Asia in an area bounded by the Mediterranean Sea in the west and the Zagros Mountains in the east. Known today as the Fertile Crescent because of the rich soils and regular rainfall that once were characteristic of the region, the area played a leading role in the domestication of wild grasses and the taming of the animals most important to humans. Of the five large mammals that have been vital to humankind for meat, milk, skins (including hair), haulage, and transportation (goats, sheep, pigs, cattle, camels, and horses), only horses were not first domesticated in Southwest Asia, though they soon spread into the area and assumed great importance.

Given the presence of so many of the wild ancestors of humankind's most valuable plants and animals, it is scarcely surprising that Southwest Asia led the agricultural revolution

and was the region in which many of the world's first major city-states appeared (see Chapter 2). An event that prepared the way was a significant warming trend that began about 13,000 years ago and resulted in a profusion of plants and animals, large numbers of which began to live closer to humans.

Around 9000 BCE, in the southern corridor of the Jordan River valley, humans began to domesticate the wild ancestors of barley and wheat. (See Map 1-5.) Many different kinds of wild grasses were already growing abundantly in this region, and barley and wheat proved the easiest to adapt to settled agriculture and the easiest to transport to new locales. Although this changeover from the mere gathering of wild cereals to regular cultivation took many centuries and was marked by failures as well as successes, by the end of the ninth millennium BCE cultivators were selecting and storing seeds and then sowing these seeds in prepared seedbeds. Moreover, as already noted, in the valleys of the Zagros Mountains on the eastern side of the Fertile Crescent, the same kind of experimentation was taking place with animals at around the same time.

One place conspicuous by its lack of involvement in the early spread of these new ways of producing food is the valley of the Tigris and Euphrates rivers, a region that became central to the story of humanity a few thousand years later. There, in what is often called "the cradle of the world's earliest urban civilization," humans lived in very small communities. They found the region's hot, dry summers and harsh, cold winters inhospitable. Annual floods were terrifying and could be highly destructive; all animals, including humans, had to retreat to safer, higher ground. In low flood years, plant life perished for want of water. In high flood years, the destruction of the physical environment from the raging waters was even more devastating. As a consequence, before 5500 BCE, the Tigris-Euphrates floodplain, like many other of the great floodplains of the Eurasian and North African landmass, showed little evidence of human habitation.

MAP 1-5   THE BIRTH OF FARMING IN THE FERTILE CRESCENT

Agriculture production first appeared in the Fertile Crescent, starting roughly at 9000 BCE. Though the process was slow, farmers and herders domesticated a variety of plants and animals over time, a process that led to the rise of large-scale, permanent settlements. What does the map reveal about the environment and natural resources in the Fertile Crescent? What relationship existed between cereal cultivators and herders of goats and sheep? Why was agriculture absent in the region of the southern Tigris and Euphrates rivers during this period?

But as the populations in the surrounding regions began to rise and competition for land and grazing lands became more intense, some enterprising communities slowly moved into the river valley. They developed primitive methods of seasonal irrigation, drawing water from feeder streams into shallow canals that the community maintained. The land was very fertile, as long as it was properly watered, and it produced extraordinarily successful harvests. As a consequence, the communities in the river valley gradually grew until some groups had created small villages and had introduced simple irrigation techniques in the region (see Chapter 2).

EMERGENCE OF AGRICULTURE IN OTHER AREAS

> → *What factors contributed to autonomous innovation in agriculture versus early borrowing?*

Similar agricultural revolutions occurred all over the world in these four or five millennia. They had much in common. The same factors of climatic change, increased knowledge about plants and animals, and the need to develop more efficient ways to feed, house, and promote the survival of larger numbers led peoples in Eurasia, Africa, and the Americas to see the advantages of cultivating plants and domesticating wildlife. In at least five of these locations, and perhaps another four areas, these agricultural revolutions were internally generated, with no influence from the outside. In some locations, notably western Europe, the new ideas and techniques were largely borrowed, and then adapted to local conditions. But wherever this agricultural and social transformation occurred, local variations were important. These variations stemmed from climate, geography, and preexisting social organizations, but they especially reflected the different plants and animals that were suitable to the particular locations. By examining early agriculture in Southeast Asia and the southern part of China in East Asia, where water and rice were critical; in western Europe, where the new cultivators borrowed much from Southwest Asia; in the Americas, which had the disadvantage of few animals that could be domesticated; and finally in Africa, where a fishing culture had many of the same features of the agricultural revolution that was taking place elsewhere, we can observe the broad array of patterns with which humans experimented as they settled down as farmers and herders.

RICE AND WATER IN EAST ASIA

When the glaciers began to melt around 13,000 BCE, and the ocean levels began to rise, environmental changes affected living and subsistence patterns for coastal dwellers in East Asia. Here, too, although under different circumstances, a revolution in food production occurred. (See Map 1-6.) As the temperature warmed, the sea level rose, creating the Japanese islands. Hunters there tracked a diminishing supply of large animals, like giant deer, but all such big game eventually became extinct. Men and women had to find other ways to support themselves, and before long they settled down and became cultivators of the soil. In this postglacial period, divergent human cultures flourished in both northern and southern Japan. In the south, hunters created relatively primitive pebble and flake tools. Those in the northernmost island of Hokkaido prepared sharper blades about a third of an inch wide. Earthenware pottery production also seems to have begun in this period in the south. Converting mud into pottery—a hard, lightweight substance that could be transported—was a major breakthrough and enabled food to be stored more easily and carried over longer distances.

Throughout the rest of East Asia, the spread of lakes, marshes, and rivers created water basins and river systems that became the habitats for large population concentrations and agricultural cultivation. Two newly formed great river basins became densely populated areas and focal points for increasingly intensive agricultural development. These were the Yellow River, which flowed from west to east through the more arid North China plain, and the Yangzi River in central China, which traversed a land of streams and lakes from west to east. Moreover, winds carried alluvial loess topsoil (a loamy soil deposited by river waters) from the northwest regions of the Yellow River, continually extending the reach of the North China coastline as the soil entered the sea. The same loess topsoil was deposited on the North China plain by fierce winter winds sweeping across the Mongolian steppe. In addition to good soil, the region had ample fresh water. Heavy rains brought by strong monsoon winds that blew in from the oceans in the spring and summer watered the crops. Much later on, farmers developed intricate irrigation systems for rice crops (see Chapter 4).

Rice in the south and millet in the north were for East Asia what barley and wheat were for western Asia—staples

> *Converting mud into pottery was a major breakthrough and enabled food to be stored more easily and carried over longer distances.*

→ *What factors contributed to autonomous innovation in agriculture versus early borrowing?*

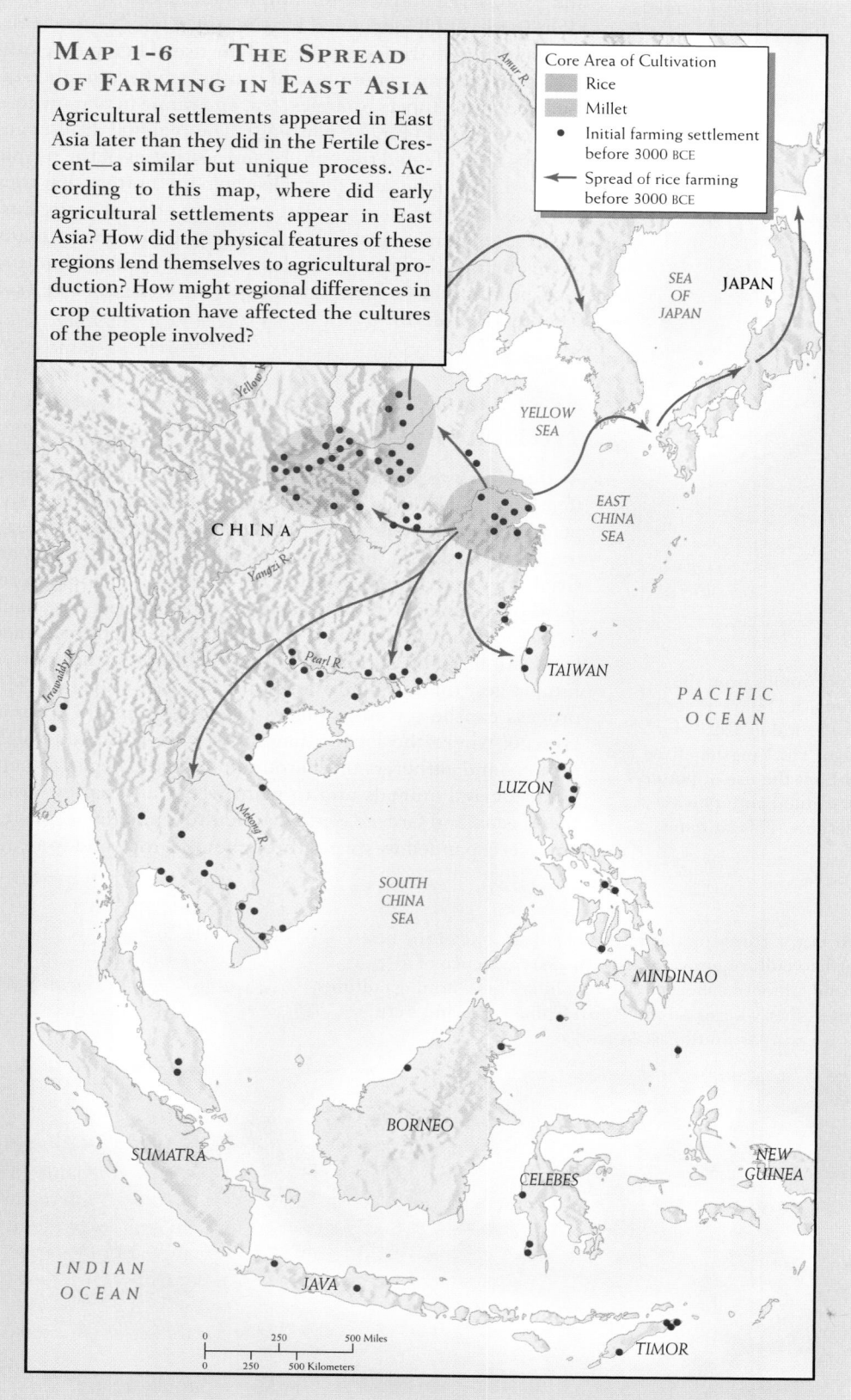

MAP 1-6   THE SPREAD OF FARMING IN EAST ASIA

Agricultural settlements appeared in East Asia later than they did in the Fertile Crescent—a similar but unique process. According to this map, where did early agricultural settlements appear in East Asia? How did the physical features of these regions lend themselves to agricultural production? How might regional differences in crop cultivation have affected the cultures of the people involved?

Core Area of Cultivation
- Rice
- Millet

• Initial farming settlement before 3000 BCE

→ Spread of rice farming before 3000 BCE

adapted to local environments that humans could domesticate. Archaeologists have found evidence of rice cultivation in the Yangzi River valley in 6500 BCE, and millet cultivation in the Yellow River valley in 5500 BCE. Rice and millet cultivation supported a much larger sedentary population. Innovations in grain production came early and spread fairly widely, thanks in part to internal migration and wider contacts. When farmers migrated east and south, they carried with them domesticated millet and rice. In the south, they also came into contact with southern strains of faster-ripening rice originally from Southeast Asia, which they adopted. There is also evidence of early plow cultivation and a wide dissemination of stone shards. Ox plows and water buffalo plowshares were the technical prerequisites for large-scale millet planting in the drier north and the rice-cultivated areas of the wetter south.

Rice was the principal staple, but millet and wheat (which spread to China around 1500 BCE from Southwest Asia) were also fundamental to the food-producing revolution in East Asia. There is some evidence that early maize was grown in China as well, although it soon dropped out of the mix. Each crop depended on ecological suitability and the human knowledge of how to manipulate plants.

The economic breakthrough in China occurred around the early eighth millennium BCE. As elsewhere, the move to settled agriculture was crucial. But also important were advances in pottery making, which enabled the harvesters to store products, and the use of polished stone axes for clearing fields. Each region struck its own adapted combination of crops and animals. Between 8000 and 5000 BCE, northern inhabitants along the Yellow River plain increasingly depended for their livelihoods on cereals, such as millet in the loess soils, and the use of hemp for clothing. In the warmer, more humid south, rice became the staple, along with tubers, oranges, tea, and ramie (a plant whose fibers were used to make clothing). The regional differences in crops also affected the culture and aesthetics of the people involved, as can be seen most clearly in the pottery that they produced for storing crops. Recent discoveries at many East Asian sites demonstrate that food was produced in many places before the more complex royal states arose limiting food production to fewer places but on a larger scale (see Chapters 3 and 4).

SPREAD OF AGRICULTURE TO EUROPE

At the far western fringe of Afro-Eurasia, in Europe, domestication was achieved by the diffusion of existing ideas and peoples from centers where it had already developed. Here, too, as in East Asia, once the new ideas and techniques arrived, they spread rapidly. By 6000–5000 BCE, people in regions of Europe close to the societies of Southwest Asia, such as Greece and the Balkans, were already being transformed from hunters and gatherers into agriculturists who exerted human control over plants and animals. (See Map 1-7.) The process can be traced in places like the Franchthi Cave in Greece, where the local inhabitants, who had been solely hunters and gatherers until around 6000 BCE, began to herd domesticated animals and to plant wheat and barley. From the Aegean and Greece, settled agriculture and domesticated animals expanded westward throughout Europe and were ac-

Large Two-handled Yangshao Pot. This pot comes from the village of Yangshao in Henan Province, along the Yellow River in Northwest China, where remains were first found in 1921 of a people who lived more than 6,000 years ago. The Yangshao lived in small, rammed-earth fortresses and, without the use of pottery wheels, created fine white, red, and black painted pottery with human faces and animal and geometric designs. This jar dates back to the third or second millennium BCE.

Pottery in Banpo Village (c. 4800–4200 BCE). This remarkable, intact village, one of the best-known ditch-enclosed settlements of Yangshao culture, provides us with clear evidence of a sophisticated agriculture based on millet and Chinese cabbage. One of China's first farming cultures, the people of Banpo interacted directly with other villages on the North China Plain and were indirectly in contact with peoples from as far away as Southeast Asia.

→ *What factors contributed to autonomous innovation in agriculture versus early borrowing?*

MAP 1-7   THE SPREAD OF AGRICULTURE IN EUROPE

The spread of agricultural production into Europe after 7000 BCE represents an example of geographic diffusion. Europeans borrowed agricultural techniques and technology from other groups and adapted those to their own situations. Through what two pathways did agriculture spread through Europe? Where did the ideas and techniques originate? How did the spread of agriculture throughout the region alter the physical and social landscape?

companied by the development of communities in which people resided in concentrated groups.

The emergence of agriculture and village life occurred in Europe along two separate paths. The first and most rapid trajectory took place along the northern rim of the Mediterranean Sea. In this area, domestication of crops and animals would have moved westward, following the prevailing sea currents of the Mediterranean, from what is now Turkey through the islands of the Aegean Sea to mainland Greece, and from there to southern and central Italy and Sicily. Whether domestication was accomplished through migration of individuals or through the spread of ideas, connections by sea quickened the pace of the transition. Once the basic elements of domestication had been introduced into the Mediterranean from Southwest Asia, the speed and ease of seaborne communications aided what were astonishingly rapid changes. Almost overnight, hunting and gathering gave way to domesticated agriculture and herding.

The second trajectory took an overland route from Anatolia, across northern Greece into the Balkans, then northwestward along the Danube River into the Hungarian plain, and from there further north and west into the Rhine River valley, in modern-day Germany. Here change was likely the result of the transmission of ideas rather than of population migrations, for community after community adapted to domesticated plants and animals and the new mode of life. This route of agricultural development was slower than that along the Mediterranean for two reasons. First, domesticated crops, or individuals who knew about them, had to travel by land, as there were few large rivers like the Danube. Second, new groups of domesticated plants and animals had to be found that could be grown or herded in the colder and more heavily forested lands of central Europe. Crops had to be planted in the spring and harvested in the autumn, rather than the other way around. Cattle rather than sheep became the dominant herd animals in this northern area.

In Europe, the main cereal crops were wheat and barley, and the main animals herded were sheep, goats, and cattle (all of which were first domesticated in Southwest Asia). Additional plants, such as olives and grape-producing vines, were later domesticated. These changes, however fundamental and important they were, did not bring dramatic material progress. The normal settlement in Europe at this time consisted of a few dozen mud huts. These settlements, although small in numbers, were often made up of typical large "long houses" built of timber and mud, designed to store produce and shelter animals during the long winters. Some settlements were larger, with perhaps sixty to seventy huts—in some rare cases, up to a hundred. Hunting, gathering, and fishing still supplemented in important ways the new settled agriculture and the herding of the newly domesticated animals. The innovators dynamically blended the new ways with the old. About 6000 BCE, hunter-gatherers in southern France, for example, adopted the idea of herding domesticated sheep, but they decided not to plant domesticated crops—*that* would have conflicted too much with their preference for a more mobile life of hunting, which was a traditional part of their economy.

By about 5000–4000 BCE, areas around rivers and in the large plains and flatlands, even where forest cover had yet to be

Franchthi Cave. This cave in southern Greece was used as a living space from about 20,000 years ago until about 3000 BCE. It is one of the most important prehistoric sites for tracing the transmission of ideas and goods from Southwest Asia and the Mediterranean into Europe. Some of the tools found here were constructed of obsidian originating from the island of Melos (well over eighty miles to the east), indicating seaborne contacts at a very early date. There is also evidence that domesticated cereal grains were used here as early as 8,000 years ago, signaling a major change from the inhabitants' previous hunter-gatherer lifestyle.

"Long House." The people who opened up the whole of central Europe to agriculture typically lived in communities of six to twelve "long houses." Although large in size (varying between 60 and 120 feet in length), long houses were built on simple principles: a framework of wooden beams and posts with walls made of mud and woven branches beneath a thatched roof. These dwellings probably sheltered large extended family or kinship units that cooperated to provide the hard work needed to carve out pioneer farming settlements along river valleys. This cutaway reconstruction of a longhouse shows the placement of wall timbers and internal support posts.

fully stripped away, had embraced the new food-producing economy. Elsewhere, notably in the rugged mountain lands that still account for much of Europe's modern-day landscape, hunting and foraging remained the dominant way that humans related to nature. But the transition to settled farming and herding brought with it an enormous rise in population. As agricultural communities produced more and more people, such communities came to be the dominant social organization.

AGRICULTURE IN THE AMERICAS

When people crossed Beringia and trekked southward through the Americas, they set off a major ecological transformation. But they also adapted to habitats that humans had not previously encountered. The flora and fauna of the Americas were different enough to induce the early settlers to devise ways of living that distinguished them from their ancestors in Afro-Eurasia. Then, when the glaciers began to melt around 12,500 BCE, and the land bridge between East Asia and America eventually was covered by water, the Americas and their peoples truly became a whole world apart.

Early humans in America made use of basic chipped blades and pointed spears, pursuing their prey among the herds of large mammals that included mastodons, large woolly mammoths, and bison. In doing so, they extended the hunting traditions they had learned in Afro-Eurasia, establishing campsites and moving with their herds. These hunters were known as "Clovis people" because the typical arrowhead point that they used was first found by archaeologists at a site near Clovis, New Mexico. They were so mobile that the remains of the weaponry are scattered in archaeological sites all over North America.

For many years, scientists thought that the Clovis communities had wiped out the large Ice Age mammals that they found in America. But recent research suggests that it is more likely that climatic change destroyed the indigenous plants and trees, and thus the feeding grounds of large prehistoric mammals, and that what was once abundant forage became scarce. The vast spruce forests that had fed the great mastodons, for instance, shrank into isolated pockets, leaving increasingly isolated and undernourished mastodons vulnerable to human and animal predators, until they vanished. The tall grassland prairies gave way to areas with short grass; and where there had been short grass, cacti took over. As in Afro-Eurasia, the advent of a long warming cycle compelled those who entered the Americas to adapt to different ecological niches and to create new subsistence strategies. Thus, in the woodland area of the present-day northeastern United States, hunters learned to trap smaller wild animals for food and furs. To supplement the protein gained from meat and fish, these people also dug for roots and gathered berries. What is important is that most communities adapted to the settled agricultural economy, but they did not fully abandon basic survival strategies of hunting and gathering.

Food-producing changes in the Americas were different from those in Afro-Eurasia because this area did not witness the same relatively sudden cluster of innovations that revolutionized agriculture in Southwest Asia and elsewhere. Tools ground from stone, rather than chipped implements, appeared in the Tehuacán Valley by 6700 BCE, and evidence of plant domestication there can be dated as far back as 5000 BCE. But villages, pottery making, and sustained population growth came later. For many of the early American inhabitants, the life of hunting, trapping, and fishing went on much as it had for millennia. The remains of ancient shell fishing can be found throughout the coastal Americas, from California to Brazil. Along the Pacific coast, for instance, communities formed around fishing cultures, many relying on dugout canoes and spears to obtain food.

On the coast of what is now Peru, people primarily found their food by fishing and gathering shellfish from the Pacific, and archaeological remains include the remnants of fishnets, bags, baskets and textile implements, gourds for carrying water, and stone knives, choppers, scrapers, bone awls, and thorn needles. Oddly enough, however, there is no evidence of watercraft used in this area. Hundreds if not thousands of villages dotted the seashores and riverbanks of the Americas. Some had made breakthroughs in the management of fire that enabled them to manufacture pottery; others devised irrigation and water sluices in floodplains. And some even began to send their fish catches inland in return for agricultural produce.

The earliest evidence of plant experimentation in Mesoamerica dates from around 7000 BCE, and it went on for a long time. Maize, squash, and beans were first found in what is now central Mexico and became staples of Mesoamerican diets. Small seeds of maize were foraged, peeled from ears that were no longer than a few inches long, and planted by early settlers. Maize offered some real advantages to its consumers. It was easily stored, relatively imperishable, nutritious, and easy to cultivate alongside other plants, though it was mostly complementary to plants like beans, which replenished the soils with nitrogen that maize plants sucked up. Nonetheless, it took fully 5,000 years, until about 2000 BCE, for farmers to domesticate maize completely—that is, to settle in one place, live there year-round, plant maize, and stay beyond a single growing and harvesting cycle. Over the years, farmers had to mix and breed different strains of maize for it to evolve from the thin spikes of seeds to cobs rich with kernels, with a single plant able to yield big, thick ears to feed a growing permanent population. Thus the agricultural

changes afoot in Mesoamerica were slow and late in maturing. The same gradual process of change was even more marked in South America, where early settlers relied even more heavily on hunting and gathering.

Across the Americas, the settled, agrarian communities, when they finally did appear, relied on a variety of crops. They found that legumes (beans), grains (maize), and tubers (potatoes) all complemented each other in keeping the soil fertile and offering a balanced diet. Yet as peoples in the Americas formed permanent communities, they did not turn to domesticated animals as an alternative source of protein. Unlike in Afro-Eurasia, where people used domesticated animals for meat or milk, in the Americas animals were not generally domesticated as a source of food (aside from some Andean camelids such as the llama and the vicuña, and the turkey in Mesoamerica). In only a few pockets of the Andean highlands in South America is there evidence of the domestication of tiny guinea pigs, which were, at best, tasty but unfilling meals.

Head of Mayan Corn God. Corn, or maize, was a revered crop in Mesoamerica, where people ritually prayed to their deities for good harvests. Notice the crown made not of precious metals and stones but of corn husks as an example of the cultural emphasis on maize.

Primary Source

A MESOAMERICA CREATION MYTH

The discovery and cultivation of maize was so central to the livelihood of Mesoamericans that the crop was seen by many as the fount of humanity. This excerpt from the Mayan classic text Popol Vuh *describes the making of the first humans from ears of corn.*

Here, then, is the beginning of when it was decided to make man, and when what must enter into the flesh of man was sought.

And the Forefathers, the Creators and Makers, who were called Tepeu and Gucumatz said: "The time of dawn has come, let the work be finished, and let those who are to nourish and sustain us appear, the noble sons, the civilized vassals: let man appear, humanity, on the face of the earth." Thus they spoke.

They assembled, came together and held council in the darkness and in the night; then they sought and discussed, and here they reflected and thought. In this way their decisions came clearly to light and they found and discovered what must enter into the flesh of man.

It was just before the sun, the moon, and the stars appeared over the Creators and Makers.

From Paxil, from Cayalá, as they were called, came the yellow ears of corn and the white ears of corn.

These are the names of the animals which brought the food: *yac* (the mountain cat), *utiú* (the coyote), *quel* (a small parrot), and *hob* (the crow). These four animals gave tidings of the yellow ears of corn and the white ears of corn, they told them that they should go to Paxil and they showed them the road to Paxil.

And thus they found the food, and this was what went into the flesh of created man, the made man; this was his blood; of this the blood of man was made. So the corn entered [into the formation of man] by the work of the Forefathers.

And in this way they were filled with joy, because they had found a beautiful land, full of pleasures, abundant in ears of yellow corn and ears of white corn, and abundant also in *pataxte* and cacao, and in innumerable *zapotes, anonas, jocotes, nantzes, marasanos,* and honey. There was an abundance of delicious food in those villages called Paxil and Cayalá. There were foods of every kind, small and large foods, small plants and large plants.

The animals showed them the road. And then grinding the yellow corn and the white corn, Xmucané made nine drinks, and from this food came the strength and the flesh, and with it they created the muscles and the strength of man. This the Forefathers did, Tepeu and Gucumatz, as they were called.

After that they began to talk about the creation and the making of our first mother and father; of yellow corn and of white corn they made their flesh; of corn meal dough they made the arms and the legs of man. Only dough of corn meal went into the flesh of our first fathers, the four men, who were created.

→ *How does this text represent the relationship between (maize) food and (human) flesh? What were the variety of ways that maize served creation?*

SOURCE: *Popol Vuh: The Sacred Book of Ancient Quiché Maya,* English version by Delia Goetz and Sylvanus G. Morley from the Spanish translation by Adrián Recinos (Norman: University of Oklahoma Press, 1950), pp. 165–67.

Nor did people in the Americas tame animals capable of protecting villages (as dogs did in Afro-Eurasia), or carrying heavy loads over long distances (as camels did in Afro-Eurasia). Only llamas could be made to haul heavy loads—but their patience and cooperation were notoriously limited. Llamas can be considered at best only semidomesticates, mainly useful for clothing. Nonetheless, the domestication of plants and animals in the Americas, as well as the concentration of population into villages and clans, does suggest a great deal of diversification and refinement of technique. But the centers

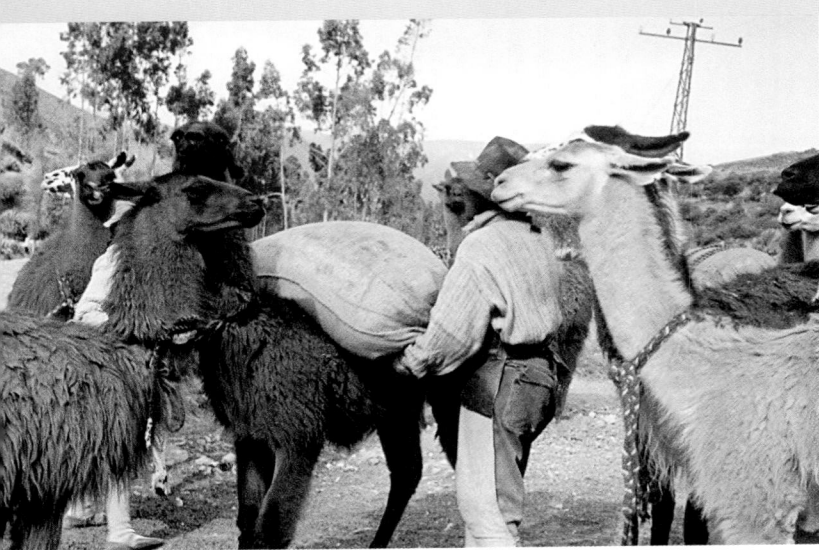

Llamas. The peoples of the Americas were unable to domesticate beasts of burden such as camels, horses, or oxen. Their closest option was the finicky llama, which had neither the strength nor the stamina of its counterparts in Afro-Eurasia. Llamas were more prized as a source of wool than as pack animals.

of this kind of activity were many, scattered, and more isolated from each other than those in Afro-Eurasia, and thus were much more narrowly adapted to local ecozones, without much exchange and learning between them. This fragmentation in human migration and communication was a major distinguishing force in the gradual pace of change in the Americas and contributed to their taking a path of development separate from Afro-Eurasia's.

AFRICA: THE RACE WITH THE SAHARA

Some societies, like those in Southwest Asia and East Asia, were autonomous innovators, while others, like those in Europe, were early borrowers. What about Africa, where the story began? The evidence for settled agriculture in different African regions is still uncertain and far from uniform. But most scholars believe that the Sahel area—a territory running across Africa just south of the Sahara Desert—was most likely the location where hunters and gatherers became settled farmers and herders without any outside help. In this area, what now appears to be a move to settled agriculture, including the domestication of larger herd animals, took place two millennia before it did along the Mediterranean in North Africa. In fact, the Sahel agricultural revolution was so early that it cannot be seen as an example of a diffusion of techniques from Southwest Asia via the Nile River valley. From this innovative heartland, Africans carried their agricultural breakthroughs elsewhere across the landmass. (See Map 1-8.)

The Sahel was colder and moister 10,000 years ago than it is today. The region was lush with grassland vegetation and

teeming with animals. Before long, the inhabitants had made sorghum their principal food crop. Yet as the world became warmer and more arid and the Sahara Desert expanded, men and women living in this region had to disperse and take their agricultural and herding skills into other parts of Africa. Some went south to the tropical rain forests of West Africa, while others trekked eastward into the Ethiopian highlands. In their new environments, farmers searched for new crops that could be domesticated. The rain forests of West Africa yielded root crops, particularly the yam and cocoyam, both of which became the principal life-sustaining foodstuffs for these populations. The enset plant, which is similar to the banana, played the same role in the Ethiopian highlands.

In sub-Saharan Africa, the area extending far southward below the Sahara Desert, where population grew it did not concentrate into major urban hubs. But in the wetter and more temperate locations in the vast Sahel region, particularly in the upland massifs and their foothills, villages and towns came into being. Residents constructed stone dwellings and underground wells and granary storage areas. In one such population center, fourteen circular houses were built facing each other so as to form a main thoroughfare, or a street. Recent archaeological investigations have unearthed remarkable rock engravings and paintings, one often composed on top of another, filling up vast expanses of the cave dwellings' walls. Many images portray in fascinating detail the changeover from hunting and gathering to pastoralism that was in full swing 5,000 to 6,000 years ago. Caves abounded with pictures of cattle, which were a mainstay of these early men and women. The cave illustrations also depict day-to-day activities, for the artists drew men and women undertaking household chores, living in conical huts, crushing grain on stone, and riding bareback on their oxen, with women always sitting behind the men. Yet, around 4,000 years ago, the warming and drying of the earth's climate drove the Sahelian inhabitants out of the region in search of a place where they could preserve their way of life.

If the definition of settled agriculture includes the systematic collection of aquatic life from lakes and streams, then it is quite possible that the move to settled agriculture, with an accompanying creation of settled village life, occurred all across the southern Sahara region approximately 11,000 years ago, even before its emergence in Southwest Asia. This, at least, is the view of Christopher Ehret, an ethnolinguistic historian of Africa. The region where Ehret believes that this agricultural revolution occurred was around the shores of Lake Chad, in the central zone of West Africa, which is today at the edge of the Sahara Desert. Then, the lake covered an area ten times its current size. Harvesting the lake's fish enabled the peoples living in this area to expand their populations, establish substantial villages, and create a distinctive way of life that included elaborate rites of passage from childhood to adult status, burial ceremonies, and an elaborate set of highly sophisticated religious beliefs. Unfortunately for Africa's first settled aquatic cultivators, the world grew hotter

MAP 1-8　　THE SPREAD OF FARMING IN AFRICA

African societies living south of the Sahara Desert developed their own version of agricultural production after 6000 BCE. Locate the Sahel region on this map. How did the expansion of the Sahara Desert affect the diffusion of agriculture in the Sahel? Compare the diffusion of agriculture in the Sahel versus that in Europe (Map 1-7). What similarities and differences are evident?

North African Cave Painting. This cave painting comes from Tassili n'Ajjer, highlands in the Sahara Desert, and dates from the second millennium BCE. In this illustration, early men and women covered the walls with pictures of daily life: children tending calves tethered to a rope. The white ovals to the left represent huts.

and more arid. Small lakes dried up, and so did rivers and streams. The largest lakes did survive, but they lacked the fish stocks that had fed expanding human populations. Apart from the extraordinary visual record that they left, Africa's first settled agrarian and fishing communities disappeared virtually without a trace, only to be discovered 11,000 years later at the hands of ingenious archaeologists.

REVOLUTIONS IN SOCIAL ORGANIZATION

> → *How did agricultural revolutions foster new communal hierarchies and interaction?*

With the domestication of plants and animals came settlement in agricultural villages. These villages were near fields for accessible sowing and cultivating, and pastures for herding livestock. Villagers worked together to clear fields, plant crops, and celebrate rituals in which they sang and danced and sacrificed to nature and the spirit world for fertility, rain, and successful harvests. They also produced stone tools to work the fields and clay and stone pots or woven baskets to collect and store the crops. As populations rose, and lands yielded surplus food, some villagers stopped working the fields to become specialized craftworkers, devoting their time to producing pottery, baskets, textiles, or

tools, which they could trade to farmers and pastoralists for food. Craft specialization and the buildup of surpluses contributed to early stratification, as some people accumulated more land and wealth while others led the rituals and sacrifices.

EARLY SETTLEMENT IN VILLAGES

The earliest dwelling places of the first settled communities were quite simple structures—little more than circular pits with stones piled on top of each other to form walls, above which was stretched a cover that rested on poles. Social structures were equally simple; they were clanlike and based on kinship networks. With time, however, population growth enabled clans to expand their size. As the use of natural resources intensified, specialized tasks evolved and divisions of labor came into being. Some members of the community procured and prepared food; others built terraces and defended the settlement. Later, walls were built and clamped together with wooden fittings. And as construction techniques changed, the shape of the houses altered from the traditional circular plan to a rectangular one. The rectangular shape is not found in nature, and it is thus a truly human mark on the landscape. Certainly this new shape reflected new mental attitudes and social behaviors. In rectangular houses, walls did more than support and protect: they also divided and separated. Because it was easier to build interior walls leaning against flat surfaces, privacy improved and family members were physically parted. Human relations would never be the same as they had been in the highly egalitarian arrangements of the mobile hunters and gatherers.

Although the food-producing changes were gradual and widely dispersed, a few communities stand out as pioneers in the long transition from hunting and gathering to agrarian and pastoral life. Around Wadi en-Natuf, located about ten miles from present-day Jerusalem, a group of people known historically as Natufians began to dig sunken pit shelters and to chip stone tools around 12,500 BCE. Over the course of the next two millennia or so, these bands stayed in one place, improving their toolmaking techniques, building circular shelters, and developing a variety of ways to preserve and prepare food. They dwelled in solidly built structures, buried their dead, and harvested grains. Although they did not plant seeds and did not give up hunting, their growing knowledge of wild plants paved the way for later breakthroughs.

It was only a matter of time before the full transition to settled agriculture and full-scale pastoralism took place. As noted above, the agricultural revolution spread in all directions. In the highlands of eastern Anatolia, the area that encompasses modern-day Turkey, large settlements were arranged around monumental public buildings with impressive stone carvings that attest to the complexity of social organization. In central Anatolia, at the site of Çatal Höyük, a dense honeycomb of settlements was filled with rooms that were covered with wall paintings and sculptures of wild bulls, hunters, and pregnant women. The use of art and imagery to provide identity and to master the powerful forces of the cosmos is a human characteristic continued unbroken from the time of the early cave artists. The difference now was that men and women made their own structures, where they gathered to worship the forces of nature and the spirit world, interacting with each other according to rituals that defined their place in society.

After 5500 BCE, people began to move into the river valley in Mesopotamia (in present-day Iraq) along the Tigris and Euphrates rivers, and small villages began to appear. They began to work together to build simple irrigation systems to water their fields. Perhaps because of the increased demands for community work to maintain the irrigation systems, the communities in southern Mesopotamia became stratified, with some people having more power than others. We can see from the burial sites and the large number of public buildings uncovered by archaeologists that for the first time, communities had people who were born into a higher status rather than acquiring high status through the merits of their work. A class of people who had access to more luxury goods, and who lived in bigger and better houses, now became part of the social organization.

The agricultural revolution created farmers and herders where once there had been only hunters and gatherers. Agriculture required settled communities and because it provided surplus food, populations could easily increase. As populations grew, they eventually began to concentrate in ever larger centers, where they formed the first towns. Settled agricultural societies could finally produce enough sustenance to feed large numbers of people who did not themselves have to produce food and could move from the countryside to urban settings. The next chapter will explore early urbanization in more detail. What is important for us to emphasize here is that changes dependent on agriculture enabled larger numbers of people to live together in denser concentrations. Rapid population expansion also followed in the wake of agriculture and herding. By 1000 BCE, the world's population had reached 50 million, and the household, with its dominant male, had replaced the small, relatively egalitarian band as the primary social unit.

MEN, WOMEN, AND THE GROWTH OF DRUDGERY

Over the 4- to 5-million-year-long history of humans and their hominid ancestors, one of the fundamental divisions manifest in the fossil remains of early hominids and humans is that between males and females. The existence of this division naturally raises questions about what relationships between the two sexes were like in prehistoric times. Certainly, for millions of years, basic differences in biology affected differences in the roles played by men and women. The fact that females gave birth to offspring and that males did not was the driving force that determined female and male actions and behaviors and attitudes toward each other, at least up to the appearance of *Homo erectus*. Thus, it is a mistake to think of male-female interactions as "gender" (social and cultural) relations when, in reality, they are biologically based sexual

Çatal Höyük. Discovered in 1958 by the British archaeologist James Mellaart, this site is notable for providing information on the global transition from hunting and gathering to urban dwelling. Çatal Höyük is located in modern Turkey and dates from the eighth millennium BCE.

MOTHERING AND MILKING

One of the dividing lines among all animals, humans included, involves child rearing and the division of labor between mothers and fathers. In this text, the renowned primatologist Sarah Blaffer Hrdy argues that breast-feeding among mammals was a major factor shaping women's fortunes.

"Is sex destiny?" When this question is posed, it's a safe bet that the underlying agenda has to do with what women *should* be doing. Should they be home caring for their children or off pursuing other interests? A comparative look at other creatures that (like humans) breed cooperatively and share responsibilities for rearing young with other group members reveals that sex *per se* is not the issue. Lactation is.

Caretakers of both sexes, wet-nurses, even "daycare"—none of these are uniquely human, nor particularly new. They are standard features of many cooperatively breeding species. As we saw, cooperative breeding is exquisitely well developed in insects such as honeybees and wasps. Shared provisioning is also common among birds such as acorn woodpeckers, bee-eaters, dunnocks, and scrub jays. Although cooperative breeding is uncommon among mammals generally, it is richly developed in species such as wolves, wild dogs, dwarf mongooses, elephants, tamarins, marmosets, and humans. In all these animals, individuals other than the mother ("allomothers") help her provision or otherwise care for her young. Typically, allomothers will include the mother's mate (often but not necessarily the genetic progenitor). Individuals other than either parent ("alloparents") also help. These helpers are most often recruited from kin who are not yet ready to reproduce themselves, or from subordinates who do not currently—or may never have—better options. In the human case, the most important alloparents are often older, post-reproductive relatives who have already reproduced.

Among mammals, the trend toward having young who require costly long-term care began modestly enough. It probably began with an egg-laying brooding reptile that started to secrete something milklike. Such egg-layers gradually developed glands especially equipped for milk production. Only among mammals did one sex come to specialize in manufacturing custom-made baby formula, to provide something critical for infant survival that the other sex could not. This peculiarity has had many ramifications, especially as infants became dependent for longer periods in the primate line.

The ante was upped substantially when primate mothers, instead of bearing litters, began focusing care on one baby at a time. These singletons were born mature enough to cling to their mother's fur, to be carried by her right from birth and for months thereafter. Whether or not this intimate and prolonged association is the mother's destiny, *sex* is not the issue. Lactation is.

What Is Lactation About?

Other forms of caretaking—fathers brooding eggs, bringing food, protecting babies—are not nearly so sex-specific. Even gestation is a function that in rare cases (for example, the sea horse) a male takes on. But not lactation. Why—with the sole exception of one rare fruit bat—does lactation appear to be exclusively female? How did these curious secretions get started?

At first glance, a mother sea horse might seem to have a sweet deal. She sallies up to her mate, injects her eggs into his belly pouch, and then, carefree, propels herself off to feed and make more eggs. Meanwhile, back at the male's pouch, the sea-mare's last batch is fertilized, toted, and kept safe in the ballooning brood chamber of the now extremely pregnant male. At birth, as many as 1,500 fully formed but still minuscule and defenseless sea-foals are sprayed out into the open ocean. The sea around them teems with predators and competitors, many bigger than they are. Forced to fend for themselves immediately after birth, almost all starve.

Viviparity means keeping infants safe inside some sealed chamber within the parent's body till they can be born alive, as opposed to protected in an egg fill hatching. But by itself, viviparity offers tiny, still helpless creatures only the slimmest toehold on posterity. Why not linger in the womb longer, and grow bigger before venturing into the world?

→ *How does human child rearing affect mothers differently from fathers? Why is the difference more marked among humans than other species?*

Source: From Sarah Blaffer Hrdy, *Mother Nature: Maternal Instincts and How They Shape the Human Species* (New York: Ballantine Books, 2000), pp. 121–23.

relations. One can speak of the emergence of "gendered" relations and roles only with the appearance of modern humans (*Homo sapiens*) and perhaps Neanderthals. Only when humans began to think imaginatively and in complex symbolic ways and when they gave voice to these perceptions in a spoken language, perhaps no sooner than 150,000 years ago, did such true gender categories as *man* and *woman* crystallize. As these cultural aspects of human life took shape, the distinction between "men" and "women," rather than between "males" and "females," began to be made, and culture joined biology in governing human interactions.

Gender roles became more pronounced and fixed in the stages leading up to and during the food-producing revolution. As human communities became larger, more stratified, and more powerful following the transition to an agriculturally based way of life, the rough gender egalitarianism of hunting and gathering societies eroded. An enhanced human power over the environment did not confer equal power on all. In one view, women were the net losers of the agricultural revolution. Women's knowledge of wild plants had contributed decisively to early settled agriculture, but women did not necessarily benefit from the transition to which their expertise contributed. Indeed, a well-known student of primate behavior, Sarah Hrdy, has called the settled agricultural transformation a "Great Leap Sideways," because advances for some people meant losses for others.

Advances in agrarian tools, notably the plow, made heavy work much more onerous for some people than for others, especially undermining the status women had held as farmers. Men, who had been more involved in hunting and gathering, took charge of yoking animals to plows, leaving to women the backbreaking and repetitive tasks of planting, weeding, harvesting, and grinding the grain into flour. Thus, although agricultural innovations augmented productivity, they also increased the drudgery of work, especially for women. The unequal effects on men and women are visible, for instance, in fossils found in Abu Hureyra, Syria, where the bones found by archaeologists displayed the evidence of a harsh working life. Damage to the vertebrae, osteoarthritis in the toes, and curved and arched femurs suggest that the work of bending over and kneeling in the fields especially took its toll on female agriculturalists. These maladies do not usually appear among the bone remains of hunters and gatherers.

The stratification of men and women during this era also affected power relations within households and communities. The senior male figure became the dominant figure in these households—and even beyond, in the new political and cultural hierarchies, where societies favored males over females in leadership positions. The agricultural revolution marked a greater division among men, and particularly between men and women. Where the agricultural transformation was most widespread, and where population densities especially began to grow in Afro-Eurasia, the social and political differences created inequalities within society, espe-cially along gender lines, and patriarchy, or the "rule of senior males" within households, began to spread around the globe.

CONCLUSION

Over thousands of generations, African hominids evolved from other primates into *Homo erectus* hominids, who then wandered very far from their native habitats to fill other landmasses. They did so in successive waves, each responding to worldwide alternations of glaciation and melting. These predecessors of humans had some common features with modern humans. They stood erect, made stone tools, lived in extended families, and, to a certain extent, communicated with each other (by means other than language). An ability to adapt to environmental change was what increasingly separated humans from other animal species. *Homo sapiens*, who had larger brains than other hominids and are what we know as "modern humans," also emerged in Africa and trickled out of the world's largest landmass about 100,000 years ago. Since *Homo sapiens* had greater adaptive skills, when a cooling cycle returned they were better prepared to face the elements, and eventually they eclipsed their genetic cousins. One critical variable was their ability to use language, to engage in abstract, representational thought, and to convey the lessons of experience to their descendants and neighbors. Thus it was that modern humans stored and shared knowledge, thereby enhancing their adaptive abilities.

While modern men and women share a recent African heritage, people adapted over hundreds of generations to the specific environments that they encountered as they began to fill the earth's corners. Some settled near lakes and took to fishing, while others hunted large mammals in northern steppes. But everywhere, the dependence on nature yielded broadly similar social and cultural structures. It took another warming cycle for people from Africa to the Americas slowly to put down their hunting weapons and begin to domesticate animals and plants.

The changeover to settled agriculture was not uniform across the world. There were some basic commonalities: reliance on wood, stone, and natural fibers to make tools, shelter, and materials for cultural expressions, as well as increasing social hierarchies, especially a status differential between men and women. But with time, the social geography of the world's regions began to vary as communities became more settled. The process of divergence between the world's parts gathered speed as humans learned to modify nature to fit their needs. The varieties of animals that could be domesticated, as well as differences in climatic conditions and topography, all shaped the early ways in which people drifted apart in spite of their recent common origins.

Still, there was one important commonality: the scale and complexity of settlements and communities across the world had a limit. The vast majority of people in the age before the agricultural revolution continued a life of foraging for food supplies. Villages grew—but they did not become cities. Moreover, although fishing and farming enabled settled communities to spring up, pastoral communities that followed moving herds of animals or migrating schools of fish also spread. These peoples moved across mountains or deserts to find fresh pastures for their animals or seek waters where fish were spawning. Around the world, the remains of rudimentary pottery, stone tools, and rustic adobe and stone villages give us pictures of worlds that were almost exclusively rural, largely horizontal in social structure, and still very much dependent on the natural flow of fresh water and fertility of soils. As we will see in the next chapter, another round of technical advances would be necessary before humans in some areas could further change their relationship to nature and in so doing create the foundations for the world's first highly complex societies.

STUDY QUESTIONS

 WWNORTON.COM/STUDYSPACE

1. Explain how evolutionary biologists and archaeologists in recent decades have transformed our understanding of human origins. What tools and discoveries led them to their conclusions?
2. Describe the evolutionary process through which *Homo sapiens* emerged. Was it a linear progression?
3. Analyze the advantages that art and language gave *Homo sapiens* over other species. How did art and language contribute to the domestication of plants and animals and the spread of agriculture?
4. List the nine regions where agricultural production first emerged. What common factors existed in all of these places that allowed for the domestication of plants and animals?
5. Explain the conditions that allowed agriculture to emerge first in Southwest Asia.
6. Analyze the advantages and disadvantages of agricultural production versus nomadic foraging. How were agricultural or pastoral communities different from those of hunters and gatherers?

FURTHER READINGS

Arsuaga, Juan Luis, *The Neanderthal's Necklace: In Search of the First Thinkers*, translated by Anthony Klatt (2002). A stimulating overview of prehistory that focuses on the Neanderthals and compares them with *Homo sapiens*.

Barker, Graeme, *Agricultural Revolution in Prehistory: Why Did Foragers Become Farmers* (2006). The most recent, truly global, and up-to-date study of this momentous event in world history.

Bellwood, Peter, *First Farmers: The Origins of Agricultural Societies* (2005). A state-of-the-art global history of the origins of agriculture including recent archaeological, linguistic, and microbiological data.

Bogucki, Peter, *The Origins of Human Society* (1999). An authoritative overview of prehistory.

Cauvin, Jacques, *The Birth of the Gods and the Origins of Agriculture*, translated by Trevor Watkins from the original French published in 1994 (2000). An important work on the agricultural revolution of Southwest Asia and the evolution of symbolic thinking at this time.

Cavalli-Sforza, Luigi Luca, *Genes, Peoples, and Languages*, translated by Mark Selestad from the original French published in 1996 (2000). An expert's introduction to the use of gene re-

Chronology

15 mya*	10 mya	5 mya	1 mya

▌ *Global climate cooling; apes move down from trees and become bipedal, 10–15 mya*

Orrorin tugenensis *appears, 6 mya* ▌

Australopithecus africanus *hominid species appears, 3 mya* ▌

Homo habilus *appears, 2.5 mya* ▌

Homo erectus *appears, 1–2.5 mya* ▌

Beginnings of Ice Age across the Northern Hemisphere ▌

Homo erectus *migration across Afro-Eurasia*

*millions of years ago

search for revealing new information about the evolution of human beings in the distant past.

Childe, V. Gordon, *What Happened in History* (1964). A classic work by one of the pioneers in studying the early history and evolution of human beings. Though superseded in many respects, it is still an important place to start one's reading and a work of great power and emotion.

Clark, J. Desmond, and Steven A. Brandt (eds.), *From Hunters to Farmers: The Causes and Consequences of Food Production in Africa* (1984). Excellent essays on the agricultural revolution.

Coon, Carleton Stevens, *The Story of Man; from the First Human to Primitive Culture and Beyond*, 2nd ed. (1962). An important early work on the evolution of humans, emphasizing the distinctiveness of "races" around the world.

Cunliffe, Barry (ed.), *The Oxford Illustrated Prehistory of Europe* (1994). The definitive work on early European history.

Ehrenberg, Margaret, *Women in Prehistory* (1989). What was the role of women in hunting and gathering societies, and how greatly were women affected by the agricultural revolution? The author offers a number of stimulating generalizations.

Ehret, Christopher, *The Civilizations of Africa: A History to 1800* (2002). Although this is a general history of Africa, the author, a linguist and an expert on early African history, offers new information and new overviews of African peoples in very ancient times.

Fagan, Brian, *People of the Earth: An Introduction to World Prehistory* (1989). An authoritative overview of early history, widely used in classrooms.

Fage, J. D., and Roland Oliver (eds.), *The Cambridge History of Africa*, 8 vols. (1975–1984). A pioneering work of synthesis by two of the first and foremost scholars of the history of the African continent. Volume 1 deals with African prehistory.

Frison, George C., *Survival by Hunting: Prehistoric Human Predators and Animal Prey* (2004). An archaeologist applies his knowledge of animal habitats, behavior, and hunting strategies to an examination of prehistoric hunting practices in the North American Great Plains and Rocky Mountains.

Gebauer, Anne Birgitte, and T. Douglas Price (eds.), *Transition to Agriculture in Prehistory* (1992). Excellent essays on the agricultural revolution, especially those written by the two editors.

Johnson, Donald, Lenora Johnson, and Blake Edgar, *Ancestors: In Search of Human Origins* (1999). A good overview of human evolution, with insightful essays on *Homo erectus* and *Homo sapiens*.

Jones, Steve, Robert Martin, and David Pilbeam (eds.), *The Cambridge Encyclopedia of Human Evolution* (1992). A superb guide to a wide range of subjects, crammed with up-to-date information on the most controversial and obscure topics of human evolution and early history.

Ki-Zerbo, J. (ed.), *Methodology and African Prehistory*, vol. 1 of the UNESCO General History of Africa (1981). A general history of Africa, written for the most part by scholars of African descent.

Klein, Richard G., and Blake Edger, *The Dawn of Human Culture* (2002). A fine and reliable guide to the tangled history of human evolution.

Leakey, Richard, *The Origin of Humankind* (1994). A readable and exciting account of human evolution, written by the son of the pioneering archaeologists Louis and Mary Leakey, a scholar of equal stature to his parents.

Lewin, Roger, *The Origin of Modern Humans* (1993). Yet another good overview of human evolution, with useful chapters on early art and the use of symbols.

Loewe, Michael, and Edward Shaughnessy (eds.), *The Cambridge History of Ancient China: From the Origins of Civilization to 221 B.C.* (1999). A good review of the archaeology of ancient China.

Mellaart, James, *Çatal Höyük: A Neolithic Town in Anatolia* (1967). A detailed description of one of the first towns associated with the agricultural revolution in Southwest Asia.

Mithen, Steven, *The Prehistory of the Mind: The Cognitive Origins of Art and Science* (1996). A stimulating discussion of the impact

200,000 ya**	150,000 ya	100,000 ya	50,000 ya	1 CE

Climate and environmental shift in Africa
Neanderthal evident in Europe, 200,000 ya

Homo sapiens emerges in Africa and migrates ∎
to other regions, 120,000–50,000 ya

Cave art develops in Europe, 30,000 ya ∎
Human migration from Afro-Eurasia to Americas begins, 18,000 ya ∎
Ice age, 16,000–10,000 BCE ∎
Beginnings of agricultural revolution in Southwest Asia, 9000 BCE ∎
Millet cultivation in Yellow River valley develops, 6500 BCE ∎
Rice cultivation in Yangzi River valley develops, 5500 BCE ∎
Domestication of plants and animals begins, 6700–2000 BCE ∎
Agricultural settlements using Southwest Asian domesticants emerges, 6000–5000 BCE ∎
Pastoralism begins in Inner Asia, 3000 BCE ∎
Maize cultivation emerges in central Mexico, 2000 BCE ∎

years ago

of biological and cultural evolution on the cognitive structure of the human mind.

Olson, Steve, *Mapping Human History: Genes, Race, and Our Common Origins* (2003). Using the findings of genetics and attacking the racial thinking of an earlier generation of archaeologists, the author writes powerfully about the unity of all human beings.

Price, T. Douglas (ed.), *Europe's First Farmers* (2000). A discussion of the agricultural revolution in Europe.

Price, T. Douglas, and Anne Birgitte Gebauer (eds.), *Last Hunters-First Farmers: New Perspectives on the Prehistoric Transition to Agriculture* (1996). An exciting collection of essays by some of the leading scholars in the field studying the transition from hunting and gathering to settled agriculture.

Scarre, Chris (ed.), *The Human Past: World Prehistory and the Development of Human Societies* (2005). An encyclopedia and an overview rolled up into one mammoth volume, written by leading figures in the field of early human history.

Shaw, Thurstan, Paul Sinclair, Bassey Andah, and Alex Okpoko (eds.), *The Archaeology of Africa: Food, Metals, and Towns* (1993). Up-to-date research on the earliest history of human beings in Africa.

Smith, Bruce D., *The Emergence of Agriculture* (1995). How early humans domesticated wild animals and plants.

Stringer, Christopher, and Robin McKie, *African Exodus: The Origins of Modern Humanity* (1996). Detailed data on why Africa was the source of human origins and why *Homo sapiens* is a recent wanderer out of the African continent.

Tattersall, Ian, *The Fossil Trail: How We Know What We Think We Know about Human Evolution* (1995). A passionately written book about early archaeological discoveries and the centrality of Africa in human evolution.

Van Oosterzee, Penny, *Dragon Bones: The Story of Peking Man* (2000). Describes how the late-nineteenth-century unearthing of sites in China containing fossils of animals used for medicinal purposes led to the discovery of the fossils of the Peking Man.

Weiss, Mark L., and Alan E. Mann, *Human Biology and Behavior: An Anthropological Perspective* (1996). The authors stress the contribution that biological research has made and continues to make to unravel the mystery of human evolution.

RIVERS, CITIES, AND FIRST STATES, 4000–2000 BCE

One of the oldest cities and first centers of society in the world was the ancient city of Uruk, known in the Bible as Erech and in modern Arabic as Warka. Located in the southernmost part of the Mesopotamian alluvium in Southwest Asia on one of the many winding branches of the Euphrates River, it had at least 10,000 inhabitants and many large public structures and temples by the late fourth millennium BCE. A temple probably dedicated to the god An, the Sumerian god of the sky, had been built before 3000 BCE. Known today as the White Temple because of its bright lime-plastered surface, it was constructed on a high platform that towered more than thirty feet above the level of the plain, with niched mud-brick walls forming stepped indentations up and down the surface. In another sacred precinct of the city dedicated to the Sumerian goddess Inanna (also called Ishtar in the semitic Akkadian language), huge administrative buildings and temples stood in courtyards defined by tall columns. The surfaces of these buildings were covered with colored stone cones arranged in elaborate geometric patterns. These buildings must have been visible from far away, making Uruk the "shining city" of the epic devoted to its later king, Gilgamesh.

The city of Uruk had once been a mere town, but over the years it grew into an immense commercial and administrative center—a location where jobs, adventure, and new ideas were to be found. A huge wall with seven massive gates surrounded the metropolis. Down the middle ran a canal whose waters had been diverted from the Euphrates River. On one side were gardens, pottery kilns, and enormous textile workshops where hundreds of men and women made beautiful clothes, fit for the goddess Inanna and her royal consorts; on the other side was the temple quarter, where the priests and their households lived, where scribes kept their records, and where the LU-GAL, or the big man, met the elders when they held their important discussions about the future of the city.

As Uruk grew, it became home to laborers, craftworkers, farmers, and scribes, as well as ruling elites. By the middle of the fourth millennium BCE, all kinds of specialists lived and worked in Uruk. Many of the industries, previously small and localized, now became centralized to address the burgeoning demand for their services and the increasing sophistication of construction and manufacturing. Potters made significant technical breakthroughs using a fast wheel that enabled them to mass-produce vessels in many different shapes. Metalsmiths, stone bowl makers, and brickmakers all worked under the centralized city administration. They, along with other workers, were paid in rations allocated from central storehouses—probably doled out in crude, standardized beveled-rim bowls that archaeologists have found by the millions at Uruk and other sites occupied during this period.

> *Uruk was the first city of its kind in world history; its appearance marked a new phase in human development.*

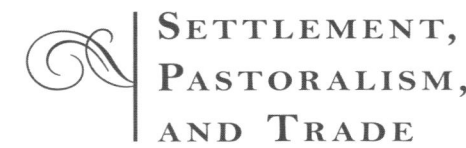

SETTLEMENT, PASTORALISM, AND TRADE

> → *What diverse strategies did people across the globe develop to live in their environments?*

Uruk was the first city of its kind in world history; its appearance marked a new phase in human development. In earlier times, humans had settled in small communities that were equal in size and distributed over the landscape at a level of density ensuring that water and land were easily accessible to all. Gradually some communities grew to a larger size, becoming focal points of trade and settlements that attracted specialists. Eventually a few of these centers became cities—centers with large populations, containing institutions of economic, religious, and political power. At these centers, most of the inhabitants would no longer be involved in producing their own food. Rather, they would be engaged in other professions or tasks necessary for the larger community. Workers would be fed with rations, and the elite would receive their support through taxes levied on those over whom they held authority.

Over many millennia, people had slowly developed strategies to make the best of their environments. But around 3500 BCE, a series of remarkable cultural changes, demographic leaps, and technological innovations gave rise to a major revolution in social organization that was relatively swift (compared to the pace of earlier developments) and that

Focus Questions RIVERS, CITIES, AND FIRST STATES

→ *What diverse strategies did people across the globe develop to live in their environments?*
→ *What role did cities play in Mesopotamian society?*
→ *Why do we know less about Harappan culture than about others in Afro-Eurasia?*
→ *How did the Nile River shape the development of early Egyptian society?*
→ *What hallmarks of urban life emerged in China during this period?*
→ *How did the growth of urban societies in river basins affect people living in the Aegean region, Anatolia, and Europe?*

 WWNORTON.COM/STUDYSPACE

Aerial View of Ur. The ancient city of Ur is now an archaeological mound, known as a Tell or Tal in Arabic. Ur was a medium-sized city in the third millennium BCE located on one of the important canals connected to the mouth of the Persian Gulf. It was there that the first true ziggurat, or temple tower, was built by Ur-Nammu, the founder of the Third Dynasty of Ur, which controlled all of Mesopotamia, Khuzistan, and the central Zagros Mountains at the end of the third millennium BCE.

fundamentally changed human life. In combination, these changes enabled complex, hierarchical societies to form, and they were reinforced in turn by the emergence of cities and the institutions that define them. The physical, social, and cultural achievements of city life would begin to have a profound impact on the human experience.

Village conglomerations arose as people gathered together to live near a reliable water source that would enable them to grow the crops so vital to feeding larger populations. Although the first groupings appeared in regions with abundant rainfall, the larger foundations of the new cities were established in drier zones, where rich alluvial soils were irrigated with river water. Equally important, a warming cycle caused temperatures around the world to rise and growing seasons to expand. These changes in the natural environment provoked a revolutionary response, fundamentally altering the very fabric of the human experience.

At the beginning, cities were scarce and could be found only in very select places. To begin with, cities required the conducive environments of stable river systems. As their waters cut through mountains, steppe lands (vast treeless grasslands), and deserts, the rivers deposited rich soils around the deltas before finally reaching the sea. The combination of fertile soils, access to water for irrigation, and the widespread availability of domesticated plants and animals made these particular places attractive for human habitation. Abundant water and arable soil made the city possible.

With the dense settlement of large numbers of people in the new cities also came labor specialization, and craftworkers began to concentrate solely on making textiles, pottery, and other goods. Soon these goods were used not only in the cities themselves but also in trade with outlying areas. Such

trade would expand over longer distances, bringing in raw materials such as metal, timber, and precious stones that could be used to construct and decorate city walls, temples, and palaces, as well as to fashion tools and weapons.

EARLY CITIES ALONG RIVER BASINS

At first, these material and social advances occurred in a remarkably short period of time in three locations: the basin of the Tigris and Euphrates rivers in modern Iraq, at the heart of Southwest Asia; the Indus River basin in modern Pakistan, in the northwest corner of South Asia; and the northern parts of the Nile River, which flows north from the heart of Africa through modern-day Egypt before it enters the Mediterranean Sea. (See Map 2-1.) In these three regions, from roughly 4000 to 2000 BCE, humans altered how they farmed and fed themselves—turning to intensive irrigation agriculture; where they lived—with more people moving to cities inhabited by rulers, administrators, priests, and specialized craftworkers; and how they organized communities—now controlled by divinely inspired monarchs and elaborate bureaucracies. They also transformed what and how they worshipped—praying to a multitude of anthropomorphic gods who communicated with believers through kings and priests living in palace complexes and temples that were the centers of the early cities. These far more complex modes of living required new means of record keeping that finally led to the invention of writing systems. The same development took place at the same time but on a smaller scale along the inland river valleys of the Iranian plateau and in central

NORTH
AMERICA

ATLANTIC
OCEAN

SAHARA

SAHEL

TEHUACAN VALLEY

PACIFIC
OCEAN

CHICAMA VALLEY

SOUTH
AMERICA

ANDES MOUNTAINS

Desert
Pastoral belt – steppe lands
Tropical rain forest
Agricultural society 3000 BCE
Riverine societies
Widespread village culture

0   1000   2000 Miles
0   1000   2000 Kilometers

MAP 2-1   THE WORLD IN THE THIRD MILLENNIUM BCE

Human societies became increasingly diversified in the third millennium BCE. Agricultural, urban, and pastoral nomadic communities expanded across time and space during this era. Why do you think cities appeared in the regions that they did and not in other areas? In what areas did pastoral nomadism emerge? What kinds of interaction developed among pastoral and sedentary agricultural societies?

Southwest Asia. About a millennium later, a similar process commenced along the Yellow River in North China in East Asia, laying the foundations for a culture that has, uniquely, flourished unbroken until this day.

As large numbers of people congregated in the new cities, new technologies appeared. It is around this time that the wheel, both as a tool for the production of pottery and as the fundamental component of vehicles used for transportation, began to be fully exploited. Metallurgy and stoneworking provided both luxury objects and utilitarian tools. With these, urbanites also developed writing systems and a new imagery of power and control, which they used to organize the increasingly complex society.

The emergence of cities as population centers created the second of history's most durable worldwide distinctions—the urban-rural divide. This division between those living in cities and those living in countrysides eventually encompassed the globe. In areas where riverine cities appeared, communities of people adopted lifestyles based on the mass production of goods and on specialized labor. In contrast, those still living in the countryside remained close to nature, cultivating the land or tending livestock; rather than specializing in particular tasks or professions, they diversified their labor and exchanged their grains and animal products for necessities available in urban centers. Therefore the new separation never implied isolation; the two lifeways were entirely dependent on one another. People from the countryside went to the cities to trade and to worship and brought with them offerings to the gods and produce to feed and to supply the urban populations. Despite the divide between the city and the countryside, the urban and rural worlds still remained closely linked through trade, politics, and religion.

Each urban culture developed its own practices and institutions, providing the social glue that enabled generation after generation living in these communities to survive and flourish.

The rise of cities in the fourth millennium BCE represented a quantum leap in increased complexity in human history—a transformation made possible by abundant water and fertile soil. Those who congregated in the river valleys of Afro-Eurasia lived close together in the cities, which were integrated into the countryside that brought them the surplus crops on which they depended. In these remarkable urban enclaves, humans made fundamental intellectual advances, including the invention of systems of writing, enabling sounds and words to be recorded and transmitted through the medium of visual signs. A cultural breakthrough of unprecedented scope, the technology of writing used the symbolic storage of words and meanings to extend human communication and memory. Oral compositions, which were eventually transformed into written annals and literature, quickly followed, telling the story of human life in these river settlements. Such cultural developments strongly shaped religion and politics, as well as the economy. Each urban culture developed its own practices and institutions, providing the social glue that enabled generation after generation living in these communities to survive and flourish.

SMALLER SETTLEMENTS AROUND 3500 BCE

Around 3500 BCE, the vast majority of people distributed in all parts of the globe were still living in small village communities close to the animals and plants they used for food. As they hunted, gathered, fished, and cultivated plants, they formed small egalitarian communities organized on the basis of clan and family allegiances. Tools were restricted mainly to wood and stone materials, though containers made of gourds were used to transport water and food over long distances. In a few special locations, early artisans regularly formed and then fired malleable clay to make vessels and dishes for storing and preparing food. More rarely still, craftworkers pounded native copper into small items of personal adornment. In such places where the population increased, divisions between artisans and manual laborers emerged, community life became more hierarchical, and villages grew into larger towns.

In other places, however, there was an environmental limit to the size of these settlements. The techniques of food production and storage, transportation, and communication restricted the surpluses available to feed those who did not cultivate the land. These communities did not grow in size and complexity. For example, in the Chicama Valley of Peru, which opens onto the Pacific Ocean, people nestled in small coastal villages to fish, to gather shellfish, to do some hunting, and to grow beans, chili peppers, and cotton to make twined textiles, which they dyed with wild indigo. By around 3500 BCE, these fishermen abandoned their rickety cane and adobe homes for sturdier houses, half underground, on streets lined with cobbles.

Hundreds if not thousands of such villages dotted the seashores and riverbanks of the Americas. Some made the technological breakthroughs required to produce pottery; others devised irrigation systems and water sluices in floodplains (areas onto which the rivers would overflow and deposit fertile soil). And some even began to send their fish catches inland in return for agricultural produce. In the remains of these villages, archaeologists have recovered ceremonial structures such as temples, hearths, fire-pit chambers, and special tombs that reveal an elaborate religious life. It was filled with communal devotion and homage to deities and with rituals to celebrate the momentous events of birth and death, as well as to perpetuate the memory of ancestors.

In the Americas, the largest population center at the time was located in the valley of Tehuacán near current-day Mexico City. The domestication of corn in this region created a subsistence base that enabled people to migrate from caves to cluster in a mosaic of pit-house villages that supported a growing population. But by 3500 BCE, the valley held nothing resembling a large city, though it teemed with inhabitants.

The same can be said of sub-Saharan Africa, where the population grew but did not concentrate into major urban communities. About 12,000 years ago, when there was more rainfall and temperatures increased, small encampments of African hunting, gathering, and fishing communities congregated around the large lakes and big rivers that flowed through what is now the largest desert in the world. Elephants, rhinoceroses, gazelles, antelopes, lions, and panthers roamed, both posing a threat to humans and providing them a source of food. Over millennia, in the wetter and more temperate locations of this vast region—particularly in the upland massifs and their foothills—permanent villages slowly came into being. As the Sahara gradually became drier, people moved to the edges of the desert, to areas along the Niger River and the Sudan. They settled along Lake Chad in what is today eastern Nigeria and southern Cameroon, where they grew yams, oil palms (a palm tree whose fruit and seeds produce oil), and plantains (a fruit similar to bananas). In the Sudan, settlers grew grains such as millet and sorghum, which later spread to areas along the Niger River as well. Residents constructed stone dwellings and dug underground wells and food storage areas. As an increasing population strained resources, groups of migrants moved south toward the Congo River and east toward Lake Victoria; there they established new farms and villages. Although population centers were often hundreds and even thousands of miles apart, they maintained trading and cultural contacts. We know of their connection because villagers from present-day Mali in the west to Kenya in the southeast used much the same style of pottery, characterized by bowls with rounded bottoms and similar wavy-line decorations.

PASTORAL NOMADIC COMMUNITIES

While many peoples continued to live in settled agricultural villages, where they fished and farmed and raised a few animals, some instead turned to pastoralism—herding and breeding sheep and goats as their primary means of subsistence. As their herds expanded, they found it necessary to move to the periphery of the settled areas to find sufficient pastures. Around 3500 BCE, western Afro-Eurasia witnessed the growth and spread of pastoral nomadic communities that herded domesticated animals whose grazing requirements were sizable. Rather than living permanently in settled com-

munities, these pastoral nomads moved their herds from highland to lowland pastures in an annual cycle. Their communities were small, and their settlements were impermanent, without substantial public buildings or infrastructure, but the herders' patterns of moving seasonally between specific pasturelands were stable. Across the vast expanse of Eurasia's great mountains (Taurus, Zagros, Himalaya, Tianshan, and Kunlun) and its desert barriers (Sahara, Gobi, and Taklamakan), and from its steppe lands ranging across inner and central Eurasia to the Pacific Ocean, these pastoral peoples lived alongside settled agrarian people when they were on their lowland pastures. The herders traded meat and animal products for the grains and pottery and tools produced in the settled agrarian communities.

As in western Afro-Eurasia, in the arid environments of Inner Mongolia and central Asia people initially engaged in a combination of herding animals and crop cultivation. But the environment on the Eurasian steppes was not conducive to large-scale farming, and they began to turn primarily to animal breeding and herding; they continued to engage in fishing and hunting and farming small plots of land in their winter pastures as secondary pursuits. Their economy centered on domesticated cattle and the sheep and horses that they raised. As their herds increased, they had to move often to new, ungrazed pastures. By the second millennium BCE, full-scale nomadic communities dominated these steppe lands. The horse-riding nomads moved their large animal herds across immense tracts of land within zones defined by rivers, mountains, and other natural features of the geography. In the arid zones of central Eurasia, the nomadic economies made horses—which enabled riders to move easily over large areas—a crucial component of survival.

THE RISE OF TRADE

Whether seeking to ensure their physical existence or providing luxury items conveying status or magical powers, humans from the time of their earliest groupings have exchanged things with one another. When they settled in one place, their need to exchange goods with those in other communities became even greater, as no one place had everything that people need. At the same time, settlements make it possible for humans to accumulate material wealth. By the advent of the earliest farming villages around 7000 BCE, trade patterns across Eurasia were well established. Most often this trade was in exotic materials such as obsidian, a black volcanic glass used to make superb chipped stone tools. Its proximity to one of the richest and best sources of this volcanic glass in all of Southwest Asia helps explain why the village at Çatal Höyük in central Anatolia (present-day Turkey) grew to such an extraordinary size (see Chapter 1). The obsidian was passed from one village to another in a process called "trickle trade" or "down the line trade."

More important to the people of the cities of southern Mesopotamia was long-distance trade. Because they lacked many basic raw materials that developed settlements require, they needed to find sources of wood, stones, and metal to augment their locally available building materials—mud and reeds. Indeed, these communities established outposts close to the sources of these materials so that they could coordinate and monitor the resources' import. In exchange, they offered manufactured goods, especially luxury textiles. This long-distance trade began around 5000 BCE, carried out by boats along the shores of the Persian Gulf. By 3000 BCE, there was extensive interaction between southern Mesopotamia and the highlands of Anatolia, the forests of the Levant (present-day Lebanon, Syria, Israel, and the Palestinian territories, bordering the eastern Mediterranean), and the rich mountains and vast plateau of Iran. (See Map 2-2.)

Throughout the millennia, trade and exchange between peoples increased. By the mid-third millennium BCE, trading communities were established in the oases (fertile areas with water in the midst of arid regions) dotting the deserts of western Syria, the plateau of Iran, northern Afghanistan, and Turkmenistan. Trading stations, or entrepôts, at the borders between several communities made possible exchanges among many partners. Caravans of pack animals—first donkeys and onagers (an Asian wild ass) and later camels—were used to take goods across long distances over land. These caravans

MAP 2-2   TRADE AND EXCHANGE IN SOUTHWEST ASIA AND THE EASTERN MEDITERRANEAN—THIRD MILLENNIUM BCE

Extensive commercial networks linked the urban cores of Southwest Asia in the third millennium BCE. According to the map, why was Mesopotamia the crossroads of Afro-Eurasia? Why do you think there were more extensive trade connections between Mesopotamians and people to their northwest and east than with Egypt to the west? How did trade shape societies living beyond urban cores in Mesopotamia, Egypt, and the Indus Valley?

would cross deserts, stopping at oasis communities where water and supplies could be exchanged for their wares. They traveled over routes that passed through deserts, steppes, and forests, carrying goods and ideas across Afro-Eurasia.

BETWEEN TWO RIVERS: MESOPOTAMIA (5500–2000 BCE)

> → *What role did cities play in Mesopotamian society?*

The common social geography of the world in 3500 BCE saw people living close to the land in small clans and settlements, some mobile, some stationary, but a breakthrough occurred in one place: the Mesopotamian river basin in Southwest Asia, where the world's first complex society came into existence. There the city and the river changed how people lived.

TAPPING THE WATERS

Mesopotamia, whose name is a Greek word meaning "[country] between two rivers," is not at first glance a hospitable place. From their headwaters in the mountains to the north and east, the Tigris and Euphrates rivers are wild and unpredictable, flooding in periods of heavy rainfall and snow, and dry during the parched months of summer. Thus, water was both scourge and blessing for the pioneers who moved to the Tigris and Euphrates river basin. It could wipe out years of hard work; but, properly handled, water could also transform the landscape into verdant fields. In retrospect, the simple irrigation systems created by the earliest Mesopotamians were nothing short of revolutionary. A large landmass that includes all of modern-day Iraq and parts of Syria and southeastern Turkey, Mesopotamia embraces a richly varied topography and a wide variety of cultures—all unified by interlocking drainage basins. Both rivers provided water for irrigation, and although hardly navigable, both served as important routes for transportation and communication by pack animal and by foot.

The first advances occurred in the foothill zones of the Zagros Mountains along the banks of the smaller rivers that feed into the Tigris. Here, men and women discovered that simple irrigation techniques enabled them to achieve higher agricultural yields and greater surpluses on these lands than were possible on rain-fed areas to the north. Gradually they ventured out of the foothills onto the southern alluvial plain of the Tigris and Euphrates River basin. There floods were larger, and the water harder to harness, but the land held greater promise of abundant harvests.

Early Mesopotamian Waterworks. From the sixth millennium BCE, irrigation was necessary for successful farming in southern Mesopotamia. By the first millennium BCE, sophisticated feats of engineering allowed the Assyrians to redirect water through constructed aqueducts, like the one illustrated here on a relief from the palace of the Assyrian king Sennacherib at Nineveh.

Converting the floodplain of the Euphrates River into a breadbasket required mastery over the unpredictable rivers. Both the Euphrates and (to an even greater degree) the Tigris, unless controlled by waterworks, were rivers profoundly unfavorable to cultivators. The annual floods and low-water seasons came at exactly the wrong times in the farming sequence. Floods occurred at the height of the growing season, when crops were most vulnerable. Irrigation waters, conversely, were needed when the floodwaters had receded and the river was at low ebb. In order to prevent the river from overflowing during the flood stage, farmers put up and maintained levees (barriers to the waters) along the river's banks, and dug ditches and canals to drain away floodwaters. To ensure a plentiful supply of water in the later growing stages, they needed highly developed water-lifting devices. In pioneering water storage, Mesopotamians were the world's first hydraulic engineers.

The great technological breakthrough in Mesopotamian societies was in irrigation, not necessarily in agrarian methods. The soils were fine and rich, constantly replenished by silt carried by the floodwaters, so soil tillage was light work. Farmers sowed a combination of wheat, millet, sesame, and especially barley (which doubled as the basis for beer, a staple of their diet), with yields possibly as high as those afforded by current-day wheat fields in Canada.

CROSSROADS OF SOUTHWEST ASIA

Though its soil was rich and water was abundant, southern Mesopotamia had few other natural resources apart from the abundant mud and marsh reeds in the immediate vicinity of the river basin that provided primitive building materials. In order to get wood, stone, metal, and all of the other raw materials on which complex settled societies relied to construct cities and the temples and palaces within them, Mesopotamians had to interact with the inhabitants of surrounding regions. They imported the cedars of Lebanon, the copper and stones of Oman, more copper from what is now Turkey and Iran, and the precious blue gemstone called lapis lazuli from faraway Afghanistan in return for textiles, oils, and other commodities. Maintaining trading contacts with their neighbors was relatively easy, given Mesopotamia's open boundaries on all sides. In this crucial respect, Mesopotamia contrasted with Egypt, whose long and narrow land was cut off by impassable deserts to the east and west, and by the Nile River rapids to the south.

Mesopotamia's natural advantages—its rich agricultural land and water combined with easy access to neighboring regions—were propitious for the growth of cities. But this very openness made the river valleys vulnerable to invaders from the deserts and the mountains. Mesopotamia thus became a crossroads for the peoples of Southwest Asia, the meeting grounds for several distinct cultural and linguistic groups of people. Among the dominant groups were Sumerians, who were concentrated in the south; Hurrians, who lived in the north; and the Semitic-speaking Akkadians, who concentrated in western and central Mesopotamia. In general, people engaged in pastoralism outside the core agricultural regions, and they provided the settled communities with animal products in exchange for agricultural produce.

FIRST CITIES

Archaeological surveys suggest that sometime during the first half of the fourth millennium BCE, a large-scale demographic transformation occurred. The population in the region had expanded as a result of its agricultural bounty, and swelling ranks of Mesopotamians migrated from the villages scattered across the countryside to particular centers that eventually became cities. The earliest of these cities, Eridu, Nippur, and Uruk, dominated their environs by 3500 BCE. Rather than appearing suddenly, the first cities in the southern part of the Mesopotamian floodplain grew gradually over about 1,000 years. Buildings of mud brick were erected in successive layers of accumulated urban development. Consider Eridu, which had first been settled as a village around 6000 BCE. Home to the Sumerian water god, Ea, Eridu was a sacred site where temples full of fish bones were built one on top of the other for more than 4,000 years. During the course of more than twenty reconstructions, the temples became increasingly elaborate, built on an ever-higher base. Eventually, the temple was raised on a platform like a mountain, looming over the featureless landscape and visible for miles in all directions. Not only had the temple grown up but the village had expanded horizontally, becoming a city, with its god overseeing its growth.

There were some thirty-five cities with major divine sanctuaries widely scattered across the southern plain of Mesopotamia. Sumerian ideology glorified a way of life and a territory composed of politically equal city-states, each with its own principal guardian deity and sanctuary, supported by its inhabitants. Local communities in these urban hubs expressed their homage to individual city gods and took great pride in the temple, the god's home.

Early Mesopotamian cities served as meeting places for peoples and their deities. In fact, it was the city's status as a devotional and economic center that elevated it over the countryside. Whether enormous, like Uruk or Nippur, or modest, like Ur or Abu Salabikh, all cities performed these complex roles as spiritual, economic, and cultural homes for Mesopotamian subjects.

Layout of Eridu. Over several millennia, temples of increasing size and complexity were built atop each other at Eridu in southern Iraq. The culmination came with the elaborate structure of level VII.

Level XVI Level IX Level VII

Ziggurat. The first ziggurat of Mesopotamia, dedicated to the moon god Nanna, was built by the founder of the Neo-Sumerian dynasty, Ur-Nammu (2112–2095 BCE). Although temples had been raised on platforms since early times, the distinctive stepped form of the ziggurat was initially borrowed from the Iranian plateau. It became the most important sacred structure in Mesopotamia.

Simply making a city was therefore not enough: it had to be made great. Urban design reflected the role of the city as a wondrous place to pay homage to the gods and their human intermediary, the king. The early cities contained enormous spaces within their walls. Initially, houses were large and separated by great plantations of date palms. Within the city limits were also located extensive sheepfolds (which became a frequent metaphor for the city). As populations grew, the fabric of the cities of Mesopotamia became denser. Even houses belonging to the well-to-do became considerably smaller. And often urbanites established new suburbs, either settling beyond the city perimeter or simply breaking through the old walls and spilling into the countryside.

The original layout of Mesopotamian cities conformed to a common pattern. Through their middle invariably ran a canal, around which neighborhoods housing specific occupational groups emerged. The temple marked the city center, while the palace and other official buildings often arose on the periphery. In separate quarters for craft production, families passed down their trades from generation to generation.

The emergence of politically autonomous and essentially equal cities was a recurring theme in lower Mesopotamia, where Sumerians and Semites lived side by side. The city-states were bound together through a common culture, intense trade, and a shared environment. Urban life and irrigated agriculture demonstrate how much ancient peoples depended on the nearby rivers to produce their distinctive cultures.

GODS AND TEMPLES

The worldview of the Sumerians and, later, the Akkadians revolved around a pantheon of gods who were believed to inhabit the lands of Sumer and Akkad, shaping political institutions and controlling everything, including the weather, fertility, harvests, and the underworld. As depicted in the *Epic of Gilgamesh,* a later composition based on a cycle of several oral tales about Gilgamesh (a historical but much mythologized king of Uruk), the gods could give, but they could also take away—with searing droughts and unmerciful floods and with natural and violent death. Gods, and the natural forces they controlled, had to be revered and feared. Faithful subjects imagined their gods as immortal, all-powerful, anthropomorphic beings whose habits were capricious, contentious, and gloriously work-free. Each of the major gods of the Sumerian pantheon had its home in a particular floodplain city, which it was believed to have created; therefore each gave his or her city its particular character, distinct institutions, and individual patterns of relationships with its urban neighbors.

Temples, and especially the main temple, were thought of as the home of the gods and the symbol of urban identity.

Cylinder Seal of Adad Carved from Green Stone. Many people in Mesopotamia involved with administration and public life had one or more cylinder seals. Cylinder seals were carved with imagery and inscriptions and were impressed into clay tablets and other documents while they were still malleable in order to guarantee the authenticity of a transaction. The cylinder seal shown here carries the inscription of the scribe Adda. The imagery includes representations of important gods of the Akkadian pantheon. The sun god Shamash rises from between the mountains in the center. Ishtar as a warrior goddess stands to the left. To the right is Ea, the god of wisdom, who is associated with flowing water and fish. Behind him is the servant Usmu, whose double face allows him to see everything. At the far left is a god of hunting.

Temples represented the ability of the gods to hoard wealth at sites where mortals exchanged goods and services. They were the single most important marker distinguishing the urban from the rural world, and rulers lavished resources on their construction and adornment to demonstrate the power of their cities. Because the temple was the symbolic focus of the entire city-state, it was important for rulers and other important members of the community to contribute to its upkeep. Communal efforts would often be channeled to temple projects. Many royal inscriptions commemorate the construction and later renovation of a temple as one of the ruler's major duties.

Inside the temple was an altar, on which the cult image was placed. Frequently benches lined the walls, with statues of humans standing in perpetual worship of the deity's images. By the end of the third millennium BCE, the elevated platform base of the temple was transformed into a stepped platform called a *ziggurat*. On top of the temple tower itself stood the main temple. Surrounding the ziggurat was a conglomeration of buildings that composed the temple precinct, which housed priests, officials, laborers, and a copious retinue of servants—all bustling about to serve the city's god.

While the temple was the god's home, it was also the god's estate. As such, temples functioned like large households engaged in all sorts of productive and commercial activities.

Their dependents cultivated cereals, fruits, and vegetables, all of which required extensive irrigation. The temples owned vast flocks of sheep, goats, cows, and donkeys. Those located close to the river employed workers to collect reeds, to fish, and to hunt. Enormous labor forces were required to maintain this high level of production. Other temples operated huge workshops (embryonic factories), where textiles and leather goods were manufactured. Temple workshops employed legions of craftworkers, metalworkers, masons, and stoneworkers. Since southern Mesopotamia lacked many raw materials, temples as well as the palaces sponsored long-distance trade, often commissioning independent merchants and traders to organize commercial expeditions to distant lands. The model of the household extended beyond the temple to all aspects of the Sumerian and Akkadian economy. The royal court was organized around the king's household; and in the private sector, large landowning extended families functioned as a household economic unit.

THE PALACE AND ROYAL POWER

The palace, both as an institution and as a set of buildings, appeared around 2500 BCE, about a millennium later than the Mesopotamian temple. But the palace quickly joined the temple as a defining landmark of city life. As life became more complex and cities grew in size, palaces began to supplement temples in upholding order and diffusing a sense of shared membership in city affairs. Over time, the palace became a source of power rivaling the temple. Palace and temple life often blurred, with rulers doubling as secular governors and sacred figures. Indeed, rulers embodied gods in such rituals as the Sacred Marriage, in which the king, as high priest, took on the role of the god Dumuzi, a Sumerian god of fertility and agrarian productivity, as in the temple he engaged in sexual relations with the high priestess, who embodied the goddess Inanna. Although located at the edge of cities in previously uninhabited locations, palaces quickly became the visible expression of permanent secular, military, and administrative authority, as distinct from the spiritual and economic power of the temples. Their builders expanded their city's influence—and thereby also disrupted the balance of power within and among Mesopotamian cities.

Rulers tied their status to their gods through elaborate burial arrangements of the kind well known from Egypt and China. The Royal Cemetery at Ur offers spectacular archaeological evidence of how Sumerian rulers dealt with death. Of the more than 2,000 graves that archaeologists uncovered in

the 1930s, 16 were the burial sites of highborn persons. The royal burials were distinguished from others by being housed in a structure of mud brick. Further, they held not only the primary remains but also the bodies of other humans who had been sacrificed. In one case, more than eighty men and women accompanied the deceased to the afterlife. Many of the graves containing human sacrifices also demonstrate the elaborateness of the burial festival rituals. From the huge vats for cooked food, the bones of animals, the drinking vessels, and the musical instruments recovered from the grave sites, we can reconstruct the lifestyle of those who were required to join their masters in the graves. Honoring the dead by including their followers and possessions in their tombs reinforced the social hierarchies—including the vertical ties between humans and gods—that were the cornerstone of these early states.

SOCIAL HIERARCHY AND FAMILIES

Social hierarchies were an important part of the fabric of Sumerian city-states. The origins of the first states and hierarchies topped by powerful elites that supported them and profited from them can be traced to the very breakthrough

The Royal Tombs of Ur. The Royal Tombs of Ur, excavated in the 1930s, contained thousands of objects in gold, silver, lapis lazuli, and shell that were buried along with elites of the First Dynasty of Ur. One tomb belonged to the king, Mes-KALAM-dug. Next to his head was a gold helmet with the bun and braid that was headdress of the ruler. In another grave, along with the skeletons of more than sixty members of a royal household, were musical instruments, including this large harp with a golden bull's head. Such instruments would have been played at the ritual meal associated with these fabulously rich burials. Pu-Abi, identified as a queen by the cylinder near her body, was buried in a separate chamber. She was interred in full regalia, including the elaborate headdress shown here.

that made the region so special: irrigation. Whereas plows and sickles—the basic implements of farming—were tools employed by individuals for their own benefit, dikes, canals, banks, and hydraulic lifts required collective effort, investment, and organization. No single individual or family could sustain the challenge. Early irrigation societies therefore created communal ways of building infrastructure and maintaining it, collecting taxes and drafting labor to expand and preserve waterworks. These efforts laid the foundations of the first Afro-Eurasian states.

City-states at first were run by assemblies of elders and young men who made collective decisions for the community. From the outset, specially empowered elites were intermittently appointed to tackle emergencies; with time, these elite power holders became permanent features of the political landscape. The social hierarchy set off the rulers from the ruled. Ruling groups secured their privileged access to economic and political resources by erecting systems of bureaucracies, priesthoods, and laws. Priests and bureaucrats served their rulers well, championing rules and norms that legitimized the political leadership.

Occupations within the cities were highly specialized. A list of professions was formalized and transmitted across the land so that everyone could know where he or she fit within the newly emerging social order. The king and priest in Sumer were at the top of the list. Following them were bureaucrats (scribes and accountants of the household economy), supervisors, and specialized craftworkers. These included cooks, jewelers, gardeners, potters, metalsmiths, and traders. The biggest group, which was at the bottom of the hierarchy, consisted of the male and female workers who were not slaves but who were dependent on their households. Frequently several households would operate as a closed economic unit, producing most of the necessities within a closed system. Property was held collectively by the family or extended household. All members were party to land transfers or sale. Movement between these economic classes was not impossible but, as in many traditional societies, it was unusual. There were also independent merchants who assumed the risk of long-distance trading ventures, hoping for a generous return on their investment.

Sumerian society was organized around the family and the household, and the Sumerian family was also hierarchical: the senior male dominated as the patriarch of the family. Most Sumerian households were made up of a single extended family, all living under the same roof. The family consisted of the husband and wife bound by a contract; she would provide children, preferably male, while he provided support and protection. Monogamy was the norm, unless a son was not produced, and in such cases it was common to take a second wife or to bring a slave girl into the house to bear male children who would be considered the married couple's offspring. Sons would inherit the family's property in equal shares, while daughters were supported through gifts that were meant to provide the dowry necessary for a successful marriage. Adoption was also a common way for a family to gain a male heir. Most women lived inside the contract of marriage, but a special class of women joined the temple staff as priestesses. By the second millennium BCE, these priestesses were allowed broad economic autonomy that included ownership of estates and productive enterprises. Yet even in the case of the female temple personnel, their fathers and brothers remained ultimately responsible for their well-being.

FIRST WRITING AND EARLY TEXTS

The first recorded words of history were set down in the cities of Mesopotamia, and they promoted the power of the temples and kings in the expanding city-states. The people who controlled the production and distribution of goods used writing to enhance communication among large numbers of individuals and to keep track of the products of their realm. Oral communication and human memory had adequately served the needs of small-scale hunting and gathering and village farming communities, but they imposed limits on a society's scale and complexity. As people developed more specialized skills and roles, they had to communicate with other specialists and convey messages over longer distances. Writing facilitated transactions and information sharing across wider spans of distance and time.

We now take reading and writing for granted, but they emerged independently in only a few locations. Mesoamerica was one such area, and China, too, saw the autonomous development of literacy. What is certain is that at approximately the same time, Mesopotamians and Egyptians became the world's first record keepers and readers. The precursors to writing appeared in Mesopotamian societies when farming peoples and officials who had been employing clay tokens and images carved on stones to seal off storage areas began to use them to convey messages. Originally intended simply to identify those responsible for the vessels and storerooms where valuable commodities were held, these images, when combined with numbers also drawn on clay tablets, began to record the distribution of goods and services.

In a flash of human genius, someone, probably in Uruk, understood that the marks, usually pictures of objects, could also represent words and then distinct sounds. A representation that transfers meaning from the name of a thing to the sound of that name is called a *rebus*. For example, a picture of a bee can be used to represent the sound "b." Such pictures opened the door to writing: a technology of symbols that uses marks to record specific discrete sounds. Before long, scribes connected symbols with sounds, and sounds with meanings. As people combined rebus symbols with other ways to store meaning in visual marks, they became able to record and transmit messages over long distances by using

THE ORIGINS OF WRITING ACCORDING TO THE SUMERIANS

One Sumerian myth records the invention of writing by the Lord of Kullaba, Enmerkar, who sought to transmit complex messages across the vast distances to the Land of Aratta, where his rival for the love of the goddess Inanna lived. Messengers would memorize their responses and deliver them orally after an arduous journey across the mountains. Enmerkar felt he could not trust the memory of his messenger to deliver one particularly complicated response, and so he invented writing in the form of cuneiform script.

His speech was substantial, and its contents extensive. The messenger, whose mouth was heavy, was not able to repeat it. Because the messenger, whose mouth was tired, was not able to repeat it, the lord of Kulaba patted some clay and wrote the message as if on a tablet. Formerly, the writing of messages on clay was not established. Now, under that sun and on that day, it was indeed so. The lord of Kulaba inscribed the message like a tablet. It was just like that. The messenger was like a bird, flapping its wings; he raged forth like a wolf following a kid. He traversed five mountains, six mountains, seven mountains. He lifted his eyes as he approached Aratta. He stepped joyfully into the courtyard of Aratta, he made known the authority of his king. Openly he spoke out the words in his heart. The messenger transmitted the message to the lord of Aratta:

"Your father, my master, has sent me to you; the lord of Unug, the lord of Kulaba, has sent me to you." "What is it to me what your master has spoken? What is it to me what he has said?"

"This is what my master has spoken, this is what he has said. My king is like a huge *meš* tree, ... son of Enlil; this tree has grown high, uniting heaven and earth; its crown reaches heaven, its trunk is set upon the earth. He who is made to shine forth in lordship and kingship, Enmerkar, the son of Utu, has given me a clay tablet. O lord of Aratta, after you have examined the clay tablet, after you have learned the content of the message, say whatever you will say to me, and I shall announce that message in the shrine E-ana as glad tidings to the scion of him with the glistening beard, whom his stalwart cow gave birth to in the mountains of the shining *me*, who was reared on the soil of Aratta, who was given suck at the udder of the good cow, who is suited for office in Kulaba, the mountain of great *me*, to Enmerkar, the son of Utu; I shall repeat it in his *ǧipar*, fruitful as a flourishing *meš* tree, to my king, the lord of Kulaba."

After he had spoken thus to him, the lord of Aratta received his kiln-fired tablet from the messenger. The lord of Aratta looked at the tablet. The transmitted message was just nails, and his brow expressed anger. The lord of Aratta looked at his kiln-fired tablet. At that moment, the lord worthy of the crown of lordship, the son of Enlil, the god I_kur, thundering in heaven and earth, caused a raging storm, a great lion, in .... He was making the mountains quake ......, he was convulsing the mountain range ......; the awesome radiance ...... of his breast; he caused the mountain range to raise its voice in joy. (lines 500–551)

→ *What aspects of Sumerian history are preserved and transmitted in the mythic story of the struggle between Enmerkar and the Lord of Aratta? "Enmerkar and the Lord of Aratta" is a text that was written down about 500 years later than the events that it describes. What other kinds of evidence do historians use to reconstruct the history of the early Sumerian period?*

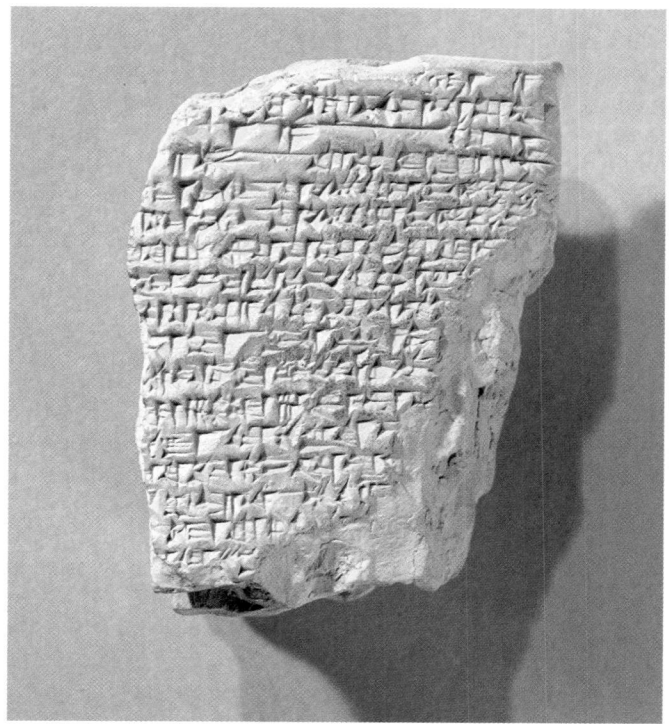

Cuneiform version of the myth "Enmerkar and the Lord of Aratta."

SOURCE: J. A. Black, G. Cunningham, E. Fluckiger-Hawker, E. Robson, and G. Zólyomi, *The Electronic Text Corpus of Sumerian Literature* (Oxford, 1998–2006), www.etcsl.orient.ox.ac.uk/. Italics signify Akkadian glosses.

Early Uruk Writing. The earliest tablets found at the site of Uruk were first impressed with cylinder seals and subsequently with wedge-shaped signs. Appearing around 3200 BCE, these earliest tablets are no more than aids to memory, recording, for example, quantities of goods transferred to workers. It is not until six hundred years later that the cuneiform script is developed enough to record complete sentences that would be read by everyone in the same way.

abstract symbols or signs to denote concepts; such signs later came to represent syllables, which could be joined into words.

From the beginning, scribes occupied a special place in Mesopotamian societies. By impressing these signs into wet clay with the cut end of a reed, the scribes engaged in a form of wedge-shaped writing that we call *cuneiform;* it could be used to fill clay tablets with information. What looked like gibberish to someone who was illiterate was actually intelligible to anyone who could decipher it—even those in faraway locations or in future generations. This Sumerian innovation powerfully enhanced the ability of urban elites to produce and trade goods, to control property, and to transmit ideas of society through literature, historical records, and sacred texts. Once again, the human experience had changed fundamentally, this time because human communication and memory were extended by being stored in the symbols of natural spoken language.

By taking these gradual steps, Mesopotamians opened the door into the world of literacy. The cuneiform script was exceedingly complicated, using a large set of signs that only a very small proportion of the population was trained to decipher. Therefore literacy, though a fundamental part of the civilizing process in cities, was a skill mastered by only a tiny but influential scribal elite.

Much of what we know about Mesopotamia rests on our ability to decipher cuneiform script. Writing that employed the rebus first appeared sometime around 3200 BCE, but not until about 700 years later could the script record spoken utterances completely. By around 2400 BCE, texts began to describe the political makeup of southern Mesopotamia, giving details of its history as well as its economy. At that time, the land of Sumer in the southern floodplain consisted of at least a dozen city-states. Northern cities also borrowed the cuneiform script to record economic transactions and political events, but in their own Semitic tongue. Cuneiform's adaptability to different languages is one of the main reasons its use spread so widely. As city life and literacy expanded, they gave rise to more than documents; they also spawned the first written narratives, the stories of a "people" and their origins.

One famous set of texts written down around 2100 BCE, "The Temple Hymns," describes the thirty-five major divine sanctuaries on the southern plain. The magnificent Sumerian King List is among the texts that recount the making of political dynasties and depict great periodic floods. Written down around 2000 BCE, it organizes the reigns of kings by dynasty, one city at a time. The Sumerian King List also refers to the Great Flood, which is just one of many traditional Mesopotamian stories that were transmitted orally from one generation to another before being recorded (this story was borrowed and incorporated into the book of Genesis as part of the traditional creation story of the Bible). The Great Flood, a crucial event in Sumerian memory and identity, explained Uruk's demise as the gods' doing. Flooding was the most riveting of natural forces in the lives of a riverine folk, and it helped shape the material and symbolic foundations of Mesopotamian societies—societies whose breakthroughs were a consequence of tapping the waters of massive rivers.

SPREADING CITIES AND FIRST TERRITORIAL STATES

Although no single state dominated the history of fourth and third millennium BCE Mesopotamia, a few stand out. Easily the most powerful, influential, and fully studied were the Sumerian city-states of the Early Dynastic Age (2850–2334 BCE) and their successor, the Akkadian territorial state (2334–2193 BCE), which was founded by the warrior king Sargon of Akkad (r. 2334–2279 BCE).

While the city-states of southern Mesopotamia flourished and competed, giving rise to the land of Sumer, the rich agricultural zones to the north inhabited by the Hurrians also became urbanized. (See Map 2-3.) Northern urbanization, beginning around 2600 BCE, was rapid and soon yielded cities comparable in size to those in the south, including ancient

Nagar and Urkesh. In western Syria, ancient Ebla (modern Tell Mardikh) was the center of another Semitic-speaking city-state. Though their inhabitants were culturally related to the Sumerians and Akkadians of the alluvium, the northern cities had economic, political, and social organizations that were distinct and independent.

It was their very success that eventually destabilized the balanced world of the early Sumerian city-states. Southern Mesopotamia contained many cities with burgeoning populations that were vying for access to agrarian lands, to increasingly scarce water, and to lucrative trade routes. As the region's bounty became known to pastoralists far and wide, they journeyed in greater numbers to Mesopotamian cities, fueling urbanization and competition. Thus, as cities grew up, they also became important crossroads.

The world's first great conqueror emerged from one of these cities. By the end of his long reign, he had successfully united the independent Mesopotamian

MAP 2-3   THE SPREAD OF CITIES IN MESOPOTAMIA AND THE AKKADIAN STATE, 2600–2200 BCE

Urbanization began in the southern alluvium of Mesopotamia and gradually spread northward during the third millennium BCE. Eventually, the entire region was united under one territorial state. Why did urbanization spread to the northern alluvium of Mesopotamia after 2600 BCE? How similar were these new urban centers to those in the southern alluvium? What were the legacies of Sargon's Akkadian territorial state for the region?

cities south of modern Baghdad by force. The legendary Sargon the Great, king of Akkad, a city-state close to modern Baghdad, brought the era of increasingly competitive independent city-states to an end. Remembered for two millennia as a conqueror, Sargon was a ruler whose remarkable achievement was not simply to dominate the southern lands but to unify their cities, forging a single political, economic, and cultural alliance in a land called Agade or Akkad. Although the unity forged by Sargon lasted only three generations, he established the first multiethnic collection of urban centers—the territorial state—capable of combining the northern and southern parts of the alluvium, thus laying the foundations for the integration of the territorial states that we describe in Chapter 3.

The most obvious legacy of the dynasty established by Sargon was sponsorship of monumental architecture, artworks, and literary works. These cultural achievements stood for centuries and were copied by many generations of builders, architects, artists, and scribes. And by encouraging contact with distant neighbors, many of whom incorporated various aspects of Mesopotamian culture into their own distinct traditions, the Akkadian kings also increased the geographic reach of Mesopotamian influence. Although his historical reputation has endured, Sargon's "empire" was short-lived. Foreign tribesmen who came out of the Zagros Mountains to the east of the Tigris River infiltrated the heartland of Akkad, conquering the capital city around 2190 BCE. As legend has it, these "barbarians" wreaked havoc on "civilization," but we will see that this interpretation was promoted by the conquered and may not have reflected the reality of the conquest (see Chapter 3). Nonetheless, this cycle of urban magnificence, punctuated by nomadic destruction, would become the stuff of epic history writing—and it continues to captivate readers to the

Naram Sin. This life-size head of a ruler cast of almost pure copper was found at Nineveh in northern Iraq in the destruction levels of the Assyrian Empire. The style and imagery of this sculptural masterpiece identify it as a ruler of Old Akkadian dynasty. While sometimes identified as Sargon, it is most likely a portrait of his grandson, Naram Sin, who consolidated and transformed the Akkadian state. It must have stood for over fifteen hundred years in the courtyard of a temple at Nineveh, before it was defaced by the Medes and Elamites, whose savage attack on Nineveh cause the Assyrian Empire to fall.

present, even while creating a myth of urban civility and rural backwardness.

INDUS VALLEY: A PARALLEL CULTURE

> → *Why do we know less about Harappan culture than about others in Afro-Eurasia?*

Mesopotamian developments had spillover effects across much of Eurasia. As an outward-looking people, Mesopotamians depended on trade for many of their most basic needs. Mesopotamian commercial trails reached across the Iranian

plateau (Jiroft culture) and beyond what is now called the Khyber Pass as far as the Indus River in present-day Pakistan and India. To the west, they reached the Mediterranean Sea and entered the floodplains of the Nile. Riverine settings, such as the Nile and the Indus rivers, produced parallel flourishing states. While in some ways influenced by Mesopotamian examples, the peoples of the Nile and Indus created their own distinctive cultures and societies.

The urban culture of the Indus and the surrounding area is called Harappan after the urban site of Harappa that arose in the third millennium BCE on the banks of the Ravi River, a tributary of the Indus. Unlike in Mesopotamia, developments in the Indus River basin reflected an indigenous tradition combined with strong influences from the peoples of the Iranian plateau, as well as indirect influences from the peoples of more distant cities on the Tigris and Euphrates rivers. Villages first appeared around 5000 BCE on the Iranian plateau along the foothills of the Baluchistan Mountains, to the west of the Indus. By the early third millennium BCE, a frontier of villages had spread from these mountains in an eastwardly direction until it reached the fertile alluvial banks of the Indus River and its numerous tributaries. (See Map 2-4.) The riverine settlements soon yielded agrarian surpluses that supported greater wealth, more trade with neighbors, and more surpluses that could be devoted to public works. In due course, urbanites of the Indus region and the Harappan peoples both began to fortify their cities and to embark on public works similar in scale to those in Mesopotamia, but strikingly different in function.

The ecology of the Indus Valley boasted many advantages, especially compared to the area near the Ganges River—the other great waterway of the South Asian subcontinent. Located in the semi-tropical latitudes, the Indus Valley had plentiful water coming from the Himalayas that ensured flourishing vegetation without suffering the torrential monsoon downpours that caused heavy flooding every year on the Ganges plain. The expansion of agriculture in this basin, like those in Mesopotamia, Egypt, and China, depended on the river's annual floods. Here the river provided the land with predictable amounts of water, drawn from the melting snow on the Himalayas and beyond, that replenished the soil and averted droughts. From June to September, the rivers inundated the plain. Once the waters receded, farmers planted wheat and barley on fertile soft alluvium. They harvested the crops the next spring as temperatures rose. And as they took advantage of the fertility created by the river, the villagers on the banks of the Indus also improved their tools of cultivation. Researchers have found evidence of furrows, probably made by plowing, that they have dated to around 2600 BCE. Farmers were soon able to achieve harvests like those of Mesopotamia—yielding a surplus that freed many of the inhabitants from having to produce food and thus allowed them to specialize in other activities.

In time, rural wealth produced urban splendor. More abundant harvests, now stored in large granaries, brought migrants into the area and supported ever-growing populations. By 2500 BCE, cities began to take the place of villages throughout the Indus River valley, and within a few generations towering granaries became prominent features of the urban skyline. Harappa and Mohenjo Daro, the two largest cities, each covered an area about 250 acres (a little less than half a square mile) and probably housed 35,000 residents. As in Mesopotamia, such population densities were unprecedented departures from the common dispersal of peoples into self-sufficient agrarian hamlets, villages, or nomadic communities.

The floodplain over which Harappan cities sprawled was vast, totaling an area of 500,000 square miles—two or three times the area covered by the Mesopotamian cultural zone.

At the height of their development, the Harappan peoples reached the edge of the Indus ecological system and came into contact with the cultures of the northern part of Afghanistan, as well as with the inhabitants of the infertile desert frontier, the nomadic hunter-gatherers to the east, and western traders.

HARAPPAN CITY LIFE

We know less about Harappan culture than about the other cultures of Afro-Eurasia of a comparable age. Many of its remains are buried today under a water table raised through years of heavy flooding and accumulated silt deposits. To complicate matters further, scholars have thus far been unable to identify the spoken language of the Indus peoples, who devised a script of about 400 symbols. Indeed, it is unclear if the script even represents a spoken language: it may instead be a nonlinguistic symbol system. Most of what remains of the Indus script is carried on some thousand or more stamp seals and small plaques, excavated from the region; these may represent the names and titles of individuals rather than complete sentences. Moreover, because the Harappans did not produce King Lists, as did the Mesopotamians and the Egyptians—and may not even have had kings—scholars are unable to chart a political history by tracing the rise and fall of dynasties and kingdoms.

What we know about Harappa is therefore not based on literary accounts. It is pieced together from archaeological reconstructions, and it is inevitably and disappointingly sketchy. The sketchiness reminds us that "history" is not what happened but only what we know about what happened. Unable to read documents from the Harappan period

MAP 2-4   THE INDUS RIVER VALLEY IN THE THIRD MILLENNIUM BCE

Historians know less about the urban society of the Indus Valley in the third millennium BCE than they do about its contemporaries in Mesopotamia and Egypt. Still, archaeological evidence affords insight into this urban complex. Where were cities concentrated in the Indus Valley? How did the environment of the region shape urban development? What functions do you think outposts such as Lothal played in Harappan society?

THE MYSTERY OF HARAPPAN WRITING

Harappa culture in the Indus Valley is one urban culture of the third millennium BCE whose writing system has not yet been deciphered. The Indus script appeared on seals and tablets, and in Dholavira, a recently discovered site, even on a board for public display. Though no one can read the script, and no one is sure which language it represents, certain of its characteristics provide scholars with fuel for speculation.

As for verbal communication through writing, it needs to be understood that no one has as yet succeeded in deciphering the Harappan script and that this will remain an unlikely eventuality unless a bilingual inscription—in Harappan and a known form of writing—is found, that incorporates the names of people or places. The Harappan script is logographic: there are 375 to 400 signs, which rules out an alphabet (where one sign stands for one vowel or consonant) because alphabets usually have no more than thirty-six signs. Often Harappan bangles or metal tools are inscribed with just one sign. Harappan writing goes from right to left, as can be made out from close examination of overlapping signs scratched on pots. Short strokes indicate numbers, and numerals precede other signs, which could mean that in the Harappan language adjectives preceded the nouns they qualified. Certain signs, computer concordances reveal, tend to occur frequently at the end of inscriptions, which points to a language using a set of phonetic suffixes.

The Harappan language was probably agglutinative, or a language which added suffixes to an unchanging root. This feature is characteristic of the Dravidian language family rather than the Indo-Aryan languages. This, and the fact that the earliest Indo-Aryan text, the *Rigveda*, shows Dravidian influence (indicating that the early Indo-Aryans in the northwest had some contact with Dravidian speakers), make it likely that the language of the Harappans was a Dravidian one. (Note, also, that Brahui, spoken in the hills of southern Baluchistan today, is a Dravidian language.)

The inscriptions on the seals being brief, on average five to six signs long, they probably gave little more than the owner's name and designation. Perhaps it was the pictorial (often solo animal) emblem, rendered with great skill, that indicated the lineage, ancestry or social origins of the owner. There is no geographic pattern to the occurrence of the various seal animals (unicorn, bull, rhinoceros, antelope, tiger or elephant), so the animal could not possibly have signified the place of origin of the seal owner. Perhaps it was this pictorial image that lent authority to any spoken message that accompanied a seal or an object stamped with one. It may be noted that so far it

is Harappa and Mohenjo-daro—and mound E rather than the 'citadel mound' AB at Harappa—that have yielded the evidence for the most intensive writing activity. These were probably centres of administration.

Harappan writing occurs on pots, seals, bullae, terracotta (stoneware) and shell bangles, copper tablets and tools, and ivory rods. Large numbers of scored goblets with pointed bases that occur at Harappa and Mohenjo-daro are important as they are one of the very few pottery forms that can occasionally carry seal impressions (as distinct from scratched signs)—their use remains a mystery. We get the impression that writing was for humdrum purposes. A striking exception to this is the occurrence of a huge "public" inscription that seems to have been set up on a street at Dholavira in Kutch, with letters about thirty-seven centimetres high cut out of stones and, R. S. Bisht suggests, fastened on a wooden board.

The most important point, however, is the enormous intellectual advance that the emergence of writing signifies. When we speak we utter sounds in one or other language using a series of sound sequences that carry specific meanings in that language. What writing does is to encode in visual form, that is, through a set of distinct symbols or signs, those sounds and sound sequences—thereby conveying meaning or information. Further, writing makes possible the storage of information or the maintenance of records for future reference. It makes communication at a distance possible. It requires of the writer knowledge of the signs and some amount of manual dexterity, and of the reader, knowledge of how the visual signs are vocalized and of course familiarity with the relevant language. Writing has been termed the most momentous invention human beings have ever made.

→ *Even though we cannot read Harappan script, why is the knowledge that the Harappans wrote in script important? Judging from the information above about Harappan writing, what language do you think the script most likely represents?*

SOURCE: Shereen Ratnagar, *Understanding Harappa Civilization in the Greater Indus Valley* (New Delhi: Tulika, 2002), pp. 60–61.

Mohenjo Daro. Mohenjo Daro, the "mound of dead," is a large urban site of the Harappan culture. The view of the city demonstrates a neat layout of houses and civic facilities such as sewer draining.

and forced to rely on fragmentary archaeological evidence, scholars have been unable to draw the rich portraits of the Harappan way of life that they have supplied for the Mesopotamians and the Egyptians.

Still, what we know is impressive. The layout of Harappan cities and towns followed the same general pattern. A fortified citadel housed public facilities, alongside which was located a larger residential area. Both the citadels and the residential areas of Harappan cities were well planned. The main street cut through the city and had covered drainage on both sides. Because the house gates and doors opened onto back alleys, the main street, flanked by blank walls of houses, probably looked rather dull. Citadels were most likely centers of political and ritual activities. At the center of the citadel of Mohenjo Daro was the famous great bath, a brick structure that was 39.3 feet by 23 feet and 9.8 feet deep. Flights of steps led to the bottom of the bath, while other stairs went up to a level of rooms surrounding it. The bath was well sealed with mortar and bitumen, and its water was supplied by a large well nearby. The water then drained through a channel leading from one corner of the bath to lower land to the west of the small mound where the bath was located. The location, size, and quality of the structures all suggest that the bath served ritual purposes.

The Harappans used brick extensively. Houses for notables, the city walls, and underground water drainage systems were all built of bricks manufactured in large ovens, where they were baked into tough, durable, but costly construction materials, made and laid so skillfully that basic structures remain intact to this day. A well-built house had private bath-

rooms, showers, and toilets that drained into durable municipal sewers—also made of bricks. Less durable, and less costly, sun-baked bricks, a ubiquitous building material throughout the southern stretches of Eurasia even today, were employed in constructing houses in small towns and villages.

TRADE

The Harappans engaged in trade along the Indus River and through the mountain passes to the Iranian plateau, as well as along the coast of the Arabian Sea as far as the Persian Gulf and Mesopotamia. They traded such resources as copper, flint, shells, and ivory, as well as pottery, flint blades, and jewelry created by their craftworkers, for gold, silver, gemstones, and textiles from afar. Some of the Harappan trading towns were located in remote but strategically important places. Lothal, a well-fortified town at the head of the Gulf of Khambhat (Cambay), was distant from the center of the Harappan society. Yet it was a vital port, providing access to the sea and to valuable raw materials. Its many workshops processed precious stones, both those available locally and those brought in by traders—especially carnelian, a red stone. The demand for these gemstones was high on the Iranian plateau and even higher in Mesopotamia, and Harappans knew that controlling their extraction and trade was essential to maintaining economic power. Carnelian was found nearby, but lapis lazuli had to be imported from what is now northern Afghanistan, and the Harappans built fortifications and settlements near its sources. Extending their

Harappan Gemstone Necklace. Beadmakers perforated lapis lazuli and other semi-precious stones using a bow drill to make tiny holes for suspension.

frontier to control resources did not stop at gemstones. Metals such as copper and silver also had strategic importance in the Afro-Eurasian commercial systems, and Harappans set up settlements near their copper mines.

Through a complex and vibrant trading system, the Harappans maintained access to mineral and agrarian resources. To facilitate trade across the Indus riverine area, rulers relied not just on Harappan script but on a system of weights and measures that they devised and standardized. Harappan seals, used to stamp commodities with the names of their owners or the nature of the goods, have been found in archaeological sites as far away as the Persian Gulf, Mesopotamia, and the Iranian plateau (see "Global Connections & Disconnections").

The high degree of uniformity in Harappan sites suggests a centralized and structured state. Unlike the Mesopotamians, however, the Harappans seem to have built neither palaces nor grand royal tombs, nor even impressive monumental structures of any kind. Unlike the Egyptians and Mesopotamians, the Harappan elites expressed their elaborate urban culture in ways that did not loudly proclaim their high standing in the world. The Harappans were as reticent as the Egyptians and Mesopotamians were boastful. This

quality has puzzled scholars, but it clearly underscores the profound differences in ancient societies: they did not all value the same things. The advent of writing, urban culture, long-distance trade, and large cities did not necessarily produce the same social hierarchies and the same ethos. What the people of the Indus River show us is how much even the urbanized parts of the world were diverging from each other, even as they borrowed from and imitated their neighbors.

THE GIFT OF THE NILE: EGYPT (5000–2000 BCE)

> → *How did the Nile River shape the development of early Egyptian society?*

The earliest inhabitants along the banks of the Nile River, where another of the great founding riverine cultures of the third millennium BCE arose, were a mixed people. Some had migrated from the eastern and western deserts in Sinai and

Harappan Seal Stamps. The stamp seals of the Indus Valley culture are distinctive. Cut from the soft stone steatite and fired to a white color to make them hard, they have a rounded boss pierced for suspension on the back. The images carved on their surface are usually animals: elephants, tigers, bulls. Occasionally human figures, perhaps deities, perhaps rulers, are depicted seated on a platform, or dancing, or surrounded by animals. Many of the stamp seals have inscriptions across the top edge. The script of the Harappan people has not been deciphered, nor has its underlying language been identified.

Libya as these areas became nearly barren. Still others came from the Mediterranean, but equally important were the peoples who trekked northward from Nubia and central Africa. Ancient Egypt was a melting pot, where early immigrants to the river basin blended cultural practices and technologies from southwestern Asia, northern Africa, the Mediterranean basin, and central Africa.

Egypt had much in common with Mesopotamia and the Indus Valley. Like them, it had densely populated areas whose inhabitants depended on irrigation for their economic well-being, employed monumental architecture, endowed their rulers with immense authority, and created a social order of great complexity. Tapping the Nile water gave rise to agrarian wealth, commercial and devotional centers, early states, and new techniques of communication.

Yet the ancient Egyptian culture was profoundly distinct from its contemporaries in Mesopotamia and the Indus Valley. To understand its unique qualities, we must begin with Egypt's geography. The country and its inhabitants were, and continue to be, dominated by the environment and the natural boundaries of deserts and river rapids and the sea. What is today the Arab Republic of Egypt, roughly the core area of the ancient Egyptians, consists of 386,560 square miles, of which only 7.5 million acres (11,720 square miles) are cultivable. And of this total, no fewer than 6 million acres are located in the Nile delta, that vast agriculturally rich alluvial land that lies between the two main branches of the Nile River as it flows north of Cairo into the Mediterranean Sea.

THE NILE RIVER AND ITS FLOODWATERS

Because knowing Egypt requires appreciating the pulses of the Nile, we must turn first to this extraordinary body of water, the world's longest river, which stretches 4,238 miles from its sources in the highlands of central Africa to its ultimate destination in the Mediterranean Sea. In this way and many others Egypt was, and remains to this day, deeply attached to sub-Saharan Africa. Not only did its life-giving irrigation waters and its rich silt come from African highlands, but much of its population originally migrated into the valley of the Nile from the south.

The Upper Nile is a sluggish river that cuts deeply through a merciless desert. Rising out of central Africa and Ethiopia, the two main branches of the Nile—the White and Blue Niles—join together at the present-day capital city of the Sudan, Khartoum, and then scour out a single riverbed 1,500 miles long to the river's outlet on the Mediterranean. The floods were annual, which gave the basin a regular injection of moisture and alluvial richness. But when the waters spilled over the banks, they did not fertilize or irrigate fields as broad as those in Mesopotamia or Harappa. Floodwaters created something more closely resembling green belts flank-

ing the thick brown waterway. The result was a society whose highly coherent culture stretched out along the navigable axis of the river and its carefully preserved banks. Further away from the banks of the river, on both sides, lay a desert, rich in raw materials but largely uninhabitable. Egypt had no vast fertile hinterland like the sprawling plains of Mesopotamia and the Indus Valley. In a sense, Egypt was the most "riverine" of the riverine cultures.

The predictability of the Nile as the source of life and abundance fundamentally shaped the character of ancient Egypt. In contrast to the wild and uncertain Euphrates and Tigris rivers, whose floods often brought great destruction, the Nile was gentle and bountiful, leading Egyptians to view the world as beneficent. The White Nile, rising in the heart of Africa and traversing the great lakes of central Africa, including Lake Nyanza, yielded Egypt a steady stream of water, varying little from one season to the next or one year to the next. The same was not true of the Blue Nile, which rose in the highlands of Ethiopia and was fed by the monsoon rains of East Africa and by melting snows. The Blue Nile provided Egypt's floodwaters, while the White Nile ensured that these would be predictable and relatively easy to regulate.

Once the Egyptians began to occupy the Nile River valley, they devised a simple but highly effective system for turning the Nile floodwaters to their advantage and rendering the area one of the most fertile spots in the world. During the summer months, as the Nile swelled, local villagers, unsupervised by any central administration, built earthen walls

Nile Agriculture. The Nile is fed by the Blue Nile, which has its source in the Ethiopian highlands, and the White Nile in southern Sudan. It rises and falls according to a regular pattern that was the basis for the ancient Egyptian agricultural cycle. Flooding the valley in August and September, the Nile recedes, depositing a rich layer of silt in which the crops were planted in the fall and harvested in April and May.

that carved the floodplain into basins. As the flood spilled over the banks the waters were trapped in the basins, where they deposited the rich silt of the Ethiopian highlands. The waters stood in the flood basins long enough to provide silt for the growing season; then the earthen dams were breached, allowing the water to drain into adjacent basins and eventually back into the river. Annual flooding meant that each year the land received a new layer of rich topsoil.

The light fertile soils made planting simple. Peasants cast seeds into the ooze and then had their livestock trample them to the proper depth. The never-failing sun, which the Egyptians worshipped, ensured that the fields would yield an abundant harvest as long as they were properly weeded. In the early spring, when the Nile waters were at their lowest and no crops were being grown, the sun dried out the soil, allowing it to shed the harmful salts that ultimately destroyed the fertility of southern Mesopotamia.

The contrasts with Mesopotamia are clear: large-scale hydraulic engineering was not required to domesticate the Nile. Because villagers and households could create and maintain the basic waterworks, the Egyptian state played no essential role in controlling the Nile flood. This is not to say that Egyptians had no need of public infrastructure provided by the state. Accordingly, the state built vast storehouses to hold grain for the next growing season.

EGYPT'S UNIQUE RIVERINE CULTURE

The peculiarities of the Nile region had effects that distinguished it from Mesopotamia and the Indus Valley. Some 2,500 years ago, the Greek historian and geographer Herodotus famously observed that Egypt was the gift of the Nile. He also noted that the Nile basin—from its first cataract (a rough river rapid), south of Aswan, to the sea—was one of the world's most self-contained geographical entities. Bounded on the north by the Mediterranean Sea, on the east and west by harsh deserts, and on the south by cataracts, Egypt was destined from its earliest days to achieve a sense of common destiny. It was a region far less open to outsiders than were Mesopotamia and the Indus River basin.

Reinforcing a sense of separation from the outside was the region's bounty: nearly all of the natural resources that the ancient Egyptians needed were available locally. In the desolate landscapes of the western and eastern deserts were abundant sources of copper, silver, lead, and other metals, as well as colorful stones like turquoise. Gold, exotic woods, plants, animals, and extra manpower were available to the south in Nubia and were transported along the Nile River in vessels with sails and oars. This was a far cry from the resource-poor alluvium of Mesopotamia, which from the fourth millennium BCE onward required copper, timber, and stones to be imported from the surrounding plateaus and mountain regions.

Yet, like the other pioneering societies, Egypt created a common culture by balancing regional tensions and reconciling regional rivalries. Ancient Egyptian history can be told as a struggle of sharply competing dualistic forces: the north or Lower Egypt versus the south or Upper Egypt; the sand, the so-called red part of the earth, versus the rich soil, described as black; life versus death; heaven versus earth; and order versus disorder. For Egypt's ruling groups—most notably the kings, known as pharaohs, at the apex of the political system—the primary task was to bring stability or order, referred to as *ma'at*, out of these antagonistic impulses. The Egyptians believed that keeping chaos, personified by the desert and its marauders, at bay through vigilant attention to *ma'at* was what allowed all that was good and right to occur.

THE RISE OF THE STATE AND DYNASTIES

Once the Nile was harnessed to agriculture, Egypt quickly developed from a scarcely inhabited area to a complex society. Whereas the pace of development in Mesopotamia and Harappa was gradual and cumulative, Egypt grew seemingly overnight; it changed from being only a few small village communities into a powerhouse, projecting its splendor along the full length of the river valley.

The king's primary responsibility was to ensure that the fundamental forces of nature, in particular the regular flooding of the Nile, continued without interruption. In addition, the king had to protect his people from the invaders of the eastern desert, as well as from the Nubians who pressed against Egypt's southern borders. These groups threatened Egypt with intolerable social chaos. As guarantors of the social and political order, the early kings depicted themselves as shepherds. In wall carvings, artists portrayed them carrying the crook and the flail, indicating their responsibility for the welfare of their flocks (the people) and of the land. Moreover, under the king, an elaborate bureaucracy organized labor and produced public works, sustaining both his vast holdings and general order throughout the realm.

The narrative of ancient Egyptian history has been organized around its dynasties—a structure that gives Egyptian history a sense of deep continuity. According to a third-century BCE Egyptian cleric named Manetho, Egypt was ruled by no fewer than thirty-one dynasties, stretching out over nearly three millennia from 3100 BCE down to its conquest by Alexander the Great in 332 BCE. Since the nineteenth century, however, scholars have found it easier to group the dynasties and recast the story of ancient Egypt around three great periods of dynastic achievement: the Old Kingdom (dynasty III or IV to dynasty VI, from 2649 to 2152 BCE); the Middle Kingdom (dynasties XI to XIII, from 2040 to 1640 BCE), and the New Kingdom (dynasties XVIII to XXI, from 1550 to 1070 BCE). At the end of each of these eras,

→ *How did the Nile River shape the development of early Egyptian society?*

cultural flourishing was interrupted by a breakdown in central authority, known respectively as the First, Second, and Third Intermediate Periods. But no other region of the world has charted its history across a continuum of such extraordinary length and durability.

RITUALS, PYRAMIDS, AND TRUE ORDER

The Third Dynasty (2649–2575 BCE) launched the long foundational period of ancient Egyptian culture known as the Old Kingdom, the golden age of ancient Egypt. (See Map 2-5.) By the time it began, the basic institutions of the Egyptian state were in place, and the ideology and ritual life that gave legitimacy to dynastic rulers were fully integrated into the region's culture.

The king as god presented himself to the population by means of impressive architectural spaces. The priestly class performed rituals that reinforced his supreme status within the natural order of the universe. The most important royal ceremony, especially in the Old Kingdom, was the Sed festival, which renewed the vitality of the king after he had ruled for thirty years (sometimes fewer). Although it focused on the vitality of the king, its origins lay in ritually ensuring the perpetual presence of water.

King Djoser (r. 2630–2611 BCE), the second king of the Third Dynasty, celebrated the Sed festival in his tomb complex at Saqqara. This magnificent monumental complex, the world's oldest stone edifice (rather than the mud brick of the temples and palaces of Mesopotamia), was

MAP 2-5   OLD KINGDOM EGYPT, 2686–2181 BCE

Old Kingdom Egyptian society was strongly influenced by its unique geographical location. How does this map offer insight into early Egyptians' view of their place in the world? Compare this map with Map 2-2. Why do you think Old Kingdom Egyptians had less contact with other societies than did their counterparts in Mesopotamia?

The Pyramids of Giza. The Pyramid Fields of Giza lie on the western side of the Nile just south of the modern city of Cairo. The Old Kingdom Pharaohs built their eternal resting places there, surrounded by the smaller pyramids and mastaba tombs of their relatives and courtiers. The largest pyramid of Khufu is to the north. Khephren's is linked to the Nile by a causeway flanked by the famous Sphinx. The smallest is that of Menkaure, the penultimate king of the glorious Fourth Dynasty.

built during his reign. It began as a huge flat structure—a *mastaba,* which means "bench" in Arabic—identical to earlier royal tombs. Remarkably, we know the name of the architect of Djoser's funerary complex: Imhotep, who was himself deified and became a mythic hero of Egyptian lore. Imhotep was not satisfied with the modest shape of earlier burial chambers. Through the course of six separate renovations, he transformed the *mastaba* into a step pyramid that in its final form rose some 200 feet above the plain, dominating the landscape as did the later Mesopotamian ziggurats. This mountainlike structure stood at the center of an enormous walled precinct that had five individual courts in which the king performed various rituals that emphasized the divinity of kingship and the unity of Upper and Lower Egypt. Because most of the structures were facades, the whole complex resembled a stage on which state rituals were performed. The symbolism of the unity of Upper and Lower Egypt was pervasive, embodied in the entwined lotus and papyrus—symbols of each region. The step pyramid complex incorporated the artistic and architectural forms that would characterize Egyptian culture for millennia.

The Egyptian pharaoh—the king as god—used the royal tomb to embody the state's ideology and the fundamental ideas of the Egyptian cosmos. The ritual of death, leading to everlasting life, became part of the cultural myth. So, too, did a common ideology that stressed the underlying unity of the distinct regions of the long river valley. The pharaoh also used symbols (for example, the dual crown representing Upper and Lower Egypt), throne names, and many descriptive titles for himself and his advisers to represent his power and that of his administrators, the priests, and the landed elite. The Egyptian cosmic order was from the beginning one of inequality and stark hierarchy. Established at the time of creation, the universe was the king's responsibility to maintain for eternity. The insistence, in Egypt and elsewhere, that the king was a god, or was like a god, has often been misunderstood as exalting the power of the king. In fact, the belief that the king was a god compelled the ruler to behave like one. And therefore, like a god, he had to be serene, orderly, merciful, and perfect. An expression of divine peace (not the angry snarl of mere human power) had always to be on his lips.

Pyramid building evolved rapidly from the step version of Djoser to the grand pyramids put up in the Fourth Dynasty (2575–2465 BCE). The Fourth Dynasty kings erected their magnificent structures at Giza, just outside modern-day Cairo and not far from the early royal cemetery site of Saqqara. The pyramid of Khufu is the largest stone structure in the world, and it was built to almost perfectly exact measurements.

Khephren's pyramid, though smaller, is even more alluring because of the protective presence of the famous recumbent sphinx. These royal tombs were surrounded on all sides by the tombs of the high officials, almost all of whom were members of the royal family. The amount of labor involved in constructing these monuments was enormous and provides another measure of the degree of centralization and the large surpluses that existed in Egyptian society at this time. The manpower was drawn from the peasants and workers who were obliged to work for the state at certain times of the year. Their numbers were augmented by slaves brought from Nubia, as well as by captured peoples from the Mediterranean.

RELIGION OF ANCIENT EGYPT

Religion stood at the center of this ancient world. All aspects of the culture of the ancient Egyptians were suffused with spiritual expression. Egyptians understood the world in which they lived to be inhabited by three groups: gods, kings, and the rest of humanity. Official records, especially pictorial but also written texts, exclusively bore representations of gods and kings. Yet rarely were kings confused with gods—at least during their lifetimes. Mortality was the bar between rulers and deities; after death, kings joined the gods whom they had represented while alive.

As in Mesopotamia, every region in Egypt had its resident god. The fate of each deity was mirrored in the history of its region. Some gods, such as Amun, who was believed to reside and be physically present in Thebes, transcended regional status because of the importance of their hometown. Over the centuries, the Egyptian gods evolved, combining often contradictory aspects into single deities who were represented by symbols: animals and human figures that often had animal as well as divine attributes. They included Horus, the hawk god; Osiris, the god of regeneration and the underworld; Hathor, the goddess of childbirth and love; Ra, the sun god; and Amun, a creator who was considered the hidden god.

Official religious practices took place in the main temples, the heart of ceremonial and festive practices. The king and his agents cared for the gods in their temples, giving them respect, adoration, and thanks. In return, the gods, who were embodied in sculptured images, maintained order and gave sustenance to the king and through him all humanity. In this contractual relationship between the gods and humans, gods were invariably passive and serene while the kings were active, a difference that reflected the inherent inequality in their relationship. The practice of religious rituals and communication with the gods formed the cult, whose goal was to preserve cosmic order—and achieving that goal required constant exertion on the part of human worshippers.

The task of upholding the cult, regulating yearly rituals according to a cosmic calendar, and mediating between gods, kings, and the rest of society fell to one specialist class: the priesthood. In the Egyptian order of things, the priesthood was more important than a cadre of tax collectors. Creating a priesthood required elaborate rules for selecting and training the priests to project the organized power of spiritual authority. And as was true of all Egyptian society, that organization was highly stratified. That the priests alone could enter the inner sanctum of the temple drove home their exceptional and exalted status. The god, embodied in the cult statue, left the temple only on the occasion of great festivals. Even then the divine image remained hidden in a portable shrine, out of sight of the general populace. This arrangement ensured that priests monopolized the channels of communication between spiritual powers and their subjects—and thereby made certain that Egyptians understood and embraced their subservience to the priesthood.

While the priesthood helped integrate Egyptians into one unified realm and focused the attention of all subjects on the central role of temple life, the priests coexisted with less visible local protectors of the divine order. Unofficial, popular religion was equally important in the cosmic system. Ordinary people in ancient Egypt matched their elite rulers in faithfulness to the gods. But their distance from temple life required that they fulfill their religious needs and duties in different ways. Common Egyptian people frequented the many scattered local shrines, just as those of higher status visited the temples. There they prayed, made requests, and left offerings to the gods.

Magic held a special importance for commoners, who attributed extraordinary powers to amulets—for example, expecting them to ward off illness and ensure safe childbirth. Marked with the images and symbols of deities, amulets were especially useful because they were easily moved, able to accompany—and therefore watch over—humble believers wherever they went. To deal with the most profound questions of life, commoners looked to omens and divination—a practice that was also used both in Mesopotamia and in ancient China to help predict and control future events.

Like Egyptian elites, commoners attributed supernatural powers to animals. Chosen animals were entitled to special treatment in life and were looked after in death. Special cemeteries and mourning rituals were reserved for Apis bulls, sacred to the god Ptah; ibises, dogs, jackals, cats, baboons, lizards, fish, snakes, crocodiles, and other beasts associated with deities enjoyed similar privileges.

A "Chosen" Animal. In the popular religion of ancient Egypt, gods were thought to be manifest through certain animals, which were mummified when they died. Bulls were sacred to several gods. The Apis bull at Memphis was considered the earthly manifestation of Ptah, the creator god through whom he gave oracles. Pious individuals would dedicate a calf to the gods as a token of their devotion. This is a typical example of such a mummy.

Egyptian Gods. Osiris (*top left*) is the dying god who rules over the netherworld. Most frequently he is depicted as a mummy wearing a white crown with plumes and holding the scepter and flagellum across his chest. The god Horus (*top right and bottom*), who was also rendered as Ra-Horakhty, is the falcon-headed Egyptian sky god. Horus is the earliest state god of Egypt and is always closely associated with the king. Horus is a member of the ennead of Heliopolis and is the son of Osiris and Isis.

→ *How did the Nile River shape the development of early Egyptian society?*

WRITING AND SCRIBES

Egypt, like Mesopotamia, was a scribal culture. A common statement that circulated among Egyptians was that peasants toiled so that scribes could live in comfort; literacy sharpened the divisions between rural and urban worlds. By the middle of the third millennium BCE, literacy was already firmly established among tiny circles of experts in the cultures of Egypt and Mesopotamia. Because it was limited to relatively few individuals, its possession heightened scribes' social status. Although in both cultures writing emerged in response to economic needs, its utility for commemorative and religious purposes was grasped immediately: as soon as literacy took hold, Mesopotamians and Egyptians were drafting historical records and literary compositions.

Both the early Mesopotamian and Egyptian scripts were complex. Indeed, one feature shared by all writing systems is that over time they became simpler and more efficient at representing the full range of spoken utterances. Only when the first alphabet appeared (to record Aramaic in the middle of the second millennium BCE) did the potential for wider literacy surface. To judge from remaining records, it seems that more Egyptians than Mesopotamians were literate. Most high-ranking Egyptians were also trained as scribes who were employed by the king's court, the army, or the priesthood. Occasionally, kings and members of the royal family also learned to write.

Two basic forms of Egyptian writing were used in conjunction throughout antiquity. *Hieroglyphs*, a term derived from a Greek word meaning "sacred carving," were employed exclusively in temple, royal, or divine contexts. From the early appearance of writing in the tombs of the First Dynasty, records were also kept in a cursive script that was written with ink on papyrus, on pieces of pottery, or on other absorbent media. This was called *demotic writing* and was the most common and practical form of writing in Egypt. Used for administrative record keeping, demotic writing was also employed in private or pseudo-private forms, like letters, and for works of literature, including narrative fiction, manuals of instruction and philosophy, cult and religious hymns, love poems, medical and mathematical texts, collections of rituals, and mortuary books.

Becoming literate required being taught by scribes, and often the skills clustered in extended families. Usually students started their training when they were young; after its completion, they entered the bureaucracy. They began by repeatedly copying standard texts in demotic cursive or hieroglyphs. After mastering these texts, students moved on to

Egyptian Hieroglyphics and "Cursive Script." The Egyptians wrote in two distinctive types of scripts. The more formal is hieroglyphics, which is based on pictorial images that carry values of either ideas (idiograms) or sounds (phonemes). All royal and funerary inscriptions, such as this funerary relief from the Old Kingdom, are rendered in hieroglyphic script. Daily documents, accountings, literary texts, and the like were most often written in a cursive script called demotic, which was written with ink on papyrus. The form of the cursive signs is based on the hieroglyphics but is more abstract and can be formed more quickly.

THE ADMONITIONS OF IPUWER

In order to maintain his power during a period of increasing drought, Pepy II (r. 2246–2152 BCE) gave away many advantages and tax exemptions to provincial nobles. At the end of his long reign, no strong successors emerged who were capable of maintaining centralized power. The collapse of the central state was traumatic, and Egyptian society was for a time reduced to chaos. This social condition was poignantly captured in a number of texts written by prophets and wise men. One of the most moving was by Ipuwer.

Behold, the fire has gone up on high, and its burning goes forth against the enemies of the land.

Behold, things have been done which have not happened for a long time past; the king has been deposed by the rabble.

Behold, he who was buried as a falcon [is devoid] of biers, and what the pyramid concealed has become empty.

Behold, it has befallen that the land has been deprived of the kingship by a few lawless men.

Behold, men have fallen into rebellion against the Uraeus, the [...] of Re, even she who makes the Two Lands content.

Behold, the secret of the land whose limits were unknown is divulged, and the Residence is thrown down in a moment.

Behold, Egypt is fallen to pouring of water, and he who poured water on the ground has carried off the strong man in misery.

Behold, the Serpent is taken from its hole, and the secrets of the Kings of Upper and Lower Egypt are divulged.

Behold, the Residence is afraid because of want, and [men go about] unopposed to stir up strife.

Behold, the land has knotted itself up with confederacies, and the coward takes the brave man's property.

Behold, the Serpent [...] the dead: he who could not make a sarcophagus for himself is now the possessor of a tomb.

Behold, the possessors of tombs are ejected on to the high ground, while he who could not make a coffin for himself is now [the possessor] of a treasury.

Behold, this has happened [to] men; he who could not build a room for himself is now a possessor of walls.

Behold, the magistrates of the land are driven out throughout the land: [...] are driven out from the palaces.

Behold, noble ladies are now on rafts, and magnates are in the labor establishment, while he who could not sleep even on walls is now the possessor of a bed.

Behold, the possessor of wealth now spends the night thirsty, while he who once begged his dregs for himself is now the possessor of overflowing bowls.

Behold, the possessors of robes are now in rags, while he who could not weave for himself is now a possessor of fine linen.

Behold, he who could not build a boat for himself is now the possessor of a fleet; their erstwhile owner looks at them, but they are not his.

Behold, he who had no shade is now the possessor of shade, while the erstwhile possessors of shade are now in the full blast of the storm.

Behold, he who was ignorant of the lyre is now the possessor of a harp, while he who never sang for himself now vaunts the Songstress-goddess.

Behold, those who possessed vessel-stands of copper [...] not one of the jars thereof has been adorned.

→ *What were the causes of the collapse of Egypt's Old Kingdom? How can we use such a document as "The Admonitions of Ipuwer" to understand what conditions were like in Egypt at the end of the third millennium BCE?*

SOURCE: Translated by John A. Wilson in *Ancient Near Eastern Texts Relating to the Old Testament*, edited by J. B. Pritchard (Princeton: Princeton University Press, 1950), pp. 442–43.

literary works. The upper classes prized the ability to read and write almost above all else, regarding it as proof of high intellectual achievement. When they died, those who had attained literacy often had their student textbooks placed alongside their corpses in tombs, as evidence of the talents they had displayed during their lifetimes. The literati produced texts mainly in temples, where these works were also preserved. Writing hieroglyphs and transmitting texts continued without break in ancient Egypt for almost 3,000 years, coming to an end only in the third century BCE.

THE PROSPERITY OF EGYPT

Under pharaonic rule, Egypt prospered. Its population grew at a steady, and in some periods spectacular, rate, swelling from 350,000 in 4000 BCE to 870,000 in 3000 BCE, 1 million in 2500 BCE, 2 million in 1800 BCE, 2.9 million in 1250 BCE, and nearly 5 million by 1500 BCE.

The success of the state depended on administering resources skillfully, and especially on managing agricultural production and labor. Everyone, from members of the most powerful elite groups to the workers in the field, was part of the system. In principle, no one possessed private property; in practice, Egyptians treated land and tools as their own—but submitted to the intrusions of the state. Indeed, a strong state exerted its control, especially over matters of taxation, prices, and the distribution of goods, with unchallenged powers. Such strength was rooted in a large bureaucracy that maintained records, watched over society, and of course regulated and stored the Nile's floodwaters. While land had to be tilled by farmers, the precious source of prosperity was African water, the gift of the gods and the exclusive right and responsibility of the rulers. Mirroring the predictability of the Nile's flow, the bureaucracy and the culture at large became highly resistant to change, counting on tried and true practices and resisting fundamental transformation.

During this period of Egypt's growing social and occupational complexity, when large urban conglomerates were appearing elsewhere, the continued absence of cities on the scale of those in Mesopotamia was extraordinary. In striking contrast to Mesopotamia, ancient Egypt was a land of extensive settlements that had many metropolitan centers. Hence, the divide between rural and urban settings was not as stark in the Nile River basin as it was in Mesopotamia. There were, to be sure, administrative headquarters, where the ruling family and the bureaucrats who supported it resided—Memphis during the Old Kingdom, and Thebes later on—but Egypt neither had nor needed massive cities. It was not nearly so vital a crossroads of trade and population movements as the Tigris-Euphrates region. Its peoples lived tightly compacted into the Nile River basin, and they could easily reach one another by boat. Because the Nile and the surrounding countryside provided most of the goods that men and women needed for a comfortable existence, those dwelling in ancient Egypt could live in communities—constructed just beyond the floodplain, safe from the Nile overflows—that were largely self-contained.

THE LATER DYNASTIES AND THEIR DEMISE

As the Old Kingdom matured and expanded without a powerful uniting or dominating city like those found in Mesopotamia or Harappa, the Egyptian state became more dispersed. The patterns of monumental architecture tell us that Fifth Dynasty policies were less centralized than those of the Fourth Dynasty. The state's expansion, driven by economic growth, led to local variation and adaptation. That private tombs were more highly decorated with images and inscriptions than before testifies to an enhanced freedom of expression. As this era came to an end, high officials were beginning to use magical spells and imagery that originally had been the sole preserve of kings. By the beginning of the Middle Kingdom, such officials began in special cases to have the same access as kings to immortality through burial rituals.

Fifth Dynasty Egypt no longer looked inward. By the Sixth Dynasty, texts, reliefs on tombs, and archaeological evidence suggest that Egypt had extended its power militarily in Palestine to the east, in Libya in the west, and in Nubia in the south. Trade also increased, and the southern Egyptian oases of El Kharga and El Dakhla bustled with traders driving caravans of donkeys loaded with goods.

Expansion and decentralization eventually exposed the weaknesses of dynastic genealogies. The shakeup resulted not from external invasion or of bickering between rival city-states but from feuding between factions of the political elite. In addition, an extended drought that began in northern Africa sometime around 2250 BCE put impossible strains on Egypt's extensive irrigation system, which could no longer water the lands that kept the population of about a million inhabitants fed. Imagery of great suffering filled the texts and depictions on the walls of the royal tombs. The long reign of Pepy II (2246–2152 BCE), at the end of the Sixth Dynasty, proved to be the swan song of the Old Kingdom. Upon his death, royal power collapsed completely. For the next hundred years, many rivals jostled for the throne; some fell within a year. Local magnates assumed hereditary control of the government in the provinces and treated the lands previously controlled by the royal family as their own personal property. Descriptions of life were filled with internecine feuding, as local leaders plunged into bloody regional struggles to keep the irrigation works functioning for their own communities. This so-called First Intermediate Period lasted roughly from 2150 to 2040 BCE.

RIVERINE PEOPLES IN EAST ASIA (5000–2000 BCE)

> → *What hallmarks of urban life emerged in China during this period?*

Like the inhabitants of Mesopotamia and Egypt, East Asian peoples tended to cluster in river basins. Their settlements along the banks of the Yellow River in the north and the Yangzi River in the south became the foundation of the future Chinese state, unlike the Jomon in Japan, who were tied to a hunting-gathering subsistence economy. Already by 5000 BCE, both millet in the north and rice in the south were being

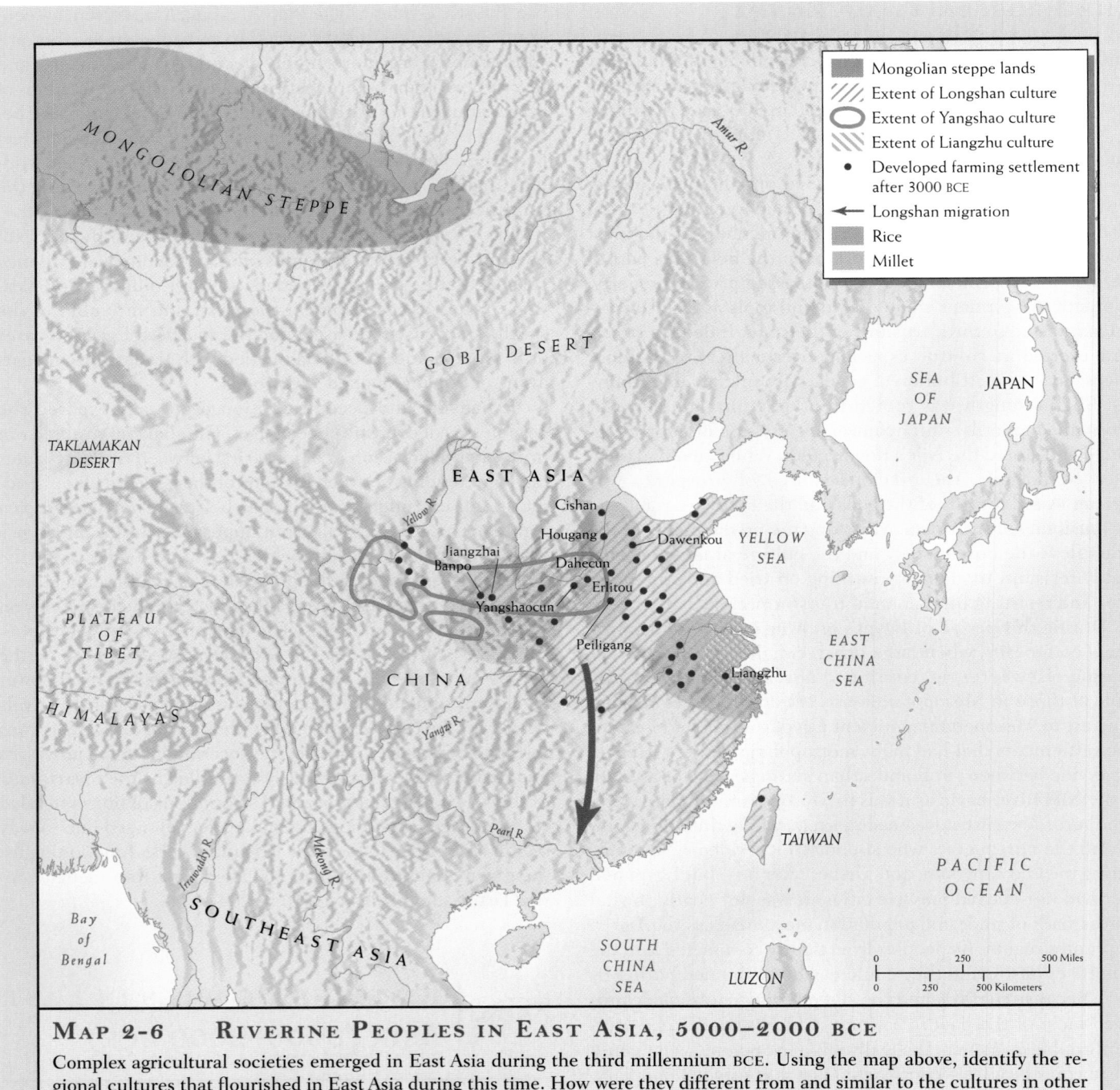

MAP 2-6   RIVERINE PEOPLES IN EAST ASIA, 5000–2000 BCE

Complex agricultural societies emerged in East Asia during the third millennium BCE. Using the map above, identify the regional cultures that flourished in East Asia during this time. How were they different from and similar to the cultures in other contemporary riverine societies? How did regional cultures in East Asia influence each other?

widely cultivated. Yet in the following three millennia, during an era when Mesopotamia, Egypt, and the Indus Valley were creating populous, socially complex, and city-based cultures, the Chinese moved more slowly. China's great riverine cultures did not arise until the second millennium BCE. (See Map 2-6.) Like the waterways in the other regions, the Yellow and Yangzi rivers also had annual floods and extensive floodplains that proved eminently suitable for high agricultural yields and capable of supporting dense populations. But in China the evolution of hydraulic works, big cities, priestly and bureaucratic classes, and a new writing system took longer.

→ *What hallmarks of urban life emerged in China during this period?*

Living conditions and the environment played a strong role in ancient Chinese society just as it did in the riverine culture of Southwest Asia. In the riverine basins of China, food was abundant and communities were spread out, encouraging localized agrarian cultures. Complex cities would come later. The early Chinese peoples simply did not feel the same kinds of pressure compared to the societies bordering the deserts in Southwest Asia. Other factors contributing to their different course of development included the paucity of easily domesticated animals and plants, as well as geography. Geography worked to isolate China, for the Himalayan Mountains and the Taklamakan and Gobi deserts prevented large-scale population movements between East Asia and Central Asia and hindered the rapid diffusion of intellectual and cultural breakthroughs occurring elsewhere in Afro-Eurasia.

FROM YANGSHAO TO LONGSHAN CULTURE

China's classical histories place the society's beginnings at the foundation of the Xia dynasty, dating from 2200 BCE. Archaeological studies of riverine environments in East Asia tell a story that challenges the traditional account. Whether or not the Xia actually existed as a historical dynasty, it is clear that our study of the Yellow River basin and Yangzi delta should begin earlier, in the two millennia from 4000 to 2000 BCE.

Although somewhat isolated in comparison to Southwest Asia, China was never completely sealed off from outside influences. Unlike the Americas, East Asia was not separated from the rest of Afro-Eurasia by great oceans. Indeed, some travelers arrived via the ocean, though not on a large scale until the invention of truly seaworthy vessels. More importantly, the Mongolian steppe provided an opening to China through which such important technologies as the chariot were introduced by nomads sometime in the second millennium BCE. Nomads were drawn to the agricultural settlements in China as they were in Mesopotamia, and they brought with them innovations and bronze and other goods from afar. Through trade and migration, nomadic cultures and technologies filtered from the steppes to communities settled on the rivers.

The combination of agrarian settlements and increasing contact with neighbors gave rise to greater cultural complexity. The telltale signs include breakthroughs in communication. Although the Chinese did not create a graphic writing system until the middle of the second millennium BCE, pre-literate signs and marks found at Jiahu, on the south banks of the Yellow River, have been dated as early as the seventh millennium BCE—long before similar systems appeared in Mesopotamia and Egypt.

Markings on red pottery, which archaeologists found in ancient sites near the village of Yangshao along the Yellow River in northwestern China, likewise represent a pioneering system of signs and symbols from as early as 5000 BCE. Some

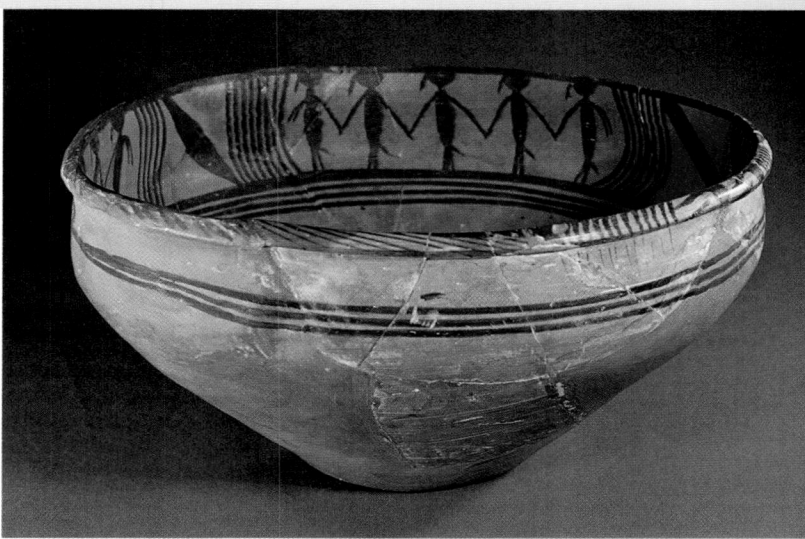

Yangshao Bowl with Dancing Figures, c. 5000–1700 BCE. The Yangshao, also referred to as the "painted pottery" culture, produced gray or red pottery painted with black geometric designs and occasionally with pictures of fish or human faces and figures. Because the potter's wheel was unknown at the time, the vessels were probably fashioned with strips of clay.

of the signs may be precursors of script. Archaeologists have also discovered analogous signs on early pottery in southern China. A complex society that required writing, such as that of the Sumerians, did not emerge until much later. Nevertheless, shamans—many of them women—in the emerging villages of the fourth and third millennium BCE may have used signs in performing rituals, music, and healing, as well as in divination to interpret omens and predict the future.

China's early riverine societies produced stone and pottery storage vessels of the sort that we associate with permanent, increasingly urban settlements. Near the village of Longshan in Shandong province on the eastern end of the North China plain, for example, archaeologists in 1931–1932 discovered highly polished black pottery and a complete town enclosure of compacted earth. Such finds contrast sharply with the simpler artifacts of the Yangshao sites in the northwest. Furthermore, Longshan residents burned deer scapulas to communicate with the dead: the cracks that formed were interpreted by diviners. This ritual was likely the precursor of the inscribed oracle bones introduced in the Shang dynasty (1600–1045 BCE), which like the deer bones were consulted by those who wished to get the advice of their dead ancestors when making important decisions.

We do not know where the Longshan people originally came from, but they likely migrated in several waves from the peripheries of East Asia to the eastern China seashore, and they helped form the many villages then dotting China. Their achievements, compared to those of the earlier Yangshao peoples, suggest marked development between 5000 and 2000 BCE. Several regional cultures in northern and southern China, which arose independently, began to produce similar

Primary Source

ARCHAEOLOGICAL EVIDENCE FOR LONGSHAN CULTURE

Over the course of a millennium, multiple cultures with strong similarities emerged in north and northwest China. Some scholars have argued that a single Longshan culture grew out of these various close-knit groups. Even if its cohesiveness did not rise to the level of forming a fully integrated interaction sphere, the changes that Longshan represented were nonetheless remarkable.

Let us take a quick look at the kind of innovations that sprouted everywhere and that, because of the similarities of style, must be interrelated:

1. Archaeologically acceptable evidence of copper objects, mostly trinkets and small tools of no agricultural value, has been unearthed in Shantung, western Honan, southern Shansi, and Ch'i-chia from archaeological horizons comparable in age. The finds do not suffice to point to a major metal industry as yet, but in light of what happened later on one must regard the Lung-shan metallurgy as worthy of note. The bronze vessel fragment from Wang-ch'eng-kang is of special significance.

2. Industrially much more important is the extremely widespread use of potter's wheels for the manufacture of ceramics. There was tremendous variation in the pottery wares of the various Lung-shan Cultures, but the overwhelming change from red to gray and the general decline of painted decoration must have been the result of a conscious choice on the part of the potters, who, armed with improved kilns and the wheel, must have represented a specialized profession in the Lung-shan society.

3. The stamped-earth construction technology and the construction of town walls using that technology are separate issues, but the town walls in Shantung, east Honan, north Honan, and west Honan indicate both the transmission of a technology and the rise of the necessity for defensive public works.

4. Related to the rise of defensive ramparts is the archaeological evidence of institutionalized violence. This takes two forms—evidence of raids or wars, such as the Chien-kou-ts'un finds of skulls and bodies in the water well; and burials of possible ritual victims relating to the construction of chiefly or royal monuments.

5. There are several manifestations of rituals, especially ones closely tied to persons of high political status. The first is the role of some animals and birds in ritual art, such as those found or identified recently in Liang-ch'eng, Shantung; the Liang-chu sites, in Kiangsu and Chekiang; and T'ao-ssu, Shansi.

6. The *ts'ung* tube, especially if associated with animals and birds, is a very distinctive ritual object manifesting a unique cosmology. Its discovery in Liang-chu on the coast and T'ao-ssu in the interior cannot be accidental; it indicates without question an interregional transmission of cosmology or even a spherewide substratum featuring that cosmology. If we include jade rings (*pi*) in this cosmological bag, the Ch'i-chia Culture also becomes involved.

7. The virtually universal occurrence of scapulimancy among the Lung-shan Cultures is another manifestation of the spherewide communication or substratum of cosmology.

8. The archaeological evidence for violence and for ritual on an institutional basis almost inevitably means a society featuring sharp political and economic divisions, and that is exactly what we find in the mortuary remains of many of the Lung-shan Cultures. We have already seen archaeological indications of social ranking in the mortuary remains of the Neolithic sites of the fifth and fourth centuries B.C. (see chapters 3–4). These trends accelerated and further intensified in the Lung-shan cemeteries. Furthermore, as the Ch'eng-tzu (Shantung) and T'ao-ssu (Shansi) cemeteries show, the economic and political polarization appears to have taken place within the framework of the unilinear clans and lineages.

All of the above happenings are plainly indicated by archaeological evidence, but they do not point to a single Lung-shan Culture. Instead, they indicate a series of interrelated changes in culture and society that took place within each of the regional cultures in the Chinese interaction sphere. From the point of view of each of the regional sequences, both the external interaction network and internal changes during a period of two thousand years were essential for its readiness, toward the end of the third millennium B.C., to step over the next threshold into the state society, urbanism, and civilization.

→ *What were the key ingredients of Longshan culture? What does the evidence of violence reveal about Longshan society?*

SOURCE: Kwang-chih Chang, *The Archaeology of Ancient China*, 4th ed. (New Haven: Yale University Press, 1986), pp. 287–88. Note: Chang uses Wade-Giles romanization.

pottery and tools and to plant the same crops, probably reflecting their contact with one another. They did not yet produce city-states, but agriculture began to flourish and small settlements covered the increasingly populated Yellow River valley in the northwest and the coastal areas.

Some of the hallmarks of the beginnings of urban life are evident. Members of the Longshan cultural complex buried their dead in cemeteries outside their villages. Several thousand graves have been uncovered in southern Shanxi province; the largest ones contain ritual pottery vessels, musical instruments made of wood, copper bells, and painted murals. Specialized shamans performed rituals employing axes of jade. Jade quarrying in particular indicated the group's highly developed technical power, as skilled craftworkers translated stone tablets into powerful expressions of ritual and military authority. The recent discovery in the middle part of the Yellow River's flow across the North China Plain of a Longshan household whose members were all scalped after being killed demonstrates the power and danger of organized violence. Attackers filled the water wells with five layers of human skeletons, some decapitated. The defensive walls that surrounded newly established villages were clearly needed.

Longshan Beaker, c. 2500 BCE. Longshan has been called the "black pottery" culture, and its exquisite black pottery was not painted but rather decorated with rings, either raised or grooved. Longshan culture was more advanced than the Yangshao culture, and its distinctive pottery was likely formed on a potter's wheel.

As communities became more centralized, contact between regions also increased. Interregional links between northern and southern China took shape in the middle of the third millennium BCE, when peoples originally from Longshan villages began to migrate along the East Asian coast to Taiwan and the Pearl River delta in the far south. Similarities in the artifacts found along the coast and at Longshan sites in northern China, such as the form and decoration of pottery and jade items, also point to a shared cultural and trading sphere. Many of the early peoples in the south, whom we also call Austronesians (a diverse group of people stretching roughly from Madagascar to Easter Island whose languages were similar), then moved by boat into the Pacific from East Asian coastal islands (see Chapter 3).

Finally, archaeologists have found evidence of small-scale, short-lived, and scattered political organizations. Although they did not aggregate into anything resembling the translocal alliances that created dynastic systems in Egypt, Mesopotamia, and the Indus Valley, they did not consist simply of chieftains ruling impoverished hamlets. These were wealthy—if localized—polities, which constituted what scholars have called the era of Ten Thousand States (*Wan'guo*). One of them, the Liangzhu, has drawn particular interest because of its remarkable jade objects.

LIFE IN LIANGZHU

The Liangzhu people, like their Longshan relatives to the north, were sophisticated agriculturalists, growing rice and fruits along the banks of the Qiantang River where it flows into Hangzhou Bay. Among their implements were flat and perforated spades, as well as rectangular and curved sicklelike knives with holes. They raised domesticated water buffalo, pigs, dogs, and sheep. Archaeologists have discovered the remains of net sinkers, wooden floats, and wooden paddles, which demonstrate that the Liangzhu were familiar with watercraft and fishing. Also surviving in wood are pieces of boats, the foundations of houses, tools, and utensils. Their stone and bone artifacts were highly developed as well. Liangzhu artisans produced a black pottery from soft paste thrown on a wheel. And like the people of the Longshan culture, they devoted much labor to creating ritual objects from several varieties of jade; they mined it in the silt-formed Great Lake (Taihu) area of the Yangzi delta, close to the Liangzhu tombs.

In the late third millennium BCE, a long drought hit China as it did Egypt, Mesopotamia, and India. The Chinese recovered during the early centuries of the second millennium BCE, creating elaborate agrarian systems along the Yellow and Yangzi rivers that in many respects were similar to the irrigation systems established earlier along the Euphrates, Indus, and Nile. Extensive trading networks and a highly stratified social hierarchy based on age and gender then emerged; like the other river basin complexes of Asia and North Africa, China became a centralized polity. Here, too, a powerful

Liangzhu Jade Axe Blade, c. 3400–2250 BCE. The Liangzhu represented the last new Stone Age culture in the Yangzi River Delta. Their culture was highly stratified, and jade, silk, ivory, and lacquer artifacts were found exclusively in elite burial sites.

monarchy eventually devised the political and military means to unite the independent communities of riverine peoples. But what developed in China was a social and political system that ideologically emphasized an idealized past and tradition represented by sage-kings. In this and numerous other ways, China diverged from the rest of Afro-Eurasia.

AFRO-EURASIAN LIFE ON THE MARGINS

> → *How did the growth of urban societies in river basins affect people living in the Aegean region, Anatolia, and Europe?*

Those who lived in river basins and who looked to cities and their hierarchies as a model of dependable order, protected by bureaucracies and strong militaries, were inclined to see outsiders—particularly those who lived in the countryside, and especially those who were nomads—as "barbarians" and primitives. The imagery and narratives produced by city peoples in which they sought to distinguish themselves from rural and nomadic folk by depicting people from the periphery as backward and less civilized should not be accepted at face value. The city folk were less concerned with accurate portraits of the nomads than with enhancing their own self-image. Certainly, those who lived on the margins would not have recognized themselves as savages who were bereft of culture, faith, and organized life. They had frequent contact with the urbanites in river basins and became adept users of the technologies that radiated from cities. (See Map 2-7.) Despite being less urbanized, settled, and stratified than city dwellers, they fashioned institutions and belief systems that were as durable as those that flourished in the metropolitan centers.

AEGEAN WORLDS

One distinctive characteristic of people who lived outside the river basins was their warrior-based ethos. The top tiers of the social ladder, to which priests and scribes rose in cities, were held by chiefs and military men in less-stratified societies. This feature could be observed with particular clarity north of the Mediterranean Sea—especially in Europe and Anatolia, where weaponry rather than writing, palisades rather than palaces, and conquest rather than commerce dominated everyday life. Here, too, the inhabitants moved beyond stone implements and hunting and gathering, but they remained more egalitarian than riverine folk and politically did not evolve much above the level of small-scale societies led by a chief.

Contact with Egypt and Mesopotamia affected the worlds around the Aegean, but it did not lead to their basic transformation. Mountains and large bodies of water kept apart communities that lacked the unifying effects of a great river. Geography stood in the way of urban conglomerations arising on the mountainous islands, on the Anatolian plateau, and in Europe. People from Anatolia, Greece, and the Levant took to boats and populated the Aegean islands in the sixth millennium BCE. Their small villages endured almost unchanged for 2,000 years, not becoming more complex until the early third millennium BCE.

On mainland Greece and on the Cycladic islands in the middle of the Aegean Sea, large fortified settlements became the habitations of local rulers who controlled a small area of agriculturally productive countryside. Metallurgy developed both in Crete and in the Cyclades. There is evidence of a more formal administration and organizations in some communities by 2500 BCE, but the norm for the region was scattered settlements separated by natural obstacles. Consider rocky and mountainous Crete, the largest island in the Aegean. Occupied by sea-

→ *How did the growth of urban societies in river basins affect people living in the Aegean region, Anatolia, and Europe?*

MAP 2-7   SETTLEMENTS ON THE MARGINS: THE EASTERN MEDITERRANEAN AND EUROPE, 5000–2000 BCE

Urban societies in Southwest Asia profoundly influenced peripheral societies in the third millennium BCE. How did the spread of flint and copper tools and weapons transform Aegean and European societies during this time? What other influences did societies in Southwest Asia have on these settlements? How does this map demonstrate the growth of distinct cultures in these regions?

faring peoples, the island had hamlets and settlements sprinkled through its rugged interior. By the early third millennium BCE, it had made intermittent contact with distant neighbors—Egypt to the south and the coastal towns of the Levant to the east. Through these contacts, Cretans brushed up against new ideas, technologies, and materials as new waves of people arrived on their shores to trade or to stay. People came in ships with goods from the coast of Anatolia and from Egypt and the Levantine

coast. They brought with them such items as stone vessels and other luxury objects, which they traded for the abundant copper that could be found on the islands.

Lacking a rich agrarian base, communities remained small villages; most had no more than 100 inhabitants, and only a few grew over time. By the middle of the third millennium BCE, a more complex society was emerging on the eastern part of the island. During the second millennium BCE, Knossos, located in the middle of a rich agricultural plain,

Global Connections & Disconnections

RITUAL OBJECTS IN THE IRANIAN PLATEAU, CHINA, AND EGYPT

An important aspect of religious practice is the interaction between the worldly and the divine, between the living and the dead, between heaven and earth. Thousands of years ago ritual objects, such as amulets, statues, or carved objects representing the gods, were tangible representations of the connection between the earthly and the sacred. Other objects carried images of important myths and other stories that helped bind people together. Such objects could be used in specific ceremonies marking major events, such as a birth or a death. They may also have acted as more permanent signs of the divine, in shrines or temples. In both cases, ritual objects represented the sacred in everyday life.

From earliest times humans have deposited symbolic objects with the dead to ease the journey to the world beyond and to provide the sustenance and tools that the deceased would need in the afterlife. Both illicit and scientific excavations in the region of Jiroft in south-central Iran have revealed thousands of symbolic objects as well as utilitarian vessels that were put in graves. Most frequently interred with the body was a jar or cylindrical vessel made of soft green stone (locally available steatite or chlorite), whose sides were carved with elaborate designs that undoubtedly carried symbolic meaning. Furniture inlays and rectangular slabs with handles were also carved from the green stone and were decorated with similar designs.

While many of the designs featured repeating patterns of a grid or depicted curls or scorpions, some carried representations of gods in human form, who wore bull horns on their head as a sign of their divinity. A common motif portrayed a bird of prey grasping a snake in its talons; a leopard confronts the snake. Both the body of the bird and the snake are covered with holes that would originally have been filled with multihued stones, making the overall pattern very colorful and lively. The struggle between forces of nature is represented by the confrontation of the snake and the leopard. Neither wins; rather, they are always seen in a perfectly balanced equilibrium.

Vessels from Jiroft have been found in the Persian Gulf and in Mesopotamia. Some historians have argued that they were objects of trade no different from semiprecious lapis lazuli and carnelian. In fact, the centrality of these very distinctive objects to the funerary cult in their homeland makes it much more likely that they were carried to distant lands by traders and craftsmen who found work and lucrative markets for their commodities in the large cities of the great river valleys. These items were carried as personal effects; there is no evidence that the objects were ever exchanged in trade.

The Liangzhu people of ancient China carefully crafted ritual objects from several varieties of jade that they mined in the silt-formed Great Lake (Taihu) area of the Yangzi delta. Many of these jade pieces were decorated with animal masks or bird designs. Especially important in these rituals were circular jade objects called *bi* discs (found in tomb sites) and *cong* tubes. The *cong* jades, used in divination practices, were round in their hollow interior but squared on the outside. The rounded portion of the tube represented heaven and the square portion the earth; the jade tubes thus signified interaction between heaven and earth, the dead and the living. Both heaven and earth were penetrated by a central axis running through the jade's shaft, which symbolized the sacred mountains dividing the land of the living from the place of the dead.

Jade was the most important precious substance in East Asia. It was associated with the qualities of being

would become the primary palace-town in an extended network of palaces. The evidence from burial sites suggests that some households belonged to an elite class, for they were buried in their gold jewelry and took other exotic objects to their graves. Aegean elites did not spurn the niceties of civilized life. At the same time, they never forgot that their power rested as much on their ability to extract a living from a rugged landscape as on self-defense and on trade and interaction with others.

ANATOLIA

The emergence of regional cultures that were focused on the control of vital trade routes and mining outposts is especially clear on the highland plateau of Anatolia, which had been populated almost from the time that humans walked out of Africa. The pace of change was slow, as people clung to their village ways and stone tools. True cities did not develop in Anatolia until the third millennium BCE; even then, they were not the sprawling, densely packed centers of humanity typi-

Egyptian Funeral Amulet. This winged scarab is a symbol of rebirth and would have been placed in the wrapping of the mummy along with other amulets to assure the successful passage of the deceased into the afterlife. The Egyptians understood the dung-beetle who pushes a ball of dung as Khepri, the divine protector of the daily solar cycle.

good, pure, lucky, and virtuous, and it was carved into such items as ceremonial knives, blade handles, religious objects, and elaborate jewelry. Because jade is an especially hard stone, its intricate carving required much time and great skill. Smaller objects, such as blades and amulets, could serve a ceremonial purpose in ancient China. Jade objects used in a funerary function might be placed in the mouths and on the eyes of the deceased, or jade ornaments, jewelry, and ritual objects might be buried with them. Men and women had different ornaments, including necklaces and headdresses, swords and seals.

In ancient Egypt, precious stones and metals shaped into jewelry and ritual objects also played an important role, especially in burying the dead. Indeed, much of what we know about Egyptian amulets rests on discoveries made in tombs. Archaeologists often find amulets and funerary jewelry placed in specific positions on the bodies of mummies. The system for preparing a body for mummification was so specialized that it mandated a special type of funerary jewelry distinct from what ordinary people wore during their lives. Funerary amulets were thought to protect a mummy from potential suffering in the afterlife. The Egyptian *Book of the Dead* contains drawings and small paintings, along with spells, explaining how certain jewelry amulets should be used.

In addition, amulets of stone or precious metal—also described in the *Book of the Dead*—could be entombed with a mummified body. Nearly every mummy archaeologists have discovered has been found with one such amulet, made variously of stone, glass, or wood, in the shape of a pillar with cross bars at its top, perhaps mimicking the form of a tree (see Carol Andrews, *Egyptian Mummies*). Other types of amulets were made to resemble parts of the body, particularly an arm or a foot, indicating that the person had suffered in that body part or that a limb was missing, and the amulet could serve as its substitute. In either case, embalmers appear to have desired to make the deceased person as whole as possible for his or her passage into the afterlife. And Egyptian amulets of this sort often complemented the features of the person with whom they were placed.

Whether they were used to express religious or social status in this world or fend off evil spirits in the next, ritual objects played a major role in the practice of religion in China and Egypt. Amulets and ritual jewelry were the ultimate way of personalizing the divine, as they represented a connection to heaven that could belong to an individual. In this way, the creation and use of ritual objects stressed the interconnectedness of worldly and spiritual life.

cal of the Mesopotamian plain. Instead, small communities that were organized around fortified citadels housing competing local rulers were the usual settlement type. The most impressive of these fortified centers were Horoz Tepe and Alaça Hüyük, which we know primarily from more than a dozen very rich graves, apparently of royalty, full of gold jewelry, ceremonial standards, and elaborate weapons.

Another important third millennium BCE site in Anatolia was Troy to the far west. Troy is legendary as the place of the famous war launched by the Greeks (the Achaeans) and recounted by Homer in the *Iliad*. Troy, the modern mound of Hissarlik, was founded around 3000 BCE on the coast of the Mediterranean in a fertile and productive plain. First investigated by the German archaeologist Heinrich Schliemann in the 1870s, Troy level I was identified as a third-millennium BCE fortified settlement with monumental stone gateways and stone-paved ramps. Troy level II was extremely rich and had five large buildings called *megarons*, the forerunners of the classic Greek temple. Here, Schliemann found gold and silver objects, vessels, jewelry, and other artifacts. Many of these are similar to the ones found in the graves at Alaça Hüyük in the east. Moreover, since they closely parallel finds in the graves at Mochlos on Crete and at sites on the Greek mainland, they indicate that Troy was active in the trade system that linked the Aegean and Southwest Asian worlds during the third millennium BCE. Precious objects such as these may have been obtained through trade, but Troy still had to be defended against predatory neighbors and pirates who attacked from the sea—a necessity that helps explain its impressive fortifications.

THE WESTERN FRONTIER: EUROPE

At the far western reaches of the Eurasian landmass was a region that contained both more temperate and more frigid climates with much smaller population densities Its peoples—forerunners of present-day Europeans—began to make things out of metal, moved into permanent settlements, and started to create complex societies. Here, too, hierarchies replaced older egalitarian ways. Yet, as in the Aegean worlds, density and complexity here also had their limits.

More strongly than in the Mediterranean or Anatolia, it was in Europe—partly because of the persistent fragmentation of the region's peoples, partly because of the type of agrarian development they pursued—that warfare dominated social development. The introduction of the plow and the clearing of woodlands expanded agriculture. Agrarian development was driven by households and communities wielding axes both for defense and to cut down trees, not city-states or dynasties organizing irrigation and settlement. Compared to the riverine societies, even those of East Asia, Europe was a wild frontier, where day-to-day confrontations and violent conflicts over resources were common.

The effects of the gradual frontier expansion of agricultural communities were cumulative and eventually reached a critical turning point. The huge growth of flint mining to an industrial level, such as the thousand shafts sunk at Krzemionki in Poland or the large flint-mining complex of Grimes Graves in England, indicate a large-scale social and economic transformation. Most important, mining output slashed the cost and increased the availability of the raw materials needed to make tools that could more efficiently clear forested lands and till them into arable fields. Agricultural communities proliferated throughout the continent; some grew into villages capable of dominating their regions.

By 4000 BCE, the more developed agrarian peoples had coalesced into large communities. They supplied labor for the construction of large fixed monuments that are visible today. In western Europe, the building of large ceremonial centers shared the same model: enormous shaped stones, sometimes weighing several tons each, were set together in common patterns—in alleyways, troughs, or circles—that we call *megalithic* (literally, "great stone") constructions. These large-scale projects were certainly evidence of some kind of

Stonehenge. This spectacular site, located in the Salisbury Plain in Wiltshire in southwestern England, is one of several such megalithic structures found in the region. Constructed by many generations of builders, the arrangement of the large stone uprights enabled people to determine precise times in the year through the position of the sun. Events such as the spring and autumn equinoxes were connected with agricultural and religious activities.

Primary Source

THE MALE WARRIOR BURIALS OF VARNA AND NETT DOWN

In the burials arranged for elite individuals across the whole region from the Black Sea to the Atlantic, we witness the kinds of precious objects and weapons associated with a competitive warrior culture. At Varna, on the Black Sea coast of Bulgaria, the lifestyle of the "big men" associated with a farming village dated to around 4000 BCE was suddenly revealed in 1972 when a farmer driving a tractor uncovered graves from an ancient cemetery. The burials at Varna seem to represent a relatively powerful and well-connected settlement of the period, since most other contemporary sites do not display such high levels of wealth. In the grave of a man who died at about age forty-five, large pots used for drinking and storage were found. Much more striking were the 990 separate gold objects: most were decorative devices sewn onto his clothing, but they also included bracelets on both arms, a necklace, and small axe with a gold handle. The weapons buried with him—daggers, axes, and spearheads, and points—were still made of flint.

A second individual burial—from the far western parts of Europe, at Nett Down in Wiltshire, England, and at the end of our period, around 2500 BCE—reveals a less highly developed culture. In this case, a young male warrior was buried in a small tomb cut into the chalk ground and covered with a small circular mound of earth. He was buried with the two most significant representative objects connected with his life: a bronze dagger and, lower down, by his hands, a large bell beaker. No gold or precious metal ornaments were found with the man, who was clearly part of a more basic and poorer society than Varna's. As one scholar has remarked, "the grave neatly encapsulates the ideal male image of drinking and fighting."

→ *What does the fact that most individualized burial sites contain male bodies tell us about gender relations in these societies? When we compare these sites to those in Egypt and China, what can we learn about the importance of burying the dead across these societies? What can we perceive more generally about the differences between these societies?*

cooperative planning and work. In the British Isles, where such developments tended to come later than those on the continent, the famous megalithic complexes at Avebury and Stonehenge probably reached their highest stages of development in the centuries just before 2000 BCE.

European societies intensified communication, exchange, and mobility among the various communities. This increased interaction was an important source of wealth, but it also sparked organized warfare, especially as peoples vied for frontier lands and sought to conquer sites that contained valuable resources. Integration of local communities, ironically, led to greater friction and produced regional social stratification. The first material sign of an emerging warrior culture was the appearance of drinking cups. The violent men who now provided the protection that these communities needed were buried ceremonially with their drinking cups and weapons. These warrior burials have been found in a huge swath of European lands, from areas in present-day France and Switzerland in the west to areas in present-day central Russia in the east. The agricultural communities now were producing surplus wealth that could be stored, boosting populations to levels at which land and resources had to be fought over, conquered, and defended from encroaching neighbors.

A rough and aggressive culture based on violent confrontations between adult males organized in larger "tribal" groups was taking shape. War cultures became deeply entrenched in all western European societies, marked by a universal presence of a new drinking instrument, the "bell beaker"—so named by archaeologists because it was shaped like an inverted bell. These cups were transported across Europe from their place of origin among armed groups on the lower Rhine River, where they were widely used to swig beer and mead that was distilled from a mixture of grains, honey, herbs, and nuts. As beer drinking spread across Europe, many local variations on beer mugs appeared, again illustrating the constant interplay between external communication and local forces.

As new tools and weapons spread across Europe, the region adopted similar cultural practices. But a split between its eastern and western flanks also began to emerge. In the millennium following 2500 BCE, western Europe witnessed a more elaborate working out of its combative ethos in which warriors battled for territory and resources. The twin pillars of agriculture and metalworking, initially in copper, became the normal supports of daily life almost everywhere.

Warfare had the ironic effect of accentuating the borrowing among the competing people of the region as each tried to best, or at least to check, all rivals. The violent warrior culture of central Europe exerted tremendous pressure to produce more effective weaponry. Warrior elites borrowed from Anatolia the technique of combining copper with tin to produce harder-edged weapons made of an alloy that we call *bronze*. The war economy also provoked universal demand for these better weapons; smiths therefore began to produce them in bulk—as evidenced by the great hoards of copper and bronze tools and weapons from the period found in several archaeological sites in central Europe. Traders used the networks of water communication offered by the rivers of central and northern Europe to exchange their prized metal products, creating one of the first widespread commercial networks that covered the continent.

Constant warfare propelled Europe to become a hugely innovative frontier society. The violent struggles between communities and emerging kinship groups fueled a massive demand for weapons, alcohol, and horses. The culture of violence and conflict that now was driving a basic agricultural economy served to integrate European kinship-based oral societies in a realm of their own, and to separate them from rather than to integrate them with the Mediterranean—a seemingly ordered world of palaces, scribes, and well-disciplined commoners.

Chronology

	5000 BCE	4000 BCE
SOUTHWEST ASIA AND NORTH AFRICA		Earliest Sumerian cities in southern Mesopotamia appear, 3500 BCE ▮
SOUTH ASIA		
EAST ASIA	▮ *Yangshao culture thrives in northwest China along Yellow River, 5000 BCE* ▮ *Longshan culture emerges in northeast Yellow River valley between 5000 and 2000 BCE* ▮ *Jomon culture in Japan, 5000–2500 BCE*	
THE EASTERN MEDITERRANEAN AND EUROPE	*Megalithic stone constructions begin in western Europe, 4000 BCE* ▮	
THE AMERICAS		*Chicama Valley along Pacific Ocean coast in modern-day Peru thrives, 3500 BCE* ▮ *Tehuacán Valley in modern-day Mexico thrives, 3500 BCE* ▮
SUB-SAHARAN AFRICA		*Dense village life by Lake Chad and Niger River, Congo River, and Lake Victoria, 3500 BCE* ▮
INNER AND CENTRAL EURASIA		*Growth and spread of nomadic pastoralism begins, 3500 BCE* ▮

CONCLUSION

Over the course of the fourth and third millennia BCE, the social geography of the world changed in remarkable ways. In a few key locations, where giant rivers irrigated fertile lands, complex human cultures began to emerge. These areas were the world's most densely populated regions, and they experienced all of the advantages and difficulties of big populations: occupational specialization; social hierarchy, with haves and have-nots; rising material standards of living; highly developed systems of art and science and centralized production and distribution of food, clothing, and other goods for expanding populations. Ceremonial sites and trading entrepôts became cities that were, in turn, the emerging cores of centralized religious and political systems. Cities became the homes for the scribes, priests, and rulers who labored to keep complex societies together. As they did so, urbanites—both men and women—sharpened the distinction between country folk and city dwellers. In effect, urbanization exemplified the many ways in which societies were becoming more complex and stratified, creating social and cultural distinctions within each of these worlds. Social distinctions affected the distinct roles of men and women, as urban families began to take different forms from the kinship groups in the countryside.

But while the riverine cultures shared basic features, the evolution of each followed a distinctive path. Where there was a single river—the Nile or the Indus—the agrarian hinterlands that fed the cities lay along the banks of the mighty waterway. In these areas, cities tended to be smaller, and the Egyptian and Harappan worlds probably enjoyed more political stability and less rivalry. In contrast, cities in the immense floodplain between the Tigris and Euphrates needed large hinterlands to sustain themselves as they became the home for larger populations. Because of their growing power and prestige and their need for resources, Mesopotamian cities vied for preeminence, and their competition often became violent. As we will see in Chapter 3, a similar pattern emerged after 1500 BCE in China, where the Yellow and Yangzi rivers provided the environmental foundations for the rapid expansion of Chinese settlements into cities.

Cities stood at one end of the spectrum of social complexity. At the other end, in most areas of the world, people still lived in relatively simple, horizontal societies, supporting themselves by hunting, gathering, and basic agriculture, as in the settlements of the Americas and Africa. In between, of course, were worlds such as Anatolia, as well as Europe and large parts of China, where towns emerged and agriculture advanced—but not with the leaps and bounds made by the great riverine cultures. Beyond these frontiers, farmers and nomads survived as they had for many centuries.

In spite of these global differences, changes in climate affected everyone and could slow or even reverse development. How—and indeed whether—cultures adapted depended on local circumstances. As the next chapter will show, the human agents of change often came from the fringes of larger settlements and urban areas.

3000 BCE	2000 BCE	1000 BCE

st Dynasty emerges in Egypt, 3100 BCE
First writing appears, 3200 BCE
Early Dynastic Age, 2850–2334 BCE
Old Kingdom Egypt, 2649–2152 BCE
Sargon's Akkadian territorial state, 2334–2193 BCE
Middle Kingdom Egypt, 2040–1640 BCE
Cities began to appear in Indus Valley, 2500 BCE

Troy founded in Western Anatolia, 3000 BCE
Fortified villages in Aegean, 2500 BCE
Stonehenge constructed in modern-day England just before 2000 BCE

Nomadic pastoral communities dominate Central Asian steppe lands by the second millennium BCE

STUDY QUESTIONS

Ⓢ WWNORTON.COM/STUDYSPACE

1. Explain how the rise of cities in the fourth millennium BCE represented a quantum leap forward in complexity in human history. How did urban dwellers shape political, economic, and cultural developments in their region?

2. Describe how cities in Mesopotamia, the Indus Valley, and Egypt differed from small village communities across the globe. Why did cities emerge in a relatively few places between 5000 and 2000 BCE?

3. Define *pastoralism*. Where in Afro-Eurasia did this form of social organization develop and thrive?

4. Identify major common characteristics that urbanites in Mesopotamia, the Indus Valley, and Egypt shared. What features distinguished each from the others?

5. Compare and contrast the ways in which early writing emerged in the urban societies between 5000 and 2000 BCE. How did each use this new technology? How common was literacy?

6. Compare and contrast early state structures in Egypt and Mesopotamia. Why was Egypt more politically unified than Mesopotamia?

7. Analyze the influence of long-distance trade on the political and economic development of urban societies in Egypt, Mesopotamia, and the Indus Valley. How was each society influenced by contacts with other people?

8. Explain East Asia's relative physical isolation from other Afro-Eurasian societies during this time period. To what extent did this isolation shape social development in this region between 5000 and 2000 BCE?

9. Identify major common characteristics shared by European, Anatolian, and Aegean settlements between 5000 and 2000 BCE. How did settlements in these regions on the margins differ from urban settlements in river basins?

FURTHER READINGS

Adams, Robert McCormick, *The Evolution of Urban Society* (1966). A classic study of the social, political, and economic processes that led to the development of the first urban civilizations.

Algaze, Guillermo, *The Uruk World System: The Dynamics of Expansion of Early Mesopotamian Civilization* (1993). A compelling argument for the colonization of the Tigris and Euphrates valley by the proto-Sumerians at the end of the fourth millennium BCE.

Andrews, Carol, *Egyptian Mummies* (1998). An illustrated summary of Egyptian mummification and burial practices.

Assmann, Jan, *The Mind of Egypt: History and Meaning in the Time of the Pharaohs* (2002). A superb analysis of the cultural and philosophical foundations of Pharaonic culture.

Bagley, Robert, *Ancient Sichuan: Treasures from a Lost Civilization* (2001). Describes the remarkable findings in Southwest China,

particularly at Sanxingdui, which have challenged earlier accounts of the Shang dynasty's central role in the rise of early Chinese civilization.

Bar-Yosef, Ofar, and Anatoly Khazanov (eds.), *Pastoralism in the Levant: Archaeological Materials in Anthropological Perspectives* (1992). Classic study of the role of nomads in the development of societies in the Levant during the Neolithic period.

Bruhns, Karen Olsen, *Ancient South America* (1994). The best basic text on pre-Columbian South American cultures.

Butzer, Karl W., *Early Hydraulic Civilization in Egypt: A Study of Cultural Ecology* (1976). The best work on how the Egyptians dealt with the Nile floods and the influence that these arrangements had on the overall organization of society.

Habu, Junko, *Ancient Jomon of Japan* (2004). Study of prehistoric Jomon hunter-gatherers on the Japanese archipelago that incorporates several different aspects of anthropological studies, including hunter-gatherer archaeology, settlement archaeology, and pottery analysis.

Jacobsen, Thorkild, *The Treasures of Darkness: A History of Mesopotamian Religion* (1976). Best introduction to the religious and philosophical thought of ancient Mesopotamia.

Kemp, Barry J., *Ancient Egypt: Anatomy of a Civilization* (1989). A synthetic overview of the culture of the Pharaohs.

Kramer, Samuel Noah, *The Sumerians: Their History, Culture and Character* (1963). Classic study of the Sumerians and their culture by a pioneer in Sumerian studies.

Kuhrt, Amelie, *The Ancient Near East c. 3000–330 BCE* (1995). Comprehensive and authoritative history through the Achaemenid period of the societies of the Ancient Near East, including Mesopotamia, Egypt, Anatolia, and Western Iran.

Lamberg-Karlovsky, Carl C., *Beyond the Tigris and Euphrates Bronze Age Civilizations* (1996). A thought-provoking essay on the social, economic, and political development of the wider Near East during the fourth and third millennia BCE.

Pollock, Susan, *Ancient Mesopotamia: The Eden That Never Was* (1999). An analysis of the social and economic development of Mesopotamia from the beginnings of settlement until the reign of Hammurapi.

Possehl, Gregory L., *Indus Age: The Beginnings* (1999). The second of four volumes analyzing the history of the Indus Valley civilization.

Postgate, J. N., *Early Mesopotamia: Society and Economy at the Dawn of History* (1992). A study of the economic and political development of the Sumerian civilization.

Preziosi, Donald, and L. A. Hitchcock, *Aegean Art and Architecture* (1999). One of the best general guides to the figurative and decorative art produced both by the Minoans and Mycenaeans and by related early societies in the region of the Aegean.

Ratnagar, Shereen, *Trading Encounters: From the Euphrates to the Indus in the Bronze Age*, 2nd ed. (2004). A comprehensive presentation of the evidence for the relationship between the Indus Valley and its western neighbors.

———, *Understanding Harappa: Civilization in the Greater Indus Valley* (2001). Harappan site archaeological data of the last century organized into a historical narrative comprehensible to the general audience.

Rice, Michael, *Egypt's Legacy: The Archetypes of Western Civilization, 3000–300 BC* (1997). The author argues for the decisive influence of Egyptian culture on the whole of the Mediterranean and its later historical development.

Roaf, Michael, *Cultural Atlas of Mesopotamia and the Ancient Near East* (1990). A comprehensive compendium of the historical and cultural development of the Mesopotamian civilization from the Neolithic background through the Persian Empire.

Shaw, Ian (ed.), *The Oxford History of Ancient Egypt* (2000). The most up-to-date and comprehensive account of the history of Egypt down to the Greek invasion.

Thorp, Robert, *The Chinese Neolithic: Trajectories to Early States* (2005). Uses the latest archaeological evidence to describe the development of early Bronze Age cultures in North and Northwestern China from about 2000 BCE.

Van de Mieroop, Marc, *A History of the Ancient Near East, ca. 3000–323 BC* (2004). A political history of Mesopotamia and its neighbors from the late fourth millennium rise of first cities through the first centuries CE.

Warren, Peter, *The Aegean Civilizations: From Ancient Crete to Mycenae,* 2nd ed. (1989). An excellent textual and pictorial guide to all the basic aspects of the Minoan and Mycenaean societies.

3

NOMADS, TERRITORIAL STATES, AND MICROSOCIETIES, 2000–1200 BCE

The big states of the river basins collapsed—and collapsed brutally—around 2000 BCE when a subsistence crisis gripped much of Afro-Eurasia. For all their achievements and complexity, urbanites existed on a precarious edge. Also severely threatened when the world entered a dry phase were people living in decentralized communities who relied on rainfall rather than on irrigation to supply water for their crops. In the homelands of the large urban cultures of the Nile, Indus, and Mesopotamian floodplains, disaster struck. The crisis was above all environmental. Many centuries of farming had degraded the soils, trees had been stripped from the land for firewood, and rains and floods had washed away layers of topsoil. And as if humanity's ability to unwittingly destroy natural resources was not enough, climatic cycles made things worse. The world entered a warming and drying cycle that converted into deserts lands that had already become less fertile. Irrigation could no longer sustain regular crops when the land became parched.

Urban worlds suffered most. In the great cities of Afro-Eurasia, food shortages led to hunger, and hunger soon gave way to famine. The decline lasted some generations, but by the end of this period of severe drought, the inhabitants of some cities, unable to procure food from their hinterlands, staggered about the streets until they collapsed. Transhumant herders—that is, those who moved their herds back and forth seasonally between microenvironments—from the desert and mountain areas and horse-riding pastoral nomads from the Inner Eurasian steppes, who moved over much longer distances, also felt the pinch. And as they searched for sustenance they more frequently raided permanent settlements. Political vacuums opened up: governing structures in Egypt, Mesopotamia, and the Indus Valley collapsed. Everywhere, in urban centers, political crises in state-level societies disrupted their two millennia of impressively rapid development. In a sense, Afro-Eurasian societies were the first to experience the inescapability of global warming: the emergence of great pioneering cities may have created unprecedented differences between elites and commoners, and between urbanites and rural folk, but everyone felt the effects of this disaster.

Such a radical loss of life-sustaining water did not destroy everything that pioneering city people had created. Writing, ideologies of kingship, architecture, skill at metalworking, and forms of transportation such as sailing vessels and wheeled vehicles were durable cultural creations not easily forgotten. When nomadic and transhumant peoples from the peripheries entered into the fabric of these weakened settled societies, they brought with them their beliefs and customs, but they were also strongly influenced by the settled people, adapting indigenous beliefs and accommodating their own cultural practices to fit with those of the people they had joined. Just as earlier cultural achievements had set the stage for a preliminary round of intense growth in social complexity, so the cultural innovations of Mesopotamia, Egypt, the

Indus River valley, and the North China plain set the stage for another cycle of human cultural development: polities would expand beyond their previous urban frontiers to encompass more cohesive territorial states. But like their riverine predecessors, the regimes that arose in the second millennium BCE created new kinds of tensions between peoples even as they augmented humanity's achievements. Much further away, among the islanders of the Pacific and the Aegean, and in the cut-off world of the Americas, regimes did not bump against each other with the same intensity—and therefore their political systems evolved differently. In those locales, the norm was small-scale micro-states.

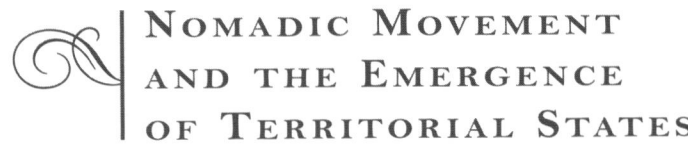

NOMADIC MOVEMENT AND THE EMERGENCE OF TERRITORIAL STATES

> → *How did nomadic groups recast the cultural landscape and geography of Afro-Eurasia during the second millennium BCE?*

Drought and food shortages led to political turbulence and the collapse of the power of kings and ruling elites throughout central and western Afro-Eurasia. Walled cities could not defend their hinterlands. Trade routes lay open to predators, and pillaging became a lucrative enterprise. Clans of pastoral nomads from the Inner Eurasian steppes (north of the Caucasus Mountains and west of the Black, Caspian, and Aral seas) moved across vast distances on horseback and increas-

Focus Questions   NOMADS AND TERRITORIAL STATES

> → *How did nomadic groups recast the cultural landscape and geography of Afro-Eurasia during the second millennium BCE?*
>
> → *What was the impact of the interactions triggered by the drought on the organization of societies?*
>
> → *How did Vedic migrations influence South Asia?*
>
> → *What methods did the Shang state employ to maintain its rule?*
>
> → *How did Austronesian migrations affect the South Pacific?*
>
> → *How did long-distance trade influence the Aegean world?*
>
> → *Why did politics remain small-scale in Europe?*
>
> → *How did the ecology of the Central Andes influence early state systems?*

 WWNORTON.COM/STUDYSPACE

NOMADIC MOVEMENT AND THE EMERGENCE OF TERRITORIAL STATES | **99**

➤ *How did nomadic groups recast the cultural landscape and geography of Afro-Eurasia during the second millennium* BCE?

ingly threatened the settled people of the mighty cities. In much the same way, transhumant herders from the borderlands of the Iranian plateau and the Arabian Desert advanced on the more densely populated areas near cities searching for food and resources for themselves and for their animals. Similar migratory patterns would also occur in the Indus River valley and the Yellow River valley, causing fundamental changes within the societies there as well. (See Map 3-1.)

The change in environmental conditions now forced humans throughout Afro-Eurasia to adapt or perish. When the pastoral nomads and transhumant herders proved able to adjust more quickly to the new dry conditions of the second millennium BCE, they provided the historic catalyst for the rise of new but still localized territorial states from pharaonic Egypt and Mesopotamia to Vedic South Asia and Shang China. Using chariots, the horse-mounted pastoral nomads introduced technologies that led to new forms of warfare whose spread transformed the ancient Afro-Eurasian world. Moreover, the state building of the new rulers produced changes in society and government that enabled humans not only to survive the climate change but even to thrive in it.

NOMADIC AND TRANSHUMANT MIGRATIONS

As noted in Chapter 2, pastoral nomads rode their horses across the steppe lands of inner Eurasia herding a wide array of livestock. They were perpetually in motion as they covered tremendous areas. Transhumant migrants tended to live closer to city-states and riverine societies; they moved from lowland to highland areas with their livestock, depending on the season of the year.

The changes in climate and landscape affected both migratory groups. The same droughts that ravaged city-states and riverine societies at the end of the third millennium BCE devastated the homelands of nomads and transhumant herders. Both types of peoples were therefore driven to search for secure water sources and pastures for their livestock. Many of them migrated onto the highland plateaus that border the Inner Eurasian steppe lands. From there, some continued into the more densely populated river valleys and soon were jostling with the farming communities over space and resources. They also came from the western and southern deserts in Southwest Asia. For example, the Amorites, pastoral nomads speaking a Semitic language, moved into southern Mesopotamia from the western Syrian Desert. Indo-European-speaking steppe peoples migrated into Anatolia (in present-day Turkey) and eastern Europe, probably entering the plateau from both sides of the Black Sea, especially through the Caucasus Mountains.

The newly arrived pastoral nomadic and transhumant populations settled in the agrarian heartlands of Mesopotamia and the Indus River valley for their tribesmen. After the first wave of newcomers, more immigrants gradually arrived by foot or in wagons pulled by draft animals. Sometimes they came looking for temporary work; sometimes they came to resettle permanently. Nomadic peoples of inner and Central Asia began to fan out across much of Eurasia, including China, Europe and South Asia, bringing with them horses and new technology that could be used for making war. They also brought with them their religious practices and languages, as well as new pressures to feed, house, and clothe an ever-growing population. Taken together, all this human motion caused major changes in the cultural landscape and geography in western Eurasia.

Not all nomadic activity took place on the land. Numerous Greek peoples took to the sea in search of new opportunities, establishing complexes across a wide range of islands in the Aegean Sea. Around the same time, Austronesians set out from the shores of East Asia, hopping from island to island in mammoth sea canoes. They would ultimately populate many of the large habitable islands throughout the Pacific Basin.

The hard-riding pastoral nomads linked disparate cities and towns of South Asia and China for the first time into regional networks connected by tribal clan relations and trade. Using weapons, the horsemen controlled trade and maintained peace in their enclaves. But they could not control how the more literate elites they conquered would write about them. Those who lost their power described the nomadic warriors as "barbaric" and inhuman, painting them as cruel and heartless enemies of "civilization." And in the annals of world history, the label *barbarian* has generally stuck to these nomads. Yet what we know of them today suggests that they were anything but barbaric.

When nomads and transhumant herders conquered settled peoples, they carried with them inventions and ideas that urban and agricultural elites adapted to revitalize and rebuild their societies. Chariots, and especially the horses that pulled them, brought by the pastoral nomadic warriors from the steppes became the favored mode of transportation for an aristocratic warrior class from the cities and for other men of power in agriculture-based societies like China. Kings learned to make alliances with chariot-driving warriors. They also came to use chariots as the centerpiece of their own armies. Control of chariot forces was the foundation of the new balance of power across Afro-Eurasia during the second millennium BCE.

HORSES AND CHARIOTS On the vast steppe lands north of the Caucasus Mountains, as early as the late fourth millennium BCE, the settled people had successfully domesticated the horse. Elsewhere, as on the northern steppes of what is now Russia, horses served as a food source. It was only during the late third millennium BCE that fashioned cheek pieces and mouth bits were used. Horses are faster than any other draft animals, but harnessing horses for

URAL MOUNTAINS

E U R A

EUROPE

Volga R.

Dnieper R.

Dnister R.

HUNGARIAN
PLAIN

Danube R.

Lake
Balkas

ARAL
SEA

Oxus R.

CENTRAL ASIA

CASPIAN
SEA

BLACK SEA

F
R
O

ANATOLIAN
PLATEAU

Tigris R.

Euphrates R.

PAMIR MTS.

HINDU KUSH MTS.

MEDITERRANEAN SEA

A
F

IRANIAN PLATEAU

ZAGROS MTS.

SOUTHWEST ASIA

H. I.

SOUT

Indus R.

Nile R.

Persian Gulf

ARABIAN
DESERT

RED SEA

ARABIAN SEA

- Spread of wheeled vehicles
- Spread of war chariots
- Dispersal of nomads
- Pastoral nomads c. 2000 – 1500 BCE
Southwest Asian Society
- Zone of urban civilization

0   500   1000 Miles

0   500   1000 Kilometers

MAP 3-1   NOMADIC MIGRATIONS IN AFRO-EURASIA, 2000–1000 BCE

How did the domestication of horses transform nomadic societies in Afro-Eurasia? How did nomadic pastoral migrations affect settled, agriculture-based societies? To what extent did pastoral peoples bring various worlds together in the second millennium BCE?

pulling is a complicated matter. Unlike cattle, onagers, or donkeys, which stretch their necks ahead when walking, a horse raises its head. The drivers needed headgear to control horses' speed and direction. In the tombs of nomads scattered around the steppe, archaeologists have found various parts of horse harnesses made from wood, bone, bronze, and iron. These reveal the evolution of headgear from simple mouth bits to full bridles with headpiece, mouthpiece, and rein.

Sometime around 2000 BCE, pastoral nomads on the far northern edge of the broad Mesopotamian plains fashioned a vehicle with one axle and two wheels, and harnessed the newly invented chariot to horses. Early versions had been attached to lumbering oxen or to onagers or donkeys. But harnessing horses was much more complicated than making bullocks draw plows and wagons. Horses were the fastest animals domesticated by human beings and remained the speediest means of transportation until the invention of the steam engine, but they were rarely used as draft animals, for they could not haul sizable loads at high speeds.

Pastoral nomads borrowed transportation techniques developed among agrarian peoples to make chariots light enough for horses to pull at high speeds. Spoked wheels demanded special wood and the carpentry skills to bend it into a circle; wheel covers, axles, and bearings were produced by settled people. The moving parts of the chariot were made of durable metal, first bronze and later—around 1000 BCE—iron. Initially iron was a decorative and experimental metal and bronze was the metal of all tools and weapons. Iron's hardness and flexibility, however, eventually made it more desirable than

copper or bronze (it was also more plentiful) for reinforcing moving parts and protecting wheels. Similarly, solid wood wheels that easily shattered gave way to spokes and hooped bronze and later iron rims. The horse chariots, properly speaking, were the result of a creative combination of the innovations of both nomadic people and agrarian people in western Afro-Eurasia. These innovations—combining new engineering skills, metallurgy, and animal domestication—and their ultimate diffusion revolutionized how humans made war and therefore changed history.

The horse chariot slashed the time it took to travel between capitals and altered the machinery of war. Slow-moving infantry gave way in the second millennium BCE to battalions of chariots. Each vehicle carried a driver and an archer, and charged into the melee of battle with deadly precision and speed. The mobility, accuracy, and shooting power of warriors in horse-drawn chariots tilted the political balance so dramatically that after the nomads perfected chariot warfare by 1600 BCE, they were able to challenge the political systems of Mesopotamia and Egypt and soon were affecting war making in regions as far removed as present-day Greece, India, China, and Sweden. Only with the advent of cheaper armor after 1000 BCE could foot soldiers—in China, armed with crossbows—recover their military importance. For much of the second millennium BCE, charioteer elites prevailed over huge swaths of Afro-Eurasia.

City dwellers in the river basins must have found their first sight of horse-drawn chariots terrifying, but they knew that war making had changed forever and scrambled to adapt. The Shang kings of China and the pharaohs in Egypt probably learned about and copied chariots from nomads or neighbors who already had them, and they came to be valued almost as highly as the throne itself. The young pharaoh Tutankhamun (c. 1350) was portrayed as a chariot archer; when he died, his chariot and other accoutrements of a warrior were laid in his tomb. A century later, horse chariots were displayed in the tombs of the Shang kings in the Yellow River valley, the heartland of agricultural China.

PASTORAL NOMADS, HERDERS, AND TRADE Transhumant herders, whose lowland pastures were often on the periphery of cities in riverine societies, traded their surplus meat and animal products for items produced by artisans in the cities. When the production of goods in the cities fell because of environmental or political pressures, the herders might instead raid the cities in order to gain access to what they needed. Drought affecting their usual pasturelands might also force them to move their herds closer to the riverine cities in order to find grass and water.

Horse-riding nomads from the steppes ranged more widely. Some of these nomads engaged in long-distance trade, traveling quickly over great expanses and bearing goods and ideas back and forth across Afro-Eurasia. Traveling by horse or camel in relatively small bands over unsettled areas, they

Horse Figurines. Around 1500 BCE, a group of people who spoke an Indo-European language, the Vedic Sanskrit, entered South Asia. These people were nomads with horse chariots, a novelty in South Asia. Because they cremated their dead and roamed around, few traces of them have survived. These horse figurines from the northwest region of South Asia, in modern Pakistan, are probably among the few material remains of the migrants.

War Chariots. *Bottom left:* A large vase typical of Mycenaean art on the mainland areas of Greece. The regular banding and presentation of scenes reflect a society that is more formally ordered and rigidly hierarchical than that on Minoan Crete. Note the presence of the horse-drawn chariot. Possessing this more elaborate means of transport and warfare characterized the warrior elites of Mycenaean society and linked them to developments over wide expanses of Afro-Eurasia at the time. *Upper left:* This wooden chest covered with stucco and painted on all sides with images of the Egyptian pharoah in his war chariot was found in the fabulously wealthy tomb of Tutankhamun in the Valley of the Kings in Egypt. The war chariot was introduced into Egypt by the Hyksos. By the reign of Tutankhamun in the New Kingdom, depictions of pharaoh single-handedly smiting the enemy from a war chariot drawn by two powerful horses were common. *Upper right:* The Shang fought with neighboring pastoral nomads from the central Asian steppes. To do this, they imported horses from central Asia and copied the chariots of nomads they had encountered. This gave Shang warriors devastating range and speed for further conquest.

could carry such prestige goods as precious stones or textiles, or metals such as copper, tin, or silver. In small bands, they also might raid trading caravans organized by merchants, or they might offer protection to such caravans for a fee. Early nomads did not write down their achievements, as did the kings of sedentary societies. Yet archaeologists have uncovered some of what the nomads accomplished as traders, for they have found jade from Central Asia's Khotan Desert in tombs at Anyang, one of the Shang capitals, and amber pieces in Greece that likely originated in Nordic lands.

THE EMERGENCE OF TERRITORIAL STATES

From the riverine cities in Mesopotamia, overwhelmed by the arrival of displaced nomadic peoples, emerged a new political form—the territorial state—that broke out of the urban confines of its predecessors. (See Map 3-2.) Power reaching from cities into distant hinterlands was the chief political innovation of this epoch. Great centralized kingdoms, organized around charismatic rulers heading large households, achieved

MAP 3-2   TERRITORIAL STATES AND TRADE ROUTES IN SOUTHWEST ASIA AND NORTH AFRICA, AND THE EASTERN MEDITERRANEAN, 1500–1350 BCE

What kind of goods did people in this region exchange? How did these commercial contacts shape interaction between the territorial states? How did commercial networks affect people living on the peripheries of these territorial states?

Legend:

- • Major Minoan settlement, 2000–1450 BCE
- Mitanni Kingdom, 1500 BCE
- New Hittite Kingdom, 1400–1300 BCE
- New Kingdom Egypt, 1400–1300 BCE
- Kassite Kingdom, 1400–1100 BCE
- Middle Assyrian Kingdom, 1350–1100 BCE
- Mycenaean civilization, 1350 BCE
- ELAM Region or territory
- ← Mycenaean trade route
- ← Eastern Mediterranean trade route

Map labels: BLACK SEA, SARDINIA, SICILY, AEGEAN SEA, ASSUWA, HATTI, ARZAWA, AHHIYAWA, LUKKA, TAURUS MTS., KIZZUWATNA, Tigris R., Ugarit, Aleppo, Euphrates R., ALASHIYA, CYPRUS, Qadesh, SYRIA, CRETE, MEDITERRANEAN SEA, Byblos, Damascus, SYRIAN DESERT, Megiddo, PALESTINE, Jerusalem, Memphis, Amarna, NORTH AFRICA, EGYPT, SAHARA DESERT, RED SEA, SO

Scale: 0 — 250 — 500 Miles; 0 — 250 — 500 Kilometers

political stability for a while by passing the torch of political command from one generation to the next. People now identified themselves as more than simply residents of cities—they felt allegiance to their territories, their rulers, and their widely dispersed linguistic and ethnic communities. These territories for the first time had identifiable borders, and those living within them began the long process of creating a shared identity.

Territorial states differed from the city-states that preceded them. The earlier city-states of the riverine societies, organized around the temple and palace, were each autonomous polities and were separated by buffer zones that were increasingly contested. The new territorial states in Egypt and Mesopotamia based their authority on divine monarchs, large and widely dispersed bureaucracies, elaborate and widely administered legal codes, large territorial expanses, definable borders, and plans for continuous expansion. Although power still emanated from central cities, the rulers had changed: the once-marginalized peoples of the Syrian Desert (the Amorites) and of the northern steppe lands and Anatolia (the Hittites) now held considerable power. Their drive to conquer and expand overcame and replaced the earlier models of competition and coexistence. Territorial states also emerged for the first time in Greece and China; there the newcomers from the outside who took power more completely adopted local ways.

Each of these societies was different, but they all shared the drive to integrate dominions within a landscape that had definable boundaries. In the second millennium BCE, when rulers created large-scale territorial states for the first time, they were literally remapping their known world and dividing it into specific areas and zones to be "governed" by an authority recognized—sometimes loved, sometimes feared—by the people. Such states brought two major changes to the lives of their inhabitants. First, people now identified themselves as part of an entity with territorial limits; those living beyond them belonged to "other" territorial states, were seen as unlike them in significant respects, and had to be dealt with (mainly through new forms of diplomacy and advanced warfare). Second, people welcomed the return of "government," which first restored and then upheld order. Achieving that order was made possible not only by the formal laws or codes developed by these territorial states, laws that all subjects were expected to obey, but also by the subjects' adherence to a shared set of norms and values. During the second millennium BCE, people came to view a good king as one who could command the respect of neighboring states and bring security to his subjects. Their feelings of safety, however, were often the result of a long and bloody process as territorial states expanded their borders to their geographical or demographic limits. It was one of the great paradoxes of the era that upheavals and surges of great violence could yield unprecedented political innovation and security.

The long-term political consequences of ecological and demographic upheavals played out during this period. The

Afro-Eurasia-wide droughts had forced peoples to move in search of new lands. Nomads from the north moved southward in pursuit of arable land, while settled peoples from the southern coastal areas went north as salt from overirrigation and the seas encroached on the land and poisoned water supplies. The resulting shift of the population axis across much of central and southwestern Asia ultimately contributed to the creation of the new territorial states. As city-states fell, undone by these climatic and demographic changes, new political structures emerged in their place.

Other regions of the world were undergoing similar developments but more slowly; they would not feel the full effects of the changes attending the formation of their states for a few more centuries. In one way, East Asia and especially the Americas were fundamentally different from the lands that stretched from North Africa to South Asia: because these regions were not as densely packed as the emerging territorial states, they experienced less rivalry and consequently less struggle over borders and populations. High density of states brought greater pressure on borders, which state builders were then forced to defend. Within those borders, ruling classes sought to integrate their dominions and thereby increase loyalty to the capital and its laws. Ever larger territorial states began the long-term process of giving the world a political map, divided into specific areas tied to different sovereign authorities.

THE RISE OF TERRITORIAL STATES IN SOUTHWEST ASIA AND NORTH AFRICA

> → *What was the impact of the interactions triggered by the drought on the organization of societies?*

Environmental pressures and conquering pastoral nomads and transhumant herders transformed the city-states of Southwest Asia and North Africa. As the newcomers became assimilated, they competed for positions of leadership and resources among themselves and with the rulers they encountered. From 2000 to 1600 BCE, small kingdoms, organized according to territorial and ethnic identity, dominated the landscape from the Aegean Sea through Mesopotamia and Iran. In 1600 BCE, a renewed wave of pastoral nomadic conquests and migrations brought the fledgling territorial kingdoms—never very stable—to their knees. After a century of turmoil, the balance of power shifted irrevocably, and a new order of territorial states based in urban capitals but

commanding large hinterlands with definable boundaries and common cultures took form.

The five great territorial states of Southwest Asia and North Africa during this period consisted of the Egyptians, who extended their power to the eastern Mediterranean and Palestine; the Hittites in Anatolia; the Mitanni (later replaced by the Middle Assyrians), who controlled Syria and northern Mesopotamia; the Kassites in southern Mesopotamia; and the Middle Elamites, who controlled the southwestern Iranian plateau. These large states were so well balanced and competed with each other so intensely that over time, they were compelled to learn the techniques of coexistence. They produced highly developed forms of statecraft and international diplomacy that served this area well for several centuries. Not so fortunate were the smaller kingdoms, such as the Syro-Palestinian vassal realms, squeezed between the major powers. They were relegated to the status of buffer zones between the regions that the large territorial powers dominated.

EGYPT

The first and probably best known of the five great territorial kingdoms of Southwest Asia was Egypt. There the pharaohs of the Middle Kingdom and later the pharaohs of the New Kingdom unified the river valley and expanded both south and north into adjacent lands. The long era of prosperity associated with the Old Kingdom of the third millennium BCE had ended abruptly when the Afro-Eurasia-wide drought brought catastrophe to the area. For several decades, the Nile did not overflow its banks, and Egyptian harvests withered. The pharaohs lost legitimacy and fell prey to internecine feuding among pretenders to the title. Regional powers took the place of a unifying, centralized state. Egypt, which had been one of the most stable corners of Afro-Eurasia, would endure more than a century of tumult before a new order emerged.

MIDDLE KINGDOM EGYPT (2040–1640 BCE)   Around 2050 BCE, after a century of drought, the floodwaters of the Nile returned to normal. Crops grew again. But who would restore order and reunite the kingdom? From about 2061 to 1991 BCE, two rulers at Thebes—far south of the Old Kingdom's seat of power in Memphis—named Mentuhotep consolidated power in Upper Egypt and began building activity in much of the country. By taming rivals and co-opting pretenders, they ushered in a new phase of stability that later historians have called the Middle Kingdom. For 350 years, the new pharaonic line built on earlier foundations to develop institutions far beyond their original forms.

GODS AND KINGS   Just as rulers of this new phase came from the margins, so too did its gods. The Twelfth Dynasty

(1991–1783 BCE), with its long, unbroken line of succession, dominated the epoch of the Middle Kingdom, in part because it brought a new sacred order to replace the chaos that had visited drought and despair on the Egyptian people. Amenemhet I (1991–1962 BCE) elevated a formerly insignificant god, Amun, to prominence. The king capitalized on the god's name, which means "hidden" in ancient Egyptian, to convey a sense of his invisible omnipresence throughout the realm.

Because Amun's attributes were largely hidden, he could with relative ease be embraced by believers in a different theological system. Amun's cosmic power was attractive to those in areas that had recently experienced impoverished independence. As the pharaoh elevated the cult of Amun, he also brought the parts of his kingdom into a more unified, if not always fully integrated, whole, thereby further empowering Amun—as well as his worldly sponsor, the pharaoh. Thus, during the Twelfth Dynasty, Amun eclipsed all of the other gods of Thebes. Grafted onto the sun god Re, Amun emerged as "Amun-Re": a supreme deity, the king of the gods. His champion among the Egyptian kings also became the ruler of the rulers. The power of the gods and kings was intertwined, increasing the sway of both. But the cult of Amun was more than simply a tool of political culture: it also had a strong spiritual impact on the pharaoh and on Egyptian society.

Amun. This sculpture of the head of the god Amun was carved from quartzite during the Eighteenth Dynasty, around 1335 BCE. At Thebes in Upper Egypt, a huge temple complex was dedicated to the combined god Amun-Re. The powerful kings of the Middle and New Kingdoms each added a courtyard or a pylon, making this one of the largest religious structures in the ancient world.

ROYAL SPLENDOR AND ROYAL CARE Middle Kingdom rulers tapped into the bounty of their kingdom, the loyalty of their subjects, and the work of untold slaves and commoners to build what would become the largest and longest-lasting public works project ever undertaken. For 2,000 years, Egyptians and slaves captured in war or raids set about erecting monumental gates, enormous courtyards, and other structures in a massive temple complex at Thebes dedicated to Amun-Re to exhibit the power of the pharaohs and the gods.

Gradually the Middle Kingdom pharaohs reasserted royal power over the regions that had broken off from the old regime, deploying ideology and administrative innovation as well as religion. Unlike the perfect and removed rulers of the Old Kingdom, the Middle Kingdom rulers nurtured a cult of the pharaoh as the good shepherd whose prime responsibility was to fulfill the needs of his human flock. By instituting charities, offering homage to gods at the palace to ensure cyclical floodwaters, and performing ritualized ceremonies to honor their own generosity, the pharaohs portrayed themselves as the stewards of their people.

MERCHANTS AND TRADE NETWORKS Prosperity gave rise to an urban class of merchants and professionals who used their wealth and specialized skills to carve out places in the cities for their own leisure and pastimes. What was new was that they did not depend directly on the kings for such benefits. Indeed, in a sign of their upward mobility and autonomy, some members of the middle class constructed tombs that they filled with representations of the material goods they would use in the afterlife as well as the occupations that would engage them for eternity—a privilege that during the Old Kingdom had been reserved exclusively for the royal family and a few powerful nobles.

Centralized and reforming kingdoms also drove the expansion of more actively extended and more wealth-producing trade networks. The Egyptian floodplains had long since been deforested. Wood had to be imported by ship, in massive quantities; especially prized were cedars from Byblos (a city in the land that would soon be known as Phoenicia, corresponding roughly to present-day Lebanon), used to make furniture for the living and coffins for the dead. Superb examples are preserved from the tombs of nobles and pharaohs. Commercial networks extended south through the Red Sea as far as present-day Ethiopia to bring back precious metals, ivory, livestock, slaves, and exotic animals such as panthers and monkeys to the pharaoh's palace. Expeditions were also undertaken to the Sinai Peninsula in search of copper and turquoise. Egyptians looked south for gold, which was highly desired for personal and architectural ornamentation. To acquire it, they crossed into Nubia, where they ran into some stiff resistance; eventually they colonized the area to broaden their trade routes and secure needed resources. A series of forts extended as far south as the second cataract of the Nile River. (See Map 2-5.)

HYKSOS INVADERS AND NEW FOUNDATIONS Pharaonic peace brought prosperity, but it did not ensure that the pharaohs' rule would continue uninterrupted. Egypt found itself open to migration and foreign invasion, coming once again from the margins. First, the very success of the new commercial networks lured pastoral nomads from the frontiers who were in search of work. Later, a new people from Southwest Asia attacked Egypt, initially destabilizing the kingdom but ultimately putting it on stronger foundations.

Beginning in 1780 BCE, large numbers of Amorites, who were Semitic-speaking transhumants, reached the banks of the Nile after being forced out of the Syrian Desert by drought. Over the course of the next century, they were absorbed into Egyptian society as agricultural workers, especially in the region of the delta in Lower Egypt, and gradually their numbers and power increased. Sometime around 1640 BCE, a western Semitic-speaking people, whom the Egyptians called the Hyksos (literally, "Rulers of Foreign Lands"), overthrew the unstable Thirteenth Dynasty. The Hyksos had mastered the art of horse chariots, and with those chariots and their superior bronze axes and composite bows (made of wood, horn, and sinew) they were able to defeat the pharaoh's foot soldiers. Yet the victors did not destroy the conquered land; if anything, they were assimilated into it. By adopting Egyptian ways, they also reinforced them. The Hyksos settled down and ruled as the Fifteenth Dynasty, taking control of the northern part of the country and transforming the Egyptian military force.

> *No longer cut off as a world apart, Egypt became a major player in the politics of Southwest Asia.*

After a century of political conflict, an Egyptian who controlled the southern part of the country, Ahmosis (r. 1550–1525 BCE), successfully used the Hyksos weaponry—horse chariots—against the invaders themselves and became pharaoh. The Egyptian rulers had learned an important lesson from the invasion: they had to pay closer attention to their frontiers, for they could no longer rely on deserts as natural buffers. Ahmosis built up large, mobile armies and drove the "foreigners" back into the Levant. Diplomats followed in the army's path, and the pharaoh initiated a strategy of interference in the affairs of the Levantine states. Such policies laid the groundwork for developing statecraft and an international diplomatic system that future Egyptian kings used to dominate the eastern Mediterranean world.

The migrants and invaders from the west introduced new ideas and techniques that the Egyptians quickly adopted to consolidate their power. The new techniques included bronze working, which the Egyptians had not perfected, preferring to import already alloyed bronze or to work with a copper arsenic alloy that was dangerous and more difficult to work. The migrants also introduced an improved potter's wheel and a vertical loom. South Asian animals such as humped zebu cattle, as well as vegetable and fruit crops, appeared on the banks of the Nile for the first time.

Probably the most significant innovations pertained to war: the horse and chariot, the composite bow, the scimitar, and other weapons associated with fighters from western Eurasia. These weapons rapidly transformed the Egyptian army from a standing infantry to a high-speed, mobile, and deadly fighting force. As Egyptian armies drove the military frontier as far south as the fourth cataract of the Nile River, the kingdom now stretched from the Mediterranean shores to Ethiopia. West Eurasian military technology enabled the pharaohs to pacify the frontiers and to maintain command over distant provinces. No longer cut off as a world apart, Egypt became a major player in the politics of Southwest Asia.

NEW KINGDOM EGYPT By the beginning of the New Kingdom (1550–1070 BCE), Egypt was projecting its interests outward: it defined itself as a superior, cosmopolitan society that drew its strength from an efficient bureaucracy run by competent and socially mobile individuals. For 100 years, Egypt expanded its control south into Nubia, a source of gold, exotic raw materials, and manpower. This expansion is most strongly identified with the reign of Egypt's most powerful woman ruler, Hatshepsut. Hatshepsut served as regent for her young son Thutmosis III, who came to the throne in 1479 BCE. When he was seven years old, she proclaimed herself "king," ruling as co-regent until she died. During her reign, there was little military activity, but trade contacts both into the Levant and Mediterranean and south into Nubia flourished.

Thutmosis III (r. 1479–1425 BCE) launched an even more expansionary phase that lasted for 200 years. The direction of Egypt's expansion was northeastward into the Levant, where Egyptians collided with the ambitions of the Mitanni and the Hittite kingdoms. At the Battle of Megiddo (1469 BCE), the first recorded chariot battle in history, Thutmosis III defeated vassals of the Mitanni and established an Egyptian presence in Palestine. Egypt was now poised to engage in commercial, political, and cultural exchanges with the rest of the region (see "The Community of Major Powers" later in this chapter).

ANATOLIA AND THE RISE OF THE HITTITES

Anatolia was an overland crossroads that linked the Black and Mediterranean seas. Like so many other semi-arid plateaus of Afro-Eurasia—high tablelands, easy to crisscross and hospitable to large-scale herding societies and clans—

Hatshepsut. The only powerful queen of Egyptian pharonic history was Hatshepsut, seen here in a portrait head created during her reign. Because a woman on the throne of Egypt would offend the basic principles of order (*ma'at*), Hatshepsut usually portrayed herself as a man, especially late in her reign. This was reinforced by the use of male determinatives in the hieroglyphic renditions of her name.

during the third millennium BCE Anatolia had become home to a number of powerful independent polities run by indigenous elites, combining pastoral lifeways, agriculture, and urban commercial centers. Before 2000 BCE, peoples speaking Indo-European languages began to infiltrate onto the plateau, probably coming from the steppe lands north and west of the Black Sea. The newcomers lived in fortified settlements and often engaged in regional warfare, and their numbers grew. Splintered into competing clans, the peoples of Anatolia fought for regional supremacy. They borrowed extensively from the cultural developments of the Southwest Asian urban cultures, especially those of Mesopotamia.

THE OLD AND NEW HITTITE KINGDOMS (1800–1200 BCE)   In the early second millennium BCE, the chariot aristocracies, which were the most powerful of the competing groups in the Anatolian area, thrived on the commercial activity between east and west. Chief among them

were the Hittites, who would form one of the five great territorial states of this period. Their chariots carried lancers and archers across vast expanses to plunder recalcitrant neighbors and enforce tax and tribute collection from those they subdued. These chariot aristocracies were finally unified during the seventeenth century BCE under the reign of Hattusilis I.

During Hattusilis's reign, the Hittite armies campaigned throughout Anatolia and met strong resistance, especially in the west. After claiming victory, Hattusilis turned his attention to the east, crossed the Taurus Mountains, and defeated the kingdom that controlled all of northern Syria from its capital (located at the site of the modern city of Aleppo). In 1595 BCE, Hattusilis and his son Mursilis I marched south along the Euphrates River as far as Babylon and sacked the city. But the occupation of Mesopotamia left the homelands exposed to domestic feuding and overstretched his army. With rebellion brewing in Anatolia, the Hittite forces soon withdrew to their plateau bastions, leaving a power vacuum in southern Mesopotamia.

It took almost two centuries for the Hittites to recover the strength that had enabled them to attack and destroy Babylon in 1595 BCE. Under the leadership of the great king Suppilulimua I (r. 1380–1345 BCE), the Hittites returned to their former glory and became one of the major powers of Southwest Asia. After conquering the small kingdoms to the southwest, the Hittites extended their control all the way to the Euphrates in the east and Syria in the south, where at Qadesh they met the Egyptians in a battle involving a vast number of chariots. The Hittites controlled much of the middle ground between Mesopotamia and the Nile, and thus the kingdom's rulers were crucial in maintaining the region's balance of power.

THE IRANIAN PLATEAU AND THE ELAMITES

As environmental conditions turned warmer and drier, the early part of the second millennium BCE saw extensive movements of people on the Iranian plateau. The people living in the valley of the Halil River, whose trade in precious stones and metals in the third millennium BCE had linked the peoples from North Africa to South Asia (see "Global Connections & Disconnections" in Chapter 2), gradually abandoned their heartland regions, some moving to the north and others to the west. During this time, the Elamites with their capital in the upland valley of modern Fars in the southwest formed into a cohesive polity that incorporated various transhumant peoples of the Zagros Mountains. When the catastrophic drought hit the Iranian plateau, some of the Elamites and the peoples of the Zagros Mountains migrated further south and westward into Mesopotamia, ultimately bringing down the Third Dynasty of Ur in 2004 BCE (see below). A century or so later, the Elamites and the Amorites were at the center of newly formed dynasties in southern Mesopotamia.

Gradually, pastoral nomads entered the Iranian plateau from the steppes of inner Eurasia. Perhaps the Kassites, who would come to rule southern Mesopotamia during the second half of the second millennium BCE, began their journey from there. Certainly the Indo-Iranian-speaking Medes and the Persians, who rose to prominence in the first millennium BCE, started their movement onto the Iranian plateau at this time. Transhumant peoples continued to dominate the lands of the Zagros Mountains and on occasion to threaten their settled neighbors to the west.

MESOPOTAMIA

The period of drought that brought down the Old Kingdom of Egypt near the end of the third millennium BCE was as damaging to Mesopotamia and the Iranian plateau. Harvests were small, the price of basic goods rose, and the social order broke down. Already short of agricultural produce, the towns of southern Mesopotamia were invaded by transhumant peoples coming from the Zagros Mountains to the east and from the Syrian Desert to the west. These herding peoples, who did not use horses or chariots, were looking for new grazing lands to replace those swallowed up by the growing deserts. As elsewhere in Afro-Eurasia, environmental changes altered the human landscape. A millennium of intense cultivation, combined with a period of severe drought, seriously damaged the productivity of the land. The rich arable soil was increasingly depleted of nutrients; at the same time, salt water from the Persian Gulf was spreading into the marshy deltas and contaminating the water table. As the main branch of the Euphrates River shifted to the west, large areas of previously arable land were no longer sufficiently watered for cultivation. As a result, many of the ancient cities lost access to their fertile agrarian hinterlands and slowly withered away. Other agrarian belts were developed along which new cities appeared. All these alterations pushed the center of political and economic gravity northward, away from the silted, marshy deltas of the southern heartland. North of Uruk and farther up the Euphrates River, Amorite pastoralists founded the city of Babylon (near current-day Baghdad) in 1830 BCE. Its establishment marked the end of the era of Sumer and Akkad and the beginning of the Old Babylonian era.

NOMADIC AND TRANSHUMANT MIGRATION TO MESOPOTAMIAN CITIES Mesopotamian urbanites called the transhumant herders from the Arabian Desert Amorites, from the Akkadian word for "west," *Amurru*. Technically speaking, the term *Amorites* does not refer to a single tribe; it was a general label for all transhumant groups who had their roots in

the western desert. City dwellers looked down their noses at these rustic folk, as the scorn in the following poetry makes clear. The Amorite is

> a tent-dweller, [buffeted] by wind and rain, [who
>   offers no] prayer,
> He who dwells in the mountains, [knows not] the
>   places [of the gods];
> A man who digs up mushrooms at the foot of the
>   mountain, who knows no submission,
> He eats uncooked meat,
> In his lifetime has no house,
> When he dies, he will not be buried;
> My girlfriend—why would you marry Martu?!
>   (Klein, "The Marriage of Martu," 89)

Transhumant herders may have been "foreigners" in the cities of Mesopotamia in the sense that they did not make their homes there, but they were not strangers to them. They had always played an important role in Mesopotamian urban life and were familiar with the culture of Mesopotamian city-states. During the winter, these rural folk spent their time in villages close to the river (their lowland pastures) to water their animals, which grazed on fallow fields. In the scorching summer, they retreated to the cooler highlands. Their flocks provided the various wools for the vast textile industries of Mesopotamia, and the herders supplied the leather, bones, and tendons that were used in other craft productions. Conversely, they admired and purchased those products created by sedentary craftworkers as well as agricultural goods. Moreover, they paid taxes, served as warriors, and labored on public works projects. Yet despite being part of the urban fabric and benefiting economically from the connection, they had few political rights within city-states.

As scarcities mounted, transhumant peoples began to press the settled communities more closely. Finally, in 2004 BCE, Amorites from the western desert joined forces with the Elamites and other allies from the Iranian plateau to bring down the Third Dynasty of Ur that had controlled all of Mesopotamia for more than a century. As in Egypt, a century of political instability followed the demise of the old city-state models of the third millennium BCE. But here, too, it was pastoral folk who finally restored order, taking the wealth of the regions they conquered and helping the cultural realm to flourish. They also expanded trade and founded new kinds of political communities: territorial states with dynastic ruling families and well-defined frontiers.

RESTORED ORDER AND CULTURE Restored order and prosperity enabled new kings to nourish a vibrant intellectual and cultural milieu. Public art and works projects were commissioned, and institutions of learning thrived. The court supported workshops for skilled artisans such as jewelers and sculptors, and it also established schools for scribes, the creators and transmitters of an expanding literary culture.

→ *What was the impact of the interactions triggered by the drought on the organization of societies?*

Culturally, Babylonians inherited and reproduced the achievements of earlier Mesopotamia. To rid themselves of the image of being rustic foreigners and to show their familiarity with the core values of the region, they studied the oral tales and written records of the earlier Sumerians and Akkadians. Scribes transcribed the ancient texts and preserved their tradition. Royal hymns, for instance, continued to be composed in the Sumerian language that had not been spoken for centuries but that was used for this form of literature. These hymns portrayed the king as a legendary hero whose status was quasi-divine.

Heroic narratives about ancient founders, which were based on a cycle of traditional stories concerning the legendary rulers of ancient Uruk, served to establish the legitimacy of the new rulers. These great poems were written not in Sumerian but in the contemporary Babylonian dialect of the Semitic Akkadian language and constituted the first epic narratives of purely human—as opposed to godly—achievement. They helped identify the history of a people with their king, constructing stories intended to circulate widely and to unify the kingdom. The most famous was the elaboration of the *Epic of Gilgamesh.*

Mesopotamian kings invested in cultural production because it enlightened them, unified their people, and distinguished their subjects from peoples in other kingdoms. Literature, the arts, and science helped delimit the kingdom's reach—beyond which lay other cultures and other polities.

TRADE AND THE RISE OF A PRIVATE ECONOMY

With restored prosperity also came a decisive shift away from economic activity dominated by the city-state and toward autonomous private ventures. The new rulers designated private entrepreneurs rather than state bureaucrats to collect taxes. People paid their taxes in the form of commodities, which the entrepreneurs exchanged for silver that they passed on to the state after taking a percentage for their profit. The result was both more private activity and wealth and more revenues flowing into state coffers.

At the same time, a reliance on labor from state impressments was giving way to contracted work. Palace and temple officials, as well as private agents, began hiring individuals on daily contracts: workers were taken on as needed and were no longer maintained year-round. While cheaper for the state in the short run, this piecework approach—mirrored in agriculture, where tenant farmers began renting land and giving a portion of their crop back to the landowners, a system known as sharecropping—did not provide for all of the needs of the workers. The result was a large destitute and disenfranchised underclass that ultimately threatened the existence of the state.

Mesopotamia was a crossroads for overland caravans leading east and west. Merchants organized donkey caravans to transport goods over long distances. When the region was peaceful and well-governed, the trading community flourished. Their ability to move exotic foodstuffs, valuable minerals, textiles, and luxury goods across Southwest Asia won Mesopotamian merchants and entrepreneurs a privileged position as they connected producers with distant consumers. Merchants also used sea routes for trade with the Indus Valley. Before 2000 BCE, mariners had

Gilgamesh. This terra-cotta plaque in the Berlin Museum is one of the very few depictions of Gilgamesh (on the left wielding the knife) and his sidekick, Enkidu. It illustrates one of the episodes in their shared adventures, the killing of Humwawa, the monster of the Cedar Forest. The style of the plaque indicates that it was made during the Old Babylonian period, between 2000 and 1600 BCE.

THE EPIC OF GILGAMESH

Gilgamesh, an early ruler of the ancient city of Uruk, was the supreme hero of Mesopotamian myth and legend. He and his deeds were the subject of epic poems composed and revised over two millennia. He was a larger-than-life figure—a successful ruler, boastful and vain, as well as a courageous adventurer and a devoted friend to his companion Enkidu. The Gilgamesh epic, constructed in the early second millennium BCE from a number of independent stories, is the oldest piece of world literature still extant. It portrays the hero as a tragic figure who is obsessed with fame and glory and whose quest for immortality necessarily ends in failure. The following excerpt from tablet X tells of his anguish on his long and ultimately fruitless journey to gain immortal life. He is speaking to an alewife (a woman who keeps an alehouse) as he continues to refuse to accept his humanity and embrace the inevitability of death.

The alewife spoke to him, to Gilgamesh,
"If you are truly Gilgamesh, that struck down the Guardian,
Destroyed Humbaba, who lived in the Pine Forest,
Killed lions at the mountain passes,
Seized the Bull of Heaven who came down from the sky,
    struck him down,
Why are your cheeks wasted, your face dejected,
Your heart so wretched, your appearance worn out,
And grief in your innermost being?
Your face is like that of a long-distance traveler,
Your face is weathered by cold and heat . . .
Clad only in a lion skin you roam open country."
Gilgamesh spoke to her, to Siduri the alewife,
"How could my cheeks not be wasted, my face not
    dejected.
Nor my heart wretched, nor my appearance worn out,
Nor grief in my innermost being,
Nor my face like that of a long-distance traveler,
My friend whom I love so much, who
Experienced every hardship with me,
Enkidu, whom I love so much, who experienced every
    hardship with me—
The fate of mortals conquered him! Six days and seven
    nights I wept over him,
I did not allow him to be buried, until a worm fell out of
    his nose.

I was frightened and . . .
I am afraid of Death, and so I roam open country.
The words of my friend weigh upon me.
I roam open country for long distances; the words of my
    friend
Enkidu weigh upon me.
I roam open country on long journeys.
How, O how, could I stay silent, how O how could I keep
    quiet
My friend whom I love has turned to clay:
Enkidu my friend whom I love has turned to clay.
Am I not like him? Must I lie down too,
Never to rise, ever again?"

→ *What does this passage from* Gilgamesh *tell us about human relationships and human nature during this period? What does it tell us about rulers and their relationship with their gods? How should historians view a work such as* Gilgamesh *that was passed on via oral tradition for many centuries before it was written down? Is it a legitimate historical source?*

SOURCE: Stephanie Dalley, *Myths from Mesopotamia: Creation, The Flood, Gilgamesh and Others* (New York: Oxford University Press, 1991), pp. 100–101.

charted the waters of the Red Sea, the Gulf of Aden, the Persian Gulf, and much of the Arabian Sea. During the second millennium BCE, shipbuilders figured out how to produce larger and larger vessels and to rig them with towering masts and woven sails—creating seaworthy craft able to carry bulkier loads to remote ports. Building ships of course required wood, particularly cedar from Phoenicia, as well as wool and other fibers from the pastoral hinterlands for the sails. Such reliance on imported materials was part of a more general trend of growing regional economic specialization and increasing interaction across western Afro-Eurasia.

Doing business in Mesopotamia was profitable but also very risky. If harvests were poor, cultivators and merchants were unable to meet their tax obligations and thus incurred heavy debts. The frequency of such misfortune is evident from the profusion of royal edicts that annulled certain kinds of tax debts as a gesture providing relief for weary subjects. Moreover, traders and goods had to pass through many lands, some of whose rulers were hostile and unwilling to protect the caravans. Taxes, duties, and bribes had to be paid along the entire route. If goods reached their final destination, they yielded large profits; if disaster struck, as often happened, investors and traders had nothing to show for their efforts. As a result, merchant households seeking to lower their risks experimented with various instruments. They formalized commercial rules, established early insurance schemes, and used extended kinship networks (relying on trusted family or clan members living in cities along trade routes and handled the family's interests there) to ensure strong commercial alliances and gather intelligence. They also cemented their ties with political authorities—indeed, the merchants who dominated the ancient city of Assur on the Tigris pumped revenues into the coffers of the local kingdom in the hope that wealthy dynasts would look out for the merchants' interests in the rough-and-tumble world of early Mesopotamian commerce.

Control over military resources was necessary to gain dominance but was no guarantee of success: the ruler's charisma also mattered.

MESOPOTAMIAN KINGDOMS The new rulers of Mesopotamia changed not only how trade was conducted but also how the state was organized. Where city-states had once prevailed, rulers from pastoral nomadic stock fashioned kingdoms that ruled over large territorial expanses. These herders-turned-urbanites hybridized their own social organization with that of the city-states to create the structures necessary to support territorial states. The basic social organization of the Amorites was tribal, dominated by a ruling chief. Tribal polities, even those extending over wide areas, were divided into clans; each claimed descent from a common ancestor, and thus drew a line between itself and all who were not kin, yet the clans were open to incorporate and exchange new members through marriage and adoption. Even the many Amorites who had given up nomadic ways and settled in the cities remained conscious of their genealogical roots. The new territorial polities were rooted in identification with the clan and tribe, with the line between own group and others now drawn on a larger scale.

The emergence of ruling cliques from among the nomadic chieftains who took power in Mesopotamia gave way to a new model of statecraft in three stages. In the first major transformation, chieftains became kings. Second, these new Mesopotamian kings turned their authority—which in the tribe had been based on their prowess on the battlefield—into an alliance with merchant magnates in exchange for revenues and for elite support. Finally, royal status became hereditary, a practice of succession that replaced the old tribal system according to which leaders were elected by influential members of the community. Yet even in this new system, kings could not rule without the support of nobles and merchants.

Over the centuries, powerful kings continued to push out the borders of their territories. They subdued weaker neighbors, coaxing or forcing them to become vassals—allies required to pay tribute in the form of luxury goods, raw materials, and manpower as part of a broad confederation of Mesopotamian polities under the king's protection. Control over military resources—access to metals for weaponry and eventually to herds of horses used to pull vast numbers of chariots—was necessary to gain dominance but was no guarantee of success: the ruler's charisma also mattered. This emphasis on personality explains why Mesopotamian kingdoms tended to be strong for certain periods, but vulnerable to ambitious rivals and neighbors when the king was weak or vacillating. It also distinguished them fundamentally from Middle Kingdom Egypt and Hittite Anatolia, territorial states in which power was much more institutionalized and durable.

The most famous of the Mesopotamian rulers of the second millennium BCE was Hammurapi (or Hammurabi), who ascended the throne as the sixth king of Babylon's First Dynasty in 1792 BCE and ruled until 1750 BCE. Continuously engaged in conflicts with powerful neighbors, he sought to centralize state authority and to create a new legal order. He used both diplomatic and military skills to become the strongest king in Mesopotamia, making Babylon the capital of his kingdom and calling himself "the king who made the four quarters of the earth obedient." After subduing his rivals, he implemented a new system to secure his power, appointing regional governors to manage outlying provinces and to deal with local elites.

Hammurapi's image as ruler was borrowed from that of the Egyptian pharaohs of the Middle Kingdom. The king was shepherd and patriarch of his people, responsible for the proper preparation of the fields and irrigation canals and for the well-being of his followers. Such an ideal recognized that being king was a delicate balancing act. While he had to curry favor among the realm's powerful merchants and elites, he was also expected to attend to the needs of the poor and disadvantaged—in part to keep from gaining a reputation for cruelty but in part to gain a key base of support should the elites become dissatisfied with his rule.

Hammurapi converted this balancing act into an art form, encapsulated in a grand legal structure—Hammurapi's Code. The code began and concluded with the rhetoric of paternal justice. For example, he concludes the code by describing

The Code of Hammurapi. The inscription on the shaft of the Code of Hammurapi is carved in a beautiful rendition of the cuneiform script. Because none of the laws on the Code were recorded in the thousands of judicial texts of the period, it is uncertain if the Code of Hammurapi presented actual laws, or only norms for the proper behavior of Babylonian citizens.

himself as "the shepherd who brings peace, whose scepter is just. My benevolent shade was spread over my city, I held the people of the lands of Sumer and Akkad safely on my lap."

The Code of Hammurapi was in fact a compilation of more than 300 edicts addressing crimes and their punishments, listing the behaviors that could bring legal sanction. One theme rings loud and clear: governing public matters was man's work, and upholding a just order was the supreme charge of rulers. Whereas the role of the gods in ordering the world was distant, the king was directly in command of ordering the relations between people. Accordingly, the code elaborated in exhaustive detail social rules that were supposed to ensure the peace of the kingdom through its primary instrument, the family, carefully outlining the rights and privileges of fathers, wives, and children. The father had the duty of treating his kin as the ruler would treat his subjects, with strict authority and care. Adultery, which represented the

supreme violation of this moral code, was considered a female crime. Any woman found with a man not her husband was bound and thrown into the river, as was her lover.

Hammurapi's order both pacified the region and stratified society. His code divided the Babylonian kingdom into three classes—each member was either a freeman (*avilum*), a dependent man (*mushkenum*), or a slave (*wardum*), and each had an assigned value and distinct rights and responsibilities.

By the end of his reign, Hammurapi had reconfigured the political map of Southwest Asia. He had established Babylon as the single great power in Mesopotamia and had reduced competitor kingdoms to mere vassals. Following his death, his sons and successors struggled to maintain control over a shrinking domain lands for another 155 years in the face of internal rebellions and foreign invasions. In 1595 BCE, Babylon was sacked by the Hittite king Hattusilis I.

KASSITE RULE As a crossroads for Afro-Eurasia, Mesopotamia continued both to benefit from and to be threatened by the arrival of nomadic and transhumant neighbors and immigrants. The Kassites, for instance, who came from the eastern Zagros Mountains, had entered southern Mesopotamia from the Iranian plateau. They began arriving in the river valley as agricultural laborers as early as 2000 BCE and gradually integrated themselves into Babylonian society by becoming bureaucrats associated with the temple. Already deeply entrenched in society, they were well placed to fill the power vacuum left when the Hittites destroyed the First Dynasty of Babylon. By 1475 BCE, Kassite rulers had reestablished order in the region; over the next 350 years they brought all of southern Mesopotamia under their control, creating one of the great territorial states within an emerging latticework of states from North Africa to South Asia.

STATES OF SOUTHWEST ASIA AND NORTH AFRICA, 2000–1200 BCE

Middle Kingdom Egypt	2040–1640 BCE
The Old Hittite Kingdom	1800–1600 BCE
Hammurapi's Babylonia	1792–1750 BCE
New Kingdom Egypt	1550–1070 BCE
The New Hittite Kingdom	1400–1200 BCE
Kassite Rule	1475–1125 BCE
Community of Major Powers	1400–1200 BCE

The Kassites presided over a golden age that was based not on militaristic expansion but on trade in such precious commodities as horses, chariots, and lapis lazuli, which they exchanged for gold, wood, and ivory. Like other immigrant communities who had come to this ancient land before them, the Kassites absorbed the traditions and institutions of Mesopotamia. Even more vigorously than their predecessors, they strove to preserve the past and transmit its institutions to posterity. Very little of their own language and customs, apart from their personal names, has been preserved. With an unrivaled thoroughness and dedication, Kassite scribes translated much of the older Sumerian literature into Akkadian. They revised and compiled texts into standard editions, from which scholars have recovered a Babylonian creation myth called the Enuma Elish. In their determination to become even more Babylonian than the Babylonians, the Kassites saved a treasure trove of historical literature and artifacts for later generations.

THE COMMUNITY OF MAJOR POWERS (1400–1200 BCE)

By the fifteenth century BCE, societies in Southwest Asia and North Africa had recovered from environmental upheaval and invasion. The five great territorial states that emerged, occupying the area between the Aegean Sea and the Iranian plateau, ultimately established an interregional system based on the concept of a balance of power. Over the course of two centuries, these major powers learned how to settle their differences through treaties and diplomatic negotiations rather than on the battlefield. Only in Syria and Palestine, where the edges of major powers met, did lesser states centered on single cities continue to exist. Jerusalem, Byblos, Damascus, Ugarit, and Aleppo were all capitals of little kingdoms tightly squeezed between the large states to the north, south, and east. Although small in size, each of these vassal kingdoms played an important role in maintaining the balance of power and thus keeping the region peaceful.

The leaders who created this international system pioneered a form of international diplomacy that would inspire rulers across the centuries. Each state, large and small, knew its place in the political pecking order of the broader interregional system. It was an order that depended on constant communication—the foundation of what we now call diplomacy. A remarkable cache of more than 300 letters discovered at Tell el-'Amârna, the capital city of the New Kingdom under the pharaoh Akhenaten, offers intimate views of these complex interactions. Most are letters from the Egyptian king to his vassals in the small tributary states of Palestine, but others were sent from Akhenaten and his father to the Babylonian, Mitanni, Middle Assyrian, Kassite, and Hittite kings. Many of these letters were written in a dialect of Akkadian, used by the Babylonian bureaucrats, that served as the diplomatic language of the era. This correspondence reveals a delicate balance, constantly shifting, between competing kings who were intent on maintaining their status and who knew that winning the loyalty of the small buffer kingdoms was crucial to political success.

Formal international treaties, although rare and usually signed only at the conclusion of serious military conflicts, reinforced diplomatic contacts. Diplomacy more commonly took the form of marriages and the exchange of specialized personnel who would reside at the court of foreign territorial states. Gifts also strengthened the peaceful relations between the major powers and signaled a ruler's respect for his neighbors. They had to be acknowledged by reciprocating gifts of equal value; anything less risked a potentially dangerous slight. At the same time, gifts introduced raw materials into regions that otherwise lacked them. According to the letters, Egypt was the sole source of gold, which it exchanged for horses and lapis lazuli from the Kassites, who certainly obtained these goods from further east. Copper came from Alashiya (the ancient name for Cyprus), and ivory and craft goods were sent from the small vassal states in Syria and Palestine.

Although each of the major powers and the vassal kingdoms had its own social order, their close-knit international relations led to the creation of an elite cosmopolitan merchant and political class. Use of the Babylonians' Akkadian dialect soon separated these elites from the lower classes. Like the royal courts on which they depended, they drew on their

Akhenaten. The pharaoh Amenhotep IV changed his name to Akhenaten to reflect his deep devotion to Aten, the god of the sun disk. The art of the period of his reign, like his religion, challenged conventions. In it, the faces of the king and queen, as well as their bodies, were extremely elongated and distorted. Some scholars think that this distortion reflects a condition that the king himself suffered from.

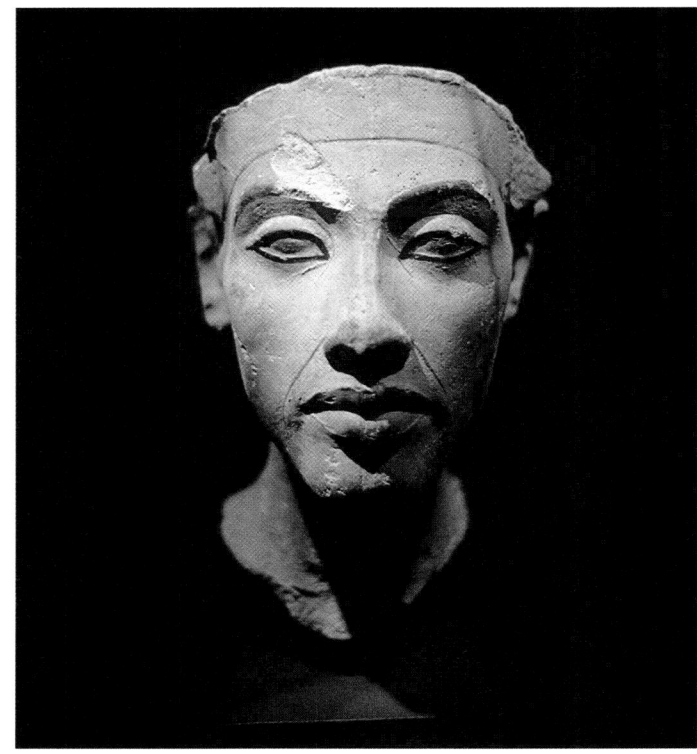

great fortunes to erect buildings, decorate their tombs, and consume goods in a conspicuous way that marked their special status. Supporting these elites were specialists, bureaucrats, scribes, and craftworkers. Military men also enjoyed high status, especially the charioteers. Standing armies provided the foundation of royal power.

The foundations of power were not always durable, however. Building the state system was ultimately the task of those at the bottom of the social pyramid, and the reliance of the ruling classes on the least privileged for their power and political authority was an intrinsic weakness of these regimes. Commoners remained tied to the land, which sometimes was owned by communities or institutions, not individual families. They paid taxes to the state, performed corvée labor (that is, labor conscripted by the state for public works such as irrigation or building projects), and served as foot soldiers. The hefty taxes and conscription were needed to sustain the state. The collapse of the international age had many causes, but one factor contributing to its demise was the disintegration of the social fabric as workers could not pay their taxes or fled their communities rather than fight in the armies of the rulers.

Indra with Buddha. The Vedic people worshipped their gods by sacrificing and burning cows and horses and by singing hymns and songs, but they never built temples or sculptured idols. Therefore we do not know how they envisioned Indra and their other gods. However, when Buddhists started to make images of Buddha in the early centuries CE, they also sculpted Indra and Brahma as attendants of the Buddha. Indra in Buddhist iconography evolved into Vajrapani, the Diamond Lord. In this plate, the one on the left holding a stick with diamond-shaped heads is Indra/Vajrapani.

NOMADS AND THE INDUS RIVER VALLEY

> → *How did Vedic migrations influence South Asia?*

Drought at the end of the third millennium BCE ravaged the Indus River valley as it did other regions. By 1700 BCE, the population of the old Harappan heartland had plummeted. Around 1500 BCE, the Vedic people, who originally came from the steppes of inner Eurasia, crossed from the northern highlands of Central Asia through the Hindu Kush and entered the fertile lowlands of the Indus River basin. (See Map 3-3.) As they moved into the Indus Valley, these nomads changed and adapted to their new environment.

The Vedic people called themselves Aryans, or "respected ones." Like other nomads who had arrived from the northern steppe into Southwest Asia, they spoke an Indo-European language—in this case Sanskrit, which literally means "perfectly made." They brought with them domesticated animals—especially horses, which they used to draw chariots and which thus were crucial to establishing their military superiority—as well as elaborate rituals for worshipping gods, which they actively used to distinguish themselves from the indigenous populations. The Vedic people did not doubt that their chief god, Indra, the deity of war, was on their side. But, as was true of so many Afro-Eurasian migrations, the arrival of outsiders led to as much fusion as conflict. While the native-born peoples eventually adopted the language of the newcomers, the new-

comers soon took up the techniques and rhythms of agrarian life. In adapting to local conditions, the Vedic steppe people developed their own world.

The Vedic people used the Indus Valley as a staging area for migrations throughout the northern plain of South Asia. As they mixed agrarian and pastoral ways and borrowed technologies such as ironworking from further west, their population grew, and they began to look for new resources. With horses, chariots, and iron tools and weapons, they marched south and east. By 1000 BCE, they reached the southern foothills of the Himalayas and gradually began to settle in the Ganges River valley. Five hundred years later, they had settlements as far south as the Deccan plateau.

Each wave of occupation was accompanied by violence, but the invaders did not simply dominate the indigenous peo-

Primary Source

VEDIC HYMNS TO THE CHARIOT RACE OF THE GODS

The Vedic people did not leave us accounts of their horse chariot races and festivals, despite the centrality of these events to their culture. However, they have left us their religious hymns praising the chariot races of gods. As we see from the following hymn, the Maruts, the storm gods under the direction of Indra, were viewed as particularly good charioteers.

1. The Maruts charged with rain, endowed with fierce force, terrible like wild beasts, blazing in their strength, brilliant like fires, and impetuous, have uncovered the (rain-giving) cows by blowing away the cloud.

2. The (Maruts) with their rings appeared like the heavens with their stars, they shone wide like streams from clouds as soon as Rudra, the strong man, was born for you, O golden-breasted Maruts, in the bright lap of P*ris*ni.

3. They wash their horses like racers in the courses, they hasten with the points of the reed on their quick steeds. O golden-jawed Maruts, violently shaking (your jaws), you go quick with your spotted deer, being friends of one mind.

4. Those Maruts have grown to feed all these beings, or, it may be, (they have come) hither for the sake of a friend, they who always bring quickening rain. They have spotted horses, their bounties cannot be taken away, they are like headlong charioteers on their ways.

5. O Maruts, wielding your brilliant spears, come hither on smooth roads with your fiery cows (clouds) whose udders are swelling; (come hither), being of one mind, like swans toward their nests, to enjoy the sweet offering.

6. O one-minded Maruts, come to our prayers, come to our libations like (Indra) praised by men! Fulfil (our prayer) like the udder of a barren cow, and make the prayer glorious by booty to the singer.

7. Grant us this strong horse for our chariot, a draught that rouses our prayers, from day to day, food to the singers, and to the poet in our homesteads luck, wisdom, inviolable and invincible strength.

8. When the gold-breasted Maruts harness the horses to their chariots, bounteous in wealth, then it is as if a cow in the folds poured out to her calf copious food, to every man who has offered libations.

➔ *What kind of gods are the Maruts? What is their heavenly job when racing on horse chariots? Why did the Vedic people try to please the Maruts by offering libations?*

SOURCE: Mandala II, Hymn 34, in Vedic Hymns, translated by Hermann Oldenberg, in vol. 32 of *Sacred Books of the East,* edited by F. Max Müller (1897; reprint, New Delhi: Motilal Banarsidass, 1979), pp. 295–96.

ples; indeed, the confrontation was a catalyst for change. Although the Vedic people despised the local rituals, they were in awe of the inhabitants' farming skills and knowledge of seasonal weather. They therefore adapted even as they

Gandhara Grave Site. Gandharan Grave Culture, an archaeological assemblage named after cemeteries and settlements in Timargarh, Pakistan, testifies that the migration to South Asia lasted more than a thousand years. The people who are buried there show many different physical types. The early graves were complete burials of bodies. Cremation, the practice of Vedic people, appeared after the fourteenth century BCE.

Global Connections & Disconnections

HOW LANGUAGES SPREAD: THE CASE OF NOMADIC INDO-EUROPEAN LANGUAGES

Language arose independently in a number of places around the world. All languages change with time, and related tongues with a common ancestral origin are grouped as "language families"; members of the same family diverged from one another at different times, varying with each family, but share grammatical features and root vocabularies.

While technically more than a hundred language families exist in the world, a much smaller number have influenced vast geographic areas. For example, the Altaic languages spread from Europe to Central Asia. The Sino-Tibetan language family includes Mandarin, the most widely spoken single language in the world. The Uralic family, which includes Hungarian and Finnish, is found mainly in Europe. The Afro-Asiatic language family contains several hundred languages spoken in North Africa, sub-Saharan Africa, and Southeast Asia, Hebrew and Arabic among them.

The family of languages that has received the most attention from linguists, and the one with the largest number of speakers, is Indo-European; it was first identified by scholars who recognized the similarities in grammar and vocabulary among classical Sanskrit, Persian, Greek, and Latin. Living languages in this family include English, Irish, German, Norwegian, Portuguese, French, Russian, Persian, Hindi, and Bengali. For the past 200 years, comparative linguists have sought to reconstruct Proto-Indo-European, the parent of all the languages in the family. They have drawn some conclusions about its grammar (hypothesizing a highly inflected language, with different endings on nouns and verbs depending on how they are used) and its vocabulary. For example, after analyzing regular patterns of linguistic change, scholars have suggested that the basic Indo-European root that means "horse"—in Sanskrit, *aśva*; Persian, *aspa*; Latin, *equus*; and Greek, *hippos* (ἵππος)—is *ekwo-.

Attempts have also been made to locate the homeland of the original speakers of Proto-Indo-European. These ef-

forts have relied heavily on the reconstructed vocabulary, which contains words for "snow," "mountain," and "swift river," as well as for animals not native to Europe, such as "lion," "monkey," and "elephant"; such terms are then mapped onto a matching geography. Other words describe agricultural practices and farming tools that date back as far as 5000 BCE. Many believe that nomadic and pastoral peoples of the Eurasian steppes took this language as well as their horses and chariots to the borderlands of what is now Afghanistan and eastern Iran.

We know that the early speakers of Indo-European languages used chariots, and they also had specific terminology for "wheel," "yoke," and "axle." The earliest pictures of horse-drawn chariots, marked on stone, are found in the region between two lakes, Van (in modern-day Turkey) and Urmia (in modern-day Iran). The chariot was the literal vehicle for cultural mingling, as reflected in the spread of the language of the people who used them. In this way, migrations of populations from distant regions created new cultural convergences.

The reasons that languages move over vast areas and alter over time are complex, and scholars argue over the importance of such factors as invasions, migrations, climatic changes, the availability of natural resources, and ways of life (hunter-gatherer vs. agriculturalist). Even within one language, the import of words changes through generations of use—for example, the original sense of the English word *nice* was "foolish, stupid"—and words from a common Indo-European root could take on very different meanings while remaining quite similar phonetically. Thus *aśura* means "demonic creature" in Sanskrit, whereas the Persian *ahura* means "Supreme God."

The study of language families and their history throughout the world can be quite revealing. The geographic, material, climactic, and demographic details of their use and penetration into different countries clearly indicate the importance of language in how cultures intermingled throughout time.

→ *How did Vedic migrations influence South Asia?*

BLACK SEA

HITTITES

MEDITERRANEAN SEA

MITANNI

Tigris R.

Euphrates R.

CASPIAN SEA

ARAL SEA

PROTO-INDO-IRANIANS

INDO-ARYAN/VEDIC

Persian Gulf

Indus R.

Nile R.

RED SEA

ARABIAN SEA

Bay of Bengal

0   500   1000 Miles
0   500   1000 Kilometers

Suggested Indo-European homeland, 3rd millennium BCE
← Spread of Indo-European speakers, 2nd millennium BCE
Indo-European speakers, 2nd millennium BCE (Hittites, Mitanni)

INDIAN   OCEAN

MAP 3-3   INDO-EUROPEAN MIGRATIONS, 2ND MILLENNIUM BCE

How did Indo-European migrations reshape the cultural landscape of Afro-Eurasia in the second millennium BCE? Compare this map to Map 3-1. Why do you think some pastoral peoples moved into more settled agricultural regions? How did Vedic Indo-European migrants contribute to the growth of a new South Asia world?

continued to expand their territory. They moved into huts constructed from mud, bamboo, and reeds. They refined the already highly developed production of beautiful carnelian stone beads, and they further aided commerce by devising standardized weights. In addition to raising domesticated animals, they planted wheat and rye on the Indus plain, and they learned to plant rice in the marshy lands after they had settled in the Ganges Valley. Eventually they mastered the use of plows with iron blades, an innovation that transformed the agrarian base of South Asia.

The turn to settled agriculture was a major shift for the pastoral Vedic people, whose staple foods were dairy products and meat and who traditionally measured their wealth in livestock—horses were valued most highly, and cows worth more than sheep. Horses were prized for their ability to draw chariots but could not be bred in South Asia's semi-tropical climate; the need to import them from central and western Asia helped support a brisk trade. But as they became an agrarian folk, the Vedic people learned from the local agriculturists among whom they now lived. In the process, they created polities and cultures that combined traits from the steppe lands with indigenous ways. We will pick up their story again in the next chapter.

RISE OF THE SHANG STATE (1600–1045 BCE)

> → *What methods did the Shang state employ to maintain its rule?*

Climatic change at the end of the third millennium BCE affected East Asia much as it had central and western Asia. As Chapter 2 detailed, this was a time of cultural integration among agricultural communities along the Yellow and Yangzi rivers. Chinese lore maintains that in this era the Xia dynasty was founded by the mythological Yu the Great. While evidence for such a kingdom is sketchy, archaeological and other evidence does confirm the later emergence, around 1600 BCE, of a territorial state called the Shang dynasty, located in northeastern China. (See Map 3-4.)

Like the ruling families in the Southwest Asian societies, the Shang handed down their own foundation myths to unify the state. Stories supposedly written on bamboo strips and later collected into what are known as the authentic "Bamboo Annals" tell of a time at the end of the Xia dynasty when the sun was dimmed, frost and ice appeared in July, and heavy rainfall and flooding were followed by a long period of drought. According to Chinese mythology, Tang, the first ruler of the Shang dynasty, defeated a cruel and despotic Xia king and then offered to sacrifice himself so that the long drought would finally end. Tang survived, however, and proved to be a just and moral ruler who strengthened his state and unified his people.

The Shang state was not as well defined by fixed and clearly established borders as were the territorial kingdoms of Southwest Asia. To be sure, it faced threats—but not in the form of rival territorial states encroaching on its peripheries. It had little need for a strongly defended central complex, though its heartland was called Zhong Shang, or "center Shang." Its capital moved as its frontier expanded and contracted. This relative security can also be seen in the Shang kings' highly personalized style of rule, as they traveled regularly around the country to meet, hunt, and conduct military campaigns with those who owed allegiance to them. Yet, like the territorial kingdoms of Southwest Asia, the Shang state had a ruling lineage (that is, a line of male sovereigns descended from a common ancestor), which was eventually set down in a written record. Like the kings of other early territorial states, Shang rulers used metallurgy and writing to reinforce their rule, as well as ancestor worship, divination, and other rituals. At the heart of their power, however, was their keen awareness of the importance of promoting agricultural growth and controlling the precious metals that could be used to wage war. All of these efforts cumulatively laid the foundation for future state formation in East Asia, shaping a system in which one regime would be dominant, surrounded by (not always happy) satellites. For the time being, spared the intense scramble for territorial control, the Shang regime had relatively little motivation to assert its hegemony, especially in comparison with contemporary Southwest Asian states.

STATE FORMATION

One of the first kingdoms of East Asia, the Shang state built upon the small agricultural and riverine village cultures of the Longshan peoples, who had set the stage for a centralized state, urban life, and a cohesive culture at the end of the third millennium BCE. The Shang state did not grow out of urban polities such as those in Mesopotamia and Egypt, for the abundant supply of food from the agriculturally rich lands in the areas around the Yellow and Yangzi rivers enabled China to maintain a more decentralized local form of life. But as the population began to grow and the number of villages multiplied, interactions—and conflicts—inevitably grew. Because of the increase in trading networks and the greater need for mechanisms to settle disagreements between towns, larger and more centralized forms of control were required. The Shang state emerged to play that larger governmental role.

Four fundamental elements that were instrumental in forming the Shang state had already been introduced by the Longshan peoples: a metal industry based on copper, pottery making, standardized architectural forms and walled towns, and divination using animal bones. To these foundations, the Shang dynasty added a lineage of hereditary rulers whose hold on power was based on their relation to their ancestors and the gods, written records, tribute, and elaborate rituals that enabled them to commune with ancestors and foretell the future. In particular, the Shang promoted large-scale metallurgy and the development of writing, major components in the advance of Chinese society in the second millennium BCE.

The Shang dynasty derived its name from the location where, over the course of several centuries, a royal ancestral temple, a city, and finally the dynasty itself were established. To expand and protect their borders, the Shang fought with neighboring states and with pastoral nomads from the central Asian steppes. Horses imported from central Asia helped the Shang dominate northern and central China. Moreover, the Shang copied the chariots of the nomads they encountered, improving them by adding bronze fittings and harnesses; this new technology gave the warriors devastating range and speed. The importance of such chariots to military victories highlights the impact of nomadic contacts across Afro-Eurasia. Here, as in Southwest Asia, chariot aristocracies emerged.

→ *What methods did the Shang state employ to maintain its rule?*

Several other large states also developed in East Asia between 1500 and 1300 BCE, formed both by relatively urban and wealthy southeastern peoples and by more rustic peoples bordering the Shang. The latter interacted with and traded with these other groups, whom they called the Fang, their label for those who lived in non-Shang areas. Other kingdoms in the south and southwest also had independent bronze industries, with casting technologies comparable to those of the Shang.

Though the Shang dynasty arose in part because greater centralization of power was needed, it was never as fully centralized a state as its contemporaries in Southwest Asia and North Africa, such as the New Kingdom in Egypt or Hammurapi's Babylonian kingdom. It did not control surrounding vassal states or even, as noted above, have a fixed capital. Sima Qian (c. 145–86 BCE), the greatest historian of ancient China, claimed that the Shang state moved its capital six

times, adding that the final and most important move to Yin (Anyang in present-day Henan) in 1350 BCE led to the dynasty's golden age. Its rulers may have moved in search of metal resources, as copper and tin were the basis of the bronze industry and thus of wealth and power for those who controlled them.

The Shang state reached its zenith around 1200 BCE. At Yin, the Shang erected massive palaces, royal neighborhoods, and bronze foundries. In workshops surrounding the palace, craftworkers decorated jade, stone, and ivory objects; wove silk on special looms; and produced bronze weapons and bronze ritual objects and elaborate ceremonial drinking vessels from which the Shang dynasts, ancient accounts say, imbibed strong drink. Based on the local abundance of metal ores, artisans were able to organize large numbers of workers into workshops where they mass-produced the large bronze vessels. The levels of urbanization reached at Yin make it

MAP 3-4   SHANG DYNASTY IN EAST ASIA

Why were there no clear territorial boundaries for the Shang state? Why do you think that control of copper and tin sources was important to Shang rulers? Compare this map to Map 3-2. How was the Shang state different from territorial states in Western Asia?

Primary Source

SIMA QIAN ON THE RULER'S MANDATE

Sima Qian was the first great historian in ancient China; he later had as much influence in East Asia as Herodotus, the first Greek historian, had in Greece and Rome. The excerpt below presents the Xia-Shang dynastic transition as an example of the transfer of the ruler's mandate.

After Emperor K'ung-chia was enthroned, he delighted in following ghosts and spirits and engaging in licentious and disorderly actions. The prestige of the Hsia-hou Clan declined and the feudal lords rebelled against him.

Heaven sent down two dragons, a male and a female. K'ung-chia was not able to care for them and he lost the support of the Huan-lung (Dragon Raising) Clan. The Yao-t'ang Clan was already in decline, [but] among their descendants one Liu Lei learned the technique of taming dragons from the Huan-lung Clan and thus obtained service with K'ung-chia. K'ung-chia bestowed on him the *cognomen* Yü-lung (Dragon Tamer) and conferred on him the people descended from the Shih-wei [Clan]. The female dragon died and Liu Lei fed it to The Hsia-hou, The Hsia-hou sent [someone] to demand [more of it], and, fearing [that he would be punished], Liu Lei moved on.

When K'ung-chia passed away, his son Emperor Kao was enthroned. When Emperor Kao passed away his son Emperor Fa was enthroned. When Fa passed away, his son Emperor Lu-k'uei was enthroned. He was known as Chieh.

From K'ung-chia's time to the time of Emperor Chieh, the feudal lords had revolted many times against the Hsia. Chieh did not engage in virtuous [government] but in military power and [this] hurt the families of the hundred cog-nomens. The families of the hundred cognomens were not able to bear him.

Chieh then summoned T'ang and jailed him in Hsia-t'ai. After a while he freed him. T'ang cultivated his virtue and the feudal lords all submitted to T'ang. T'ang then led troops to attack Chieh of Hsia. Chieh fled to Ming-t'iao and subsequently was exiled and died there. Before he died he said to someone, "I regret failing to kill T'ang in Hsia-t'ai; that is what has brought me to this."

T'ang then ascended the throne of the Son of Heaven and received the world's homage in The Hsia's place. T'ang enfeoffed the descendants of the Hsia. In the Chou dynasty they were enfeoffed at Ch'i.

→ *Does Sima Qian's first-century BCE account confirm the existence of the Xia [Hsia] dynasty in the third millennium BCE? What role did morality play in Sima Qian's description of the transfer of the Xia ruler's mandate to the Shang dynasty?*

SOURCE: "The Hsia, Basic Annals" 2, in *The Grand Scribe's Records*, edited by William H. Nienhauser, Jr., translated by Tsai-fa Cheng, Zongli Lu, William H. Nienhauser, Jr., and Robert Reynolds, vol. 1 (Bloomington: Indiana University Press, 1994), pp. 37–38.

---

clear that the Shang also collected tribute from their agrarian heartlands and used these resources to support the city's nobles, priests, and dependent artisans and metalworkers. The Shang state simultaneously promoted both the writings of elite scribes and the productions of common artisans.

METALWORKING, AGRICULTURE, AND TRIBUTE

Small-scale metalworking first emerged in northwestern China; pre-Shang sites such as Erlitou reveal that casting techniques were being used as early as 1800 BCE. Because both copper and tin were accessible from the North China plain, only short-distance trade was necessary to obtain the resources needed by a bronze culture. Access to copper and tin and to the new technology that used them to make bronze war and ritual objects gave the Shang unprecedented power as they dealt with their neighbors. The Shang used an alloy of copper, lead, and tin to produce bronze, from which they made weapons, fittings for chariots, and ritual vessels. They created hollow clay molds into which they poured the molten metal alloy and then removed the desired bronze objects after the liquid metal had cooled and solidified. Casting modular components that could later be combined made possible huge increases in production and fueled the extravagant uses of bronze vessels by royal elites for burials. For example, in 1975 archaeologists found a tomb at Anyang that held a bronze vessel weighing 1,925 pounds that was produced in the Shang workshops around 1200 BCE. Another Anyang tomb from the same period contained 3,500 pounds of cast bronze.

The bronze industry in the second millennium BCE shows the high level in ancient China not only of material culture—that is, the actual physical objects produced—but also of cultural development. The Shang metalworking that emerged around 1500 BCE in the Yellow River valley required extensive mining (and thus a large labor force), efficient casting, and a reproducible artistic style. The extraction of the resources was separated from their conversion into goods. And while highly valuing its artisans, the Shang state treated its copper miners as lowly tribute laborers.

By closely controlling access to tin and copper and to the production of bronze, the Shang kings managed to prevent their rivals from forging bronze weapons and thus increased their own power and legitimacy. With their metal weapons, Shang armies could easily destroy armies equipped with wooden clubs and stone-tipped spears. Moreover, the ruler

also enhanced his power by hiring artisans to record his feats for posterity. Shang workers produced large and small bronze vessels that they then delicately inscribed with images of important events, particularly those in which the ruler played a significant role, such as a battle, a wedding, the birth of an heir, or an astrological sighting.

The Shang dynasts also understood the importance of agriculture to winning and maintaining power and did much to promote agrarian development. The activities of local governors and the masses revolved around agriculture. The rulers controlled their own farms, which supplied food to the royal family, craftworkers, and army. New technologies enabled food production to rise. Farmers opened up previously untilled land by draining low-lying fields or clearing forested areas so that they could expand the cultivation of millet, wheat, barley, and possibly some rice. Farm implements included stone plows, spades, and sickles. In addition, farmers cultivated silkworms and raised pigs, dogs, sheep, and oxen. To best use the land and increase production, they tracked the growing season. And to record the seasons, the Shang

Bronze. At the height of the Shang state, circa 1200 BCE, its rulers erected massive palaces at the capital of Yin, which required bronze foundries for its wine and food vessels. In these foundries, skilled workers produced bronze weapons and ritual objects and elaborate ceremonial drinking and eating vessels.

Bronze Head. Other large states such as Sanxingdui emerged in East Asia between 1500 and 1300 BCE, showing that the Shang rulers were not unique. These kingdoms in the south and southwest had their own metallurgy and casting technology. From Sanxingdui in particular we have spectacular gold masks and bronze sculptures that present unprecedented human—as opposed to purely graphic—forms.

developed a twelve-month, 360-day lunar calendar; it contained leap months inserted as necessary to maintain the proper relationship between months and seasons. The calendar also relieved fears about seemingly anomalous events such as solar and lunar eclipses by rendering them predictable.

As in other Afro-Eurasian states, the ruler's wealth and power depended on tribute from elites and allies. Elites supplied warriors and laborers, as well as horses and cattle. Allies sent foodstuffs, soldiers, and workers and "assisted in the king's affairs"—perhaps hunting, burning brush, or clearing land—in return for such help as providing defense against invaders and predictions about the harvest. Commoners sent their tribute to the elites, who held the land as fiefs from the king. Farmers transferred their surplus crops to the elite landholders (or to the ruler himself if they worked on his personal landholdings), making payments in kind on a regular schedule. Commoners also made labor (corvée) payments: some became workers attached to the royal workshops that produced vast quantities of bronze ritual vessels as well as bronze armaments, such as dagger-axes, arrowheads, spearheads, helmets, shields, and chariot fittings; others labored to drain fields, clear land, build palaces, excavate tombs, or construct walls to protect towns or the capital.

Tribute could also take the form of turtle shells and cattle scapulas, which the Shang used for divination. The ability to divine the future was a powerful way to legitimate royal power—and then to justify the right to collect yet more trib-

ute. By placing themselves symbolically and literally at the center of all exchanges, Shang kings reinforced their power over others.

Shang Society and Beliefs

Both metalworking and agriculture contributed to the wealth of the state and supported a complex social structure. The organizing principle of Shang society was a patrilineal ideal: descent was traced back through the generations to a common male ancestor. Grandparents, parents, sons, and daughters lived and worked together. Their property was held in common, and male family elders took precedence. Women from other patrilines married into the family, winning honor when they became mothers, particularly of sons.

The social hierarchy was also reflected in the death ritual, which involved sacrificing humans to accompany the deceased in the next life. A member of the royal elite was often buried with his full entourage, including his wife, consorts, servants, chariots, horses, and drivers. The inclusion of personal slaves and servants indicates a belief that the familiar social hierarchy would continue to exist in the afterlife. Modern Chinese historians have described the Shang as a "slave society," but its economy was not primarily based on owning slaves and using their labor. Instead, the driving force was the tribute labor of the commoners who made up most of society, particularly as delivered in metalworking and farming.

The Shang state can best be described as a patrimonial theocracy: the ruler at the top of the hierarchy was believed to derive his authority from the guidance from ancestors and gods. Rulers therefore had to find ways to communicate with ancestors and foretell the future, and they relied mainly on divination. When diviners applied intense heat to the shoulder bones of cattle or to turtle shells, they cracked. Diviners would then interpret those cracks as an auspicious or inauspicious sign from the ancestors regarding royal plans and actions. Scribes subsequently inscribed the queries they had asked of the ancestors on these so-called oracle bones to confirm that the cracks had been understood. Thus, Shang writing began as a dramatic ritual performance in which the living responded to their ancestors' oracular signs.

In Shang theocracy, the ruler was also head of a unified clergy; and because the Shang theocratic ruler simultaneously embodied religious and political power, no independent priesthood emerged to challenge the power of the royal family as happened in Egypt and Mesopotamia. Diviners and scribes were subordinated to the ruler and the royal pantheon of ancestors he was thought to represent: unlike in the regimes of Mesopotamia and Egypt, diviners were never entrusted with independent action. Ancestor worship sanctified Shang control and legitimized the lineage of rulers, ensuring that all political and religious power was held by the ruling family.

Primary Source

THE ORACLE BONE

About 3,000 years old (c. 1200 BCE), the oracle bone below dates from the Shang dynasty reign of King Wu Ding, the husband of Lady Fu Hao. Oracle bones enabled diviners to access the other world and provided the ruler with important information about the future. Because Shang kings wished to plan ahead, they often relied on divination to predict the weather and make current political or military decisions or justify future ones.

A partial translation of the left-hand side of this oracle bone reads

[Preface:] Crack making on *gui-si* day, Que divined:

[Charge:] In the next ten days there will be no disaster.

[Prognostication:] The king, reading the cracks, said, "There will be no harm; there will perhaps be the coming of alarming news."

[Verification:] When it came to the fifth day, *ding-you*, there really was the coming of alarming news from the west. Zhi Guo, reporting, said, "The Du Fang [a border people] are besieging in our eastern borders and have harmed two settlements." The Gong-fang also raided the fields of our western borders.

→ *Why did Shang kings rely on oracle bones? With whom were the diviners communicating through the medium of oracle bones?*

SOURCE: This translation follows, with slight modifications by Bryan W. Van Norden, David N. Keightley, *Sources of Shang History* (Berkeley: University of California Press, 1978), p. 44.

Because the Shang gods were ancestral deities, all the Shang rulers were deified when they died and ranked in descending chronological order. Thus, the primary Shang deity was Di, the High God (Shangdi), who was the founding ancestor of the Shang royal family. The Shang ruler who became a god was closer to the world of humans than the supreme Egyptian and Mesopotamian gods, and he served to unite the world of the living with the world of the dead. Much as the Egyptian pharaohs were thought to be born of human mothers and godlike fathers, who had ascended into heaven after their deaths, so the Shang kings moved into a parallel other world when they died.

THE DEVELOPMENT OF WRITING IN CHINA

Although Shang scholars did not invent writing in East Asia, they certainly perfected it. Oracle bones, which were so central to political and religious authority, are our primary evidence of early writing in China. Archaeologists have found oracle bones with inscriptions of Chinese script dating from the Shang dynasty, around 1300 to 1200 BCE. Divinations were inscribed on an imperishable material, bones. Other early written records may have been committed to materials that did not survive through the centuries. Thus accidents of preservation may explain the major differences between the ancient texts in China (primarily divinations) and in the Southwest Asian societies that impressed cuneiform on clay tablets (primarily economic transactions, literary and religious documents, and historical records).

The extant inscriptions on oracle bones and bronzes leave no doubt that the Shang surpassed the other states and peoples in northwestern China in their ability and determination to leave records; their governmental institutions and religious rituals were more complex and sophisticated than those of the peoples living nearby. But in comparison with Mesopotamia and Egypt, here the transformation of record keeping (for example, questions and answers to ancestors, lineages of rulers, or economic transactions) to literature (for example, mythological tales about the founding of states) was slower.

As noted above, Shang kings used writing to reinforce their position at the top of the hierarchy of royal families. Priests used writings on the oracle bones to address the other world and gain information about the future. Because the North China climate entered a warmer and wetter phase in the twelfth and eleventh centuries BCE, their divinations were often aimed at predicting rainfall for the sustenance of crops—particularly the Shang staple of millet, often mentioned on the oracle bones. The priests presented the living Shang ruler as the religious pivot between Di, the High God (who controlled the ever-important rain cycles), the ancestors, and their royal descendants.

In addition, like the Babylonian dynasts, later Shang rulers organized a wide range of ceremonial and bureaucratic routines that depended on detailed written records to integrate their urban capital with tributary states and peoples. In these records, the court kept track of foods, wines, bronze vessels, and livestock, thereby demonstrating that a centralized "royal household" had emerged. During this period, the original archaic script evolved into the preclassical script used on many of the bronze vases discussed above, which in turn was the precursor to the formal character-based system that has endured among elites to the present day and that sets apart the later Chinese, Japanese, Korean, and Vietnamese societies in East Asia from the cultures in Mesopotamia and the Mediterranean that rely on syllable- and alphabet-based writing.

THE SOUTH PACIFIC (2500 BCE–400 CE)

> → *How did Austronesian migrations affect the South Pacific?*

As Eurasian populations grew, and migration and trade brought cultures together, some of the peoples of East Asia left the mainland and took to the waters in search of opportunities or refuge. By comparing the vocabularies and grammatical similarities of languages spoken today by the tribal peoples in Taiwan, the Philippines, and Indonesia, we can trace the ancient Austronesian-speaking peoples back to their origins in coastal South China in the fourth millennium BCE. Apparently that first migration, which reached the islands of Polynesia, was followed by another from Taiwan around 2500 BCE, which then extended into the South Pacific. By 2000 BCE these peoples had replaced the earlier inhabitants of the East Asian coastal islands, the hunter-gatherers known as the Negritos. The latter had migrated south from the Asian landmass around 28,000 BCE, during an ice age when the coastal Pacific islands were still connected to the Asian mainland.

Using their remarkable double-outrigger canoes, which were 60 to 100 feet long and bore huge triangular sails, the early Austronesians successfully crossed the Taiwan Straits and colonized the key islands in the Pacific. Their vessels represented a major advance beyond the earlier simple dugout canoes used in inland waterways. In good weather, double-outrigger canoes could cover more than 120 miles in a day. The invention of a stabilization device for deep-sea sailing sometime after 2500 BCE triggered further Austronesian expansion into the Pacific. By 400 CE, these nomads of the sea had reached most of the South Pacific except for Australia and New Zealand.

Their seafaring skills enabled the Austronesians, like the Phoenicians in the eastern Mediterranean during the middle of the first millennium BCE, to monopolize trade wherever they went. Among their specialized craftworkers were potters, who produced a distinctive kind of pottery called Lapita ware on offshore islets or in coastal villages. We know from archaeological finds that these canoe-building people also served as inter-island traders in New Guinea after 1600 BCE. By four hundred years later, according to the evidence of Lapita potsherds and remains of animals typically domesticated by the Austronesians—pigs, dogs, and chickens—they had also made their way to Fiji, Samoa, and Tonga.

Pottery, stone tools, and domesticated crops and pigs characterized Austronesian settlements throughout the coastal islands and in the South Pacific. These unique cultural markers reached the Philippines from Taiwan. By 2500 BCE, according to archaeologists, the same cultural features had spread to the islands of Java, Sumatra, Celebes, Borneo, and Timor. Austronesians arrived in Java and Sumatra in 2000 BCE; by 1600 BCE they were in Australia and New Guinea, although they failed to penetrate the interior, where descendants of the indigenous peoples still survive. The Austronesians then ventured further eastward into the South Pacific, apparently arriving in Samoa and Fiji in 1200 BCE and on mainland Southeast Asia in 1000 BCE. (See Map 3-5.)

Because the lands along the equator in the South Pacific have a tropical or subtropical climate and, in many places,

MAP 3-5 AUSTRONESIAN MIGRATIONS

How did Austronesian speakers migrate to these various locations? How have historians traced this migration across time and space? Why, unlike other migratory people during the second millennium, did Austronesian settlers in Polynesia become a world apart?

rich soils left by the ash from volcanoes, Austronesians successfully cultivated dry land crops (yams, and sweet potatoes), irrigated crops (yams, which grew more prolifically in paddy fields or on land where water was supplied by rainfall or by supplemental irrigation), and tree crops (breadfruit, bananas, and coconuts). In addition, the areas that were colonized off the Asian landmass, such as the islands of Indonesia, provided the inhabitants and newcomers with labyrinthine coastlines rich in maritime resources, including coral reefs and mangrove swamps full of wildlife. Island hopping certainly led the adventurers to encounter new food sources, but the shallow waters and reefs teemed with sufficient fish and shellfish for their needs.

In the South Pacific, the Polynesian descendants of the early Austronesians shared a common culture, language, technology, and stores of domesticated plants and animals. These later Polynesian seafarers came from many disparate island communities (hence the name *Polynesian*, or "belonging to many islands"), and after they settled down their numbers

grew. Their crop surpluses allowed more densely populated communities to support craft specialists and soldiers. The size of the island and its resources determined how much specialization the islanders required. Most settlements created ceremonial buildings to promote local solidarity and forts to provide defense. On larger islands, communities often cooperated and organized workforces to enclose ponds for fish production and to build and maintain large irrigation works for agriculture. Politically, Polynesian communities ranged from tribal or village units to multi-island alliances that on occasion invaded other areas.

The Austronesians reached the strategically located Marquesas Islands in the central Pacific around 200 CE; over the next few centuries, some moved on to Easter Island to the south and Hawaii to the north. The immense thirty-ton stone structures on Easter Island, for example, represent the monumental Polynesian architecture produced after their arrival. In separate migrations they traversed the Indian Ocean, heading westward, and arrived at the island of Madagascar by

Austronesian Canoe. Early Austronesians crossed the Taiwan Straits and colonized key islands in the Pacific using double-outrigger canoes from sixty to one hundred feet long equipped with triangular sails. In good weather, such canoes could cover more than 120 miles in a day.

the sixth century CE; along the way, they transmitted crops such as the banana to East Africa.

The expansion of East Asian peoples throughout the South Pacific and their trade back and forth did not, however, integrate the archipelagos of islands closely into the mainland culture. Expansion south and east could not overcome the underlying tendency of these societies, physically dispersed across a huge ocean, toward fragmentation and isolation.

Easter Island. By the fifth century BCE the Austronesians had reached Easter Island to the south of the Marquesas. The thirty-ton stone structures on Easter Island represent the monumental Polynesian architecture produced after the arrival of the Austronesians.

THE AEGEAN IN THE SECOND MILLENNIUM BCE

> → *How did long-distance trade influence the Aegean world?*

In the region around the Aegean Sea, the islands and the mainland of what is now Greece, no single power emerged before the second millennium BCE. Settled agrarian communities developed into local polities linked by trade and culture but not by an integrated central government. Fragmentation was the norm, perhaps as a consequence of the landscape itself, which lacked a single riverine axis or common plain. In this sense, the island world of the eastern Mediterranean initially resembled that of the South Pacific.

One unintended benefit of the lack of centralization was that there was no single regime to collapse when the droughts ushered in the new millennium. Thus, in the second millennium BCE, peoples of the eastern Mediterranean did not struggle to recover lost grandeur. Rather, they enjoyed a remarkable though gradual development, making advances that drew on the many influences that they absorbed from Southwest Asia, Egypt, and Europe both by land and by sea. It was a time when the people of such islands as Crete and Thera engaged in extensive trade with the Greek mainland and with Egypt and the Levant. It was also a time of the migration and movement, sometimes peaceful but sometimes violent, of peoples from the region of the Danube and central Europe into the Mediterranean. Groups of these peoples moved into settlements in mainland Greece in the centuries after 1900 BCE; modern archaeologists have named them "Mycenaeans," after the famous palace at Mycenae that dates to this era. Once settled in their new environment, the Mycenaeans quickly turned to the sea to look for resources and interaction with their neighbors.

SEABORNE TRADE AND COMMUNICATION

At the outset, the dominant influence on the Aegean world came from the east by sea. As the institutions and ideas that had developed earlier in Southwest Asia moved westward, they found a ready reception along the coasts and on the islands of the Mediterranean. Like the ships and the trade products that preceded them, these innovations followed the sea currents in the eastern Mediterranean, moving counterclockwise up the eastern seaboard of the Levant, then to the island of Cyprus and along the southern coast of Anatolia, and finally westward to the islands of the Aegean Sea and to Crete. Trade was the main bearer of eastern influences—and the sea-lanes were busy, with vessels carrying cargoes from island to island and up and down the commercial centers along the coast. (See Map 3-6.)

The islands in the Mediterranean were important meeting points that brought together the mainland peoples of western

MAP 3-6 THE AEGEAN SEA WORLDS

What does the distribution of the Aegean Islands tell us about how trade most likely developed? Given their geographic locations, why do you think that the Mycenaeans eventually conquered the Minoans? If an Egyptian trade item reached Mycenae, what do you think was the most likely route it took?

Seaborne Trade. The size of the seaborne trade is revealed most spectacularly in the shipwrecks recovered by underwater archaeologists. One of these ships, sunk off the southern coast of Anatolia around 1325 BCE, was transporting ten tons of copper in 354 oxhide-shaped ingots, as well as more than a hundred amphorae (large two-handled jars) containing all kinds of high-value commodities.

Asia and Europe with the islanders, thereby serving as places from which eastern influences spread into Europe. By 1500 BCE, the islands were booming. Trade centered heavily on the precious metals of tin and copper, both essential for making bronze, the primary metal used in making tools and weapons. Islands located in the midst of these active sea-lanes flourished. Because Cyprus, the largest island in the eastern Mediterranean (followed closely by Crete), straddled the main sea-lane, it was a focal point of trade. It also possessed large and easily workable reserves of copper ore, which suddenly began to be intensely exploited around 2300 BCE. By 2000 BCE, major harbors on the southern and eastern sides of the island were shipping and transshipping goods, along with copper ingots, as far west as Crete, east to the Euphrates River (Mari), and south to Egypt. So identified was this island with the metal that the English word *copper* is in fact derived from "Cyprus."

Crete, too, had copper and was an active trading node in the Mediterranean, connected to networks reaching as far east as Mesopotamia. Around 2000 BCE, a large number of independent palace centers began to emerge on Crete, at Knossos and elsewhere. Modern scholars have named the people who built these elaborate centers the Minoans, after the legendary King Minos, said to have ruled Crete at this time. The Minoans sailed back and forth across the Mediterranean, and by 1600 they were planting colonies around the

Palace at Knossos. An artist's reconstruction of the Minoan palace at Knossos on Crete. This complex, the largest such center on the island, covered more than six acres and contained more than thirteen hundred rooms. Its main feature was a large open-air central courtyard, around which were arranged the storage, archive, ritual, and ceremonial rooms. Rather than the complex cities that would emerge later, the urbanized centers on Crete were represented by these large complexes, similar to palace complexes in contemporary Levantine sites.

LINEAR A AND B—WRITING IN THE EARLY MEDITERRANEAN WORLDS

On the island of Crete and on the mainland areas of Greece, documents of the palace-centered societies were written on clay tablets in two scripts that, unlike the Cretan pictographs of c. 2000 BCE, were linear. These were first discovered on Crete in 1900 by the British archaeologist Arthur Evans. Linear A script, apparently written in Minoan, has not yet been deciphered. Linear B was first deciphered by Michael Ventris, a brilliant young British architect and freelance scholar, in the early 1950s. In the process he discovered that contrary to the assumptions of almost all classical scholars, these tablets were inscribed by speakers of Mycenaean, an early form of Greek. Massive numbers of these records, kept on clay tablets by palace scribes, have survived. Carefully noting every detail of the goods and services managed by the palace bureaucracy, they contain lists short and long of persons or things—about as interesting as modern grocery or laundry lists. The following tablet from the Pylos on the Greek mainland notes how much seed grain the bureaucrats were distributing to rural landholders who were dependent on the ruler.

The plot of Qelequhontas: this much seed: 276 l. of wheat

R. slave of the god, holds a lease: so much seed: 12 l. of wheat

W. the priest holds a lease: so much seed: 12 l. of wheat

Thuriatis, female slave of the god, dependant of P. the old man: so much seed: 108 l. of wheat

The plot of Admaos, so much seed: 216 l. of wheat. . . .

T. slave of the god, holds a lease: so much seed: 32 l. of wheat

The plot of A . . .eus, so much seed: 144 l. of wheat. . . .

The plot of T. slave of the god, holds a lease: 18 l. of wheat

The plot of R., so much seed: 138 l. of wheat. . . .

The plot of Aktaios, so much seed: 384 l. of wheat. . . .

→ *What does this document suggest is the function of writing in these societies? What does this kind of information tell us about these societies? What doesn't it tell us?*

SOURCE: M. Ventris and J. Chadwick, *Documents in Mycenaean Greek*, 2nd ed. (Cambridge: Cambridge University Press, 1973), doc. 116.

An example of the earlier Linear A writing, used to write the non-Greek language of the Minoans. This script was used for record keeping, but it was used only on Crete and is therefore closely connected solely with the early Minoan palatial centers on the island. This example was found at the small palace site at Hagia Triada.

This is a typical Linear B document inscribed on clay with linear signs representing syllables and signs. The clay tablet was dried and stored in a palace archive. This particular tablet was found in the excavations of the Mycenaean palace at Pylos on the mainland of Greece.

islands of the Aegean that became trading and mining centers. The Minoans' wealth soon became a magnet for the Mycenaeans, their mainland competitors, who took over Crete around 1400 BCE.

MINOAN CULTURE

Although they were connected to the people of Southwest Asia, these far-flung islands and coastal communities had their own distinctive cultural elements. To be sure, the monumental architecture so characteristic of Southwest Asia found small-scale echoes in the Aegean world, notably in the Minoan palace complexes built between 1900 and 1600 BCE; the largest and most impressive of these palaces was at Knossos. But religion was a prime example of cultural differences.

Worship on the islands focused on a female deity, the "Lady," but the communities have left no traces of the large temple complexes that were common in Mesopotamia, Anatolia, and Egypt. Nor, apparently, was there any priestly class of the type so central to running the temple complexes of Southwest Asian societies. Scholars disagree about whether these societies had full-time scribes. Moreover, significant regional diversity existed even within this small Aegean world. The most intense and complex developments were found on islands. On Thera, for example, archaeologists have uncovered a splendid trading city in which large private houses contained bathrooms with toilets and running water and were decorated with exotic wall paintings. One such painting depicted a flotilla of pleasure, trading, and naval vessels. On the

island of Crete, the palace-centered communities were civil societies of a high order of refinement, confident in their wealth and power. None of the large palaces was fortified or even built in a locale with natural defenses. They were light, airy, and open to their surrounding landscapes.

MYCENAEAN CULTURE

Migrating to Greece from central Europe, the Mycenaeans brought with them their Indo-European language along with their horse chariots and their metalworking skills. Their move to Greece was gradual, lasting from about 1850 to 1600 BCE, but they came to dominate the indigenous population. Known for their exceptional height, they maintained their dominance with their powerful weapon, the chariot, until 1200 BCE, and horse chariots remained important in their mythology and cultural tradition. The battle chariots and festivities of chariot racing described in the epic poetry of Homer, which date from a time after the collapse of Mycenaean societies, contain memories of the importance of chariots that echo similar stories in Vedic legends, told among the speakers of another Indo-European language who had settled in South Asia.

The population centers on the Mycenaean Greek mainland were much more oriented toward war and conflict than were the Minoan centers. In this respect, they resembled settlements of the Southwest Asian mainland kingdoms. The Mycenaeans possessed a less refined material culture than that of the Minoans: it emphasized displays of weaponry, por-

Aegean Fresco. This is one of the more striking wall paintings, or frescoes, discovered by archaeologists in the 1970s and 1980s at Akrotiri on the island of Thera (Santorini) in the Aegean Sea. Its brilliant colors, especially the blue of the sea, evoke the lively essence of Minoan life on the island. Note the houses of the wealthy along the port and the flotilla of ships that reflects the seaborne commerce that was beginning to flourish in the Mediterranean in this period.

Mycenaean Sword. The hilt and engraved gold pommel of a sword from the regal burials at the site of Mycenae. The presence of this weaponry, both depicted in the art of the period and preserved in artifacts buried with the dead, was typical of a violent society with a warrior elite. The riveted hilt and the bronze sword blade are of a kind found widely distributed in the Mediterranean, following the patterns of Mycenaean trade routes.

traits of armed soldiers, and illustrations of violent conflicts. The main palace centers at Tiryns and Mycenae were the hulking fortresses of warlords, who surrounded themselves with huge rough-hewn stone walls and lived on the top of large rock outcroppings. The Mycenaeans amassed an amazing amount of wealth and carried some of it with them to their graves. Their tombs contain many gold vessels and decorations; most ostentatious were the gold masks. The many amber beads found by archaeologists indicate that the warriors had contacts with inhabitants of the coniferous forest regions in northern Europe.

Southwest Asian economic and political structures shaped the coastal sites where the Mycenaeans settled, such as Tiryns and Pylos. Massive stone fortresses and fortified palaces dominated these urban hubs. A preeminent ruler (*wanax*) stood atop a complex bureaucratic hierarchy run by various officials; he was aided by a large number of subordinates, some of whom were slaves. At the heart of the palace

society were the scribes, who kept records of the goods and services that the palace organizations allotted to local communities of farmers, shepherds, and metalworkers, among others.

Mycenaean expansion eventually reached and overwhelmed the Minoans; as noted above, they ultimately occupied Crete. The Mycenaeans also sought to create colonies and trading settlements, reaching as far as Sicily and southern Italy. In this fashion, "Greek" trade and language created a veneer of unity linking the dispersed worlds of the Aegean Sea.

At the close of the second millennium BCE, the eastern Mediterranean faced large-scale internal and external convulsions that brought an end to the flourishing heyday of these exotic micro-societies. Most notably, a series of sometimes violent migrations of peoples from central Europe moved through the whole of southeastern Europe, Anatolia, and the eastern Mediterranean between 1250 and 1150 BCE (see Chapter 4). The invasions, as destructive as they were, did not extinguish but rather reinforced the creative potential of this frontier area. Following the upheaval at the close of the millennium, yet another new kind of social order emerged, destined to have an even greater brilliance and influence. Because theirs was a closed maritime world—in comparison with the wide-open Pacific—the Aegean peoples quickly reasserted a dominance in the eastern Mediterranean that Austronesians could not match in Southeast Asia or Polynesia.

EUROPE—THE NORTHERN FRONTIER

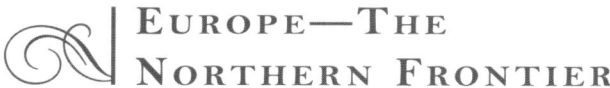

→ *Why did politics remain small-scale in Europe?*

The transition to settled agriculture and the raising of domesticated animals proved to be an altogether slower and more arduous process in the western flank of Afro-Eurasia than in the rest of the landmass. It took two millennia, from 5000 to 3000 BCE, before settled agriculture became the dominant economic form in Europe. In large areas of the continent, hunters and gatherers were reluctant to give up their traditional ways. Even this frontier, however, was visited by peoples driving horse chariots during the second millennium BCE.

The northern area of the far western stretches of Europe, dominated by cold and forbidding evergreen forests, remained thinly populated and was slow to implement any of the new ways. The new agricultural communities appeared first as frontier settlements in which pioneers struggled to break new land. Surrounded by hunting and foraging communities, these innovators lived hard lives in harsh environments, overcoming their isolation only by creating regional alliances. They were unstable and too weak to initiate or sustain long-distance trade. These were not fertile grounds for creating powerful kingdoms.

The early European cultivators adopted the techniques for controlling plants and animals pioneered in Southwest Asia; but rather than establishing large, hierarchically organized and centralized societies they used them to create self-sufficient communities. They did not incorporate the other cultural and political features that characterized the societies of Egypt, Mesopotamia, and the eastern Mediterranean. Innovations such as the working of metal (initially, copper), the manufacture of pottery, and the use of the plow occurred sporadically and had little impact on local conditions. Throughout this period, Europe was hardly a developed cultural center. Instead, it was a wild frontier in which new agriculturalists struggled, often unsuccessfully, to open up new lands, in the process undoubtedly engaging in violent confrontations with each other and with the indigenous inhabitants.

Two significant changes were decisive in the northern frontier zone: the domestication of the horse and the emergence of wheeled chariots and wagons. Both became instruments of war and enabled humans to adapt to the expanses of steppe lands across the southern face of inner and central Europe, a vast open zone where pasturing animals in large herds proved profitable. The success of this horse culture created several frontiers, including those bearing the kinds of agriculturally self-sustaining communities discussed above.

These new agriculturalists seeking to cultivate the land faced constant challenges not just within Europe but also eastward, as they looked toward the rolling grasslands that stretched across central Eurasia. Their attempts to enter this zone were usually countered successfully by men on horseback, who could rapidly marshal an overpowering mobile force. The inhabitants of the great flat steppelands north of the Black Sea gradually shifted from a primitive agriculture to an economy based on the mobile herding of animals. In this zone, the domestication of the horse encouraged the development of a highly mobile culture in which whole communities moved on horseback or by the use of large wheeled wagons. These pastoral nomads in the east were constantly attracted to the richer agricultural lands in central Europe, producing a source of constant hostility between the two worlds. Although in most cases agricultural communities could defend themselves when these nomadic raiders looked to Europe, its agricultural heart continued to draw their attacks. The constant struggles between settlers, hunter-gatherers, and nomadic horse riders created cultures with a strong warrior ethos at their core. The fullest development of this mounted horse culture is found in the centuries after 1000 BCE, when the Scythian peoples in the steppelands engaged in rituals like the drinking of blood, in which male warriors forged bonds of blood brotherhood that were central to their

aggressive and violent behavior. This rough-and-tumble frontier gave its people an appetite to borrow more effective means of waging war. Europeans desired the nomadic people's weaponry, and over time, their interactions with the horsemen included trade as well as violence. As a result of these trading contacts with nomadic steppe peoples to the east, Europeans adopted horses and finer metalworking technologies from the Caucasus. Of course, such trade only made their battles even more lethal. And while the connections between this northern frontier zone and other parts of the Afro-Eurasian world began to multiply, it was still too dispersed and unruly a region to give rise to integrated kingdoms. At a time when the rest of Afro-Eurasia was developing, Europe was still a land of warmaking small chieftainships. Politics there remained a small-scale, rivalrous affair.

EARLY STATES IN THE AMERICAS

> → *How did the ecology of the Central Andes influence early state systems?*

Across the Americas, river valleys and coasts filled in with villages and towns drawing their sustenance from the rich resources in their hinterlands. But without beasts of burden or domesticated animals able to carry loads or plow fields, local communities could produce only limited surpluses. Trade from one community to the next was therefore restricted to luxuries and symbolic trade goods, such as shells, feathers, hides, and precious metals and gems.

In the Central Andes, however, archaeologists have found evidence of early state systems that transcended local communities to create "confederations," or alliances of towns. These were not as well integrated as many of the territorial states of Southwest Asia, the Indus Valley, and China; they more closely resembled settlements in Europe and the eastern Mediterranean, where towns engaged in a form of trade in basic goods, and in some cases joined together to defend themselves against outside aggressors.

Facilitating the development of Central Andean confederations was the region's ecological mix. Along the arid coast of what is now Peru, fishermen learned to exploit the currents that teemed with large and small fish; they brought in good hauls of a basic staple that could be dried to make it less perishable and more easily transported. The rivers that flowed down the Andean mountains cut through the desert, often creating basins suitable for agriculture. And as the mountains rose from the Pacific, rainfall and higher altitudes favored the creation of extensive pasturelands, known as *puna*, used by wild ruminants such as llamas and alpacas—difficult to use as beasts of burden but valuable for the wool that was needed for textile production. Such ecological diversity within a relatively limited area promoted greater trade between subregions and towns, and the interchange of manioc, chili peppers, dried fish, and wool created the commercial networks that could support political ones.

Communities on the coast, in the riverbeds, or in the mountain valleys were not large but they were numerous. They took shape around central plazas, most of which had large platforms with special burial chambers built for elders and persons of importance, surrounded by clusters of dwellings. Much of what we know about political and economic transactions between communities—and the confirmation of longer-distance trade and statecraft—comes from the offerings and ornaments left in these burial chambers. Painted gourds, pottery, and fine textiles illustrate the degree to which complex cultures were increasingly in contact with each other, and often bound in alliances. Marriage, for instance, between noble families of scattered communities, was a common means of strengthening a pact or confederation.

One early site known as Aspero reveals how a local community had evolved into a form of chiefship, with a political elite and diplomatic and trading ties with neighbors. The large temple at the center was heavily ornamented, temples straddled the top of the raised platform, and there is plenty of evidence that smaller communities around Aspero sent crops (like fruits) and fish (especially anchovies) as part of an intercommunity system of mutual dependency. But not all politics among the valley peoples of Peru consisted of trade and diplomacy. In the Casma Valley, some 300 feet from the Pacific coast, excavation of a clay and stone architectural complex at Cerro Sechín has revealed a much larger sprawl of dwellings and plazas, dating back to 1700 BCE. The community's central structure was surrounded by a wall composed of hundreds of massive stone tablets, carved with ornate etchings of warriors, battles, prisoners, executions, and many human body parts. Warrior clothing was simple and rustic, and the main weapon appears to have been nothing more than a club. Clearly, the first expressions of statecraft in the Americas were accompanied by warfare.

 CONCLUSION

The second millennium BCE was an unprecedented era of migrations, warfare, and the building of territorial kingdoms in Afro-Eurasia. Emerging riverine societies had marked the fourth and third millennia BCE in Mesopotamia, Egypt, and the Indus Valley, but in the second millennium BCE humans confronted the dire ecological challenges that droughts and deserts posed for their agricultural and pastoral economies.

The drought would trigger large-scale migrations across Afro-Eurasia. In their search for arable land and water sources, transhumant herders first entered into the riverine societies and thereby changed the social and political fabric of these communities. Soon following, and for similar reasons, were horse-riding nomads from steppe communities in inner Eurasia; they conquered and settled in the agrarian states, bringing with them a number of key innovations. Chief among them were the horse chariots, which became an irresistible military catalyst sparking the evolution from smaller states and polities to larger-scale kingdoms that linked crowded, endangered cities to their vast hinterlands. These nomads and transhumant herders did not simply impose their ways on those they conquered, but instead adopted many of the beliefs and customs of the settled people. Land and sea nomads also created zones of interaction in which long-distance trade by sea and land linked agrarian societies.

The Nile Delta, the basin of the Tigris and Euphrates rivers, the Indus Valley, and the Yellow River basin were worlds apart before 2000 BCE. Through trade and conquest, nomadic groups provided means of bringing these early societies into closer contact, sometimes for the first time. The result was a political transformation and the makings of the first territorial states. The alliance of farmers and warriors united agrarian wealth and production with political power to create and defend boundaries around communities living under common laws and customs. The new arrangements overshadowed the historic role of nomads as predators and enabled them to become military elites at the top of social hierarchies that ruled territorial states.

This unique partnership created armies of foot soldiers and elite charioteers who protected and spurred the expansion of farmers' villages. Through their taxes and drafted labor, the villagers repaid their rulers for local security and state-run diplomacy. Their symbiotic relationship with warrior elites fostered trade and commerce. Their cooperation, not always voluntary, with the ruling elite made possible the first great territorial states and kingdoms of Afro-Eurasia.

The rhythms of state formation differed where regimes were not as closely packed together. In East Asia, one state was coming into its own, but the absence of strong rivals allowed the Shang to accumulate strength more gradually. Where landscapes had much sharper divisions, whether in the island archipelagos of the South China Sea, in Europe, or elsewhere, the political arrangements were much more decentered, as people lived in what resembled a tapestry of micro-states. This was true above all in the Americas, where the lack of wheeled vehicles and horses made long-distance communication and movement much more challenging—and therefore inhibited the territorial ambitions of rulers. Here, too, micro-states were the norm during the second millennium. But we must recall that fragmentation is not the same as isolation. Even peoples on the fringes and the subjects of micro-states were not absolutely secluded from the increasing flows of technologies, languages, goods, and migrants.

STUDY QUESTIONS

Ⓢ WWNORTON.COM/STUDYSPACE

1. Explain the differences between nomadic pastoral and transhumant migrations. How did each shape Afro-Eurasian history during the second millennium BCE?

2. Analyze the impact of the domestication of horses on Afro-Eurasia during the second millennium BCE. How did this development affect both nomadic and settled societies?

3. Define the term *territorial state*. Where in Afro-Eurasia did this new form of political organization emerge and thrive?

4. Compare and contrast political developments in Mesopotamia and Egypt during the second millennium BCE. To what extent did outside groups influence each region?

5. Identify the five great territorial states of western Asia and North Africa during the second half of the second millennium BCE and describe their relationships with each other. How did they pioneer international diplomacy?

6. Compare and contrast Austronesian and Indo-European migrations. What impact did each people have on the regions it settled?

7. Describe the Shang state in East Asia. How was it similar to and different from the territorial states of western Afro-Eurasia?

8. Compare and contrast the islands of the South Pacific to those in the eastern Mediterranean during the second millennium BCE. Why were societies in the South Pacific more fragmented and isolated than those in the eastern Mediterranean?

9. Explain why state structures were smaller and less integrated in Europe and the Central Andes than the territorial states that arose elsewhere during the second millennium BCE. How similar and different were state structures in both regions?

FURTHER READINGS

Allan, Sarah, *The Shape of the Turtle: Myth, Art and Cosmos in Early China* (1991). Explains the roles of divination and sacrifice in artistic representations of the Shang cosmology.

Allen, James P., *Middle Egyptian: An Introduction to the Language and Culture of Hieroglyphs* (2000). An introduction to the system of writing and its use in Ancient Egypt.

Arnold, Dieter, *Building in Ancient Egypt: Pharaonic Stone Masonry* (1996). Details the complex construction of monumental stone architecture in ancient Egypt.

Chronology

	MAJOR TRENDS	2000 BCE	1900 BCE	1800 BCE	1700 BCE	1600 BCE	1500 BCE	1400
NORTHERN AFRICA	*Global warming and drying cycle beginning 2000 BCE*	▪*Middle Kingdom in Egypt, 2010–1640 BCE* ▪ *Development of chariot technology, 2000 BCE*				▪ *Hyksos rule in Egypt, 1640–1550 BCE* *New Kingdom in Egypt, 1550–1070 BCE*▪			
SOUTHWEST ASIA		▪*Kassite, Median, and Persian migration begins, 2000 BCE*		▪ *Old Hittite Kingdom in Anatolia, 1800–1600 BCE* ▪*Hammurapi's Babylonia, 1792–1750 BCE*		*Kassite rule, 1475–1125 BCE* ▪ *New Hittite Kingdom in Anatolia, 1400–1200 BCE* ▪		
SOUTH ASIA							*Vedic migration into Indus River valley begins, 1500 BCE* ▪	
EAST ASIA						*Shang State emerges, 1600 BCE* ▪		
THE AEGEAN		▪*Minoan culture, 2000–1600 BCE* ▪*Mycenaean culture, 1850–1200 BCE*						
SOUTH PACIFIC		▪*Austronesian migration to East Asian coastal islands begins, 2500 BCE*						
EUROPE					▪*Frontier zone with Southwest Asia and horse culture in Eastern Europe emerge*		▪ *Rise of small chiefta*	
CENTRAL ANDES					▪ *Emergence of small-scale political confederations, 1700 BCE*			

Baines, John, and Jaromir Málek, *Atlas of Ancient Egypt* (1980). Useful compilation of information on ancient Egyptian society, religion, history and geography.

Beal, Richard H., *The Organization of the Hittite Military* (1992). A detailed study based on textual sources of the world's first chariot-based army.

Bogucki, Peter, and Pam J. Crabtree (eds.), *Ancient Europe 8000 BC–AD 1000: Encyclopedia of the Barbarian World*, 2 vols. (2004). An indispensable handbook on the economic, social, artistic, and religious life in Europe during this period.

Bruhns, Karen Olsen, *Ancient South America* (1994). The best basic text on pre-Columbian South American cultures.

Castleden, Rodney, *The Mycenaeans* (2005). One of the best current surveys of all aspects of the Mycenaean Greeks.

Chadwick, John, *The Decipherment of Linear B,* 2nd ed. (1968). Not only a retelling of the story of the decipherment of the Linear B script but an introduction to the actual content and function of the tablets themselves.

Cline, E. H., *Sailing the Wine-Dark Sea: International Trade and the Late Bronze Age Aegean* (1994). An excellent account of the trade and contacts between the Aegean and other areas of the Mediterranean, Europe, and the Near East during the late Bronze Age.

Cunliffe, Barry, *Facing the Ocean: The Atlantic and Its Peoples, 8000 BC–AD 1500* (2001). An in-depth, highly useful treatment of western Europe during this period.

Cunliffe, Barry (ed.), *Prehistoric Europe: An Illustrated History* (1997). A state-of-the-art treatment of first farmers, agricultural developments, and material culture in prehistoric Europe.

Davis, W. V., and L. Schofield, *Egypt, the Aegean and the Levant: Interconnections in the Second Millennium BC* (1995). A discussion of the complex interactions in the eastern Mediterranean during the "international age."

Doumas, Christos, *Thera: Pompeii of the Ancient Aegean* (1983). A study of the tremendous volcanic eruption and explosion that destroyed the Minoan settlement on the island of Thera.

Drews, Robert, *Coming of the Greeks: Indo-European Conquests in the Aegean and the Near East* (1988). A good survey of the evidence for the "invasions" or "movements of peoples" that reconfigured the world of the eastern Mediterranean and Near East.

Finley, M. I., *The World of Odysseus,* 2nd rev. ed. (1977; reprint, 2002). The classic work that describes what might be recovered about the world of the social values and behaviors of men and women in the period of the so-called Dark Ages of early Greek history.

Frankfort, Henri, *Ancient Egyptian Religion: An Interpretation* (1948; reprint, 2000). A classic study of Egyptian religion and culture during the pharaonic period.

Keightley, David N., *The Ancestral Landscape: Time, Space, and Community in Late Shang China, ca. 1200–1045 B.C.* (2000). Provides insights into the nature of royal kinship that undergirded the Shang court and its regional domains.

1300 BCE	1200 BCE	1100 BCE	1000 BCE	900 BCE	100 BCE	1 CE	100 CE	200 CE	300 CE	400 CE	500 CE

▌*Vedic migration into Ganges River valley begins, 1000 BCE*

▌*Austronesian migration to Samoa and Fiji, 1200 BCE*

▌*Austronesian migration to Southeast Asia, 1000 BCE*

Austronesian migration to Madagascar, 500 CE ▌

▌*Austronesian migration to Polynesia, 200 CE*

Kemp, Barry J., *Ancient Egypt: Anatomy of a Civilization* (2006). A definitive presentation of the history, culture, and religion of ancient Egypt.

Klein, Jacob, "The Marriage of Martu: The Urbanization of 'Barbaric' Nomads," in *Mutual Influences of Peoples and Cultures in the Ancient Near East,* ed. Meir Malul (1996).

Kristiansen, Kristian, *Europe Before History* (1998). The finest recent survey of all the major developmental phases of European prehistory.

McIntosh, Jane, *Handbook to Life in Prehistoric Europe* (2006). Highlights the archaeological evidence that enables us to re-create the day-to-day life of different prehistoric communities in Europe.

Preziosi, Donald, and L. A. Hitchcock, *Aegean Art and Architecture* (1999). One of the best general guides to the figurative and decorative art produced both by the Minoans and Mycenaeans and by related early societies in the region of the Aegean.

Quirke, Stephen, *Ancient Egyptian Religion* (1992). A highly readable presentation of ancient Egyptian religion that summarizes the roles and attributions of the many Egyptian gods.

Ratnagar, Shereen, *Understanding Harappa: Civilization in the Greater Indus Valley* (2001). A cogent and meaningful summary from one of the leading archaeologists of Harappan society.

Robins, Gay, *The Art of Ancient Egypt* (1997). The most comprehensive survey to date of the art of pharaonic Egypt.

———, *Women in Ancient Egypt* (1993). An interesting survey of the place of women in Ancient Egyptian society.

Romer, John, *Ancient Lives: Daily Life in Egypt of the Pharaohs* (1990). A discussion of the economic and social lives of everyday ancient Egyptians.

Sandars, N. K., *The Sea Peoples: Warriors of the Ancient Mediterranean* (1985). A readable discussion of a very complex period of Levantine history.

Simpson, William Kelly (ed.), *The Literature of Ancient Egypt: An Anthology of Stories, Instructions, and Poetry* (1972). A compilation of the most important works of literature from Ancient Egypt.

Thorp, Robert L., *China in the Early Bronze Age: Shang Civilization* (2005). Reviews the archaeological discoveries near Anyang, site of two capitals of the Shang kings.

Warren, Peter, *The Aegean Civilizations: From Ancient Crete to Mycenae,* 2nd ed. (1989). An excellent textual and pictorial guide to all the basic aspects of the Minoan and Mycenaean societies.

Wilson, John A., *The Culture of Ancient Egypt* (1951). A classic study of the history and culture of pharaonic Egypt.

Yadin, Yigael, *The Art of Warfare in Biblical Lands in the Light of Archaeological Discovery* (1963). A well-illustrated presentation of the machinery of war in the second and first millennium BCE.

Chapter

4

FIRST EMPIRES AND COMMON CULTURES IN AFRO-EURASIA, 1200–350 BCE

Sennacherib—the ruler of the vast Assyrian Empire, which at the height of its power at the beginning of the seventh century BCE ruled over much of Southwest Asia—tells us in his annals that at the end of his successful campaign against Hezekiah, the king of Judah, he took "200,150 people great and small, male and female, horses, mules, asses, camels and sheep, without number, I brought away from them and counted them as spoil." Similarly, he forced other peoples whom he had conquered and who would not submit to his rule, especially the Arameans who lived in the Levant, to leave their lands and to migrate to Assyria. With such people, Sennacherib rebuilt and greatly expanded his capital city of Nineveh and developed immense irrigation works to open up new agricultural lands.

From early on, Assyrian kings' policy of moving large numbers of people over great distances was a foundation of their rule. The Assyrians pushed the establishment of power a step further than previous regimes: whereas their predecessors had annexed territory, they redistributed populations to create more homogeneity within their territory and to settle more productive regions of the dominion. Those they had uprooted were assimilated into the social fabric as the equals of Assyrian citizens. In small rural communities, these new inhabitants increased the agricultural potential of the empire and populated new cities. They were a source of manpower for the army, and many became elite troops. Their numbers included not only military men and laborers but also scribes and skilled craftworkers. Through these practices, the Assyrian rulers both punished those who were not subservient and integrated their enormous and diverse populations.

While nomadic pastoralists and transhumants moved between pasturelands, most agrarian people at the end of the second millennium BCE remained in the same place for all of their lives. Yet further climatic change and political conquests spurred the migration—in effect, mass resettlements —of people who might otherwise have never left their lands. From the Mediterranean region, some people traveled by sea to the Levant, Egypt, and Anatolia, spreading before them disruption and political upheaval. Similarly, transhumant herders from the Syrian Desert moved on land toward the riverine cities in Mesopotamia in search of water and pastures for their animals. And in China, as in the Assyrian Empire, conquerors from beyond the borders took aim at obstinate local elites and forced them to submit—or move. The new rulers relocated valued workers such as metalworkers skilled in making bronze so that their special knowledge could be applied to building a new imperial capital. Throughout Afro-Eurasia, large-scale population movements were becoming part of the regional integration of new imperial states.

FORCES OF UPHEAVAL AND THE RISE OF EARLY EMPIRES

> → *What were the agents of change that facilitated the rise of culturally integrated early empires?*

Beginning around 1200 BCE, another warming phase gripped the Afro-Eurasian landmass. As had happened a thousand years earlier, in some areas prolonged drought brought about social upheavals and human migration. In other regions, population growth and the exhaustion of marginal soil forced many people to leave their homes in search of food and fertile land. (See Map 4-1.) These renewed migratorial incursions overturned urban societies as fierce warriors attacked capitals and cities and destroyed the administrative centers of kings, priests, and dynasties, leaving the way open for new states. Some of these states became the world's first empires, precursors of the giant empires we will encounter in later chapters.

Invaders came from loosely organized peripheral societies rather than from neighboring states. Marauders from the Mediterranean and from the Syrian Desert attacked the territorial kingdoms of the Levant, Egypt, Anatolia, and Mesopotamia, upsetting the diplomatic relations among these states and disrupting the elaborate system of international trade that had linked this area. In East Asia, rugged nomadic people from the steppes of Inner Eurasia tangled with Shang

Focus Questions   FIRST EMPIRES AND COMMON CULTURES IN AFRO-EURASIA

→ *What were the agents of change that facilitated the rise of culturally integrated early empires?*

→ *What distinguished the Neo-Assyrian Empire from earlier territorial kingdoms?*

→ *In what ways was the Persian Empire similar to the Neo-Assyrian Empire, and in what ways was it different?*

→ *How did the growth of the first empires in western Afro-Eurasia affect societies in the Levant and the Aegean? What influence did they have on the broader region?*

→ *How did South Asia become more socially and culturally integrated despite the absence of an imperial state?*

→ *To what extent was the Zhou state similar to contemporary empires in western Afro-Eurasia in its structure and its impact on its neighbors?*

WWNORTON.COM/STUDYSPACE

authorities in the Yellow River valley and eventually overwhelmed the regime in the eleventh century BCE. In the Indus Valley, waves of nomadic invaders likewise pressed down from the northwest, lured by the wealth of the fertile lands to the south. Once there, they discarded their nomadic ways and became an agrarian folk. This was a process that took centuries, but by the time of Alexander the Great (see Chapter 6), the splendor of India had become legendary.

The resultant intermixing and intermingling of these nomadic and urban societies impelled many rulers to expand beyond the old territorial kingdoms; warrior kings deployed troops that conquered independent and culturally distinct kingdoms and subjugated their people. With these conquests, different regions became more integrated, connected by a common language (or by individuals fluent in multiple languages), joint political structures, and shared religious beliefs. Local worlds were beginning to converge. But convergence did not yield homogeneity, as local customs, languages, and gods persisted even as common administration, laws, calendars, and ritual practices were instituted. In a few places, the prophet emerged as an important new agent of social change but prophets like Jesus and Mohammed and the universalizing religions that followed them would not appear until the beginning of the next millennium, and would take nearly another millennium to be fully established across all of Afro-Eurasia.

Some regions, like South Asia, were united less by shared political systems than by shared cultures and beliefs about the gods and ritual practices. Other regions had no political integration but were instead connected through extensive trade; for example, coastal cities such as Byblos and Tyre had commercial and cultural tentacles that reached as far as, and sometimes farther than, the empires' military conquests. There remained a great deal of variation within and across worlds.

In a few places, the prophet emerged as an important new agent of social change.

The rise of empires in the first millennium BCE depended on the expanded use of pack camels and ships for trade, iron tools for cultivation, and iron weapons for conquest. Innovations involving iron production were thus a major catalyst for change. The first millennium empires were highly centralized and militarized states that successfully expanded their boundaries by using force and the threat of force to absorb the wealth of neighboring states. They were based on the interaction and integration of the conquerors with their conquered peoples.

The role of iron was crucial in these advances. Although far more abundant and widely distributed in nature than are the tin and copper used to make bronze, iron is a harder substance to mold and hammer into shape. To make iron implements, metalworkers learned to apply intense heat to soften the ore and to remove its impurities. A further breakthrough occurred when they discovered how to add carbon to the iron, thereby making an early form of steel. When the technology to smelt and harden iron advanced, iron tools and weapons rapidly replaced those made in bronze. The new ability to use iron—a cheap and highly durable metal accessible to all— was a technological breakthrough that quickly leaped across territorial and cultural borders.

Iron also contributed to a shift in agrarian techniques— one that produced an agrarian revolution analogous to the leap forward earlier stimulated by irrigation engineering. Innovators learned to tip their plowshares with edges of forged iron that could be shaped and resharpened with ease. With the aid of the iron-tipped plow, for instance, cultivators could clear the dense jungle of the Ganges plain and repeatedly till the topsoil to keep it clear of weeds and to enhance its quality. Increasingly, farmers did not have to rely on regular floods to restore layers of rich loess soil to their fields for planting; they could break the sod and turn it over to bring up fertile subsurface soils. The effects of this transformation are easy to miss, but together they drove the agrarian frontier far beyond the traditional floodplains of riverine settings. Agricultural developments thus provided the technological underpinning to support larger, more integrated societies linked by roads and canals.

The camel became the chief overland agent of change during this period. Employed as a beast of burden since around 1700 BCE, the animal was now used to open up new overland trade routes across the Syrian and the Arabian deserts. The domestication of the camel, which is able to carry heavy loads over long distances, contributed significantly to the growth of overland trade—especially across deserts. The fat stored in camels' humps helps them survive long journeys and the harsh conditions of deserts, and thick pads under their hoofs enable them to walk smoothly over sand. First to be domesticated, around 4000 BCE, was the one-humped and more streamlined-looking camel called the *dromedary,* or Arab camel, native to the Sahara Desert. Other peoples, probably in central Asia, independently domesticated the bigger, two-humped Bactrian camel sometime before 2500 BCE. A stockier and hardier animal, it was better able than the dromedary to survive the scorching heat of northern Iran and the frozen winters along the route from China that would become the Silk Road (so named because silk was one of the major products carried along this route).

The final developments driving change were innovations in military and administrative control. The expansion of the first empires was based on military might. For example, using a standing army equipped with the most advanced weapons and armor, the Assyrian king led annual campaigns to establish and reinforce his absolute control over the countryside.

NORTH SEA

BALTIC SEA

URAL MOUNTAINS

EUROPE

ARAL SEA

Dnieper R.

Danube R.

Dniester R.

Volga R.

CASPIAN SEA

CENT

BLACK SEA

ANATOLIA

MYCENEANS

AEGEAN SEA

Troy

Tiryns

CRETE

CYPRUS

MEDITERRANEAN SEA

HITTITES

MITANNI

Tigris R.

Nineveh

Ashur

ELAMITES

ZAGROS MTS

IRANIAN PLATEAU

ASIA

SYRIAN DESERT

Euphrates R.

Babylon

Tyre

LEVANT

Jericho

Jerusalem

SOUTHWEST

Persian Gulf

NORTH AFRICA

A

F

R

El Amarna

EGYPT

Thebes

ARABIAN PENINSULA

Sub-Saharan periphery: Increased population and gradual adoption of agriculture

SAHARA

Nile R.

RED SEA

NUBIA

Niger R.

SUB-SAHARAN AFRICA

Congo R.

Lake Victoria

Tropical woodlands: Yams and palm nuts cultivated

ATLANTIC OCEAN

	Urban cores
	Vedic settlement by 900 BCE
→	Nomadic incursions (sea peoples)
→	Nomadic incursions (pastoralists)
■	Destroyed site
●	City

MAP 4-1   AFRO-EURASIA, 1200 BCE—URBAN CORES AND NOMADIC INVADERS

Nomadic incursions shattered the social and political status quo in Afro-Eurasia at the end of the second millennium BCE. While destroying old polities, these migrations fostered a new social and political order in a variety of regions. What caused migrations across Afro-Eurasia toward the end of the second millennium BCE? Where did nomadic groups originate and to where did they migrate? Why do you think historians' knowledge of these nomadic incursions is limited and sketchy?

Dromedary Camels. Dromedary camels look neat and tidy. They are good draft animals for travel and domestic work in the deserts of Arabia, Afghanistan, and India.

Two-hump Camels. Two-hump camels are much bigger and messier than dromedary camels. They are more suited to the extreme dry and cold weather in Iran and Central Asia.

Deportations were another strategy regularly used to break the unity of resisters. They also served to provide slave labor to parts of the empire in need of manpower and to integrate the imperial enterprise. Throughout the 300 years of Assyrian hegemony, an infrastructure of roads, garrisons, and relay stations was constructed throughout the entire expanse of the territory, making it easier to communicate information and move troops. Moreover, the Assyrians required subject peoples to send tribute, which they used to build imperial cities and to enrich the royal coffers, as well as to bolster their dominance over those they had conquered. In the coming centuries, these practices would become common among empires, widely varying degrees of brutality used as a method of control.

This remarkable period of integration and interaction did not simply evolve from the kingdoms of the previous age. The prosperity and bounty of the first millennium BCE were the fruits of a spasm of disorder across Afro-Eurasia caused by migrations of nomadic and settled peoples, as well as by invasions by neighboring states. The orders of the previous millennium trembled and collapsed; their successors were replacements, not descendents. The key factor shaping human development was now war, not the environment. As these new hybrid societies formed, they produced fresh, written ideologies and doctrines, some sacred, some secular, that also contributed to integration in this era in Vedic parts of South Asia, in Zhou China, in Assyria, and in Persia. Under the protection of fierce warriors, cities and hinterlands were joined under a single ruler. Farming yields again increased, and populations grew. The expansion of territorial power via conquest contributed to the regional integration of larger and larger states, some of which took the form of the first empires—the bigger, the better.

THE NEO-ASSYRIAN EMPIRE

> → *What distinguished the Neo-Assyrian Empire from earlier territorial kingdoms?*

When stability returned to Southwest Asia and North Africa, around 950 BCE, the societies were entirely restructured, and the balance among many large and small powers soon gave way to a regional superpower. The Neo-Assyrian Empire directly dominated or more indirectly affected all the area's populations, even those living in the Mediterranean. (See Map 4-2.)

The third and second millennia BCE had seen expansionary territorial states, such as those of Babylonia and Egypt, but the scale and extent of the Neo-Assyrian state—"new" (neo-) in distinction to the "Old" and "Middle" Assyrian states, which had existed in the second millennium BCE—made it the Afro-Eurasian world's first empire. Neo-Assyrian rulers had ambitions beyond governing their own people. They also wanted to subordinate and exploit peoples who lived in distant lands, controlling their resources and trading cities and commanding the trade routes. By the time that full-scale expansion was under way, all institutions of the Neo-Assyrian state were focused on the goal of territorial expansion into an empire. They had succeeded by the middle of the seventh century BCE with the conquest of the entirety of Southwest Asia and parts of North Africa, including Egypt.

EXPANSION INTO AN EMPIRE

The Neo-Assyrian Empire lasted for three brutal centuries. It became legendary for its ruthless efficiency and particularly for its reliance on terror (through harsh punishments, such as the cutting off of ears, lips, and fingers; castration; and mass executions), large-scale deportations, and systematic intimidation to crush its adversaries.

The heartland of Assyria was a small area centered on the ancient cities of Ashur and Nineveh on the upper reaches of the Tigris River. Unlike the surrounding regions, during the disturbances of the eleventh century BCE Middle Assyria had managed to fend off the invading peoples, kept at bay by trained warriors loyal to the royal house. By the ninth century BCE, the turmoil had subsided, and soon the Assyrians renewed their westward expansion. By 824 BCE, the Assyrians again dominated the land and inhabitants all the way to the shores of the Mediterranean and thus controlled trade and tribute from these areas.

The Assyrians had several advantages. Their armies were made up of well-trained and ruthlessly disciplined professional troops led by officers who, in the empire's later years, rose high in the ranks because of their merit, not their birth. They perfected the combined deployment of infantry and cavalry (horse-mounted warriors equipped with iron weapons) together with horse-drawn chariots that were armored with iron plates and carried archers. They were also siege warriors par excellence, using iron to build massive wheeled siege towers and to cap their battering rams. No city walls could stand against them for long. Finally, Assyrian armies were massive. At the height of their power in the ninth century BCE, the rulers sent 120,000 soldiers on the annual campaign to the west. Chinese armies would not reach this scale for another 500 years.

In the first stage of imperial expansion, the king himself participated in the annual campaigns. Not surprisingly, such pressure provoked fierce opposition, particularly from the small independent states in the west, but the resisting populations were devastated —they were relocated through forced deportations, their lands annexed. The Assyrian state grew even more ambitious when a talented military leader usurped the throne. Naming himself Tiglath Pileser III (r. 745–728 BCE), after an

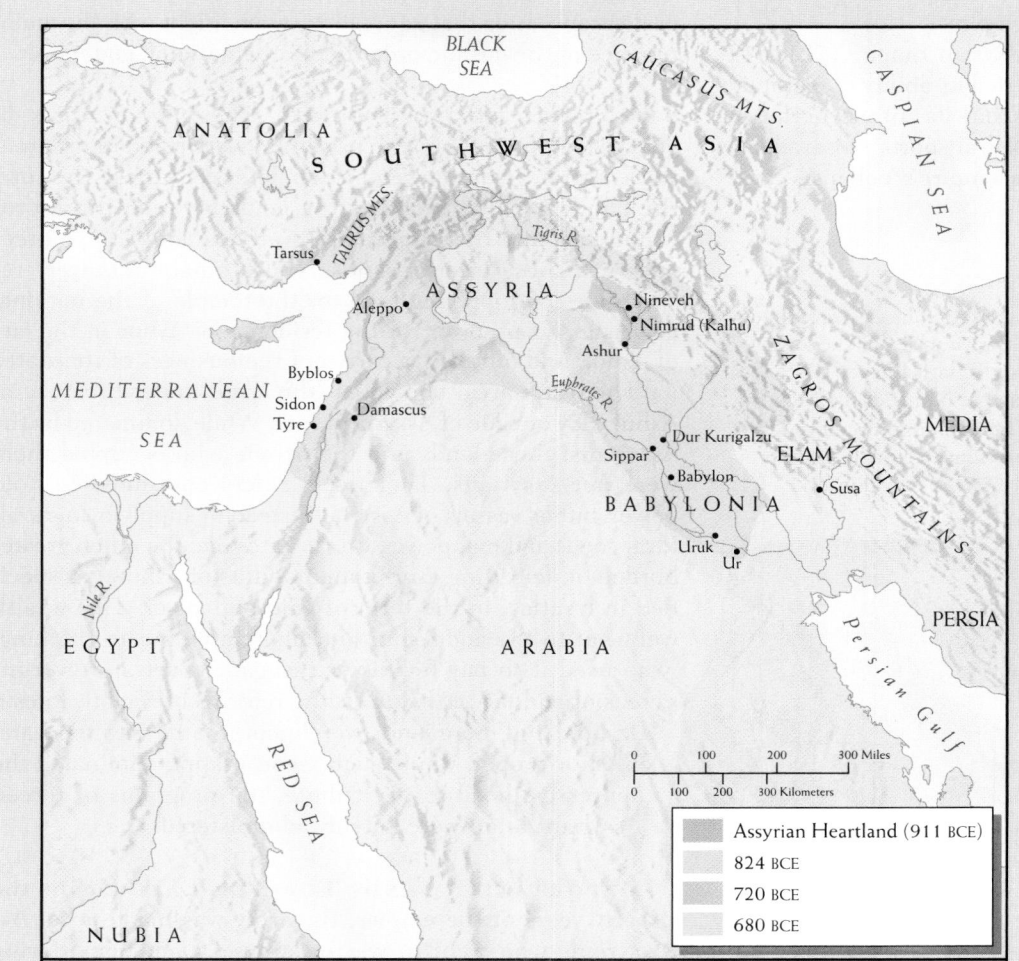

MAP 4-2 THE NEO-ASSYRIAN EMPIRE

The Neo-Assyrians built the first strong regional empire in Afro-Eurasia. In the process of building their state, they faced the challenge of promoting order and stability throughout their diverse realm. Where did the Neo-Assyrian empire expand? Which parts of the Neo-Assyrian Empire were "the Land of Ashur" and which were "the Land under the Yoke of Ashur"? How did the Assyrian state govern each of these areas? Why do you think expansion after 720 BCE led to the destruction of the empire?

Legend:
- Assyrian Heartland (911 BCE)
- 824 BCE
- 720 BCE
- 680 BCE

earlier reform-minded Assyrian king, he completely reorganized the Assyrian state in order to centralize power in royal hands and thus prepared the empire for a second phase of imperial expansion and consolidation. He took away the rights of the nobility to own and inherit land and other wealth. He abolished the old system of hereditary provincial governors, whom he replaced with officials who were annually appointed and directly controlled by the center of the empire. He reinstated the practice of aggressive, expansionary annual military campaigns. But the destruction and mass deportations carried out by his armies intensified the conquered peoples' hatred of the Assyrians. While they occasionally employed diplomacy in their dealings with other peoples, the Assyrians increasingly relied on state-sponsored terror in governing their empire.

In the final phase of the Neo-Assyrian Empire (721–612 BCE), the state's expansion far exceeded its ability to maintain effective control, given the limits that its infrastructure—particularly the roads and means of transportation available—imposed on its integration. The empire's collapse came swiftly and without warning.

Tiglath Pileser III. The walls of the Assyrian palaces were lined with stone slabs carved with images of the victories of the king. This fragmentary slab from the palace of Tiglath Pileser III originally decorated the wall of his palace at Nimrud. It shows in two registers the inhabitants and their herds being forced to leave after the defeat of their town by the Assyrians. Below is Tiglath Pileser III, shaded by his royal umbrella, in his war chariot.

INTEGRATION AND CONTROL OF THE EMPIRE

The idea of conquest was not new. We have seen episodes of warfare and expansion before. But the Neo-Assyrian Empire was distinguished from earlier territorial kingdoms and nascent empires by its idea of conquest and subjugation of other peoples. Conquered peoples were forced to obey and to pay tribute to their new imperial masters, as they were integrated into a cohesive empire. This system was based in part on the rulers' ability to employ brutality to break the will of defeated peoples, destroying their identity by removing them from their homes through mass deportations. It also depended on elaborate propaganda that equated Assyrian might with the maintenance of the cosmic order under the national god Ashur.

STRUCTURE OF THE EMPIRE The Assyrian rulers divided their empire into two parts that were ruled in different ways, a strategy used by empires in later centuries. The core, the Land of Ashur, included the lands between the Zagros Mountains and the Euphrates River. The king's appointees governed these interior lands, whose inhabitants were responsible for supplying food for the temple of the national god Ashur, manpower for the residence of Ashur in the city of Ashur, and officials to carry out the business of the state.

The other area, known as "the Land under the Yoke of Ashur," lay outside of Assyria proper. While dominated by the Assyrians, these lands and the people who occupied them were not Assyrians. Their local rulers continued to hold power, but as vassals of Assyria. Instead of supplying agricultural goods and manpower, vassal states had the much greater burden of delivering exorbitant amounts of tribute, as specified in treaties, in the form of gold and silver. This wealth went not to the god Ashur and his temple but to the king, who used it to pay for his extravagant court and ever-increasing military costs. After the reforms of Tiglath Pileser III, more and more lands were incorporated into the Land of Ashur proper. While such incorporation eliminated the oppressive need to pay tribute, the programs of forced Assyrianization were harshly administered.

DEPORTATION AND FORCED LABOR In the early years of the empire, the army was made up of Assyrians who went to war on annual campaigns during the summer months. Later, when the demands of campaigning became year-round, the army grew to several hundred thousand men mobilized to protect and extend the vast imperial holdings. These later forces included not only Assyrians but also men from the conquered peoples. By the seventh century BCE, different ethnic groups under Assyrian rule were assigned to specialized military functions. The Phoenicians from the Levant provided the ships and sailors for battle in the Mediterranean; the Medes,

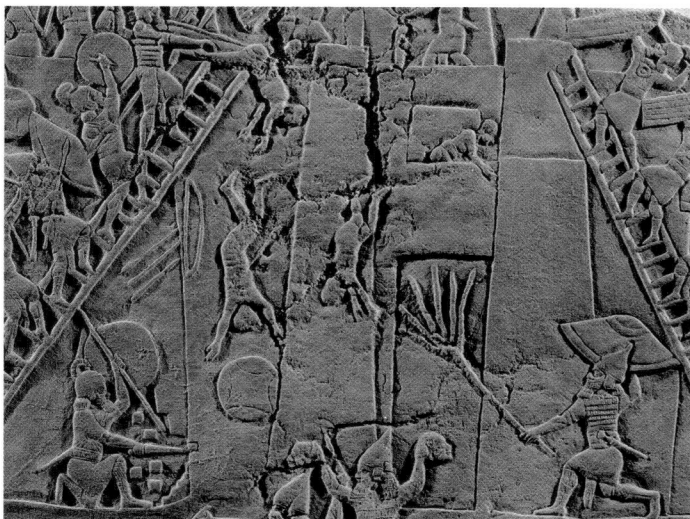

Capture of an Egyptian City. This stone panel from the palace in Nineveh shows warriors scaling walls with ladders during Ashurbanipal's campaign against Egypt (mid-seventh century BCE).

Defeat of Arab Tribes. In Room L of the North Palace of Ashurbanipal at Nineveh, the wall slabs were carved with three registers showing the defeat of rebellions in various parts of the realm. This slab shows with great artistry and detail the defeat of the Arab tribes who resisted the Assyrian war machine in the very south of Mesopotamia. The Arabs, like the Amorites and the Arameans before them, arrived in the riverine valley from the western desert. They were a formidable foe as they conducted war from the back of dromedary camels.

from the Iranian plateau, served as the king's bodyguards; and charioteers from Israel fought against rebellious western provinces.

In order to accomplish its goals, the Assyrian state had to organize huge labor forces for agricultural work and for enormous building projects. Since so many Assyrians went into the army, most of the agricultural and construction workers were recruited from conquered peoples, who often had to be relocated to the areas where their labor was needed. During the three centuries of the Neo-Assyrian Empire, the state moved more than 4 million people, a practice that not only supported work projects but also undermined local resistance efforts.

ASSYRIAN IDEOLOGY AND PROPAGANDA The Neo-Assyrian Empire, like all others, had a propaganda machine that promulgated an imperial ideology to support and justify its system of expansion, exploitation, and pervasive inequality. Even in the late second millennium BCE, when Assyrian expansion was first beginning, Assyrian inscriptions and art projected a strong sense of divinely determined destiny that drove the regime to swell westward toward the Mediterranean Sea. According to the state ideology, the national god Ashur commanded all Assyrians to support the endless and forcible growth of the empire, whose goal was to establish and maintain order and keep an ever-threatening cosmic chaos at bay. Only the god Ashur and his agent, the king, could bring universal order out of the cosmic chaos. The king as the *sangu*, or priest, of Ashur conducted holy war to transform the entire known world into the well-regulated Land of Ashur, and he intensified his campaign of terror and territorial aggrandizement with elaborate and far-reaching propaganda. This state

propaganda, based on a detailed historical record of countless military and political victories, assured the people that Assyria's triumph was inevitable. It was directed primarily at the nobles, whose complete devotion to and support of the king and the empire were crucial. Both verbal and visual programs were developed to reinforce their loyalty to the empire.

The rulers devised three distinct but mutually reinforcing varieties of propaganda campaign. First, as in Egypt and China, elaborate architectural complexes serve to stage ceremonial displays of pomp and power. Second, many different types of texts were composed that glorified the king and the empire. These were spoken at state occasions, inscribed on monumental surfaces, written in annals that detailed the military campaigns and achievements of the Assyrian kings, and buried at propitious places in public buildings, where they could be viewed only by the eyes of the god Ashur. Finally, visual images glorifying the king and the might of the Assyrian army were placed on palace walls. They graphically depicted the overwhelming force of the Assyrian army, showing all who resisted being smashed into submission—their towns burned; their men killed, impaled on stakes, or flayed for all to see; and their women and children taken into captivity and physically deported to faraway lands with any male survivors.

The commitment to "accurately" depict the triumphal events of the regime was visible not only on palace walls but also in the refinement of a particularly Assyrian literary form

Primary Source

THE BANQUET STELE OF ASSURNASIRPAL II

From the third millennium BCE onward, the rulers of Mesopotamia used architecture as one of the most effective means of signaling their power to their subjects. When a change of dynasty or other fundamental reorganization of power took place, rulers would build new palaces; sometimes they would even move their capital city. In the ninth century, Assurnasirpal II established Assyria as an imperial power that intended to expand and consolidate its economic and political control of surrounding peoples. After moving the capital and building a new palace and royal precinct, he called all of the people of the empire to a celebration to mark the transformation of the polity; it lasted for ten days. This remarkable event was commemorated by an inscribed stele that he erected in the chamber next to the throne room.

(102) When Ashur-nasir-apli, king of Assyria, consecrated the joyful palace, the palace full of wisdom, in Kalach (and) invited inside Ashur, the great lord, and the gods of the entire land; 1,000 fat oxen, 1,000 calves (and) sheep of the stable, 14,000 . . . -sheep which belonged to the goddess Ishtar my mistress, 200 oxen which belonged to the goddess Ishtar my mistress, 1,000 . . . -sheep, 1,000 spring lambs, 500 *ayalu*-deer, 500 deer, 1,000 ducks (*iṣṣū rū rabûtu*), 500 ducks (*usū*), 500 geese, 1,000 wild geese, 1,000 *qaribu*-birds, 10,000 pigeons, 10,000 wild pigeons, 10,000 small birds, 10,000 fish, 10,000 jerboa, 10,000 eggs, 10,000 loaves of bread, 10,000 jugs of beer, 10,000 skins of wine, 10,000 containers of grain (and) sesame, 10,000 pots of hot . . . , 1,000 boxes of greens, 300 (containers of) oil, 300 (containers of) malt, 300 (containers of) mixed *raqqatu*-plants, 100 (containers of) *kudimmus*, 100 (containers of) . . . , 100 (containers of) parched barley, 100 (containers of) *ubuḫšennu*-grain, 100 (containers of) fine *billatu*, 100 (containers of) pomegranates, 100 (containers of) grapes, 100 (containers of) mixed *zamrus*, 100 (containers of) pistachios, 100 (containers of). . . , 100 (containers of) onions, 100 (containers of) *garlic*, 100 (containers of) *kunipḫus*, 100 *bunches* of turnips, 100 (containers of) *ḫinḫinu*-seeds, 100 (containers of) *giddū*, 100 (containers of) honey, 100 (containers of) ghee, 100 (containers of) roasted *abšu*-seeds, 100 (containers of) roasted *šu'u*-seeds, 100 (containers of) *karkartu*-plants, 100 (containers of) *tiatu*-plants, 100 (containers of) mustard, 100 (containers of) milk, 100 (containers of) cheese, 100 bowls of *mīzu*-drink, 100 *stuffed oxen*, 10 homers of shelled *dukdu*-nuts, 10 homers of shelled pistachios, 10 homers of . . . , 10 homers of *ḫabbaququ*, 10 homers of dates, 10 homers of *titip*, 10 homers of *cumin*, 10 homers of *saḫūnu*, 10 homers of . . . , 10 homers of *andalšu*, 10 homers of *šišanibu*, 10 homers of *simberu*-fruit, 10 homers of *ḫašú*, 10 homers of fine oil, 10 homers of fine aromatics, 10 homers of . . . , 10 homers of *naṣṣabu*-gourds, 10 homers of *zinzimmu*-onions, 10 homers of olives; when I consecrated the palace of Kalach, 47,074 men (and) women who were invited from every part of my land, 5,000 dignitaries (and) envoys of the people of the lands Suhu, Hindanu, Patinu, Hatti, Tyre, Sidon, Gurgumu, Malidu, Hubushkia, Gilzanu, Kumu, (and) Musasiru, 16,000 people of Kalach, (and) 1,500 *zarīqū* of my palace, all of them – altogether 69,574 (including) those summoned from all lands and the people of Kalach – for ten days I gave them food, I gave them drink, I had them bathed, I had them anointed. (Thus) did I honour them (and) send them back to their lands in peace and joy.

→ *Compare the use of such display with the architectural practices of Egypt, ancient China, and the polities of the New World. What techniques, as reflected in the text of the Banquet Stele, did Assurnasirpal use to build loyalty among his subjects?*

SOURCE: *Assyrian Royal Inscriptions, Part 2: From Tiglath-pileser I to Ashur-nasir-apli II*, compiled and translated by Albert Kirk Grayson, vol. 2 of Records of the Ancient Near East, edited by Hans Goedicke (Wiesbaden: Otto Harrassowitz, 1976), pp. 175–76.

The Annals of Ashurbanipal. This baked clay faceted cylinder carries a portion of the annals of Ashurbanipal. It was found at Nineveh along with thousands of other tablets preserved in his famous library. The annals of Ashurbanipal were detailed, almost novelistic accounts of his military and civic achievements. Unlike earlier annals, there is first-person discourse, indirect discourse, flashbacks, and lively description of events and places. These annals are invaluable for our understanding of the Assyrian Empire.

called *annals*. A major milestone in human history, these documents illustrate the ways in which communication and writing served state formation from a very early stage. The annals were inscribed in cuneiform, both across carved stone slabs and on tablets and clay cylinders. The scribes of the Assyrian court entered a record of each successful campaign (and all were by definition successful) into the yearly report of the achievements of the Assyrian king. These written compositions, like the images, never gave any indication that the Assyrians did or could lose a battle in the struggle to extend and maintain their control of the land.

ASSYRIAN SOCIAL STRUCTURE AND POPULATION

The iron-fisted rule of the Assyrians rested on a rigid social hierarchy. Alone at the top was the king, who as the sole agent of the god Ashur conducted war to expand the Land of Ashur. Beneath the king were seven powerful officials who executed the king's commands and ensured the smooth functioning of the state. The governors of the provinces were originally members of ancient Assyrian families, and the office was passed down from father to son. For a time, nobles vied with the monarch for control over resources and power. But this competition ended with the reforms of Tiglath Pileser III.

The state handsomely rewarded its military elites who surrounded the king for their service, plying them with land grants, silver, and exemptions from royal taxes. Over time, they became the noble class and intimates of the king, replacing the older landed elites who had lost their hold on resources after Tiglath Pileser III reorganized the empire's landholdings. Elites often controlled vast estates that included both the land and the local populations who worked the fields and orchards. The bulk of the population consisted of peasants owned by the throne or by elites. These workers fell into different categories, with different privileges. Those who were enslaved because of an inability to pay their debts were allowed to marry free partners, engage in financial transactions, and even own property with other slaves attached. In contrast, foreigners enslaved after being captured in war had no rights; they were forced to undertake hard manual labor constructing the state's monumental building projects. Those forcibly relocated were not slaves but they became attached to the new lands that they were required to work. The little evidence we have indicates that families were small and lived on small plots of land, where they raised vegetables and planted vineyards.

Women in Assyria were far more restricted and controlled than their counterparts in the earlier periods of Sumerian and Old Babylonian Mesopotamia. Under the patriarchal social norms of the Assyrians, women had almost no control over their lives. Because all inheritance in the Assyrian system passed through the male line, it was crucial that a man be certain of the paternity of the children borne by his wives. As a result, all interactions between men and women outside of the family were highly restricted. The Middle Assyrians introduced the practice of veiling in the thirteenth century BCE, requiring it of all respectable women. Indeed, the veil was expressly forbidden to prostitutes who serviced the men of the army and worked in the taverns, so that their revealed faces and hair could signal their disreputable status to all. Any prostitute found wearing the veil would be taken to the top of the city wall, stripped of all of her clothing, and flogged. In certain circumstances, she could even be killed.

The queens of Assyria were bound by the same social norms, but their lives were more comfortable and varied than those of commoners. They dwelled in a separate part of the palace and were served by women or by eunuchs, whose role throughout the Assyrian court became increasingly important. Though Assyrian queens rarely wielded genuine power, they usually enjoyed respect and recognition, especially in the role of mother of the king. A queen could serve as a regent for her son, however, if the king died while the heir to the throne was still a child. Such was the case of Sammuramat, a queen who served as regent from 810 to 806 BCE, successfully ruling the empire until her son came of age.

THE INSTABILITY OF THE ASSYRIAN EMPIRE

At their high point, the Assyrians had conquered most of the lands stretching from Persia to Egypt. This was an awesome feat, but the empire was also unstable. Imperial expansion brought political headaches. Assyrian commanders had to position occupying armies far and wide to keep subjects in line. The propaganda machine ramped up, but so did the discontent among the regime's nobility. To compound the internal unrest, subject peoples also rose up—often using the iron weapons on which their tormentors had relied. Once a successful rebellion had challenged the Assyrian worldview of invincibility, the empire's fall was inevitable. Although successor states would temporarily fill the Assyrian political vacuum, the three-millennia-long culture of Mesopotamia was essentially dead. In 612 BCE, the Neo-Assyrian Empire collapsed as Nineveh was conquered.

 # THE PERSIAN EMPIRE

> → *In what ways was the Persian Empire similar to the Neo-Assyrian Empire, and in what ways was it different?*

The Assyrians were not the only people to push territorial states to their limits. Nor were they alone in feeling the pressures of nomadic incursions, which both shook up the existing system and gave its successors access to new resources, especially military and other technologies. The Persians were one of the nomadic groups speaking an Indo-Iranian language who arrived on the Iranian plateau from central Asia during the last centuries of the second millennium BCE. The Medes before them had settled on the central plateau and formed a large polity that stretched from the Zagros Mountains in the west to at least as far east as the modern city of Tehran. The Persians arrived in the region of Pars in the southwestern part of the Iranian plateau during the early centuries of the first millennium BCE. For many years, both the Medes and the Persians had warred with and paid tribute to the Assyrians, and later the Neo-Babylonians. Expert horsemen, they shot arrows with deadly accuracy while on horseback. Until Cyrus the Great (r. 559–529 BCE) took the reins of power, the Medes had dominated the Persians. But Cyrus

united the Persian tribes and defeated the Medes, incorporating them and their lands in Anatolia into his empire. In 546 BCE, his armies defeated the Lydians in southwestern Anatolia and took over their gold mines, land, and trading routes; he next gained ascendancy over the Greek city-states on the Aegean coast of Anatolia.

Cyrus's conquests set the stage for a vast and multicultural empire that spread from Europe to South Asia. His capture and incorporation of Babylon changed the nature of empire. In place of the Assyrians' reliance on brutal control, the Persians created a political system that used persuasion to impose their will on subject populations—though they kept the threat and reality of physical coercion close to hand. And because their ancestors were pastoralists, the Persians had no highly developed urban tradition of their own to draw on. Instead, they adapted the ideology and institutions of the Elamites, the Babylonians, and the Assyrians, modifying them to better fit their own customs. They thereby created the Persian institutions that formed the basis of the new empire, which would last until the arrival of Alexander the Great in 331 BCE.

THE INTEGRATION OF A MULTICULTURAL EMPIRE

Cyrus, the founder of the Persian Empire, traced his ancestry back to a legendary king, Achaemenes, and used his heritage to legitimate his empire-building campaign. By defeating the Median and Babylonian kings, Cyrus assumed control of much of Southwest Asia. From their base on the Iranian plateau, over the next 200 years the Persian rulers expanded their domain into an enormous empire that extended from the Indus Valley to northern Greece, and from Central Asia to the south of Egypt. (See Map 4-3.)

Cyrus was a benevolent ruler who liberated his subjects from the oppression of their own kings. He pointed to his victory in Babylon as a sign that the city's gods had turned against its king, Nabonidus, as a heretic. According to the cuneiform text known as the Cyrus cylinder, the Babylonians greeted him "with shining faces." At the same time, as will be discussed below, Cyrus released the Jews from their fifty-year captivity in Babylon. They, too, considered him a savior who, having freed them on the orders of their God, allowed them to return to Jerusalem and to rebuild their temple, and they acclaimed him as the Lord's anointed (see Isaiah 45:1). Even the Greeks, who later defeated the Persians, saw Cyrus as a model ruler.

Following the death of Cyrus on the battlefield, Darius I (r. 521–486) put the nascent empire on a solid footing. In his first two years of rule, Darius put down revolts across the lands, recording this feat on a monumental rock relief at Beisitun on the road to his capital city, Persepolis. Then he conquered territories held by seventy different ethnic groups,

→ *In what ways was the Persian Empire similar to the Neo-Assyrian Empire, and in what ways was it different?*

MAP 4-3   THE PERSIAN EMPIRE, 550–479 BCE

Starting in the sixth century BCE, the Persians succeeded the Assyrians as rulers of the large regional empire of Southwest Asia and North Africa. Compare the Persian Empire's territorial domains to those of the Neo-Assyrian Empire in Map 4-2. Geographically, how did the Persian Empire differ from the Neo-Assyrian state? How does this map help explain Persian strategies for promoting order and stability in their empire? Which groups proved most resistant to Persian rule?

stretching from the Indus River in the east to the Aegean and Mediterranean seas in the west, from the Black, Caspian, and Aral seas in the north to the Nile River in the south. To manage this huge domain, Darius introduced innovative and dynamic administrative systems that enabled the empire to flourish for another two centuries. The Persian Empire brought together people of many different cultures, languages, and backgrounds in its new bureaucracy, which successfully combined central and local administration to exploit the strengths of local tradition, economy, and rule—rather than attempting to force Persian tradition and customs on subject people via rigid central control in the manner of the Assyrians.

This empire was both centralized and multicultural. The Persians believed that all subject peoples entered it on an equal footing; the only demand on them was that they give the king their loyalty and pay tribute—which was considered an honor, not a burden. The Persians' lack of administrative

experience and urban traditions may have contributed to their political flexibility. When they came to power, the Persian ruling classes simply adapted the bureaucratic practices of the peoples whom they conquered.

Local Persian administrators used local languages: thus in Iran, the authorities employed Elamite; in Babylon, they used Akkadian; and in Egypt, they used Egyptian, written in hieroglyphs and demotic scripts. In time, Aramaic, a dialect of a Semitic language long spoken in Southwest Asia, became the empire's lingua franca because many of its literate scribes came from Mesopotamia. Aramaic was written on parchment or papyrus in an alphabetic script, and its use spread quickly throughout the empire. The language of the emperors, Old Persian, was now written down for the first time. Monumental inscriptions were usually recorded in three languages, Elamite, Akkadian, and Old Persian; by order of Darius, the last was rendered in a script known as alphabetic cuneiform.

Cyrus the Great. This great Genius with four wings was preserved in the doorjamb of Gate R at the palace of Cyrus the Great at Pasargadae. When Cyrus forged the Persian Empire from Media, Assyria, Babylonia, and Egypt, there was no coherent imperial imagery to represent the new political entity. His court artists borrowed freely from the realms that he had brought into his empire. The image is a combination of features borrowed from Egypt (the headdress), Assyria (low relief representation on a stone slab and the four wings), and Babylonia (the long garment).

Much like Tiglath Pileser III of Assyria, Darius understood that the empire could not be expanded without reorganization and centralization. His method for ensuring that the wealth of the provinces came to the imperial center was to establish a system of provinces, or satrapies, each ruled by a satrap (a governor) who was a relative or an intimate associate of the king. The local bureaucrats and officials who ran the government and administration were closely monitored by military officers, tax collectors from the center, and spies (the so-called eyes of the king) who enforced the satrap's loyalty. Further, Darius put in place a system of fixed taxation and formal tribute allocations; when needed, he instituted economic reforms. Moreover, he promoted trade throughout the empire by building roads, establishing a standardized currency including coinage, and introducing standard weights and measures.

ZOROASTRIANISM, IDEOLOGY, AND SOCIAL STRUCTURE

Like the Assyrians, the Persians established their ideology of kingship on religious foundations. The supreme god, Ahura Mazda, was believed to have appointed the monarch as ruler over all the people and lands of the earth and charged him with maintaining a perfect order on earth from which all would benefit. Thus, according to Darius, one reason Ahura Mazda made him king was that the earth "was in commotion" and Darius "put it down." Unlike their Mesopotamian neighbors, the Medes and the Persians drew their religious ideas from their pastoral and tribal roots, which reflected the same traditions of warrior and priestly classes as those preserved in the Vedic texts of the Indus Valley. The effects of the Persian Empire's religious ideas would be powerful and lasting. As was true of so much else in this age of increasing integration,

Darius's Relief at Beisitun. At Beisitun, high above the Royal Road through the Zagros Mountains, Darius carved a relief on the face of the cliff commemorating his victories over Gaumata (the false Smerdis) and nine rebel kings. The kings are roped together at the neck, and Baumata lies under Darius's feet. Above the rebels is a figure of a winged disk, probably the god Ahuramazda. Darius had his scribes develop a version of cuneiform script to represent Old Persian. In a trilingual inscription (Old Persian, Elamite, and Babylonian), he recorded in detail this victory, which allowed him to consolidate and expand the empire founded by Cyrus. This inscription, which was copied between 1835 and 1847 by Sir Henry Creswicke Rawlinson, provided the key for the decipherment of Babylonian cuneiform.

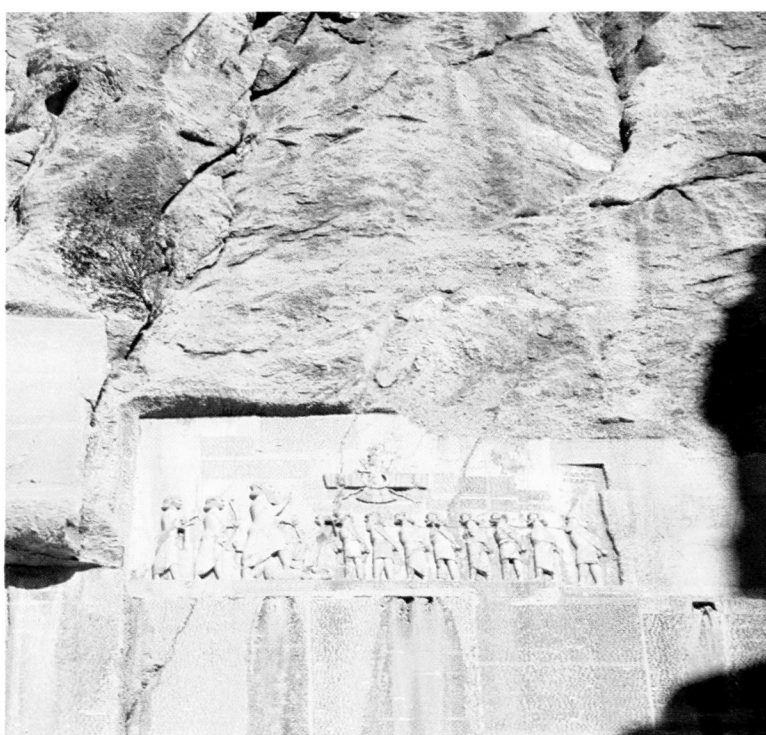

Primary Source

BEISITUN INSCRIPTION

To commemorate his consolidation of power over the Persian state, Darius I commissioned a pictorial relief of himself as victor high above the main road leading from Mesopotamia to Ecbatana. The images are surrounded by a long text, inscribed in three languages—Old Persian, Akkadian, and Elamite. This is the earliest Old Persian inscription; it is written in a version of the cuneiform script that Darius had devised specially for this occasion.

4.31–2. Saith Darius the King: These IX kings I took prisoner within these battles.

4.33–6. Saith Darius the King: These are the provinces which became rebellious. The Lie made them rebellious, so that these (men) deceived the people. Afterwards Ahuramazda put them into my hand; as was my desire, so I did unto them.

4.36–40. Saith Darius the King: Thou who shalt be king hereafter, protect thyself vigorously from the Lie; the man who shall be a Lie-follower, him do thou punish well, if thus thou shalt think, "May my country be secure!"

4.40–3. Saith Darius the King: This is what I did; by the favor of Ahuramazda, in one and the same year I did (it). Thou who shalt hereafter read this inscription, let that which has been done by me convince thee; do not thou think it a lie.

4.43–5. Saith Darius the King: I turn myself quickly to Ahuramazda, that this (is) true, not false, (which) I did in one and the same year.

4.45–50. Saith Darius the King: By the favor of Ahuramazda and of me much else was done; that has not been inscribed in this inscription; for this reason it has not been inscribed, lest whose shall hereafter read this inscription, to him what has been done by me seem excessive, (and) it not convince him, (but) he think it false.

4.50–2. Saith Darius the King: Those who were the former kings, as long as they lived, by them was not done thus as by the favor of Ahuramazda was done by me in one and the same year.

4.52–6. Saith Darius the King: Now let that which has been done by me convince thee; thus to the people impart, do not conceal it: if this record thou shalt not conceal, (but) tell it to the people, may Ahuramazda be a friend unto thee, and may family be unto thee in abundance, and may thou live long!

4.57–9. Saith Darius the King: If this record thou shalt conceal, (and) not tell it to the people, may Ahuramazda be a smiter unto thee, and may family not be to thee!

4.59–61. Saith Darius the King: This which I did, in one and the same year by the favor of Ahuramazda I did; Ahuramazda bore me aid, and the other gods who are.

4.61–7. Saith Darius the King: For this reason Ahuramazda bore aid, and the other gods who are, because I was not hostile, I was not a Lie-follower, I was not a doer of wrong---neither I nor my family. According to righteousness I conducted myself. Neither to the weak nor to the powerful did I do wrong. The man who cooperated with my house, him I rewarded well; whoso did injury, him I punished well.

4.67–9. Saith Darius the King: Thou who shalt be king hereafter, the man who shall be a Lie-follower or who shall be a doer of wrong---unto them do thou not be a friend, (but) punish them well.

4.69–72. Saith Darius the King: Thou who shalt hereafter behold this inscription which I have inscribed, or these sculptures, do thou not be destroy them, (but) thence onward protect them; as long as thou shalt be in good strength!

→ *Do you think that all imperial states must go through similar stages of reorganization to preserve themselves? Throughout the millennia, local and imperial rulers on the Iranian plateau used rock reliefs such as the Beisitun inscription to project their power and to mark boundaries. Often these were high and completely inaccessible. Who would see these monuments, and what messages would they receive? What other methods did rulers use to inscribe their political power?*

SOURCE: Roland G. Kent, *Old Persian: Grammar, Texts, Lexicon*, 2nd rev. ed. (New Haven: American Oriental Society, 1953), pp. 131–32.

those ideas came not from the urban cores of ancient kingdoms but from the hinterlands.

Zoroaster (also known as Zarathustra), who is thought to have taught sometime after 1000 BCE in eastern Iran, was most responsible for crystallizing the region's traditional beliefs into a formal religious system. The eastern tribes of the Iranian plateau spread the ideas of Zoroastrianism to the Iranian peoples living in the west, and Zoroastrianism became the religion of the Persian Empire. (The archaeological record is too sketchy to give us a clear sense of how this came about.) The main source for the teachings of Zoroaster is the Avesta, a compilation of holy works transmitted orally by priests for more than a millennium before they were written down in the sixth century CE. It has much in common linguistically with the Vedic texts of the people of the Indus Valley, even though deities with the same names played different roles when they were worshipped in different parts of the world.

Zoroaster's teachings endeavored to wean the Iranian faithful away from their earlier animistic nomadic beliefs. He was radical for the age and place in promoting belief in one god, Ahura Mazda, who had created the world and all that was good. Though rare, monotheism was also found during this time in Judah; it had briefly been the official religion of Egypt, when Akhenaten (r. 1375–1350 BCE) had imposed

Sasanian Coin. Fire worship is central to the Zoroastrian faith. On the reverse of a coin of the Sasanian king Shapur II, two images of kings flank a fire altar. Fire altars of this shape are known from as early as the seventh century BCE in Iran.

Panel from the Palace of Darius. The Palace of Darius at Susa was elaborately decorated with glazed bricks. This panel shows human-headed winged lions in a heraldic seated posture. Above them is a winged disk with tendrils and a human bust. This symbol, which borrows from Assyrian and Egyptian imagery, is thought to represent the Zoroastrian god Ahuramazda.

worship of Aten, the sun, on his subjects during the New Kingdom period. This initial effort to impose monotheism on Egyptians failed primarily because the people remained devoted to their old gods, and because the new religion lacked a single key component: the attraction of an afterlife. Persians came to believe that the universe was fundamentally dualistic: Ahura Mazda was good and capable only of good, whereas his adversary, Ahiram, was deceitful and wicked. These two forces were engaged in a cosmic struggle for the universe. Ahura Mazda was destined to save the earth from darkness, to deliver Ahiram to the dark place (akin to hell), and to enable the dead to rise for their final judgment.

Unlike the fatalistic religions of Mesopotamia, Zoroastrianism treated humans as independent actors, capable of choosing between good and evil and of engaging in good works or sinful acts. Their choices had consequences—rewards or punishments in the afterlife. Strict rules of behavior determined the fate of each individual. For example, because animals were good, they deserved to be treated well. Intoxicants, widely used in tribal religions, were strictly forbidden. The treatment of the dead was carefully prescribed. To prevent the sacred elements of earth, fire, and water from being contaminated by death, it was forbidden to bury, burn, or drown the dead. Instead, corpses were exposed to the elements to be devoured by beasts and birds of prey. Apparently, this practice was borrowed from the Median priestly class, known as the Magi. These priests enjoyed great prestige throughout the region; indeed, the reported appearance of *magoi apo anatolōn* (the "wise men from the east" of Matthew 2:1) to honor the newborn Jesus was viewed by Christians as evidence that he was the messiah.

Persian kings enjoyed absolute authority. But in return, they were expected to exercise power according to moral and political tenets that reflected Zoroastrian notions of ethical behavior. As the embodiment of the positive virtues that made them fit to hold power, they were to be just rulers, fair in bestowing rewards and in meting out punishments, displaying insight and the ability to distinguish right from wrong so that they might preserve justice and maintain social order. In addition, kings were required to demonstrate physical superiority that mirrored their moral standing. Kings had to be awe-inspiring horseman and peerless in wielding bows and

→ *In what ways was the Persian Empire similar to the Neo-Assyrian Empire, and in what ways was it different?*

spears. These were qualities valued by all Persian nobles, who continued to prize the virtues of their nomadic ancestors. The ancient Greek historian Herodotus tells us that Persian boys were taught three things only: "to ride, to shoot with the bow, and to tell the truth."

Persians divided their social order into four large and quite diverse groups: priests, nobles, and warriors; scribes/bureaucrats and merchants; artisans; and peasants. Members of each contributed to the welfare of the state by paying taxes and performing their required duties. Surrounding the king was the powerful Persian hereditary nobility, whose support was crucial to the success of the empire. These men had vast landholdings and often served the king as satraps or advisers. Also close to the king were wealthy merchants who orchestrated trade across the vast empire. The king's obligations to them required that he take his wives only from their families and grant them exemptions from certain taxes. But in order to consolidate his hold on the throne, Darius diminished the real political power of aristocrats; by exerting direct control over all appointments, he ensured that the nobles would be his puppets. At the same time, he allowed them to maintain their high status in a society in which birth and royal favor counted for everything.

Royal gifts solidified the relations between king and nobles, reinforcing the king's place at the top of the political pyramid. Vessels of gold, elaborate textiles, and jewelry were presented in public ceremonies designed to reward the recipient's loyalty and underscore his dependence on the crown. Most often these gifts were specially made in the court workshops from gold and silver obtained through tribute, and they reminded those to whom they were given of their continual obligation to the ruler. Any kind of failure would result in the king withdrawing his royal favor; should such failures be serious or treasonous, the offenders faced torture and death.

PUBLIC WORKS AND IMPERIAL IDENTITY

Given the enormous size of the empire, good roads and a system of rapid and dependable communication were absolute necessities. A key element in unifying the land was the Royal Road, which followed age-old routes 1,600 miles, from Sardis in western Anatolia to Susa at the heart of the empire in southwestern Iran. It continued to the east along the traditional route across the northern reaches of the Iranian plateau and beyond into central Asia. The Royal Road was used by traders and by the Persian army (and later by other warriors), as well as by those taking tribute to the king and by couriers carrying messages from the king to his satraps and imperial armies. As the Assyrians had done, the Persians placed way stations with fresh mounts and provisions for the messengers along the route at regular intervals.

In addition to the Royal Road, the Persians also built other infrastructures to connect the far reaches of the empire with its center in southwestern Iran. Under Darius, a canal was built that was some 150 feet wide and more than 50 miles long and linked the Red Sea to the Nile River. One of the most ingenious contributions of the Persians was the invention of *qanats,* underground tunnels through which water, vital for irrigation and society, could flow for long distances without evaporating or being contaminated. Later adopted by many cultures, this system is still used today to

Persepolis. In the highland valley of Fars, the homeland of the Persians, Darius and his successors built a capital city and ceremonial center at the site of Persepolis. On top of a huge platform, there were audience halls, a massive treasury, the harem, and residential spaces. The building was constructed of mudbrick. The roof was supported by enormous columns with bull protome capitals.

The King and His Courtiers. Leading to the Apadana (reception hall) are two monumental staircases that are faced with low-relief representations of the king and his courtiers, as well as all of the delegations bringing tribute to the center of the empire. The lion attacking the bull is a symbolic rendering of the forces of nature. Above the central plane is the winged disk of Ahuramazda and the human-headed lion griffins.

move water across arid lands. These feats of engineering were by and large built by laborers from the local populations, who worked on them as their civic obligation.

Until Cyrus's time, the Persians had been nomadic pastoralists and had no traditions of monumental architecture, visual arts, or written literature or history. Cyrus began to define a Persian court style, which drew on the talents of his subjects. It was Darius, however, who was most responsible for forging visual and physical expressions that were uniquely Persian.

The vast capital at Persepolis was the clearest expression of this new imperial identity. On the highland plain of Fars, near the capital of Cyrus the Great at Pasargadae, Darius built an immense complex that complemented the administrative center at Susa in the lowlands. Skilled craftworkers were gathered from all over the empire to work on the complex, and their distinct cultural influences were melded into a new Persian architectural style. He erected his city, designed for celebrations and ceremonies, on a monumental terrace that covers more than thirty acres. Into the cliffs behind it, Darius and his successors cut their eternal resting places from the rock. Persepolis was also an important administrative hub, where archaeologists have found more than 30,000 tablets; written in Elamite cuneiform script, they describe in meticulous detail the bureaucracy and the activities of the great empire.

For their monumental architecture, Persians borrowed from the Urartians (in modern Armenia) and the Medes the use of grand columned halls. These huge open spaces provided reception rooms for thousands of representatives arriving from all over the empire and bringing tribute to the Persian king. Not only did this central place serve as the treasury for the court, but it also helped integrate disparate peoples by connecting them all to one imperial authority located at the center of the realm. In the palace, three of the columned halls were placed on raised platforms that were reached through monumental processional stairways, lined with endless repeating images of the peoples of the empire taking gifts and tribute to the king. This elaborate architectural decoration was a highly refined program of visual propaganda. The carved relief images showed the Persian Empire not as a homogenized state but as a rich conglomeration of gladly obedient peoples. The carvings on the great stairway of Persepolis offer a veritable ethnographic museum frozen in stone. Each group carries its own distinctive tribute—the Armenians bringing precious metal vessels, the Lydians from Anatolia bringing gold armlets and bowls, the Egyptians bringing exotic animals, and the Sogdians from Central Asia bringing horses. Gateway figures and protective relief images copied from the palaces of Assyria represented the grandeur of the occasion and the power of the king—but the borrowings in this visual propaganda underscore the contrast with their originals. While both the Persians and the Assyrians aspired to and realized their dreams of creating substantial empires, the methods they used for achieving their goals were quite different.

Persian Water-Moving Technique. The Perisans perfected the channeling of water over long distances through underground channels called "qanats." This technique, an efficient way to move water without evaporation, is still used today in hot, arid regions. In this example near Yazd, in central Iran, the domed structure leading to the underground tunnel is flanked by two brick towers called "badgir," an ancient form of air conditioning that cools the water using wind (*bad* in Persian).

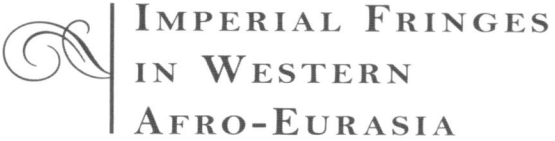

IMPERIAL FRINGES IN WESTERN AFRO-EURASIA

> → *How did the growth of the first empires in western Afro-Eurasia affect societies in the Levant and the Aegean? What influence did they have on the broader region?*

Although the first empires of Southwest Asia proclaimed their control over vast territories, their power was never as total or as far-reaching as their propagandists claimed. Peoples living on the edges of the empires or well beyond their reach in western Afro-Eurasia and around the northern and southern shores of the Mediterranean Sea were equally dynamic actors, often intruding on the empires themselves. More important, they developed their own political and cultural systems. Their powerful neighbors greatly affected their societies, yet they retained their own languages, belief systems, and local arrangements for ruling themselves. Despite establishing large bureaucracies, priestly classes, and armies that enabled them to rule over large expanses of land, the apparatus of empire did not eradicate differences. In fact, the very smallness and intimacy of communities on the fringes of the big empires enabled them to project their own kind of power and influence.

MIGRATIONS AND UPHEAVAL

Demographic upheavals and migrations around 1200 BCE enhanced the ability of the smaller fringe communities to wield an influence perhaps out of proportion to their size. In earlier millennia, influences and ideas had moved rapidly up the Danube River basin into Central Europe, provoking a shift to an economy based on agriculture (see Chapter 3). Among the consequences of these east-to-west communications were a rapid rise in population and advances by the peoples of Central Europe to develop their own natural resources, including an advanced metallurgy in a new metal, iron. At the end of the second millennium, this surplus population armed with its new metal weapons moved in large groups back down the river highway of the Danube into southeastern Europe, the Aegean, and the eastern Mediterranean. Advancing quickly over southwestern Asia and the Mediterranean, the invaders threw the existing societies into turmoil. These huge movements considerably weakened the power of empires and regimes in the region, increased the value of mobility and communication as peoples vied for resources, and opened

The Naval Battle against the Sea Peoples. The walls of Egyptian temples were covered with images in sunk relief, a technique that allows them to stand out in the bright sunlight. On the temple of Ramses III at Medinet Habu at Thebes, the North Wall is covered with scenes of the naval battle against the Sea Peoples. The Sea Peoples invaded both Egypt and the cities of the Levant during the last centuries of the second millennium BCE.

Mycenaean Arms and Armor. A Mycenaean vase that illustrates the central role of arms and war to the societies on mainland Greece in the period down to 1200 BCE. The men bear common suits of armor and weapons—helmets, corsets, spears, and shields—most likely supplied to them by the palace-centered organizations to which they belonged. Despite these advantages, they were not able to mount a successful defense against the land incursions that destroyed the Mycenaean palaces toward the end of the thirteenth century BCE.

new spaces in which smaller, more innovative communities could gain sway.

These invasions brought about the collapse of even the most highly developed societies in the region. The first of the big states in the region to fall were the Hittites, who had once dominated the central lands of what is today Turkey (see Chapter 3); they could not retain power in the face of violence and social chaos.

Once they reached the Mediterranean, migrants from the north appeared to have adopted boats as their primary means of transportation, hugging the coasts of the Aegean and the eastern Mediterranean seas. For this reason, these communities on the move are sometimes known as the Sea Peoples. The Egyptians knew them as the Peleset, and it was only by marshalling all the resources of their land that the pharaohs Merneptah in the 1220s BCE and Ramses III in the 1180s BCE managed to repel them, thereby securing the traditional order of Egyptian society for several more centuries. Still, Egypt's survival was achieved at considerable cost. And outside Egypt, the former major states and kingdoms suffered heavily from the ravages of these violent freebooters. Settling along the southern coast of the Levant, where they became known as the Philistines, the Sea Peoples considerably weakened local Canaanite communities—and that weakness allowed another tribe from the fringes of empire, the Israelites, to move in and settle the interior of the country.

From 1100 to 900 BCE, a prolonged economic downturn unsettled the major kingdoms, as well as the coastal cities of the eastern Mediterranean and the Aegean islands. During this time, artistic representation, large-scale construction, the development of urban centers, trading and shipping on any significant scale, writing and record keeping, and much else disappeared; societies were now characterized by smaller-scale, technically simpler, materially impoverished, illiterate, and certainly more violent rural communities.

In the Mediterranean, the intrusions of the Sea Peoples shook up the social order of the Minoans on the island of Crete and of the Mycenaeans in mainland areas of Greece. Agricultural production declined, and populations moved to other islands in the Aegean and to southwestern Anatolia. The basis of the complex social order of the second millennium—the large palace-centered bureaucracies and priesthoods, which maintained elaborate written records—vanished, and a more violent society, reliant on the iron weapons used by the newcomers, emerged. This was the culture of individual warrior-heroes that was evoked in the *Iliad,* an epic poem about the Trojan War composed centuries after the events it purports to describe. Like many retrospective accounts, the *Iliad* reflected concerns of later years, but it was based on oral tales passed down and embellished for generations. The Greeks told these stories about a hazily recalled war that may have occurred around 1200 BCE at Troy, a city in Anatolia, during a time of seismic political and social upheaval.

For the long-established kingdoms and states of Southwest Asia and the Mediterranean, these rapid transformations were destructive and traumatic. But they were also creative: they shattered long-established ways of doing things, wiping the social slate clean. Violent change was the first step toward completely new patterns of human relations.

PERSIA AND THE GREEKS

The contact between empires and peoples on their fringe sometimes led to coexistence, sometimes to conflict. But contact always created a political borderland between the imperial cores and emerging regimes on the periphery. It was in such zones of contact that great shifts in the political centers of gravity were most keenly felt. Consider the example of the western fringe of the Persian Empire, where by the sixth century BCE, the influence of the urban cultures of Anatolia and Mesopotamia had waned, replaced by stronger associations with the people of the Mediterranean. The peoples known as Greeks are a good example of these borderland dynamics. In the area of contact with the Persian empire, Greek-speaking people in different cities sometimes cooperated with the Persians, even borrowing their ideas and styles, but sometimes strongly resisted them.

In 499 BCE, some Greek city-states joined with others in the eastern Mediterranean in a revolt against the Persians in Anatolia. The struggle went on for five years until the Per-

WAR IN HOMER'S *ILIAD*

The great epic poem, more than 15,500 lines long, called the Iliad—about the war that took place at Ilium, a Greek name for the city of Troy—was attributed by the later Greeks to a single poet named Homer. The written text that we have, however, is actually the end result of generations of oral singers who composed different versions of this story in the ninth and eight centuries BCE. The story of the Iliad takes place during just three days of fighting on the plains in front of the city of Troy. It is the story of a war, but it focuses on a few prominent individual warriors—men such as Achilles and Odysseus on the side of the Achaeans and Hector and Paris on the Trojan side. There have been many debates among historians about the historical reality of the story in the Iliad, but almost all agree on the site of the ancient city it describes.

Antiphus hurled at *him*—
the son of Priam wearing a gleaming breastplate
let fly through the lines but his sharp spear missed
and he hit Leucus instead, Odysseus' loyal comrade,
gouging his groin as the man hauled off a corpse—
it dropped from his hands and Leucus sprawled across it.
Enraged at his friend's death Odysseus sprang in fury,
helmed in fiery bronze he plowed through the front
and charging the enemy, glaring left and right
he hurled his spear—a glinting brazen streak—
and the Trojans gave ground, scattering back,
panicking there before his whirling shaft—
a direct hit! Odysseus struck Democoon,
Priam's bastard son come down from Abydos,
Priam's racing-stables. Incensed for the dead
Odysseus speared him straight through one temple
and out the other punched the sharp bronze point
and the dark came swirling thick across his eyes—
down he crashed, armor clanging against his chest.
And the Trojan front shrank back, glorious Hector too
as the Argives yelled and dragged away the corpses,
pushing on, breakneck on. But lord god Apollo,
gazing down now from the heights of Pergamus,
rose in outrage, crying down at the Trojans,
"Up and at them, you stallion-breaking Trojans!
Never give up your lust for war against these Argives!
What are their bodies made of, rock or iron to block
your tearing bronze? Stab them, slash their flesh!
Achilles the son of lovely sleek-haired Thetis—
the man's not even fighting, no, he wallows
in all his heartbreak fury by the ships!"
So he cried
from far on the city's heights, the awesome god Apollo.
But Zeus's daughter Athena spurred the Argives on—
Athena first in glory, third-born of the gods—
whenever she saw some slacker hanging back
as she hurtled through the onset.
Now Amarinceus' son
Diores—fate shackled Diores fast and a jagged rock
struck him against his right shin, beside the ankle.

Pirous son of Imbrasus winged it hard and true,
the Thracian chief who had sailed across from Aenus . . .
the ruthless rock striking the bones and tendons
crushed them to pulp—he landed flat on his back,
slamming the dust, both arms flung out to his comrades,
gasping out his life. Pirous who heaved the rock
came rushing in and speared him up the navel—
his bowels uncoiled, spilling loose on the ground
and the dark came swirling down across his eyes.
But Pirous—
Aetolian Thoas speared *him* as he swerved and sprang away,
the lancehead piercing his chest above the nipple
plunged deep in his lung, and Thoas, running up,
wrenched the heavy spear from the man's chest,
drew his blade, ripped him across the belly,
took his life but he could not strip his armor.
Look, there were Pirous' cohorts bunched in a ring,
Thracians, topknots waving, clutching their long pikes
and rugged, strong and proud as the Trojan Thoas was,
they shoved him back—he gave ground, staggering, reeling.
And so the two lay stretched in the dust, side-by-side,
a lord of Thrace, a lord of Epeans armed in bronze
and a ruck of other soldiers died around them.
And now
no man who waded into that work could scorn it any longer,
anyone still not speared or stabbed by tearing bronze
who whirled into the heart of all that slaughter—
not even if great Athena led him by the hand,
flicking away the weapons hailing down against him.
That day ranks of Trojans, ranks of Achaean fighters
sprawled there side-by-side, facedown in the dust.

→ *What does this selection reveal about the style of combat used in this period? What does it tell us about the weapons used? What can we surmise about the cultures from which these soldiers come?*

SOURCE: Homer, *The Iliad*, translated by Robert Fagles (1990; reprint, New York: Penguin, 1998), pp. 160–63.

sian coalition gained mastery over the rebellious Greek cities. In this same struggle, however, there were Greek communities that sided with the Persians and were condemned by other Greeks as "Medizers"—Greeks who sided with the Medes or Persians. On the mainland, further away from the contact zone, most Greek cities exhibited a more hostile attitude, actively resisting the Persian king's authority. So, in 492 BCE, Darius sent his fleet to subdue Athens and Sparta, the two big city-states on the mainland, but the ships were destroyed in a storm. Two years later, Darius and his vast army invaded mainland Greece but were soundly defeated by the much smaller force of Athenians at Marathon, just to the northeast of Athens. The Persians wisely retreated to nurse their wounds, waiting another decade before daring to hit their western foe again. Meanwhile, Athens emerged as a major sea power.

Under the leadership of Themistocles in the 480s BCE, Athens became a naval power whose strength was in the fleet of its triremes, or battleships. This great shift was fundamental to the future relationship between the Greeks and the Persians and to the rise of Athens as a great power. When the two militaries met again in 480 BCE, the Persians were able to burn Athens but lost the pivotal naval battle of the invasion at Salamis. A year later, they were decisively defeated on land and eventually lost the war. But in a way that was typical of the close and intertwined relationships between the two cultures, Themistocles, the hero of Salamis, later finished his career in the service of the Persian king.

The major Persian defeats changed the balance of power, and for the next 150 years Persia continually lost ground to the Greeks, who gradually regained territory in southeastern Europe and western Anatolia. During this time, palace intrigues and ongoing rebellions throughout the empire preoc-

The Sea Battle at Salamis. A modern artist's reconstruction of the sea battle at Salamis in which the Greek ships led by Athens defeated a large invading fleet commanded by King Xerxes of Persia. The trireme—so-called because of its three banks of oars—was the state-of-the-art battleship of the time. Drawing on their long experience of sailing on the Mediterranean and using the fleet of triremes built under Themistocles, the Athenians gained a critical victory over the Persians and asserted ascendancy over the eastern Mediterranean.

cupied the Persian court. The Greek historian Xenophon wrote that "whereas the king's empire was strong in that it covered a vast territory with large numbers of people, it also was weak because of the need to travel great distances and the wide distribution of its forces, making it vulnerable to a swift attack." In the end, the fatal blow against Persian rule would come from the most remote of the Greek outposts in the eastern Mediterranean, Macedonia; its armies, led by Alexander the Great, would range as far as India in their quest for empire (see Chapter 6).

THE PHOENICIANS

The effects of integration on the fringes went beyond resistance. Some peoples who lived on the borderlands of empire, such as the Phoenicians, seized opportunities to coexist with and to flourish under imperial rule—and to create their own autonomous dominions. Particularly successful were those living on the western edges of the emerging Assyrian and later Persian empires. (See Map 4-4.)

Engaging in trade and retaining their autonomy, albeit as imperial vassals, were the people who called themselves the Chanani—called "Canaanites" in the Bible, but better known by the name that the Greeks gave them, probably because they manufactured and widely traded throughout the Mediterranean an expensive purple dye: the Phoenicians, or literally the "Purple People." These Phoenicians were a mixture of the local population and the Sea Peoples who had arrived in recent centuries. As traders, they were more socially opportunistic than politically ambitious; they preferred opening up new markets and new ports to subduing frontiers. Their coastal cities made the Phoenicians ideally situated to develop trade in the whole of the Mediterranean basin. Inland from their cities was an extraordinary forest of massive cedars—perfect timber for making large, seaworthy craft and a highly desirable export to the treeless heartlands of Egypt and Mesopotamia.

Innovations in shipbuilding and seafaring enabled the Phoenicians to sail as far west as present-day Morocco and Spain, carrying huge cargoes of such goods as timber, dyed cloth, glassware, wines, textiles, metal ingots, and finished goods, as well as carved ivory. They established trading colonies all around the southern and western rim of the Mediterranean, including Carthage in modern-day Tunisia on the North African coast. The Phoenician cities were full-scale trading ports that attracted goods from their respective interiors that were then shipped throughout the Mediterranean.

During the height of Assyrian power in the eighth and seventh centuries BCE, the Phoenicians supplied the empire with special commercial services and were able to continue their business without Assyrian interference. They accommodated their powerful neighbors rather than resisting them. Phoenician kings signed treaties with the Assyrian

→ *How did the growth of the first empires in western Afro-Eurasia affect societies in the Levant and the Aegean?*

MAP 4-4   THE LEVANTINE BORDERLAND, 1000–400 BCE

Peoples on the borderlands of the great regional empires of Southwest Asia and North Africa demonstrated strong influence beyond their borders, despite their political marginalization. Though politically dwarfed by the Neo-Assyrian and Persian empires in the first millennium BCE, various groups in the Levant displayed strong cultural and economic power. Why are the Phoenicians and Judeans of the Levant called *borderland communities*? What kind of relationship did they have with the large regional empires and with other peoples of western Afro-Eurasia? How did they contribute to the cultural integration of the wider region?

kings that required the Phoenicians to pay tribute with luxury goods in return for some political autonomy. Phoenician merchants and citizens established and colonized port cities along the Mediterranean coasts and sent ships to the colonies full of goods from the east. On their return trips, they carried new goods that would meet the demands of the Assyrian elites for exotic luxuries. At precisely the same time, Greek merchants were spreading eastward and establishing colonies on the northern rim of the Mediterranean. As the two groups competed and interacted intensely, many ideas of the advanced cultures of Southwest Asia were transferred across the Mediterranean.

The Phoenicians were part of the larger Mesopotamian culture, whose shared gods, laws, units of measurement, and science all proved useful to their entrepreneurship. But the Phoenicians themselves developed a groundbreaking innova-

The Phoenician Alphabet. The first alphabet was written on clay tablets using the cuneiform script. It was developed by Phoenician traders who needed a script that was easy to learn and could represent their form of west Semitic language. This tablet was found at the port town of Ugarit (Ras Shamra) in Syria and is dated to the fourteenth century BCE.

tion that revolutionized communication and commerce between and within societies: the alphabet, first introduced in the second millennium BCE in the western Levant, where it provided a simplified record of spoken languages. Around 800 BCE, this new method of writing was transmitted to the west, probably through Greek traders who lived and worked in Phoenician centers. The alphabet made it possible for educated men to communicate directly with each other, dramatically reducing the need for the professional scribes of Western Afro-Eurasian societies.

ISRAEL AND JUDAH

To the south of the mountains of Lebanon (the homeland of the Phoenicians), in an area that extended to the borders of Egypt, lay southern Canaan, the land that would become the nations of Israel and Philistia. The origins of Israel are disputed, but ultimately unknown. According to the biblical account, the Israelites entered the land from Egypt in approximately 1400 BCE, killing all the native inhabitants. In fact, Egypt controlled southern Canaan in 1400, and there is no evidence that a new population group arrived during this period. More recently, scholars have hypothesized that the Israelites arrived in the 1200s, or that they were originally Canaanites who moved into the central hill country (the heart of biblical Israel) during the late 1200s. However they arrived, the people who would eventually call themselves Israel gradually spread outward from their base in the central hills, until by 1000 BCE they had established a kingdom under the rule of David.

Around 1100 BCE, the Sea People, possibly natives of Cyprus, arrived on the southwest coast of Canaan, where they became known as the Philistines. Though later famous as the birthplace of Judaism, a religion already taking shape in this period, around 1000 BCE Israel was just another small frontier kingdom, intermittently controlled for much of the period by the Assyrian and Persian empires. This micro-region was a borderland that became the center of yet another way of understanding the world.

Israel did not have the special status of the trader-state Phoenicia, but it did figure as one of the micro-states on the borderlands of the Assyrian system. Israel was not a source of irrepressible resistance, as were the Greek borderlands. It was in essence a hybrid society, for it merged aspects of the Mesopotamian states with its own distinctive traits—uneasily surviving on the fringes of Assyrian power. A centralized monarchy emerged under David (r. 1000–960 BCE) and his son Solomon (r. 960–931 BCE), who used their military skill and creative diplomacy to unify the local populace. The size and importance of Israel under David and Solomon are impossible to reconstruct; biblical narrative portrays heroes whose achievements were grand, but archaeological remains suggest a kingdom of more modest size and wealth.

PHŒNICIAN	ANCIENT GREEK	LATER GREEK	ROMAN

Comparative Alphabets. The forms of the letters in the Phoenician alphabet of the first millennium BCE are based on signs used to represent the Aramaic language. These Phoenican letters were then borrowed by the ancient Greeks. Our alphabet is based on that used by the Romans, who borrowed their letter forms from the later Greek inscriptions.

The kingdom founded by David proved short-lived. By 925 BCE, civil war had split the nation into the rival kingdoms of Israel in the north and Judah in the south. By the middle of the ninth century BCE, both kingdoms had come under the control of the Neo-Assyrian Empire. After successive attempts at rebellion, the northern kingdom was destroyed by the Assyrians, with much of its population dispersed throughout the Assyrian Empire. Judah, the southern kingdom, had remained loyal to Assyria, and so remained an Assyrian vassal until shortly after the fall of Nineveh in 612 BCE, when it became a vassal of Assyria's successor, Babylon. Judah, however, soon

rebelled against its new overlords, and in 587 BCE the Babylonian forces of Nebuchadrezzer destroyed Jerusalem. The Babylonians deported large numbers of Judeans from Jerusalem and other cities to exile in Babylon. Later, following the collapse of Babylon, when in 539 Persians under Cyrus the Great swept into Mesopotamia, many Judeans straggled home, where they rebuilt their ancient temple and began the process of reuniting and restoring their society in what is known as the Postexilic or Second Temple period.

The origins of the Judeans' religious beliefs are closely tied to these historical developments. What we can piece together from the Hebrew Bible (Old Testament) and archaeological evidence suggests that Israelite religion, in a period spanning well over half a millennium, underwent a tumultuous transformation: during this time, it would establish its own identity as one of the world's earliest and most enduring monotheistic religions. The early Israelites, like their neighbors, had worshipped many gods, including their national god, Yahweh. By the period of the Babylonian exile, however, they had clearly moved into a stage of monolatry, in which most people worshipped Yahweh alone, without denying the existence of other gods.

From an early period, Israelite prophets urged the people to worship only Yahweh, as well as announcing that Yahweh demanded justice, especially for the poorest members of the society. Unlike diviners who could be hired to forecast the future, the prophets whose words are recorded in the Hebrew Bible were primarily concerned with the moral well-being of the people.

The Israelites saw Yahweh as both the all-powerful creator of the universe and a personal god who expected his followers to subscribe to moral precepts, rituals, and taboos. The moral precepts at their broadest level were outlined in the Ten Commandments, which included injunctions against murder, adultery, and lying. The Bible also prescribes ritual requirements, such as not working on the seventh day of the week. These laws for proper living would be further specified and codified in the coming centuries. Ultimately, religious leaders compiled them into a set of religious scriptures and teachings known as the Torah (literally, "Law" or "Instruction"), which would become the central text of Judaism.

Through their lengthy period of oppression by and resistance to the Neo-Assyrians, which began in the ninth century BCE, and the Babylonian captivity, which ended in the sixth century BCE, Judeans did not turn away from Yahweh. Instead, they elevated his standing to that of the one true God, beside whom all others were false. Their turn toward monotheism and their striking of a covenant with Yahweh—in which he promised deliverance to them in exchange for their devotion and adherence to his "Law"—helped them to survive as a people and to establish a strong identity during this extended period of suffering.

From the practice of this small and otherwise insignificant borderland community, the idea of worshipping a single

Phoenician Inscription. This detail of a basalt slab carries an inscription written in the Phoenician alphabetic script that recounts how Eshumanazar and Amashtarte (servant of Astarte) built the temples to the gods of Sidon.

god spread over the rapidly developing Mediterranean world. Soon, one omnipotent god would take the place of the pantheons of gods in religions across much of Afro-Eurasia.

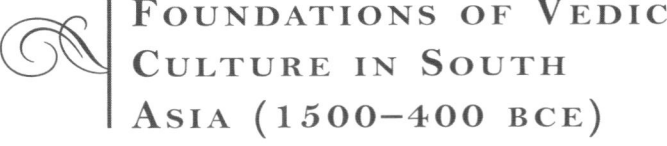

FOUNDATIONS OF VEDIC CULTURE IN SOUTH ASIA (1500–400 BCE)

> → *How did South Asia become more socially and culturally integrated despite the absence of an imperial state?*

The origins of Vedic culture in South Asia do not follow the patterns found in Southwest Asia and the Mediterranean lands, where nomads pressed on older civilizations. In Southwest Asia, nomads adapted to metropolitan ways as they created integrated states and sometimes imperial systems. The polities of Mesopotamia built on earlier cultural and technological achievements, military machinery, laws, religions, and trading networks. By contrast, rulers in the region stretching from the Indus River to the Ganges plain did not have previous polities to draw on; the earlier Harappan urban centers in the Indus River valley had been pushed into decline by floods and earthquakes and ultimately died out, vanishing several hundred years before the nomads arrived from the northwest. When nomadic charioteers (who called them-

selves Aryans), speaking their Indo-European languages, gradually entered South Asia through passes in the Hindu Kush Mountains around 1500 BCE, they neither encountered states to conquer nor were united.

Like the Persians, the new migrants lacked an urban tradition. And because the Harappan urban centers had long since disappeared, they had no existing cities to emulate. But they did bring with them many of the cultural traits that characterized Indo-European nomadic communities living on the Inner Eurasian steppe lands and in central Asia. The early Aryan settlers were herders who measured their wealth by the number of cattle they had, and cattle raids often led to conflicts. Rituals were extremely important to them; they attached great significance to the formal sacrificing of cattle, horses, and sheep to their numerous gods, gathering together at festivities to sing hymns, make animal sacrifices, burn *ghee* (clarified butter) for the gods, and share a meal. Priests conducted the ceremonies (for which they received payment in cows). Moreover, they composed rhymes, hymns, and explanatory texts called the Vedas (literally, "wisdom," "knowledge") as part of their rituals. The Vedas were initially passed on orally. Because the newcomers did not develop a writing system for at least 800 years, the Vedas became their most sacred religious works. They were eventually written down in Sanskrit, in which form they have survived into modern times. Because the Vedas became the cultural authority for these new migrants to South Asia, historians call this group of Indo-Europeans the Vedic peoples.

Although they did not find states or urban centers when they first arrived in the Indus Valley, the migrants did encounter indigenous people—a number of whom were likely the descendants of the Harappans—who lived in agricultural settlements or were herders like themselves. The migrants allied with some of the indigenous people who showed them how to live and prosper in their new environment; they made enemies of others, with whom they fought for territory and dominance. As they encountered people speaking different languages and following different cultural practices, the Vedic people held on to their own language and rituals to their gods but also absorbed local vocabulary into their language and deities into their pantheon. Accepting Vedic culture—a culture modified in the South Asian environment—was the price paid by both allies and defeated enemies who were absorbed into their society. By the middle of the first century BCE, the Vedic peoples covered all of what is now northern India, and their language and rituals had become dominant in the area.

In occupying the Indus Valley and later migrating into and settling on the Ganges plain, the newcomers mingled among local farming people, who came to adopt their rituals and their gods as well as their language. Yet while the Vedic migrants changed the social geography and culture of the region, they did not give it greater political coherence, as they did not create a single, unified regional kingdom. To the extent that this world grew more integrated, it did so because of a shared culture: its inhabitants adhered to a set of basic principles and norms inscribed in the Vedas. In contrast, political affairs brought Southwest Asian societies together by imposing political practices and institutions.

Initially, the material culture of Vedic society was very rudimentary. Even the chiefs and elite warriors enjoyed few luxuries. Early trade was based not on importing sumptuous goods but rather on obtaining horses, which could not be bred or trained in the lands newly settled by the Vedics. These former nomads still highly prized horses, and their importation from the northwest beyond the Hindu Kush—from *asvika* "the country of horses"—never ceased to be a major preoccupation of the ruling elite. It eventually drove the creation of the long-distance route across the North Indian plain that stretched from the Khyber Pass to the lower Ganges. Moreover, while engaging in the horse trade in the northwest, the Vedic people encountered the Persians, who by the end of the sixth century BCE had extended their suzerainty all the way to the upper Indus.

As the Vedic people entered the fertile river basins, they gradually settled down and gave up their roaming ways. They cultivated the land and kept herds of animals. Their turn to agriculture was made easier because from peoples to the west they had gained access to the iron plow, which was crucial for tilling the Ganges plain in the east and transforming the Deccan plateau into croplands. The word for plow (*lāngala*), however, is not Indo-European in origin. In other words, Vedic people learned agricultural practices from locals but applied them with new, more effective tools. In the drier north, they cultivated wheat, barley, millet, and cotton, while wet rice paddies filled the lowlands; farmers also produced such tropical staples as sugarcane and spices (pepper, ginger, and cinnamon). Over time, the agrarian frontier filled in, and regions that had been sparsely populated became crowded.

As farming became the dominant way of life, and urban settlements spread across the region, overland and riverine trade also blossomed. Trade between urban settlements developed as the agricultural surpluses grew. Grain was transported to towns to feed their residents; sugarcane was pressed into sugar in the cities, then sold back to people in the agricultural villages.

SPLINTERED STATES

The region's social and economic integration offered a stark contrast to its persistent political disintegration. In the process of fanning out from the Punjab, the region of the five tributaries of the Indus River, and settling along the Ganges River, the Vedic peoples created regional oligarchies and chieftainships. And as much as they fought with the indigenous peoples, they fought even more fiercely among themselves. Such aggression reinforced the importance of warriors and of Indra and Agni, the gods of war and fire respectively. As in the Mycenaean societies, the tribal societies of the Iranian plateau, and the society of Zhou China, the warriors were the elite, battling each other and the farmers for land and other resources.

Their chieftainships eventually became fragmented kingdoms, grounded in kin and clan structures. Inhabitants were bound to each other through lines of descent from a common ancestor, tracing that lineage through blood ties, marital alliances, and, in many cases, invented family affinities. The earliest Vedic society was divided into two main lineages: the Chandravamsha, or the lunar lineage, and the Suryavamsha, or the solar lineage. Each had its own creation myth, ancestors, language, and rituals. The lineages included many clans, ordered in a hierarchy determined by seniority. The Vedic people absorbed many of the clans of the indigenous people into their lineages. Clans that adopted their culture were made part of the lineage (through marriage or fictive ties) and were considered insiders; clans that had other languages and rituals were considered outsiders, beyond the pale of so-called civilized people. Roughly contemporaneous parallels to this notion of the civilized versus uncivilized could be found in Zhou China.

As much as the Vedic people fought with the indigenous peoples, they fought even more fiercely among themselves.

These lineages ceased to be the basis of the social structure with the rise of urban society and states, but they continued to live on in two major epics that recounted tales of the Vedic people: the *Mahabharata*, which relates the last phase of the lunar lineage, and the *Ramayana,* which focuses on a hero of the solar lineage. Later rulers would continue to exploit the memory of these two ancient lineages, legitimizing their regimes by claiming blood links with them.

Nomadic communities on the steppe lands of Inner Eurasia attached more importance to kinship than to landed territory. This heritage lived on in their lineage systems, in which some clans had higher status than others and senior members of a clan enjoyed higher individual status. Such individuals became the chiefs of the clans, and in the more unified Vedic regimes chiefs (*rajas*) took on the characteristics of kings, bequeathing their authority to their offspring.

The senior clan of a lineage was called *Rajanya*, meaning "the group of brilliant ones," and the lesser clans were known as *Vis. Rajanya* were protectors of the entire lineage, while *Vis* herded cattle. As the Vedic society expanded from the Punjab to the Upper Ganges, the clans of the solar lineage tended to stay together in the same geographical area. In contrast, the clans of the lunar lineage split into many branches, as some migrated east to the Ganges River valley and others south to the northern Deccan plain. Though separated by distance, the dispersed groups maintained their relationship through marriage. Within kin-bound clan structures, hierarchies and divisions established each member's location in the political and social order.

CASTES IN A STRATIFIED SOCIETY

When the Vedic peoples first spread out across South Asia, their herding societies were quite homogeneous. But as these herders settled down and created state structures, more complex and stratified arrangements became the norm. Thus, the development of settled agriculture after 1000 BCE led to an increasing discrepancy between those who controlled land and those who worked it—and the differences were represented in castes (inherited social classes) that were associated with specific lineages. Dominant clan members became Kshatriyas, who had power and controlled the land (originally the warrior caste). Meanwhile, lesser clan members became Vaishya, householders whose obligation was to work the land and tend the livestock. Moreover, as rice production expanded and labor-intensive paddy cultivation took hold, households often supplemented the family workforce by hiring laborers and using slaves. Such workers and slaves came from outside the Vedic lineages and were known as Shudras, literally "the small ones." They constituted the lowest caste.

In this way, the late Vedic social system came to consist of four strata, or castes, known as *varna*: the Kshatriyas, who controlled the land and were the ruling caste; the Vaishyas, who were agrarian commoners; and finally the Shudras, who were servants and menial laborers. The Shudras included those who had no lineage, as defined by Vedic society; they were outsiders who joined households as hired or enslaved laborers. The fourth layer was above the Kshatriyas: the priests or Brahmans, who performed rituals and communicated with gods. Some of them continued to function as priests for the chiefs and some were *rishi*, sages who chose to live as ascetics in forests, where they discussed philosophical questions with their students. Their ability to communicate with the heavens, the most coveted of skills, elevated them to the apex of the social pyramid. As communicators with the deities, ritual experts, and Vedic intellectuals, the Brahmans guided a society in which the proper relationship with the forces of nature as represented by the deities was seen as the cornerstone of prosperity. As agriculture became more and more important, Brahmans acted as agents of Agni, the god of fire, to purify the new land for cultivation.

In settling down, the Vedic people created stratified societies that bore little resemblance to those of their egalitarian, pastoral ancestors. Powerful monarchies emerged around hereditary kings (*rajas*), who ruled in conjunction with councils of elders. Kings were also aided by Brahmans, who turned the customary social sanctions and practices into formal legal codes. Much later (c. 100 BCE–100 CE), one or several sages, using the collective name of Manu (Sanskrit for "human being"), gathered these laws into a single text (see Chapter 8 for full discussion). Unlike Hammurapi's code, which was a creation of the ruler, the Laws of Manu and numerous similar documents compiled before and after it were the handiwork of Brahmans. These legal books served both to guide the king and to regulate the behavior of the king's subjects.

VEDIC WORLDS

A Vedic culture, transmitted by the Brahman caste, unified what political rivalries had divided. Belief in Indra and other gods, a common language (Sanskrit), and shared cultural symbols linked the communities dispersed across the northern half of the region and gave the Vedic peoples a collective sense of destiny. Though Sanskrit was an imported tongue, it was the language in which the Vedas were orally transmitted. The Vedas contained the sacred knowledge of the people—prayers and hymns praising gods and goddesses and fixing the rules for making sacrifices to them—and the Sanskrit language, with its beautiful rhythms and rhymes, was thus the means of passing on the people's culture.

As the priests of Vedic society, the Brahmans were responsible for memorizing every syllable and tone of the Vedic works. During the time when the Vedic people had evolved from being predominantly pastoral nomads into a society of settled agriculturists, the Brahmans had compiled numerous commentaries on the older sacred works. Before long, the Brahman priests and scholars had developed a new set of rules and rituals, which became a full-scale theology that explained their new settled, farming environment. In addition to promoting cultural unity and pride through common ritual practices and support for hereditary *raja* kingdoms, the Brahmans did not neglect the non-Sanskrit-speaking peoples, many of whose beliefs and farming practices were incorporated into the Vedas. The *Atharva Veda*, the last and latest of the four Vedas, is full of charms and remedies from indigenous traditions. Although the Vedic period of South Asian history has not left impressive buildings and artifacts, it created a wealth of thinking about cosmology and human society, thereby laying the foundations of the religion for coming generations.

The main corpus of Vedic literature includes the four Vedas: the Rig-Veda (the earliest), Yajur-Veda, Sama-Veda, and Atharva-Veda (the most recent). These foundational literatures consist of hymns recited at sacrificial rituals to the gods, as well as formulas and spells dealing with calamities and diseases. The Sanskrit-speaking people worshipped and sacrificed to a large number of gods. A strict oral tradition required every word and sound to be learned by heart so that recitations would be errorless.

Primary Source

BECOMING A BRAHMIN PRIEST

When the Vedic people became farmers, many of them started to question the validity of sacrificing cows, the draft animals valued for their use in cultivation. Around the seventh century BCE, some thinkers abandoned Vedic rituals and chose to live simply in forests as they debated the meaning of life and the structure of the universe. Those sages were Brahman rishis, highly respected priests in their society. However, not every one of the famous Brahmans was born a Brahman.

1. Satyakâma, the son of Gabâlâ, addressed his mother and said: 'I wish to become a Brahmakârin (religious student), mother. Of what family am I?'

2. She said to him: 'I do not know, my child, of what family thou art. In my youth when I had to move about much as a servant (waiting on the guests in my father's house) I conceived thee. I do not know of what family thou art. I am Gabâlâ by name, thou art Satyakâma (Philalethes). Say that thou art Satyakâma Gâbâla.'

3. He going to Gautama Hâridrumata said to him, 'I wish to become a Brahmakârin with you, Sir. May I come to you, Sir?'

4. He said to him: 'Of what family are you, my friend?' He replied: 'I do not know, Sir, of what family I am. I asked my mother, and she answered: "In my youth when I had to move about much as a servant, I conceived thee. I do not know of what family thou art. I am Gabâlâ by name, thou art Satyakâma," I am therefore Satyakâma Gâbâla, Sir.

5. He said to him: 'No one but a true Bráhmana would thus speak out. Go and fetch fuel, friend, I shall initiate you. You have not swerved from the truth.'

Having initiated him, he chose four hundred lean and weak cows, and said: 'Tend these friend.'

He drove them out and said to himself. 'I shall not return unless I bring back a thousand.' He dwelt a number of years (in the forest), and when the cows had become a thousand.

↬ *Satyakama became a well-known Brahman teacher after his study. Judging from this story, which section of the society was he from? At that time, was membership in the Brahman caste strictly exclusive?*

SOURCE: *The Upanishads,* translated by F. Max Müller, vol. 1 of *Sacred Books of the East,* edited by F. Max Müller (1900; reprint, New Delhi: Motilal Banarsidass, 1981), pp. 60–61.

During the middle of the first millennium BCE, thinkers felt that the Vedic rituals were no longer adequate for their fast-changing society; the result was a collection of works known as the Upanishads, or the supreme knowledge. The Upanishads, which take the form of dialogues between disciples and a sage, record explorations and discussions of questions of deep concern to the people of that time. Out of these conversations came a set of didactic lessons that offered insights into the fundamentals of the social order. Indeed, the social order and the religious order were fully intertwined; the term *Brahma* refers to a universe composed of the earth, the sky, and the heavenly bodies beyond the sky. In this universe, an eternal being, *atman*, exists everywhere, in the smallest creature as well as in the entire universe. In the Upanishads, the term *atman* does not name a supreme

deity. While all living creatures are destined to die, the *atman* never perishes but is reborn when it transmigrates into another life. Reincarnation was therefore a cornerstone of the late Vedic belief system. According to one philosophical school, the Vedanta (literally, "the end of the Veda"), people did not die but simply appeared in different life forms, governed by the eternal cosmic order.

These unique Vedic views of life and the universe were transmitted as principles of faith, bringing spiritual unity to the northern half of South Asia. The peoples of the Indus Valley and Ganges plain would follow a different path forward than those in the societies of Southwest Asia and North Africa. Here in this array of localized kingdoms, the common Vedic culture rather than larger-scale polities would be the unifying bond.

PROPHETS AND FOUNDING TEXTS—
COMPARING JEWISH AND VEDIC SOURCES

Reliance on sacred texts is one of the defining traits of religious movements. Writing helped make possible the transmission of beliefs from generation to generation. The stories, historical material, and parables contained in religious texts contributed to forming belief systems that have become the backbone of religious identity for many of the major faiths. In many faiths, we find one core immutable text, such as the Bible, for Jews and Christians; or the Vedas, for Hindus; or the Koran, for Muslims. In addition, we also often find supplementary texts that discuss, clarify, or expand on the ideas expressed in the core texts. In the Jewish tradition, such textual exegesis is known as *midrash*.

Like many other religions, Judaism is based on a revealed scripture, thought to have been transmitted directly from God to his prophets. These were the core works over whose interpretation rabbis argued for centuries; their discussions were passed on orally through their students. Judaism is thus built on a series of texts that include debates about the Bible by generations of scholars.

The name *Bible* was not originally used by Jews themselves; instead, a common term was *Tanakh,* an acronym derived from the Hebrew titles of the text's three major parts:

1. Torah (literally, "Instruction"). The Torah is usually referred to as the law of the Jewish people; it encompasses five books, also called the Pentateuch, whose authorship was traditionally ascribed to Moses.

2. Nevi'im (Prophets). This term is associated with texts ascribed to various prophets who preached and warned the people about how to live their lives in accordance with the law.
3. Ketuvim (Writings). It includes the Psalms and Proverbs.

According to Jewish tradition, the Tanakh consists of twenty-four books: five in the Torah, eight in the Nevi'im, and eleven in the Ketuvim. They took their canonical written form gradually, beginning with the Torah in the sixth century BCE. Determined to ensure their religion's survival and restoration in Jerusalem, priests in exile in Babylon combined and finalized writings that had begun to be recorded in the tenth century BCE. The entire canon was not closed until the first or second century CE, at a time when Jewish scholars again felt that their religion was imperiled, now by the enormous social and religious upheaval that followed the destruction of the second temple in Jerusalem by the Romans in 70 CE. The huge compilation of oral law, the Talmud, was finally written down (in two versions) around the fifth and sixth centuries BCE. Taken together, these texts express the ability of the Jewish community to adapt and persevere, turning to the written word to determine how to respond and shape their lives when historical conditions changed.

Vedic culture also had foundational texts at its core, and developed traditions for their use in religious rituals. There are four Vedic texts: the Rig-Veda, Sama-Veda, Yajur-Veda, and Atharva-Veda. The Rig-Veda, the earliest text in the

THE EARLY ZHOU EMPIRE IN EAST ASIA (1045–771 BCE)

> → *To what extent was the Zhou state similar to contemporary empires in western Afro-Eurasia in its structure and its impact on its neighbors?*

China also felt the effects of incursions from nomadic neighbors. Around the same time that western Afro-Eurasian states

and societies went through a cycle of upheaval and reconsolidation, invasion and warfare were setting the stage for a reconfiguration of the political and social map of East Asia. The Zhou initially swore allegiance to the Shang and allied with them in their fight against nomadic incursions on the western borderlands. But they eventually turned against the Shang, assembling superior military forces in the northwest and using chariots and archers to defeat them in about 1045 BCE.

According to Korean and Chinese legends, a disgruntled Shang prince refused to cede power to the Zhou when Anyang, the capital city, fell. He led remnants of the Shang garrisons east toward modern-day Pyongyang and established corpus, is a collection of hymns praising the gods, including Indra (god of war), Agni (god of fire), and Varuna (god of water). Though every major god receives attention, Indra stands out as the most powerful and important, as he is the one who set the order of the universe and made life possible. Priests would recite hymns from the Rig-Veda during sacrifices in which hundreds of cows and several horses were slaughtered and clarified butter was burned in the name of the gods. The Sama-Veda is a textbook of songs to be performed by the priest at a sacrifice; most of their stanzas had already appeared in the Rig-Veda. The Yajur-Veda is a prayer book for the priest who conducted rituals for chariot racing, horse sacrifices, or the king's coronation. The Atharva-Veda, the most recently composed of the four, includes charms and remedies for major and minor difficulties; many address problems related to agriculture, a central aspect of life.

Brahmans, the priests and intellectuals of Vedic society, composed works—the Brahmanas and Aranyakas—to explain how and when the hymns and chants of the Vedas should be recited, during the ritual performances and to elucidate the rituals' secret meanings. However, as Vedic peoples embraced settled agriculture and abandoned the lifeways of herding nomads by the middle of the first millennium BCE, some thinkers seriously doubted the validity of Vedic sacrificial rituals that were based on gods driving chariots and began to reflect on the meaning of life and the universe. Scholars then composed the Upanishads, mystic speculative works whose concepts of life and death,

time and space, geography and the cosmos laid the foundations for most, if not all, of South Asia's later schools of thought, including Buddhism and Jainism.

Vedic literature, both hymns and rules for rituals, long remained an oral tradition. Brahman masters taught their pupils to recite and remember every syllable. Even after Buddhists started to write down texts in the late first millennium BCE, Brahmans resisted the temptation to make copies of the Vedas, fearing that they would lose exclusive control of their sacred works. It is possible that sometime after the beginning of the common era, Brahmans started to copy Vedic passages onto palm leaves, which soon decay in the tropical climate of South Asia, only to aid their memory: they still considered oral teaching the most reliable. When Brahmanism was reborn as Hinduism during the first half of the first millennium CE, a host of new deities became objects of cults of worship and gave rise to new genres of Sanskrit literature, such as Puranas (stories of the past) and epics. The Vedas are still considered the final authority of Hinduism, though most Hindus find their contents incomprehensible and of little relevance to their lives.

In both Jewish and Vedic traditions, the pressures of a changing world, and especially the inability to carry out sacrificial rituals in traditional ways, created a new relationship between oral culture, texts, and interpretation. Though their old systems of religious practice were abandoned, Jewish and Vedic worshippers continued to interpret sacred texts as they made sense of their lives, passing from religions of oral tradition to those of the written word.

the first Korean kingdom. According to Sima Qian's much later but well-researched account, the son of the last Shang ruler declared his allegiance to the new Zhou ruler. In return, he received the title of the Prince of Yin and was permitted to retain nominal control of Yin, the Shang capital where he could continue to perform rituals in honor of his ancestors. In fact, he remained a thorn in the side of the Zhou regime and eventually joined a rebellion against the Zhou ruler, only to be killed in the fighting. With that victory, the Zhou consolidated their military power and also ensured their cultural supremacy over the Shang, thereby becoming the dominant kingdom in East Asia at the end of the second millennium BCE. (See Map 4-5.)

When the Zhou took over power from the Shang, China was not yet a fully integrated empire. Like Vedic South Asia, China under the Zhou dynasty was at first a decentralized polity split into regional powers; but as we will see, China's political substructure gave it more unity. The Shang dynasty had exerted control in northeastern China from its capital at Anyang or Yin. The unifying dynastic institutions that it created were emulated by the Zhou: a patrimonial state centered on ancestor worship, as the rulers' power was transmitted through genealogies (from their ancestors and, ultimately, the gods). The Zhou also continued and expanded on the Shang state's tribute system, under which allied regional leaders paid tribute to the Shang, including the provision of warriors and laborers, in

MAP 4-5 THE ZHOU DYNASTY, 2200–256 BCE

Toward the end of the second millennium BCE, the Zhou state supplanted the Shang dynasty as the most powerful political force in East Asia. Using the map above, compare and contrast the territorial reach of the Zhou state with that of the Shang. What factors account for the Zhou state's larger geographic influence? How effectively did the Zhou state control the various groups living in all of this territory? Compared to the large regional empires in western Eurasia during the first millennium, to what extent did the Zhou politically integrate the peoples of East Asia?

return for land, divinations, and protection from the incursions of nomads or other states. On such a foundation—notably absent in Vedic South Asia—an integrated and remarkably durable political structure could gradually be built. In some respects, the creation of integrated war-making regimes, more productive modes of agriculture, and common legal norms re-

sembled the Assyrian and Persian models. But China was not a crossroads for invaders, and thus the Chinese under the Zhou never faced the kinds of rivals or powerful neighbors that would eventually bring down the Assyrian and Persian states.

Able to adopt the local political organization of the Shang and spared the assaults and intrigues of rivals, the Zhou began

Zhou Chariots. After swearing allegiance to the Shang, the Zhou assembled superior military forces in the northwest, in part by emulating Shang chariots. The Zhou subsequently used their own chariots and archers to defeat the Shang in about 1045 BCE. The regional lords who owed allegiance to the Zhou king distinguished themselves in the aristocratic hierarchy by using chariots for travel and battle.

the extended process of integration that formed "China proper" in East Asia. Bit by bit, without a decisive conquest, regional aristocracies joined into a hierarchical system under a single ruler. It was a balancing act between a dynastic central ruler and powerful local lords, however. Using cultural symbols and the art of statecraft rather than religion, the Zhou peoples in the north established a single dynasty, one with broad geographic influence but with limited power over its regional states. This was integration, but not quite unification.

ZHOU SUCCESSION AND POLITICAL FOUNDATIONS

The rise of the northwestern neighboring state of the Zhou and the demise of the Shang distinguished Chinese political successions from western Afro-Eurasia's conquest model of outsiders taking power. Emerging from west of the Shang heartland in the valley of the Wei River, which flowed into the Yellow River as it entered the North China plain, the Zhou

may have had ties to the bronze-producing peoples in the northwest who had preceded the Shang. For many years, the Zhou and Shang peoples lived side by side, westerners and easterners trading and interacting. Indeed, as noted above, they often allied to fend off raiders from the far west. Though initially less advanced in writing and technology than the Shang, the Zhou learned and borrowed from them. And when the Zhou became strong enough, they overcame the Shang.

The Zhou rulers sought to legitimize their takeover of Shang wealth and territories by claiming moral superiority. The rich array of textual and material evidence uncovered from this period indicates that a powerful ruler, commanding wide cultural respect and political loyalty, established Zhou control in northwestern China and also expanded north toward what is now Beijing and southward toward the Yangzi River valley. Under the Shang, the regional lords had been princes of preexisting states who gave their allegiance to the Shang ruler; now the Zhou ruler held the allegiance both of the lords of older states and of new lords whom he installed in new states in the east and north that had been annexed and colonized over time. Rewarding his relatives and key followers with lands that they could pass on to their descendents was an important means of exerting control over strategic areas. Often, the new colonies consisted of a garrison town (containing what they called the "people of the state," or the Zhou colonizers) surrounded by fields containing the local inhabitants (the "people of the field," or the farmers). As under the Shang, Zhou regional lords were required to supply military forces as needed, to pay tribute, and to appear at the imperial court to pledge their continuing allegiance to the king.

THE ZHOU "MANDATE OF HEAVEN" AND THE LEGITIMATION OF POWER

To establish their superiority over the vanquished Shang and their theocratic state, the Zhou dynasts elaborated an ideology to support a morally correct transfer of power, which they called the "mandate of heaven." At first the mandate of heaven (*tianming*) was a religiously based compact between the Zhou people and their supreme god in heaven, known as *tian* (literally, the "sky god"), but it evolved in the first millennium BCE into a fundamental Chinese political doctrine. The Zhou argued that since worldly affairs were supposed to align with those of the heavens, heavenly powers conferred legitimate rights to rule on their chosen representative. The ruler was then duty-bound to uphold heaven's principles of harmony and honor. Any ruler who lapsed from this duty, who let instability creep into earthly affairs, or who let his people suffer would lose his "mandate." In this conception of politics, it was the prerogative of spiritual authority to withdraw support from wayward dynasts and find another, more worthy agent. Thus the Zhou sky god legitimated regime change.

Primary Source

ZHOU SUCCESSION STORY

The early Zhou dynasty is often glamorized in Chinese lore as an era of sage rulers such as King Wu and the Duke of Zhou. The Shangshu (Book of History) account, however, shows that the transition of power from the founder King Wu to the Duke of Zhou was fraught with difficulty, as was often the case in early states. It reveals how the Duke of Zhou tried simultaneously to protect his reputation as regent to King Wu's young son and to preserve Zhou rule. This document also represents one of the first major efforts in Chinese history to provide a historical narrative of events.

After he had completed the conquest of the Shang people, in the second year, King Wu fell ill and was despondent. The two lords, the duke of Shao and Tai-kung Wang, said, "For the king's sake let us solemnly consult the tortoise oracle." But the duke of Chou [King Wu's younger brother, named Tan] said, "We must not distress the ancestors, the former kings?"

The duke of Chou then offered himself to the ancestors, constructing three altars within a single compound. Fashioning one altar on the southern side facing north, he took his place there, holding a jade disc and grasping a baton of jade. Then he made this announcement to the Great King, to King Chi, and to King Wen, his great grandfather, grandfather, and father, and the scribe copied down the words of his prayer on tablets:

"Your chief descendant So-and-so [King Wu's personal name is tabooed] has met with a fearful disease and is violently ill. If you three kings are obliged to render to Heaven the life of an illustrious son, then substitute me, Tan, for So-and-so's person. I am good and compliant, clever and capable. I have much talent and much skill and can serve the spirits. Your chief descendant has not as much talent and skill as I and cannot serve the spirits! . . . "

Then he divined with three tortoises, and all were auspicious. He opened the bamboo receptacles and consulted the documents, and they too indicated an auspicious answer. The duke of Chou said to the king, "According to the indications of the oracle, you will suffer no harm."

[The king said,] "I, the little child, have obtained a new life from the three kings. I shall plan for a distant end. I hope that they will think of me, the solitary man."

After the duke of Chou returned, he placed the tablets containing the prayer in a metal-bound casket. The next day the king began to recover.

[Later, King Wu died and was succeeded by his infant son, King Ch'eng. The duke of Chou acted as regent and was slandered by King Wu's younger brothers, whom he was eventually forced to punish.]

In the autumn, when a plentiful crop had ripened but had not yet been harvested, Heaven sent great thunder and lightning accompanied by wind. The grain was completely flattened and even large trees were uprooted. The people of the land were in great fear. The king and his high ministers donned their ceremonial caps and opened the documents of the metal-bound casket and thus discovered the record of how the duke of Chou had offered himself as a substitute for King Wu. The two lords and the king then questioned the scribe and the various other functionaries, and they replied, "Yes, it is true, But his lordship forbade us to speak about it."

The king grasped the document and wept. "There is no need for us to make solemn divination about what has happened," he said. "In former times the duke of Chou toiled diligently for the royal house, but I, the youthful one, had no way of knowing it. Now Heaven has displayed its terror in order to make clear the virtue of the duke of Chou. I, the little child, will go in person to greet him, for the rites of our royal house approve such action."

When the king came out to the suburbs to meet the duke of Chou, Heaven sent down rain and reversed the wind, so that the grain all stood up once more. The two lords ordered the people of the land to right all the large trees that had been blown over and to earth them up. Then the year was plentiful. (*Chin t'eng.*)

→ *Why was the Duke of Zhou [Chou] willing to die in place of his older brother, King Wu? Why did King Wu's son and successor suspect that his uncle, the Duke of Zhou, coveted the throne himself? What do the direct speeches tell us about the place of religion and divination in Zhou politics?*

SOURCE: Translated in Burton Watson, *Early Chinese Literature* (New York: Columbia University Press, 1962), pp. 35–36.

In using this creed to justify their overthrow of the Shang, the Zhou rulers had to acknowledge that any group of rulers, themselves included, could be ousted as illegitimate if they lost the mandate of heaven because of their illicit and improper practices. By breaking the Shang line of succession in the eleventh century BCE, the Zhou made the full-scale deification of rulers problematic. Henceforth, dynastic legitimacy depended on ruling in accordance with the principles of good governance and upright behavior. China's rulers, unlike the theocracies of Southwest Asia and the later emperor system of Japan, created political and ideological tools that favored a secular empire based more on politics, military power, and morality than on religious legitimacy.

The early Zhou kings contended that heaven had favored their triumph over "all under heaven" (*tianxia*) because the last Shang kings had been evil men whose policies had brought pain to the people. Thereafter, the mandate became a political tool. The mandate of heaven was a compelling way to defend continuity of political structures, if not rulers, in the name of preserving a natural order. It helps explain why the break from the Zhou to the Shang did not result in an abrupt overhaul of political and cultural institutions.

The Shang had employed writing to communicate with the divine world, and the Zhou continued this practice. But the Zhou also expanded the use of writing, recording matters from royal divinations (omens, predictions, and questions for the gods) to a variety of political practices, such as kingly speeches, grants of official offices, and rewards that we can tie directly to the early Zhou state. Other texts—notably the *Zhouli* (*Rituals of Zhou*), which described the organization and administration of government, and the *Yi Li* (*On Ceremonies and Rituals*)—were said to have been prepared by the Duke of Zhou but were actually from a much later period. They thus cannot be taken as proof of how effectively the Zhou used writing to legitimate their power by providing a basis for government and a guide to behavior.

When King Mu (r. 956–918 BCE) put in place a more formal system of bureaucratic governance, restructuring the court and military by appointing officials, supervisors, and military captains who were not related to him and instituting

Zhou Wine Vessel and Sword. Under the Zhou, bronze metallurgy depended on a large labor force. Many workers initially came from Shang labor groups, who were superior to the Zhou in technology. The use of bronze, such as for this wine vessel and sword, exemplified dynastic continuity between the Shang and Zhou.

a formal legal code, writing became even more essential: bureaucratic records, including archives of appointments and legal verdicts, had to be kept. Increasingly, a pool of scribes and scholars joined the entourage of royal diviners, using their mastery of writing to find patrons at court and among regional powers. Using powerful rhetoric, they tied many of the new changes to the early Zhou founding myth.

One of the duties and privileges of the king was to create a royal calendar, which defined times for undertaking agricultural activities and celebrating rituals. The calendar also served as an impartial gauge of the ruler's success or failure. Anomalies such as unpredicted solar eclipses or natural calamities threw into question the ruling house's authority. Since they claimed that their authority was derived from heaven, the Zhou rulers believed it important to gain accurate knowledge of the stars and to perfect the astronomical system on which the calendar was based. By creating a calendar that improved on the Shang's version, they enhanced their public legitimacy. Advances in astronomy and mathematics enabled Zhou astronomers to precisely calculate the length of a lunar month (29.53 days) and measure the length of the solar year (365.25 days). But a year of twelve lunar months is 354.36 days long; to resolve the discrepancy, the Zhou occasionally inserted a leap month. Scribes dated the reigns of kings by days and years within a repeating sixty-year cycle, which was said to match the cosmological interaction between heaven and earth.

Zhou legitimacy also derived indirectly from Shang material culture—that is, from the use of bronze ritual vessels, statues, ornaments, and weapons. The Zhou emulated the Shang's large-scale production of ceremonial bronzes, which they employed in announcements of official appointments, gift-giving, and rituals. The Zhou's extensive bronze metalworking depended on a large force of tribute labor. Many of its members were Shang, who long maintained their superiority to the Zhou in technology, written language, and sociopolitical organization, if not on the battlefield. These Shang craftworkers were sometimes forcibly transported to new Zhou towns to produce the bronze ritual objects.

Such continuity was not merely an uncritical clinging to old ways. The Zhou revered their predecessors and devised elaborate rituals to underscore the importance of inheritance and thereby justify their power. Ancestor worship was a critical component of political life, which celebrated the resilient influence of the past on the present.

SOCIAL STRUCTURE AND ECONOMIC TRANSFORMATION

Accompanying the consolidation of an integrated order was greater social differentiation within Chinese society. Directly under the Zhou ruler and his royal ministers were the hereditary nobles, divided into five ranks (*gong, hou, bo, zi,* and

Zhou Cooking Vessel. Zhou bronze workers began by using Shang decorative designs, such as those that highlighted dragon and animal motifs.

nan, somewhat but not exactly equivalent to the later English titles duke, marquis, earl, viscount, and baron, respectively). These regional lords had landholdings of different sizes, with the largest being held by overlords or dukes. They all owed allegiance to the Zhou king, and they supplied warriors to fight in the king's army and laborers to clear land, drain fields, and do other work as needed. They periodically appeared at court and took part in complex rituals to reaffirm their allegiance to the king. Below the regional lords were a number of high officers at the Zhou court, as well as ministers and administrators who were supposed to supervise the work of the people. A military caste, the *shi,* consisted of aristocratic warriors at the bottom of the noble hierarchy during the first centuries of Zhou rule.

Initially, most of the population worked as farmers on fields owned by great landholding families. Some commoners were artisans, such as those who produced valuable bronze vessels used in rituals, or weavers who spun delicate silk textiles. Over time, according to contemporary accounts, an elaborate ladder of occupational strata appeared, dividing people by function into landholders who produced grain, growers of plants and fruit trees, woodsmen, breeders of cattle and chickens, artisans, merchants, weavers, servants, and those with no fixed occupation. These same sources claimed that this system was held together by the central government, which supposedly controlled how each group did its work—for example, telling landholders what crops to plant, when to harvest, and when to irrigate their lands. To be sure, these efforts to burnish the Zhou's image as a well-organized state by applauding its success as China's integrator overstated the true reach of the early government. Still, the Chinese state played a major role in pulling the region and its diverse peoples together in ways attempted by none of Eurasia's other great regimes.

One of the important methods of integration was the political and legal use of family structures. In their patrilineal society, the Zhou perpetuated an elite organized around kinship principles, which established strict hierarchies for both men and women. The filial son who honored his parents was celebrated in both art and literature. Men and women played out different roles in family and ceremonial life. On landholdings, men farmed and hunted, while women produced silk and other textiles and made them into clothing. Wealth increasingly trumped gender and class distinctions, however. In particular, rich women who were highly placed in the Zhou aristocracy were likely to be permitted a greater range of actions than others of their sex. Wealthy merchants in emerging cities challenged the hegemony of local lords.

What has been remarkable about China throughout history is how its integration progressed in small steps, not in a single, triumphal bound. Zhou achievements likewise were incremental, rooted in a transformation of the countryside. Both princes and peasants began the process of expanding

Shang-Zhou Axe Head. The Zhou dynasty was one of the first empires in the first millennium BCE that expanded its territory by relying on new weaponry, in addition to monopolizing trade and creating new institutions. The Shang-Zhou axe head shown here represents the important role that bronze weaponry played in the invasions and warfare that set the stage for reconfiguring the political and social map of East Asia after 1045 BCE.

the agrarian frontier inland. Wooden and, much later, iron plows enabled farmers to break the hard sod of lands beyond the river basins, and in due course cultivators learned the practice of field rotation to prevent the nutrients in their soils from being exhausted. A great advance occurred in the middle of the first millennium BCE as regional states organized local efforts to regulate the flow of the main rivers. They built long canals to promote communication and trade, and dug impressive irrigation networks to convert arid lands into fertile belts. Some of these systems remain in use today. A slow-motion agrarian revolution enabled the Chinese population to soar—reaching perhaps 20 million by the late Zhou era. Thus already this region was arguably the world's most densely populated.

Over the course of the first millennium BCE, under the Zhou dynasty, landowners and rulers organized the construction of dikes and irrigation systems to control the floodplain of the Yellow River. They particularly concentrated their efforts in the Wei River valley surrounding the Zhou capital at Chang'an (present-day Xi'an), transforming it into a fertile area for the cultivation of crops. For centuries, peasants labored over the floodplain of the Yellow River and its tributaries—building dikes, digging canals, and raising levees as the river flowed to its destination in the sea. When their work was done, the bottom of the floodplain looked like a latticework of rich, well-watered fields, with carefully manicured terraces rising in gradual steps to higher ground. This enormous undertaking was the work of many, many generations. Eventually, irrigation works grew to such a scale that they could be managed only by powerful territorial rulers, the Zhou dynasts centered in the Wei River valley, and by their skilled engineers. The engineers also designed canals that connected rivers and facilitated commerce and internal exchanges. Such canals were dug by tens of thousands of corvée workers, paying their tribute to the state in the form of labor. Other dynasties in Afro-Eurasia similarly provided the resources for massive building works. We have seen in Chapters 2 and 3 how both Egypt and Mesopotamia depended on the labor of thousands to tame the Nile and the Tigris and Euphrates rivers so that their peoples might survive and flourish.

Increasingly, the canals linked China's two breadbaskets: the fields of wheat and millet in the north and the rice fields in the south. The Yangzi River in the south, which also fell under the dynasty's reach, was likewise controlled by engineers. So wealthy was China that its influence was even starting to be felt in the distant steppe lands to the north and west. Nomads living on the edge of Zhou frontiers or in mountainous areas within the Zhou lands, who often engaged in conflict with the Zhou ruler and his regional lords, were now becoming dependent on their trade with the fertile heartlands. In return for the pastoral produce they provided to the Zhou, they received textiles, metal tools and weapons, and luxury items.

LIMITS AND DECLINE OF ZHOU POWER

At its center, the Zhou state had great influence, but its power outside its immediate domains was limited. The rulers' control of their allies in the Yellow River should not be exaggerated. The Zhou state was powerful, but unlike Assyria and Persia it never evolved into a superpower. The dynasty relied instead on culture (its bronzes) and statecraft (the mandate of heaven) to maintain its leadership role among competing powers and lesser principalities. Rather than having absolute control of an empire, the Zhou state was first among many regional economic and political allies.

The Zhou dynasty ruled over a much larger expanse than did the Shang dynasty, but its government displayed little increase in centralization. It relied on local authorities—the regional lords, who in this regard resembled Persian satraps—to hold provinces in line. Military campaigns continued to be fought by the Zhou rulers seeking to expand into new lands or to maintain their holdings when attacked by enemy peoples (often labeled "barbarians," simply because they were not part of the Zhou state). Rulers attempted to keep neighbors and allies in line by giving them power, by protecting them from others' aggression (especially the repeated incursions from the steppe lands), and by the tried-and-true method of intermarriage between Zhou dynastic family members and local nobles. The Zhou's subordinates had more than autonomy; they had genuine resources that they could turn against dynasts at opportune moments.

The power of the Zhou royal house over its regional lords declined in the ninth and eighth centuries BCE. In response, the Zhou court at its impressive capital at Chang'an introduced ritual reforms. The earlier Zhou family rituals that had focused on small sets of ritual bronzes were replaced by grandiose ceremonies performed by specialists employing large bronze vessels, newly standardized. Yet this assertion of centralized control of rituals and of bronze metalworking did nothing to address the regime's growing political weakness in dealing with its steppe neighbors and internal regional lords. For the most part, the Zhou court became a theater state, hoping that impressive rituals would conceal its lack of military might.

The facade began to crumble as wars, their attendant social dislocations, and changes in landholding shook the system's social and political foundations. The Zhou dynasts managed to cling to their authority over their vast domains until 771 BCE, when northern steppe invaders forced the Zhou to flee their western capital at Chang'an. The Zhou dynastic period, like the Shang, was later idealized by historians such as Sima Qian. He portrayed this period as a golden age of wise kings and sage officials. Even more than the Shang, the Zhou model of government, culture, and society became the standard for later generations. As a result, a tradition emerged in China of upholding political continuity and social stability; the regime's fundamental legitimacy was seen as resting on the moral bonds between ruling families, who were at the top of a carefully managed social pyramid, and those in the orderly layers beneath them. Though the Mesopotamian and Persian superpowers were capable of greater expansion during this period, China was sowing the seeds of a more durable state.

CONCLUSION

Upheavals in the territorial states of Afro-Eurasia led to the emergence of more extensive political powers—in Egypt, Mesopotamia, and China—during the first half of the first millennium BCE. For a total of seven centuries, both the Assyrian Empire based in Mesopotamia and the Persian Empire based in Iran stood as superpowers whose reach continued to grow. These first empires pioneered ways of expanding territorial states beyond their "ethnic" or linguistic

Chronology

	1100 BCE	1000 BCE	900 BCE
SOUTHWEST ASIA AND NORTH AFRICA			∎ *Neo-Assyrian Empire, 950–612 BCE*
THE MEDITERRANEAN			
SOUTH ASIA		∎ *Vedic migrations* ∎ *Development of settled agriculture after 1000 BCE* ∎ *Emergence of caste system after 1000 BCE*	
EAST ASIA	∎ *Zhou state, 1045–771 BCE (Western Zhou)*		

homelands, and eventually provided means for parts of Afro-Eurasia to intensify their interactions and exchanges. Driving these changes were the incursions of nomadic people, new weaponry, trade, and new administrative strategies and institutions.

The Assyrian and Persian empires marked a new stage in the history of the world's polities. Despite the numerous borrowings by their rulers, they differed fundamentally from the previous city-states and territorial states that had flourished in this area earlier. Assyrians and Persians created ideologies, political institutions, economic ties, and cultural ways that facilitated their unceasing territorial expansion across very large regions. They also established more forceful control over outlying regions than their predecessors had achieved; their strong imperial institutions permitted the systematic exploitation of the human and material resources at great distances from the imperial centers.

We should not treat the Assyrian and Persian empires as models of durable integration, however. In this regard they differed from the gradual and sustained evolution of cultural continuity in South Asia or the slow development of dynastic statecraft in China. For all their majesty and power, these first empires tended to be highly unstable, because they created enormous concentrations of power and ruthlessly extracted resources from local populations. The study of world history suggests that the rise of empires can follow distinct trajectories. In the most common, illustrated by Assyria and Persia, an initial period of expansion is followed by a radical administrative restructuring of institutions in order to further territorial expansion and consolidate control over dispersed dominions. Next, the polities undergo a period of decline, occasioned by problems within the core of the regime that are aggravated by external shocks. As time passes, what is remembered is an age of imperial grandeur.

The empires of Assyria and Persia had distinctive features, but they shared core ideological and institutional characteristics. A single absolute ruler, claiming legitimacy from a supreme divine being, lay at the heart of their imperial ideologies. Both saw the link between the god and the ruler as unique and irrevocable; the ruler maintained imperial order to secure cosmic well-being, a task mandated by the god. These imperial enterprises were founded on moral imperatives: both the ruler and his subjects deemed the state's success to be an unmitigated good, and resistance to empire to be always bad.

But there were other models of expansion that did not yield political empires—at least at first. Core beliefs and principles did not everywhere encourage political integration. In the Vedic world of the Indus Valley and Ganges plain, commonality of values and revered texts did not lead even to a single state. The unparalleled degree of integration across northern South Asia was cultural and economic rather than political. Centuries would pass before a regime would layer a state over this shared cultural world.

In China as well, a core of cultural and political beliefs developed. As in Persia and the Indus Valley and Ganges plain, shared ideas and values circulated across a wide geographic area. But unlike in Vedic South Asia, a powerful political system emerged in China when the Zhou dynasts sought to integrate their empire. It could not last, however; although the Zhou transformed China in many ways, they could not overcome the power of local nobles or fully protect the western frontier from nomadic predators—and thus the regime could never command military and fiscal powers as great as those that characterized the empires of southwestern Afro-Eurasia. But Zhou efforts had the longer-term consequence of establishing the foundations of a political and ruling culture that would serve the ambitions of later imperial dynasts.

Empire building was not occurring around the globe at this time. Indeed, the vast majority of the world's people lived in smaller polities. Sub-Saharan Africa and the Americas—which were worlds apart from the first empires of Afro-Eurasia—aside, those expanding empires left many Afro-Eurasian areas completely untouched. Nor did the might of Assyria and

800 BCE	700 BCE	600 BCE	500 BCE
			▮ *Persian Empire, 550–479* BCE
▮ *Phoenician colonization, 8th and 7th centuries* BCE			
	Greek colonization ▮	*Greek/Persian battles, 499–480* BCE ▮	

Persia necessarily crush all who came into contact with imperial rulers, soldiers, and traders; the nomadic peoples who lived in the northern steppes and in southern desert locations throughout the Afro-Eurasian landmass continued to enjoy their autonomy.

Significant political developments were taking place among peoples living in Vedic Indus Valley and Ganges plain, the river valleys of China, and around the eastern Mediterranean shore. Here, men and women developed their own sophisticated state structures in relative isolation from Assyria and Persia. The new state structures of China, Vedic South Asia, and the Mediterranean did not leave as many impressive monuments as did the Assyrian and Persian empires. But they promoted the agrarian revolutions in China and Vedic South Asia and the precocious commercial life of the Mediterranean, which served to make their worlds more integrated.

The peoples living on the eastern Mediterranean shore, in the Vedic society in South Asia, and in the Zhou kingdom in China made distinctive and enduring contributions to the cultural and religious history of humanity. A budding monotheism sprouted from the land of Judah, the concept of cyclic universal time in the form of rebirth or reincarnation developed in late Vedic South Asia, and an ideal of statecraft and social order took shape in late Zhou China. All evolved into powerful cultural forms that in time spread their influences well beyond their sites of origin.

Thus, in the first millennium BCE a crucial transformation occurred. Even as Assyrians and Persians were erecting monuments to political centralization, southwestern Asia clearly was becoming less central to world history. Up to the first millennium BCE, much of recorded human history was concentrated in Mesopotamia and its environs. But by the close of the first millennium BCE, many other, fully independent sources of writing, science, and legal and spiritual thought had emerged, based near the Yellow River and in the Ganges plain, and scattered over the hills of Judah and the Greek islands of the eastern Mediterranean. We thus can see the ongoing tension within and between worlds as they came together, while also standing apart. Moreover, the Afro-Eurasian world was breaking out of a very long cycle in which urban culture was synonymous with a couple of great river systems in Mesopotamia and Egypt. As the next chapter shows, small-scale but innovative places of human discovery were proliferating around the globe.

STUDY QUESTIONS

 WWNORTON.COM/STUDYSPACE

1. Explain how migrating populations paved the way for greater cultural integration across Afro-Eurasia after 1200 BCE. Where did migrants come from, and where did they invade?

2. Analyze the extent to which political integration in the form of regional empires led to cultural integration in western Afro-Eurasia in the first millennium BCE. What other factors contributed to cultural convergence?

3. Compare and contrast the statecraft of the Neo-Assyrian and Persian empires. How did each strive to integrate their multicultural realms?

4. Analyze the role of the peripheral societies in the Aegean and Levant in western Afro-Eurasia during the first millennium BCE. How did they contribute to cultural integration and expansion during this time?

5. Explain the role of clans and castes in Vedic society in South Asia during the first millennium BCE. To what extent did these social institutions sustain a culturally integrated and distinct world in the absence of political unity?

6. Compare and contrast the Zhou state to the regional empires in western Afro-Eurasia in the second millennium BCE. What legacies did each leave to their respective regions?

7. Compare and contrast the process of regional integration in East Asia, South Asia, and western Afro-Eurasia. What primary agents encouraged these processes in each region? How important to regional integration was the role played by states?

FURTHER READINGS

Ahlström, Gosta W., *The History of Ancient Palestine from the Paleolithic Period to Alexander's Conquests* (1993). An excellent survey of the history of the region by a renowned expert, with good attention to the recent archaeological evidence.

Allen, J. P., *Middle Egyptian: An Introduction to the Language and Culture of Hieroglyphs* (2000). An introduction to the system of writing and its use in Ancient Egypt.

Arnold, Dieter, *Building in Ancient Egypt: Pharaonic Stone Masonry* (1996). Details the complex construction of monumental stone architecture in ancient Egypt.

Aubet, Maria Eugenia, *The Phoenicians and the West*, 2nd ed. (2001). The basic survey of the Phoenician colonization of the western Mediterranean and Atlantic, with special attention to recent archaeological discoveries.

Baines, John, and Jaromir Málek, *Atlas of Ancient Egypt* (1980). A useful compilation of information on ancient Egyptian society, religion, history, and geography.

Briant, Pierre, *From Cyrus to Alexander: A History of the Persian Empire*, trans. Peter T. Daniels (2002). A complex and comprehensive history of the Persian Empire by its finest modern scholar.

Bright, John, *A History of Israel,* 4th ed. (2000). An updated version of a classic and still very useful overview of the whole history of the Israelite people down to the end of the period covered in this chapter.

Cook, J. M., *The Persian Empire* (1983). An older but still useful, and highly readable, standard history of the Persian Empire.

Falkenhausen, Lothar von, *Chinese Society in the Age of Confucius (1000–250 BC): The Archaeological Evidence* (2006). A timely reassessment of early Chinese history that compares the literary texts on which it has traditionally been based to the new archaeological evidence.

Frankfort, Henri, *Ancient Egyptian Religion* (1948). A classic study of Egyptian religion and culture during the pharaonic period.

Frye, Richard N., *The Heritage of Persia* (1963). This classic study of ancient Iran gives the political and literary history of the Persians and their successors.

Grayson, A. K., "Assyrian Civilization," in *Cambridge Ancient History,* vol. 3, pt. 2, pp. 194–228. The Assyrian and Babylonian empires and other states of the Near East, from the eighth to the sixth centuries BCE.

Isserlin, Benedikt J., *The Israelites* (1998). A very well-written and heavily illustrated history of all aspects of life in the regions of the Levant inhabited by the Israelites, equally good on the latest scholarship and the archaeological data.

Kemp, Barry J., *Ancient Egypt: Anatomy of a Civilization* (1989). A definitive presentation of the history, culture, and religion of ancient Egypt.

Lancel, Serge, *Carthage: A History*, trans. Antonia Nevill (1997). By far the best single-volume history of the most important Phoenician colony in the Mediterranean (the first three chapters are especially relevant to materials covered in this chapter).

Lemche, Niels Peter, *Ancient Israel: A New History of Israelite Society* (1988). A quick, readable, and still up-to-date summary of the main phases and themes.

Lewis, Mark Edward, *Writing and Authority in Early China* (1999). A work that traces the changing uses of writing to command assent and obedience in early China.

Markoe, Glenn E., *Phoenicians* (2000). A thorough survey of the Phoenicians and their society as it first developed in the Levant and then expanded over the Mediterranean, with excellent illustrations of the diverse archaeological sites.

Matthews, Victor H., and Don C. Benjamin, *Social World of Ancient Israel, 1350–587 BCE* (1993). A thematic overview of the main occupational groups and social roles that characterized ancient Israelite society.

Oates, Joan and David, *Nimrud: An Assyrian Imperial City Revealed* (2001). A fine and highly readable summary of the state of our knowledge of the Assyrian Empire from the perspective of the early capital of Assurnasirpal II.

Oded, Bustenay, *Mass Deportations and Deportees in the Neo-Assyrian Empire* (1979). A detailed textual examination of the deportation strategy of the Assyrian kings. Good for in-depth research of the question.

Potts, D. T., *The Archaeology of Elam: Formation and Transformation of an Ancient Iranian State* (1999). The definitive study of the archaeology of western Iran from the Neolithic period through the Persian Empire.

Quirke, Stephen, *Ancient Egyptian Religion* (1992). A highly readable presentation of ancient Egyptian religion that summarizes the roles and attributions of the many Egyptian gods.

Robins, Gay, *The Art of Ancient Egypt* (1997). The most comprehensive survey to date of the art of pharaonic Egypt.

———, *Women in Ancient Egypt* (1993). Interesting survey of the place of women in ancient Egyptian society.

Romer, John, *Ancient Lives: Daily Life in Egypt of the Pharaohs* (1990). A discussion of the economic and social lives of everyday ancient Egyptians.

Shaughnessy, Edward L., *Sources of Western Zhou History: Inscribed Bronze Vessels* (1992). Detailed work on the historiography and interpretation of the thousands of ritual bronze vessels discovered by China's archaeologists.

Simpson, W. K. (ed.), *The Literature of Ancient Egypt: An Anthology of Stories, Instructions, and Poetry* (1972). Compilation of the most important works of literature from ancient Egypt.

Thapar, Romila, *From Lineage to State* (1984). The only book on early India that uses religious literature historically and analyzes major lineages to reveal the transition from tribal society to state institutions.

Tubb, Jonathan N., *Canaanites* (1998). The best recent survey, well illustrated, of one of the main ethnic groups dominating the culture of the Levant.

Wilson, John A., *The Culture of Ancient Egypt* (1951). A classic study of the history and culture of pharaonic Egypt.

Chapter

5

WORLDS TURNED INSIDE OUT, 1000–350 BCE

The sixth century BCE was an age of violent conflicts. Regional lords attacked other regional lords; communities fought neighbors. The struggle for power and territory gripped societies from China to Africa. In the midst of this mayhem, Master Kong Fuzi of China gathered his disciples and instructed them on how best to govern, saying: "Guide them by edicts, keep them in line with punishments, and the people will stay out of trouble but will have no sense of shame. Guide them by virtue, keep them in line with the rites, and they will, besides having a sense of shame, reform themselves" (Confucius, *The Analects*, II, 3). Master Kong, better known to us by his Latinized name, Confucius (c. 551–479 BCE), represented a new breed of highly influential leaders—teachers and thinkers, not nobles, kings, warriors, or priests—who relied on words and ideas to persuade and mobilize large numbers of people. They sought to instruct rulers on how to govern in an orderly and just way, and tried to teach ordinary individuals how to live an ethical life. Instead of fighting wars of conquest, they conducted wars of ideas. In doing so, they began to integrate regional worlds with

183

shared identities and beliefs, not just institutions or rulers. In this process, regional cultures distinguished themselves from others—so as regions grew more integrated, they also became more self-conscious of their difference from other regions.

How did teachers and prophets reshape the world? As paradoxical as it might seem, thinkers emerged from a world in which unremitting warfare fostered first political conflict and then large-scale integration. China's Eastern Zhou king had no real power—his primary function was to enact rituals and lead ceremonies. Genuine power was wielded by regional lords, who took what they wanted, paying only lip service to morality or the welfare of the common people. Many of them made sacred covenants that they broke at a whim, willing to bribe, to betray, and to kill anyone (including relatives) who got in their way or displeased them. Armed conflict was endemic, and the common people saw the land they farmed pillaged during times of both war and peace. As the states fought for territory and competed for economic resources, the larger states often annexed their smaller neighbors. Warfare shook up societies. Nobles among the ranks of the defeated—like Confucius himself—fell to the bottom of the aristocratic hierarchy, while upward mobility proved a boon to many commoners. As the bonds of servitude that had tied them to their local lords were broken, the former peasants became independent, taxpaying farmers whose sons served in the vast infantries of their regional lords. A new political and social order was emerging; in many parts of the world, societies were being turned inside out.

> *Thinkers emerged from a world in which unremitting warfare fostered first political conflict and then large-scale integration.*

A teacher and an aspiring official (he hoped to attain an appointment as a minister to a regional lord), Confucius wanted to end the chaos of the times and restore order by promoting education, moral behavior, and the performance of ritual. He thought that cooperation rather than conflict, ethical behavior rather than reckless actions, merit rather than heredity, and concern with the welfare of the others rather than self-aggrandizement should be the basis of society and government. The good life was, in effect, an ethical one, pursued to protect the welfare of the family and society. This was an age in which great sages—philosophers and teachers in a range of societies—expressed many similar concerns as they explored what it meant to live an ethical life. For example, in the Greek city-state of Athens, Socrates not only questioned the political order but also challenged people to justify what they claimed to know. Rather than accepting the status quo, he called on individuals to reform their own moral world by constantly examining their lives and their values. These new ideas were the product of a turbulent world; but by providing new ways of viewing the world, they were intended to lead societies out of that turbulence. Beginning in this age, philosophers would change humanity, not immediately, of course, but forever. This chapter is about how an age of political turmoil in many places of the world was also an era of great intellectual and cultural creativity. From this ferment emerged a new global cultural geography of regions from Mesoamerica to China that developed shared notions and beliefs and became more aware of the differences between themselves and others.

Focus Questions WORLDS TURNED INSIDE OUT

→ *How did "second-generation" cultures expand the social, political, and cultural options available to men and women?*

→ *In what ways did scholars propose ending the incessant warfare and chaos of China's Spring and Autumn and Warring States periods?*

→ *How did political and social transformations encourage new beliefs and dissident thinkers in South Asia?*

→ *How did cultural integration develop in the Andes and Mesoamerica in the absence of political unity?*

→ *How did the spread of iron smelting shape the social landscape of sub-Saharan Africa?*

→ *In what ways did city-states integrate the geographically dispersed settlements of the Mediterranean?*

WWNORTON.COM/STUDYSPACE

ALTERNATIVE PATHWAYS AND IDEAS

> → *How did "second-generation" cultures expand the social, political, and cultural options available to men and women?*

During the first millennium BCE, societies along the peripheries of regional empires started to follow their own innovative paths, defying the ways of the dynastic regimes they often envied. (See Map 5-1.) They tinkered with new types of political and social organization, new ideas, and new ways of fighting and expanding borders. Such innovation occurred, for example, in Eastern Zhou China, where nearly constant warfare and power struggles culminated in the formation of several large and powerful territorial states. Radical changes also took place in Greece and in the Levant, where the period of chaos and economic decline caused by the onslaught of the Sea Peoples was followed by the emergence of city-states.

In regions as far apart as the great river valleys of East and South Asia, the Caribbean coast of Mexico, and the coasts of the Mediterranean, new complex societies arose. These societies developed cultural and political ideas that were radically different from those of the large regional empires of Southwest Asia. As they did so, the communities of China, the Indus Valley, the Americas, and the Mediterranean demonstrated that they could rely more on their own innovations than on patterns inherited from such older, well-established societies as those of Egypt and Mesopotamia. In the Indus Valley, for example, new complex societies were based on sacred categories (especially caste, which determined every individual's status, occupation, and spouse) and new religious experiences. These communities revolved around small-scale monarchies and urban oligarchies dominated by elite families. In China, small polities held by regional lords under the Zhou king gave way to powerful and ever more centralized and belligerent states. In the Americas, the Olmecs in Mesoamerica and the Chavín peoples of the Andes ordered their lives around dispersed settlements that relied on simple agricultural technology, but they produced complex and increasingly hierarchical social orders. Around the Mediterranean Sea, new social forms were taking shape in independent cities. Some elements in these new communities were borrowed from the older complex societies, but more often, they developed in place to match their environments.

These new communities were not just extensions of old lifeways. In each, dramatic innovations in how inhabitants expressed cultural and religious beliefs expanded the social, political, and cultural options available to men and women. Although the cultures were clearly different from one another, we might call these all "second-generation" societies,

simultaneously building on their predecessors and representing a departure from ancient legacies. They were marked by a competitiveness in which literary warfare and battles of ideas produced political and social innovations and encouraged intellectual curiosity. The new communities harbored bold thinkers who devised new ways of looking at politics and society. They were present in China during the time of Confucius (who looked to the past but transformed its meaning) and in the Ganges Valley during the age of the Buddha (who questioned the dominance of kings and priests), and their ideas have reverberated down through the ages. The Greek city-states produced a generation of skeptical and questioning philosophers who influenced later Western political, moral, and scientific thinkers, as well as many Muslim scholars. The new cultural centers in Afro-Eurasia encouraged probing and reflective inquiries into who human beings were, how human behavior was to be explained, and to what end it was directed. Their theological and philosophical questions, and their answers, are still relevant today.

The new engagement with ideas by no means bred consensus: the age of great ideas was in fact characterized by magnificent disputes over what was best for humanity. For instance, thinkers disagreed over the very political and moral status of the individual. In Greece, they worried about the possibility of gaining and transmitting true or reliable knowledge of the world. Their new and more skeptical forms of thinking led them to doubt the permanence of the social order and ponder the relationship between humans and the cosmos. In Eastern Zhou China, beset by constant warfare, they debated how best to restore order; some advocated engagement while others urged withdrawal from government. In the Ganges Valley, philosophers questioned the rituals of the Brahmans and sought new ways of exhibiting moral behavior and attaining enlightenment. Whereas many Greek philosophers endorsed skepticism for its own sake, thinkers in Eastern Zhou China and in the Ganges Valley at the time of the Buddha tended to debate the issues in the name of ultimate truths that would end all controversy and yield a unitary vision of state and society.

EASTERN ZHOU CHINA (770–221 BCE)

> → *In what ways did scholars propose ending the incessant warfare and chaos of China's Spring and Autumn and Warring States periods?*

The first millennium BCE was a time of political and cultural innovation in China, as it was in the Ganges Valley and the Mediterranean. But unlike the South Asian and Greek

ROCKY MOUNTAINS

NORTH

AMERICA

NOMADIC HUNTERS

Great Lakes

Mississippi R.

St. Lawrence R.

CELTIC PEOPL

IBERIANS

La
citi

Carl

ATLANTIC
OCEAN

Gulf
of
Mexico

OLMEC

MESOAMERICA

La Venta

Monte Alban

WEST INDIES

SAHAR

SAHAR
PEOPL

SAHEL

Niger R.

PACIFIC
OCEAN

CHAVÍN

ANDES

NOMADIC HUNTERS

Amazon R.

SOUTH

AMERICA

MOUNTAINS

	Persian Empire
	Zhou China
	South Asian states
	Nubia
	Kush
	Nok
	Olmec
	Chavín
	Mediterranean colonies
•	City
NOK	State
SLAVS	People

0   1000   2000 Miles

0   1000   2000 Kilometers

MAP 5-1   THE WORLD, C. 500 BCE

By the middle of the first millennium BCE, complex agriculture-based societies beyond Southwest Asia and North Africa contributed to the flowering of new cultural pathways and ideas. According to this map, where did more culturally integrated societies appear? Which societies had greater opportunities for cultural borrowing and mixing and which were more isolated? How did proximity to others or relative isolation shape these societies' development?

intellectuals, the new Chinese leaders and thinkers did not rise up to challenge the old cultural orthodoxy. Instead, they looked to the past as a golden age that could show them how to govern complex states; they stressed elaborately regulated court protocol and ritual, as well as the importance of maintaining hierarchies of authority and deference within families and the state. By the middle of the millennium, however, political innovations were taking place on a much broader geographical scale in China and involved larger numbers of people than did comparable developments in the Mediterranean, or even in the Indus Valley. As Chapter 4 noted, their defeat by northern steppe invaders forced the Zhou to flee their western capital at Chang'an. The beginning of the Eastern Zhou dynasty, centered on Luoyang, was known as the Spring and Autumn period (722–481 BCE); it was marked by great competition, fierce fighting among regional states and their ruling lords as they sought to acquire land and expand their borders, and the beginning of political and social transformations. A chronicle allegedly written at this time by Confucius, expressing his despair over the demise of high Zhou ideals, gave the period its name. The Eastern Zhou dynasty ended with the Warring States period (403–221 BCE), when seven major regional states consolidated their power into territorial states. The result was a multistate system that manifested revolutionary developments in agriculture, government, politics, and society, including new transportation networks, changes in landownership, universal military service, and the growth in importance of scholar-officials and merchants.

THE SPRING AND AUTUMN PERIOD

China was far from being politically unified: at the outset of the Spring and Autumn period, there were 148 Zhou tributary states. Though many were simply garrison towns and their surrounding lands, some were quite large and powerful. The central states on the North China plain clustered on or near the Yellow River and were the bastions of Zhou culture. The peripheral states were more aggressive than the central states and eagerly sought control of neighboring Zhou states as well as non-Zhou borderlands, where the cultural outsiders or "barbarians" lived; they therefore engaged in nearly constant warfare.

During the Spring and Autumn period, anarchic violence led to a series of major transformations in politics and society. The regional states, which wielded more power than the Zhou ruler, forged alliances and met at interstate conferences under a *ba* (a hegemon or "senior one," who led the alliance); new administrative units were formed in the countryside to conscript men for fighting and to collect taxes; landownership was no longer based on a tribute system, in which the regional lords had their holdings legitimated by the Zhou king; the rulers of the states were advised by ministers who gained their positions through their merit and wile rather than ties

of kinship; and the southern states of Chu, Wu, and Yue came to recognize Zhou culture. Throughout the dynasty, the major states competed for power and land, but they still acknowledged the Zhou dynasty's mandate of heaven and nominally accepted the authority of the Zhou ruler. In effect, the fractured political system in China inverted the normal pattern of strong central states with weaker satellites. Instead, the central states served as a buffer zone between the large peripheral states to which they were forced to swear allegiance. They became the battlefields on which larger states fought for dominance.

Increasing political anarchy coincided with technological breakthroughs. As new smelting techniques to remove metallic impurities from iron were devised and became known across China, bronze weaponry gave way to stronger iron swords and armor. Zhou kings tried hard to monopolize iron production and to maintain control of stockpiles, but to no avail. The spread of cheaper and more lethal weaponry accelerated the shift in influence away from the central government to local authorities. Indeed, the regional states became so powerful that they were able to engage in large-scale projects that earlier had been feasible only for empires. As regional states undertook the construction of dikes and of drainage and irrigation systems, they brought greater areas of land under cultivation. New canals linked rivers, and the networks spurred transformation. For example, in 486 BCE the regional lord of the Wu state began to build what would eventually become the thousand-mile-long Grand Canal, tying the Yellow River in the north and the Yangzi River in the south. Stretching several hundred miles, Wu's canal functioned as an artificial Nile, making it possible for the economies of all the states to begin to be more highly integrated. Like all the grand infrastructure projects of this era, it was constructed by peasants whom the Zhou regional lords pressed into corvée labor in lieu of tax payments.

THE WARRING STATES PERIOD

By the beginning of the Warring States period, seven large territorial states had come to dominate the Zhou world in a multistate system; several smaller states on the Central Plain remained part of the sphere of influence of the major powers. (See Map 5-2.) All of these states were still under the formal overlordship of the Zhou ruler, although they continued to have more real power than the Zhou king. Beginning in the fifth and fourth centuries BCE, their vying for dominance would devour the Zhou dynasty from within. The wars of conquest of the seven major states and the shifting political alliances among them involved the mobilization of huge armies and resources unprecedented in scale anywhere in the world, far surpassing the Assyrian armies at the height of their power. Qin was the greatest state, and it would ultimately replace the Zhou dynasty in 221 BCE.

→ *In what ways did scholars propose ending the chaos of China's Spring and Autumn and Warring States periods?*

The Warring States alternatively formed bonds or fought with each other; they engaged in diplomacy or battle, depending on which seemed to further their interests at the moment. Thus statecraft emerged, similar to that which developed between major states in Southwest Asia in the second millennium BCE (see Chapter 3). Trained diplomats traveled on missions to persuade rulers of other states to ally with the ruler they represented, and if dismissed by their first employer they would offer their services to another. The Warring States sought to maintain a balance of power and would re-form their coalitions if one state appeared to be becoming too powerful. Moreover, impersonal legal codes, which established uniform punishments based on the specific crime committed rather than the social status of the perpetrator, enhanced the rulers of these states at the expense of the remaining aristocratic elites. There can be little doubt that intrigues, alliances, and wars of conquest were also instrumental in the emergence of the large-scale states that dominated China during the Zhou decline.

Overall, the conception of central power changed dramatically in the Warring States era, as royal appointees replaced hereditary officeholders. Moreover, by the middle of

MAP 5-2   ZHOU CHINA IN THE WARRING STATES PERIOD

The Warring States period initially witnessed a fracturing of the Zhou dynasty into a myriad of states, followed centuries later by the emergence of even more durable and enduring dynasties. What about this map tells us why diplomacy was so important during this period? What does this map tell us about the relationships between "civilized" and "barbarian" peoples in East Asia? How do you think so many smaller polities could survive when surrounded by three large and powerful states (Qin, Qi, and Chu)?

the fourth century BCE, power was so concentrated in the hands of the rulers of the major states that each began to call himself "king," a title formerly held only by the Zhou ruler. Despite the incessant warfare, scholars, soldiers, merchants, peasants, and artisans were able to thrive in the midst of an expanding agrarian economy and interregional trade. At the same time, major innovations, largely begun during the Spring and Autumn period, were taking place in government, warfare, culture, economy, and society. Despite the warfare and chaos—or perhaps because of them—many of the fundamental beliefs, values, and philosophies that would become the foundation for later dynasties were formulated during this period. By the middle of the first millennium BCE, China's political activities and innovations were involving larger numbers of people, spread over a much broader area, than comparable developments in South Asia and the Mediterranean.

INNOVATIONS IN STATE ADMINISTRATION

Beginning in the Spring and Autumn period, many of the states reorganized their administrative structure to concentrate central power in the hands of the ruler, to obtain natural resources and men for their armies, and to oversee conquered areas; this trend continued in the Warring States period. The major states created administrative districts, each with stewards, sheriffs, and judges; a system of registration of peasant households was instituted to facilitate both tax collection and the provision of conscripts for the ruler's armies. Keeping such records enabled officials to closely monitor the rural population and punish those who did not comply with their obligations. The officials were drawn from the *shi*, who under the Western Zhou had been knights but were now bureaucrats in direct service to the ruler. Confucius and other classical masters called them "gentlemen," or "superior men" (*junzi*), and considered them partners of the ruler in state affairs. Officials were paid in salaries of grain and sometimes received gifts of gold and silver, as well as titles and seals of office, from the ruler.

Of all the ministers who aimed at enhancing the power and size of central government, none was more successful than Shang Yang of Qin. The ministerial reforms that he carried out after he arrived in Qin in 361 BCE expanded the power of the Qin domain and positioned it to become the dominant state of its time. He divided the state into administrative *xian* (districts) and appointed their magistrates, vice magistrates, military commanders, and overseers, thereby extending the ruler's authority into the hinterland and using the districts for universal military recruitment. He divided the land into blocks that would be farmed by individual households, and he introduced a capitation, or head tax, ensuring that households containing two or more adult sons would pay more in taxes than families with only one adult

son. He rewarded those who distinguished themselves in war (as determined by the number of enemy killed in battle) with titles and land; conversely, nobles who failed to distinguish themselves in war lost their status. He introduced a harsh penal code that stressed collective responsibility. For example, those who harbored criminals had their bodies cut in two. The legal code applied to both government officials and peasants, with severe punishments for violent crimes, theft, use of nonstandard weights and measures, or wrongdoing in office. Paradoxically, Shang Yang was later trapped by his own regulations when his ruler charged him with sedition; he tried to flee Qin, but he was captured and executed.

INNOVATIONS IN WARFARE

The most powerful and successful states in China ruled over millions of people, and by 221 BCE, they were able to boast of million-man armies. The contrast with Athens, which at the height of its ascendancy in the fifth century BCE was the largest and most powerful city-state in the Mediterranean, is obvious: with a whole population of 250,000, it could field an army of just 20,000 men. Only Rome, just beginning to assert itself in the Mediterranean at around this time and later to become a mega-state, could possibly compete with China's scale. With administrative reform came reforms in military recruitment and warfare. As noted above, one purpose of registering the rural population was to guarantee their military service. During the Spring and Autumn period, rulers began to rely on men from the countryside to expand their armies, recruiting some into corps of personal bodyguards. During the Warring States period, as such practices persisted, the conscription of peasants provided rulers with ever larger military organizations.

In earlier battles, the nobles had shot arrows from chariots while some peasants from their lands stood and fought beside them. But the Warring States relied instead on massed infantries of peasants bearing iron lances, who fought fiercely and to the death, unconstrained by their relationships with nobles. Rather than 30,000 nobles fighting from chariots, war was now waged by huge state armies reported to contain as many as one million commoners in the infantry, supported by 1,000 chariots and 10,000 bow-wielding cavalrymen. During the Spring and Autumn period, one state's entire army would be massed against another state's; now, armies could be divided into separate forces and fight several battles simultaneously.

Vast campaigns involving hundreds of thousands of replaceable peasant soldiers led by a professional officer corps were common. Armies also contained elite professional troops who wore heavy iron armor and helmets, carried iron weapons, and were trained to use the recently invented crossbow. The crossbow's tremendous power, range, and accuracy, with its ingenious trigger mechanism, enabled archers to eas-

Bronze Spearhead. Although bronze weaponry gave way to stronger iron swords and armor during the Warring States era, stylized bronze spearheads were still prized by Zhou kings and regional lords.

ily kill lightly armored cavalrymen or charioteers at a distance. The technology of siege warfare also advanced in response to the growing importance given to defensive walls along frontiers and around towns. Enemy armies used counterweighted siege ladders (called "cloud ladders" by the Chinese) to scale urban walls or dug tunnels under them; those defending their city often pumped smoke into the tunnels to thwart the attackers. The rhythms of warfare also changed; rather than lasting a season, campaigns could stretch over a year or even longer. As commanders of armies seeking conquest plotted their strategies (determining which troops should be placed where, the kind of terrain best suited for battle, and how to outmaneuver opposing armies), military action and thought became ever more sophisticated.

ECONOMIC, SOCIAL, AND CULTURAL CHANGES

Rather than being a drain on the economy, the incessant warfare of both the Spring and Autumn period and the Warring States period spurred China's economic growth to remark-

able heights. A veritable agricultural revolution on the North China plain along the Yellow River made possible rapid population growth, and the inhabitants of the Eastern Zhou reached approximately 20 million—the largest number of people then living in a single state in the world. These dramatic demographic changes affected the environment, however; greater numbers of people required more fuel, and the deforestation that resulted as trees were cut down to supply it led to erosion of the fields. In addition, many animals were hunted to extinction; others, like the elephant, found their open range sharply curtailed.

Economic changes began in the Spring and Autumn period when rulers of some of the states gave peasants the right to their land in exchange for paying taxes and providing military service. Because the peasants could enjoy the benefits of their labor, their productivity increased. Innovations in the technologies of agriculture also raised productivity: crop rotation was introduced (millet and wheat in the north, and rice and millet in the south), and farmers began using iron plowshares harnessed to oxen to prepare their fields.

With larger harvests and advances in bronze and iron casting came trade in surplus grain and in pottery and ritual objects, and thus the beginning of a market economy. Grain and goods were shipped along roads, rivers, and canals. Peasants continued to rely on barter as they exchanged goods, but minted coins began to circulate among elites and rulers. Early coins were made of bronze, and were formed in a variety of shapes, some resembling spades. Private traders and merchants also appeared during this time.

During the Warring States period, these changes continued. The new bargain with the peasants—allowing them private ownership of land in exchange for their taxes and military service—undergirded the economies of all the Warring States. A strong emphasis on the military aided the polities more broadly. Infrastructure benefited directly, as roads and walls, forts and towers were built to defend against invading armies.

Knife Coin. Zhou dynasty coins, like the later Han coin shown here, were made of bronze and produced in a variety of shapes, some resembling spades and knives, depending on the region. Each of the Warring States had its own currency.

In addition, rulers and administrators applied the skills gained in organizing the military to devising public projects: powerful states undertook large-scale irrigation projects, built canals and dikes, and drained low-lying lands, which opened up more acreage for agriculture. Moreover, military conscripts worked on these large-scale municipal and irrigation projects during periods when they were not needed for fighting.

Economic growth helped the rulers attain a high level of cultural sophistication, as reflected in their magnificent palaces and burial sites. At the same time, social relations became more fluid during the Warring States period as commoners gained power and aristocrats lost it. In Qin, for example, as noted above, peasants who served in the ruler's army were rewarded for killing enemy soldiers; their military success fueled their advance through the ranks, and could win them land, houses, and slaves, and a change in status. Officials were also rewarded with lands and gifts that enhanced their status and wealth. Officials, ministers, and diplomats traveled far and wide during this period, but peasants were required to stay in their fields and villages, leaving them only to fight in the ruler's army.

While class relations had a revolutionary fluidity, gender relations became more inflexible for elites and nonelites alike as the value ascribed to male-centered kinship groups grew. The resulting separation of the sexes and heightened male domination within the family naturally affected the position of women. An emphasis on monogamy, or at least the primacy of the first wife over additional wives (concubines), also emerged. Relations between the sexes were increasingly ritualized and were marked by heavy moral and legal sanctions against any behavior that appeared to threaten the purity of authoritarian male lineages.

Recently discovered archaeological evidence about the daily lives of people of the time reveals that commoners and elites were both concerned with restoring order and stability in their lives through religion, medicine, and statecraft. Rites of divination to predict the future and medical recipes to heal the body among elites were paralleled by commoners' use of ghost stories and astrological almanacs to understand the meaning of their lives and the significance of their deaths. Elites recorded their political discourses on wood and bamboo slips that were tied together to form scrolls. They also prepared military treatises, the arts of persuasion, ritual texts, geographic works, and poetry this way. Moreover, social changes were occurring. Even commoners could now purchase bronze metalwork, for example, when previously only Zhou rulers and aristocrats could afford to do so.

NEW IDEAS AND THE "HUNDRED MASTERS"

As states came and went under the Eastern Zhou dynasty during both the Spring and Autumn and the Warring States pe-

Pendant. Gender relations became more inflexible because of male-centered kinship groups. Relations between the sexes were increasingly ritualized and were marked by heavy moral and legal sanctions against any behavior that appeared to threaten the purity of powerful lineages. This pendant depicts two women who formed a close relationship with each other in the "inner chambers" of their homes.

riods, the losers among the political elites sought to replace their former aristocratic advantages with status gained through new types of service—not just political but also social and intellectual. In this fashion, political conflict was conducive to intellectual creativity, and important teachers emerged, each with disciples attracted to what was presented as an independent school of thought. The most prominent of the "hundred masters" of the age was Confucius; other masters either expanded on Confucian thought or formulated opposing ideas about human nature and the role of government. Their philosophies are now known as the Hundred Schools of Thought.

Confucius taught hundreds of students, but historian Sima Qian claims that during his lifetime he had seventy-seven core disciples. Like the Greek philosopher Socrates, Confucius left no writings of his own; the followers of each sage—in Confucius's case, working anonymously—compiled and transmitted his teachings after his death. *The Analects,* which collected Confucius's ethical teachings and cultural ideals, had an extraordinary influence on many of the leading scholar-officials who came after him. In his effort to persuade society to again embrace what he saw as the lost ideals of the early Zhou, Confucius set forth a new moral framework, stressing correct performance of ritual (*li*), responsibility and loyalty to the family (*xiao*), and perfection of moral character to become a "superior man" (*junzi*)—that is, a man defined by *ren* (benevolence, goodness) rather than by the pursuit of profit. Confucius believed that government should be the purview of these superior men; in such a society, coercive laws and punishment would not be needed to achieve order. He taught these concepts to those who were highly intelligent and willing to work, whether their backgrounds were noble or humble; thus any man could gain the education needed to become a gentleman of the ruling class. This was a dramatic departure from past centuries, when only nobles were believed to be capable of ruling. Nonetheless, Confucius's clear distinctions between gentlemen-rulers and commoners continued to support a society based on social hierarchy, though

Iron Spoon Stamp. Zhou courtiers used geomancy (*fengshui*) to determine sites for burials and palaces. Elites and commoners also used geomancy to site their homes and graves. As the image proudly heralded on this modern stamp reveals, by the third century BCE, the Chinese had discovered that an iron spoon on a bronze surface would always point south, the cardinal direction for the Zhou king and his regional lords. Such a "compass" served as a reliable siting device for what we might call a "spiritual ecology."

Chinese Calendar. This Han period calendar for 63 BCE is formed from sixteen slips of wood with handwritten characters; each begins with day one, day two, and so on; the calendar is to be read from right to left.

an individual's position in that hierarchy might rest more on education than on birth.

One competing school of thought, later called Mohism, derived from the teachings of Mozi, also known as Mo Di (c. 479–438 BCE). This writer and craftsman-builder lived after Confucius, just before the Warring States period; he believed that each man should feel obligated and responsible to all other people, not just to his own family and friends. Thus, whereas ritual or art or music was associated with Confucianism, he instead emphasized practical concerns of good government; in his view, government should promote social order, material benefits for its people, and population growth. He opposed wars of conquest, arguing that they wasted life and resources and interfered with productivity and fair distribution. His relatively utilitarian philosophy appealed mainly to city dwellers, and he recognized the need for strong urban defenses to keep out marauders.

Another philosophy that took shape during this time was Daoism, which distinguished itself sharply from the credo of Confucius and his followers, scorning what was seen as the Confucian emphasis on rigidly prescribed rituals and social hierarchies. Its ideas were first formulated by someone known to us as Master Lao (Laozi, literally, "Old Master"), who—if he actually existed—may have been a contemporary of Confucius. His sayings were collected in writings titled *The Daodejing,* or *The Book of the Way and Its Power* (c. third century BCE). His book was then elaborated by Master Zhuang (Zhuangzi, c. 369–286 BCE). Daoism stressed the *dao* (the

Primary Source

WARRING IDEAS: CONFUCIANISM VERSUS DAOISM

Normally historians who compare the influence of Confucianism and Daoism focus on their strictures for individuals—moralist and laissez-faire, respectively. Though Daoists and Confucians similarly viewed the world of political power as perilous, their competing teachings also offered regional Chinese rulers a choice in political philosophies.

Initially, Confucius's call for moral rigor had little appeal to those in power. But some saw the attractions of his humanistic beliefs after they realized that a tyrannical government that punished its citizens harshly could be brought down by a peasant rebellion.

In one exchange with a student, Confucius described the core foundations of government:

> Zigong asked about government. The Master said, "Sufficient food, sufficient military force, the confidence of the people." Zigong said, "If one had, unavoidably, to dispense with one of these, which of them should go first?" The Master said, "Get rid of the military." Zigong said, "If one had, unavoidably, to dispense with one of the remaining two, which should go first?" The Master said, "Dispense with food: Since ancient times there has always been death, but without confidence a people cannot stand." (*Analects* 12.7)

Many who sought power were drawn more to Daoism, whose teachings warned that the state was easily ruined by overly assertive rulers. Thus, the *Daodejing* (*The Book of the Way and Its Power*, c. third century BCE), a famous Daoist work attributed to Master Lao (Laozi), argued that long-term rule should be based on "doing nothing" (*wuwei*):

If one desires to take the empire and act on it,
I say that he will not succeed.
The empire is a sacred vessel,
That cannot be acted upon.
In being acted upon, it is harmed;
And in being grasped, it is lost.
For among living things some move ahead and others
     follow,
Some breathe easily and others hard,
Some are strong and others are weak,
Some rise up and others are brought low.
Thus the sage rejects the excessive, the extravagant,
     the extreme.

(*The Book of the Way and Its Power*, Vol. 1, p. 86)

→ *Why did Confucius think that culture trumped politics and the military in government?*
→ *Why did he believe that a cruel tyrant could not remain in power for very long?*
→ *Why did the Legalists find Daoism more appealing than Confucianism as a practical political philosophy?*

SOURCE: Wm. Theodore De Bary and Irene Bloom, comp., *Sources of Chinese Tradition*, 2nd ed. (New York: Columbia University Press, 1999).

Way) of nature and the cosmos: the best way to live was to follow the natural order of things. Its main principle was *wuwei*, "doing nothing"—what mattered was spontaneity, noninterference, and acceptance of the world as it is rather than attempting to change it by entering politics and government. In Laozi's vision of politics, the ruler who interfered least in the natural processes of change was the most successful. Zhuangzi focused on the enlightened individual, who lived spontaneously and in harmony with nature, free of eth-

ical rules and laws as defined by society and viewing life and death as simply different stages of existence.

Legalism, or Statism, another major way of understanding how best to live an orderly life, grew out of the writings of Master Xun (Xunzi, 310–237 BCE), who lived toward the end of the Warring States period. He believed that men and women were innately bad, and therefore required moral education and authoritarian control. In the decades leading up to the Qin victory over the Zhou, the Legalist thinker Han

Fei, Han state minister and Xunzi disciple (280–233 BCE), agreed that human nature was primarily evil. He imagined a state with a ruler who followed the Daoist principle of *wuwei*, detaching himself from everyday governance but only after setting an unbending standard—strict laws, accompanied by harsh punishments—for judging his officials and people. For Han Fei, the establishment and uniform application of these laws would ensure that the evil nature of all people would be kept in check. As we will see in Chapter 7, the Qin state, before it became the dominant state in China, was particularly draconian in enforcing its laws, as it systematically followed the Legalist philosophy.

The inseparability of scholars and the state, so vital a feature of Chinese society through many centuries, began in this age. Scholars became state functionaries dependent on the patronage of rulers. In return, the rulers recognized the expertise of scholars in matters of punishment, ritual, astronomy, medicine, and divination. Because philosophers and priests in Greece and South Asia did not exclusively serve the state and its rulers and had no interest in justifying the existence of a particular ruler, they felt free to speculate on a wide range of issues; they also tended to see the world as constantly changing. In Zhou China and later dynasties, in contrast, philosophical deliberations focused on the need to maintain order and stability by preserving the state and tended to view the world as static. The close bonds that rulers forged with their scholarly elites distinguished governments in Warring States China from the other Afro-Eurasian polities of this period.

The growing importance of scholars as bureaucrats and philosophers promoted the use of writing as a fundamental tool of statecraft and philosophical discourse. Indeed, even though the evolving Chinese script was not standardized until 221 BCE, its use in the philosophical debates that raged between various schools across many states and regions helped foster cultural unity at a time of intellectual pluralism, a diversity of thinking inspired not by skepticism but by a vision of empire and unity. Scholar-diplomats and scribes in each of the Warring States debated and attacked each other in clear and forceful prose, as they argued over how to create a stable and harmonious society; some nine to ten thousand graphs or signs became required for writing. The active participation in these debates by men holding high political office—scholar-bureaucrats—set China apart from other societies of this period.

Over the coming centuries, the ideas of Confucianism, Daoism, and Legalism gradually merged into a unified story about the crucial role that the ancient sage-kings had played in empire building. This account invoked the concept of the mandate of heaven (see Chapter 4), but scholars embellished it with details of how the dynastic cycle of history worked. The Qin imperial victors—Statists who at first relied on raw military power and strictly applied Legalist approaches to running the state and achieving order—drew on the discourses of their rivals, the Daoists, whom they had scorned for simply "leaving things alone," and the Confucians, whom they derided as overly concerned with ritual and "preachy." This new formulation of history described the evolution of state power as a natural process, as small states grew into a unified empire, and thus gave the chaotic Warring States period a coherent shape and a virtuous, moral purpose aiming toward unity.

THE NEW WORLDS OF SOUTH ASIA

> → *How did political and social transformations encourage new beliefs and dissident thinkers in South Asia?*

Following their gradual migration into South Asia around 1500 BCE, the Vedic peoples fought with the indigenous population as well as with each other as they established and sought to enlarge new states. Around 1000 BCE, they began to expand eastward from the Indus River valley into the mid-Ganges plain, where they created new polities. Here, as in Eastern Zhou China and in the Mediterranean, warfare and expansion led to political, social, and ideological transformations in the first millennium BCE. At the same time that scholar-officials in Zhou China were developing theories about the role of government, conceiving new ways of administering states, and devising economic and social innovations, the Vedic peoples were also forging new political institutions, new economic activities, and new ways of viewing the natural and supernatural worlds. In Vedic societies, these transformations were driven by warriors and upper-class intellectuals, with kin groups and caste organizations the primary agents of social transformation.

THE RISE OF NEW POLITIES

Significant political and social transformations in South Asia began about 600 BCE, after the Vedic peoples had expanded eastward into the mid-Ganges plain—around the same time that major changes were occurring in Zhou China and the Mediterranean. The leading force in reclaiming the new lands in the east were the Brahmans, an upper class of priests and scholars. The area into which the Vedic peoples migrated was a monsoon region where abundant rainfall made the land suitable for cultivating rice in paddies; in contrast, the appropriate crops in the Indus River valley were wheat and barley. The migrants cleared the land by setting fire to the forests and using iron tools—fashioned from the abundant supplies of iron ore in the mid-Ganges plain—to remove what was left of the jungle.

Gradually, between 1000 and 600 BCE, settlements and towns evolved into small territorial states; as in China, it was a time of constant feuding. Sixteen polities known as *mahajanapadas* (great countries) quarreled for territory and dominance and gave their name to the era: the Sixteen State period. None could completely overpower the others to establish a unified state. (See Map 5-3.) It was also a time marked by new thinking—most dramatically, the rise of Buddhism as a challenge to the authority of Vedic sacrifices and the leadership of the Brahmans.

There were two major kinds of states in the mid- and lower Ganges plain: those ruled by hereditary monarchs and those ruled by a small, elected elite, or oligarchies. One such oligarchy was the Vrijji Confederacy, also called *ganasangha,* meaning "a gathering of a large number." As described in Chapter 4, the South Asian city-states were led by a class of warriors and officials called the Kshatriya. The rulers of kingdoms assumed the title *raja,* a word usually translated "king." But in the oligarchic communities, which were ruled collectively, each adult freeborn male head of a family was called a *raja.* Nonetheless, the Kshatriya aristocracy alone controlled the land and other resources in the ganasangha states. At regular gatherings in their meeting halls, they both performed religious rituals and discussed and made decisions on important issues.

Powerful as they were, the *rajas* in the kingdoms often came from low-status clans that gained power with their military strength. Their land and wealth made it unnecessary for them to claim Ksha-

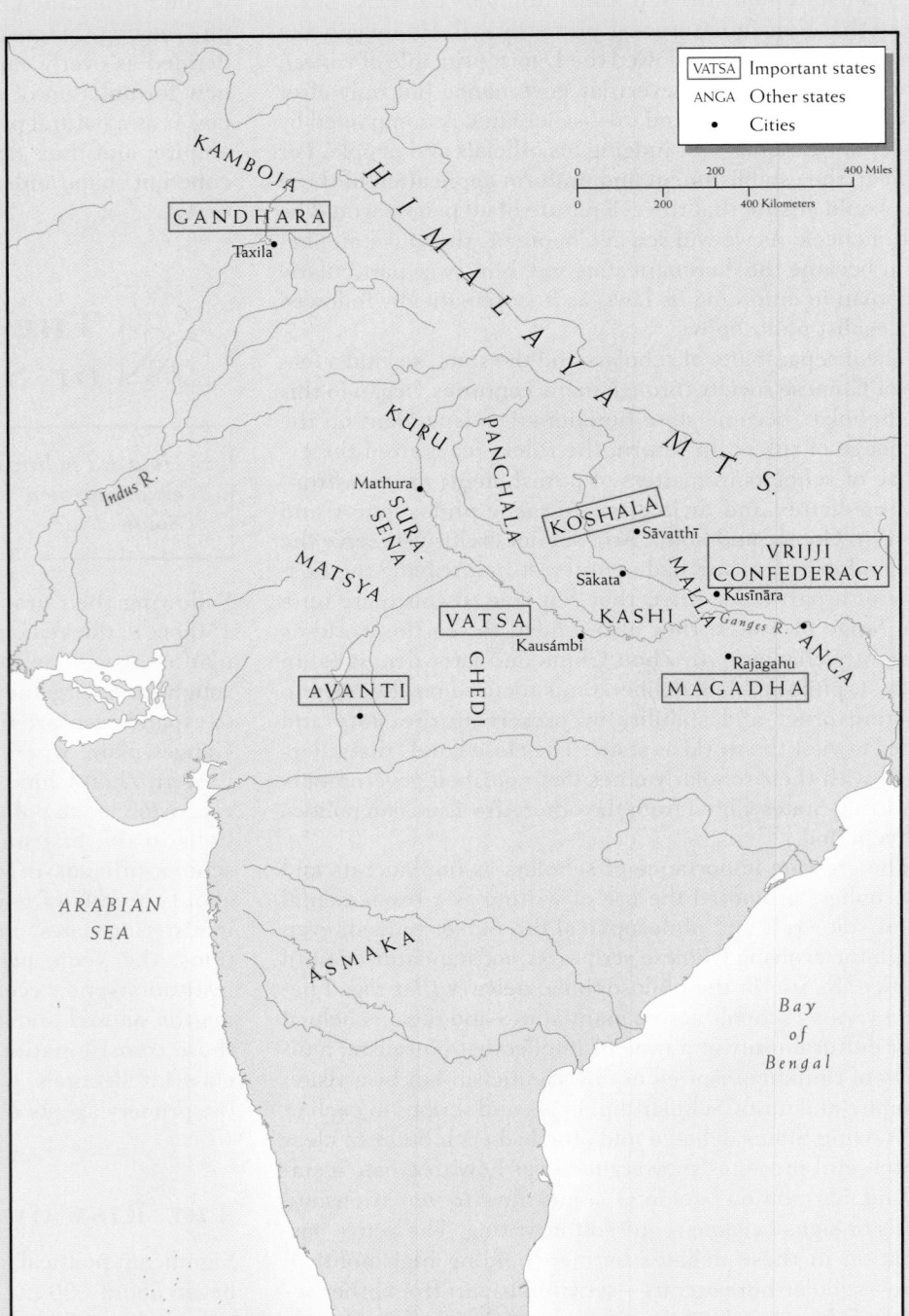

MAP 5-3   SIXTEEN STATES IN THE TIME OF THE BUDDHA IN SOUTH ASIA

South Asia underwent profound social, cultural, and political transformations in the first millennium BCE that reflected growing urbanization, increased commerce, and the emergence of two types of states. Where did new states and cities appear? What regional features encouraged social and cultural integration? According to this map, what other regions had influence on South Asia, and where might South Asian culture spread?

triya status as the basis of their authority. Such a *raja* would often elevate his status by marrying a woman from a high-status clan. For example, according to the *Jatakas*, a Buddhist text, Pasenadi, the ruler of Koshala, sought to gain status by marrying a princess of the prestigious Shakya family. Although unhappy at the prospect of a daughter marrying beneath her station, the Shakya feared offending their powerful neighbor. But one man came up with an ingenious plan: his daughter born to a slave woman (hence not a real princess) could be married to Pasenadi, thereby preserving both the honor and safety of the Shakya. Unfortunately for them, Vidudabha, the prince born of this marriage, learned the truth of his mother's birth on a visit to her homeland, where the elders failed to accord him the respect due a prince. Outraged, he returned home, only to encounter more humiliation when the people of Koshala learned that his mother was slave-born. He later usurped the throne of Koshala and took his revenge on the Shakyas, organizing four military expeditions against the small mountainous state—which the young Koshala king eventually destroyed.

EXPANSION OF THE CASTE SYSTEM

Though the kingdoms and oligarchic republican cities had different political structures, they shared many social features, including the caste system. As they migrated eastward, the Vedic peoples brought elements of the caste system into the Ganges plain. The traditional *varna* scheme of Brahmans (scholars and priests), Kshatriyas (warriors), Vaishyas (commoners), and Shudras (laborers and servants) expanded in an economy centered on farms that were worked by extended families. Many more Shudras, clans outside the Vedic lineages, joined the agricultural economy as *jatis*, or subcastes of laborers. Cows were no longer the main draft animals because they could not work in rice paddies and therefore were replaced by water buffaloes; some plows required six or eight animals to pull them. Moreover, cultivating rice paddies was highly labor-intensive, since water had to be constantly supplied to the fields from distant rivers through elaborate irrigation canals that needed constant maintenance.

Households therefore came to rely on hired workers and slaves, who probably differed little in their status and economic conditions. Either as tenants of the householders or as cultivators of small pieces of land, Shudra peasants now appeared as a distinct status group. While men in the three *varnas* above them—Brahmans, Kshatriyas, and Vaishyas—were "twice-born" by virtue of having experienced a second, ritual birth around age twelve, this ceremony—together with the status it brought—was denied to Shudras, who therefore remained outsiders in the Brahman-dominated society. The Shudras then invented their own social hierarchy based on kinship and religious rituals. When the Vedic landowners incorporated them into the farming economy as laborers, ten-

ants, or cultivators, they joined the communities as a unit and maintained their communal structure by marrying inside their group. Such a group became known as a *jati* (literally, "born"—that is, the group into which a person was born). The *jatis* became the lower orders (the "subcastes") of an expanding caste system. A further expansion of the caste system occurred as the booming agricultural economy generated more labor specialization. Carpenters and ironsmiths were needed to make the tools for tilling the land, to build irrigation systems, and to fashion utensils for daily life. Carpenters were usually residents of the villages, while ironsmiths as a rule traveled. Those specialists formed their own *jatis*

Brahman Recluse. When Buddhists started to tell their stories in sculptures and paintings, Brahmans were included when appropriate. This character in Gandharan Buddhist art probably represents a Brahman who lived as a recluse, instead of as a priest. He is not shaved or dressed, but his expression is certainly passionate.

through marriage networks. Although ironsmiths were essential to the economy, even Shudra peasants looked down on them as itinerant craftsworkers.

There were also *jatis* of traders and artisans, who were viewed as Vaishya or commoners, in the Brahmans' *varna* scheme, but the relative ritual status among these *jatis* varied by their profession. Traders were usually considered "purer" than artisans, while those engaged in making gold utensils had a higher status than those who made copper or iron ones. But as they gained wealth, even these subcastes began to monopolize skills and resources by banning intermarriage with outsiders, thus preventing the leak of knowledge—a significant change in the highly stratified Vedic society.

New Cities and an Expanding Economy

Supported by rice agriculture, around 500 BCE cities began to emerge on the Ganges plain. These cities became centers of commercial exchange. Some, such as Shravasti and Rajagriha, also thrived as artisanal centers. Others in the northwest, like Taxila—not far from present-day Peshawar, on the border between Pakistan and Afghanistan—engaged in trade with Afghanistan and the Iranian plateau.

As agricultural production increased, surplus grain, sugarcane, and rice became available for trade with towns and cities over longer distances. Farmers needed markets in which to sell their products and to purchase manufactured wares from the cities. Specialized goods were produced in some of the new towns and cities, and trade in these goods expanded beyond the local area in which they were produced.

In the middle of the first millennium BCE, cities in northern India grew as their commercial activities flourished, but they arose with little planning. Alleys leading from the main streets zigzagged between houses built with pebbles and clay. Yet though development was haphazard, civic authorities showed great interest in sanitation. Garbage bins were placed in squares all over the city, and dirty water was channeled deep underground. Streets were graded so that they could be cleaned by rainfall. Because most of the cities settled during this period have been continuously inhabited, they are difficult sites in which to conduct archaeological digs. Taxila, destroyed in the fifth century CE, is an exception: it was excavated in the twentieth century, providing much of our knowledge of urban life in early South Asia.

These new cities opened up exciting opportunities for the adventurous. Rural householders who moved into them prospered by importing rice and sugarcane from villages to sell in the markets; they then transported such processed and manufactured goods as sugar, salt, and utensils back to their villages. Those who already possessed capital became bankers, financing trade and industry. The less affluent turned to craftwork, fashioning textiles, tools such as needles, fine pottery,

Taxila. *Top:* Taxila became the capital of Gandhara at the time that it was occupied by the Persian Empire in the fifth century BCE. Dharmarajika was one of the most important monasteries. The walkway around the stupa was covered with glass tiles, and the stupa itself was decorated with jewels. *Bottom:* This corner of a stupa exhibits a variety of the architectural styles that prevailed in Gandharan art at its height. Both square and round columns are covered by Corinthian capitals. The right arch gate shows the style of Sanchi, the famous stupa in central India.

copper plates, ivory decorations, and gold and silver utensils. Traders and artisans formed guilds (associations of people with similar interests) to regulate competition, prices, and wages; to provide support for destitute members and their families; and to set standards to which all members had to comply. To protect their trading and manufacturing monopolies, guilds required their members to marry within their organizations. By following this practice, the guilds were eventually transformed into *jatis*.

The leaders of traders' guilds wielded financial influence over the new urban communities. Even kings had to heed their advice when deciding on issues as important as war and peace. Coins came into use at about the same time that they appeared in Greece and China. Traders and bankers established municipal bodies that issued the coins and vouched for their worth. Made of silver, they had irregular shapes but specific weights, which determined their value; they were punched-marked, or stamped with symbols of authority on one side.

Cities generated many new professions: they supported physicians, launderers, barbers, cooks, tailors, and entertainers. Complex financial transactions necessitated accountants and professional scribes to keep accurate records, but unfortunately no writing from this period has survived; kings had yet to learn to have their achievements inscribed on stone, while religious teachers taught orally.

The new cities were melting pots that allowed considerable social mobility despite the rigidity of the caste system, as the story of the famous physician Jivika illustrates. Jivika lived during the time of the Buddha, whose good friend he became, in the mid–sixth century BCE. His mother was a courtesan in the great city of Rajagriha in the lower Ganges Valley, beautiful and highly accomplished in dancing, singing, and playing the lute; her fame spread far and wide, attracting business to the city. When she found herself pregnant, she hid away until the baby was born; then, under cover of darkness, she had her maid carry the infant in a basket to a trash dump. The next morning, the baby's crying attracted the attention first of a crowd and then of a prince named Abhaya, who sent a servant to find out the reason for the uproar. When he learned that the newborn boy was alive, he adopted the child as his own and named him Jivika, meaning "alive." Prince Abhaya did raise the boy like a son, but after learning of his low birth Jivika decided to earn his own livelihood. From his hometown of Rajagriha, Jivika set out for Taxila. He traveled more than 800 miles along the Ganges River, journeying from city to city—a long journey well worth the effort, for Taxila was widely known as a center of learning. There Jivika received the best training available in medicine, and after he returned to Rajagriha his knowledge and skill soon earned him a brilliant reputation in all of northern India.

The opportunities provided by the new cities and states did not ensure success for everyone. Royal warfare expanded polities but disrupted lives. Many who lost their land and livelihood entered cities in search of work, and some fared better than others. Householders who turned to commerce and finance risked losing everything. As a whole, the society had more material wealth, but individual lives were far more

Indian Coins. Coinage appeared in India at about the same time as in the Greek world and China. Although standard in weight, the silver punch-marked coins were not regular in shape.

uncertain. In addition, the demands of urban life created a new status of person: those who did the dirtiest jobs, such as removing garbage and sewage, and were therefore viewed as physically and ritually impure. They were thought to be so polluting that a daughter of a decent householder was expected to go home to wash her eyes after seeing one of these outcastes, known as "untouchables." Even though their work kept the cities clean and healthy, they were forced to live in shantytowns outside the city limits.

Yet some among these untouchables were dissatisfied with the lot assigned to them. In times of rapid change, when thinkers were putting all varieties of authority into question, some of them joined dissident sects to protest their oppression. The turbulence and ferment in the new cities affected even the most abject of their inhabitants. Residents of the dynamic and cosmopolitan cities would offer those challenging the Vedic rituals and Brahman priests their most receptive audiences.

BRAHMANS, THEIR CHALLENGERS, AND NEW BELIEFS

The South Asian wise men found urban life in the fast-changing society to be profoundly unsettling. Traditional priests viewed cities as dirty and polluting places, where castes mixed indiscriminately, where lowborn persons were able to raise their status by acquiring wealth or skill, and where the oral traditions that they had monopolized were threatened by writing. These Brahmans were not happy when an alphabetic script appeared around 600 BCE, for it undermined their ability to control the definition of right and wrong and thus weakened the moral legitimacy of the order they dominated. Because all of Vedic literature had been memorized, only the brightest of the Brahmans, free from the need to do productive labor, could master the tradition. The newer, simpler writing made sacred knowledge more accessible. To the Brahmans, nothing about the cities seemed good.

Frightened by these chaotic conditions, Brahmans sought to strengthen their relationships with the rajas by establishing the idea of a king endowed with divine power. Kingship had been unnecessary according to Brahman writings in a long-ago golden age; but over time the world deteriorated, until "fish ate fish" and the pure mixed with the impure. Then the gods decided that people on earth needed a king to maintain order. The gods selected just such a king, calling him Manu—literally, "Man"—but Manu did not want to accept the difficult job. To win his consent, the gods promised him one-tenth of the grain harvest, one-fiftieth of the cattle, one-quarter of the merits earned by the good behavior of his subjects, and the most beautiful woman in his domain. In this account of how kingship began, royal power has a divine origin: the gods chose the king and protected him. Moreover, priests and Vedic rituals were essential to royal power, since it was validated through ceremonies carried out by Brahman priests.

> *Since land could not be cultivated without killing insects, the extreme nonviolence of Jainism automatically excluded peasants.*

This emphasis on divine kingship created tensions within Vedic South Asian society. The Brahmans' claim to moral authority came to be resented by many of the Kshatriyas—especially those in the oligarchic republics, whose leaders did not claim divine power through sacrificial rituals. Merchants and artisans, as members of subcastes in growing cities, also came to chafe at the power and superiority of the Brahmans, whose performance of rituals served only the kings. Such resentments provoked members of these other groups to challenge the Brahmans' domination. Some thinkers in South Asia, like those in China and in the Greek cities experiencing similar upheavals around this time, believed that they were in an age of acute crisis because their culture's ancient harmony had been lost. And like many contemporary scholars and philosophers elsewhere, a new group of South Asian scholars and religious leaders took on the new challenges by developing their own answers to questions about human existence.

DISSIDENT THINKERS As the Brahmans had feared, the spread of writing led to questioning of the order over which they presided. Dissident South Asian thinkers challenged the religious foundations of the Brahmans' worldview by refusing to recognize the gods that populated the Vedic world. Some of these rebels sprang from inside of the Vedic tradition; though Brahmans, they rejected the idea that sacrificial rituals pleased the gods. Their discussions and teachings about the universe and life resulted in the collection called the Upanishads (see Chapter 4). Others, from non-Vedic cultural traditions, challenged the Brahmans more directly, though some adopted and developed ideas expressed in the Upanishads.

MAHAVIRA AND JAINISM Jainism and Buddhism were the two most influential schools that set themselves against the Brahmans. The doctrines of Jainism, which emerged in the seventh century BCE, were popularized in the sixth century BCE by Vardhamana Mahavira (c. 540–468 BCE), who drew on the teachings from the Upanishads but emphasized interpretation for everyday human life rather than trying to provide deeper understanding of the fundamentals of the social order of the universe. Born into the Kshatriya caste in an oligarchic republic, Mahavira left home when he was thirty years old to seek the truth about life; he spent twelve years as an ascetic, meaning one who denies themselves of material possessions and physical pleasures, wandering around the Ganges Valley before reaching enlightenment. He taught his disciples that the universe obeys its own everlasting rules and could not be affected by any god or other supernatural being. Meanwhile, he believed that the purpose of life was to purify one's soul through asceticism, or *ahimsa,* and to attain a state of permanent bliss. The Jains' religious doctrines emphasize asceticism over knowledge: strict self-denial enables one to avoid harming other creatures and thereby purify the soul. Moreover, the doctrine of ahimsa—literally, "no hurt"—held that every living creature has a soul. Killing even an ant would incur demerits and thus an unfavorable rebirth and further away from permanent bliss. Therefore, believers had to watch every step to avoid inadvertently becoming a murderer.

Since land could not be cultivated without killing insects, the extreme nonviolence of Jainism automatically excluded peasants from its devotees; it became a religion of traders and other city dwellers whose occupations allowed them to follow its precepts. The teachings of Mahavira were originally transmitted orally by his followers; but around the fifth century CE, a thousand years after his death, his followers wrote down his teachings. The strictly nonviolent doctrine, though originally intended only for followers of Jainism, has profoundly affected the thinking of inhabitants of South Asia down to modern times.

BUDDHA AND BUDDHISM The most direct challenge to traditional Brahman thinking came from Siddhartha Gautama (c. 563–483 BCE), usually called the Buddha (the Enlightened One), a contemporary of Mahavira as well as of Confucius in China. The Buddha not only objected to the traditional Brahman rituals and sacrifices; he also denied the elaborate cosmology described by the Brahmans and the preference for kingship so important to the power of the priestly class. His teachings provided the peoples of South Asia and elsewhere with alternatives to established traditions that eventually themselves became established. In this respect, Buddhism in South Asia functioned much as did Confucianism in China.

Known as the wise man of Shakya, the Buddha came from a small Kshatriya community in the foothills of the Himalayas; in this oligarchic republic, his father was one of the *rajas* (though he may have been elected to head the oligarchs of his state, he was not a king). Like many other thinkers, Siddhartha was dismayed at the misery and political carnage of his age, and he left home at the age of twenty-nine in search of truth and enlightenment. Traveling through the Ganges region, he lived first as a beggar and then as a hermit, and finally, according to legend, meditated for forty-nine days until he understood how to eliminate suffering from the world.

His wanderings and ascetic life led him to create a new credo. He delivered his first sermon at Sarnath, or the Deer Garden, near Banaras. His teachings can be summarized as the Four Truths: first, life, from birth to death, is full of suffering; second, all sufferings are caused by desires; third, the only way to rise above suffering is to renounce desire; and fourth, it is only through adherence to the Noble Eightfold Path that individuals can rid themselves of desires and the illusion of separate identity and thus reach a state of contentment, or *nirvana*. The elements of the Eightfold Way can be grouped into three overarching categories: wisdom (right views and right intentions), ethical behavior (right conduct, right speech, and right livelihood), and mental discipline (right effort, right thought, and right meditation). Because these principles were simple and clear, the Four Truths of the Buddha had a powerful appeal. Like the teachings of Mahavira, the doctrines of the Buddha left no space for the supernatural, which was a prominent feature in classical Brahmanical thinking. His logical explanation of human suffering and his guidelines for renouncing desire appealed to many—though, not surprisingly, Brahman potentates frowned on this disturbing new development.

For people outside South Asian culture, the major barrier to accepting the Buddha's teachings was the concept of *nirvana*—literally, "nonexistence." For people not familiar with the Indian conception of life and death, nirvana at its most simplistic level could be interpreted as the end of life, or nonexistence, which implicates death. Just as unappealing was Buddha's pessimistic belief that life is bad and that we must endure cycles of endless suffering and deaths in order to ultimately liberate our souls. Buddhism's appeal becomes more understandable in the context of a belief in reincarnation of the soul. If life itself is suffering, and death leads simply to rebirth into another life, then the cycle of time brings endless suffering. Attaining *nirvana,* a state reached only after accumulating many merits, was the sole means of achieving a final liberation from life's troubles.

Like the other dissident thinkers of this period who challenged the authority of the Brahmans, Buddha delivered his message in Pali, a colloquial dialect of Sanskrit that all could understand. He soon attracted many followers, who formed a community of monks called a *sangha* (literally, "gathering"). Unlike the Brahmans, the Buddha and his followers preferred cities, wandering from one to another on the Ganges plain. The cities provided larger audiences for his preaching as well as the alms needed to sustain his expanding *sangha*. It is not surprising that the Buddha's most influential patrons were urban merchants. And in struggles between the oligarchs and kings, the Buddha sided with the oligarchs—reflecting his upbringing in an oligarchic republic. He inevitably aroused the opposition of the Brahmans, who favored monarchical government. While the Buddha himself did not seek to erase the *varna* hierarchy, the Buddhist *sangha* provided an escape

The Buddha's Footprints. Before his followers came to regard Buddha as a god, they were reluctant to make an idol of him—the footprints were an early representation of Buddha. They were carved in a limestone panel in a first-century BCE stupa in India.

WARRING IDEAS: THE BUDDHA VERSUS THE BRAHMANS

Great Election

This passage is from one of the earliest Buddhist texts, Dialogues of the Buddha. *Here the Buddha explains to one of his
disciples, Vāseṭṭha, how the state and king came into being.
Early in our existence, human beings were pure, but they became
greedy and chaotic. As a result they elected one person, typically
someone capable and handsome, as king to maintain order. The
one chosen is rewarded with a share of their rice.*

When they had ceased rice appeared, ripening in open
spaces, without powder, without husk, pure, fragrant and
clean grained. Where we plucked and took away for the
evening meal every evening, there next morning it had
grown ripe again. Where we plucked and took away for the
morning meal, there in the evening it had grown ripe again.
There was no break visible. Enjoying this rice, feeding on
it, nourished by it, we have so continued a long long while.
But from evil and immoral customs becoming manifest
among us, powder has enveloped the clean grain, husk too
has enveloped the clean grain, and where we have reaped
is no re-growth; a break has come, and the rice-stubble
stands in clumps. Come now, let us divide off the rice fields
and set boundaries thereto! And so they divided off the rice
and set up boundaries round it.

Now some being, Vāseṭṭha, of greedy disposition, watching over his own plot, stole another plot and made use of it.
They took him and holding him fast, said: Truly, good being,
thou hast wrought evil in that, while watching thine own
plot, thou hast stolen another plot and made use of it. See,
good being, that thou do not such a thing again! Ay, sirs, he
replied. And a second time he did so. And yet a third. And
again they took him and admonished him. Some smote him
with the hand, some with clods, some with sticks. With
such a beginning, Vāseṭṭha, did stealing appear, and censure and lying and punishment became known.

Now those beings, Vāseṭṭha, gathered themselves together, and bewailed these things, saying: From our evil
deeds, sirs, becoming manifest, inasmuch as stealing, censure, lying, punishment have become known, what if we
were to select a certain being, who should be wrathful
when indignation is right, who should censure that which
should rightly be censured and should banish him who deserves to be banished? But we will give him in return a
proportion of the rice.

Then, Vāseṭṭha, those beings went to the being among
them who was the handsomest, the best favoured, the
most attractive, the most capable and said to him: Come
now, good being, be indignant at that whereat one should
rightly be indignant, censure that which should rightly be
censured, banish him who deserves to be banished. And
we will contribute to thee a proportion of our rice.

And he consented, and did so, and they gave him a proportion of their rice.

Chosen by the whole people, Vāseṭṭha, is what is
meant by Mahā Sammata; so Mahā Sammata (the Great
Elect) was the first standing phrase to arise [for such an
one]. Lord of the Fields is what is meant by Khattiya; so
Khattiya (Noble) was the next expression to arise. He
charms the others by the Norm—by what ought (to charm)
—is what is meant by Rāja; so this was the third standing
phrase to arise.

The Duties of a King

Unlike their legal codes, such as the Laws of Manu, *the Brahmans' early law was not very specific about daily duties of a
monarch. Gautama, a Brahman thinker, nevertheless made
clear that "the king is master of all, with the exception of
Brahmanas." His main duties include sponsoring Brahmans
to carry out rituals and maintaining the hierarchy of castes.*

Chapter XI

1. The king is master of all, with the exception of Brâhma*n*as.

2. (He shall be) holy in acts and speech,

3. Fully instructed in the threefold (sacred science) and in logic,

4. Pure, of subdued senses, surrounded by companions possessing excellent qualities and by the means (for upholding his rule).

5. He shall be impartial towards his subjects;

6. And he shall do (what is) good for them.

7. All, excepting Brâhma*n*as, shall worship him who is seated on a higher seat, (while they themselves sit on a) lower (one).

8. The (Brâhma*n*as), also, shall honour him.

9. He shall protect the castes and orders in accordance with justice;

10. And those who leave (the path of) duty, he shall lead back (to it).

11. For it is declared (in the Veda) that he obtains a share of the spiritual merit (gained by his subjects).

12. And he shall select as his domestic priest (purohita) a Brâhma*n*a who is learned (in the Vedas), of noble family, eloquent, handsome, of (a suitable) age, and of a virtuous disposition, who lives righteously and who is austere.

13. With his assistance he shall fulfil his religious duties.

14. For it is declared (in the Veda): 'Kshatriyas, who are assisted by Brāhma*n*as, prosper and do not fall into distress.'

15. He shall, also, take heed of that which astrologers and interpreters of omens tell (him).

16. For some (declare), that the acquisition of wealth and security depend also upon that.

17. He shall perform in the fire of the hall the rites ensuring prosperity which are connected with expiations (sânti), festivals, a prosperous march, long life, and auspiciousness; as well as those that are intended to cause enmity, to subdue (enemies), to destroy (them) by incantations, and to cause their misfortune.

18. Officiating priests (shall perform) the other (sacrifices) according to the precepts (of the Veda).

19. His administration of justice (shall be regulated by) the Veda, the Institutes of the Sacred Law, the A*ṅ*gas, and the Purâna.

20. The laws of countries, castes, and families, which are not opposed to the (sacred) records, (have) also authority.

21. Cultivators, traders, herdsmen, money-lenders, and artisans (have authority to lay down rules) for their respective classes.

22. Having learned the (state of) affairs from those who (in each class) have authority (to speak he shall give) the legal decision.

23. Reasoning is a means for arriving at the truth.

24. Coming to a conclusion through that, he shall decide properly.

→ *The Buddha and Brahmans gave different explanations of how states arose in late Vedic India.*

→ *Why did the Buddha suggest that the first king was elected by people to end the chaos?*

→ *Why did the Brahman lawmakers make the king the masters of everyone but themselves?*

SOURCE: *Dialogues of the Buddha, Part iii*, vol. 4 of *Sacred Books of the Buddhists*, translated by T. W. Rhys David and C. A. F. Rhys David (London: Oxford University Press, 1921), pp. 87–88; *The Sacred Laws of the Âryas as Taught in the Schools of Âpastamba, Gautama, Visishtha, and Baudhâyaa*, translated by Georg Bühler, vol. 2 of *The Sacred Books of the East*, edited by Friedrich Max Müller (1879; reprint, Delhi: Motilal Banarsidass, 1975), pp. 234–37.

Global Connections & Disconnections

PROPHETS AND THE FOUNDING TEXTS:
COMPARING CONFUCIUS AND THE BUDDHA

Throughout history, universalizing religions have been defined not just by their sacred texts but also by central figures whose lives inspired and shaped movements and long-lasting traditions. Stories about them and their religious experience have often become a primary method of transmitting beliefs. In Confucianism and Buddhism, we find key leaders who inspired the faiths that were subsequently named for them.

Although famous for claiming that as a thinker he was a "transmitter who invented nothing," Confucius was one of ancient philosophy's great innovators. Born in China near the northern city of Qufu, he elaborated a code of behavior that put the highest value on individual performance of traditional rituals and on governmental morality based on correct social relationships, sincerity, and justice. Seeing division and war between rival states, he wished to restore the mandate of heaven to the declining Zhou dynasty and reunify China, but peace and prosperity would not come to the region until long after his death.

Though Confucius never held a high government post himself, over the centuries both the method and substance of his teaching, with many revisions, became the mainstream ideology of imperial China. His idea that the state should be modeled on the patriarchal family—that is, the ruler should respect the heaven as if it was his father, and protect his subjects as if they were his children—became the foundation of Chinese political theory. His philosophy of teaching could be summarized in three statements: "I teach whoever wants to learn with no regard to his birth," "The best educated men should serve the government," and "Those who work with their mind should rule, and those who work with their manual labor should be ruled." In short, each man was perfectible if he received the proper training. Confucius wanted people to perform the rituals bequeathed by the early Zhou and to emulate the actions of the great men who had ordered the world according to principles of civility and culture.

These ideas directly affected his immediate disciples and prominent Chinese philosophers of later generations, who did not always agree on how they should be interpreted. One school of Confucianists was represented by Mencius (372–289 BCE), who held that while recognizing the tendency of people to be led astray by worldly appetites and ambitions, Confucius believed in the inherent goodness of human nature. To recover that innate goodness required moral training. But according to Xunzi, Confucius saw humans as evil and lacking an innate moral sense. They therefore had to be controlled by education, ritual, and custom—an argument that later would be embraced by the founders of Legalism. Xunzi's pessimistic understanding seemed to better fit the experience of those who lived through the Warring States period and its imperial aftermath, the rise and fall of the short-lived Qin Empire.

Nevertheless, both Mencius and Xunzi embraced—though for different reasons—Confucius's dictum that the people were perfectible by being educated and by practicing the proper rules of conduct. All Confucians, whether pessimists or optimists, viewed the moral cultivation of the individual through education as the heart of the Confucian civilizing process, and they ensured that his ideas remained a vital force throughout Chinese history. Confucius's teachings, innovative and new during his life, in-

---

from the oppressive *varna* system and the tremendous prestige that it afforded the Brahman caste.

Thus, in South Asia as in China, the first millennium BCE was a time of innovation as well as warfare. Until the fourth century BCE, South Asia remained a confusing mass of warring territorial states. But out of the competition between these states came social transformations, including expansion of the caste system, the rise of cities and trade, and new philosophies and religions. Political unification would eventually follow in 321 BCE, followed by the conversion of the most powerful emperor of the new empire to Buddhism (see Chapter 6).

COMMON CULTURES IN THE AMERICAS

> → How did cultural integration develop in the Andes and Mesoamerica in the absence of political unity?

For many thousands of years, the original inhabitants of the Americas lived in small groups and villages as they engaged in hunting, gathering, and farming. Having wiped out the influenced all Chinese, both high and low, to focus on bettering their lives in this world through education and cultural pursuits. To become a "Confucian" meant to put into daily practice the civilized ideals of the past in order to achieve a vision of the highest good.

Though Buddhism cannot match Confucianism's long incorporation into state ideology, the teachings of the Buddha, like those of Confucius, had a far-reaching influence. The two thinkers were roughly contemporary, and both formulated their ideas in response to what they perceived as social chaos and degeneration. The Buddha, who had grown up in an oligarchic republic whose leaders (*rajas*) did not claim their authority to rule as divinely sanctioned by the Brahmans' rituals, presented a vision of society that challenged the Brahmanical order, although that order—in the form of caste hierarchy and monarchical polities—continued to thrive in South Asia. Indeed, Buddhist *sangha,* or communities of monks, had nearly vanished from the subcontinent after the first millennium CE. Nevertheless, Buddhism shaped the views of life and death and the scheme of time and space of the universe in South Asia. It also had a profound impact on peoples outside the region and even replaced Confucianism as the dominant religion in China for a few hundred years.

The Buddha offered a logical approach in the form of a unified system underlying the universe, instead of invoking divine intervention, to understanding the universe and social life at a time of rapid political development. As the Upanishads taught, he believed that the universe and individual lives all go through eternal cycles of birth, death, and rebirth, and the Buddha focused on and elaborated the

concept of *karma* (literally, "fate" or "action"), a universal principle of cause and effect. The birth of every living being, human or animal, reflects actions taken in his or her past lives. Karma embodies the sins and merits of each individual, establishing his or her status in the current life—and deeds in the current life, in turn, affect that karma and thus determine suffering and happiness in the next life. Buddhist believers therefore focused not on pleasing gods who threatened punishment for misdeeds but on the consequences of their own actions: through their own behavior, they could attain better future lives. The Buddha's teachings, recorded as his dialogues with disciples in the vernacular dialect of Pali, were collected in *Nikayas* (*Collections*) and *Vinayas* (*Disciplines*). Several centuries later, when Buddhists rewrote his teachings in Sanskrit, the more poetic rhetoric obscured many of his original ideas.

Confucianism and Buddhism, much like the Vedic, Brahmin, and Judaic faiths discussed in Chapter 4, emerged during periods of great turmoil and change. All four faiths are undoubtedly products of their historical circumstances, and all were initially transmitted orally; later adherents created a written record of their teachings so that they might spread more widely. From their inception to the present, the basic principles and teachings of each have been debated by their believers. But Buddhism and Confucianism differ from the other two faiths in that they have founders whose identification with their belief systems remains their single most defining characteristic. We will see this phenomenon again with the rise of Christianity (from the teachings of Jesus) and Islam (from the teachings of Muhammad) as we continue our discussion of universalizing religions.

digenous large animals—not just the woolly mammoth but proto-camels and horses as well—the first Americans lacked domesticable animals; unlike members of early Afro-Eurasian societies, they could not mount horses, yoke oxen, or herd sheep. They therefore also lacked any impetus to invent a working wheel that an animal could pull to transport heavy loads. The result, quite apart from the obvious divergence in lifeways between American and the Afro-Eurasian peoples, was that basic communications between settlements in the Americas relied on human feet for locomotion on land; on water, they relied on canoes. These restrictions limited the

distances that individuals traversed and the cargoes that they could haul.

There was some evidence for seaborne contact among native Americans dating from 1500 BCE. Buoyed in canoes, they paddled up and down the shorelines of the Pacific Ocean and the Gulf of Mexico. Strikingly similar chambered tombs, for instance, appear from the Pacific coast of Mexico, where the earliest instances have been found, all the way down to South America to coastal Peru. Early clothing, ceramic bottles, and other common items with shared features are likewise scattered across the Pacific coast of the Americas. For the most

El Lanzón. The Chavín excelled at elaborate stone carvings with complex images of their deities. This image of El Lanzón is a good example. At the center of one of the Chavín peoples' greatest temples is this massive gallery with a giant monument in the middle, etched with images of snakes, felines, and humans combined into one hybrid supernatural form. Observe the hands and feet with claws and the eyebrows that turn into serpents.

part, however, communications were intermittent, though recent excavations suggest that settlements may have been established on the coast of present-day Ecuador by colonists from western Mexico. Regional diversity, influenced by only sporadic long-distance communication and exchange, dominated the lifeways of the inhabitants of the Americas.

THE CHAVÍN IN THE ANDES (1400–200 BCE)

In this world of extreme localization and diversity, the steep mountainsides and deep fertile valleys of the Andes Mountains became the home of a distinctive people called the Chavín. In what is now northern Peru, farmers and pastoralists began to share a common belief system around 1400 BCE. With time, their artistic influence and spiritual principles touched a broad expanse of Andean folk. Like the peoples of South Asia and others in Afro-Eurasia, the Chavín peoples were united by culture and faith much more than by any political structure.

The Chavín peoples literally organized their societies vertically. Communities and households spread their trading systems up the mountainsides: valley floors yielded tropical and subtropical produce, further up the mountains maize and other crops were grown, and in the highlands, potatoes became a staple, and llamas were domesticated to produce wool

and dung (as fertilizer and fuel) and eventually to serve as beasts of burden. But because llamas could not transport humans, the Chavín migratory and political reach remained limited: no empire would emerge in the Andes for another millennium. The ecological diversity of the vertical societies of the Chavín enabled them to find all necessities close at hand, but they did undertake some long-distance trade, restricted mainly to dyes and precious stones, like obsidian. By 900 BCE, the Chavín were erecting elaborate stone carvings, using advanced techniques to weave fine cotton textiles, and making gold, silver, and copper metal goods. Scholars have found evidence that by 400 BCE, trade in painted textiles, ceramics, and gold objects spanned the Pacific coast, the Andean highlands, and the watershed eastward to the tropical rainforests of the Amazon basin. But these networks were not extensive and restricted themselves to conveying light precious goods.

There was a great deal of heterogeneity and fragmentation among the Chavín. But unifying their communities was a shared artistic tradition motivated by devotion to powerful deities; their spiritual capital was at the central temple complex of Chavín de Huántar, in modern Peru's northeastern highlands. The temple boasted a U-shaped platform, whose opening to the east surrounded a sunken, circular plaza; from its passageways and underground galleries, priests could suddenly emerge during ceremonies. The priests took hallucinogenic drugs, which were believed to enable them to become

> *How did cultural integration develop in the Andes and Mesoamerica in the absence of political unity?*

jaguars—the largest and most dangerous of the predators in the region—and to commune with the supernatural. Pilgrims brought tribute to Chavín de Huántar, where they worshipped and feasted together.

The Chavín drew on influences from as far away as the Amazon and the Pacific coast as they created devotional cults that focused on wild animals as representatives of spiritual forces. Carved stone jaguars, serpents, and hawks, baring their large fangs and claws to remind believers of the powers of nature, dominated the spiritual landscape. The "Smiling God" at Chavín de Huántar, El Lanzón, shaped from a slab of white granite fifteen feet high, had a human form but a fanged, catlike face, hair made of snakes, feet ending with talons, and hands that bristled with claws. This supernatural image was set on an awe-inspiring stage: dimly lit from above so that his face would glow from the reflection of polished

mirrors, the god stood over a canal, and the vibrations and deep rumbling sounds of the rushing water below helped convey a sense of the spiritual forces in the world. Though they borrowed from neighbors and refined existing sculptural techniques, the Chavín created the first great art style of the Andes; their cult finally gave way around 400 BCE to multiple local cultural heirs. Still, elements of it survived, taken up by successor religions adopted by stronger states further south.

THE OLMECS IN MESOAMERICA

Further to the north, in Mesoamerica, the first complex society emerged around 1500 BCE in the region between the highland plateaus of central Mexico and the Gulf Coast around modern-day Veracruz. (See Map 5-4.) The Olmecs

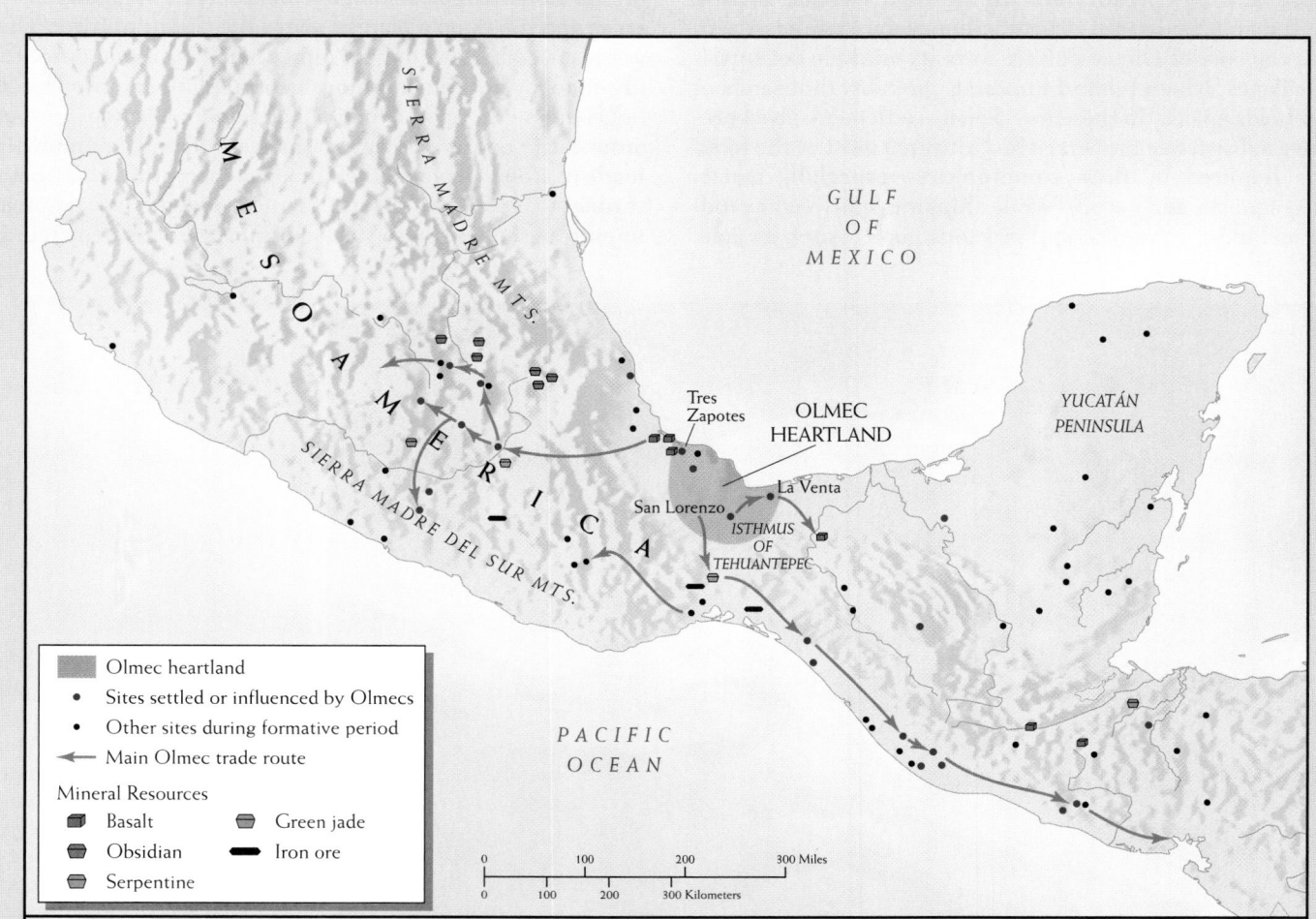

MAP 5-4   THE OLMEC WORLD

The Olmecs had a strong impact on Mesoamerica's early cultural integration. According to this map, how did they influence people living beyond the Olmec heartland? What factors limited the extent of Olmec influence? Why do you think the Olmec never became a politically unified regional empire?

provide an example of a first-generation small-scale community endeavoring to create new political and economic institutions while trying to answer the most profound questions about the nature of humanity and the world beyond.

Unlike the territorial states of Mesopotamia, these native American peoples had no preexisting high cultures from which to draw inspiration. Rather, the Mesoamerican cultures were something new, created out of local village roots. The peoples of this region formed themselves into a loose confederation of villages, scattered from the coast to the highlands and in large part nestled in river valleys and along the shores of swampy lakes. Their residents traded with each other, shared a common language, and worshipped the same gods. These were the Olmecs, a name meaning "inhabitants in the land of rubber"—one of their basic staples exported from the lowlands. Around 1500 BCE, the residents of hundreds of hamlets began to integrate themselves into a single culture and to spread elements of their beliefs, artistic achievements, and social structure far beyond their heartland.

At the core of Olmec culture were its multiple decentralized villages, which housed hundreds, possibly thousands of households apiece. In these low-density settlements lived productive subsistence farmers, who cultivated most of the foodstuffs required by their communities—especially maize, beans, squash, and cacao—while shipping lightweight products including ceramics, and precious goods (such as jade,

obsidian, or quetzal feathers, obtained from outlying areas and used to create masks and ritual figurines) to other villages. Most of these highly valued objects were intended for religious purposes rather than everyday consumption. The Olmecs also forged a network of exchange of sacred ritual objects among fellow believers.

CITIES AS SACRED CENTERS Despite their dispersed social landscape, the Olmec peoples created shared belief systems, a single language, and a priestly class who ensured that villagers adhered to highly ritualized practices. Their primary cities, including San Lorenzo, La Venta, and Tres Zapotes, were not large compared to the urban centers of Afro-Eurasia, but they were religious and secular hubs that bound together the surrounding agrarian hamlets. They were built around specialized buildings that featured massive earthen mounds, platforms, palaces, and capacious plazas. The rulers of San Lorenzo, for instance, constructed a high city of terraces and ridges on a plateau above the Chiquito River. Their vassals used baskets to haul more than 2.3 million cubic feet of soil to lay out the enormous central platform, two football fields in length, upon which palaces and workshops rose. All around the courtyards and paths were massive monuments made of stone—colossal heads, jaguar sculptures, and basalt thrones—as well as clusters of large wooden busts. Arranged to portray scenes, these vast sculpture gardens depicted the

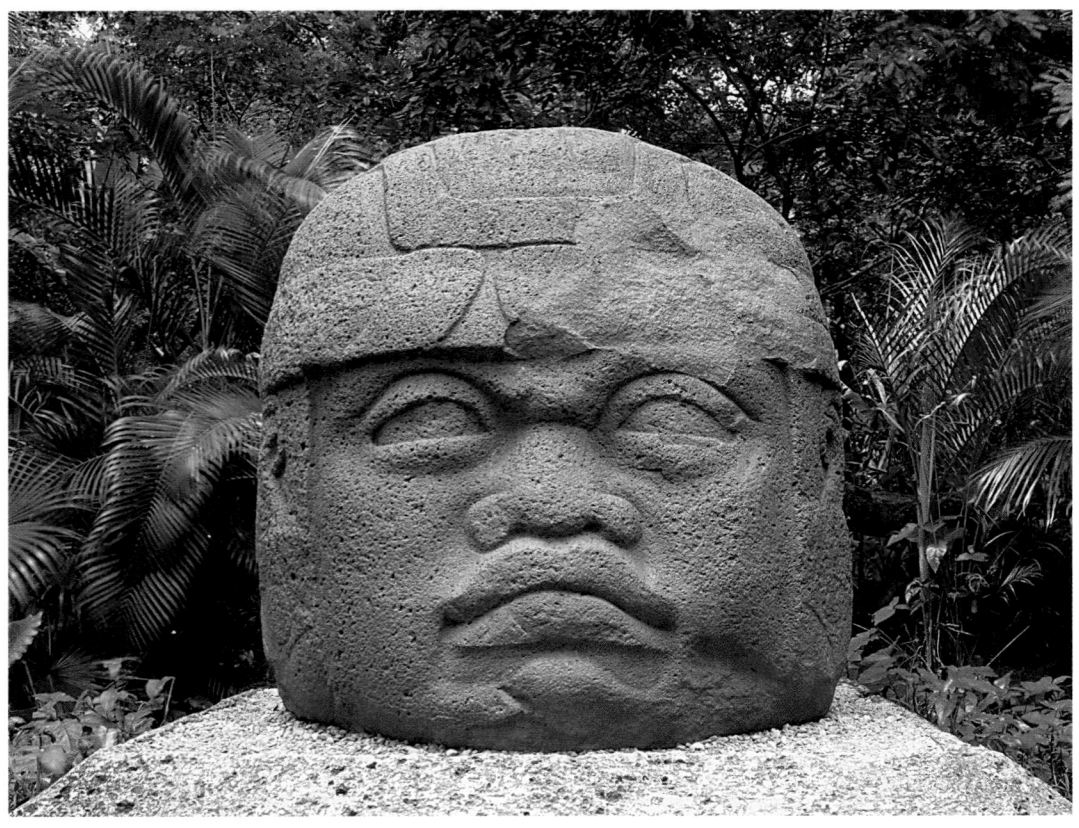

Olmec Head. At La Venta, in Tabasco State in Mexico, four colossal heads rest on the ground, remnants of a field of monumental figures that once ornamented this Olmec site. Nine feet high and weighing up to twenty tons, the giant helmeted heads are the source of much speculation. Carved from single boulders, they are thought to be portraits of great kings or legendary ballplayers. Each head bears distinctive elements in homage to its subject.

OLMEC ART AS IDEOLOGY

Olmec ideology put great emphasis on the ties between the natural, supernatural, and the human worlds. It was also an ideology crafted to influence and possibly convert the Olmecs' neighbors. Known for their great monumental architecture and artwork, Olmec craftsworkers also made portable objects, icons, and miniature figures that unify their belief systems and that could be transported long distances to convey a religious message to non-Olmecs and bring them into their cultural sphere of influence. Such works were designed to expand the spiritual frontier of Olmec belief throughout Mesoamerica.

Consider one of the most famous of these surviving portable spiritual icons, called "Young Lord" by some archaeologists and "Slim Jim" by others because of his elongated figure. Although most icons represent a single deity or power, Young Lord combines many of the basic elements of Olmec belief into a single, beautiful figurine. Standing about two feet tall, Young Lord was a diplomatic artifact, intended to spread the influence of a complex belief system far and wide.

Look closely at the photograph of Young Lord. He is fierce. Holding two scepters against his chest, and himself carved in the form of a scepter, he is meant to con-

vey power and influence—but the power and influence of what?

See if you can "read" the delicate incisions around his body. Note his pose: rigid and tall, like a ruler who is the axis mundi, the turning point who joins the earthly and the supernatural worlds. The images you see represent ceremonial practices—rituals that Young Lord oversees, and that enable him to exercise his shamanic powers over believers. His face, for instance, is covered by a mask that evokes classic Olmec shamanic images; his mouth snarls like a jaguar's and his nose resembles an eagle's beak. The mask and its carvings suggest that this lord is capable of transforming into a jaguar or an avian hunter to conduct sacrificial rites, a surmise confirmed by the extensive incisions over his body.

Bloodletting and human sacrifice dominate the cicatrices and underscore the importance of the scepters, used to draw blood. These sacrifices were intended to please the forces of the supernatural world, which would reward believers with rain. Notice the arms and hands, covered with images of ritual performers and victims. His legs are adorned with figures of serpentlike creatures, monsters with gaping jaws, fangs, and forked tongues.

The statue as a whole is divided horizontally into three, signifying the three layers of the cosmos—the supernatural, the terrestrial, and the underworld—which Young Lord has the power to travel between as he brings messages to believers and nonbelievers alike. This is a powerful image, one meant to drive home the authority of Olmec rulers to their subjects and neighbors.

→ *What kind of power and influence does Young Lord represent?*
→ *What do the various symbols on his statue tell us about various spiritual aspects of Olmec society?*
→ *What kinds of spiritual objects would Christians, Muslims, or Buddhists draw on to propagate their faith, as the Olmecs did with Young Lord?*

human rulers and deities to whom the Olmecs paid homage and offered sacrifice. Artificial lagoons and channels criss-crossed the precinct. Beneath these mounds archaeologists have found axes, knives made of sharpened obsidian, other tools, and simple yet breathtaking figurines made most often of jade, buried as tokens for those who dwelled in the super-natural world. San Lorenzo was not a capital city, with a large permanent population whose rulers made laws throughout Olmec territorial dominions. Rather, it was a devotional cen-ter, the influence of whose monumental architecture and art was felt throughout the Olmec hinterlands.

Paying homage to their gods and rulers was part of the Olmecs' daily life. While devotional activity took place on the shores of lakes, in caves, on mountaintops, and in other nat-ural settings, it occurred above all in the primary cities. In La Venta, huge pits (one was thirteen feet deep and seventy-seven feet wide) contained the devotees' massive offerings of hundreds of tons of serpentine carved blocks. Olmec art speaks to the powerful influence of devotion on creativity. Many images were dominated by representations of natural and supernatural entities—not just animals such as snakes, jaguars, and crocodiles but also certain humans called *shamans,* who were believed to have special powers to com-mune with the supernatural and the ability to transform themselves wholly or partly into beasts (as also seen in im-ages at Chavín sites). A common figurine, for instance, is of the "were-jaguar," a being that was part man, part animal. Shamans representing jaguars invoked the Olmec rain god, a jaguarlike being, to bring rainfall to the land and thereby se-cure its fertility. The ceremonial life of the Olmecs revolved around agricultural and rainfall cycles. Throughout the Olmec heartland, we see evidence of a distinct and shared iconography—an integrated culture that transcended eco-logical niches.

The Olmecs' major cities were not just centers of pure de-votion. They were also athletic hubs where victorious teams paid homage to their deities. Intricate ball courts made room on the sidelines for fans to applaud and jeer at the sweating contestants, who struggled to bounce hard rubber balls off parallel side walls and their bodies and into a goal. Noble players, bearing helmets and heavy padding, could touch the six-pound rubber ball only with their elbows, hips, knees, and buttocks, and were honored when they knocked the ball through the stationary stone hoop. Massive sculptures of hel-meted heads carved out of volcanic basalt suggest that famous ballplayers gained more renown by being monumen-talized. At La Venta, a huge mosaic made out of greenstone served as an elegant ball court; at its center was a portal that was thought to open out into the otherworld. Olmec archae-ological sites are now filled with the remains of game equip-ment and of the trophies awarded to the victors. Some trophies were buried in the tomb of a dead ruler so that he could play ball with the gods in the otherworld. Ritual ball games, for all their entertainment value, were integral to Olmec devotional culture. It was in honor of the powerful rain god that players struggled to win.

What added to the thrill of the ball court was that they were dangerous yet fecund places associated with water and agricultural fertility, for an equally important aspect of devo-tional culture was the practice of human sacrifice. Indeed, it is likely that athletics and sacrifice were blended in the same rituals. Many monuments depict a victorious and costumed ballplayer (sporting a jaguar headdress or a feathered serpent helmet) atop a defeated, bound human, though it is not known whether the losers were literally executed. Rainmak-ing rites also included other forms of human sacrifice. Captives—we do not know how they were selected or seized —were executed and dismembered. There is increasing evi-

Olmec Ballplayer. Ball-playing was an important ceremonial and athletic activity among the Olmec. Games were occasions for human competitors to display their skills to deities, and also against the gods themselves. Playing the sport was intimately tied to fertility. This figure exemplifies the Olmec's skill at refined stone carving.

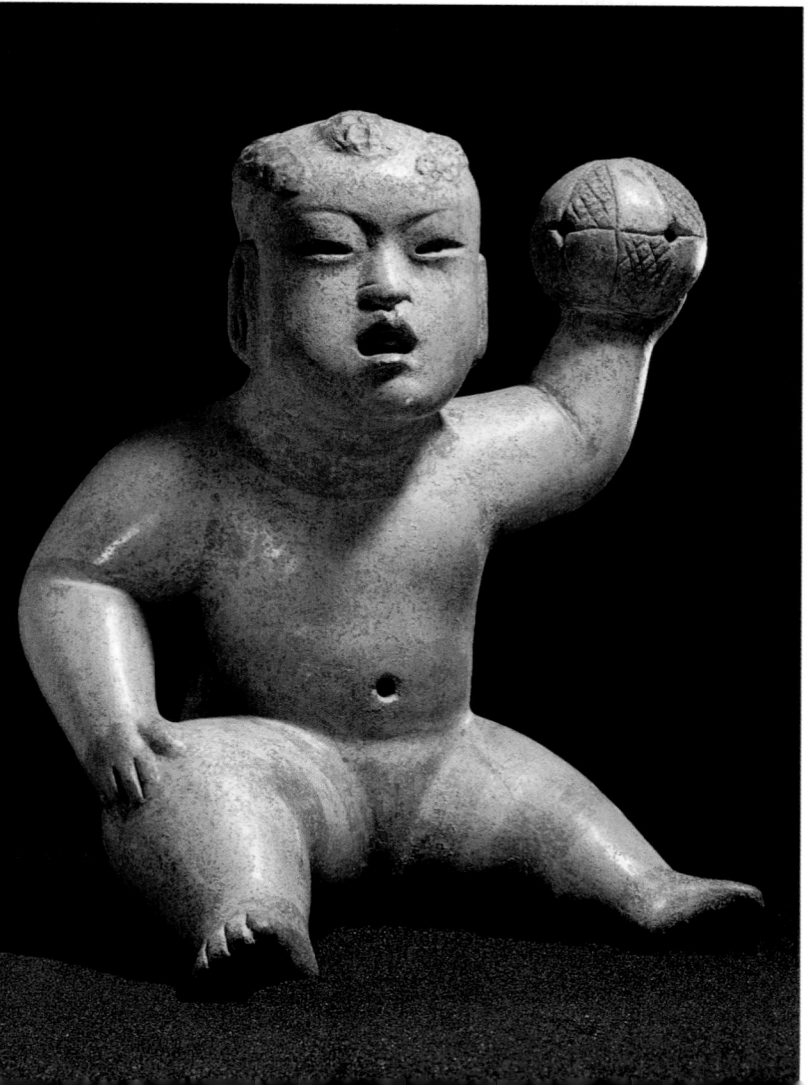

dence that the Olmecs practiced ritual warfare to supply rulers with humans whose death and torture was meant to ensure that the soil would be fertile and the rains would continue. At El Manatí, select offering sites alongside a spring and the shore of a boggy lake are filled with the bones of children slaughtered for the gods. Across the artistic landscape of the Olmecs are representations of human victims fed to the gods and to the rulers who embodied them.

MAN, NATURE, AND TIME   The Olmec cosmology also assumed a basic relationship between the natural and supernatural worlds, with the latter dictating the motions of the former. Olmec culture is saturated with belief in the power of supernatural forces and with tales of shamans controlling the supernatural. But the Olmecs were hardly a simple, superstitious folk; indeed, their conviction that the supernatural pervaded the natural world drove them to learn more about nature so that they might know with more certainty what the gods wanted. By systematically observing the natural world, they might discover godly meanings. There was no hard-and-fast line between what we now consider the separate arenas of "faith" and "science." The way that rulers reckoned time reflects this belief system, for they were convinced that the gods defined calendric passages, and therefore seasons and rainfall patterns that so decisively shaped the livelihoods of agrarian peoples. Priests, charting celestial movements, devised a complex calendar that marked the passage of seasons and generations. As in China and Mesopotamia, a flowering of culture encouraged priests and scholars to study the world around them—and the heavens—so that they might accurately chart the rhythms of the terrestrial and celestial worlds.

A WORLD OF SOCIAL DISTINCTIONS   It is easy to forget, as we consider all the remarkable effigies, artwork, and evidence of early scientific observation and writing, that Olmec centers were also communities where people went about their daily business. Daily labor kept Olmecs busy. The vast majority worked the fertile lands as part of household units, children and parents alike toiling in the fields with wooden tools, fishing in streams with nets, and hunting turtles and other small animals. Most Olmecs had to juggle the needs of their village neighbors, their immediate families, and the taxes imposed by rulers.

The Olmecs present us with an enigma. We often think of dispersed and decentralized agrarian cultures as simple and egalitarian. Increasingly, however, archaeologists of the Olmecs are finding the reverse. Not only did the Olmecs have an elaborate cultural system, they had many tiers of social rankings. The priestly class, raised and trained in the palaces at La Venta, San Lorenzo, and Tres Zapotes, directed the exchanges of sacred ritual objects between farming communities. Because these exchanges involved immense resources, the engagement of the ruling families was necessary and their involvement with these objects buttressed their claim to be

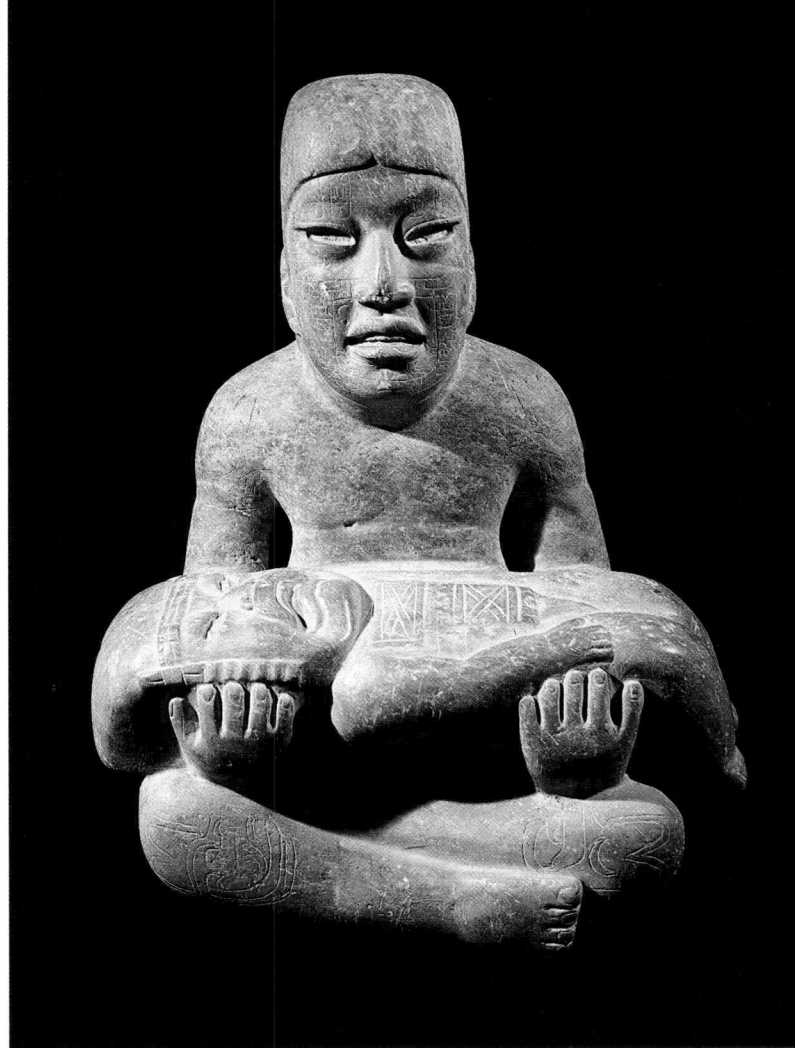

The Las Limas Monument. The were-jaguar was an important figure in the pantheon of Olmec deities. This sculpture, known as the Las Limas monument, represents a youth holding a limp were-jaguar baby. We do not know what these figures represented exactly—most likely they refer to spiritual journeys. Some have argued that this monument harkens to child sacrifice. Notice the faces of supernatural forces incised on the knees and shoulders of the youth, common Olmec motifs.

descended from divine ancestors. At the same time, their control of the commerce in precious secular goods added to their fortunes. In this fashion, dominant families blurred the line between the everyday and the religious, the profane and the sacred heritages, and thereby legitimized their domination of their subjects.

Alongside the priestly elite, a secular one emerged composed of chieftains who supervised agrarian transactions among farmers, oversaw a class of artisans, and accepted tribute from inhabitants of their villages. They set up specialized workshops, managed by foremen who answered to them,

La Mojarra Stela. This monument bears the inscription of the Long Count Olmec calendar. It is called "Long Count" because it is nonrepeating and vigesimal (base-20, in contrast to our decimal system). It also relied on the use of a zero as a place-holder, represented by a small glyph, one of the earliest uses of the concept of zero. We still have only partial knowledge of how the Olmec kept temporal records, but their system was the basis of future calendric systems across Mesoamerica. The calendar is part of a narrative about astronomy, rituals or accession, warfare, and bloodletting.

where craftsworkers carved, created pots, painted, sculpted, and wove; stones and gems were imported from surrounding villages. Those at the top of the hierarchy of chieftainships could command villages scattered over the approximate area of a territorial state. The larger the domain, the greater the ability to ship the produce of workshops and fields to the chiefs' centers or priests' capitals.

The combination of an integrated culture and a complex social structure gave the Olmecs a degree of cohesion unprecedented in the Americas. With this cohesion and the ability to transmit goods and services up the social ladder, rulers at the top had access to vast resources. Olmec influence radiated well beyond their heartland. Without an urge to con-

quer or colonize, the Olmecs nonetheless shaped the social development of much of Mesoamerica. As their population centers grew and their arts expanded, their demand for stones such as obsidian and jade, seashells, plumes, and other precious goods drove them to find suppliers at an ever greater remove. Nor were the Olmecs merely importers. They exported rubber, cacao, pottery, ceramics, figurines, refined jaguar pelts, and crocodile skins, all of which found purchasers throughout Mesoamerica. Importing and exporting were probably in the hands of a merchant class—about whose size and wealth we know little. What is more, as the evidence of the Young Lord suggests (see Primary Source box), the Olmecs also conveyed their belief system to neighbors, if not to convert them, at least to influence them and reinforce a sense of superiority.

THE LOSS OF CENTERS   The breakdown of the Olmec culture is shrouded in mystery. The decline was uneven, abrupt in some centers and protracted in others. At La Venta, for instance, the altars and massive basalt heads were defaced and buried—the ultimate ignominy for the people and gods they were meant to represent, indicating a dramatic shift. And yet, there is little evidence of a spasm of war, a peasant uprising, a demographic cataclysm, or civil conflict between factions of the ruling classes. Indeed, in many parts of the Olmec heartland, the religious centers that had once served as the hubs of the Olmec world were abandoned but not destroyed. Much of the Olmec hinterland remained heavily populated and highly productive.

The machinery for drawing resources into Olmec capitals eventually failed. As the bonds between rulers and their subjects weakened, so did the networks of exchange of ritual objects that had enlivened the Olmec centers and made them magnets for obedience and piety. Olmec hierarchies then collapsed. Without a sacred elite to transmit the cosmology, it too faded. What was left of the Olmec heritage passed on to other Mesoamericans—especially those of the central plateaus and the tropical lowlands of the Yucatán peninsula, where new centers of power eventually arose that bore traces of their Olmec predecessors.

COMMON CULTURES IN SUB-SAHARAN AFRICA

> → *How did the spread of iron smelting shape the social landscape of sub-Saharan Africa?*

Africa's most significant historical development in the first millennium BCE was the continued desiccation of the northern and central parts of the landmass, and the emergence of the great Sahara Desert, the largest desert on the planet, as its primary geographical and population barrier. (See Map 5-5.) Large areas that had once supported abundant plant and animal life, including human settlements, now became more sparsely populated. Moreover, the peoples living in Africa began to coalesce in a few locations; the most important of these was the Nile Valley, which may have held more than half of the landmass's population at this time. Climatic change divided the whole of Africa from the Equator northward to the Sahara Desert roughly into four distinct geographical and human zones. Moving from north to south, the first zone was the Sahara Desert itself, which never completely emptied out, despite its extreme heat and aridity. Its oases supported pastoral peoples, like the ancestors of the modern Tuareg tribal communities, who raised livestock and promoted contacts between the northern and the western parts of Africa. Further south of the Sahara was the Sahel, literally the coast (Arabic *sahil*) of the great ocean of sand. In time, some of Africa's great commercial cities, like Timbuktu, would arise in this zone; but in the first millennium BCE no city of great size had yet made its appearance.

The next zone was the Sudanic savanna region, an area of high grasslands stretching all the way from present-day Senegal along the Atlantic Ocean in the west to the Nile River and the Red Sea in the east. Many of West Africa's kingdoms emerged there, since the area was free of the tsetse fly, which was as lethal to animals as to humans, killing off livestock, including cattle, horses, and goats. The fourth and final ethnogeographical zone was the

western and central African rain forests, a region characterized by small-scale societies. In this period, it was sparsely populated.

Although there was contact across the Sahara, Africa below the Sahara was markedly different in many ways from

MAP 5-5   AFRICA, 500 BCE

The first millennium BCE was a major period of social, cultural, economic, and political integration for North and sub-Saharan Africa. What effect did the presence of the Greek and Phoenician colonies have on Africa? What main factor integrated Nubia and Egypt? Does the map reveal a relationship between the rise of Sudanic culture and the spread of ironworking? If so, what is it?

North Africa and Eurasia. It did not develop a plough agriculture; its farmers depended on hoes. Also, in most parts of sub-Saharan Africa, except for densely populated regions, land was held communally and never regarded as having as much value as labor. African peoples could always move into new locations. They had more difficulty finding workers to till the soil.

Distinctive ways of life that were to become associated with these areas from 1000 CE onward were only beginning to appear during the first millennium BCE. In the savanna area, millet and sorghum were the primary food crops; in the rain forests, yams and other root crops dominated. Relatively large populations were confined mainly to the Sudanic savanna region, the sole area for which substantial historical records for this period exist. Here, in fact, a way of life that can be called Sudanic began to crystallize.

These peoples of the first millennium BCE were not completely dependent on their feet to get around, as were their counterparts in the Americas. They had domesticated several animals, including cattle and goats, and even possessed small horses (about the size of today's ponies). Although their communities were scattered widely across Africa, some 4,000 miles from west to east, they had much in common. They all tended to adhere to a cosmology dominated by a high god, and their polities were led by sacred kings; servants were buried alongside their rulers in the belief that the rulers would be resurrected in the afterlife and would need to be served by those who had been loyal to them in this life. They were skilled cultivators and weavers of cotton, which they had domesticated from a wild plant indigenous to the area. At

first, archaeologists and historians believed that these Sudanic peoples had borrowed their institutions, notably their sacred kingships, from their Egyptian neighbors to the north; but linguistic evidence and especially their custom of burying servants along with the rulers make it clear that the Sudanic communities had developed these practices on their own.

MEROE: BETWEEN SUDANIC AFRICA AND PHARAONIC EGYPT

Without doubt, the most highly developed of these Sudanic sacred kingdoms was the state of Meroe, located in what is now Sudan. Meroe arose in the southern part of an area known historically as Nubia, a region lying between the first Nile cataract (located at the present-day city of Aswan) and the sixth and last cataract (just north of present-day Khartoum, where the Blue and the White Nile come together). From at least the fourth millennium BCE onward, and perhaps earlier, peoples in this region were in contact with both the northern and southern parts of the African landmass. It was one of the few parts of sub-Saharan Africa known to the outside world. The Greek poet Homer described its inhabitants as "the remotest nation, the most just of men; the favorites of the gods." Nubia's historical connection to Egypt was obvious: it was Egypt's corridor to sub-Saharan Africa; a source of ivory, gold, and slaves; and an area that expansionist Egyptian monarchs wanted to dominate. The best known of the conquerors from Egypt was Rameses II, who left his imprint on the culture of this area with his magnificent monuments at

The Temple of Ramses II. The temple of Ramses II at Abu Simbel was constructed during the reign of Ramses II between 1304 and 1237 BCE. It was cut out of the rock and featured four colossal statues of the king, each of which was twenty meters high. When the Aswan High Dam was built in the 1960s, the monument had to be cut into large stone slabs and moved to higher ground so that it would not be submerged under the waters of Lake Nasser, which the High Dam formed.

Primary Source

WRITING THE HISTORY OF PRELITERATE AFRICAN PEOPLES

Traditionally, historians have relied on written records and have had difficulty reconstructing the history of preliterate societies. Hence, African history has come of age only in recent times as scholars devised new techniques for uncovering past narratives.

The sources used in African history are varied and in many ways unconventional. They include art, pottery, linguistic analysis, oral traditions, and many other elements that most historians have not commonly worked with. Here are two such vital but unusual historic sources. The first is Nok terra-cottas. These terra-cottas were discovered just before and during World War II in the middle belt region of modern-day Nigeria. The figurines themselves probably were created in the common era, but they are part of a vibrant culture that dates back to the fifth century BCE.

The second source comes from the kingdom of Meroe, located between the fifth and sixth Nile cataracts. Meroe flourished for nearly a millennium, from the fifth century BCE to the fifth century CE. Though in close contact with Egypt, it lay within sub-Saharan Africa. The Egyptian influences were profound and obvious—for example, the use of the term *pharaoh* to refer to the king, borrowed religious beliefs, and the use of hieroglyphics. The African influences were more subtle and less easily discerned, but important nonetheless.

Nok figurine.

Burial pyramids at the Royal Necropolis of the ancient kingdom of Kush.

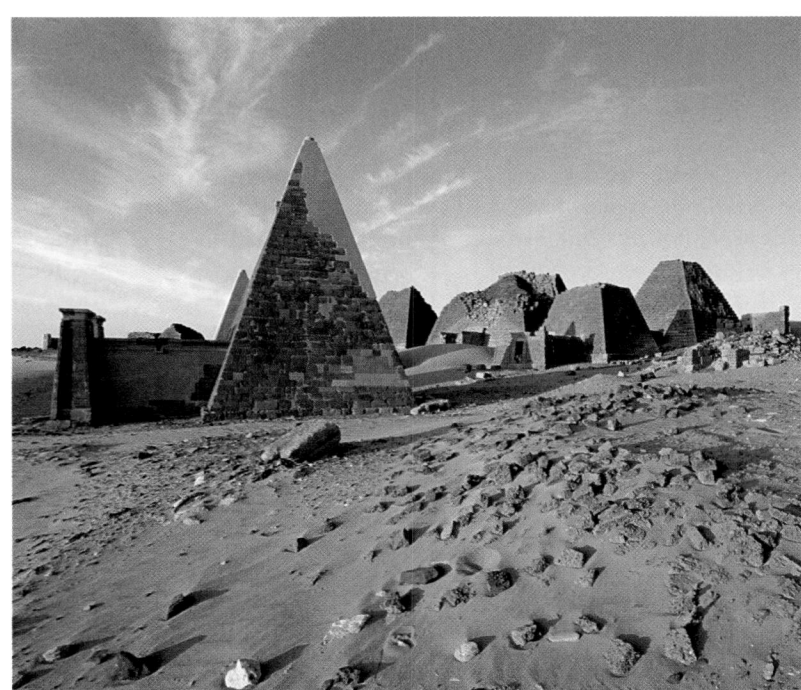

→ *How do the Nok figures help scholars understand the very ancient culture of West Africa?*

→ *Do they provide insight into the artistic abilities of the people living in this region?*

→ *What can they tell us about how people dressed and how they looked?*

→ *Can you see the Egyptian influence in the photograph of the Kush burial pyramids?*

Abu Simbel. Such connections with Egypt have long been stressed by historians, especially Egyptologists, but only recently have scholars become aware of just how deeply the peoples and states in Nubia were influenced by the cultures of sub-Saharan Africa.

Building on the earlier foundations of kings that had ruled Nubia, the Meroe kingdom came into being in the fourth century BCE and flourished until 300 CE. The rulers of Meroe were much influenced by the pharaonic culture, even to the point of adapting hieroglyphs, erecting pyramids in which they buried their rulers, viewing their kings as divine, and worshipping the Egyptian god Amun. But Meroe was equally a part of the Sudanic way of life that flourished across Africa's savanna lands. In order to assert their autonomy from the powerful Egyptians to the north, the rulers of Meroe moved their capital city about 300 miles upstream (to the south), where it commanded the whole of the Nile region between the fifth and sixth Nile cataracts.

Meroe soon became a thriving center of production and commerce. The residents of the city were especially skilled in iron smelting and the manufacture of textiles, and their products were widely circulated throughout Africa. The capital city itself covered a square mile; at its center was a royal city, surrounded by a rectangular wall 300 yards long and half as wide. The royal city featured monumental and highly decorated buildings, which were built, according to the custom of this area, not in stone but in mud bricks.

WEST AFRICAN KINGDOMS

Meroe was not the only sacred kingship in the Sudanic savanna lands of Africa. Similar polities thrived in West Africa, among peoples living in the Senegal River basin and among the Mande peoples living inland around the western branch of the Niger River. They established settlements at such places as Jenne and Gao, which would expand to become large trading centers. In these areas, artisans smelted iron ore and wove textiles, and merchants engaged in long- distance trade.

Even more spectacular was the Nok culture, which arose in the sixth century BCE in an area that is today the geographical center of Nigeria. Though slightly south of the Sudanic savanna lands of West Africa, it was (and still is) in regular contact with that region. At a place called Taruga, near the present-day village of Nok (which gave this cultural system its name), early iron smelting occurred in 600 BCE. Taruga may well have been the first place in western Africa where iron ores were smelted. Undeniably ironworking was significant for the Nok peoples, who made the move from using stone materials directly to iron, bypassing the customary intermediate stage of working in bronze and copper. They made iron axes and hoes, iron knives and spears, and luxury items that could be traded. Ironworking had spread east to-

ward Egypt and Nubia and south to the Congo River by 300 BCE. Moreover, Bantu-speaking people from Nok migrated southward into the equatorial rain forests, where they cleared land for farming; from there, some moved on to southern Africa. Yet Nok is famous not for its iron-smelting prowess but rather for its magnificent terra-cotta figurines, discovered only in the 1940s in the tin-mining region of central Nigeria. These naturalistic figures, with features that are striking in their resemblance to modern inhabitants of the region, date back to at least 500 BCE. They were altarpieces, produced in connection with a cult associated with the fertility of the land. Placed next to new lands that were being brought into cultivation, they were believed to have the power to bless the soil and to enhance its productivity.

During the first millennium BCE, sub-Saharan Africa remained a highly diverse area ecologically and culturally, with many different peoples living in a wide variety of climates and ecologies. Simple hunting and gathering peoples dwelled in the tropical forests at the same time that Bantu people from sophisticated farming societies cleared land to grow millet and sorghum; raised cattle, sheep, and goats; organized themselves into clans with chiefs; conducted complex religious rituals; and engaged in extensive trade within and across regions. Perhaps the most telling development in sub-Saharan Africa in this period was the widespread improvement in iron-smelting techniques. It would be these advances in metalworking that would enable larger settled communities to develop. With better and stronger tools made with iron, settled communities could improve their farming techniques—and as a result, they had more food and could sustain larger communities. Indeed, in the period between 400 BCE and the new millennium, the estimated population of sub-Saharan Africa shot up from 3.5 million to more than 11 million people. This would be the first of many major population explosions that would transform sub-Saharan Africa and its inhabitants.

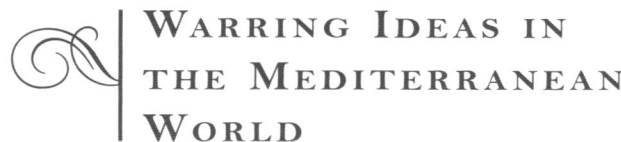

WARRING IDEAS IN THE MEDITERRANEAN WORLD

> → *In what ways did city-states integrate the geographically dispersed settlements of the Mediterranean?*

The tortuous and widespread movements of peoples that convulsed large parts of southern Europe and Southwest Asia around 1200 BCE (see Chapter 4) also brought marauding armed bands into the well-settled regions of the Mediterranean. The combined impact of large population movements and social destruction radically transformed the existing social organizations and cultures throughout the region. Thus, as in Eastern Zhou China and Vedic South Asia, the first millennium BCE in the Mediterranean was a time of political, economic, and social changes, as well as of new ideas.

The violent upheavals at the end of the second millennium BCE had a great impact on the borderland areas west of the highly developed societies of Southwest Asia. As noted in Chapter 4, these areas comprised the northern region of the Levant (approximately the area of modern-day Lebanon), the coastal lands of Anatolia (in modern-day Turkey), the islands of the Aegean and Mediterranean seas, and mainland Greece. The inhabitants of these regions had always been in contact with the most highly developed societies in Southwest Asia, and they had experienced the power of the Assyrians and Persians. But the disorder and chaos of the time freed them from the domination of those large regional states. More on their own than ever before, these communities were now able to experiment with new cultural ideas and new types of social and political organization. Thus, around 1000 BCE, the peoples in these lands (many of whom were new settlers from the north and west) not only absorbed the rapidly changing cultural and technical knowledge but also devised new and challenging ways of organizing their societies—creating what could be considered second-generation societies, hybrids that mix the old and the new.

The seaborne peoples from all around the Mediterranean Sea basin—Phoenicians, Greeks, Cretans, Cypriots, Lydians, Etruscans, and many others—shared common characteristics. As they sailed through the Mediterranean, they carried with them not just trade goods but also new ideas about the virtues of self-sufficient cities in which power was shared more widely (even more democratically) than before. Inventions that proved valuable in one place, such as the use of money and the alphabet in trading transactions, usually spread rapidly throughout the entire region; the result was an uncommonly high degree of intercommunication, drawing together the diverse communities of the region.

Increased knowledge and refinements in maritime technology were crucial to the expansion of trade and the rapid, large-scale population movements that took place in the first millennium BCE. In the ninth and eighth centuries BCE, improved design and construction of ships, better deployment of sail and rowing technology, and, above all, better practical knowledge of winds, currents, and shorelines made it possible for sailing peoples to transform the seaborne world of the Mediterranean.

Homer's *Odyssey* (composed in the eighth century BCE about events that had occurred centuries earlier) was the epic tale of the wanderings of Odysseus as he sailed through the Mediterranean on his way back to his island home of Ithaca after the siege of the city of Troy. It tells of his encounters with pirates, traders, adventurers, witches, monsters, powerful barons, and wealthy and exotic kings and queens, and suggests that the Greeks were premier seafarers. Yet the Greeks were far from being the first, the only, or even the best masters of the seas. Around 800 BCE, the Phoenicians began sailing westward in the Mediterranean in search of metals and trade (see Chapter 4). Some historians even believed that Phoenician sailors had circumnavigated Africa around 600 BCE. Even if this claim was an exaggeration, it is certain that as early as 750 BCE Phoenicians *had* sailed across the Mediterranean and had ventured into the Atlantic Ocean—and that they had also sailed through the Red Sea and down the eastern coast of Africa. Hanno, a general from the Phoenician city of Carthage in the western Mediterranean (near present-day Tunis), is said to have set sail from Carthage in 500 BCE with a fleet of sixty-seven fifty-oared ships filled with a large number of men and women. His mission was to explore and settle the Atlantic coast of Africa, and he reports finding elephants, gorillas, and wild people along the way. The stories of Odysseus and Hanno reflect the new kinds of mobility and transforming encounters outside their own sphere that people from Mediterranean communities enjoyed in the first millennium BCE.

> The stories of Odysseus and Hanno reflect the new kinds of mobility and transforming encounters that people from Mediterranean communities enjoyed in the first millennium BCE.

A NEW WORLD OF CITY-STATES

In the ninth and eighth centuries BCE, order was reestablished and the population returned to levels that had been achieved in earlier periods. But when these larger numbers of people began to congregate in more concentrated settlements, they did not revive the old palace and temple organizations of the Mycenaeans and Minoans. Instead, they created something quite novel: the independent, self-governing city-state. These city-states were characterized by intense competition both between them and inside them. Furthermore, they became commercial centers managing exchange and trade, and they established colonies throughout the Mediterranean.

SELF-GOVERNMENT AND DEMOCRACY The self-governing city-state was a new political form that had a profound impact on the whole of the Mediterranean. First found among the Phoenicians (see Chapter 4) and in their settlements in the western Mediterranean like Carthage, but ultimately associated most strongly with the Greeks, these new urban communities had multiplied throughout the

Mediterranean by the sixth century BCE. This new urban entity that we call a city-state—known by the Phoenicians as a *qart*, the Greeks as a *polis*, and the Romans as a *civitas*—is perhaps best understood by what it was *not*. Unlike the great urban centers in the empires of Southwest Asia, the new city-states were not organized by a critically important class of scribes or run by directives issued by high priests, monarchs, or their subordinates. Record keeping and the administration of goods and services by a central authority were very minor, often unimportant elements in their day-to-day operation.

The new principles of rulership were revolutionary. Ordinary residents or "citizens" of these cities—cities such as Athens, Thebes, Sparta, or Corinth among the Greeks, Caere and Rome on the Italian peninsula among the Etruscans (and later among the Romans themselves), or Carthage and Gadir (modern-day Cádiz in Spain) among the Phoenicians—governed themselves and selected their leaders. Their self-government took various forms. One kind was rule by a popularly approved political head of the city, called a *tyrannis* (tyrant) by the Greeks. Another was rule by a restricted number of wealthy and powerful citizens—the "few" or *oligoi*, as the Greeks called them (hence the modern concept of "oligarchs" and "oligarchies"). The most inclusive type of government involved all free adult males in a city—in Greek, a *dēmokratia* (democracy; see below). The wealthiest landowners often formed the power elite in these new city-states, but farmers, craftsworkers, shopkeepers, merchants, soldiers, and traders were the backbone of the citizenry. The inhabitants of the burgeoning number of new Mediterranean communities ran the city's affairs, decided when they would go to war, and set their own priorities for the development of their communities. This approach contrasted with that in Mesopotamia, where the much smaller number of cities of the second millennium BCE had been administered from the top down: the power of kings largely determined whether new cities were founded and how they grew.

The new cities of the Mediterranean basin were made up of communities of adult male citizens, other free persons (including women, who could not vote or hold office), foreign immigrants, and large numbers of unfree persons (including slaves and Sparta's helots, people tied to the land who could not vote or fight for the polis). Those enjoying full citizenship rights—the adult freeborn males—in each community were able to decide for themselves what was to be done (what tasks would be undertaken by the city-state) and how it was to be done (what kind of government and laws would be adopted by the city-state). Consequently, these cities differed markedly from one another.

FAMILIES AS THE FOUNDATIONAL UNITS   Within all these cities the small family unit, called an *oikos* (household) by the Greeks and a *familia* by the Romans, was the single most important social unit. Indeed, thinkers like Aristotle regarded the state as a natural outgrowth of the household. To

Hetaira. The painting on this vase by the artist Oitos is of a "companion" woman—called by the Greeks an *hetaira*—putting a sandal on her foot. Proper Greek women were protected and enclosed within their households; they were modest and always fully clothed. Women who were so bold as to be out in public, talking and otherwise associating with men—like the woman portrayed here—were deemed immoral. The artist therefore had no problem portraying this *hetaira* in the nude.

Aristotle, the *oikos* embodied the fundamental power relationships found in cities, where free men and citizens were lords over their wives and children, and masters of their slaves. The free adult male was head of the household and fully entitled to engage in the city's public affairs.

In contrast, adult women of free birth were permanently enclosed within the private world of the family and had no standing to debate policy in public, vote, or hold office. Women who did carry on intelligent conversations with men in public about public matters were castigated as *hetairai* (courtesans—literally, "female companions"). Spartan women were a partial exception to all of these rules, and their unusual behavior, such as exercising in the nude in public (as did men) or holding property in their own right, evoked humor and hostility from men in the other Greek city-states.

COMPETITION AND ARMED WAR Because centralized governments exerted little control over the actions and thoughts of the inhabitants of these new city-states, they were comparatively freewheeling and competitive places, sometimes bloodily so. Their histories are filled with violent rivalries between individuals, social classes, and other groups. Among the larger Greek city-states, only Sparta avoided most of this internal strife, achieving greater calm by a radical and rigorous program of social discipline and military organization that cut the city and its people off from many external influences. The Spartans rejected coined money and chattel slavery (see below), thereby avoiding what they saw as the "corruption" of cities with more mercantile interests. However successful it was as a military state, Sparta was widely viewed by the other Greeks as a very unusual polis.

Competition for honor and prestige—a "good strife," as the Greek poet Hesiod called it—was one of the moral values that shaped the behavior of individuals in the city-states. Such an extreme competitive ethic, which might easily take bad forms such as murder and feuds, could find a benign outlet in organized sporting events, or *agōnes* (struggles). Almost from the moment that Greek city-states emerged, athletic contests sprang up—both on a small scale, as an essential part of life in all cities, and in large, centralized events in which all Greeks could participate. The greatest of these competitions were the Olympic Games, which were staged for the first time in 776 BCE at Olympia in southern Greece.

Hoplites. Most battles between Greek city-states took place on land between massed formations of infantrymen, or "hoplites" [*hoplon* meaning shield]. Serving the community in this way defined one's right to citizenship or membership in the city. Since hoplites wore the same armor and contributed equally to the battle line, the nature of hoplite warfare helped to define the democratic ethos of the individual citizen.

Greek Boxers. Greek athletic contests or struggles (*agones*) were less games in our sense than all-out attempts to decide who was superior in a given competition, such as this one between two boxers. Since the point was to decide on a winner, there were no rounds and few restrictions regarding the level of violence. The men simply hit each other as hard as possible until one went down or gave up. The winner received glory, fame, and material rewards.

This competitive spirit existed not just between individuals on the athletic field but also between communities, where it took the more dangerous and destructive form of armed conflicts over borderlands, trade, minerals, religious shrines, prestige, and other valuable resources. Wars of one sort or another were characteristic of city-state relations, as they were of relations between states in Eastern Zhou China and Vedic South Asia during the same period. Almost no year enjoyed complete peace, and the incessant battles fueled new developments in military equipment, such as the heavy armor that gave its name to the hoplites, or infantrymen, and in tactics, such as the standard blocklike configuration (called a *phalanx* by the Greeks) in which the regular rank and file fought.

These wars were so destructive that they threatened to destabilize the world of the city-states. The bigger the states and the more resources that they had, the more likely their embroilment in warfare, even to the detriment of their own people. The longest and most famous of these conflicts was the Peloponnesian War (431–404 BCE), fought between Athens and Sparta, the two largest and most powerful of the Greek city-states. It dragged on for decades, eating away the resources of both of these great polities and the numerous cities that allied themselves with one side or the other; Athens never fully recovered from its defeat. On the other hand, the superiority in land warfare developed in the course of the persistent clashes between the Greek city-states enabled them to defend themselves successfully against external enemies who outnumbered them, sometimes against considerably larger armies. Earlier in the fifth century BCE, the Greek cities, led by Athens, had managed to defeat Persians Darius I and Xerxes, though the kings mounted huge expeditions against Greece that spanned more than a decade (see Chapter 4).

ECONOMIC INNOVATIONS AND POPULATION MOVEMENT

Besides novel political structures, the Mediterranean communities also created economic innovations, such as the alphabet, coins, and the central marketplace, which facilitated trade and were well adapted to the fragmented and yet interconnected human ecology of the Mediterranean. As a result, city-states entered into a period of accelerated economic growth in the ninth and eighth centuries BCE. Even more spectacular than the obvious signs of expansion, such as population growth and rapid urbanization, was the speed with which these city-states began to establish colonies throughout the Mediterranean, wherever they found resources and trade. Their superior military technology, developed and tested in intense conflicts among themselves, enabled them to easily defeat any local resistance to their land takeovers. Moreover, in the course of trade and colonization, the

Mediterranean peoples also came to buy or capture as slaves the inhabitants of frontier communities to the north. The labor of these slaves further contributed to the city-states' wealth and growth.

FREE MARKETS AND MONEY-BASED ECONOMIES Since they were not living within a top-down bureaucratic and administrative structure, the residents of the new cities of the Mediterranean had to devise new ways to run their own affairs. They developed open trading markets and a system of money that enabled buyers and sellers to know the precise value of commodities so that exchanges worked quickly and efficiently. The Greek historian Herodotus, who journeyed widely throughout the eastern Mediterranean and Southwest Asia in the mid–fifth century BCE, observed that the new city-states had at their center a marketplace (*agora*), a large open area in which individuals bought and sold commodities. He found no such public commercial spaces set aside in Egypt or the cities of Babylonia.

Soon most transactions involving goods required money rather than barter or gift exchange; coins also were used to buy services, and such payment may have been used at first mainly to hire mercenary soldiers. In the absence of large bureaucracies to manage commerce, the new Mediterranean cities relied on money to connect the producers and buyers of goods and services with each other, often over long dis-

The Agora. The agora, or central open marketplace, was one of the core defining features of Mediterranean city-states. At its center, each city had one of these open-air plazas, the heart of its commercial, religious, social, and political life. When a new city was founded, the agora was one of the first places that the colonists measured out. The large rectangular-shaped open area in this picture is the agora of the Greek colonial city of Cyrene (in modern-day Libya).

→ *In what ways did city-states integrate the geographically dispersed settlements of the Mediterranean?*

Mediterranean Coins. From the sixth century BCE onward, money in the form of precious metal coins began spreading through the city-states of the Mediterranean, beginning with the Greek city-states in the western parts of what is today Turkey, then spreading to the other Greek *poleis* and beyond. On the left here is the classic tetradrachm (four-drachma piece) coin of Athens with its owl of the goddess Athena; on the right is a silver coin of shekel weight produced by the city of Carthage in the western Mediterranean.

tances. By the end of the fifth century BCE, a striking variety of coins was being issued by Greek city-states, and the use of coins spread to non-Greek peoples nearby, including the Phoenicians, Etruscans, and Persians. During the same period, around 500 BCE, money was independently developed and also came into common use in Vedic South Asia and in Eastern Zhou China.

TRADE AND COLONIZATION The search for high-value commodities, especially such metals as silver, iron, copper, and tin, drove the first traders westward across the Mediterranean. Early Greek traders and settlers were attracted to the western coast of Italy by its iron deposits.

By about 500 BCE, the Phoenicians, Greeks, and others who had set sail from their homes in the eastern Mediterranean had planted new city-states around the shores of the western Mediterranean and the Black Sea; historians and archaeologists have identified dozens attributable to the Phoenicians and hundreds that were Greek. Once established, these offshoots became completely independent entities, and their independence enabled them to spread rapidly. These colonial communities transformed the coastal world. City-based life became common everywhere, from southern Spain and western Italy to the Crimea on the Black Sea.

With amazing speed, seaborne communications helped create a Mediterranean-wide urban culture embraced by the wealthy and powerful elites across the region. This cultural movement witnessed the spread of material elements from the east to cover the whole of the Mediterranean. Found among the local elites of Tartessos in southern Spain, among Gallic chiefs in southern France, and among the Etruscan and Roman nobles of central Italy, the new shared aristocratic culture featured similar public displays of wealth—richly decorated chariots, elaborate armor and weapons, high-class dining ware, elaborate houses, and public burials. From one end of the Mediterranean to the other (and also around the Black Sea), we can see the gradual emergence not just of city-state communities but also of a culture founded on alphabetic scripts, market-based economies, and private property.

HUMANS FOR SALE: SLAVES AND SLAVERY The explosion of buying and selling that accompanied the rise of the city-state and the expansion of trade and colonization also produced an ethos in which all the different things that the city dwellers needed, even human beings, were given a monetary value. Turning men, women, and children into objects of commerce, bought and sold on a large scale in markets, created something novel—a new form of slavery called *chattel slavery*, as human beings were treated as property. This

Prisoners of War. Constant warfare both among the Greek city-states and with their "barbarian" neighbors produced prisoners of war. The Greek convention was to permit the ransoming of fellow Greeks—as in this illustration of Spartans captured by the Athenians in the Peloponnesian War. Prisoners taken from "barbarians," however, were almost inevitably sold into slavery.

chattels for the next 2,000 years. This trade in humans was immensely profitable. Indeed, it was one of the most profitable businesses of the entire Mediterranean.

ENCOUNTERS WITH FRONTIER COMMUNITIES The forces creating the new world of the Mediterranean cities obviously changed the lives of the people living in them and in the rural lands immediately around them, as the new identity of the individual citizen and his family took shape. But these same forces significantly affected those much further away, in the lands of northern and central Europe, whose inhabitants lived in ethnic groups. Whether they wished it or not, peoples as diverse as the Celts and Germans in western Europe and the Scythians to the north of the Black Sea became integrated into the expanding cities' networks of violence, conquest, and trade.

In the rural lands and mountainous regions surrounding this mosaic of urban communities scattered around the Mediterranean Sea was a different world of tribes and ethnic groups. In these frontier communities, people lived in roaming nomadic bands, in isolated settlements, or in small villages. By this time, most of Europe—including Spain in the west, most of France, and the lands along and north of the Danube River—had created a culture based on bronze- and ironworking technologies. Kinship and cooperation held these communities together, but they were just as likely to resort to violence to settle their differences as were the cities of the Mediterranean. Here, change took place much more slowly, impeded by the densely wooded forests, mountainous terrain, and inhospitable climates that challenged easy movement and communications by land—and also hindered by pervasive illiteracy.

Increasingly drawn to the wealth of the city-states and wanting what the city-states produced—money, wine, ornate clothing, weapons—the tribal peoples often became an armed threat to the core societies of the Mediterranean, as they sometimes tried to acquire the desired commodities through force rather than through trade. These frontier peoples convulsed the settled urban societies of the Mediterranean in repeated wavelike incursions that fell most severely between 2200 and 2000 BCE, then again between 1200 and 1000 BCE, and finally between 400 and 200 BCE. Called "barbarians" (*barbaroi*), a mocking name given by the Greeks to foreigners unable to speak their language, the invaders in fact were not much different from the Phoenicians or Greeks who themselves had sought new homes and a better future by large-scale migrations. In colonizing the Mediterranean, they too had violently dispossessed the original inhabitants. The Celts, Gauls, Germans, Scythians, and other northerners came to the Mediterranean first as conquerors. Later, when Mediterranean empires grew more powerful and could successfully keep them at bay, they were imported as slaves. Because the Greeks and the western Phoenicians regarded these external peoples with whom they came into contact as uncivilized and savage, the lands of these outsiders could be seized and col-

commercial type of slavery spread quickly. Where additional labor was needed, especially for dangerous and exhausting tasks like mining, slave laborers were purchased and owned by the freeborn citizens. The proportion of slaves in different places could vary considerably: in Athens, the largest and most economically powerful of the Greek city-states, slaves may well have formed a fifth, or even a quarter, of the whole population. But whatever their absolute or relative numbers, slaves were essential to every one of the new city-states, providing manual and technical labor of all kinds and producing the agricultural surpluses that supported the urban population.

The new seaborne communications networks of the Mediterranean greatly enhanced the ability to acquire and to transport the slaves that the urban economies demanded. At this time, supply lines were first established to what would become the main sources for slaves, especially the lands around the Black Sea—zones that would furnish human onized. And these "barbarians" (as they regarded them) could be captured and sold as commodities in the new marketplaces of the Mediterranean.

NEW IDEAS

As we have already seen, new ways of thinking about the world emerged from the competitive atmosphere found inside each Greek city-state, as well as from the rivalries between them. Moreover, since the Mediterranean city-states imposed very few top-down controls, such as existed in the kingdoms of Southwest Asia, their citizens had to devise methods for managing and directing their own affairs. In the absence of monarchical or priestly rule, ideas and beliefs were free to arise, circulate, and clash. Individuals seeking to establish the validity of their thinking about the nature of the gods, the best state, what is good, or even whether or not to go to war, argued publicly with those holding other and sometimes strongly opposing views. In these cities, there was no final authority—whether a god-king, a holy priest, or a huge bureaucracy—to give any particular idea a final stamp of approval and force its general acceptance.

NATURALISTIC SCIENCE AND REALISTIC ART Given these new opportunities, some curious and daring persons in the new city-states developed novel ways of perceiving the cosmos and representing the environment. Rather than seeing everything around them as the handiwork of all-powerful deities, they took a naturalistic view of humans and their

The Human Form. The human body as it appeared naturally, without any adornment of clothing or accessories, became the ideal set by Greek art. Even gods, as perfect beings, were portrayed in this same natural nude human form. These are two divine portraits produced by Praxiteles: a statue of the god Dionysos and the child Hermes (*left*) and one of the god Apollo (*right*). Such bold nude portraits of humans and gods were sometimes shocking to other peoples.

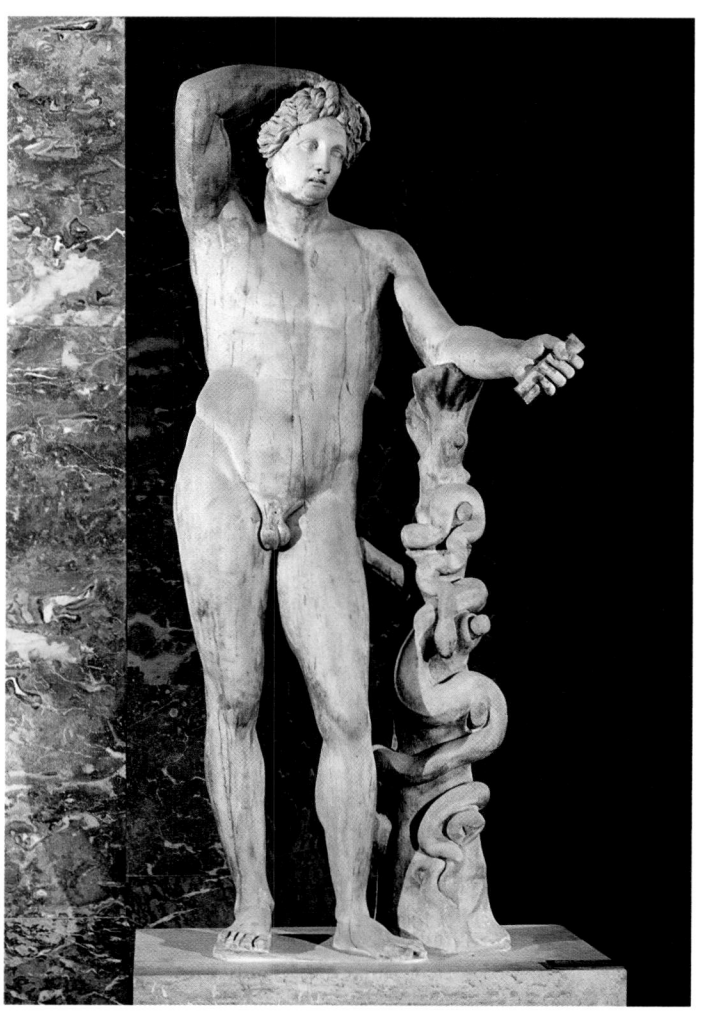

Primary Source

WARRING IDEAS: PLATO VERSUS ARISTOTLE

Great debates raged among Greek thinkers during the fifth and fourth centuries BCE over the essence of the world that we live in and how we can have knowledge of it. They began by rejecting religious explanations that posited the existence of creator gods and goddesses, and instead began to seek explanations elsewhere. Some looked to the material world (in primary substances like water), while others turned to abstractions. For example, Pythagoras suggested that numbers were at the basis of everything—a far more revolutionary notion then than it might seem today. Some later thinkers, most notably Plato, took this line of argument further and argued that all existence, and therefore all human knowledge, is based on absolute concepts that are like numbers, existing independent of time and place. Each of them he called an idea, a word whose meanings in Greek include "shape," "form," and "appearance" (its root is the verb "to see").

In a number of Plato's dialogues, his teacher, Socrates, tries to explain this theory:

Socrates: I am going to try to explain to you the theory of causes that I myself have thought out. . . . I assume that you admit the existence of absolutes like "beauty" and "good" and "size" and the rest. If you admit that these absolutes exist, then I can hope with their help to show you what causes are. . . . I remain obstinately committed . . . to the explanation that the one thing that causes a thing to be "beautiful," for example, is the existence in it of "the beautiful" or its sharing in "the beautiful"[;] . . . and so, is it not also the case that things that we call "big" are big because they share the idea of "bigness" and similarly that things that we call "small" are small because they share in the idea of "smallness"? [Socrates then goes on to dismiss the claim that in calling things "tall" or "small" we are simply describing them in relation to other things.]

Phaedo: I believe that Socrates has persuaded us of these matters and that we have agreed that these different ideas do exist; and he has also persuaded us that the reason why specific things in our world are named after these ideas is that they share in the existence of the specific idea. (Phaedo 99d–102b)

Still other thinkers drew on some of the very first Greek *philosophoi* (knowledge lovers, philosophers) in the sixth century BCE to argue that the basis of all existing things was, quite simply, other things. They rejected the proposal that all the things that we feel, see, hear, and otherwise perceive with our senses are poor copies of permanent ideas of them that exist in a separate, unchangeable sphere of existence. Human knowledge was in fact acquired through the careful observation of existing things and through the

place in the universe. Evidence for this concept of the world comes from their art, which placed an ideal form of the natural world as perceived by human eyes at its center. Artists increasingly attempted to picture the world in a more "natural" way, representing humans, objects, and landscapes not in hyperreal, abstract, or formal ways but rather more or less as they appeared to the human eye of the time in these cities. Even gods increasingly were portrayed as being more or less like humans. Later, these more objective and natural views of humans and nature were themselves turned into ideals, the highest of which was the unadorned human figure: the nude became the centerpiece of Greek art. The public display of the uncovered human body, both in artistic representations and in everyday life (notably in men's athletic training and competition, which normally took place in the nude) signaled

the sharp break between the moral codes of the older traditional societies of the east and those of the revolutionary cities of the Mediterranean. Vase painters such as Exekias (sixth century BCE), spurred on by a desire to be famous, signed their works and became known as individual artists. Sculptors like Praxiteles (mid–fourth century BCE) became famous as artists in their own right. But no less assertive were creative writers, such as the poets Archilochus (fl. c. 700 BCE) and Sappho (born c. 612 BCE), who wrote individual lyrics exploring their own emotions.

Perhaps nothing more vividly evokes this new sense of the individual cut free of the restraints of an autocratic state or a controlling religious system than these poems of Sappho and her peers. In them we see the individual human expressing nothing but his or her own self.

meticulous collection of data about them. Thus in the following passage, in a fundamental statement of his purpose, Aristotle rejects Plato's concept of ideas:

> For the moment, we can simply dismiss the followers of Pythagoras. It is good enough that we have dealt with them briefly. As for the followers of Plato who claim that "ideas" (or "shapes") are the causes or origins of all things, this too is objectionable. First of all, in their struggle to find causes for things that exist in our world of sense perceptions, they simply introduce as many new things into the equation as they are attempting to explain[;] . . . so their "ideas" are as many . . . as the things whose causes they are seeking to explain and for which reason they were led to invent these ideas. They must do this because they must create an idea to match every substance that exists in our real everyday world . . . and also one in the realm of the eternal heavenly entities. Not one of the arguments by which they try to demonstrate that these ideas actually exist can demonstrate or prove their claim. From some of their arguments, indeed, no real conclusions follow. From other arguments of theirs it only follows that there must be ideas of things for which they themselves hold no such ideas can exist. (*Metaphysics* 1.9, 990a–b)

In other works Aristotle further contested Plato's claims and put forth his own views about how humans could gain reliable knowledge of the world in which they lived:

> All teaching and learning by means of rational argument is based on our existing knowledge and observations; . . . and

I think that we have reliable knowledge of each thing . . . when we think that we have found the cause because of which that thing exists—what is the cause of that thing and of nothing else, with the result that this thing or this fact cannot be other than it is. That this is real knowledge of something is very clear—just look at those people who falsely claim to know [i.e., the followers of Plato and others] as opposed to those who possess real knowledge. . . . We know what we do by demonstration, by showing that it is true. By demonstration I mean an argument that produces real knowledge, . . . all of which is based on a knowledge and observation of facts and things . . . of these things the most important are the prior ones. By prior I mean those objects that are closer to human sense perceptions which are better known to us. . . . But I also say that not all real knowledge can in fact be demonstrated or proved. (*Posterior Analytics* 1.1–3, 71a–72b)

→ *What factors in the makeup of these Mediterranean city-states encouraged such debates over fundamental values and concepts?*

→ *Other than the philosophical debates themselves, what provoked Plato and Aristotle to advance such different concepts of knowledge?*

→ *Might such factors be linked to other major developments of the time, occurring not just in the Greek city-states but elsewhere (in South or East Asia, for example)?*

SOURCE: Plato, *Phaedo*, 99d–102b; Aristotle, *Metaphysics*, 1.9 = 990a–b; *Posterior Analytics*, 1.1-3 = 71a–72b. All translations are by Brent Shaw.

NEW THINKING AND GREEK PHILOSOPHERS These new thinkers, however, were deeply influenced by existing ideas on the gods, the environment, and the cosmos developed in Southwest Asia. Not surprisingly, the first generation of new thinkers came from eastern Anatolia, a contact zone in which Greeks had the greatest exposure to ideas from the Persian Empire. Armed with their own ideas and with this borrowed knowledge, thinkers in cities such as Miletus and Ephesus did not accept the earlier explanations of how and why things came to be the way they were in the universe. Rather than focusing on the role of the gods, they looked to nature itself, which many held to be made up of some fundamental substance (usually one of the traditional elements: earth, air or breath, fire, or water). Thales (c. 636–546 BCE), the earliest known theorist of these ideas, believed that water

was the primal substance from which all other things were created. He was also said to have predicted the eclipse of the sun on May 28, 585 BCE.

As each thinker competed to outdo his peers in offering persuasive and comprehensive explanations, the theories became ever more radical. Men like Xenophanes (c. 570–480 BCE), from the city of Colophon, even came to doubt the very existence of gods as they had been portrayed and, rather, asserted that there was only one general divine aura that suffused all creation. He pointed out that each ethnic group in fact produced images of gods that were more or less like themselves. Ethiopians made representations of their gods with dark skins and broad noses, while Thracians depicted their gods as blue-eyed redheads. Such variation in human beliefs about the attributes of the divinities suggested that the gods existed only in the human imagination.

Some of the new thinkers proposed that the real world had some physical and tangible basis. Among them was Democritus (c. 460–370 BCE), who claimed that everything that humans saw was made up of small and ultimately indivisible particles. Since the particles were indivisible, Democritus called them *atoma* (uncuttables), or atoms (a word that we have come to use in a similar sense). Even more radical were thinkers like Pythagoras from Samos, who held that a wide range of physical phenomena in the world, from masks to music, were in fact based in numbers; thus in a sense he foreshadowed the modern-day digital revolution. He devoted himself to studying numbers, though the famous "Pythagorean theorem" attributed to him was already known to Babylonian priests and mathematicians—and was borrowed from them, along with other eastern ideas.

Such thinkers may in some respects appear eerily modern, but in many others they remained men of their time. Although Democritus did produce a primitive atomic theory, he did not view the cosmos with the eyes of a scientist of today: like other ancient theorists, he regarded it as a single great huge organism, living and breathing. And most still considered the particles and elements of nature to be suffused with profound divine powers. Yet they challenged commonly accepted values and ideas, including traditional religious beliefs. Very soon these new ideas spread far from their birthplace in the eastern Aegean through the web of Greek and Phoenician city-states to the whole of the Mediterranean.

The competition between ideas led to a more aggressive mode of public thinking. The Greeks called this new speculation *philosophia* (love of wisdom), and the professional thinkers who were good at it *philosophoi* (philosophers). Some of the earliest recorded debates dealt with the nature of the cosmos, the environment, and the physical elements of human existence. But by the fifth century BCE, philosophers were focusing on humans and their place in society. These debates were lively dialogues—a term that itself derives from a Greek verb meaning "to speak alternately"—deeply informed by the identities of those engaged in them: autonomous human beings, who were almost always adult male citizens of a city-state. They argued about the fundamental questions of human existence much as they debated civic policy in their political assemblies.

In the early fourth century BCE, the prolonged and unremitting conflicts between the major city-states created greater economic difficulties: poverty became more widespread, cities had fewer resources for benefits for their citizens, and social discontent and civil violence were on the rise. Responses to these social and economic problems varied, but the crisis provoked skepticism about the political viability of independent cities. What *was* to be done?

Some thinkers tried to describe an ideal city, possessing harmonious relationships among all of its parts and therefore free from corruption and political decline. Socrates (469–399 BCE), a philosopher in Athens, asked questions designed to encourage people to reflect on ethics and morality; he stressed the importance of honor and integrity as opposed to wealth and power, as had Confucius in Eastern Zhou China and the Buddha in Vedic South Asia. Plato (427–347 BCE) was a student of Socrates who presented Socrates' philosophy in a series of dialogues (much as Confucius's students had

Chronology

	1500 BCE	1400 BCE	1300 BCE	1200 BCE	1100 BCE	1000
THE AMERICAS	▮ Olmec culture emerges and diffuses throughout Mesoamerica, 1500–400 BCE					
	▮ Chavín culture flourishes in Central Andes of South America, 1400–400 BCE					
SUB-SAHARAN AFRICA						
SOUTH ASIA					Sixteen State period, 1000–600 BCE ▮	
					Vedic migrations ▮	
THE MEDITERRANEAN					Migration of Sea Peoples ▮	
EAST ASIA						

written down his thoughts). In *The Republic*, Plato described his vision of a perfect city that would be ruled by philosopher-kings. He thought that if fallible humans could imitate this model city more closely, they could create polities less susceptible to the decline and decay that affected the Greek city-states of his own day. This belief was an outgrowth of his more general theory of "ideas"—eternal archetypes that are only imperfectly copied by their instantiations in the real world. For the followers of Socrates and Plato, these perfect conceptions provided a guide to pursuing not just state and government affairs but all forms of human knowledge. The more closely that faulty and error-prone human constructions could be made to match these eternal, perfect, and unchanging models, the better.

In the next generation, Plato's most famous pupil answered the same question differently. Aristotle (384–322 BCE) was deeply interested in the natural world; he believed that by collecting all the ascertainable facts about a given thing—no matter how imperfect they might be—and studying them closely, it was possible to achieve a better understanding of the general patterns in the world around him. Those patterns could reveal what ways of living were most successful both in nature and in culture. Following this inductive approach, Aristotle collected evidence from more than 150 Greek city-states, and in *The Politics* he described the institutional responses and codes of moral conduct that he believed would enable urban communities to function better. Neither Plato nor Aristotle, however, was able to promote and preserve the city-state as the exemplary civilized society. Indeed, during their lives, the world of the independent city-state was to change dramatically, as new forms of bigger states emerged and later became dominant.

CONCLUSION

Afro-Eurasia's four great river basin areas—the Tigris-Euphrates, the Nile, the Yellow and Yangzi, and the Indus—were still important in the first millennium BCE. But their time as centers of world cultures, the hubs of pioneering civilizations, was passing. They had to yield some of their leadership to regions that had previously been on the fringes of their worlds. In those peripheral regions, smaller-scale polities came into being; and the increased face-to-face contacts fostered by these city-states (in the Mediterranean world), smaller territorial states (in China), and smaller kingdoms and oligarchies (in Vedic South Asia) created great social dynamism. In time, the new polities were destined to expand and be incorporated into massive empires. The Mauryan Empire, later established by the Magadha kingdom (see Chapter 6), would grow out of the turbulent political competition in northern India and eventually spread over almost the whole of South Asia. The Warring States of China prepared the way for the later Qin and Han empires.

The later developments in each region can be traced back to small beginnings in this period. Thinkers came to the fore with perspectives quite different from those that had dominated the great river basin civilizations. The Greek philosophers put forward new views about nature, about their political world, and about human relations and values, all based on secular rather than religious ideas. They introduced new concepts captured in a new vocabulary, as the terms *democracy*, *philosophy*, and *politics* became part of this new discourse. In South Asia, dissident thinkers challenged the prevailing Brahmanic

0 BCE	800 BCE	700 BCE	600 BCE	500 BCE	400 BCE	300 BCE	200 BCE

■ *Nok culture in West Africa (early iron smelting)*, 600 BCE

Meroe kingdom in Nubia, 4th century BCE–3rd century CE ■

■ *Cities emerge on Ganges plain*, 500 BCE

■ *Vardhamana Mahavira (540–468 BCE) popularizes Jainism*

■ *Siddhartha Gautama (c. 563–483 BCE) develops Buddhist principles*

■ *Phoenician settlements and trade networks emerge*, c. 800 BCE

■ *Greek and other city-states flourish*

Socrates, Plato, and Aristotle teach in Athens, 5th and 4th centuries BCE ■

■ *Peloponnesian War*, 431–404 BCE

■ *Eastern Zhou dynasty*, 770–221 BCE

■ *Mozir*, c. 479–438 BCE

■ *Spring and Autumn period of Eastern Zhou dynasty*, 722–481 BCE

■ *Zhuangzi*, c. 369–286 BCE

Laozi (founder of Daoism), c. 605–520 BCE ■

Warring State period, 403–221 BCE ■

■ *Xunzi, fl.* 298–238 BCE

■ *Confucius*, c. 551–479 BCE

Han Fei, 280–233 BCE ■

spiritual and political order, and the Buddha, the region's leading religious figure, created a new belief system, much less hierarchical than its Vedic predecessor. In China, the political instability of the Warring States gave scholars like Confucius an opportunity to insert themselves into the political debate, where they promoted a political and social philosophy that stressed respect for social hierarchy.

Around the world, distinctive regional cultures defined by shared faiths, texts, and the teachers and prophets who recited them were on the rise. Even where the contacts with other societies were much less intense, as in the Americas and sub-Saharan Africa, a great deal of innovation and trail blazing occurred. Indeed, in this period we see the origins of many social developments to come. In the Americas, the Olmecs came to terms with their environment by developing a view of the world in which angry gods had to be appeased through human sacrifice and elaborate temples were erected to allow the peoples of a vast region of villages to pay homage to the same deities. In sub-Saharan Africa as well, pockets of settled peoples began to devise complex cultural foundations for community life that would extend well beyond local districts. The Mediterranean and Egyptian cultures continued to expand their influence up the Nile through the Nubian corridor into sub-Saharan Africa. The most spectacular example of a sub-Saharan and Egyptian synthesis was the polity and culture of Meroe. There pharaonic influences mixed with those of tropical Africa. There, too, merchants intensified contacts with North Africa and other parts of Sudanic Africa. In addition, the Nok peoples of West Africa promoted interregional trade and cultural contact, as the peoples of sub-Saharan Africa, like those living in Eurasia and North Africa, expanded their geographical horizons.

The world was being carved up into culturally distinct regions. All these ideas newly forged in Afro-Eurasia, the Americas, and sub-Saharan Africa were to long endure. In whatever region of the world they were created, they had a continuing and powerful impact on the societies that later emerged.

STUDY QUESTIONS

Ⓢ WWNORTON.COM/STUDYSPACE

1. Explain how small states created new cultural and social pathways and ideas in Afro-Eurasia in the first millennium BCE. What alternative approaches to philosophy, economics, and religion emerged in East Asia, South Asia, and western Afro-Eurasia?

2. Explain the "war of ideas" that occurred during the first millennium in China. How did Legalism, Confucianism, and Daoism influence political developments during the Warring States period?

3. Analyze the impact of commerce and urbanization on the Vedic belief system in South Asia during the first millennium BCE. Why were urban audiences more receptive to Buddhist and other challenges than to Vedic concepts?

4. Compare and contrast Buddhist and Confucian philosophies. What problems and issues did they address, and what solutions did they propose?

5. Explain the broad cultural features that united Olmec and Chavín society in the Americas in the first millennium BCE. To what extent did each cultural group leave an imprint on their respective regions?

6. Analyze the extent to which the diverse peoples of sub-Saharan Africa were connected to each other and the larger world during the first millennium BCE. What processes brought various groups together, and what kept them apart?

7. Describe the political and economic innovations in the Mediterranean world in the first millennium BCE. What impact did these ideas have on peoples living on the periphery of that world?

8. Analyze how the use of coins shaped economic systems in Afro-Eurasia during the first millennium BCE. Which regions adopted this practice?

9. Compare and contrast the Greek philosophers Socrates, Plato, and Aristotle with Confucius in China and the Buddha in South Asia. What was similar and what was different in their proposals for creating a better world?

FURTHER READINGS

Adams, William Y., *Nubia: Corridor to Africa* (1977). The authoritative historical overview of Nubia, the area of present-day Sudan just south of Egypt and a geographical connecting point between the Mediterranean and sub-Saharan Africa.

Aubet, Maria Eugenia, *The Phoenicians and the West*, 2nd ed. (2001). The basic survey of the Phoenician colonization of the western Mediterranean and Atlantic, with special attention to recent archaeological discoveries.

Barker, Graeme, and Tom Rasmussen, *The Etruscans* (1998). The most up-to-date introduction to this important pre-Roman society in the Italian peninsula, with strong emphasis on broad social and material patterns of development as indicated by the archaeological evidence.

Burkert, Walter, *Greek Religion*, trans. John Raffan (1985). The best one-volume introduction to early Greek religion, placing the Greeks in their larger Mediterranean and Near Eastern contexts.

Burns, Karen Olsen, *Ancient South America* (1994). A very useful overview of recent debates and conclusions about pre-Columbian archaeology in South America, including both the Andes and the lowland and coastal regions.

Cartledge, Paul (ed.), *The Cambridge Illustrated History of Ancient Greece* (2002). An excellent history of the Greek city-states down to the time of Alexander the Great.

Chakravarti, Uma, *The Social Dimensions of Early Buddhism* (1987). A description of the life of Buddha drawn from early Buddhist texts.

Cho-yun, Hsu, *Ancient China in Transition* (1965). An account of the political, economic, social, and intellectual changes that occurred during the Warring States period.

Coarelli, Filippo (ed.), *Etruscan Cities* (1975). A brilliantly and lavishly illustrated guide to the material remains of the Etruscans: their cities, their magnificent tombs, and their architecture, painting, sculpture, and other art.

Coe, Michael, et al. (eds.), *The Olmec World: Ritual and Rulership* (1996). A collection of field-synthesizing articles with important illustrations, based on one of the most comprehensive exhibitions of Olmec art in the world.

Confucius, *The Analects (Lun Yü)*, trans. D. C. Lau (1979). An outstanding translation of the words of Confucius as recorded by his major disciples. Includes valuable historical material needed to provide the context for Confucius's teachings.

Garlan, Yvon, *Slavery in Ancient Greece*, trans. Janet Lloyd (1988). A treatment of the emergence, development, and institutionalization of chattel slavery in the Greek city-states.

———, *War in the Ancient World: A Social History*, trans. Janet Lloyd (1976). A discussion of the emergence of the forms of warfare, including male citizens fighting in hoplite phalanxes and the development of siege warfare, that were typical of the Greek city-states.

Finley, M. I., and H. W. Pleket, *The Olympic Games: The First Thousand Years* (2005). A fine description of the most famous of the Greek games; it explains how they exemplify the competitive spirit that marked many aspects of the Greek city-states.

Iliffe, John, *Africans: The History of a Continent*, 2nd ed. (2007). A first-rate scholarly survey of Africa from its beginnings, with a strong emphasis on demography.

Kagan, Donald, *The Peloponnesian War* (2004). A vivid description of the major war that pitted the major Greek city-states, including Athens and Sparta, against each other over the latter half of the fifth century BCE.

Lancel, Serge, *Carthage: A History*, trans. Antonia Nevill (1997). By far the best single-volume history of the most important Phoenician colony in the Mediterranean.

Lewis, Mark Edward, *Sanctioned Violence in Early China* (1990). An analysis of the use of sanctioned violence as an element of statecraft from the Warring States period to the formation of the Qin and Han empires in the second half of the first millennium BCE.

———, *Writing and Authority in Early China* (1999). A revisionist account of the central role of writing and persuasion in providing models for the invention of a Chinese world empire.

Lloyd, G. E. R., *Early Greek Science: Thales to Aristotle* (1970). An especially clear and concise introduction to the main developments and intellectuals that marked the emergence of critical secular thinking in the early Greek world.

Lloyd, G. E. R., and Nathan Sivin, *The Way and the Word: Science and Medicine in Early China and Greece* (2002). A comprehensive rethinking of the social and political settings in ancient China and city-state Greece that contributed to the different views of science and medicine that emerged in each place.

Murray, Oswyn, *Early Greece*, 2nd ed. (1993). One of the best introductions to the emergence of the Greek city-states down to the end of the archaic age.

Osborne, Robin, *Archaic and Classical Greek Art* (1998). An outstanding book that clearly explains the main innovations in Greek art, setting them in their historical context.

———, *Greece in the Making, 1200–479 BC* (1999). The standard history of the whole early period of the Greek city-states characterized by an especially fine and judicious mix of archaeological data and literary sources.

Pallottino, Massimo, *The Etruscans,* rev. ed., trans. J. Cremona (1975). A fairly traditional but still classic survey of all aspects of Etruscan history, political and social institutions.

Redford, Donald B., *From Slave to Pharaoh: The Black Experience of Ancient Egypt* (2004). A description of Egypt's twenty-fifth dynasty, which was made up of Sudanese conquerors.

Schaberg, David, *A Patterned Past: Form and Thought in Early Chinese Historiography* (2002). A comprehensive study of the intellectual content of historical anecdotes by the followers of Confucius collected around the fourth century BCE.

Schaps, David, *The Invention of Coinage and the Monetization of Ancient Greece* (2004). A new analysis that offers a broad overview of the emergence of coined money in the Near East and the eastern Mediterranean and its effects on the spread of money-based markets.

Sharma, J. P., *Republics in Ancient India, c. 1500 B.C.–500 B.C.* (1968). Relying on information from early Buddhist texts, this book first revealed that South Asia had not only monarchies but also alternative polities.

Shaw, Thurston, *Nigeria: Its Archaeology and Early History* (1978). An important introduction to the early history of Nigeria by one of that country's leading archaeologists.

Shinnie, P. L., *Ancient Nubia* (1996). An excellent account of the history of the ancient Nubians, who, we are discovering, had great influence on Egypt and also on the rest of tropical Africa.

Snodgrass, Anthony, *Archaic Greece: The Age of Experiment* (1981). A good introduction to the archaeological evidence of archaic Greece.

Taylor, Christopher, Richard Hare, and Jonathan Barnes, *Greek Philosophers* (1999). A fine, succinct one-volume introduction to the major aspects of the three big thinkers who dominated the high period of classical Greek philosophy: Socrates, Plato, and Aristotle.

Torok, Laszlo, *Meroe: Six Studies on the Cultural Identity of an Ancient African State* (1995). A good collection of essays on the most recent work on Meroe.

Welsby, Derek A., *The Kingdom of Kush: The Napatan and Meroitic Empires* (1996). A fine book on these two important Nubian kingdoms.

SHRINKING THE AFRO-EURASIAN WORLD, 350 BCE–250 CE

*I*n the burning August heat of 324 BCE, at a town on the Euphrates River that the Greeks called Opis but the local Babylonians called Upî (not far from modern Baghdad), Alexander the Great's crack Macedonian troops declared that they had finally had enough. They had been fighting away from their homeland, in northern Greece, for more than a decade. They had marched from the Mediterranean, forded wide rivers, traversed great deserts and vast plains, trudged over the high mountain passes of present-day Afghanistan, and slogged through the rain-drenched forests of South Asia. Along the way, they had defeated large armies, including those armed with fearsome war elephants. Some had taken wives from the cities and tribes of the vanquished, and the army soon became a giant swarm of ethnically mixed families. This was an army like no other. It did more than just defeat neighbors and rivals—it forcefully connected entire worlds, bringing together peoples and lands.

But conquering in the name of building a new world was not what the soldiers had bargained for. They loved their leader, but many thought that he had gone too far. They had lost companions and grown weary of war. Some had mutinied at Hyphasis, a tributary of the Indus, halting Alexander's advance into South Asia. At Opis, they threatened to desert him altogether. They wanted to return to their families and their homeland. Plucking up their courage, they voiced these resentments to their supreme war commander. Alexander's response was immediate and inspired. In persuading his rebellious troops not to desert him, he evoked the great military triumphs and history-making achievements that he and they had accomplished —his personal rule, stretching from Macedonia to the Indus Valley. It was a monumental achievement to bring together such dispersed places. This grand new far-reaching and land-mass-uniting political vision came to an sudden end with Alexander's death at Babylon a year later, in June of 323 BCE, when he was only thirty-two. But even in his own short lifetime, he set in motion cultural and economic forces that would transform Afro-Eurasia.

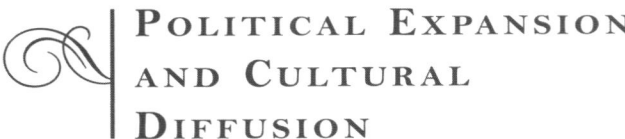

POLITICAL EXPANSION AND CULTURAL DIFFUSION

> → *How did political expansion enable a variety of exchanges between different parts of the Afro-Eurasian world?*

Alexander's armies, linked to Greek population movements throughout Afro-Eurasia, ushered in an age of thinking and practices that transformed Greek achievements into a com- mon portable culture that is called "Greek-based," or Hellenistic. While this cultural movement did not eradicate local cultures, its influence spread outward from Greece to all shores of the Mediterranean, into parts of sub-Saharan Africa, and across Southwest Asia and through the Iranian plateau into central and south Asia; it even had echoes in China. As a cultural system that linked widely removed areas and forced other cultural systems to respond to its unifying aspirations, Hellenism was a new phenomenon. By diffusing well beyond its homeland, Hellenism brought worlds together; it did not lead to a single common culture, but it did provoke shifts and adjustments in the cultures it contacted. In that process, many of the world's regions, from China to Africa, became more internally integrated.

What Alexander did, along with conquering, was to lay the foundations for state systems and introduce some institutional stability for, and protection and patronage of, trading systems. Instead of plundering, governments promoted trade. With their fear of attack reduced, cities could thrive. And increasingly, states encouraged the use of money and a common language for contracts, both innovations that aided commercial transactions. In effect, the early passageways that carried small bands of traders were replaced by major commercial arteries. Political expansion became an important enabling condition for all kinds of exchanges, among them commercial, between different parts of the Afro-Eurasian world. One consequence was the emergence of what is called the Silk Road, an artery that for nearly a thousand years would serve as the primary commercial network linking East Asia and the Mediterranean world.

It is impossible to make sense of Alexander and this Hellenistic movement without acknowledging the importance of some underlying ways in which the distinct parts of the world were already in contact and in some places converging. In-

Focus Questions SHRINKING THE AFRO-EURASIAN WORLD

> → *How did political expansion enable a variety of exchanges between different parts of the Afro-Eurasian world?*
>
> → *How did the spread of Hellenism reshape the Mediterranean world?*
>
> → *How did Hellenistic and pastoral nomadic cultures influence central and South Asia?*
>
> → *In what ways did the transformation of Buddhism represent cultural integration in South Asia?*
>
> → *How did long-distance exchanges alter the cultural geography of Eurasia and North Africa?*
>
> → *What factors contributed to the growth of the Indian Ocean sea trade?*

WWNORTON.COM/STUDYSPACE

deed, political expansion driven by military conquest followed a period of extensive migration, trade, and technological diffusion over very long distances. Alexander's conquests did not take arbitrary pathways; long-distance trading and cross-cultural exchanges had laid the trails for him. Yet cross-cultural contacts were limited by the weakness of institutional ties. In the absence of armies, legal codes, and governors to integrate vast regions, cultural and economic influences lacked protection and promotion, and thus could not spread over long distances. Such expansion would accelerate with the emergence of a powerful—if fleeting—center that would unite parts of Asia and Africa. Slowly a new idea took hold: the world's parts could be integrated by common cultures and shared commodities. Political expansion occurred from Macedonia in northern Greece to the Buddhist worlds of South Asia, first under the Persians and then under Alexander. And just as Hellenistic influences followed on the heels of Alexander's conquests, so Buddhist influences followed the conquests of the Mauryan dynasty in South Asia. Backed by a major dynasty, with its belief systems carried outward by powerful armies and legions of magistrates and monks, Buddhism spread far and wide. From the corners of South Asia, Buddhism now became the world's most expansive religious system.

From the corners of South Asia, Buddhism now became the world's most expansive religious system.

The interconnections of trade and cultural diffusion therefore enhanced regional integration, which unfolded in specific political contexts—marking a shift to territorial kingdoms (states ruled by powerful monarchs). The changes were mutually reinforcing: the Persian, Macedonian, and Mauryan conquests were made possible by some existing links across long distances, and the political shakeups and political integration they caused created immense opportunities for other ways of absorbing societies, notably trade, migration, and religious conversion. Conquests yielded to new kinds of contacts and stimulated old ones, as traders, moving goods by sea and land, quickly took advantage of the institutional links forged across long distances. The first long-distance caravan trading, and even fleets, began to ply regular trade routes, setting up commercial hubs that would crisscross the landmass from China to the Mediterranean. Merchants joined with monks and administrators in helping to tie disparate parts of Afro-Eurasia into a more interconnected whole, thereby enabling busy sea-lanes and the Silk Road to flourish.

This chapter examines how peoples from the western end of Afro-Eurasia sent shock waves east, and how the Hellenistic movement created new ways of imagining societies in far-flung regions. Its influences, both direct and indirect, were enormous. A few centuries after his conquests, the world looked very different from the realms Alexander had traversed.

THE EMERGENCE OF A COSMOPOLITAN WORLD

> → *How did the spread of Hellenism reshape the Mediterranean world?*

The armed campaigns of a minor Greek people, the Macedonians, and their leader, Alexander the Great, began a drive for empire from the west. Alexander's rapid and novel use of new kinds of armed force in a series of lightning attacks on the Persian Empire broke down earlier barriers between the Mediterranean world and the rest of Southwest Asia. The massive transfers of wealth and power that resulted from his conquests sped up the development of the Mediterranean into a new, more unified world of common economic and cultural exchanges. The whole period and the cultural movement associated with it are called Hellenistic (a term derived from the Greeks' name for themselves, *Hellēnes*). Alexander's ambition drove Hellenistic influences as far as Vedic South Asia and contributed to the flourishing of a new power, the Mauryan Empire, which united the smaller warring states in South Asia.

CONQUESTS OF ALEXANDER THE GREAT

The story of Alexander the Great has been recounted by many historians and biographers, yet it remains one of the most fascinating in world history. Alexander, who came from the small frontier state of Macedonia, to the north of Greece, was a pathbreaking conqueror who transformed the Mediterranean world. For a dozen years, between 334 and 323 BCE, he commanded a compact and highly mobile force that was armed with the advanced military technologies developed in the incessant warfare between Greek city-states.

Under Alexander's predecessors—especially his father, Philip II—Macedonia had developed into a large ethnic and territorial state. Philip had unified Macedonia and then gone on to conquer neighboring states, one of which had gold mines that he used to finance new military technology and a disciplined, full-time army. Heavily armored infantry in closely arrayed phalanxes, allied with the large-scale shock cavalry formations from his native land, were paid for not just with the huge income from the local gold mines but with the enormous profits of a slave trade that passed directly through Macedonia. By the early 330s BCE, Philip had crushed the old

MAP 6-1   AFRO-EURASIA IN 250 BCE

Alexander of Macedonia never created one large politically unified empire, but his conquests did bring various Afro-Eurasian worlds together. Use this map to identify various Hellenistic states that emerged in the wake of Alexander's conquests. What did these states have in common? Which states on the map did Greeks not rule? How did the spread of Hellenism affect them?

EMPIRE OF THE XIONGNU

GOBI DESERT

AECO–CTRIA

Lake Balkas

Tashkent

Kokand

Sogdian Rock

TAKLAMAKAN DESERT

TIBETANS

Taxila

HIMALAYA MOUNTAINS

Ganges R.

Pataliputra

Sanchi

Ujjain

MAURYAN EMPIRE

Yellow R.

Xianyang   Luoyang

QIN EMPIRE
(221 BCE)

Yangzi R.

SEA OF JAPAN

JAPAN

SINITIC PEOPLES

Mekong R.

SOUTH CHINA SEA

PACIFIC OCEAN

OCEAN

MALAYS

MALAYS

AUSTRALIAN ABORIGINES

- Campaigns of Alexander the Great
- Conquests of Alexander the Great
- Qin Empire
- Greek City State
- Carthage
- Area of Roman control
- Macedonia
- Ptolmaic Empire
- Seleucid Empire
- Graeco-Bactria
- Mauryan Empire
- Empire of Xiongnu

Battle of Issus. Mosaic of the Battle of Issus between Alexander the Great of Macedon and Darius, the king of Persia (found as a wall decoration in a house at Pompeii in southern Italy). Alexander is the bareheaded figure to the far left; Darius is the figure to the right, gesturing with his right hand. The men represent two different types of warfare. On horseback, Alexander leads the cavalry-based shock forces of the Macedonian Greeks, while Darius directs his army from a chariot in the style of the great kings of Southwest Asia.

Greek city-states to the south, including the great city of Athens. After Philip's assassination in 336 BCE, his son Alexander used this new military machine in a series of sudden and daring attacks, beginning in 334 BCE, on the apparently invincible power of the Persian Empire and its king, Darius III.

Like many other successful conquerors, Alexander owed a considerable part of his success to his readiness to take risks. In his initial series of forays into Southwest Asia, he simply outpaced and outflanked his adversaries, repeatedly taking them by surprise. Through these rapid assaults, he brought under the rule of his Greek-speaking elites all the lands of the former Persian Empire that extended from Egypt and the shores of the Mediterranean to the interior of what is now Afghanistan as well as to the Indus River valley.

The result of this lightning, violent rampage was hardly an empire, given that Alexander did not live long enough to put in place the institutions needed to hold these distant lands together. But Alexander's military campaigns smashed the barriers that had separated the peoples on the eastern and western ends of Afro-Eurasia. Indeed, the conqueror modeled himself as a new universal figure, a bridge between distant cultures. He epitomized this vision in his choice of wife, Roxana, the daughter of a Bactrian chief from Central Asia, and turned Balkh into a center of operations for two years, reinforcing the long-term importance of the new kingdoms of the Kushan rulers, who would emerge as powerful brokers in the new east-west axis between Asia and the Mediterranean.

Alexander opened a door that changed Afro-Eurasia forever. His conquests exposed Syria, Palestine, Egypt, and Mesopotamia to the commodities of the Mediterranean, to the development of money-based economies (both Philip and Alexander issued gold coins to pay for their invasions), and to the bundle of cultural ideas associated with the Greek city-states. Alexander founded dozens of new cities named after himself, the most famous of which was Alexandria in Egypt.

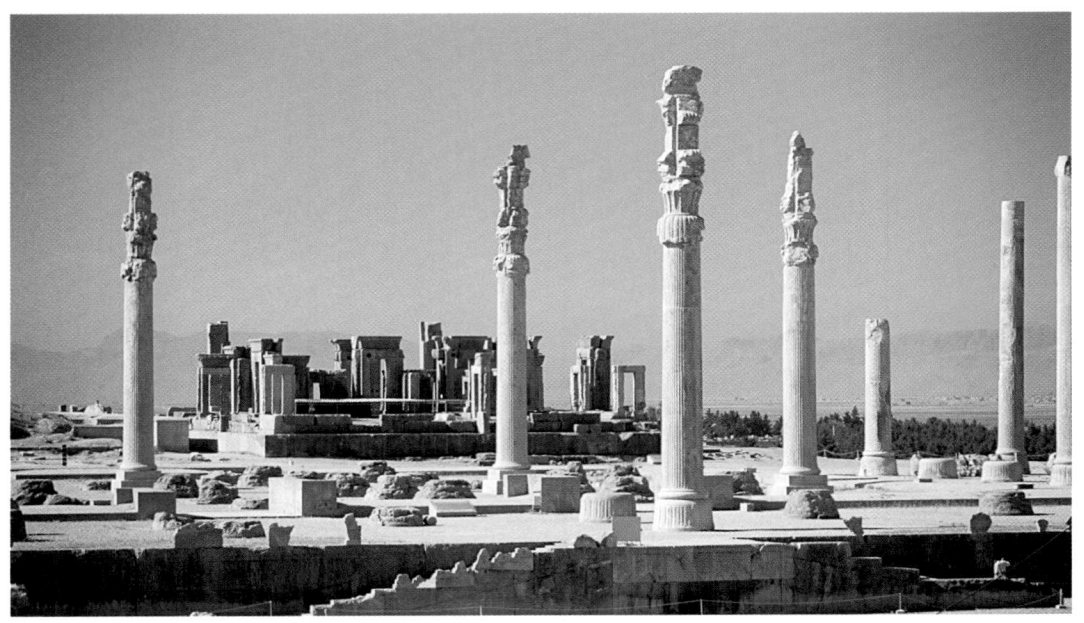

Palace of Darius. The remains of the great palace of Darius I of Persia at Persepolis, modern Tatchara in southwestern Iran. This is part of the so-called Appadana, or royal audience hall of the king. Construction of this palace began about 520 BCE and continued for several decades. This view shows only a small part of the complex, which covered dozens of acres and included hundreds of rooms in addition to the grand stairways and royal reception rooms. The palaces of Near Eastern monarchs physically represented the huge extent of their power.

→ *How did the spread of Hellenism reshape the Mediterranean world?*

Primary Source

CLASH OF EMPIRES: THE BATTLE OF GAUGAMELA (331 BCE)

The following passage, taken from the Greek historian Arrian, delineates the makeup of the army of Darius as it marshaled to confront Alexander and his forces. In describing the size of the army—much larger than that of the largest Greek city-state, Athens—Arrian mentions the various ethnic groups of the Persian Empire that contributed troops to it. Arrian is as reasonably trustworthy a writer as we can get on these matters, even though he was writing more than four centuries after the events in question. Note that army contingents come from lands as far-flung as Bactria (near modern-day Afghanistan), Scythia (in the broad geographical area from Ukraine to Kazakhstan), Armenia, Cappadocia (in east-central Turkey), and Caria (what is today southwestern Turkey), as well as from lands close to the Red Sea.

Darius's army was so large because it had been reinforced with Sogdians, with Bactrians, and with Indian peoples from the borderlands of Bactria, all under the command of Bessus, the satrap [i.e., the regional governor] of Bactria. There were also units of the Sakai—who were part of the Scythians who are found in Asia. They owed no loyalty to Bessus, but were still allies of Darius. These soldiers were mounted bowmen commanded by one Mauaces. The Arachotoi and the hillmen from India were commanded by Barsaentes, the satrap of Arachosia. The Areioi were commanded by their satrap, Satibarzanes; the Parthians, the Hyrcanians, and Tapeiroi, all cavalrymen, were commanded by Phrataphernes. The Medes, to whom were attached the Kadousioi, the Albanoi, and Sakesinai, were commanded by Atropates the Mede. All the units from the lands near the Red Sea were commanded by Orontobates, Ariobarzanes, and Orxines. The Ouxioi and Sousianoi were commanded by Oxathres, son of Aboultius. The men from Babylon, to whom were attached the Siracenioi and Carians, were commanded by Boupares—these Carians had been resettled in the empire by a mass transfer of their people. The Armenians were commanded by Orontes and

Mithraustes; the Cappadocians, by Ariaces. The Syrians from Hollow Syria [i.e., the Bekáa Valley in modern Lebanon] and from Mesopotamia were commanded by Mazaeus. The total number of men in the army of Darius was reported to be 40,000 cavalry, 1,000,000 infantry, 200 scythed chariots [i.e., war chariots with blades mounted on both ends of the axle], and some war elephants—the Indians who came from this side of the Indus River had about fifteen of them.

→ *Does the ability of both Xerxes, in the early fifth century* BCE, *and Darius, in the late fourth century* BCE, *to command ethnic loyalties across the huge landmass of Southwest Asia tell us something important about the nature of communications across this immense area?*

→ *Do you think that the mobilizing of military force on this scale by a large empire contributed in important ways to these communications?*

→ *Do you think that it also contributed to transfers of types of knowledge beyond what pertains to military concerns?*

SOURCE: Arrian, *The History of Alexander* 3.8; translated by Brent Shaw.

While it is true that some of these new colonial cities had little long-term impact, the linkage of Afro-Eurasian societies from East Asia to the Mediterranean world was never again to be broken.

One of Alexander's most significant acts was to seize the accumulated wealth stored by the Persian kings in their immense palaces, especially at Persepolis, and to disperse it into the money economies of the Mediterranean city-states. This massive redistribution of wealth, like the post-Columbian exploitation of the Americas, in turn fueled a huge economic expansion in the Mediterranean (along with price inflation, the downside of such rapid expansion).

ALEXANDER'S SUCCESSORS AND THE TERRITORIAL KINGDOMS

Alexander died in Babylon at the age of thirty-two—struck down by massive overconsumption of alcohol and other physical excesses of a piece with his larger-than-life personality and the war culture of the Macedonian male. His death in 323 BCE brought on the collapse of the regime he had personally held together. The conquered lands fragmented into large territories over which his generals fought incessantly for control.

Alexander's generals became his successors. Seleucus, Ptolemy, Antigonus, Lysimachus, and others did not think of themselves as citizens, even very important ones, of a Greek city-state, but rather modeled themselves on the regional rulers whom they had defeated. The emergence of kingdoms created by these men in the Eastern Mediterranean worlds not only imported Alexander's predilection for absolute rulership into the region but also unified large blocks of territory under the control of single, powerful rulers.

One effect of powerful families placing themselves in charge of whole kingdoms was that a few women were now able to hold great power, a prospect that had been completely closed to them in the democracies of the city-states. Queens in Macedonia, Syria, and Egypt, whether independent or co-regents with their husbands, established new public roles for women. Berenice of Egypt (c. 320–280 BCE) was the first of the powerful royal women who helped rule over the kingdom of the Nile; the line was to end with the most famous of them all, Cleopatra, in the 30s BCE.

The old city-states of the Mediterranean, such as Athens and Corinth, still continued to thrive, but they now had to function in a world dominated by much larger power blocs. In the eastern Mediterranean, three large territorial states overshadowed this new Greek world: Syria, ruled by the Seleucids (the dynasty established by Seleucus); Macedonia, ruled by the Antigonids (the dynasty established by Antigonus); and Egypt, ruled by the Ptolemies (the dynasty established by Ptolemy). In the interstices between these larger states, middle-sized kingdoms emerged—for example, Pergamum, in the northwestern part of what is today Turkey. Elsewhere, polities banded together in order to survive in this new world; on mainland Greece, larger confederations like the Achaean League or the Aetolian League now forced the previously independent city-states to join with them.

In general, therefore, political states became bigger and began to coalesce into larger operating units that displayed a uniformity unknown in the governments of the earlier city-states. The impulse to standardization during this period can be seen not just in its politics but in every aspect of ordinary daily life. Unlike the first empires we described in Chapter 4, which sought to prevail over neighbors by subordinating them as colonies or tribute states, these kingdoms expanded their frontiers by integrating neighboring peoples as fellow sub-

Berenice. Portrait head of Berenice, wife and consort of Ptolemy I, the first Macedonian king of Egypt after its conquest by Alexander the Great. Berenice was one of the women who, as queens of huge empires, wielded power and commanded wealth in their own right.

jects. They believed, unlike their predecessors, that they possessed cultural assets that could be disseminated across much broader geographic areas. They were Alexander's successors in their certainty that their culture could transcend the place where it was born and make all peoples within a vast state the worthy subjects of powerful monarchs.

Competition in war remained an unceasing fact, even in the new world of expanding states. But the wars between the kingdoms established by the successors of Alexander were bigger in size and more complex in organization than ever before. The adversaries fought some of the largest-scale battles that the Mediterranean was ever to witness. At the same time, the relative parity in strength of each of the large states meant that warfare never achieved much. Every big state had access to much the same advanced military technology. Rulers simply went out into the marketplace and acquired the highly trained soldiers, mercenaries, generals, and military advisers required to run their armies. After battles that killed tens of thousands, and severely injured and wounded hundreds of thousands, the three major kingdoms, and even the minor ones, remained largely unchanged.

The great powers therefore settled into a prolonged centuries-long game of carefully watching each other and balancing threats with alliances. What emerged was a fierce competition that dominated international relations, with diplomacy and endless treaty making replacing actual fighting—an equilibrium reminiscent of the first international age in the second millennium BCE (see Chapter 3). Long periods of peace began to exist between the extremely violent and destructive wars waged by the new kingdoms.

HELLENISTIC CULTURE

Just as large-scale uniformity in politics and war trumped the small size and diversity of the old city-state, so too the individuality of the cultures of the earlier city-states now gave way to a new uniform culture that stressed the common identity of all who embraced Greek ways. This homogenized culture emphasized the common denominators of language, style, and politics to which anyone, anywhere in the Afro-Eurasian world, could have access.

Following already existing commercial networks, Greek culture spread rapidly through the whole of the Mediterranean basin. It was an alluring package, and ruling elites in all the regions that came into contact with it were strongly attracted to its powerful modes of thinking and behaving. This Greek city-state culture included secular disciplines from history to biology, philosophical and political thinking, popular entertainment in theaters, competitive public games, and secular art for art's sake in all kinds of media. No other society at the time had such a complete package of high culture: hence its obvious appeal and its diffusion into distant corners. Archaeologists have found a Greek-style gymnasium and theater in the town of Aï Khanoum in modern Afghanistan and adaptations of Greek sculptures made at the order of the Vedic king Sandrakottos (better known as Chandragupta); we know of Carthaginians in North Africa who became "Greek" philosophers, and Gallic and Moorish chieftains, from the far west of France and Morocco, who had fine Greek drinking vessels buried with them.

Hellenistic cultural forces provoked varying responses in different parts of the Afro-Eurasian world as they came into contact with preexisting cultures and ruling groups. Hellenism had its most decisive impact and produced its strongest reactions in the home territory of the Greeks, the Mediterranean. A segment of the Jewish population of the region then called Judea resisted it violently, seeing it as a lethal threat to the identity of their culture and to their reli-

gious beliefs. The inhabitants of the rising city of Rome, in contrast, regarded the mastery of Greek ways as a vehicle for advancing the status of Rome throughout the Mediterranean. And the Carthaginians took the new Greek influence in stride, promoting its spread throughout the larger Mediterranean world and seeing it as an aid to their economic and cultural well-being.

COMMON LANGUAGE A common language had widespread appeal, for it replaced the numerous idiosyncratic dialects of Greek, each with relatively few speakers, found in the world of the early city-states with a new, everyday form of Greek that could be understood anywhere. Known as "common," or *koine,* Greek, it became the international language of its day.

Most of the peoples who came into contact with this language, and with the culture accompanying it, accepted the benefits of Greek language and culture in expanding a wide network of communication and exchange. Peoples living in Egypt, Judea, Syria, and Sicily, who all had their own languages and cultures, were now able to communicate more easily with each other, to worship Greek deities such as Dionysus, and to enjoy the same dramatic comedies in their theaters and new common forms of art and sculpture. But—as would generally be the case throughout history—cultural dominance was not achieved without considerable local resentment and resistance. As noted above, some of the Jews in Judea rejected the push to "become Greek": local Jewish religious leaders rebelled against Hellenism's common language, music, gymnasia, nudity, public art, and secularism, believing that the new culture was deeply immoral and threatening to local beliefs. Yet despite pockets of resistance, overall the Hellenizing movement was remarkably successful in spreading a shared Greek culture throughout the Mediterranean and into Southwest Asia.

COSMOPOLITAN CITIES Much as Athens had been the model city of the age of the Greek city-state, the city of Alexandria in Egypt became exemplary in the new age. Whereas fifth-century BCE Athens had zealously maintained an exclusive civic identity, Alexandria was a multiethnic city that was built from scratch by immigrants, who rapidly totaled half a million as they streamed in from all over the Mediterranean and Southwest Asia in search of new opportunities. Members of its huge and dynamic population, representing dozens if not hundreds of Greek and non-Greek peoples, communicated with each other in the new common language, which supplanted their original dialects. A new urban culture emerged to meet the needs of so diverse a population.

The culture of the Hellenistic movement supplanted local art forms. In the previous city-state world, comic playwrights had written plays for their city and its culture, basing their art on local languages, local foibles and problems, and local well-known politicians; in this new connected world, however,

Primary Source

THE COSMOPOLITAN CITY OF ALEXANDRIA

According to legend, Alexander both selected the site of Alexandria and named the city after himself. As a result of Alexander's personal influence and its strategic location, Alexandria quickly grew into a megalopolis that attracted an immense and diverse immigrant population from the entire Mediterranean world. In the following description of the city, the Greek geographer Strabo, who was writing in the time of the first two Roman emperors, Augustus and Tiberius (between about 25 BCE and 20 CE), emphasizes the city's function as an enormous entrepôt for trade and commerce across Eurasia. (Entrepôts are ports that had become transshipment centers where cargoes were unloaded from seafaring vessels and then sent elsewhere, by sea or by land.) By Strabo's time, it was the second-largest city in the Mediterranean, surpassed only by Rome itself. Alexandria's commercial reach was enormous. From the upper regions of the Nile in what is now Sudan it received ivory, slaves, and animal skins, many of which its merchants transported to other Mediterranean locations in North Africa, Europe, and Southwest Asia.

As for the Great Harbor at Alexandria, it is not only wonderfully well closed in and protected by artificial levees and by nature, it is also so deep that even the largest ships can be moored right at the stairs along its quayside. This Great Harbor is divided up into several minor harbors. . . . Even more exports are handled than imports. Anyone who might happen to be at Alexandria and at Dichaiarchia [the large Italian port on the Bay of Naples] would easily see for himself that the cargo ships sailing from here are bigger and more heavily laden. . . . The city itself is crisscrossed by streets that are wide enough for riding horses and driving chariots, and intersected by two main roads very much broader than the others. Its streets and avenues cut across each other at right angles. The city also boasts exceedingly beautiful public parks and its royal quarters take up a quarter, perhaps even a third of the whole city. . . . In earlier times, not even twenty ships would dare to go as far as the Arabian Gulf and manage to get a look outside its straits. But now large fleets of ships are sent out as far as India

and to the furthest lands of the Ethiopians, from which the most valuable cargoes are brought to Egypt and then sent out again to other regions of the world. Double charges are collected on these shipments—both when they come in and when they go out—and the duties are especially high on luxury goods . . . for Alexandria alone does not just receive trade goods of this kind from all over the world, but it also furnishes supplies to the whole of the world outside.

→ *If you consider the historical circumstances of the city's foundation by Alexander the Great, what factors might have led to the sudden, even explosive, growth in its size and population?*

→ *Looking at the city's location on a map, can you think of other factors connected with communication, travel, trade, and supply that would have further encouraged the city's tremendous expansion?*

SOURCE: Strabo, *Geography* 17.1.6, 7, 8, 13; translated by Brent Shaw.

---

entertainment had to appeal to bigger audiences and had to be accessible to a wider variety of people. Plays were now staged in any city where Greek influence existed, and they were understood in any environment. Distinctive regional humor or local characters gave way to dramas populated by stock characters with whom a vast Afro-Eurasian audience

could identify: the miser, the old crone, the jilted lover, the golden-hearted whore, the boastful soldier, the befuddled father, the cheated husband, and the rebellious son. Such plays could be performed anywhere in the Mediterranean, and the laughter would be just as loud in Syracuse on the island of Sicily as in Scythopolis in the Jordan Valley of Judea.

→ *How did the spread of Hellenism reshape the Mediterranean world?*

The Theater at Syracuse. The great theater in the city-state of Syracuse in Sicily was considerably refurbished and enlarged under the Hellenistic kings. It could seat 15–20,000 persons. Here the people of Syracuse attended plays written by playwrights who lived on the far side of their world, but whose works they could understand as if the characters were from their own neighborhood. In the common culture of the Hellenistic period, plays deliberately featured typecast characters and situations, thereby broadening their audience.

Ways of thinking changed to match this newly unified world. The new ideas took into account that individuals were no longer citizens (*polites*) of a particular city (*polis*): they were the first "cosmopolitans," belonging to the whole world or "universe" (*kosmos*). The new political style was relentlessly cosmopolitan, radiating out of cities not just into local hinterlands but also to distant (and often rivalrous) cities.

Kingdoms and states had become so big that individuals could relate to it only through the personality of kings or rulers and their families. Rulership was personality, and personality and style bound together large numbers of subjects. For example, Demetrius Poliorcetes, the ruler of Macedonia, wore high-platform shoes and heavy makeup, and he decorated his elaborate, flowing cape with images of the sun, the stars, and the planets. In the presence of a powerful and solitary sun king like Demetrius, ordinary individuals felt small, inconsequential, and personally isolated. In response, an obsessive cult of the self arose, as Hellenistic religion and philosophy increasingly focused on the individual and his or her place in the larger world.

PHILOSOPHY AND RELIGION This new concern with the individual self was expressed in many different ways. One was personified in Athens by the philosopher Diogenes (c. 412–323 BCE), who was originally from Sinope on the Black Sea. He sought self-sufficiency and freedom from the laws and customs of society, rejecting all the cultural norms of his society as human-made inventions not in tune with nature and therefore false. He masturbated in public in order to "relieve himself" (it was, after all, a "natural need"), as well as to

show his disdain for the artificial sexual mores of the city. He lived with no clothing in a wooden barrel in the public square, or agora, of Athens, with his female companion in her barrel beside him. Other teachers were also rejecting the values of the city-state, although with more finesse and less contentiousness than Diogenes. Nonetheless, all recognized that a new orientation was required now that the old world of the city-state, with its face-to-face relationships, had vanished. In a world turned larger and more threatening, many sought answers within the individual.

The self was similarly emphasized by the teacher Epicurus (c. 341–279 BCE), the founder of a school in Athens that he called The Garden. He set out his ideal of a community centered on The Garden and stressed the importance of sensation, saying that pleasurable sensations were good and painful sensations were bad. Epicurus was seen as a personal savior (*sōtēr*) and his students were taught to pursue a life of contemplation and ask themselves, "What is the good life?" The Epicureans struggled to develop a sense of "not caring" (*ataraxia*) about things in their life and to view them as not mattering, so as to find peace of mind. In Epicurus's cult, none of the social statuses of the old city-state had more value than any other: women, slaves, and others in the underclass were equally welcome in The Garden as worshippers.

Epicurus and his followers acquired adherents throughout the Mediterranean, but they were hardly alone. Unrestrained by the controls of any one city-state, other new cults and schools of philosophy emerged. Of these, Stoicism was perhaps the most widespread and effective. It was initiated by a man named Zeno (c. 334–262 BCE), from Citium on the island of Cyprus, and a large number of other cosmopolitan figures across the Hellenistic world—from Babylon in Mesopotamia to Sinope on the Black Sea—developed its beliefs; their mission was to make individuals better able to understand their place in the cosmos. Zeno taught his ideas in the Stoa Poikilē, a decorated roofed colonnade that opened onto the central marketplace of Athens and gave his followers their name. For the Stoics, everything was grounded in nature itself, which was held to be the ultimate, permanent world. Cities and kingdoms were human-made things, important but transient. Being in tune with nature and living a good life required understanding the rules of the natural order and being in control of one's passions and thus indifferent to pleasure or pain.

Greek colonial control of other lands and cultures transformed long-established religions, which were then reexported to cities throughout the Mediterranean. The Greeks in Egypt drew on the cult of Osiris and his consort Isis, once a vital element in pharaonic temple rituals, to fashion a new narrative, employing the story of Osiris's death and rebirth to represent personal salvation from death. Isis became a supreme goddess whose lists of "excellencies" or "supreme virtues" encompassed the powers of dozens of other Mediterranean gods and goddesses. Believers experienced personal revelations and out-of-body experiences (*exstasis*, "ecstasy").

A ritual of dipping in water (*baptizein*, "to baptize") marked the transition of believers, "born again" into lives devoted to a "personal savior" who produces an understanding of a new life by direct revelation. These new religious beliefs, like the worship of Isis, emphasized the spiritual concerns of humans as individuals, rather than the collective worries of towns or cities.

HELLENISM AND THE ELITES Once high Greek culture coalesced, its appeal to elites in widely dispersed communities along the major communication routes became almost irresistible. Social elites in such communities believed that they could enhance their position by adopting Hellenistic culture, the only culture that had standing above the level of local values. This attitude was taken by Syrian, Jewish, and Egyptian elites in the eastern Mediterranean, as well as by Roman, Carthaginian, and African elites in the western Mediterranean. The later Roman high culture was itself a form of Greek culture. Of the Romans' extensive borrowings from the Greeks, not the least important was a belief—unusual at that time—in the value of a written history. They, too, began writing about contemporary events and their past. Secular plays, philosophy, poetry, competitive games, and art followed, all based on Greek forms or on local imitations of them. North African kings, ruling polities located in the area

The Painted Stoa. An artist's reconstruction of the Stoa Poikilē, or "Painted Stoa," in the city-state of Athens of the fourth century BCE. In the manner of a modern-day strip mall, this business and administrative center ran along the northern side of the agora, or central business and marketplace of the city. Philosophers and their students would hang out at the Stoa, lounging in the shaded areas under the colonnade as they debated the ideas flowing into Athens from all over the Hellenistic world. The painted wall decoration behind the columns (from which the Stoa received its name) depicts the Battle of Marathon.

of present-day Algeria and Tunisia, similarly decked themselves out in Greek dress, built Greek-style theaters, imported Greek philosophers, and wrote history. Now they, too, had "culture."

The Hellenistic influence penetrated deeply into sub-Saharan Africa, where the kingdom of Meroe (see Chapter 5), while decisively influenced by pharaonic forms, displayed many of the characteristics of Greek culture. Both Meroe and its rival, Axum, located in the Ethiopian highlands, used Greek stelae to boast of their military exploits. Not surprisingly, Greek influences were extensive among the Meroe, whose continuous interaction with the Egyptians exposed its people to the world of the Mediterranean. Herodotus mentions that the citizens of Meroe "worshipped Zeus and Dionysus alone of the gods, holding them in great honor. There is an oracle of Zeus there, and they make war according to its pronouncements, taking from it both the occasion and the object of their various expeditions." The rulers of Meroe, understanding the advantages of the Greek language, employed many Greek scribes to record the accomplishments of the kings on the walls of Greek-Egyptian temples. In this way, the kingdom and culture of Meroe provided a remarkable mix of Greek, Egyptian, and African cultural and political elements. Of all of the archaeological finds in Meroe, perhaps the most stunning is the bronze head of the Roman emperor Augustus that was discovered in front of the royal temple in the capital city of Meroe and frequently has been used to illustrate books on Nubia.

JEWISH RESISTANCE TO HELLENISM

The Jews in Judea, a small land squeezed between Egypt to the south and the superstates of Mesopotamia to the north and east, offer a striking case of resistance to the universalizing forces of Hellenistic culture. The focal point of all Jewish culture was the temple in Jerusalem. The people of Judah had first been unified under King David in the early tenth century BCE. And it was his son and successor, King Solomon, who masterminded the building of the new temple, designed by a Phoenician architect, as well as an even more elaborate royal palace. These two structures were in the new city of Jerusalem, where a high priesthood ordered the affairs of the single supreme deity of the whole people, who in effect defined themselves in opposition to all of the powers impinging on their small world. After the seventh century BCE, however, Judah and the Jews were almost constantly subject to one or another of the major powers dominating the region—first the Assyrians and then the Babylonians, who finally destroyed the city and its temple in 587 BCE. The Jews therefore had a long schooling in surviving and resisting foreign rule. The defeat of Babylon by the Persians was followed by a royal edict of restoration issued by the Persian monarch Cyrus in 538 BCE and the sub-sequent integration of what was now a province, Judea, into the Persian Empire. As the Jews who had been forced to move to Babylon returned to Judea, the process of rebuilding Jerusalem began.

The reconstruction of the temple was finally completed in 516 BCE. It was under the aegis of Nehemiah, a Jewish eunuch in the Persian court of Artaxerxes I, that permission and resources were given to rebuild the fortification walls around the city (440–437 BCE). Around this same time, the physical rebuilding of Jerusalem was complemented by a restoration of the religious community, with stricter adherence than ever before to the cultural and ritual regulations that defined the Jewish people (for example, no marriage with "outsiders") and to the laws of their God. Yet all of this rebuilding of local Jewish society occurred within the confines of another great Southwest Asian empire, that of the Achaemenids, where Persian toleration of local customs and beliefs supported the restoration of Jewish tradition. It took Alexander's lightning defeat of the Persian Empire in the 330s BCE to suddenly make possible the transformation of political relationships and a new and shocking openness to the cultural innovations of the Mediterranean world. Hellenism came in the wake of Alexander's sweep through the region.

Some parts of the ruling elite of Jewish society began to adopt Greek ways—to wear Greek clothing; to introduce the culture of the gymnasium, with its cult of male nudity; to produce images of gods as art. When a full-scale armed revolt, led by the family of the Maccabees, broke out in 166 BCE after the Syrian overlords issued edicts forbidding the practice of Judaism and deliberately profaned the temple, the rebels consciously rejected the imported culture of the Hellenists. Though they succeeded in establishing an independent Jewish state centered on the temple in Jerusalem, they did not entirely overcome the impact of the new universal culture. By the beginning of the first century BCE, descendants of the Maccabees were calling themselves kings, were minting coins with Greek legends, and were presiding over a largely secular kingdom. Moreover, a huge Jewish society that existed outside Judea in the new Hellenistic city of Alexandria in Egypt fully embraced the new culture; there scholars produced a Bible in koine Greek, and historians, like Jason of Cyrene, and philosophers, like Philo of Alexandria, wrote in Greek, imitating Greek models.

ROMAN HELLENISM AND THE BEGINNINGS OF THE ROMAN EMPIRE

Other cities were less reluctant than Jerusalem to follow Hellenistic ways. Early on, the Romans saw the Greek model as offering them opportunities to increase their importance in the Mediterranean world. In the 330s and 320s BCE, when Alexander's conquests were uniting the whole of the eastern Mediterranean, a city-state on the Tiber River in central Italy took the first critical military actions to unify Italy; eventually, it would bring together the rest of the Mediterranean and parts of Southwest Asia. Rather than beginning as a kingdom like Macedonia, Rome mutated from a Mediterranean city-state into a large territorial state. In this transformation, it adopted, bit by bit, many of the elements of the new uniform Hellenistic culture: Greek-style temples, elaborately decorated Greek-style pottery and paintings, and an alphabet based on that of the Greeks, all of which had appeared in the fifth and fourth centuries BCE.

Romans saw immersion in Greek culture and language as enabling them to appear to the rest of the world as "civilized." Yet this notion was not accepted by the Roman elites without struggle, resistance, and much worry and debate. The Roman senator Cato the Elder (234–149 BCE), one of the best-known figures in this transitional age, reveals the extreme tensions and adaptations that these changes required. Although he was devoted to the Roman past, the Latin language (his extant prose works are among the oldest that survive in Latin), and the ideal of small-scale Roman peasant farmers

Roman Mosaic. Although this colorful mosaic comes from a later period of Roman history (third-century CE Gaul; it was found at Saint-Germain-en-Laye in modern-day France), it shows a constant theme of Mediterranean history—the annual cycle of hard work required of Roman peasants. Here the peasants are ploughing the land in the spring—the farmer to the right is driving the pair of oxen drawing the plough—and seeding the crop—the farmer to the left is throwing seed from a wicker basket into the furrows made by the plough.

and their families, he embraced many of the new Hellenistic influences. He wrote a standard how-to manual for the new economy of slave plantation agriculture (discussed below), invested in shipping and trading, learned Greek rhetoric (both speaking and writing the language), added the genre of history to Latin literature, and much more. In some ways, Cato blended an extreme devotion to tradition and the solid and unchanging Roman past, manifest in his public statements, with bold innovations in most aspects of his day-to-day life.

CARTHAGE

In contrast to Rome, whose inhabitants assimilated Greek ways to elevate their status in the larger Mediterranean world, cities that were prosperous and well integrated into the world economy welcomed Hellenistic culture because it facilitated communication and exchange. The ideas and new economic forces that the Romans and Cato experienced so powerfully in the second century BCE spread throughout the Mediterranean; when they reached the great city of Carthage in present-day Tunisia, they were adapted without great fanfare but with much success. Not only did Carthage's merchants trade with other Phoenician colonies in the western Mediterranean, but its ruling families assumed direct control over western Sicily and Sardinia. Remains of pottery and other materials unearthed by archaeologists demonstrate that the Carthaginians' trading contacts extended far beyond other Phoenician settlements to towns of Etruscans and Romans in Italy, to the Greek trading city of Massilia (modern Marseilles) in southern France, and to Athens in the eastern Mediterranean. In addition, the Carthaginians expanded their commercial interests into the Atlantic, moving north along the coast of Iberia and south along the coast of West Africa—which, as noted in Chapter 5, a great Carthaginian commander, Hanno, explored and colonized. Pushing their influence along the littoral, they even established a trading post at the island of Mogador, more than 600 miles down the Atlantic coast of Africa.

Carthaginian culture—or Punic culture, to use the Romans' name for the people with whom they would soon be embroiled in warfare—also shared important parts of the common Hellenistic culture of the time. Carthaginians went to Athens to become philosophers. The design of their sanctuaries, temples, and other public buildings reveals a marriage of modes and styles: Greek-style pediments and columns mixed with Punic designs and measurements, and local North African motifs and structures were added to the mix. The fine jewelry worn by Phoenician women reflected influences and styles coming from Egypt. The finest tableware and pottery were imported from Etruscans in Italy, and coinage and ideas came from the Greek city-states.

Aerial View of Punic Carthage. Carthage was located on a promontory in the Bay of Tunis. In the lower foreground of this artist's reconstruction is a rectangular area of water and above it a circular-shaped one. These were the two major harbors of Carthage—the rectangular one was the commercial port and the circular one was the military harbor. Above these harbors are the main market square and the high central point named the Byrsa. To the left is the twenty-mile-long wall that defended the city on its land side.

ECONOMIC CHANGES AND MEDITERRANEAN UNITY: PLANTATION SLAVERY AND MONEY-BASED ECONOMIES

Perhaps the fundamental economic innovation that accompanied the unification of the Mediterranean world was the use of very large numbers of slaves in agricultural production, especially in Italy, Sicily, and the regions of North Africa close to Carthage. The conquests of Alexander and the political rise of Rome produced unprecedented wealth for a small elite living in the Mediterranean cities. These men and women, in turn, used their riches to acquire huge tracts of land and to purchase slaves—either individuals who had been kidnapped or peoples conquered in warfare—on a scale and with a degree of detailed managerial organization never seen before.

The slave plantations, wholly devoted to the production of surplus crops for profit, became one of the engines driving a new Mediterranean economy. The estates created vast wealth for their owners, though at a heavy price to others. Reliance on slave labor forced the free peasants who previously had worked the fields into overcrowded cities where employment was hard to find. The results of the sudden importing of such large numbers of slaves and working them in such harsh conditions should have been anticipated but were not. Between 135 and 70 BCE, authorities on the island of Sicily and in southern Italy were challenged by three massive slave uprisings against owners, led by the religious seer and prophet Eunus in 130 and the slave gladiator Spartacus in the late 70s. These were among the greatest slave wars known in world history.

The circulation of money reinforced the effects of forced labor. With more cash in the economy, wealthy landowners, urban elites, and merchants could more easily do business. The increasingly widespread adoption of Greek-style coins to pay for goods and services, in place of a barter system, promoted the importation of such cultural commodities as wine from elsewhere in the Mediterranean region. As coined money became more and more available, it was increasingly used as the main means for facilitating commercial exchanges. The forced transfer of precious metals to the Mediterranean from Southwest Asia by Alexander's conquests actually caused the price of gold to fall. In the west, Carthage now began to mint coins of its own on a large scale, at first mainly in gold but later in other metals. Rome moved to a money economy at the same time. By the 270s and 260s BCE, the Romans created their first major issues of coins and then moved decisively toward the

Early Roman Coin. Coins like this one were the standard means by which the state paid its expenditures, and they later were widely used in ordinary commercial dealings. This coin features the prow of a ship with its "evil eye" decoration and armed beak for ramming other ships. The legend ROMA stamped on the bottom signals that Rome is a state with the power and autonomy to have its own money.

Roman Slaves. One of the most profitable occupations for peoples living beyond the northwestern frontiers of the Roman Empire, in what was called Germania, was that of providing bodies for sale to Roman merchants. In this relief from Roman Moguntiacum on the Rhine River (modern-day Mainz), we see chained German prisoners whose fate was to become slaves in the empire. This stone picture supported columns in front of the headquarters of the Roman fortress at Mainz-Kästrich.

general use of money under the pressures of their first full-scale war with Carthage (264–241 BCE). By the end of the third century, even borderland peoples such as the Gauls in their kin-based kingdoms had begun to mint coins, using the galloping-horse images found on Macedonia's gold coins issued by Philip II. So, too, did the kinship-based African kingdoms in North Africa, where the coins of the kings Massinissa and Syphax were imprinted with the same Macedonian royal imagery. By the end of this period, inhabitants of the whole of the Mediterranean basin and of the lands immediately around it were using coins to buy and sell all manner of commodities.

To pay for the goods made desirable by their newly acquired tastes, Celtic chieftains in the regions covered by modern France were willing to sell their own people in the expanding slave markets of the Mediterranean. Slavery and slave trading also became central to the economies of the

Iberian Peninsula, especially in the hinterlands of large river valleys like the Ebro, where local elites founded urban centers imitating Greek styles and forms in the fourth and third centuries BCE. If Alexander's more immediate triumphs were the broadcast of political and, especially, military influences from the Hellenistic world, the more influential aftershocks were economic and cultural. From North Africa to South Asia and beyond, Hellenistic influences and the very idea of a universal culture that might incorporate all urban, settled peoples reverberated across Afro-Eurasia.

CONVERGING INFLUENCES IN CENTRAL AND SOUTH ASIA

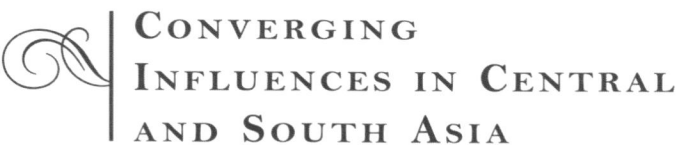

→ *How did Hellenistic and pastoral nomadic cultures influence central and South Asia?*

The mountains of what is today known as Afghanistan are formidable but permeable. Their passes, between the high plateau of Iran to the west and the towering ranges of Tibet to the east, are pinched like the narrow neck of an hourglass —but they offer the shortest route through the mountains.

By crossing those passes Alexander's armies opened a route between two worlds, the eastern and western portions of Afro-Eurasia, fashioning a new land bridge that has remained open to this day. It created avenues for an unprecedented sort of cross-cultural exchange that eventually remapped whole regions. Conquerors moving from west to east, like Alexander, and from east to west, like the later nomads from central Asia, were drawn southward, through the mountains, into the rich plains of the Indus and Ganges River valleys. South Asian trade and, above all, South Asian religions moved northward toward the trade routes that ran from west to east along what became known as the Silk Road. As a result, the politics, economics, and cultures of Afro-Eurasia, between China and the eastern regions of the empire of Alexander, were profoundly influenced by the incorporation of central Asia and South Asia into this east-west axis. The new links set the stage for exchanges that would first touch and penetrate North Africa, and then over time work their way into East Africa and parts of sub-Saharan Africa.

INFLUENCES FROM THE MAURYAN EMPIRE (321–184 BCE)

Alexander's occupation of the Indus Valley, though it lasted only two years (327–325 BCE), helped pave the way for

The Bolan Pass. The formidable Bolan Pass separated India from the highland of Baluchistan. It was both an artery for transportation and a strategic military spot.

India's most powerful and durable polity before the Common Era. Previous to the arrival of Alexander's forces, India had been a conglomerate of small warring states. This political instability came to an abrupt halt when, in 321 BCE, an ambitious young man named Chandragupta Maurya ascended the throne of the Magadha kingdom and launched a series of successful military expeditions in what is now northern India. Magadha, located on the lower Ganges plain, held great advantages over other states. It contained rich iron ores and fertile rice paddies. On the nearby northeast Deccan plateau, ample woods supported herds of elephants, the mainstay of the potent Magadha cavalries. The Mauryans did not start out as a distinguished ruling family in north India, but economic strength and military acumen elevated them over their rivals. The retreat of Alexander created a momentary political vacuum: it was an opportunity for the

shrewd Mauryans to extend the dynasty's claims to the northwest areas of South Asia, the region previously controlled by the Persian Empire.

Chandragupta's expanding regime, called the Mauryan Empire by late historians, constituted the first large-scale empire in the history of South Asia and served as a model for later Indian empire builders. This empire was known to the contemporary Greek world as "India," the country stretching from the Indus River eastward. Indeed, the Mauryan regime began to etch out the territorial contours of what would many centuries later become modern India. Chandragupta, who ruled from 321 to 297 BCE, used his military resources to reach beyond the Ganges plain to the northwest into the Punjab, pushing up to the border with the Seleucid kingdom, the largest successor kingdom of Alexander's ephemeral empire. Its king, Seleucus Nicator, fretted about his neighbor's challenge and invaded Mauryan territory—only to run into Chandragupta's impregnable defenses. Soon thereafter, a treaty between the two powers gave a large portion of Afghanistan—including Kandahar, one of the Alexandrias—to the Mauryan Empire. The territory that the Mauryans wrested from the Seleucids, especially Kandahar, remained Greek-speaking for centuries, and some urban locations developed from garrison towns into genuine Greek-style poleis. The treaty yielded a round of gift exchanges and diplomacy. One of the daughters of Seleucus went to the Mauryan court at Pataliputra, accompanied by a group of Greek women. Seleucus also sent an ambassador, Megasthenes, to Chandragupta's court. Megasthenes lived in India for years, and he gathered his observations of Indian life in a book titled *Indica*. In return, Mauryans sent Seleucus many Indian valuables, including hundreds of elephants, which the Greeks soon learned to use in battles.

The Mauryan Empire reached its height during the reign of the third king, Aśoka (ruled 268–231 BCE), Chandragupta's grandson. Aśoka's lands comprised almost the entirety of South Asia, including the Deccan plateau; the tip of the peninsula alone remained outside his control. In 261 BCE, the eighth year of his long reign, Aśoka waged the dynasty's last campaign: the conquest of Kalinga, a kingdom on the east coast of the Indian peninsula. It was a gruesome and despicable operation. The Mauryan army triumphed but at a high price. About 100,000 soldiers died in battle, and many more perished in its aftermath; some 150,000 people were uprooted and forcibly relocated. Aśoka himself, when he learned of the devastation, was shocked and appalled at his own handiwork, and in a fit of guilt issued a famous edict renouncing his brutal ways.

Aśoka was a faithful follower and patron of Buddhism. Indeed, the Kalinga campaign redoubled his fealty to Buddhism, which informed his peaceable edict. All over his domain he built stupas, or Buddhist dome monuments, which marked the burial sites of relics of the Buddha. In the Kalinga edict, he claimed to rule over his subjects according to

AŚOKA'S KALINGA EDICT

After the Kalinga war, Aśoka issued an edict to express his regret at the miseries it had caused his people. From this edict, we can tell that Aśoka knew that he was ruling a country of many different cultures and religions.

Beloved of the Gods, is that those who dwell there, whether brahmans, *śramaṇas*, or those of other sects, or householders who show obedience to their superiors, obedience to mother and father, obedience to their teachers and behave well and devotedly towards their friends, acquaintances, colleagues, relatives, slaves, and servants—all suffer violence, murder, and separation from their loved ones. Even those who are fortunate to have escaped, and whose love is undiminished [by the brutalizing effect of war], suffer from the misfortunes of their friends, acquaintances, colleagues, and relatives. This participation of all men in suffering weighs heavily on the mind of the Beloved of the Gods. Except among the Greeks, there is no land where the religious orders of brahmans and *śramaṇas* are not to be found, and there is no land anywhere where men do not support one sect or another. Today if a hundredth or a thousandth part of those people who were killed or died or were deported when Kaliṅga was annexed were to suffer similarly, it would weigh heavily on the mind of the Beloved of the Gods.

The Beloved of the Gods believes that one who does wrong should be forgiven as far as it is possible to forgive him. And the Beloved of the Gods conciliates the forest tribes of his empire, but he warns them that he has power even in his remorse, and he asks them to repent, lest they be killed. For the Beloved of the Gods wishes that all beings should be unharmed, self-controlled, calm in mind, and gentle.

The Beloved of the Gods considers victory by *Dhamma* to be the foremost victory. And moreover the Beloved of the Gods has gained this victory on all his frontiers to a distance of six hundred *yojanas* [i.e., about 1500 miles], where reigns the Greek king named Antiochus, and be-

yond the realm of that Antiochus in the lands of the four kings named Ptolemy, Antigonus, Magas, and Alexander; and in the south over the Colas and Pāndyas as far as Ceylon. Likewise here in the imperial territories among the Greeks and the Kambojas, Nābhakas and Nābhapanktis, Bhojas and Pitinikas, Andhras and Pārindas, everywhere the people follow the Beloved of the Gods' instructions in *Dhamma*. Even where the envoys of the Beloved of the Gods have not gone, people hear of his conduct according to *Dhamma*, his precepts and his instruction in *Dhamma*, and they follow *Dhamma* and will continue to follow it.

What is obtained by this is victory everywhere, and everywhere victory is pleasant. This pleasure has been obtained through victory by *Dhamma*—yet it is but a slight pleasure, for the Beloved of the Gods only looks upon that as important in its results which pertains to the next world.

This inscription of *Dhamma* has been engraved so that any sons or great grandsons that I may have should not think of gaining new conquests, and in whatever victories they may gain should be satisfied with patience and light punishment. They should only consider conquest by *Dhamma* to be a true conquest, and delight in *Dhamma* should be their whole delight, for this is of value in both this world and the next.

→ *Aśoka promised to rule his people with Dhamma (Dharma in Sanskrit). Is this Dhamma the Buddhist doctrine or a general moral standard for all religious and ethnic communities?*

Source: Romila Thapar, *Aśoka and the Decline of the Maurya*, 2nd ed. (Delhi: Oxford University Press, 1973), 255–57.

---

dhamma, or a general set of moral regulations that applied to all—including the priestly Brahmans, Buddhists, and members of other religious sects, and even the Greeks. To explain and implement this *dhamma,* Aśoka regularly issued decrees, which he had displayed on stone pillars and boulders

in every corner of his domain; occasionally, he also issued edicts to explain his own Buddhist faith. All were inscribed in local languages. While most of his decrees were written in dialects of Sanskrit, those published in northwestern regions were in Greek or in Aramaic, the administrative script of old

Persia. Aśoka's legal pronouncements helped give legitimacy to the Greek-speaking population that had entered the country with Alexander and now resided in Greek-style towns.

The works of art created under Aśoka's patronage celebrated the copious cultural and economic exchanges between the Greeks, Persians, and Indians. The most famous monument of this kind was the edict pillar that Aśoka erected in Sarnath at the Deer Garden, where the Buddha gave his first sermon. Atop the pillar, four lions sat facing four directions. Beneath the four lions, four wheels representing universal rule were separated by a bull, a horse, elephants, and another lion. The majestic images of lions, animals not found in the Ganges plain, represented an Indian version of the Persian royal symbol. Its technique displayed Greek influence as well, in vivid, animated style.

Lion Pillar. Aśoka had his edicts carved on this kind of pillar all over India. The majestic lion as the capital of the pillar shows the influence of Persian art, in which the lion was the symbol of royalty.

The Stupa at Sarnath. Buddhist legend claims that Aśoka placed relics of the Buddha into the many stupas he had built. The stupa at Sarnath is the best-preserved one from the time of Aśoka.

THE SELEUCID EMPIRE AND GREEK INFLUENCES

Alexander's Asian military thrust reached as far as the Punjab (literally "Five Rivers," the area around the upper stream of the Indus where four tributaries joined it); there, he defeated several rulers of Gandhara in 326 BCE. In the course of this campaign, he planted many garrison towns. Their highest concentration was in eastern Iran, northern Afghanistan, and the Punjab, where many encampments were needed to protect his easternmost new territory. A large number of these eastern outposts, such as those at Ghazni, Kandahar, Kapisi, and Bactra (modern Balkh), became major Hellenistic cities, sporting the characteristic features of a Greek polis—a colonnaded main street lined by temples to patron gods or goddesses, a theater, a gymnasium for education, a palace administration center, a marketplace.

After the death of Alexander, Seleucus Nikator (358–281 BCE), the ruler of the Hellenistic successor state in this area, built more Greek garrison towns throughout the region. Seleucus, who also controlled Mesopotamia, Syria, and Persia, named sixteen cities Antioch after his father, five Laodiceas after his mother, nine Seleucia after himself, three Apamea after his wife Apama, and Stratonicea after another wife. Though many of these towns or cities, especially those located in Iran, have vanished without a trace, the remains of several have been found in modern-day Afghanistan, the easternmost corner of the Hellenistic world. These cities were originally stations for soldiers, but they soon also became centers of Hellenistic culture.

Most of the Greek invaders integrated themselves into the local societies. Once the soldiers realized that they would be spending their lives in a country far from their homeland, they married local women and started families. They brought their ways to the local populations and established the institutions familiar to them from the polis. Greek was the official language, but because local women used their native tongues in daily life, subsequent generations were bilingual. The traditional Greek institutions, and especially Greek language and writing, survived many political changes and much cultural assimilation in a long strip of land stretching from the Mediterranean to South Asia, providing a common basis of engagement for many different lands and people across several centuries.

THE KINGDOM OF BACTRIA AND THE YAVANNA KINGS

Hellenistic influences were even more pronounced in the successor regimes of central Asia of the late third century BCE. The Seleucid state took over the entire Achaemenid Persian realm, including its central Asian and South Asian territory. The Hellenistic kingdom of Bactria, located west of the Hindu Kush in modern-day Afghanistan and Uzbekistan, broke away from the Seleucids to establish a strong state, which included the Gandhara region in modern Pakistan, around 200 BCE. As Mauryan power receded from the northwestern region of India, the Bactrian rulers extended their conquests into this area, drawn by the prospects of obtaining even more fertile territories. Because the cities that the Bactrian Greeks founded included a substantial number of Indian residents, and thus were a mix of cultural influences, they have been called "Indo-Greek." Those in Gandhara incorporated familiar features of the Greek polis, but inhabitants kept a reverence for Indian patron gods and goddesses.

Hellenistic Bactria served as a bridge between South Asia and the Greek world of the Mediterranean. Among the many goods that the Bactrians sent west were elephants, which were vital to the Greek armies. The Greeks' fascination with Indian war elephants is demonstrated by their frequent appearance in Greek art. The Greek king Demetrius invaded India around 200 BCE and had himself portrayed on his coins as wearing an elephant cap (i.e., a headdress with an elephant's trunk). In the following decades, Bactrian Greek in-

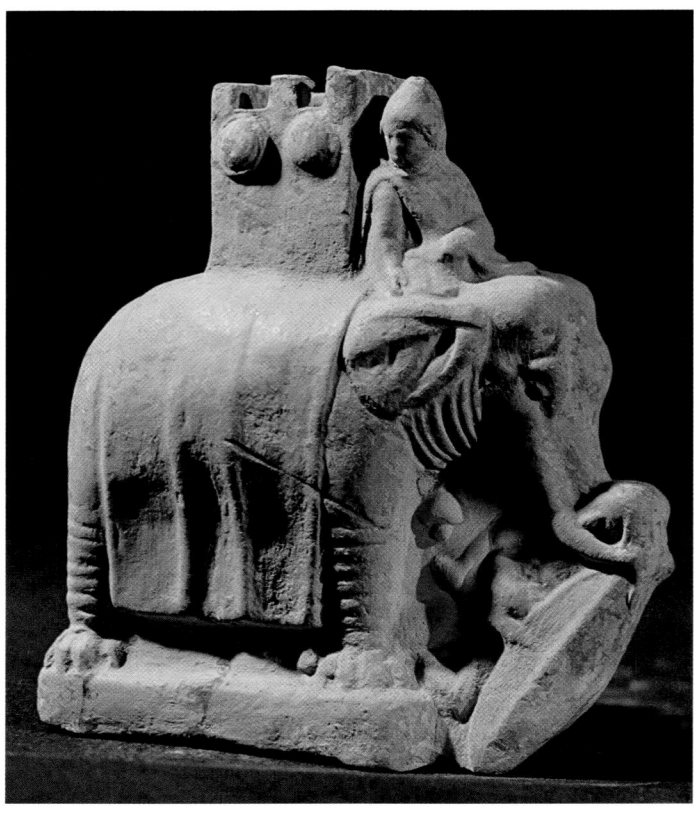

Elephant Cavalry. As shown by this terra-cotta statuette from 200 BCE, elephant cavalry was an important component of the Greek military. In their exchanges with India, Hellenist states demanded numerous elephants for their army.

vaders not only revived the cities in India left by Alexander but also founded several new Hellenistic cities in the Gandhara region. Demetrius entrusted the extension of his territorial empire in northern India to his generals, many of whom became independent rulers after his death. In Sanskrit literature, these Greek rulers were known as the Yavana kings—a word derived from Ionia, a region of western Asia Minor whose name was extended to all those who spoke Greek or came from the Mediterranean.

Remains of a Greek garrison town, unearthed under the site of ancient city of Samarkand in Uzbekistan, attest to the strength of Hellenistic influences even in cities far removed from the Greek homelands. In the 1960s, archaeologists working at Aï Khanoum on the Oxus River (now the Amu) in present-day Afghanistan were stunned to find the ruins of nearly an entire Greek city, largely undisturbed. Miraculously, Aï Khanoum had avoided the reconstructions and devastations that had befallen so many other Hellenistic cities in this region. We do not know its Greek name, but it was certainly an administrative center, if not the capital city, of the Bactrian state. The Greek-style architecture and inscriptions indicate that the original residents of the garrison city were soldiers from Greece. They followed the typical pattern: they married local women and stayed, but they also established the fundamental institutions of a Greek polis.

Aï Khanoum had many characteristic Greek structures: a palace complex, a gymnasium, a theater, an arsenal, a citadel on the acropolis, several temples, and elite residences. Built with marble columns with Corinthian capitals, the palace contained an administrative section, storage rooms, and a library. Though far from Greece, the elite Greek residents read poetry and philosophy. The baths in the palace had a mosaic floor made of colored pebbles,which were readily available from the nearby riverbank. At the city's theater, Greek dramas were performed. Grape cultivation made possible a festival of wine drinking, associated with the god Dionysus. The main temple housed a gigantic marble statue of an unknown deity; only its huge marble foot has survived the ravages of time. The remains of various statues make clear that the residents not only revered the Greek deity Athena and the demigod Heracles but also paid homage to the Zoroastrian religion and worshipped the gods of Mesopotamia.

Thus, Alexander's Asian conquests implanted Greek culture in what is modern Uzbekistan, Afghanistan, and northern India, connecting settlements there with communities in the Mediterranean basin. Although the residents of these Asian Hellenistic cities often worshipped different patron gods and were fluent in local languages, they too were influenced by the ideals of the Greek polis. Most men and women spoke and wrote some Greek, often as a second language.

The Hellenistic cities tried to maintain Greek culture by educating young people in gymnasia and by performing Greek dramas in their theaters. Their temples housed various deities —some Greek in origin, some not. Because Greek religious practices were inclusive, temples were suitable places for cultural assimilation; there, local deities donned Greek garb to protect the city. When Greeks moved into the new areas, they planted crops familiar to them from their homeland, and vineyards and olive orchards flourished. A material culture, such as tableware associated with wine drinking, also thrived. Cities and kings issued coins with Greek inscriptions, or legends, in the standard weights of the Greek world. Perhaps the most adept at mingling Greek and Indian influences was Menander, the best-known of the Yavana city-state kings in India in the mid–second century BCE and ruler over a large area stretching from Mathura on the Yamuna River to the Gulf of Khambhat (Cambay), located on the Indian Ocean. Using images and legends on coins to promote both traditions among his new subjects, Menander claimed his legitimacy as an Indian ruler but also cultivated Greek cultural forms. On the face of his coins, he had his regal image surrounded by the Greek words *Basileus Sōtēr Menandros* (King, Savior, Menander). The reverse side of these coins featured the Greek goddess Athena; her image was accompanied by the king's title in the local Pakrit language, written in Karoshthi letters (the alphabetic script developed in northwest-

ern India). These legacies, some obvious and others more subtle, persisted long after the collapse of the Hellenistic regimes. Greek language, letters, and coinage remained essential elements in the communication and trade around the Indian Ocean rim until at least the third century CE.

NOMADIC INFLUENCES OF PARTHIANS, SAKAS, AND KUSHANS

A wave of invasions and migrations from central Asia during the last three centuries BCE weakened Hellenistic influences in Iran and central Asia but did not completely eradicate them. The Seleucid state in Iran, having lost control of Bactria, now came under relentless pressure from the nomadic peoples living on the steppes to the north. The first to prey on them were the Parthians, a horse-riding people, who pushed southward around the middle of the second century BCE and wiped out the Greek kingdoms in Iran. The Parthians extended their power all the way to the Mediterranean, where they would ultimately encounter the expanding Roman Empire in Anatolia and Mesopotamia.

The original heartland of the world's first cities was becoming a borderland between the emerging powers of the Mediterranean and West Asia. Parthia and Rome were both strong, expansionist states and became archenemies: they confronted each other in Mesopotamia for nearly four centuries, until the Sasanian kings replaced the Parthians as the rulers of Iran in 224 CE. Because the Parthians probably did not have their own writing system when they became rulers of settled agricultural communities, their empire left no historical record; it is known to us only through the descriptions of Greek observers who had remained in central Asia after the retreat of Greek powers. According to these sources, the Hellenistic caravan cities on the eastern frontier of the Roman Empire continued to trade with the east in spite of the conflicts between the Romans and the Parthians. From the eastern shore of the Mediterranean all the way to Afghanistan, Greek was still the lingua franca for commercial activities.

During a second major wave of invasions after the Parthians invaded in the middle of the second century BCE, nomadic peoples swept out of Mongolia and central Asia into India around 130 BCE. They filled some of the vacuum left by the disintegration of Alexander's and Aśoka's empires, infusing the societies of South Asia with the nomadic and equestrian values of the steppe. In the process, they blended both Hellenism and Buddhist religious thought with a culture that glorified nomadic and pastoral ways and institutions. A modified Hellenistic culture and the Greek language became even more vital than before; even as its connections to Greece became more attenuated, its influence over Buddhism and other South Asian cultures grew. The famous Gandharan Buddhist art of this period clearly demonstrates a Hellenistic imprint.

Permanent Hellenistic settlement
SCYTHS Nomad confederacy
HAN Contemporary settled culture
Great Wall of China, 1st century BCE

The new rulers came down from the dry northern steppe in waves, each driving its predecessor before it in search of new tribal domains. In the second century BCE, a vast tribal confederacy called the Xiongnu emerged as a dominant force in the east Asian steppe lands. While consolidating their power, the Xiongnu forced many other pastoral groups out of their homelands. One of these groups, the Saka tribes, moved toward the southwest into India; they conquered the area from Mathura to the western coast of India and gradually es-

tablished many states. Meanwhile, the Parthians, who had supplanted the Greek Seleucids in Iran, also entered the Indus Valley—from the northwest, through the mountain passes of Baluchistan.

India's new Central Asian rulers were proud horse-riding peoples, possessing different cultural and linguistic backgrounds than the indigenous inhabitants. Like the Parthians, all lacked their own system of writing. Once they entered Bactria and the Indus Valley, they imitated the sedentary

MAP 6-2   NOMADIC INVASIONS, 800 BCE–100 CE
Interaction between nomadic and settled societies was a major engine of change in Afro-Eurasia in the first millennium BCE. According to the map, where did nomadic and settled societies interact? How did both groups change as a result of this interaction? How did this interaction shape cross-cultural processes (the spread and diffusion of goods, peoples, and ideas) during the first millennium?

surrounded by the same legend—but here in the script of northwestern India.

The most dynamic and powerful of all of the northern nomadic groups to migrate into South Asia were the Yuezhi-Kushans, who arrived in 50 CE, about 150 years after the Yuezhi had entered Bactria. Led by their chief, Kujula Kadphises, the Yuezhi unified all the tribes of the region and immediately set up the Kushan dynasty. The Kushans' empire embraced a large and diverse territory and played a critical role in the formation of the Silk Road.

Like the Sakas and the Parthians, the Kushans were an illiterate people, but they adopted Greek as their official language. The face of a gold coin of Wima Kadphises (the second Kushan king to rule South Asia) features the king's bust, surrounded by Greek legends. The reverse side of the coin contains the image of the Hindu god Shiva, with his cow. Up to the end of the Kushan Empire in the early third century CE, Greek letters continued to be displayed on Kushan coins, sometimes on both sides but always on the face. The Kushan rulers kept alive the influence of Hellenism in Afghanistan and northwestern India in an area strategically located on the Silk Road, even though by this time few Greek speakers were left in the population. Mediterranean traders arrived in the Kushan markets to purchase silks from China, as well as Indian gemstones and spices; they carried out their transactions in Greek. The coins they used—struck to Roman weight standards (themselves derived from Greek coinage) and inscribed with Greek inscriptions—answered their needs perfectly.

The coming of the many nomadic groups did not undermine local cultural traditions or the Hellenistic heritage, but it brought in a powerful new cultural ingredient: equestrianism.

rulers such as Menander, issuing coins, collecting taxes, and facilitating trade. The legends and images on the coins vividly demonstrate how these nomadic chiefs used the Hellenistic cultures of their conquered subjects. For example, one of the silver coins issued by the Saka ruler Maues, dated around 100 BCE, carries an image of Zeus, surrounded by the Greek inscription ΒΑΣΙΛΕΩΣ ΒΑΣΙΛΕΩΝ ΜΕΓΑΛΟΥ ΜΑΥΟΥ (King of Kings, the Great Maues). The reverse side of the coin shows the image of the Greek goddess Nike (Victory),

Three Coins. *Top:* Wearing an elephant cap, Demetrius of Bactria titled himself the king of Indians as well as Greeks. On the other side of the coin is Hercules. *Middle:* The king Menander is remembered by Buddhists for his curiosity about their theology. His image appears on one side of the coin with a Greek legend of his name and title. On the other side, Athena is surrounded by Kharoshthi script, an Indian writing. *Bottom:* The Scythian king Maues used Greek to claim "King of Kings" on one side of his coin. On the other side, the goddess Nike is surrounded by Kharoshthi letters.

The Sakas and Kushans were proud nomads, who carried their horse-riding skills into India. In spite of the hot climate, the Sakas and Kushans continued to wear cone-shaped leather hats, knee-length robes, trousers, and boots as a way to set themselves off from the indigenous inhabitants. Since the time of the Vedic invaders (see Chapter 3), horses had been valued imports into the region—and with the advent of the Kushans, they became the most prestigious status symbol of the ruling elite. At the same time, the Kushans began consuming exotic goods that arrived from as far east as China and as far west as

the Mediterranean, as they enjoyed a highly diversified material culture. Their successful rule also stabilized the trading routes through central Asia that stretched from the steppes in the east to the Parthian Empire in the west. This would become one of the major segments of the Silk Road.

THE TRANSFORMATION OF BUDDHISM

> → *In what ways did the transformation of Buddhism represent cultural integration in South Asia?*

While India was undergoing noteworthy political and social change caused by the incursions of nomadic tribes, it was also experiencing dramatic cultural change in the religious sphere. Perhaps the most surprising repercussion of the spread of Hellenism after Alexander was the mutation of Buddhism. Like the Romans, the Indians were profoundly impressed with Hellenistic thought, and they sought to blend it with their own ethical and religious traditions—the most important of which was Buddhism.

A merger of belief systems began first among the Yavana city-states in the northwest, where Buddhism's sway was most pronounced. Here, for example, Menander, the Yavana king who ruled from Mathura on the Ganges plain, went far beyond promoting the belief that the Buddha was an inspired ethical philosopher: he held instead that the Buddha was a god. The most important step in this direction was the publication of *Milindapunha* (*Questions of King Milinda*), a text that featured a discussion between the king and a sophisticated Buddhist sage named Nagasena. According to this account, composed during his reign, Menander asked many questions about Buddhist theology and Nagasena explained away all his doubts. Nonetheless, the transformation of Buddhism into a religion with Hellenistic influences and wide-ranging support in other states was far from complete when Menander died around 130 BCE. It would occur only after other influences, and other gods and beliefs, were accommodated.

INDIA AS A SPIRITUAL CROSSROADS

Hellenism spread through many lands and cultures, but it was not the sole cultural movement to make a virtue of reaching out to other cultures, if only to subdue or transform them. Hellenism disrupted traditional political institutions and threatened existing religions wherever it went. In India, the nomads added another layer to this transformation, as did Arab and other seafarers whose mastery of the monsoon trade winds opened the Indian Ocean to commerce (see below) and made

Primary Source

THE QUESTIONS OF KING MILINDA

The Indo-Greek king Menander is a famous patron of Buddhism, as described in the Questions of King Milinda. *The book, written in Pāli, begins with a description of the kingdom of Milinda, the Pāli name for Menander. The country is Yonakas (the Pāli name for Greeks, derived from Ionia, a region in western Asia Minor). This kingdom, according to the following passage from* The Questions of King Milinda, *is a center of prosperous trade and people of many different creeds, with a city whose glory rivals that of "the city of the gods."*

Thus hath it been handed down by tradition—There is in the country of the Yonakas a great centre of trade, a city that is called Sâgala, situated in a delightful country well watered and hilly, abounding in parks and gardens and groves and lakes and tanks, a paradise of rivers and mountains and woods. Wise architects have laid it out, and its people know of no oppression, since all their enemies and adversaries have been put down. Brave is its defence, with many and various strong towers and ramparts, with superb gates and entrance archways; and with the royal citadel in its midst, white walled and deeply moated. Well laid out are its streets, squares, cross roads, and market places. Well displayed are the innumerable sorts of costly merchandise with which its shops are filled. It is richly adorned with hundreds of almshalls of various kinds; and splendid with hundreds of thousands of magnificent mansions, which rise aloft like the mountain peaks of the Himâlayas. Its streets are filled with elephants, horses, carriages, and foot-passengers, frequented by groups of handsome men and beautiful women, and crowded by men of all sorts and conditions, Brahmans, nobles, artificers, and servants. They resound with cries of welcome to the teachers of every creed, and the city is the resort of the leading men of each of the differing sects. Shops are there for the sale of Benares muslin, of Koṭumbara stuffs and of other cloths of various kinds; and sweet odours are exhaled from the bazaars, where all sorts of flowers and perfumes are tastefully set out. Jewels are there in plenty, such as men's hearts desire, and guilds of traders in all sorts of finery display their goods in the bazaars that face all quarters of the sky. So full is the city of money, and of gold and silver ware, of copper and stone ware, that it is a very mine of dazzling treasures. And there is laid up there much store of property and corn and things of value in warehouses—foods and drinks of every sort, syrups and sweetmeats of every kind. In wealth it rivals Uttara-kuru, and in glory it is as Âlakamandâ, the city of the gods.

→ *The city Sâgala is in the country Yonakas, that of the Greeks. Judging from the references to elephants, horses, and the Himalayas, where approximately would it have been located?*

→ *What kind of people lived there?*

SOURCE: *The Questions of King Milinda*, translated by T. W. Rhys Davis (1890; reprint, Delhi: Motilal Banarsidass, 1975), 2–3.

India the hub for long-distance ocean traders and travelers. All land and sea roads seemed to lead to India. Not surprisingly, during this era the region became a melting pot of ideas and institutions, from which a powerful and expansionist new spiritual synthesis emerged. Taken together, these influences—Hellenism, nomadism, and Arab seafaring culture—profoundly transformed one of India's most characteristic and indigenous spiritual and philosophical systems, Buddhism.

The Kushans, as rulers from the steppe, courted the local population by patronizing local religious cults. In so doing, they accommodated to the ways of their vanquished subjects. For example, in Bactria, where they encountered the shrines of many different gods, the Kushan kings had the images of various deities cast on the reverse side of their coins. They further demonstrated their acceptance of local belief systems by donating generously to shrines of Zoroastrian, Vedic, and particularly Buddhist cults. Around Kushan political centers, religious shrines mushroomed, and sculptural works reached a high artistic level. Kushan kings also had royal dynastic shrines built, beside which they placed statues of themselves, as patrons of the deities honored. Governors and generals followed their example of patronizing religions, as did traders, artisans, and other urbanites. Wealth flowed into religious institutions, especially Buddhist monasteries.

As a result, Buddhism changed dramatically from the days in the sixth and fifth centuries BCE when the Buddha walked from city to city preaching to his community of followers (*sangha*). In the first century CE, under the Kushan rule of northwestern India, the Buddhist *sangha* grew so rich because of India's growing commercial prosperity that monks

began to live in elegant monastic complexes. The center of each was a stupa decorated with sculptures depicting the life and teachings of the Buddha. Such monasteries provided generously for the monks' well-being, with halls in which they gathered and worshipped and rooms in which they meditated and slept. During this age, Buddhist monasteries also opened themselves up to the public as places for worship.

THE NEW BUDDHISM: THE MAHAYANA SCHOOL

The mixing of new ways—nomadic, Hellenistic, Persian, and Mesopotamian—with traditional Buddhism produced a spec-

Stupa Staircase. These risers from the staircase of a large stupa in the Gandhara region display scenes from Buddhist stories. The upper one shows men in nomads' clothing playing music, including the Greek-style lira. On the middle one, men and women in Greek clothing drink and make merry. The people on the lower riser wear little clothing but are as happy as those on the other two panels.

> → *In what ways did the transformation of Buddhism represent cultural integration in South Asia?*

Buddhist Cave Temple at Ajanta. Buddhists excavated cave temples along the trade routes between ports on the west coast of India and places inland. Paintings and sculptures from Ajanta became the models of Buddhist art in Central Asia and China.

tacular spiritual and religious synthesis. A new Buddhist school of theology, Mahayana, appeared at this time, marking a new stage in the evolution of the religion. For at least a hundred years, Buddhist learned men had debated the question of whether the Buddha was a god or a wise human being. The Mahayana Buddhists resolved this dispute in the first two centuries of the Common Era with a ringing affirmation: the Buddha was, indeed, a deity. This deification merged older Buddhist doctrines with Hellenism and cultural influences imported from the northern steppes. Mahayana Buddhism was at once worldly and accommodating, a spiritual pluralism that positioned Indian believers as a cosmopolitan, open people—welcoming contacts with peoples from other parts of Afro-Eurasia and laying the spiritual foundations for a region that had emerged as a crossroads of world cultures.

The religious appeal of Mahayana Buddhism was greater among lay followers than had been the earlier form of Buddhism, which had stressed that life was full of suffering and that people had to renounce desire to end their suffering and achieve *nirvana*. Indeed, as we saw in Chapter 5, the appeal of *nirvana* was difficult to understand for those without a belief in reincarnation. Newcomers such as migrants or traders were unlikely to embrace the nonexistence offered by *nirvana*, since they saw no need to escape painful cycles of birth, growth, death, and rebirth. In the vision of the Mahayana Buddhists, bodhisattvas (enlightened demigods who were ready to reach *nirvana* but delayed so that they might help others attain it) prepared "buddha-lands" and heavens—spiritual halfway points, like the Western Pureland of Amitabha—to welcome deceased devotees not yet ready to let go of desires and enter *nirvana*. The universe of the afterlife in Mahayana Buddhism thus was colorful and pleasant, promising an attractive variety.

Mahayana—literally, "Great Vehicle"—Buddhism was so named because it was viewed as enabling all individuals, the poor and powerless as well as the rich and powerful, to move from a life of suffering into a happy existence. Yet to suffering devotees, the Buddha, who was now considered a god and had moved on to *nirvana*, could provide little relief. Mahayana

Stone Frieze from Ajanta. The figures flanking the Buddha should be bodhisattvas. However, the iconography of bodhisattvas was not clearly established at the time that this frieze was carved.

Buddhism featured a religious world peopled by bodhisattvas, still living in the world, whose primary purpose was to help all ranks of the human race. One of these bodhisattvas, Avalokiteshvara, proclaimed his willingness to stay in this world to guide people out of trouble, especially those who traveled in caravans and had the misfortune of running into robbers or those who had to navigate ships through storms.

The new image of the Buddha and the bodhisattvas also appeared in a new genre of Buddhist literature: Sanskrit Buddhist texts. Aśvaghosa (80?–150? CE), a great Buddhist thinker and also the first known Sanskrit writer, wrote a biography of the Buddha. In this work, known as the Buddhacarita, Aśvaghosa set the life story of the Buddha within the Kushan Empire instead of in the Shakya republic in the foothills of the Himalayas, where he had actually lived. Aśvaghosa said that the Buddha was born as a prince into a life of extreme luxury, becoming aware of human suffering only after heavenly revelations. To escape his mundane life, the young prince left home in the middle of the night, riding on his white horse. This new, largely fictive, version of the Buddha's life story quickly became canonical, spreading throughout India as well as to other countries in which people accepted Buddhism. Aśvaghosa's foundational spiritual text gave Buddhist beliefs more uniformity across South Asia.

CULTURAL INTEGRATION

Sanskrit Buddhist texts of the first centuries CE created a colorful set of images that gave rise to a large repertoire of Buddhist sculptural art and drama. On Buddhist stupas and shrines, artisans carved scenes of the Buddha's life, figures of bodhisattvas, and statues of patrons and donors. Buddhist sculptures from the northern part of Kushan territory, fashioned from gray schist rock, are called Gandharan art, and those from the southern part are called Mathuran art, created mainly from the local red sandstone. Gandharan Buddhist art shows strong Greek and Roman influences, whereas the sculptural style of the Buddha and bodhisattvas in the Mathura region evolved from the carved idols of folk gods and goddesses.

In spite of their stylistic differences, the schools shared themes and cultural elements. Both took the bold step, inspired by Hellenistic art and religious tradition, of sculpting the Buddha and bodhisattvas in realistic human, rather than symbolic, form, such as a bodhi tree. The Buddha of the Gandharan artists took on a Greek look, while the Buddha of Mathura appeared more Indic, yet both were serene. Though the Buddha wore no decorations, since he had cut off all his links to the world of endless death and rebirth, bodhisattvas were dressed as princes because they were still in this world, generously helping others. What was important was bringing the symbolic world of Buddhism closer to the people.

Bronze Buddha. This bronze Buddha often strikes viewers as a Jesus Christ. Greco-Roman influence on the iconography of Buddha was probably responsible for the Gandharan-style attire and facial expression of Buddhas and bodhisattvas.

Buddhist art depicted a society of diverse populations, as befit a spiritual system that appealed to peoples of many different cultural backgrounds. Take, for example, the clothes of the patron figures. For men and women alike, the garments represented simple and well adapted to tropical climates. Those indigenous to the semi-tropical land dressed in a fashion that left their upper bodies nude; their lower bodies were covered by a wrapping akin to the modern dhoti, or loincloth. Jewelry adorned the headdresses and bodies. By contrast, their cone-shaped leather hats, knee-length robes, trousers, and boots made it easy to spot the nomadic peoples and identify their traditional garb. Figures with Greek clothing demonstrate continuing Hellenistic influence, and the appearance of Roman togas makes clear that imperial Rome's influence had reached the Indian subcontinent. In fact, the loose toga-like robes that adorn many statues of the Buddha suggest a mix-

Mathuran Buddha. This Mathuran Buddha of Gupta times is more refined than the Buddhas of the Kushan era. The robe is so transparent that the artist must have had very fine silk in mind when sculpturing.

ing of Roman and Buddhist themes. The jumble of different clothing styles makes visible the appeal of Buddhism to peoples of diverse backgrounds, who could share a faith while retaining their ethnic or regional differences.

The many peoples who lived under Kushan rule, Buddhist or not, had important cultural traits in common. They preferred Hellenistic or pseudo-Hellenistic architecture, particularly favoring columns, and they reveled in Greek music and dance. Although we do not know the songs that they sang at their festivals, we can recognize many of their musical instruments: the lira (a small version of the harp), the flute, the cymbal, the drum, and the xylophone. They were wine drinkers, and celebrated wine's intoxicating pleasures by using grape and grape-leaf motifs in their carvings. Carvings in the vicinity of Buddhist shrines often highlight festive drinking scenes. The horse was also celebrated in the story of

the Buddha. Under the Kushans, Buddhist monasteries were cosmopolitan organizations, where Greco-Roman, Indic, and steppe nomadic cultural themes blended together.

Long-distance and regional trade contributed to the transformation of Buddhism as well. Traders brought incense and jewels, which adorned bodhisattvas and stupas. Mahayana texts describe how these commodities became sacred to Buddhism. At the same time, monastic organizations became hospitable to traders who converged on India over mountain passes or from the Indian Ocean.

THE FORMATION OF THE SILK ROAD

↠ *How did long-distance exchanges alter the cultural geography of Eurasia and North Africa?*

By 300 BCE, Afro-Eurasia was in the throes of a major transformation. Traders, migrants, and marauders, as well as conquerors, took to the roads and waterways with unprecedented zeal. They forged connections between distant areas, transporting products and ideas that would alter societies.

Overland routes, focusing on the spice trade (the trade in frankincense and myrrh from the Arabian Peninsula) and on the exchange of metals (copper, tin, and iron) and precious commodities (precious stones and textiles), had been traveled by merchants and traders in earlier periods, but they now expanded to link the lands from South Asia to the Mediterranean. In the first century BCE, early overland trade routes stretching from China to central Asia and then from central Asia to the Mediterranean would be joined in what was later labeled the Silk Road—though many commodities flowed back and forth on caravans, it was silk that came to exemplify the commercial integration of the Afro-Eurasian world. Traders would travel specific segments of the route, passing their goods on to others who would take the goods further along the road and, in turn, pass them on.

Also effective in promoting long-distance trade were waterways. The Egyptians had used the Nile River to transport goods and to trade for thousands of years, and coastal trade between ports thrived from very early times. Sea routes arose, following the coastlines of Iran, the Persian Gulf, and the Arabian Sea into the Red Sea, stretching down the shore of East Africa. Initially, mariners relied on land-based markers to orient themselves; but toward the end of the first millennium BCE, as navigational techniques improved and larger, more seaworthy craft were built, Arab traders ventured out into the Indian Ocean, and trade expanded. Once a large body of water such as the Indian Ocean could safely be crossed, the possible connections, exchanges, and accumulated knowledge

NORTH SEA

ROMAN EMPIRE

SCYTHIANS

BLACK SEA

ANATOLIA

URAL MTS.

ARAL SEA

CASPIAN SEA

from the West to India and China:

Rome

Athens

Antioch

Dura Europos

Palmyra

PARTHIAN EMPIRE

Merv

Buk

B

IRANIAN PLATEAU

ZAGROS MTS.

Tigris R.

Euphrates R.

Oxus R.

Carthage

MEDITERRANEAN   SEA

Alexandria

Petra

NABATAEAN KINGDOM

EGYPT

ARABIAN

DESERT

Persepolis

Persian Gulf

from India to the We

A/D

Barba

from Arabia to India:

SAHARA DESERT

Niger R.

Nile R.

Berenice

NUBIA

Meroe

RED SEA

from Arabia, Ethiopia and East Africa to the West:

LF

ARABIAN STATES

from Arabia and Ethiopia to India and Cl

I

ARABIA

AXUMITE KINGDOM

from the West to India and Southeast Asia:

G □ LT

Lake Victoria

INDIAN

Bhapta

MADAGASCAR

Legend:

- ——— Silk Road
- ——— Other trade routes
- SCYTHS   Nomad group
- ——— Boundary of empires, states, and kingdoms
- •   Port/trading town
- ⌇⌇⌇   Great Wall of China

Traded Goods

A/D	Aromatics and drugs	○	Jewelry and cut gems
Cu	Copper	▱	Laquerware
○	Coral	LF	Luxury foods
◿	Everyday textiles	LT	Luxury textiles
◤	Fine cotton/garments	●	Peacocks
◉	Fine stone and metal vessels	○	Pearls
✕	Furs	◥	Silk
G	Glassware	⬤⬤⬤	Slaves
⬠	Gems	S	Spices
▢	Gold	▯	Statuary
Y	Grain	Sn	Tin
H	Horses	●	Tortoiseshell
I	Incense	◳	Wine
○	Ivory	▲	Wood

MAP 6-3 AFRO-EURASIAN TRADE, C. 150 CE

During the time period covered in this chapter, trade and commerce increasingly brought Afro-Eurasian worlds together. This map highlights important commercial pathways and economic linkages between various societies. According to the map, what role did nomadic pastoral peoples play in the creation of long-distance trade routes? How did mariners develop ocean-based commercial links? How did trade facilitate the spread of Buddhism during this time? Where and how did it spread?

of the human communities linked by its currents increased dramatically.

The expansion of commerce and contacts between the Mediterranean and South Asia built on and then reinforced a frenetic rise in commercial activity within each region. Over land and across the seas, traders loaded textiles, spices, and precious metals onto the backs of camels and into the holds of oceangoing vessels destined for distant markets. Trade thereby strengthened the ongoing political, intellectual, and spiritual shift: other areas that had once been on the fringes of the old Southwest Asian heartlands were coming to the fore as heartlands in their own right.

The compound effects of long-distance exchanges altered the political geography of Afro-Eurasia. The former cradles of the most highly developed cultures, Egypt and Mesopotamia, were fading as sources of innovation and knowledge, becoming instead a crossroads for the peoples on either side of them. The former borderlanders, in turn, ceased to be outsiders on the fringes of dynastic regimes, creating new centers as their own empires grew. These people became great merchants, whose private trade networks helped connect societies even as political institutions devised by state builders were integrating those societies. What we now call the Middle East literally became a commercial middle ground between emerging centers of culture and political expansion of the Mediterranean in the west and India in the east.

Eastern Afro-Eurasia, principally China, finally connected with the Mediterranean via central Asia and South Asia; through China, a connection was then made with Japan, Korea, and Southeast Asia, whose traders penetrated Bali and other islands of Indonesia by the first century BCE. The silk trade brought China into direct contact with central Asia and indirectly the Mediterranean world, and Chinese historians systematically recorded important events and customs of the "Western Regions." However, China remained politically and culturally a mysterious land to those from the Mediterranean. Alexander had gotten as far as the Indus Valley, to be sure, but the Himalayas and Pamir Mountains insulated the Chinese from ambitious conquerors from the west. Silk—a word derived from the Greek and Roman name for the people of northwestern China, *Sēres*—revealed that on the other side of Afro-Eurasia lay an advanced society, though the Greeks and Romans knew little about it.

NOMADS, FRONTIERS, AND TRADE ROUTES

Long-distance trade routes grew out of the activities of the horse-riding nomads from Inner Eurasia, the steppe lands stretching from the Caspian Sea all the way to present-day Mongolia, accustomed in the course of their migrations to carry supplies over great distances in order to survive. Gradually, they learned to trade goods from one region for goods produced elsewhere. They were the pioneers of a slow but powerful commercial transformation of Afro-Eurasia. In the second millennium BCE, as noted in Chapter 3, the arid central Asia homelands of the nomadic horsemen became deserts, and they sent out conquering armies. These so-called foreign barbarians played a vital role in history and in trade, for they alone traversed the entire region and had an impact on all the peoples living there.

One other advantage proved crucial to the nomads' interactions with other populations. Because of their movements from place to place, they were exposed to—and thus acquired resistance to—a greater variety of microbes than did sedentary peoples. Their relative immunity to disease aided the launch of early overland trade routes across Afro-Eurasia in the middle of the second millennium BCE, at the time when chariots first appeared in central Asia and pastoral groups began to link the North China plain to Turkestan (Xinjiang) as well as to Mongolia and Manchuria. Around 600 BCE, nomads on the steppe became skillful archers on horseback, gaining an advantage in fighting that emboldened them to range farther from their homelands. These long-distance marauders eventually learned the skills of mediating between cultures, blending terror and traffic to bring disparate Afro-Eurasian worlds together.

These long-distance marauders eventually learned the skills of mediating between cultures, blending terror and traffic to bring disparate Afro-Eurasian worlds together.

The commercial transformation that would sweep across Afro-Eurasia in the coming centuries had political antecedents in the routes that Alexander's armies had opened up, but more important were the ways in which nomads raced into the political vacuum and created new regimes that would link northwest China and the Iranian plateau. The most powerful and intrusive of the nomadic peoples were the Xiongnu (Hsiung-nu) pastoralists, originally from the eastern part of the Asian steppe in modern Mongolia. They had appeared along the frontier with China in the late Zhou dynasty, and by the third century BCE they had become the most powerful of all the pastoral communities in that area. Their mastery of bronze technology enabled them to produce highly effective war weapons, notably bronze daggers, knives, and axes. As they grew in strength, they menaced their neighbors, and many fled before the Xiongnu war-making machine.

After the Xiongnu attacked their Yuezhi neighbors, they made the Yuezhi king's skull into a drinking vessel used in making sacrifices to the supreme god of the steppe lands. The humiliated Yuezhi, still a force of 100,000 to 200,000 horse-riding archers, galloped along the pastoral land north of the Tianshan Range until they reached the banks of the

Oxus. Their desire for revenge on the Xiongnu was tempered by their fear of yet more carnage. Besides, from their camp along the river they could see the fertile Bactrian plain dotted with Hellenistic cities. The Yuezhi continued their retreat westward, into Bactria and then into South Asia proper, where they would form the mighty Kushan Empire. As described above, the Kushans, occupying a large and diverse territory in northern and western India, played a key role in creating the infrastructure of the Silk Road during the first century CE and thus providing the key link between supply in the east and the rising market demand of the Roman Empire in the west.

What emerged was a political bridge that brought parts of Afro-Eurasia together. Both the land routes linking the Roman trading depot of Palmyra to central Asia and the sea routes carrying ships from the Red Sea to ports on the western coast of India had to pass through the territory of the Kushan Empire. At the eastern end of this chain of political and commercial contacts, the Chinese state was also beginning to protect trading outposts and frontiers, thereby enabling caravans to move about more easily. Chinese silk textiles were reaching the Roman market, and glassware from the Mediterranean, incense from the Arabian Peninsula, and precious stones from India were reaching China. The Silk Road connected the Mediterranean and Pacific coasts.

EARLY OVERLAND TRADE AND CARAVAN CITIES

As nomads moved southward, exposing new regions to their trading and migrating habits, they pushed the axis of commerce further south, beyond the original overland routes of central Asia—into the valleys and across the mountain passes east and west of India. The result was a new set of networks, parallel to and south and west of the original systems.

With this surge in trade came a new kind of commercial hub: the caravan city, established at strategic locations—often at the edges of deserts, or in oases—where vast trading groups would assemble before beginning their arduous journeys. Some of these caravan cities in the mountains and deserts of Southwest Asia, having begun as Greek garrison towns, became centers of Hellenistic culture, displaying such staples of the polis as public theaters. Even those depots founded by Arab traders had a Hellenistic tinge, as local traders often admired Greek culture and in any case had frequent commercial interactions with the Mediterranean world. They wrote in Greek, sometimes speaking it in addition to their native tongues.

A number of important caravan cities emerged at the northern end of a route that led through the deserts of Arabia. At the extreme southwestern tip of the Arabian Peninsula, in what is now known as Yemen, was a land watered by the same rains responsible for the annual flooding of the Nile. The area was a wonder of its own, a vivid patch of green at the

end of 1,200 miles of desert. Its prosperity was in part due to its role as a major gathering place both for long-distance spice traders about to transport frankincense and myrrh north through the Arabian Desert and for sailors, whose ships early on traveled the Red and the Arabian Seas, and later crossed the Indian Ocean.

The southern Arabian Peninsula had long been famous for its frankincense and myrrh, products used by Greeks and Romans to make perfume and incense; they reached their buyers via an overland route sometimes called the Incense or Spice Road. The Sabaeans, who lived in southern Arabia, became fabulously wealthy from these sales and from the Indian Ocean spice trade. The traders who transported the spices and fragrances to the Mediterranean were another Arabic-speaking people: the Nabataeans, sheepherders who eked out a living in the Sinai Desert and the northwestern Arabian Peninsula.

Because the Greeks and later the Romans needed large quantities of incense to burn in worshipping their gods, the trade passing through this region was extremely lucrative. But the camel caravans had a difficult journey through the rock ravines stretching from the Dead Sea to the Red Sea's Gulf of Aqaba. Here, Nabataean herders had learned to cut cisterns out of solid stone to catch rainwater and to provide themselves with cave shelters. Nabataeans profited by supplying water and food to the travelers. In one of the valleys through which travelers frequently passed, in what is now southwest Jordan, the Nabataeans built their capital—a rock city called Petra ("rock" in Greek is *petros*)—which displayed abundant Greek influences. Many of the houses and shrines were cut out of the mountains. Their colonnaded facades and tombs, constructed for common people as well as the nobles, projected Hellenistic motifs. The most striking building of this kind was the vast theater. The entire structure—the stage

Petra. This beautiful building is known as El-Khaznah, or The Treasury, at Petra, the capital of the Nabataean kingdom, located in the southern part of modern-day Jordan. The wealth created by the region's long-distance trade is manifest in the magnificent buildings at the center of the city. Both the face of the building and its interior are cut out of the sandstone rock that forms the cliffs surrounding Petra.

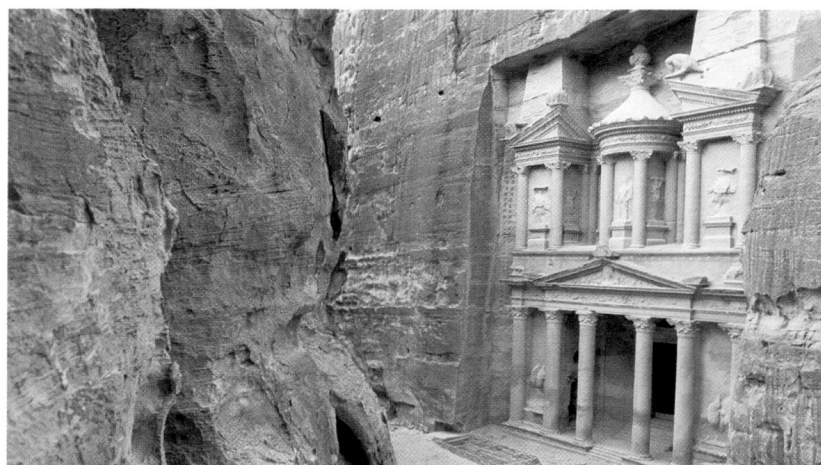

Primary Source

THE CARAVAN CITY OF PETRA

Petra was a city cut out of the pink rock cliffs in the valley between the Dead Sea and the Red Sea. The Nabataeans, an Arabic-speaking people, built the city to host traders from west and east; from here, caravans were sent to trading entrepôts in the Mediterranean and on the Iranian plateau. Petra was totally dependent on the spice and perfume trade, and its good fortune ran out under the Roman Empire when the silk trade favored another caravan city, Palmyra. Yet even today, the rock structure of the city shining in the sun is an imposing sight.

Much has already been written about Petra and I do not wish to repeat what has already been said. I am tempted almost to liken the city to some wonder from the *Arabian Nights*. When one descends into the valley from the surrounding heights towards the place where the river has cut for itself a passage between the dark-red rocks, one seems to be gazing at some large and fantastic excrescence—a piece of reddish-mauve raw flesh set between the gold of the desert and the green of the hills. It is a most extraordinary sight, which becomes even more extraordinary when the cavalcade slowly descends into the river valley, and the rocky walls of the ever-narrowing gorge tower up to the right and left, speckled with red, orange, mauve, grey, and green layers. Wild and beautiful they are, with their contrasts of light and shade; the light blinding, the shadows black. And there is seldom even anything to remind the visitor that this gorge served for centuries as a main road, trodden by camels, mules, and horses, and that along it rode Bedouin merchants who must have felt like ourselves its horror and its mystic fascination. Yet suddenly one may be confronted with the façade of a tomb-tower

with dog-tooth design, or with an altar set high up on one of the vertical walls, bearing a greeting or prayer to some god, inscribed in the Nabataean tongue. Our caravan advanced slowly along the gorge, until an unexpected bend disclosed to us an apparition sparkling pinky-orange in the sun, which must once have been the front of a temple or tomb. Elegant columns joined by fascinating pediments and arches form the frames of the niches in which its statues stand. All this rose up before us dressed in a garb of classicism yet in a style new and unexpected even by those well acquainted with antiquity. It was as though the magnificent scenery of some Hellenistic theatre had appeared, as though a Pompeian wall-painting, not of the fourth but of the second period, had been chiselled in the rock.

→ *What specific features in the description of the gorge leading to Petra and the monuments in and around the city remind you of the* Arabian Nights?

SOURCE: M. Rostovtzeff, *Caravan Cities* (Oxford: Clarendon Press, 1932), 42–43.

platform, orchestra, and forty-five rows of seats—was carved out of the sandstone terrain and could accommodate an audience of 6,000 to 10,000 people (up to one-third of the city's population). Plays were at first invariably performed in Greek, and later in Latin, for being cosmopolitan required participating in the language of high culture.

Petra's power and wealth, at its height from the mid–second century BCE to the early second century CE, outlasted the Hellenistic Seleucids' control of the region. The Greek language persisted as the lingua franca critical to Petran mer-

chants seeking to maintain their trading ties. The caravan traders, the ruling elite of the rock city, controlled the supply of spices and fragrances from Arabia, North Africa, and India to the ever-expanding Roman Empire. During these years, Nabataean caravan traders based in Petra traveled throughout the eastern Mediterranean, erecting temples wherever they established their trading communities. Yet the glory of this commercial people dimmed with the coming of the Romans, who took over the province of Arabia—and with it, the profitable Spice Road trade.

THE WESTERN END OF THE SILK ROAD: PALMYRA

As central Asia became dotted with overland trading hubs, these new commercial cities thrived in Southwest Asia as well. Indeed, they soon came to overshadow the older political or religious capitals. With Petra's decline during the Roman period, another settlement took its place as the most important caravan city at the western end of the Silk Road: Palmyra. (Palmyra's local name was Tadmor, which means "palm.") Rich citizens of Rome relied on the Palmyran traders to procure luxury goods for them, importing Chinese silks for women's clothing and incense for the worship of their gods, as well as gemstones, pearls, and many other precious items.

Administered by an oligarchy composed of the chiefs of local tribes, Palmyra was able to maintain a great deal of local autonomy, even under formal Roman control. Although the Palmyrans used a Semitic dialect in daily life, state affairs and business were conducted in Greek. Their merchants had learned the language when the region came under Seleucid rule, and it remained useful to them when they did business with caravans from afar, long after the political influences of Hellenism had waned. Palmyran traders handled many kinds of textiles, including cotton from India and cashmere wool that originated in Kashmir or nearby in the highlands of central Asia. The many silk textiles that archaeologists have discovered at this site were produced in Han China (see Chapter 7), providing material evidence that the Silk Road had, by the first century CE, reached the Mediterranean. While the oligarchs retained some of the exquisite silks for themselves, most were shipped on to the more profitable markets in the Mediterranean. The Romans not only purchased silk cloth but also started to have silk woven to order in eastern Mediterranean cities such as Beirut and Gaza. Silk yarns and dyes have also been found at Palmyra.

The earnings from this lucrative trade enabled the people of Palmyra to build a splendid marble city in the desert. A colonnade, theater, senate house, agora, and major temples formed the metropolitan area of the city. The Palmyrans worshipped many deities, both local and Greek, but they seemed most concerned about their own afterlife. Like Petra, Palmyra had a cemetery as big as its residential area, and the marble sculptures on the tombs depicted the life of the city. Many tombs showed the master or the master and his wife reclining on a Greek-style couch, holding drinking goblets in their hands. The clothes on those marble statues appear more Iranian than Greek: robes with wide stripes whose hems were decorated with exquisite designs. Sculptures of camel caravans and horses tell us that the deceased were caravan traders in this world and were looking forward to continuing their rewarding occupation in the afterlife.

Left alone to conduct its business, Palmyra rapidly grew into a commercial powerhouse. The city not only provided supplies and financial services to passing caravans but also hosted self-contained trading communities, or *fondûqs*—complexes of hostels, storage houses, offices, and often temples. Palmyra achieved its golden age at the same time that the Silk Road in central Asia was flourishing as the major

Palmyran Tomb Sculpture. This relief was part of the tomb sculptures for a wealthy trader from Palmyra. The camel to the left of the men—a dromedary, a one-humped camel renowned for its speed—was truly the ship of the desert, able to haul huge loads of commercial goods over the big trade routes of Southwest Asia. Merchants, like these two men, became wealthy from the transcontinental exchange of luxury goods.

Palmyran Tomb Sculpture. This tombstone relief sculpture shows a wealthy young Palmyran, attended by a servant—probably a household slave. Palmyra was at the crossroads of the major cultural influences traversing southwestern Asia at the time. The style of the clothing—the flowing pants and top—and the couch and pillows reflect the trading contacts of the Palmyran elite, in this case with India to the east. The hairstyle and mode of self-presentation signal influences from the Mediterranean to the west.

route for the shipment of silk and other luxuries from China to the eastern rim of the Indian Ocean. Some of the goods went across the Iranian plateau, reaching the Mediterranean by way of Syria's desert routes. Another major artery went via Afghanistan, the Indus, and the west coast of India, then across the Indian Ocean to the Red Sea. Aiding the success of the Silk Road was the pervasive shared culture of Hellenistic influences, lingering centuries after Greek political power had vanished from this region.

REACHING CHINA ALONG THE SILK ROAD

The Chinese economy was growing rapidly at the eastern end of the trans-Afro-Eurasian networks of commerce. Chinese artisans produced the most sought-after commodity of long-distance trade: silk. The country grew rich from the Silk Road and the ships that plied the South China Sea. Silkworms, carefully bred, produced silk, which was China's most valuable export. It was also used to conduct diplomacy with the nomadic kingdoms on the western frontiers and to underwrite its armies. Chinese rulers used silk to pay off neighboring nomads and borderlanders, buying both peaceful borders and horses with the fabric. During the Zhou dynasty, it served as a precious medium of exchange and trade. Silk has always been highly valued as a material for clothing—

while cloth made from hemp, flax, and other fibers tends to be rough, silk looks and feels rich. Moreover, it was both cool against the skin in hot summers and warm in the winter. Silk also had immense tensile strength, useful for bows, lute strings, and fishing lines; spun into a tight fabric, it could be made into light body armor or light bags to transport liquids (particularly useful for long-distance traders, who traveled across arid expanses). Before the invention of paper by the Chinese sometime after 100 CE, silk was widely used as writing material, more durable than bamboo or wood. Brush writing on silk was the medium of choice for correspondence, maps, and illustrations, and important texts written on silk often joined other funerary objects in the tombs of aristocratic lords and wealthy magnates. No wonder it was such a prized commodity!

Thousands of bales of silk made their way to Indian, central Asian, and Mediterranean markets, where they became extraordinarily valuable trade goods—an exotic luxury that could be obtained only from China. The ultimate prestige commodity of the ruling classes from India to the Mediterranean, silk naturally gave its name to the trade route along which its precious bales traveled. Pliny the Elder noted: "The *Seres* [the Chinese] are especially well known for a wool-like substance in their trees. After soaking it in water, they comb a white-colored substance from the down of the leaves. . . . The work involved is so complex, and the goods sought out from a place so distant in our world, all so that Roman women can appear in public in transparent clothing" (*Natural History* 6.20.54; trans. Brent Shaw).

Economic life in ancient China had centered on the agricultural manors of rich and powerful landowners. After 300 BCE, however, independent farmers increasingly produced commercial crops for the expanding marketplaces now scattered across the landscape along key land routes as well as rivers, canals, and lakes. As the market economy grew, merchants organized themselves into influential family lineages and specialized occupational guilds. Increasingly, power shifted away from older agrarian elites and into the hands of urban financiers and traders. They benefited from the improvement in roads and waterways, which eased the transportation of local products such as grain, hides, horses, and silk from the villages to the new towns and cities. By the second century BCE, wealthy merchants such as the Fan family were ennobled as local magnates and wore the clothing that marked their official status. Bronze coins of various sizes and shapes (such as the spade-shaped money of a number of semi-autonomous Warring States; see photo in Chapter 5), as well as cloth and silk used in barter, also aided the growth in long-distance trade. As commerce expanded, regional lords opened local customs offices to extract a share of the money and products for themselves.

Chinese and other merchants expanded trade across the Silk Road and the South China Sea. Local tollgates and customhouses sprang up to tax this commerce along land routes and waterways, but facilitating trade was also a key concern of the state. To protect traders, the merchant ships were joined by military boats, able to cover some seventy-five miles in a day and carry fifty soldiers and supplies for a three-month voyage. Though China still had little intellectual interaction with the rest of Afro-Eurasia, its commercial exchanges skyrocketed. Southern silk was only the first of many Chinese commodities that reached the world beyond the Taklamakan Desert. China also became an export center for lacquer, hemp, and linen. From Sichuan came iron, steel, flint, hard stone, silver, and animals, while jade came from the northwest. At the same time, China was importing Mediterranean, Indian, and central Asian commodities.

Despite its early development of commerce, China still had no major ports on the east coast that might compare to Palmyra. Internal, interregional trade predominated; it eventually fed into the emerging Silk Road through much more decentralized networks. Cities in the landlocked north were usually administrative centers where farmers and traders gathered to take advantage of the regional states' political and military protection. The larger ones had gates that were closed between sunset and sunrise, and during the night, mounted soldiers patrolled the streets. Newer towns along the seacoast in the southeast still looked upriver to trade with inland agrarian communities, which also produced the silk that made it to the Mediterranean via Central Asia. Later, China would become the site of massive trading centers.

The Chinese people and the Chinese state remained little affected by Hellenism and Mahayana Buddhism, the intellectual globalizing influences so important elsewhere in Afro-Eurasia during this period. China went about dealing with its own crises, laying the foundations for the magnificent Han Empire that eventually expanded into the Silk Road in the middle of the first century BCE (see Chapter 7). But through trade, the emergence of long-distance exchange and increasingly globalized contacts did powerfully influence the

Silk Texts. Before the invention of paper, silk was widely used as writing material because it was more mobile and durable than bamboo or wood for correspondence, maps, illustrations, and important texts included as funerary objects in the tombs of aristocrats. The Mawangdui silk texts shown here are from a Hunan tomb that was closed in 168 BCE and opened in 1973. Daoist philosophical texts and medical works were found in the tomb.

Zhou Coins. The diversity of bronze coinage during the late Zhou represented the growing autonomy of the Warring States from the declining Zhou dynasty. Not until the Qin unification would a centralized government again issue a unified bronze currency.

region. The booming trade that rippled through China would reshape its social and political structures.

THE SPREAD OF BUDDHISM ALONG THE TRADE ROUTES

Conquest and commerce brought the edges of Afro-Eurasia together. The pathways that took shape with the migrations of nomads, and had become the routes followed by armies, now were secured, enabling merchants to expand their business. But more than just commercial opportunity coursed through the trade arteries. Monks also plied these roads to spread the word of new religions to far-flung peoples. The chief expansionist faith in this period came out of India, inspired in part by the successful spread of Hellenism (which had, for the most part, diffused itself through secular institutions) and taking advantage of the great new trade links that crisscrossed Afro-Eurasia. The Buddha was no longer just a sage departed to the state of *nirvana*, but was also a god who could be worshipped like any Greek deity.

Under Kushan patronage during the first centuries CE, Buddhism reached out from India to China and central Asia,

following the Silk Road. Commercial networks became the channels for spreading religious beliefs. Monks from the Kushan Empire accompanied traders to Luoyang, the eastern capital of the Han Empire. There they started to translate Buddhist texts into Chinese, aided by Chinese converts who were mostly also traders. Buddhist ideas were slow to gain acceptance, however. It took several centuries, and a new wave of nomadic migrations, for Buddhism to take root in China.

Buddhism fared less well when it tried to follow the same commercial arteries westward. Although Buddhists did make efforts to gain followers in the Parthian Empire—indeed, some early Buddhist preachers in China were Parthians—the religion never became established on the Iranian plateau and made no further headway toward the Mediterranean. The main barrier to its westward movement was Zoroastrianism, which had been a state religion in the Achaemenid Empire during the fifth and fourth centuries BCE; by the time Buddhism's aspirations took a global form, it had long been well established in Iran. Iranian Hellenism had done little to weaken the power of Zoroastrianism, whose adherents, like their Buddhist counterparts, formed city-based religious communities affiliated primarily with traders. Following the Silk Road, Zoroastrian traders traveled both eastward to China and westward to the coast of the Mediterranean and were another impediment to the westward spread of Buddhism.

TAKING TO THE SEAS: COMMERCE ON THE RED SEA AND INDIAN OCEAN

> → *What factors contributed to the growth of the Indian Ocean sea trade?*

Land routes were the tried-and-true avenues followed by migrants, traders, and wayfarers. But they carried only what could be borne on the backs of humans and animals; travel on them was slow, and they were vulnerable to marauders. With time, some risk takers found ways of moving about on waterways and thereby connecting regions together—eventually on an unprecedented scale and with an ease unimaginable to earlier merchants. These risk takers were Arabs, from the commercial middle ground of the emerging Afro-Eurasian trading system.

Arab traders had long carried such spices as frankincense and myrrh to the Egyptians, who used them in religious and funerary rites, and later to the Greeks and Romans. Metals such as bronze, tin, and iron were carted by traders over land routes from Anatolia, as were gold, silver, and chlorite from

THE WORLDS OF *PERIPLUS*

A particularly revealing periplus that has survived was written in Greek by an Egyptian sailor and trader toward the end of the first century CE. *Periplus Maris Erythraei*, or *Periplus of the Red Sea*, was much more than a guide to the Red Sea trade. Its author, a shrewd businessman, keen observer, and experienced navigator, described the whole world of commerce of the Red Sea, the Mediterranean, and the Indian Ocean. He catalogued the navigable routes and listed the various goods that were available and marketable in the ports; starting from the Red Sea, he moved southward along East Africa's coast and then eastward all the way to India. The result is the first historical record of the city-states existing along the coast of East Africa and one of the earliest accounts of Africa south of the Sahara. Throughout, he supplied data on currencies, customs, and the political regimes that controlled the ports and radiated into their hinterlands.

The author's voyage began from Berenice. After leaving this Red Sea port, he encountered tribal countries on his right hand, the coastal lands of today's Sudan and Eritrea. The *Periplus* named the region Barbaria, the land of barbarians, and identified its inhabitants with such labels as "eaters of fish" and "eaters of wild animals." Further south, the author noted the coastal area of a former Ptolemaic Egyptian colony that had fallen into decline and now exported only tortoise shells and ivory. On the other side of the Red Sea lay the coast of Arabia, where the waters were so calm that ships did not need to be anchored but where pirates from the Nabataean tribes preyed on passing ships.

Once it sailed out of the narrow strait, the ship entered the Gulf of Aden, famed as the land of frankincense and myrrh. The author of the *Periplus* dubbed the northern coast of modern Somalia "the Far-side Country." Beyond the territory from which incense was exported, traders brought ivory, tortoise shells, and slaves to the markets. The Somalia ports received cargoes of staple goods from India such as rice and ghee (clarified butter), sesame oil, cotton textiles, and sugar. The southernmost port along the east coast of Africa known to the author was Rhapta, somewhere near modern Dar es Salaam and nearly 3,000 miles from Berenice. This region had fallen under the influence of Arabs—specifically, the Sabaeans— through intermarriage and trade.

The trading ships left the southern Arabian coast with the monsoon winds behind them, heading for the entrepôts of India. With the emergence of long-distance trade, entrepôts became a new kind of urban hub on the social landscape. Barbaricum, at the mouth of the Indus, was the first Indian port reached from the west. On their arrival there, traders unloaded linen textiles, red coral, glassware, wine, and money from the Mediterranean and Egypt, as well as frankincense and storax, aromatic gum resins from Southwest Asia that the traders had purchased on their journey. These cargoes were shipped to the upper Indus region of the Punjab and Gandhara. While at harbor in India, traders loaded their ships with treasures from the east: fragrances or spices from the Himalayas and India, such as costus root and bdellium, turquoise from Khorasan in Iran, lapis lazuli from Badakhshan in Afghanistan, indigo dye and cotton textiles from India, furs from central Asia, and silk textiles and yarn from China.

The most important Indian port at the time of the *Periplus* was Barygaza on the Gulf of Khambhat (Cambay), near the modern city of Broach in Gujarat, but its harbor was very difficult to navigate. The coast was rugged, the sea bottom was uneven, and the tidal waves were high and variable. Local fishermen under the king's service came out to guide foreign ships to the harbor. In fact, the entire northwestern and western parts of India were connected to the Mediterranean through Barygaza. Here the descriptions in the *Periplus* concentrate on the abundance of Greek influences. For example, the author noted that in the market of Barygaza old drachmas of the Indo-Greek kings Apollodotus and Menander, inscribed with Greek letters, were still circulating. Although he often garbled the names of places and people, his general point was clear enough: Greek culture played a critical role in the long-distance trade of India.

Map of the Periplus.

the Iranian plateau. Gold, ivory, and other goods from northern India passed through Taxila (the capital of Gandhara) and the Hindu Kush Mountains into Persia as early as the sixth century BCE. Following the expansion of the Hellenistic world, however, ships increasingly engaged in long-distance trade by sea, sailing down the Red Sea and across the Indian Ocean as they carried goods between the tip of the Arabian Peninsula and the ports of the Indian subcontinent.

Arab seafarers led the way into the Indian Ocean, forging the links that joined East Africa, the eastern Mediterranean, and the Arabian Peninsula with India, Southeast Asia, and East Asia. Such voyages involved longer stays at sea and were far more dangerous than sailing in the Mediterranean. Yet by the first century CE, Arab and Indian sailors were transporting Chinese silks, central Asian furs, and fragrances from the trees of the Himalayas across the Indian Ocean. The city of Alexandria in Egypt soon emerged as a key transit point between the Mediterranean Sea and the Indian Ocean. Boats carried the main Mediterranean exports of olives and olive oil, wine, drinking vessels, glassware, linen and wool textiles, and red coral up the Nile, stopping along the river at Koptos and other port cities from which camel caravans took the goods to the Red Sea ports of Myos Hormos and Berenice. For centuries, Mediterranean merchants considered the Arabian Peninsula to be the end of the Spice Road. But after Alexander's expedition and the establishment of numerous colonies between Egypt and Afghanistan, they began to appreciate the wealth and opportunities that lay along the shores of the Indian Ocean.

Arab sailors who ventured into the Indian Ocean took advantage of new navigational techniques, especially celestial bearings (using the position of the stars to determine the position of the ship and the direction to sail). They used large ships called *dhows,* whose sails were rigged to easily capture the wind; these were the forerunners of modern cargo vessels, capable of long hauls in rough waters. Beginning about 120 BCE, mariners came to understand the seasonal rain-filled monsoon winds, which blow strongly from the southwest be-

Chronology

	400 BCE	300 BCE	200 BCE
SOUTHWEST ASIA AND NORTHERN AFRICA		▪ *Conquests of Alexander the Great, 334–323 BCE* ▪ *Emergence of Hellenistic "successor kingdoms" beginning in 323 BCE* ▪ *Parthian kingdom, 240 BCE–224 CE*	
THE MEDITERRANEAN		▪ *Roman expansion in the Italian Peninsula beginning in 330s and 320s BCE* ▪ *Roman-Carthage war (continued Roman territorial expansion), 264–241 BCE*	
CENTRAL ASIA		▪ *Conquests of Alexander the Great, 334–323 BCE* ▪ *Bactrian kingdom, 250–130 BCE*	
SOUTH ASIA		▪ *Mauryan Empire, 321–184 BCE* *Yavana kings emerge around 200 BCE* ▪	*Saka invasions* ▪ *Han expands into the Silk Road*
EAST ASIA	▪ *Warring States period, 403–221 BCE*	*Xiongnu Confederacy in the Mongolian steppes, 2nd or 3rd century BCE* ▪ *Unification of China under the Qin dynasty, 221 BCE* ▪ *Emergence of Han Empire, 206 BCE* ▪	

tween October and April and then from the northeast between April and October—knowledge that gave a huge impetus to the maritime trade connecting the Mediterranean with the Indian Ocean.

The new sailing knowledge was reflected in the books—each called a *periplus,* or a "sailing around"—in which sea captains recorded the landing spots and ports between their two destinations. The revolution in navigational techniques and knowledge dramatically reduced the cost of long-distance shipping and multiplied the ports of call around large bodies of water such as the South China Sea, the Indian Ocean, and the Mediterranean Sea. Some historians have argued that there were now two Silk Roads: one by land and one by sea.

 CONCLUSION

Alexander's bloody campaigns, which reached the frontiers of South Asia, had effects more profound than any military or political regime that had preceded them. To be sure, the regime created by his conquests depended so much on Alexander himself that it fragmented almost immediately after his death. Nevertheless, the political, social, and cultural significance of those conquests was lasting, for they ultimately helped transform Afro-Eurasia culturally and economically. Alexander's military forces carried with them Greek institutions and culture, and they promoted the establishment of Greek-speaking communities across Eurasia and North Africa. For at least five centuries after the breakup of Alexan-

der's short-lived rule, Hellenistic culture reverberated from Rome in the west all the way to the Ganges in the east. Appropriately, the Hellenistic cultural movement was most strongly represented by the Greek language, which was linked to Greek culture, institutions, and trade. We should not lose sight of the fact, however, that many of the Greek-speaking peoples and their descendants who stayed on in parts of Southwest and Central Asia integrated cultural practices and traditions with their own Greek ways creating a series of diverse and rich cultures. The influences of culture flowed both ways. The economic story is equally a complex one. Let us remember that we should not give all the credit to Alexander and his successors. In many respects, they followed pathways long established by previous kingdoms and empires. If anything, Alexander's successors helped strengthen and expand the existing trade routes and centers of commercial activity, which ultimately led to the formal creation of the Silk Road.

Although this cultural movement that we call Hellenistic lasted longer than most cultural systems and had a wider appeal than any previous set of philosophical and spiritual ideas, it did not sweep away everything before it. Indigenous cultures made their accommodations with this movement or fought against it with all their might, fearing the loss of their own cultural identities. Others took from it what they liked and discarded the rest. The citizens of Rome admired its achievements and steeped themselves in it while fashioning their own Latin-based culture. Eventually, they created an imperial polity that outdistanced Alexander's in expanse, depth, and durability. In North Africa, the culturally sophisticated and commercially talented Carthaginians saw some

100 BCE	1 CE	100 CE	200 CE

■ *Transformation of Buddhism, 1st century* CE

■ *Kushan kingdom, 1st–3rd centuries* CE *(established 60* CE*)*

of these Greek means of expression as advantageous and useful for new elites of the Mediterranean like themselves.

Of all the peoples brought under the sway of Hellenistic thinking, the South Asian peoples produced the most varied responses because Hellenism struck a region that was already riddled with a multitude of cultures. Once opened to the external influences of Macedonian invaders, steppe nomads, and Arab seafarers, South Asia became the confluence of the currents that were moving so swiftly and decisively across Afro-Eurasia. The most telling of the South Asian responses took place in the realm of spiritual and ethical norms, where the doctrines of a compelling teacher of the sixth and fifth centuries BCE, the Buddha, evolved in the direction of a full-fledged world religious system, which in turn spread through the commercial networks that crisscrossed Afro-Eurasia.

Greater political integration helped fashion highways for commerce. Nomads left their steppe lands and exchanged wares across great distances. As they continued to find greater opportunities for business, their trade routes shifted further south, radiating out of the oases of central Asia. Eventually merchants, rather than the trading nomads, created new ventures and seized the opportunities provided by new technologies, especially in sailing and navigation. These commercial transformations connected distant parts of Afro-Eurasia. Accompanying the spread of Greek ways—indeed, fueling the diffusion of Hellenism—was the opening of trade. Alexander's campaigns had followed some of the trade routes east, and his conquests opened up the channels of exchange permanently. In the wake of conquests, the Silk Road and proliferating sea-lanes connected ports and caravan towns from North Africa to South China, creating new social classes, producing new urban settings, and ultimately supporting the emergence of powerful new polities. In this sense, long-distance trade began the process of bringing distant parts of the world together and fostering awareness of other cultures. The paradox of the era discussed in this chapter is that although growing trade and migration encouraged greater contact between the regions of Afro-Eurasia, it also ushered in the beginnings of new universalist ideas of a "people" bound by customs and faith, if not by loyalty to a leader. As people began to adopt these varying creeds, they also became increasingly aware of their differences.

STUDY QUESTIONS

WWNORTON.COM/STUDYSPACE

1. Analyze the impact of Alexander's conquest on the Afro-Eurasian world. How did his military pursuits, and those of his successors, bring together various worlds?
2. Describe the influence of Hellenism on societies outside the Greek homeland during this time period. What aspects of Hellenistic culture held broad appeal for diverse groups?
3. Compare and contrast Judean, Roman, and Carthaginian responses to Hellenistic influences. How receptive was each society to Greek cultural influences?
4. Explain how South Asia (or India) became a melting pot for the intellectual, political, and economic currents sweeping across Afro-Eurasia between 350 BCE and 250 CE. How did this development affect Buddhist doctrine?
5. Analyze the extent to which long-distance trade routes connected societies across Afro-Eurasia during this time period. Which societies were involved in these exchanges? How did commercial linkages affect those societies involved?
6. Analyze the influence of nomadic pastoral societies in Afro-Eurasia during this time period. What role did they play in integrating cultures and economies?
7. Explain how interregional contacts transformed Buddhism during this time period. How did Buddhism expand across a variety of cultures?
8. Explain how art, architecture, and other forms of material culture in various Afro-Eurasian societies reflected broader patterns of cultural, political, and economic integration during this period. In particular, how did caravan cities along long-distance trade routes reflect new cultural configurations?

FURTHER READINGS

Bradley, Keith, *Slavery and Rebellion in the Roman World, 140 B.C.–70 B.C.* (1989). A description of the rise of large-scale plantation slavery in Sicily and Italy, and a detailed account of the three great slave wars.

Browning, Iain, *Palmyra* (1979). A narrative of the history of the important desert city that linked eastern and western trade routes.

Casson, Lionel, *The Periplus Maris Erythraei* (1989). An introduction to a typical ancient sailing manual, this one of the Red Sea and Indian Ocean.

———, *Ships and Seamanship in the Ancient World* (1995). The classic account of the ships and sailors that powered commerce and war on the high seas.

Colledge, Malcolm, *The Art of Palmyra* (1976). A well-illustrated introduction to the unusual art of Palmyra with its mixture of eastern and western elements.

Fowler, Barbara H., *The Hellenistic Aesthetic* (1989). How the artists in this new age saw and portrayed their world in new and different ways.

Green, Peter, *Alexander to Actium: The Historical Evolution of the Hellenistic Age* (1990). The best general guide to the whole period in all of its various aspects, and well illustrated.

Habicht, Christian, *Athens from Alexander to Antony,* trans. Deborah L. Schneider (1997). The authoritative account of what happened to the great city-state of Athens in this period.

Holt, Frank L., *Thundering Zeus: The Making of Hellenistic Bactria* (1999). A basic history of the most eastern of the kingdoms spawned by the conquests of Alexander the Great.

Hopkirk, Peter, *Foreign Devils on the Silk Road* (1984). A historiography of the explorations and researches on the central Asian Silk Road of the nineteenth and early twentieth centuries.

Juliano, Annette L., and Judith A. Lerner (eds.), *Nomads, Traders and Holy Men Along China's Silk Road* (2003). A description of the travelers along the Silk Road in human terms, focusing on warfare, markets, and religion.

Lane Fox, Robin, *Alexander the Great* (1973). Still the most readable and in many ways, the sanest biography of the world conqueror.

Lewis, Naphtali, *Greeks in Ptolemaic Egypt* (1986). An account of the relationships between Greeks and Egyptians as seen through the lives of individual Greek settlers and colonists.

Liu, Xinru, *Ancient India and Ancient China* (1988). The first work to connect political and economic developments in India and China with the evolution and spread of Buddhism in the first half of the first millennium.

Long, Antony A., *Hellenistic Philosophy: Stoics, Epicureans, Sceptics*, 2nd ed. (1986). One of the clearest guides to the main new trends in Greek philosophical thinking in the period.

Martin, Luther H., *Hellenistic Religions: An Introduction* (1987). An introduction to the principal new Hellenistic religions and cults that emerged in this period.

Mendels, Doron, *The Rise and Fall of Jewish Nationalism* (1992). A sophisticated account of the various phases of Jewish resistance in Judah to foreign domination.

Miller, James Innes, *The Spice Trade of the Roman Empire, 29 B.C. to A.D. 641* (1969). A first-rate study of the spice trade in the Roman Empire.

Pomeroy, Sarah B., *Women in Hellenistic Egypt: From Alexander to Cleopatra* (1990). An highly readable investigation of women and family in the best-documented region of the Hellenistic world.

Ray, Himanshu P., *The Wind of Change, Buddhism and the Maritime Links of Early South Asia* (1994). Ray's study of Buddhism and maritime trade stretches from the Arabian Sea to the navigations between South Asia and Southeast Asia.

Rosenfield, John, *The Dynastic Art of the Kushans* (1967). Instead of focusing on the Gandharan Buddhist art itself, Rosenfield selects sculptures of Kushan royals and those representing nomadic populations in religious shrines to display the central Asian aspect of artworks of the period.

Rostovtzeff, Michael Ivanvovich, *Caravan Cities,* trans. D. and T. Talbot Rice (1932). Though published more than seven decades ago, this small volume contains accurate descriptions of the ruins of many caravan cities in modern Jordan and Syria.

———, *The Social and Economic History of the Hellenistic World* (1941). A monumental achievement. One of the great works of history written in the twentieth century. An unsurpassed overview of all aspects of the politics, social and economic movements of the period. Despite its age, there is still nothing like it.

Schoff, Wilfred H. (ed. and trans.), *The Periplus of the Erythraean Sea* (1912). An invaluable tool for mapping the names and places from the Red Sea to Indian coastal areas during this period.

Shipley, Graham, *The Greek World after Alexander, 323–30 B.C.* (2000). A more up-to-date survey than Peter Green's work (above), with more emphasis on the historical detail in each period.

Tarn, W. W., *Greeks in Bactria and India* (1984). The most comprehensive coverage of Greek sources on Hellenistic states in Afghanistan and northwest India.

Thapar, Romila, *Ashoka and the Decline of the Mauryas* (1973). Using all available primary sources, including the edicts of Ashoka and Greek authors' accounts, Thapar gives the most authoritative analysis of the first and the most important empire in Indian history.

Vainker, Shelagh, *Chinese Silk: A Cultural History* (2004). A work that traces the cultural history of silk in China from its early origins to the twentieth century and considers its relationship to the other decorative arts. The author draws on the most recent archaeological evidence to emphasize the role of silk in Chinese history, trade, religion, and literature.

Wood, Francis, *The Silk Road: Two Thousand Years in the Heart of Asia* (2004). Illustrated with drawings, manuscripts, paintings and artifacts to trace the Silk Road to its origins as far back as Alexander the Great, with an emphasis on its importance to cultural and religious movements.

Young, Gary K., *Rome's Eastern Trade: International Commerce and Imperial Policy, 31 BC–AD 305* (2001). This study examines the taxation and profits of eastern trade from the perspective of the Roman government.

7

HAN DYNASTY CHINA AND IMPERIAL ROME, 300 BCE–300 CE

I n the third century BCE, the Eastern Zhou state of Qin absorbed the remaining Warring States in China and set the stage for the vast empire of the succeeding Han dynasty. The chief minister of the Qin state, Li Si, urged his king to take actions based on the pragmatic notions of power politics. He tried to press on the king the need to seize opportunities: a man who aimed at great achievements must relentlessly exploit the advantages offered to him. With the armed might of the Qin and his own virtues, the king could sweep away his regional rivals as if he were removing the dust from a kitchen stove—he could annihilate them all. In this way he could establish a truly imperial rule and unify the whole world. "This is the one moment in ten thousand ages," Li Si advised. The king listened carefully and acted.

We have already seen in Chapter 5 how the Qin state emerged as the dominant "warring state" in Zhou China because of its unprecedented military power and strong agrarian economy. Now, seizing that "one moment in ten thousand ages," the Qin king relied on his massive army of conscripted peasant farmers to make himself China's First Emperor. Thus, in 221 BCE, the Qin emerged as the dominant power over the other Warring States and created a new political structure for a new era. No longer a mere regional power, the Qin became the first great land-based empire in East Asia. But the Qin Empire quickly collapsed in 207 BCE, and soon the Han Empire took its place. Following the Qin model for imperial power—as did all subsequent Chinese dynasties—the Han defeated other regional groups and established the first long-lasting Chinese empire.

The cultural identity of the Han dynasty became synonymous with "China" as the "Middle Kingdom." A subject of Han felt he or she was participating in an ideal society whose four estates of land-holding literati elites, millions of free farmers, trained artisans, itinerant traders, and urban merchants were all part of a new era that emulated the statecraft ideals of antiquity, unlike the pragmatic and cruel Qin. To be "Han Chinese" meant that elites shared a common written language based on the Confucian classics, which qualified them for public office. It also meant that commoners from all walks of life shared with those elites a common cultural framework based on family-organized ancestor worship, ritual practices in which an appropriate decorum and dress reigned for each estate, and a view that the Han as an agrarian-based empire was organically a microcosm of the entire cosmos. Those who lived beyond the pale of the Han were uncivilized peoples whose pastoral ways and primitive beliefs marked them as outsiders.

At the other end of Afro-Eurasia, another great state, imperial Rome, similarly met its rivals in war, ultimately emerging victorious and consolidating its power over the lands around the Mediterranean into an empire. The Romans achieved this feat of political unification by the use of violent force on a scale hitherto unseen in their part of the globe. The result was a state of huge size, astonishingly unified and stable. Living in the Roman Empire in the mid-70s CE, a man of middle rank, Pliny the Elder, could write glowingly about the unity of the imperial state that he served. Praising its communications network, he noted that not just people but even plants moved around the empire, traveling through the whole of the Roman world as they were taken from their orig-

inal regions to be transplanted in new ones. As he saw it, all of this was for the general welfare of humankind. In Pliny's eyes, all of the benefits that flowed from the unimpeded movement of humans, animals, and even plants were owed to the boundless greatness of a peace that joined diverse peoples, beliefs, and customs under one benevolent emperor. He fervently prayed that this gift of the gods might last forever. The gods, he thought, seemed to have intended the Romans as a gift to all humans, to shine, as it were, as a second sun for them.

Just as in China, the expansion of empire changed what it meant to be a Roman. In the beginning, being a Roman was just like belonging to any other city-state in the Mediterranean. Like "being an Athenian," it meant having citizenship in a city and sharing in that urban community's language and culture. So in the fifth century BCE, being a Roman meant being a member, a citizen, of the city of Rome, speaking Latin—the regional language of central Italy of the time—and eating and dressing like Latin-speaking people. By the end of the second century BCE, however, as the Roman state had expanded its control over Italy and parts of the Mediterranean, the concept of citizenship was also expanded to include not just members of the city of Rome, but anyone who had been granted formal membership in the new larger territorial state that the Romans were building. By the beginning of the third century CE, even this bigger view was no longer true. Now being a Roman meant simply being a subject of the Roman emperors. This even more general idea of who a Roman was became so deeply rooted that when the western parts of the empire disintegrated in the fifth century CE, the inhabitants of the eastern parts of the empire that survived, who had no connection with the city of Rome, who did not speak Latin, and who did not dress or eat like the original Romans, still considered themselves to be "Romans" (or *Rhomaioi*, in the Greek language that they spoke). In this way, the creation of a huge territorial empire had created a new and very much larger idea of what it was to be Roman.

Put very simply, the mere existence of these two states, much larger than any that had existed before, mattered a great deal. At least one out of every two human beings living in Afro-Eurasia fell directly under the control of China or

Focus Questions HAN DYNASTY CHINA AND IMPERIAL ROME

→ *How did the Roman and Han empires differ from earlier large states?*

→ *What policies did the Qin leaders use to integrate their empire?*

→ *How did Han leaders promote peace and stability?*

→ *Were the policies and institutions involved in integrating the Roman Empire similar to those of the Han dynasty in China?*

 WWNORTON.COM/STUDYSPACE

Rome, and still more fell under their influence. In addition, these empires made it possible for their subjects to live more predictable and peaceful lives than anyone had known before. The long period of several centuries of settled conditions established by the Roman Empire, for example, is rightly known as the *Pax Romana,* or "the Roman peace." So it is natural that by Pliny's time, further large-scale expansion of the Roman Empire mattered less than did the rational use of force and administration to maintain stable conditions of existence for the empire's subjects. Moreover, the general patterns of imperial expansion were broadly similar both in East Asia and in the Mediterranean. The Roman Empire in western Eurasia and the Han Empire in East Asia fully exploited the ecological limits of their agrarian base and human resources. They then became more interested in consolidating power within these limits than in expanding beyond them. In effect, each empire brought the provinces of their dominions together into regimes of unprecedented scale, and therefore enhanced the integration of local worlds into a common legal (and eventually cultural) framework, and had economic effects even further afield. They were big. They were, for a long time, indomitable. But they were not yet like the empires that would step on to the global stage after 1300, empires that pulled distant overseas lands under one roof.

At least one out of every two human beings living in Afro-Eurasia fell directly under the control of China or Rome, and still more fell under their influence.

CHINA AND ROME: HOW EMPIRES ARE BUILT

> → *How did the Roman and Han empires differ from earlier large states?*

The massive new empires in the Mediterranean and East Asia emerged toward the end of the first millennium BCE, rising out of preexisting territorial kingdoms and states located on the edges of Eurasia. Though there had been regional empires before them, the Roman and the Han empires represented a different scale and quality of empire building. And they left huge imprints that lasted for centuries after their demise. Did common ecological factors, such as increasing population growth and expanding long-distance trade, feed these impulses to empire building? Or was the concurrent emergence of two great imperial systems just a coincidence? Whatever the causes, the most salient characteristic of these new empires was their sheer size.

The scale of the Han dynasty was unprecedented. A land survey made by the imperial government in 2 CE revealed a registered population of 12,233,062 households, or a grand total of around 58 million people. These households paid taxes, provided recruits for the military, and produced laborers for public works. At its height, the Han Empire covered some 3 million square miles of land in China proper and, for a while, another 1 million square miles in Central Asia. The extent of the system of the two big rivers—the Yellow River and the Yangzi River—dominated by the Han Empire was similarly unprecedented, as each was almost as long as the Nile. The Yellow River was nearly 3,500 miles long and drained an area of a third of a million square miles in the north, while the Yangzi River drained a basin of three- quarters of a million square miles in the south as it flowed almost 4,000 miles from Central Asia to the East China Sea.

The new empires of Asia and the Mediterranean united huge landmasses and extraordinarily diverse populations. The Roman Empire governed an area and a population that were as great as those of Han China. These new states were empires in the sense that we usually think of empires today: superstates of enormous size and power that are wholly dominant in their own worlds. The Han and Roman empires achieved new heights of cultural, economic, and administrative control over vast numbers of people whom they made subjects of their rule.

Despite their similarities, the Roman and Han empires had separate patterns of development and different representative types of public servants: the civilian magistrate and the bureaucrat were typical of the Han Empire, while the citizen, the soldier, and the military governor stood for the Roman Empire. Their ideals of the best kind of government were also different. In China, dynastic empires were constructed according to the models of past empires. The Chinese envisaged imperial culture as an ideal from the past that had to be emulated. By contrast, Rome began as a collectively ruled city-state—a "republic," as the Romans called it—and pursued a pragmatic road to the domination of its world. Only by a long, sometimes violent process of trial and error did the Romans finally work their way to a political system of one-man rule by emperors. Nonetheless, they, like the Chinese, were strongly traditional. They also idealized their ancestors, or *maiores.* But they were less fascinated with the earlier major powers of their world. What characterized Roman expansion and empire building was a process of continual experimentation, innovation, and adaptation.

Both empires created indelible ideas of what it was to be an empire and to behave imperially. Although the Han Empire collapsed in the third century CE and the Western Roman Empire disintegrated in the fifth century CE, they survived as models, displacing earlier large states from the center of political and cultural debates and discourse about empire. Successor states in the Mediterranean sought to become the Second Rome. And, after the Han dynasty fell, as a people the Chinese always identified themselves and their language simply as "Han." Both empires enabled people throughout Afro-Eurasia to elevate their idea of what life could be to a new level—now they saw that they could share a common identity on a much larger scale than ever before. It was a vision that would never be lost, even if the empires were.

THE QIN DYNASTY

> → *What policies did the Qin leaders use to integrate their empire?*

The Qin and the Han were the dynasties that established the groundwork to make China a unified state. (See Map 7-1.) They created the political, social, economic, and cultural

structures that would thereafter characterize imperial China. Through conquest and a strong bureaucracy, the Qin managed to forge a central state that was far more powerful than the Zhou state had been even at its most potent. The administrative organizations and laws, and standardized measures and procedures, put in place by the Qin rulers would last well beyond their own rule.

King Zheng of Qin succeeded in defeating the remaining Warring States between 230 and 221 BCE, thereby ending one of the most violent periods in Chinese history. With the help of able ministers and generals and with a large conscripted army, as well as a system of taxation that provided revenues to finance all-out war, he assumed the mandate of heaven from the Zhou and unified the states into a centralized empire, declaring himself Shi Huangdi (First August Emperor)—much as the first emperor of Rome was also to call himself Augustus. He took the title of emperor (*di*) to distinguish himself from both the Zhou ruler and the rulers of the states, all of whom had been referred to as kings (*wang*). To further consolidate his power, he forced the defeated states' rulers and their families to move to Xianyang, the capital of Qin, where he could assure himself that they were not gathering armies to rebel against him. As noted at the start of this chapter, the Qin ruler also had a clearer and more ruthless vision of empire building than did his more conservative enemies.

Qin Warriors. As part of the tax quota, all able-bodied males were expected to serve in the army and to build border walls, roads, canals, and palaces. Terra-cotta warriors were buried with the Qin emperor in the expectation that they would join in his military campaigns in the next life.

→ *What policies did the Qin leaders use to integrate their empire?*

MAP 7-1   EAST ASIA, 206 BCE-220 CE

Both the Qin and the Han dynasties consolidated much of the population of East Asia into one large regional empire in the last two centuries of the first millennium BCE. According to the map, what physical features imposed an ecological limit to this territorial expansion? What impact did the pastoral Xiongnu have on each empire's effort to consolidate a large territorial state? How did each respond? Why did the Han leaders expand their imperial influence further west than the Qin?

ADMINISTRATION AND CONTROL

After securing the loyalty of the rulers from the defeated states, the First Emperor proceeded to systematically divide up China so that the new dynasty could effectively rule the massive new state. Ultimately, the emperor parceled China into thirty-six provinces, called commanderies (*jun*), which

he then subdivided into counties (*xian*). Each commandery had a civilian and a military governor, both of whom answered to an imperial inspector. Importantly, the regional and local officials also answered directly to the emperor, who could dismiss them whenever he pleased. Civilian governors would not serve in their home areas and would be frequently reassigned to new posts, policies designed to prevent them from building up their own power. Clerks registered the common people in order to observe, to control, and to punish them. Registration, required of all males when they reached maturity (at age sixteen or seventeen, and five feet in height), provided the lists from which men were taxed and conscripted. All able-bodied males were expected to serve in the army and to provide labor for public works: to build border walls, imperial roads, water canals, and huge palaces in the capital. Imperial rule was harsh, and censorship was rife. Unauthorized books were banned, and allegedly many scholars were executed in an effort to eliminate criticism of the government. Social order and control were reestablished after nearly two and a half centuries of warfare and chaos.

To further unify the divergent systems that had survived from the time of the Warring States, the Qin emperor also established standard weights and measures, and a standard currency: circular coins with square holes in the center replaced the coins shaped like miniature spades or knives that had been used in different states.

The Qin began to extend China's boundaries in the northeast to the Korean Peninsula, in the south to present-day Vietnam, and in the west into Central Asia. Han Fei, a minor official from the state of Han, first voiced the notion of a "grand unity" that the Qin rulers and ministers embraced as their guiding political idea. The chief minister of the Qin Empire, Li Si, used it to justify the harsh measures that he enacted to join the various states of the Central Plain into an empire and to establish a centralized administrative structure.

Both Han Fei and Li Si subscribed to the principles of Legalism developed during the Warring States period of the previous Zhou dynasty (see Chapter 5). This philosophy accorded the highest value to written law codes, administrative regulations, and set punishments rather than to rituals and ethics (as emphasized by the Confucians) or spontaneity and the natural order (as stressed by the Daoists). They were both disciples of the Confucian Xunzi, a moralist who had favored solutions based on rational statecraft over the unpredictable vagaries of human nature (see Chapter 5). They believed that strict laws and punishments would lead to stability and order in a turbulent society. They therefore enacted unambiguous laws and regulations, as well as harsh punishments (including beheading, mutilation by cutting off a person's nose or foot, tattooing, shaving off a person's beard or hair, hard labor, and loss of office and rank) that applied to anyone who violated the law, regardless of rank or wealth. They registered people in groups of five and ten, and made all of them responsible for each other and hence subject to punishment for a crime committed by any one of them.

The Qin also devised systems to make communication more efficient. They built roads connecting the Qin capital to all parts of the new empire. These were immense thoroughfares, 115 feet wide and divided into three lanes to accommodate vehicles, pedestrians, animals, and, most importantly, soldiers. Their thick embankments of soil were reinforced with metal poles and planted with pine trees to check erosion. Officials required vehicles to have a standard axle length so that all wheels would fit in the same dirt ruts.

Just as crucial to bringing unity to the empire was the Qin effort to standardize the diverse forms of writing used in the Warring States period. Regional variants in written characters had appeared in different states under the Eastern Zhou dynasty, but the Qin banned these alternative versions. In their place, scribes and ministers throughout the empire were required to adopt the "small seal script"; its characters, smaller and simpler than those used previously, eventually evolved into the less-complicated clerical style of bureaucratic writing prominent during the Han dynasty.

The new, standardized script helped the Qin disseminate their idea of the state and eliminate the competing political ideas that had been so prominent during the Warring States era. It made uniform the style of writing employed by regional elites and clerks, who now served as bureaucratic intermediaries transmitting oral and written communications between the imperial capital and local government. Standardization also eliminated aberrant ideas that might disturb the new imperial unity. In 213 BCE, a Qin decree ordered officials to confiscate and to burn all books in residents' private possession (technical works dealing with medicine, divination, and agriculture were exempt). In addition, the court prosecuted teachers who used the newly outlawed classical books, including some of Confucius's works that could be used to criticize the Qin regime. Education and learning were now entrusted exclusively to state officials.

Qin Coin. After centuries of distinctive regional currencies, the Qin unified the currency as part of its general unification policy. Thereafter bronze or copper cash was the standard imperial currency in China.

Roof Tiles. Roof tiles (*wadang*) with molded designs were manufactured beginning in the late Zhou. The use of stylized characters as architectural ornaments began during the Warring States Period and continued during the Qin and Han dynasties.

A QIN LEGAL DOCUMENT: MEMORIAL ON THE BURNING OF BOOKS

When the first emperor of Qin came to power, his minister, Li Si, devised a cultural policy to enhance state power by creating a unified political ideology. Any traditions of learning that differed from the Qin orthodoxy were thus considered heterodox and targeted for elimination. The most serious threat to Qin power came from the Five Classics, *said to have been compiled by Confucius, which contained teachings that urged the importance of moral rectitude, personal character, and political responsibility while holding office. Such texts were an affront to imperial power, Li thought, and should therefore be destroyed, and the scholars who defended such teachings in public should be executed.*

In earlier times the empire disintegrated and fell into disorder, and no one was capable of unifying it. Thereupon the various feudal lords rose to power. In their discourses they all praised the past in order to disparage the present and embellished empty words to confuse the truth. Everyone cherished his own favorite school of learning and criticized what had been instituted by the authorities. But at present Your Majesty possesses a unified empire, has regulated the distinctions of black and white, and has firmly established for yourself a position of sole supremacy. And yet these independent schools, joining with each other, criticize the codes of laws and instructions. Hearing of the promulgation of a decree, they criticize it, each from the standpoint of his own school. At home they disapprove of it in their hearts; going out they criticize it in the thoroughfare. They seek a reputation by discrediting their sovereign; they appear superior by expressing contrary views, and they lead the lowly multitude in the spreading of slander. If such license is not prohibited, the sovereign power will decline above and partisan factions will form below. It would be well to prohibit this.

Your servant suggests that all books in the imperial archives, save the memoirs of Qin, be burned. All persons in the empire, except members of the Academy of Learned Scholars, in possession of the *Classic of Odes,* the *Classic of Documents,* and discourses of the hundred philosophers should take them to the local governors and have them indiscriminately burned. Those who dare to talk to each other about the *Odes* and *Documents* should be executed and their bodies exposed in the marketplace. Anyone referring to the past to criticize the present should, together with all members of his family, be put to death. Officials who fail to report cases that have come under their attention are equally guilty. After thirty days from the time of issuing the decree, those who have not destroyed their books are to be branded and sent to build the Great Wall. Books not to be destroyed will be those on medicine and pharmacy, divination by the turtle and milfoil, and agriculture and arboriculture. People wishing to pursue learning should take the officials as their teachers.

→ *Why did Qin fear the teachings of Confucius about gentlemen of moral purpose and proper behavior?*
→ *Why were writings dealing with medicine, pharmacy, and agriculture exempt from this policy of book burning?*

SOURCE: *Sources of Chinese Tradition,* vol. 1, *From Earliest Times to 1600,* compiled by Wm. Theodore de Bary and Irene Bloom, 2nd ed. (New York: Columbia University Press, 1999), pp. 209–10.

ECONOMIC AND SOCIAL CHANGES

The Qin rulers expanded their agrarian empire through conquest. During the Warring States period, landownership had shifted from the great aristocratic clans to a new Chinese peasantry, who were now free of the burden of paying tribute—in money, commodities, and services—to regional lords. An agrarian bonanza created wealth that could be taxed by the state, and increased tax revenues supplied the resources that enabled the central state to impose order on the country. Government support for agriculture continued under the Qin Empire; the government established rules on working the fields (with severe penalties for failure to follow its regulations), taxed individual households that farmed the land, and conscripted laborers to build irrigation systems and canals in order to provide even more land that could be cultivated. Whereas the Greek city states and the Roman Empire relied heavily on slave labor, the Qin and later the Han dynasties championed free farmers and successfully conscripted able-bodied sons into their huge armies. Free to work their own land, and required to pay only a relatively small portion of their crops in taxes, peasant families were the economic foundation of the Chinese empires.

The Qin dynasty's consolidation of central power was accompanied by major economic changes: self-sufficient local royal manors increasingly were replaced by farms producing goods for exchange in the marketplace and buying necessities from merchants. As production rose, landowners—some of them peasants—began to focus on profiting from their surpluses. Increasingly, public royal domains and private employers used contracts and money to strike bargains with laborers and with each other. A similar shift toward a reliance on contracts occurred more generally in Chinese society and government. Previously, ties of blood had been all-important, but with the growth in trade and commercial ways, nonroyal newcomers such as farmers and traders were coming to dominate public and private business.

Agricultural surpluses fueled long-distance commerce—yet another source of wealth and revenues. The growth of a money economy gave rise to a class of merchants in China's cities, which became market centers rather than fortresses and created a new world of region-based networks. Merchants handled foodstuffs as well as weapons, metals, horses, dogs, hides, furs, silk, and salt. They traded specialized goods produced in different regions of the empire. Moreover, the new roads and canals between rivers not only aided the movements of soldiers but also promoted commerce, carrying both goods and the tax revenues sent from the commanderies throughout the empire. Nonetheless, the central government, believing that trade produces nothing of lasting value, continued to value and encourage the production of crops and goods over trade, and imposed ever-higher taxes on goods in transit and in the markets.

THE XIONGNU AND THE QIN ALONG THE NORTHERN FRONTIER

Both the Qin dynasty and later the Han dynasty grappled not only with the problems of governing their empires but also with the need to expand and defend their borders. During the last centuries of the Warring States period, states along the northern border had enlarged their domains by conquering nomadic frontier peoples (see Chapter 6). When the Qin dynasty united the states into an empire and sought to further extend its borders to the north and west, it faced direct contact with nomadic warrior peoples—especially the Xiongnu, the dominant people in the Asian steppe regions. Like the Qin, the Han faced the same ecological limits. Despite its huge financial resources, the Han dynasty's identity as an empire of sedentary farmers who tilled the soil in thousands of permanent villages petered out on the Asian steppe where the

Xiongnu and their migrating herds of horses and sheep were in their element.

The Xiongnu were horse-riding pastoral nomads who traveled within a large zone of the Inner Eurasian steppe in search of pastures for their herds. Their warrior elites fought for pasturelands with other nomadic tribes and strove to protect those lands from the northern Zhou states and then from the conscripted armies of the Qin Empire. Yet archaeological evidence indicates that they also engaged in trade and diplomacy with the people of China's Central Plain, the Yellow River valley (see Chapter 6). Thus, during the fourth century BCE the nomads exchanged their horses, cattle, sheep, and furs for gold necklaces, beads of precious stones, sculpted silver animals, and coins from the settled population. The rich burial sites of the Xiongnu that have been excavated contain hundreds of gold and silver objects and reveal a society sharply divided by social distinctions, for it was only the aristocratic rulers who were entombed with precious goods.

A precarious balance existed between these nomadic peoples of the steppe and the Chinese until 215 BCE, when the newly founded Qin Empire expanded north into the middle of the Yellow River basin. At that time, the First Emperor sent troops against the Xiongnu in the north in order to seize their pasturelands for his empire. To make these new lands more secure for settlement, the Qin officials built a road between the frontier and the nearest city. They also used conscripts and criminals sentenced to hard labor to build a massive defensive wall along the northern border (the beginnings of the Great Wall of China, though considerably to the north of the current wall, which was constructed more than a millennium later). As a result of these imperial efforts, in 211 BCE the Qin settled 30,000 colonists in the steppe lands of Inner Eurasia.

The Xiongnu ultimately regrouped; in response to the expansion of Qin imperial power into the steppe and the economic crisis created by the loss of their pasturelands, they

Qin Crossbow. This is a reproduction of one of the formidable crossbows carried by the Qin terra-cotta kneeling archers. The bronze arrowhead and trigger mechanism in this reproduction were found with the terra-cotta army.

Primary Source

THE "FAULTS OF THE QIN" BY JIA YI

After the Qin dynasty disintegrated in 207 BCE, Confucians sought reasons to explain the fall of so strong a military power that had unified China just fourteen years before. In one notable account, Jia Yi tied the Qin dynasty's collapse to its autocratic rule and mean-spirited policies. Rather than blame the imperial system itself, Jia blamed the immorality of the Qin penal code and the first Qin emperor's totalitarian policies for his loss of the mandate of heaven. If the empire had been ruled according to Confucian teachings and ritual guidelines, he contended, it would have endured.

[Later] when the First Emperor ascended [the throne] he flourished and furthered the accomplishments of the six generations before him. Brandishing his long whip, he drove the world before him; destroying the feudal lords, he swallowed up the domains of the two Zhou dynasties. He reached the pinnacle of power and ordered all in the Six Directions, whipping the rest of the world into submission and thus spreading his might through the Four Seas. . . . He then abolished the ways of ancient sage kings and put to the torch the writings of the Hundred Schools in an attempt to keep the people in ignorance. He demolished the walls of major cities and put to death men of fame and talent, collected all the arms of the realm at Xianyang and had the spears and arrowheads melted down to form twelve huge statues in human form—all with the aim of weakening his people. Then he . . . posted capable generals and expert bowmen at important passes and placed trusted officials and well-trained soldiers in strategic array to challenge all who passed. With the empire thus pacified, the First Emperor believed that, with the capital secure within the pass and prosperous cities stretching for ten thousand *li,* he had indeed created an imperial structure to be enjoyed by his royal descendants for ten thousand generations to come.

Even after the death of the First Emperor, his reputation continued to sway the people. Chen She was a man who grew up in humble circumstances in a hut with broken pots for windows and ropes as door hinges and was a mere hired field hand and roving conscript of mediocre talent. He could neither equal the worth of Confucius and Mozi nor match the wealth of Tao Zhu or Yi Dun, yet, even stumbling as he did amidst the ranks of common soldiers and shuffling through the fields, he called forth a tired motley crowd and a mob of several hundred to turn upon the Qin. Cutting down trees to make weapons, and hoist-

ing their flags on garden poles, they had the whole world come to them like gathering clouds, with people bringing their own food and following them like shadows. These men of courage from the East rose together, and in the end they defeated and extinguished the House of Qin.

Actually, the Qin empire was by no means small and weak, having always been secure within the pass in Yongzhou. Moreover, Chen She's position was far below the level of respect commanded by the rulers of Qi, Chu, Yan, Zhao, Han, Wei, Song, Wei, and Zhongshan. His weapons made of farm implements and thorny tree branches were no match in battle against spears and halberds, his roving conscripts in no way compared to the armies of the nine states. In matters of strategy and tactics, and other military arts, Chen was no match for the men of the past. . . . Qin, from a tiny base, had become a great power, ruling the land and receiving homage from all quarters for a hundred-odd years. Yet after they had unified the land and secured themselves within the pass, a single common rustic could nevertheless challenge this empire and cause its ancestral temples to topple and its ruler to die at the hand of others, a laughingstock in the eyes of all. Why? Because the ruler lacked humaneness and rightness; because preserving power differs fundamentally from seizing power.

→ *How was the mandate of heaven used to justify the defeat of the Qin by rebels?*

→ *Why did Jia Yi seek to preserve the imperial government that the Qin had created, even while he attempted to eliminate the Legalist ideology informing its political policies?*

SOURCE: *Sources of Chinese Tradition,* vol. 1, *From Earliest Times to 1600,* compiled by Wm. Theodore de Bary and Irene Bloom, 2nd ed. (New York: Columbia University Press, 1999), pp. 229–30.

Qin Archer. This kneeling archer was discovered in the tomb of the First Emperor. Notice his breastplate. The wooden bow he was holding has disintegrated.

founded a state in 209 BCE in the form of a loose confederacy among various steppe tribes. When the Qin fell in 207 BCE and civil war broke out, the new Xiongnu confederacy pushed across the defensive lines and reconquered their old pasturelands. They continued to threaten the Han rulers who would emerge as leaders of a new empire.

In their warfare, the sedentary Chinese and the nomadic warriors exhibited a dynamic symbiotic relationship that was both political and ecological; that is, the locally fixed agrarian villages of the Chinese peasants contrasted with the vast steppe grasslands traversed by the Xiongnu (see the section on the Han Empire, below). This pattern persisted for centuries, until later nomads challenged the hegemony of the Chinese dynastic system along the frontiers of the Inner Eurasian steppe and agricultural settlements connected to the Yellow River valley. Thereafter, long-term trade relations and diplomatic contacts between the Chinese and the nomads were frequently punctuated by armed hostilities.

THE QIN DEBACLE

For all of its military power, the Qin dynasty collapsed quickly. Qin rule weighed heavily on taxpayers because of constant warfare, which required not just massive tax revenues but also huge numbers of corvée and forced laborers, the latter drawn from petty criminals. Dissension at court became apparent: Chief Minister Li Si was implicated in a conspiracy and executed. When desperate conscripted workers mutinied in 211 BCE, they were joined by descendants of the nobles from the Warring States, local military leaders, and influential merchants. The rebels gained thousands of supporters with their call to arms against the "tyrannical" Qin. Shortly before the First Emperor died in 210, even the educated elite, who had grown tired of Qin social and cultural repression, joined with former lords and regional vassals in revolt. The second Qin emperor was forced to commit suicide early in 207, and his weak successor promptly surrendered to the leader of the Han forces later that year.

In the aftermath of the fall of the Qin, the leader of the insurgents, Xiang Yu, tried to restore the Zhou system of powerful regional states that had existed before the Qin dynasty, establishing nineteen feudal states. In the ensuing civil war between them, an unheralded commoner and former policeman named Liu Bang (ruled 206–195 BCE) declared himself the prince of his home area of Han. In 202 BCE, after Xiang Yu committed suicide, Liu declared himself the first Han emperor.

Emphasizing his peasant origins, Liu demonstrated his initial disdain for intellectuals by urinating into the hat of a court scholar. But Liu quickly learned that power would be kept only with better manners. Confucian scholars loyal to the Han were employed to justify Liu Bang's victory by depicting his Qin predecessors as cruel and oppressive dynasts and as ruthless despots. They painted the Qin in dark colors to exaggerate the purity of the succeeding Han. The Han court and its officials denied any link to the Qin. Instead, they affirmed the Confucian idea of the moral and cultural foundations of state power. In his essay titled "The Faults of the Qin," the scholar Jia Yi (c. 200–168 BCE) argued that the Qin had fallen "because the ruler lacked moral values." Under the cover of receiving the mandate of heaven, the Han construed the Qin as evil, even as they adopted the Qin's bureaucratic system. In reality—as we can see from the cache of Qin penal codes and administrative ordinances, written on some 1,000 bamboo slips, that was discovered in 1978—Qin laws were not especially any more cruel or arbitrary than those of the later Han. Punishments suited the crimes, and the laws themselves actually closely resembled the later Han penal code.

THE HAN DYNASTY

> → *How did Han leaders promote peace and stability?*

The Han dynasty, which lasted from 206 BCE to 220 CE, became China's formative empire. (See Map 7-2.) Han armies had some 50,000 lethal crossbowmen, who fought with mass-produced weapons made from bronze and iron. Armed with the crossbow, foot soldiers and cavalry (mounted archers) extended Han imperial lands in all directions. Following the Qin practice, the Han relied on a huge conscripted labor force for special projects such as building canals, roads, or defensive walls. State revenues came from state lands and a land tax, though the latter was reduced to gain the peasants' support for the dynasty.

MAP 7-2 *PAX SINICA:* THE HAN EMPIRE IN THE FIRST CENTURY BCE
Agriculture, commerce, and industry flourished in East Asia during the first century BCE under Han rule. According to the map, what Han policies contributed to this period of peace and prosperity? How did the Han organize their vast domains? How did they integrate them economically?

The 400 years of Han rule were characterized by both change and continuity. The first part of the Han dynastic cycle, known as the Western (or Former) Han dynasty (206 BCE–9 CE), was marked by economic prosperity and the expansion of the empire, especially under Emperor Wu or Wudi, who was known as the "Martial Emperor" because of his many military campaigns (ruled 140–87 BCE). After Wu's reign, however, poor harvests, heavy taxes, and increased debt forced many peasants to sell their land to the wealthy, and social tensions grew. A usurper who tried to introduce land reforms took power from 9 to 23 CE, but he was overthrown by a coalition of landowners and peasants who restored the Han dynasty to power. Liu Xiu reconsolidated the Han Empire as the Eastern (or Later) Han dynasty, which lasted from 25 to 220 CE. He moved the capital eastward from its former location, Chang'an, to Luoyang on the North China plain. Out of the experience of the Han, the Chinese produced a political narrative known as the dynastic cycle. Dynasties rose and fell, and heaven could, potentially, grant its mandate to anyone who unified the empire. Indeed, the imperial continuity established by the Han was extraordinarily long-lasting, enduring more than 2,000 years, until 1911.

FOUNDATIONS OF HAN POWER

The Han and Roman empires, like all subsequent big imperial states, relied on political institutions, ideological supports, and control of economic assets to maintain power. Yet they differed in the places assigned to civil bureaucracy, the military, and the ideologies designed to ensure the consent of the governed. The Han Empire was distinguished by the tight-knit alliance that existed between the imperial family and the new elite—the scholar-gentry class—who united in their determination to impose order on the rank and file of the Chinese population. Economic and social supports, as well as a strong military and bureaucratic administration, also contributed to the strength, expansion, and longevity of the Han Empire.

POWER AND ADMINISTRATION The first Han emperors were compelled to compromise with the aristocratic groups who had helped overthrow the Qin. To win their favor, Liu Bang provided land grants to his military supporters as well as to his relatives. His brothers and sons became regional lords, and military leaders and selected high officials were set up as local lords. Initially, two-thirds of the land in the empire was governed by royal relatives or supporters, and only one-third was directly administered by the emperor's officials.

Power emanated from the ruling family, whose dynasts combined the decentralized aristocratic institutions of the Zhou with the centralized bureaucratic system of the Qin. Kin of the imperial family were made nobles and were given lands over which they had direct power, while governors ap-

Emperor Wudi. This idealized representation of Emperor Wudi (156–87 BCE, ruled 141–87 BCE) welcoming a man of letters was one of a series of seventeenth-century silk paintings of Chinese emperors.

pointed by the emperor administered the commanderies that remained under central control. A "grand counselor," chosen by the emperor, headed a civil bureaucracy whose members were drawn from educated men representing powerful local communities. At the outset of the Han dynasty, the central government refrained from interfering with regional communities. The court followed the same flexible policy toward border peoples, using marriage alliances to gain control over their territories. Han administration was therefore marked by complex compromises between the ruling household and the rest of the Chinese population. The emperor, his family, and the court represented a strong centralized, hierarchical, and autocratic monarchy. But practical considerations always restrained the ruler's power.

The Han state developed a more highly centralized bureaucracy than did Rome, and that structure became the source of its enduring power. As under the Qin, the bureaucracy affected individuals through requirements that all males register, pay taxes, and serve in the military. At first, regional officials seldom intervened at the local level, simply supervising the local officials and making sure that they sent tax revenues and army conscripts. But the Han court was quick to tighten its control over regional administration. From 177 to 155 BCE, the court successively removed several pow-

Primary Source

HAN LEGAL PHILOSOPHY FROM DONG ZHONGSHU

The Qin legal system was presented as more brutal than its predecessors in its application of uniform punishments against criminals. It had allegedly not allowed for any extenuating circumstances whatsoever. Scholars claimed that all crimes under the Qin were punished equally, regardless of the accused's motive or social status. Under the Han emperor Wudi, Dong Zhongshu devised an ingenious way to humanize such laws in the Han penal code using Confucian philosophy, so that the social statuses of those involved in litigation and the personal motives behind allegedly criminal behavior could be considered. In essence, Dong as a Confucian argued that the spirit of the law took precedence over its letter when true justice was the goal.

At the time, there were those who questioned the verdict saying: "A had no son. On the side of the road, he picked up the child B and raised him as his own son. When B grew up, he committed the crime of murder. The contents of the accusation [against B] included [the fact that] A had concealed B [after the crime]. What should be the judgment regarding A?"

Tung Chung-shu passed judgment saying: "A had no son. He restored [B] to life and raised him [as his own son]. Although B was not A's natural son, who would think of seeing [B] as anyone but [A's] son? The *Poetry* [*Classic*] says: 'The mulberry-tree caterpillar has little ones, but the wasp raises them.' According to the intent of the *Annals*, a father must cover up for his son. A accordingly concealed B. The verdict: A does not deserve to be punished."

→ *Why did the Han state maintain a penal code that drew on the Qin legal system?*

→ *How could the penal code serve the ritual needs of the new Han dynasty?*

SOURCE: Pan Ku, *Han-shu* 3:1714 (*chüan* 30); quoted in Benjamin A. Elman, *Classicism, Politics, and Kinship: The Ch'ang-chou School of New Text Confucianism in Late Imperial China* (Berkeley: University of California Press, 1990), p. 262.

erful princes, crushed rebellions, and took over the areas controlled by regional lords. As princes lost power, regional officials came to govern these aristocratic enclaves as commanderies of the empire. The empire, according to arrangements put in place in 106 BCE by Emperor Wu, was made up of thirteen provinces under imperial inspectors, who each oversaw between four and ten commanderies. Governors-general were appointed during emergencies such as floods or famine.

A civilian official and a commandant for military affairs administered each commandery. The responsibilities of such officials were immense, far exceeding the duties of their counterparts in the Roman Empire. The total populations of commanderies, which covered vast landmasses and were inhabited by diverse ethnic groups, ran into millions of people. These officials, like their Roman equivalents, were responsible for political stability and for the regular and efficient collection of taxes. But in light of the immense numbers that came under their jurisdiction and the heavy duties that fell on them, the local administrative staff was skeletal and in many respects inadequate.

Government schools that promoted the scholar-official ideal became a major source for the recruitment of local officials. To provide an adequate number of educated officials to fill the many positions in the bureaucracy, the Han established formal institutions of learning. Emperor Wu founded a college for classical scholars in 136 BCE and soon expanded it into the Imperial University. It had 30,000 members by the second century CE, completely dwarfing the number of students in even the largest of Roman schools. Not only did they study the classics, but Han scholars were also naturalists and inventors, making important medical discoveries, inventing the magnetic compass and developing high-quality paper, which replaced silk, wood, and bamboo strips as the most

The Wuliang Shrine. This rubbing of a Wuliang Shrine stele depicts Han scholars sitting on mats on the floor. Chairs were not used until late medieval times.

convenient medium for communicating laws, ideas, rituals, and technical knowledge.

Officials selected students on the basis of recommendations and exempted them from corvée labor, military service, and the poll tax so that they could concentrate on their studies. At graduation, the young men began their careers in the lower ranks of the bureaucracy. The Han state school system was a precursor of the later civil examination system. Increasingly, local elites encouraged their sons to become masters of the classical teachings in Confucianism. This practice not only became one of the most widely accepted ways of entering the ruling class but also made the Confucian classics the heart of the imperial state.

Gradually a bureaucratic political culture emerged that balanced the interests of the authoritarian emperor and his officials, without whom he could not rule. The court tried to control its elites. At the same time, the elites brazenly used the government to enhance their social status and economic assets. Rather than exercising absolute despotic power, the Han rulers ended up by creating a remarkable partnership between the imperial government and China's educated and economic elites—a collaboration emulated by all later dynasties that ruled China.

CONFUCIAN IDEOLOGY AND LEGITIMATE RULE
The Han used Confucian thought as the primary ideological buttress of the empire. According to official Han political philosophy, the welfare of the people was the foundation of legitimate rule. When the Confucian scholar and official Jia Yi wrote that "the state, the ruler, and the officials all depend on the people for their mandate," he was describing the role that "the primacy of the people" played in affirming the mandate of heaven. Claims like these promoted devotion to classical political principles of civilizing the people as well as supporting local elites. Such principles did *not* imply, as they did in the Greek-city states, that the people actually chose their own leaders. The only power given to the people was that of turning away from rulers who failed to promote general well-being.

By 50 BCE, Han officials made the Confucian ideals of honoring tradition, respecting the lessons of history, and emphasizing the emperor's responsibility to heaven the official doctrine of the empire. Confucians now tutored the princes, and the grand historian Sima Qian provided a historical vision of good and evil Shang and Zhou rulers for the Han dynasty to mark the lessons of the past. By embracing Confucian political ideals, the Han rulers established a polity based on the mandate received from the people and created a careful balance between two arms of government—the emperor and his officials—that enabled the officials to provide a counterweight to the emperor's autocratic strength. Of course, when the interests of the court and the bureaucracy clashed, the will of the emperor was paramount. But classical political teachings empowered officials to criticize bad government and even to impeach corrupt leaders.

THE NEW SOCIAL ORDER AND THE ECONOMY The Han Empire slowly established a new imperial order. The genius of the Han was their ability to win the support of diverse social groups that had been in conflict for centuries. They did so by working with them and by forming alliances with key leaders. The Han allowed some aristocratic survivors of the Qin collapse to reacquire some of their former power and status. They also encouraged enterprising peasants who had worked the lands of nobles to become local leaders in the countryside. Successful merchants were permitted to extend their influence in cities or towns, and in local areas scholars became de facto masters when their lords were removed.

A massive agrarian base provided the Han with tax revenues and labor for military forces and public works. The Han court also relied on revenues from special state-owned imperial preserves, mining, and mints; tribute from outlying domains; household taxes on the nobility; and additional contributions of surplus grains from wealthy merchants who sought noble ranks, official appointments, or a decrease in their tax burdens. Emperor Wu established state monopolies in salt, iron, and wine to fund his expensive military campaigns. He supported policies that encouraged growth in silk

Primary Source

"RESPONSIBILITIES OF HAN RULERSHIP" BY DONG ZHONGSHU

In the early Han dynasty, officials sought to enhance the legitimacy of the imperial government by replacing the Legalist defense of an autocratic state with a Confucian notion that presented the ruler as the moral and cosmological foundation of the government. Thus the philosopher Dong Zhongshu provided a new theory of legitimation for the Han dynasty, while criticizing the Qin's mismanagement of the imperial government. Under the guidance of Confucian officials, Dong argued, the imperial system would nourish the people and promote upright officials who would maintain the Han dynasty's mandate to govern, rather than ruling through fear and intimidation.

He who rules the people is the foundation of the state. Now in administering the state, nothing is more important for transforming [the people] than reverence for the foundation. If the foundation is revered, the ruler will transform [the people] as if a spirit. If the foundation is not revered, the ruler will lack the means to unite the people. If he lacks the means to unite the people, even if he institutes strict punishments and heavy penalties, the people will not submit. This is called "throwing away the state." Is there a greater disaster than this? What do I mean by the foundation? Heaven, Earth, and humankind are the foundation of all living things. Heaven engenders all living things, Earth nourishes them, and humankind completes them. With filial and brotherly love, Heaven engenders them; with food and clothing, Earth nourishes them; and with rites and music, humankind completes them. These three assist one another just as the hands and feet join to complete the body. None can be dispensed with because without filial and brotherly love, people lack the means to live; without food and clothing, people lack the means to be nourished; and without rites and music, people lack the means to become complete. If all three are lost, people become like deer, each person following his own desires and each family practicing its own customs. Fathers will not be able to order their sons, and rulers will not be able to order their ministers. Although possessing inner and outer walls, [the ruler's city] will become known as "an empty settlement." Under such circumstances, the ruler will lie down with a clod of earth for his pillow. Although no one endangers him, he will naturally be endangered; although no one destroys him, he will naturally be destroyed. This is called "spontaneous punishment." When it arrives, even if he is hidden in a stone vault or barricaded in a narrow pass, the ruler will not be able to avoid "spontaneous punishment."

One who is an enlightened master and worthy ruler believes such things. For this reason he respectfully and carefully attends to the three foundations. He reverently enacts the suburban sacrifice, dutifully serves his ancestors, manifests filial and brotherly love, encourages filial conduct, and serves the foundation of Heaven in this way. He takes up the plough handle to till the soil, plucks the mulberry leaves and nourishes the silkworms, reclaims the wilds, plants grain, opens new lands to provide sufficient food and clothing, and serves the foundation of Earth in this way. He establishes academies and schools in towns and villages to teach filial piety, brotherly love, reverence, and humility, enlightens [the people] with education, moves [them] with rites and music, and serves the foundation of humanity in this way.

If these three foundations are all served, the people will resemble sons and brothers who do not dare usurp authority, while the ruler will resemble fathers and mothers. He will not rely on favors to demonstrate his love for his people nor severe measures to prompt them to act. Even if he lives in the wilds without a roof over head, he will consider that this surpasses living in a palace. Under such circumstances, the ruler will lie down upon a peaceful pillow. Although no one assists him, he will naturally be powerful; although no one pacifies his state, peace will naturally come. This is called "spontaneous reward." When "spontaneous reward" befalls him, although he might relinquish the throne and leave the state, the people will take up their children on their backs and follow him as the ruler, so that he too will be unable to leave them. Therefore when the ruler relies on virtue to administer the state, it is sweeter than honey or sugar and firmer than glue or lacquer. This is why sages and worthies exert themselves to revere the foundation and do not dare depart from it.

→ *Why was the emperor so important in Dong Zhongshu's vision of Han political culture after the fall of the Qin?*
→ *What role did public officials play in transmitting the policies of the state to the people so that they could live out their lives in peace and prosperity?*

SOURCE: *Sources of Chinese Tradition*, vol. 1, *From Earliest Times to 1600*, compiled by Wm. Theodore de Bary and Irene Bloom, 2nd ed. (New York: Columbia University Press, 1999), pp. 299–300.

Wuzhu Coin. This copper coin was issued by Emperor Xuandi during the Western Han Dynasty, 73–49 BCE. *Wuzhu*, which means "five grains," refers to the weight of the coin (1 wuzhu = 5 grains = 4 grams). The wuzhu was in circulation until 621.

production and iron production—especially iron weapons and everyday tools—and sought to control profiteering by instituting central price controls. He also minted standardized copper coins and exacted stiff penalties for counterfeiting. All these efforts were undertaken to expand the Han economy and to support the emperor's imperial ambitions.

Later Chinese monarchs took their cue from the Han, using government monopolies to undercut the independence of merchants. Merchants in this way became partners of the rulers, responsible for the management of peasants and artisans and for the transfer of agrarian and industrial products to the state, yet they never submitted entirely to state policy. They used their financial resources to become officials and secured state protection for their wealth and property. That wealth was often displayed in their lavish urban homes.

Laid out in an orderly grid, Han cities—particularly capitals—mainly reflected their political functions. Markets were strategically placed south of the palace complex and served as the only public areas. The palaces of the court became forbidden inner cities, off-limits to all but those in the imperial lineage or in the government. Monumental architecture in China was associated with the palaces and tombs of rulers rather than with sites of mass entertainment, like the Colosseum in Rome.

Wealthy families lived in houses of several stories built with richly carved crossbeams and rafters. They covered their floors with embroidered cushions, wool rugs, and mats. Fine embroideries hung as drapes, and screens in the rooms secured privacy for the inhabitants. Women and children were cloistered in inner quarters, as the patriarchal gender ideology encouraged lineage heads to protect their mothers, wives, and children from the harsher society at large. Elite women were often literate and managed to win respect for their talents as teachers and managers within the family while their husbands served as officials away from home. Women who were commoners led less-protected lives; many worked in the fields, and some joined troupes of entertainers to sing and dance for food at the open markets.

Silk was abundant and worn by members of all classes, though in winter only the rich wore furs, while everyone else was dressed in woolens and ferret skins. The rich were also distinctive in their footwear, clad in slippers inlaid with leather or lined with silk. No longer were wine and meat reserved only for festivals, and critics decried the prodigal and indecorous ways of the well-to-do. In the cooked-meat stalls in the markets, those who could afford them pushed and shoved to buy their piglets, dog cutlets, or chopped liver. Such tasty victuals were served to the wealthy on vessels fashioned with silver inlay or golden handles. Carriages transported rich families up and down the wide avenues, and they paid dearly for the privilege: keeping a horse required as much grain as a family of six could consume.

Entertainment for those who could afford it included performing animals, tiger fights, and foreign dancing girls. Some gambled, betting for high stakes at *liubo,* a board game that involved shaking bamboo sticks out of a cup. Music was fre-

Han Man with Fish. A terra-cotta sculpture of a chef or fishmonger during the Han Dynasty.

Model of a Han House. Elite families in Chang'an and other Han cities typically lived in two-story houses with carved crossbeams and rafters and enclosed courtyards. The floors were covered with embroidered cushions, wool rugs, and mats for sitting. Screens were used for privacy. Women and children were cloistered in the inner quarters.

quently played at homes, and rich families kept their own orchestras, complete with bells and drums. Such events during the Zhou dynasty were tied to formal, ritual occasions; now, Han elites called on the gods for their own earthly happiness. Funerary rites were still taken very seriously, however; the finest wood was used for the coffins of the rich, and the poor managed to have at least their coffin lids painted.

At the base of Han society was a free peasantry—farmers who owned and tilled their own land. The Han court held to an agrarian ideal: peasants were honored for their productive labors, while merchants were subjected to a range of controls, including regulations on luxury consumption, and were belittled for not engaging in physical labor. For their own reasons, Confucians and Daoists supported this hierarchy, but we will

see below that the Daoists later challenged the status quo. The Confucians, for instance, envisioned scholar-officials as working hard for the ruler to enhance a moral economy in which the profiteering of merchants would be kept to a minimum. In reality, however, the first century of Han rule perpetuated powerful elites. At the apex were the imperial clan and nobles, followed, in order, by the high-ranking officials and scholars, the great merchants and manufacturers whose wealth placed them on an equal level with nobles, and a regionally based class of local magnates. Below these elites, lesser clerks, medium and small landowners, free farmers, artisans, small merchants, poor tenant farmers, and hired laborers eked out a living. The more destitute became government slaves and relied on the state to supply their food and clothing. At the

The Wuliang Shrine. This rubbing of a stele from the Wuliang Shrine shows musicians performing on typical Han Dynasty stringed instruments.

bottom was a thin layer of convicts and private slaves, who made up less than 1 percent of the total population.

Between 100 BCE and 200 CE, scholar-officials whose Confucian learning encouraged them to seek civil service appointments emerged as the empire's most loyal and most formidable social group, the ultimate bulwark of imperial authority and legitimacy. At first, they used their political clout and cultural prestige to complement the power of landlords and large clans, but over time they increased their political and economic autonomy, gaining independent wealth as they acquired private property. In their official capacity, they linked the imperial center with local society. Their power survived the fall of the Han, and they emerged as the dominant aristocratic clans in post-Han China.

In the long run, the imperial court's struggle to limit the power of local lords and magnates failed. Indeed, any central ruler would have been hard-pressed to monitor every corner of so huge a realm; dynasts had to rely on local officials to legitimate and enforce their rule, but those local officials could rarely stand up to the powerful men they were supposed to be governing. And when central rule proved too onerous for local elites, they always had the option of rebelling. Local uprisings against the Han that began in 99 BCE forced the court to relax its measures and left landlords and local magnates as dominant powers in the empire's provinces. Below these privileged strata, increasingly disenfranchised agrarian groups turned to Daoist religious organizations to provide the organizational framework that crystallized into potent cells of dissent and revolt.

RELIGION AND OMENS Under Wu, Confucianism slowly took on religious overtones. Dong Zhongshu, Wu's chief minister, advocated a new and more powerful view of Confucius, promoting texts that turned Confucius into a man who possessed aspects of divinity. An apocryphal treatise on Confucius's *Spring and Autumn Annals* portrayed him not as a humble teacher but as an uncrowned monarch, and even as a demigod and a giver of laws.

Classical learning was not just state orthodoxy—it also informed popular religion. Although the world of the early

Han Entertainment. Han entertainment included dancing, particularly by foreign girls, and acrobatics, for which the Chinese remain famous today. Music was often played at the homes of rich families, who kept their own orchestras complete with bells and drums.

→ *How did Han leaders promote peace and stability?*

Han Musicians. Musical events became so popular, for both the entertainers (note the faces in these Han statues) and the entertained, that performances ceased being only somber ritual occasions.

Han was dominated by social elites, religion was the universal element that linked scholars and officials to the peasantry. Classical learning remained the orthodox monopoly of the Confucians at court, but many in local communities practiced forms of a remarkably dynamic popular Chinese religion.

Imperial cults, magic, and sorcery reinforced the court's interest in astronomical omens such as the appearance of a nova (a suddenly bright star), solar halos, and meteors, in addition to periodic lunar and solar eclipses. Celestial events that imperial officials could not predict, as well as earthquakes and famines, were portents that pointed to the emperor's lack of virtue, and powerful ministers exploited them to restrain and to intimidate their ruler. A cluster of calamities, prodigies, and heavenly omens was usually taken to mean that the emperor had lost the mandate of heaven. Similarly, witchcraft was taken very seriously; believed to manip-

ulate natural events and to interfere with the will of heaven, it was feared by high and low alike.

EXPANSION OF THE EMPIRE AND THE SILK ROAD

Empires cannot be maintained by shared political and cultural beliefs alone. They invariably survive by force, and the Han Chinese, like their Roman counterparts, created a powerful, even ruthless military machine that expanded the borders of the empire and created stable conditions that permitted the safe transit of goods by caravans over the Silk Road. Emperor Wu did much to transform the military forces and set them on the path of territorial conquest. Following the Qin precedent, he again made military service compulsory. Most conscripts served in their own local areas. The

Reconstruction Drawings of Composite Ritual Hall in the Suburbs of Chang'an. After taking the throne in 9 CE, Wang Mang rebuilt the Ritual Hall in the former Han palace by following the six cardinal directions (N-S, E-W, Up-Down), which enabled the building and its rooms to correspond to the tenets of popular religion and elite philosophy. The court's interest in astronomical omens and natural disasters also meant that the Ritual Hall represented the cosmological confluence of heaven and earth.

number of men under arms at any one time was stunning: some 100,000 crack troops formed the Han Imperial Guard and were stationed in the capital, and the standing army totaled more than a million. In contrast, the armies of Athens, the largest of the Greek city-states, rarely exceeded 20,000 men; the Hellenistic kingdoms that arose later were sometimes able to field double these numbers but still nowhere near as many soldiers as the Chinese. Even the Roman field armies rarely exceeded 30,000 men. The Han simply created armies on an entirely different scale.

EXPANDING BORDERS Like all large empires, the Han dynasty used military force to expand its frontiers. During the reign of Emperor Wu, between 138 and 111 BCE, power struggles among the Yue people, then living in the Yangzi delta in southeastern China, enabled the Han to absorb several kingdoms in this region. Han control thereafter extended from southeastern China to northern Vietnam. Because of similar strife in the northeast, pro-Han-dynasty Koreans could appeal for Han help against their rulers in their internal squabbles. Emperor Wu sent an expeditionary force that defeated the Korean king, and four Han commanderies were set up in northern Korea in 108 BCE. Incursions into Sichuan and the southwestern border areas were less successful, as the Han armies were hampered both by the mountainous terrain and by malaria, which was endemic to the region. Much like the steppe horsemen of later invasions, the Han infantry and cavalry moved easily from east to west. But because of their lack of resistance to semitropical "miasmas," the viral infections prevalent in more southerly latitudes wrought havoc when they ventured into those areas. Nevertheless, a commandery was established in southern Sichuan in 135 BCE, and it opened trading routes to S. E. Asia.

THE XIONGNU, THE YUEZHI, AND THE HAN DYNASTY For the Han, the most serious military threat came from the nomadic peoples living in the north, especially from the Xiongnu. The Han inherited from the Qin a symbiotic relationship with the nomads outside the defensive wall along the northern frontier. As under the Qin, mutual dependence between the Xiongnu and the Han Empire brought silk cloth and thread, bronze mirrors, and lacquerware to the nomadic chiefs, and furs, horses, and cattle to China's settled farming communities. It also took Chinese textiles to the west along the Silk Road.

At the beginning of the Han dynasty, the battles against the Xiongnu intrusion were defensive, and the Han often suffered humiliation at the nomads' hands. Under Emperor Wu, however, the Han Empire started offensive campaigns against the Xiongnu. In addition to sending military expeditions to the Mongolian steppe to push the nomadic raiders from the frontier, Wu also looked for allies on the steppe. To the west of the Xiongnu territory of central Mongolia, a Turkic nomadic people called the Yuezhi roamed on pastoral lands. The Yuezhi people had long had friendly relationships with the farming societies in China. They had supplied jade from Khotan, a Taklamakan Desert oasis, to Shang rulers (who preferred jade even to gold), as well as large, strong horses for the horse chariots and cavalry of the northern Warring States. The Yuezhi detested the Xiongnu and had frequent armed clashes with them. In 177 BCE, the Xiongnu invaded their lands; in 162 BCE, the Yuezhi were soundly defeated and their chief killed. Humiliated, the 100,000 to 200,000 Yuezhi horse-riding archers left the area; as described in Chapter 6, they eventually reached the bank of the Oxus River, on the border between present-day Afghanistan and Tajikistan.

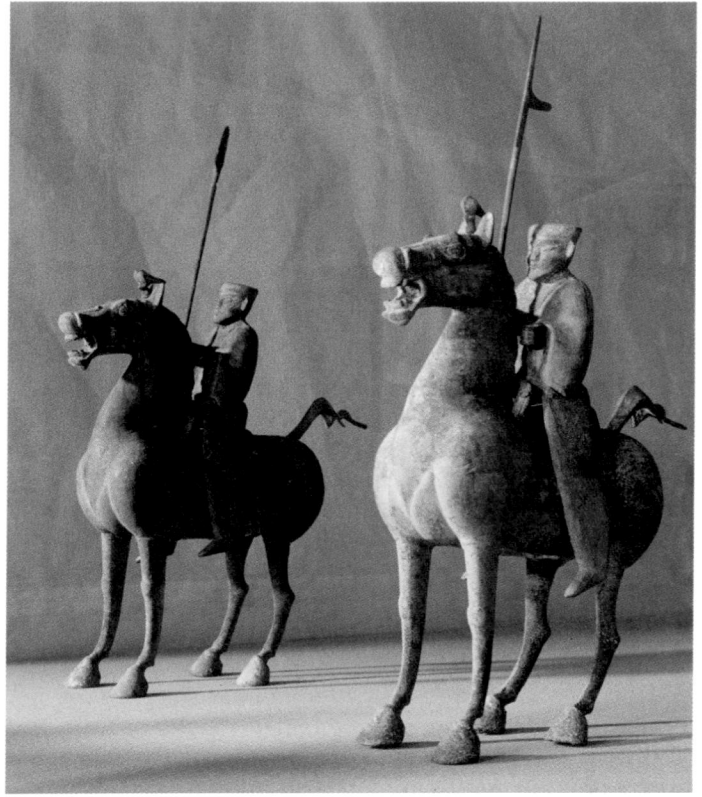

Bronze Horsemen. Two bronze horsemen holding *Chi*-halberds from the Later Han Dynasty, circa second century CE. These statues were excavated in 1969 in Gansu along the Silk Road. Note the size and strength of these Ferghana horses from Central Asia.

Between 129 and 124 BCE, the Han repelled several Xiongnu invasions. In campaigns from 123 to 119 BCE, Han forces of more than 100,000 men penetrated deep into Xiongnu territory, reaching as far as the northern Mongolian steppe. Eventually, the Han armies split the Xiongnu tribes in half. The southern tribes surrendered, but the northern Xiongnu tribes moved westward away from Han forces, toward the Mediterranean, where they were eventually to threaten the stability of the eastern flank of the Roman Empire.

THE CHINESE PEACE: TRADE, OASES, AND THE SILK ROAD The military expansion of the Han Empire resulted in the submission or retreat of the Xiongnu and other nomadic peoples and made the years from 149 to 87 BCE the most peaceful and prosperous of the entire Han epoch. China achieved a *Pax Sinica* that had many of the same features as the *Pax Romana* in the west. Long-distance trade flourished, cities increased in size, material standards of living rose, and the population grew, although not everyone benefited from the expansion of the empire and trade. As a result of their military campaigns, Emperor Wu and his successors became

monarchs enjoying tribute from vassal peoples far outside Han territories. Normally, the Han did not intervene in the domestic policy of vassal states unless they rebelled. Instead, the Chinese preferred to rely on trade and markets to induce their vassals to work within the tribute system and become prosperous satellite states within the Han political sphere of influence.

The clash of cultures between the nomadic Xiongnu and sedentary Chinese farmers frequently led to local conflict. But even more often, Chinese-outsider tributary relations in the borderlands produced benefits for both sides. Han expansion coincided with the flourishing of the Silk Road during which the Xiongnu nomads served as necessary middlemen. In the first century BCE, trade along the eastern half of the Silk Road enabled the Chinese to export silk in exchange for Central Asian horses, furs, and jade.

When the Xiongnu were no longer a threat on the northern border of the empire, Wu decided to extend his territory to reach the exotic products from further west. By 100 BCE, he had the northern defensive wall extended along the corridor between the Tianshan Mountains and the Gobi Desert. Along the wall were stationed signal beacons to send emergency messages, and it contained gates that opened periodically for trading fairs. The westernmost gate was called the Jade Gate, since jade from the Taklamakan Desert passed through it. Wu also had a series of garrison cities built at oases to protect the trade routes through the region; the farthest west of these garrisons was Dunhuang, which would later become a famous polyglot center of Buddhist culture.

Han Crossbow. The Han created huge armies to maintain and expand its borders. Between 138 and 111 BCE, Emperor Wu used his archers and cavalry to absorb kingdoms from southeastern China to northern Vietnam to Central Asia. At its height, the Han had about fifty thousand crossbowmen.

The Jade Gate Pass. From the Jade Gate Pass, the most significant pass on the Silk Road, foods, fruits, and religions of the "Western Regions" were introduced into central China during the Han Dynasty. Chinese inventions, such as paper during the Later Han and then the compass and gunpowder, traveled in the opposite direction.

To maintain a strong military force in such a remote and barren country was expensive. Wu thus initiated the practice, followed by many later Chinese rulers, of establishing military and farming settlements in the semi-desert region. Soldiers were encouraged to bring their families to settle on the frontier. As warfare in these territories was then relatively infrequent, soldiers could spend much of their time digging wells, building canals, and reclaiming wastelands. The government gave the soldiers seeds, tools, and technical support.

Soon after its military power had expanded outside the Jade Gate, the Han government set up a similar system of oases on the rim of the Taklamakan Desert. With irrigation, agriculture on the oases developed and attracted many more settlers. Traders now could find food and fodder for their animals in the oases along what was increasingly becoming the Silk Road as the Xionghu fled westward. As trade routes passing through deserts and oases took shape, they became safer and more reliable than the steppe routes, which they gradually replaced. These new desert routes would continue to flourish for another century, until the distant Han frontiers were challenged by fierce Tibetan Qiang tribes in the second and third centuries CE. Local tribes and magnates filled the power vacuum, and Chinese power and influence in Central Asia became dormant for a span of six centuries.

SOCIAL CONVULSIONS AND THE USURPER

Emperor Wu's dramatic military expansions required that Han soldiers be stationed in large garrisons stretching all the way from Central Asia to the Pacific and from Korea to Vietnam. But further conquests failed to add new wealth to the state coffers, and the huge expenditures required to maintain a standing army of over a million men exhausted the reserves of the imperial treasury. Wu raised taxes, which put a strain on the small landholders and peasants, who were the foundation of the empire. The strains continued after his death, and by the end of the first century BCE, the Chinese empire was drained financially. In this epoch, large segments of the population experienced a dramatic economic decline, as natural disasters led to crop failures. These further exacerbated the plight of poor farmers, whose taxes were based not on their crop yield but on the size of their holdings. Unable to pay their taxes, many free peasants fell into debt and were consequently forced to sell their land to large landholders; they became tenant farmers and sometimes even slaves. As local landlords rebuilt their power and their landholdings, they accumulated even more wealth, which enabled them to obtain classical educations and begin careers as government officials. As a fast-growing population confronted the shortage of land in the countryside, the social fabric of Han society finally tore. In desperation, the ever-increasing number of dispossessed peasants turned to rebel movements.

This crisis led Wang Mang (ruled 9–23 CE), who had served as a Han minister and then regent to a child emperor, to take over the throne and establish a new dynasty, as he believed that the Han had lost the mandate of heaven. After usurping power, Wang Mang attempted to enact reforms to help the poor. He tried to foster economic activity by confiscating gold from wealthy landowners and merchants and by depreciating the value of state coinage so that peasants would have more money to pay their taxes and their debts. He sought to break up large estates, placing limits on the amount of land each family could own, and even prohibited the purchase and sale of land. His goal was to redistribute excess land equitably among the people on the basis of an ancient ideal of a "well-field" land system: all families would work their own parcels of land and also share in cultivating a communal plot whose crops would be set aside as tax surplus for the state. Wang Mang imposed higher taxes on artisans, hunters, fisherman, and silk weavers in order to pay for a storehouse system that was intended to help alleviate grain shortages, and he forbade slavery. Unfortunately, his reforms did not succeed.

NATURAL DISASTER AND REBELLION

Wang Mang was unseated by a violent upheaval that united peasants and large landholders against central authority. Bad luck also played a part in his fall. Up to 5 million Chinese lived along the great northern plain south of the Yellow River—whose course, unluckily for Wang, changed greatly soon after he assumed power. In 11 CE, the river broke its dikes; rather than bending northward on the Central Plain, it now flowed due south toward the Yellow Sea. This demographic catastrophe, which plunged the entire region into famine and banditry, would be played out several more times in Chinese history. Each time it changed its course from north to south and then back again, "China's Sorrow," as the Yellow River was called, unleashed enormous flooding that caused mass death and vast migrations outside the region. Peasant impoverishment and revolt followed with chilling regularity. Researchers estimate that these floods affected some 28 million Chinese, or half of China's population. The recorded population in China declined from 58 million in 2 CE to 49 million in 140 CE, the next time we have reliable figures.

Not surprisingly, Wang Mang's reforming regime proved incapable of coping with a cataclysm of such a magnitude. Rebellious peasants, led by Daoist clerics (who ministered to peasants in their religious communities in the countryside), used the disaster as a pretext to march on Wang's capital at Chang'an. The peasants painted their foreheads red and called themselves Red Eyebrows in imitation of demon warriors, who were believed to have red eyelids. Their leaders spoke to them through inspired religious mediums. By 23 CE, they had overthrown Wang Mang, whom they considered a usurper.

Wang's enemies attributed this natural disaster to the emperor's unbridled exercise of power. They created a history of legitimate Han dynastic power that Wang Mang had illegitimately overturned, and soon Wang was cast as the model of the evil usurper. The fall of Wang Mang also brought an end to his reformist policies, as the statecraft tradition of the first half of the Han was forgotten. Instead, a conservative ethos emerged during the Later Han dynasty that favored the hereditary privileged elite, who used Wang Mang's sudden fall to justify their own social and political status and power.

THE LATER HAN DYNASTY (25–220 CE)

The Later Han dynasty restored Han rule by accepting existing social, political, and economic inequalities. After Wang Mang's fall, these problems fatally diluted the central power of the emperor and the court. As a result, the Later Han followed a hands-off economic policy that enabled large land-owners and merchants to amass great wealth and more property. Decentralizing the regime was also good for local business and long-distance trade, as international trade along the Silk Road continued to grow. Chinese silk became familiar to people as far away as the Roman Empire. In return, China received glass, jade, horses, precious stones, tortoise-shells, and fabrics.

By the second century CE, landed elites were enjoying the fruits of their success in manipulating the Later Han tax sys-tem, which granted them so many land and labor exemptions that the government never again firmly controlled its human and agricultural resources as Emperor Wu had. As the court refocused on the new capital in Luoyang, local power devolved into the hands of great aristocratic families, who concentrated even more privately owned land in their own hands and turned free peasants into tenants.

This kind of prosperity was accompanied by greater social inequity, creating a new source of turmoil. Pressure grew on tenants to pay high rents, on free peasants to pay most of the taxes, and on poor migrant workers—called by the Chinese the "floating population"—to provide laborers. As the Later Han state's political arm weakened, its ritual tasks became more formalized (a similar symbolic compensation for the loss of real power had also occurred under the Eastern Zhou dynasty). The tensions between large landholders and peasants, who had briefly been mollified by Wang Mang's reforms, erupted in a full-scale rebellion in 184 CE. Popular religious groups such as the Red Eyebrows, who had helped overthrow Wang Mang, championed new ideas among commoners and elites during the Later Han dynasty. Confucius was replaced as the exemplary figure: the new models were a mythical Yellow Emperor, who was extolled as the inventor of traditional Chinese writing and medicine, and the Daoist sage Master Laozi, who was presented as the voice of naturalness and spontaneity. Laozi was now treated as a god. Although scholars denigrated folk cults and magical practices, these beliefs persisted in rural communities among both the common people and local magnates.

At this propitious moment, Buddhist clerics arrived in northern China from Central Asia, preaching a new religion of personal enlightenment for the elite and millennial salvation for the masses. Their message was warmly welcomed by an increasingly disaffected population. The rise of Buddhism

Jade Burial Shroud. Shown here is the jade burial suit of Princess Tou Wan, late second century BCE.

in China thus parallels the rise of Christianity in Roman Empire in the Mediterranean world. Yet the most powerful challenge to the Later Han came not from the Buddhists but from Daoists. Idiosyncratic Daoist masters challenged Confucian ritual conformity, advancing their ideas in the name of a theocracy that would redeem all people. Officials who were unhappy with Wang Mang's usurpation and other political outcasts who had retreated to local areas became leaders of strong dissident groups. They eventually formed local religious movements. Under their leadership, religious groups such as the Yellow Turbans—so called because of the yellow scarves that they wrapped around their heads—emerged across the empire and championed Daoist millenarian movements.

Proclaiming the Daoist millenarian belief in a "Great Peace" in the future, the Yellow Turbans demanded fairer treatment by the Han state and, more importantly, an equal distribution of all farm lands. When agrarian conditions further deteriorated, widespread famine ensued, a catastrophe that, in the view of the Daoist rebels, demonstrated the emperor's loss of the mandate of heaven. The economy disintegrated when the people refused to pay taxes or to provide forced labor, and internal wars engulfed the Han dynasty. After the 180s CE, three competing states replaced the Han: the Wei in the northwest, the Shu in the southwest, and the Wu in the south. A unified empire did not return until three centuries later with the emergence of the Tang dynasty in 618 CE. Unlike the post-Roman world in Europe, with its multitude of small kingdoms and states, East Asia clung to the ideal of a united, powerful empire. The Chinese viewed the waxing and waning of empires as inevitable. In the words of the opening line of the fourteenth-century classical novel *Romance of the Three Kingdoms*, which depicted this post-Han period, "Long united, the empire must divide. Long divided, the empire must unite." Bigger remained better.

THE ROMAN EMPIRE

> → *Were the policies and institutions involved in integrating the Roman Empire similar to those of the Han dynasty in China?*

The other large empire of the time was found at the other end of Eurasia. There, Rome had established itself as a great power ruling 60–70 million subjects. The Roman Empire at its height encompassed lands from the highlands of what is now Scotland in the northwest to the lower reaches of the Nile River in what is today Egypt and part of Sudan in the southeast, from the borders of the Inner Eurasian steppe in what is today Ukraine and the Caucasus in the northeast to the Atlantic shores of North Africa in what is today Morocco

in the southwest. (See Map 7-3.) It was comparable in size and scale to Han dynasty China.

Centered on the Mediterranean, the world's largest inland sea, the Roman Empire dominated lands around the sea;

→ *Were the policies and institutions involved in integrating the Roman Empire similar to those of the Han dynasty in China?*

MAP 7-3   ROMAN EXPANSION TO 120 CE
Roman expansion continued for several centuries before reaching its peak in the second century CE. What factors contributed to Rome's conquest of the Mediterranean world? Why did Romans not expand their empire further into eastern Europe or Southwest Asia? What were the ecological limits to Rome's expansion?

China, in contrast, dominated an enormous continental landmass. But like Han China, the Romans had relied on an unprecedented exercise of violence to acquire command over their world. Through their almost unceasing wars waged against their neighbors, by the first century CE the Romans were able to forge an unparalleled number of ethnic groups and minor states into a single large political state. This achievement was so unusual and so striking that the Jewish historian and general Josephus, writing in the 90s CE, saw the empire as the unchallengeable work of God on earth. We can easily see how the Latin word that the Romans used to designate their power of command over their subjects—*imperium*—became the source for the English words *empire* and *imperialism*.

FOUNDATIONS OF THE ROMAN EMPIRE

The emergence of the Romans as a world-dominating power was a surprise. Although the Romans might have looked to the Persians or to Alexander the Great to provide imperial models, they did not. Unlike the Han, in their own world in the western Mediterranean, the Romans had no great imperial ancestors on whose shoulders they could stand. Down to the 350s BCE, the Romans were just one of a number of Latin-speaking communities in Latium, a small region south of the Tiber River in the center of the Italian peninsula. Not much was exceptional about them. Although Rome was already one of the largest urban centers on the Italian peninsula, it was still only a city-state, and one that had to ally itself with about thirty other Latin-speaking towns for the purposes of self-defense. Beginning in the middle of the fourth century BCE, however, Rome suddenly began an extraordinary phase of military and territorial expansion; by 265 BCE, it had taken control of most of the Italian peninsula. At least two factors contributed to this achievement. One, a migration of foreign peoples, had little to do directly with the Romans. The other consisted of the military and political innovations created by the Romans themselves.

POPULATION MOVEMENTS Between 450 and 250 BCE, great movements of peoples in northern and central Europe brought large numbers of Celts from the north to settle in lands in the Mediterranean. They convulsed the northern face of the Mediterranean, staging armed forays into lands from what is now Spain in the west to present-day Turkey in the east.

One of these large movements in the late fifth and early fourth century BCE involved dozens of different Gallic peoples in a series of violent incursions into northern Italy that ultimately—around 390 BCE—led to the seizure of the city of Rome. The important result for the Romans was not the capture of their own city, which was temporary and brief (the Gauls were paid to go away), but the permanent destruction and dislocation that the invading Gauls inflicted on the city-

states of the Etruscans, who until that time were the dominant people in the Italian peninsula. The Etruscans did survive and, with great effort, finally succeeded in driving the invading Gauls north back into the Po Valley. But the Etruscan cities never recovered their ability to dominate other peoples in Italy, including the Romans. This great population movement, over which the Romans had no control, removed one of the most formidable roadblocks to their growth and expansion in Italy.

MILITARY INSTITUTIONS AND CONQUESTS To grasp the full nature of the unparalleled expansion of Rome, we must also understand the military and political institutions developed by the Romans themselves. In brief, the Romans were more successful and more efficient in killing other humans than were any other people in their part of the world. They created their unassailable military power by organizing the communities that they conquered in Italy into a system that provided huge and unprecedented reservoirs of manpower for their army. This development began decisively in the years between 340 and 335 BCE, when the Romans faced a concerted attack by their fellow Latin city-states. By then, the Latins had come to see Rome not as a brotherly ally in a system of mutual defense but as a growing threat to their own independence. After overcoming the nearby Latins, the Romans went on to defeat one community after another in Italy. The main demand that the Romans made of their defeated enemies was to provide men for the Roman army every year. The result was a snowball-like accumulation of military manpower: with each new community that the Romans conquered on the Italian peninsula, they automatically increased the size of their army.

By 265 BCE, Rome controlled the Italian peninsula. It next turned outward, entering into a series of three wars with the Carthaginians, the major power located in the region of present-day Tunisia. The First Punic War (264–241 BCE) was a prolonged naval battle over the island of Sicily. With their victory, the Romans acquired a dominant position in the western Mediterranean. But the Second Punic War, beginning in 218 BCE, revealed the real strength and might of Roman arms. The great Carthaginian general Hannibal had the insight that if the Carthaginians were to have any hope of victory, the Italian peninsula itself would have to be attacked. But the new Roman military system made a Roman victory almost certain. Whereas the resources of Carthage were those of a large city-state, like classical Athens, the resources of Rome had taken on a qualitatively different character. Like a modern nation-state, Rome could draft military

> *Beginning in the middle of the fourth century BCE, Rome suddenly began an extraordinary phase of military and territorial expansion; by 265 BCE, it had taken control of most of the Italian peninsula.*

THE ROMAN EMPIRE | **301**

→ *Were the policies and institutions involved in integrating the Roman Empire similar to those of the Han dynasty in China?*

manpower from a huge population. Hannibal moved his foot soldiers and his cavalry from southern Spain, which Carthage had conquered, toward the Italian peninsula. After the heroic feat of crossing the Pyrenees and the Alps mountain ranges with his war elephants, Hannibal entered Italy in the spring of 217 BCE with a force of about 20,000 men. Because of the innovative system of recruiting that Rome had developed in Italy, it could draw on reserves of more than three-quarters of a million men for its armed confrontation with Hannibal. With those numbers, Roman commanders could afford to lose battles—which they proceeded to do, suffering casualties of about 60,000 to 80,000 dead in three great encounters with the able Carthaginian general—and still win the war. They finally did so in 201 BCE. In the end, not even a strategic and tactical genius like Hannibal could prevail against them.

In addition to enjoying an overwhelming advantage in manpower, the Romans cultivated an unusual war ethos among their male citizens. Roman adult males were driven by a heightened sense of honor to push themselves into battle again and again, and never to accept defeat. They were educated to imitate the example of such soldiers as Marcus Sergius. Wounded twenty-three times in battle, Sergius was crippled in both hands and both feet. In the war with Hannibal, he lost one hand but continued to serve in the military, using a false right hand made out of iron. He was twice taken prisoner by Hannibal, each time managing to escape despite being kept in chains. Going into action four times with his artificial hand tied to the stump of his arm, Sergius helped to rescue major Roman cities from siege by the Carthaginians—

and twice the horse that he was riding was cut out from under him. Such men set a high standard of commitment to war. What also controlled and formed Roman soldiers was an unusual regime of training and discipline, which held that minor infractions of duty were punishable by death (in Greek armies, misconduct merely drew fines). Disobedience by a whole unit led to a savage mass execution called decimation, in which every tenth man was arbitrarily selected and killed. For men like Sergius, the annual campaign in the spring of every year, in the month dedicated to Mars (still called March today), the Roman god of war had an almost biological rhythm to it.

Displaying an unrelenting compulsion to war, the Romans continued to draft, train, and put into the field extraordinary numbers of men. The percentage of young men that they pressed into army service in western Afro-Eurasia was not matched until the later modern mass drafts of Napoleon in France in nineteenth-century Europe. In the late Republic, in the centuries after 220 BCE, about 10 percent of the whole adult male population (about one-fifth of all adult male citizens) was drafted into service. Soldiers, conscripted at age seventeen or eighteen, could expect to serve for periods of up to ten years at a time. Since such large numbers of young men were devoted to war for such long spans, the ethos of battle became deeply embedded in the ideals of every generation. It was this successful war machine that was unleashed on the kingdoms of the eastern Mediterranean after 200 BCE—with devastating results. In one year, 146 BCE, Romans achieved the final extermination of what was left of the city of Carthage in the west and the parallel obliteration of the great Greek city-state of Corinth in the east: their monopoly

War Elephants. There are no contemporary illustrations of the elephants that Hannibal brought when he invaded Italy in 217 BCE. Hannibal was influenced by the Hellenistic armies in the east who had borrowed the idea of war elephants, and the elephants themselves, from Indian rulers. This painting, by an artist from the school of the Renaissance painter Raphael, highlights the terrifying aspect of the elephants and reduces the human warriors to bit players. In fact, the elephants were not decisive in the winning of any major battle in Italy in the Second Roman-Carthaginian War. Hannibal won them all by superior generalship.

EMPIRES, ALLIES, AND FRONTIERS

Both the Han and the Roman empires faced threats on their frontiers, and both relied on allies as much as on their own military prowess to counter such threats. Keeping good relations with frontier allies was essential to the statecraft of empires. It could also yield important intelligence for rulers in capitals.

Consider first the ways in which the Han dealt with their enemies, the Xiongnu. Emperor Wu decided to send a special envoy to the Yuezhi, whom he thought would be willing to ally with him against the Xiongnu. His emissary was Zhang Qian, who had volunteered to undertake the journey into the unknown and dangerous steppe. In 139 BCE, Zhang set out with a group of 100 people; one was a former slave from the steppe, Ganfu, who proved invaluable, guiding the travelers and using his bow to kill wild animals when they ran out of food. Aware of the envoy's purpose, the Xiongnu chief detained the group when they tried to pass through his territory. The Xiongnu kept Zhang Qian for ten years, during which time he married a Xiongnu woman and had children. Zhang learned much of steppe life and geography, but he did not forget his mission; together with Ganfu, he eventually managed to escape. At last, they reached the Yuezhi camp on the northern bank of the Oxus River.

Unfortunately, Zhang Qian did not succeed in enlisting the support of the Yuezhi. Their surviving leaders had little inclination to return to the steppe to again battle the fierce Xiongnu, especially as they could see before them the fertile Bactrian plain dotted with Hellenistic cities (see Chapter 6). Zhang Qian accompanied the Yuezhi court in crossing the Oxus and touring the land of Bactria. After consuming a year in futile negotiations with the Yuezhi leaders, Zhang set out for home, bearing much information about the cultures and products of Bactria and regions beyond, including India and Persia. On his way back, he was again captured by the Xiongnu. One year later, the Xiongnu chief died, and as the camp was thrown into chaos, Zhang was able to slip away. He finally reached Chang'an, the Han capital, together with his family and Ganfu, thirteen years after beginning his expedition. Although he had failed in his diplomatic mission, Zhang had collected invaluable information for Wudi about the frontier areas in central Asia, and the emperor was pleased by his report, which told of all the wonders he had seen and heard in his journey to the Western Region.

The Romans also had to deal with their frontiers; to the north, they contended with "barbarians," and to the east, they ran up against the powerful kingdoms of the Parthians and the Sasanians (discussed below). But the Romans did have occasional contacts with kingdoms far to the east of the empire. For example, in the reign of the first emperor, Augustus (ruled 27 BCE–14 CE), an embassy came from Poros, a king in India. In a letter carried by his ambassadors, Poros described himself as the king over 600 other kings, and he offered any help that the emperor Augustus might want of him. With the letter, according to Strabo, came gifts carried by eight slaves, naked except for their scented loincloths: a "freak," a number of large snakes, a huge turtle, and a partridge larger than a vulture.

Although embassies of this sort did bring information from far afield, Rome knew little of communities outside the empire to the east except for the peoples and provinces of the Parthian and Sasanian empires, which were closest to its frontiers. And most of this knowledge was very local in nature, gained not through formal channels but in contacts between the two states over specific military or territorial problems or from merchants and other travelers passing between the two regions. Diplomacy did exist—emperors from Nero (ruled 59–68 CE) to Justinian (ruled 527–565 CE) intervened to manage affairs within the kingdom of Armenia—but the Roman empire had nothing like a modern diplomatic service and certainly had no centralized bureaucratic office to collect and manage intelligence reports.

Still, that diplomacy of some kind did exist raises the question of how much contact the Romans and Han had via their intermediaries. The evidence is scant. It is reported by the Roman historian Florus that once an ambassador of the Seres (i.e., the Han Chinese) made it all the way to Rome in the reign of Augustus. More important than the practice of statecraft were exchanges along the Silk Road that regularly brought news, rumors, and impressions of distant empires. The Chinese were the source of the single most expensive item in the Roman Empire: the greatly desired and highly valued commodity silk. But in Roman eyes, the Chinese were still very remote, unknown, and therefore barbaric, as Pliny the Elder wrote: "Though mild in character, the Chinese still resemble wild animals in that they shun the company of the rest of humankind, and wait for trade to come to them." Although connected, the two empires that so dominated their own worlds were still worlds apart.

of power over the whole of the Mediterranean basin was now unchallenged.

During the last centuries BCE, the prodigious war capabilities of the Romans both overwhelmed the organized and highly structured city-states of the Mediterranean and systematically pulverized the warrior-based societies along the periphery of the empire, such as those in Iberia and Gaul. Roman military forces were led by men who knew they could win not just glory and territory for the state but also enormous personal rewards. They were talented men driven by burning ambition, from Scipio Africanus (d. 183 BCE) in the 200s BCE, the conqueror of Carthage—a man who claimed that he personally communicated with the gods—to Julius Caesar, the great general of the 50s BCE. A man of prodigious abilities, the greatest orator of his age, and a writer of boundless persuasion, Julius Caesar (100–44 BCE) allegedly was able to dictate seven letters simultaneously to his secretaries while attending to other duties. He was also a mass killer who kept an exact body count: he knew that he had killed precisely 1,192,000 men in his wars. And that number did not include his fellow citizens, whose murders during civil war he refused to acknowledge or add to the total. The eight-year-long cycle of his wars in Gaul—that is, modern-day France and the Rhine valley—between 58 and 50 BCE was one of the most murderous of his expeditions. By Caesar's own estimation, his army killed more than 1 million Gauls and enslaved another million. War on this scale had never been witnessed in the Western world; it had no equal anywhere, except in China.

POLITICAL INSTITUTIONS AND INTERNAL CONFLICT

The conquest of the Mediterranean placed new and unprecedented power and wealth into the hands of a few men in the Roman social elite. The rush of battlefield successes, one following another, had kept Romans and their Italian allies constantly preoccupied with the demands of army service overseas. Once this process of territorial expansion slowed, social and political problems that had been lying dormant back home in the Italian peninsula began to resurface. Following the traditional date of its foundation in 509 BCE, the Romans had lived in a state that they called the "public thing" or *Res publica* (i.e., republic), in which policy and rules of behavior were determined by the Senate—a body of permanent members, 300 to 600 of Rome's most powerful and wealthy citizens—and by popular assemblies of the citizens. The Republic was to remain the only form of Roman government for the next five centuries. Every year the citizens voted to elect the officials of state, principally two consuls who held power for a year and commanded the armies. In addition, the people annually elected ten men who, as tribunes of the plebs (literally, "the common people"), had the special task of protecting their interests against those of the rich and the powerful. In severe political crises, the Romans sometimes chose one man to hold absolute power over the state, a man whose words, or *dicta,* were law—so he was called a *dictator.* But

Julius Caesar. This full-size statue represents Caesar as a high-ranking Roman army commander and conveys some of the power and influence that a charismatic military and political leader like Caesar had over both soldiers and citizen voters. Caesar belonged to a generation of Roman politicians who were immensely attentive to their public images.

ordinarily he could hold those powers for no longer than six months. The problems with using these institutions, originally devised for a city-state, to rule a Mediterranean-sized empire became glaringly apparent by the second century BCE.

Rome's power elite seized the influx of wealth that poured into Italy from Rome's Mediterranean conquests to acquire huge tracts of land in Italy and Sicily, and then imported enormous numbers of slaves from lands all around the Mediterranean to work them. This process drove the poorer free citizen farmers, the backbone of the army, off their lands and into the cities. The result was a severe agrarian and recruiting crisis. In 133 and 123–21 BCE, two tribunes, the brothers Tiberius and Gaius Gracchus, attempted to institute land reforms that would guarantee to all of Rome's poor citizens a basic amount of land that would qualify them for army service. Both men were assassinated by their political

Roman Farmers and Soldiers. In the late Republic most Roman soldiers came from rural Italy, where small farms were being absorbed into the land holdings of the wealthy and powerful. In the empire, soldiers were recruited from rural provincial regions. They sometimes worked small fields of their own and sometimes worked the lands of the wealthy—like the domain in the Roman province of Africa (in modern-day Tunisia) that is depicted in this mosaic.

enemies. From this point onward, poor Roman citizens increasingly looked not to the established institutions of the state but rather to army commanders, to whom they gave their loyalty and support, to provide them with land and a decent income. These generals thus became increasingly powerful in their own right and began to compete directly with each other, ignoring the Senate and the traditional rules of politics. As they sought control of the state and their supporters lined up on opposite sides, a long series of civil wars began in 90 BCE: the tremendous resources built up during the conquest of the Mediterranean were now turned inward by the Romans on themselves. These civil wars were of a scale and ferocity that threatened to tear the empire to pieces from the inside.

EMPERORS, AUTHORITARIAN RULE, AND ADMINISTRATION

It is perhaps strange that the most violent and warlike of all the ancient Mediterranean states was responsible for creating the most pervasive and long-lasting peace of its own time—often called the *Pax Romana* (Roman Peace). Worn out by half a century of savage civil wars, by the 30s BCE the Romans, including their warlike governing elite, were ready for basic changes in their fundamental values. The Romans were now prepared to embrace the virtues of peace.

But political stability came with its own price: authoritarian one-man rule. Peace depended on the power of one man

who possessed enough authority to enforce an orderly competition among Roman aristocrats. Ultimately, Julius Caesar's adopted son, Octavian (63 BCE–14 CE), would reunite the fractured empire by the year 30 BCE and emerge as the new undisputed master of the whole Roman world. Octavian concentrated most of the state's surplus wealth, the most important official titles, and positions of power in his own hands. To signal the transition to a new political order in which he and he alone would control the army, the provinces, and the political processes in Rome, in 27 BCE he assumed a new name, Augustus (the Revered One). He also assumed a series of titles: *imperator,* or "commander in chief" (compare the English word *emperor*), *princeps* or "first man" (whence the English *prince*), and *caesar* (pronounced "kai-sar" in Latin and the source of the words *tsar* in Russian and *kaiser* in German). Augustus had become the first of dozens of men who, over the next five centuries, were to rule the Roman empire as emperors.

Rome's subjects always tended to see and to cultivate these emperors as heroic or semi-divine beings in life, and to think of the good ones among them as becoming gods on their death. This propensity to deify good emperors prompted the Emperor Vespasian's famous deathbed joke: "Dear me, I think I'm turning into a god!" Yet emperors were always careful to present themselves as civil rulers whose power ultimately depended on the consent of Roman citizens and the power of the army. They deliberately contrasted themselves with the image of the "king," or absolute tyrannical ruler, whom the Romans for centuries had been taught to detest. The powers possessed by emperors were nevertheless immense. Moreover, quite a few of them deployed those powers arbitrarily and whimsically, thereby exciting a profound fear of emperors in general. One such emperor was Caligula (ruled 37–41 CE), who presented himself as a living god on earth, engaged in casual incest with his sister, and kept books filled with the names of persons whom he wanted to kill. His violent behavior was so erratic that he was thought to suffer from serious mental disorders; those who feared him called him a living monster.

Being a Roman emperor was a delicate high-wire act that required finesse and talent, and few succeeded at it. Of the twenty-two emperors who held power in the most stable period of Roman history—between the first Roman emperor, Augustus, and the beginning of the third century—fifteen met their end by murder or suicide, a sign of their failure at this difficult task. As powerful as he might be, no individual emperor could alone govern an empire of such great size and population, encompassing a multitude of different languages and cultures. He needed institutions and competent people to help him. In terms of sheer power, the most important institution was the army. The emperors, beginning with Augustus, systematically transformed the army into a full-time professional force. Men now entered the imperial army not as citizen volunteers for a limited (albeit lengthy) span but rather as paid experts who signed up for life and swore loyalty to the emperor and his family. And it was part of the emperor's image to present himself as a victorious battlefield commander, inflicting defeat on the "barbarian" peoples who threatened the frontiers of the empire. Such a warrior emperor, like Trajan, was a "good" emperor.

For most emperors for most of their time, however, governance was a long daily chore of listening to complaints, answering petitions, deciding court cases, and hearing reports from civil administrators and military commanders. By the second century CE, the empire was divided into more than forty provinces or administrative units; as in Han China, each was headed by a governor personally appointed or approved by the emperor. In turn, these governors depended on lower-ranking officials to help them. Compared with the Chinese imperial state, however, with its ranks of senior and junior officials, the Roman empire of this period was relatively underadministered by its central government. The emperor and his provincial governors had to depend very much on local help, sometimes aided by elite slaves and freedmen (ex-slaves) who served as government bureaucrats. With these few full-time assistants and with an entourage of amateur friends and acquaintances, the governor would be expected to guarantee peace and collect taxes for his province. But for many essential tasks, especially the collection of imperial taxes, even these helpers were not sufficient: the state had to rely on private companies to perform these necessary governmental functions, setting up a constant tension between the profit motives of the publicans—the men in the companies that took up government contracts—and expectations of fair and just government among the empire's subjects.

TOWN AND CITY LIFE

Above all, the emperor had to count on the local elites of the empire to see him as a presence that guaranteed the stability of their world and their personal well-being. Because of the unusual concentration of wealth made possible by imperial unity, core areas of the empire—central Italy, southern Spain,

Symbols of Roman Power. Roman power was conveyed to people as much by symbols as by actual words. In this piece of sculpture from Santo Omobono in Rome dating to the third century BCE, we see symbols of imperial power. The winged figures to the left and right of the military shield represent the idea of Victory; the eagle on the shield, holding bundles of lightning bolts in its claws, represents brute power; and the garland around the top of the shield represents the wealth and rewards of empire. These powerful images have been copied by many modern states in the West.

A Roman Municipal Charter. This bronze tablet inscribed in Latin is part of a group of six bronze tablets discovered in 1981 at the Roman town of Irni, near modern Molino del Postero, in southern Spain. Charters like this one, set up for public display in the forum or central open area of the town, displayed regulations for the conduct of public life in a Roman town, from rules governing family inheritance and property transfers to the election of town officials and definitions of their powers and duties. For some of these rules, see the Primary Source box on the facing page.

northern Africa, and the western parts of what is today Turkey—had surprising densities of urban settlements. Perhaps up to one in every twenty persons in these regions lived in a town. To the extent that these towns imitated Roman forms of government, they provided the backbone of local administration for the empire. This world of municipalities was to be one of the permanent legacies left by Roman govern-

A Roman Town. Roman towns featured many of the standard elements of modern towns and cities. Streets and avenues crossed at right angles; streets were paved; sidewalks ran between streets and houses. The houses were often several stories high and had wide windows and open balconies. All these elements can be seen in this street from Herculaneum, nicely preserved by the pyroclastic flow that ran down the slopes of nearby Mount Vesuvius when its volcano erupted in August of 79 BE, burying the town and its inhabitants.

ment to the Western world. Some of our best records of how these towns were run come from Spain, later to become one of the great colonial powers that exported Roman forms of municipal life to the Americas.

Some of the best physical records of such towns are offered by Pompeii and Herculaneum in southern Italy, which were almost perfectly preserved by the ash and debris that buried them in the explosion of a nearby volcano, Mount Vesuvius, in August 79 CE. Their excavation by archaeologists has provided us with a great deal of information. Towns would often be walled, and inside those surrounding walls, streets and avenues ran at regular right angles. A large, open-air, rectangular area called the *forum* dominated the center of the town. Around it were arranged the town's main public buildings: the markets, the main temples of the principal gods and goddesses, and the building that housed the city administrators. Residential areas featured regular blocks of houses, usually tiled with bright red roof tiles, closely packed together and fronting directly on the streets. Larger towns like Ostia, the port city of Rome, contained large apartment blocks that were not much different from the four- and five-story buildings in any modern city. In the smaller towns, sanitary and alimentary conditions were usually reasonably good. Human skeletons discovered at Herculaneum in the 1970s revealed people in good health, with much better teeth than many people have today—a difference explained largely by the lack of sugar in their diet.

The great imperial metropolis of Rome was another matter. With a population of well over a million inhabitants, it was an almost grotesque exaggeration of everything good and bad in Roman city life. The only other urban centers of com-

MUNICIPAL CHARTER OF A ROMAN TOWN

Towns in the Roman Empire gradually came to be governed according to standard sets of rules and regulations that were developed during the Roman conquest of Italy. These uniform sets of laws were sometimes imposed on and sometimes voluntarily adopted by cities and towns in the provinces of the empire, and determined how they were to run their affairs. One of the most detailed copies of these town regulations was discovered in 1981, in southern Spain at Molino del Postero (a place called Irni in Roman times). The rules on administering the town, publicized by the Roman governor of Spain in 81 CE, were incised on ten plates of bronze that were publicly displayed in the town's forum. Only six of the original ten tablets have been recovered, but they reveal how the lives of people in the municipality of Irni were regulated. By following these rules, the indigenous people of a Spanish community learned how to behave like Romans.

[19] ON AEDILES: The aediles [the two town business managers] . . . are to have the right and power of managing the grain supply, the sacred buildings, the sacred and holy places, the town and its roads and neighborhoods, the drains and sewers, the baths, the marketplace, and of checking weights and measures; and also of setting a night watch if the need arises.

[20] CONCERNING THE RIGHT AND POWER OF QUAESTORS: The quaestors [the two town financial officers] . . . are to have the right and power of collecting, spending, storing, administering, and managing the common funds of the municipality at the discretion of the *duumviri* [the two town mayors]. And they are allowed to have the public slaves belonging to the municipality to help them.

[21] HOW ROMAN CITIZENSHIP IS ACQUIRED IN THE MUNICIPALITY: When those who are senators, decurions [town councillors], or conscripted town councillors who have been or are chosen as town magistrates according to the terms of this law, have completed their term of office, they are to become Roman citizens, along with their parents and wives and any children who have been born out of legal marriages and who are in the power of their parents, and likewise grandsons and granddaughters born to a son. . . .

[28] CONCERNING THE FREEING OF SLAVES BEFORE THE MAYORS: If any citizen of the municipality of Flavian Irni . . . in the presence of a *duumvir* [mayor] of that municipality in charge of the administration of justice sets free his male or female slave from slavery into freedom or orders him or her to be free . . . then any male slave who has been manumitted or ordered to be free in this way is to be free, any female slave who has been manumitted or ordered to be free in this way is also to be free. . . . Someone who is under twenty years of age may manumit his or her slave only if the number of town councillors necessary for decrees passed under this law to be valid decides that the grounds for said manumission are proper.

→ *What are some of the characteristics of the typical Roman town or municipality?*

→ *What different types of persons are assumed to be part of the normal social structure?*

→ *In what ways did inhabitants of towns such as Irni become Roman citizens?*

→ *Why would making small towns uniform in design and function be important to the Roman Empire?*

SOURCE: J. González, "The *Lex Irnitana*: A New Copy of the Flavian Municipal Law," *The Journal of Roman Studies* 76 (1986): 147–243; translated by Brent Shaw.

parable size at the time were Chang'an and Luoyang, the Han capitals, each with a population of between 300,000 and 500,000. Rome's inhabitants were privileged, because there the power of the emperor and the wealth of the empire assured them of a basic food supply. Thirteen huge and vastly expensive aqueducts provided the city with a constant and dependable supply of water, sometimes brought from very great distances. A basic amount of wheat (and, later, olive oil and pork) was given regularly to many of its adult citizens—about a quarter of a million of them at the height of these

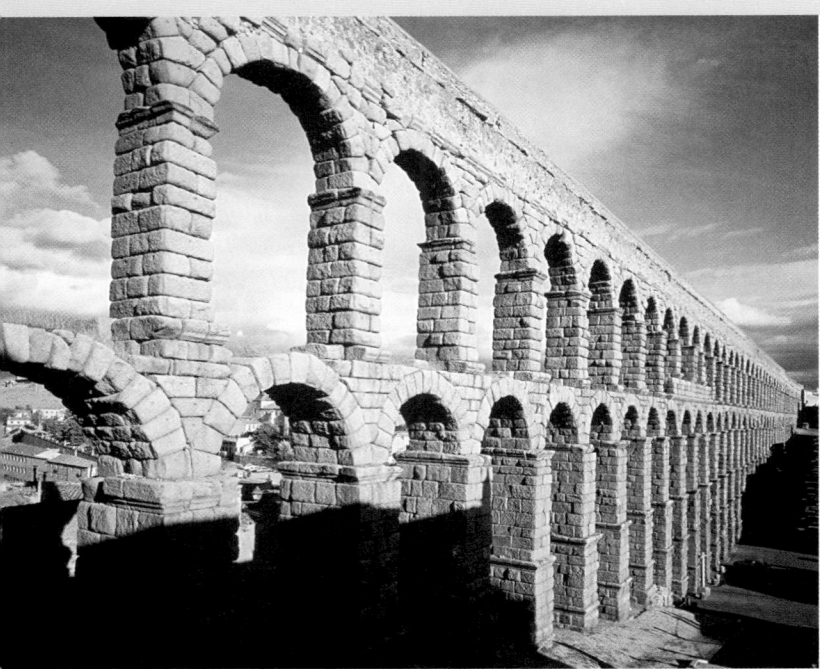

Aqueduct. The Romans built aqueducts to transport to Rome the huge amounts of water needed to sustain the city's population of over a million. The idea soon spread to the provinces, where these expensive structures were built to bring water to Roman-style cities developing in the peripheral regions of Roman rule. This aqueduct at Segovia in modern Spain is one of the best preserved.

free distributions. But living conditions were often appalling, with large numbers of people jammed into ramshackle high-rise apartments that threatened to collapse on their renters or go up in flames. And Romans constantly complained of rampant crime and violence. Worse than all of these problems, however, was the city's terrible lack of sanitary conditions—despite the sewage and drainage works that were wonders of their time. Like most premodern cities in early-modern Europe, Rome was disease-ridden; its inhabitants died from infection at a fearsome rate—malarial infections were particularly bad—and so the city required a constant input of a large number of immigrants every year just to maintain its population.

MASS ENTERTAINMENT

Every self-respecting Roman town had at least two major entertainment venues. One of these was an adoption from Hellenistic culture—a theater devoted to staging plays, dances, and other kinds of popular entertainments. The other was a Roman innovation that combined two horseshoe-shaped theaters in the form of a more elaborate structure called an amphitheater—literally, a "surround theater." A much larger seating capacity than in a regular theater surrounded the oval performance area at its center. The emperors Vespasian and

Titus completed the Flavian Amphitheater in Rome and dedicated it in 80 CE. It is the vast structure that today is known as the Colosseum, after the colossal statue of the emperor Nero that formerly stood beside it. It was a state-of-the-art entertainment facility whose floor area, the arena, could be used to put on elaborate hunts of exotic wild animals, such as giraffes and elephants. The arena area could also be flooded to stage naval battles in which hostile fleets attacked each other, to the delight of the audience, or it could provide a venue for a Roman invention, gladiatorial games: expensive public entertainments in which heavily armed and well-trained men—most of them slaves and prisoners of war, but sometimes even free men who volunteered—fought each other, wounding or killing for the enjoyment of the huge crowds of appreciative spectators. People from the West tend to think of these structures for public entertainment as ordinary and normal. Seen from a contemporary Chinese perspective, however, they look strange and unusual. Among the Han, local elites and the imperial family created gigantic palace complexes across the empire, complete with hunting parks to impress and to amuse themselves, not the general

North African Amphitheater. After the original Colosseum was built in Rome under the Flavian emperors in the 70s CE, the idea that an important Roman town anywhere in the empire must have an amphitheater took hold. This huge amphitheater is in the remains of the Roman city of Thysdrus in North Africa (the town of el-Jem in modern-day Tunisia). The wealth of the Africans under the empire enabled them to build colossal entertainment venues that competed with the one at Rome in scale and grandeur.

Roman Gladiators. In this brilliant mosaic from Rome, we see two gladiators at the end of a full combat in which Astacius has killed Astivus. The Greek letter theta, or "th" (the circle with crossbar through it), beside the names of Astivus and Rodan indicates that these men are dead—*thanatos* being the Greek word for "death."

public. In contrast, the public entertainment facilities of a Roman town were there precisely because of the distinctive cultural and political developments that stressed the importance of the citizen public in town life.

SOCIAL AND GENDER RELATIONS

Political forums and game venues were just two key constituent elements of a Roman community. Even more significant were the personal relations that linked the rich and powerful with the mass of average citizens in these towns. Men and women of wealth and high social status acted as "patrons," protecting dependents or "clients" of a lower class. From the emperor at the top to the local municipal man at the bottom, these popular relationships were reinforced by generous distributions of food and entertainments made by wealthy men to their people. The bonds that linked these two groups in each city were formalized in legal definitions of the responsibilities of patrons to clients; at the same time, the informal social code raised expectations that the wealthy would engage in do-gooding as public benefactors. For example, a senator, Pliny the Younger, constructed for his hometown of Comum a public library and a bathhouse, and supplied the money needed to furnish and run them both; supported a teacher of Latin; and established a fund to support the sons and daughters of former slaves. The emperors at the very top were no different. Augustus documented the scale of his gifts to the Roman people in his autobiography, gifts that exceeded hundreds of millions of sesterces in expenditures made out of his own pocket. A later emperor, Trajan (ruled 98–117 CE), under whose rule the empire reached its greatest extent, was responsible for establishing a social scheme for feeding poor Roman citizen children in Italy—a benefaction that he advertised on coins and in pictures on dramatic arches in Beneventum and other towns.

But the essence of Roman civil society was less the informal system of patronage than the presence of formal relationships governed by Rome's system of laws and courts. Disputes were brought to the public courts, and decisions were made by judges and sometimes by large juries. By the last century BCE, the Roman state's complex legal system featured not only a rich body of written law but also institutions for settling legal disputes and a growing number of highly educated men who specialized in the interpretation of the law. The apparatus of Roman law eventually appeared in every town and city of the empire, creating a deeply entrenched civil culture that affected the lives of most ordinary subjects. It is no surprise that this legal infrastructure of empire persisted long after the empire's bigger political and military institutions had disappeared.

Municipal charters and the civil laws—as well as secular philosophers and, later, Christian writers—placed the family at the very foundation of the Roman social order. In its purest ideal, the authoritarian *paterfamilias* (father of the family) headed the family. Legally speaking, he had near total power

Primary Source

BIRTHDAY INVITATION OF CLAUDIA SEVERA

The ability to write in Latin became widespread under the Roman Empire; even its distant frontier areas could boast some level of basic literacy. The discovery at the Roman army base at Vindolanda, in northern England, of a large cache of documents written on thin sheets of wood has revealed the normal use of Latin writing for a very wide range of day-to-day activities in the last decades of the first century CE. Roman women married to officers on the base were as skilled in writing as the men. One of these elite women, Claudia Severa, sent a letter to a good friend of hers (whom she addresses affectionately as her "sister"), inviting the woman to her birthday party. The elegant handwriting found on several of these documents is almost certainly that of Claudia Severa herself. The second letter is a reply by her friend, Sulpicia Lepidina.

Claudia Severa to her Sulpicia Lepidina. Greeting.

My sister, I am sending an invitation to you to attend my birthday festivities on the third day before the Ides of September [September 11 in our calendar]—just to make sure that you come to visit us. Your presence will make the day all the more enjoyable for me. Please convey my greetings to your Cerialis [i.e., Lepidina's husband]. My Aelius and our little son send him their warmest greetings.

I await your arrival, my sister.

I bid you goodbye, my sister, my dearest soul. Be well. [Address on the outside:] To Sulpicia Lepidina, wife of Cerialis, from Severa.

[Sulpicia Lepidina to Claudia Severa] Greeting.

Just as I had told you, my sister, and had promised that I would ask your Brocchus [i.e., Claudia Severa's husband, Aelius Brocchus] for permission to come to visit you, he replied to me that I was, of course, always most welcome to come. . . . [I shall try] to come to you by whatever way I can, for there are certain things that we must do . . . on which matter you will receive a letter from me so that you will know what I am going to do. . . .

Farewell, my sister, my dearest and most-desired soul . . .

→ *What does the very existence of these letters tell us about Roman women?*

→ *What does the writing of letters in Latin at this far edge of the empire at this time tell us about Roman culture?*

→ *Does the ordinariness of the letters—a birthday invitation and its reply—tell us anything about the extent and nature of written communications in the Roman world?*

SOURCE: Alan K. Bowman and J. David Thomas, with contributions by J. N. Adams, *The Vindolanda Writing-Tablets (Tabulae Vindolandenses II)* (London: British Museum Press, 1994), nos. 291 and 292, pp. 256–62. Translated by Brent Shaw.

over his dependents, including his wife, children, grandchildren, and the slaves whom he owned. Imperial society heightened the importance of the basic family unit of mother, father, and children in the urban centers, whose growth it fostered. As in Han dynasty China, the Roman state regularly undertook a detailed census, rigorously counting the inhabitants of the empire and assessing their property for tax purposes—a process that more clearly than ever defined the family as the core unit of society.

In this Roman system, women might seem to be under the domineering rule of fathers and husbands. That is certainly the picture presented in the repressive laws that Roman men drafted and in the histories that Roman men wrote. But compared with women in most Greek city-states,

→ *Were the policies and institutions involved in integrating the Roman Empire similar to those of the Han dynasty in China?*

Roman women, even those of only modest wealth and status, had much greater freedom of action and much greater control of their own wealth and property. Thus Terentia, the wife of the Republican senator Cicero, bought and sold properties of some scale on her own, made decisions regarding her family and wealth without so much as consulting her husband (much to his chagrin—he later divorced her), and apparently fared perfectly well following her separation from Cicero. Her behavior, so far as we can see, was normal for a woman of her status: she was well educated, literate, well connected, and in control of her own life—despite what the laws and ideas of Roman males might suggest. The daily lives of ordinary women that are well documented in the papyrus documents from the Roman province of Egypt, for example, show them buying, selling, renting, and leasing with no sign that the constraints written into laws that tried to subject them to male control had any significant effect on their dealings.

Terentia reminds us of Ban Zhao, the younger sister of the historian Ban Gu (32–92 CE). She became the first female Chinese historian and lived her life relatively unconstrained. After marrying the local resident, Cao Shishu, at the age of fourteen, she was called Madame Cao at court. Subsequently, she completed her elder brother's *History of the Former Han Dynasty* when he was imprisoned and executed in 92 for dealings with the dowager empress's family. In addition to completing the first full dynastic history in China, Ban Zhao also wrote a work entitled *Lessons for Women*, in which she described the status and position of elite women in society and presented the ideal woman in light of her virtue, her type of work, and the words she spoke and wrote.

ECONOMY AND NEW SCALES OF PRODUCTION

At the most basic level, families and the state depended for their existence on the workings of the economy: production and consumption. Although Rome never transformed economic relations in the Mediterranean sufficiently to create a modern industrial economy, it did achieve staggering transformations of scale in the production of agricultural, manufactured, and mined goods. Public and private demand for metals, for example, led the Romans to mine lead, silver, and copper in Spain in operations so massive that traces of the air pollution they generated can easily be detected today in ice core samples taken in far distant Greenland. The evidence from Mediterranean shipwrecks similarly indicates that goods were transported by sea in the Mediterranean on a scale never seen before. The area of land carefully surveyed and brought under cultivation rose steadily throughout this period, as Romans reached into arid lands on the periphery of the Sahara Desert to the south, and opened up heavily forested regions in present-day France and Germany to the north. (See Map 7-4.)

The Romans also built an unprecedented number of roads to connect the various parts of their empire. Although many of these roads did not have the high quality—flagstone paving and excellent drainage—exhibited by the major highways in Italy, such as the Via Appia, many of them were systematically marked, for the first time in this part of the world, with milestones that indicated to travelers their precise location and the distance to the next town. Also for the first time, complex land maps and itineraries were prepared on which all of the major roads and distances between towns were specified. Adding to the roads' significance was their deliberate coordination with the sea routes of the Mediterranean to support the flow of traffic, commerce, and ideas through the empire on land and at sea more smoothly and safely than had previously been possible.

The mines produced the valuable metals—copper, tin, silver, and gold—out of which the Roman state and its agents produced the most massive coinage known in the Western world before early modern times. Coinage greatly facilitated the exchange of commodities and services, which could now be assigned standard values. Throughout the Roman Empire, from small towns on the edge of the Sahara Desert to army towns along the northern frontiers, goods were appraised, purchased, and sold in coin denominations. Taxes were assessed and hired laborers were paid day wages in coin. Although not fully money-based in a modern sense, the

Roman Roads. Like Qin and Han China, the Roman Empire was characterized by large-scale road building, which began as early as the late fourth century BCE. Roads eventually connected most land areas and larger urban centers in the empire, considerably easing ordinary travel, as well as trade and commerce. Here we see part of the Via Appia, the great highway that connected Rome with the southern parts of Italy.

economy of the empire in its leading sectors functioned more efficiently because of the government's production of coins on an immense scale—indeed, on a scale paralleled only by Han dynasty China and its successors.

Roman mining, as well as other sizable operations, relied significantly on chattel slaves—human beings purchased as private property. The unprecedented concentration of wealth and slaves at the center of the Roman world led to the first large-scale commercial plantation agriculture, along with the first technical handbooks on how to run such large operations for profit. These *latifundia* (literally, "broad estates") as they were called, specialized in products destined for the

big urban markets: cash crops such as wheat, grapes, and olives, as well as cattle and sheep raised on a huge scale. And all these economic developments rested on a bedrock belief that private property and its ownership were sacrosanct. Indeed, the Roman senator Cicero argued that the defense and enjoyment of private property were the basic reasons for the existence of the state. Roman law more clearly defined and more strictly enforced the rights of the private owner than had any previous legal system. The enormous extension of the private ownership of land and other property to regions that previously had little or no knowledge of it—Egypt in the east, Spain in the west, the lands of

MAP 7-4 *PAX ROMANA:* **THE ROMAN EMPIRE IN THE SECOND CENTURY CE**

The Roman Empire enjoyed remarkable peace and prosperity in the second century CE. Economic production increased and Roman culture expanded throughout the realm. According to the map, what Roman policies contributed to these conditions? Where did threats to the empire's peace exist? With what groups did Romans trade beyond their empire? How did the *Pax Romana* promote the spread of Christianity?

THE ROMAN EMPIRE | 313

→ *Were the policies and institutions involved in integrating the Roman Empire similar to those of the Han dynasty in China?*

Coin Hoard. The use of coins for a wide spectrum of economic exchanges became common in the Roman Empire. Looking at the batches that people buried for safekeeping gives us some idea of the range of coins in circulation at any one time. This coin hoard was found near Didcot in Oxfordshire, England. Buried about 165 CE, it contained about 125 gold coins minted between the 50s and 160s CE and represents the equivalent of about eleven years' pay for a Roman soldier. Gold coins were used only for very expensive transactions or to store wealth. Most ordinary purchases or payments were made with silver or brass coins.

western Europe—was one of the most enduring, if less visible, effects of the Roman Empire.

RELIGIOUS CULTS AND THE RISE OF CHRISTIANITY

The political unification of the Mediterranean under one empire also suggested that the beliefs of its peoples might be unified. The world of gods, spirits, deities, and demons remained hugely important, even as the region had experienced the general spread of new religions as part of the Hellenistic movement. Indeed, the municipal charters of Roman towns required the local town councilors to institute and maintain the support of a wide variety of official and semi-official cults of different gods and goddesses.

But if there was any religion of empire, it was Christianity, whose spread followed the geopolitical movement of the other big Mediterranean-wide religious cults. Its foundations lay in the specific context of a direct confrontation and dialogue with Roman imperial authority: the trial of Yeshua ben Yusef (Joshua son of Joseph), who had preached the new doctrines of what was originally a sect of Judaism and who is known to us today by the Greek form of his name, Jesus. Jesus was tried by a Roman governor, Pontius Pilatus, in a typical form of Roman provincial trial; found guilty of sedition; and executed, along with two bandits, by a standard Roman penalty—crucifixion.

We know of Jesus only after his death. No reference to him survives from his own lifetime. Two years after his crucifixion, Jesus was believed by Paul of Tarsus, a Jew and a Roman citizen from a city in southeastern Anatolia, to have appeared to him in full glory outside the city of Damascus. Paul and the communities to whom he preached between 40 and 60 CE were the first to call Yeshua "Jesus." They also referred to him as "the Christ"—*ho Christos*—or the Anointed One (i.e., the Messiah), and thought of him as a god.

Paul had not been one of Jesus' original disciples. Only much later did four of those men—Matthew, Mark, Luke, and John—attempt to write about his life and to record his sayings in accounts that came to be called the Gospels, an early English word that directly translates their name in the original Greek, *Evangeliai* (Good News). While they varied greatly, they had in common the need to tell the world not what Jesus had said, but who he had been. They were written as answers to the question that Jesus was reported to have asked his disciples a few months before he died: "Who do people say that I am?" (Mark 8:27).

Jesus' preachings could not have been more Jewish. God is the father of his people—a people of sinners, who are always liable to fall away. But God is like a good shepherd to them. Scrambling down dangerous ravines, the good shepherd seeks those who have gone astray, carrying home with joy on his shoulders even a single lost lamb (see John 10:1–18). We have already met the ancient image of the great king as shepherd of his people in both Egypt and Mesopotamia (see Chapter 3). This image also passed through the Psalms and the books of the prophets of Israel (Psalm 23:1, Isaiah 40:11). With Jesus, this ancient image took on a new intimacy. Not a distant monarch but a preacher, Jesus had set out, on God's behalf, to gather a new, small flock. Jesus' teachings—like the teachings of the Buddha—comforted people who lived at a distance from power, such as scholars, merchants, and farmers.

To his followers, Jesus was a man who had slowly revealed to them an awesome, hidden identity. Jesus was crucified not for what he had preached but for what he (or others) claimed that he was. Through the preaching of Paul in Greek and the textual portraits carefully painted in the Gospels, also in Greek, this image of Jesus rapidly spread beyond the local confines of Palestine—where Jesus had preached to Jews only and only in the local language, Aramaic—and entered the religious bloodstream of the Mediterranean.

Just half a century after his crucifixion, the followers of Jesus saw in his life not the wanderings of an amiable Jewish charismatic but a moment of head-on conflict between "God" and "the world." Jesus had "overcome" the "world." He had even broken the boundaries of the human condition: he had been raised by God from the dead. This was the chief thing that Paul wished his followers in Corinth and elsewhere to know about Jesus: "If Christ has not been raised, your faith is futile [and] we are truly to be pitied" (1 Corinthians 15:17,

CICERO ON THE ROLE OF THE ROMAN STATE

Greek thinkers debated ethics and morals, the role of the good life, the nature of the universe, and how we know things, but it is perhaps natural to expect the Romans, given their more pragmatic attitudes and their possession of a huge empire, to have deliberated more about the nature of government and the role of the state. In the following passage, Marcus Tullius Cicero, one of the leading politicians in Rome from the 60s to the 40s BCE, discusses how the politician—the man who holds public office in the state (in this case, the Roman state)—has a fundamental duty to defend the state's main function.

That man who undertakes responsibility for public office in the state must make it his first priority to see that every person can continue to hold what is his and that no inroads are made into the goods or property of private persons by the state. It was a bad policy when Philippus, when he was tribune of the plebs [about 104 BCE], proposed an agrarian reform law. When his law was defeated, he took the defeat well and was moderate in his response. In the debates themselves, however, he tried to curry popular favor and acted in a bad way when he said, "In our community there are not more than two thousand men who have real property." That speech ought to be condemned outright for attempting to advocate equality of property holdings. What policy could be more dangerous? It was for this very reason—that each person should be able to keep his own property—that states and local governments were founded. Although it was by the leadership of nature herself that men gathered together in communities, it was for the hope of keeping their own property that they sought the protection of states. . . . Some men want to become known as popular politicians and for this reason they engage in making revolutionary proposals about land, with the result that owners are driven from their homes and money lent out by creditors is simply given free to the borrowers with no need for repayment. Such men are shaking the very foundations of the state. First of all, they are destroying that goodwill and sense of trust which can no longer exist when money is simply taken from some people and given to others [by the state]. And then they take away fairness, which is totally destroyed if each person is not permitted to keep what is his own. For, as I have already said, it is the peculiar function of the state and of local government to make sure that each person should be able to keep his own things freely and without any worry.

➔ *According to Cicero, what is the main function of the Roman state?*

➔ *How does the very important role given to the protection of private property rights of individuals determine the claims that citizens had on their rulers?*

➔ *And how does this differ from the role of the state as envisioned in contemporary Han dynasty China?*

SOURCE: *De Officiis (On Duties)*, 2.21.73, 22.78; translated by Brent Shaw.

19). Thus, the preaching that the followers of Jesus brought to confront this world was no longer the preaching of a man. It was the message of a god—a god who, for thirty years, half a century before, had moved (largely unrecognized) among human beings. And the followers formed a church, an *ekklēsia:* a permanent gathering committed to the charge of leaders chosen by God and by their fellow believers. For these leaders and their followers, death—death for Jesus—was the hallmark of their faith. In dying they witnessed for the faith. Indeed, the central defining experience for Christians remained that of the Roman trial and the idea of "witnessing" to God. The Greek word *martus* means a witness in a trial. From this came the English term *martyr* and the concept of martyrdom.

The persecutions of Christians were sporadic and intensely local in nature. Like imperial power itself, they were a series of responses to local concerns. Not until the emperor Decius, in the mid-third century CE, was a formal empire-wide attack on Christians directed by the state as a whole. And that attempt failed in its objective. Decius died within the year and Christians, not unnaturally, interpreted the death of their persecutor as evidence of the hand of God in human affairs. By the last decades of the third century, Christian communities of various kinds, reflecting the different strands of their movement through the Mediterranean as well as the background of local cultures into which they settled, were present in every local society in the empire.

→ *Were the policies and institutions involved in integrating the Roman Empire similar to those of the Han dynasty in China?*

THE LIMITS OF EMPIRE

The empire both defined and labeled outsiders as those whom it excluded. A crucial part of that process was the successful exercise of force in extending its borders. (See Map 7-5.) Thus the limitations of that force determined who belonged in the empire and was subject to it, and who was outside it and therefore excluded. For two of the four phases of the empire, there was not much question about such deter-

minations. To the west, the Romans pushed their authority to the shores of the Atlantic Ocean, and to the south they drove it to the edges of the Sahara Desert. In both cases, they extended their control to its ecological limits: in those directions, little further land was available that the empire could dominate to its own profit. To the east and north, however, things were different.

On Rome's eastern frontiers, powerful Romans such as Marcus Licinius Crassus in the mid-50s BCE and Mark

MAP 7-5   POPULATION OF ROMAN WORLD IN 362 CE

Roman frontiers at the northern and eastern limits of the empire were persistent sources of anxiety and concern for imperial leaders. While not as densely populated as the Roman Empire, these regions contained large population centers as well. Name some of the major groups of peoples that lived just beyond Roman rule in the areas of eastern Europe and Southwest Asia. What kinds of political and social organization did these societies develop? Why were Roman armies never able to subdue these neighboring peoples?

Wooden Tablet Letter. This wooden tablet from Vindolanda in northern England contains a text, not in neat Latin print but in the natural longhand writing of the time. On the tablet is a letter from two men, Niger and Brocchus, to their friend Cerialis. They wish him success in all that he is about to do. The large cache of letters found at Vindolanda has expanded our vision of the role and place of writing in distant parts of the empire.

Antony in the early 30s BCE wished to imitate the achievements of Alexander the Great and conquer the arid lands beyond Judea and Syria. But they failed miserably, stopped by a barrier that would limit the ability of any Mediterranean state to extend its influence east of the Mediterranean periphery: the empire of the Parthians, who had moved south from present-day Turkmenistan and settled in the region covered by the modern-day states of Iraq and Iran. Unlike the Persians before them, the Parthians were a people whose social order was founded on nomadic pastoralism and whose war power was based on the technical advances in mounted horseback warfare made on the great plains of Inner Eurasia. Reliance on horses made their style of fighting highly mobile,

and it was ideally adapted to the arid plains and deserts. They perfected the so-called Parthian shot: the arrow shot from a bow with great accuracy, at long distance, and from horseback at a gallop. On the flat, open plains of Iran and Iraq, the Parthians had a decisive advantage over the slow-moving, cumbersome Roman mass infantry formations that had been developed for war in the Mediterranean.

The Sasanians, who in the mid-220s CE succeeded the Parthians as the major power in this region, improved on and expanded these same technical advantages. King Shapur I (Shabuhr), their greatest monarch (ruled 240–272 CE), was able to exploit the weaknesses of the Roman Empire in the mid–third century, even capturing the Roman emperor Valerian in 260 CE. On the other hand, as successful as Parthians and Sasanians were in fighting the Romans, they could never equal the Romans' sway. Their relatively different political structure—built up out of modular units, mainly of local ethnic groups—set limits of a different kind on their empires. And though the Parthian and Sasanian militaries were very successful in their own desert environment, they were ill-suited to fighting around the Mediterranean. Thus these states, centered in the arid lands to the east, never posed a serious threat of long-term military domination over the Mediterranean world to the west.

In the lands across the Rhine and Danube, to the north, the limits imposed on empire were largely determined by ecological conditions. The long and extremely harsh winters, but excellent soil and growing conditions, produced hardy populations clustered densely across vast distances. They formed illiterate, kin-based agricultural societies that had changed little since their emergence in these regions over the first millennium BCE. And because their warrior elites still engaged in armed competitions, it is hardly surprising that war and vio-

Chronology

	400 BCE	300 BCE	200 BCE	100 BCE
THE MEDITERRANEAN		▌ *Roman city-state expansion in Italian peninsula, 350–265 BCE* *Rome defeats Carthage in three Punic Wars and* ▌ *incorporates Carthaginian territory, 265–146 BCE*		*Civil wars divide Romans, 90–30 B*
SOUTHWEST ASIA			*Parthian Empire established in Southwest Asia, 129 BCE* ▌	
EAST ASIA		*Qin Empire, 221–207 BCE* ▌ *Han dynasty, 206 BCE–220 CE* ▌ *Western (Former) Han, 206 BCE–9 CE* ▌ *Expansion of Han Empire under Emperor Wu, 140–87 BCE* ▌ *Zhang Qian leads western expedition in a failed attempt to form a Han alliance with Yuezhi tribes, 139 BCE* ▌ *Imperial University founded, 136 BCE* ▌		

Soldier versus Barbarian. On the frontiers of the empire, the legionary soldiers faced the non-Roman 'barbarians' from the lands beyond. In this piece of a stone-carved picture from the northwestern frontier, we see a civilized and disciplined Roman soldier, to the left, facing a German 'barbarian'—hair uncut and unkempt, without formal armor, his house a thatched hut. Frontier realities were never so clear-cut, of course. Roman soldiers, often recruited from the 'barbarian' peoples, were a lot more like them than was convenient to admit; and the 'barbarians' were influenced by and closer to Roman cultural models than this picture indicates.

lence characterized their connections with the empire. As the Roman Empire fixed its northern armed frontiers along the Rhine and Danube rivers, the relationship of the empire to the large populations of Germans and Goths north of the rivers was determined by two factors. First, these small kinship-based societies had only one major commodity for which the empire was willing to pay: human bodies. The slave trade out of the land across the Rhine and Danube was immense, and gold, silver, coins, wine, arms, and other luxury items of high value flowed in one direction in exchange for slaves in the other. Second, their wars were unremitting, as it came to be expected of every emperor that he would deal harshly with these northern tribal peoples whom the Romans considered to be "barbarians." These fundamental connections, involving arms and violence, were to enmesh the Romans ever more tightly with the northern tribal societies. Indeed, they overlapped, as the internal conflicts within the Roman Empire prompted increasing recourse to the use of "barbarians" as soldiers and officers who served the empire.

CONCLUSION

China and Rome were similar in their construction of empires of immense and unprecedented scale and duration. In many ways, however, they were fundamentally different. Having initially less numerous and, more important, a less dense population than China, Rome relied on slaves and "barbarian" immigrants to expand and to diversify its workforce. While about 1 percent of the Chinese population was enslaved, more than ten times this proportion were slaves in the Roman Empire. The Chinese rural economy was based

1 CE	100 CE	200 CE	300 CE

Julius Caesar conquers Gaul, 58–50 BCE

■ *Jesus preaches in Judea, 1st century CE*

■ *Augustus reigns as first Roman emperor, 27 BCE–14 CE*

Christianity expands to broader Roman Empire by 2nd and 3rd centuries CE

■ *Roman Empire reaches greatest territorial extent under Emperor Trajan, 98–117 CE*

Sasanid Empire supplants Parthia, 224 CE ■

■ *Red Eyebrows uprising, 23 CE*

■ *Wang Mang usurps the Han throne, 9–23 CE*

■ *Eastern (Later) Han, 25–220 CE*

■ *Yellow Turbans uprising, 184 CE*

■ *Popular rebellions against Han rule, 184 CE*

almost solely on a huge population of free peasant farmers; this enormous labor pool, together with their remarkable bureaucracy, enabled the Han to achieve great political stability. The millions of peasant farmers who were the backbone of rural society in the Roman Empire were much more loosely integrated into the structure of the state. They never had the sense of belonging to a cohesive social whole, and they never unified to revolt against their government and overthrow it, as did the raging millenarian peasant movements of Later Han China.

By Chinese standards, the Roman Empire was relatively fragmented and underadministered. What is more, philosophy and religion never underpinned the Roman state in the way that Confucianism served the dynasties of China. But both empires were aided by the spread of a uniform language and imperial culture. This process was more comprehensive in China than in Rome, whose empire tended to divide into a two-language world—Latin was dominant in the western Mediterranean, Greek in the east. Both states fostered the development of a common imperial culture, at nonelite as well as elite levels of society, and once entrenched, these cultures and languages lasted well after the end of empire and formed deep-seated links between one imperial age and the next.

Their basic differences in human resources, languages, and ideas led the Roman and Han states to evolve in unique ways. In both places, however, the faiths of outsiders, Christians and Buddhists, eclipsed the secular classical ideals that grounded their respective states. And the transmission of the ideas of these new faiths was considerably assisted by the new communications networks fashioned to serve the empires' interests. These new religions added to the cultural mix that succeeded the Roman Empire and the Han dynasty. Yet despite their cultural and social significance, neither Christianity nor Buddhism ever challenged the political status quo, nor did they offer viable alternatives to the state systems that the Roman Empire and Han China had perfected.

At their height, Rome and Chang'an exercised uniform rule over vast expanses of land and large numbers of people for great lengths of time—a huge step beyond the scale of anything yet witnessed on the globe. Each state surpassed its forebears by translating unprecedented military power into the fullest form of state-based organization, as large, well-trained standing armies enforced its will. The complex organization of the state was supported by the systematic control, counting, and taxing of its population. In both cases, the general increase of the population, the growth of huge cities, and the success of long-distance trade contributed to the new scales of magnitude. The Han would not be superseded in East Asia as the model empire until the Tang dynasty in the seventh century. In western Afro-Eurasia, the Roman Empire would not be surpassed in scale or intensity of development until the rise of powerful European nation-states more than a millennium later.

STUDY QUESTIONS

 WWNORTON.COM/STUDYSPACE

1. Compare and contrast the labor systems in the Qin and Han dynasties of East Asia with that of the Roman Empire in the Mediterranean world. To what extent did each rely on systems of forced labor?

2. Analyze the impact of Xiongnu pastoralists on imperial policies of the Qin and Han dynasties of East Asia. How did each dynasty attempt to counter the threat of nomadic incursions into their territorial heartlands?

3. Compare and contrast the methods through which Han and Roman leaders enlisted the support of those they governed. What emphasis did each dynasty place on ideology, civil bureaucracy, and military organization?

4. Explain the influence of Confucian ideas on East Asia during the Han dynasty. How did Confucian ideas shape political and social hierarchies during their empire?

5. Explain the concepts of the *Pax Sinica* and *Pax Romana*. How did Han and Roman leaders promote long periods of peace and prosperity in Eastern and Western Afro-Eurasia, respectively?

6. Describe the process through which the Roman city-state created a vast empire in the Mediterranean world. How did Roman attitudes toward military service influence the growth of the empire?

7. Compare and contrast the concept of emperor in the Han dynasty with that in the Roman Empire. What role did each emperor play in the governing structure of his respective empire?

8. Explain the social and legal hierarchies that governed Roman urban life. To what extent did residents of towns and cities enjoy personal autonomy?

9. Describe the appeal of early Christianity in the Roman Empire. How did the *Pax Romana* promote the spread of Christian communities?

10. Compare and contrast Roman strategies for promoting peace and stability along its borders with those of the Han dynasty. How different were the threats that each empire faced from borderland peoples?

FURTHER READINGS

Bodde, Derk, *China's First Unifier: A Study of the Ch'in Dynasty as Seen in the Life of Li Ssu (280?–208 B.C.)* (1938). A classic account of the key Legalist adviser who formulated the Qin policy to enhance its autocratic power.

Bowman, Alan K., *Life and Letters on the Roman Frontier: Vindolanda and Its Peoples* (1994). An introduction to the exciting discovery of writing tablets at a Roman army base in northern Britain.

Bradley, Keith, *Slavery and Society at Rome* (1994). The best single overview of the major aspects of the slave system in the Roman empire.

Chevallier, Raymond, *Roman Roads,* trans. N. H. Field (1976). A guide to the fundamentals of the construction, maintenance, administration, and mapping of Roman roads.

Coarelli, Fillipo (ed.), *Pompeii,* trans. Patricia Cockram (2006). A lavishly illustrated large volume that allows the reader to sense some of the wondrous wealth of the buried city of Pompeii.

Colledge, Malcolm A. R., *The Parthians* (1967). A bit dated but still a fundamental introduction to the Parthians, the major power on the eastern frontier of the Roman empire.

Cornell, Tim, *The Beginnings of Rome: Italy and Rome from the Bronze Age to the Punic Wars, c. 2000 to 264 B.C.* (1995). The single best one-volume history of Rome through its early history to the first war with Carthage.

Cornell, Tim, and John Matthews, *Atlas of the Roman World* (1982). A history of the Roman world; much more than simply an atlas. It is provided not only with good maps and a gazetteer but also with marvelous color illustrations and a text that guides the reader through the basics of Roman history.

Csikszentmihalyi, Mark, *Readings in Han Chinese Thought* (2006). A volume presenting a representative selection of primary sources to illustrate the growth of ideas in early imperial times; a useful introduction to the key strains of thought during this crucial period.

Dixon, Suzanne, *The Roman Family* (1992). The best one-volume guide to the nature of the Roman family and family relations.

Garnsey, Peter, and Richard Saller, *The Roman Empire: Economy, Society, and Culture,* (1987). A perceptive and critical introduction to three basic aspects of social life in the empire.

Giardina, Andrea (ed.), *The Romans,* trans. Lydia Cochrane (1993). Individual studies of important typical figures in Roman society, from the peasant and the bandit to the merchant and the soldier.

Goldsworthy, Adrian, *The Roman Army at War: 100 B.C.– A.D. 200* (1996). A summary history and analysis of the Roman army in action during the late Republic and early Empire.

Goodman, Martin, *The Roman World: 44 B.C.– A.D. 180* (1997). A newer basic history text covering the high Roman Empire.

Harris, William, *Ancient Literacy* (1989). A basic survey of what is known about communication in the form of writing and books in the Roman Empire.

Hopkins, Keith, *Death and Renewal: Sociological Studies in Roman History,* vol. 2 (1983). Innovative studies on Roman history, including one of the best on gladiators and another on death and funerals.

———, *A World Full of Gods: Pagans, Jews and Christians in the Roman Empire* (1999). A somewhat unusual but interesting and provocative look at the world of religions in the Roman Empire.

Juliano, Annette L., and Judith A. Lerner (eds.), *Nomads, Traders and Holy Men Along China's Silk Road* (2003). A description of the travelers along the Silk Road in human terms, focusing on warfare, markets, and religion.

Kraus, Theodore, and Leonard von Matt, *Pompeii and Herculaneum: The Living Cities of the Dead,* trans. Robert E. Wolf (1975). A huge, lavishly illustrated compendium of all aspects of life in the buried cities of Pompeii and Herculaneum as preserved in the archaeological record.

Loewe, Michael, *The Government of the Qin and Han Empires: 221 BCE–220 CE* (2006). A useful overview of the government of the early empires of China. Topics include the structure of central government, provincial and local government, the armed forces, officials, government communications, the laws of the empire, and control of the people and the land.

Millar, Fergus, *The Crowd in the Late Republic* (1998). An innovative study of the democratic power of the citizens in the city of Rome itself.

———, *The Emperor in the Roman World, 31 B.C.–A.D. 337* (1992). Everything you might want to know about the Roman emperor, with special emphasis on his civil role as the administrator of an empire.

Potter, David, *Roman Empire at Bay: A.D. 180–395* (2004). A new basic text covering the later Roman Empire, including the critical transition to a Christian state.

Potter, David S., and David J. Mattingly (eds.), *Life, Death, and Entertainment in the Roman Empire* (1999). A good introduction to basic aspects of Roman life in the empire, including the family, feeding the cities, religion, and popular entertainment.

Qian, Sima, *Records of the Grand Historian: Qin Dynasty,* trans. Burton Watson, 3rd ed. (1995). The classic work of Chinese history in a readable translation. The Han dynasty's Grand Historian describes the slow rise and meteoric fall of the Qin dynasty from the point of view of the succeeding dynasty, which Sima Qian witnessed or heard of during his lifetime.

Southern, Pat, *The Roman Army: A Social and Institutional History* (2006). A fundamental guide to all aspects of the Roman army.

Todd, Malcolm, *The Early Germans,* rev. ed. (2004). A basic survey of the peoples in central and western Europe at the time of the Roman Empire.

Vainker, Shelagh, *Chinese Silk: A Cultural History* (2004). A work that traces the cultural history of silk in China from its early origins to the twentieth century and considers its relationship to the other decorative arts. The author draws on the most recent archaeological evidence to emphasize the role of silk in Chinese history, trade, religion, and literature.

Wells, Peter S., *The Barbarians Speak: How the Conquered Peoples Shaped Roman Europe* (1999). The cultures of the peoples of central and northern Europe at the time of the Roman Empire and their impact on Roman culture.

Wood, Francis, *The Silk Road: Two Thousand Years in the Heart of Asia* (2004). A work illustrated with drawings, manuscripts, paintings, and artifacts to trace the Silk Road to its origins as far back as Alexander the Great. The author stresses the importance of the Silk Road to cultural and religious movements.

Woolf, Greg (ed.), *The Cambridge Illustrated History of the Roman World* (2005). A good guide to various aspects of Roman history, culture, and provincial life.

Chapter 8

THE RISE OF UNIVERSAL RELIGIONS, 300–600 CE

Around 180 CE, a group of relatively humble persons (three men and three women) stood trial before the provincial governor at Carthage. They claimed to be Christians, and their only crime was a refusal to worship the gods who protected the Roman Empire. The governor was unimpressed; his god was "the protecting spirit of our lord the emperor." To this, one Christian retorted that his god was also an emperor, but that he could not be seen, for he stood "above all kings and of all nations." There was an unbridgeable gap between the governor and the Christians. The governor had no choice but to read out a death sentence, ordering their immediate execution. "Thanks be to God!" cried the Christians, and straightaway they were beheaded.

As the centuries unfolded, the tables would turn dramatically. Old ideas of the supremacy of an emperor-lord gave way to those of the Lord God as emperor. This period witnessed the conjunction of religions with universal aspirations spreading across different geographic zones. It was the combination of a different kind of spiritual fervor with more numerous social and political contacts that gave religious beliefs their powerful significance. In

321

effect, religiosity became a powerful integrative force, while also setting in motion a long-term process of creating new world divides. This advent of religion as a global influence was anything but simple. It also built on the expansive reach of the Roman and Han empires and the closer commercial and intellectual connections that bound east and west together. But how did new religious movements shape political structures? Were those structures reinforced, or were they undercut? How did this process remap relations between world societies?

UNIVERSAL RELIGIONS AND COMMON CULTURES

> → *How did religion bring worlds together and drive them apart?*

In the three centuries from 300 to 600 CE, the whole of the Afro-Eurasian landmass experienced a surge of religious ferment. In the West, Christianity became the state faith of the Roman Empire. In India, Vedic religion (Brahmanism) evolved into a far more formal spiritual system that came to be called Hinduism, while in northern India, all across central Asia, and even in China, Buddhism, originally a code of ethics enunciated by an inspired individual, became a religion. Across much of the world, spiritual concerns became more and more important to everyday life, integrating dispersed communities into shared faiths.

Politics shaped religion, and religion shaped politics. Indeed, the new Afro-Eurasian spirituality took shape within imperial frameworks. Christianity arose in western Europe alongside a decaying Roman state. In the eastern Mediterranean it provided inspiration and strength for a revived eastern Roman *imperium*, Byzantium. In India, Hinduism and Buddhism vied for cultural preeminence; in central Asia and China, Buddhism flourished as the old polities foundered.

Elsewhere, in sub-Saharan Africa and the Americas, dynamic and mobile populations demonstrated that universalistic religions were not essential for creating empires of the mind. They, too, reached beyond local communities and wove them together into common spiritual worlds. In Africa a relatively small group of Bantu-speaking peoples, residing in the southeastern corner of present-day Nigeria, began to spread themselves and their way of life throughout the entire southern half of the landmass. Their latter-day ancestors became the dominant peoples in central, eastern, and southern Africa. Similarly, in the Americas, the Mayans established political and cultural institutions over a large portion of Mesoamerica.

A wide variety of societies around the world were caught up in various forms of spiritual ferment. By writing of "spiritual ferment" we do not mean that people became more excitable, more otherworldly, or more escapist. Rather, the phrase implies that religion touched more areas of society and culture than before and that it touched them in different, more demanding ways. People felt deeply about religion because it was through religious filters that they processed the meaning of what had always been important to them. Issues of truth, of loyalty, and of solidarity were discussed in religious terms, and framed by religious leaders who claimed to know the truth about an invisible other world.

Focus Questions THE RISE OF UNIVERSAL RELIGIONS

→ *How did religion bring worlds together and drive them apart?*

→ *How did empires such as the Roman and Sasanian help religions such as Christianity become universalizing?*

→ *How did the actions and activities of central Asians influence the geographic spread of universal religions and other cross-cultural developments during this time?*

→ *To what extent did South Asia develop a widespread common culture despite the region's political, religious, and social diversity?*

→ *To what extent did new influences from other parts of Afro-Eurasia transform Chinese culture and politics during this era?*

→ *How similar and different were spiritual developments in worlds apart from Afro-Eurasia during this time?*

WWNORTON.COM/STUDYSPACE

It helps to step back and consider how many questions in our own world are assumed to be answerable by science. In many respects, religion functioned in that age as science does in ours. It claimed to give clear answers about the nature of human beings, about why they lived in society, about why they married and had children, about whom they should obey, and about the degree of allegiance they owed to something unseen (God, the gods, or a supernaturally guaranteed code of conduct) rather than to any ruler. Even more, as the case of the Christian martyrs showed, it was religion that told them what they should die for.

Because religion claimed to enable its followers to distinguish sharply between right and wrong, it freed people from the past. The extreme age of local religious practices that might have existed since time immemorial did not make the old beliefs true. As this shift reverberated, and cultures shrugged off their older heritages bound to local customs and traditions, the new religious belief systems enabled people to bond together into new identities shaped by a shared faith, across much broader scales than hitherto imaginable. As we will see in this chapter, some religious systems, such as Buddhism and Christianity, would spread far and wide because they professed universal precepts; later, Islam would follow the same pattern (see Chapter 9).

The new spiritual ferment also freed individuals from the restraints imposed by preexisting social bonds. Knowing—and believing in—sharp distinctions between right and wrong drew new lines between peoples. In this way, religion provided a new wedge to drive worlds apart, as absolute conviction left little room for tolerance. Centuries of harmonious interaction offered few protections to neighbors now perceived to be "wrong" in their beliefs—and because of their errors, they could be ostracized, exiled, or killed. For wrong beliefs were held to be as dangerous as today's counterfeit medicines. Like noxious drugs, they had to be removed from circulation as quickly as possible. Conflict, even violence and religious persecution, went with this new sense of certainty.

Moreover, like science, religious beliefs were held to apply equally from one end of Afro-Eurasia to the other. Religious leaders, carrying written texts (books, scrolls, or tablets of wood or palm leaf), often traveled widely, and wherever they were, what they said and read was both true and relevant. Everywhere, universal religions were on the move. That Christians from Persia went to China demonstrates the fundamental error of associating Christianity exclusively with "Europe." Buddhism also migrated, journeying from South Asia to Afghanistan and the caravan routes of Central Asia, and to China. In 643, the Chinese Buddhist Xuanzang brought back to Chang'an (at the time, the world's largest city) an entire library of Buddhist scriptures—527 boxes of writings and 192 birch-bark tablets—that he had collected on a pilgrimage, begun in 630, to Buddhist holy sites in South Asia. He lodged them in the Great Wild Goose Pagoda, which

still towers above the city, and immediately began to translate every line of them into Chinese. He had traveled 10,000 miles to bring these books to China. Here was the "truth" of Buddhism—propositions as true, in Xuanzang's opinion, as anything found in a modern science textbook, and as exciting and as healing when they reached distant China as when Buddhist thinkers had first elaborated them in northern India, more than 5,000 miles away.

Voyages, translations, long-distance pilgrimages, and sweeping conversion campaigns remapped the spiritual landscape of the world. New religious leaders were the brokers of more encompassing but also more intolerant worldviews, premised on a new relationship between gods and their subjects. Religions and their brokers profoundly integrated societies. But they also created new ways to drive them apart.

Xuanzang. This painting c. 900 CE, which survives in the caves of Dunhuang along the Silk Road, portrays the Chinese pilgrim Xuanzang accompanied by a tiger on his epic travels to South Asia to collect important Buddhist scriptures.

NORTH AMERICA

ROCKY MOUNTAINS

Great Lakes

Mississippi R.

St. Lawrence R.

ATLANTIC OCEAN

Gulf of Mexico

Teotihuacán

MAYAN CITY STATES

WEST INDIES

PACIFIC OCEAN

CHAVIN

Amazon R.

SOUTH AMERICA

ANDES MOUNTAINS

CELTIC PEOPLES

GERMA

KINGDOM OF THE VISIGOTHS

Cart

KINGDOM OF THE VANDALS

SAHAR

SAHA PEOF

Niger R.

	Qi
	Toba
	Ruanruan
	Hephthalites
	Sasanian
	Gupta
	Eastern Roman
	Mayan
VANDALS	Kingdom
BANTU	People
•	City

0   1000   2000 Miles

0   1000   2000 Kilometers

ARCTIC OCEAN

FINNO-UGRIANS

TURKIC

ARAL
SEA

GOBI DESERT

EMPIRE OF THE RUANRUAN

BLACK SEA
Constantinople

CASPIAN SEA

Merv

EMPIRE OF THE
HEPHTHALITES

TAKLAMAKAN
DESERT

TOBA
EMPIRE

SEA
OF
JAPAN

EASTERN ROMAN
EMPIRE

Tigris R.

SASANIAN
EMPIRE

Bactra

Taxila

Yellow R.

Luoyang

Chang'an

YELLOW
SEA

Jerusalem

Euphrates R.

Ctesiphon

Indus R.

HIMALAYA MTS

GUPTA
EMPIRE

Ganges R.

Yangzi R.

QI
EMPIRE

Alexandria

RED SEA

ARABS

Persian Gulf

ARABIAN
SEA

PACIFIC
OCEAN

DESERT

Nile R.

Mekong R.

SOUTH
CHINA
SEA

Lake
Victoria

Lake
Tanganyika

BANTUS

INDIAN
OCEAN

KALAHARI
DESERT

AUSTRALIAN ABORIGINES

MAP 8-1   EMPIRES AND COMMON CULTURES FROM
300 TO 600 CE

The period between 300 and 600 CE was a time of great political change around the
world. Which polities are new? Which polities have disappeared? Which have expanded
or contracted? What fundamental historical factors are driving these changes in the
political landscape?

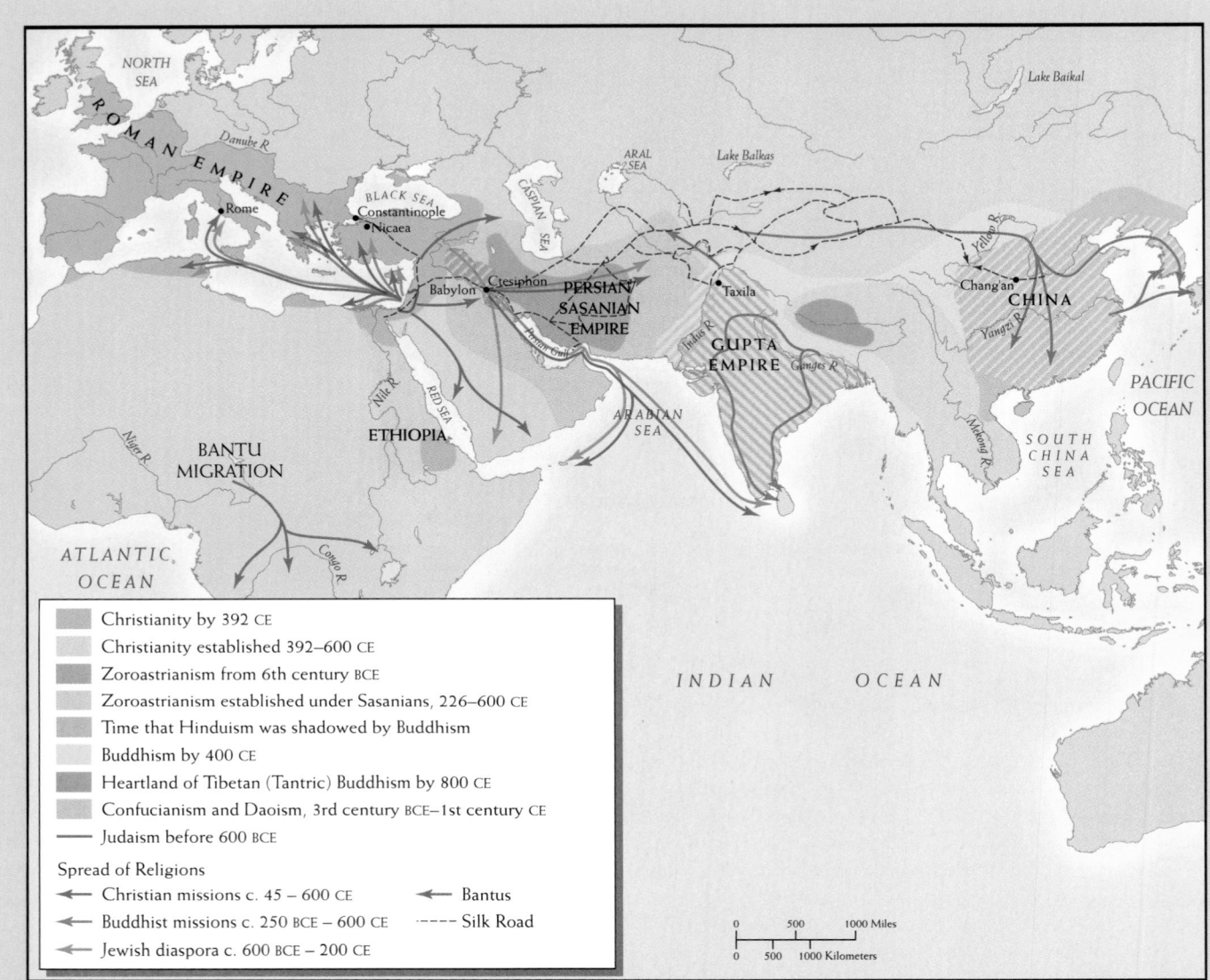

Spread of Religions

Christianity by 392 CE
Christianity established 392–600 CE
Zoroastrianism from 6th century BCE
Zoroastrianism established under Sasanians, 226–600 CE
Time that Hinduism was shadowed by Buddhism
Buddhism by 400 CE
Heartland of Tibetan (Tantric) Buddhism by 800 CE
Confucianism and Daoism, 3rd century BCE–1st century CE
Judaism before 600 BCE

Christian missions c. 45 – 600 CE
Buddhist missions c. 250 BCE – 600 CE
Jewish diaspora c. 600 BCE – 200 CE
Bantus
Silk Road

0   500   1000 Miles
0   500   1000 Kilometers

MAP 8-2   THE SPREAD OF UNIVERSAL RELIGIONS IN AFRO-EURASIA, 300–600 CE

The spread of universal religions and the shifting political landscape of Afro-Eurasia in the first half of the first millennium were intimately connected. Using Map 8-1, identify the major polities in Afro-Eurasia during this era. How did these political configurations differ from those in the era covered in Chapter 7? Compare and contrast Map 8-1 with Map 8-2. Where did Hinduism, Buddhism, and Christianity emerge, and where did they spread? How did the rise and fall of empires affect the expansion of universal religions? To what extent did the polities identified in Map 8-1 use universal religions to establish their legitimacy?

EMPIRES AND RELIGIOUS CHANGE IN WESTERN AFRO-EURASIA

> → *How did empires such as the Roman and Sasanian help religions such as Christianity become universalizing?*

In the western region of Afro-Eurasia, the Roman Empire reigned supreme in 300 CE, but it was hardly the political and military juggernaut it had been 300 years earlier. Surrounded by peoples who coveted its great wealth while resisting its power, Rome was in the process of fragmenting. Rome's endurance proved a boon to new religious ferment, which took hold in its decaying structures. The populations of the western parts of the Roman Empire were eventually overrun by the barbarians on their peripheries, but in many ways they continued to feel "Roman." They looked to the new faith of Christianity to maintain order and continuity with the past, eventually founding a papacy in Rome to rule the remnants of empire.

This Christian empire split almost from the start. In Rome's east, on the other hand, a powerful successor state appeared in the form of the Byzantine Empire based at Constantinople. Its claim to be the political arm of Christianity seemed more viable than that of the western European Christian church based in Rome. But it faced a new foe still further east. The Sasanian Empire of Persia, like the papacy at Rome and the Byzantine state, was unlike the previous polities of the area. Indeed, these states represented something new in Afro-Eurasian polities. They claimed the blessing of new (or transformed) religions, and their rulers were concerned that their subjects should worship the correct gods in the correct manner. Those who did not were treated as outsiders, both in this life and in the next—where hell awaited them.

THE RISE OF CHRISTIANITY

It is one of the paradoxes of Western history that the most crucial change ever to happen to the Roman Empire had little to do with distant frontier wars. Instead, it grew from a religious war fought, from the bottom up, in the peaceful and tightly administered towns that were the nerve centers of the Roman Mediterranean.

The rise of Christianity coincided with the appearance of a new figure in matters of spiritual belief. Those who were executed by Roman authorities were called *martyrs* by the Christians, and many of them were indeed remarkable wit-

Saint Perpetua in Heaven. The Christian martyr Perpetua came to be represented as an upper-class Roman matron with carefully covered hair. Set in a circle of bright blue, in the golden dome of a church, she looks out from a distant, peaceful Heaven.

nesses to their faith. In 203, a well-to-do mother in her early twenties, Vibia Perpetua, faced a horrible punishment for her refusal to sacrifice to the gods. Denied even the benefit of a human executioner, she and her companions were condemned to be exposed to wild beasts in the amphitheater of Carthage. The amphitheater is still there, a little to the south of modern Tunis. It is a mean, small place—not a gigantic stadium. The condemned and the spectators would have had eye contact with each other throughout the fatal encounter.

Before her death, Perpetua dictated to her fellow Christians a prison diary that is unique in Roman literature. Here a woman speaks to us with a full religious message. She described her relief at being allowed to have her baby stay with her: "My prison had suddenly become a palace, so that I wanted to be there rather than anywhere else." More important, she recounted powerful visions of the next world, from which she and her companions derived strength and courage. Perpetua stepped every night into paradise, which appeared to her as a place of peace and abundance. "I saw an immense garden," she related, "and in it a gray-haired man sat in a

RELIGIOUS DEBATE AND CHRISTIAN UNIVERSALISM

The spread of religious ideas in the Roman Empire changed how people viewed their present existence. Believing implied that something bigger and more important loomed behind the world of physical matter. Feeling contact with this "other" world gave individual worshippers a sense of worth; it guided them, in this life, and they would eventually meet their guides and spiritual friends there. This was the power of Perpetua's visions. But it is important to note that the sharp taste for paradise had developed even beyond Christian circles. The fervor was potent enough that a little more than a century after Perpetua's execution, a Roman emperor, Constantine, considered that he had been led to military victory by a vision sent to him by Christ. From 312 onward, Constantine and his successors would place the huge authority of the Roman state behind a Christian church that up to then had been marginal and, often, persecuted.

Religion was no longer something that could be taken for granted—instead, it was supposed to engage the minds of those who practiced it. The reform of Judaism by the rabbis, which was also under way between 200 and 600 CE, took part in the same movement of ideas. As they struggled to rethink their religion after the loss of the Temple of Jerusalem (destroyed by the Romans in 70 CE), they recast time-honored oral traditions into the codified written volumes of the Talmud of Jerusalem, produced by the rabbis of Galilee around 400 CE. The efforts of the rabbis were intended to enable Jews to create, in their own homes and in their synagogues, "virtual temples" echoing the solemnity and purity of a temple that no longer existed. Even more influential was the Babylonian Talmud—the famous Bavli—produced by the rabbis of Mesopotamia sometime between 500 and 600 CE. Polytheists, Jews, and Christians alike unleashed their intellectual energies not, as had the ancient Greeks, in debates on how best to live in the polis but in fierce arguments about how to live in relation to God or the gods.

Religion was coming to take a form more familiar to modern Westerners. The gods were no longer local powers who had to be placated by dimly understood, archaic rituals associated with specific sacred places. Many gods became omnipresent figures to whom human beings might come close through loving attachment (similarly, as described below, the rise of *bhakti* piety among India's Hindus at this time brought individual gods closer to their worshippers). Humans might even hope to meet these divine beings again in another, happier world—and thus the sense that there must be an afterlife became stronger.

Above all, at this time, the gods expected to be obeyed, as one would obey a human lord. And it was on the issue of obedience to God rather than to a human ruler that the Christians entered with zest into a Mediterranean-wide debate on the nature of religion. Like the Jews, the Christians

Criminals and Martyrs. This detail from a mosaic found in a Roman circus in North Africa shows a criminal tied to a stake and being pushed on a little cart toward a lunging leopard. Christian martyrs were treated much the same as criminals: they were executed—exposed to animals without even the "privilege" of suffering at the hands of a human executioner.

shepherd's garb; tall he was, and milking sheep. And around him were many thousands of people clad in white garments. He raised his head, looked at me and said: 'I am glad you have come, my child.'"

Other religions, including Judaism and later Islam, honored martyrs who died for their faith. But because Christianity saw itself as being based directly on "the blood of martyrs," in the words of Tertullian (197 CE), martyrdom took on unusual significance in the Christian church in its early centuries. Moreover, the remembered heroism of women martyrs—as numerous as men—acted as a constant imaginative balance to the increasingly all-male leadership (the bishops and clergy) of the institutionalized Christian church.

→ *How did empires such as the Roman and Sasanian help religions such as Christianity become universalizing?*

claimed to possess divinely inspired scriptures in which their God had told them what to believe and what to do, even when those actions went against the laws of the empire. The little group of martyrs who appeared in Carthage carried into court a satchel containing "books and letters of a righteous man called Paul"—the Gospels and the letters of Saint Paul.

In their emphasis on texts, the Christians were moving with the times. After 200 CE, new forms of published writings, directed toward a wider audience, made their appearance in the Roman world. By 300 CE, a revolution in book production had taken place. The scroll that all ancient readers had used (and that still survives in the Torah scrolls of Jewish synagogues) was replaced by the codex: separate pages bound together to form what is the modern book. The English word "code" comes from the Latin *codex,* and even today it connotes a set of legally binding regulations ("the federal tax code") or of technical requirements ("a house built according to code"). Christians spoke of their scriptures as "a divine codex." Bound together in a compact volume (or, more usually, a set of volumes)—a form that, unlike the unwieldy

scrolls, made quick reference to precise pages quite easy—this was, in their view, the definitive Code of God's law.

THE CONVERSION OF CONSTANTINE

Born sometime after 280 CE in Naissus (Niš), in modern southern Serbia, near the Danubian frontiers of the empire, Constantine belonged to a class of professional soldiers whose careers took them a long way from the Mediterranean. He had been proclaimed emperor by his troops in the far north, in York, in 306 after the death of his father, the emperor Constantius. It was a time of political confusion, with two co-emperors and sub-emperors, and several claimants fought for power. In 312, Constantine's armies closed in on Rome in his first bid to rule the heartlands of the Mediterranean.

Like other Roman emperors before him, Constantine looked for signs from the gods and put great credence in them when they came. Before the decisive battle for the control of Rome, he claimed to have had a dream in which he was shown an emblem bearing the words "In this sign conquer."

Scroll and Codex. (*Left*) The Torah scroll still used in Jewish synagogues is the same as that used in the ancient world. Sheets of papyrus were carefully glued together to produce a continuous roll. (*Right*) The codex of the Christian Scriptures is written in simple letters. Each column of text is put on a separate page, and the pages are then bound together to form a book.

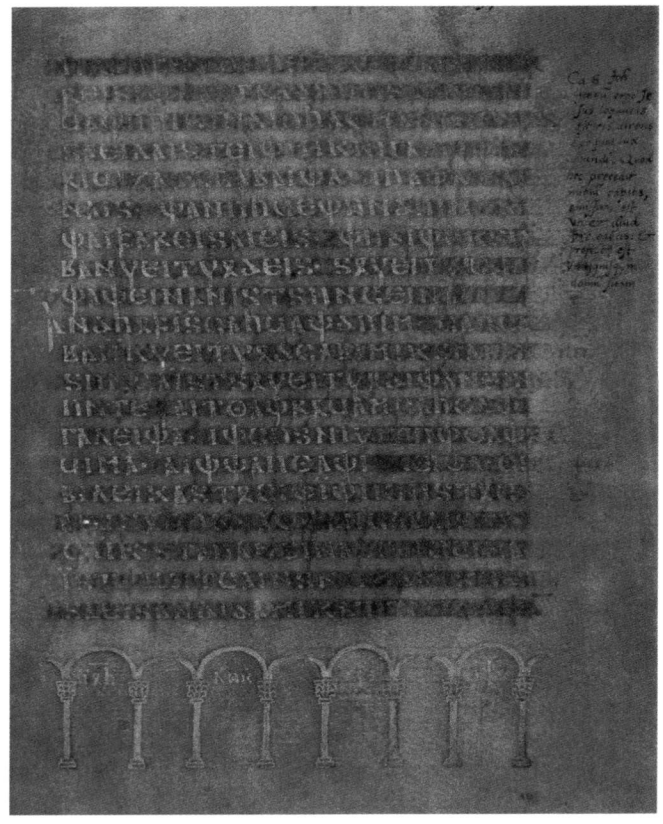

He was told to place this mysterious sign—later known as the *labarum*—on the shields of his soldiers. It took the form of an X (the Greek letter chi, representing a "ch" sound) placed over P (the Greek letter rho, or "r")—the opening letters of the name of Christ—and it soon became known all over the Roman world.

The recently persecuted Christian Church was the immediate beneficiary of Constantine's strange vision. In 313 CE, he issued a famous proclamation, exalting the work of Christian bishops and giving them tax exemptions for their services. But the significance of this edict was much broader. It was the first public evidence for what was soon labeled the "conversion" of Constantine, and it took a typically Roman approach to a powerful new god: it gave privileges to a favored religious group who were responsible for that god's worship. The order displayed no direct intention to make Christianity into a majority religion, still less to make it the exclusive religion of the empire. But, as is so often the case, an act's unintended effects were long-lasting; it would be through the institutions and across the byways of the Roman Empire that Christianity would spread.

Christians, taking Constantine's conversion as evidence of total victory for their faith, exploited their new privileges with fierce alacrity. Though still a minority within the empire (10 percent of the population, at most), they reacted to their earlier victimization by strenuously pushing their rights to the fore, even at the expense of others. Thus, as the century proceeded, the other religions of the Roman world felt the consequences of Constantine's conversion. Some resisted better than others. Notably, Judaism did not wither away. The archaeology of modern Israel and elsewhere has shown that Jewish communities remained proud and prosperous, despite the hostility of Christian emperors and Christian local violence, which was more frequent than any assaults by pagans against the Jews.

In 400, most inhabitants of the empire were still polytheist, but they were simply declared by Christians not to count. Christians in the Latin world gave them the pejorative name *pagani* (pagans), a word previously applied to those who were outside the privileged class of imperial officials (and who thus were second-class citizens). Being a *paganus* also meant to be a "local"—a person tied to his or her *pagus* (village), as in the modern French *paysan*, Spanish *paesano*, and English *peasant*. By using this name, Christians placed the entire world of ancient polytheism on a lower level than their own universal, urbane religion, which had taken shape from the preaching and reading of Christians in towns all over the Roman Empire.

The Conversion of Constantine. In this painting, the seventeenth-century artist Rubens uses "period" details for historical accuracy: the XP (the first letters of the name of Christ in Greek) in the sky; beneath them, the "dragon" standard of the Roman cavalry of the year 312 (the standard came from China and passed to Rome via the cavalry-nomads of Central Asia); beside the dragon, the eagle of the traditional Roman standard.

CHRISTIANITY IN THE CITIES

It took a long time for Christianity to become the majority religion of the Roman world. But Christianity soon established itself at the top of society, and it became a majority religion in the cities.

After 312 CE, the large churches built in every major city, many with the help of imperial funding, were a sign of Christianity's growing strength. They were gigantic meeting halls, often with room for more than a thousand worshippers. Called *basilicas,* from the Greek *basileus* (king), the solemn halls were indeed worthy of royalty. But unlike the ancient temples, which housed the gods inside (often in a small, dark sanctuary chamber) while the people milled around in the outdoors, they were open to all. Those entering a basilica found a vast enclosed space, shimmering with the light of oil lamps playing on shining marble and mosaics. Rich silk hangings, swaying between the rows of columns, increased the sense of mystery and directed the eye to the far end of the building—a semi-circular apse furnished with particular splendor. They had come into a different world. This was heaven on earth.

And it was a very orderly heaven. The bishop and priests sat at the very end of the building, under the dome of the apse, which represented the dome of heaven itself. The bishop had a special throne, called his *cathedra* (the Latin word regularly used both for a teacher's seat and for the throne of a governor). The space around the bishop and clergy was holy, marked off from the rest of the building by low marble screens and especially vivid floor mosaics. (The church at Verona even had under-floor heating in this area!) Ordinary members of the congregation would stand, as a gesture of respect, while the bishop sat and preached, usually from his space in the apse.

Such churches became the new urban public forums. They were ringed with spacious courtyards in which every city's poor would gather. In return for the tax exemptions that Constantine had given to the bishops of "his" church, the bishops were made responsible for the metropolitan poor, becoming in effect their governors. Christian poor relief helped the cities of the Mediterranean to weather financial crises in the fourth and fifth centuries.

Bishops also became judges. Constantine turned the process by which Christian bishops had acted as arbiters in disputes between fellow Christians into a more formal kind of small claims court. It was by such means—offering the poor shelter, quick justice, and moments of unearthly splendor in grand new basilicas on the holy days and festivals of the Christian year—that the bishops in the cities of the Roman world built up for themselves a position that would last (in many areas within and beyond Europe) until modern times. In many societies of Afro-Eurasia, as we will see, the weakening of grandiose imperial institutions often favored

Basilica Interior. The interior of a basilica was dominated by rows of ancient marble columns and was filled with light from upper windows, so that the eye was led directly to the apse of the church, where the bishop and clergy would sit under a dome, close to the altar.

the rise of local power blocs formed by religious groupings, who could hold the hearts and minds of smaller communities that discovered they were living in an increasingly dangerous world. In western Europe, those power blocs were headed by the Christian bishops. In their basilicas, "Rome" lived on for centuries after the empire had disappeared.

THE CHRISTIAN EMPIRE

Here was a universalizing religion and its practices. But how did it spread across parts of Southwest Asia, Africa, and Europe? Constantine and his successors were impressed by the Christian Church's unity and emphasis on expansion. Christianity was spreading into the hinterlands of Africa and Southwest Asia as part of a drive to reach out from the cities, where Greek or Latin predominated, to broader, more ethnically diverse populations. These efforts required the breaking of language barriers. After around 300 CE, the Christian clergy in Egypt replaced the hieroglyphs that were still being used to write the language—a system that only a few temple priests could read—with a more accessible, "modern" script, based on Greek letters: it is known today as Coptic (from the Greek word meaning "Egyptian," *Aigyptios*). With this innovation, the Christian clergy also brought the countryside and

Primary Source

EUSEBIUS

Eusebius declared that the Roman Empire had always owed its success to divine providence. He viewed the birth of Christ during the rule of the emperor Augustus as no coincidence: it showed God's choice to come to earth at a time when the preaching of his message could coincide with an almost uncanny era of peace and unity in the Roman world. Christianity had ridden to its favored position on the providential tide of a unified world empire.

Now formerly all the peoples of the earth were divided, and the whole human race cut up into provinces and tribal and local governments, states ruled by despots or by mobs. Because of this continuous battles and wars, with their attendant devastations and enslavements, gave them no respite in countryside or city. . . .

But now two great powers—the Roman Empire, which became a monarchy at that time, and the teaching of Christ—proceeding as if from a single starting point, at once tamed and reconciled all to friendship. Thus each blossomed at the same time and place as the other. For while the power of our Savior destroyed the multiple rule and polytheism of the demons [the old gods] and heralded the one kingdom of God to Greeks and barbarians and all men to the furthest end of the earth, the Roman Empire, now that the causes of manifold governments had been abolished, subdued the visible governments of, in order to merge the entire race into one unity and concord. . . .

Moreover, as One God and one knowledge of this God is heralded to all, one empire has waxed strong among men, and the entire race of mankind has been re-directed into peace and friendship as all acknowledged each other as brothers. . . . All at once, as if sons and daughters of one father, the One God, and children of one mother, true religion, they greeted and received each other peaceably, so

that from that time the whole inhabited world differed in no way from a single well-ordered and related household. It became possible for anyone who pleased to make a journey and to leave home for wherever he might wish with all ease. Thus some from the East moved freely to the West, while others went from here [the East] back there, as easily as if traveling to their native lands.

→ *What do you think of this praise of Constantine as the first Christian emperor, which comes from a seventy-year-old bishop who had witnessed the "Great Persecution" of Christians (launched by the emperor Diocletian in 303 CE)?*

→ *What elements in the history of Christianity at this time would have led Eusebius to emphasize its role as a unifying force in the Roman world?*

→ *Was his belief in a relation between the expansion of a world religion and the expansion of an empire an assumption that was unique to Christians?*

SOURCE: Eusebius, *Tricennial Oration* 16.2–7 [Jubilee Oration on the Thirtieth Year of the Reign of Constantine, delivered on July 25, 336], translated by H. L. Drake in *In Praise of Constantine: A Historical Study and New Translation of Eusebius' Tricennial Orations* (Berkeley: University of California Press, 1976), pp. 119–21.

its local languages closer to the towns and the towns to the countryside. A similar pattern unfolded in Africa along the Nile, not just in Egypt but also in Nubia and Ethiopia, each of which developed its own scripts and language under Christian influence. And in the crucial corridor that joined Antioch to Mesopotamia, Syriac, an offshoot of the Semitic language Aramaic, became a major Christian language. Christianity also spread further east, to Georgia in the Caucasus and to

Armenia, and Christian clergy, around 450 CE, created the written languages that are still used in those regions.

Constantine hoped to increase the unity of his empire by fostering the universal outreach of the Christian Church. In 325 CE, he celebrated his final conquest of the eastern provinces in Southwest Asia by summoning all the bishops to a gathering at Nicaea (modern Iznik in western Turkey), where he himself presided. Though their religion has since produced many denominations, all Christians still look back to the Council of Nicaea as the foundational moment when the Christian faith was first summed up in what is now known as a "creed"—from the Latin *credo*, "I believe." The belief that the essence of an entire religion could be captured in a written formula (rather than carried by memory, as was the case for oral societies and most "pagan" cults) typified the high hopes that the intellectual revolution of the third century had inspired. It was a statement of religious belief formulated in technical, philosophical terms. Jews and, later, Muslims expected believers to make formal statements that their God was the only God; Christians asked believers to balance three separate Gods in terms that required an expert to explain.

The effort did not succeed: Christians found themselves unable to come to universal agreement on such crucial questions as how Jesus could be both human and God in human form. More than a century later, the Council of Chalcedon (451 CE) fared no better. These were not issues that could be solved by a committee, even one backed by a Roman emperor; bishops did not always think alike. But, at Nicaea, they agreed on one crucial point: they agreed to hold Easter, the day on which Christians celebrated the resurrection of Christ from the tomb after his crucifixion, on exactly the same day in every church of the Christian world.

Constantine died in 337 CE. His legacy was monumental: he had converted to Christianity, but he had done so in such a way that Christianity itself was converted to the Roman Empire. Writing in the very last years of Constantine's reign, an elderly bishop of Caesarea in Palestine, Eusebius (c. 263–339?), presented a vision of the Roman Empire that would have surprised the martyrs of Carthage, who had died (less than a century and a half before) rather than recognize any "empire of this world."

From the time of Constantine onward, many Christians—especially in the Greek-speaking provinces of the empire, where Christianity was stronger and the empire was more secure—loudly trumpeted Eusebius's view of the history of Rome. Around the eastern Mediterranean, at least, Christians came to believe that Christianity, empire, and culture had flowed together.

But after the year 400 CE, Christians had to confront a new issue. What was the relative position of the "Christian" Mediterranean in a far wider sphere, where the world empire of Rome (which Christians such as Eusebius had come instinctively to identify with "civilization") was subject to increasing challenge from its own margins?

THE FALL OF ROME: A TAKEOVER FROM THE MARGINS

After 400 CE, the Roman world began to fall apart. The western European provinces went their own way, because there

the frontiers had never been borders in the modern sense. They did not constitute a clear defensive line, separating the inhabitants of the empire from the tribal world outside it. Indeed, over the centuries, the presence of Roman armies and of Roman cities along the Rhine and Danube had blurred the boundary between the Roman and the non-Roman world. A common zone had emerged, as Roman skills and the impact of the Roman economy reached deep into Germany and as non-Roman customs reached deep into Roman territory—including the shocking "barbarian" custom of wearing trousers. The ancient Roman dress code, which insisted on the loosely folded toga for civilians, gave way, in the course of the fourth century, to a tight, brightly embroidered shirt and trousers covered by a great cloak, itself pinned to one shoulder by brooches that were now of exquisite barbarian workmanship. This became the fashion favored by top military personnel in the Roman armies. The men who wore such attire might be Romans, but they were proud to look like warriors drawn from the tribes across the frontier.

WHO WERE THE BARBARIANS?

Romans and non-Romans were drawn together along the Rhine and the Danube through an active market in military manpower. In the societies that bordered the empire, young men grew up knowing that their personal status (the precious freedom of a male warrior in Germanic societies) depended on their ability to fight. In the absence of a strong state, order was maintained by the blood feud. Hence fighting was a part of everyday life as well as military campaigns. Such societies produced surplus warriors almost as a modern country in the developing world produces cash crops with export value (for example, bananas or coffee). So, too, non-Roman soldiers were exports sold for Roman gold. In the course of the third and fourth centuries, every civil war within the Roman Empire had been accompanied by massive immigrations of manpower from across the frontier that supplemented the armies of the rival claimants to the position of emperor.

What is often referred to as the "barbarian invasions" of the late fourth and fifth centuries were simply a more violent and chaotic form of this steady immigration. Today we use *barbarian* to label someone uncultivated or savage, but the core meaning of the word is simply "foreigner" (with overtones of inferiority). The inhabitants of the western provinces had become used to non-Roman soldiers from across the frontiers, and for them *barbarian* was virtually synonymous with "soldier." Soldiers could be destructive, and Roman civil wars were murderous affairs. But nobody feared that the presence of barbarians fighting in armies on Roman territory would bring the end of Roman culture.

As arresting as the popular image of bloodthirsty barbarian hordes streaming into the Roman Empire might be, it bears little resemblance to reality. In fact, the barbarians

MAP 8-3   WESTERN EURASIA: WAR, IMMIGRATION, AND SETTLEMENT IN THE ROMAN WORLD, 375–450 CE

Invasions and migrations brought about the reform and reconstitution of the Roman Empire beginning in the fourth century CE. Describe the people who migrated to or invaded the Roman Empire during this era. Where were they from, and where did they go? How did they reshape the political landscape of western Afro-Eurasia? Was the Roman depiction of these groups as "barbarians" a fair assessment?

were sucked into the empire in ever greater numbers by the Roman need for soldiers. The process reached a crisis point when, in 376 CE, Visigothic tribes from across the Danube petitioned the emperor Valens (ruled 365–378 CE) to let them immigrate into the Roman Empire. In need of manpower, Valens encouraged their entrance. But the Roman authorities failed to feed their new guests. It was famine and anger at the breakdown of supplies from the Roman side—and not innate bloodlust—that turned the Visigoths against Valens. When Valens marched against them at the flat plains outside Adrianople (modern Edirne, in European Turkey) in the hot August of 378 CE, he was not seeking to halt a barbarian invasion. Rather, he had come to teach a lesson in obedience to his newly recruited military stoop laborers. But the Visigoths, driven to desperation by famine, had brought with them cavalry from the steppes north of the Danube, and the charge of this cavalry proved decisive. Valens and a large part of the Roman army of the East vanished in a cloud of red dust, trampled to death by the men they had hoped to hire.

Even the most notorious incidents of the so-called barbarian invasions follow a similar pattern, as most involved armies from across the frontier drawn into the empire by Roman civil wars. Intermittent and murderous civil wars had long been a feature of Roman society, but the Roman state could not survive this bout, constantly fed by non-Roman recruits. The "fall" of the Roman Empire in western Europe was not a sudden collapse; instead, it was the culmination of a long process—the result of what historians have called overextension. Rome could never be nearly as strong along its frontiers as it was around the Mediterranean, because those frontiers were simply too far away. Despite the deservedly famous Roman roads, travel time between the Rhine border and Rome was more than thirty days. Because the Romans did not have the vast network of canals that enabled the Chinese emperors to move goods and soldiers by water, Roman power could be felt in the north only at the cost of constant effort and high taxes. After 400 CE, neither men nor funds were available to exert that power.

It became plain that the western emperors could no longer raise the taxes required to maintain control of the provinces. While some loss of revenue was attributable to military defeat and the perpetual disruption brought about by civil wars, the primary cause may have been the rise of an aristocracy of great Roman landowners throughout the provinces of the West. Their imposing villas dominated the landscape outside the cities. Often fortified with strong towers on every corner, these buildings were harbingers of the castles that would rise in medieval Europe. Those who lived in them controlled their peasantry for miles around as completely as the later feudal lords would. They could manage, if need be, without an empire.

In 418 CE, the Visigoths finally settled in southwest Gaul, between present-day Bordeaux and Toulouse. Ruled by their own king, who kept his military following in order, they were welcomed by the local landowners. The Goths, as they were more generally known, became a form of local militia, capable of maintaining law and order. In particular, they were able to suppress the peasants' revolts that had begun occurring with alarming frequency along the margins of Gallic society. Though never as savage or as widespread as the uprisings that had brought about the end of the Han dynasty in China, they created a mood of emergency. The threat of chaos made the Roman landowners of Gaul and elsewhere anxious to ally themselves with new military leaders rather than face the worse disruption that would follow social revolution and the raids of even more dangerous armies. The Goths came as allies of the aristocracy, not as enemies of Rome.

> *The "fall" of the Roman Empire in western Europe was not a sudden collapse; instead, it was the culmination of a long process—the result of what historians have called overextension.*

CONTINUITY IN CHANGE

Such accommodation ensured that a "Roman" style of life survived around the western Mediterranean long after the empire that had claimed to protect it had vanished. Even today, the names of some of the most famous vineyards in the valley of the Garonne and Bordeaux in southwestern France, such as Loupiac and Paulliac (the villages of Lupus and Paulinus) outside Bordeaux, still bear the names of the Romans who owned them around the year 400. Across the Mediterranean, outside Carthage, the chance discovery of a cache of estate documents written in careful Latin in 497 (twenty years after the departure of the last Roman emperor of the West) show that little had changed on the ground. Large estates made up of olive plantations continued to produce stunning wealth for local landowners with Roman names. The olive trees were still being rented out, sold, and planted according to legal rulings that went back more than 350 years, to the age of the emperor Hadrian.

Romans, and the non-Romans with whom they had allied and fought, also drew together because both suddenly confronted a common enemy. As happened many times in the history of Afro-Eurasia, a nomad confederation—in this case, that of the Huns, from eastern Inner Asia—reached out along the steppe corridor north of the Black Sea (modern Ukraine) to bring a new style of warfare and a new political ideology to the very edge of western Europe. For twenty chilling years, from 433 to 453, a single king, Attila, imposed himself as sole ruler of all the Hunnish tribes. His euphemistic name—"little Daddy," in Gothic—did nothing to soften the reality: he was a harsh overlord who frightened the Germanic peoples even more than he frightened the Romans. The Romans had walls to hide behind—Hadrian's Wall, town walls, villa walls, city walls. In the open plains north of the Danube, however, the Hunnish cavalry found only scattered villages and open fields, whose harvests they would plunder on a regular basis, reducing the Germanic population to starvation.

Attila was so formidable because he intended to be a "real" emperor. Having seized (perhaps from the Chinese empire) the notion of a "mandate of heaven"—in his case, a divine right to rule the tribes of the north—he fashioned the first opposing empire that Rome ever had to face in northern Europe. Its traces clearly remain in the archaeology of Ukraine, of Hungary, and of central Europe. Spectacular jewelry of a Hunnish style, often bearing dragon motifs that had come all the way from China, showed that a true warrior-aristocracy could exist across the Rhine and the Danube. Rather than having to sell his people's services to Rome, Attila extracted thousands of pounds of gold coins from the Roman emperors in the form of tribute. With Roman gold, he could dominate the barbarian world. The result: the Roman empire in the West vanished only twenty years after the death of the great Hun. In 476, the last Roman emperor of the West, a young boy with the pretentious name of Romulus Augustulus —namesake of both Rome's heroic founder and, as "Mini-Augustus," its first emperor—resigned to make way for a so-called barbarian king in Italy.

Rule from Rome was over, but not its legacies. Future rulers had to make alliances with the landowning classes that had prospered during the days of the empire. The Roman landowners of southern Europe had survived, and among them, by the year 500, the Visigoths felt fully at home. Their king could call himself Alaric II, proudly underscoring his connection to the man who had sacked Rome in 410. At the same time, he could also now count on the warm support of the great Roman landowners, some of whom claimed to be descended from members of the ancient Roman Senate stretching back to the time before the empire was established. In 506, Alaric II even issued for them a simplified code of imperial law that owed nothing to the non-Roman world. This carefully chosen condensation of the essence of Roman law provided his Roman subjects with all that was necessary to maintain a Roman way of life in a world without empire.

Such an alliance was not unique. In China as well, the great landowning families survived the passing of the Han empire. From 200 to 550 CE, they stood for a way of life that was sufficiently well-rooted in the land to outlive the unwieldy political superstructure of a unified empire. In Europe, as in China, there was a price to pay: alliance with outsiders. Non-Romans had been stereotyped, for centuries, as "barbarians"—violent, foreign, lacking all culture. But the landowners in Roman territories, as in China, proved to be adaptable realists. Though they now lacked an empire, they remained confident of the superiority of their "Roman" way of life. Nevertheless, they lived in a poorer world: the huge cities and the extensive trade networks that had characterized the Roman Empire at its height were drastically curtailed. The population of Rome itself dropped vertiginously —from half a million in 350 CE to about 80,000 in 500. Smaller, weaker states that were ruled by a warrior upper class became the norm.

The sense of unity of the Roman Empire was replaced by a sense of the continued unity of the church. This process is dramatically exemplified by the well-known story of the "Apostle of Ireland"—Saint Patrick (died c. 470). A Roman-Briton, he was first brought to Ireland as a slave, but he later returned to the island as a missionary. He believed that in making the Irish people Christian, he also made them "Romans." Once baptized, he argued, they were no longer "barbarians." They were then entitled to the same respect as any other "Roman" Christian. The "Catholic" (literally, "universal") Church became the one institution to which all Chris-

tians in western Europe, Romans and non-Romans alike, felt that they belonged. As a result, the bishops of Rome eventually emerged as "popes"—as the symbolic head of the western Christian churches. Rome ceased to be an imperial capital. Instead, it became a spiritual capital. By 700 CE, the great Roman landowning families had vanished (unlike the more tenacious families of China). They were replaced in the power structure by religious leaders, who wielded vast moral authority—a clergy that was often descended from them and that continued to regard Latin culture as the only culture suited to an international Catholic Church.

BYZANTIUM, ROME IN THE EAST: THE RISE OF CONSTANTINOPLE

The collapse of empire in the fifth-century West was a development restricted to a small corner of Afro-Eurasia. Elsewhere, the Roman Empire was alive and well. From the borders of Greece to the borders of modern Iraq, and from the Danube River to the future location of the Aswan Dam in Egypt and the borders of Saudi Arabia (over a territory now occupied by ten separate modern states), the Roman Empire survived undamaged. Rich and self-confident, it saw itself as a new and more fortunate version of Old Rome.

The new Roman empire of the East already had its own Rome. In 324 CE, a year before he assembled the Christian bishops at Nicaea, Constantine decided to build a grandiose new city on the European side of the straits of the Bosporus, which separated Europe from Asia. He chose the site of the ancient Greek city of Byzantium; he first called it New Rome, but it soon took on his own name, "Constantine's City" (in Greek, *Kōnstantinou polis*).

In the next centuries, Constantinople grew explosively, becoming not just a new Rome but a bigger and better Rome. By 500 CE, when Rome itself had dwindled to fewer than 80,000 inhabitants, its population numbered more than half a million. It was one of the most spectacularly successful cities in Afro-Eurasia, boasting 4,000 new palaces. Every year, more than 20,000 tons of grain were shipped in from Egypt, to a dockside one and a half miles in length along the Bosporus and in the sheltered inlet of the Golden Horn. A gigantic hippodrome (a deliberate echo of Rome's Circus Maximus) straddled the central ridge of the city, flanking an imperial palace whose opulent, carefully enclosed spaces stretched down the hillside to the busy shore of the Bosporus. As in Rome, the emperor would sit in his imperial box, witnessing the chariot races as rival teams careened around the stadium. The Hippodrome was also the place where eastern imperial might was put on display. Ambassadors came to the Hippodrome, on bended knees, from as far away as central Asia, northern India, and Dongola in Nubia (modern Sudan).

Constantinople also had the resources of a world capital. In the early sixth century (long after their western colleagues had been declared bankrupt), the emperors of Constantinople had a yearly budget of 8,500,000 gold pieces. On his death in 518 CE, the emperor Anastasius left a surplus of 23 million gold pieces. No other state west of China had tax revenues so gigantic or regular. It is important to recall that by Roman standards, nowhere could be more "Roman" than Constantinople. Constantinople was a predominantly Greek city. But Greeks had accepted Roman rule for half a millennium. They were proud (and obliged) to be ruled by Roman law, a circumstance that made them "Romans"—*Rhomaioi*. This was the Constantinople to which the future emperor Justinian came, as a young man from an obscure village in the Balkans, to seek his fortune around 510 CE. He became emperor in 527 CE. He thought of himself as the successor of a long line of forceful Roman emperors—and he believed that he would outdo them.

First, Justinian reformed the Roman laws. Working at headlong speed, by 533 CE a commission of lawyers created the *Digest*: a solid volume of 800,000 words that condensed the contents of 1,528 Latin law books. It was accompanied by the *Institutes*, which was to serve as a teacher's manual in the schools of Roman law. The best ones had long been not in Rome but in Beirut, on the eastern Mediterranean coast of ancient Phoenicia. These works were the foundation of what all later ages came to know as "Roman law," as followed both in eastern and in western Europe.

Justinian was equally determined to reassert the authority of the Roman emperors in the western Mediterranean. Relying on formidable naval superiority and small regiments of his crack troops, which included units of Hunnish horse archers armed with the most advanced bows, he crushed the once-formidable Vandals in Africa. In 533 CE, Carthage became part of the "true" Roman empire once again. He then turned his attention to the heart of the old empire, wresting Rome itself from the Ostrogoths in 536 CE and reclaiming the former imperial capital of Ravenna in northern Italy, beside the Adriatic, in 540 CE.

Our only portraits of Justinian and his wife, Theodora, come from a mosaic that he set up in the church of San Vitale in Ravenna to celebrate his brisk reconquest of Italy. In brilliant colors, the emperor is shown, surrounded by his entourage, as he advances beside the bishop to offer his gifts at the altar. His remarkable wife—a former strip dancer in the Hippodrome turned high-class courtesan (so her enemies said)—stands on the other side, swathed in imperial finery, bringing a large chalice up to the silken veils of the sanctuary. The two portraits, carefully placed on either side of the holiest part of the basilica, are still there, a reminder that Justinian did not only fashion himself the successor of Augustus and the reformer of Roman law, but also as the direct heir of Constantine. Justinian's empire was victorious because it was a Christian empire.

The perfect example of the marriage of Christianity and empire was the building of the church of the Hagia Sophia at the far end of the Hippodrome. With characteristic boldness and energy, Justinian took advantage of the burning in 532 CE of the city's old basilica church, destroyed in the course of a riot that started in the Hippodrome and almost cost him

Justinian and Theodora. These portraits face each other on either side of the altar in the apse of the church of San Vitale at Ravenna. Both Justinian and Theodora are shown presenting lavish gifts. As emperor, Justinian heads the procession. On his left are the clergy; on his right are guards with Constantine's XP symbol on their shields and his lay advisers. Thus, both church and state line up behind their leader, the emperor. Theodora is more secluded. She is surrounded by ladies with veiled heads and by beardless eunuchs, who draw back the curtains for her to make her appearance.

The Hagia Sophia. After the conquest of Constantinople by the Muslim Ottomans in 1453, the Hagia Sophia was made into a mosque by having minarets (slender, high towers) added to each corner. Otherwise, it looks exactly as it did in the days of Justinian. In modern times, it became the model for the domed mosques that appear all over the Islamic world.

his throne. Finished within a few years, Hagia Sophia (literally, "Holy Wisdom") would have come as a complete surprise to those who first entered it. No church of this size had ever been seen in the world; few buildings so large had been constructed in Roman times. The nave was twice the span of the former basilica—230 feet wide—and the new church was more than twice as high as its predecessor. The largest church built by the emperor Constantine, the basilica of Saint Peter in Rome, would have reached only as high as its lower galleries. Above all, the solemn straight lines of the traditional Christian basilica were transformed. Great cliffs of stone, sheathed in multicolored marble and supported on gigantic columns of green and purple granite, rose to a dreamlike height. Audaciously curved semi-circular niches placed at every corner made the entire building seem to dance. Instead of a pitched or flat wooden roof, a spectacular dome, in which light was trapped in the refulgent depths of gold mosaics, floated almost 200 feet above it all.

In later centuries, Hagia Sophia was called, by the Greek and non-Greek Christians of the East, "the eye of the civilized world." It represented in stone the flowing together of Christianity and imperial culture that, for another thousand years, would be the distinctive feature of the eastern Roman empire of Constantinople.

SASANIAN PERSIA

Justinian had the misfortune of having to rule an empire at the western edge of Asia when Asia itself was changing dra-

matically. To begin with, the contacts between east and west intensified. The first, most unexpected, and most deadly reminder of the influence of the east was a sudden onslaught of the bubonic plague—the grim gift of the Indian Ocean, a region of latent plague. In 542 CE, the plague first appeared in the Egyptian port of Pelusium (near modern Port Said and the outlet of the modern Suez Canal), which linked the Mediterranean to the commercial route that reached down the Red Sea and across the Indian Ocean, to Kerala and Ceylon. We are not sure of the actual origin of the plague—whether it was South Asia or the Great Lakes region of Africa—but it quickly emptied the cities of the Mediterranean. A third of the population of Constantinople died of bubonic plague within a few weeks. Justinian himself survived and lived until 565 CE, but he was forced to rule an empire whose traditional heartland had been crippled.

The quick spread of epidemic diseases was one reminder of the growing interconnectedness of distant Afro-Eurasian worlds; another was border clashes between empires whose frontiers bumped up against each other. Rivalry for territorial control escalated. Justinian's empire was locked in conflict with a formidable eastern rival for the control of Southwest Asia. Beginning at the Euphrates River and stretching for eighty days of slow travel by land across the modern territories of Iraq, Iran, Afghanistan, and much of central Asia—a distance of more than 1,500 miles—a great landbased empire, the Sasanian empire of Persia, extended across the land routes of western Asia.

KING OF KINGS OF ERAN AND AN-IRAN

As we saw in Chapter 7, the Sasanians had replaced the less ambitious Parthians as the rulers both of the Iranian plateau and of the rich lands of Mesopotamia by the mid-220s CE. For the sake of convenience, westerners (Romans included) tended to call their domain the empire of Persia, but its precise title is more revealing. The Sasanian ruler was the King of Kings of Eran and An-Eran—of the Iranian and the non-Iranian lands. A royal dynasty and an aristocracy drawn from the heartlands of the Iranian plateau claimed to rule, by divine right, the non-Iranian territories of Mesopotamia. The ancient, carefully irrigated fields of what is modern Iraq were very different from the stark, dry plateau of Iran itself. They were the economic heart of the empire. The Sasanians placed their capital—Ctesiphon—where the Tigris and the Euphrates Rivers come close, only twenty miles south of modern Baghdad. The presence of the King of Kings at Ctesiphon was symbolized by a vast vaulted arch (more than 110 feet high, with a span exceeding 75 feet) framed by a high facade, decorated with rows of windowlike arches. Though it may have been built as early as 300 CE, the great arch was known throughout the Middle Ages as the Taq-e Kesra, the "arch of

EMPIRES AND RELIGIOUS CHANGE IN WESTERN AFRO-EURASIA | **339**

→ *How did empires such as the Roman and Sasanian help religions such as Christianity become universalizing?*

Kesra/Kisra," from the name of Justinian's exact contemporary and rival, Khusro I Anoshirwan—Khusro of the Righteous Soul—who reigned from 530 to 579 CE.

In Southwest Asia during this period, Khusro Anoshirwan stood for the model ruler, and his name was identified with strong, just rule. Khusro's image in the east, as an ideal monarch and the personification of justice, was quite as glorious as that enjoyed by Justinian in the west, as the epitome of a Christian Roman emperor. For both Persians and Arab Muslims of later ages, the Arch of Khusro was as awe-inspiring and as seemingly indestructible as Justinian's Hagia Sophia appeared to be to Christians.

As Khusro's long reign unfolded, it became increasingly obvious that the vast Sasanian Empire was more than the equal of the Mediterranean empire of Rome, for it controlled the crossroads of Afro-Eurasia. Sasanian control of the western oases of central Asia ensured that the precious Silk Road passed through Iran before it reached the Romans at Antioch. But the control of trade was only part of the story. The flat lands around the Oxus River were the military laboratory of Afro-Eurasia, and developments there were studied keenly by Persians and Chinese alike. The Chinese emperors demanded "blood-sweating horses" from the plains of eastern central Asia for their own cavalry.

Christian forces met their match in the form of Iranian heavily armored cavalry, a fighting machine adapted from many years of Persian competition with the nomads of central Asia. On the plains of Syria, the Romans marched into a slaughterhouse. Covered from head to foot in flexible scale armor (small plates of iron sewn on to leather), these Persian horsemen were true harbingers of the medieval knight. More important still, the Sasanians had gleaned from northern India the art of making steel: their swords and armor were light and flexible. With such cavalry behind him, Khusro captured and sacked Antioch in 540 CE. The unexpected campaign proved to be no more than a smash-and-grab raid, and Khusro returned to Persia with vast plunder. But it was a warning, at the height of Justinian's glory in the west, that (as in the days of the Assyrians and then of the Achaemenids) Mesopotamia could reach out, once again, to conquer the shoreline of the eastern Mediterranean.

Under Khusro II, "the Victorious" (590–628 CE)—the grandson of Khusro I—the confrontation between Persia and Rome escalated into the greatest war that Southwest Asia had seen for centuries. Between 604 and 628 CE, Khusro II's armies conquered Egypt and Syria and even reached the threshold of Constantinople. Khusro II was finally defeated by the emperor Heraclius (ruled 610–641 CE) in a series of brilliant campaigns in northern Mesopotamia. Never had either empire reached so far into the heart of the other, and the effort exhausted both. For that reason, both fell easily to the Arab invasion that would occur only a few years later (see Chapter 9).

AN EMPIRE AT THE CROSSROADS

In their confrontations with Rome, Khusro I and Khusro II were helped by many factors. Culturally, Southwest Asia was already more united than its political boundaries implied. The political frontier between the two empires cut across an

The Great Arch. For a Persian king-of-kings, the prime symbol of royal majesty was the great arch marking the entrance gate of his palace. Here, in a Middle Eastern tradition that reached back for millennia, the king would appear to his subjects to deliver judgment. This building was associated with Khusro I, who came to be remembered as an ideal ruler.

MAP 8-4   SOUTHWEST ASIA, 300–600 CE

Southwest Asia remained the crossroads of Afro-Eurasia between 300 and 600 CE in a variety of ways. Trade goods flowing back and forth between west and east passed through this region, as did competing universal religions. How did religious communities interact during this time period? How did religious geography correspond to political geography? How was Southwest Asia affected by other regions, such as sub-Saharan Africa and central Asia, and how did it in turn shape developments in other these regions? The question mark in eastern Africa indicates our uncertainty about the origination of the plague.

exuberant common zone, in which Syriac was spoken and into which Christianity had spread. Strong Christian communities were established, under Sasanian rule, in northern Mesopotamia; to the south, at the head of the Persian Gulf; and along the trade routes of central Asia. The Sasanians themselves remained loyal to the Zoroastrian religion, which they had inherited from the distant past, calling it "the Good Religion." But they were forbearing rulers. Jews and Christians enjoyed a tolerance in Mesopotamia that no Christian emperor had extended to any non-Christians within the territories of the autocratic Christian Roman Empire. Protected by the King of Kings, the rabbis of Mesopotamia compiled the monumental and definitive Babylonian Talmud at a time when their western peers, in Roman Palestine, were beginning to feel the cramping pressure of a Christian state.

Christians particularly throve in this empire. Named by their enemies "Nestorian" Christians (from Nestorius, a former bishop of Constantinople, deposed for heresy because he emphasized the human rather than the divine qualities of Jesus), these members of the "Church of the East," based in Ctesiphon, made full use of the horizons opened up by Sasan-

ian trade and diplomacy to spread their faith more widely. As Nestorian merchants passed along the Silk Road, they settled communities across Asia; by 635 CE, they had established monasteries and a church in Chang'an in China. Earlier, Christian merchants operating out of the Persian Gulf founded colonies on the west coast of southern India. Those colonists have survived up to today, known as "Saint Thomas's Christians" because they claimed to be descended from Christians converted by Thomas the Apostle, the companion of Jesus. In fact, they were the product of the wide economic outreach of the Persian Empire.

Tolerance paid off. When, in a burst of Christian zeal, Justinian finally forbade "pagans" to teach philosophy in Athens in 527 CE, the philosophers promptly went to Ctesiphon—and were made welcome by Khusro. At the same time, the Sasanian court embraced offerings from northern India, including the *Pancantantra* stories (moral tales played out in a legendary kingdom of the animals), polo, and the game of chess. Khusro's was truly an empire of Afro-Eurasia's crossroads, where the cultures of central Asia and India met the Greek culture of the eastern Mediterranean.

RELIGIOUS CONFLICT IN IMPERIAL BORDERLANDS

Through the Persian Gulf, the Sasanian Empire reached out to control the trade on the Indian Ocean. This effort brought Persians into conflict with Roman merchants, who had striven to reach India from the Red Sea. The entire region bounded by present-day Ethiopia, at the western end of the Red Sea; Yemen, in southern Arabia; and the Persian Gulf became a field of conflict between the Roman and Sasanian empires.

Their clash took religious as well as commercial and political form. Both Ethiopia (then known as Axum) and Himyar (modern-day Yemen) were rich lands. They were amply watered by the same rains from equatorial Africa that caused the annual rising of the Nile. Both regions had embraced monotheism, expressed in the worship of a Most High God, known as al-Rahmānān (the Merciful One). In Ethiopia, this monotheism was Christian. As in the empire of Constantine and his successors, Christ was seen as the protector of the kings of Ethiopia and the Cross of Christ was their talisman in battle. The leaders of Yemen and the southern coast of Arabia were Jewish, and they dismissed Jesus as a crucified sorcerer.

The kings of Axum occupied the African side of the southern end of the Red Sea, looking down on the sea from the foothills of the well-watered and populous mountains of Ethiopia. Their formidable warrior-kingdom stretched as far as the Nile to the northwest, south into equatorial Africa, and eastward across the Red Sea to southern Arabia and Yemen. Axum's rulers, who became Christian around 340 CE, celebrated their victories on gigantic granite obelisks; larger than any known in the Roman Empire, they were monuments to a God that was very much a god of battles.

Faced by the aggressive Christian kingdom of Axum, the Sasanians reached out to support the kings of Himyar, who since 380 CE had been Jewish. Thus two monotheisms faced each other across the narrow southern opening of the Red Sea. Each was associated with a rich and aggressive kingdom. Each was backed by a Great Power—Ethiopia by Christian Rome and Himyar by the Persians.

Between 522 and 530 CE, a Jewish king of Himyar popularly known as Dhu-Nuwas (the Man with the Forelock) drove the Ethiopian Christian garrisons out of southern Arabia. He turned churches into synagogues (just as, in the Christian empire far to the north, many synagogues had been turned into churches). In 523 CE, the Christians of the oasis city of Najran were ordered to become Jewish. After all, Dhu-Nuwas told them, it was not as if he was asking them to become "pagans." They simply had to worship the One God, whom Jews and Christians shared, and to agree that Jesus of Nazareth had been a mere man—for, he insisted somewhat disingenuously, "All countries understand that he was a man and not a God." Those who refused to become Jews, Dhu-Nuwas burned on pyres of brushwood piled into a deep trench.

Swept by these rivalries, the Arabian peninsula was no longer a world apart, seemingly shut off from "civilization" by its cruel deserts and by the nomadic lifestyle of its inhabitants. Far from it. Arabia had become a giant soundboard that amplified claims about the pros and cons of Judaism and Christianity, argued over in Arabic and among Arabs, with unusual intensity for an entire century. The "nonaligned" Arabs of the intermediate regions (between southern Arabia and Mesopotamia) still worshipped their ancestral tribal gods. But they had heard much, of late, about Jews and Christians, Romans and Persians. Arab tribes around Yathrib (modern Medina) adopted Judaism and remained in touch with the rabbis of Galilee along the caravan routes of northern Arabia. Here was a new kind of borderland between empires and between religions, stretching from the West Coast of Africa to the Red Sea. It would be from this borderland that a new religion and a new prophet would emerge. His name was Muhammad.

THE SILK ROAD

> → *How did the actions and activities of Central Asians influence the geographic spread of universal religions and other cross-cultural developments during this time?*

Crucial to the growing interconnectedness of the Afro-Eurasian landmass was the region of central Asia. Through its mountain passes and across its difficult terrains, merchants, scholars, and travelers joined the two ends of Afro-Eurasia. They helped transmit the commodities, technologies, and ideas that flowed with increasing rapidity between the Mediterranean worlds and China and across the Himalayas into northern India. Although the zone of Afro-Eurasia from the Mediterranean to Iran and from the Caucasus to Ethiopia was dominated by the rivalry of Rome and Persia, the widely distant regions of East Asia were connected to each other by trade, imperial ambitions, and the spread of world religions. In particular, the Sogdian peoples, residing in central Asia's commercial entrepôts, maintained the stability and accessibility of the Silk Road.

It was only through central Asia that the peoples of the Mediterranean world and China could learn about each other. This sharing of knowledge began in earnest during the period when Christianity and Buddhism were spreading, and when traditional Vedic religion (Brahmanism) was also developing a scholarly written tradition. Early evidence of a heightened eastern Roman interest in the area can be seen in the dispatch of ambassadors from Constantinople to the nomads of eastern central Asia. Attempting to circumvent the Sasanian Empire, in 568 CE these emissaries brought back firsthand reports of the great empire of China. Long known for the fabulous wealth of its silk, China struck them as a miraculously stable state.

Chinese observers were also impressed by the eastern and western Roman empires. They caught a distant echo of a strong and prosperous military empire, governed by rulers who (in the western empire, in the fifth century) came and went in rapid succession. According to the "History of the Later Han Dynasty," written by Fan Ye in the fifth century, "They have no permanent rulers, but when an extraordinary calamity visits the country, they elect a new king."

It was the political and economic dynamism of central Asia, as described in previous chapters, that enabled the empires at the opposite ends of Afro-Eurasia to be visible to one another. The trading links provided the routes through which universalistic religious movements could flow, and in so doing helped reinforce cross-cultural connections. This was a region of great oasis cities. The Sasanians controlled Merv in the west (in modern-day Turkmenistan), and the Sogdian

cities of Samarkand and Panjikent in the east (on the edge of the Tienshan Mountains, in today's Uzbekistan and Tajikistan) were absorbed into ambitious nomadic kingdoms. The first of these was the kingdom of the Hephthalites or "White Huns," who had crossed the Altai Mountains into Sogdiana around 400 CE. After 560 CE, the Hephthalites were replaced by an equally wide-ranging Turkish confederacy, which would eventually leave the name Turkistan—the region of the Turks—on the countries north of Afghanistan.

As the Kushan kingdom of central Asia had previously done (see Chapter 6), these confederacies joined western and eastern Afro-Eurasia by patrolling the Silk Road between Iran and China. Like the Kushans, they also joined north to south, as they passed through the mountains of Afghanistan into the plains of northern India. As a result, central Asia between 400 and 600 CE was the hub of a system of Afro-Eurasia-wide contacts. The religious and cultural aspects of these contacts are essential for understanding the spread and appeal of universalistic religious ideals in this period.

BETWEEN IRAN AND CHINA: THE SOGDIANS AS LORDS OF THE SILK ROAD

The nomadic confederacies of Central Asia made possible a remarkable contribution of borderlanders to world history. Sogdians in the large oasis cities of Samarkand and Panjikent served as human links between the two ends of Afro-Eurasia. Their religion was a syncretic blend of Zoroastrian and Mesopotamian beliefs, inflected with Brahmanic influences. Their language was the common tongue of the early Silk Road, and their shaggy camels bore the commodities that moved back and forth, east to west, through their oasis trading hubs. The splendid mansions of the Sogdians (recently excavated at Panjikent) show that they shared fully in the epic culture of the warrior-aristocracy of Iran. The palace walls are covered with gripping frescoes of armored riders, such as had revolutionized the art of cavalry warfare from Rome to China. But the Sogdians were known as far away as China as merchants. They were the first to organize the caravan trade

Simurgh, the legendary dog-headed bird of Persian mythology, as shown on this seventh-century silver plate from Sasanian Persia, was a favored motif on textiles, sculptures, paintings, and architecture from the Byzantine Empire to Tang China.

A LETTER FROM A SOGDIAN MERCHANT CHIEF

Perhaps the clearest demonstration of how the Sogdians brought the ends of Eurasia together is a vivid document discovered in western China. In the year 313 CE (that is, a year after Constantine's famous "conversion" outside distant Rome), a Sogdian merchant chief, Nanai-vandak, wrote a letter from a station in modern Gansu, China, to his partner in Samarkand, his homeland some 2,000 miles to the west. He describes a state of civil war made more violent by the involvement of barbarian armies, much as had happened in the Roman Empire in the fifth century. He also describes the "business as usual" attitude of traders. The letter never reached Samarkand, however. It was among several Sogdian letters in a mailbag found in one of the guard posts of the Great Wall of China, near Dunhuang.

And sirs, it is three years since a Sogdian came from "inside" [i.e., from China]. And now no one comes from there so that I might write to you about the Sogdians who went inside, how they fared and which countries they reached. And, sirs, the last emperor, so they say, fled from Luoyang because of the famine and fire was set to his palace and to the city, and the palace was burnt and the city [destroyed]. Luoyang is no more, Ye is no more! And sirs, we do not know whether the remaining Chinese were able to expel the Huns [from] Chany'an, from China, or whether they took the country beyond . . .

And from Dunhuang up to Jincheng . . . to sell, linen cloth is going [selling well?], and whoever has made cloth or woolen cloth . . .

And, sirs, as for us, whoever dwells in the region from Ji[ncheng] up to Dunhuang, we only survive so long as the . . . lives, and we are without family, old and on the point of death. . . .

. . . Moreover, four years ago, I sent another man named Artikhu-vandak. When the caravan left Guzang, Wakhushakk . . . was there, and when they reached Luoyang . . . the Indians and the Sogdians there had all died of starvation.

➢ *What does the letter tell us about the nature of long-distance travel and trade along the Silk Road?*
➢ *What does it tell us about the relationship between the Han Chinese and the "barbarian" Huns?*
➢ *What does it tell us about the lives of the foreign traders in Han China?*

SOURCE: Annette L. Juliano and Judith A. Lerner (eds.), *Monks and Merchants: Silk Road Treasures from Northwest China Gansu and Ningxia, 4th–7th Century* (New York: Harry N. Abrams with the Asia Society, 2001), p. 49.

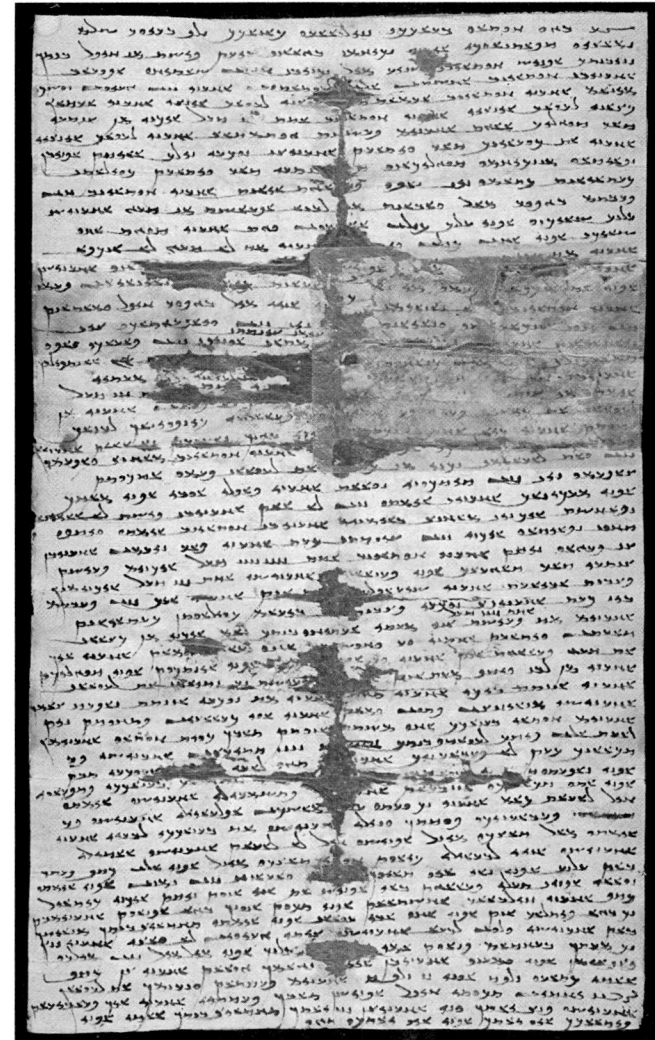

across the Taklamakan Desert to Chang'an, which served as the eastern terminus of the Silk Road in northwest China. To the Chinese, they were persons "with honey on their tongues and gum on their fingers"—to sweet-talk money out of others' pockets and to catch every stray coin.

Through the Sogdians, the products from West Asia and North Africa came into China. Goods decorated with Persian motifs—such as the legendary simurgh bird and prancing rams with the fluttering ribbons that, in Iran, were the symbol of good fortune and royalty—joined Roman glass, produced in the cities of the Mediterranean. Along with Sasanian silver coins and even gold pieces minted in Constantinople, these exotic products of the Western Lands traveled as far east as Japan, where some can still be seen in the treasury of the Shoso-in at Nara.

BUDDHISM ON THE SILK ROAD

Unstable political systems did not hinder the flow of ideas or commodities. On the contrary, the civil wars that marked the end of the Han Empire simply rendered China more open to the populations and the cultures of its far western regions. South of the Hindu Kush Mountains, in northern India, the conquests of the Hephthalite White Huns made the roads from India into central Asia safe to travel. It was over the mountainous corridor of Afghanistan that a new Buddhism came to spread, transforming the Chinese empire almost as dramatically as Christianity had transformed the world of Rome. That spread made Buddhism, for the first time, a major world religion. Buddhism in this era involved monks bearing holy books, offering salvation to the average layperson (to use a Christian term), traveling widely, and establishing themselves more securely in their host communities than did armies, diplomats, or even merchants.

In Bamiyan, a valley of the Hindu Kush Mountains that stretches off the road from northern Afghanistan and central Asia to Kabul, two gigantic statues of the Buddha—one 121 feet and another 180 feet in height—were hewn from the stone face of the cliff during the fourth to the fifth centuries CE. Until their destruction in 2001, they looked out over a high, vividly green valley of intensive cultivation. Standing at one of the major entrances to South Asia, the colossal Buddhas beckoned travelers from far away to the Buddhist monasteries that lay at their feet.

Starting at Bamiyan, Buddhist cave monasteries accompanied the traveler all the way through the oases on the edges of the Taklamakan Desert to North China. For China, in those centuries, was also ruled by emperors of nomadic origin drawn from the steppes of the "lands of the West"—from Inner Asia—much as Germanic warriors had been sucked into the provinces of the western Roman empire. The emperors of the Northern Wei (c. 386–534 CE), successors to the Han dynasty, came from a nomadic group known as the Xianbei, who represented a federation of non-Han groups; of these groups, the Tuoba were the most important. They commissioned five huge Buddhas—carved from cliffs, like the Buddhas of Bamiyan—which were fashioned in Yungang during the late fifth century. Two have survived: one is about 55 feet high, the other about 45 feet. While those at Bamiyan

Yungang Buddha. This is one of the five giant statues of the Buddha in Yungang, created under the emperors of the Northern Wei, a dynasty built by nomads who invaded and occupied north China. Sitting at the foothills of the Great Wall, the Buddhas marked the eastern destination of the Central Asian Silk Road.

Legend:
- Buddhist heartland
- Silk Road and connecting trade routes
- The travels of Xuanzang
- Spread of Buddhism and Mahayana Buddhism
- Buddhist centers
- Buddhist rock-carved temples
- Sacred Buddhist mountain

MAP 8-5 BUDDHIST LANDSCAPES, 300–600 CE

Buddhism spread from its heartland in northern India to central and East Asia during the first millennium CE. According to the map, what role did increasingly extensive trade routes play in pushing this movement? What was the relationship between Buddhist centers and rock-carved temples, trade routes, and the spread of this universal faith? How did the travels of Xuanzang symbolize growing connections between East and South Asia? To what extent did each region share a common culture?

had stood with royal majesty, the Buddhas of Yungang are shown seated, in meditation postures. Surrounding the Buddhas, more than fifty caves shelter more than 50,000 statues, representing both Buddhist deities and patrons who subsidized the construction. The Yungang Buddhas, seated

just inside of the Great Wall, welcomed travelers to the market in China. They marked the eastern end of the central Asian Silk Road.

These two groups of the Buddhas, placed more than 2,500 miles apart, are a reminder that at this time, in both the western and the eastern stretches of Afro-Eurasia, religious ideas had taken on a momentum of their own as they began to create world empires of the mind. Religions such as early Christianity and Buddhism saw themselves as not belonging to the kingdom of this world. They claimed to bring a universal message, contained in holy scriptures, and they were endowed with greater reach and greater cultural flexibility than the ponderous empires that *were* of this world—whether Roman, Hephthalite, or Chinese. Religion traveled light and traveled faster than did armies.

But as the conversion of the emperor Constantine showed, at the other end of Afro-Eurasia, "otherworldly" religions were not indifferent to the world. They were employed to validate ambitious new political structures. The sense of enjoying the blessing of Christ had encouraged Constantine to create nothing less than a New Rome on the Bosporus. Similarly, when the barbarian emperor Xiaowen moved the imperial capital of China from Pingcheng, at the foothills of the Great Wall, to Luoyang in the Yellow River valley in 494 CE, he formed a new religious center by having giant statues of the Buddha carved on the cliffs of Longmen, near the new capital. The nomadic rulers of the Northern Wei claimed that they were the incarnations of the Buddha, entitled by their identification with a new, divine world figure to rule their Chinese subjects in their own way. They could rule non-Chinese populations who were fellow Buddhists and could expect the Chinese to tolerate non-Chinese "barbarians" as fellow believers.

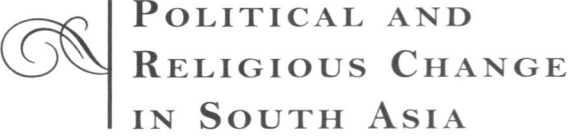

POLITICAL AND RELIGIOUS CHANGE IN SOUTH ASIA

> → *To what extent did South Asia develop a widespread common culture despite the region's political, religious, and social diversity?*

South Asia, especially the area that is now India, was also swept up in the religious enthusiasm of this period. Its major cultural system, Brahmanism (Vedic religion), did not claim to be a universal faith, with aspirations to reach outside India. But it did strive to meet all needs and to explain all theological problems, much as its rival, Buddhism, had done. Like Christianity in the Mediterranean and Southwest Asia, and Buddhism in China, religion in India helped unify diverse peoples. And here as in those regions, political opportunities aided the spread of spiritual forces.

Religious change in South Asia took a dramatic turn during the Gupta dynasty. The largest political entity in South Asia from the early fourth to the mid-sixth century—a sev-

A Gold Coin of Chandragupta II. The Gupta dynasty, based in the middle and lower Ganges plain, was known for its promotion of indigenous Indian culture. Here, Chandragupta II, the most famous king of the dynasty, is shown riding a horse in the style of the invaders from the Central Asian steppes.

enth century historian suggests there may have been as many as 70 states at this time—it provided the political stability that facilitated commercial and cultural exchange, much as the Roman Empire had done in its united territories. Chandra Gupta (ruled c. 320–335 CE)—who shared his name with Chandragupta, the founder of the Mauryan Empire 600 years earlier—titled himself "King of Kings, Great King." His son, Samudra Gupta (ruled c. 335–375 CE), expanded the Gupta territory to the entire northern Indian plain and even made a long expedition to southern India. Military achievements made the third king of the Gupta line, Chandra Gupta II (ruled c. 375–413 CE), the most famous, as did his generous patronage of many poets and singers in his court. Among them was Kalidasa, the poet and playwright whose works included *Sakuntala,* a famous play about a romantic encounter between a king and a daughter of an ascetic dwelling in a forest, and *Meghaduta (Cloud Messenger),* a lyric about a Yaksha, a man of a tribe outside of mainstream society, who sent a message through the monsoon cloud to his beloved wife in their faraway home while describing the cities and landscape —virtually all of India—on the cloud's route. Kalidasa and other poets of the time took episodes from the two great epics *Mahabharata* and *Ramayana*—finally set down in classical Sanskrit during this period—to write drama and narrative poems. The epics were no longer just lyrics for entertainment but a religious canon. All stories in the epics and derived works embodied *dharma,* or religious teachings. Hinduism was developing into a truly inclusive cultural complex.

THE TRANSFORMATION OF THE BUDDHA

In the centuries known as the Gupta period, the two main contemporary schools of Buddhism underwent fundamental changes as they increasingly took on universalistic features. From being regarded by his disciples as a contemplative atheist, the Buddha came to be worshipped as a god. The doctrines of both schools of this period—the Mahayana (Greater Vehicle) and the Hinayana (Lesser Vehicle)—had become quite different from what the Buddha had preached in the sixth to the fifth centuries BCE. As we saw in Chapter 5, the historical Buddha was a sage of the Shakya people who was believed to have entered *nirvana,* ending the pain of consciousness. In the earliest Buddhist doctrine, there was no god and no room for supernatural powers. But by 200 CE, as noted in Chapter 6, a crucial transformation had taken place in Buddhism: his followers had begun to view the Buddha as a god. Mahayana also extended worship to mediating demigods, the many bodhisattvas who bridged the gulf between the serene perfection of the Buddha and the world's sadly imperfect peoples. Some Buddhists, though, fully accepted Buddha as the god but could not accept the divinity of bodhisattvas; these adherents belonged to the school of Hinayana. It was especially in the wider, more inclusive form of Mahayana that Buddhism became a universal religion, whose adherents now worshipped divinities rather than simply acknowledging the worth of great men. Spreading along the Silk Road, this new religion, with claims to universality that rivaled Christianity's, would eventually appeal to peoples all over East Asia.

THE HINDU TRANSFORMATION

The ancient Vedic religion associated with the Brahmans responded to the new challenges of world religion with a revival and transformation of its own. Like Christianity, Buddhism and Jainism (another influential challenge to Brahmanic thinking, as described in Chapter 5) had become dominant in cities and in commercial communities. Ascetic and highly intellectual (and furnished with written scriptures), these two urban religions had pushed their rivals to one side, relegating the more conservative Brahmans and their religious practices to rural India.

Under this pressure, the Brahmanic (Vedic) religion changed profoundly, emerging to dominate Indian society as what we know today as Hinduism. Hinduism is a modern word coined from *Hindu,* the people who live in Hind, the Arabic word for India. People in India did not call themselves Hindus. In this new form of Brahmanical religion, the Brahmans became vegetarians, forsaking the animal sacrifices that had been so important to their earlier rituals. With this important change, totally abandoning the customs associated with pastoralists and nomads and absorbing in the process Buddhist and Jain practice, the Brahmans came to identify themselves with agricultural culture. Their new rituals were linked to self-sacrifice—denying themselves meat rather than offering up massive gifts of slaughtered animals to the gods, as they had in previous centuries. Three major deities, Brahma, Vishnu, and Siva, formed a trinity, representing both the three consecutive phases of the universe—birth, existence, and destruction, respectively—and the three expressions of the eternal self, known as the *atma.*

The Hindu trinity made it possible for believers to claim to be monotheists, since the three gods that they worshipped were thought to be embodiments of a single god, Atma. This belief also created a hierarchy around which to organize the numerous deities inherited from Vedic times. Vishnu, who embodied the present, was undoubtedly the most popular of the three. He came to the world in various avatars or incarnations, such as Krishna, the dark-skinned cowboy of Mathura who was the charioteer of the ancient hero Arjuna. Even the Buddha was adopted by Hindus as yet another avatar of Vishnu. The next most popular was Siva, who stood for the future. All three had female consorts—some beautiful goddesses, others fierce-looking.

The new Hindu pantheon was larger and more accessible than the Vedic one, enabling more believers to be incorporated into a single faith. Hindus did not wish to approach the gods only through sacrificial rituals, at which Brahmans alone could officiate. They sought to devote their passion and faith to an individual form of each one of the great gods. This religious practice of personal devotion to gods was called *bhakti. Bhakti* attracted Hindus of all social strata to the many deities, while a great body of mythological literature wove the deities into an intriguing heavenly order presided over by the trinity.

A CODE OF CONDUCT INSTEAD OF AN EMPIRE

Besides setting heaven in order, the Brahmans in this era also set about establishing a "correct" social order on earth. What emerged were new ways of thinking about governance and

Hindu Statue. This huge statue of a three-headed god in a cave on a small island near Mumbai (Bombay) represents the monotheistic theology of Hinduism. Brahma, the creator, Vishnu, the keeper, and Shiva the destroyer are all from one *atma,* or the single soul of the universe.

Primary Source

THE LAWS OF MANU

The Laws of Manu were compiled during the first or the second century CE, when the Kushan Empire ruled over much of South Asia. The compiler was a Brahman or a group of Brahmans. Among the many law codes that appeared in different periods of Indian history, that of Manu holds the most authority among the Hindus, as its coverage is the most comprehensive. It not only describes the origins of the four castes but also designates the occupations that provide members of each with their livelihood, as the following passage shows.

87. But in order to protect this universe He, the most resplendent one, assigned separate (duties and) occupations to those who sprang from his mouth, arms, thighs, and feet.

88. To Brâhmanas he assigned teaching and studying (the Veda), sacrificing for their own benefit and for others, giving and accepting (of alms).

89. The Kschatriya he commanded to protect the people, to bestow gifts, to offer sacrifices, to study (the Veda), and to abstain from attaching himself to sensual pleasures;

90. The Vaisya to tend cattle, to bestow gifts, to offer sacrifices, to study (the Veda), to trade, to lend money, and to cultivate land.

91. One occupation only the lord prescribed to the Sûdra, to serve meekly even these (other) three castes.

→ *The Brahmans, Kshatriyas, Vaishyas, and Shudras are the major four categories in the Hindu religious hierarchy. How are the differences in religious status reflected in the jobs that the people in different castes can take?*

SOURCE: *The Laws of Manu*, I.87–91; translated by G. Bühler, vol. 25 of *The Sacred Books of the East* (Oxford: Clarendon Press, 1886), p. 24.

the bonds between rulers and subjects. They were not enough to transcend the political fissures that crisscrossed the region. But they laid the foundation for an alternative ethic of statecraft, steeped in a universalizing faith, that would eventually bring legitimacy to an integrated polity. Unlike China and Rome, India did not have a centralized empire that this new ethic could revitalize. The empires that arose in central Asia, after the fall of the Mauryan Empire in the second century BCE left a vacuum in northern India, were governed by rulers who had no contact with the populations from whom they collected taxes and tariffs. Largely untouched by the empires' elaborate political structures, the local populations relied on religious and social institutions such as castes and guilds to maintain civic order during periods of frequent warfare and regime change (much as, in the west, Christian bishops had provided guidance and protection to Roman city dwellers and thereby spread their religion). To maintain order,

the Brahmans compiled many law codes, drawing their inspiration from Hindu moral precepts and customary law. Among them, the Laws of Manu, which were probably compiled in the first or the second century CE, stood out as the most comprehensive and widely valid. In Hindu mythology, Manu was the father of the human race (in Sanskrit, *manu* means "human"), and the Laws of Manu were considered applicable to all persons, irrespective of the states in which they lived. Kingdoms might come and go; but the "true" order of society, appropriate to "true" human beings and summed up in the Laws of Manu, remained the same.

Above all, the Laws of Manu offered clear guidance for living in a caste system, whose origins lay centuries earlier, in ways that embraced the entire complicated society. They ruled that every member of a certain caste could marry only within the caste and must follow the profession and dietary rules of that particular caste in order to perpetuate its status.

Thus tremendous social and religious pressure, but not government coercion, was exerted to keep all individuals within specific categories, obeying the social norms.

Though seemingly rigid, the Laws of Manu offered those who obeyed them a way to cope with a constantly changing Indian society, for the code's purview extended far beyond the frontiers of the major states of northern India. In providing the regulations and the mechanisms for absorbing new groups into the caste system, it helped Hinduism propagate into areas that the state could not control or even reach. Further, the *bhakti* form of religious devotion made Hinduism especially absorptive. Deities of folk religion joined the Hindu pantheon as new objects of worship were created. At the same time, the basic text or code reinforced what it meant to belong to a community of believers, especially as the faithful no longer lived close to one another. For with the universalizing of religious systems came the challenge of establishing norms and rules, principles set forth in writing and enforced by a priestly class. In this sense, the Laws of Manu functioned very much like the Jews' Torah, the Confucian Analects, the more recent "New Testament," and eventually the Muslim Quran, laying out basic precepts about religious life. These texts were also, it bears repeating, easily transported—they were certainly more mobile than armies or populations. Such holy scriptures could be conveyed great distances to those who were not yet members of the community of believers, potent weapons in the arsenal of religious conversion.

Behind these developments was a remarkable movement of internal colonization, as settlers from northern India pushed ever more southward, into lands that had formerly been outside the Brahmans' domain. In these territories south of the Deccan plateau, Brahmans met Buddhists as equals. Buddhist teachers were expected (like Brahmans) to speak refined Sanskrit, the "perfect" language, and they used the same vocabulary as the Brahmans while debating with them many topics, ranging from theology to theories of the structure of the universe to mathematics, logic, and botany. In essence, large Buddhist monasteries—such as Nalanda, with about 10,000 residential faculty and students in northeast India—became universities, responsible for both the spiritual and the intellectual growth of young men. Brahmans followed the models of Buddhist practice and established schools called *matha*. The meetings, often in open spaces sponsored by kings, were decisive historically, as the constant debates that they provoked helped to create a shared "Indic" culture. Most people spoke a dialect with imperfect grammar, but they could still understand the essentials of the debate in perfect Sanskrit. Although divided politically and religiously, the peoples living in what is now the country of India began between the fourth and sixth centuries to fashion a common culture organized around a shared vocabulary on crucial subjects such as concepts of the universe and the cyclical time scheme of life and death.

This widespread cultural unity physically covered no fewer than one million square miles (equaling the greatest extent of the Roman Empire) and affected a large and diverse population whose exact numbers are still not known. Although India was not under one polity (as was the case in China), or dominated by a single religious system (as would happen in the Christian Roman Empire and in medieval western Europe), it was becoming a region held together by a distinctive common culture—as outsiders clearly recognized. Xuanzang, a Chinese Buddhist pilgrim, began his account of a visit to India in the 630s and 640s CE by discussing the name *Indu*. For him and others, Indu, or what we today would refer to as India, began after a traveler crossed the valley of the Hindu Kush (modern Afghanistan). Geographically it was bounded by oceans on three sides (the east, south, and west) and by the snowy mountains of the Himalayas to the north. Politically, the region was split into more than seventy states. Yet it was culturally cohesive. Throughout this large land, Xuanzang observed, the Brahmans were the highest caste, and he thus suggested that it could also be called "the land of the Brahmans." In short, Xuanzang described India as an area of great diversity of regimes, climates, and local customs, but still a unity—possibly even a country.

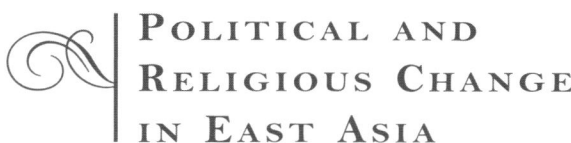

POLITICAL AND RELIGIOUS CHANGE IN EAST ASIA

> → *To what extent did new influences from other parts of Afro-Eurasia transform Chinese culture and politics during this era?*

In the first century CE, Han China had been the largest state in the world, with a population of approximately 60 million registered taxpayers (as great a population, that is, as the Roman Empire at its height). Its emperor ruled an area of 4 million square miles (more than twice the size of the Roman Empire) and regularly extracted an annual income of millions of pounds of rice and bolts of cloth and conscripted millions of regular and emergency corvée laborers. The end of the Han Empire (after 200 CE) was regarded, by later Chinese, as great a disaster as the end of the Roman Empire came to be viewed by western Europeans. Successive generations looked back to the centuries after the fall of the Han as a period marked by the barbarization of the Chinese world.

In reality (as was also true of the Roman Empire in the west), "barbarization" meant the opening up of a proud society to the cultures of the wider world that had grown up along its margins. In the case of post-Han China, the Silk Road, the military talents of the nomads, and the religious skills of proselytizing Buddhist monks from what the Chinese called the Western Regions provided new inspiration and new influences. In this invasion from the west, Buddhism took much the same role as Christianity played in Rome, adapting itself to the Chinese empire and gaining in strength and popularity as a result of imperial and elite patronage. Here Buddhism evolved into a Chinese religion with universalistic appeal—even extending its reach beyond China into Korea and Japan (as discussed in Chapter 9).

DOWNSIZING: NORTHERN AND SOUTHERN CHINA

After the fall of the Han in 220 CE, several kingdoms—initially three, though at times as many as sixteen—competed for total power. The Shu state in the southwest (Sichuan), the Wu kingdom in the south (the lower Yangzi region), and the Wei state in the northwest region all sought to restore the Han Empire and to monopolize political power to further their own interests. Civil wars raged between these three powerful states and their allies from 220 to 589 CE, a time often called the Six Dynasties period, when no single state was able to conquer more than half of China's territory. One of the major turning points of this era came in 311, when the Xiongnu confederacy from the northern steppes of Inner Eurasia, which had played a central role in forming the Silk Road and in bringing down the Han dynasty, sacked the former Han capital of Luoyang. Ultimately, the most successful regime was that of the Tuoba, a people originally from Inner Mongolia on the eastern edge of the steppe lands. Nearly seventy-five years after their first contact with the northern Chinese rulers, the Tuoba founded the Northern Wei dynasty in 386; it lasted one and half centuries, ending in 534 CE. As a result of the northern invasions, China was divided by polity, culture, and ethnicity for nearly three centuries. But the idea that it should be united still endured.

The northern and southern divide was the most pronounced. Many of the powerful families in the south were the descendants of aristocratic northerners and their supporters who had fled in disgust and fear at the thought of being ruled by barbarians from the steppes such as the Xiongnu and the Tuoba. The southerners thus regarded themselves as the true representatives of Chinese culture, and they scorned the allegedly barbarian rulers who had usurped power in the north. The flow of migrants from the north never stopped, but life in the southern reaches of China over the next several centuries proved difficult. The hot and wet climate of the southern region of China was ideal for growing rice, but it also fostered diseases—especially malaria—that ravaged the population. The exiles tried to return, but their military expeditions to reconquer the north were like the efforts of the emperor Justinian to reconquer Italy and re-create the "true" Roman Empire: despite some initial successes, they ultimately failed.

Undeterred by the contempt of the Han peoples and scholars for their rough manners, the "barbarian" rulers in northern China—first the Xiongxu, then the Tuoba—maintained many of their preconquest forms of state and society. Because they had lived within the Chinese imperial orbit as tributary states before they conquered North China, they were "civilized" by imperial standards—yet still, in the minds of the Han, inferior. Nevertheless, they maintained many Chinese traditions of statecraft and court life; thus, they taxed land and labor on the basis of a census, conferred official ranks and titles, practiced court rituals, preserved historical archives, and promoted classical learning and the use of classical Chinese for record keeping and political discourse. Though they were nomadic warriors, they adapted their large standing armies to city-based military technology, which required large-scale public works such as dykes, fortifications, canals, and walls. Following the Qin-Han Chinese precedent, they drafted huge numbers of workers as corvée to complete such enormous projects as rebuilding a new capital city at Luoyang for the Northern Wei dynasty.

Rulers of the Northern Wei dynasty faced many challenges, including the need to consolidate authority over their own highly competitive nomadic people. One approach to bringing more control and order to their society, pursued strenuously but with little success over the course of nearly a century, was to make their own government more "Chinese." Emperor Xiaomen (ruled 471–499) encouraged Tuoba warriors to emulate Chinese society and customs. The royal family changed their name, adopting the Chinese family name of Yuan. All court officials were required to speak Chinese and wear Chinese clothing. The Tuoba families resisted these policies, continuing to speak in their native tongues and to wear native clothing. At the same time, the Wei rulers sought to cultivate stronger relationships with the great Han families of Luoyang that had not migrated to southern China, hoping that offers of more political power (greater opportunities to serve as officials in the Wei bureaucracy) and more land might persuade these families and their supporters to stay in the north.

A key figure in attempting to sinicize, or "make more Chinese," Tuoba rule and to win support of the Han Luoyang

> *As a result of the northern invasions, China was divided by polity, culture, and ethnicity for nearly three centuries. But the idea that it should be united still endured.*

families was the Dowager Empress Fang (regent 476–490 CE), grandmother of Emperor Xiaomen. Her most substantial initiative on this front centered on a series of progressive land reforms. The need for the Han Chinese families to continue growing crops was urgent, both to feed the city dwellers and to maintain a strong tax base (the nomadic Tuoba were not required to pay land taxes). Under the land reform policies, young men who agreed to cultivate the land would receive two allotments of land, one at the age of eleven and one at fifteen, which they could pass on to their heirs. After age seventy, they would no longer be required to pay taxes on the land. But even this rather appealing plan, pursued over several decades, failed to bridge the cultural divides between the "civilized" Han of Luoyang and the "barbarian" Tuoba Wei because the latter showed no interest in farming. The boldest attempt to unify northern China would be made by Emperor Xiaomen, who rebuilt the old Han capital of Luoyang and made it the seat of his government in an effort to recapture the glory of the Han dynasty. His untimely death in 499 CE cut short his efforts to unify the north. Several decades of intense fighting among military rulers followed, leading ultimately to the downfall of the Northern Wei dynasty.

BUDDHISM IN CHINA

By the third and fourth centuries CE, when Chinese imperial power had reached a low point, Buddhist travelers arriving from central Asia had already become frequent visitors in the streets and temples of the competing Chinese capitals of the various warring states: Chang'an, Luoyang, and Nanjing. Great movements of peoples swept fascinating individuals

into China. For example, in 383 CE, regional Chinese forces in the northwest seized Kucha (now Xinjiang), then under Tibetan rule. There they found Kumarajiva (344–413 CE), a renowned Buddhist scholar and missionary, whom they brought back to China proper. Beginning in 401 Kumarajiva resided at the court in Chang'an, where he both taught and practiced magic rituals and became known as a promoter of Buddhist holistic medicine.

Spreading the universalizing faith required brokers, endowed with texts or codes, to convey its message. Kumarajiva was the right man, in the right place, at the right time to spread Buddhism in China, where it already had toeholds but coexisted with many other faiths. He was, above all, a bearer of exotic holy books (not unlike the Christians of the Roman Empire), and his influence on Chinese Buddhist thought was critical. Not only did he translate previously unknown Buddhist texts into Chinese, including many of the most important titles in the Chinese Buddhist canon, but he also clarified Buddhist terminology and philosophical concepts for Chinese adepts. He and his disciples established a Mahayana branch known as Madhyamika (Middle Way) Buddhism in China, which used irony and paradox to show that reason was limited. They sought enlightenment through transcendental visions and spurned experiences in the material world of sights and sounds.

Kumarajiva represented just the beginning of a major cultural shift. After 300 CE Buddhism began to expand in northwestern China, taking advantage of imperial fragmentation and the decline of state-sponsored classical learning. The Buddhists stressed devotional acts and the saving power of the Buddha and the saintly bodhisattvas. They encouraged the Chinese to join the clergy. The idea that persons could be

Amitabha. This exquisite tapestry is an illustration for the *Amitabha Sutra*, the "Sutra of the Western Pureland." Since the text was translated into Chinese by Kumarajiva in the fourth century CE, Amitabha has been one of the most popular bodhisattvas in China. A devotee who invokes the name of Amitabha ten times before death would be saved to this Western Pure Land, where the Seven Treasures decorated the quiet landscape.

defined by faith rather than kinship was not entirely new in Chinese society, as the Han dynasty Daoist rebels showed (see Chapter 7), but it had special appeal in a time of unprecedented crisis. In the south, the immigrants from the north found that membership in the Buddhist clergy and monastic orders offered a way to restore their lost prestige.

Even more important, in the northern states—now part-Chinese, part-barbarian—Buddhism provided legitimacy. The presence of Buddhists at "Sino-barbarian" courts—taking prominent positions in government, medicine, and astronomy—enabled the ruling houses in northern states to espouse a philosophy and worldview that could provide them a defense against the Han Chinese who favored classical learning and despised "barbarians" for their lack of culture and education.

Despite its appeals to universalism, Buddhism, which did not have a central ecclesiastical authority, took on different forms in the different regions of South and East Asia as it adapted to realities on the ground. It did not have the hard edges that defined Christianity in the Roman Empire as a religion that was the same in all places and at all times. On the contrary, as the expression of a cosmic truth as timeless and as varied as the world itself, Buddhism easily took on new appearances in new places. It absorbed as its own the gods and the wisdom of every country into which it came. A particularly interesting variant emerged in South China, where Buddhism and Daoism borrowed many common practices from each other. In fact, there the two faiths became so amalgamated that quite often only scholars could elucidate the fine distinctions between them and explain the origins of various practices. In effect, Buddhism in South China had taken on a Chinese tinge through its borrowing from Daoist practices.

DAOISM, ALCHEMY, AND THE TRANSMUTATION OF THE SELF

Daoism had gained ground as a popular Chinese religion during the Han period. At that time, Daoist clergy challenged the Confucian state and its scholar-officials, first as leaders of rebellious local groups and, later, as leaders of massive armies. Beginning in the period of disunity, however, Daoism quickly lost its political edge and adapted to the society then in place. Two new traditions of Daoist thought flourished in this era of self-doubt in China. The first was community-oriented and involved heavenly masters guiding local religious groups or parishes. Followers sought salvation through virtue, confession, and liturgical ceremonies. Through ecstatic and orgiastic initiation rites, which were often achieved through an "external alchemy"—that is, using drugs and chemicals to cause transformations (in this context, in the self)— the Daoist clergy brought believers into contact with the divine.

A second Daoist tradition was more individualistic. In the Yangzi delta, personal expressions of religious faith emerged. Ge Hong (283–343 CE), a student of esoterica, sought to reconcile Confucian classical learning with Daoist religious beliefs in the occult and magical. He focused on "internal alchemy": that is, the use of trance and meditation alone to control human physiology. Through such mental and physical exertions, an adept accumulated enough religious merit to prolong his life. The quantification of merit and demerit in Daoist circles had important affinities with the Buddhist notion of karmic retribution (the cosmic assessment of the sum total of one's acts in this life that determines whether one will be reborn into a better or worse next life; see Chapter 5).

The Shaolin Monastery. This monastery on Mount Song, Henan province, is famous for its martial art, or "gongfu." But the martial art tradition was established quite a few hundred years after the monastery came into being in c. 495 CE, under the Northern Wei dynasty. In 527, an Indian priest, Bodhidharma, arrived there to initiate the Zen school of Buddhism in China. The more than 230 small pagodas contain relics of the head monks who managed the monastery in the last 1500 years.

THE ART OF RELIGIOUS FERVOR IN CHINA

Above all, the religious fervor of this period changed the visual environment of China. The decorations for pottery and metal objects from this time show strong central Asian and Sasanian influences, which were transmitted primarily through Buddhism. The impact on architecture was even more striking. In India, Buddhists had adapted a form of dome-shaped tombs called stupas into shrines used to house relics of the Buddha. Huge pagodas represented a Chinese attempt in wood to imitate stone and brick stupas in India. Regarded by Koreans and Japanese (and later by Westerners) as quintessentially Chinese, the pagoda was in fact a distant echo, on Chinese soil, of northern Indian Buddhism. Similarly, the complexes of cave temples at Longmen and Yungang were inspired by Indian and central Asian examples. In these ways, a universal religion created common artistic themes that stretched from central to East Asia.

One site that featured the work of central Asian artisans was the oasis city of Dunhuang. Located along the Silk Road, it contained a number of cave temples. Since 400 CE, they had been adorned with paintings and statues, and between the fifth and eighth centuries hundreds of cave chapels were decorated with wall paintings. Some illustrated Buddhist legends, and others depicted scenes of paradise. The caves were sealed in 1035 to save them from raiding Tibetans, and they have survived to this day. In 1900, the cave housing the great Buddhist library at Dunhuang was found unopened. The dry climate had preserved thousands of manuscripts, including Buddhist texts and works of popular literature.

→ *What do the architectural links from India to China, Japan, and Korea tell us about Buddhism?*
→ *Why are the Dunhuang caves so essential to our understanding of Chinese Buddhism in medieval times?*

Pagoda on Mount Song. This is probably the earliest pagoda in China. The solid stone structure shows the influence of pagodas in the contemporary eastern part of India, such as the one in Mahabodhi Monastery in Bodhgaya.

The Western Pure Land. This mural painting of the Western Pure Land is from Dunhuang, close to the eastern end of the Silk Road. The facial features of the celestial beings and the art style are more Chinese than Indian. Lazulite blue, a pigment made from lapis lazuli from Badakshan, Afghanistan, is the dominant color here, as it is on all the cave art along the central Asian Silk Road.

For the Daoists, however, eternal life—not the Buddhist ideal of release from the cycle of rebirth—was the ultimate goal. Older alchemical writings were reinterpreted in light of notions of Daoist breath control and the meditation techniques introduced by Buddhists. Both external and internal alchemy thus relied on natural processes for creating perfected substances to ingest or for creating a new self by practicing meditation. Each could confer eternal life.

By 400 CE China had more than 1,700 Buddhist monasteries and about 80,000 monks and nuns. By contrast, in 600 CE (after two centuries of monastic growth), Gaul and Italy—the two richest regions of western Europe—had, altogether, only 320 monasteries, many of them with fewer than thirty monks. In this emphasis on the cloister, the two ends of Afro-Eurasia resembled each other. Both in China and in large regions of Europe, the principal bearers of the new religion were monks, set apart from "worldly" affairs in their refuges, where they were piously supported by royal courts and by warriors whose lifestyle differed sharply from their own. Yet in China, the Buddhists were challenged as the major cultural force in the region, though their religion was one of the most dominant.

We will see in Chapter 9 that when the Chinese empire was reunified under the Sui (581–618) and Tang (618–907) dynasties, its officials brought Confucianism back into ascendancy. They spearheaded a renaissance based on the classical teachings that Buddhism and Daoism had overshadowed since the fall of the Han dynasty.

FAITH AND CULTURES IN THE WORLDS APART

→ *How similar and different were spiritual developments in worlds apart from Afro-Eurasia during this time?*

Sub-Saharan Africa was only loosely connected to the Eurasian and North African landmass, and the Americas were wholly separate. Where these worlds stood apart, ideas, institutions, peoples, and commodities did not circulate easily and quickly. Cultures that were based on world religions or principles held to apply everywhere in the world were therefore more difficult to create; as we have observed, however, Christianity spread up the Nile through the Nubian corridor into Ethiopia and the Sudan, two parts of sub-Saharan Africa that had always maintained close contacts with North Africa and many other parts of Eurasia. But elsewhere, we do not see the development of universalizing faiths. Rather, belief systems and their deities were localized. This is not to say that sub-Saharan Africa and the Americas lacked the elements for creating profound and integrated cultural systems

around communities of faith. Indeed, Africans and Americans alike had prophetic figures who were said to have communicated with the deities and brought to humankind divinely prescribed rules of behavior. Moreover, peoples in both regions had canonical beliefs and rules that, though not preserved in texts, were passed down orally from generation to generation. They, too, were intended to guide behavior and to establish social mores. The calendar of rituals across these regions was closely governed by relationships with deities in whose hands Africans and Americans believed their fortunes to lie.

BANTUS OF SUB-SAHARAN AFRICA

Almost all of Africa south of the Equator is inhabited today by peoples speaking some variant of more than 400 Bantu languages, no more distinct from each other than are the Germanic languages of northern Europe. Early Bantu history is shrouded in mystery. At present, scholars using oral traditions and linguistic evidence can trace the narrative of these peoples no further back than 1000 CE. The first Bantu speakers apparently lived in the southeastern part of modern Nigeria, where they began to shift from a hunting, gathering, and fishing economy to practicing settled agriculture. The areas into which they spread as they began to move about 4,000 or 5,000 years ago demanded an immense amount of work. To ready a new acre of land in the tropical rain forest for cultivation required the removal of some 600 tons of moist vegetation, and the early migrant groups brought to this task only simple tools (mainly machetes and billhooks). In fact, their most effective technique for the initial clearing was controlled bush burning, but it left a great deal of burned vegetation to be removed. Moreover, the African equatorial forests, the primary zones of Bantu habitation, were almost totally devoid of indigenous food plants. Yams were native to Africa, but new varieties were later introduced from Southeast Asia, as were bananas; and maize, manioc, and sweet potatoes arrived only after the Europeans had reached the Americas. As a consequence, these peoples had to make do with woodland plants such as yams and mushrooms, as well as palm oils and kernels.

Bantu migrants traveled out of West Africa along river beds and elephant trails, in two great population waves. One group moved eastward across the Congo forest region to East Africa, aided early in their migration by their knowledge of iron smelting, which enabled them to use iron tools in their agricultural activities. Because the habitats into which they moved permitted them to maintain a mixed economy of animal husbandry and sedentary agriculture, they became relatively prosperous. The second branch moved southward through the rain forests in present-day Congo, eventually reaching the Kalahari Desert, but they were not so fortunate. Their tsetse fly–infested environment did not permit them to rear livestock, and thus they were limited to subsistence farming. They learned to use iron later than those who had moved to the east.

Precisely when these Bantu migrations began cannot yet be known with certainty, but once under way, the travelers moved with extraordinary rapidity. Genetic and linguistic evidence demonstrates that they swept all else before them, absorbing most of the hunting-and-gathering populations who had originally inhabited these areas. A few remnants of the earlier residents do survive, however, most notably the pygmy hunters and cultivators in the Ituri forest of central Africa and the Khoisan hunters of the Kalahari Desert in southern Africa.

What enabled the Bantus to prevail and then to prosper was their skill as settled agriculturalists. They knew how to cultivate the soil, and they were able to adapt their farming to widely different environments. They thrived equally well in the tropical rain forests of the Congo River basin, the high grasslands around Lake Nyanza, and the highlands of Kenya,

MAP 8-6 BANTU MIGRATIONS

The migration of Bantu speakers throughout much of sub-Saharan Africa in the first millennium CE dramatically altered the cultural landscape of the region. According to the map, where were the Bantu speakers' migrations? What skills did they possess that enabled them to populate the lands they migrated to and dominate the peoples who were already living there? Did the Bantu migrations create a common culture below the Sahara Desert during this time?

even though they had to grow different crops in each of these locations.

For the Bantu of the equatorial rain forests of central Africa, known as the Western Bantu, the introduction of the banana plant was decisive. Linguistic evidence suggests that it first arrived in the Upper Nile region, and from there it was carried into the rest of Africa by small groups migrating from one favorable location to another; the earliest proof of its presence is a record from the East African coast dated to 525 CE. Eventually it spread into the equatorial rain forests, where its adaptability to local conditions was unmatched. Not only did it provide more nutrients than the yam crop, which it ultimately replaced, but it better withstood heavy rainfalls. In addition, banana plantings required farmers to clear fewer trees from the land than did yam cultivation and created an environment that was free of the anopheles mosquito, the

carrier of malaria. Taking full advantage of the benefits of banana cultivation, the Western Bantu filled up the equatorial rain forest areas of central Africa—perhaps as early as 500 CE, certainly by 1000 CE.

But did these peoples create a Bantu culture, as some scholars claim? Clearly, they could not establish the same political, social, and cultural institutions in widely different ecological zones. The Great Lakes in eastern Africa presented them with savanna lands, which allowed for relatively easy communications. Here, they eventually created centralized polities whose kings ruled by divine right. Mostly, however, they moved into heavily forested areas—tropical rain forests similar to those they had left in southeastern Nigeria. These locations supported a distinctive way of life that remained fundamentally unaltered for perhaps a millennium and a half (400 to 1900), withstanding the impact of the Atlantic slave

Primary Source

INSTRUCTIONS TO A YOUNG MAN IN WEST AFRICA

The words that were traditionally spoken to a young man coming of age in the Cameroons in West Africa reflect the importance that families attached to being a strong and enterprising individual.

The grandfather gave an ivory bracelet and said:

> "This elephant which I put on your arm, become a
> man of crowds,
> a hero in war, a man with women
> rich in children, and in many objects of wealth
> prosper within the family, and be famous
> throughout the villages."

The grandmother gave a charm of success as a belt and said:

> "Father, you who are becoming a man
> Let toughness and fame be with you as this sap of the
> *Baillonella toxisperma* tree is glued to this thread.

> Become dominant, *a great man,*
> a hero in war, who surpasses strangers and visitors;
> prosper, Have us named!"

➤ *Why were gifts in these coming-of-age ceremonies typically charms?*

➤ *Why did the sub-Saharan peoples organize themselves around "big men" rather than kings or other sorts of rulers?*

SOURCE: Jan Vansina, *Paths in the Rainforests: Toward a History of Political Tradition in Equatorial Africa* (Madison: University of Wisconsin Press, 1990), pp. 73–74.

---

trade and withering only under European colonialism in the twentieth century. The western Bantu-speaking communities of the lower Congo rain forests formed small-scale societies that relied on family and clan connections. They organized themselves socially and politically into age groups, the most important of which were the ruling elders. Within these age-based networks, individuals of demonstrated talent in warfare, commerce, and politics regularly came to the fore and provided decisive leadership.

Lacking chiefs and kings, the highly fluid and loosely organized Bantu societies rallied around these so-called big men, whose talents inspired others and attracted followers, thereby promoting territorial expansion. In the rain forest, land was relatively abundant but labor was in short supply. Hence, individuals able to attract a large community of followers and to marry many women and sire many children could lead their bands into new locations and establish dominant communities.

Although dispersed, these rain forest communities embraced a common view of the world. They believed that the natural world was inhabited by spirits, many of whom were

their own heroic ancestors. These spiritual beings intervened in people's lives and required constant attention and appeasement. Diviners helped men and women understand the ways of the spirits, and charms warded off the misfortune that aggrieved spirits might wish to inflict. Both diviners and charms were also important in protecting people from the injuries that living beings—witches and sorcerers—could inflict on them. Much of the misfortune that occurred in the world was thought to be the work of these malevolent forces, especially as wielded by witches and sorcerers. Indeed, the big men were often thought to control such forces and to use them to punish opponents and reward friends. These beliefs, like the rest of the Bantu worldview, would survive unchallenged for well over a millennium.

The Bantu migrations filled up an immense part of Africa, not less than half of its landmass. The diverse population groups that moved out from their original location in southeastern present-day Nigeria introduced settled agriculture into all corners of the southern part of the landmass. They brought with them a political and social order based on family and clan structures that at the same time allowed considerable leeway for individual achievement—and maintained an intense relationship to the world of nature that they believed, for good or ill, was shot through with supernatural forces.

MESOAMERICANS

As in sub-Saharan Africa, the process of settlement and expansion in Mesoamerica differed from that in the large empires of Afro-Eurasia. In the case of Teotihuacán, the first major community to emerge since the Olmecs, we see the growth of a city-state that ruled over a large, mountainous valley in present-day Mexico. While it did not evolve into a territorial state, it traded as well as warred with neighboring peoples, and created a smaller-scale common culture. In the case of the more famous Mayans, we witness the emergence of a "big" common culture, one that also ruled over large stretches of Mesoamerica; it was composed of a series of kingdoms, each built around ritual centers rather than cities. The Mayan people aggressively engaged neighboring peoples in warfare and trade, expanding their borders through tributary relationships. The extraordinary feature of Mayan society was that its people were defined not by a great ruler, or great capital city, but by their shared religious beliefs, worldview, and sense of purpose. But there is a mystery at the heart of Mesoamerican societies. For as great as were the early so-

cieties of the Olmecs, the people of Teotihuacán, and the Mayans, there was less carryover from one society to the next. Cultural development was much less cumulative here than in Afro-Eurasia, where new regimes built on the old—in part because frequently they absorbed their predecessors. In the Americas, decline often set in before newcomers could take advantage of the learning and breakthroughs of those who had preceded them. As a result, in Mesoamerica empires and common cultures did not emerge on the same scale as in Afro-Eurasia before 1000 CE.

The factors responsible for the repeated interruptions in development remain a mystery. Some argue that the lack of domesticated beasts of burden limited humans' ability to control nature and amass resources. Others point out that what was so essential to Afro-Eurasian developments—the constant contact with neighbors and strangers that fostered learning from others—here vanished once the land bridge across the Bering Straits sank. Inhabitants of the Americas were thereafter on their own, truly in a world apart.

TEOTIHUACÁN Around 300 BCE, the people of the central plateau and the southeastern districts of Mesoamerica, where the dispersed villages of an Olmec culture had risen and fallen, began to gather in larger concentric settlements and to create state systems. The growing scale of political and social integration led to city-states, the largest of which was Teotihuacán, in the heart of the fertile valley of central

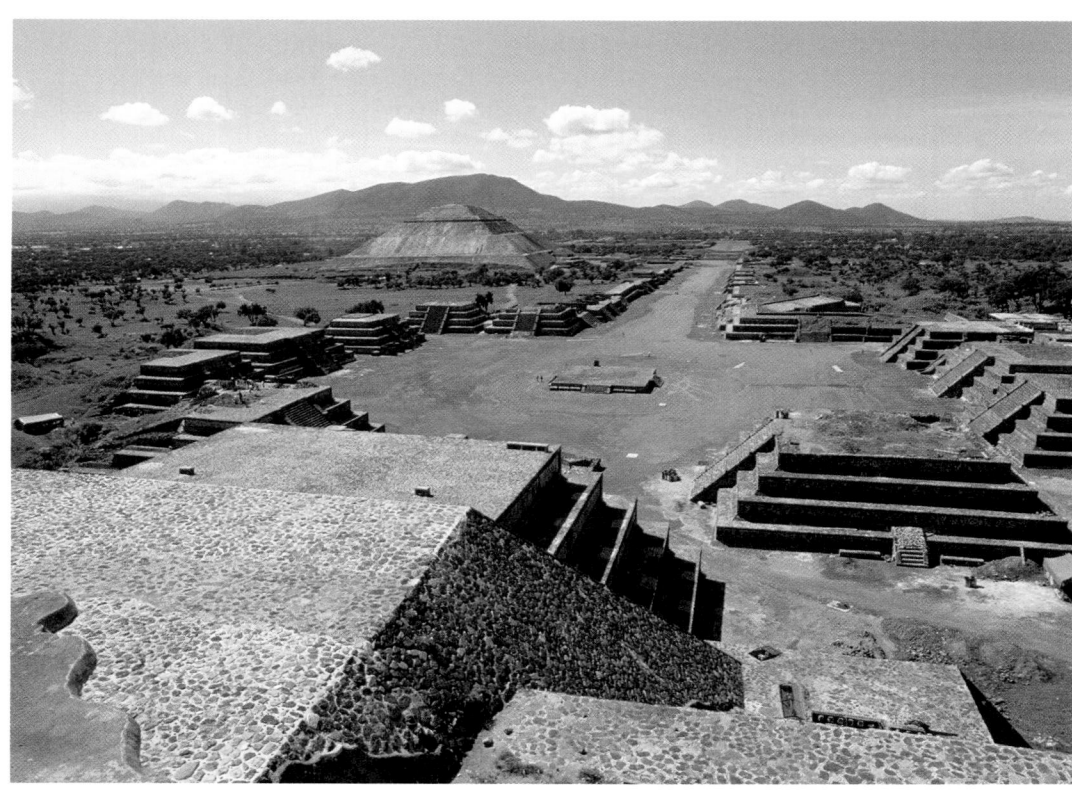

Teotihuacán. The ruins of Teotihuacán convey the importance of monumental architecture to Aztec culture. In the foreground is the Plaza of the Moon, leading to the Street of the Dead, with the Pyramid of the Sun to the left. These massive structures were meant to confirm the importance of spiritual affairs in urban life.

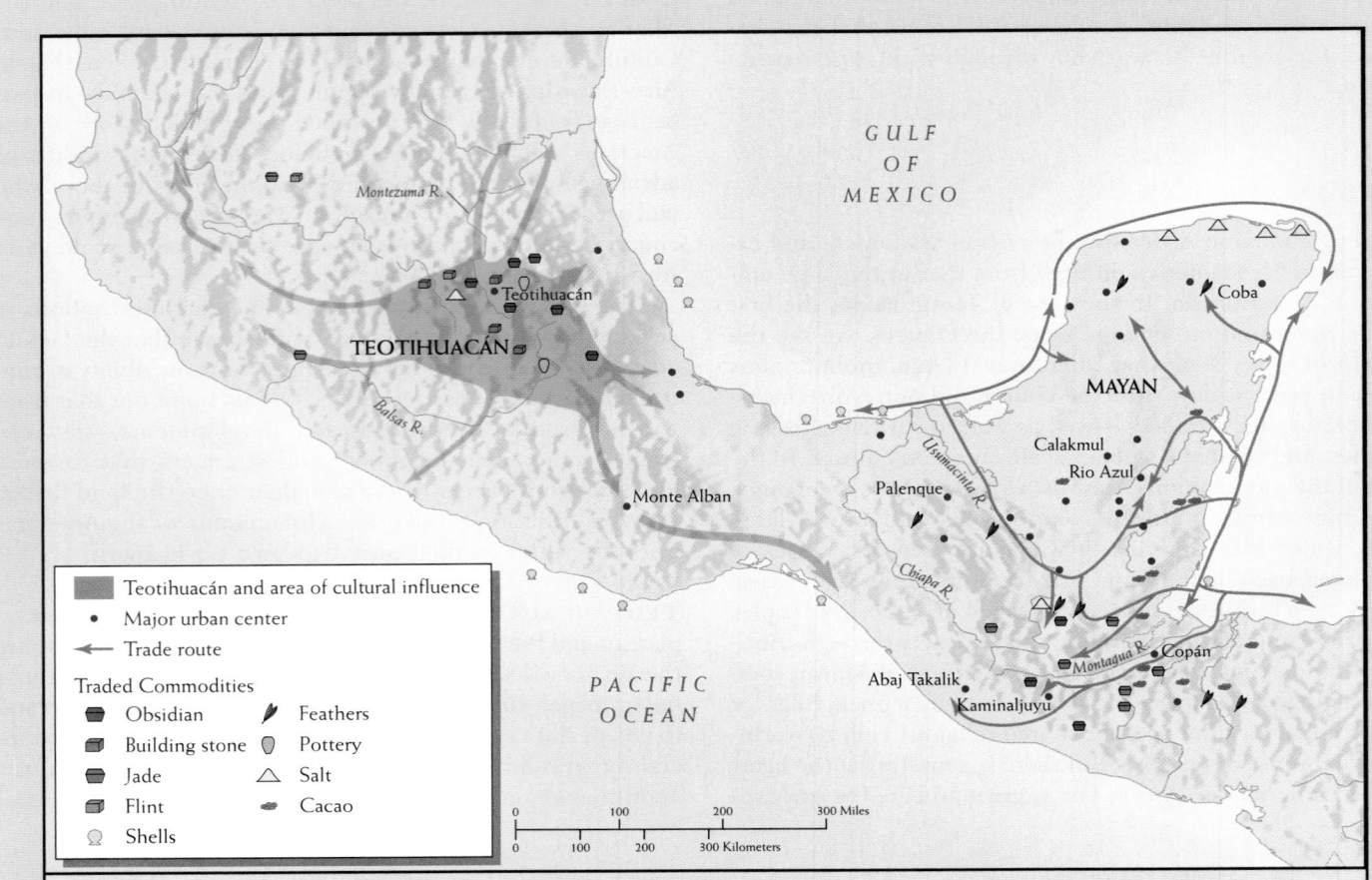

MAP 8-7 MESOAMERICAN WORLDS, 200–700 CE

In the first millennium, two cultural groups dominated Mesoamerica: one was centered at the city of Teotihuacán in the center, and the other, the Mayans, was in the south. According to the map, how did each group create a common culture in surrounding regions? Do common trade goods suggest common cultural outlooks? To what extent do you believe the people of the Teotihuacán and Mayan worlds influenced each other?

Mexico; indeed, it became by far the largest center of the Americas before the Aztecs almost a half-millennium later. Its influence was felt across Mesoamerica, from the deserts in the north to the jungles of the south, and from the Gulf Coast to the Pacific.

The fertility of Teotihuacán's land and the ample supply of water from the marshes and lakes of the valley fostered high agricultural productivity, though the methods of cultivation were still technologically primitive. At the city's zenith, the local food supply sustained a metropolis of probably 100,000 people (as many as 200,000, by some estimates), living in more than 2,000 apartment compounds lined up and down the city's streets. At one corner were the massive pyramids of the sun and the moon, the focus of spiritual life for the city dwellers. The city's center was given over to the huge royal compound, or Ciudadela; it contained its own stepped stone pyramid, the Temple of the Feathered Serpent, whose grandeur and refinement were famed throughout Mesoamerica at the time and probably influenced Mayan pyramid builders. The awesome promenade, known as "the Street of the Dead," culminated in the hulking Pyramid of the Moon, where, as archaeologists have discovered, foreign warriors and dignitaries were mutilated, sacrificed, and often buried alive to consecrate the holy structure, an edifice designed to raise believers closer to their deities.

Teotihuacán was a powerful city-state that did not mutate into an empire. Though it did not conquer vassal states or create a centralized bureaucracy, its military muscle was imposing. Its rivals were soon either overwhelmed or annexed; by 300 CE, Teotihuacán controlled the entire basin of the Valley of Mexico. It dominated its neighbors and demanded gifts, tribute, and humans for ritual sacrifice. Its massive public architecture was adorned with art commemorating decisive battles, defeated neighbors, and captured

→ *How similar and different were spiritual developments in worlds apart from Afro-Eurasia during this time?*

Quetzalcoatl. The artisans of Teotihuacán decorated the sides of their monumental buildings with sculptures. Here, feathered serpents, denoting the god Quetzalcoatl, burst from the sides of a wall to stare menacingly at passers-by.

fighters. Warfare was instrumental for the city's command of distant hinterlands, even if the vanquished were not made into formal provinces of Teotihuacán.

But the city's political influence beyond the basin was limited. Far more important was its cultural and economic diffusion. Teotihuacán's merchants traded throughout Meso-america, outside its formal sphere of control. Ceramics, ornaments of marine shells, and all sorts of decorative and valued objects (especially of highly prized green obsidian) made by Teotihuacano artisans were shipped out on the backs of porters and exchanged far and wide. For instance, a modest Mayan community near the coast of present-day Belize used Teotihuacán green obsidian objects, such as elegant figurines that resembled the Temple of the Feathered Serpent, in burial offerings. At the same time, Teotihuacán imported pottery, feathers, and other goods from distant lowlands.

This kind of expansion therefore left much of the political and cultural sovereignty of neighbors intact, with only the threat of force keeping them in check. But as that threat began to wane, Teotihuacán ran into trouble. Reasons for the demise of the city remain unclear. It likely fell at the hands of invaders near the end of the fifth century, probably after a generations-long decline that left it vulnerable to attack. Whatever the precise circumstances, invaders attacked the city, burned it, and smashed the carved figurines of the central temples and palaces, targeting their destructive energies at its institutional and spiritual core; Teotihuacán's gods, helpless or resigned, watched the assailants' rampage.

THE MAYANS Teotihuacán's power eventually spread as far as the Caribbean region of the Yucatán and its interior hinterlands. These became the areas occupied by the Mayan

people, who expanded gradually from about 250 CE to reach their zenith in the eighth century. The Mayans have been a never-ending mystery to historians and archaeologists. They lived in an inhospitable region—hot, with infertile soils, lacking large navigable river systems, and vulnerable to periodic hurricanes. Still, they managed to develop large concentrations of peoples, trade over long distances, and make stunning scientific and mathematical innovations. They were also great artists and builders, and it is largely from the remains of their prodigious constructions that we know much about them. Like the Olmecs before them, the Mayans accomplished magnificent things, only to collapse, leaving their ancient centers deserted for centuries and entire provinces utterly depopulated.

In contrast to those who dwelled in Teotihuacán (or in Baghdad or Constantinople, for that matter), the Mayans achieved greatness without founding a single great metropolis. Instead, they settled across present-day southern Mexico to western El Salvador. In this region divided by many ecological zones, hundreds, possibly thousands, of agrarian villages sprang up; their people shared the same Mayan language and were connected by trade. Villages were also linked together through tribute payments, chiefly from lesser settlements to central, mainly sacred, towns, in honor of deities and family rulers. Because the population growth rates were high and sustained for many centuries, at their peak the Mayans may have numbered as many as 10 million—a figure that certainly qualifies them as a "big" culture. Bigness in a cultural system without big cities made them unique.

The Mayans were divided into a variety of kingdoms that revolved around major hubs and their hinterlands. Palenque,

Palenque. Deep in the Lacandon jungle lies the ruin of the Mayan city of Palenque. Its pyramid, on the left, overlooks the site; on the right, the Tower of the Palace shadows a magnificent courtyard where religious figures and nobles gathered. There is no mistaking how a city like Palenque could command its hinterland with religious authority.

Copán, and Piedras Negras, for instance, were closer to the model of a city-state with hinterlands, similar in some respects to the Mesopotamian city-states surrounded by the transhumant societies; they were politically sovereign but culturally and economically interconnected. Some larger polities, such as Tikal and Kalak'mul, became substantial, sprawling cities with dependent provinces. The ambitions of rulers in these larger states frequently and repeatedly embroiled them in hostilities.

Thus a single culture was internally divided into about a dozen kingdoms, with shifting borders, that shared many features. Each was highly stratified, displaying an elaborate class structure. At the center was a shamanistic king who legitimated his position by extolling his lineage, which reached back to a founding father and ultimately the gods, and who promoted public ceremonies to honor him as well as his ancestors. Kings sponsored elaborate rituals to reinforce their divine lineages, including ornate processions down the main boulevards of their cities to pay homage to gods and their descendants, the rulers. Lords and their wives performed ritual blood sacrifice to feed their ancestors. Though a priestly ruling caste has sometimes been credited with great powers, the pillars of these societies were their scribes, legal experts, military advisers, and skilled artisans. Indeed, many artists and scribes rose to high political positions because they bestowed an aura of greatness on rulers whose grasp on power was often insecure.

Most of the Mayan people remained tied to the land, which was capable of sustaining a high population but not in concentrated settlements. In much of the region, the soil was poor and quickly exhausted. Limited water was also an impediment to large-scale agriculture, as major rivers or irrigation systems were lacking. Mayans therefore employed a combination of agrarian systems adapted to the ecology. Where possible, they created terraces and drained fields—thereby allowing more intensive cultivation. But in much of the region they relied on swidden (slash and burn) agriculture, which pushed the arable frontier further into the dense jungle of Mesoamerica. Either way, farmers could not become too specialized. The result was largely a subsistence economy of diversified agrarian production. Villagers cultivated maize, beans, and squash, rotating them to prevent soil nutrients from being depleted. Where possible, some farmers supplemented these staples—and their diets—with root crops such as sweet potato and manioc. Cotton was the basic fibrous staple used for robes, dresses, and blouses; it was frequently grown amid rows of other crops as part of a diversified mix.

Commerce connected the dispersed Mayan worlds, as did a shared culture: a common set of beliefs, codes, and values that rulers supported. Villagers spoke dialects of roughly the same language. Writing developed very early, though only very recently have epigraphers been able to make sense of the Mayan script—and that new knowledge has revolutionized modern understanding of the Mayan world. The advent of

Wood Tablet. This detail of a wood-carved tablet from a temple in the city of Tikal (c. 741 CE) is a fine example of the ornate form of scribal activity, which combined images and portraits with glyphs that tell a narrative.

writing created an important caste of scribes, who were vital to the integration of Mayan society. Rulers handsomely rewarded scribes with great titles and honors, as well as material comforts, for their ability to write grand epics telling the story of dynasties and their founders, great battles, marriages, deaths, and sacrifices. Such writings taught generations of Mayan subjects that they shared common histories, beliefs, and gods, and that these were associated with the narratives of ruling families.

The Mayans also were skilled in mathematics, which they used in devising a calendar and pursuing the study of astronomy. Keen readers of the stars, they charted regular celestial movements with amazing accuracy. They clearly had developed a method for marking the passage of time by precise lunar as well as solar cycles. By counting and watching the stars, the Mayans could map heavenly motions onto their sacred calendars and rigorously observe their rituals at the proper times.

Here was a world riven by political divisions and often crippling warfare, but with common religious and cultural features. A common faith provided a powerful human resource that rulers could exploit. Cities, and even their rem-

POP	UO	ZIP	ZOTZ	TZEC
XUL	YAXKIN	MOL	CHEN	YAX
ZAC	CEH	MAC	KANKIN	MUAN
PAX	KAYAB	CUMHU	uayeb	

Mayan Pictograms. The Mayans were famous for keeping records of time with an elaborate calendar. Pictograms, each with a separate image, represented the months of the year. All literate Mayans would have recognized this index.

nants after intense periods of warfare, reflected a ruler's ability to summon his subjects to work and contribute to the greatness of the kingdom. Mayan cities lacked street grids. Instead, plazas, ball courts, terraces, and palaces were simply added on to existing neighborhoods, in an early form of urban sprawl. The hubs of activity revolved around royal palaces, whose sophistication was intended to manifest a ruler's grandeur, and massive ball courts, where teams of players met before enthusiastic audiences in a contest that was more religious ritual than game. Moreover, great rulers exhorted their people to build not just outward but upward. The Mayans excelled at the building of skyscrapers—especially as tombs. In Tikal, for instance, surviving buildings include six steep funerary pyramids, whose massive superstructures are made of thick masonry walls and contain grand corbel-vaulted ceilings and chambers; the tallest temple soars above the treetops, more than 220 feet high. The outsides are embellished with giant carvings and paintings, and deep within are the crypts that held the bodies of royal family members.

The elites were obsessed with blood: spilling it was a way to honor dynastic lineages while paying homage to gods. This rite led to chronic warfare, especially among the high-ranked members of rival dynasties, to capture victims whose blood could be shed. Rulers also would frequently shed their own blood at intervals set by the calendar. Royal wives drew blood from their tongues; men underwent a more delicate ritual, as it involved using a stingray spine or sharpened bone to perforate the ruler's penis. Such bloodletting was undertaken only by those of noble descent, with the aid of instruments that were adorned and sanctified; beautiful scenes carved and painted on stelae portrayed blood cascading from the mutilated bodies of great rulers.

Warfare could cut two ways. It enabled rulers to consolidate control over subjects. It brought tribute, sacrificial victims, and honor to commanders. It also led to the grandeur of some of the sovereign polities and their hinterlands. But constant seesawing across the Mayan region among the sub-states also brought constant territorial flux. The frontiers of each kingdom expanded and contracted in the jostling with neighbors. Such shifts help explain why the Mayan era lasted for so long—in fact, kingdoms rose and fell during this time. Neighbors eclipsed each other in sequence across seven centuries even though we now treat them all as part of "Mayan" culture. Some lesser states became dependencies of greater ones and were expected to bestow honor on their patrons with royal visits, gifts, eligible marital partners, and subjects for sacrifice.

The spiral of warfare doomed the Mayans, especially after the ravages of devastating wars between Tikal and Kalak'mul between the fourth and seventh centuries. With each outbreak of more encompassing war, rulers drafted larger armies and insisted on sacrificing greater numbers of captives, and their resolve only fueled the carnage. Crops were ruined. People fled. Food supplies began to dwindle. After centuries of spreading misery, it began to seem as if the gods themselves were abandoning the Mayan people and their rulers. This appears to have been the cycle that contributed to their ultimate demise.

Warfare therefore engulfed the fractured Mayan polities. With the collapse of ruling households, entire states fell. The cycle of violence destroyed the cultural underpinnings of elite rule that were so important for keeping the Mayan world together. There was no single catastrophic event, no great defeat by a rival power. Spiritual centers of Mayan cultures were abandoned; cities became ghost towns. As populations declined, jungles overtook temples. Eventually, the hallmark of Mayan unity—the ability to read a shared script—was lost.

CONCLUSION

The breakdown of two ancient imperial systems—Rome around the Mediterranean and Han China in East Asia—provided the opening to an era in which religion and shared common culture rather than political structure and institutions became the social and cultural glue holding together large areas of Afro-Eurasia. The demise of these empires yielded to new efforts to bring peoples together, relying more on faith and culture than on military conquest and incorporation. Between 300 and 600 CE, the unity of the Roman Empire gave way to a religious unity, first represented by Christian dissenters and then co-opted by the emperor Constantine. This sense of a unity not limited by the frontiers of any empire formed the basis of a universal church in western Europe, which called itself "Catholic" and believed that it was the true religion that should be spread to all peoples. In the eastern Mediterranean, where the Roman Empire had survived, Christianity and empire coalesced to reinforce the feeling that true religion, high culture, and empire went hand in hand. This Christianity called itself "Orthodox," convinced that beliefs about God and Jesus were given their most correct and most splendid expression within the eastern Roman empire and in its capital, Constantinople. At this time, it showed little interest in evangelizing.

Similarly, in East Asia, the weakening of the mighty Han dynasty enabled Buddhism to become a dominant force in Chinese culture. Without a unified state in China, Confucian officials languished in obscurity, while Buddhist priests and monks gained wide patronage from regional rulers, local warriors, and commoners seeking solace and legitimation in an age of decentralized political and social units. In India, too, a political vacuum helped make possible the unfolding of a new culture. The Brahman elites were also aided by the movement of populations into new territories beyond the reach of the old power structures as they set the agenda for the ritual organization of daily life on every level of society.

By the same token, differences in belief could also create new divides. Not all regions of the world felt the spread of universalizing religions. In sub-Saharan Africa and the Americas, where long-distance transportation was harder, where language systems had not yielded texts that could be shared with and easily conveyed to neighboring cultures of nonbelievers, belief systems were much more localized. But spiritual life was no less profound an influence governing daily existence. What is more, in both Bantu regions of sub-Saharan Africa and in Mesoamerica, religion could integrate peoples far more effectively than political or military influences—which often tended to fracture states rather than centralize them. In these two more distant regions, it was the strong sense of a shared worldview, a shared sense of purpose, and a shared sense of faith that enabled common cultures to develop. Indeed, the Bantus and Mayans would become large-scale common cultures, but ones that were ruled at the local level. This bottom-up approach in sub-Saharan Africa and Mesoamerica created the longer-term means to integrate both regions under similar cultural and religious frames.

Chronology

	1 CE	100 CE	200 CE	300 CE	400 CE
THE MEDITERRANEAN AND NORTH AFRICA		Christianity spreads among peoples of the Roman Empire ∎	Christianity becomes dominant in Roman cities after 312 CE ∎ / Emperor Constantine legalizes Christianity in Roman Empire, 313 CE ∎	∎ Nicaean Creed developed, 325 / "Barbarian" invasions of Roman Empire, late 4th and 5th cent	
SOUTHWEST ASIA	Sasanians create empire in Iran, Mesopotamia, 220s ∎	∎ Buddhism spreads through Central Asia	Constantine establishes new Roman capital at Constantinople, 324 CE ∎	Jewish Talmud produced in the Levant, 400 CE ∎	
CENTRAL ASIA		Sogdian merchant communities dominant trade routes through Central Asia ∎ / ∎ Buddhism spreads through Central Asia		Hephthalites rule much of Central Asia, 400–560 CE ∎	
SOUTH ASIA	∎ Transformation of Brahmanism to Hinduism begins, 1st or 2nd centuries CE / Gupta dynasty rules much of northern India, 320–550 CE ∎				
EAST ASIA	Buddhism spreads among Chinese society, 300–600 CE ∎		∎ Han Empire collapses, c. 220 CE / ∎ Six Dynasties Period, 220–589 CE / Daoism reforms and revives in popularity ∎		
SUB-SAHARAN AFRICA					
MESOAMERICA	City of Teotihuacán dominates valley of Mexico, 300 CE to late 5th century ∎ / Early Classic Mayan Period begins in Yucatan Peninsula, 250 CE ∎				

Hence, the three centuries from 300 to 600 CE were marked by the emergence of three great cultural units in Afro-Eurasia, each defined in religious terms: Christianity in the Mediterranean and Southwest Asia, Brahmanism in South Asia, and Buddhism in East Asia. They gave the world a new set of markers and signposts that would illustrate the ways in which peoples were converging under larger and larger religious tents, while at the same time becoming more clearly distinguished from each other. Although these religions did not always replace imperial institutions, they provided transitional alternatives in each region from one form of empire to the next. Universal religions, whether Christian or Buddhist, and universal codes of behavior, such as the Brahmanic Laws of Manu, offered people a way to define themselves, their families, and their loyalties. But this pattern would soon change, when empire returned to East Asia in the form of the mighty Tang and when the inhabitants of a zone stretching from Morocco to central Asia found themselves suddenly united in a gigantic imperial system, created by the unexpected conquests of the Arab followers of the Prophet Muhammad.

STUDY QUESTIONS

 WWNORTON.COM/STUDYSPACE

1. Describe the spread of universal religions in Afro-Eurasian societies between 300 and 600 CE. How did this process reshape, remap, and realign cultural configurations between and among a variety of societies?
2. Describe the connections between the growth and power of Christianity and the political reconfiguration of the Roman Empire between 300 and 600 CE. How did the popularity of Christianity reshape identities among societies in western Asia?
3. Analyze the role of the Sasanian Empire in the spread of universal religions and the development of common cultures in Afro-Eurasia between 300 and 600 CE. How did the geographic context of the empire heighten its role in cross-cultural dissemination?
4. Explain the role of Sogdians and other central Asian peoples in the geographic dispersion of universal religions between 300 and 600 CE. How and through what means did they influence East Asian societies in particular?

500 CE	600 CE	700 CE	800 CE	900 CE	1000 CE

▌Collapse of Roman authority in western empire, 5th century CE

▌Byzantine Empire flourishes in the eastern part of former Roman Empire by 500 CE

　　▌Emperor Justinian revises Roman law, attempts to revive Roman Empire, 533–540 CE

　　▌Justinian commissions construction of Hagia Sophia in Constantinople, 532 CE

　　　▌Bubonic plague ravishes Southwest Asia starting in 542 CE

　　　　▌Sasanian/Byzantine Wars

　▌Rock temple at Bamiyan constructed, 507 and 554 CE

　　　▌Turkish Confederacy rules much of Central Asia beginning 560 CE

 orian Christianity spreads along the Silk Road, 5th–7th centuries CE

　　　　▌Xuanzang, Chinese Buddhist pilgrim, visits South Asia, 630s, 640s

　　　▌Sui dynasty revival of Confucianism begins, 581 CE

　▌Tuoba Wei dynasty rules northern China to 534 CE

　　　　　Bantu migrations from West Africa into Central and Southern Africa occur over centuries, 3000 BCE–1000 CE ▌

　　　▌Mayan culture reaches its zenith, 8th century

5. Describe how South Asian Brahmanism (Vedic religion) evolved into Hinduism during this era. What factors contributed to this development?

6. Identify key changes in Buddhist thought and practice in South Asia during this era. How did these refinements aid the spread of this religious outlook outside Buddhism's South Asian homeland?

7. Explain the role of written texts such as the Laws of Manu, the Talmud, the Analects, and the New Testament in universalizing religion in this era. How did these texts reshape social attitudes toward spiritual behavior and identity?

8. Analyze how political decentralization affected the growing popularity of Buddhist and other religious ideas in East Asia between 300 and 600 CE. To what extent did they challenge Confucian ideas on social and political organization?

9. Analyze the impact of the Bantu migration on the social and cultural geography of sub-Saharan Africa. Did a common set of beliefs unite societies in this region of the world during this time?

10. Compare and contrast Mayan society with that of Teotihuacán in Mesoamerica. To what extent did each represent a common religious and cultural outlook in this region at different times?

11. Analyze the extent to which universalizing religions and the enlargement of common cultures fostered common artistic themes among a variety of societies during this era. How, in particular, did a common artistic theme accompany the geographic spread of Buddhism in this period?

12. Analyze the extent to which universal religions brought worlds together and pushed worlds apart. To what extent did religion create new cultural boundaries and rivalries in Afro-Eurasia during this era?

FURTHER READINGS

Bowersock, Glen W., Peter Brown, and Oleg Grabar, *Late Antiquity: A Guide to the Postclassical World* (1999). Essays and items for the entire period 150–750 CE. The volume covers the Roman, East Roman, Sasanian, and early Islamic worlds.

Brown, Peter, *The Rise of Western Christendom: Triumph and Diversity,* A.D. *200–1000,* 2nd ed. (2003). The rise and spread of Christianity in Europe and Asia, with up-to-date bibliographies on all topics, maps, and time charts.

———, *The World of Late Antiquity: From Marcus Aurelius to Muhammad,* AD *150–750* (1989). A social, religious, and cultural history of the late Roman and Sasanian empires, with illustrations and a time chart.

Bühler, G. (trans.), *The Laws of Manu* (1886). The classic translation of one of India's most important historical, legal, and religious texts.

Coe, Michael D., *The Maya,* 6th ed. (1999). A work by the world's most famous Mayanologist, with up-to-date evidence, analyses, and illustrations.

Cowgill, George L., "The Central Mexican Highlands and the Rise of Teotihuacan to the Decline of Tula," in Richard Adams and Murdo Macleod (eds.), *The Cambridge History of the Native Peoples of the Americas,* vol. 2, *Mesoamerica, Part 1* (2000). The most recent and thorough review of findings about urban states in central Mexico.

Fash, William L., *Scribes, Warriors and Kings: The City of Copan and the Ancient Maya* (2001). A fascinating and comprehensive study of one of the most elaborate of the Mayan city-kingdoms.

Fowden, Elizabeth Key, *The Barbarian Plain: Saint Sergius between Rome and Iran* (1999). The study of a major Christian shrine and its relations to Romans, Persians, and Arabs.

Fowden, Garth, *Empire to Commonwealth: The Consequences of Monotheism in Late Antiquity* (1993). A study of the relation between empire and world religions in western Asia.

Gombrich, Richard F., and Sheldon Pollack (eds.), *Clay Sanskrit Library* (2005–2006). All major works from the Gupta and post-Gupta periods, in both Sanskrit and English versions. During the Gupta period, classical Sanskrit literature reached its apex, with abundant drama, poetry, and folk stories.

Gordon, Charles, *The Age of Attila* (1960). The last century of the Roman Empire in western Europe, vividly illustrated from contemporary sources.

Harper, Prudence, *The Royal Hunter: The Art of the Sasanian Empire* (1978). The ideology of the Sasanian Empire as shown through excavated hoards of precious silverware.

Heather, Peter, *The Fall of the Roman Empire: A New History of Rome and the Barbarians* (2006). A military and political narrative based on up-to-date archaeological material.

Herrmann, Georgina, *Iranian Revival* (1977). The structure and horizons of the Sasanian Empire as revealed in its monuments.

Hillgarth, Jocelyn (ed.), *Christianity and Paganism, 350–750: The Conversion of Western Europe,* rev. ed. (1986). A collection of contemporary sources.

Holcombe, Charles, *In the Shadow of the Han: Literati Thought and Society at the Beginning of the Southern Dynasties* (1994). A clear and concise account of the evolution of thought in China after the fall of the Han dynasty in 220 CE. The book presents the rise of Buddhism and Daoism as popular religions as well as elite interests in classical learning in a time of political division and barbarian conquest in North and South China.

La Vaissière, Étienne de, *Sogdian Traders: A History,* trans. James Ward (2005). A summary of historical facts about the most important trading community and their commercial networks on the Silk Road, from the early centuries CE to their demise in the ninth century CE.

Liu, Xinru, and Lynda Norene Shaffer, *Connections across Eurasia: Transportation, Communication, and Cultural Exchanges on the Silk Roads* (2007). A survey of trade and religious activities on the Silk Road.

Maas, Michael, *Readings in Late Antiquity: A Source Book* (1999). Well-chosen extracts that illustrate the interrelation of Romans and non-Romans, and of Christians, Jews, and pagans.

Maas, Michael (ed.), *The Cambridge Companion to the Age of Justinian* (2005). A survey of all aspects of the eastern Roman empire in the sixth century.

Moffett, Samuel, *A History of Christianity in Asia*, vol. 1 (1993). Particularly valuable on Christians in China and India.

Munro-Hay, Stuart, *Aksum: An African Civilization of Late Antiquity* (1991). The origins of the Christian kingdom of Ethiopia.

Murdock, George P., *Africa: Its Peoples and Their History* (1959). A vital introduction to the peoples of Africa and their history.

Oliver, Roland, *The African Experience: From Olduvai Gorge to the Twenty-First Century* (1999). An important overview, written by one of the pioneering scholars of African history and one of the leading authorities on the Bantu migrations.

Pregadio, Fabrizio, *Great Clarity: Daoism and Alchemy in Early Medieval China* (2006). An examination of the religious aspects of Daoism. The book focuses on the relation of alchemy to the Daoist traditions of the third to sixth centuries CE and shows how alchemy was integrated into the elaborate body of doctrines and practices of Daoists at that time.

Tempels, Placide, *Bantu Philosophy* (1959). A highly influential effort to argue for the underlying cultural unity of all the Bantu peoples.

Vansina, Jan, *Paths in the Rainforests: Toward a History of Political Tradition in Equatorial Africa* (1990). The best work on Bantu history.

Walker, Joel, *The Legend of Mar Kardagh: Narrative and Christian Heroism in Late Antique Iraq* (2006). Christians and Zoroastrians in northern Iraq and in Iran.

Wells, Peter, *The Barbarians Speak: How the Conquered Peoples Shaped the Roman Empire* (1999). A view, based on archaeology, of the Roman Empire from the non-Roman side of the frontier.

Yarshater, Ehsan, *Encyclopedia Iranica* (1982–). A guide to all aspects of the Sasanian Empire and to religion and culture in the regions between Mesopotamia and central Asia.

Zürcher, E., *The Buddhist Conquest of China: The Spread and Adaptation of Buddhism in Early Medieval China*, 3rd ed. (2007). A reissue of the classic account of the assimilation of Buddhism in China during the medieval period, with particular focus on the religious and philosophical success of Buddhism among Chinese elites in South China.

Chapter

9

NEW EMPIRES AND COMMON CULTURES, 600–1000 CE

In 754 CE, when the Muslim caliph al-Mansur (ruled 754–775 CE) began his search for a new capital city, Islam was already more than a century old and into its second dynasty, the Abbasids. Al-Mansur wanted to relocate his primary city from Damascus, the capital of Islam's first dynasty, in order to shift the center of imperial power toward the Iranian plateau, the Abbasids' home region. Traveling the length and breadth of the Tigris and Euphrates rivers, the caliph eventually decided to build near a small, unimposing village called Baghdad, located along the west bank of the Tigris.

He had good reasons for his selection. The site lay between Mesopotamia's two great rivers, where they were only twenty-five miles apart and were linked by canals. As one contemporary observer noted, the area was "surrounded by palm trees and near water so that if one district suffers from drought or fails to yield its harvest in due season, there will be relief from another" (Hodges, *Mohammed*, p. 126). Al-Mansur also knew that his metropolis would arise close to the illustrious ancient capital of the Sasanian Empire, Ctesiphon, where the old Arch of Khusro was still standing. This was also the site of earlier Sumerian and

Babylonian imperial power. Rulers decided to build at Baghdad with the intention of reaffirming Mesopo- tamia's centrality in the Afro-Eurasian world, and in so doing exalting the universalizing ambitions of Islam. Al-Mansur proceeded with the vigor that characterized the new Abbasid regime. He laid the first brick in 762 CE; within five years, a set of towering inner city walls surrounded what soon became known as the "round city."

Al-Mansur's choice was inspired. As the new capital of Islam, Baghdad also became a crossroads for Africa and Eurasian commerce; as the nexus of a universalizing faith, it also became an economic point of world convergences. Overnight, this city turned into a bustling world emporium. Chinese merchants supplied it with silk, paper, and porcelain. Indian traders shipped it pepper, and East Africa was its source for gold, ivory, and slaves. While Chinese goods arrived by land and sea, commodities originating in Inner Eurasia came via the well-traveled Silk Road from Khurasan. Large camel caravans wound across Baghdad's western desert, linking the capital with Syria, Egypt, North Africa, and even southern Spain. In effect, the unity that the Abbasids imposed with their impressive capital at Baghdad redoubled the movement of peoples, ideas, innovations, and commodities. Baghdad's reputation quickly spread. Seen as the "navel of the earth," Baghdad attracted people "from all countries far and near, and people from every side have preferred Baghdad to their own homelands." To its inhabitants and visitors, Iraq was "the most elegant country," from which goods "can be procured so readily and so certainly that it is as if all the good things of the world were sent there, all the treasures of the earth assembled there, and all the blessings of creation reflected there" (Yaqubi and Muqaddasi, in Lewis, p. 70).

These were the words of the ninth-century Arab Muslim intellectuals Yaqubi and Muqaddasi. For them, Baghdad's eminence and prosperity needed no explanation. After all, the city was the center of the Islamic world, which in turn was

God's gift to his believers. The transformation was remarkable. Here was a tribal people from a distant and remote part of the Arabian Peninsula, founders of a religion that by 762 CE had sliced through the territory of the once dominant Christian Byzantine Empire and totally absorbed the Zoroastrian Sasanian Empire. Here was an empire that replaced the eastern and southern regions of the old Roman Empire and that represented a polity as powerful as the Tang empire in China. The rise of Islam is yet another example of how religion and empire entwined to create the foundations of the world's modern social geography.

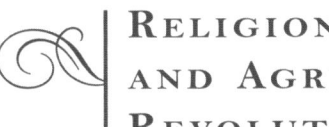

RELIGIONS, EMPIRES, AND AGRICULTURAL REVOLUTIONS

> → *How did the growth of Islamic empires lead to a revolution in agriculture across Afro-Eurasia?*

But Islam's origins illustrate how the entwinings of religion and empire were not all the same. Islam alters the pattern displayed by the ascent of Christianity and Buddhism. As we saw in Chapter 8, empire served as the main vehicle for the growth of those two universalizing religions. Moreover, they played significant political and spiritual roles in societies weakened by the breakdown of the Roman, Mauryan, and Han empires. In the case of Islam, in contrast, it was religion that led to the creation of empires. Having swept aside their predecessors in Southwest Asia, Muslim leaders had to form their own imperial system. Although they borrowed liberally from the Byzantines and Persians, their underlying reason for

Focus Questions   NEW EMPIRES AND COMMON CULTURES

- → *How did the growth of Islamic empires lead to a revolution in agriculture across Afro-Eurasia?*
- → *What factors created a common cultural outlook among Muslim communities in Afro-Eurasia during this era?*
- → *How did the Tang state balance its desire to restore Confucian principles to China with the growth of new universal religions in East Asia?*
- → *To what extent did Japanese and Korean states and societies emulate Tang China during this era?*
- → *How did two Christianities come to exist in western Eurasia?*

 WWNORTON.COM/STUDYSPACE

establishing an imperial system was new: to secure, defend, and spread their religion. Christianity and Zoroastrianism converted empires to their own views; Islam created its empire from scratch.

When we consider how religions had pervaded the lives of the Afro-Eurasian populations in the previous three centuries, we should not be surprised that a charismatic and prophetic figure would arise among the Arabs, proclaiming new religious precepts. By this time, religions had become the currency of life. Christianity and Buddhism were now laying claim to universal truths, and groups seeking to compete with them in making a mark on the Afro-Eurasian landmass at the end of the sixth century had to speak their language of universal religion. The Tang dynasty in China alone withstood the universalizing claims of religion that swept across the region in this period, as Confucianism and Daoism responded to the upsurge of Chinese Buddhism—proving again that China would follow a somewhat different path from the other Afro-Eurasian empires by maintaining its commitments to its past traditions and customs.

At the same time that Islam was spreading, the Muslim world was experiencing significant developments in agriculture. Islam may well have been a crucial factor in this transformation. As a syncretic culture, it assimilated the ideas, institutions, and beliefs of many different peoples and geographical zones—a feature that was as fully apparent in

Most of the new cultigens had their origins in Southeast Asia, made their way only gradually to India, and dispersed from there throughout the Muslim world.

the agricultural realm as in other areas of culture. Farmers in the early Muslim empire became agricultural innovators, introducing a host of new crops and employing new agrarian techniques that made possible rapid population growth, rising standards of living, and urbanization.

By the dawn of the Common Era, India had replaced Mesopotamia as the source of a wide range of new crops. In fact, most of the new cultigens in Afro-Eurasia in the first millennium CE had their origins in Southeast Asia, made their way only gradually to India, and dispersed from there throughout the Muslim world. Southeast Asia provided Indian cultivators with rice, taro, sour oranges, lemons, limes, and most likely coconut palm trees, sugarcane, bananas, plantains, and mangoes. Sorghum and quite possibly cotton and watermelons arrived from Africa. Only the eggplant was indigenous to India. Although many of these crops spread quickly and easily to East Asia, where they became staples in the Chinese diet, their movement westward was not so rapid. A few crops made their way into Sasanian Persia and the Arabian Peninsula, but it was not until the Muslim conquest of Sindh in the lower Indus region of northern India in 711 CE that the territories to the west were fully opened up to the crop innovations pioneered in South Asia.

Writing in the fourteenth century, the Arab historian Ibn Khaldun once observed about his peoples that "all of their customary activities lead to travel and movement" (Ibn Khaldun, *Prologomena*). India fascinated them, and their travelers, merchants, scholars, and landed gentry exploited the new agriculture of India to the hilt. Between 700 and 1000 CE nothing less than a revolution in cultigens and diet swept through the Muslim world. Sorghum supplanted millet and the other grains of antiquity because it was hardier, had higher yields, and required a shorter growing season. Citrus trees added flavor to the diet and provided refreshing drinks during the heat of the summer, and the spread of cotton cultivation led to increased demand for textiles.

During the first three and half centuries after the appearance of Islam, farmers from northwest India in the east to Spain, Morocco, and West Africa in the west used these new cultigens to expand the area under cultivation; they increased agricultural output, became a more productive workforce, slashed fallow periods, and grew two and sometimes even three crops on lands that had previously yielded only one. (See Map 9-1.) The results were impressive. Farmers could feed larger urban communities and offer consumers more diversified and healthier diets. We lack population figures for this period, but the evidence from Arab travelers and geographers is incontrovertible. Cities grew, and the countryside became more densely populated and more productive. According to one writer, the Fayyum region of Egypt had no fewer than 360 villages, each of which, by his account, was so productive that its cultivators could provision the whole of Egypt for a day. Once Islam began to consolidate its command over much of the region spanning North Africa to the edges of India, it acted as a massive conveyor belt of these agrarian breakthroughs, with dramatic repercussions for the peripheries of Eurasia and Africa. In the long run, the Afro-Eurasian world was set on a path of population increase and ever-larger cities; its growth accelerated after 1000 CE and was not interrupted until the fourteenth century, when the Black Death produced dying and suffering on a scale that few had seen before.

The transformation also swept through East Asia. China, too, experienced an agricultural surge between 600 and 1000 CE, receiving—often directly from Southeast Asia rather than through India—the same crops that Islamic cultivators were carrying westward. Rice was critical. New varieties entered China from the south; as populations migrated down from the north, fleeing the political turmoil that followed the collapse of the Han empire, they eagerly took up the new crops. By the eleventh century, Chinese farmers had become the world's most intensive wet-field rice cultivators. Early- and

MAP 9-1(A & B) THE SPREAD OF ISLAM AND AGRICULTURAL DIFFUSION IN THE FIRST MILLENNIUM

The second half of the first millennium saw a revolution in agriculture throughout Afro-Eurasia. As the map on page 371 demonstrates, agriculturalists across the landmass increasingly cultivated similar crops. How does the map suggest these cultigens diffused across a wider geographic area? What role did the spread of Islam and the growth of Islamic empires play in this process? How did the spread of this new religion act as a massive conveyor belt for crop diffusion? How did this process shape the history of Afro-Eurasia?

late-ripening seeds made it possible to harvest two or three plantings during a single year. Champa rice, introduced from central Vietnam, was the most widely used. It was drought resistant, had low gluten content, and ripened faster than the older strains.

The introduction of new grains and new technologies opened vast new arable lands in China's south to feed an expanding populace. In 742 CE, 60 percent of China's 80 million people lived in the wheat- and millet-producing areas of the Yellow and Wei rivers in the north and northwest. By 980, only 38 percent of China's 100 million people still lived in the north. This shift was made possible by improvements in irrigation techniques and the expansion of the road and water transportation system. Rice needs ample supplies of water, and Chinese hydraulic engineers designed water-lifting devices while peasant farmers built more canals linking lakes and rivers and drained swamps, alleviating the malaria that had long troubled the region. These developments created a booming and constantly moving rice frontier. (See Map 9-2.)

Europe was the exception to these agricultural breakthroughs. Most of the new crops were tropical and semitropical cultigens, suited only to the Mediterranean basin. Moreover, cultivators in northern Europe were still in the early stages of clearing the primeval forest. The critical ingredients for agricultural growth in Europe were the axe, the steel plow, and the harnessed horse; in China they were new seeds, dams, sluice gates, and sophisticated hydraulic devices. In Europe, agrarian innovation lagged and took longer to flourish, but it, too, would soon come, as the next chapter will illustrate.

So it was that a vibrant new universalizing faith erupted onto the Afro-Eurasian stage just as an agrarian transformation was about to spread across the middle latitudes of the landmass. The two movements—the diffusion of a rural revolution and a spiritual riptide—reinforced each other and heightened the potential of each to change the cultural, political, and economic geography of the world. They did so in league with new imperial formations in the heartlands, integrating the dis-

Original Source Areas of Staple Crops	Spread of Staple Crops	Areas to Which Crops Had Spread by 1500
Bananas	← Bananas	Bananas
Sugarcane	← Sugarcane	Sugarcane
Cotton	← Cotton	Cotton
Sorghum	← Sorghum	Sorghum

persed peoples of the middle of Southwest Asia and North and East Africa into an increasingly common cultural system. The long-term effect was to strengthen the linkages across even longer distances, from China to Africa. These linkages were the interlocking effects of three significant changes: an agrarian revolution (which fostered more commerce and denser populations), the resurgence of empires in the wake of Roman and Han collapses (which created institutional structures with greater unity to facilitate some stability within polities), and the appearance of a new, vibrant universalizing faith in the region straddling western and eastern Afro-Eurasia. It was the ascent of Islam out of Arabia, its unifying effects on the territories between the two other spreading universal faiths—Christianity and Buddhism—and its provision of the spiritual foundations for a new empire in Southwest Asia and Africa that brought the world together in historically unprecedented ways. It also laid the basis for a new set of divisions that would drive worlds apart, as a politicized Islam created internal and external sources of conflict across these regions.

THE ORIGINS AND SPREAD OF ISLAM

→ *What factors created a common cultural outlook among Muslim communities in Afro-Eurasia during this era?*

Any explanation of Islam's emergence as a universalizing religion that sowed the seeds for a widespread common culture must begin where Islam's story began: inside Arabia. Despite its remoteness and sparse population, by the sixth century CE Arabia was feeling the influence of outside currents of long-distance trade, religious disputation, and imperial politics. Toward the end of the sixth century, as we learned in Chapter 8, Byzantine and Sasanian imperial pressures had intruded deeply into Arabia. Commodities from Egypt, Syria,

MAP 9-2 THE SUI DYNASTY CANALS

China, like the Islamic world, experienced an explosion in population during this period (see the discussion on page 370). What role did the building of the Sui dynasty canals play in this growth? What role might the canals have played in fostering massive internal migrations in China? What other advantages might the presence of these canals provide to the Chinese state and its peoples?

and Iraq circulated in local markets, and learned men debated the doctrinal tenets of Christianity and Judaism. The Hijaz, the western region of Arabia bordering the Red Sea, was connected to the outside world by trading routes that led all the way up the coast to the Mediterranean. Yet without the actions of a deeply inspired and powerful religious leader, the Prophet Muhammad, it is doubtful that the peoples of Arabia would have entered the mainstream of world history so forcefully.

Mecca, in the Hijaz, was not an imposing place. A pre-Islamic poet wrote of it that "winter and summer are equally intolerable. No waters flow . . . [and there is] not a blade of grass on which to rest the eye; no, nor hunting. [Here there are] only merchants, the most despicable of professions" (Peters, p. 23). Hardly more than a village, Mecca was composed of simple mud huts whose inhabitants sustained themselves less as traders than as caretakers of a revered sanctuary, the kaaba, an otherwise unprepossessing collection of unmortared

→ *What factors created a common cultural outlook among Muslim communities in Afro-Eurasia during this era?*

rocks piled one on top of the other that local peoples regarded as the dwelling place of deities. But it was here that a great prophet was born.

A VISION, A TEXT

Born in Mecca around 570 CE into a well-respected tribal family, Muhammad enjoyed only moderate success in his career as a trader. Little in his early life suggested the momentous events that were in the offing. Then came a revelation, one that would convert this broker of commodities into a proselytizer of a new faith. In the year 610 CE, while he was on a monthlong spiritual retreat in a cave on Mount Hira (near Mecca), God himself, or possibly the angel Gabriel, came to him in a vision and commanded him to recite the following words, which eventually became Sura 96 of the Quran:

> Recite in the Name of the Lord who createth,
> Createth man from a clot
> Recite: And thy Lord is the most Bounteous who
>   teacheth by the pen
> Teacheth man that which he knew not.

Further revelations followed. The early ones were like the first: short, powerful, and full of instructions for his fellow Meccans. Note in particular the injunction to teach, to carry the message to nonbelievers. They were eminently memorable, an important feature in an oral culture where no art form was more highly prized than poetry recitation. Muhammad's early preaching had a sharp and clear message. He enjoined his followers to act righteously, to set aside false deities, to submit themselves to the one and only true God, and to care for the less fortunate, for the Day of Judgment was imminent. Muhammad's most insistent message was the oneness of God, a belief that has remained at the core of the faith ever since.

When finally compiled into a single authoritative version sometime around 650 CE, more than a decade after the Prophet's death, the Quran consisted of 114 chapters, known as suras, which were arranged in descending order of length; the longest ran to 300 verses and the shortest, a mere three. According to Arab historians, the verses were at first written down on "bits of parchment, thin white stones, leafless palm branches, and the bosoms of men" (Arberry, p. viii). Accepted as the very word of God, they were transmitted without flaw through God's perfect instrument, thee Prophet Muhammad.

Like basic works described in earlier chapters, such as the Jewish Torah, the Christian Bible, and other foundational texts, this was one meant to inscribe the tenets of a faith to unite a people and to convey a set of stable messages to other cultures, to expand the frontiers of the new faith. Here was one God, one set of lessons, one text, and a providential purpose to spread the word.

Muhammad saw himself as the last of the long line of prophets—or, as he said, the seal of the prophets. He believed that he was in the tradition of Moses, other Hebrew prophets, and Jesus and that he communicated with the same God that they did. As we have seen, Christian and Jewish religious ideas and communities existed in the Arabian peninsula at the time of Muhammad. A substantial Jewish community resided in the city of Yathrib (later called Medina). Just how deeply Muhammad understood the tenets of Judaism and Christianity is difficult to determine, but his professed

Mecca. At the great mosque at Mecca, which many consider the most sacred site in Islam, hundreds of thousands of worshippers gather for Friday prayers. Many are performing their religious duty to go on a pilgrimage to the holy places in the Arabian Peninsula.

Primary Source

THE QURAN

These two suras from the Quran are relatively short ones, but they provide some of the essence of Muhammad's message and the faith of Islam. The Quran opens with a sura known as the fatiha, *which in its powerful prayerlike quality lends itself to frequent recitation. Sura 87, "The Most High," provides a deeper insight into the nature of humanity's relationship with God.*

THE EXORDIUM

IN THE NAME OF GOD THE COMPASSIONATE THE MERCIFUL

Praise be to God, Lord of the Universe,
The Compassionate, the Merciful,
Sovereign of the Day of Judgement!
You alone we worship, and to You alone we turn for help.
Guide us to the straight path,
The path of those whom You have favoured,
Not of those who have incurred Your wrath,
Nor of those who have gone astray   (1.1–1.7)

THE MOST HIGH

IN THE NAME OF GOD, THE COMPASSIONATE, THE MERCIFUL

Praise the Name of your Lord, the Most High, who has created all things and proportioned them; who has ordained their destinies and guided them; who brings forth the green pasture, then turns it to withered grass.

'We shall make you recite Our revelations, so that you shall forget none of them except as God pleases. He has knowledge of all that is manifest, and all that is hidden.

We shall guide you to the smoothest path. Therefore give warning, if warning will avail. He that fears God will heed it, but the wicked sinner will flout it. He shall burn in the gigantic Fire, where he shall neither die nor live. Happy shall be the man who purifies himself, who remembers the name of his Lord and prays.

Yet you prefer this life, although the life to come is better and more lasting.

All this is written in earlier scriptures; the scriptures of Abraham and Moses.   (87.1–87.19)

→ *What themes can you glean from these passages about humanity's relationship to God?*
→ *Do you find any similarities to the tenets of Judaism and Christianity as you have encountered them in this volume?*

SOURCE: *The Koran*, trans. with notes by N. J. Dawood (London: Penguin, 1993), pp. 9, 424.

---

indebtedness to and affiliation with their tradition is a part of Islamic belief.

THE MOVE TO MEDINA, 622 CE

Muslims date the beginning of the Muslim era from the year 622 CE, when Muhammad and a small group of followers, persecuted by the leaders of Mecca, escaped to Yathrib (later renamed Medina)—an event known as the Hegira (in Arabic *Hijra,* "breaking off of relations" or "departure"). The perilous 200-mile journey accomplished more than a flight. It yielded an entirely new form of communal unity: the *umma* (band of the faithful), which supplanted traditional family, clan, and tribal affiliations with loyalty to Muhammad as the one and true Prophet of God. Medina became the birthplace of a new faith, called Islam, which means "submission" (to the will of God), and a new collectivity, called Muslims (literally, "those who submit"). Its believers accepted the prophecy of Muhammad. From Medina Muhammad's adherents broadcast their new faith and their new mission, first to the recalcitrants of Mecca and then, after Mecca had been converted, to all inhabitants of Arabia and even beyond—to the larger world of Asia, Africa, and Europe. In this way, Islam joined Christianity in seeking to bring the whole known world under its authority—asserting a logic of world integration,

The Battle of Badr. This image depicts the battle of Badr, which took place in 624 and marked the beginning of Muhammad's reconquest of Mecca from his new base in the city of Medina.

but also laying out a fundamental new division between the worlds of believers and nonbelievers.

CONQUESTS, 632–661 CE

In 632, in his early sixties, the Prophet passed away. Islam could easily have withered. What kept the new religious movement moving forward were the inspiration of the founder himself and the energy of the early leaders—especially the first four successors to Muhammad, referred to in later Muslim accounts as the "rightly guided caliphs." The word caliph, or *khalīfa,* means "successor" in Arabic, and in this context it referred to the successors to Muhammad as political rulers over the Muslim peoples and the expanding state.

The expansive spiritual force of Islam galvanized its imperial political authority. Muhammad's successors decided to implement the Prophet's plans to send Arab-Muslim armies into Syria and Iraq. Spurred on by religious fervor and a desire to enrich their growing empire with the wealth of conquered territories, Muslim soldiers embarked on military conquests; this expansion of the Islamic state was one aspect of the struggle that they referred to as *jihad* (another aspect focuses on the daily personal struggle for faith). Within a decade and a half they had control over Syria, Egypt, and Iraq. These centerpieces of the Byzantine and Sasanian empires then became the pillars of an even larger new Islamic empire. Mastery of desert warfare and inspired military leadership help explain these astonishing exploits, but equally important was the exhaustion of the Byzantine and Sasanian empires after generations of continuous warfare. The Byzantines saved the core of their empire by pulling most of their troops back to highlands of Anatolia, where they had more defensible frontiers, and conceding the more distant and discontented parts of their territories. In contrast, Sasanian rulers gambled all on a final effort: they hurled their remaining military resources against the armies of the Muslim believers, only to be crushed and then to collapse. Having lost Iraq and unable to defend the Iranian plateau, the Sasanian Empire passed out of existence, its remnants absorbed into a new imperial regime.

AN EMPIRE OF ARABS, 661–750 CE

When the last of the first four caliphs, Ali, was assassinated in 661 CE, new men took over. A political vacuum had opened, and a branch of one of the Meccan clans, the Umayyads, seized the opportunity to lay claim to Ali's legacy. As the governors of the province of Syria under Ali, this first dynasty moved the core of Islam out of Arabia and introduced the principle of a hereditary monarchy to resolve leadership disputes. Cosmopolitan traders who were adaptable in their outlook, they ruled from the city of Damascus until they were overthrown by the Abbasids in 750 CE.

By then, the core practices and beliefs of every Muslim had already crystallized and were known early on as the five "pillars" of Islam. These tenets built on long-standing practices. In addition to a declaration of a belief in one God and in the role of Muhammad as Messenger, ritual prayer, fasting, pilgrimage, and alms were prescribed in the text of the Quran, and were similar to either familiar Jewish practices or old Arabian customs. They became solid parts of Islamic practice in the first decades of Muhammad's career as a prophet.

In its early days, converting to Islam was a simple affair. The religion was also open to blending with older belief systems, an openness that enhanced its ability to spread by adaptation. Rather than insisting that followers abandon all of their former ways of life, the new faith called on them to add adherence to its key beliefs, which involved allegiance to Muslim authorities and payment of alms. Another major incentive to convert was a reduction in the *jizra,* or "toleration tax." The simplicity of these core doctrines, especially the first and essential pillar affirming a belief in one God and the prophecy of Muhammad, may have attracted early converts, but Islam in fact made many demands on its faithful, particularly after the full elaboration of its legal system, the sharia, a century after Muhammad's death.

There was, however, a political limit to Islam's ability to integrate others. Although tolerant of conquered populations, the ruling groups during the Umayyad dynasty did not permit non-Arabic-speaking converts to rise to high political offices. The overthrow of Umayyad rule ended the "Arabs only" empire, paving the way for the incorporation of non-Arab populations into the Islamic core. This changed the nature of the incipient empire. For as the political center of Islam moved out of Arabia to Syria, and then with the Abbasids to Mesopotamia, it sacrificed ethnic purity for geographic expansion. So while this universalizing religion spread the word to create a more common spiritual world, it became more and more diverse within the Islamic world. To be sure, obstacles to converts' acceptance still existed, and the pace of conversion was often slow—fastest in Persia, sluggish in Egypt. By the middle of the eighth century, probably less than 20 percent of the peoples residing in the Islamic empire were Muslims.

THE ABBASID REVOLUTION

As the Umayyad dynasty spread Islam beyond Arabia to integrate more people and provinces, it created resistance to its authority. The province of Khurasan in central Asia contained many who had accepted the Islamic faith and resented discrimination at the hands of the Arab peoples. Here, religious reformers and political dissidents stressed doctrines of religious purity and depicted the Umayyads as irreligious and politically repressive. A coalition emerged led by the Abbasi family, which claimed descent from the Prophet's family. Disgruntled provincial authorities and their military allies joined the Abbasid movement, which also found strong support among the non-Arab converts to Islam—individuals known as *Mawali,* or freedmen, who had made themselves clients to Muslim Arabs, embraced Islam, and learned Arabic, only to discover that they were still regarded as second-class citizens. This coalition amassed a sizable military force and trounced the Umayyad ruler in 750 CE. The Abbasid triumph in turn shifted the center of the caliphate to Iraq, signifying the eastward sprawl of the faith and of its empire. It also represented a success for non-Arab ethnic groups within Islam without entirely eliminating Arab influence at the center of the new dynasty, as indicated by the Abbasids' decision to make Baghdad in Arabic-speaking Iraq the capital of their empire.

Muslim lands by 634 CE
Muslim lands by 656 CE
Muslim lands by 756 CE
Muslim raid, with date
Muslim victory, with date
Muslim defeat, with date
656 Date of Muslim conquest
Further expansion of Islam
Byzantine Empire, 610 CE
Sasanian Empire, 610 CE
Frankish Empire, 610 CE
City

→ *What factors created a common cultural outlook among Muslim communities in Afro-Eurasia during this era?*

MAP 9-3   THE SPREAD OF ISLAM DURING THE FIRST MILLENNIUM

Islam emerged in the Arabian Peninsula in the seventh century. Within 150 years, leaders of this religious community had conquered a vast amount of territory. Identify the areas that came under Islamic armies' control by the eighth century. How were Arab armies able to defeat their Byzantine and Sasanian counterparts? To what extent did Islamic conquests lead to widespread conversion to the religion among those they conquered during this era? How did Islam expand beyond these areas of conquest?

But conversion to Islam rested on the zeal of evangelizers and the appeal of the new faith to converts. Some turned to it for practical reasons, seeking a reduction in their taxes or aspiring to exercise power. Others were impressed with the message of Islam. They regarded the new way of life as offering superior answers to a range of secular and spiritual questions. Not only did the Abbasids move aggressively to open Islam to Persian peoples, they also encouraged the Islamic world to embrace Greek and Hellenistic learning, Indian science, and Chinese innovations. No doubt the origins of the Abbasid dynasty broadened their worldview, as peoples along the Silk Road in central Asia were exposed to elements from all major cultures. The result was to make Islam in the Abbasid period truly cosmopolitan. It successfully merged the contributions of peoples from vastly different geographical expanses and widely different intellectual backgrounds into a rich yet unified culture.

> *Not only did the Abbasids move aggressively to open Islam to Persian peoples, they also encouraged the Islamic world to embrace Greek and Hellenistic learning, Indian science, and Chinese innovations.*

RALLYING POINTS: THE CALIPHATE One of the first questions that the Abbasid rulers had to answer was how traditional or "Arab" they could be and still rule over so vast an empire. They chose to retain the bedrock political institution of the early Islamic state—the caliphate, a political and spiritual head of the Islamic community—which the early Islamic community had recognized as the successor to the incandescent leadership of Muhammad. Although from the outset the caliphs exercised temporal and spiritual authority over the Muslim community, Muhammad's successors did not inherit his prophetic powers. Nor were they expected to exercise authority in the realm of religious doctrines: that power was reserved to specialist religious scholars, called *ulama* (the Arabic plural of *alim*, meaning "scholar"). But the Abbasid caliphs differed from their predecessors, the Umayyads and the first four Meccan caliphs, in leadership style. The new approach revealed how syncretic imperial Islam had become. Exposure to Byzantine and Persian political influences significantly altered what the community of believers expected of their rulers and how they were chosen. The Persians stressed the leader's absolute authority, such as that wielded by the rulers of the Achaemenid Empire. And like Byzantine rulers, Abbasid caliphs lived in secluded palaces, cut off from their subjects and protected by eunuchs and professional bodyguards.

The rulers of imperial Islam mingled practices of absolute authority with decentralized exercise of power through their envoys in the provinces. It was a delicate and ultimately unsustainable balancing act. As the empire grew it became increasingly decentralized, making it possible for regional governors and even counter-caliphates in Spain and Egypt to take hold. The political result was an Islamic world characterized by multiple nodes of power, nominally led by a weakened Abbasid caliphate. But as its political center shifted in the coming centuries, the spiritual center of the faith always remained fixed in Mecca.

RALLYING POINTS: THE ARMY The Abbasids, like all rulers, relied on force to integrate their empire; and for imperial Islam, as was true of the Romans, the exercise of military power necessitated the involvements of warriors and soldiers from different ethnic backgrounds from across Afro-Eurasia. How "Arab" should the Muslim armies be? In the early stages of conquest, leaders had conscripted their military forces from local Arab populations, creating, in effect, citizen armies. But as Arab populations settled down in new garrison cities, the rulers turned to professional soldiers. The Abbasids looked to the peripheries of the empire for their military forces, recruiting from the Turkish-speaking communities in central Asia and from Berbers and black Africans in the West. Their reliance on these foreign (non-Arab) groups as the core of their military, much like that of the second- and third-century Romans on the Germanic peoples and Goths, represented a major historical shift in the Islamic world. Not only did the change bring new populations into the empire, but by the ninth and tenth centuries these groups had begun to wield decisive political authority, just as the "barbarians" had done in the last centuries of the Roman Empire. Having begun as an Arab state and then incorporated strong Persian influence, the Islamic empire now embraced Turkish elements from the pastoral belts of Inner and central Asia. So, as the universalizing religion spread, it became increasingly multicultural while uniting diverse peoples into a single community of believers. Like other universalizing religions, this faith brought people together in more integrated political and religious structures, and in doing so created polities that were more ethnically and culturally diverse. The presence of the nomadic Turkish warriors in particular reminds us of the important role that pastoral peoples continued to play throughout the history of the early world. Ultimately, the Ottoman Turks would become the successor state to the Umayyad dynasty and rule over stretches of southern Europe and Southeast Asia for more than eight centuries.

RALLYING POINTS: ISLAMIC LAW (THE SHARIA) AND THEOLOGY In the Abbasid period, not just the caliphate but also a crucial foundation of Islam—Islamic law, known as the *sharia*—took shape. Sharia law covers all aspects of practical as well as spiritual life, providing legal principles for marriage contracts, trade regulations, and religious prescriptions such as prayer, pilgrimage rites, and ritual fasting. It was the work of generations of religious scholars, rather than of men of the sword, courtiers, and bureaucrats—and its life has continued until today all over the Muslim world, independent of empires.

The early Muslim communities prepared the ground for the sharia, endeavoring (guided by the Quran) to handle legal matters in ways that they thought Muhammad would have wanted. But because the Quran dealt mainly with family concerns, religious beliefs, and social relations—not legal questions—local judges exercised their own judgment where the Quran was silent. The most influential of these early legal scholars was an eighth-century Iraqi, al-Shafi'i, who was determined to make the laws of the empire entirely Islamic. He insisted that the laws that Muhammad had laid out in the Quran, with the addition of the Prophet's sayings and actions that were written down in later reports known as *hadith*, provided all the legal guidance that Islamic judges needed.

The triumph of scholars such as Shafi'i marked an important development in the Muslim world. It placed the ulama, the Muslim scholars, at the heart of Islam. Ulama, not princes and kings, became the lawmakers, insisting that the caliphs could not define or make religious law. Only the scholarly class had the right to interpret the Quran and determine which hadith were authentic. The emergence of the ulama opened a sharp division within Islam between the secular realm, where the caliphs and their representatives exercised power, and the religious sphere, where a wide range of religious officials and scholars—judges (*qudah,* or qadis), experts on Islamic jurisprudence or *fiqh,* teachers, and holy men (*a'immah,* or imams)—held forth.

RALLYING POINTS: GENDER IN EARLY ISLAM An area in which early Islam adapted new rules to older arrangements was its handling of the relations between men and women. Pre-Islamic Arabia was one of the last regions in Southwest Asia where patriarchy had not triumphed. Instead, men still married into women's families and moved to their wives' locations, as was common in tribal communities. Some women were known to engage in a variety of occupations and even, if they became wealthy, to marry more than one husband. But here, too, the status of women was changing, as the communities of Arabia became more settled and entered into closer contact with the rest of Southwest Asia.

Muhammad's own personal biography and his evolving relations with women reflected the changes that were occurring around him. As a young man, he married a woman fifteen years his senior—Khadija, an independent trader—and took no other wives before she died. During some of the crucial battles between Mecca and Medina, he allowed women to fight at his side. Later in life, however, he took younger wives and insisted on their veiling. He married his favorite wife, Aisha, when she was only nine or ten.

Hence, by the time that Islam spread through Southwest Asia and North Africa, where strict gender rules existed and where women had already become deeply subordinated to men, the new faith had already begun to accommodate itself to the already-established patriarchal way of life. Muslim men could divorce freely; women could not. A man could take four wives and numerous concubines, while a woman could have only a single husband. Well-to-do women were veiled and lived secluded from male society. Still, the Quran did offer women some protections. Men were required to treat each wife with respect if they took more than one. Women could inherit property, although only a half of what a man received. Infanticide was prohibited. Marriage dowries were paid directly to the bride rather than to the bride's guardian, indicating that women had independent legal standing; and while a woman's adultery was harshly punished, its proof required eyewitness testimony. The result was a legal system that helped reinforce the dominance of men over women but gave to magistrates superior powers to oversee the definition of male honor and proper behavior.

THE BLOSSOMING OF ABBASID CULTURE

The arts flourished during the Abbasid period, a blossoming that left its imprint throughout society. Within a century, Arabic had superseded Greek as the world's most widely used language in poetry, literature, medicine, science, and philosophy. Like Greek, it spread beyond its native speakers to become the language of the educated classes. Arabic scholarship made many important contributions to the world of learning, including the preservation and extension of Greek and Roman thought and the transmission of Greek and Latin treatises to Europe. Scholars at Baghdad translated the principal works of Aristotle; essays by Plato's followers; many works by Hippocrates, Ptolemy, and Archimedes; and above all the medical treatises of Galen, the second-century CE court physician. This extensive borrowing exemplified the most substantial effort by one culture to assimilate the learning of other peoples since the Roman conquest of Greece. To house these and other scholarly manuscripts, the patrons of the arts and sciences, including the caliphs themselves, opened massive—and magnificent—libraries.

The acts of borrowing, translating, storing, and diffusing written works helped bring worlds together. The Muslim world in this period absorbed the scientific breakthroughs of China and other areas and circulated them throughout thee Islamic world and beyond, incorporating into its societies the use of paper from China, siege warfare from China and Byzantium, and knowledge of plants from the old Greek texts. From Indian sources, scholars borrowed a numbering system based on the concept of zero and units of ten—what we today call Arabic numerals. Arab mathematicians were pioneers in

Global Connections & Disconnections

Libraries invariably accompanied urbanization, centralized governments, and writing. Not surprisingly, in the ninth and tenth centuries the biggest, most carefully organized, and most actively used were found in the Islamic and Chinese empires. These were the great centers of learning and government; their cultures extolled the written word. Respect for books and libraries was especially plentiful in the Islamic world, for in the Quran Muhammad had brought the very words of God to his followers. Later generations added to Islam's religious traditions by collecting sayings attributed to the Prophet and the Prophet's companions and the early caliphs (hadith), writing treatises on religious law (the sharia), and assimilating the knowledge of the Greeks, Persians, Indians, and Chinese when they overran their territories or came into contact with their merchants, travelers, and scholars. Moreover, since Egypt and Southwest Asia had seen the world's earliest writing, these areas—the heartland of Islam—already had strong literary and library traditions in place.

The world's very first libraries arose, predictably, in Mesopotamia, where writing itself first appeared. These libraries were quite different from modern repositories of learning. They did house literary masterpieces, like the Sumerian *Epic of Gilgamesh,* but their principal function was to serve as government archives, holding the important records of the kings and the state to which future rulers and government bureaucrats might need to refer. The library often considered to be the first storehouse of written materials was that created by King Ashurbanipal II of Assyria, who ruled over the Assyrian Empire from his capital city at Nineveh in the seventh century BCE. Like other monarchs aspiring to universal sway, he set about to collect all significant literary works. His library, which numbered perhaps as many as 25,000 tablets, contained omens, incantations, and hymns; it also held the literatures of the many Mesopotamian languages, including Assyrian, Sumerian, Ugaritic, and Aramaic.

Because the "books" of King Ashurbanipal II's library were clay tablets etched in cuneiform, hardened through baking in kilns, they were safe from the destroyer of many later libraries—fire. Those in its famous successor in Alexandria were not so fortunate. That magnificent library was established by Ptolemy I and Ptolemy II (ruled 323–285, 285–246 BCE), two enlightened kings who believed that the arts, sciences, and literature of the Greeks were unmatched in the world and had to be preserved for future generations. They set their administrators the task of collecting anything written in Greek. Though the size of Alexandria's holdings (housed in several buildings) is unknown, it was by all estimates almost unimaginably large for this period, whether as little as 40,000 scrolls or, at the other extreme, half a million separate works. But beginning in the first century BCE, these collections were repeatedly subject to burning and looting. By the fourth century CE, an immense body of literature had been almost wiped out, and the peoples of this region in Afro-Eurasia were forced to start over again.

The Muslims led the way, as impressive and large libraries arose in the heartland of Islam. They appeared first in the early mosques, including those in Cairo, Damascus, and Baghdad. But book and manuscript collecting spread rapidly to the outskirts of the Islamic world, where libraries

arithmetic, geometry, and algebra, and they expanded the frontiers of plane and spherical trigonometry.

ISLAM IN A WIDER WORLD

As Islam spread and became more decentralized, it gave rise to a series of dazzling and often competitive dynasties in Spain, North Africa, and points further east in central Asia. Each of these dynastic states put on display the Muslim talent for achieving high levels of artistry in locations far from the political and cultural heartland. Spreading the message brought more and more peoples under the roof provided by the Quran, its priests, and its scholarly interpreters. Such expansion invigorated a world of Islamic learning and science. But the growing diversity of peoples gave rise to a problem: the political structures Islam invented could not hold its widely dispersed believers under a single regime. Many legal elements were shared, especially those controlled by Islamic texts and its enforcers. But when it came to secular power, Islam was deeply divided—and remains so to this day. (See Map 9-4.)

in Timbuktu in West Africa, Samarkand in central Asia, and Jakarta in Southeast Asia earned deservedly high reputations for their extraordinary collections of religious and scientific treatises.

Compared with those in Christian Europe, the Muslim libraries were immense. The library at Cordova in Muslim Spain at the end of the tenth century was reported to hold 600,000 books, or more than two books for every household in the city. Ibn Sina, the great Muslim scholar of the eleventh century, marveled at the library holdings at the Saminid court in Persia. There he found Greek books that he had not seen anywhere else and that most of the best Muslim scholars barely knew of. Probably the largest collection of them all was Cairo's vast library, known as the House of Learning, assembled over time by the Fatimid caliphs. At its height at the beginning of the eleventh century, when the caliph al-Hakim merged his collection with that of one of his predecessors, the caliph al-Aziz, the collection was said to number 1.5 million books. By contrast, Germany's Reichenau, one of the largest monastic libraries in Christian Europe, the West, had only 450 volumes in parchment—almost one-third of them prayer books. It did, however, have a catalog and a system of interlibrary loans that served monasteries spread across Germany, northern Italy, and France.

As befit another empire that had a strong literary tradition and relied on written records for administrative purposes, China was very much the equal of the Islamic world in its wealth of libraries. Indeed, the Chinese had many advantages over the western neighbors with whom they shared the Afro-Eurasian landmass. They had invented paper during the Western Han Dynasty and printing during the Tang era. As a result, scholarship, book production, and libraries became vital ingredients of the cultural fabric of China. Accompanying the highbrow classical works printed for literati during the Tang and Song dynasties were lowbrow works of popular literature and primers that circulated more widely among a commoner audience.

The Chinese infatuation with the printed word and book collecting led to the emergence of a small, elite class of bibliophiles. These individuals located source materials and created the reference works necessary to found coherent scholarly disciplines. Although Chinese libraries housed printed books, unpublished manuscripts formed a more substantial portion of many collections.

During the Han, private libraries did not exceed 10,000 "rolls" (each holding about a chapter) of books or manuscripts. But in the Tang era, many Buddhist monasteries accumulated thousands of books and religious sutras. Some 30,000 rolls, for example, survived in the precious Buddhist grottoes of Dunhuang along the Silk Road, which were made public in 1907. The largest collection was gathered at the emperor's command to form the imperial library in the capital. Bibliophiles played an important role in creating the Tang imperial library, which was staffed by tens of scholars who as collators and editors recompiled the Confucian classics and dynastic histories for the examination system and for posterity. The Tang imperial catalog indicates that by the early eighth century, the imperial library contained some 54,000 unique titles and, including duplicates, about 200,000 rolls. Then as now, libraries were crucial repositories of knowledge and culture.

SPAIN One such Muslim state that vied with the others arose in Spain under that region's most dynamic ruler, Abd al-Rahman III, al-Nasir (the Victorious), who reigned from 912 until 961 CE. The Muslim kingdom in Iberia had been founded at the time of the Abbasid revolution of 750 CE, when a member of the defeated Umayyad family fled Damascus and established an independent kingdom in Spain. Abd al-Rahman brought peace and stability to a frontier region whose commerce and intellectual exchanges had been disrupted by civil conflict and much violence. His evenhanded approach to governance facilitated amicable relations among the Muslims, Christians, and Jews, and his extensive diplomatic relations with Christian potentates as far away as France, Germany, and Scandinavia promoted prosperity among all of the communities of western Europe and North Africa. He expanded and beautified the capital city of Cordova, and his successor, al-Hakim II, made the Great Mosque of Cordova one of Spain's most stunning sites. With room for 20,000 worshippers, it could have comfortably held the total population of Paris in the mid–tenth century!

As in the Mediterranean lands and Southwest Asia after Alexander the Great, competition between rival rulers spurred

MAP 9-4 POLITICAL FRAGMENTATION IN THE ISLAMIC WORLD, 750–1000
By 1000, the Islamic world was politically fractured and decentralized. The Abbasid caliphs still reigned in Baghdad, but they wielded very limited political authority. Why were Abbasid caliphs unable to create and sustain political unity in the Islamic world? In what regions, according to the map, did other Islamic powers emerge? How did the Sunni-Shiite schism among the Islamic faithful contribute to political decentralization?

creativity in the arts. By the tenth century, the Islamic world resembled a series of dazzling lanterns, each vying to exceed the brightness of the others as each powerful center strove to outdo the others in glory. Abd al-Rahman built an extravagant city, Madinat al-Zahra, next to Cordova; it was intended to overshadow the splendor of Islam's most fabled cities, including Baghdad and al-Qayrawān, the great North African city in northeast Tunisia. He surrounded the main administrative offices and mosque of its city center with gardens, pools, fountains, and aqueducts. Madinat al-Zahra was meant to be paradise on earth.

A CENTRAL ASIAN GALAXY OF TALENT At the other end of the Islamic empire, 8,000 miles east of Spain, the region beyond the Oxus River in central Asia experienced an equally spectacular cultural flowering in the eighth and ninth

centuries. In a territory where Greek culture had once sparkled and where Sogdians had emerged as the leading intellectuals, Islam now became the dominant faith and the source of intellectual ferment. The Abbasid rulers in Baghdad delighted in surrounding themselves with learned men from this region in whose accomplishments they took great pride. The famous Barmaki family, who for several generations held high administrative offices during the Abbasid caliphate, came from the central Asian city of Balkh. They had been Buddhists living close to the great carved Buddhas of Bamiyan (see Chapter 8). The Barmakis prospered under Islam and enjoyed remarkable influence in Baghdad. According to the tenth-century Arab historian Ali al-Mas'udi, the Barmaki family was responsible for building the Abbasid bureaucratic system and opening the Islamic world to many inventions from Central Asia, including papermaking. Loyal

The Great Mosque of Cordova. The great mosque of Cordova was built in the tenth century by the caliph al-Hakim II, who succeeded Abd al-Rahman III, considered by many historians to have been the most powerful and effective of the Spanish Umayyad caliphs.

servants of the caliph, they ensured that all the wealth and talent from the crossroads of Asia made their way to Baghdad, as they themselves had done.

In turn, the Barmakis aided their native region as patrons of the arts. They collected and had Arabic translations made of Persian, Greek, and Sanskrit manuscripts, and they encouraged scholars from central Asia to enhance their learning by moving to Baghdad. One of their protégés, the highly regarded Islamic cleric al-Bukhari (d. 870 CE), from Bukhara, was Islam's most dedicated collector of hadith, which provided vital knowledge about the Prophet's life.

Others from the area made notable contributions to science and mathematics. Al-Khwarizmi (c. 780–850 CE) modified the Indian digits into Arabic numerals, wrote the first book on algebra, and through the Latinized version of his name is the source of the word *algorithm*. He became one of the most valued members of Baghdad's famous translation center, the House of Knowledge, using his deep familiarity with the geography of the regions described by the Alexandrian polymath Ptolemy (fl. 127–148 CE) to correct many of Ptolemy's mistakes. The renowned Abbasid philosopher al-Farabi (d. 950 CE), from a Turkish military family, also made his way to Baghdad, where he studied Hellenistic Christian teachings. Although he regarded himself as a Muslim, he thought formal religions were for the common people, not

Materia Medica. A page from an Arabic translation of the classical text of Dioscorides, *Materia Medica*. The translated text is dated to 1224 and comes from Iraq, which was one of the centers for the translation of classical Greek and Roman works into Arabic.

the intellectual elite. In his view, good societies would naturally embrace the idea of a single God, but they would succeed only if their rulers implemented the political tenets espoused in Plato's *Republic*. He championed a virtuous "first chief" to rule over an Islamic commonwealth in much the same way that Plato had favored a philosopher-king.

As the power of the Abbasid caliphate began to decline in the eleventh century because of the same problems that had faced the Roman Empire—overextension and the influx of outsider groups—scholars from central Asia no longer made the trek to the caliph's court at Baghdad. Yet the intellectual vitality of central Asia did not suffer, for young men of learning began to find patrons among local rulers. Consider Ibn Sina, known in the West as Avicenna (980–1037 ce). He never made it to Baghdad; he grew to adulthood in Bukhara, practiced medicine in the courts of various Islamic rulers, and spent the last fifteen years of his life in Isfahan, in central Persia. Schooled in the Quran, the Arabic secular literature known as *adab,* philosophy, geometry, and Indian and Euclidean mathematics, Ibn Sina had mastery over many disciplines. His *Canon of Medicine* was the standard medical text in both Southwest Asia and Europe for centuries.

ISLAM IN SUB-SAHARAN AFRICA Islam also crossed the Sahara and entered Africa, carried by traders and scholars rather than by soldiers. (See Map 9-5.) Its movement depended largely on camels, which were domesticated well before the Common Era but were not used for crossing the Sahara Desert until the third century CE; these animals, able to carry heavy loads and to go weeks without water, enabled long-distance traders to traverse the deserts with almost as much ease as they traveled through settled areas and across seas. By the seventh and eighth centuries, large numbers of Islamic adventurers were arriving in sub-Saharan West Africa, where in exchange for weapons and textiles they received gold, salt, and slaves. The lively trading networks included the old city of Jenne in modern-day Mali, whose archaeological remains can be dated to around 400 BCE. Four centuries later, it had become a bustling entrepôt, with residences and town buildings taking up about 100 acres and surrounded by a large protective wall.

Trade did more than join West Africa to North Africa. It also generated wealth, which in turn facilitated the creation of centralized political kingdoms in West Africa. The most celebrated of these kingdoms was Ghana, located north and east of the modern country of that name, in the eastern region of modern Mauritania. It lay at the terminus of North Africa's major trading routes.

Of Ghana, we know little. The first to mention it was the Baghdadi scholar al-Fazari, who in the eighth century described Ghana as "the land of gold." A century later, the Arab traveler and geographer al-Yaqubi wrote of "the kingdom of Ghana, the king of which is very powerful. In his country there are gold mines. Under his authority are other kingdoms

Ibn Sina. Ibn Sina was a versatile scholar, most famous for his *Canon of Medicine,* which was for centuries the standard medical text in Southwest Asia and Europe.

. . . and gold is found in all of these regions" (Fage, p. 15). Although Muslim traders frequented the state, its rulers were not Muslims. Still, the pomp and power of the state impressed visitors; in 1067–1068, the Andalusian geographer al-Bakri wrote of a powerful and resplendent king who heard "grievances against officials in a domed pavilion around which stand ten horses covered with gold-embroidered materials.

➔ *What factors created a common cultural outlook among Muslim communities in Afro-Eurasia during this era?*

MAP 9-5   ISLAM AND TRADE IN SUB-SAHARAN AFRICA, 700–1000

Islamic merchants and scholars, not Islamic armies, carried Islam into sub-Saharan Africa soon after their religion emerged. According to the map, what kinds of goods were Islamic merchants seeking below the Sahara? How did increased trade with the broader Afro-Eurasian world affect societies below the Sahara? How did trade and commerce lead to the further geographic expansion of the Islamic faith?

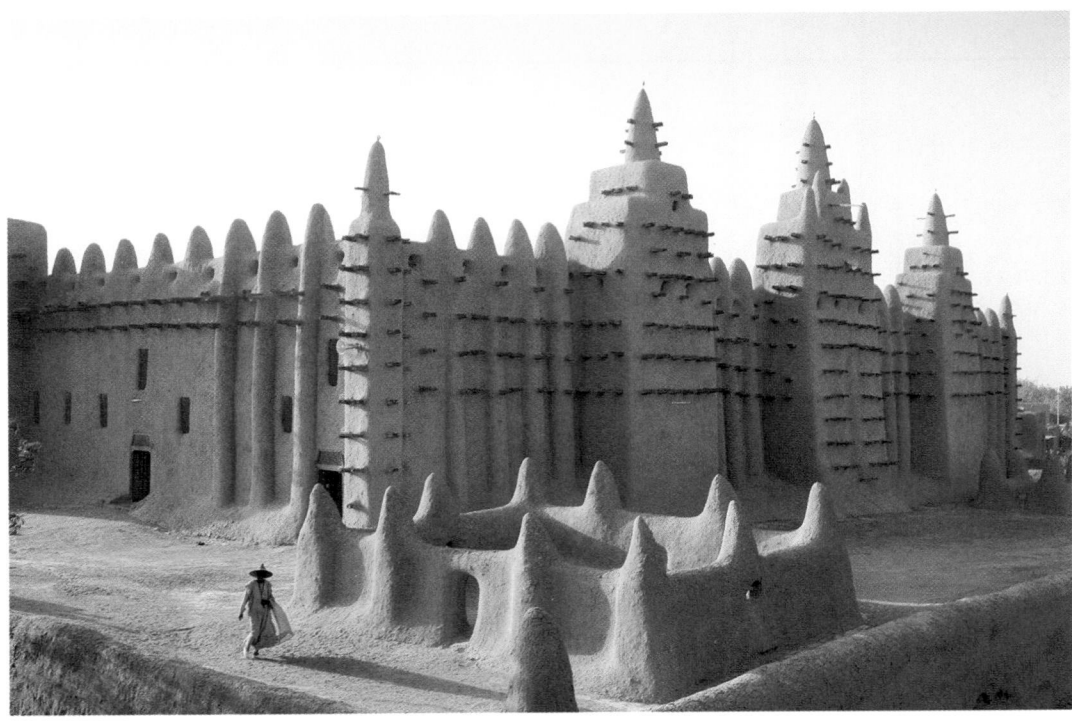

Jenne Mosque. This fabulous mosque arose in the kingdom of Mali when it was at the height of its power. It speaks to the depth and importance of Islam's roots in the Malian kingdom.

Behind the king stand ten pages holding shields and swords decorated with gold and on his right are the sons of the (vassal) kings of his country wearing splendid garments and their hair plaited with gold" (Levtzion and Spaulding, p. 16).

Seafaring Muslim traders carried Islam into East Africa as Islam became a dominant mercantile force in the Indian Ocean. A small Islamic trading community had come into being in the eighth century at Lamu, along the northern coast of present-day Kenya. By the middle of the ninth century, other East African coastal trading communities had sprung up. On the island of Pate, off the coast of Kenya, the inhabitants of Shanga constructed the region's first mosque, a simple structure replaced 200 years later by a mosque capable of holding all of the adult members of the community when they gathered for their Friday prayers. These communities, an amalgam of African and Arab populations, exported ivory and possibly slaves. Already by the tenth century, the East African coast featured a mixed African-Arab culture. The evolving Bantu language of the region took in Arabic loanwords—at first a few and later, especially after the fifteenth century, many more—and before long was given a new name, Swahili (derived from the Arabic plural of the word meaning "coast").

OPPOSITION WITHIN ISLAM, SHIISM, AND THE RISE OF THE FATIMIDS

Islam's whirlwind rise generated internal tensions from the start. Such a powerful religious movement fostered a shared reverence for a basic text and a single God. But there was not much else that was shared. The divisions were apparent from the time of Muhammad's proselytizing campaigns, and only grew deeper as Islam spread into new corners of Eurasia and Africa. Once the charismatic Prophet died, in 632 CE, the latent fissures came to the surface as believers disagreed over who should take his place and how to preserve some authority. Strains associated with the selection of the first four caliphs after Muhammad's death left a legacy of protest; to this day, they represent the greatest challenge facing Islam in its efforts to create a unified culture.

Early and spirited opposition originated during the seventh century among a group calling itself the Kharijites, who came together in Arabia during the dispute over the succession to Muhammad. Spurning all of the conservatives' choices for caliphs, the Kharijites believed that the rulers of Islam should only be individuals of impeccable religious credentials—individuals who most resembled Muhammad himself. The doctrine found support especially among those peoples who felt deprived of power, appealing to the highlander Berber peoples of North Africa and the inhabitants of lower Iraq, who complained that the leaders of the faith discriminated against them, despite the teaching that all Muslims belonged equally to the community of believers.

The Kharijite movement died out. It was too individualistic to challenge the authority of established political elites. But another, more powerful, movement of opposition arose in many of the same areas where Kharijism had been influential. In North Africa, lower Iraq, and the Iranian plateau, the mat-

Primary Source

GHANA AS SEEN BY A MUSLIM OBSERVER IN THE ELEVENTH CENTURY

The following excerpt is taken from a manuscript written in the eleventh century by a Muslim serving under the Umayyad regime in Spain. Its author, Abdullah Abu Ubayd al-Bakri, produced a massive general geography and history of the known world, as did many of the most accomplished Muslim scholars of this period. This manuscript has special value because it provides information about West Africa, a region in which the Spanish rulers had a great interest and into which Islam had been spreading for several centuries.

Ghana is the title of the king of the people. The name of the country is Aoukar. The ruler who governs the people at the present time—the year 460 AH (after the Hijra and 1067–68 CE)—is called Tenkamein. He came to the throne in 455 AH. His predecessor, who was named Beci, began his reign at the age of 85. He was a prince worthy of great praise as much for his personal conduct as for his zeal in the pursuit of justice and his friendship to Muslims. . . .

Ghana is composed of two towns situated in a plain. The one inhabited by Muslims is large and contains twelve mosques, in which the congregants celebrate the Friday prayer. All of these mosques have their imams, their muezzins, and their salaried readers. The city possesses judges and men of great erudition. . . . The city where the king resides is six miles away and carries the name el-Ghaba, meaning "the forest." The territory separating these two locations is covered with dwellings, constructed out of rocks and the wood of the acacia tree. The dwelling of the king consists of a chateau and several surrounding huts, all of which are enclosed by a wall-like structure. In the ruler's town, close to the royal tribunal, is a mosque where Muslims come when they have business with the ruler in order to carry out their prayers. . . . The royal interpreters are chosen from the Muslim population, as was the state treasurer and the majority of the state ministers. . . .

The opening of a royal meeting is announced by the noise of a drum, which they call a *deba*, and which is formed from a long piece of dug-out wood. Upon hearing the drumming, the inhabitants assemble. When the king's coreligionists appear before him, they genuflect and throw dust on their heads. Such is the way in which they salute their sovereign. The Muslims show their respect for the king by clapping their hands. The religion of the Negroes is paganism and fetishism. . . . The land of Ghana is not healthy and has few people. Travelers who pass through the area during the height of the agricultural season are rarely able to avoid becoming sick. When the grains are at their fullest and are ready for harvesting is the time when mortality affects visitors.

The best gold in the land comes from Ghiarou, a town located eighteen days journey from the capital. All of the gold found in the mines of the empire belongs to the sovereign, but the sovereign allows the people to take gold dust. Without this precaution, the gold would become so abundant that it would lose much of its value. . . . It is claimed that the king owns a piece of gold as large as an enormous rock.

→ *From this excerpt, how much can you learn about the kingdom of Ghana?*
→ *What influence did Islam have in the empire?*
→ *What elements of Ghana most interested the author, al-Bakri?*

SOURCE: Abou-Obeïd-el-Bekri, *Description de l'Afrique septentrionale*, revised and corrected edition, translated by [William] Mac Guckin de Slane (Paris: A. Maisonneuve, 1965), pp. 327–31; translated from the French by Robert Tignor.

ter of who should succeed the Prophet and how the succession should take place was a source of fundamental disagreement from the outset. Some repudiated the Umayyad and Abbasid rulers and the claims to succession defended by those who came to be known as Sunnis (from the Arabic word meaning "tradition"). Among the earliest dissidents were the Shiites (literally, members of the party of Ali), who believed that the proper successors to the Prophet should have been Ali, who had married the Prophet's daughter Fatima, and his descendants. Shiites also believed that Ali's descendants, whom they called imams, had religious and prophetic power as well as political authority and should enjoy spiritual primacy even over

Muslim scholars with more extensive religious training. Like Kharijism, Shiism appealed to groups whom the Umayyads and Abbasids had excluded from power; it became Islam's most potent dissident force and created a permanent divide within Islam. Shiism was well established in the first century of Islam's existence.

But not until the tenth century, after nearly 300 years of struggling, did the Shiites finally seize power. Repressed in Iraq and Iran, Shiite activists made their way to North Africa, where they joined with dissident Berber groups to bring down several rulers. In 909 CE, a Shiite religious and military leader, Abu Abdallah, overthrew the Sunni ruler in North Africa. Thus began the Fatimid regime; after conquering Egypt in 969 CE, it set itself against the Abbasid caliphs of Baghdad, refusing to acknowledge their legitimacy and claiming authority to speak for the whole of the Islamic world. The Fatimid rulers established their capital in a new city that arose alongside al-Fustat, the old Umayyad capital. They called this place al-Qahira (or Cairo), "the Victorious." Although intended simply as a royal refuge, Cairo soon overshadowed al-Fustat, and the Fatimid rulers promoted its beauty. One of their first acts was the founding of a place of worship and learning, the Azhar mosque, which attracted scholars from all over Afro-Eurasia and spread Islamic learning outward from Egypt; they also built other elegant mosques and centers of learning. The Fatimid regime remained in power until the end of the twelfth century, though its rulers made little headway in persuading the Egyptian population to embrace their Shiite beliefs.

By 1000 CE Islam had become the dominant political and cultural force in the middle regions of the Afro-Eurasian landmass. At Afro-Eurasia's peripheries, its armies, merchants, and scholars had finally run out of energy, leaving much of western Europe and China outside the Islamic domain. Moreover, by the beginning of the new millennium Muslims were ceasing to be a minority within their own lands. A rapidly increasing rate of conversions reduced the Christian, Jewish, and other non-Muslim populations living in polities ruled by Muslim kings and princes. Yet the political unification of the whole Muslim world had not followed. Although the Abbasid caliphate made claims to universal political power, breakaway regimes disputed these claims. Powerful separatist Muslim states emerged in Spain and North Africa.

THE TANG STATE

> → *How did the Tang state balance its desire to restore Confucian principles to China with the growth of new universal religions in East Asia?*

The rise of the Sui (581–618 CE) and Tang (618–907 CE) empires in China and their pervasive impact on Korea and Japan paralleled Islam's explosion out of Arabia in the seventh cen-

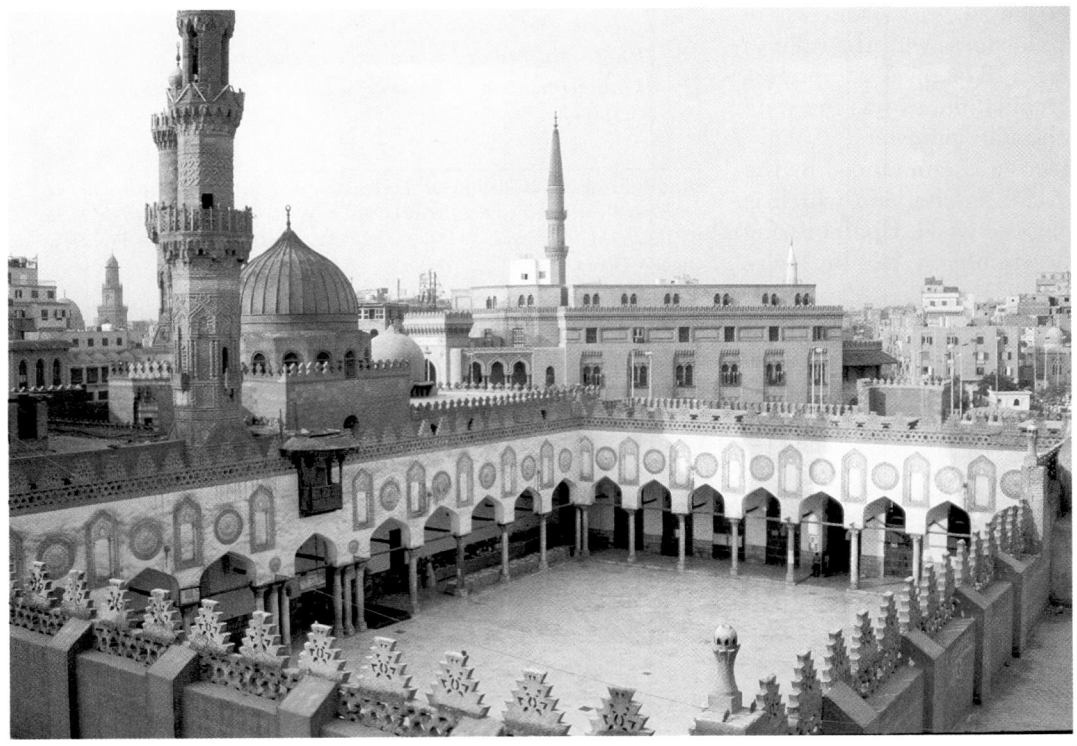

Al-Azhar Mosque. The mosque of al-Azhar is Cairo's most important ancient mosque. Built in the tenth century by the Fatimid conquerors and rulers of Egypt, it quickly became a leading center for worship and learning, frequented by Muslim clerics and admired in Europe.

tury and its rise to prominence throughout Afro-Eurasia in the eighth, ninth, and tenth centuries. Once again, the Afro-Eurasian landmass had two centers of power. Islam, stretching to Africa and Iberia, replaced the Roman Empire in providing a counterbalance to the power and wealth of China.

But in one fundamental way, this bipolar world differed from that of the Roman and Han empires: in the centuries since their waning, Eurasian and African worlds had been brought much closer together by trade, conversion, and more regular political contacts. The two most powerful political and cultural systems of Afro-Eurasia now had common borders. They converged and then competed for dominance in central Asia, were influenced by one another and even shared populations, admired features of the other, and encouraged travelers and traders to share information about the other society. The world had, indeed, become smaller. Peoples, ideas (especially technological innovations), and commodities moved rapidly across political boundaries.

Yet in China, religion did not play the role in shaping the formation of states and empires seen in the rest of Afro-Eurasia. Instead, its religious and political histories ran on separate but not parallel rails. China's political fortunes did not rest nearly as much on sacred foundations as did the smaller dynasties of India or Europe, or the powerhouse of the caliphate and Islam. Underneath a single dynastic and imperial culture in China lay a plurality of religions and sects—an amalgamation of belief systems rather than a single integrated culture functioning as the polity's bulwark. In this regard, China exemplifies the many ways in which Eurasian and African worlds balanced the forces of integration and diversity as they neared the end of the first millennium.

China was both at the receiving end of foreign influences and a source of influences on its neighbors. Indeed, it was becoming the hub of East Asian integration. Like the Umayyads and the Abbasids, the Tang promoted a cosmopolitan culture that absorbed and digested many new cultural elements arising at a great distance. Buddhism, medicine, and mathematics from India via central Asia gave China's chief cities an international flavor. Buddhist monks from Bactria; Greeks, Armenians, and Jews from Constantinople; Muslim envoys from Samarkand and Persia; Vietnamese tributary missions from Annam; chieftains of nomadic tribes from the Siberian plains; officials and students from Korea; and monkish visitors from Japan rubbed elbows in the streets of the dual Tang capitals at Chang'an and Luoyang, previously the Qin and Han capitals. Ideas floated to the east as well—notably in the middle of the first millennium CE, when the early societies and states in Korea and Japan emerged in the shadow of China. Even when China was disunited politically after the fall of the Han, the impact of Chinese religions, particularly Daoism and Buddhism, in Korea and then Japan was marked. Similarly, Chinese statecraft—as enunciated principally through the Confucian classics—seemed to the early Korean and Japanese scholars and courtiers to provide the best and most universally applicable model for their own state building.

Yet conversely, even during the Tang dynasty (608–907 CE), when the Chinese empire revived as never before, China's impact on Korea and Japan was limited. The latter never became "little Chinas." Each culture adapted and appropriated Chinese institutions, values, and religions in ways that suited its own political and social conditions. To be sure, for the sake of trade relations each paid lip service to the Middle Kingdom's efforts to define them as subordinate states that had to pay tribute in their economic and diplomatic exchanges with China. But each maintained cultural autonomy and often turned Chinese learning and cultural and political concepts to its own purposes, sometimes with unexpected consequences.

Throughout its history, China was the "Middle Kingdom" (*Zhongguo*), but this name mainly differentiated between those who considered themselves Chinese and those who were seen as outsiders. During the Warring States era (see Chapter 5), the key states were referred to in aggregate as "Zhongguo," that is, the "middle states." Under the Tang, the name differentiated the "Middle Kingdom" of China proper from her non-Chinese provinces. During the Song and thereafter, the term demarcated the Middle Kingdom (and its Han civilization) from the steppe barbarians (and their allegedly uncivilized ways). The Mongol and Manchu conquests of China made this last distinction moot, as they both equated their dynasties with the Middle Kingdom.

CHINESE TERRITORIAL EXPANSION UNDER THE SUI AND TANG DYNASTIES

After the fall of the Han in 220 CE, China faced a long period of political instability (see Chapter 8). But it was only a matter of time before a new set of the rulers (the Sui and Tang) took advantage of military weaknesses and political fragmentation to restore Han models of empire building. Their claims that a big imperial system could outperform small states found a receptive audience in a populace fatigued by internal chaos. Both dynasties expanded the boundaries of the Chinese state and reestablished China's dominance in East and central Asia.

Leading the way back to empire was Yang Jian, who had served as an official of the militarily strong Northern Zhou dynasty (557–580 CE). His struggles for unification ended in the Sui dynasty, which heralded the revival of Han imperial ideals. The Sui reunification continued reforms begun at the Northern Zhou court that were aimed at enhancing the state's power over the aristocracy. The two emperors of Sui, Wendi (ruled 581–604 CE) and Yangdi (ruled 605–616 CE), father and son, championed the notion that bigger is better as they channeled the state's domestic energy into territorial expansion into Korea, Vietnam, Manchuria, Tibet, and central Asia. Yet those efforts, particularly the costly and disastrous military campaigns undertaken against Silla Korea in the early seventh century, fatally weakened the dynasty. In addition, as so often occurred throughout Chinese history (e.g., see Chapter 7), a precipitous change in the course of the Yellow River, causing extensive flooding on the North China plain, led to popular revolts; they set the stage for Li Yuan, a Sui general, to march on Chang'an and take the throne for himself. Li Yuan promptly established the new Tang dynasty in 618 CE and began building a powerful central government. He increased the number of prefectures and counties and expanded the bureaucracy. By doubling the number of government offices, the emperor tightened his control over individual governors. By 624 CE the initial steps needed to found the new Tang dynasty had been completed. (See Map 9-6.)

THE ARMY AND IMPERIAL CAMPAIGNING

An expanding Tang state required a large and professionally trained army, capable of defending far-flung frontiers and squelching recalcitrant populations. The military organization created by the Tang emperors consisted of aristocratic cavalry and peasant soldiers. The aristocrats were used primarily on the northern steppes in Inner Eurasia to deal with nomadic peoples, who similarly fought mounted; at its height the Tang military had some 700,000 horses. At the same time, between 1 and 2 million peasant soldiers garrisoned the south and were also used for public work projects.

MAP 9-6   THE TANG STATE IN EAST ASIA

The Tang dynasty, at its territorial peak in 750, was the most powerful, most advanced, and best administered empire in the world. It controlled a state that extended from central Asia to the East China Sea. How did Tang rulers promote order and stability in such a diverse realm? In particular, how did they foster and try to control the growth and spread of religious communities? According to the map, how did Tang policies promote an economic revolution in China? To what extent did the empire influence other peoples in Afro-Eurasia not ruled directly ruled by the Tang state?

Much like the Islamic forces, the Tang's frontier armies, especially those that operated beyond the Great Wall—newly repaired now that China was reunified—became increasingly reliant on pastoral nomadic soldiers from the Inner Eurasian steppe. Notable among them were the Uighurs, Turkish-speaking steppe peoples who had moved into the Tarim basin in western China and who by 750 CE had become the most potent military force in the empire. The Tang military also enabled the westward expansion of the state, which brought the first Chinese penetration of parts of Tibet, then emerging as a powerful centralized kingdom in the southwest and along the Silk Road. The Red River valley in northern Vietnam and Manchuria in the north came under Chinese suzerainty as well. Briefly, Tang authority stretched from Tibet and central Asia to Korea.

Though it rested on earlier imperial foundations, the Tang's spread into East and central Asia was no less dramatic than the expansion of Islam. By 650 CE, as Islamic armies were moving toward central Asia, the Tang were already the new colossus of the region, claiming to have surpassed even the Han in scope and scale. At this empire's height, Tang armies controlled more than 4 million square miles of territory—an area that was as large as and was much more centrally administered than the whole of the Islamic world in the ninth and tenth centuries. The Tang population of more than 80 million surpassed the Han peak of 60 million and was far greater than the populations under Islamic rulers in the eighth and ninth centuries. Once the Tang administrators had brought the rich farmlands of South China under cultivation—draining swamps, building an intricate network of canals and channels to complement those in the north, and connecting lakes and rivers to the rice lands—the state was able to collect taxes from no fewer than 10 million families in agricultural labor, representing 57 million individuals.

In spite of the Abbasid Empire's precocious spread, China in 750 CE was the most powerful, most advanced, and best administered empire in the world. Korea and Japan, its neighbors in East Asia, recognized its superiority in every material aspect of life. Muslims were among the people who arrived from the four corners of the world to pay homage. Persians, Armenians, and Turks brought tribute and merchandise via the busy Silk Road or by sea, and other travelers and traders came from Southeast Asia and Japan.

This was the peak of Chinese power—at the very moment that the Abbasids were expanding into the Tang portions of central Asia. The map of Afro-Eurasia was now connected by bordering empires on the east and west, filling in the political landscape with powerful states, some of them bursting with religious energy. The rivalry for Afro-Eurasian supremacy brought the worlds together, but not peaceably. Muslim forces drove the Tang from Turkistan in 751 CE at the battle of Talas, and their success emboldened new groups such as the Sogdians and Tibetans to challenge the Tang in the west. As a result, the Tang were forced to retreat from central Asia

and mainland Southeast Asia into the old heartlands of China along the Yellow and Yangzi rivers. Even in the Wei River valley, Chinese rulers saw their capital in Chang'an fall to invading Tibetans and Sogdians in the middle of the eighth century. Misrule, court intrigues, economic exploitation, and popular rebellions weakened the empire, but the dynasty held on for over a century more until northern invaders brought an end to it in 907 CE. The next half century saw the fragmentation of China into five northern dynasties and ten southern kingdoms, a brief repeat of the era of disunity after the fall of the Han dynasty in 220 CE. Wars and rebellions devastated the population.

ORGANIZING AN EMPIRE

The Tang empire was a worthy successor to the Han and deservedly ranks as one of China's great dynastic polities. In its nearly 300-year tenure, it was exceeded only by the Han (202 BCE–220 CE) and it surpassed the Ming (1368–1644) and Qing (1644–1912) dynasties, China's other long-lasting empires. Although Tang rulers emulated the Han in many ways, including the compilation of their own legal code (which drew heavily on that of the Han) in 624 CE, they also introduced new institutions, the most significant and enduring of which was the imperial examination system. Moreover, as an empire in an age of universalistic and proselytizing religions, the Tang had to deal with the arrival of global religions inside their borders and accommodate these new religious institutions and agents within their imperial framework. Its methods for achieving and maintaining power often differed from those employed by the Abbasid Empire, Afro-Eurasia's other superpower at this time.

CONFUCIAN ADMINISTRATORS Even though the Tang ultimately relied on military force, their day-to-day control of

China Trade. In this seventh-century silk painting, we see envoys from the busy Silk Road bearing tribute to gain access to the lucrative China trade.

the empire depended on an efficient and loyal civil service. Unlike the multilingual, multiethnic, and even multireligious Islamic empire, which was held together by a shared spiritual commitment to Islam, the Tang had to devise other formulas for integrating their remote territories and diverse ethnicities and linguistic groups. Instead of a single universalizing faith, the Tang provided the political framework for a spiritual mosaic of Buddhism, Confucianism, and Daoism. In some areas, local deities continued to flourish. Rather than relying on a world religion to anchor their empire, to maintain order the Tang created a formidable and unifying political culture based on Confucian teachings composed in the classical written language that was mastered by Mandarin-speaking officials and China's educated elites.

Chinese integration began at the top. To enter the ruling group required knowing the ideas of Confucius and all of the subsequent commentaries on the classics that he had transmitted to his disciples. It also entailed handling the intricacies of the classical Chinese language, in which all such literature was written. These skills were as powerful in forging cultural and political solidarity as Islam was for the Abbasid state or Christianity for Europe and the Byzantine Empire. Thus a common written language (classical Chinese) and a common philosophy (Confucianism) served as a surrogate for the universalistic religions that created common cultures elsewhere in Eurasia and Africa. Confucian thought, learned and embraced by a privileged group of individuals from elite families, provided a set of common characteristics for the rulers and administrators of Tang society. Indeed, we have seen that the adoption of a common language—Latin, Greek, Arabic—at least among elites, can be a powerful element unifying an empire.

Of the highest importance in exalting the powers of the Tang state was the world's first written civil service examination system. Examinations now became the mechanism for making knowledge of a specific language and the Confucian classics the only route to power and the means of uniting the Chinese state, and no innovation was more significant for promoting the obedience and loyalty of state appointees. Candidates for office, whom local elites recommended, gathered in the capital to take qualifying examinations that required them to know the classics and display highly developed literary skills. Those who were successful underwent further trials to evaluate their character and determine the level of their appointments. New officials were selected from the pool of examination graduates on the basis of deportment, eloquence, skill in calligraphy and mathematics, and legal knowledge. When Emperor Li Shimin (ruled 627–649 CE) first observed the new officials obediently parading out of the examination hall, he slyly noted, "The heroes of the empire are all in my pocket!" (Miyazaki, *China's Examination Hell*, 13).

Having assumed the mandate of heaven (see Chapter 4), the Tang rulers and their supporters were intent on estab-

Tang Official. Tang officials were selected through competitive civil examinations in order to limit the power of Buddhist and Daoist clerics. This painted clay figure of a Tang official c. 717 was excavated in 1972.

lishing a common code of moral values for the whole empire. Building on Han models, they expanded the state school in the capital into an empire-wide hierarchy of select state schools that prepared those who had already mastered the required Confucian texts for the civil examinations. But Tang rulers and officials also favored the continued use of the Daoist classics as texts for the examinations, because the rulers and many elites still regarded the early Daoists as an important stream of ancient wisdom. What the Tang managed to do was to amalgamate this range of texts, codes, and

> → *How did the Tang balance restoring Confucian principles with the growth of universal religions in East Asia?*

Primary Source

INTEGRATING EMPIRE BY EXAMINATION

The young and old competed equally in the Tang examination market, bringing different experiences into the examination halls. The rituals of success looked alluring to youths, while the tortures of failure were common among their older competitors still seeking an elusive degree. For all, however, the emotional tensions they felt when the list of successful candidates was posted—following years of preparation for young boys, and even more years of defeat for old men—were the private, human response to success or failure. The few that passed would look back on that day with relief and pride.

In the Southern Court they posted the list. (The Southern Court was where the Board of Rites ran the administration and accepted documents. All prescribed forms together with the stipulations for each [degree] category were usually publicized here.) The wall for hanging the list was by the eastern wall of the Southern Court. In a separate building a screen was erected which stood over ten feet tall, and it was surrounded with a fence. Before dawn they took the list from the Northern Court to the Southern Court where it was hung for display.

In the sixth year of Yuanhe [AD 811] a student at the University, Guo Dongli, broke through the thorn hedge. (The thorn hedge was below the fence. There was another outside the main gate of the Southern Court.) He then ripped up the ornamental list [*wenbang*]. It was because of this that afterwards they often came out of the gateway of the Department [of State Affairs] with a mock list. The real list was displayed a little later.

> → *Why were the stakes so high in the civil examinations?*
> → *Was the Tang civil examination system an open system that tested talent—that is, a meritocracy?*
> → *What happened to those that failed?*

SOURCE: Wang Dingbao (870–940), quoted in Oliver J. Moore, *Rituals of Recruitment in Tang China* (Leiden: Brill, 2004), p. 175.

tests into a common intellectual and cultural credo for the governing classes.

CHINA'S FIRST FEMALE EMPEROR Not all Tang power brokers were men. Women also played influential roles in the court, usually behind the scenes—but sometimes publicly. Consider the example of Empress Wu, who dominated the Tang court in the late seventh and early eighth centuries. She deftly used the examination system to check the power of aristocratic families and helped consolidate courtly authority by creating cadres of loyal bureaucrats, who in turn preserved loyalty to the dynasty at the local level.

Born into a rich and noble family, Wu Zhao (626–706 CE) played music and mastered the Chinese classics as a young girl. By thirteen, because she was witty, intelligent, and beautiful, Wu was recruited to Li Shimin's court, where she soon became his favorite concubine. She also became enamored of his son. When Li Shimin died, his son assumed power and became the Emperor Gaozong (ruled 649–683 CE). Wu quickly became the new emperor's favorite concubine as well and gave birth to the sons he required to succeed him. As the mother of the future emperor, Wu's prestige in court was heightened, and her political power grew. Subsequently, she took the place of Gaozong's Empress Wang by accusing her—falsely—of killing Wu's newborn daughter. Gaozong believed Wu and married her.

When Emperor Gaozong suffered a stroke in 660 CE, Wu Zhao became administrator of the court, a position equal to the emperor's. She created a secret police force to spy on her opposition, and she jailed or killed those who stood in her way, including the unfortunate Empress Wang. Upon the emperor's death, Wu outmaneuvered her eldest sons and placed her youngest son in power; she named herself as his regent. Shortly afterward she seized power in her own right as Empress Wu (ruled 684–705 CE), becoming the first and only female ruler in Chinese history, though initially reigning in the name of her son. She expanded the military and recruited her administrators from the civil examination candidates to oppose her enemies at court.

Challenging Confucian beliefs that subordinated women, Wu elevated their position. She ordered scholars to write biographies of famous women, and she empowered her mother's clan by giving her relatives by marriage high political posts. Later, she moved her court away from the seat of traditional power in Chang'an to Luoyang, where she tried to establish a new "Zhou dynasty" in imitation of the time of Confucius.

Despite the ruthlessness of her climb to power, her rule proved to be benign and competent. During her reign, Empress Wu elevated Buddhism over Daoism as the favored state religion. She invited the most gifted Buddhist religious scholars to her capital at Luoyang, built Buddhist temples, and subsidized the building of spectacular cave sculptures, particularly in northwest China. Chinese Buddhism achieved its highest officially sponsored development in this period.

As she grew older, Empress Wu lessened the power of her secret police, but she became superstitious and fearful. Sor-

Empress Wu. When she seized power in her own right as Empress Wu, Wu Zetian became the first and only female ruler in Chinese history. Although ruthless toward her court enemies, she expanded the military and recruited administrators from the civil examination candidates. She also challenged Confucian beliefs that subordinated women.

cerers and corrupt court favorites flattered her. Finally, in 705 CE, she gave up the throne in favor of her third son. Later that year, she died in retirement at age eighty.

Although official careers were in theory open to anyone of talent, in practice members of many groups were excluded. Despite Empress Wu's prominence, women were not permitted to serve, nor were sons of merchants and those who could not afford a classical education. The Tang restored the Han dynasty state school in the capital, but because there were still no public schools, initially many candidates—as in Zhou and Han times—still came from aristocratic families. Tang civil examinations over time forced aristocrats to compete with rising southern families, commoners whose economic wealth and new educational resources made them the equals of the old elites. Under the banner of a classical meritocracy that Empress Wu enforced, a new aristocracy of academic ability emerged in the upper echelons of the Tang government. Through examinations, this new elite of southern commoners eventually outdistanced the sons of the landed northern aristocracy in the Tang government.

The system also indirectly benefited the poor by impressing on them the value of an education as the primary avenue for entering the ruling elite. Even poor families sought the best classical education they could for their sons. Although few from the ranks of the less well-off succeeded in the civil service examinations, many boys and even some girls learned the fundamentals of reading and writing. The Buddhists played a crucial role in extending education across society, for their temple schools introduced many children to primers based on classical texts as part of their charitable empire-wide mission. Relatively few of these students became fully literate in classical Chinese, but in a society containing nearly 16 million families and 80 million people in 750 CE, many were at least functionally literate.

EUNUCHS Abbasid and Tang rulers alike defended themselves and their most valued possessions, including their womenfolk, from opponents and enemies by surrounding themselves with loyal and well-compensated men. The caliphs in Baghdad chose young male slaves, frequently Turks, as their personal guards, although males known as eunuchs, who were surgically castrated as youths to perform a specific social function, also protected the harem. Similarly, Tang emperors in Chang'an and Luoyang relied on castrated males from the lower classes to guard the harem and protect the royal family because they were rendered sexually impotent. By the late eighth century, however, eunuchs in China were fully integrated into the empire's institutions, wielding a great deal more court power than those of the male slaves in Baghdad.

The numbers provide a sense of their growing power: in 820 CE the Tang government included 4,618 eunuchs, and 1,696 of them served at the highest administrative grade. The Chief Eunuch controlled the military, and through him the military power of court eunuchs extended to every province

Eunuchs. Castrated males, known as eunuchs, guarded the harem and protected the royal family of Tang emperors. By the late eighth century, eunuchs were fully integrated into the government and wielded a great deal of military and political power.

Tang Court Women. This tenth-century painting of elegant ladies of the Tang imperial court enjoying a feast and music tells us a great deal about the aesthetic tastes of elite women in this era. It also shows the secluded "inner quarters," where court ladies passed their daily lives far from the hurly-burly of imperial politics.

and garrison station in the empire, forming an all-encompassing network. In effect, the eunuch bureaucracy mediated between the emperor and provincial governments.

Under Emperor Xianzong (ruled 806–820 CE), eunuchs acted as a third pillar of the government, working alongside the official bureaucracy and the imperial court. By establishing clear career patterns for eunuchs that paralleled those in the civil service, Xianzong empowered them and sparked a striking rise in their levels of literacy and their cultural attainments. More eunuchs acquired enough classical training to handle imperial documents and official reports. Yet by 838 CE, the delicate balance of power that had existed between the throne, eunuchs, and civil officials had evaporated. Eunuchs became an unruly political force in late Tang politics, and their machinations equaled those of the slaves guarding the Abbasid caliph and his harem.

AN ECONOMIC REVOLUTION

In the Abbasid caliphate and in Tang China, political stability fueled remarkable economic achievements. Rising agricultural production based on an egalitarian land allotment system for peasant farmers, an increasingly fine handicrafts industry, a diverse commodity market, and dynamic urban life highlighted China's dramatic successes. The Sui had started this economic progress by building canals—especially the Grand Canal linking North and South China—throughout the country (see Map 9-2). The Tang continued the canal-building endeavor, centering their efforts on the Grand Canal and the Yangzi River, which flows from west to east. These new waterways aided communication and transport to all parts of the empire and helped raise living standards. Granaries built along the canals enabled the Tang to transport rice from the south to the north. The south grew richer, largely through the hard work of northern immigrants. Fertile land along the Yangzi became China's new granary, and areas south of the Yangzi became the demographic center of the Chinese empire.

Chinese merchants took full advantage of the Silk Road to trade with India and the Islamic world; but when mid-eighth-century rebellions in northwest China and the rise of Islam in central Asia jeopardized the land route, the "silk road by sea" blossomed. From all over Asia and Africa, merchant ships arrived in South China ports bearing cargos of spices, medicines, and jewelry; they left carrying Chinese silks and porcelain. The capital, Chang'an, became the richest and arguably the most populous city in the world. Its million or so residents included minorities from many countries. Fortified with a wall and moat, the city was divided into government and residential quarters; in its two main markets full of shops and stores, more than 200 types of businesses sold a wide variety of domestic and international goods.

Tang Tripod Jar. Tricolor glazed stoneware was all the rage in the early and middle Tang court and among elites in Chang'an, Loyang, and the provinces. This glazed jar from the eighth century imitated ancient Zhou bronzes (see Chapter 4). Such stoneware was displaced in the late Tang by the exquisite jadelike porcelains made in high-fired kilns.

In the larger cities of the Yangzi delta—debatably the world's first industrial heartland—workshops proliferated; they were admired far and wide for the elegance of their wares, which included brocades, fine paper, printed woodblocks, iron casts, and high-fired porcelains. Chinese industrialists used locally grown cotton to produce clothing of the highest quality. The textile industry prospered as painting and dyeing technology improved, and superb silk products were a major source of tax revenue. Asian art collectors valued what became known as Tang "tricolor porcelain," decorated with brilliant hues of yellow, green, white, brown, and blue. Many of these pieces moved through the river and lake systems of the middle Yangzi region to major urban centers and then on to Chang'an and Luoyang in the northwest. Conspicuous consumption of manufactured fineries stimulated Tang producers of high-value textiles and porcelain. Chinese luxuries dominated the domestic and international trading networks that reached Southwest Asia, Europe, and Africa via the Silk Road and Arab ships from the Indian Ocean.

DEALING WITH WORLD RELIGIONS

The Confucian ideology at heart was secular. Although it posited a heaven from which the ruling dynasty claimed the

authority to govern, it did not hold out the promise of an afterlife or threaten unbelievers with eternal damnation. Not surprisingly, therefore, the early Tang emperors tolerated a remarkable amount of religious diversity. Nestorian Christianity (originally based in the old Persian capital of Ctesiphon), Zoroastrianism, and Manichaeanism (a radical Christian sect) had entered China through central Asia from Persia at the time of the Sasanian Empire. Islam came later. These—together with Buddhism and the indigenous teachings of Daoism and Confucianism—spread throughout the empire and were not at first viewed as conflicting with state power.

THE GROWTH OF BUDDHISM Buddhism, in particular, thrived under Tang rule. Many foreign students from Korea and Japan journeyed to China in the early years of the dynasty to study it.

Emperor Li Shimin distrusted Buddhist monks because they avoided serving the government and paying taxes. Yet once Buddhism was accepted as one of the "three ways" of learning—joining Daoism and Confucianism—Li endowed monasteries, sent emissaries to India to collect texts and relics, and commissioned Buddhist paintings and statuary. To provide devotional sites where the people could practice Buddhism through good works and prayer, huge monasteries were built with imperial patronage. Giant carvings of the Buddha in northwestern temple sanctuaries dotted the trading routes to central Asia, and less monumental temples filled with ornate statuary provided sites for religious refuge throughout South China. Such temples provided shelter, and gave some measure of autonomy to commoners and women burdened by the rigid Tang social hierarchy. Chinese pilgrims braved the Silk Road and the heights of the Pamirs to travel to India, where they learned Sanskrit; when they returned, they brought back Buddhist texts. One of these pilgrims was Xuanzang, whose story was told in Chapter 8. On returning, Xuanzang won many followers in Japan as well as in China. His life inspired the widely read novel *Journey to the West* (c. 1590), a classic of the Ming dynasty.

ANTI-BUDDHIST CAMPAIGNS By the middle of the ninth century, the Tang empire contained nearly 50,000 monasteries and hundreds of thousands of Buddhist monks and nuns. By comparison, the Carolingian Empire under Charlemagne in France had only 700 major monasteries (see the following section). Such success by a foreign religion, in conjunction with the beginning of the decline of the Tang dynasty in the mid–eighth century, threatened the Confucian and Daoist leaders. They therefore attacked Buddhism, arguing that its values were at variance with Confucian and Daoist traditions.

One example of a Confucian response comes from the scholar-official Han Yu (768–824 CE). Han Yu represented the rising literati from the south, who championed ancient writing forms based on Confucian classics. Han Yu's Memorial of 819 protested the emperor's plan to bring a relic of the Buddha to the capital for exhibition. Striking a xenophobic note that would have been inconceivable during the cosmopolitanism of the early Tang, Han Yu attacked Buddhism as a foreign doctrine of barbarian peoples who were different in language, culture, and knowledge. For raising these objections, Han was exiled to the southern province of Guangdong. Yet, two decades later, the state began suppressing Buddhist monasteries and confiscating their wealth.

Secular rulers grew more and more concerned that religious loyalties would undermine political ones. Increasingly intolerant Confucian scholar-administrators argued that the Buddhist monastic establishment threatened the imperial order. They accused Buddhists of undercutting kinship values and undermining the cardinal family relations of father and son, husband and wife, and so on. They claimed that the clergy were conspiring to destroy the state, the family, and the body—a conspiracy that they labeled the "Three Destructions" of Buddhism.

Piecemeal measures against the monastic orders gave way in the 840s CE to open persecution. Emperor Wuzong (ruled 841–847 CE) closed more than 4,600 monasteries and destroyed 40,000 temples and shrines. More than 260,000 Buddhist monks and nuns were forced to return to secular life, and the state parceled out monastery lands to taxpaying landlords and peasant farmers. Two important points can be made about the persecution of Buddhism in this period. First, in China the Tang government brought the Buddhist monastic communities under its control; in Latin Europe, in contrast, the Christian church dominated feudal states. Second, because the Chinese bureaucracy was steeped in the traditions of Confucianism and Daoism, its traditions had a power base that Buddhism lacked. China's most prominent universalizing religion was thus vulnerable once Emperor Wuzong began to persecute it.

To expunge the cultural impact of Buddhism, classically trained literati emphasized the revival of ancient prose styles and the teachings of Confucius and his followers. Linking classical scholarship, ancient literature, and Confucian morality, they constructed a cultural fortress that reversed the early Buddhist successes in China. Scholars such as Liu Zongyuan (773–819 CE) claimed that skill in writing ancient prose verse forms was still the best measure of talent and should remain the core of the civil examinations. The Tang poets Li Bai (701–761 CE), Du Fu (c. 712–c. 770 CE), and Bo Juyi (772–846 CE) extolled verse, always popular with the literate population, as the most effective genre for expressing moral concerns and personal emotions, thereby obviating the need to turn to the Buddhist religion for solace.

Among the many remarkable feats of the Tang era was the triumph of the homegrown ideologies of Confucianism and Daoism over the universalistic ethos of Buddhism. The result was persistent religious pluralism within China. Tang China stands out in this age of world religions as the one cultural zone that remained committed to a secular common culture and that resisted the pressures to embrace universalistic religions.

THE FALL OF TANG CHINA

China's deteriorating economic conditions in the ninth century resulted in peasant uprisings, some led by failed examination candidates. These revolts, which began in 859 CE, ultimately brought down the dynasty. In the tenth century, China fragmented into as many as ten regional states. The result was a new era of decentralization, which even the Song dynasty that emerged in 960 CE could not overcome. Only the Mongols, invading steppe peoples, were later able to restore the glory of the Han and Tang empires.

 EARLY KOREA AND JAPAN

> → *To what extent did Japanese and Korean states and societies emulate Tang China during this era?*

At the same time that China was opening up to the cultures of its western regions, such as Chinese Turkestan, versions of its culture colored by Buddhism (and thereby rendered more flexible and less distinctly Chinese) reached out to the east—to Korea and, eventually, to Japan. (See Map 9-7.) To comprehend Korean and Japanese history of this era, we need to gain some understanding of the developments that predated the Koryo kingdom and the Japanese experience of the ninth and tenth centuries.

EARLY KOREA

Chinese cultural influences in Korea can be documented as early as the third century BCE, when Chinese immigrants from the northeast helped locals set up a small state called Lelang (also called Lolang) at the present-day site of Pyongyang. By the fourth century CE, three independent states had emerged on the peninsula that jutted into the Yellow Sea: Koguryo in the north, Paekche in the southwest, and Silla in the southeast. Koguryo subsequently expanded its influence northward into Manchuria. By contrast, because of its location on the southwest coast facing the Yellow Sea and Shandong province in China, Paekche had close ties with North China. This division into what was known as the "Three Kingdoms" of Korea lasted until 668 CE, when the southeastern kingdom of Silla gained control over the entire peninsula and unified it for the first time. During this period, Japan also maintained a small enclave on Korea's southern coast at Kaya (also called Mimana).

Extent of Silla power, 670–935 CE
Extent of Nara state by 600 CE
⊙ Capital
• City
🏯 Buddhist temple
✪ Shinto shrine
▲ Holy mountain
Bohai

MAP 9-7   BORDERLANDS: KOREA AND JAPAN, 600–1000

The Tang dynasty held great sway and power over emerging Korean and Japanese states in East Asia, although it never directly ruled either region. Study the map above. How did state formation evolve in Korea and Japan between 600 and 900? What connections existed between these states and the Tang empire during this era? To what extent did Korean and Japanese states adapt Tang traditions and customs during this time?

Silla's unification of Korea after 670 CE enabled the Koreans to establish a unified government modeled on the Tang Chinese imperial state. Silla dispatched annual embassies to the Chinese capital at Chang'an, as well as regularly sending students and monks to China. Like Latin among diverse populations in Europe, literary Chinese became the written language of Korean elites. Koreans later devised a phonetic system for writing their own language that simplified Chinese characters, but most official writing remained in Chinese. Early Korean society, like China's, was based on a hereditary aristocracy who monopolized official posts. But like Japan, Korea initially resisted the classical meritocracy that would be introduced into Tang China through the civil service examinations.

Silla's own fortunes were entwined with those of the Tang. In the wake of the Tang decline, the state of Silla also began to fragment. In 936 CE, Wang Kon, a rebel leader, absorbed Silla into the northern-based Koryo kingdom (918–1392 CE), an act that tenuously reunified the country. The Koryo dynasty, from which the country's modern name derives, began to construct a new cultural identity for itself by enacting an unprecedented bureaucratic system aimed at replacing the archaic tribal system that had continued under the Silla. Unlike in Japan, Tang dynasty–style civil service examinations to select the most capable officials to govern at court and in the provinces were successfully put in place in Korea. Wang Kon's heirs consolidated control over the peninsula and strengthened its political and economic foundations by more closely following the bureaucratic and land allotment systems of Tang China.

Yet during this period, Korea, like Tang China itself, was harassed continuously by northern tribes such as the Khitan people. As we will see in Chapter 10, the Khitan also took advantage of the fall of the Tang dynasty to control northern Chinese lands after 907 CE, establishing the rival Liao dynasty (907–1126 CE) in northeast China. During this troubled period, Korean artisans anxiously carved wooden printing blocks for 81,258 scriptures from the Buddhist canon as an offering to the Buddha to protect them from invading enemies—but in vain. After being overwhelmed by the Khitan in 1010, the Koryo dynasty revived, only to be invaded by the Mongols in 1231 (see Chapter 10). Despite these temporary invasions, the dynasty managed to last until 1392.

EARLY JAPAN

Beginning in the Ice Age, tribal groups known as the Jomon (from 10,000 years ago to 400 BCE; see Chapter 2) and succeeding Yayoi peoples (400 BCE–250 CE) dominated prehistoric Japan. Subsequently, in the middle of the third century, a warlike group from northeast Asia arrived by sea from Korea and aggressively imposed their military and social power on southern Japan. These conquerors, known today as the "Tomb Culture" because of their elevated necropolises near present-day Osaka, unified Japan by extolling their imperial ancestors and maintaining the social hierarchy that they had brought with them from Korea and Manchuria. They also brought with them a belief in the power of female shamans, who married into the imperial clans; like Himiko, discussed below, these women became de facto rulers of early Japanese kinship groups, combining religious and political power.

Chinese dynastic records describe the early Japanese, with whom imperial China had contact in this period, as a "dwarf" people who maintained a rice and fishing economy. The Japanese farmers had also mastered Chinese-style sericulture. According to the Chinese, the Japanese were united under a shaman-queen, Himiko, who sent an envoy in 239 CE to the state of Wei—one of the Three Kingdoms in China after the fall of the Han. The complex aristocratic society that developed under the leaders of the Tomb Culture became the basis of an emerging Yamato Japanese state, which in successive waves incorporated many natives and Korean migrants. The rise of the Japanese state coincided with the Three Kingdoms era in Korea; they were linked for a long time and at least until 688 CE, when Silla, with Tang military help, occupied the Japanese enclave of Kaya on the Korean peninsula. Many Koreans, along with Japanese who had fought on the side of Paekche, crossed the straits and settled in the island kingdom.

THE YAMATO EMPEROR AND THE ORIGINS OF JAPANESE SACRED IDENTITY Ancestor worship, though influenced by China, was native to Japan and lay at the heart of a belief system that emerged after the fourth century. Ancestral rites that predated the influx of Buddhism and Confucianism from Paekche in the sixth century underwent significant transformation in the hands of the early Japanese aristocratic clans. For the early Japanese, a person's *tamashii*, his or her soul or spirit, became a *kami* or local deity when it was fully nourished and purified through the proper rituals and festivals after death. Before the imperial Yamato clan

Tomb Culture. Daisenryo Kofun, in Osaka, is allegedly the tomb of Emperor Nintoku, dating from the fifth century.

Creation Myth. Tsukioka Yoshitoshi (1839–1892) depicted Japan's creation myth in "Amaterasu Appearing from the Cave." To entice Amaterasu, the goddess of the sun, out so that light would be returned to the world, the other gods performed a ribald dance.

became dominant, each clan had its own pantheon of ancestral deities; but after 500 CE, the ancestors of the Yamato clan were increasingly worshipped by all Japanese. Other regional ancestral deities were later subordinated to the Yamato deities, who claimed direct lineage from Amaterasu, the Sun Goddess and creator of the sacred islands of Japan.

After 587 CE, the Soga kinship group—originally from Korea—became Japan's leading family and controlled the Japanese court. The Soga were particularly sympathetic to the Buddhist religion of the southwestern kingdom of Paekche, which also faced China, and sympathy flowed the other way as well. From the polity's inception, aristocratic birth and kinship, tied to descent lines from the *kami*, were the overriding qualification for social status and advancement within the Yamato imperial clan. The imperial line justified it-

self by embracing a tradition that used both Buddhism and Shinto to sacralize the Japanese state and Japanese society.

The political developments in Japan differed strikingly from those in China or Korea, where a more secular state took hold: the Yamato scribes wove together a unique historical blend that presented their emperor as the living embodiment of Japan and its peoples. They created a sacred past in which the divine and human realms coalesced in the imperial state to form the "way of the deities" (Shinto). Its divine characteristics placed the Yamato aristocratic families at the top of the Japanese state and its aristocratic society.

PRINCE SHOTOKU AND THE TAIKA POLITICAL RE-FORMS By 600 CE, just as the new Sui dynasty (581–618 CE) was bringing together North and South China under a single ruler for the first time in 300 years, the Japanese had gained a sense of themselves as a distinct and unified people. Looking back on this era a century later, and eager to believe that they owed little or nothing to outside influences, the Soga kinship group attributed everything that was innovative in the culture of the early Japanese Yamato state to their own creative young Prince Shotoku (574–622 CE). Contemporary Japanese scribes claimed that Prince Shotoku rather than Korean immigrants had introduced Buddhism to Japan and that his illustrious reign had touched off Japan's rise as an exceptional and powerful island kingdom in East Asia. Indeed, the Japanese Buddhists saw in Prince Shotoku what the Christians of the Roman Empire saw in Constantine: the founding religious figure and chief political icon. But Shotoku's actual historical role remains, at the very least, overstated.

When the Sui dynasty took power, Prince Shotoku allegedly sent envoys to China to inquire about their strengths, and Chinese artists, craftsmen, and clerks were brought to help Japan reshape its institutions. In addition, Shotoku was given credit for preparing a seventeen-article treatise in 1604 that promoted governmental reforms along the Chinese lines; then, the model was the Sui dynasty. At the end of Prince Shotoku's regency, Japan's neighbor underwent a momentous change, as the Sui dynasty quickly gave way to the Tang. For Korea and Japan, such success transformed the Tang empire into a model for up-to-date statecraft, culture, religion, the arts, and society in East Asia.

As in China, Japanese rulers tolerated, and even promoted, a mosaic of religions. Increasing political integration was cover for growing religious pluralism. Shotoku promoted Buddhism and Confucianism; though the groundwork for their growth had been laid by Korean immigrants the century before, he was given credit for introducing them into a native religious culture, Shintoism, which had been wholly Japanese. The prince's prestige has also been associated with several Buddhist temples modeled on Tang pagodas and massive halls; one of these, built in Nara (near present-day Kyoto and Osaka), was the Horyuji Temple; it is still extant, the oldest surviving wooden structure in the world. Its frescoes include figures derived directly from the art of Iran and central Asia. They are a reminder that within two centuries, Buddhism had dispersed its visual culture along the full length of the Silk Road, from Afghanistan to China, and then on to Korea and the island kingdom of Japan in the Pacific Ocean. In Japan, it contributed to the variety of religions.

Political integration was not necessarily the same as political stability. In 645 CE, another leading kinship group known as the Nakatomi came to power via a violent coup d'état that eliminated the Soga and their allies. The leader of the coup, Nakatomi no Kamatari (614–669 CE), and his family used their power over the throne to enact the Taika Reform edicts, which were based on Confucian principles of government allegedly first enunciated by Prince Shotoku in

Taishi. Prince Shotoku Taishi was instrumental in the establishment of Buddhism in Japan, although his actual historical role was overstated. In this hanging scroll painting from the early fourteenth century, he is idealized as a sixteen-year-old son, holding an incense censer and praying for the recovery of his sick father, the Emperor Yomei (r. 585–87).

604 CE. These reforms were sponsored by Nakatomi courtiers in the Yamato court who advanced a new Japanese imperial ideology. According to these edicts, the ruler was no longer simply an ancestral kinship group leader. Instead he became an exalted "emperor" (*tenno*) who ruled by the mandate of heaven, as in China, and exercised absolute authority.

By adapting the Chinese notion of the mandate of heaven, the Yamato court elevated the religious prestige of the Japanese emperor. But not all aspects of Chinese culture were welcomed. Even when Tang institutions of governance were introduced during the Taika reforms of 645, the Japanese court refused to institute the Chinese civil service examination system for fear that doing so would destabilize the aristocrats in power. In the early eighth century, the imperial court at the first Japanese capital of Nara prepared a political narrative about themselves, written in classical Chinese. They linked religious reverence for earlier imperial Yamato ancestors with legitimate political power in Japan.

MAHAYANA BUDDHISM AND THE SANCTITY OF THE JAPANESE STATE Religious influences continued to flow into Japan, contributing to spiritual pluralism while bolstering its rulers. Although Prince Shotoku and later Japanese emperors turned to Confucian models for government, they also dabbled in the occult arts and in Daoist purification rituals. In addition, the Taika edicts under the Nakatomi promoted Buddhism as the state religion of Japan, following Shotoku's lead. Though the imperial family did not cease to support native Shinto traditions, association with Buddhism gave the Japanese state extra status by affiliating it with a universal religion whose appeal stretched to Korea, China, and India.

State-sponsored spiritual diversity led native religions to formalize credos of their own. The introduction of Confucianism and Buddhism to Japan motivated the adherents of native Shinto cults to organize what had been an amorphous body of religious practices into something comparable to these two well-organized belief systems—much as Buddhism had spurred a transformation of Vedic religion in distant India a few centuries earlier. Shinto priests now collected ancient liturgies, and Shinto rituals were incorporated into the official Department of Religion.

The Japanese did not fully accept the traditional Buddhist view of the state as purely a vehicle to protect and propagate moral and social justice for both the ruler and his subjects. The Japanese emperor was the object of more explicit worship as the sacred ruler, one in a line of luminous Shinto gods. He was not simply the temporal ruler who turned the wheel of the law (*dharmaraja*) and patronized the Buddhist monasteries from afar. Unlike rulers in Korea and China, the Japanese emperor was a supreme *kami*—a divine force in his own right. Buddhism as a universal religion imported from China and Paekche was adapted and spread in Japan to also serve the interests of the state, much as Christianity would be used by

European monarchs and Islam by the various Islamic dynasties. But in one respect Japan fundamentally differed from Christianity and Islam. Whereas a single faith—splintered and fractious, to be sure—integrated the latter, Shinto and Buddhism became symbiotically intertwined in the political and religious life of the Japanese. Moreover, unlike in China, emperors in Japan rarely wielded direct power themselves. We will see in Chapter 10 that other individuals, whether next of kin or warrior elites, usually invoked the religious aura of the emperor to legitimate their own political protection of the imperial line.

THE CHRISTIAN WEST, 600–1000 CE

> → *How did two Christianities come to exist in western Eurasia?*

Seen from the Mediterranean and the Islamic world, post-Roman Europe during the period from 600 to 1000 CE seemed little more than a warrior-dominated world. In the fifth century, the mighty Roman military machine gave way to a multitude of warrior leaders whose principal allegiances were local affiliations. Indeed, ever since the days of the ancient Celts, small societies of farmers and herders (living in scattered homesteads or in villages with populations rarely larger than 300) had been dominated by warlords. Yet, here, too, major innovations were under way. The leading force was Christianity, and the leading agents of the Christianization of the European peoples were missionaries and monks. The political ideal of the Roman Empire cast a vast shadow over the western Europeans, but the inheritor of the mantle of Rome was increasingly a spiritual institution—the Roman Catholic Church—whose powerful head, the pope, was based in Rome.

CHARLEMAGNE'S FLEDGLING EMPIRE

In 802 CE, Harun al-Rashid, the ruler of Baghdad, sent the gift of an elephant to Charlemagne, the king of the Franks, in northern Europe. The elephant, named Abuldabaz—after Abu Abbas, Harun's ancestor and the founder of the Abbasid dynasty—caused a sensation among the Franks, who saw the gift as an acknowledgment of Charlemagne's power. In fact, Harun, like the Sasanian King of Kings centuries before him, often sent rare beasts to distant rulers as a gracious reminder of his own formidable power. In his eyes, Charlemagne's "empire" was a minor principality. Indeed, the region would have struck those accompanying the elephant from Baghdad as

profoundly underdeveloped. Northern Europe contained few cities—the largest, Paris, had only 20,000 inhabitants—and they were smaller than the long-deserted Roman settlements now in ruins.

This was an empire that Charlemagne ruled with tireless energy from 768 to 814 CE, often traveling 2,000 miles a year on campaigns of plunder and conquest. By 802 CE, he controlled much of western Europe, lands reaching across the Pyrenees Mountains as far south as Catalonia in modern-day Spain, as far east as across the Alps, and as far south as Naples in modern-day Italy. Yet, compared with the rulers of the Islamic world, he was a political lightweight. His empire had a population of less than 15 million; he rarely commanded armies larger than 5,000; and he had only the most rudimentary tax system. At a time when the palace quarters of the caliph at Baghdad covered nearly 250 acres, Charlemagne's newly built palace at Aachen was merely 330 by 655 feet. (Baghdad itself was almost 40 square miles in area, whereas there was virtually no "town" outside the palace at Aachen.) Constructed in 796 CE (only a generation after the foundation of Baghdad), it was little more than a large country house set in the middle of open countryside, close to the

Charlemagne's Throne. From this raised throne, Charlemagne presided over services performed by the clergy. Constructed of slabs of marble transported all the way from Rome to Aachen, the throne showed that Charlemagne was the "new" emperor of the West and heir of the emperors of Rome.

Charlemagne's Palace and Chapel. Though not large by Byzantine or Islamic standards, Charlemagne's palace and chapel were heavy with symbolic meaning. A royal hall for banqueting in Frankish, "barbarian" style was linked by a covered walkway to the imperial domed chapel, which was meant to look like a miniature version of the Hagia Sophia of Constantinople. Outside the chapel was a courtyard, like that outside the shrine of Saint Peter at Rome.

woods of the Ardennes where Charlemagne and his Franks loved to hunt wild boar on horseback.

He and his men were representatives of the warrior class that had come to dominate post-Roman western Europe. Set against the broader history of northern and western Europe, there was nothing unusual about the Franks. Roman rule, which inaugurated a period when large towns were privileged over the countryside and educated civilians valued over warriors, had briefly imposed an alien way of life. That Mediterranean empire had withdrawn, and from 500 CE onward, war became, once again, the duty and the joy of the aristocrat: buoyed up by their chieftains' mead—a heavy beer made with honey, "yellow, sweet and ensnaring"—young men were expected to follow their lords into battle, "among the war horses and the blood-stained armor" (Aneirin, *Y Gododin*, ll. 102, 840).

And though the Franks vigorously engaged in trade, that trade was based on war: Europe's principal export at this time was Europeans. The Frankish empire was financed by the massive sale of prisoners of war. From Venice, which grew rich from its role as middleman in human trafficking, the captives were sent across the sea to Alexandria, Tunis, and southern Spain. The main victims of this trade were Slavic-speaking peoples, tribal communities of hunters and cultivators whose populations had slowly grown in eastern Europe. Their long oppression is preserved in the English language,

for the medieval Latin *sclavus* (which originally meant "Slavic") replaced the classical Latin *servus* to denote "slave"; *servus,* by contrast, was applied to those who stayed at home and became the English word "serf"—a peasant tied for life to the estates of the aristocracy.

Yet in this seemingly uncivilized and inhospitable zone, a religion with universalistic aspirations—Christianity—began to sink down roots. Although its worldwide expansion did not occur for centuries, its spiritual conquest of the European peoples established institutions and fired enthusiasms that would later drive believers to carry its message to faraway lands.

A CHRISTIANITY FOR THE NORTH

Charlemagne's empire was unquestionably primitive when compared with the Islamic empire or the Tang empire of China. But what mattered most about it was *where*, not what, it was. Far removed from the old centers of high culture, it had left the Roman Mediterranean behind. Charlemagne's empire was a polity of the borderlands. It was also based on an expansionist and proselytizing Christianity that drew energy from its rough frontier mentality. (See Map 9-8.)

As the fuzzy frontier lines between the Roman Empire and the territories to its north vanished forever, Christianity was pulled into a new world profoundly different from the Mediterranean cities in which it had taken form.

Through its evangelizing efforts, the Christianity of the West bridged the ancient gulf between the Mediterranean world and the non-Roman world of the north. As a result, Christians felt that theirs was the only truly universal religion. It could bring hitherto opposed groups into a single "catholic" church that, as we have seen, had begun to replace a political unity lost in western Europe when the Roman Empire fell.

As far back as 410 CE, reacting to the Visigothic sack of Rome, the great Christian bishop Augustine of Hippo (a seaport in modern Algeria) had laid down the outlines of this belief. Of Augustine's many books, the most important for future centuries was his *City of God.* He wrote it to persuade contemporary Christians that the barbarian takeover already happening around them was not the end of the world. The "city of God" was represented on earth by the Catholic Church, and the Catholic Church was not for Romans only— it was for all times and for all peoples, "in a wide world which has always been inhabited by many differing peoples, that have so many different customs and languages, so many different forms of organization and so many languages, and who have had so many different religions" (Augustine, *The City of God*, 14.1). Nonetheless, only one organization would bring them all to paradise: the Catholic Church.

Such confidence may appear paradoxical. After all, around 800 CE barely 25 percent of the Christians in the

MAP 9-8   CHRISTENDOM, 600–1000

The end of the first millennium saw much of Europe divided between two versions of Christianity, each with different traditions and histories. Identify the regions where each version of Christianity held sway. Why do you think the Catholic Church based in Rome was successful in expanding its influence in the west, but not the east? Why did the Orthodox version of Christianity based in Constantinople expand into eastern Europe, but not the west? How influential was Charlemagne's empire in promoting this division?

world were found in western Europe. Most lived in the richer and more populous Byzantine Empire—the eastern Roman empire of Constantinople—or in the large and sophisticated Christian communities that were thriving under a relatively tolerant Muslim rule. Independent Christian kingdoms still flourished in Africa, in Nubia on the Upper Nile and in the highlands of Ethiopia. Beyond the Islamic lands, to the east, Nestorian Christianity was a major presence on the Silk Road. Yet none of these offshoots of Christianity felt quite the certainty of being truly, and exclusively, the one universal

Primary Source

CHRISTENDOM ON THE EDGE: A VIEW OF EMPIRE IN IRELAND

A young Christian Briton of Roman citizenship who lived near Hadrian's Wall experienced the pull of Christianity around 400. In his teens, Patricius was captured by Irish slave raiders and spent six years herding pigs on the Atlantic coast of Mayo. He escaped and years later decided to return in order to convert his former captors to Christianity. He believed that in making the fierce Irish Christians, he also made them "Romans." He thus brought Christianity to the Atlantic edge of the known world. Patricius, who died around 460, is remembered today as Saint Patrick.

16 But after I reached Ireland, well, I pastured the flocks every day. . . . I would even stay in the forests and on the mountain and would wake to pray before dawn in all weathers, snow, frost, rain. . . .

17 And it was in fact there that one night while asleep I heard a voice saying to me: 'You do well to fast, since you will soon be going to your home country;' and again, very shortly after, I heard this prophecy: 'See, your ship is ready.' And it was not near at hand but was perhaps two hundred miles away, and I had never been there and did not know a living soul there. And then I soon ran away and abandoned the man with whom I had been for six years. . . . till I reached the ship.

23 And again a few years later I was in Britain with my kinsfolk. . . . And it was there that I saw one night in a vision a man coming as it were from Ireland . . .

with countless letters, and he gave me one of them, and I read the heading of the letter, 'The Voice of the Irish,' and as I read these opening words aloud, I imagined at that very instant that I heard the voice of those who were beside the forest of Foclut which is near the western sea; and thus they cried, as though with one voice: 'We beg you, holy boy, to come and walk again among us.'

→ *What does this passage tell us about life in the Celtic worlds?*

→ *What does this passage reveal to us about how St. Patrick's spiritual experiences compare to those of priests in the older Christian communities in the Mediterranean worlds of Rome and Constantinople?*

SOURCE: *St. Patrick: His Writings and Muirchu's Life*, edited and translated by A. B. E. Hood (London: Phillimore, 1978), pp. 41, 44–46, 50.

church that was enjoyed by the Catholic Church of Europe in the age of Charlemagne.

Several developments helped give rise to this attitude. First, the arrival of Christianity in northern Europe had provoked a cultural revolution. Preliterate societies made contact, for the first time, with a sacred text in a language that seemed utterly strange to them. Latin became a sacred language, and books themselves became charged vehicles of the holy. As we saw in Chapter 8, Roman Christians had already moved from the clumsy scroll to the bound codex, but it was still a messy object. Written on papyrus, the codex had none of the features that Europeans today associate with a modern book—no divisions between the words, no punctuation, no

paragraphs, and no chapter headings. The reader was assumed to know Latin well enough (as a spoken language) that no further aids to understanding were needed. The same assumption could not be made of an Irishman, a Saxon, or a Frank who had never spoken Latin but wished to read and understand the Bible. Hence the care lavished in the new Christian north on the Latin scriptures. The few parchment texts that circulated in northern Europe were carefully prepared, with the words in them separated, the sentences correctly punctuated and introduced by uppercase letters, and chapter headings provided: they were far more like the book you are reading now than anything available to Romans at the height of the empire.

Celtic Bible. Unlike the simple codex of early Christian times, the Bible came to be presented in Ireland and elsewhere in the northern world as a magical book. Its pages were filled with mysterious, intricate patterns, which imitated on parchment the jewelry and treasure for which early medieval warlords yearned.

Second, those who produced the new Bibles were starkly different from ordinary men and women. They were monks and nuns. Monasticism, which had been a feature of Mediterranean Christianity since 300 CE, had originated in Egypt, and its technical terms underscore its eastern source. The root of "monastic" (and of "monk") is the Greek *monos*, "alone": a man or a woman who chose to live alone, without the support of marriage or family. And "hermit" derives from the Greek *herēmos*, "man of the desert," for zealous Christians had retired to the desert to find solitude.

Monasticism had been immensely popular in Egypt, Syria, and elsewhere, but it also suited the missionary tendencies of Christianity in northern Europe particularly well. It placed small, well-organized groups of men and women in the middle of societies with which they had nothing in common.

Monasticism rapidly took hold because it appealed to a deep sense that precisely the men and women who had least in common with those whose lives were "normal" were best able to mediate between the believer and God. Just as in Buddhism, in the monastic Christianity of western Europe the relation between the members of religious orders and the laity was grounded in religious "merit," or spiritual credit. Lay persons gave gifts to the monasteries and offered their protection. In return for these righteous acts, they gained the prayers of the monks and nuns and the very real reassurance that although they themselves were warriors and men of blood, the monks' and nuns' intercessions would keep them from going to hell.

With the spread of monasticism, the Christianity of the north took a decisive turn. In Muslim (as in Jewish) societies, religious leaders tended to emphasize their commonalities with those around them: many of the greatest scholars, theologians, and mystics of Islam were married men, including merchants and courtiers. In the Christian West, the opposite was true: preliterate warrior societies honored small groups of men and women who were utterly unlike themselves—unmarried, unfit for warfare, and intensely literate in an incomprehensible tongue. Even their hair looked different. Unlike warriors, these men were close-shaven; by contrast, the Orthodox clergy of the eastern Roman empire sported long, silvery beards (signifying wisdom and maturity and not, as in the West, the warrior's masculine strength). The heads of Catholic monks and priests were shaved as well, in a rite known as "tonsure." Such deliberate differentiation shows that the Catholic Church of northern Europe owed its ambitious horizons, as a missionary religion, to the same principles that explained the spread of Buddhism in central and Inner Asia (and later in Japan): it was a religion of monks, whose communities represented an otherworldly alternative to the warrior societies in which they found themselves. By the year 800 CE, few regions of northern Europe were without great monasteries, many of which held more than 300 monks or nuns (they were larger, that is, than the local villages). Supported by thousands of serfs donated to them by kings and local warlords, these were powerhouses of prayer, which kept the regions safe.

Northern Christianity also gained new ties to an old imaginative center. As the cleric leading the gigantic former capital of the empire, the Christian bishop of Rome had always enjoyed much prestige around the Mediterranean. But he was only one bishop among many. He was often overshadowed and contradicted by his peers in Carthage, Alexandria, Antioch, and Constantinople. Though he was spoken of with respect as *papa*, as "the grand old man," many others shared that title.

By the year 800 CE, this picture had dramatically changed. As believers looked down into the Mediterranean from the distant north, they saw only one *papa* left in western Europe: Rome's pope. The papacy as we know it rose because of the

St. Gallen Monastery. The great monasteries of the age of Charlemagne were like Roman legionary settlements. Placed on the frontiers of Germany, they were vast, stone buildings, around which entire towns would gather. Their libraries, the largest in Europe, were filled with parchment volumes, carefully written out and often lavishly decorated in a "northern," Celtic style. Though dwarfed by the Islamic libraries of the same time, they were the places where Latin literature was preserved. All Latin "classical" texts known to us survive because they were copied by monks in such monasteries at this time.

fervor with which the Catholic Church of western Europe united to support a single and exclusive symbolic center, represented by the popes at Rome. This movement had begun at the time of the collapse of the Roman Empire in the west, and sometime after 750 CE it achieved its goal. The popes owed their position in the Christian West to two developments: the Arab conquests, which had removed Rome's competition by abruptly slicing the Mediterranean in two, and the increased need of new Christians who had grown up in the northern borderlands to create a more vibrant, more exclusively religious focus for their hopes.

Charlemagne recognized this need very well. In 800 CE, he went out of his way to celebrate Christmas Day by visiting the shrine of Saint Peter at Rome. There, Pope Leo III acclaimed him as the new "emperor" of the West. The hurried ceremony added nothing to his power, but it ratified the aspirations of an age. A "modern" Rome—inhabited by popes, famous for the shrines of the martyrs, and protected by a "modern" Christian monarch from the north—and not the "ancient" Rome of pagan emperors was what his subjects wanted.

Stone Beehive Huts. Monasticism was also about the lonely search for God at the very end of the world, which took place in these Irish monasteries on the Atlantic coast. The cells, made of loose stones piled in round domes, are called "beehives." Beyond, in the ocean, is the rock of Saint Michael (Skellig Michál), a place of total isolation for monks known as "hermits"—men of the deep desert. Having no deserts, the Irish turned to offshore rocks and islands to find a place to be alone with God.

THE AGE OF THE VIKINGS, 800–1000 CE

Harun's elephant died in 813—one year before Charlemagne himself. Abuldabaz's death was recorded because the Franks viewed it as an omen of coming disasters. The great beast keeled over when he was marched out to confront the army

The Coronation of Charlemagne. This is how the coronation of Charlemagne at Rome in 800 was remembered in medieval western Europe. This painting stresses the fact that it was the pope who placed the crown on Charlemagne's head, thereby claiming him as a ruler set up by the Catholic Church for the Catholic Church. But in 800 contemporaries saw the pope as recognizing the fact that Charlemagne had already deserved to be emperor. The rise of the papacy to greater prominence and power in later medieval Europe caused this significant "re-remembering" of the event.

of a Viking king from Denmark. In the next half century, the Vikings from Scandinavia exposed the weakness of Charlemagne's self-confident regime. His once powerful empire of borderland peoples met its match on the widest border of all: that between the European landmass and the mighty Atlantic. (See Map 9-9.)

The motives of the Vikings were simple and announced in their name, which is derived from the Old Norse *vik,* "to be on the warpath." The Vikings sought to loot the now wealthy Franks and replace them as the dominant warrior class of northern Europe. It was their turn to extract plunder and to

Oseberg Ship. The Viking ship was a triumph of design. It could be rowed up the great rivers of Europe, and, at the same time, its sail could take it across the Atlantic.

sell droves of slaves across the water. They succeeded because of a deadly technological advantage: ships of unparalleled sophistication, developed by Scandinavian sailors in the Baltic Sea and the long fjords of Norway. Light and agile, with a shallow draft, they could be rowed up the rivers of northern Europe and even carried overland from one river system to another. Under sail, the same boats could tackle open water and cross the hitherto unexplored wastes of the North Atlantic.

In the ninth century, the Vikings set their ships on both courses. They emptied northern Europe of its treasure, sacking the great monasteries that had sprung up in precisely those places most vulnerable to attack from the sea—along the Atlantic and North Sea coasts of Ireland and Britain and on the banks of the Rhine and the Seine, great, slow rivers that led into the very heart of Charlemagne's Frankish empire. At the same time, Norwegian adventurers colonized first the hitherto uninhabited island of Iceland, and then Greenland. By 982 CE, they had even reached the New World and established a substantial settlement at L'Anse aux Meadows on the coast of Labrador. Viking goods have been found as far west as the Inuit settlements of Baffin Island to the north of Hudson Bay, carried there along intricate trading routes by Native Americans.

The consequences of this spectacular reach across the ocean to the coast of America were short-lived, but the penetration of eastern Europe by Viking ships had lasting effects. Ruthless and supremely well equipped to penetrate long river systems, the Vikings sailed east along the Baltic and then turned south, edging up the rivers that flowed into the Baltic to cross the watershed of central Russia, where the Dnieper, the Don, and the Volga begin to flow south into the Black Sea and the Caspian. By opening this link between the Baltic and what is now Kiev in modern Ukraine, they created an av-

MAP 9-9   THE AGE OF VIKINGS AND THE SLAVE TRADE, 800–1000

Vikings from Scandinavia dramatically altered the history of Christendom in the late first millennium. What impact did Viking raiders have on western Christendom during this era? Was their influence on the communities of eastern Europe similar or different? What influence did Vikings have on people beyond the Afro-Eurasian world? What role did the Vikings and the Holy Roman emperors play in expanding the slave trade during this period?

enue of commerce that, for the first time, linked Scandinavia and the Baltic directly to Constantinople and Baghdad. What they added was yet more slaves; Muslim geographers bluntly called this newly opened route "The Highway of the Slaves." The fortified trading posts of the Scandinavians would eventually form the spine of medieval Russia.

THE SURVIVAL OF THE CHRISTIAN EMPIRE OF THE EAST

On reaching the Black Sea, the Vikings made straight for Constantinople. In 860 CE, more than 200 of their long ships gathered ominously in the straits of the Bosporus, beneath the walls of the city. What they found was not Charlemagne's rustic Aachen but a proud city with a population exceeding 100,000, surrounded by well-engineered late Roman walls.

The Vikings had come up against a state hardened by battle. For two centuries on end, the empire of East Rome, centered on Constantinople, had held Islamic armies at bay. Once Southwest Asia as a whole had fallen to the Islamic empire of Baghdad, the East Romans fought across Anatolia and the eastern Mediterranean for their own survival. From 640 to 840 CE they faced almost yearly campaigns launched by an empire that grew to be ten times greater in extent than their own, with a budget fifteen times greater. For years on end, Muslim armies and navies came within striking distance of Constantinople. Each time they failed, outmaneuvered by highly professional generals and unable to prevail against a skillfully constructed line of fortresses that controlled the roads across Anatolia. Muslim writers took the Christian empire of East Rome—Rûm—seriously, as they never took the Franks. The Christian empire of East Rome fought the caliphs of Baghdad to a draw.

Jelling Stone. Carved on the side of this great stone, Christ appears to be almost swallowed up in an intricate pattern of lines. For the Vikings, complicated interweaving like serpents or twisted gold jewelry was a sign of majesty: hence, in this, the first Christian monument in Denmark, Christ is part of an ancient pattern of carving, which brought good luck and victory to the king.

Moreover, this empire had its own technological advantage, one used to deadly effect in naval warfare: Greek fire, a combination of petroleum and potassium that, when sprayed from siphons, would explode in a great sheet of flame on the water. In 717 CE, the emperor Leo III used it for the first time to destroy the Muslim fleet as it lay at anchor within sight of the imperial palace of Constantinople. A century and a half later, the experience and weaponry of East Rome were too much for the Vikings, and their raid was a spectacular failure.

In the long run, the sense of having outlasted an endless series of military emergencies bolstered the morale of East Roman Christianity and led to its unexpected flowering in distant lands. Not just Constantinople but Justinian's glorious church, the Hagia Sophia, its heart, had survived. That great building and the solemn Greek liturgy that was performed in it might not impress Catholic Franks. But Scandinavian adventurers from the new slave markets of Kiev and the Volga— like their medieval Russian successors—were prepared to be immensely impressed. Here was the central church of a Christian empire that for half a millennium had represented all that was most dignified and venerable in the Christian tradition. In the tenth century, as Charlemagne's empire collapsed in western Europe, large areas of eastern Europe became Greek Orthodox, not Catholic. As a result, Greek Christianity gained a spiritual empire that eventually offset the losses of the eastern Roman empire in Southwest Asia.

The conversion of Russian peoples and the Balkan Slavs to Orthodox Christianity was a complex process. But it was based on an admiration for Constantinople, on the part of Russians, Bulgarians, and other Slav princes, as intense as that of any Western Catholic for the Roman popes. This admiration amounted to awe, as shown by the famous story, preserved in a Russian chronicle, of the conversion to Greek Christianity in 987 CE of the rulers of Kiev (descendants of Viking adventurers from the Baltic):

> The envoys reported[,] . . . "We went among the Germans [the Catholic Franks] and we saw them performing many ceremonies in their churches; but we beheld no glory there. Then we went to Greece [in fact, to Constantinople and Hagia Sophia], and the Greeks led us to the edifices where they worship their God, and we knew not whether we were in heaven or on earth. For on earth there is no such splendor or such beauty, and we are at a loss to describe it. We only know that God dwells there among men, and their service is fairer than the ceremonies of other nations. For we can not forget that beauty. (Cross and Sherbowitz-Westor, *The Russian Primary Chronicle*, 111)

By 1000, two Christianities existed: one was the new and confident "borderland" Catholicism of western Europe, and the other was an ancient Greek Orthodoxy, protected against constant threat of extinction by the iron framework of a "Roman" state inherited directly from Constantine and Justinian. Western Catholics believed that their church was destined to expand everywhere. East Romans were less euphoric but more tenacious. They believed that their Christian empire would, somehow, forever survive the regular ravages of invasion. It was a significant difference in attitudes, and neither side liked the other. East Romans considered the Franks barbarous and grasping: "no one deserves to have a Frank as their neighbor" was an East Roman proverb of the age of Charlemagne. For their part, Western Catholics contemptuously called the East Romans "Greeks" and condemned them for "Byzantine" cunning—failing to recognize that the generals and diplomats of Constantinople managed for centuries to fend off Baghdad's aggression largely by living by their wits. And locked in this confrontation, both Catholics and Orthodox tended to forget the sizable Christian communities to the east and south of them, from Ethiopia to Armenia, who continued under Muslim rule or on the frontiers of the Islamic empire, largely unaffected by what happened in either Europe or Byzantium.

Thus, like Islam, the Christian world was divided, though in this case the main division was into just two distinct entities—Western and eastern Christianity. Their differences

Viking Longhouse. A simple turf bunker was built by the Vikings on the coast of Canada. Low-lying for protection against wind and snow, it was built as a permanent settlement and trading post with the Eskimos. Viking trade goods appear far to the north in Baffin Island.

at that time were not doctrinal, like those of Shia and Sunni Islam. They were differences in heritage, customs, and levels of civilization. At that time, the orthodox world was considerably more ancient and more cultured than that of the Catholic west. Both encountered the expansionist ambitions of Muslim warriors, but they dealt with Islam differently. At Constantinople, capital of eastern Christianity and heir to the eastern part of the Roman Empire, Christianity held off Muslim forces that constantly threatened the integrity of the great city and its Christian hinterlands. In the west, on the other hand, Muslim expansionism ran its course confined to the Iberian Peninsula, behind the Pyrenees Mountains. Western Christendom, led by the Roman papacy, did not feel the same degree of political and cultural intimidation from Islam. It set about the task of spreading Christianity to the pagan tribes to the north, and as the period drew to a close it began to contemplate retaking lands from the Muslims.

Also like Islam, western Christianity expanded its geographic reach into new frontiers by harnessing faith to empire. (Byzantine Christianity tended to keep within its own frontiers and used the religion only for matters of interstate diplomacy.) In this fashion, universalizing religions reinforced the claims to power of aspiring rulers; but they also relied on rulers' armies to subdue or incorporate nonbelievers into the expanding circle of common spirituality. But much more than in Islam, where conquering armies more effectively centered the faith in Baghdad, Christendom was cleaved between east and west, and within the west it was splintered among rivalrous warrior provinces with only nominal allegiance to popes and other central authorities. Religion adapted itself to the localized political structures. And in contrast to China, where new rulers rebuilt integrated empires using traditional means

of rulership while accommodating and even promoting growing religious pluralism, in Christendom, especially in the west, we see increasing religious homogeneity and common faith, but no recovery of the bygone power of Rome—to which ambitious pretenders continued to aspire.

CONCLUSION

The four centuries from 600 to 1000 CE were marked both by extraordinary fluidities and by striking rigidities. Eurasian and North African societies witnessed a radical reordering of their political and cultural maps that encouraged movement across cultural boundaries and over long distances while at the same time insisting on the distinctiveness and often the superiority of individual political and cultural systems. Commodities, technological innovations, ideas, travelers, merchants, adventurers, and scholars moved with unusual rapidity from one end of Afro-Eurasia to the other, and up and down coastal Africa. This mercantile activity was accompanied by missionizing into new frontiers. The proximity and relatively porous boundaries of the two great political and cultural units of this period—Abbasid Islam and Tang China—abetted the movement of people and commodities; in this regard, the two empires stood in glaring contrast to their two powerful predecessors, Han China and Rome, which had occupied the far corners of the Afro-Eurasian landmass and were separated by great distances. The Silk Road was now even more widely traveled than in the previous centuries. And the agrarian revolution that swept much of middle Afro-Eurasia only fueled the bounty and population growth.

Yet in spite of the circulation of peoples and ideas throughout Eurasia and Africa, a new set of political and cultural boundaries were developing that would split this landmass in ways that it had not known before. The most important of these dividing forces was the new universalistic religion, Islam, which emerged in the first half of the seventh century and immediately challenged and slowed the spread of an equally determined universalistic religion, Christianity. As a consequence, Afro-Eurasia's highly differentiated major cultural zones now began to compete with one another in their universalistic religious and cultural doctrines. The Abbasid empire pushed back the borders of the Tang empire. But the intensity of interimperial conflict grew particularly high between the Islamic and Christian worlds, where the clash involved faith as well as frontiers.

The Sui and Tang empires revived Confucianism, insisting on its primacy within the Chinese political and moral system as the foundation of a new imperial order; and they embraced the classical written language as another unifying element in a new common culture. They thereby successfully counteracted the powerful global forces that brought foreign religions, notably Buddhism but also Islam, into the Chinese state. The same adaptive strategies, promoting religious amalgamation of new and old belief systems while elevating the powers of centralizing dynasties, also influenced the creation of new systems on the Korean Peninsula and in Japan.

Chronology

	MAJOR TRENDS	200 CE	300 CE	400 CE	500 C
THE ISLAMIC WORLD	*Afro-Eurasian agricultural revolution begins*				
EAST ASIA		▮ *Three Kingdoms dominate Korea from the 3rd century*		*Yamato clan becomes dominant in Japan, 500* ▮	
EUROPE					

There were, therefore, many ways to cope with the emergence and spread of universalizing religions across Eurasia and Africa, but all were linked to empire. In some circumstances, faith followed empire and relied on rulers' support or tolerance, as well as some measure of political stability, to spread the word. This was the case especially in East Asia. At the opposite extreme, empire followed faith, as in the case of Islam, whose believers imagined an empire out of new cloth. To be sure, emerging dynasts exploited older symbolic resources, like the allure of a "restored" Mesopotamian centrality. But for the most part, the Islamic empire—and its successors—represented a new force on the world stage: expanding political power backed by one God whose instruc-

tions to believers was to spread his message. In the worlds of Christianity, a common faith yielded to elements of a common culture (shared books, a language for learned classes), but in the west only in name did rulers overcome the intense allegiance to local sources of political authority.

While this was an age in which universalizing religions expanded and common cultures grew, especially among literati and learned groups who aligned themselves with state power, there was also enormous debate and dissent within each religion over basic principles. In spite of the diffusion of basic texts inscribed in "official" languages, many variations of Christianity, Islam, and Buddhism existed, proliferating even more as each of these belief systems spread into new

600 CE	700 CE	800 CE	900 CE	1000 CE

- Muhammad born in Mecca, 570
- Muhammad and small group of followers flee Mecca for Medina, 622
- Death of Muhammad, 632
- Arab armies conquer Southwest Asia, North Africa, Spain, Central Asia, and parts of South Asia, 650–750
- Ummayad caliphate rules from Damascus, 661–750
- Shiism emerges as major dissident force within Islam, late 7th century
- Abbasid caliphate rules from Baghdad, 750–1258
- Al-Khwarizmi (c. 780–850) writes first book on algebra
- Fatimid Shiite regime forms, based in Egypt, 969
- Ibn Sina (980–1037) produces Canon of Medicine

- Prince Shotoku (574–622) initiates Taika political reforms
- Sui state unites much of China, 581–618
- Tang state emerges in China, 618
- Tang dynasty establishes strong influence on Central Asia by 650
- Silla state unifies Korea, 668
- Empress Wu reigns over Tang state, 690–705
- Tang army loses battle of Talas in 751 to Islamic forces, beginning Tang retreat from Central Asia
- Tang state embarks on anti-Buddhist campaigns
- Peasant uprising begins, 859
- Tang dynasty disintegrates, 906
- Koryo kingdom assumes control of Korea, 918
- Khitan invasion

- Arab armies conquer much of Byzantine Empire's lands in Southwest Asia, but the empire survives, 632–661
- Missionaries and monastic orders begin converting much of northern Europe into Christian communities loyal to the popes in Rome (had been converted by 800)
- Catholic Church based in Rome dominates Christian West
- Charlemagne (768–814) unites much of western Europe into a short-lived kingdom
- Vikings plunder northern Europe, 9th century
- Vikings establish strong commercial links across eastern Europe to Constantinople
- Vikings reach North America, 982
- Russian leaders convert to Orthodox Christianity, 987

regions. As the first millennium drew to a close, religion, re-inforced by prosperity and imperial resources, was a means to bring peoples together in unprecedented ways. But it was also, as the next chapter will illustrate, a new means to drive them apart in bloodcurdling confrontations.

STUDY QUESTIONS

 WWNORTON.COM/STUDYSPACE

1. Analyze the impact of the spread of Islam on the various societies of Afro-Eurasia. How did the emergence of a large Islamic empire shape the movement of peoples, ideas, innovations, and commodities across the vast landmass?

2. Describe the process through which the spread of Islam fostered an agricultural revolution in Afro-Eurasia. What crops and cultivation techniques were involved in this process?

3. Compare and contrast the spread of Islam, Christianity, and Buddhism between 600 and 1000. What was the geographic range of each religious community? Through which methods did each religion gain new converts?

4. Explain the origins and basic concepts of Islam. How similar to and different from other religions that began in Southwest Asia, such as Judaism, Christianity, and Zoroastrianism, was this new religious outlook?

5. Analyze the successes and failures of Islamic leaders in creating one large empire to govern Islamic communities. What opponents emerged to challenge this goal?

6. Describe the Tang dynasty's attempts to restore political unity to East Asia. How did Tang leaders react to the growth of universal religions within their realm?

7. Explain the significance of the year 751 in world history. How did the battle of Talas shape the history of Afro-Eurasia?

8. Describe the state structure that emerged in Korea and Japan during this era. How were these new states shaped by other developments in Afro-Eurasia, such as the growth of universal religions?

9. Compare and contrast Christian communities in western Europe to those in eastern Europe and the Byzantine Empire. What factors contributed to each region's distinctiveness?

10. Analyze the impact of Viking communities on world history during this era. How did Vikings shape developments in the Christian world especially?

FURTHER READINGS

Ahmed, Leila, *Women and Gender in Islam* (1992). A superb overview of the relations between men and women throughout the history of Islam.

Aneirin, *Y Gododdin: Britain's Oldest Heroic Poem*, ed. and trans. A. O. H. Jarman (1988). A sixth-century Welsh text that describes the battle of the last Britons against the invading Anglo-Saxons.

Arberry, Arthur J., introduction to *The Koran Interpreted: A Translation*, trans. Arthur J. Arberry (1986). One of the most eloquent appreciations of this classical work of religion.

Augustine, *The City of God*, trans. H. Bettenson (1976). An excellent translation of Augustine's monumental work of history, philosophy, and religion.

Berkey, Jonathan P., *The Formation of Islam: Religion and Society in the Near East, 600–1800* (2005). A recent overview of the history of Islam before the modern era. It is particularly sensitive to the influence of external elements on the history of the Muslim peoples.

Bol, Peter, *This Culture of Ours: Intellectual Transitions in T'ang and Sung China* (1994). A study tracing the transformation of the shared culture of the Chinese learned elite from the seventh to the twelfth centuries.

Brown, Peter, *The Rise of Western Christendom: Triumph and Diversity, AD 200–1000*, 2nd ed. (2003). A description of the changes in Christianity in northern Europe and the emergence of the new cultures and political structures that coincided with this development.

Bulliet, Richard W., *Conversion to Islam in the Medieval Period: An Essay in Quantitative History* (1979). A determined and largely successful effort to measure the rate at which the populations overrun by Arab conquerors in the seventh century CE embraced the religion of their rulers.

Cook, Michael, *The Koran: A Very Short Introduction* (2000). A useful overview of Islam's holy book.

———, *Muhammad* (1983). A brief but careful life of the Prophet that takes full account of the prolific and often controversial preexisting scholarship.

Cross, S. H., and O. P. Sherbowitz-Westor, trans., *The Russian Primary Chronicle* (1953).

Donner, Fred M., *The Early Islamic Conquests* (1981). The best account of the Arab conquests in the Persian and Byzantine empires in the seventh century.

Fage, J. D., *Ghaua: A Historical Introduction* (1966). A brief but authoritative history of Ghaua from earliest times to the present.

Fisher, Humphrey J., *Slavery in the History of Muslim Black Africa* (2001). A general history of the relations between North Africa and black Africa, focusing on one of the most important aspects of contact—the slave trade.

Graham-Campbell, James, *Cultural Atlas of the Viking World* (1994). A positioning of the Vikings against their wider background in both western and eastern Europe.

Hawting, G. R., *The First Dynasty of Islam: The Umayyad Caliphate, A.D. 661–750* (2000). The essential scholarly treatment of Islam's first dynasty.

Herrmann, Georgina, *Iranian Revival* (1977). The structure and horizons of the Sasanian Empire as revealed in its monuments.

Hillgarth, J. N. (ed.), *Christianity and Paganism, 350–750: The Conversion of Western Europe*, rev. ed. (1986). A collection of contemporary sources.

Hodges, Richard and David Whitehouse, *Mohammed, Charlemagne, and the Origins of Europe* (1983). A spirited comparison of Islam and the rise of Europe.

Hodgson, Marshall G. S., *The Venture of Islam: Conscience and History in a World Civilization* (1977), 3 vols. A magnificent history of the Islamic peoples. Its first volume, *The Classical Age of Islam*, is basic reading for anyone interested in the history of the Muslim world.

Holdsworth, May, *Women of the Tang Dynasty* (1999). An account of women's lives during the Tang dynasty.

Hourani, Albert, *History of the Arab Peoples* (2002). The best overview of Arab history.

Jones, Gwynn, *The Norse Atlantic Saga* (1986). The Viking discovery of America.

Kennedy, Hugh, *The Prophet and the Age of the Caliphate: The Islamic Near East from the Sixth to the Eleventh Century* (2004). A very good recent synthesis.

Lee, Peter, et al. (eds.), *Sources of Korean Tradition*, vol. 1 (1996). A unique view of Korean history through the eyes and words of the participants or witnesses themselves, as provided in translations of official documents, letters, and policies.

Levtzion, Nehemia, *Ancient Ghana and Mali* (1980). The best introduction to the kingdoms of West Africa.

Levtzion, Nehemia, and Jay Spaulding, *Medieval West Africa: Views from Arab Scholars and Merchants* (2003). An indispensable source book on early West African history.

Lewis, Bernard, *The Middle East: Two Thousand Years of History from the Rise of Christianity to the Present Day* (1995). A stimulating introduction to an area that has seen the emergence of three of the great world religions.

——— (trans.), *Islam from the Prophet Muhammad to the Caphre of Constantinople* (1974). Vol. 2: Religion and Society. A fine collection of original sources that portray various aspects of classical Islamic society.

Middleton, John, *The Swahili: The Social Landscape of a Mercantile Community* (2000). An exciting synthesis of the Swahili culture of East Africa.

Miyazaki, Ichisada, *China's Examination Hell* (1981).

Nurse, Derek, and Thomas Spear, *The Swahili: Reconstructing the History and Language of an African Society, 800–1500* (1984). A work laying out what we know at present about the history of the Muslim peoples who lived along the coast of East Africa.

Peters, F. E., *Muhammad and the Origins of Islam* (1994). A work that explores the early history of Islam and highlights the critical role that Muhammad played in promoting a new religion and a powerful Arab identity.

Schirokauer, Conrad, et al., *A Brief History of Japanese Civilization*, 2nd ed. (2005). A balanced account; chapters focus on developments in art, religion, literature, and thought as well as on Japan's economic, political, and social history in medieval times.

Smith, Julia, *Europe after Rome: A New Cultural History, 500–1000* (2005). A vivid analysis of society and culture in so-called Dark Age Europe.

Twitchett, Denis, *The Birth of the Chinese Meritocracy: Bureaucrats and Examinations in Tang China* (1976). A description of the role of the written civil examinations that began during the Tang dynasty.

———, *Financial Administration under the Tang Dynasty* (1970). A pioneering account—based on rare Dunhuang documents that survived from medieval times in Buddhist grottoes in central Asia—of the political and economic system undergirding the Chinese imperial state.

Whittow, Mark, *The Making of Byzantium, 600–1025* (1996). A study on the survival and revival of the eastern Roman empire as a major power in eastern Europe and Southwest Asia.

Wood, Ian, *The Missionary Life: Saints and the Evangelization of Europe, 400–1050* (2001). The horizons of Christians on the frontiers of Europe.

10

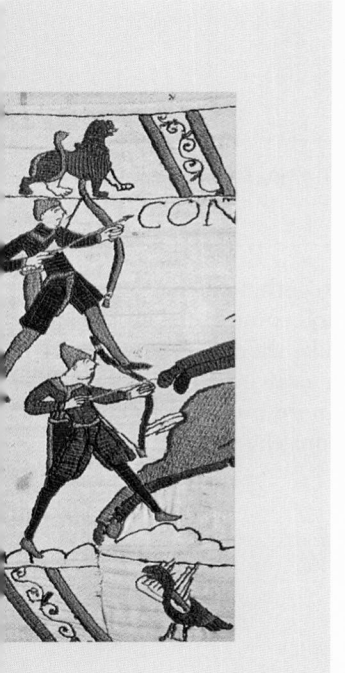

BECOMING "THE WORLD," 1000–1300 CE

In the late 1270s, two Christian monks, Bar Sāwmā and Markōs, voyaged into the heart of Islam. They were not Europeans. They were Uighurs, a Turkish people of central Asia, among whom the Nestorian Christians had established churches in the seventh century CE. Sent by the mighty Mongol ruler Kubilai Khan on the eve of his becoming the first emperor of China's Yuan dynasty (1280–1368), the monks were supposed to worship at the temple in Jerusalem. But the Great Khan also had political ambitions—he had his eyes on conquering Jerusalem, held by the Muslims. Accordingly, he dispatched the monks to help make alliances with Christian kings of western Afro-Eurasia and to gather intelligence on his potential enemy's readiness in Palestine.

By 1280, conflict and conquest had transformed many parts of the world. But friction was simply one manifestation of cultures around the world brushing up against each other. Another had become more important: trade. Indeed, Bar Sāwmā and Markōs were delayed at the magnificent trading hub of Kashgar in what is now far western China, where caravan routes of Afro-Eurasia converged in a market for jade, exotic spices, and precious silks. They were following the pathways of traders and migrants who were bringing Afro-Eurasian worlds into greater contact with each other. The monks detoured to Baghdad, and from there they parted ways. Bar Sāwmā himself visited Constantinople (where the king gave him gold and silver), Rome (where he met with the pope at the shrine of Saint Peter), and Paris (where he saw that city's university, teeming with students), before deciding to return to China, where the Christians of the East awaited his reports. In the end, neither monk ever returned. Yet their voyages exemplified the crisscrossing of people, money, and goods along the trade routes and sea-lanes that connected the world's parts. For just as religious conflict was a hallmark of this age, so too was a surge in trade, migration, and global exchange.

During the period from 1000 to 1300, people from distant regions often borrowed ideas, tools, and norms from other cultures. It was an era of great population growth, rising wealth, and social transformation, which propelled the world's cultures into heightened cross-cultural contact—a far cry from the common view that the world moved in slow motion before 1500 and the advent of modern institutions and technologies. But it was equally an age of conflict, carnage, and colonization, in which warfare fractured old states and created militarized new ones. Economic splendor, social change, and political upheaval entwined in the first three centuries of the second millennium in the Common Era. Commerce, conflict, and conquest did not make the world's people at the beginning of the second millennium more alike, however. To the contrary: contact and exchange reinforced

the sense of difference across cultures and created a feeling of apartness, of living within bounded cultural worlds that would soon come to be called "Europe," or "China," or "India." Even the minimal contact with other cultures experienced by the more separate areas of the world, such as sub-Saharan Africa, Japan, and the Americas, strengthened their identities. The paradoxical result was that the world was becoming more interconnected, while its regions became more clearly differentiated. The more geographical boundaries were crossed, the more they were reinforced by distinct cultural identities—which began to map out the world's regions as we recognize them today.

COMMERCIAL CONNECTIONS

> → *What factors led to the explosion of global trading activity between 1000 and 1300?*

The pace of economic change started to gather speed during this period. The effects of the agrarian and commercial breakthroughs of earlier periods began to make themselves felt in hitherto remote regions of Afro-Eurasia, drawing them closer together and making them more and more interdependent. The Americas, a region truly apart from the structures of

Focus Questions BECOMING "THE WORLD"

→ *What factors led to the explosion of global trading activity between 1000 and 1300?*

→ *How did trade and migration affect sub-Saharan Africa between 1000 and 1300?*

→ *How did trade and migration affect the Islamic world between 1000 and 1300?*

→ *In what ways did India remain a cultural mosaic?*

→ *What transformations in communication, education, and commerce contributed to the emergence of a distinct Chinese identity during this era?*

→ *How were Southeast Asia, Japan, and Korea influenced by sustained contact with other regions in this era?*

→ *How did Christianity produce a distinct identity among the diverse peoples of Europe?*

→ *Where did societies in the Americas demonstrate strong commercial expansionist impulses?*

→ *How did Mongol conquests affect cross-cultural contacts and regional development in Afro-Eurasia?*

Ⓖ WWNORTON.COM/STUDYSPACE

long-distance trade and migration, also saw greater regional trade, urbanization, and population growth. The most visible sign of these prosperous times was the global explosion of trading activity.

REVOLUTIONS AT SEA

In the centuries after 1000 CE, traders took to the seas. By the tenth century, sea routes were eclipsing old land-based trading networks for long-distance trade. The combination of improved navigational aids, refinements in shipbuilding, better mapmaking, and breakthroughs in commercial laws and accounting practices made shipping easier and slashed the costs of seaborne long-distance trading. The numbers testify to the power of the maritime revolution: while a porter could carry about 10 pounds of commodities over long distances, and animal-drawn wagons could move 100 pounds of goods, the large Arab dhows that plied the Indian Ocean were capable of transporting as many as 5 tons of cargo. The result was that some small coastal ports, like Mogadishu in present-day Somalia, on the east coast of Africa, became in the eleventh century vast transshipment centers for a thriving trade across the Indian Ocean.

A new instrument made available to navigators was crucial in this boom: the needle compass. This Chinese invention was initially intended to find auspicious locations and orientations for houses and tombs, but it was also employed by sailors from Canton in the eleventh century to help guide them on the high seas. Use of the device spread rapidly from there. By the early thirteenth century, the compass was a vital tool on all vessels plying the sea-lanes between Southeast Asian and Indian trading hubs. Not only did it make sailing under cloudy skies possible—thus opening up the Mediterranean, which in Roman times had been too dangerous to travel from November to March, to year-round travel—but it made mapmaking less arduous and more accurate. And, of course, it made all the oceans, including the Atlantic, easier to navigate.

Shipping became less dangerous. Navigators relied on their trusty vessels—lateen-rigged dhows between the Indian Ocean and the Red Sea, heavy junks in the South China seas. They could also rely on the protection of political authorities, such as the Song dynasts in China, in guiding the trading fleets in and out of harbors. The Fatimid caliphate (909–1171 CE) in Egypt, for instance, profited from the maritime trade and therefore agreed to defend merchant fleets from pirates. Armed convoys of five or three ships escorted com-

Dhow. This modern dhow in the harbor of Zanzibar displays the characteristic triangle sail. The triangle sail can make good use of the trade monsoon and thus has guided dhows on the Arabian Sea since ancient times.

mercial fleets, a system called *karim* that regularized the traffic on the Indian Ocean and Red Sea. Because of its success, the system soon spread west to North Africa and southern Spain. *Karimi* firms were often family-based, and they sent young men of the family, sometimes servants or even slaves, to work in India. Housewives in Cairo could expect gifts from their husbands to arrive with the *karim* fleet.

Antique Chinese Compass. Chinese sailors from Canton started to use needle compasses in the eleventh century. By the thirteenth century, needle compasses were widely used on ships in the Indian Ocean and were starting to appear in the Mediterranean.

The needle compass and changes in navigation ushered in the slow demise of the overland routes. Just as the merchants of the Silk Road had adapted by moving to southern routes in earlier centuries, so they eventually pulled up their stakes from the camel trains, fragrant caravansaries, and oasis hubs as they abandoned the road for the sea-lanes. It took centuries for the shift to be completed, but overland routes and camels were no commercial match for multiple-masted cargo ships laden with tons of silks, spices, and even more basic tradable staples. As the end of the first millennium drew near, a new interregional and increasingly global set of connections emerged on the high seas, bringing the parts of the world together, and thereby also creating new divisions.

COMMERCIAL CONTACTS

The opening of the sea-lanes sparked a commercial transformation. It also tapped into changes occurring in world agriculture. Agricultural development in Afro-Eurasia, and especially in western Europe, altered the nature of trade and transportation. (See Map 10-1.)

For a long time it was thought that agriculture remained primitive, not much more advanced than in Neolithic times, until the introduction of modern husbandry and the application of science. This view, we now know, misses the gradual and fundamental shifts occurring by 1000. The centuries of great irrigation works began to yield their enormous returns.

MAP 10-1   AFRO-EURASIAN TRADE, 1000–1300

During the early second millennium, Afro-Eurasian merchants increasingly turned to the Indian Ocean to transport their goods. Larger commercial flows profoundly shaped the history of the region. What revolutions in maritime travel facilitated this development? Why were ocean-based commercial routes more lucrative than land-based routes? Identify Quilon, Alexandria, Cairo, and Guangzhou. What role did they play in connecting the peoples of Afro-Eurasia?

→ *What factors created a common cultural outlook among Muslim communities in Afro-Eurasia during this era?*

Farmers learned how to rotate their crops to preserve soil fertility. The development of new strains of cereals, especially of barleys, ryes, and oats, and in the Americas the refinement of maize, enabled the cultivation of grains in vast areas that had formerly been too cold and arid to sustain them. Clover, alfalfa, and newly domesticated grasses of other sorts became fodder for grazing healthier, stronger, and fatter animals. Agriculture pushed into new regions, buoying population growth and yielding surpluses in many provinces—surpluses that now could be shipped great distances.

The Silk Road had conveyed luxuries, such as gemstones, fragrances and spices, silk textiles, woolen rugs, and tapestries. Their value was high, and they were light and easily carried. But now rice and other agrarian staples joined manufactured goods such as porcelains and silks in the long-distance trading systems. Ships made it feasible and lucrative to transport bulky and lower-value commodities—goods whose shipment was impossible or impractical when technologies of distribution were less developed: tea, rice, palm oil, woolen linen, and cotton textiles. Some goods, like the popular celadon porcelain ware, were not only heavy but fragile; they often shattered when carried on the backs of camels. Ships were a better means of conveying such delicate commodities to distant markets. In addition, the weight of porcelain added ballast necessary for long-distance sailing vessels.

GLOBAL COMMERCIAL HUBS

Long-distance trade spawned a new kind of metropolis: the commercial city. These hubs, the meeting points between distant cultures that we call entrepôts, became cosmopolitan nerve centers of an increasingly integrated world. Beginning in the late tenth century, three places emerged as the major anchorages of the maritime trade linking the landmasses of Afro-Eurasia, including the islands of Southeast Asia and Africa. In the west, the city of Cairo-Fustat (old Cairo) was a commanding headquarters for commerce between the Mediterranean and the Indian Ocean through the Red Sea. In the east, Quanzhou was the major port handling China's international trade. And Quilon, a port near the tip of Indian peninsula, which pushed deeply into the Indian Ocean's shipping lanes, functioned as the way station for voyages between the South China Sea and the Red Sea. All of these great trading centers thrived, in part because the free-for-all of trade and market life flourished under the political stability provided by big, powerful dynasts who recognized that the wealth created by trade would benefit their regimes.

THE EGYPTIAN ANCHORAGE The Egyptian cities of Cairo and Alexandria were Europe's main maritime commercial centers with ties to the Indian Ocean and beyond. Cairo, some 100 miles up the Nile, was home to numerous Muslim and Jewish trading firms, and Alexandria was their lookout

Persian Book. Books, such as this hand-copied one written in Kufic style, were traded in the Afro-Eurasian market starting in the tenth century.

post on the Mediterranean. These trading firms were kin-based, made up of family members, servants, and even slaves; they therefore took form within a single religion and conducted business according to rules set by their respective religious authority. Yet Jews, Muslims, and Christians were close partners in trade. On the Indian Ocean, Muslim firms owned most of the ships ferrying cargoes of Jewish traders to India.

Silk yarn and textiles were the most commonly traded commodities. It was through Alexandria that Europeans acquired silks from China, especially the coveted *zaytuni* (satin) fabric from Quanzhou. Spanish silks also passed through Alexandria on their way to eastern Mediterranean markets. But the entrepôts handled much more. Traditional goods from the Mediterranean included olive oil, glassware, flax, corals, and various metals. Gemstones and aromatic perfumes made from plants and animals poured in from India. Long-distance traders also shipped many staples such as minerals and chemicals for dying textiles or tanning skins, and raw materials such as timber and bamboo. The real novelties were paper and books. Hand-copied Bibles, Talmuds, works of legal and moral instruction, grammars in various languages, and Arabic books became the first best sellers of the Mediterranean.

Cairo and Alexandria prospered because Islamic leaders created sophisticated commercial institutions. Success began with the states that took seriously their obligation to protect merchants from predators. As noted above, the powerful Fatimid caliphate began regularly dispatching armed convoys to escort commercial fleets in the Mediterranean and the Red Sea, enabling the *karimi* firms and their family members to send goods and information on schedule. So regular were these fleets that they soon became the basis of an effective postal system. Thus, when an Egyptian trader who had traveled to Quilon around 1100 was delayed on his journey home, he could send a consoling message to his wife in Cairo. He could also send tokens of his love. In his letter he apologized for his absence from home but promised several gifts, including pearl bracelets, garments of red silk, a bronze basin, a ewer, and a six-year-old slave girl: "I shall send them, if God wills it, with somebody who is traveling home in the *Karim*" (Goitein, "New Light," 179).

The Islamic legal system also was involved in creating an environment favorable to conducting business. Those efforts are perhaps best exemplified in the techniques that specialists in law employed to get around the rule that would probably have brought commerce to a halt—the injunction in the sharia against usury, which prohibited earning any interest on loans. With the blessing of the clerics, Muslim traders formed partnerships, called *commenda* in medieval Europe, between those who had capital to lend and those who needed money to expand their businesses. These partnerships enabled owners of capital or merchandise to entrust their money or commodities to agents who, after their work was done, returned the initial investment and a share of the profits to the owners, keeping the rest as their reward. The English word "risk" derives from the Arabic *rizq*, the extra allowance paid to merchants in lieu of interest.

> *The English word "risk" derives from the Arabic* rizq, *the extra allowance paid to merchants in lieu of interest.*

THE ANCHORAGE OF QUANZHOU At the other end of Afro-Eurasia, in China, Quanzhou was as busy as the cities of Cairo and Alexandria, although trade there was not a free-for-all. The Song government set up offices of Seafaring Affairs in its three major ports: Canton, Quanzhou, and an area near present-day Shanghai in the Yangzi delta. In return for taking a portion of the taxes, these offices registered and examined cargoes, sailors, and traders, while archers employed as guards kept a keen eye on the traffic.

All foreign traders were guests of the governor, who doubled as the Chief of Seafaring Affairs. Part of his mandate was to host an annual ritual intended to summon favorable winds for ships. Unlike in the Arabian Sea, where monsoons make the wind direction predictable, winds in the Taiwan Strait do not fall into regular seasonal patterns. Every year, the governor took his place on a high perch facing the harbor, in front of a rock cliff filled with inscriptions that recorded the wind-calling rituals. Traders of every origin witnessed the rite, then joined the governor and local dignitaries for a large banquet. Quanzhou sailors, foreigners as well as Chinese, also frequently sought protection at the shrine of the goddess Mazu. According to the local legend, before assuming godhood Mazu had lived from 960 to 987 and had performed many miracles. Her temple became prominent after 1123, when the governor of Quanzhou survived a bad storm at sea while returning home from Korea. Ever since then, sailors as well as their wives and mothers regularly burned incense for the goddess and prayed for her aid in keeping them safe at sea.

Ships departing from Quanzhou and other Chinese ports were junks—large flat-bottomed ships with internal sealed bulkheads and stern-mounted rudders. Those from Quanzhou headed for Srivijaya, or Java, in the Malay Archipelago, navigating through the Strait of Melaka, a choke point between the South China Sea and the Indian Ocean. The final destination was Quilon, on the Malabar Coast of southwest India. Traders wishing to go further west unloaded their cargo and boarded small Arabian dhows, to make passage in Arab-dominated seas. Conversely, traders from Islamic countries arriving at Quilon in dhows and wishing to travel further east had to change to big Chinese ships.

Chinese traders had the best ships in the world. Multiple watertight compartments increased their stability and seaworthiness, and the larger ships contained as many as four decks, six masts, and a dozen sails and could carry 500 men. Navigators used up-to-date charts and compasses to reach foreign ports.

The traders who arrived at Chinese ports on junks were not all Chinese. Arabs, Persians, Jews, and Indians traded at Quanzhou, and quite a few stayed on to manage their businesses. Perhaps as many as 100,000 Muslims lived in Quanzhou's trading communities during the Song dynasty. Foreign traders could become power brokers in their own right. Consider the Pu family, which owned several hundred ships that plied the routes between India and Islamic countries. To promote good relationships in the community, it made large donations over several generations for public projects such as bridges, and the contributions even garnered official positions for some male family members. After the Mongols conquered the Southern Song in the late thirteenth century, Pu Shougeng, the patriarch of the family, turned over all the ships and the city of Quanzhou. The new emperor, Kubilai, was pleased with his services—and granted him the position of administrating the port's overseas trade.

Foreign merchants did not stay in isolated neighborhoods, apart from the rest of the city. Indeed, their residences and graves were scattered throughout Quanzhou. However, they had their own buildings for religious worship and indicated their faith on their gravestones. A well-built mosque from this period is still standing on a busy street. Hindu traders who lived in Quanzhou worshipped in a Buddhist shrine, Kaiyuan Si, where statues of the Hindu deities Hanuman and Krishna stand beside Buddhist gods. Like so many of the new global entrepôts, Quanzhou was simultaneously a power base in its own state and a home for world traders and travelers.

THE TIP OF INDIA In the tenth century, the Chola dynasty in modern Tamil Nadu rose as a major power in south India. It supplied the political support and protection for a new commercial nerve center for maritime trade between

China and the Red Sea and the Mediterranean. As the Chola dynasts profited from their commercial ventures, they expanded their reach. Following their conquest of Sri Lanka, they moved on to extend their influence over key ports on the southern Malay Peninsula, Sumatra, and eventually to the all-important Strait of Malacca, the seagoing gateway to Southeast and East Asia (see more on the islands of Southeast Asia below).

A commercial revolution swept the Indian Ocean as networks of Chola traders fanned out to establish entrepôts around the sea's rim. Indian merchant ships benefited from the Chola patronage to sail to Chinese ports. However, the Chola golden age lasted only about two generations. Indian Ocean trade continued to flourish after the Chola hegemony. Beginning in the mid–eleventh century, Islamic traders, both Arabs and Iranians, made adjustments to their trading arrangements. Many Muslim traders settled in Malabar, on the southwest coast of the Indian peninsula, and Quilon became a major hub. Dhows arrived, laden with goods from the Red Sea and Africa, and unloaded their cargoes. Passengers, traders, sojourners, and fugitives also disembarked and made Quilon into a cosmopolitan city. Big Chinese junks entered the port to unload their wares of silks and porcelain, and to pick up passengers and commodities for East Asian markets. Sailors and traders strictly observed the customs of this entrepôt; as they knew well, it was good business to respect others' norms and values while engaging in commerce with them.

Muslims constituted the largest foreign community, living in their own neighborhoods. They shipped horses from Arab countries to India and southeast islands. Kings of the tropical countries viewed horses as symbols of royalty, and because the animals could not survive long in those climates the demand was constant. Elephants and cattle from tropical countries were also sold in Quilon, though the bulk of the goods traded were spices, perfumes, and textiles. Traders who frequented Quilon knew each other well, and personal relationships were key in their transactions. When trying to strike a deal with a local merchant, a Chinese trader would mention his Indian neighbor in Quanzhou and the residence of that family in Quilon. Global commercial hubs relied on friendship and family to keep their businesses humming across religious and regional divides.

SUB-SAHARAN AFRICA COMES TOGETHER

> → *How did trade and migration affect sub-Saharan Africa between 1000 and 1300?*

The dawn of the new millennium produced dramatic transformations in sub-Saharan Africa's relationship to the rest of the world, while heightening North Africa's integration into an emerging global economy. Before 1000 CE, sub-Saharan Africa had never been a world truly apart, but after this date its integration became firmer. Africans and outsiders now became more determined to overcome the sea, river, and desert barriers that had blocked the peoples who lived below the Sahara Desert from participating in long-distance trade and intellectual exchanges. (See Map 10-2.) During this period, hardly a region within Africa escaped the effects of the outside world, though many inhabitants who lived far away from the new routes bearing trade and culture were unaware of how events outside of Africa were now altering their lives.

WEST AFRICA AND THE MANDE-SPEAKING PEOPLES

Ever since the camel had bridged the great Sahara Desert (see Chapter 9), trade, commodities, and ideas linked Africa south of the Sahara to the Muslim world of North Africa and Southwest Asia. As the savanna region of West Africa became increasingly connected to Afro-Eurasian developments, the mobile Mande-speaking peoples emerged as the primary agents for integration within and beyond West Africa, using their expertise in commerce and political organization to edge out other groups living in the area. The Mande languages are a branch of the large Niger-Congo family, which contains most of the African languages below the Sahara (including those in the Bantu branch). But Mande was more than a linguistic category. It was also associated with a way of life, as its speakers shared a common culture.

The home to the Mande or Mandinka peoples was, and continues to be, the vast area between the bend in the Senegal River to the west and the bend of the Niger River to the east (1,000 miles wide), a territory stretching from the Senegal River in the north to the Bandama River in the south (a distance of more than 2,000 miles). This was the locale in which the kingdom of Ghana had come into being around the eighth century and where Ghana's successor state—the Mandinka state of Mali, discussed below—emerged around 1100 CE.

The Mande-speaking peoples were constantly on the go, and they were marvelously adaptable. By the eleventh century they were spreading their cultural, commercial, and political hegemony from the high grasslands of the West African savanna southward into the woodlands and the tropical rainforests that stretched to the Atlantic Ocean. Those who lived in the rain forests of West Africa organized themselves into small-scale societies led by local councils, while those who occupied the savanna lands of the interior of West Africa became adept at centralized forms of government. It was in these high grasslands that the Mande and other groups developed an institution that marked the centralized polities of West Africa: sacred kingships. The inhabitants of these polities believed that their kings had descended from the gods

MAP 10-2 SUB-SAHARAN AFRICA, 1300

Increased commercial contacts continued to influence the religious and political geography of sub-Saharan Africa between 1000 and 1300. Compare this map to Map 9-5 (p. 385). Where had strong Islamic communities emerged by 1300 and what factors facilitated their growth? How did Mande speakers heighten the cultural integration of sub-Saharan societies? To what extent had sub-Saharan Africa "come together"?

Legend:

— Trans-Saharan trade routes
— Maritime trade routes
State nucleus and sphere of influence
Islamic areas
➤ Spread of Islam
Gold deposits
Copper deposits
▲ Salt
Ivory
Slaves

0   250   500   750   1000 Miles
0   500   1000 Kilometers

and that they enjoyed the blessing of the gods. As the Mande broadened their territory from the interior of West Africa all the way to the Atlantic coast, they gained access to the tradable items much sought after in the interior, notably kola nuts and malaguetta peppers, for which they exchanged iron products and textile manufactures. By 1300, the Mandinka merchants had followed the Senegal River to its outlet on the northern coast of present-day Senegal, and then pushed their commercial frontiers further inland and down the coast. Thus, even before the arrival of European explorers and traders in the middle of the fifteenth century, West African peoples had created dynamic trading networks that linked the African hinterlands with coastal trading hubs.

In the period from the eleventh century to the end of the fifteenth century, the most vigorous and profitable businesses were those that stretched across the Sahara Desert. The Mande-speaking peoples, with their far-flung commercial networks and highly dispersed populations, dominated this trade as well. Here one of the most prized items of trade was salt, mined in the northern Sahel, around the city of Taghaza; it was in demand on both sides of the Sahara. Another highly valued commodity was gold, mined within the Mande homeland itself and borne by camel caravans to the northern societies on the far side of the Sahara, where it was exchanged for a variety of manufactures. Equally important in West African commerce were slaves, who were shipped to the settled Muslim communities of North Africa and Egypt.

THE EMPIRE OF MALI

Booming trade spawned new political organizations. The empire of Mali was the Mande successor state to the kingdom of Ghana. Founded during the first half of the twelfth century, it exercised political sway over a vast area up until the fifteenth century, when it gave way to yet another sprawling Muslim state, Songhai, whose center was based further to the east. The Mali Empire represented the triumph of horse warriors, and its origins have long been enshrined in an epic involving the dynasty's founder, the legendary Sundiata. According to *The Epic of Sundiata,* a powerful but deformed youngster eventually overcame unjust and irreligious rulers to install a righteous Islamic state in the new capital city of Niamey. Many historians believe that an individual named Sundiata actually existed, noting that the famed Arab historian Ibn Khaldun referred to him by name a full century later and reported that he was "their [Mali's] greatest king. He overcame the Susu, conquered their country, and seized the power from their hands" (Levtzion, p. 64). He—or if not he, then someone very much like him—lived in the early part of the thirteenth century, and his triumph, as narrated in *The Epic,* marked the victory of the new cavalry forces over traditional foot soldiers. Henceforth, horses—which had always existed in some parts of Africa—became prestige objects of the savanna peoples, the essential symbols of state power.

Asanti Gold. Although this gold head from the kingdom of Asante was made in the eighteenth century, it nicely shows the artistic abilities of the West African peoples. The head probably belonged to the Asante ruler, known as the Asantehene, and symbolized his power and wealth.

The Mali Empire was a thriving polity, and its commerce was in full swing in the fourteenth century. Because Mande trade routes ran through the rain forests to the Atlantic Ocean and crossed the Sahara Desert, West Africa was no longer a distant, isolated periphery of the central Muslim lands. The noted Arab traveler Ibn Battuta, who visited Mali in the early thirteenth century, praised the Muslims of the area for their punctuality in carrying out the five daily prayers required of the faithful. Mali's most famous sovereign, Mansa Musa, who ruled from 1312 until 1332, made a celebrated hajj, the pilgrimage to Mecca, in 1325–1326, traveling through Cairo and impressing crowds of merchants and clerics with the size of his retinue and with his displays of wealth, which usually featured items made from gold.

The Mali Empire boasted two of West Africa's largest cities. Jenne, an ancient northern commercial entrepôt, was a vital assembly point for caravans of salt, gold, and slaves about to set out on their long journeys west to the Atlantic Ocean coastal area and north over the Sahara. An urban settlement first appeared here around 200 BCE, and from that time on it became an important gathering place for traders. The town itself arose as the area became more arid and was no longer subject to annual Niger River flooding. The first

AN AFRICAN EPIC

The traditional story of the founding of the kingdom of Mali is long and complex; it was passed down orally from generation to generation by griots, counselors, and other official historians to the royal family. Only in 1960 was it finally written down in French. Because the narrative involves many complicated stories as it recounts the life of Sundiata, the heroic founder of the Mali state, no single excerpt can fully capture its flavor. The following short passage provides some insight into the role of the narrator (the griot) in the Malian kingdom and identifies the qualities of good and bad rulers.

We are now coming to the great moments in the life of Sundiata. The exile will end and another sun will arise. It is the sun of Sundiata. Griots know the history of kings and kingdoms and that is why they are the best counsellors of kings. Every king wants to have a singer to perpetuate his memory, for it is the griot who rescues the memories of kings from oblivion, as men have short memories.

Kings have prescribed destinies just like men, and seers who probe the future know it. They have knowledge of the future, whereas we griots are depositories of the knowledge of the past. But whoever knows the history of a country can read its future.

Other peoples use writing to record the past, but this invention has killed the faculty of memory among them. They do not feel the past any more, for writing lacks the warmth of the human voice. With them everybody thinks he knows, whereas learning should be a secret. The prophets did not write and their words have been all the more vivid as a result. What paltry learning is that which is congealed in dumb books!

I, Djeli Mamoudou Kouyaté, am the result of a long tradition. For generations we have passed on the history of kings from father to son. The narrative was passed on to me without alteration and I deliver it without alteration, for I received it free from all untruth.

Listen now to the story of Sundiata, the Na'Kamma, the man who had a mission to accomplish.

At the time when Sundiata was preparing to assert his claim over the kingdom of his fathers, Soumaoro was the king of kings, the most powerful king in all the lands of the setting sun. The fortified town of Sosso was the bulwark of fetishism against the word of Allah. For a long time Soumaoro defied the whole world. Since his accession to the throne of Sosso he had defeated nine kings whose heads served him as fetishes in his macabre chamber. Their skins served as seats and he cut his footwear from human skin. Soumaoro was not like other men, for the jinn had revealed themselves to him and his power was beyond measure. So his countless sofas [soldiers] were very brave since they believed their king to be invincible. But Soumaoro was an evil demon and his reign had produced nothing but bloodshed. Nothing was taboo for him. His greatest pleasure was publicly to flog venerable old men. He had defiled every family and everywhere in his vast empire there were villages populated by girls whom he had forcibly abducted from their families without marrying them.

→ *Are you able to understand the function of the griot after reading this passage?*

→ *How reliable do you think this kind of oral history is?*

→ *Soumaoro was the adversary of Sundiata and exemplified the characteristics of a bad ruler. Sundiata, in contrast, prevailed because he embodied good kingly qualities. What were they?*

→ *Comment on the role of religion in the founding of this empire.*

SOURCE: *Sundiata: An Epic of Old Mali*, translated by D. T. Niane (Harlow: Longman Group, 1965), pp. 40–41.

houses were made of mud, but most of these had been replaced by 1000 CE with more substantial brick structures. Around the city, running for more than a mile, was an impressive wall more than eleven feet thick at its base. Even more spectacular than Jenne was the city of Timbuktu; founded around 1100 as a seasonal camp for nomads, it grew in size and importance under the patronage of different Malian kings. By the fourteenth century the city was a thriving commercial and religious center, famed for its two large mosques, which are still standing. In addition to being a

King of Mali. This 1375 picture shows the king of Mali on his throne, surrounded by images of gold. The Europeans considered the interior of West Africa to be an important source of gold.

booming commercial center, it was also renowned for its intellectual vitality. Here, West African Muslim scholars congregated to debate the tenets of Islam and to ensure that Islam even when distant from the Muslim heartland was rigorously practiced, with no taint of pagan observances. These clerics acquired learned treatises on Islam from all over the world for their personal libraries, remnants of which remain to this day.

EAST AFRICA AND THE INDIAN OCEAN

Eastern and southern African regions were also integrated into long-distance trading systems. The monsoon winds, blowing from the southwest in January and the northeast in July, had made East Africa a logical end point for much of the Indian Ocean trade; Swahili peoples living along that coast became active brokers intermediating between the peoples of the Arabian Peninsula, the Persian Gulf territories, and the west coast of India. The city of Kilwa soon caught up with the booming port of Mogadishu as a great entrepôt. Merchants in Kilwa, along the coast of present-day Tanzania, brought ivory, slaves, gold, and other items from the African interior and shipped them to destinations around the Indian Ocean.

The most valued commodity for Swahili traders was gold. It was the key to the commercial revolution along the East African coast—and fueled the extravagant success of the In-

dian Ocean trading system. Located in the highlands between the Limpopo and Zambezi rivers, gold was mined by Shona-speaking peoples, who had established their dominance in the region around 500 CE. By the beginning of the new millennium, the Shona had already founded as many as fifty small centers of religious and political significance; each was dominated by stone structures that displayed its political and religious power and was surrounded by many small peasant villages. Around 1100 one of these centers, Great Zimbabwe, emerged as supreme among the Shona peoples. It was built on the fortunes made from gold, and its most impressive landmark was a massive elliptical building—32 feet high, 17 feet thick in parts, and stretching for more than 800 feet—made of stone so expertly that its fittings needed no grouting. The buildings of Great Zimbabwe were probably intended to house the king, known as *monomotapas*, whose religious and political powers were greatly extolled and feared. They probably also contained the smelters for melting down the gold that had been mined or panned nearby.

The commercial integration of the Swahili and Shona peoples enabled gold and other products to flow from the interior of eastern and southern Africa across the Indian Ocean. Before Europeans accidentally happened upon the Americas, Africa was the world's largest source of precious metals.

One of the great meeting grounds of the Indian Ocean trading system was the island of Madagascar—the fourth-largest island of the world, lying just 150 miles off the coast of East Africa. Indeed, during this period so intense was the

Great Zimbabwe. These walls surrounded the city of Great Zimbabwe, which was a center of the gold trade between the East African coastal peoples and traders plying the Indian Ocean. Great Zimbabwe flourished during the thirteenth, fourteenth, and fifteenth centuries.

interchange of peoples, plants, and animals from mainland Africa and around the rest of the Indian Ocean that Madagascar became one of the most intermixed and multicultural places in the world. The minority population came from Bantu-speaking peoples, who by then dominated the southern part of the African landmass (see Chapter 8); the majority were of Malay-Indonesian origin. Early seafarers from Indonesia, plying large, seaworthy outrigger canoes, hugged the shores of the Indian Ocean as they sailed from their homes past Sri Lanka and South Asia, and were carried by the monsoon winds to the African coast. Then they sailed south, perhaps picking up Bantu-speaking peoples along the way, and finally arrived at the island of Madagascar. The first evidence of human settlement does not occur until the eighth century CE. Thereafter, the island became a regular stopover point, as well as an import-export market, for traders crossing the Indian Ocean.

THE TRANS-SAHARAN AND INDIAN OCEAN SLAVE TRADE

African slaves were as valuable as African gold in shipments to the Mediterranean and Indian Ocean markets. Unlike gold, slave populations left a permanent imprint, since they eventually merged into the North African and Indian Ocean communities. There had been a busy trade in African slaves, mainly from Nubia, into pharaonic Egypt well before the Common Era. After Islam spread into Africa and sailing techniques improved, the slave trade across the Sahara and Indian Ocean boomed. As noted above, slaves were an important component of West African commerce.

This slave system was unlike the chattel slavery found much later in the Americas (the form of slavery most familiar to us today). The Prophet Muhammad had found slavery to be a well-established institution in the Arabian Peninsula when he was promulgating his message in the seventh century. The Quran attempted to mitigate its severity, requiring Muslim slave owners to treat their slaves with kindness and generosity and praising the manumission of slaves as an act of piety. Nonetheless, the African slave trade flourished under Islam, and slaves filled a great variety of roles in the slave-importing societies.

African slaves were obtained in this period much as they were later on: some were taken in wars; others were judged to be criminals and sold into slavery as punishment. Their duties in slave-importing societies were quite varied. Some slaves were pressed into military duties, rising in a few instances to positions of high authority. Others were valued for their seafaring skills and were used as crewmen on dhows or dockworkers servicing dhows in the Indian Ocean's port cities. Still others, mainly women, were domestic servants, and not a few African slave women became concubines of powerful Muslim political figures and businessmen. African slaves were also used on plantations, the most notorious and oppressive being the agricultural estates of lower Iraq—very early forerunners of the plantations of the antebellum South in the United States; there slaves worked under fearsome discipline and carried out a revolt in the ninth century. Yet in this era, such labor was more the exception than the rule. Slaves were more prized as adjuncts to family labor or as status symbols for their owners. Although the precise numbers are not known, the Arab Muslim slave traders transported many millions of Africans across the Sahara or the Indian Ocean from the beginning of the seventh century until the end of the nineteenth century. Slavery was therefore widespread. But in the words of the American historian Ira Berlin, these were societies with many slaves rather than slave societies—that is, societies whose basic economic fortunes and social structures rested on the widespread ownership of human beings as a source of labor.

Slave Market. Slaves were a common commodity in the marketplaces of the Islamic world. Turkish conquests during the years from 1000 to 1300 put many prisoners into the slave market.

ISLAM IN A TIME OF POLITICAL FRAGMENTATION

> → *How did trade and migration affect the Islamic world between 1000 and 1300?*

Islam underwent the same burst of expansion, prosperity, and cultural diversification that swept through the rest of the Afro-Eurasian world in the three centuries after 1000. (See Map 10-3.) However, in contrast to many other regions, where prosperity fostered greater integration, the peoples of Islam remained politically fractured despite sharing a common faith and culture. The Islamic empire's population at the turn of the millennium (excluding India and Africa below the Sahara) was well below that of China and India at this time—a mere 34 million, just slightly less than that of Europe (including European Russia). This was a paradoxical age, in which the dream of a unified Islam became precisely that: a dream nurtured in a bountiful present by the sense of a glorious past. As in China, efforts to unite under a common rulership failed, giving way to defeats by marauding outsiders. The attempt to uphold centralized rule ended cataclysmically in 1258 with the Mongol sacking of Baghdad and the execution of the last Abbasid caliph.

Islam responded to its political fragmentation not by turning inward but by undergoing major changes, many prompted by contacts (and conflicts) with neighbors. Commercial networks, sustained by active Muslim merchants, carried the word of the Quran far and wide. As Islam spread, it attracted more converts. But new converts often carried on many traditions that the ulama and other Islamic leaders condemned as incompatible with the religion. This conflict between orthodox Muslims and newer converts threatened to divide the wider Islamic community. At the same time (as discussed below), many Sufi orders emerged that blended orthodox and unorthodox practices in a fashion that held broad appeal and linked diverse communities. Also, as the commercial revolution driven by the dramatic expansion of Afro-Eurasian trade within the old Islamic heartlands brought urban and peasant masses into trading relations, it introduced them to a faith that previously had been shared mainly by political, commercial, and scholarly elites. In these three centuries, Islam became an even more open and accommodating religious system, embracing Persian literature, Turkish ruling skills, and Arabic language contributions in the fields of law, religion, literature, and science. In this way the world acquired another "core" region centered in what we now call the Middle East—the lands between the "Far East" of China and Japan and the "Near East," or the countries of the eastern Mediterranean—united by a shared faith and pulsating with frenetic commercial energies.

But by the thirteenth century, India and China, rather than the Islamic world, were the most technologically advanced and prosperous agrarian societies. Cultivation in Islamic societies began to stagnate and, in some places, even decline. Trade became the main source of prosperity when the agrarian innovations that Islam had so dynamically spread across Afro-Eurasia stalled. Muslim merchants became the world's premier traders in this era; the old Islamic heartland became the crossroads for Afro-Eurasian commercial networks.

AFRO-EURASIAN MERCHANTS

The peoples most responsible for integrating the sprawling Islamic worlds were long-distance merchants. They also were the main cultural brokers mediating between Islamic peoples and the rest of the world. Afro-Eurasia's expanding populations and rising material prosperity offered unprecedented opportunities for the merchants of Islam to enrich themselves; Southwest Asia was poised at the center of the Afro-Eurasian landmass, its merchants settled in key nodal points.

These merchants were as diverse as their businesses. Islam's lack of violent turmoil, the spread of the Arabic

MAP 10-3 (A & B)   THE ISLAMIC WORLD IN A TIME OF INSTABILITY, 1000–1100 AND 1200

The Muslim world experienced political disintegration in the first centuries of the second millennium. According to the maps, what was a major force in this collapse of central authority and shifting political configurations? How did Muslim communities respond to this political challenge? What forces helped integrate the Islamic world in the face of political instability?

language, and Islamic law enabled entrepreneurs of many different ethnic and religious backgrounds to flourish. While Muslims played a major part in the brisk long-distance trading of this period, Armenian, Indian, and Jewish traders who were based in Islam's major cities and connected with families in North Africa and Central Asia also expanded their commercial networks. Documents discovered in a Jewish synagogue in Cairo that date back to this era reveal how voluminous and far-reaching this trade was. Jewish merchants, residing in major cities from Morocco to India, oversaw a booming trade from intermediate points such as Aden.

Long-distance trade surged because it was supported by a highly sophisticated legal framework. Traders drew up elaborate contracts; and when the contracts were breached, merchants took their cases to the courts. Although disputes involving Jewish, Armenian, or Christian coreligionists were often resolved by local religious tribunals, many merchants appeared before Islamic *qadis* (judges), who presided over the Islamic courts and whose expertise in commercial matters was greatly admired. Yet, in truth, merchants rarely needed to seek legal recourse. The mercantile community was self-policing; its members severely punished those who violated trust, sometimes ending their careers. Relying on partner-

ships, using letters of credit, and possessing knowledge of local trading customs and currencies, traders and their customers were confident that agreements made in India would be honored in Southeast Asia, Egypt, and North Africa.

DIVERSITY AND UNIFORMITY IN ISLAM

Not until the ninth and tenth centuries did Muslims become a majority within their own recently ascendant Abbasid Empire. From the outset, Muslim rulers and clerics had to deal with large non-Muslim populations, even as these populations were gradually converting to Islam. Borrowing freely from subject peoples and regarding those with their own scriptures as fellow "peoples of the book," Muslim rulers accorded non-Muslims religious toleration as long as they accepted Islam's political dominion. Jewish, Christian, and Zoroastrian communities were permitted to choose their own religious leaders and to settle internal disputes in their own religious courts. They were, however, obligated to pay a special tax, called the *jizya,* and to be properly deferential to their rulers. Especially in times of heightened religious tension, such deference could entail wearing special clothing and dismounting from horses when they passed important Muslim personages.

These regulations, which shaped what was known as the *dhimma* system, granted protections to religious minorities. They therefore spared the Islamic world some of the religious conflict that afflicted other areas. Non-Muslims were free to worship in their traditional ways and were encouraged to make significant contributions to the economic and political well-being of Islamic lands. Such tolerance helped make Islamic cities hospitable environments for traders from around the world.

Still, Islam was an expansionist faith. Some intense proselytizing carried the sacred word to new frontiers, and in the process reinforced the spread of Islamic institutions that supported more commercial exchanges. There were also moments of intense religious passion within Islam's frontiers, especially when Muslim rulers feared that Christian minorities would make common cause with the Europeans who were pressing on their borders. Ugly incidents erupted, and some churches were burned. Pressures to convert to Islam were unremitting at this time; after a surge of conversions to Islam from the ninth century onward, the Christian Copts of Egypt shrank to a small community and never recovered their numbers.

Islam was hardly uniform. One strong element was the mystical movement known as Sufism, a name derived from the wool garments (*suf* in Arabic) that many of its adherents wore. By performing such ecstatic rituals as repeating over and over again the name of God, dancing, and most notably whirling, they sought to liberate the soul from the body and even to come face to face with God. It was inside the Sufi brotherhoods (*turuq* in Arabic) that Islam truly became a religion for the people. Indeed, Sufi orders brought about mass conversions from Christianity to Islam.

The formalizing of Sufi brotherhoods did little to lessen mystics' desire to experience the love of God. Some expressed that desire in poetry, and several of Islam's most highly regarded mystical love poets belonged to Sufi orders. The most admired of all, Jalal al-Din Rumi (1207–1273), was the spiritual founder of the Mevlevi Sufi order, famed for the ceremonial dancing of its whirling dervishes. Rumi, who wrote in Persian, celebrated all forms of love, spiritual and sexual, and preached a universalistic religious message:

> What is to be done of Muslims? For I do not recognize myself,
> I am neither Christian, nor Jew, nor Gabr [Zoroastrian], nor Muslim.

Primary Source

THE MERCHANTS OF EGYPT

The most comprehensive collection of eleventh- and twelfth-century commercial materials from the Islamic world comes from a repository originally connected to the Jewish synagogue in Cairo. It was the custom of the Jewish community to preserve all texts that mention God in a special store-room called a geniza. *A huge collection of such documents came to light just before 1890 when the Cairo Geniza became known to the outside world. Most of these papers, which are a rich source of information about the Jewish community in Egypt at that time, were purchased for the University Library of Cambridge University. The documents touch on all manner of activities: cultural, religious, judicial, political, and commercial. The following letter is addressed to Joseph ibn 'Awkal, one of Egypt's leading merchants in the eleventh century.*

Dear and beloved elder and leader, may God prolong your life, never take away your rank, and increase his favors and benefactions to you.

I inform you, my elder, that I have arrived safely. I have written you a letter before, but have seen no answer. Happy preoccupations—I hope. In that letter I provided you with all the necessary information.

I loaded nine pieces of antimony (kohl), five in baskets and four in complete pieces, on the boat of Ibn Jubār—may God keep it; these are for you personally, sent by Mūsā Ibn al-Majjānī. On this boat, I have in partnership with you—may God keep you—a load of cast copper, a basket with (copper) fragments, and two pieces of antimony. I hope God will grant their safe arrival. Kindly take delivery of everything, my lord.

I have also sent with Banāna a camel load for you from Ibn al-Majjānī and a camel load for me in partnership with you—may God keep you. He also carries another partnership of mine, namely, with 'Ammār Ibn Yijū, four small jugs (of oil).

With Abū Zayd I have a shipload of tin in partnership with Salāma al-Mahdawī. Your share in this partnership with him is fifty pounds. I also have seventeen small jugs of s[oap]. I hope they arrive safely. They belong to a man [called . . .]r b. Salmūn, who entrusted them to me at his own risk. Also a bundle of hammered copper, belonging to [a Muslim] man from the Maghreb, called Abū Bakr Ibn Rizq Allah. Two other bundles, on one is written Abraham, on the other M[. . .]. I agreed with the shipowner that he would transport the goods to their destination. I wish my brother Abū Nasr—may God preserve him—to take care of all the goods and carry them to his place until I shall arrive, if God wills.

Please sell the tin for me at whatever price God may grant and leave its "purse" (the money received for it) until my arrival. I am ready to travel, but must stay until I can unload the tar and oil from the ships.

I have no doubt that you have sent me a letter containing all the quotations.

I have learned that the government has seized the oil and that Ibn al-Naffāt has taken the payment upon himself. I hope that this is indeed the case. Please take care of this matter and take from him the price of five skins (filled with oil). The account is with Salāma.

Al-Sabbāgh of Tripoli has bribed Bu 'l-'Alā the agent, and I shall unload my goods soon.

Kindest regards to your noble self and to my master [. . . and] Abu 'l-Fadl, may God keep them.

→ *What can you learn from the letter about the commodities traded?*
→ *What does the letter tell us about the ties among merchants, and about how they conducted their business?*

Source: *Letters of Medieval Jewish Traders,* translated with introductions and notes by S. D. Goitein (Princeton, NJ: Princeton University Press, 1973), pp. 85–87.

Another Sufi mystic and advocate of the universality of religions, the Spanish Muslim poet Ibn Arabi (1165–1240), wrote in Arabic:

> My heart has been of every form; it is a pasture for
>   gazelles and a convent for Christian monks.
> And a temple for idols and the pilgrim's kaaba, and the
>   tables of the Torah and the book of the Quran.

↬ *How did trade and migration affect the Islamic world between 1000 and 1300?*

Dervishes. Today, the whirling dance of dervishes is almost a tourist attraction, as shown in this picture from the Jerash Cultural Festival in Jordan. Though Sufis in the early second millennium CE were not this neatly dressed, the whirling dance was an important means of reaching union with God.

POLITICAL INTEGRATION AND DISINTEGRATION, 1050–1300

Just as the Islamic faith was increasing its global reach from Africa to India and ultimately into Southeast Asia, its political bulwarks collapsed. Islam's religious and cultural influences transcended its political powers. For a century, from 950 to 1050, it appeared that Shiism would be the vehicle for uniting the whole of the Islamic world. While the Fatimid Shiites established their authority over Egypt and much of North Africa (see Chapter 9), the Abbasid state in Baghdad fell under the sway of the Shiite Buyid family. Each created universities—in Cairo and Baghdad, respectively—thereby ensuring that Islam's two leading centers of higher learning in the eleventh century were Shiite. But the divisions also sapped Shiism; Sunni Muslims began to challenge Shiite power and to establish their own strongholds. The last of the Shiite Fatimid rulers gave way to a new Sunni regime in Egypt. In Baghdad, the Shiite Buyid family surrendered to an unrelated group of Sunni strongmen.

Those strongmen were mainly Turks, who had been migrating into the Islamic central core from the steppe lands of Asia since the eighth century, bringing with them superior military skills and an intense devotion to Sunni Islam. Ensconced in Baghdad, they established outposts in Syria and Palestine, and then moved into Anatolia after defeating Byzantine forces at the battle of Manzikert in 1071. But this Turkish state also crumbled, as Turkish-speaking tribesmen quarreled with one another for preeminence. Thus, by the thirteenth century the Islamic core area, stretching from Morocco in the west to the Oxus River in the east, was fractured into three distinctive regions. In the east (central Asia, Iran,

and eastern Iraq), the remnants of the old Abbasid state persevered. Here, caliphs succeeded one another, still claiming to speak for all of Islam yet lacking the ability to enforce their directives. They deferred without fail to their Turkish military commanders. Even in the central core of the Islamic world (Egypt, Syria, and the Arabian Peninsula), where Arabic was the primary tongue, military men of non-Arab origin held the reins of power. Further west, in the Maghreb, Arab rulers prevailed—but there the influence of Berbers, some from the northern Saharan region, was extensive. Islam was a vibrant faith, but its polities were splintered.

WHAT WAS ISLAM?

Buoyed by Arab dhows on the high seas and carried on the backs of camels, following commercial networks, Islam evolved from Muhammad's original goal of creating a religion for Arab peoples. By 1300, its influence was spreading across Eurasia and Africa. It lacked only an American toehold. It attracted urbanites and rural peasants alike, as well as its original audience, desert nomads. Its extraordinary appeal to such diverse populations generated an intense Islamic cultural flowering at the turn of the millennium in 1000 CE.

Some worried about the preservation of Islam's true nature. The Arabic language ceased to be the idiom of Islamic believers. True, the devout read and recited the Quran in its original tongue, as the religion mandated. But Persian was now often employed in Muslim philosophy and art, and Turkish in law and administration. Moreover, Jerusalem and Baghdad no longer stood alone as Islamic cultural capitals. There were now many important cities, and consequently many universities and centers of learning, boasting alternative, vernacular versions of Islam. In fact, some of the most dynamic thought came from Islam's fringes. To confront the question of Islam's identity meant dealing with its great—and ever growing—heterogeneity.

At the same time, heterogeneity fostered cultural efflorescence, as was apparent in all fields of high learning. Arabic remained a preeminent language of science, literature, and religion in 1300. Indicative of Islam's and Arabic's prominence in thought was the culture's most influential and versatile thinker—the legendary Ibn Rushd (1126–1198). Known as Averroës in the Western world, where scholars pored over his writings, he wrestled with the same theological issues that troubled Western scholars. Steeped in the writings of Aristotle, Ibn Rushd became Islam's most thoroughgoing rationalist. His knowledge of Aristotle was so great that it influenced the thinking of the Christian world's leading philosopher and theologian, Thomas of Aquino (Thomas Aquinas, 1225–1274). Above all, Ibn Rushd believed that faith and reason could be compatible. He also argued for a new kind of social hierarchy, in which learned men would command influence akin to Confucian scholars in China or Greek philosophers in Athens. Ibn Rushd believed that the proper forms of reasoning had to be entrusted to the educated class—in the case of Islam, the ulama—who would serve the common folk.

Equally powerful works were produced in Persian, which by the eleventh century was seen as a language capable of expressing the most sophisticated ideas of culture and religion. The intellectual who best represented the new Persian ethnic pride was Abu al-Qasim Firdawsi (920–1020), a devout Muslim who also believed in the importance of pre-Islamic Sasanian traditions. In the long epic poem *Shah Namah*, or *Book of Kings*, he celebrated the origins of Persian culture and narrated the history of the peoples of the Iranian highlands from the dawn of time to the Muslim conquest. As part of his effort to extol a pure Persian culture, Firdawsi attempted to compose the whole of his poem in Persian unblemished by other languages, avoiding Arabic loanwords.

By the fourteenth century, Islam had achieved what early converts would have considered unthinkable. No longer a religion of a minority of peoples living amid larger Christian, Zoroastrian, and Jewish communities, it had become the people's faith. The agents of conversion were mainly Sufi saints and Sufi brotherhoods and not the ulama, whose exhortations and knowledge of legal and philosophic texts had little impact on common people. The Sufis had carried their faith to the Berbers of North Africa, to villagers living on the plateaus of Anatolia, and to West African animists. Indeed, Ibn Rushd worried about the growing influence and appeal of what he considered an "irrational" piety. But his message failed, because he did not appreciate that Islam's expansionist powers rested on its appeal to common folk. While the sharia was the core of Islam for the educated and scholarly classes, Sufism spoke to the religious beliefs and experiences of ordinary men and women.

INDIA UP FOR GRABS

→ *In what ways did India remain a cultural mosaic?*

Trade and migration affected India, just as it did the rest of Asia and Africa. As in the case of Islam, however, prosperity led to growing social and cultural interconnections; but there was little political continuity or integration. Under the large canopy of Hinduism, India remained a cultural mosaic; in fact, in this period the Islamic faith joined with others in South Asia to make the region even more of a cultural mosaic. (See Map 10-4.) India, in this sense, was a crossroads of various parts of Eurasia and Africa; it illustrates how integration into long-distance, cross-cultural networks can just as easily preserve diversity as promote internal unity.

Turks spilled into India as they had the Islamic heartlands, carrying with them their newfound Islamic beliefs. But in India, these newcomers, like all previous invaders, encountered an existing ethnic and religious mix to which they would add something new without greatly upsetting the balance. India became an intersection for the trade, migration, and culture of Afro-Eurasian peoples—a vital nerve center of the world. Moreover, with 80 million inhabitants in 1000,

Hindu Temple. When Buddhism started to decline in India, Hinduism was on the rise. Numerous Hindu temples were built, many of them adorned with ornate carvings like this small tenth-century temple in Bhubaneshwar, east India.

→ *In what ways did India remain a cultural mosaic?*

MAP 10-4   SOUTH ASIA IN 1300

As the fourteenth century began, India was a blend of many cultures. Politically, Muslim Turks dominated the region. To what extent did the rulers of the Delhi Sultanate integrate India into the broader Islamic world during this era? What factors accounted for Hinduism's continued appeal despite the political power of Muslim leaders? How did Muslim communities integrate themselves into the larger cultural mosaic in South Asia?

India had the second-largest population in Afro-Eurasia at the time, not far behind China's 100 million but well ahead of Islamic Southwest Asia and North Africa (34 million) as well as Christian Europe (36 million).

India was rich, but it remained splintered into the rivalrous chiefs called *rajas*. By the end of the tenth century, their constant struggles had left them all exhausted. So, when northern invaders began encroaching on their frontiers, both the will and the resources to put up a fight were scarce. Before large-scale invasions by the Turks, central Asian invaders to India did not seek to conquer all the rajas; instead they accommodated and reinforced local rajas' power bases. Claiming *kshatriya* (warrior) status, the invaders cemented an alliance with the local rajas through marriages. Meanwhile, rajas old and new solicited support from high-caste Brahmans by making land concessions to them. Much of the land was not under cultivation. Brahmans took the leadership in reclaiming the wastelands. First they built temples, and then they converted the indigenous hunter-gatherer peoples to the Hindu faith. Then they showed the new converts how to cultivate the land. The Brahmans simultaneously spread their faith and greatly expanded the agrarian tax base for themselves and the rajas. Brahmans reciprocated for their good fortunes by compiling elaborate genealogies for the rajas, endowing them with a lengthy (and therefore legitimizing) ancestry. For their part, the rajas demonstrated that they were well-versed in Sanskrit culture, including equestrian skills and courtly etiquette, and they became the patrons of artists and poets. Ultimately, many of the warriors and their heirs became Indian rajas. However, Turkish invaders were armed with Islam, so the conquerors remained sultans instead of becoming rajas.

INVASIONS AND CONSOLIDATIONS

Turkish warlords entered India in a series of waves that began in the tenth century, introducing their customs into the fertile lands between the Indus and Ganges basins, while also accepting many of the existing political structures. Concerned to uphold their image as promoters of Islamic culture, they constructed grandiose mosques and built impressive libraries where scholars could toil and share their wisdom with the court. The first wave of invaders did not intend to stay in India. Mahmud of Ghazna (971–1030), who launched many expeditions from the Afghan heartland into the wealthy northern provinces of India, was one such conqueror, seeking to make his capital, Ghazni, a great center of Islamic learning in order to win status within Islam. The booty of his invasions—especially the jewels and precious goods plundered from the Hindu temples—also helped boost his status. Worse than Mahmud, Muhammad Ghuri in the 1180s led another wave of Islamic Turkish invasions from Afghanistan and dispersed across the Delhi region in north India. Wars over the control of the plains between the Indus and Ganges rivers raged until one by one, all the way to the lower Ganges valley, the fractured kingdoms toppled.

The now land-bound Turkish Muslim regime of northern India was known as the Delhi Sultanate (1206–1526), and its rulers strengthened the cultural diversity and tolerance that had already become a hallmark of the Indian social order. Although the Delhi sultans knew how to exploit a rich agricultural society, they had little knowledge of or interest in the flourishing commercial life that had sprung up along the Indian coast. They therefore permitted these areas to develop on their own. Persian Zoroastrian traders settled on the Konkan coast in the northwest, around modern-day Mumbai (Bombay). The Malabar Coast to the south became the preserve of Arab traders, who further developed the trade that their ancestors had started. The Delhi Sultanate was a rich and powerful regime that brought political integration but did not enforce cultural homogeneity.

WHAT WAS INDIA?

The entry of Islam into India made the region more of a cultural mosaic, not less. The local Hindu population treated the arrival of the Turks in India as they had done earlier invaders from central Asia: they expected to assimilate their conquerors. The Turks cooperated, but only up to a point. They became Indians but retained their Islamic beliefs and their steppe ways. They behaved as they had in their highland redoubts, wearing their distinctive trousers and robes and riding their horses. The Turks also did not eliminate all the rajas. Some rajas continued to rule certain areas under the sultans.

Although the sultans spoke Turkish languages, they regarded Persian literature as a high cultural achievement and made Persian the sultanate's courtly and administrative language. Meanwhile, most of their Hindu subjects continued to speak local languages that had evolved out of Sanskrit and to

Lodi Gardens. The Lodi Dynasty was the last Delhi sultan dynasty. Lodi Gardens, the cemetery of Lodi sultans, places Central Asian Islamic architecture in the Indian landscape, thereby creating a scene of "heaven on the earth."

follow their caste regulations in daily life. Moreover, they adhered to their local adaptations of the Hindu faith. The sultans did not meddle with the beliefs and cultures of the conquered but merely collected the special *jizya* tax that they paid.

Despite the reluctance of most people in India to embrace Islam, the faith flourished. Islam did not have to be a conquering religion to prosper. As rulers, sultans granted lands to Islamic scholars, the ulama, and Sufi saints, much as Hindu rajas had earlier granted lands to Brahmans. Prestigious scholars and saints in turn attracted followers to their large estates and forests to enjoy the benefits of membership in this community of believers.

The Delhi sultans built strongholds to defend their conquests. Every new sultanate built a fortress in the Delhi region, employing both local workers and foreign artisans from central Asia and Iran. The curves of domes and arches on mosques, tombs, and palaces, formed in the shape of the lotus flower, were uniquely South Asian in flavor. As expenditures at court attracted traders and artisans of all sorts, the palaces and fortresses quickly evolved into prosperous cities.

Although newcomers and locals lived in separate worlds, their customs began to merge. Delhi sultans maintained their steppe lifestyle and equestrian culture, and they were delighted when conquered peoples adopted nomadic customs and artifacts. They realized, however, that they had to learn the local language to rule the country effectively. Court scholars and Sufi holymen started to use local dialects to write and teach. Hindustani, an Indian language full of Persian and Arabic words, was taking shape and became the ancestral language of both Hindi and Urdu. Foreign artisans who arrived with their rulers produced the silk textiles, rugs, and appliances to irrigate gardens that the leading families of Delhi so cherished. Their talents spread beyond the palaces and influenced the manufacturing techniques of the local population. Before long, Indians had learned from the Muslim workers how to extract long filaments from silk cocoons and were themselves weaving fine silk textiles. The merging of cultures became even more apparent when the common people began to wear Turkish–style trousers and robes and when the Persian wheel, a water-lifting device, became widely used by farmers.

By this period, Buddhism in India had already been in decline for centuries. When Vedic Brahmanism evolved into Hinduism (see Chapter 8), it absorbed many doctrines and practices from Buddhism, such as the doctrine of *ahimsa* (non-killling) and the practice of vegetarianism. The two religions became so similar that Hindus simply considered the Buddha to be one of their deities—specifically, an incarnation of the great god Vishnu. Many Buddhist moral teachings were mixed and became Hindu stories. Artistic motifs were similarly adopted and adapted. Following the onslaught of the Turkish invaders, who destroyed many monasteries in the thirteenth century, several leading Buddhist scholars re-

Vishnu. With Buddhism disappearing from India, Buddha was absorbed by the cult of Vishnu and became one of the incarnations of the Hindu god. This late-twelfth-century Angkor Wat style sculpture from Cambodia shows Vishnu asleep; from his nostril sprouts the lotus that will give birth to Buddha.

treated to Tibet, where they helped lead a flowering of Buddhism on the plateau. Bereft of local spiritual leaders and lacking dynastic support, Buddhists in India were assimilated into the Hindu population or converted to Islam.

SONG CHINA, 960–1279

> → *What transformations in communication, education, and commerce contributed to the emergence of a distinct Chinese identity during this era?*

The preeminent world power in 1000 CE was still China, despite its recent experience of turmoil. That turbulence would give rise to a long era of stability and splendor—a combination that made China one of the main regional engines of Afro-Eurasian prosperity. After the end of the Tang dynasty (907 CE), China entered the Five Dynasties period. For two centuries the Tang dynasty's power had waned until North and South China broke into a series of regional kingdoms, usually led by military generals. But one of those generals, Zhao Kuangyin, put a stop to the fragmentation in 960 CE. Overthrowing the boy emperor of his own kingdom, Zhao moved quickly to reunify China by conquering three more of the seven major regional kingdoms between 963 and 975 CE. He was succeeded after his death in 976 CE by his younger brother, who finished the reunification effort by annexing the last three kingdoms. Thus, the Song dynasty took over the mandate of heaven.

The three centuries of Song rule in China would witness many economic and political successes, but powerful nomadic tribes in the far northern stretches of China kept the Song from completely securing their reign. (See Map 10-5.) Their efforts to fight off or pay off these warriors from the north would ultimately prove unsuccessful, and in 1127, the Song finally would lose control of northern China to the nomadic Jurchen, the ancestors of the Manchu. After reconsti-

tuting their dynasty in southern China, the most populous and economically robust region of their empire, they would enjoy another century and a half of rule before falling to the Mongols in 1276.

A CHINESE COMMERCIAL REVOLUTION

China's commercial revolution during this period had agrarian roots. Without vast fields of rice, the population would never have reached 120 million in the twelfth century—doubling its size from the previous millennium. Agriculture

MAP 10-5 (A & B)   EAST ASIA, 1000–1300

Several states emerged in East Asia between 1000 and 1300, but none as strong as the Song dynasty in China. What geographic and political factors contributed to the Song state's economic dynamism? What factors contributed to the Song state's loss of territory to the Jurchen Jin dynasty? How did the Jin state demonstrate the continued impact of pastoral groups on East Asian history in this era?

→ *What transformations contributed to the emergence of a distinct Chinese identity during this era?*

benefited from breakthroughs in metalworking. China's farmers were able to employ new and stronger iron ploughs, which they harnessed to sturdy water buffalo, to break the tough soil in the south, and to extend the farming frontier. In 1078, for example, total Song iron production peaked somewhere between 75,000 and 150,000 tons, roughly the equivalent of European iron production at the start of the eighteenth century. The Chinese piston bellows were a marvel of the age, of a size unsurpassed anywhere in the world until the nineteenth century.

Manufacturing flourished. In the early years of the tenth century, Chinese alchemists were mixing saltpeter with sulfur and charcoal to produce a product that would burn and

could be deployed on the battlefield. By 1040, the first gunpowder recipes were being written down. Over the next 200 years, Song entrepreneurs invented a remarkable array of incendiary devices that flowed from their mastery of techniques for controlling explosions. Song Chinese also devised an "eruptor," a weapon that functioned like a cannon, and it was quickly emulated by their enemies. This was not the only manufacturing breakthrough to astonish the world. Building on their predecessors' techniques, Song artisans produced lighter, more durable, and stunningly more beautiful porcelains. Before long, Song porcelain (now called "china") had become the envy of all Afro-Eurasia. China's artisans also produced vast amounts of clothing and handicrafts from the hemp, mulberry, and cotton that its farmers were growing in great abundance. In effect, the Song Chinese brought about the world's first manufacturing revolution, producing finished goods on a large scale for consumption far and wide.

The growth of commerce transformed the role of money and its worldwide circulation. By the middle of the eleventh century, the Song government was annually minting nearly two million strings of currency—each string containing 1,000 copper coins—far in excess of the Tang maximum of about 300,000 strings. Indeed, the inability of the supply of metal currency to keep pace with demand fueled East Asia's thirst for East African gold in this era. At the same time, merchants began to tinker with printed paper certificates; their guilds in northwestern Shanxi developed the first letters of exchange, which were called "flying cash." These letters linked northern traders with their colleagues in the south. The paper habit spread, and by the thirteenth century printed money had eclipsed coins. Even the government became heavily dependent on paper currency, as it found itself now able to collect more than half of its tax revenues in cash rather than in grain and cloth. The government also turned to its own printing presses to issue more and more notes to pay its bills—a practice that ultimately contributed to the world's first case of runaway inflation, which destabilized the Song and later the Yuan regimes.

NEW ELITES

The commercial revolutions enabled the early Song emperors to champion civilian rule over military values and to usher in a period of social and cultural vitality. The Song undercut the powers of the hereditary aristocratic elites, establishing instead a society governed by a central bureaucracy of scholar-officials chosen through competitive civil service examinations whose scope exceeded that of the Tang. The shift of loyalties from aristocratic clans to the ruling house solidified during the reign of Zhao Kuangyin, also known as Emperor Taizu (ruled 960–976 CE), who in 973 himself administered the final test for all those who had passed the highest-level palace examination. In subsequent dynasties, the emperor became the nation's premier examiner, symbolically demanding oaths of allegiance from successful candidates for public office. Civil officials were now drawn almost exclusively from the ranks of learned men, and by 1100 they had accumulated sufficient power to become China's new ruling elite.

NEGOTIATING WITH NEIGHBORS

As the Song flourished, nomads on the outskirts eyed Chinese successes closely. At the dynasty's northern borders, Khitan, Tungusic, Tangut, and Jurchen nomadic societies formed their own dynasties and adapted Chinese techniques to their

Song Civil Service. Song emperors championed civilian rule to undercut the remaining Tang aristocratic elites. A civil service composed of scholar-officials selected through competitive examinations in both the provinces and the capital took hold. Here we see a painting of an examination being administered during Emperor Renzong's reign (1023–1031).

own advantage. Located within the boundaries of the "greater China" established by the Han and Tang dynasties, these non-Chinese polities watched with envy as China's core amassed extraordinary wealth and prestige. It was only a matter of time before nomadic armies such as those of the Khitan and Jurchen saw China proper as an object of conquest.

In one important way the Song dynasts were weak: they had limited military power, despite their sophisticated weapons. Steel tips increased the effectiveness of Song arrows used with crossbows, and Song armies also boasted flamethrowers and "crouching tiger catapults" for lobbing incendiary bombs at their enemies. But none of these breakthroughs was secret. Warrior neighbors on the steppe, such as the Khitan tribal confederation and Jurchen, mastered the new arts of war more fully than did the Song dynasts themselves.

China's strength as a manufacturing powerhouse made economic diplomacy an option. To keep borderlanders at bay, the Song relied on "gifts" and generous trade agreements with the peoples on the fringes. Defeated militarily by the Liao dy-

Trebuchet. Derived from the sling, the trebuchet served as a siege engine to smash masonry walls or throw flaming projectiles over them. Trebuchets were invented in China in about the fourth century BCE and came to Europe in the sixth century CE. All trebuchets were made of wood and could fling a three hundred–pound (140 kg) projectile at high speed. The illustration here shows a Song Dynasty naval river ship c. 1044 equipped with a traction trebuchet catapult.

nasty in 1004, the Song agreed to make annual payments of 100,000 ounces of silver and 200,000 bolts of silk. The treaty enabled the Song to live in relative peace for more than a century. Another Inner Asian tribal confederation, the Tangut, pressed on the Song's northwestern border. The Tangut state also received an annual subsidy from the Song when an agreement was reached in 1044. Securing peace meant emptying the state coffers—and thus the state turned to its printing presses to make more paper money. The resulting runaway inflation added economic instability to military weakness, making the Song an easy target when the Jurchen invaders made their final assault.

WHAT WAS CHINA?

Paradoxically, the increasing contact and exchange between outsiders and insiders within China hardened the lines that divided them. This was a pattern displayed centuries earlier, in the entanglements of the nomadic Northern Wei rulers with the Han people in China proper (see Chapter 8). The exchanges that did take place, and there were many, wound up nurturing a "Chinese" identity for those who considered themselves true insiders and referred to themselves as Han.

Thus, transformations in communications and education intensified the sense among the Han Chinese that they were authentically Chinese, and that outsiders were radically different. Driven from their ancient homeland in the north beginning in the eleventh century, the Han Chinese grew increasingly suspicious and resentful toward the outsiders living in their midst. They once again called them "barbarians" and treated them accordingly, drawing a dividing line between the nomadic warrior cultures of the Eurasian steppe and their own society based on the large-scale cultivation of grain and rice. Yet these identities were not completely fixed: Han Chinese and non-Han barbarians, insiders and outsiders, were in fact mutually dependent. For long periods, the two groups had easily coexisted, particularly in northwestern and northern China, with much interchange of cultures and technologies. But despite the nomadic borrowing of Chinese ways, and the assimilation of warrior elites to Han Chinese ways, the differences between civilized "China" and the barbarian "other" became a durable stereotype. To be authentically Chinese, even if ruled by outsiders, meant valuing civilian mores, especially for those educated Chinese who were steeped in the civil examination system. It meant being literate—able to read, write, and live by codes inscribed in foundational texts.

Of all the Afro-Eurasian societies in 1300, the Chinese had created the most advanced print culture. The Song government published a wide variety of works, using its plentiful supply of paper to print books, especially medical texts, and to distribute calendars. The private publishing industry also expanded, and printing houses sprang up throughout the country. They produced the Confucian classics, works on

Chinese and Barbarian. After losing the north, the Han Chinese grew resentful of outsiders. They drew a dividing line between their own agrarian society and the nomadic warriors, calling them "barbarians." Such identities were not fixed, however. Chinese and so-called barbarians were mutually dependent.

history, philosophical treatises, and literature, all of which were employed in the civil examinations, which were administered not just centrally but in provincial capitals throughout the country. In Fujian province alone, some 17,000 to 18,000 candidates gathered in the coastal capital city triennially to take the provincial examination. Buddhist publications were also available everywhere. Song printing directly influenced the precocious Koryo dynasty (918–1392) in Korea, which also made great headway in printing by developing movable metal type in 1234, about two centuries before its independent invention in Europe.

CHINA'S NEIGHBORS, 1000–1300

> ✦ *How were Southeast Asia, Japan, and Korea influenced by sustained contact with other regions in this era?*

Under its Song rulers, China became the most populous and wealthiest of the world's regions. Its population of more than 120 million in 1100 projected the influence of Chinese culture, through trade and migration, across all of Afro-Eurasia, especially into Korea, Japan, and Southeast Asia. Chinese commodities found ready markets in neighboring cultures, as local elites had a growing appetite for manufactured textiles, porcelains, and other luxuries. In return, they shipped staples to Chinese cities along the coast, both foodstuffs and industrial inputs. The Koryo rulers in Korea, for example, actively imitated Song culture, religions, and technology, which they passed on to Japan. Their capital, Kaesong, was one of the world's most impressive cities. Koryo rulers ordered the construction of hundreds of Buddhist temples in the Tang-Song style, as well as the creation of countless religious artworks.

THE RISE OF WARRIORS IN JAPAN

As China became an economic and political powerhouse, the cultures around its rim were forced to adapt. They could not help but feel the gravitational pull of China. Often these neighbors responded by consolidating internal political authority to resist being swallowed up, while increasing their participation in commercial transactions. In Japan, rulers had to resolve some endemic problems to create a stable regime out of feuding warrior factions. Their solution was to amalgamate the Heian court's imperial authority with the military power of the more rusticated provincial warriors in the east.

The pattern of regents ruling in the name of the sacred emperor was repeated many times in Japanese history, but it began in the Heian period (794–1185). First court nobles—an entrenched aristocracy—in the new capital of Heian (today's Kyoto) dominated Japan, and later rough-and-ready warriors followed their model in literally winning possession of the throne to "protect" its sanctity as an object of popular veneration. They captured it to gain the symbolic power of the emperor, which was transferred to his protectors.

By intermarrying with and ruling through the Heian imperial family for two centuries, the influential Fujiwara family added considerably to the power of their ancestors, the powerful Nakatomi kinship group in Nara (described in Chapter 9). The Fujiwara nobles presided over a refined Heian culture of flower and tea ceremonies. They also exchanged poetry written in classical Chinese and their native language and dressed in the elegant costumes that have influenced Japanese public life and private taste up to this day.

Political marriages enabled the Fujiwara to control the throne, but the rise of large private estates (called *shōen*) outside the capital shifted the balance of power from the court to the regional elites in the provinces. A hierarchy of land tenures emerged in the countryside: peasant cultivators were at the bottom, managers and estate officials in the middle, and absentee patrons at the top. By 1100 more than half of Japan's rice land was controlled by these large estates, and the revenue and power of the state fell considerably. In the midst of such privatization, Heian became for aristocrats a theater state—politically weak but culturally influential—while the hinterlands provided their economic wealth.

Heian aristocrats ruled through political stealth and artistic style and disdained the military. In 792—even before Heian became the capital—the conscription system to raise imperial armies was abolished. In the provinces, however, trained warriors affiliated with specific kinship groups gathered strength. The rural elites were expert horsemen who fought in armor, and they defended their private estates by relying on their skill with the bow and sword. As incipient samurai, they formed local warrior organizations in the outlying regions, particularly on Kantō Plain (where today's Kamakura and Tokyo are located), well to the east of the capital.

Japan became the home to multiple sources of power: an aristocracy, an imperial family, and local warriors (known as samurai). It was a combustible mix, a recipe for intrigue and double-dealing. Although the sanctity of the Japanese emperor and the Heian aristocracy remained intact, outside warrior groups such as the Minamoto and Taira families provided a new bridge between the elites of the capital and the nouveaux riches in the provinces. Using native Japanese script developed in the Heian era, Lady Murasaki Shikibu (c. 976–c. 1031) described the elegant lives and sordid affairs of the courtiers and their women in *The Tale of Genji*, Japan's—and possibly the world's—first novel. Neither nobles nor warriors refrained from political intrigue, as they grasped at any and all possible alliances that would propel them into power. First, beginning in 1168, the Taira kinship group ruled as

→ *How were Southeast Asia, Japan, and Korea influenced by sustained contact with other regions in this era?*

Heiji Rebellion. This illustration from the Kamakura period depicts a battle during the Heiji Rebellion, which was fought between rival subjects of the cloistered emperor Go-Shirakawa in 1159. Riding in full armor on horseback, the fighters on both sides are armed with devastating long bows.

samurai elites in the name of the emperor. Next General Yoritomo (1147–1199) led his Minamoto kin (also called the Genji) to a dramatic victory over the Taira at the sea battle of Dan no Ura off the southern island of Shikoku in 1185. Ultimately, it was the alliance of local potentates and military commanders under the Kamakura shoguns (1192–1333)—generalissimos who served as military "protectors" of the ruler in Heian—that brought more stable rule to Japan. The Kamakura age thus provided the fierce warriors who successfully fended off the Mongol naval invasions of 1274 and 1281. Moreover, the shogunate form of military government remained intact under the theoretical sovereignty of the Japanese emperor in Heian until 1868.

THE CULTURAL MOSAIC OF SOUTHEAST ASIA

Southeast Asia, like India, became a crossroads of Afro-Eurasian influences. (See Map 10-6.) Its population was still relatively low (probably not more than 10 million in 1000), especially when compared with that of its nearest neighbors, China and India. Certainly, the dominance of island life and island culture, particularly as developed on the lands that were to become Indonesia in modern times, set the peoples of this unique geographical area off from others. But the Southeast Asian communities were not immune to the influences of the peoples that flocked into this region. Like India, the archipelago became a cultural mosaic, its sea-lanes (and peoples) connecting China with Asia and Africa. The elongated Malay Peninsula became the home to many trading ports and stopovers for traders shuttling between India and China, and thus connected the Bay of Bengal and the Indian Ocean with the South China Sea.

Indian influence had been prominent both on the Asian mainland and in island portions of Southeast Asia since 800 CE. Islamic expansion into the islands that comprised maritime Southeast Asia after 1200 gradually superseded these cultural influences. Only Bali and a few other outlying islands located far to the east of the Malayan crossroads, for example, were able to preserve their Vedic religious origins relatively intact. Elsewhere in Java and Sumatra, Islam irrevocably became the universalistic religion of the islands. In Vietnam and northern portions of mainland Southeast Asia, Chinese cultural influences and northern schools of Mahayana Buddhism were especially prominent.

The prosperity and cultural vitality of the heavily populated regions of China and India spilled over into the maritime and Asian mainland worlds of Southeast Asia, especially benefiting the Thai, Vietnamese, and Burmese peoples who gradually emerged as the largest population groups on the mainland. Island residents of the Malay Archipelago—especially of Java and Sumatra—controlled much of the region's maritime activity. Each population group adjusted as Chinese and Indian influences rose and fell, selecting those aspects of "Indo-Chinese" civilization that they found compatible with local

THE TALE OF GENJI

Lacking a written language of their own, Heian aristocrats adopted classical Chinese as the official written language while continuing to speak Japanese. Men at the court took great pains to master the Chinese literary forms imported from the Tang dynasty via the Heian tributary missions periodically sent to Chang'an. Japanese court ladies, however, were not expected to master Chinese writing. For example, Lady Murasaki, the author of The Tale of Genji, *went to great pains to hide her knowledge of Chinese, fearing that she would be criticized for being unladylike. In the meantime, the Japanese developed a syllabary for their own language by simplifying Chinese written graphs and tying them directly to native sounds. Using this syllabary, Lady Murasaki began a diary in Japanese that she kept up for two years. In it she gave vivid accounts of Heian court life, whose frivolity she herself disliked. Lady Murasaki noted that some might also view writing fiction as frivolous, but she made clear that fiction could be as truthful as a work of history in capturing human life and its historical significance.*

So saying she pushed away from her the book which she had been copying. Genji continued: "So you see as a matter of fact I think far better of this art than I have led you to suppose. Even its practical value is immense. Without it what should we know of how people lived in the past, from the Age of the Gods down to the present day? For history-books such as the *Chronicles of Japan* show us only one small corner of life; whereas these diaries and romances which I see piled around you contain, I am sure, the most minute information about all sorts of people's private affairs. . . ." He smiled, and went on: "But I have a theory of my own about what this art of the novel is, and how it came into being. To begin with, it does not simply consist in the author's telling a story about the adventures of some other person. On the contrary, it happens because the storyteller's own experience of men and things, whether for good or ill— not only what he has passed through himself, but even events which he has only witnessed or been told of—has moved him to an emotion so passionate that he can no longer keep it shut up in his heart. Again and again something in his own life or in that around him will seem to the writer so important that he cannot bear to let it pass into oblivion. There must never come a time, he feels, when men do not know about it. That is my view of how this art arose.

"Clearly then, it is no part of the storyteller's craft to describe only what is good or beautiful. Sometimes, of course, virtue will be his theme, and he may then make such play with it as he will. But he is just as likely to have been struck by numerous examples of vice and folly in the world around him, and about them he has exactly the same feelings as about the pre-eminently good deeds which he encounters: they are more important and must all be garnered in. Thus anything whatsoever may become the subject of a novel, provided only that it happens in this mundane life and not in some fairyland beyond our human ken.

"The outward forms of this art will not of course be everywhere the same. At the court of China and in other foreign lands both the genius of the writers and their actual methods of composition are necessarily very different from ours; and even here in Japan the art of storytelling has in course of time undergone great changes. There will, too, always be a distinction between the lighter and the more serious forms of fiction. . . . Well, I have said enough to show that when at the beginning of our conversation I spoke of romances as though they were mere frivolous fabrications, I was only teasing you. Some people have taken exception on moral grounds to an art in which the perfect and imperfect are set side by side. But even in the discourses which Buddha in his bounty allowed to be recorded, certain passages contain what the learned call *Upāya* or 'Adapted Truth'—a fact that has led some superficial persons to doubt whether a doctrine so inconsistent with itself could possibly command our credence. Even in the scriptures of the Greater Vehicle there are, I confess, many such instances. We may indeed go so far as to say there is an actual mixture of Truth and Error. But the purpose of these holy writings, namely the compassing of our Salvation, remains always the same. So too, I think, may it be said that the art of fiction must not lose our allegiance because, in the pursuit of the main purpose to which I have alluded above, it sets virtue by the side of vice, or mingles wisdom with folly. Viewed in this light the novel is seen to be not, as is usually supposed, a mixture of useful truth with idle invention, but something which at every stage and in every part has a definite and serious purpose."

→ *What does this account tell us about the relation between historical fact and fictional romance?*

→ *How are "truth and error" displayed in religious writings, which, like novels, use stories in pursuit of their didactic purpose?*

SOURCE: *Sources of Japanese Tradition*, compiled by Ryūsaku Tsunoda, Wm. Theodore de Bary, and Donald Keene (New York: Columbia University Press, 1964), vol. 1, pp. 177–79.

MAP 10-6   SOUTHEAST ASIA, 1000–1300

Cross-cultural influences strongly shaped the development of Southeast Asian societies between 1000 and 1300. According to the map, how did East and South Asian societies influence various communities in Southeast Asia? What aspects of Chinese and Indian culture did Southeast Asian societies import? In this chapter, the term "cultural mosaic" is used to describe both South and Southeast Asia. How did the mosaic in Southeast Asia differ from that in India during this era?

state formation and cultural activities. Chinese and Indian peoples also became part of the new trading milieu.

Cambodian, Burmese, and Thai peoples founded powerful mixed polities along the Mekong, Salween, Chaophraya, and Irriwaddy river basins of the Asian mainland. The important Vedic and Buddhist kingdoms of the Khmer (today's Cambodia), Pagan (today's Burma), and Siam (today's Thailand) emerged as political buffers between the strong states in China and India. These Southeast Asian kingdoms were

soon robust enough to consolidate their hold on these borderlands, thereby bringing stability and furthering the commercial prosperity of the region.

Consider the great kingdom that ruled Angkor in present-day Cambodia. With their capital in Angkor, the Khmers (889–1431) created the most powerful and wealthy empire in Southeast Asia between the tenth and thirteenth centuries. Countless water reservoirs enabled the Khmers to flourish on the great plain to the west of the Mekong River. Public works

Aerial View of Angkor Wat. Mistaken by later European explorers as a remnant of Alexander the Great's conquests, the enormous temple complexes built by the Khmer people in Angkor borrowed their intricate layout and stupa architecture from the Brahmanist Indian temples of the time. As the capital, Angkor was a microcosm of the world for the Khmer, who aspired to represent the macrocosm of the universe in the magnificence of Angkor's buildings and their geometric-astronomic layout.

and magnificent temples dedicated to the glory of the revived Vedic gods from India went hand in hand with the earlier influence of Indian Buddhism in mainland Southeast Asia. Eventually the Khmer kings gathered enough military strength to unite adjacent kingdoms and extend Khmer influence to the Thai and Burmese states along the Chaophraya and Irriwaddy rivers.

One of the greatest temple complexes in Angkor exemplified the heavy borrowing by the Khmer peoples from Indian temples and architecture. By this time, the Brahmanist revival of Vedic religion in India circa 1000 CE had eclipsed Buddhism there, except on the island of Ceylon. Angkor aspired to represent the universe in the magnificence of its buildings. As signs of the ruler's power, the pagodas, pyramids, and terra-cotta friezes presented the life of the gods on earth. The royal palace alone extended 1,970 feet east to west and 820 feet north to south; it was crowned by the magnificent Vaishnavite temple of Angkor Wat, measuring about a mile square and probably the largest religious structure ever built. The buildings and statues represented the revival of the Hindu pantheon of gods in the Khmer royal state, such as Shiva and Vishnu, in great detail and with great artistry, but far less Buddhist influence is visible.

Because of its strategic location and proximity to Malayan tropical produce, Melaka became perhaps the most international city in the world. Indian, Javanese, and Chinese merchants and sailors spent months at a time in such ports selling their goods, purchasing a return cargo, and waiting for the winds to change so that they might reach their next destination. Seasonal shifts in the monsoon winds across the Bay of Bengal, the South China Sea, and the Java Sea al-

lowed Chinese and Japanese ships to arrive from January to March and then return home in August. Ships from India came from May to early October and sailed back west in winter. During peak season, Southeast Asian ports were filled with foreign sailors and traders from all over Asia who accompanied their own merchandise. They gathered in large numbers at crossroads where agriculture sustained the local population and maritime trade routes converged.

CHRISTIAN EUROPE

> → *How did Christianity produce a distinct identity among the diverse peoples of Europe?*

In the far western corner of the Afro-Eurasian landmass, a people were building a culture revealingly different. (See Map 10-7.) Although their numbers were still relatively small compared with the rest of Afro-Eurasia in 1000 (36 million in Europe, compared to 80 million in India and 100 million in China), their population was rapidly rising and would soar to 80 million before the arrival of the Black Death at the beginning of the fourteenth century.

This was a region of contrasts. On the one hand, the first three centuries of the second millennium witnessed an intense localization of politics. There was no successor to the Roman or Carolingian empires (see Chapter 9). On the other hand, the territory was ever more united by a progressively

MAP 10-7 LATIN CHRISTENDOM IN 1300

Catholic Europe expanded geographically and integrated culturally during this era. According to this map, into what areas did Western Christendom successfully expand? What factors contributed to the growth of a widespread common culture and shared ideas? How did long-distance trade shape the history of the region during this time?

greater shared sense of its place in the world. Indeed, in these years some even began for the first time to believe in the existence of something called "Europe," whose inhabitants were increasingly referring to themselves as "Europeans."

A WORLD OF KNIGHTS

The collapse of the Carolingian empire (768–814 CE) had exposed much of northern Europe to invasion, principally from the Vikings, and left the region's peasantry with no central authority to protect them from the power of local warlords. These warlords collected taxes and imposed forced labor. Armed with new and more deadly weapons, the warrior class came to stand out as the unchallenged rulers of society. In this growth of a warrior aristocracy, northern France led the way. The Franks (who gradually came to be called "Frenchmen" in this period) were the self-proclaimed trendsetters of eleventh- and twelfth-century western Europe.

The most important change was the subjugation of the peasantry to the knightly class. Previously, well-to-do peasants

The Bayeux Tapestry. This tapestry was prepared by a queen and her ladies to celebrate the victories of William the Conqueror. It shows the fascination of the entire "feudal" class, even women, with the sinews of war on which they depended—great horses, tightly meshed chain mail, long shields, and the stirrups that made such cavalry warfare possible.

had carried arms, and doing so had marked themselves as "free" men. The moment the farmers lost their right to carry arms, they were no longer free. They slipped back to being mere agricultural laborers. Each peasant was under the authority of a lord, who controlled every detail of his or her life. This was the basis of a system known as feudalism.

Assured of control of the peasantry, feudal lords watched over an agrarian breakthrough—which formed the basis of a commercial transformation that would link Europe to the rest of the global trading networks. This breakthrough was largely due to massive deforestation, which, in turn, implied more advanced use of metal tools (axes and ploughs) and heavier livestock to pull the ploughs that turned the heavy, root-infested sods of northern Europe. Above this stood the castle—a threatening presence that ensured that (unlike many other regions of the world) the peasantry did not simply vanish into the woods that they had cleared. They stayed within range of the collector of rents and services for the lords and of tithes for the Church. In this blunt way, "feudalism" harnessed agrarian energy to its own needs. The population of western Europe as a whole leaped forward, most spectacularly in the north. By 1300, northern Europe contained almost half of Europe's inhabitants. As a result, northern Europe (from England to Poland) finally ceased to be an underdeveloped barbarian appendage of the Mediterranean.

EASTERN EUROPE

Nowhere did pioneering peasants develop more land than in the wide-open spaces of eastern Europe, the region's land of opportunity. Between 1100 and 1200, some 200,000 farmers emigrated from Flanders (modern Belgium), Holland, and northern Germany into eastern frontiers. Well-watered landscapes, covered with vast forests, in what are now Poland,

the Czech Republic, Hungary, and the Baltic states filled up. "Little Europes," whose castles, churches, and towns echoed the landscape of France, sprang up to replace economies that had been based on gathering honey, hunting, and the slave trade. In Silesia (western Poland), for instance, 1,200 villages were founded within a century. For a thousand miles along the Baltic Sea, from the city of Lübeck in Germany to Riga in present-day Latvia, forest clearings dotted with new farmsteads and small towns edged inward from the coast up the river systems.

The social structure in eastern Europe was a marriage of convenience between migrating peasants and local elites. Western European peasants sought to enjoy, in a different land, some of the freedoms that had been lost to their feudal overlords. Eastern Europe offered the promise of freedom from arbitrary justice and from the imposition of forced labor.

Olavinlinna Castle. This castle in Finland was the easternmost extension of a "western," feudal style of rule through great castles. It was built at the very end of the Baltic, to keep away the Russians of Novgorod.

Even the harsh landscape of the eastern Baltic (where the sea froze every year and vast forests blocked the way of settlers from the coast) was preferable to life in the feudal west. For their part, the elites of eastern Europe—the nobility of Poland, Bohemia, and Hungary and the princes of the Baltic—wished to live well, in the "French" style. But they could do so only if they attracted manpower to their vast lands by offering peasants and townspeople a liberty that they had no hope of enjoying in the west.

THE RUSSIAN LANDS

In Russian lands, western settlers and knights met an eastern brand of Christian devotion. This was a world that had chosen to look toward Byzantium. Russia was a giant borderland between the interior steppe lands of Afro-Eurasia and the booming feudalisms of Europe, bridging east and west. Its cities lay at the crossroads of overland trade and migration, and Kiev became one of the greatest cities of Europe. Standing on a bluff above the Dnieper River, it straddled newly opened trade routes. With a population of well over 20,000, partly made up of merchants drawn from all over eastern Europe, western Europe, and the Middle East, Kiev was larger than Paris—larger even than the much-diminished city of Rome.

Kiev looked south to the Black Sea and to Byzantium. Under Iaroslav the Wise (1016–1054), it was carefully re-built so as to become a small-scale Constantinople on the Dnieper. A stone church called St. Sophia was placed (as in Constantinople) beside the imperial palace. Indeed, with its distinctive "Byzantine" domes, it was a miniature Hagia Sophia. Almost a hundred feet high from the floor to the top of the dome, it was at its completion the largest structure ever built in Europe east of the Elbe. Splendid mosaics covered the walls with images of Byzantine saints, which faithfully echoed the religious art of Constantinople. But the message was political as well as religious, for the ruler of Kiev similarly was cast in the mold of the emperor of Constantinople. He was now called *tsar* from the ancient Roman name given to the emperor, Caesar. From this time onward, *tsar* was the title of rulers in Russia.

The Russian form of Christianity embraced the Byzantine style of churches and replicated them up the great rivers leading to the largely independent trading cities of the north and northeast. These were not centers of growing agrarian settlement and dense populations but entrepôts, the hubs of expanding long-distance trade across Afro-Eurasia. Each city became a small-scale Kiev, and thus became a smaller-scale echo of the Great City—Constantinople. The Orthodox religion associated with Byzantium's Hagia Sophia, and not the Catholic religion associated with the popes in Rome, was their form of Christianity. Russian Christianity remained the Christianity of a borderland—a series of vivid oases of high culture, set against the backdrop of vast forests and widely

Hagia Sophia, Novgorod. The cathedral of Novgorod (as that of Kiev) was called Hagia Sophia. It was a deliberate imitation of the Hagia Sophia of Constantinople, showing Russia's roots in a glorious Roman/Byzantine past that had nothing to do with western Europe.

Primary Source

VOICES FROM THE PAST: THE BIRCH BARK LETTERS OF NOVGOROD

From 1951 onward, the excavations of Russian archaeologists in Novgorod have revealed almost a thousand letters and accounts scratched on birch bark. Written on wood, they were preserved in the sodden, frequently frozen ground. Reading them we realize what a remarkable place Novgorod must have been in the twelfth and thirteenth centuries.

First, we meet the merchants. Many letters are notes by creditors of the debts owed to them by trading partners. The sums are often expressed in precious animal furs. They contain advice to relatives or to partners in other cities:

> Giorgii sends his respects to his father and mother: Sell the house and come here to Smolensk or to Kiev: for the bread is cheap there.

Then we meet neighborhood disputes:

> From Anna to Klemiata: Help me, my lord brother, in my matter with Konstantin. . . . [For I asked him,] "Why have you been so angry with my sister and her daughter. You called her a cow and her daughter a whore. And now Fedor has thrown them both out of the house."

There are even glimpses of real love. A secret marriage is planned:

> Mikiti to Ulianitza: Come to me. I love you, and you me. Ignato will act as witness.

And a poignant note from a woman was discovered in 1993:

> I have written to you three times. What is it that you hold against me, that you did not come to see me this Sunday? I regarded you as I would my own brother. Did I really offend you by that which I sent to you? If you had been pleased you would have torn yourself away from company and come to me. Write to me. If in my clumsiness I have offended you and you should spurn me, then let God be my judge. I love you.

→ *What does the range of people writing on birch bark tell us about these people?*

→ *What does the final note tell us about the expression of love among the peoples from the northern stretches of Afro-Eurasia?*

SOURCE: A. V. Artsikhovskii and V. I. Borkovski, *Novgorodskie Gramoty na Bereste*, 11 vols. (Moscow: Izd-vo Akademii nauk SSSR, 1951–2004), document nos. 424, 531, 377, and 752.

---

scattered settlements. As the settlement frontier pushed outward, it merged with the shamanistic cultures of the Arctic and Siberia, and, in the south, with the nomad corridor that linked Europe to central Asia along the coast of the Black Sea.

WHAT WAS CHRISTIAN EUROPE?

In this era, Catholicism became a mass faith, a transformation that shaped the emergence of the region then coming to be known by some as "Europe." The Christianity of post-Roman Europe had been a religion of monks, and its most dynamic centers were great monasteries. Members of the laity were expected to revere and support their monks, nuns, and clergy, but they were not encouraged to imitate them. By 1200, all this had changed. The internal colonization of western Europe—the clearing of woods and the founding of villages—ensured that parish churches arose in all but the wildest landscapes. Their spires could be seen and their bells could be heard from one valley to the next. The graveyards around the churches were the only places where a good Christian could be buried; criminals and outlaws were piled into "heathen" graves outside the cemetery walls. Even the bones of the believers helped make Europe Christian.

The clergy reached more deeply into the private lives of the laity. For the first time in Christian history, marriage and

UNIVERSITIES AND INTELLECTUALS During this era, Europe acquired its first class of intellectuals. Since the end of the twelfth century, scholars had tended to come together in Paris. There they formed a *universitas*—a term borrowed from the merchant communities, where it denoted the equivalent of the modern "union." Those who belonged to the *universitas* were protected by their fellows and were allowed to continue their trade. Similarly protected by their union, the scholars of Paris set about wrestling with the new learning from Arab lands. And when in 1212 the bishop of Paris forbade this undertaking, they simply moved to the Left Bank of the Seine, so as to place the river between themselves and the officials of the bishop, who lived around the cathedral of Notre Dame.

The ability of the scholars to organize themselves gave them an advantage not enjoyed by their Arab contemporaries, despite the latter's immense cultural resources. For all his genius, Ibn Rushd had to spend his life courting the favor of

Amiens Cathedral. The cathedrals of northern France and elsewhere in Europe were built largely by local townsmen with the wealth that came to them through trade and industry. Each town strove to build its own cathedral ever higher and higher. No building was as high in Roman times. Even the Hagia Sophia was dwarfed by these light and lofty marvels of engineering.

Medieval Lecture. Crowded lecture halls, open to a wide audience, were a creation of the medieval university. Previously, learning had taken place in small groups over long periods of time.

divorce (which had been treated, by aristocrats and peasants alike, as family matters over which the clergy had no jurisdiction) became a full-time preoccupation of the church. Sin, for instance, was no longer dealt with as an offense that just happened to the laity. It was a matter that the laity could do something about, preferably on a day-to-day basis. After 1215, for the first time ever, regular confession to a priest was made obligatory for all Catholic, western Christians. The followers of Francis of Assisi (1182–1226)—a man from a merchant background, whose father traded wool in northern France—emerged as an order of preachers who brought to the towns a message of repentance. They did not tell their audiences to enter the monastery (as would have been the case in the early Middle Ages). Instead, the listeners were to weep, to confess their sins to their local priests, and to try to be better Christians. Franciscans instilled in the hearts of all believers a new, Europe-wide Catholicism, based on daily remorse and on the daily contemplation of the sufferings of Christ and his mother, Mary. From Ireland to Riga and Budapest, Catholic Christians shared a common piety.

individual monarchs to protect him from conservative fellow Muslims. Frequently his books were burned. Ironically, European scholars congregating in the Schools of Paris could quietly absorb the most persuasive elements of Arabic thought, like Ibn Rushd's. Yet, at the same time, they endeavored to show that everything gradually converged to prove that Christianity was the only religion that fully met the aspirations of all rational human beings. Such was the message of the great teacher and intellectual Thomas Aquinas, born in southern Italy, whose *Summa contra Gentiles* (*Summary of Christian Belief against Non-Christians*) was written in 1264.

The Europe of 1300 was more culturally unified than it had been in previous centuries. It was more fully permeated by a version of its dominant Catholicism, made more accessible than ever before to the laity of the new towns through preachers such as Saint Francis and through stunning monuments such as the new Gothic cathedrals of northern France. Its leading intellectuals extolled the virtues of Christian learning and thought. Such a confident region was not, however, a happy place for heretics, Jews, or Muslims.

TRADERS Western Europeans were expanding frontiers around the Mediterranean and pushing beyond it. Great trading hubs emerged, most famously Venice and Genoa, as the nodes of commerce and finance linking Europe, Africa, and Asia. Powerful families commanded trading fleets and used their deep pockets to influence dealings far and wide. They also possessed the means to meddle in political affairs. Indeed, both Venice and Genoa set their sights on the waning power of Constantinople and on its eastern trade, vying for access to Asia Minor, the Black Sea, and the thriving commercial hinterlands of Afro-Eurasia. The Genoese showed, on a worldwide stage, what urban magnates could do when they combined sea power with a zest for organization. By 1300, Genoese ships had linked the Mediterranean to the coast of Flanders through regular sailings along the Atlantic coast of Spain, Portugal, and France. In 1291, some ventured as far as the Azores in the Atlantic, only to be lost as they pushed further southwest. Genoese maps displayed the entire coast of West Africa—including the kingdom of Mali, ruled by Mansa Musa (see above), which was the source of the gold dust that was now carried across the Sahara to the coast of North Africa.

CRUSADERS By the tenth and eleventh centuries, Europe had gained a strong enough sense of its separate identity that its elites and even many of its common folk regarded the area as a distinct region. Western Christianity was on the move. It spread into Scandinavia, southern Italy, the Baltic, and eastern Europe. Its ambitions to reconquer Spain and Portugal, which had been under Islamic control since the eighth century, demonstrated one of the effects of the flourishing of feudal power: the self-confidence of lords, their belief in their

military capability, and their pious sense of manifest destiny were all inflated. Besides, the wealth of the east, fueled by the prosperity of trading cities, was irresistible to those whose piety was entwined with an appetite for plunder. Nor were feudal lords alone in mixing opportunism and a passion for sacred causes. The leaders of the eastern and western churches were keen to recover or gain strength. Rome and Byzantium both sought to gain the upper hand in the scramble for religious command in Europe; each considered a blow to the "infidel" a cunning ploy to out-do the other. Yet the two Christendoms formed an uneasy alliance to roll back the expanding frontiers of Islam.

Crusader. Kneeling, this Crusader promises to serve God (as he would serve a feudal lord) by going to fight on a crusade (as he would fight for any lord to whom he had sworn loyalty). The two kinds of loyalty—to God and to one's lord—were deliberately confused in Crusader ideology. Both were about war. But fighting for God was unambiguously good, while fighting for a lord was not always so clearcut.

Global Connections & Disconnections

THE CRUSADES FROM DUAL PERSPECTIVES

In 1095, at the Council of Clermont, Pope Urban II called for the First Crusade in the following words:

> Oh, race of Franks, race from across the mountains, race chosen and beloved by God, as shines forth in very many of your works, set apart from all nations by the situation of your country, as well as by your Catholic faith and the honor of the Holy Church! To you our discourse is addressed, and for you our exhortation is intended. We wish you to know what a grievous cause has led us to your country, what peril, threatening you and all the faithful, has brought us.

The "grievous cause" was the occupation of the Holy City of Jerusalem by the Islamic empire. Formed within the complex relationship between the Byzantine Empire and the western Christian papacy and kingdoms of Europe, the religious motivation behind the Crusades became the subject of many literary renditions of the tumultuous events. It also generated emotionally stirring and polemical writing, depicting either a Muslim or Christian enemy (depending on the work's author).

Polemics are often passionate, harsh, and emotional. They are also often meant to inspire and reinforce the conviction of fellow believers, with little concern for the accuracy of their portrayals. Thus authors of polemic in the time of the Crusades were usually too biased, too distant from the events or people they described, or simply too misinformed to present accurate portraits of the enemies against whom they were pitting themselves. But occasionally, firsthand accounts in the form of chronicles and histories offer us unique glimpses into Christian-Muslim relations in the age of the Crusades.

Consider Usāmah ibn Munqidh (1095–1188), the deeply learned ruler of the city of Shaizar on the Orontes River in western Syria. Skirmishes, truces, and the ransoming of prisoners were part of his daily life, and Usāmah socialized with his Frankish neighbors quite as much as he fought with them. He offers a dismissive opinion of his enemies. Basically, they struck him as "animals possessing the virtues of courage and fighting, but nothing else." In particular, their medical practice appalled him. More strange yet, the Franks allowed their wives to walk about freely and to talk to strangers unaccompanied by male guardians. How could men be at once so brave and yet so lacking in a proper, Arab sense of honor, which would lead a man to protect his women? In fact, sexual laxity seemed to be one of the aspects of Frankish life that most appalled Usāmah, who claimed that the Franks were "void of all zeal and jealousy," meaning that they were unconcerned with relatively loose sexual mores. Unlike other Muslim authors of his time, however, Usāmah does not refer to the Franks in derogatory terms such as "infidels" or "devils." In fact, he occasionally refers to some of them as his companions, and writes in one case of a Frank who used to call him "my brother" (*An Arab-Syrian Gentleman and Warrior in the Time of the Crusades*, 16).

Christian authors had similar interests in documenting the habits and customs of their enemies in battle. Jean de Joinville (1224/1225–1317) was a chronicler of medieval France. He also composed a biography of King Louis II, at the request of Jeanne of Navarre, the queen. In 1309 Joinville completed his work on the *Histoire de Saint Louis*, which documents how he himself had been in the service of the king. During the crusade launched from 1248 to 1254, Joinville, one of the king's confidants, had occasion to note the social behavior of the Muslims:

> Whenever the Sultan was in the camp, the men of the personal Guard were quartered all round his lodging, and appointed to guard his person. At the door of the Sultan's lodging there was a little tent for the Sultan's door-keepers, and for his musicians, who had Arabian horns and drums and kettledrums; and they used to make such a din at daybreak and at nightfall that people near them could not hear one another speak, and that they could be heard plainly all through the camp. The musicians never dared sound their instruments in the daytime unless by the order of the Chief of the Guard. Thus it was, that whenever the Sultan had a proclamation to make he used to send for the Chief of the Guard, and give him the order; and then the Chief would cause all the Sultan's instruments to be sounded; and thereupon all the host would come to hear the Sultan's commands.

Although we should regard literary renditions of the events described with a certain degree of caution, they are useful for gleaning personal details that may be left out of other types of works. The colorful accounts by authors such as Usāmah ibn Munqidh and Joinville have proven invaluable as resources for the social and cultural history of the Crusader era.

The result was that Europeans took war outside their own borders on a mass scale. In the late eleventh century, western Europeans launched the wave of attacks that we now know as the Crusades. The First Crusade began in 1095, when Pope Urban II appealed to the warrior nobility of France to put their violence to good use. They should combine their role as pilgrims to Jerusalem with that of soldiers and free Jerusalem from Muslim rule. What the pope and clergy proposed, in effect, was a novel kind of war. Previously, the clergy had regarded war as a dirty business and a source of sin (not unlike sex). Now the clergy told the knights that good and just wars were possible. Such wars could cancel out the sins of those who waged them.

Starting in 1097, an armed host of around 60,000 men—a force larger than any "barbarian" wave at the end of the Roman Empire—moved all the way from northwestern Europe to Jerusalem. In all, there would be four "crusades," over the course of two centuries. They cannot be described as successful. Only a small proportion of Crusaders stayed behind to guard the territories they had won. No more than 1,200 knights remained to defend the Kingdom of Jerusalem after the First Crusade. Most knights returned home, their epic pilgrimage completed. The fragile network of small Crusader lordships could only occasionally pose a threat to the true heartlands of the Islamic world. On July 4, 1187, the Frankish heavy cavalry was lured on to the dry plateau above the Sea of Galilee, where they were slaughtered in the blazing heat by Saladin (Salah ad-Din, "Righteous in Faith"), the Kurdish commander who had made himself ruler over Egypt. Subsequent forays were equally disastrous. Stretched thin, with feeble supply lines, the dwindling forces of Christian occupiers (or "liberators," depending on one's perspective) were too easy to pick off, surround and besiege, or simply overrun. Against such odds, western Christian forces took out their frustrations against other Christians and allies. In one infamous "crusade" Frankish armies went on a rampage in the Byzantine capital and sacked Constantinople in 1204. According to one Byzantine monk, "nothing worse than this has happened nor will happen." When news reached the far-off Scandinavian world, Christian I, king of Norway and Denmark, saw it as a signal of the forthcoming apocalypse, when the beast would rise from the waters, as described in the New Testament.

Muslim leaders did not see the Frankish knights as much of a threat to their heartland. From the point of view of the Muslim Middle East, the Crusades were largely irrelevant. As far as the average Muslim of the region was concerned, the Crusaders had blundered into a no-man's-land of little importance. The principal long-term effect of these assaults was to harden Muslim feelings against the *Ferangi* (Franks) of the West and to bring about a worsening of the condition of many millions of non-Western Christians who had previously lived peacefully in Egypt and Syria.

Other Crusade-like campaigns of Christian expansion undertaken around this time were considerably more successful. Rather than being overseas ventures, these were launched from a secure home base. In this period, the Spanish Reconquista got under way. Beginning with the capture of Toledo in 1061, the Christian kings of northern Spain (who could count on support from their immediate Christian neighbors across the Pyrenees) slowly but surely pushed back the Muslims. Eventually, they reached the rich heart of Andalusia and in 1248 they conquered Seville, a victory that permanently added more than 100,000 square miles of territory to Christian Europe. Another force from northern France crossed Italy to conquer Muslim-held Sicily in 1091, thereby ensuring that a rich island only seventy-five miles away from the coast of Africa and in a position to control the middle of the Mediterranean was subject to Christian rule. These two conquests accomplished in less than a century, and not the fragile foothold of the Crusaders on the edge of the Middle East, were the events that truly turned the tide in the relations between Christian and Muslim power in the Mediterranean.

THE AMERICAS

> → *Where did societies in the Americas demonstrate strong commercial expansionist impulses?*

Alone in the world, untouched by the increasing connections across the Afro-Eurasian regions, were the Americas. Simply put, the revolution in communications did not enable Asian, African, or European navigators to cross the large oceans that separated the Americas from other lands. However, isolation did not mean that the Americas were stagnant. Many of the commercial and expansionist impulses that swept the rest of the world occurred independently in the Western Hemisphere and similarly brought the peoples of the Americas into closer contact with each other.

ANDEAN STATES

Growth and prosperity in the Andean region led to the formation of South America's first empire. Known as the Chimú Empire, it developed during the first century of the second millennium in the fertile Moche Valley, bordering the Pacific Ocean. (See Map 10-8.) At its height, the Moche people had expanded their influence across a number of valleys—and thus incorporated a wide number of ecological zones, from pastoral highlands to rich valley floodplains to the fecund fishing grounds of the Pacific Coast. As their geographical reach grew, so did their wealth. The Chimú regime lasted until Incan armies invaded the coastal strongholds in the 1460s and incorporated the Pacific state into its own immense empire.

The Chimú economy was successful because it was highly commercialized. Agriculture was its base, and complex irrigation systems turned the arid coast into a string of fertile oases capable of feeding an expanding and far dispersed population. Cotton became a lucrative export to distant markets along the Andes. Parades of llamas and porters lugged these commodities up and down the steep mountain chains that are the spine of South America. As in China, a large, well-trained bureaucracy was responsible for constructing and maintaining canals, with a hierarchy of provincial administrators to watch over commercial hinterlands.

Between 850 and 900 CE, the Moche peoples founded their biggest city, Chan Chan, with a core population of 30,000 inhabitants. A sprawling metropolis surrounded by twenty-six-foot-high walls, covering nearly ten square miles with extensive roads circulating through adobe neighborhoods, it had ten huge palaces at its center. These were residence halls, protected by thick walls thirty feet high, whose prestige and opulence demonstrated the rulers' power over other Moche subjects. Within the compound, emperors erected mortuary monuments, which became stores for their accumulated riches. In them archaeologists have found

MAP 10-8   ANDEAN STATES

Although the Andes region of South America was isolated from Afro-Eurasian developments before 1500, it was not a stagnant region. Indeed, political and cultural integration brought the peoples of this region closer together. What kind of empire was the Chimú? What kinds of ecological niches did it govern? How did each polity encourage greater cultural and economic integration?

Chan Chan. This is what is left of Chan Chan. The city covered fifteen square miles and was divided into distinct neighborhoods for nobles, artisans, and commoners, with the elites living closest to the hub of governmental and spiritual power. Adobe was the basic construction material; it held up well in the arid conditions of the Peruvian coast.

Tihuanaco Buildings. The buildings of Tihuanaco were made of giant, hand-hewn stones assembled without mortar. Engineers had not discovered the principle of curved arches and keystones and instead relied on massive slabs atop gateways. Gateways were important symbolic features, for they were places where people acknowledged the importance of sun and moon gods. In this building, a giant monolith stood in the gateway that looked out over the Andean horizon.

treasures of fine cloth, gold and silver objects, splendid *Spondylus* shells, and piles of other high-status goods. Around the emperors' compound were neighborhoods for nobles and artisans; in the further reaches of the city stood small rows of houses for Moche commoners.

The Andes also saw its first highland empires during this period. On the shores of the high plateau lake Titicaca, the people of Tiahuanaco forged a high-altitude state. Though neither as large nor as wealthy as the Chimú Empire, it was complex, and it converted the seemingly inhospitable highlands into an environment where farmers and herders thrived. There is, moreover, extensive evidence of long-distance trade between the highland peoples and neighbors in semitropical valleys, and even signs of highlanders migrating down to the lowlands to set up agrarian colonies to produce staples for their kin in the mountains. Dried fish and cotton came from the coast; fruits and vegetables came from lowland valleys. Trade was active enough to sustain an enormous urban population of up to 115,000 people. Looming over the skyline of

Lake Titicaca. This is the setting for the first great Andean polity of Tihuanaco (Tiwanaku). Surrounded by the glacial peaks of the Andes, Tihuanaco grew up near the shores of Lake Titicaca, a source of water, fish, and legends about the birth of gods. To cultivate the steep mountainsides, farmers developed complex terrace systems. Most settlements were nestled, like these ruins, on valley floors or by the shores of the lake.

Tiahuanaco was an imposing pyramid of massive sandstone blocks; its advanced engineering system conveyed water to the summit, from which the liquid flowed in an imitation of rainfall down the carefully carved sides—an awesome spectacle of engineering prowess in such an arid region.

North American Connections

By 1000 CE, Mesoamerica had seen the rise and fall of several complex societies. Caravans of porters worked the intricate roads that connected the coast of the Gulf of Mexico and the Pacific, and the southern lowlands of Central America to the arid regions of modern Texas. (See Map 10-9.) Its heartland was the rich valley of central Mexico. The Toltecs rose to power with great rapidity because they were able to fill the political vacuum left by the decline of the great city of Teotihuacán (see Chapter 8) and tap into the commercial network that radiated from the valley.

The Toltecs themselves were hybrids—a combination of migrant groups, refugees from the south, and farmers from the north—who settled northwest of Teotihuacán as the city waned. Their capital was Tula, growing in the shadow of the Mesoamerican metropolis. The Toltecs relied on a maize-based economy, supplemented by beans, squash, and dog, deer, and rabbit meat, as local agrarian production covered the population's needs. Rulers, however, relied on the enterprise of merchants to provide them with status goods such as ornamental pottery, rare shells and stones, and precious skins and feathers.

Tula was a commercial hub. But it was also a political capital and a ceremonial center. While the city's layout differed from Teotihuacán's, many features revealed borrowings from other Mesoamerican peoples. Temples were made of giant pyramids topped by colossal stone soldiers, and the ball courts where subjects and conquered peoples alike played their ritual sport were ubiquitous. The architecture and monumental art bespoke the mixed and migratory origins of the Toltecs: a combination of Mayan and Teotihuanacu influences decorated the city's great public works. At its height, the Toltec capital was home to around 60,000 people—a huge metropolis by contemporary European standards.

Cities at the hubs of trading networks could be found all across North America. North of Tula, the largest was Cahokia, by the shores of the Mississippi River (near modern-day East St. Louis), a city of about 15,000 (which would make it about the size of London at the time). Farmers and hunters settled in the region around 600 CE, attracted by the combination of good soil, availability of woodlands for fuel and game, and access to the trading artery of the mighty Mississippi. Eventually, fields planted with rows of maize (their main staple) and other crops fanned out into the horizon. The hoe replaced the trusty digging stick, increasing yields, and smaller satellite towns put up granaries to hold foodstuffs.

Cahokia became a commercial center for regional and long-distance trade. The hinterlands produced staples for urban consumers. In return, Cahokia's crafts were exported, carried inland on the backs of porters and to distant North American markets in canoes. The city's woven fabrics and ceramics were desired by faraway consumers. In exchange, traders brought to the rich city mica from the Appalachian Mountains, seashells and sharks' teeth from the Gulf of Mexico, and copper from the upper Great Lakes. Indeed, Cahokia became more than an importer and exporter: it was the

Toltec Temple. Tula, the capital of the Toltec Empire, carried on the Mesoamerican tradition of locating ceremonial architecture at the center of the city. The Pyramid of the Morning Star cast its shadow over all other buildings. And above them stood columns of the Atlantes, carved Toltec god-warriors, the figurative pillars of the empire itself. The walls of this pyramid were likely embellished with images of snakes and skulls. The north face of the pyramid has the image of a snake devouring a human.

MAP 10-9   COMMERCIAL HUBS IN MESOAMERICA AND NORTH AMERICA, 1000

Both Cahokia and Tula, shown on the map above, represented commercial hubs of vibrant regional trade networks between 1000 and 1300. What kinds of goods do your readings suggest circulated through these cities? How much political influence on the surrounding region do you think each city maintained? Do you think that the trade networks anchored by each city ever interacted with each other during this time?

entrepôt for an entire regional commercial network, containing many trading nodes where salt, tools, pottery, woven stuffs, jewelry, and ceremonial goods could be procured from traders from other places.

Cahokia's urban landscape was dominated by mounds, really big mounds (which is one reason Cahokians are often known as "mound people"). These earth monuments were delicately maintained: Cahokians enveloped their shells with layers of sand and clay to prevent their foundations from drying and then cracking. It was from these great artificial hills that Cahokians paid homage to spiritual forces. Of course, building this kind of infrastructure without draft animals, hy-

draulic tools, or even wheels was labor-intensive. To solve this problem, Cahokians recruited other North Americans to serve in working brigades. Around the city was an endless palisade made from neighboring forests, to protect the metropolis from marauders and enemies.

In the end, the city outgrew its environment. The woodlands were cleared and arable soil began to lose nutrients. Timber and food became scarce. Because the city lacked a means of transportation to ship bulky items over long distances, Cahokia's success bred its downfall. When the creeks that fed its water system could not keep up with demand, engineers changed their course, to no avail. By 1350, the city

Cahokia Mounds. This is all that is left of what was once a large city organized around temple mounds in what today is Illinois. The largest of the temples, known as Monks' Mound, was likely a burial site, with four separate terraces for crowds to gather. Centuries of neglect and erosion have taken their toll on what was once the largest human-made earthen mound in North America.

was practically empty. Nevertheless, Cahokia represented the growing networks of trade and migration across North America, and it demonstrated the ability of North Americans to organize vibrant commercial societies and powerful states.

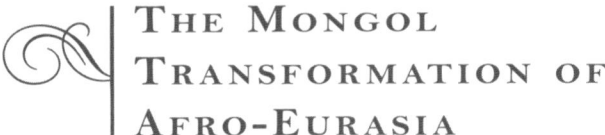

THE MONGOL TRANSFORMATION OF AFRO-EURASIA

> → *How did Mongol conquests affect cross-cultural contacts and regional development in Afro-Eurasia?*

The world's sea-lanes grew crowded with ships; ports buzzed with activity. Commercial networks were clearly one way to integrate the world. But just as long-distance trade connected people, so could conquerors—as we have seen throughout the history of the early world. In this instance, these transformative conquerors came from the inner Eurasian steppe lands, the same place where horse-riding warriors such as the Xiongnu originated centuries earlier (see Chapters 6 and 7). Like the Xiongnu and the Kushans before them, the Mongols would both conquer peoples and intensify trade and cultural exchange. By setting up a latticework of states across northern and central Asia, the Mongols created a new empire that straddled the east and west. (See Map 10-10.) It was unstable, and not as durable as other dynasties. It did

not even have a shared faith; the mother of the conquering emperors, Hulagu and Kubilai Khan, was a devout Christian, reflecting the success of Nestorian missionaries who had been laboring for centuries to bring about conversions among the animistic nomads. Many Europeans hoped and prayed that the entire empire would convert. But it did not; the Mongols were a religious patchwork of Afro-Eurasian belief systems. Yet the Mongols succeeded in bringing parts of the world together.

Who were these conquerors of territories so much larger than their own? The Mongols were a combination of forest and prairie peoples. Residing in circular, felt-covered tents, which they shared with some of their animals, the Mongols lived by a combination of hunting and livestock herding. A mobile society, they changed campgrounds with the seasons, hunting game and herding livestock south in winter and north in summer. Life on the steppes was a constant struggle, which meant that only the strong survived. Their food, consisting primarily of animal products from their herds or from game they hunted, provided high levels of protein, which built up their muscle mass and added to their strength. Always on the march, the Mongols created a society that resembled a perpetual standing army. Their bands were organized into strictly disciplined military units led by commanders chosen for their skill. Mongol archers, using a heavy compound bow, made of sinew, wood, and horns, could fire an arrow more than 200 yards at full gallop with accuracy. Mongol horses were stocky, and capable of withstanding extreme cold. Their saddles had high supports in front and back, enabling the warriors to ride and maneuver at high speeds. Iron stirrups permitted the riders to rise in their saddles to shoot their arrows without stopping. The Mongols were expert horsemen, who could remain in the saddle all day and night, even sleeping while their horses continued on the move. Each warrior kept many horses, enabling Mongol armies to travel as many as sixty or seventy miles per day. Between military campaigns, soldiers kept sharp by engaging in winter hunting.

Mongol tribes were imperialists in a special way: while they conquered they also adjoined their conquests by extending kinship networks. In this fashion, the empire was made of a confederation of familial tribes. The tents (households) were interrelated mostly by marriage; that is, they were alliances sealed by exchange of daughters. Conquest involved marrying conquering men to the women of the conquered, and selecting conquered men to marry the conqueror's women. Chinggis Khan is said to have had more than 500 wives, most of them daughters of tribes that he conquered or that sought alliance with him. As a result a great proportion of steppe chiefs were kin. Patrimony was king, but empire was achieved through the exchange of women.

Women in Mongol society were responsible for child-rearing as well as shearing and milking livestock and processing their pelts for clothing. But women also took part in

MAP 10-10   MONGOL CAMPAIGNS AND CONQUESTS

Mongol campaigns and conquests brought Afro-Eurasian worlds together as never before. What cultural groups were conquered, partially conquered, or invaded by Mongol armies? How did the Mongol armies treat and govern those they conquered? Were the Mongols capable of eradicating cultural distinctions that had emerged in Afro-Eurasia over the previous millennium?

SIBERIA

Lake Baikal

MONGOL ANCESTRAL HOMELAND

Karakorum

GOBI DESERT

CHAGATAI

Shangdu (Xanadu)

Dadu

Khanbaliq (Beijing)

Kaifeng

KHANATE OF THE GREAT KHAN (YUAN EMPIRE)

TIBET

Yangzhou

Hangzhou

KORYO

SEA OF JAPAN

KAMAKURA SHOGUNATE

Kyoto

JAPAN

BURMA

Guangzhou

ANNAM

CHAMPA

KHMER EMPIRE

SOUTH CHINA SEA

PACIFIC OCEAN

SUMATRA

BORNEO

JAVA

0   500   1000 Miles
0   500   1000 Kilometers

← Mongol campaigns
/// Area of loose or temporary Mongol control

Mongols on Horseback. Even after the Mongols became the rulers of China, the emperors remembered their steppe origin and maintained the skills of horse-riding nomads. This detail from a thirteenth/fourteenth-century silk painting shows Kubilai Khan at hunting.

that each son acquired a different second language that would aid in administrating conquered lands. She gathered Confucian scholars to prepare Kubilai Khan to rule China. Chabi, Kubilai's senior wife, followed a similar pattern, offering patronage to Tibetan monks who set about converting the Mongol elite in China to Tibetan Buddhism.

At least initially, the nomads' desire for conquests may have been fueled by their need for grazing lands. Then, as the Mongols moved into new lands, they were able to increase their wealth enormously by extracting taxes through their tributary system. Trade disputes were also a powerful spur to their expeditions. The Mongols were dependent on trade with settled peoples, seeking especially grain but also manufactured goods (including iron for tools, wagons, weapons, bridles, and stirrups), and their first expansionist forays followed caravan routes. Here were opportunities to raid instead of trade.

The nomads' expansionist thrust began in 1206, when a cluster of tribes joined into a united force. A large gathering of clan heads acclaimed one of those present as Chinggis (Genghis) Khan, or Supreme Ruler. Chinggis (c. 1155–1227) subsequently launched a series of conquests southward across the Great Wall of China, and westward through central Asia to Afghanistan and Persia. The Mongols also launched a massive invasion of Korea in 1231. Although the Korean armies fiercely resisted, the Koryo state was no match for the well-organized horsemen from the northern steppe. The armies of Chinggis's son and first successor reached both the Pacific Ocean and the Adriatic Sea. His grandsons founded dynasties in China, Persia, and on the southern Eurasian steppes east of Europe. One of them, Kubilai Khan, enlisted thousands of Koryo men and ships for ill-fated invasions of Japan in 1274 and 1281. Thus, a realm took shape that was more than 6,000 miles wide and touched all four of Afro-Eurasia's main worlds.

Mongol raiders built a permanent empire by incorporating conquered peoples and by absorbing some of their ways. By stretching their power across the northern arch of Afro-Eurasia, horsemen bypassed the Pamir watershed, which divides central Asia into eastern and western portions. This unification was far more surprising and sudden than the ties developed incrementally by traders and travelers on ships. Now, Afro-Eurasian regions were connected by land and by sea, in historically unparalleled ways.

MONGOLS IN CHINA

In 1200, the north of China was still under the control of the Jin dynasty (1115–1234), which was led by Jurchen, who had driven the Song into the south. The Song court and its Chinese followers had regrouped in the south and called themselves the "Southern Song." As the political and military upheaval continued in the north, much of the economic ac-

battles. Kubilai Khan's niece Khutulun became famous for besting men in wrestling matches and claiming their horses as spoils. Although women were often bought and sold, Mongol wives had the right to own property and even to divorce. Elite Mongol women played important political roles. Sorghaghtani Beki, Kubilai Khan's birth mother, helped to engineer the rule of her sons. Illiterate herself, she made sure

→ *How did Mongol conquests affect cross-cultural contacts and regional development in Afro-Eurasia?*

Mongolian Warriors. This miniature painting is one of the illustrations for *History* by Rashid al Din, the most outstanding scholar under the Mongol regimes. Note the relatively small horses and strong bows used by the Mongol soldiers.

tivity of trade and finance moved southward and focused on their new capital, Hangzhou. This former provincial seaport became the political center of the Chinese people in their ongoing struggles with northern steppe nomads. It also became one of China's gateways to the rest of the world via the South China Sea. Agrarian staples and precious manufactures poured out of southern China to feed and clothe people in distant markets, as Chinese precious goods were coveted by elites far and wide.

The Jin fell fairly quickly in 1234 because of the Mongols' superiority in cavalry on the North China Plain. But below the Yangzi River, the climate and weather changed, no longer favoring the Mongol horsemen against Southern Song forces. They grew ill from diseases such as malaria, and their horses perished from the heat. To conquer the semitropical south, the Mongols increasingly took to boats and fought along rivers and canals, as Chinese had done since the Three Kingdoms period and during the Sui and Tang reunifications. Kubilai, Chinggis's grandson, completed the conquest of the grandest prize of all—southern China—after 1260. His generals marched their cavalries through the higher plateaus of Sichuan and Yunnan in southwest China, and then attacked South China's economic heartland from the west. The Southern Song army, composed of hired mercenaries, proved unable to withstand the onslaught of warriors who were armed with the latest gunpowder-based weapons (developed from a technology originally invented by the Chinese themselves).

Still, Mongol armies pressed south until they reached the outskirts of Hangzhou; this last Song capital succumbed to the invaders in 1276. Rather than see the invaders pillage the city and the tombs of the emperors, they bowed to the inevitable. The Song court was in disarray: the young emperor had died suddenly in 1274, and all his heirs were minors. The new regents for the successor and the Empress Dowager were unable to handle the internal chaos and the advancing army. Meanwhile, Kubilai Khan's most trusted and able commander, Bayan, led his crack Mongol forces as they seized town after town, ever closer to the capital. The Empress Dowager tried to buy off the invaders, as the Chinese had often done in the past, proposing regular and substantial tribute payments—250,000 taels of silver and 250,000 bolts of silk—but Bayan had his eye on the prize: Hangzhou.

On the eve of the city's fall in 1276, the Empress Dowager presented Bayan with the Song dynasty's seal, the sign that she had given up. Later the Song emperor appeared in person and submitted to the new masters of the city. Bayan was magnanimous in his victory. He ordered his men to conduct a census of Hangzhou and register its granaries and treasury. He also prohibited his men from plundering the suburban tombs of the Southern Song emperors—in contrast to the Jin conquerors, who in 1127 had pillaged the Northern Song tombs outside Kaifeng. Bayan also escorted the Song emperor and the Empress Dowager to Beijing, where Kubilai treated them with honor. Pockets of resistance persisted after 1276, but within three years Song China's defeat was complete. Having extended their military sway over all of South China, the Mongols established the Yuan dynasty (1280–1368) with a new capital at Dadu ("Great Capital," present-day Beijing).

Global Connections & Disconnections

THE TRAVELS OF MARCO POLO AND IBN BATTUTA

Although no traveler crossed the Atlantic or Pacific oceans, an increasing number ventured through the lands of Africa, Europe, and Asia. The most famous of these thirteenth- and fourteenth-century travelers, Marco Polo and Ibn Battuta, encountered a world tied together by trade routes that crossed the Afro-Eurasian landmass and the Indian Ocean that often had as their ultimate destination the imperial court of the Great Khan in China. These two men and similar, though less-celebrated travelers, observed worlds that were both highly localized and yet had culturally unifying features.

In 1271, Marco Polo (1254–1324), the son of an enterprising Venetian merchant, set out with his father and uncle on a journey to East Asia. Making their way along the fabled silk route across central Asia, the Polos arrived in Xanadu, the summer capital of the Mongol empire, after a three-and-a-half year journey. There they remained for more than two decades. When they returned to their home in Venice in 1295, fellow townsmen greeted them with astonishment, so sure were they that the Polos had perished years before. So, too, Marco Polo's published account of his travels generated an incredulous reaction. Some of his European readers considered his tales of Eastern wonders to be mere fantasy, yet others found their appetites for Asian splendor whetted by Polo's descriptions.

A half-century after Polo commenced his travels, the Moroccan-born scholar Muhammad ibn Abdullah ibn Battuta (1304–1369) embarked on a journey of his own. Then just twenty-one, Ibn Battuta vowed to visit the whole of the Islamic world without traveling the same road twice. It was an ambitious assignment, for Islam's domain extended from one end of the Eurasian landmass to the other and far into Africa as well. On his journey, Ibn Battuta eventually covered some 75,000 miles and traveled through West and East Africa, across the interior of Asia, and beyond the realm of Islam to China. Along his way, he claimed to have met at least sixty rulers, and in his book he recorded the names of more than 2,000 persons whom he knew personally.

Marco Polo and Ibn Battuta provide a wealth of information on the well-traversed lands of Africa, Europe, and Asia. What they and other travelers observed was the extreme diversity that characterized the peoples living in Afro-Eurasia, where numerous ethnicities, many political formations, and varied religious faiths and practices prevailed. In addition, they observed that the vast majority of people lived deeply localized lives, the primary goal of which was to obtain the basic necessities of everyday living. Yet, they were also aware that these very same societies, however local their orientations, welcomed and even encouraged contact, trade, and cultural exchange over long distances and between regions. In fact, they wrote most eloquently about the way in which each of the four major cultural systems of the Afro-Eurasian landmass—Christian, Muslim, Indian, and Chinese—struggled to articulate definitions of themselves. Interestingly, if Ibn Battuta and Marco Polo had been able to travel in the "unknown" worlds—the African hinterlands, the Americas, and Oceania—they would have witnessed to varying degrees similar phenomena and challenges.

The exploits of Marco Polo and Ibn Battuta suggest that a few men and women, mainly merchants and scholars, routinely traversed immense distances. These travelers used and strengthened existing trade routes between regions and fostered contacts across cultural boundaries. Their journeys revealed a Eurasian world linked from the Mediterranean in the west to China in the east. Along the trade routes, merchants, travelers, commodities, and ideas circulated freely through great port cities such as Surat and Calicut along the Malabar coast in India; Zanzibar and Kilwa in East Africa; and Genoa, Venice, and Alexandria along the northern and southern shores of the Mediterranean Sea.

Although it fell in 1276, Hangzhou survived the Mongol conquest reasonably intact. However, the tombs of the Song royal family were ransacked for valuables in 1285 to raise funds for the construction and renovation of Buddhist monasteries and temples. It was still, when the Venetian traveler Marco Polo visited it in the 1280s and the Muslim traveler Ibn Battuta in the 1340s, one of the greatest cities in the world. They both agreed that neither Europe nor the Islamic world had anything like it.

After defeating the Jin in northern China in 1234 and the Southern Song by 1280, the Mongol conquest changed the political and social landscape. The population in the north, especially in Kaifeng, already had begun to drop precipitously under the Jin. When the demand for iron ores and coal dried up, steel production declined; it came to almost a total halt after the Yellow River shifted south in 1194, severing Kaifeng, as the key industrial city in the north, from its iron mines and smelters. By 1330, now under the Mongols, the once magnificent Kaifeng, with a population once exceeding a million, had become a ramshackle town of fewer than 90,000 inhabitants.

Mongol rule did not involve the imposition of rough ways of the steppe lands on "civilized" urbanite Chinese (though such was the view of Han ideologues). True, China acquired a new ruling hierarchy. Chinese Confucian insiders were relegated to a subordinate station—and withdrew to exercise power, to the extent they were permitted, at the local level. Outsiders, non-Chinese known as the *semu* (categorized peoples), took over political control. They themselves were a heterogeneous group of Afro-Eurasian peoples—Mongols, Tanguts, Khitan, Jurchen, Muslims, Tibetans, Persians, Turks, Nestorians, Jews, Armenians—a new conquering elite that ruled over a vast Han majority. The result was a segmented ruling system, in which incumbent Chinese elites governed locally while newcomers who came from around Afro-Eurasia handled the levers of the central dynastic polity and collected taxes for the Mongols.

MONGOL REVERBERATIONS IN SOUTHEAST ASIA

Southeast Asia was also whiplashed by the Mongol conquests. Circling Song defenses along the rivers and lakes in South China, the Mongols marched into the southwest and conquered the states of Dali and Pyu in Yunnan and Burma. From there, in the 1270s, the armies turned back to China, heading directly east into the soft underbelly of the Song state. In this sweep, portions of mainland Southeast Asia became part of the Mongol empire and thus were annexed to China for the first time. As the kingdom of Dali and other polities became prefectures of Mongol-ruled China, the autonomy that the southwest had enjoyed since the Han and Tang dynasties came to an end. Even the distant Khmer regime felt the consequences of the Mongol conquest of the Song dynasty when

the Mongol fleet passed by on the way to attack and take Java—unsuccessfully, as it turned out—in 1293.

THE FALL OF BAGHDAD

As in China, in Islamic lands the brunt of foreign invasions was borne by the empire's core. By this time Baghdad had become a mere shadow of its former glorious self, though caliphs continued to sit on the throne, proclaiming their dominion over all the Islamic world. From their earlier attacks on the Islamic borderlands of central Asia, Mongol raiding parties learned of the weaknesses and divisions of Islamic rulers in the heartlands.

In the thirteenth century, Mongol tribesmen streamed west out of the eastern steppes, crossing the whole of Asia and entering into the eastern parts of Europe. Mongke Khan, a grandson of the great Mongol unifier and war leader Chinggis, made clear the Mongol aspiration for world domination, appointing his brother Kubilai to rule over China, Tibet, and the northern parts of India and commanding another brother, Hulagu, to add the western territories of Iran, Syria, Egypt, Byzantium, and Armenia to the Mongol imperium.

When Hulagu reached Baghdad in 1258, he encountered a feeble foe: merely 10,000 horsemen faced his army of 200,000 soldiers, who were eager to acquire the booty of a wealthy city at the crossroads of Afro-Eurasian commerce. Even before the battle had taken place, Baghdadis knew the fate that awaited them. Poets were composing elegies for the dead and mourning the defeat of Islam.

The slaughter was vast, and few were spared. Hulagu himself boasted to one of the European kings that he had taken the lives of at least 200,000 people. The Mongols gave no quarter, pursuing their adversaries everywhere. They hunted them in wells, latrines, and sewers and followed them into the upper floors of buildings, killing them on rooftops until, as the Iraqi Arab historian Ibn Kathir observed, "blood poured from the gutters into the streets. . . . The same happened in the mosques and . . . Baghdad, which had been the most civilized of all cities, became a ruin with only a few inhabitants" (Lewis, pp. 82–83). In a few weeks of sheer terror, the venerable Abbasid caliphate was demolished. Hulagu's forces showed no mercy to the caliph himself, who was rolled up in a carpet and trampled to death by horses, his blood soaked up by the rug so it would leave no mark on the ground. With Baghdad crushed, the Mongol armies pushed on to Syria, slaughtering Muslims along the way. A succession crisis in the Mongol heartland pulled Hulagu away from the front, however.

In the end, the Egyptian Mamluks, an Islamic regime built by slave-soldiers, stemmed the advance of the Mongol armies in 1261, thereby preventing Egypt from falling into Mongol hands. The Mongol empire had reached its outer limits. Better at conquering than controlling, defeating rather than governing, the Mongols struggled to rule their vast possessions in makeshift states. But bit by bit, and with gathering speed, they ceded control to local administrators and dynasties who promised to govern as their surrogates. There was also chronic feuding among the Mongol dynasts, especially between jealous sons. In China and in Persia, Mongol rule collapsed in the fourteenth century.

Mongol conquest reshaped the social landscape of Afro-Eurasia. Islam was decisively transformed: never again would it have a unifying authority like the caliphate or a powerful center like Baghdad. Though not sundered in quite the way Islam's heartland was, China was divided and changed in other ways. The Mongols introduced many Persian, Islamic, and Byzantine influences on China's architecture, art, science, and medicine. The Yuan policy of benign tolerance for foreign creeds and consistent contacts with western Asia also brought elements from Christianity, Judaism, Zoroastrianism, and Islam into the Chinese mix. The Mongol thrust into China thus led to a flowering and great opening, as fine goods, traders, and technology would flow unstintingly from China to the rest of the world in the ensuing centuries. Finally, the Mongol state, after its bloody conquests, settled down and promoted an Afro-Eurasian interconnectedness that this huge territorial landmass had not known before and would not experience again for many centuries. Out of conquest and translandmass warfare would come centuries of trade, migration, and increasing contacts among Africa, Europe, and Asia.

Chronology

	700 CE	800 CE	900 CE	1000 CE
SUB-SAHARAN AFRICA				
THE AMERICAS		Toltec Empire in Mexico Valley, c. 900–1100 ∎	Moche people found Chan Chan, c. 900 ∎	Cahokia flourishes as a commercial hub in Mississippi River valley, c. 1000 ∎
				Chimú Empire, 1000–1460 ∎
THE ISLAMIC WORLD				Muslims become a majority in Abassid caliphate ∎
SOUTH ASIA				Turkish invasions from Central Asia begin ∎
EAST ASIA		∎ Heian period in Japan, 794–1185	Song dynasty founded, 960 ∎	
			Koryo dynasty rules, 918–1392 ∎	
			Lady Shikibu (c. 976–c. 1031) writes The Tale of Genji ∎	
			Gunpowder invented ∎	
SOUTHEAST ASIA			Khmer kingdom, 899–1431 ∎	
CHRISTIAN EUROPE				Iaroslav the Wise (1016–1054) rebu Kiev as a small scale Constantino

CONCLUSION

Between 1000 and 1300, the world of Afro-Eurasia was being divided into large cultural spheres. At the same time, as people traded and migrated across longer distances, the regions of Afro-Eurasia prospered and became more integrated. In the center of Afro-Eurasia, Islam was firmly ensconced, its merchants, scholars, and travelers taking full advantage of their location to serve as commercial and cultural intermediaries joining the entire landmass together. As Indian Ocean seaborne trade expanded, India, too, became a commercial crossroads. Merchants set up businesses in the Indian port cities and welcomed traders who arrived from the Arab lands to the west, from China, and from Southeast Asia. China also boomed, pouring its manufactures into trading networks that encompassed all of Afro-Eurasia and reached into African frontiers.

Trade helped delineate the parts of the world. The prosperity it brought also helped create new classes of peoples—thinkers, writers, and naturalists—who more clearly defined what it meant to belong to the regions of Afro-Eurasia. By 1300, learned priests and writers had begun to reimagine each of the world's regions as more than just territories: they were ideas that were now maturing into cultures with definable—and defensible—geographic boundaries. More and more these intellectuals sought to deliver their messages to commoners as well as to rulers.

1100 CE	1200 CE	1300 CE	1400 CE
▮ Kingdom of Mali emerges	▮ Swahili emerges as a distinct language linking the coast of East Africa		
▮ Great Zimbabwe	▮ Mandinka merchants establish vast commercial networks linking West Africa		
	King Mansa Musa of Mali (ruled 1312–1332) completes the hajj, 1325–1326 ▮		
▮ Turkish forces defeat Byzantine armies at Manzikert, 1071			
▮ Ibn Rushd (1126–1198) refines rationalist philosophy			
	▮ Jalal al-Din Rumi (1207–1273) spreads Sufi ideas		
	▮ Mongol forces sack Baghdad, end Abassid caliphate, 1258		
	▮ Turkish warriors found Delhi Sultanate in northern India, 1206–1526		
	▮ Buddhism loses almost all influence in India		
		▮ Japan fends off Mongol invasions, 1274–1281	
▮ Song iron production peaks, 1078		▮ Mongols conquer Southern Song dynasty, 1279	
▮ Song dynasty loses North China to Jurchen Jin dynasty, 1127		▮ Mongol invasions of Korea	
Kamakura shogunate, 1192–1333 ▮		▮ Yuan dynasty, 1280–1368	
	▮ Islamic influence increases in city-states		
	▮ Mongols invade southwestern China and Burma		
		▮ Mongol fleet attacks Java, 1293	
	▮ Francis of Assisi (1182–1226) preaches message of repentance		
	▮ Genoese ships link northern and southern Europe by sea		
▮ Spanish Reconquista, 1061–1492	▮ Half of Europe's population lives in its west		
▮ Crusades, 1095–1272			
▮ Roman Catholic farmers migrate from the western to central and eastern European frontier zones			

While Afro-Eurasia was increasingly carved up into large cultural blocs with more rigid identities and boundaries, neither the Americas nor sub-Saharan Africa saw quite the same degree of integration. But trade and migration in these areas of the world did have profound effects. Great African cultures flourished as they came into contact with the commercial energy of trade on the Indian Ocean. Indeed, Africans' trade with one another grew, bringing together coastal and interior regions into an ever-more integrated world. American peoples also built great cities that dominated large cultural areas and thrived through long-distance and regional trade. American cultures shared significant common features—reliance on trade, maize, and the exchange of similar status goods, such as shells and precious feathers. And larger and larger areas honored the same spiritual centers.

By 1300, trade, migration, and conflict were making the Afro-Eurasian regional worlds interconnected in unprecedented ways. When Mongol armies swept into China, into Southeast Asia, and into the heart of Islam, they applied a veneer of political integration to these dispersed parts and built on strong commercial links that already existed. But it is worth reminding ourselves that most people lived local lives, governed by the perennial need for subsistence and by the micro-level powers of spiritual and governmental agents who acted at the behest of distant and very remote authorities. Still, locals could see and hear the evidence of cross-cultural exchanges everywhere—in the clothing styles of provincial elites, such as Chinese silks in Paris or Quetzal plumes in northern Mexico; in enticements to move (and forced removals) to new frontiers; in the news of faraway conquests or advancing armies. In these ways, worlds were coming together within themselves and across their territorial boundaries, while remaining apart as they sought to maintain their own identity and traditions. In Afro-Eurasia especially, as the movement and goods and peoples shifted from ancient land routes to sea-lanes, these long-distance contacts were more frequent and far-reaching. Never before had the world seen so much activity that connected its parts. Nor within those parts had it ever seen so much shared cultural affinity—linguistic, religious, legal, and military. Indeed, by the time of the rise of the Mongol empire, the regions that composed the globe were those that we now recognize as the cultural spheres of today's world.

STUDY QUESTIONS

 WWNORTON.COM/STUDYSPACE

1. List the major cultural regions that existed in the thirteenth century that are explored in this chapter and explain where they were. Which of these regions were "together" and which were "apart"? How were regions connected?

2. List the four major cultural regions in Afro-Eurasia and briefly explain the defining characteristics of each. What did the various people and groups in these geographic areas all have in common that distinguished them from others?

3. Explain the role of global commercial hubs in India, China, and Egypt in fostering global commercial contacts across Afro-Eurasia. How did they reflect revolutions in maritime transportation?

4. Explain which areas of sub-Saharan Africa were parts of the larger Afro-Eurasian world by 1300. How did contact with other regions shape political and cultural developments in sub-Saharan Africa?

5. Describe the cultural diversity within the Islamic world during this era. How were these diverse communities integrated into a uniform regional identity?

6. Analyze the impact of Muslim Turkish invaders on India between 1000 and 1300. To what extent did India remain distinct from the Islamic world in this era?

7. Describe how the Song dynasty reacted to the military strength of its pastoral neighbors. How did these relationships foster a separate and distinct Chinese identity during this era?

8. Compare and contrast cultural and political developments in Korea, Japan, and Southeast Asia during this era. How were these societies influenced by other regional cultures?

9. Describe how Christianity expanded its geographic reach during this era. How did this expansion affect Latin Christianity in western Europe and Orthodox Christianity in eastern Europe?

10. Analyze the extent to which peoples in the Americas established closer contact with each other during this era. How extensive were these contacts compared with those in the Afro-Eurasian world?

11. Describe the empire created by the Mongols in the thirteenth century. How did Mongol policies bring the various regions of Afro-Eurasia into greater contact with each other?

FURTHER READINGS

Allsen, Thomas, *Commodity and Exchange in the Mongol Empire: A Cultural History of Islamic Textiles* (1997). A study that uses golden brocade, the textile most treasured by Mongol rulers, as a lens through which to analyze the vast commercial networks facilitated by the Mongol conquests and control.

———, *Culture and Conquest in Mongol Eurasia* (2001). A work that emphasizes the cultural and scientific exchanges that took place across Afro-Eurasia as a result of the Mongol conquest.

Bartlett, Robert, *The Making of Europe: Conquest, Colonization and Cultural Change, 950–1350* (1993). The modes of cultural, political, and demographic expansion of feudal Europe along its frontiers, especially in eastern Europe.

Bay, Edna G., *Wives of the Leopards: Gender, Politics, and Culture in the Kingdom of Dahomey* (1998). A work that stresses the role of women in an important West African society and dips into the early history of this area.

Beach, D. N., *Shona and Zimbabwe, 900–1850: An Outline of Shona History* (1980). A good place to start for exploring the history of Great Zimbabwe.

Brooks, George E., *Landlords and Strangers: Ecology, Society, and Trade in Western Africa, 1000–1630* (1993). A survey assembled from primary sources of early West African history that stresses transregional connections.

Buzurg ibn Shahriyar of Ramhormuz, *The Book of the Wonders of India: Mainland, Sea and Islands*, ed. and trans. G. S. P. Freeman-Greenville (1981). A collection of stories told by sailors, both true and fantastic; they help us imagine the lives of sailors of the era.

Chappell, Sally A. Kitt, *Cahokia: Mirror of the Cosmos* (2002). A thorough and vivid account of the "mound people"; it explores not just what we know of Cahokia but how we know it.

Christian, David, *A Short History of Russia, Central Asia, and Mongolia*, vol. 1, *Inner Eurasia from Prehistory to the Mongol Empire* (1998). Essential reading for students interested in interconnections across the Afro-Eurasian landmass.

Curtin, Philip, *Cross-Cultural Trade in World History* (1984). A groundbreaking book on intercultural trade with a primary focus on Africa, especially the cross-Saharan trade and Swahili coastal trade.

Dawson, Christopher, *Mission to Asia* (1980). Accounts of China and the Mongol Empire brought back by Catholic missionaries and diplomats after 1240 CE.

Foltz, Richard C., *Religions of the Silk Road: Overland Trade and Cultural Exchange from Antiquity to the Fifteenth Century* (1999). A study of the populations and the cities of the Silk Road as transmitters of culture across long distances.

Franklin, Simon, and Jonathan Shepherd, *The Emergence of Rus: 750–1200* (1996). The formation of medieval Russia between the Baltic and the Black Sea.

Gibb, Hamilton A. R., *Saladin: Studies in Islamic History*, ed. Yusuf Ibish (1974). A sympathetic portrait of one of Islam's leading political and military figures.

Goitein, S. D., *Letters of Medieval Jewish Traders* (1973). The classic study of medieval Jewish trading communities based on the commercial papers deposited in the Cairo Geniza (a synagogue storeroom) during the tenth and eleventh centuries; it explores not only commercial activities but also the personal lives of the traders around the Indian Ocean basin.

———, *A Mediterranean Society: An Abridgment in One Volume*, rev. and ed. Jacob Lassner (1999). A portrait of the Jewish merchant community with ties across the Afro-Eurasian landmass, based largely on the documents from the Cairo Geniza (of which Goitein was the primary researcher and interpreter).

———, "New Light on the Beginnings of the Karim Merchant," *The Journal of Social and Economic History of the Orient* 1 (1958). Goiten's description of Egyptian trade.

Harris, Joseph E., *The African Presence in Asia: Consequences of the East African Slave Trade* (1971). One of the few books that looks broadly at the impact of Africans and African slavery on the societies of Asia.

Hartwell, Robert, "Demographic, Political, and Social Transformations of China, 750–1550," *Harvard Journal of Asiatic Studies* 42 (1982): 365–442. A pioneering study of the demographic changes that overtook China during the Tang and Song dynasties, which are described in light of political reform movements and social changes in this seminal era.

Historical Relations across the Indian Ocean: Report and Papers of the Meeting of Experts Organized by UNESCO at Port Louis, Mauritius, from 15 to 19 July, 1974 (1980). Excellent essays on the connections of Africa with Asia across the Indian Ocean.

Hitti, Philip, *An Arab-Syrian Gentleman and Warrior in the Period of the Crusades: Memoirs of Usāmah ibn-Munqidh* (1929). The Crusaders seen through Muslim eyes.

Holt, P. M., *The Age of the Crusades: The Near East from the Eleventh Century to 1517* (1984). The Crusades period as seen from the eastern Mediterranean and through the lens of a leading British scholar of the area.

Hymes, Robert, and Conrad Schirokauer (eds.), *Ordering the World: Approaches to State and Society in Sung Dynasty China* (1993). A collection of essays that traces the intellectual, social, and political movements that shaped the Song state and its elites.

Ibn Battuta, *The Travels of Ibn Battuta*, trans. H.A.R. Gibb (2002). A readable translation of the classic book, originally published in 1929.

Ibn Fadlan, Ahmad, *Ibn Fadlan's Journey to Russia: A Tenth Century Traveler from Baghdad to the Volga River,* trans. with commentary by Richard Frye (2005). A coherent summary of the firsthand observations by an envoy who traveled from Baghdad to Russia.

Irwin, Robert, *The Middle East in the Middle Ages: The Early Mamluk Sultanate, 1250–1582* (1986). Egypt under Mamluk rule.

Lancaster, Lewis, Kikun Suh, and Chai-shin Yu (eds.), *Buddhism in Koryo: A Royal Religion* (1996). A description of Buddhism at its height in the Koryo period, when the religion made significant contributions to the development of Korean culture and monasteries of great beauty were constructed.

Levtzion, Nehemia, and Randall L. Pouwels (eds.), *The History of Islam in Africa* (2000). A useful general survey of the place of Islam in African history.

Lewis, Bernard (trans.), *Islam from the Prophet Muhammad to the Caphre of Constantinople* (1974). Vol. 2: Religion and Society. A fine collection of original sources that portray various aspects of classical Islamic society.

Lopez, Robert S., *The Commercial Revolution of the Middle Ages, 950–1350* (1976). An account focusing on the development around the Mediterranean of commercial practices such as the use of currency, accounting, and credit.

Maalouf, Amin, *The Crusades through Muslim Eyes*, trans. Jon Rothschild (1984). The European Crusaders as seen by the Muslim world.

Marcus, Harold G., *A History of Ethiopia* (2002). An authoritative overview of the history of this great culture.

Mass, Jeffrey, *Yoritomo and the Founding of the First Bakufu: The Origins of Dual Government in Japan* (1999). A revisionist account of how the Kamakura military leader Minamoto Yoritomo established the "dual polity" of court and warrior government in Japan.

McDermott, Joseph, *A Social History of the Chinese Book: Books and Literati Culture in Late Imperial China* (2006). The history of the book in China traced since the Song dynasty, with comparisons to the role of books in other civilizations, particularly the European.

McIntosh, Roderik, *The Peoples of the Middle Niger: The Island of Gold* (1988). A historical survey of an area often omitted from other textbooks.

Moore, Jerry D., *Cultural Landscapes in the Ancient Andes: Archaeologies of Place* (2005). The most recent and up-to-date analysis of findings based on recent archaeological evidence, emphasizing the importance of local cultures and diversity in the Andes.

Niane, D. T. (ed.), *Africa from the Twelfth to the Sixteenth Century,* vol. 4 of *General History of Africa* (1984). The general UNESCO history of Africa's volume on four centuries of African history. This work features the scholarship of Africans.

Oliver, Roland (ed.), *From c. 1050 to c. 1600,* vol. 3 of *The Cambridge History of Africa,* ed. J. D. Fage and Roland Oliver (1977). Another general survey of African history. This volume draws heavily on the work of British scholars.

Parry, J. H., *The Age of Reconnaissance: Discovery, Exploration and Settlement, 1450–1650* (1981). This book connects intellectual and technological developments of the Renaissance to the explorations of the new world.

Peters, Edward, *The First Crusade* (1971). The Crusaders as seen through their own eyes.

Petry, Carl F. (ed.), *Islamic Egypt, 640–1517,* vol. 1 of *The Cambridge History of Egypt,* ed. M. W. Daly (1998). A solid overview of the history of Islamic Egypt up to the Ottoman conquest.

Polo, Marco, *The Travels of Marco Polo,* ed. Manuel Komroff (1926). A solid translation of Marco Polo's famous account.

Popovic, Alexandre, *The Revolt of African Slaves in Iraq in the 3rd/9th Century,* trans. Leon King (1999). The account of a massive revolt against their slave masters by African slaves taken to labor in Iraq's mines and fields.

Scott, Robert, *Gothic Enterprise: A Guide to Understanding the Medieval Cathedral* (2003). The meaning and social function of religious building in medieval cities in northern Europe.

Shaffer, Lynda Norene, *Maritime Southeast Asia to 1500* (1996). A history of the peoples of the southeast fringe of the Eastern Hemisphere, up to the time that they became connected to the global commercial networks of the world.

Shimada, Izumi, "Evolution of Andean Diversity: Regional Formations (500 BCE–CE 600)," in Frank Salomon and Stuart Schwartz (eds.), *South America,* vol. 3 of *The Cambridge History of the Native Peoples of the Americas* (1999), part 1, pp. 350–517. A splendid overview that contrasts the varieties of lowland and highland cultures.

Steinberg, David Joel, et al., *In Search of Southeast Asia: A Modern History* (1987). An account of the emergence of the modern Southeast Asian polities of Cambodia, Burma, Thailand, and Indonesia.

Tyerman, Christopher, *God's War: A New History of the Crusades* (2006). The balance of religious and nonreligious motivations in the Crusades.

Waley, Daniel, *The Italian City-Republics,* 3rd ed. (1988). The structures and culture of the new cities of medieval Italy.

Watson, Andrew, *Agricultural Innovation in the Early Islamic World: The Diffusion of Crops and Farming Techniques, 700–1100* (1983). An impressive study of the spread of new crops throughout the Muslim world.

11

CRISES AND RECOVERY IN AFRO-EURASIA, 1300s–1500s

W hen Mongol armies besieged the Genoese trading outpost of Caffa on the Black Sea in 1346, they not only damaged old trading links between East Asia and the Mediterranean, they also unleashed an even more devastating, invisible force. Mongol troops entered the city and brought with them a disease picked up in the Gobi Desert: the bubonic plague. Defeated Genoese merchants and soldiers withdrew, inadvertently taking the germs with them aboard their ships. By the time they arrived in Messina, Sicily, half the passengers were dead. The rest were dying. Those who waited eagerly on shore were horrified at the sight and turned the ship away. Desperately, the ship's captain went to the next port, only to face the same fate. Despite this, the Europeans were unable to keep the plague (referred to as the Black Death) from reaching their shores. As it spread from port to port, it eventually contaminated all of Europe, killing about one-third of its population.

This story exemplifies one of the many disruptive effects of the Mongol invasions on societies across the Afro-Eurasian landmass. These invasions ushered in an age in which people of dispersed worlds engaged in greater communication and contact

473

across cultural and political borders. But in establishing and extending channels of exchange, the Mongols unwittingly created conduits for the flow of microbes to follow the land trails and sea lanes of human voyagers. These germs devastated societies even more decisively than did the Mongols. They were the real "murderous hordes" of world history, infecting people from every community, class, and culture they encountered. So staggering was the magnitude of the Black Death's toll that Afro-Eurasia did not regain the population densities of the thirteenth century for another 200 years. It shook many communities to their very cores. The interconnectedness that the Mongols had fostered fell apart. The most severely affected were those regions and populations that the Mongols had brought together. Settlements and commercial hubs along the old Silk Road and around the Mediterranean Sea and the South China Sea became places of dying. While segments of the Indian Ocean trading world experienced death and disruption, South Asian societies, which had escaped the Mongol conquest, were also spared the wholesale dying and political disruptions associated with the Black Death.

During the fourteenth and fifteenth centuries, following population loss, political crises, and widespread social disorders often caused by the plague, many Afro-Eurasian societies recovered their political vitality. They improved new means to rebuild their communities and attempted to build new dynasties—rule by royal hereditary households—to restore order and stability. The new rulers, merchants, and scholar-bureaucrats not only revived the old links between communities but also pioneered new commercial networks. In so doing, they created new polities, economic institutions, and social hierarchies across Afro-Eurasia—a world in which imperial dynasties became ever more important.

This chapter explores how Afro-Eurasian societies coped with and responded to the long-term impact of the Mongol invasions and the Black Death. We leave for subsequent chapters the discussions of political changes beyond Afro-Eurasia. Here, we focus on how Afro-Eurasian societies rebuilt their political orders, creating centralized power structures that lasted for centuries and that shaped their encounters with peoples and polities in Africa, the Americas, and Oceania. Here, too, we highlight several defining events and decisions that had far-reaching, if hardly predictable, consequences for reshaping the power relations between different parts of the world.

COLLAPSE AND INTEGRATION

> → *What were the key factors in rebuilding political societies?*

While the Mongol invasions overturned political systems, the plague devastated society itself. Afro-Eurasia's rulers could explain the assaults of outside "barbarians" to their people, but it was much harder for them to make sense of the invisible enemy. Many concluded fatalistically that mass death was God's wish. The upheaval wrought by the plague, however, provided rulers the opportunity to consolidate and centralize their power by making dynastic matches, putting in place new armies and taxes to support them, and establishing new systems to administer their states.

THE BLACK DEATH

The spread of the Black Death out of Mongolia in East Asia and other adjoining parts of central Asia was the single most significant historical development for much of the Afro-Eurasian world in the fourteenth century. The disease stemmed from a combination of bubonic, pneumonic, and septicaemic plague strains and resulted in a frightening loss of life. Among infected populations, death rates ranged from 25 to 50 percent.

Focus Questions CRISES AND RECOVERY IN AFRO-EURASIA

> → *What were the key factors in rebuilding political societies?*
> → *What were the major differences among the three Islamic dynasties?*
> → *Why did Europe remain disunited (and have difficulty recovering from the Black Death)?*
> → *How did the Ming centralize their authority?*

WWNORTON.COM/STUDYSPACE

How did the Black Death spread so far? One explanation seems to have been the climatic changes of this period. A drying up of the central Asian steppe borderlands may have forced rodents out of their usual dwelling places and also pressed the pastoral peoples who carried the strains, to move south into closer proximity to settled, agricultural communities. So, it is thought, began the migration of microbes. But what spread germs across Afro-Eurasia was the Mongols' economic and political grid. Breaking out first around the 1320s in the Yunnan province of southwestern China, the plague spread throughout China and then traversed the major Afro-Eurasian trade routes (see Map 11-1). The main avenue of transmission was across central Asia to the Crimea and the Black Sea, and from there by ship to the Mediterranean Sea and the Italian city-states. Secondary routes were by sea, one from China to the Red Sea and another across the Indian Ocean, through the Persian Gulf, and into the Fertile Crescent and Iraq. All routes terminated at the Italian port cities, where ships with dead and dying men aboard arrived in October 1347. From there, what Europeans at the time called the Pestilence or the Great Mortality spread across the western end of the Afro-Eurasian landmass.

The Black Death struck an expanding Afro-Eurasian population, made vulnerable because its members had no immunities to the disease and because its major cultural realms were now connected through more intensively used trading networks. Rodents, mainly rats, carried the plague bacilli that caused the disease. Fleas transmitted the bacilli from rodent to rodent, as well as to humans. The epidemic was terrifying, for the disease had not been seen for centuries and its causes were unknown at the time. The infected died quickly, sometimes overnight, and with great suffering, coughing up blood and oozing pus and blood from ugly black sores the size of eggs. Some European wise men attributed the ravaging of their societies to astrological forces; they suspected an unusual alignment of the planets Saturn, Jupiter, and Mars as the cause. Many believed that God was angry with man. The Florentine historian Matteo Villani compared the plague to the biblical Flood and believed that the end of mankind was imminent.

The Black Death wrought devastation throughout much of the Afro-Eurasian landmass. Entire populations perished. The Chinese population plunged from around 120 million to 80 million over the course of a century. Europe saw its numbers reduced by one-third. When farmers were afflicted, food production collapsed. As a result, famine often followed the disease, thereby killing off the weak survivors. But the worst afflicted were those in the crowded cities, especially in the ports along the Afro-Eurasian coast, which had been the hubs of trade and migration and where settlement was most dense. Some cities lost up to two-thirds of their population. Refugees from the cities fled their homes, seeking security and food in the countryside. The shortage of food and other necessities led to rapidly rising prices, strikes, and unrest across Afro-

Plague Victim. The plague was highly contagious and quickly led to death. Here the physician and his helper cover their noses to avoid the unbearable stench emanating from the patient; they can do little to help the victim as they do not understand what causes the boils, internal bleeding, or violent coughing that afflict him.

Eurasia. Political leaders added to their unpopularity by repressing unrest. The great Arab historian Ibn Khaldun (1332–1406), who lost his mother and father and a number of his teachers to the Black Death in Tunis, underscored the sense of desolation in the wake of the plague: "Cities and buildings were laid waste, roads and way signs were obliterated, settlements and mansions became empty, dynasties and tribes grew weak," he wrote. "The entire world changed."

REBUILDING STATES

Starting in the late fourteenth century, Afro-Eurasians began the task of rebuilding their political order and reconstructing their trading networks. Rebuilding military and tax administrations could not be tackled without political legitimacy.

SCANDINAVIA
• 1349

NORTH SEA

BALTIC SEA

Novgorod

MUSCOVY
• Moscow
1351

BRITAIN
Edinburgh
(1350)
Dublin
(1349)
Oxford
(1348)
London
(1348)

Danzig

Lübeck
(1349)

Bremen
(1349)

Cologne
(1349)

Amiens
(1348)

Paris
(1348)

EUROPE

Cracow

Kiev

Rostov

New Sarai

KHANATE OF THE
GOLDEN HORDE

ARAL
SEA

Bordeaux
(1348)

Avignon
(1347)

Genoa
(1347)

Venice
(1347)

Florence
(1347)

Siena
(1347)

Pisa
(1347)

Buda
(1349)

BLACK

Caffa
(1346)

SEA

CASPIAN
SEA

Silk route

Bukhara

Barcelona
(1348)

Marseille

Madrid

Naples

Constantinople
(1347)

Trebizond

Tabriz

Lisbon
(1349)

SPAIN
• 1348

Palermo
(1347)

Messina
(1347)

Athens
(1347)

Aleppo
(1347)

Baghdad
(1347)

Isfahan

PERSIA

IL-KHANA

Ceuta
Fez

Algiers

Tunis

Tripoli
(1348)

MEDITERRANEAN

SEA

Damascus
(1347)

Basra

Shiraz

Marrakesh
(1349)

Alexandria
(1347)

Cairo
(1347)

Hormuz

Persian Gulf

AFRICA

RED SEA

Mecca
(1348)

ARABIA

ARABIA

Aden
(1351)

Mogadishu

IND

ATLANTIC

OCEAN

Progress of bubonic plague
Trade routes
• Known areas of major outbreaks
* Modern Chinese provincial names for
regions affected by outbreak of plague

MAP 11-1   THE SPREAD OF THE BLACK DEATH

The Black Death was an Afro-Eurasian pandemic of the fourteenth century. Use the map to identify its place of origin. Can you explain why certain parts of Afro-Eurasia were more severely affected than others? Why were its major places of outbreak located in China and western Europe? The Black Death spread across the whole of the Mongol Empire. Can you offer any explanation why the Mongol states were so involved?

In much of Afro-Eurasia, this was the challenge of the fourteenth century. In the wake of disease, rulers needed to revive confidence in themselves and their polities, which they did by fostering beliefs and rituals that confirmed their legitimacy and by increasing their control over subject peoples.

The basis for power was the dynasty—the hereditary ruling family that passed power from one generation to the next. Dynasties sought to establish their legitimacy in three fundamental ways: First, the ruling families insisted that they belonged in power as a calling from above. The Ming emperors in China traditionally claimed a "mandate of heaven," while European monarchs claimed to rule by "divine right." Either way, ruling households claimed to be closer to the gods than to commoners. Second, leaders attempted to prevent squabbling and fighting among potential heirs by promulgating clear rules about succession to the throne. Clear-cut succession made it difficult for contenders to challenge the authority of the heir to the throne; many European nations tried to standardize succession by passing titles down to the eldest male heir, but in practice there were many complications and quarrels over the right to the throne. In the Islamic world, successors could be designated by the incumbent or elected by the community; but here too, struggles over succession occurred regularly. Third, ruling families elevated their power through conquest or alliance—sending armies to extend their domains or having princes and princesses marry the rulers of other states or members of other elite households. Once it established its legitimacy, the royal family would seek to consolidate its power by enacting coercive laws and punishments and sending royal emissaries to govern far-flung territories. It would also establish standing armies and set up new administrative structures to collect taxes and to oversee building projects that would proclaim royal power.

State-building in the wake of great devastation varied across Afro-Eurasia but usually drew upon older traditions. Some areas, like South Asia, had been spared the ravages of the Black Death, and some, like western Europe, had avoided conquest by the Mongols. In China, the Ming renounced the Mongol legacy, extolling their pure Han Chinese identity and repudiating the Mongol eagerness to expand. Two of the successor Islamic states, the Ottoman Empire and the Safavid state, had to deal with a large influx of Turkish-speaking peoples stemming from the Mongol invasion of the Islamic world; the third Islamic state, the Mughal Empire in South Asia, replaced the Delhi Sultanate, which had been seriously weakened, not by a Mongol army, but by Turkish warriors. Many of these regimes lasted for centuries; their political institutions and cultural values became deeply embedded in

Many of these regimes lasted for centuries; their political institutions and cultural values became deeply embedded in the fabric of their societies.

the fabric of their societies and influenced the actions of rulers and subjects at home and abroad.

ISLAMIC DYNASTIES

> → *What were the major differences among the three Islamic dynasties?*

In 1258 the Mongols sacked the great city of Baghdad, capital of the Abbasid Empire.

In doing so the Mongols had effectively destroyed older Islamic political regimes, but they failed to establish enduring dynasties. Part of their problem was that they were unable to shed their military orientation. The original Mongol state was organized for military action; economic advancement and cultural development occupied a decidedly secondary status in the minds of these military men, who were unwilling to share power with other groups. The Persian Il-khans made Maraghah in Azerbaijan their capital, even though it was little more than an enlarged military encampment, in preference to the great administrative center of Baghdad. They continued to employ terrorizing military tactics in dealing with their opponents, leveling recalcitrant villages and intimidating their subjects by parading the heads of their enemies on pikes before sullen resisters. Mongol rule was doomed because the Mongol rulers were unsuccessful at unifying warriors and pastoral peoples—and their enormous herds—with settled farmers.

Although they did not leave behind them institutional foundations for a new order, the Mongols did clear the political slate of the old order in much of the Islamic world. And then came an even more devastating killer: the Black Death. It reached Baghdad by 1347, carried there, perhaps, by an Azerbaijani army that besieged the city in that year. By the next year, the plague had come to Egypt, Syria, and Cyprus; one report from Tunis in June 1348 records the deaths of more than 1,000 people a day in the North African city. Animals too were heavily afflicted; one Egyptian writer commented: "The country was not far from being ruined. . . . One found in the desert the bodies of savage animals with the bubos under their arms. It was the same with horses, camels, asses, and all the beasts in general, including birds, even the ostriches." In the eastern Mediterranean, too, the Black Death left much of the Islamic world in a state of near political and economic collapse.

As new polities emerged from this economic and demographic crisis, they had to build from the ground floor. Warrior chiefs and charismatic religious leaders vied with one another to fill the political vacuum. The new rulers who appeared as Mongol power waned in the fourteenth century, notably the Ottomans in Anatolia and the Safavids in western Persia, operated out of strategic locations in the Islamic heartland. These new rulers gradually rebuilt state institutions.

Through migration, warfare, and eventually the consolidation of post-Mongol states, the boundaries of Islam's domain spread. Prior to the Mongol incursions, the political, economic, and cultural centers of the Islamic world were to be found in Egypt, Syria, and Iraq. The majority of the inhabitants of these regions spoke Arabic, the language of the Prophet, and hence the language of Islamic devotion and theology. These areas, along with the Arabian peninsula, contained Islam's most holy cities: Mecca, Medina, Jerusalem, Damascus, Cairo, and various religious cities in Iraq. Even before the Mongol invasions, Turks had begun to migrate into these regions, and Persian had started to emerge as a rival language of Islamic poetry and philosophy. Yet, it was the Mongol invasions of the thirteenth century, with the devastation that they brought to Persia and Iraq and the influx of nomadic peoples, which opened the door for a new Islamic world to appear. The new world of Islam, based now to a much larger extent than before on Turkish- and Persian-speaking populations, emerged in a vast geographical triangle that stretched from Anatolia in the west to Khurasan in the east and to the southern apex at Baghdad. Of course, the old Arabic-speaking Islamic world did not die out, but it had to cede some of its hegemony to the new rulers and the new religious men who now came to the fore.

At the beginning of the sixteenth century, three new and powerful dynasties dominated much of the old Islamic world. Eventually, they grew powerful enough to become empires. Between them, the Ottoman, Safavid, and Mughal empires used and developed the rich agrarian resources of the regions of the Indian Ocean and the Mediterranean Sea basin and benefited from a brisk seaborne and overland trade. Of these three, the Ottomans were in full flourish at the beginning of the sixteenth century; the Safavids and Mughals were just beginning to emerge.

By the middle of the sixteenth century, the Mughals dominated the northern Indus River valley, the Safavids Persia, and the Ottomans Anatolia, the Arab world, and large parts of southern and eastern Europe. Sharing core Islamic beliefs, each empire had unique political features. The most centralized and powerful, the Ottoman Empire, occupied the pivotal expanse between Europe and Asia. The Ottomans embraced a Sunni, or orthodox, view of Islam, while adopting pre-existing Byzantine ways of ruling and finding innovative ways to integrate the many new peoples who inhabited their ever-expanding territories. The Safavids were adherents of Shiism and ardently devoted to the pre-Islamic traditions of Persia (present-day Iran). While the Safavids were an internally cohesive Turkish people, Safavid rulers were less effective at expanding their mission beyond their Persian base. The Mughals ruled over the wealthy but divided realm that is much of today's India, Pakistan, and Bangladesh and carried even further the already well-developed South Asian religious and political traditions of assimilating Islamic and pre-Islamic Indian ways. Their very wealth and the decentralization of their domain made the Mughals constant targets for internal dissent and eventually for external aggression.

THE RISE OF THE OTTOMAN EMPIRE

Although the Mongols had little interest in Anatolia, a borderland region of little economic importance to them, their military forays against the Anatolian Seljuk Turkish state opened the region up to new political forces in the late thirteenth century. The ultimate victors in Anatolia proved to be the Ottoman Turks, who succeeded in transforming themselves from Islamic warrior bands operating on the borderlands between the Islamic and Christian worlds into rulers of a settled state and finally into sovereigns of a far-flung, highly bureaucratic empire.

Under their chief, Osman (ruled 1299–1326), the Turkish Ottomans developed a stern and disciplined warrior ethos, and they triumphed over other warrior bands because, unlike their rivals, they succeeded in mastering the techniques of settled administration. Other warrior bands, composed of young men who lived off the land and fought for booty under the leadership of charismatic military leaders, typically had little place in their societies for artisans, merchants, bureaucrats, and clerics. By contrast, the Ottomans, based in the city of Bursa in western Anatolia, realized that their consolidation of power depended on attracting just these groups. This they did with great skill, and in time, not only did the Ottoman state win the favor of Islamic clerics, but it also became the champion of Sunni, orthodox Islam throughout the entire Islamic world.

By the middle of the fourteenth century, the Ottomans had expanded beyond their regional base in Anatolia and moved into the Balkans, becoming the most powerful force in the eastern Mediterranean and western Asia. The state controlled a vast territory, stretching in the west to the Moroccan border, in the north to Hungary and Moldavia, in the south through the Arabian peninsula, and in the east to the Iraqi-Persian border (see Map 11-2). At the top of the Ottomans' elaborate hierarchy sat the sultan. Below him was a military and civilian bureaucracy, whose task was to exact obedience and revenue from subjects. The Ottoman bureaucracy allowed the sultan to expand his realm, which in turn forced him to invest in a larger bureaucracy.

MAP 11-2   THE OTTOMAN EMPIRE, 1300–1566

This map charts the expansion of the Ottoman state from its inception in the late thirteenth century under its founder, Osman, through the reign of Suleiman, the empire's most illustrious ruler. Against whom did the Ottomans fight? What were the geographic limits of the empire? How did Ottoman rulers promote unity among such a diverse population?

THE CONQUEST OF CONSTANTINOPLE   The Ottoman Empire's spectacular expansion was first and foremost a military affair. To recruit followers, the Ottomans promised wealth and glory to new subjects. This was expensive, but territorial expansion generated vast financial and administrative rewards. Moreover, by spreading the spoils of conquest and lucrative positions in the emerging state, rulers bought off potentially discontented subordinates. Still, without military might, the Ottomans would not have enjoyed the successes of the fifteenth century that were associated with the brilliant reigns of Murad II (ruled 1421–1451) and his aptly named successor, Mehmed the Conqueror (ruled 1451–1481). Mehmed vowed, shortly after his coronation as emperor in 1451, to capture Constantinople, capital of the

Byzantine Empire and a city of strategic and commercial importance. He knew he would need a large and well-armed fighting force to take Constantinople, for the heavily fortified city had kept the Turks at bay for almost a century. First he built a fortress of his own, on the European bank of the Bosporus Strait; here he could prevent European vessels from reaching the capital. Then, by promising his soldiers free access to booty and portraying the conquest of Constantinople as a holy cause, he amassed a huge army that outnumbered the defending force of 7,000 by more than tenfold. His troops bombarded Constantinople's massive walls, with artillery that included enormous cannons built by Hungarian and Italian engineers, for forty days. On May 29, 1453, Ottoman troops overwhelmed the surviving soldiers and took the ancient

Roman and Christian capital of Byzantium, which Mehmed promptly renamed Istanbul.

Many of the Christian survivors fled the city for ports to the west, taking with them their knowledge of Greek, which had virtually died out in western Europe. Some also carried classical and Arabic manuscripts. These refugees would be instrumental in reviving the study of ancient texts in Europe. Meanwhile, Mehmed made Istanbul the Ottoman capital, adopting Byzantine bureaucrats and administrative practices to solidify his newly enlarged state. From Istanbul, Mehmed and his successors would continue their expansion, eventually seizing all of Greece and the Balkan region. Ottoman navies increasingly controlled sea lanes in the eastern Mediterranean, curtailing European access to the rich ports through which the goods of the lucrative caravan trade were traded. By the end of the fifteenth century, Ottoman forces were menacing another of Christendom's great capitals, Vienna, and European merchants had grown fearful that never again would they be able to obtain the riches of Asia by the traditional overland route.

THE TOOLS OF EMPIRE-BUILDING Having penetrated the heartland of Christian Byzantium in southeastern Europe in the fourteenth and fifteenth centuries, the Ottomans turned their expansionist designs to the Arab world in the next century. What Osman had begun, a sixteenth-century Ottoman successor, Suleiman (ruled 1520–1566), consolidated. During Suleiman's reign, the Ottomans reached the height of their territorial expansion, and the sultan himself led the army on thirteen of its major military campaigns and many of its minor engagements. An exceptional military leader, Suleiman was an equally gifted administrator. He garnered accolades from his subjects, who called him "the Lawgiver" and "the Magnificent," in recognition of the attention he lavished on civil bureaucratic efficiency and justice for his people. His fame spread to Europe, where he was known as "the Great Turk." Under Suleiman's administration, the Ottoman state ruled over some 20 to 30 million people. When Suleiman died in 1566, the Ottoman Empire bridged Europe and the Arab world. Istanbul became a busy imperial hub, dispatching bureaucrats and

The Conquest of Constantinople. In 1453, the Ottoman Turks, led by Sultan Mehmed, later called the Conqueror, broke through the defenses of the city of Constantinople and incorporated this bastion of Byzantine Christian civilization into the Ottoman Empire. They changed the city's name to Istanbul and made it their own capital.

military men from the capital to administer and control the vast domain.

Ottoman dynastic power was, however, not only military; it also rested on a religious foundation. At the center of this empire were the Ottoman sultans, who combined a warrior ethos with an unwavering devotion to Islamic beliefs. Describing themselves as the "shadow of God" on earth, sultans claimed to be caretakers for the welfare of the Islamic faith. Around the empire, the sultans devoted substantial resources to the construction of great mosques and to the support of Islamic schools. As self-appointed defenders of the faithful, the sultans assumed the role of protectors of the holy cities on the Arabian peninsula and of Jerusalem, defending the internal cohesion of the realm and defining the borders demarcating heretics and infidels. Thus the Islamic faith helped to unite a diverse and sprawling imperial populace, with the sultan's power fusing the sacred and the secular.

Suleiman and Territorial Expansion. Sultan Suleiman, at the center of this illustration, leads his army as it is about to embark on a campaign to conquer Europe.

ISTANBUL AND THE TOPKAPI PALACE   Istanbul reflected the splendor of this powerful empire. After the Ottoman conquest, the sultans' engineers rebuilt the city's crumbling walls, while their architects redesigned homes, public buildings, baths, inns, and marketplaces to display the majesty of Islam's new imperial center. To crown his achievements, Suleiman Mehmed II ordered the construction of the Suleymaniye Mosque, which sat across from Hagia Sophia, a domed Byzantine cathedral that was formerly the most sacred of the Christian cathedrals, the largest house of worship in all Christendom, but which Suleiman Mehmed II had turned into a mosque. The Ottoman dynasts welcomed, indeed, forcibly transported, thousands of Muslims and non-Muslims to the city and revived Istanbul as a major trading center. Before its conquest, the city's population had fallen to 30,000. Within twenty-five years of its conquest by the Ottomans, its population had more than tripled, and by the end of the sixteenth century Istanbul's population numbered 400,000, making it the world's largest city outside China.

Istanbul's Topkapi Palace neatly displayed the Ottomans' view of governance, the importance the sultans attached to religion, and the continuing influence of Ottoman household and familial traditions, even in the administration of a far-flung empire. Laid out by Constantinople's conqueror, Mehmed II, and largely completed by the middle of the sixteenth century, the palace complex reflected Mehmed's vision of Istanbul as the center of the world. As a way to exalt the magnificent power of the sultan, the architects designed the various palaces and courtyards so that the buildings that housed the imperial household would be nestled behind layers of outer courtyards, in a mosaic of mosques, courts, and special dwellings for the sultan's harem.

The growing importance of the Topkapi Palace as the command post of empire represented an important transition in the history of Ottoman rulers. Not only was the palace the place where future bureaucrats were trained; it was also the place where the chief bureaucrat of the realm, the grand vizier, carried out the day-to-day running of the empire. Whereas the early sultans had led their soldiers into battle personally and had met face-to-face with their kinsmen, the later rulers withdrew into the sanctity of the palace, venturing out only occasionally for grand ceremonies. Still, every Friday, subjects queued up outside the palace to introduce their petitions, ask for favors, and seek justice. If they were lucky, the sultans would be there to greet the people—but they did so behind grated glass, issuing their decisions by tapping on the window. The palace thus projected a sense of majestic, distant wonder, a home fit for semidivine rulers.

Home Topkapi was, for the increasingly sedentary sultan and his harem. Among his most cherished quarters were those set aside for women. At first, the influence of women in the Ottoman polity was slight. But as the realm consolidated, women became a powerful political force. The harem, like the rest of Ottoman society, had its own hierarchy of rank

The Suleymaniye Mosque. Built by Sultan Suleiman to crown his achievements, the Suleymaniye Mosque was designed by the architect Sinan to dominate the city and to have four tall minarets from which the faithful were called to prayer.

and prestige. At the bottom were slave women; at the top were the sultan's mother and his favorite consorts. As many as 10,000 to 12,000 women lived in the palace, often in cramped quarters. Those who had the ruler's ear conspired to have him favor their own children, which made for widespread intrigue. When a sultan died the entire retinue of women would be dispatched to a distant palace poignantly called the Palace of Tears, because the women who occupied it wept at the loss of the sultan and their banishment from power.

DIVERSITY AND CONTROL IN THE OTTOMAN EMPIRE Ruling the realm through conquest and conversion did not entirely efface cultural differences in distant provinces. Take the example of the Ottomans' language policy. From the fifteenth century onward, the Ottoman Empire was more multilingual than any of its rivals. Although Ottoman Turkish was the official language of administration, Arabic was the lingua franca of the Arab provinces, the common tongue of street life. Within the European corner of the empire, various languages also continued to be spoken.

In politics, as in language, the Ottomans showed flexibility and tolerance. The imperial bureaucracy permitted a high degree of regional autonomy. In the course of imperial expansion, the Ottoman military cadres perfected a technique for absorbing newly conquered territories into the empire by parceling out these territories as revenue-producing units among loyal followers (including Christian converts) and kin. Regional appointees could collect local taxes, part of which they earmarked for Istanbul and part of which they kept for themselves. As we shall see, this was a common administrative device for many world dynasties trying to rule extensive domains.

Like other expansive realms, the Ottoman state was perennially in danger of losing control over its provincial rulers. As provincial rulers learned to operate independently

The Topkapi Palace. A view of the inner courtyard of the seraglio, where the sultan and his harem lived.

from central authority, local authorities kept larger amounts of tax revenues than Istanbul deemed proper. To clip local autonomy, the Ottomans established a corps of infantry soldiers and bureaucrats (called janissaries) who owed direct allegiance to the sultan. The system as it operated at its high point involved a conscription of Christian youths from villages in the European lands of the empire. This conscription, called the *devshirme,* required each village to turn over to the state a certain number of young males between the ages of eight and eighteen. Uprooted from their families and villages, selected for their fine physiques and good looks, these young men were converted to Islam and were sent to farms to build up their bodies and learn Turkish. A select few were then sent to Topkapi Palace to learn Ottoman military, religious, and administrative techniques. Some of these men went on to exceptional careers in the arts and sciences, as did the architect Sinan, who designed the Suleymaniye Mosque. Recipients of the best education available in the Islamic world, trained in Ottoman ways, instructed in the use of modern weaponry, and shorn of all family connections, the boys recruited through the *devshirme* were thus prepared to serve the sultan, and the empire as a whole, rather than the interests of any particular locality or ethnic group.

The Ottomans were thus able to artfully balance the decentralizing tendencies of far-flung regions with the centralizing forces of the imperial capital. Relying on a careful mixture of faith, patronage, and tolerance, Ottoman sultans curried loyalty and secured political stability. Indeed, so strong and stable was the polity that the Ottoman Empire dominated the much coveted and highly contested crossroads between Europe and Asia for many centuries.

A Harem. An interior room of an opulent Turkish palace. This image comes from the late nineteenth century but captures the arrangements employed by wealthy and elite members of Turkish society to seclude women in their own parts of a house or a palace.

Primary Source

QALANDAR DERVISHES IN THE ISLAMIC WORLD

The Qalandar dervish order came into being in Damascus, Syria, and Egypt in the thirteenth century and spread rapidly throughout the Islamic world into Arab and Ottoman lands in reaction to the unrest of the times. Renouncing the world and engaging in highly individualistic practices as they moved from place to place, the Qalandars were condemned by the educated elite, who believed them to be ignorant hypocrites living on alms obtained from gullible common folk. Giovan Antonio Manavino, a European observer of Ottoman society in the late fifteenth century, gives an obviously biased account of the Qalandars, whom he called the torlaks.

Dressed in sheepskins, the *torlaks* [Qalandars] are otherwise naked, with no headgear. Their scalps are always clean-shaven and well rubbed with oil as a precaution against the cold. They burn their temples with an old rag so that their faces will not be damaged by sweat. Illiterate and unable to do anything manly, they live like beasts, surviving on alms only. For this reason, they are to be found around taverns and public kitchens in cities. If, while roaming the countryside, they come across a well-dressed person, they try to make him one of their own, stripping him naked. Like Gypsies in Europe, they practice chiromancy, especially for women who then provide them with bread, eggs, cheese, and other foods in return for their services. Amongst them there is usually an old man whom they revere and worship like God. When they enter a town, they gather around the best house of the town and listen in great humility to the words of this old man, who, after a spell of ecstasy, foretells the descent of a great evil upon the town. His disciples then implore him to fend off the disaster through his good services. The old man accepts the plea of his followers, though not without an initial show of reluctance, and prays to God, asking him to spare the town the imminent danger awaiting it. This time-honored trick earns them considerable sums of alms from ignorant and credulous people. The *torlaks* . . . chew hashish and sleep on the ground; they also openly practice sodomy like savage beasts.

→ *Why do you think Manavino is so critical of the Qalandars?*
→ *Why do you think the Qalanders chose individualistic practices rather than communal living?*

SOURCE: Ahmet T. Karamustafa, *God's Unruly Friends: Dervish Groups in the Islamic Later Middle Period, 1200–1550* (Salt Lake City: University of Utah Press, 1994), pp. 6–7.

THE EMERGENCE OF THE SAFAVID EMPIRE IN IRAN

The Ottoman dynasts were not the only rulers to extend the political domain of Islam in Afro-Eurasia. In Persia, too, a new empire arose in the aftermath of the Mongols. The Safavid Empire, like the Ottoman Empire, rested its legitimacy on an Islamic foundation. But the Shiism espoused by Safavid rulers was quite different from the Sunni faith of the Ottomans, and these contrasting religious visions shaped distinct political systems.

Even more so than in Anatolia, the Mongol conquest and decline brought terrible destruction and political instability to Persia. Initially, Mongol conquerors refused to embrace the Islamic faith of the majority of the area's population. Instead, from 1221 to 1295, Mongol rulers practiced a form of religious toleration. Various Mongol autocrats permitted Jews to serve the state as viziers (administrators) and employed Christians as auxiliary soldiers. But in 1295, the Great Khan of the Persian state, Ghazan, adopted Islam as the state religion. When the Mongol order slipped into decline soon after, no power arose to dominate the area. The region between Konya

The *Devshirme*. A miniature painting from 1558 depicts the *devshirme* system of taking non-Muslim children from their families in the Balkan Peninsula as a human tribute in place of cash taxes, which the poor region could not pay. The children were educated in Ottoman Muslim ways and prepared for service in the sultan's civil and military bureaucracy.

three great Islamic empires, the Safavid state became the most single-mindedly religious, persecuting those who did not follow its Shiite form of Islam. When in 1501 the most dynamic of Safi al-Din's successors, Ismail (ruled 1501–1524), acceded to power in Tabriz, he required that the call to prayer announce that "there is no God but Allah, that Muhammad is His prophet, and that Ali is the successor of Muhammad." Ismail rejected the pragmatic counsels of his advisers to tolerate the Sunni creed of the vast majority of the city's population and made Shiism the official religion of the Persian state. He offered the people a choice between conversion to Shiism or death, exclaiming at the moment of conquest that "with God's help, if the people utter one word of protest, I will draw the sword and leave not one of them alive." Under Ismail and his successors, the Safavid shahs succeeded in restoring Persian sovereignty over the whole of the region traditionally regarded as the homeland of Persian speakers (see Map 11-3).

In 1502, Ismail proclaimed himself the first shah of the Safavid Empire. In the hands of the Safavids, Islam assumed an extreme and often quite militant form. The Safavids revived the traditional Persian idea that rulers were ordained by God, believing the shahs to be divinely chosen. But some Shiites went so far as to affirm that there was no God but the shah. Moreover, Persian Shiism fostered an activist clergy, the so-called turbaned classes, who, in contrast to Sunni clerics, cast themselves in the role of political and religious enforcers against any heretical authority. They compelled Safavid leaders to rule with a sacred purpose. Because the Safavids did not tolerate diversity within their realm, unlike the Ottomans, they never had as expansive an empire. Whatever territories they conquered, the Safavids ruled much more directly, based on central—and theocratic—authority.

THE DELHI SULTANATE AND THE EARLY MUGHAL EMPIRE

A quarter century after the Safavids seized power in Persia, another new Islamic dynasty, the Mughals, emerged to the east in South Asia. Like the Ottomans and Safavids, the Mughals created a new regime destined to last for many centuries. But unlike those other Islamic empires, the Mughals did not replace a Mongol regime. Instead, they erected their state on the foundations of the old Delhi Sultanate, which had come into existence in 1206.

In 1303, when Mongol forces had moved toward South Asia, the Delhi Sultanate was at the height of its powers. Its formidable military force extended imperial authority to large parts of the northern Indus River valley and cast a shadow over the political map of the south. The reigning sultan, Alaud din Khalji (ruled 1296–1316), was able to raise a sufficiently powerful army to drive the Mongols, who were

in eastern Anatolia and Tabriz in Persia and including Iraq fell into even greater disorder, with warrior chieftains fighting one another for preeminence. Adding to the volatility of the region were various populist Islamic movements that appeared at this time. Some of these urged followers to withdraw from society or encouraged devotees to parade around without clothing. Among the more prominent movements was a Sufi brotherhood led by Safi al-Din (1252–1334), which gained the backing of religious adherents and Turkish-speaking warrior bands. However, his later successors, known as Safaviyeh or Safavids, embraced Shiism.

The Safavid aspirants to power rallied support from tribal groups in badly devastated parts of Persia by promising to restore good governance to the region, and steeped themselves in the separatist sacred tradition of Shiism. As a result, of the

→ *What were the major differences among the three Islamic dynasties?*

MAP 11-3   THE SAFAVID EMPIRE, 1500–1722

The Safavid Empire rose to prominence alongside the Ottoman state. Where did it originate? What were the territories over which the Ottomans and Safavids battled? Did the Safavids have any other political enemies?

was a force led by Timur (Tamerlane), a Turkish warrior from central Asia, whose army succeeded where the Mongols had not. Sweeping down from the northwest, Timur's army sacked Delhi in 1398 and pillaged and annexed the Punjab. Death and destruction engulfed the city and much of the northern Indus River valley. Thousands were taken prisoner and carried off as slaves. Artisans and stonemasons who had built Delhi's beautiful buildings were carted away to beautify the conqueror's city of Samarkand (in present-day Uzbekistan). Yet, as the summer of 1399 approached, a time when semi-arid Delhi gets dusty and the temperature hovers between 100 to 110 degrees, Timur abandoned the hot plains of northern India and returned home. Still, Timur's conquest accelerated the fragmentation of the Delhi Sultanate.

A wave of religious revival followed in the wake Timur's conquests. Some of the more radical movements, like Persia's Shiism, adopted an intransigent stance against central rulers and official credos. Religious reaction stood in the way of re-creating powerful state structures. Bengal broke away from Delhi and

threatening the northwestern cities of the sultanate, back toward Afghanistan. The Mongols never again disturbed the tranquility of the sultanate.

Although military strength was the foundation of the sultanate's power, it was also its Achilles' heel. Toward the close of the fourteenth century, a decline in the government's revenues, from military campaigns of conquest and plunder and tax yields from the rural economy, and a rise in expenditures, on buildings and charitable institutions, combined to reduce the resources for the military. Intrigues and quarreling among nobles further weakened the Delhi Sultanate and left it vulnerable to a new Turkish, rather than Mongol, invader. This

was soon engulfed in a Sufi form of mystical Islam, extolling personal union with God. Here, too, a special form of Hinduism, called Bhakti Hinduism, put down deep roots. Its devotees preached the doctrine of divine love. In the Punjab, previously a core area of the Delhi Sultanate, a new religion, Sikhism, came into being, which largely followed the teachings of Nanak (1469–1539), who while born a Hindu was inspired by Islamic ideals and called on his followers to renounce the caste system and to treat all believers as equal before God.

Following Timur's attack, rival kingdoms and sultanates asserted their independence, leaving the Delhi Sultanate a mere shadow of its former self. It became just one of several

Primary Source

NANAK'S TEACHINGS IN INDIA

Nanak, generally recognized as the founder of Sikhism, lived from 1469 to 1539 in the Punjab in northern India, where he surrounded himself with disciples and participated in the religious discussions that were such a prominent feature of the fifteenth century. This was a period, much like that in western Europe and Islamic Southwest Asia, of political turmoil and intense personal introspection. As the following excerpts of hymns and poems from his writings demonstrate, Nanak exposed the failings of the age and used spiritual ideas drawn from Islamic and Hindu thought to elaborate his own unique spiritual perspective as a bulwark against the travails of the period. Nanak stressed the unity of God, an emphasis that reflected Islamic influences. Nonetheless, his insistence on the comparative unimportance of prophets ran counter to Islam, and his belief in rebirth was strictly Hindu.

There is but one God, whose name is true, the Creator, devoid of fear and enmity, immortal, unborn, self-existent; God the great and bountiful. Repeat His Name.

Numberless are the fools appallingly blind;
Numberless are the thieves and devourers of others' property;
Numberless are those who establish their sovereignty by force;
Numberless the cutthroats and murderers; Numberless the liars who roam about lying;
Numberless the filthy who enjoy filthy gain;
Numberless the slandered who carry loads of calumny on their heads;
Nanak thus described the degraded.
So lowly am I, I cannot even once be a sacrifice unto Thee. Whatever pleaseth Thee is good.
O Formless One, Thou art ever secure.

The Hindus have forgotten God, and are going the wrong way.
They worship according to the instruction of Narad.
They are blind and dumb, the blindest of the blind.
The ignorant fools take stones and worship them.
O Hindus, how shall the stone which itself sinketh carry you across?

What power hath caste? It is the reality that is tested.
Poison may be held in the hand, but man dieth if he eat it.
The sovereignty of the True One is known in every age.
He who obeyeth God's order shall become a noble in His court.

Those who have meditated on God as the truest of the true have done real worship and are contented;
They have refrained from evil, done good deeds, and practiced honesty;
They have lived on a little corn and water, and burst the entanglements of the world.
Thou art the great Bestower; ever Thou givest gifts which increase a quarterfold.
Those who have magnified the great God have found Him.

→ *How does Nanak's conception of God differ from the Hindu conception?*
→ *Why does Nanak call for the end of the caste system?*

SOURCE: William Theodore de Bary, *Sources of Indian Tradition* (New York: Columbia University Press, 1958), pp. 536–38.

---

competing regional powers in northern India, ruled first by the Sayyids (1414–1451) and then by the Afghan dynasty of the Lodis (1451–1526). Surrounded by resurgent Hindu and Islamic polities, the truncated sultanate experienced something of a revival in the Lodi era. But the attempt by the last sultan, Ibrahim Lodi, to consolidate his power by clipping the wings of the Afghan nobility provoked the governor of the Punjab to invite the Turkish prince Babur (the "Tiger") to India in 1526. A great-grandson of Timur, Babur traced his lineage to both the Turks and the Mongols (he was said to be a descendant of Chinggis Khan). For years, Babur had longed to conquer India. So, he accepted the invitation and marched against Sultan Ibrahim. Massing an army of Turks and Afghans and armed with matchlock cannons, he easily breached the wall of elephants put together by Ibrahim. Delhi fell, and the sultanate came to an end. Babur proclaimed himself emperor (ruled 1526–1530), and he spent the next few years snuffing out the remaining resistance to his rule (see Map 11-4). Thus was laid the foundation of the Mughal Empire, the third great Islamic dynasty (discussed in detail in Chapter 12).

By the sixteenth century, then, the Islamic heartland had seen the emergence of three new empires. Although these states did not hesitate to go to war against each other, they shared similar styles of rule. All established their legitimacy by using military prowess, religious backing, and a loyal bureaucracy to balance sacred and secular authority. This combination of spiritual and military weaponry enabled emperors, carrying Muhammad's preachings across the Afro-Eurasian landmass, to lay claim to vast domains. Islam also bound rulers and ruled together and gave them a common cause and a singular view of the world. This shared Islamic religious culture fostered the movement of goods, ideas, merchants, and scholars across political boundaries, even across Islam's most divisive boundary, that along the border between Sunni Iraq and Shiite Persia.

MAP 11-4   THE MUGHAL EMPIRE, 1530

Compare the Mughal state with the other major Asian empires of this period, notably the Ming, Safavid, and Ottoman states. What distinguishes the Mughal state at this time from these others? From what part of the Afro-Eurasian landmass did the new state arise, and what effect would its place of origin have on the nature of Mughal rule? To what religious traditions did the Mughals need to be sensitive?

Raid on Delhi. Timur's swift raid on Delhi in 1398 was notable for the death and destruction it caused. This sixteenth-century miniature captures the plunder and violence.

Babur in Battle. Following his victory over the Delhi sultan, Ibrahim Lodi, in the Battle of Panipat (1526), Babur battled with Rajput chieftains in north India. Artists chronicled these events in paintings. This miniature shows Babur's army locked in fierce fight with Rana Sanga, a Rajput chief. The painting records the use of field guns, bombards (an early type of cannon, which fired stones), and swords. The red elephant head on the left may be horse armor used to trick and frighten the enemy.

WESTERN CHRISTENDOM

> → *Why did Europe remain disunited and have difficulty recovering from the Black Death?*

On the western side of the Afro-Eurasian landmass, a period of prosperity, population growth, and cultural flowering known as the High Middle Ages ended abruptly with the coming of famine, plague, and war in the fourteenth century. The Black Death and its aftermath reversed the gains that Europe had made in the twelfth and thirteenth centuries. Between about 1100 and 1300, Europe's population had increased, and new prosperity had allowed for spectacular advances in the arts, technology, learning, building, cities, and banking. Economic and social lives focused on the family, and growing households had to crowd under the same roof. Wives worked with their husbands, especially in commerce and farming. Though excluded from many crafts and professions, women were increasingly important in retail trades, weaving, and food production.

Europe's 80 million inhabitants still resided, overwhelmingly, on rural estates, but towns and cities were growing rapidly and were allowing Europeans to widen their horizons onto the world. Between the late eleventh and early thirteenth centuries, universities had come into being in Bologna, Paris, Oxford, and Cambridge, and a few scholars began to appreciate the learning of the Arabs and the earlier achievements of the Greeks and Romans. Thomas Aquinas (1225–1274), the leading philosopher and theologian of the age, had laid out the main tenets of western Christianity and resolved questions of faith and reason to the satisfaction of clerical and secular intellectuals. New devices like mechanical clocks and the compass had improved the accuracy of measurements on sea and on land, while spinning wheels increased the pace of cloth production.

REACTIONS, REVOLTS, AND RELIGION IN EUROPE

At the beginning of the fourteenth century, Europe's rising fortunes halted, with climatic changes instigating a decline. Beginning around 1310, extremely harsh winters and rainy summers shortened the growing seasons and played havoc with harvests, especially in northern zones. Diminished and exhausted soils no longer supplied the resources to feed and clothe growing urban and rural populations. Nobles squeezed the peasantry hard in an effort to maintain their luxurious way of life. States raised taxes to keep revenues in balance with their growing expenditures. In this context, Europe endured the first of its fourteenth-century disasters: famine. Famine appeared in 1315 and did not let up until 1322, by which time millions had died of outright starvation or diseases against which the malnourished population could offer little resistance. But this would be merely the prelude to a century and more of ceaseless warfare, epidemic disease, famine, and social unrest.

In the wake of famine came the Black Death. The pandemic began around 1347, and soon ravaging the Italian peninsula moved on to France, the Low Countries, Germany, and England. Although no part of Europe was spared, the cities were particularly vulnerable because of their overcrowding and unsanitary conditions. London, with a population of about 60,000 residing within its walls and another 10,000 or 15,000 living outside, groaned under the weight of the death toll. Often in the poorer sections as many as twelve residents slept together on the floor in a single room. The disease spared few in these crowded quarters. Nor did it ignore their social betters if they hesitated to flee to their country estates.

No one had seen dying on such a scale. Anywhere from 25 to 50 percent of Europe's total population (between 19 and 38 million) perished within five years of the original outbreak. But the dying did not end then, for severe outbreaks occurred in 1361–1362, 1369, and then every five to ten years for the rest of the fourteenth century, as well as sporadically through the entire fifteenth century. The European population continued on a precipitous decline until by 1450 many areas had only one-quarter the number of people they had supported a century earlier. Indeed, it took three centuries for Europe to recover to population levels that existed prior to the Black Death.

Disaster on this scale had a number of enduring psychological, social, economic, and political effects. Many individuals, recognizing life's brevity, turned to pleasure, even debauchery, determined to enjoy themselves before it came their turn to die. Others retreated into a personal spirituality, convinced that they needed to put their lives in order before they passed on to the next life. Occasionally, like-minded individuals joined together and created eccentric groups. The Beghards or Brethren of the Free Speech claimed to be in a state of grace that allowed them to do as they pleased—from adultery, free love, and nudity to murder. By contrast, the Flagellants were so sure that man had incurred the wrath of God through his wayward ways that they whipped themselves to show their readiness to atone for human sin. But they also bullied communities that they visited, demanding to be housed, clothed, and fed in style.

For many who survived the plague, Thomas Aquinas's rational Christianity no longer appealed, and disappointment with the clergy was widespread. Famished peasants resented priests and monks for living lives of luxury in violation of church tenets. In addition, they despaired at the absence of clergy when they were so greatly needed. In fact, many clerics had perished while attending to their parishioners. Others, however, had simply deserted to rural retreats far from the ravages of the Black Death, leaving their followers to fend for themselves.

In the aftermath of famine and plague, religious authorities struggled to reclaim their power. The late medieval western church found itself divided at the top (at one point in the fourteenth century there were three popes!) and challenged from below, both by individuals pursuing alternative kinds of spirituality and by increasing demands on the clergy and church administration. In response to challenges to its right to define religious doctrine and practices, the church rigorously identified all that was suspect and demanded strict obedience to the true faith. This entailed the persecution of heretics, Jews, Muslims, homosexuals, prostitutes, and "witches." But in this period, the church was also expanding its charitable and bureaucratic functions, providing alms to the urban poor and registering births, deaths, and economic transactions.

Persecution and administration cost money. As the church had no easy way to raise new funds, the needs as well as the extravagances of the clergy spurred the undertaking of ques-

Primary Source

FLAGELLANTS IN ENGLAND

Like the Qalandar dervishes in the Islamic world, European Flagellants renounced the world and engaged in violent acts of public self-punishment in reaction to the warfare, famines, and plagues of the fourteenth century. The Flagellants carried whips (flagella) with metal pieces run through knotted thongs, which they used to beat and whip themselves until they were bruised, swollen, and bloody. Robert of Avesbury here describes the actions of Flagellants in England during the reign of King Edward III.

In that same year of 1349, about Michaelmas [29 September], more than 120 men, for the most part from Zeeland or Holland, arrived in London from Flanders. These went barefoot in procession twice a day in the sight of the people, sometimes in St Paul's church and sometimes elsewhere in the city, their bodies naked except for a linen cloth from loins to ankle. Each wore a hood painted with a red cross at front and back and carried in his right hand a whip with three thongs. Each thong had a knot in it, with something sharp, like a needle, stuck through the middle of the knot so that it stuck out on each side, and as they walked one after the other they struck themselves with these whips on their naked, bloody bodies; four of them singing in their own tongue and the rest answering in the manner of the Christian litany. Three times in each procession they would all prostrate themselves on the ground, with their arms outstretched in the shape of a cross. Still singing, and beginning with the man at the end, each in turn would step over the others, lashing the man beneath him once with his whip, until all of those lying down had gone through the same ritual. Then each one put on his usual clothes and, always with their hoods on their heads and carrying their whips, they departed to their lodgings. It was said that they performed a similar penance every night.

↳   *Why do you think Flagellants whipped themselves?*
↳   *How do the Flagellants differ from the Qalanders?*

SOURCE: Robertus de Avesbury de Gestis Mirabilibus Regis Edwardi Tertii, in *The Black Death*, translated and edited by Rosemary Horrox (Manchester, England: Manchester University Press, 1994), pp. 153–54.

---

tionable new money-making tactics. Among the most controversial of these fund-raising mechanisms was the selling of indulgences (certification that one's sins had been forgiven). This sort of unconventional fund raising, and the growing gap between the church's promises and its ability to actually bring Christianity into people's everyday lives, more than the persecutions, eventually sparked the Protestant Reformation.

Just as the mayhem of the fourteenth and fifteenth centuries unleashed a wave of popular hostility toward the church, it also undermined the legitimacy of the feudal order, especially in France and England. Since the Roman era, peasant protests and uprisings had occasionally erupted. Yet, in the wake of the catastrophes of the fourteenth century, these everyday defiances escalated into large-scale insurrections. In France and England, massive revolts broke out, in which peasant rebels expressed their resentment against lords who failed to protect them from marauding military bands and their defiance of feudal restrictions that now seemed—for the few survivors of plague and famine—onerous. In 1358, the French revolt, or *Jacquerie*—a term derived from "Jacques Bonhomme," a name used by contemptuous masters as a blanket term for all peasants—broke out. Armed with only knives and staves, the French peasantry went on a rampage, killing a few of the hated nobles and higher clergy and burning and looting all the property they could get their hands on. At issue was the peasants' insistence that they should no longer be tied to their land or have to make payments for the tools they used in their agricultural pursuits.

A far better organized uprising took place in England in 1381. Although what became known as the English Peasants'

Peasant Revolts. Long before the French Revolution, European peasants vented their anger against their noble masters. Lacking armaments and supplies, they usually lost—as this image of the brutal suppression of the French Jacquerie of 1358 depicts.

Revolt began as a protest against a poll tax levied to raise money for a war on France, it was also fueled by post-plague labor shortages, with serfs demanding the freedom to move about and free farm workers calling for higher wages and lower rents. When landlords balked at these demands, huge numbers of aggrieved and restless peasants joined the cause, finally assembling at the gates of London. The protesters pressed for the abolition of the feudal order, but King Richard II, assembling his nobles, ruthlessly suppressed the rebellious peasants. Nonetheless, despite these defeats in both France and England, a free peasantry gradually emerged as labor shortages made it impossible to continue to bind peasants to the soil.

> *It took several centuries for Europe's polities to reorganize themselves into a series of centralized monarchies, interspersed with a sprinkling of city-states.*

STATE-BUILDING AND ECONOMIC RECOVERY IN EUROPE

In the wake of famine, plague, and peasant uprisings, Europe's rulers (and would-be rulers) tried to rebuild their polities and consolidate their power. Their efforts at state-building, however, paled in comparison with those of the empires rising in Asia. Although one family, the Habsburgs, provided emperors for the Holy Roman Empire from 1440 to 1806, they never succeeded in restoring an integrated empire to western Europe, as Chinese dynasts had done time and again by basing their claims to legitimate rule on the universally recognized concept of the mandate of Heaven and creating a sense of a universal identity by referring to themselves as a people, the Han, or referring to their state as the Middle Kingdom. Moreover, language did not unite Europeans. While the written literary Chinese script remained a key administrative tool for the dynasts for centuries to come, and in the Islamic world Arabic was commonly accepted as the language of faith, Persian the language of poetry, and Turkish the language of administration, in Europe Latin was gradually displaced as rulers chose one of the regional dialects to be the official state language at court. In 1450, Europe had no central government, no official tongue, and only a few successful commercial centers, most of them in the Mediterranean basin. Fledgling banking systems had fallen apart during the fourteenth century's chaos. In the political sphere, feudalism had left a legacy of political fragmentation and enshrined privileges, which made the consolidation of a unified Christian Europe even more difficult to achieve.

Those who sought to rule the emerging regional states faced numerous obstacles. Feudal dues paid to other landholders in their realms made it possible for rival claimants to the throne to finance the formation of private armies. The clergy demanded and received privileges and sometimes meddled in politics themselves. The printing press became available after the 1460s, and despite governments' attempts at censorship, clandestine presses and anonymous pamphlets circulated religious and political views quite different from those championed by the king and his ministers. Some states had consultative bodies, such as the Estates General in France, the Cortès in Spain, or Parliament in England, in which princes formally asked representatives of their people for advice and, in the case of the English Parliament, for consent to new forms of taxation. Where such bodies existed, they gave no voice to most nonaristocratic men and virtually no representation to women of any social class. But they did allow for the collective expression of grievances against highhanded monarchical policies.

It took several centuries for Europe's polities to reorganize themselves into a series of centralized monarchies, interspersed with a sprinkling of city-states. Consolidation of these polities occurred sometimes as a result of strategic marital alliances but often involved warfare, both between homegrown princely families and with outsiders seeking territorial gains for themselves. Political stabilization was swiftest in southern Europe. These economies would also prove quickest to rebound, for they enjoyed unique access to the increasingly vibrant Mediterranean trade with the Levant. The stabilization of Italian city-states such as Venice and Florence and of monarchical rule in Portugal and Spain allowed for a period of Mediterranean economic and cultural flowering we know as the Renaissance (see below).

POLITICAL CONSOLIDATION AND TRADE IN PORTUGAL

The fortunes of Portugal under the House of Aviz demonstrate the ways in which political stabilization and the revival of trade were interrelated. Spain, England, and France followed the Portuguese example and established national monarchies following the chaos of the fourteenth century. In Spain and Portugal, warfare against Muslims would help unite Christian territories, and Mediterranean trade would add valuable income to state coffers. In northern Europe, by contrast, lack of access to lucrative trade routes, in addition to internal feuding, regional warfare, and after 1517, religious fragmentation, would delay recovery for decades (see Map 11-5).

Through the fourteenth century, Portuguese Christians had fought Muslim occupants of the Iberian peninsula. But in 1415, the Portuguese crossed the Strait of Gibraltar and captured the Moorish Moroccan fortresses at Ceuta, in North Africa. They could now sail between the Mediterranean and the Atlantic without Muslim interference. With the Muslim threat diminished, the enemy was now perceived to be Portugal's neighbor, Castile (part of what is now Spain). Under João (John) I (ruled 1385–1433), the Castilians were defeated, and the monarchy could now seek new territories and trading opportunities in the North Atlantic and along the coasts of West Africa.

One of João's sons, Prince Henrique (1394–1460), later known as "Henry the Navigator," never ruled as king, but he further expanded the family's domain by supporting Portuguese expeditions down the coast of Africa and offshore to the Atlantic islands of the Madeiras and the Azores. The west and central coasts of Africa and the islands of the North and South Atlantic, including the Cape Verde Islands, São Tomé, Principe, and Fernando Po, soon became Portuguese ports of call.

The Portuguese monarchs allocated the Atlantic islands to nobles, granting them as hereditary possessions on condition that the grantees colonize these new lands. Soon the colonizers were establishing lucrative sugar plantations on the islands. In gratitude, noble families and merchants threw their political weight behind the king. Subsequent monarchs continued to reduce the traditional power of local nobles and to ensure the smooth succession of members of the royal family. This political consolidation enabled Portugal to thrive in the wake of the Black Death.

DYNASTY BUILDING AND RECONQUEST IN SPAIN

The road to dynasty in Spain was arduous. Medieval Spain was fragmented into various kingdoms, each controlled by noble families that quarreled ceaselessly with each other. Nor was Spain a country of religious uniformity; Muslims, Jews, and Christians lived side by side, in relative if not perfect harmony, and Muslim armies still occupied strategic posts in the south. Over time, however, marriages and the formation of kinship ties among nobles and between royal lineages slowly allowed for the consolidation of a new political order. One by one, the major houses of the Spanish kingdoms intermarried, culminating in the most fateful wedding of Iberian royal heirs: the marriage of Isabella of Castile and Ferdinand of Aragon in 1469. Thus, Spain's two most important provinces were joined, and Spain became a state to be reckoned with.

By the time Isabella and Ferdinand married, Spain was recovering from the miserable fourteenth century. Castile and Aragon's population, for instance, rebounded from about 6 million in 1450 to 8.5 million in 1482. This was more than just a marriage of convenience. Castile was wealthy and populous; Aragon enjoyed an extended trading emporium in the Mediterranean, including access to Italian and especially Genoese financiers. Together, the new monarchs brought unruly nobles and distant towns under their domain. They topped off their achievements by marrying their children into other European royal families, especially the House of Habsburg, the most powerful dynasty in central Europe.

The new rulers also sent Christian armies south to push out Muslim forces; by the middle of the fifteenth century, only Granada, a strategic lynchpin overlooking the straits leading from the Mediterranean to the Atlantic, remained in Muslim hands. After a long and costly siege, the Christian forces entered the fortress of Granada. When Granada fell in 1492, it was a victory of enormous symbolic importance, as joyous as the fall of Constantinople was depressing. Pope Alexander recognized the triumph and praised the monarchs of Spain. In Spain many people thumped their chests in pride—unaware, or unconcerned, perhaps, that at the same time, Ottoman armies were conquering large sections of southeastern Europe.

As did the rulers of the Safavid Empire, Isabella and Ferdinand sought to eliminate all traces of heterodoxy and infidelity from Spain. Already in 1481, they had launched the Inquisition, taking aim especially against the *conversos*, converted Jews and Muslims, whom they suspected were Christians only in name. When the walls of Granada fell, the crown ordered the expulsion of all Jews from Spain. By the terms of the treaty ending the war, the Moors (a term used to denote Muslims who inhabited the western Sahara and Iberia) were allowed to remain and to practice their religion. But, in 1609, they too would be formally expelled. All told, almost half a million people were forced to pack what possessions they could carry and flee the Spanish kingdoms.

→ *Why did Europe remain disunited and have difficulty recovering from the Black Death?*

MAP 11-5   EUROPE, 1400–1500

Europe was a region divided by dynastic rivalries during the fifteenth century. Which regional dynasties were the strongest? What parts of Europe were under Turkish rule? Would you be able to predict on the basis of this map which European territories and polities would become powerful in subsequent centuries and which would not?

Those who converted and stayed behind faced torture and mass burnings before jeering crowds if they were found to be heretics or secret Jews or Muslims. Fueling this giant expulsion was a conviction that the struggle against Islam and Judaism constituted a just war.

Such was the tide of Spanish optimism and fervor by late 1491 that the monarchs listened now to a Genoese navigator whose pleas for patronage they had previously turned down. The navigator, Christopher Columbus (1451–1506), followed the Spanish monarchs to their camp below the besieged walls of Granada and promised them the riches that could pay for their military campaigns and that could bankroll a final and decisive crusade to liberate Jerusalem from Muslim hands. Off he sailed with a royal patent that guaranteed the Spanish

The Court of Spain. The court of Ferdinand and Isabella of Spain at the time of Columbus's first voyage in 1492.

monarchs a share of all he discovered. By the mid-1490s, the Spanish economy was reorienting itself toward the Atlantic, and Spain's merchants, missionaries, and soldiers were readying themselves for conquest and profiteering in what had been, just a few years before, a blank space on the map.

THE STRUGGLES OF FRANCE AND ENGLAND AND THE SUCCESS OF SMALL STATES

Warfare and strategic marriages allowed the Portuguese and Spanish monarchies to consolidate state power and to lay the foundations for the revival and flourishing of commerce. But by no means were all states immediately successful. In France and England, the great age of European monarchy had yet to dawn. When the French finally pushed the English back across the English Channel in the Hundred Years' War (1337–1453), the French House of Valois began a slow process of consolidating royal power. Once again, diplomatic marriages helped the French crown expand its domain, though the local nobility remained extremely powerful. It would take a further two centuries of royal initiatives and civil war to tame it. In England, even thirty years of civil war (1455–1485) between the houses of Lancaster and York did not settle which dynastic house would take the throne. Both families in this War of the Roses ultimately lost out to a new family, the Tudors, who seized the throne in 1485.

Even where stable states did arise, their populations remained quite small, and the boundaries of their states were fairly compact compared to the Ottoman and Ming empires. In the middle of the sixteenth century, Portugal and Spain, Europe's two most expansionist states at the time, had populations of 1 million and 9 million, respectively. England, excluding Wales, was a mere 3 million in 1550. Only France with 17 million had a population close to the Ottoman Empire's 25 million. And these numbers paled in comparison with Ming China's population of nearly 200 million in 1550 and Mughal India's 110 million in 1600.

But in Europe, small was, at least for a time, successful; Portugal's relatively small population proved an advantage, for the Portuguese nobility and crown had a less diverse population to instill with loyalty and obedience. The most successful merchants of the era were the inhabitants of the even smaller Italian city states and, a bit later, of the cities of the northern Netherlands. The Florentines developed sophisticated banking techniques and created extensive networks of agents—many of them family members—throughout Europe and the Mediterranean; intermarriage among other powerful merchant families kept the competition from getting out of hand. Venetian merchants enjoyed a unique role in the exchange of silks and spices from the eastern edge of the Mediterranean to European ports. Venice, in fact, became the leading entrepôt—a commercial hub for long-distance trade—for the flow of commodities between east and west Afro-Eurasia. It was in these small and prosperous city-states that the Renaissance began.

THE RISE OF A CHARISMATIC LEADER IN A TIME OF SOCIAL TURMOIL: JOAN OF ARC

The immense historical impact made by a French peasant girl, Joan of Arc, demonstrates the importance given to rare and charismatic individuals, even women leaders in predominantly male-dominated societies, during periods of social turmoil. Europe in the late fourteenth and early fifteenth centuries was beset by plagues, famines, and war. Its people, thus, were willing to look for help to the special talents of women, even in areas like warfare, where women had been largely excluded. Indeed, if not for Joan of Arc, the country we know today as France might not exist. Appearing on the scene in 1429, as the English seemed to have gained the upper hand in the Hundred Years' War, she rallied the French against the English occupiers and turned the tide of the war. Although by no means a patriot in the nineteenth-century sense of the term, by giving religious sanction, as well as military succor, to the Valois monarch Charles VII, she made possible the consolidation of France and left Europe an inspiring, yet enigmatic, image of the female warrior-saint.

The world of Joan's childhood was a chaotic one, in which English lords were laying claim to various French-speaking principalities. By 1420, Valois authority had been greatly eroded. Important French lords soon began to sense the wind blowing in the English direction, and English armies gradually conquered more and more French towns. In 1428, the English laid siege to Orléans, a large town in north-central France; to contemporaries, it seemed a symbolic battle: as Orléans went, they thought, so the war would go—and so would God wish it to go.

This is the point at which the paths of a seventeen-year-old peasant girl and the monarch of France crossed. Beginning at about age thirteen, the shy girl had received visions of saints who instructed her to come to rescue Orléans and conduct France's ruler to be crowned king at Reims Cathedral (he had not been crowned there, in the tradition of all French kings, because the English armies controlled Reims, Paris, and northern France). For five years, Joan resisted, but at last she agreed to obey her celestial advisers. Granted an audience with Charles VII in 1429, Joan impressed him with her piety and her passionate devotion to the Valois crown. He concluded that God really had sent her to serve France's cause—and his own. Joan was given command of 7,000 to 8,000 men and, wearing a suit of armor and brandishing a sword, she marched to relieve Orléans. Joan directed the assault with brilliance and inspired the French forces; her charisma came not only from a tradition of female Christian "seers," but also from the peculiarity of her appearance (a young woman in male attire) and her appeal to French speakers who preferred their local French lords and customs to rule by English "outsiders." On Sunday, May 8, she drove the English from Orléans, and then pressed on to Reims; here, thanks to her military victories, Charles VII was crowned, fulfilling her visions. He was now king of France—and though the war continued, the tide now turned in favor of the French.

The tide for Joan, however, began to turn for the worse. Although she continued to direct the troops with remarkable savvy, she failed to force open the gates of Paris, and jealous courtiers around Charles began to question her divine authority. She was wounded, then taken prisoner. After a year in English captivity, she was tried by the Inquisition and found guilty—at the hands of jealous and pro-English judges—of heresy, on the grounds that her visions were false and misleading. On May 30, 1431, she was burned at the stake in the marketplace in the town of Rouen. Since that time, she has been seen as a heroic and charismatic martyr, and her name has very often been employed by the French in attempts to awaken French patriotism against foreign threats.

The fact that this young, illiterate woman played such an important role in the history of European warfare and state formation testifies to the fact that even in these spheres, male aristocrats, intellectuals, and clerics were not the only important actors. At the right place, at the right time, a woman could use courage, faith, and intelligence to make her visions prevail. Joan's followers believed that female magic could restore order to their lives, even while fearing witchcraft. They accepted her cross-dressing and personalist style of political and military leadership as proof of her calling. Yet, her death at the stake is a reminder that every charismatic heroine may be, for the opposing side, a heretic.

EUROPEAN IDENTITY AND THE RENAISSANCE

Europe's political and economic revival from the catastrophes of the fourteenth century included a powerful outpouring of cultural achievements, which was strongly linked to the rise of new polities. Much later, in the nineteenth century, scholars coined the word *Renaissance* (rebirth) to characterize the expanded cultural production of the Italian city-states, France, the Low Countries, England, and the Holy Roman Empire in the period between about 1430 and 1550. Although some Greek and Roman texts were known in Europe, and certainly had been known in the Islamic world throughout the medieval period, new ones now became accessible. Moreover, the use to which Europeans put this knowledge was new. The term *Renaissance* captures contemporaries' sense that they were making a break with the church-centered medieval world and witnessing a rebirth of classical culture. Humankind's achievements and errors in *this* world, it was now felt, were worthy of study. Looking back to ancient texts, scholars and artists found non-Christian models for geography and poetry, rhetoric and philosophy, medicine and natural history. In the process, they developed a new aesthetic and a secular foundation for elite education. The ancients became the yardstick against which modern ideas and arts could be judged, and the products of this new education, the humanists, who best knew the Latin and Greek sources, became admired authorities on subjects ranging from physiology to military operations.

Economic prosperity, the increasing pace of book circulation (after Europeans made their own printing presses in the 1460s), and interstate competition spread Renaissance culture throughout Europe by the late sixteenth century. Many princes now sought to display their wealth and power by buying paintings and sculptures. Philip II of Spain purchased more than 1,000 paintings during his reign. Courtiers followed suit, building up-to-date palaces and inviting learned scholars to live on their estates. Italian merchants, whose patronage of scholars had been very important in the Renaissance's early years, were now joined by German, French, and Dutch merchant patrons. While buying cultural goods did not make them equal to aristocrats, certainly the commercial elite was able to show, by cultivating the arts and educating its sons, that it was becoming socially influential. Even the church found Renaissance art and scholarship appealing. The artists Raphael and Michelangelo often worked for the pope; several of the great sixteenth-century humanists—such as Desiderius Erasmus (1466–1536) and Philipp Melanchthon (1497–1560)—contributed much to the launching of the Renaissance.

The relationship between Renaissance humanists and artists and their patrons in politics and the church was not always an easy one. Indeed, since political and religious power were not united in Europe, as they were in China and the

Florence. This 1480 painting of Florence shows a bird's-eye view of the city during the Renaissance. Florence expanded its territory and trade after the Black Death. Note the density of the urban area, as well as the profusion of church spires and the prominence of waterways.

Islamic world, scholars and artists had the opportunity to play one side against the other, or alternatively, to suffer both clerical and political persecution. Erasmus criticized the church, but he survived happily on the patronage of English, Dutch, and French supporters; the popes had their own, very large, stable of lawyers and humanists, who ably defended the church against critics or secular claimants to church lands. As competition grew, artists and scholars could move from state to state in search of sympathetic patrons. As they did so, the educated elite became more and more cosmopolitan, as it had in China and in the Islamic empires. Scholars met one another in royal palaces and cultural centers like Florence, Antwerp, or Amsterdam. They began to correspond, asking for specialized information or rare books.

Thus, gradually, a network of educated men and women formed that was not wholly dependent on either the church or the state, but which, increasingly, had the power to debunk old truths and create new beauties. Some families and religious institutions offered women access to the new learning, and some men encouraged their sisters, daughters, and wives to expand their horizons. The well-educated nun Caritas Pirckheimer (1467–1532) exchanged learned letters and books with important male humanists in the German states; the accomplished Latinist and moral philosopher Laura Cereta (1469–1499) composed a volume of 82 letters defending the rights of women to participate in the arts and sciences. Though Cereta's letters remained unpublished until the seventeenth century, they did circulate in manuscript form during her lifetime. If humanism often confirmed the status quo, it also would prove to be a means by which authority—political, clerical, and aesthetic—could be tested by individuals other than princes and priests.

In some cases, humanists and commercial entrepreneurs came together, creating strikingly new visions of governance. In Florence, a new self-image emerged after the devastation of the Black Death. As the plague subsided, the remaining residents devoted their skills and relatively enhanced fortunes to the expansion of Florentine territory, trade, banking networks, and textile production. They exported woolens and silks to Southwest Asia as well as to Europe and served as the bankers of preference to the popes and all major European entrepôts. Florentine citizens amassed new disposable wealth—and gladly embraced a legacy rediscovered for them by the scholarly elite. Emphasizing the city's origins in Roman Republican times and its success in commerce, Florentines pioneered a kind of secular, civic patriotism that inspired, for example, the production of the first secular histories and eloquent discourses on liberty and civic virtue. But it was also a Florentine, Niccolò Machiavelli, who wrote the most famous treatise on the maintenance of authoritarian power, *The Prince*, in 1513. He argued that political leadership was not about obeying God's rules but about mastering the amoral means of modern statecraft. Holding and exercising power could be ends in themselves.

Neither in Florence nor elsewhere did the Renaissance produce a consensus about who should rule: its artists and scholars simply reproduced (and sometimes exacerbated) rivalries between polities, between church and state, and increasingly between wealthy merchants and titled aristocrats. Instead, the Renaissance produced a culture of critics and competitive individuals, who looked to many sources of authority and power—ancient texts as well as modern princes, wealth as well as blood—for support. It also produced an image of the "good Europe," one in which all these rivalries would produce not warfare, but legitimate, stable government, not patrons who protected intellectuals because they were useful to them, but real freedom of thought. It was this dream of a good, "civilized" Europe, in combination with the crusaders' desire to spread the true faith, that would, in the following centuries, be endlessly contrasted to the "barbarism" of the rest of humankind.

MING CHINA

> → *How did the Ming centralize their authority?*

Like Europeans, people in China long conceived outsiders as barbarians, and like Europeans, the stability of the Chinese world view and political order was severely shaken by the cataclysms of human and bacterial invasions. Together, the Mongols and the Black Death upended the political and intellectual foundations of what had appeared to be the world's most integrated society. The former brought the Yuan dynasty to power; the latter devastated the Middle Kingdom and prepared the way for the emergence of the Ming dynasty in 1368.

China had been ripe for this pandemic. Its numbers had increased significantly under the Song dynasty (960–1279). Indeed, Mongol rule initially sustained Chinese prosperity and population growth. But by 1300, hunger and scarcity began to spread as resources were stretched thin. A weakened population was especially vulnerable to plague. For seventy years, the Black Death ravaged China. The death and destruction brought by the disease were unprecedented and shattered the Mongol dynasty's claim to a mandate from heaven. In 1331, the Black Death may have killed 90 percent of the population in Hebei province. From there it spread throughout the Chinese provinces, reaching Fujian and the coast at Shandong. By the 1350s, severe outbreaks occurred in most of China's large cities.

The reign of the last of the Yuan Mongol rulers, Toghon Temür (ruled 1333–1368), was a time of utter chaos. Even as the Black Death was sweeping over large parts of China, bandit groups and dissident religious sects were undercutting the power of the state. In China, as in other realms desolated by the plague, popular religious movements arose and spoke of impending doom. The most prominent of these was the Red Turban Movement, which took its name from the red headbands that its soldiers wore. The Red Turbans blended China's rich and diverse popular cultural and religious traditions, including Buddhism, Daoism, and other faiths. Its leaders imposed strict dietary restrictions on followers, engaged in penance and ceremonial rituals, in which the sexes freely mixed, and spread the belief that the world was drawing to an end.

In these chaotic times, only the emergence of a powerful military movement capable of overpowering other groups could restore order. That intervention came from a poor young man who had acquired his early training in the Red Turban Movement: Zhu Yuanzhang (ruled 1368–1398). Zhu came from the humblest of backgrounds. He was an orphan from a peasant household in an area devastated by disease and famine and a former novice at a Buddhist monastery. In 1352, the twenty-four-year-old Zhu joined the Red Turbans and rose quickly within its ranks to become a distinguished commander. Eventually, he defeated the Yuan and drove the Mongols from China.

With his ascendance, it became clear that he had a much larger design for all of China than the ambitions of most warlords. When Zhu took the important city of Nanjing in 1356, he renamed it Yingtian, meaning "In response to Heaven." With his successful military campaigns, Zhu felt strong enough by 1368 to proclaim the founding of the Ming ("brilliant") dynasty. In September of that year his troops met lit-

tle resistance when they seized the Yuan capital of Beijing. The Mongol emperor fled to his homeland in the steppe. It would, however, take Zhu close to another twenty years to reunify the entire country.

CENTRALIZATION UNDER THE MING

Zhu and successive Ming emperors had to rebuild a devastated society from the ground up. In the past, China had experienced natural catastrophes, especially flooding (see discussion on "China's Sorrow," the great flood of the Yellow River in 11 CE, in Chapter 7), depopulation, wars, and social dislocation. But the plague in the fourteenth century brought devastation on an unprecedented scale, leaving the new rulers to reconstruct the bureaucracy, rebuild the great cities, and restore respect for the ruling elites.

The rebuilding process began under Zhu, who called himself the Hongwu ("expansive and martial") Emperor and ruled in a grand style. He displayed imperial grandeur in the extravagant scale of his newly constructed capital at Nanjing. When the third emperor of the dynasty, Zhu Di, known as the Yongle Emperor (ruled 1403–1424), relocated the capital to its present-day site of Beijing, he was set on a still more grandiose style. Construction in Beijing mobilized around 100,000 artisans and 1 million laborers. The city had three separate walled enclosures. Inside the outer city walls was the section known as the imperial city; inside its walls was the palace city, often called the Forbidden City. The traffic within the walled sections navigated through boulevards lead-

The Forbidden City. The Yongle Emperor relocated the capital to Beijing, where he began the construction of the Forbidden City, or imperial palace. The palace was designed to inspire awe in all who saw it.

Chinese Irrigation. Farmers in imperial China used sophisticated devices to extract water for irrigation, as depicted in this illustration from the Yuan Mongol period.

ing to the different gates, which were marked by imposing towers. The palace compound, within which the imperial family resided, had more than 9,000 rooms. Anyone standing in the front courts, which measured more than 400 yards on a side and were adorned with marble terraces and carved railings, was struck by a sense of awesome power. That, of course, was precisely what the Ming emperors (just as the Ottoman sultans in building the Topkapi Palace) had in mind.

Marriage and kinship buttressed the power of the Ming imperial household. The founder of the dynasty married the adopted daughter of one of the leading Red Turban rebels against the Yuan Mongol regime (her father, according to legend, was a convicted murderer), thereby consolidating his power and eliminating a threat. Empress Ma, as she was known, became Hongwu's principal wife and was known for her compassion. She emerged as the kinder, gentler face of the regime, tempering the harsh and sometimes cruel disposition of her spouse.

In addition to Empress Ma, Hongwu had numerous other consorts, including Korean and Mongol women, who bore him twenty-six sons and sixteen daughters. He initially sought to rule the empire through his many kinsmen. He gave imperial princes large stipends, command of large garrisons, and significant autonomy in running their own domains. His ini-

tial idea was that kinship solidarity would provide strong support for the ruling household. But when the power of the princes became too great and threatening to the court, Hongwu cut their stipends to one-fifth, reduced their overall privileges, and took over control of their garrisons. Instead of depending on the princes, he established an imperial bureaucracy beholden to him and to his successors (as in the Ottoman Empire). These officials and bureaucrats were appointed based on their performance on a reinstated civil service examination.

The emperor put in place bureaucrats to oversee the manufacture of porcelain, cotton, and silk products, and the collection of taxes. Hongwu reestablished the Confucian school system as a means of selecting a loyal cadre of officials (not unlike the Ottoman janissaries and administrators), who would be obedient to the emperor. He also set up local networks of villages to rebuild irrigation systems and to supervise reforestation projects to prevent flooding. The amount of land reclaimed rose from 575,965 hectares in 1371 to 1,485,572 hectares in 1379. Historians estimate that about 1 billion trees were planted during Hongwu's reign, including 50 million sterculia trees, palm trees, and varnish trees in the area of the capital, Nanjing, in 1391. The products of these trees were used for building the maritime expedition fleet in the

Primary Source

THE HONGWU EMPEROR'S PROCLAMATION

This proclamation of the founding ruler of the Ming dynasty, the Hongwu Emperor (ruled 1368–1398), reveals how he envisioned the reconstruction of a devastated country as his own personal project. He distrusted his officials and berated them for their numerous shortcomings. He sought a return to a more austere world by denouncing the corrosive effect of money and material possessions on the morals of his subjects. Although frustrated in his efforts, Hongwu nonetheless set the tone for the centralization of power in the person of the emperor.

To all civil and military officials:

I have told you to refrain from evil. Doing so would enable you to bring glory to your ancestors, your wives and children, and yourselves. With your virtue, you then could assist me in my endeavors to bring good fortune and prosperity to the people. You would establish names for yourselves in Heaven and on earth, and for thousands and thousands of years, you would be praised as worthy men.

However, after assuming your posts, how many of you really followed my instructions? Those of you in charge of money and grain have stolen them yourselves; those of you in charge of criminal laws and punishments have neglected the regulations. In this way grievances are not redressed and false charges are ignored. Those with genuine grievances have nowhere to turn; even when they merely wish to state their complaints, their words never reach the higher officials. Occasionally these unjust matters come to my attention. After I discover the truth, I capture and imprison the corrupt, villainous, and oppressive officials involved. I punish them with the death penalty or forced labor or have them flogged with bamboo sticks in order to make manifest the consequences of good or evil actions. . . .

Alas, how easily money and profit can bewitch a person! With the exception of the righteous person, the true gentleman, and the sage, no one is able to avoid the temptation of money. But is it really so difficult to reject the temptation of profit? The truth is people have not really tried.

Previously, during the final years of the Yuan dynasty, there were many ambitious men competing for power who did not treasure their sons and daughters but prized jade and silk, coveted fine horses and beautiful clothes, relished drunken singing and unrestrained pleasure, and enjoyed separating people from their parents, wives, and children. I also lived in that chaotic period. How did I avoid such snares? I was able to do so because I valued my reputation and wanted to preserve my life. Therefore I did not dare to do these evil things. . . .

In order to protect my reputation and to preserve my life, I have done away with music, beautiful girls, and valuable objects. Those who love such things are usually "a success in the morning, a failure in the evening." Being aware of the fallacy of such behavior, I will not indulge such foolish fancies. It is not really that hard to do away with these tempting things.

→ *What does Hongwu's proclamation tell us about the importance of education?*

→ *Why would a Chinese emperor issue a decree that focuses on defining moral behavior?*

SOURCE: Patricia Buckley Ebrey (ed.), *Chinese Civilization: A Sourcebook*, 2nd ed., revised and expanded (New York: The Free Press, 1993), pp. 205–06.

---

early fifteenth century. For water control, 40,987 reservoirs were repaired or constructed in 1395.

Under this revamped system, the imperial palace not only projected the image of a power center, it *was* the center of power. Every official of the administration was appointed by the emperor through the Ministry of Personnel. Hongwu also eliminated the previously important post of prime minister in 1380 after he executed the man who held the post. Henceforth, Hongwu ruled directly. Ming bureaucrats literally lost their seats and had to kneel before the emperor. In one eight-day period, he reputedly reviewed over 1,600 petitions dealing with 3,392 separate matters. The drawback, of course, was that the emperor had to keep tabs on this immense system, and his bureaucrats were not always up to the task. Indeed, Hongwu constantly juggled personal and impersonal forms of authority, sometimes fortifying the administration, sometimes undermining it lest it become too autonomous. In due course, Hongwu nurtured a bureaucracy far more extensive than those of the Islamic empires. The Ming thus established the most highly centralized and rationalized system of government of all the monarchies of this period.

RELIGION UNDER THE MING

The Ming zeal to centralize and rationalize extended to the religious pantheon as well. The emperor revised and strengthened the elaborate protocol of rites and ceremonies that had undergirded dynastic power for centuries. As well as underscoring the emperor's centrality, official rituals, such as those related to the gods of soil and grain, reinforced local political and social hierarchies. Under the guise of "community" gatherings, the performance of rites and sacrifices solidified the Ming order. Ming rulers claimed to be moral and spiritual benefactors of their subjects. On at least ninety occasions each year, the emperor engaged in rites of sacrifice, providing symbolic communion between the human and the spiritual worlds. Lavish sacred festivities were occasions for the Ming rulers to reinforce their image as mediators between otherworldly affairs of their gods and worldly concerns of their subjects. The gods were on the side of the Ming household.

The emperor sanctioned official cults which were either civil or military, then further distinguished them into great, middle, or minor, as well as celestial, terrestrial, or human categories. Official cults, however, often collided with local faiths. Such conflicts revealed the limits to Ming centralism. Consider Dongyang, a small, hilly interior region of the realm. As was common in Ming China, the people of Dongyang supported Buddhist institutions. Guan Yu, a legendary martial hero killed in the year 217, was enshrined in a local Buddhist monastery. But he was also worshipped as part of a state cult. The problem was that the state cult and the Buddhist monastery were separate entities, and according to imperial law, the demands of the state cult were supposed to prevail over those of the local monastery. Local magistrates in Dongyang kept a watchful eye on local religious leaders, though they refrained from tampering directly in Dongyang's Buddhist monastery. While the dynasty insisted that people honor their contributions to the state, people in Dongyang delivered most of their funds to the Buddhist monks. So strong were local sentiments and contributions that even officials siphoned revenues to the monastery.

Ming Deities. A pantheon of deities worshipped during the Ming, demonstrating the rich religious culture of the period.

MING RULERSHIP

Overall, sacred sources of political power were comparatively less essential for the Ming dynasty than for the Islamic dynasties. Conquest and defense helped establish the realm; a bureaucracy kept it functioning. The remarkable scale of the Ming realm (see Map 11-6) meant the establishment of a complicated administration. To many outsiders, especially Europeans whose own end of Afro-Eurasia was in a state of constant war, Ming stability and centralization appeared to be political wizardry.

As we consider the structures underlying Ming power, we must not overlook the usual dynastic dilemmas. The emperor

MAP 11-6   MING CHINA, 1500s

The Ming state was one of the largest empires at the beginning of the sixteenth century and the most populous. It had a long seacoast and even longer internal borders. Does the map offer any clues as to where the Ming rulers expected the greatest threat to their security? How did the rulers enhance the security of the state against these threats? How did the Ming rulers view foreign contact and exchange during this period?

wished to be seen as the special guardian, or patriarch, of his subjects. He wanted their allegiance, as well as their taxes and their labor. During hard times, poor farmers were reluctant to provide resources—taxes or services—to distant officials. For these reasons alone, Hongwu preferred to entrust the management of the rural world to local leaders, whom he appointed as village chiefs, village elders, or tax captains. One popular Chinese proverb was: "The mountain is high and the emperor is far away." Within these village communities, the dynasty cre-

ated a social hierarchy based on age, sex, and kinship. While women's labor remained critical for the village economy, the government reinforced a gender hierarchy by promoting a cult of female chastity and constructing commemorative arches for widows who refrained from remarrying. The Ming thus produced a more elaborate system for classifying and controlling subject peoples than did the other dynasties on the Afro-Eurasian landmass, although the system began to show strains as early as the beginning of the fifteenth century.

The Ming Empire, like the European and Islamic states, also had to cope with periodic unrest and rebellions. Rebels were often inspired by their own brand of religious beliefs, just as local elites resented the encroachment of central authority. Outright terror helped stymie threats to central authority. In a massive wave of carnage, Hongwu slaughtered anyone who posed a threat to his authority, from the highest of ministers to the lowliest of scribes. From 1376 to 1393, four of his purges condemned close to 100,000 subjects to execution. Purge victims included civil and military officials, landowners, local leaders, and their families. Yet, despite the immense power of the emperor, the Ming Empire remained undergoverned; there were too few loyal officials to handle local affairs as the number of people in the realm multiplied. By the sixteenth and the early seventeenth centuries, for example, some 10,000 to 15,000 officials had responsibility for a population exceeding perhaps 200 million people. But Hongwu bequeathed a set of tools for ruling to his descendants, tools that enabled the Ming Empire to draw on the subjects' direct loyalty to the emperor and the workings of a powerful bureaucracy. This enabled his successors to balance local sources of power with centralizing ambitions. It was, of course, imperfect. But, for the times, this was a very powerful dynasty.

TRADE UNDER THE MING

In the fourteenth century, China began its economic recovery from the devastation of disease and political turmoil. Gradually, political stability allowed trade to revive. China and the new dynasty's merchants reestablished their preeminence in long-distance, commercial exchange. Chinese silk and cotton textiles, as well as fine porcelains, ranked among the most coveted luxuries in the world. Wealthy families from Lisbon to Kalabar wished to wash their hands in delicate Chinese bowls and to make fine wardrobes from bolts of Chinese dyed linens and smoothly spun silk. When a Chinese merchant ship sailed into port, local trading partners and onlookers gathered to watch the unloading of the precious cargoes. During the Ming period, Chinese maritime traders based in ports along the southern coast, in Hangzhou, Quanzhou, and Guangzhou (Canton), were as energetic as their Muslim counterparts in the Indian Ocean. These ports were home to many prosperous merchants and the point of convergence for vast sea lanes. Leaving the mainland ports, Chinese merchants carried their wares to offshore islands, the Pescadores, and Taiwan. From there, they extended their commercial activities to the ports of Kyūshū, the Ryūkyūs, Luzon, and maritime Southeast Asia. As entrepôts for global goods, East Asian ports flourished. Former fishing villages evolved into major urban centers.

The Ming dynasty viewed overseas expansion with suspicion, however. Hongwu feared that too much commerce and contact with the outside world would cause instability and undermine the authority of his rule. In fact, Hongwu banned private maritime commerce in 1371. But enforcement of this prohibition was lax, and by the late fifteenth century maritime trade along the coast once again surged. Because so much of the thriving business of the South China Sea ports was conducted in defiance of official edicts, it led to ongoing friction between government officials and maritime traders. Although the Ming government, under pressure from the mercantile communities, did relax its ban and agreed to issue

Zheng He's Ship. A testament to centuries of experience in shipbuilding and maritime activities, the largest ship in Zheng He's armada in the early fifteenth century was about five times the length of Columbus's *Santa Maria* (pictured next to Zheng's ship) and had nine times the capacity in terms of tonnage. It had nine staggered masts and twelve silk sails, all designed to demonstrate the grandeur of the Ming Empire.

licenses for overseas trade in the mid- sixteenth century, it continued to vacillate in its policies. To Ming officials, the sea ultimately represented problems of order and control rather than opportunities.

The spectacular exception to the Ming government's general attitude to maritime trade was a well-known series of officially sponsored maritime expeditions in the early fifteenth century. It was the ambitious Yongle Emperor who took the initiative. One of his loyal followers was a Muslim captured by the Ming army when he was a boy. He was castrated (as a eunuch, he could not continue his family line and so theoretically owed sole allegiance to the emperor) and sent to serve at the court. The boy, Zheng He (1371–1433), grew up to be a powerful and important military leader, entrusted by the emperor in 1405 with venturing out to trade, collect tribute, and display China's power to the world. From 1405 to 1433, Zheng He commanded the world's greatest armada and led seven naval expeditions. His larger ships reached 400 feet long (compared to Columbus's puny *Santa Maria*, which was 85 feet long), carried many hundreds of sailors on four tiers of decks, and maneuvered with sophisticated balanced rudders, nine masts, and watertight compartments. The first expedition set sail with a flotilla of 62 large ships and over 200 lesser ones. There were 28,000 men aboard, pledged to promote the cause of Ming glory.

Zheng He and his entourage aimed to establish tributary relations with far-flung territories—from Southeast Asia to the Indian Ocean ports, to the Persian Gulf, and to the east coast of Africa (see Map 11-7). A central goal of these expeditions was not territorial expansion but rather control of trade and tribute. Zheng traded for ivory, spices, ointments, exotic woods, and even some wildlife, including giraffes, zebras, and ostriches. He also used his considerable force to intervene in local affairs, exhibiting the might of China in the process. If a community refused to pay tribute to the emperor, Zheng's fleet would attack it. Rulers or envoys from Southeast Asia, India, Southwest Asia, and Africa were encouraged to visit China. When local rulers proved to be uncooperative,

MAP 11-7   VOYAGES OF ZHENG HE, 1405–1433

Compare the voyages of Zheng He with the travels of Ibn Battuta and Marco Polo described in Chapter 10 and with the voyages of the European explorers discussed in Chapter 12. What were the goals of these voyages? Did Zheng He travel across routes that were familiar to others at this time? Why did Chinese expeditions not have the same impact as European voyages of exploration toward the end of the fifteenth century?

Zheng might seize them and drag them all the way to China to face the emperor, as he did the rulers of Sumatra and Ceylon.

Although many of the items gathered on the voyages delighted the court, most were not the stuff of everyday commerce. The expeditions were, in short, glamorous but very expensive, and they came to a rather abrupt halt in 1433. Never again did the Ming undertake such large-scale maritime ventures. In fact, as early as 1424, when the Yongle Emperor died, the official expeditions had already lost their most important and enthusiastic patron. Moreover, by the mid-fifteenth century, there was a revival of military threats from the north. In 1449, the Ming court was shocked to discover that during a tour of the frontiers, the emperor had been captured and held hostage by the Mongols. Mindful of how the maritime-oriented Song dynasty had been eventually overrun by invaders from the north, officials withdrew imperial support for maritime ventures and instead devoted their energies to overland ventures and defense.

If Chinese maritime commerce continued without official patronage, the decision to abandon imperial support for oceanic exploration led to the decline of Chinese naval power and opened the way for newcomers and rivals. Southeast Asians took advantage by constructing large oceangoing vessels, known as "jong," which plied the regional trade routes from the fifteenth century to the early sixteenth century. These ships weighed an average of 350 to 500 tons, but they could be as big as 1,000 tons, with 1,000 men on board. They carried cargoes and passengers not only to southern China, but also to the Indian Ocean as far west as Calicut and the Red Sea. Muslims also occupied the vacuum left by the Chinese, sailing from ports like Calicut across the Indian Ocean west to Mombassa and Mogadishu, and east to Melaka (Malacca). In addition, Japanese pirates took over some of the trade and made the work of Chinese overseas merchants that much more difficult. The Chinese decision after 1450 to focus on internal trade and defending northern borders just at the time others began to look outward and overseas was, in its way as monumental as that of Mehmed to take Constantinople, or that of an obscure Genoese voyager, Christopher Columbus, to attempt a perilous westward voyage across "the Ocean Sea."

 CONCLUSION

Comparisons help us to understand complex institutions and historical events like those that took place in Afro-Eurasia in the two centuries after the Black Death. The ascent of new dynasties, except for the Mughals, stemmed, in the first instance, from the impact of the Mongol invasions and the Black Death. These states were shaped by varying local conditions—the ambition of a Ming warlord, the military expansionism of Turkish households on the edge of the Christian empire of Byzantium, the unifying vision of Mughal rulers in the northern part of India, and the desire of a variety of rulers to consolidate power in smaller states within Europe. But interactions between peoples also mattered. An eagerness to reestablish and expand trade networks following the Mongol invasions and the Black Death and the desire to convert unbelievers to "the true faith" set many of the peoples of the world in motion.

The great dynasties that came to the fore in this period all had to deal with a common set of problems. They had to create legitimacy for themselves, had to ensure smooth procedures of succession to the throne when a monarch died, had to come to terms with religious groups, and had to establish working relationships with the nongovernmental elements in society, especially nobles, townspeople, merchants, and peasants. Yet, the states developed distinctive traits. The new Afro-Eurasian polities were a combination of outright political innovation, the use of well-known ways of ruling handed down within their own communities, and avid borrowing from nearby polities. The monarchies of Europe were in the process of achieving a high degree of internal unity, although this unity was often brought about through warfare with neighbors and in the context of a burgeoning cultural Renaissance. The Ottoman rulers perfected techniques for ruling a far-flung and ethnically and religiously diverse empire. They were able to move military forces swiftly, to allow local communities a degree of autonomy and at the same time to train a civil and military bureaucracy dedicated to the Ottoman and Sunni Islamic way of life. The Ming fashioned an imperial system based on a Confucian-trained bureaucracy and intense subordination, if not loyalty, to the emperor so that it could cope with the mammoth task of ruling over 200 million subjects. The rising monarchies of Europe, the Shiite regime of the Safavids in Persia, and the Ottoman state were all fired by religious fervor and sought to eradicate or subordinate the beliefs of other groups.

Afro-Eurasian societies and states recovered from the Mongols and the Black Death with greater political and economic powers than before. The Islamic states, the Ming Empire, and the emerging monarchies in Europe were all founded on military prowess and keen to ensure stable hierarchies and secure borders and, if possible, to expand their domains. Each recognized the importance of vigorous commercial activity. Each used dynastic marriage and succession, religion, and administrative bureaucracies to legitimize its rule. By the sixteenth century, societies across Afro-Eurasia were seeking to expand trade with their neighbors or to conquer them. The Islamic regimes especially, and their far-flung traders, increasingly engaged in long-distance commerce, and, by conquest and conversion, extended and strengthened their holdings, especially in the eastern Mediterranean.

Ottoman conquests provoked Europeans to seek alternative trade routes to Africa and Asia. After the ravages of the plague it took more than a century for Europeans to establish new commercial connections to the east, south, and most unexpectedly, west. The consequences of their new toeholds would be momentous—just as the Chinese decision to turn *away* from overseas exploration and commerce marked a turning point in world history. Both decisions would be instrumental in determining which worlds would be brought together—and which would remain apart.

STUDY QUESTIONS

 WWNORTON.COM/STUDYSPACE

1. Explain how the Black Death, or bubonic plague, spread throughout Afro-Eurasia in the fourteenth century. What human activity facilitated the diffusion of this pathogen?

2. Describe the long-term consequences of the bubonic plague for the Afro-Eurasian world. What were the plague's social, political, and economic ramifications in the various parts of Afro-Eurasia?

3. List the Islamic dynasties that emerged in Afro-Eurasia after the bubonic plague. How were they similar, and how were they different?

4. Describe how the Ming dynasty centralized its power in China in the fourteenth and fifteenth centuries. What new political innovations did it pursue and what traditions did it sustain in the Middle Kingdom?

5. Describe the goals of the Ming dynasty's maritime exhibitions during this time. Why did the government later abandon them?

6. Explain why the bubonic plague undermined the feudal order of the Catholic church. How were regional monarchs in Europe able to capitalize on this development?

7. Analyze the connection between the rise of regional dynasties and the European Renaissance. How did regional centralization foster new modes of expression and thinking?

FURTHER READINGS

Bois, Guy, *The Crisis of Feudalism: Economy and Society in Eastern Normandy, c. 1300–1550* (1984). A good case study of a French region that illustrates the turmoil in fourteenth-century Europe.

Brook, Timothy, *Praying for Power: Buddhism and the Formation of Gentry Society in Late Ming China* (1994). An analysis of the role of a significant religious force in the political and social developments of the Ming.

Dardess, John, *A Ming Society: T'ai-ho County, Kiangsi, Fourteenth to Seventeenth Centuries* (1996). A work that covers the different changes and developments of a single locality in China through the centuries.

Dols, Michael W., *The Black Death in the Middle East* (1977). One of the few scholarly works to examine the Black Death outside Europe.

Dreyer, Edward, *Early Ming China: A Political History, 1355–1435* (1982). A useful account of the early years of the Ming dynasty

Chronology

	1300		1400
EUROPE		▪ Famine in Europe, 1315–1322	
		▪ Hundred Years' War in France, 1337–1453	
		▪ Black Death reaches Italian port cities, 1347	
		▪ Jacquerie Revolt in France, 1358	
			▪ English Peasants' Revolt, 1381
SOUTH ASIA	▪ Delhi Sultanate army repulses Mongols, 1303		▪ Timur sacks Delhi, 1398
EAST ASIA		▪ Black Death begins in China, 1320	▪ Reign of Hongwu Emperor in China (Ming dynasty), 1368–1398
		Reign of Yongle Emperor in China, 1403–1424 ▪	
		Zheng He's voyages from China, 1405–1433 ▪	
THE ISLAMIC WORLD	▪ Osman begins to build Ottoman Empire, 1299–1326		Murad II expands the Ottoman Empire, 1421–1451 ▪

Finkel, Caroline, *Osman's Dream: The Story of the Ottoman Empire, 1300–1923* (2005). The latest and most authoritative overview of Ottoman history.

Hale, John, *The Civilization of Europe in the Renaissance* (1994). A beautifully crafted account of the politics, economics, and culture of the Renaissance period in western Europe.

Hodgson, Marshall, *The Venture of Islam: Conscience and History in a World Civilization*, vol. 3 (1974). A good volume on the workings of the Ottoman state.

Itzkowitz, Norman, *Ottoman Empire and Islamic Tradition* (1972). Another good book on the Ottoman state.

Jackson, Peter, *The Delhi Sultanate* (1999). A meticulous, highly specialized, political and military history.

Jackson, Peter, and Lawrence Lockhart (eds.), *The Cambridge History of Iran*, vol. 6 (1986). A volume that deals with the Timurid and Safavid periods in Iran.

Jones, E. L., *The European Miracle* (1981). A provocative work on the economic and social recovery from the Black Death.

Kafadar, Cemal, *Between Two Worlds: The Construction of the Ottoman State* (1995). A thorough reconsideration of the origins of one of the world's great land empires.

Karamustafa, Ahmed, *God's Unruly Friends: Dervish Groups in the Islamic Later Middle Period, 1200–1550* (1994). A book that describes the unorthodox Islamic activities that were occurring in the Islamic world prior to and alongside the establishment of the Ottoman and Safavid empires.

Levathes, Louise, *When China Ruled the Seas: The Treasure Fleet of the Dragon Throne, 1405–33* (1994). A book that provides a lively account of the Zheng He expeditions.

Lowry, Heath W., *The Nature of the Early Ottoman State* (2003). New perspectives on the rise of the Ottomans to prominence.

McNeill, William, *Plagues and Peoples* (1976). A pathbreaking work with a highly useful chapter on the spread of the Black Death throughout the Afro-Eurasian landmass.

Morgan, David, *Medieval Persia, 1040–1797* (1988). Contains an informative discussion of the Safavid state.

Peirce, Leslie, *The Imperial Harem: Women and Sovereignty in the Ottoman Empire* (1993). A work that describes the powerful place that imperial women had in political affairs.

Pirenne, Henri, *Economic and Social History of Medieval Europe* (1937). A classic study of the economic and social recovery from the Black Death.

Reid, James J., *Tribalism and Society in Islamic Iran, 1500–1629* (1983). A useful account of how the Mongols and other nomadic steppe peoples influenced Iran in the era when the Safavids were establishing their authority.

Russell, Peter, *Prince Henry "the Navigator"* (2000). A close examination of the formation of the Portuguese kingdom of the House of Aviz.

Singman, Jeffrey L. (ed.), *Daily Life in Medieval Europe* (1999). An introductory description of the social and material world experienced by Europeans of different walks of life.

Tuchman, Barbara W., *A Distant Mirror: The Calamitous Fourteenth Century* (1978). A book that shows, in a vigorous way, how war, famine, and pestilence devastated Europeans in the fourteenth century.

Wittek, Paul, *The Rise of the Ottoman Empire* (1958). A work that contains vital insights on the emergence of the Ottoman state amid the political chaos in Anatolia.

1500	1600

▌ *War of the Roses in England, 1455–1485*

    ▌ *Castile and Aragon united, 1469*

        ▌ *Tudors seize English throne, 1485*

            ▌ *Spaniards take Granada from Muslims, 1492*

                ▌ *Babur founds Mughal Empire in India, 1526*

Mehmed II expands the Ottoman Empire, 1451–1481

Ottoman armies conquer Constantinople, 1453

        ▌ *Shiism becomes Safavid state religion, 1501*

        ▌ *Shah Ismail reigns over Safavid Empire, 1501–1524*

            ▌ *Suleiman consolidates Ottoman Empire, 1520–1566*

Chapter 12

CONTACT, COMMERCE, AND COLONIZATION, 1450S–1600

On September 20, 1519, a fleet of five ships under the command of Ferdinand Magellan set out from the Spanish port of Sanlúcar de Barrameda. Nearly three years later, a single vessel returned home, having successfully circumnavigated the globe. This achievement had come at a high cost. Four ships had been lost, and only eighteen men, from an original complement of two hundred and sixty-five, staved off scurvy, starvation, and stormy seas to complete the journey. Magellan himself had died in a battle with inhabitants of the Philippines. But the survivors of Magellan's voyage had become the first true world travelers. In contrast to earlier adventurers who confined their primarily overland treks to Eurasia and Africa, Magellan's transoceanic passage connected these worlds with those that, from Afro-Eurasia's viewpoint, had been apart—the Americas.

Mongol armies had run up against barriers, natural and human, in their land-based expansion connecting much of Afro-Eurasia; most famously, Mongol-led forces had drowned when trying to cross the sea to Japan. After the Mongol downfall, land-based interconnections persisted, but more significant were the sea-based ties that developed or deepened: across the Indian Ocean, across the Atlantic, and around the Pacific as well as the South China Sea. The voyages of Magellan and other European mariners brought westerners into contact with the already vibrant commercial networks in Asia and gave Europeans access to new resources in the region they proclaimed to be the "New World." The "discovery" of the Americas was not what Christopher Columbus had in mind when he headed west across the Atlantic looking for Asia. But his voyages did convince Europeans that there were, still, vast new territories to exploit and, if possible, convert.

In the conquest and colonization of the Americas, Europeans also drew heavily on connections with West Africa.

Spanish and Portuguese attempts to exploit African territories set the stage for experiments in the New World. African laborers became increasingly vital to agricultural production and to extracting precious metals. For European merchants, it was a lucky accident and powerful motivation that, just as they gained control over these new resources, the world's demand for silver, sugar, and (a bit later) cotton was beginning to grow. By the mid-sixteenth century, the riches of the New World were making prominent participants in the vibrant commercial circuits of Afro-Eurasia.

Through the sixteenth century, the mightiest Asian empires—the Ming (in China), the Mughal (in South Asia), and the Ottoman (straddling West Asia, North Africa, and southeastern Europe)—maintained their economic prowess and retained control over all but small pockets of their expansive realms. If, by 1600, the impact of the European conquest and colonization of the Americas was being felt around the globe, these empires still had little to fear from their upstart competitors.

THE OLD TRADE AND THE NEW

> → *What was old and what was new in sixteenth-century world trade?*

Well before the products of the Americas entered the circuits of Afro-Eurasian trade, long-distance commerce had staged an impressive recovery from the destruction wrought by the Black Death. Just as political leaders had rebuilt their states by mixing traditional ideas with innovative ones, so, too, merchant elites in Asia and Europe revived old trade patterns while establishing new networks. Increasingly, traffic across seas supplemented, if not supplanted, the overland transportation of goods across long distances. In the fifteenth century, the Indian Ocean and China Seas were the focal points of Afro-Eurasia's maritime commerce. Across these waters, an assortment of goods moved from one point to another, their shipment and exchange directed by Arab, Persian, Indian, and Chinese merchants who often settled in far-off diaspora communities and established cross-cultural liaisons.

European mariners and traders, searching for new routes to South and East Asia, began exploring the Atlantic coast of Africa. Lured by spices, silks, and slaves and aided by advances in maritime technology, Portuguese expeditions made their way around Africa and to India in the last decade of the fifteenth century. At almost the same time, neighboring monarchs in Spanish kingdoms sponsored Christopher Columbus's bid to reach Asia by sailing west across the Atlantic. Both Portuguese and Spanish ventures shared similar motivations: to convert "heathen" peoples to Christianity and to

Focus Questions CONTACT, COMMERCE, AND COLONIZATION

> → *What was old and what was new in sixteenth-century world trade?*
> → *How did the Portuguese attitude toward trade enable the Portuguese to take advantage of and dominate their trading partners?*
> → *What did European conquerors adopt and change from the New World traditions they encountered?*
> → *What military and maritime technologies advanced Portuguese exploration?*
> → *How was Europe transformed politically and spiritually?*
> → *Why did trade expand and wealth increase in sixteenth-century Asia?*

 WWNORTON.COM/STUDYSPACE

reap the riches to be found in Asian ports. Although Europeans still had little to offer would-be trading partners in Asia, they did begin to develop the capability and interest in long-distance, overseas trade that would lay the foundations for a new kind of global commerce.

THE REVIVAL OF THE CHINESE ECONOMY

Crucial to Afro-Eurasia's growing economies and populations was the dynamism of China. In the fifteenth century under the Ming dynasty, commerce rebounded from the devastation of Mongol invasions and the Black Death, and the Chinese achieved impressive economic expansion. China's development, in turn, stimulated the other economies across Afro-Eurasia.

China's vast internal economy, not external trade, was the mainspring of the country's progress. The Ming dynasty transferred its capital from coastal Nanjing to the interior city of Beijing ("northern capital"), homeland of the Ming Yongle Emperor and a place better suited for defense against the Mongols. This move inland allowed Chinese merchants, artisans, and cash crop farmers to take advantage of a rapidly growing population and domestic market that had gone largely untapped when the capital and most commerce were situated on the eastern coastline of China. Over the three centuries of Ming rule, the Chinese populace doubled and increasingly congregated in large cities. The reconstruction between 1411 and 1415 of the Grand Canal, which stretched from Hangzhou in the south to Beijing in the north, opened a major artery that enabled food and riches from the lower Yangzi region to provision Beijing and the northern border cities. China's urban centers, such as Nanjing with a population approaching a million and Beijing at half a million, became massive and lucrative markets. The growth of other urban centers in the lower Yangzi area such as Suzhou and Yangzhou further challenged, and then eclipsed, Hangzhou's preeminence. Farther south, the sister cities of Guangzhou (Canton) and Foshan together had as many residents as the whole of Europe's urban population around 1600.

China's elaborate trading networks distributed silk and cotton textiles, rice, porcelain ceramics, paper, and many other products all over the country. The Ming state's concern over the autonomy of China's merchant classes did not dampen internal trade, and the dynasty's efforts to curb overseas commerce, following Zheng He's voyages (see Chapter 11), were largely unsuccessful. As long as merchants did not disturb the Ming order, they were tolerated. And in spite of the government's strictures on engaging in overseas trade, coastal cities remained active harbors (see Map 12-1).

The Chinese manufactured brocaded silks and porcelain ceramics to the highest standards of workmanship. Many Chinese cities produced silk textiles, but the city that acquired the reputation for producing the best quality was Suzhou, south of the Yangzi River. So important were the products of the Suzhou artisans to the Ming budget that taxes on their silks often provided one-tenth of state revenues. The second of the most-prized commodities was porcelain, whose single biggest consumers, with the deepest of pockets, were the Ming rulers themselves. The great imperial ceramic works at Jingdezhen produced internationally recognized "blue on white" Ming ware depicting motifs from central Asia, Persia, and India (all of which were linked to China via enhanced trade). Potentates of the court developed an almost insatiable appetite for porcelains of high quality. With their access to the fiscal reserves of the government, courtiers purchased nearly all of its most beautiful products, leaving the rougher and more durable porcelains for less discerning foreign buyers.

Although the Chinese kept the best for themselves, their silks and porcelain were coveted by wealthy persons across Afro-Eurasia. But buyers outside China faced a severe problem: What did they have to trade with the Chinese?

The answer was silver, which became essential to the smooth functioning of the Ming monetary system. Ming predecessors had used paper money and copper coinage, but Ming consumers and traders mistrusted anything other than silver or gold for commercial transactions (coins of varying quality continued to circulate for ordinary market exchanges). Silver also became a mainstay of the Ming fiscal system. Especially once the rulers adopted the precious metal as a means of tax payment in the 1430s, silver became the predominant medium for larger commercial transactions.

But China did not produce sufficient amounts of silver for its growing needs. Indeed, silver and other precious metals were about the only commodities for which the Chinese were willing to trade their highly valued manufactures.

Chinese Porcelain Box. The shape, coloring, and texture of this Chinese porcelain writing box are a tribute to the exquisite craftsmanship that went into its production. It was also a symbol of the flourishing world trade and a typical example of what the French then called "chinoiserie," the possession of which was considered a hallmark of taste and cultivation among the rich and the status-conscious in Europe.

MAP 12-1   TRADE AND PRODUCTION IN MING CHINA

The Ming Empire at the beginning of the seventeenth century was the world's most populous state and arguably its wealthiest. What were the main items involved in China's export-import trade and who purchased Chinese exports? Why was China the world's leading importer of silver in the seventeenth and eighteenth centuries? How important was export trade to the prosperity of the empire?

Foreigners learned to exploit this need. Through most of the sixteenth century, China's main source of silver was Japan, which one Florentine merchant referred to as the "silver islands." Both Chinese and European merchants plied the routes from Japanese ports to the Chinese mainland.

After the 1570s, however, the Philippines also became a gateway for silver from the New World. The Ming had over-

seen construction of a merchant marine (using trees planted by the first Ming emperor in the 1390s), enabling Chinese merchants to ship silks, cotton, and porcelain to Manila in the Philippines in exchange for silver, as well as firearms, sugar, potatoes, and tobacco. Despite modest official attempts to control trade, China became the final repository for much of the world's silver from the beginning of the sixteenth cen-

Making and Painting Porcelain. The production of porcelain, for both domestic and external markets, became a highly sophisticated enterprise during the Ming dynasty. The most famous center was the cluster of workshops at Jingdezhen, where there was a clear division of labor among the artisans, each specializing in a particular part of the production process, including decorating and glazing porcelain cups and bowls as shown here.

tury until the end of the eighteenth century. According to one estimate, one-third of all the silver mined in the Americas wound up in Chinese hands. The influx of silver allowed China to continue its phenomenal economic expansion. New World silver also allowed Europeans to gain greater access to China's coveted goods.

REVIVAL OF INDIAN OCEAN TRADE

Chinese economic expansion took part in the broader revival of Indian Ocean trade in the fifteenth century. Many of the same merchants who sought to trade with China developed a brisk commerce that tied the whole of the Indian Ocean together. As a result, ports in East Africa and the Red Sea were again linked with the coastal cities of India and South Asia and the Malay Peninsula. Muslims dominated the Indian Ocean trade, and Islam provided a unifying religion and a judicial system, but many merchants were Hindus.

India was the geographic and economic center of these trade routes. Its population expanded as rapidly as that of China, and it also had large cities, such as Agra, Delhi, and Lahore, each of which had nearly half a million residents. India's manufacturing center was Bengal, which exported silk and cotton textiles and rice to the rest of the subcontinent and throughout Southeast Asia. Like China, India had a favorable trade balance with Europe and West Asia, exporting textiles and pepper, the spice most coveted by Europeans, in exchange for silver.

In dealing with China, Indian merchants faced the same problem as Europeans and West Asians: they had to pay for Chinese silks and porcelains with silver. This made Indian merchants as dependent on gaining access to silver as the rest of those seeking inroads into Chinese commerce. But unlike Chinese merchants, Indian and Islamic traders in the commercial hubs from the Red Sea to Melaka did not obey a single overarching political authority. This gave them considerable autonomy from political affairs and allowed them to occupy strategic positions in the long-distance trade of Afro-Eurasia. Rulers all along the Indian Ocean flourished by taking customs duties, while they used the luxury goods from afar to flaunt their status. For glorifying sovereigns and for worshiping deities, luxuries such as silks, porcelains, ivory, bullion, diamonds, spices, frankincense, myrrh, and incense were in high demand. Thus did the Indian Ocean trade connect a vast array of consumers and producers long before Europeans arrived on the scene.

Of the many port cities that connected the peoples and commodities of the Indian Ocean, none was more important than Melaka, located at a choke point on the Malay Peninsula between the Indian Ocean and the South China Sea. Unlike other trading places in this region, Melaka had no hinterland of farmers to support it. Instead, it thrived exclusively as an emporium for world traders, thousands of whom resided in the city or passed through it. Indeed, Melaka's merchants were a microcosm of the Indian Ocean's diverse community of traders. Arabs, Indians, Armenians, Jews, East Africans, Persians, and eventually western Europeans established themselves there to participate in and profit from the commerce that moved in and out of Melaka's port.

OVERLAND COMMERCE AND OTTOMAN EXPANSION

The growth of seaborne commerce eclipsed but did not eliminate overland caravan trading. Along some routes, overland commerce thrived anew. One well-trafficked land route linked the Baltic Sea, Muscovy, the Caspian Sea, the central Asian oases, and China. Other land routes carried goods to the ports of China and the Indian Ocean, which then crossed to the Ottoman Empire's heartland and went on land farther into Europe.

Of the many great entrepôts (commercial hubs for long-distance trade) that grew up along caravan routes, none enjoyed a more spectacular economic success than Aleppo in Syria. Thanks to its prime location at the end of the caravan routes from India and Baghdad, Aleppo came to overshadow its other Syrian rivals, Damascus and Homs. A vital supply point for Anatolia and the Mediterranean cities, Aleppo by the end of the sixteenth century had become the most important commercial center, particularly for silk, in the whole of the Middle East.

Overland Caravans and Caravanserais. Muslim governments and merchants' associations constructed inns, or caravanserais, along the major trading routes. These areas were capable of accommodating a large number of traders and their animals in great comfort.

The Aleppans, like others within the Ottoman Empire, revered successful merchants. Rich merchants were extolled as "paragons" and celebrated, in popular stories such as *The Thousand and One Nights,* as shrewd men who had amassed enormous wealth by mastering the intricacies of the caravan trade. Those close to the trade recognized how difficult the merchant's task was. The caravans gathered on the edge of the city, where animals were hired, tents sewn, and saddles and packs arranged. Large caravans involved 600 to 1,000 camels and as many as 400 men; smaller parties required no more than a dozen animals. Whatever the size, a good leader was essential, for only someone who had knowledge of difficult desert routes and the confidence of the Bedouin (derived from the Arabic term for desert dweller and referring to pastoral nomads) tribes that provided safe passage for a fee could hope to make the journey profitable.

Ottoman authorities also took a keen interest in the caravan trade, since the state gained considerable revenue from taxes on it. To facilitate and secure the movement of caravans, the government maintained refreshment and military stations along the route. The largest and most ornate of these stations or caravansarais were made of stone and had individual rooms to accommodate the chief merchants. Some were so vast that they provided overnight lodging for 800 travelers and could feed and care for all their animals. Gathering so many traders, animals, and cargoes could also attract marauders, especially from among desert tribesmen. To stop the raids, authorities and merchants offered large cash payments to tribal chieftains as "protection money."

Revenue from the overland caravan trade helped finance the Ottoman Empire's expansion, underwriting the armies and allowing development of a powerful navy. The many tribes that were knitted together into Ottoman land forces by trade, plunder, and conquest had by the middle of the fifteenth century overrun the great commercial centers of the Afro-Eurasian trade.

The Muslim conquest of Constantinople, the European gateway to the east (Chapter 11), sent shock waves through Christendom. European merchants worried that the fall of Constantinople would mean that the Ottoman sultans would deprive them of safe passage through the newly named Instanbul, and that Christendom's overland route to lucrative Asian markets would be cut off. In 1560, to defend their commerce, Europeans gathered a massive armada of ninety ships and 12,000 men, but, in a naval battle that lasted only a few hours, Ottoman forces sank half of the fleet off the island of Djerba and later captured 10,000 survivors who had sought refuge on the island. The defeated soldiers were marched through the streets of Istanbul. With the Mediterranean and the overland routes to Asia increasingly in the hands of powerful Ottoman loyalists, how were the Europeans to acquire spices and textiles from Asia? Europeans would have to find alternative ways to Asian riches.

EUROPEAN EXPLORATION AND EXPANSION

→ *How did the Portuguese attitude toward trade enable the Portuguese to take advantage of and dominate their trading partners?*

Ottoman power prompted Europeans to probe unexplored links to the east. Some opted for territorial expansion against weaker neighbors. Muscovite tsars, for instance, presided over both defensive and commercial expansion across the Urals into Siberia. This stretched Christendom's eastern flank overland (see Chapter 13). Others in Europe looked south and west—and to the seas. The Portuguese were the first to see potential profits—as well as souls to be saved—across the Mediterranean, in Africa.

THE PORTUGUESE IN AFRICA AND ASIA

Europeans had long believed that Africa was a storehouse of precious metals. A fourteenth-century map, the Catalan Atlas from 1375–1380, illustrated a single black ruler, depicted as controlling a vast quantity of gold, in the interior of Africa. The fifteenth-century cartographic depiction of Africa, the so-called map of Columbus, also placed gold in the middle of the African landmass. Thus, as the price of gold skyrocketed during and after the Black Death, it made good sense, ambitious men thought, to venture southward in search of this commodity and its twin, silver.

NAVIGATION AND MILITARY DEVELOPMENTS The first Portuguese sailors had set out expecting, from stories and myths, to encounter giants and Amazons, seas of darkness, and distant lands of savages and cannibals. To some extent, these tales shaped their views of the places and peoples they encountered, which, thanks to the development of new maritime technology and the borrowing of information from other mariners, included lands around the tip of Africa and into the Indian Ocean. The Portuguese knew that great riches awaited them there.

Of the Portuguese ships, one, called a carrack, worked well on bodies of water like the Mediterranean, while a second, the caravel, was more suited for nosing in and out of estuaries and navigating unpredictable currents and winds. Often, however, their vessels blended elements of carrack and caravel, which allowed Portuguese mariners to overcome some of the hazards that oceanic voyages had always presented. Only by using highly maneuverable caravel vessels and perfecting the technique of tacking (sailing into the wind

The Catalan Atlas. This 1375 map shows the world as it was then known. Not only does it depict the location of continents and islands, it also includes information on ancient and medieval tales, regional politics, astronomy, and astrology.

rather than before it) were the Portuguese able to advance far along the West African coast. In addition, the Portuguese had become expert in the use of the compass and the astrolabe, which enabled them to determine their latitudes. The Portuguese success also owed to knowledge they had absorbed from ancient Greeks and Arabs and from the assistance they received from Muslim mariners, whom they had taken aboard and who had wide experience in Africa and the Indian Ocean.

The success of Portuguese ships in the Indian Ocean was also in part the result of a revolution in military technology and tactics that had been gathering momentum for a long

time—and owed much to borrowings from Asia. This began with the adaptation of a Chinese technology: gunpowder. The Ottomans had made use of this technology to conquer Constantinople in 1453 with enormous cannons filled with gunpowder and 800-pound cannonballs. In like fashion in 1492, Christians used cannons to breach the walls of Granada. Europeans also used explosive smaller cannons, which were more mobile and could propel iron balls in relatively flat trajectories to lay ruin to old fortifications. These cannons could also be mounted against the gunwales of warships, to bombard ports and rival navies, or merchant vessels, to shift the nature of ocean commerce toward more military ends.

Within Europe, the main beneficiaries of this revolution in warfare were the dynastic rulers, who commanded the financial resources to equip large fighting forces with new armaments. In 1492, what was then a huge force of 60,000 Christian soldiers drove Islam's army out of Granada; two centuries later, such an army would have been dwarfed by the hundreds of thousands of men fielded by the most powerful European states. So, too, tactics shifted. In medieval Europe, a day of combat or a short siege of castles often settled matters. By the middle of the sixteenth century, battles often involved protracted and usually inconclusive struggles. This way of war, more costly in terms of money and manpower, gave an advantage to larger, centralized states.

SUGAR AND SLAVES Africa and the islands along its coast proved to be far more than a stop-off en route to India or a source of precious metals. Africa became a valued trading area, and its islands became prime locations in which to grow sugarcane, a crop that had exhausted the soils of Mediterranean islands where it had been cultivated since the twelfth century. Along what they called the Gold Coast, the Portuguese established many fortresses and ports of call. Having taken over islands off the West African coast, notably São Tomé, Principe, and Fernando Po, they introduced the cultivation of sugarcane on relatively large-scale plantations and used slave labor brought in from the African mainland.

The Madeira, Canary, and Cape Verde archipelagos in particular became laboratories for plantation agriculture. Their rainfall and fertile soils made these islands ideally suited for growing sugarcane. Moreover, large numbers of workers were needed to cultivate, harvest, and process the sugarcane; hence, the availability of a supply of slave labor in the vicinity enabled Portugal and Spain to build sizeable plantations in their first formal colonies. Thus, in the fifteenth century, these islands off the coast of West Africa saw the beginnings of a plantation built on a system of slavery that was to be transported across the Atlantic in the following century.

The Portuguese did not restrict the export of slaves to these West African possessions. As early as 1441, Portuguese merchants had brought a shipload of African slaves back to Portugal, where they were pressed into service as domestic workers. The slave trade to Portugal increased throughout the fifteenth and into the sixteenth century, so that by 1551 the city of Lisbon, with a population of over 100,000, was reported to have 10,000 African slaves.

COMMERCE AND CONQUEST IN THE INDIAN OCEAN Having explored the African coast and established plantation colonies off it, Portuguese seafarers ventured into the Indian Ocean and inserted themselves into its thriving commerce (see Map 12-2). The Portuguese seaborne empire never aspired to direct rule or colonization. Rather, these Europeans

Coupe d'un Amiral de 104 pieces de Canon auec ses principales proportions et les noms des pieces du décans.

Caravels. Caravels became the classic vessel for European exploration. They combined castlelike defenses with many decks and plenty of portholes for cannon, could house a large crew, and had lots of storage for provisions, cargo, and booty.

GREENLAND

NORTH AMERICA

FROBISHER 1576

CARTIER 1534–1541

NEWFOUNDLAND (1497)

CABOT 1497–1498

ENGLAND

FRAN

PORTUGAL SPAIN
Lisbon
Seville
Cadiz
Ceuta
(1415)

ATLANTIC OCEAN

AZORES

MADEIRA

CANARY ISLANDS

DRAKE 1577–1580

St. Augustine

CORTÉS 1519

Zacatecas

Havana (1492)

COLUMBUS 1492

CUBA

Tenochtitlán

YUCATAN

HISPANIOLA (1482)

COLUMBUS 1493–1494

CAPE VERDE ISLANDS

FERNANDO P

AZTEC EMPIRE

VESPUCCI 1501–1502

MAGELLAN 1519

CABRAL 1500

DIAZ 1487–1488

GOLD COAST
Elmina

Panama

SÃO TOMÉ

PACIFIC OCEAN

Quito (1534)

SOUTH AMERICA

VASCO DA GAMA 1497–1498

DEL CANO (after Magellan's dea

Lima (1535)

Bahia

INCA EMPIRE

Cuzco

Potosí

DRAKE 1577–1580

1521–1522

MAGELLAN AND DEL CANO 1520

Rio de Janeiro

PIZARRO 1531

CABRAL 1500

Santiago
Buenos Aires (1535)

Line of Tordesillas 1494

Straits of Magellan

Cape Horn

- → Portuguese exploration
- → Spanish exploration
- → English exploration
- → French exploration
- Portuguese controlled islands
- Spanish controlled islands
- • Portuguese controlled cities
- • Spanish controlled cities

MAP 12-2   EUROPEAN EXPLORATION, 1420–1580

In the fifteenth and sixteenth centuries, sailors from Portugal, Spain, England, and France explored and mapped the coastline of most of the world. Why did Portuguese explorers concentrate on Africa and the Indian Ocean whereas their Spanish counterparts focused on the Americas? How did each dynasty exploit its maritime and military advancements in each region? To what extent does this map preview the changes in global trade patterns that stemmed from these maritime voyages of exploration over the next century?

ARCTIC OCEAN

RUSSIAN EMPIRE

SIBERIA

Istanbul

Beijing

JAPAN

OTTOMAN EMPIRE

Aleppo
Homs
Damascus

Isfahan

SAFAVID EMPIRE

MING CHINA
Nanjing

Nagasaki (1542)

ARABIA

Gombrun   Hormuz

Delhi
Agra

MUGHAL EMPIRE

Guangzhou
(Canton)

PACIFIC OCEAN

Mecca

Muscat

Macao

AFRICA

Aden
(1513)

COVILHÃO 1487–1489

Goa
(1510)

Manila

DEL CANO (after Magellan's death)
1521–1522

ARABIAN SEA

Calicut (1498)
Cochin (1502)
CEYLON
(1518)

PHILIPPINES

ETHIOPIA

SWAHILI COAST
Malindi

Mombasa (1498)

Kilwa (1505)

VASCO DA GAMA 1497–1498

CABRAL 1500

SEQUEIRA 1509–1510

PERESTRELLO 1514–1516

MALAY PENINSULA

Melaka (1511)

DRAKE 1577–1580

BORNEO

MALUKU
(1511)

NEW GUINEA

ABREU 1511

SUMATRA

Mozambique (1507)

Sofala (1505)

ZIMBABWE

MADAGASCAR
(1500)

JAVA

INDIAN OCEAN

AUSTRALIA

Delagoa Bay

Cape of
Good Hope

DRAKE 1577–1580

0   1000   2000 Miles

0   1000   2000 Kilometers

Primary Source

PORTUGUESE VIEWS OF THE CHINESE

When the Portuguese arrived in China in the early sixteenth century, they encountered a vast empire whose organizational structure and ideological orientation were quite different from their own. Written in 1517, this Portuguese report is replete with misrepresentations that were to characterize many Europeans' views of China for centuries to come. It also signaled a new and aggressive phase of European expansionism, in which the use of brute force was celebrated as a legitimate means to destroy and conquer those who stood in the way.

God grant that these Chinese may be fools enough to lose the country; because up to the present they have had no dominion, but little by little they have gone on taking the land from their neighbors; and for this reason the kingdom is great, because the Chinese are full of much cowardice, and hence they come to be presumptuous, arrogant, cruel; and because up to the present, being a cowardly people, they have managed without arms and without any practice of war, and have always gone on getting the land from their neighbors, and not by force but by stratagems and deceptions; and they imagine that no one can do them harm. They call every foreigner a savage; and their country they call the kingdom of God. Whoever shall come now, let it be a captain with a fleet of ten or fifteen sail. The first thing will be to destroy the fleet if they should have one, which I believe they have not; let it be by fire and blood and cruel fear for this day, without sparing the life of a single person, every junk being burnt, and no one being taken prisoner, in order not to waste the provisions, because at all times a hundred Chinese will be found for one Portuguese. And this done, Nanto must be cleared, and at once they will have a fortress and provisions if they wish, because it will at once be in their power; and then with the whole fleet attack Aynãcha, which lies at the bar of Tãcoam, as I have already said above having a good port. Here the ships, which cannot enter the river, will be anchored, and whatever craft they may have will be burnt; and after it has been taken if it seem good the town can be burnt, in order to terrify the Chinese. . . .

→ *What do you think was the main purpose of this report?*
→ *How could this observer's views be so inaccurate?*

SOURCE: Letters from Canton, translated and edited by D. Ferguson, *The Indian Antiquary* 31 (January 1902), in J. H. Parry, *European Reconnaissance: Selected Documents* (New York: Walker, 1968), p. 140.

extracted benefits by exploiting Asian commercial networks and trading systems.

The first Portuguese mariner to reach the Indian Ocean was Vasco da Gama (1469–1524). Like Columbus, da Gama was a relatively unknown sailor before he commanded four ships around the Cape of Good Hope in 1497. He then spent four months exploring the east coast of Africa but did not encounter either friendly traders or great riches. What he did encounter was a vast network of existing commercial ties spanning the Indian Ocean and skilled Muslim mariners who knew the currents, winds, and ports of call. Vasco da Gama took on board a Muslim pilot at Malindi, on the coast of East Africa, to instruct da Gama on how to navigate in the winds and currents of the Indian Ocean. Da Gama then sailed straight for the Malabar coast in southern India, one of the most important trading areas in the whole region, arriving there in 1498.

To the Portuguese—who traded in the name of their crown—commercial access was worth fighting for. Da Gama was briefly taken hostage in Pantalayini, near Calicut, and though he was eventually allowed to load his ships with a valuable cargo of spices and silks, he was incensed. On his exit from southern India, da Gama roughed up whomever he came across, making sure local fishermen watched and spread the news.

On the difficult voyage back to Lisbon in 1499, da Gama lost more than half of his crew, but he had proved the feasibility—and profitability—of trade via the Indian Ocean. When da Gama returned to Calicut in 1502—with a beefed-up contingent—he asserted Portuguese supremacy by boarding the twenty ships in the harbor and cutting off the noses, ears, and hands of their sailors, then burning the ships with the mutilated sailors on board. The Portuguese repeated their shows of force throughout the region's strategic locations, especially the three great naval choke points: Aden at the base of the Red Sea, Hormuz in the Persian Gulf, and Melaka at the tip of the Malay Peninsula. Having ensconced themselves in the area's chief commercial ports, the Portuguese attempted to take over the trade themselves, or failing this, to tax local merchants. Although they failed to hold Aden for long, they did solidify their trading networks by establishing their control in Sofala, Kilwa, and other important port cities on the East African coast, Goa and Calicut in India, and Macao in southern China. From these strongholds, the Portuguese soon commanded the most active sea lanes of the Indian Ocean.

To assert their imperial domain over Indian Ocean trade (west of the Melaka Strait), the Portuguese introduced a pass system (the cartaz) that required that ships pay for cartazes, documents that stated the name of the ship's captain, size of the ship and crew, and its cargo. But some Indian Ocean rulers and merchants got cartazes for free, showing the limits of Portuguese "dominion." Others calculated it was cheaper to pay than risk losses at sea from unpredictable "retribution." Sometimes local rulers submitted to the Portuguese because it was an opportunity to free themselves of a bigger realm's rule and taxes. The big rulers, in turn, saw the Portuguese as useful for subordinating smaller fiefs. The distinctiveness of the Portuguese presence in the Indian Ocean world was that they did not interrupt the flow of luxuries among Asian and African elites—rather, they skimmed off the top.

Between 1500 and 1634, fewer than four vessels per year sailed around the Cape back to Portugal. As the products of the Indian Ocean made their way back to Lisbon, that city eclipsed the great Italian ports such as Venice that had previously been the prime entrepôts for Asian goods. Even so, spices were far less important in Europe than *within* the Indian Ocean world, where the Portuguese became an important player. Only with the discovery of the Americas and the conquest of Brazil did Portugal become an empire with large overseas colonies. For this to transpire, the Atlantic Ocean itself had to be traversed.

THE ATLANTIC WORLD

> → *What did European conquerors adopt and change from the New World traditions they encountered?*

Western European Christendom, in opening new sea lanes in the Atlantic, set the stage for an epochal transformation in world history. New technologies certainly aided European expansion, but diseases made the difference. In their encounters with the peoples of the Americas, Europeans introduced more than new cultures to this isolated world; they also brought devastating new pathogens. The catastrophic decline of Amerindian populations enabled Europeans to colonize the Americas and reap advantage from their natural resources.

Most of the people who made the Atlantic voyage after 1500 were not Europeans but Africans. The decimation of Indians in many areas deprived Europeans of an indigenous labor force and drove them to seek workers elsewhere. As a supplier of slave labor, Africa became the third corner in a triangular order. Born of the links between the peoples and resources of Europe, Africa, and the Americas, this emerging "Atlantic Ocean system" enriched Europeans. Through conquest and resettlement in the New World, Europeans gained access to the precious metals of the Americas. New World silver provided Europeans with the means to offer something to their trading partners in Asia.

The crossing of the Atlantic Ocean was a feat of monumental importance in world history. But it was not accomplished with an aim to discover new lands; Columbus had wanted Spanish royal patronage to support a voyage into the "Ocean Sea" (the Atlantic) and to thereby open a more direct—and more lucrative—route to Japan and China. Fired by their victory at Granada, Ferdinand and Isabella had agreed to finance his trip, hoping for riches with which to bankroll a final and decisive crusade to liberate Jerusalem from Muslim hands. Just as Columbus had no idea he would find a "New World," in 1491, Spain's monarchs, not to mention its merchants, missionaries, and soldiers, never dreamed that in a few short years they would be readying themselves for conquest and profiteering in what had been, just a few years before, a blank space on the map.

Columbus's "discovery" was, therefore, something of an accident. Still, while the idea of creating an entirely new world system of trade was unintended, it took scarcely a generation for Europeans to realize the significance of their accidental discoveries. News of Columbus's voyage spread quickly through Europe, and, especially in the Iberian ports, ambitious mariners prepared their vessels to sail west. Other ships on the way to the east also found the New World by accident. For example, in 1500, Pedro Alvares Cabral and his Portuguese fleet, on a voyage originally intended for India, were blown west in the Atlantic and landed instead on the bulge of South America that is now Brazil. By 1550, all of Europe's powers were scrambling, not just for a share in the Indian Ocean action, but also for the spoils of the Atlantic. In the process, they began destroying the societies and the great dynasties of the New World. The devastation of the peoples of the Americas coincided with a sharpening of European rivalries.

WESTWARD VOYAGES OF COLUMBUS

Few figures in history have come to embody their age more than Christopher Columbus. His tiny fleet of three ships set

Columbus. As Columbus made landfall and encountered Indians, he planted a cross to indicate the spiritual purpose of the voyage and read aloud a document proclaiming the sovereign authority of the king and queen of Spain. Quickly, he learned there was barter for precious stones and metals.

sail from Spain in early 1492, stopped in the Canary Islands for supplies and repairs, and cast off into the unknown. When he walked onto the beach of San Salvador (in the Bahamas) on October 12, 1492, Columbus ushered in a new era in world history. He did not, however, return with the precious commodities of Asia that he had expected. Columbus would search in vain in three subsequent voyages for the valuable products of the South China Sea and the Indian Ocean.

It is important to see Columbus as a man of his time. Like other expansion-minded Europeans, he aimed to Christianize the world while enriching himself (and his backers). These twin goals, to save souls and to make money, drove the European colonization of the Americas and the formation of an Atlantic system. Still, it is worth reminding ourselves that Columbus's voyages aimed not to create something new but to generate revenues to pay off debts incurred in the conquest of Granada and in the reconquest of the Holy Land. To his dying day, Columbus never believed that he had discovered anything new.

FIRST ENCOUNTERS

When Columbus made landfall in the Caribbean, he unfurled the royal standard of Ferdinand and Isabella and claimed the "many islands filled with people innumerable" for Spain. Fit-

tingly, the first encounter with Caribbean inhabitants, in this case the Tainos, drew blood. As Columbus noted in his journal, "I showed them swords and they took them by the edge and through ignorance cut themselves." The Tainos certainly had their own weapons but did not forge steel—and thus such sharp edges were unknown to them.

For Columbus, the naiveté of the Tainos in grabbing his sword symbolized the child-like primitivism of these people, whom he would mislabel "Indians." In Columbus's view, the Tainos had no religion, but they did have at least some gold (found initially hanging as pendants from their noses). Likewise, Pedro Alvares Cabral wrote to his own king that the people of Brazil had all "the innocence of Adam" and were ripe for conversion, and the soils "if rightly cultivated would yield everything." But, as with Africans and Asians, Europeans also developed a contradictory view of the peoples of the Americas. From the Tainos, Columbus learned of another people, the Caribs, who, according to his informants, were savage, warlike cannibals. For centuries, these contrasting images—innocents and savages—provided the two competing visions that structured European (mis)understandings of the indigenous peoples of the Americas.

We know less about what the Indians thought of Columbus or other Europeans on their first encounters. Certainly the appearance of Europeans and their technologies often inspired awe. The Tainos of San Salvador fled into the forest at the approach of European ships, which they thought were giant monsters; others thought that approaching European ships were floating islands. European metal goods, in particular weaponry, were assumed to be otherworldly. The strangely dressed white men seemed godlike to some, although many Indians soon abandoned this view. Many found the newcomers different not for their skin color (only Europeans drew the distinction based on skin pigmentation), but for their hairiness. Indeed, the beards as well as the breath and bad manners of Europeans repulsed their Indian hosts. The inability of the Europeans to live off the fruit of the land also stood out.

In due course, the Indians realized that the strange, hairy people bearing metal weapons were not just odd trading partners, but that they meant to stay and to force the native population to labor for them. By the time Indians were aware of the dislocations and upheaval brought by the Spaniards, however, it was too late. The explorers had become conquerors (conquistadors).

FIRST CONQUESTS

After the first voyage, Columbus claimed that on the island of Hispaniola (present-day Haiti and the Dominican Republic) "he had found what he was looking for"—gold. That was sufficient inducement to persuade the Spanish crown to invest in larger, costlier expeditions. Whereas Columbus first sailed with three small ships and 87 men, ten years later the Spanish outfitted an expedition with 2,500 men.

Between 1492 and 1519, the Spanish experimented with institutions and practices of colonialism on Hispaniola, creating a model to be modified and applied in the rest of the New World colonies. Here, the Spaniards faced problems that would recur. The first was Indian resistance. As early as 1494, starving Spaniards raided and pillaged Indian villages. When the Indians revolted, Spanish soldiers replied with punitive expeditions and began enslaving the native population to work extracting gold. The crown began to systematize grants (*encomiendas*) to the conquistadors for control over Indian labor. This created a rich class of *encomenderos* who enjoyed the fruits of the system. True, the placer gold mines soon ran dry, but the model of granting favored settlers the right to coerce Indian labor endured. In return, those granted the labor rights paid special taxes on the precious metals that were extracted. Thus, both the crown and the *encomenderos* shared in the benefits of the extractive economy. The same cannot be said of the Indians, who were dying in great numbers due to disease, dislocation, malnutrition, and overwork.

> *In both Mesoamerica and the Andes, large polities began to take shape, creating the foundations of subsequent Aztec and Incan empires.*

Not surprisingly, conquests were followed by quarrels over the spoils. The family of Columbus, in particular, had been granted a commercial monopoly on his discoveries, but some of the settlers objected and challenged Columbus's authority. To prevent insurrection, the crown granted more *encomiendas* to other Spanish claimants. As special grants became a common feature of Spanish colonialism, less favored settlers grew disenchanted. When the Indians and the gold supplies began to disappear, many settlers pulled up their stakes and returned to Spain. Others looked for new untapped territories that might be rich in precious metals.

Not all joined the rush for riches or celebrated conquistadors and *encomenderos*. Dominican friars protested the abuse of the Indians, seeing them as potential converts, equal to the Spaniards in the eyes of God. In 1511, Father Antonio Montesinos accused the settlers of barbarity: "By what right do you wage such detestable wars on these people who lived idly and peacefully in their own lands, where you have consumed infinite numbers of them with unheard-of murders and desolations?" Dissent and debate would be a permanent feature of Spanish colonialism in the New World.

THE AZTEC EMPIRE AND THE SPANISH CONQUEST

As Spanish colonists saw the bounty of Hispaniola begin to dry up, they set out to discover and conquer new territories.

Finding their way to the mainlands of the American landmasses, they encountered larger, more complex, and more militarized societies than the ones they had quickly overrun in the Caribbean. On the mainland, great civilizations had arisen centuries before, boasting large cities, monumental buildings, and riches based on wealthy agrarian societies. In both Mesoamerica, starting with the Olmecs (see Chapter 5), and the Andes, somewhat later with the Chimu (see Chapter 10), large polities began to take shape, creating the foundations of subsequent Aztec and Incan empires. They were powerful. But they also represented the evolution of states and commercial systems untouched by Afro-Eurasian developments; as worlds apart, they were simply unprepared for the kind of assaults that European invaders had honed. In Mesoamerica and then the Andes, warfare was more ceremonial, less inclined to wipe out enemies than to annex them as tributary subjects. As a result, the wealth of these empires made them irresistible to outside conquerors they never knew, and their habits of war made them vulnerable to conquests they could never foresee.

AZTEC SOCIETY In Mesoamerica, the ascendant Mexicas (see the discussion of the Toltecs in Chapter 10) had created an empire and named it "Aztec" after the foundational story of the people who migrated from the mythic town of Aztlan. Around Lake Texcoco, Mexica cities grew and formed a three-city league in 1430, which then expanded outward through the Central Valley of Mexico to incorporate neighboring peoples. Over the course of the fifteenth century, the Aztec empire united numerous small, independent states under a single monarch who ruled with the help of counselors, military leaders, and priests. By the end of the fifteenth century, the Aztec realm may have embraced 25 million people and Tenochtitlán, the primary city, situated on an island in Lake Texcoco, ranked among the world's largest with a population estimated at between 200,000 and 300,000.

Tenochtitlán spread in concentric circles, with the main religious and political buildings in the center and residences radiating outward. As the city was built on an immense island, its outskirts connected a mosaic of floating gardens producing food for urban markets. Canals constantly irrigated the land, waste was used as fertilizer, and the tremendously high yields were easily transported to markets. Entire households worked: men, women, and children all had roles in Aztec agriculture.

Extended kinship provided the scaffolding for Aztec statehood. Marriage of men and women from different villages solidified alliances and created clan-like networks. In Tenochtitlán, powerful families married their children to each

Tenochtitlán. At its height, the Aztec capital Tenochtitlán was as populous as Europe's largest city. *(Left)* As can be seen from this map, it spread in concentric circles, with the main religious and political buildings in the center and residences radiating outward. *(Right)* As the city was built on an immense island, its outskirts connected a mosaic of floating gardens producing food for urban markets. Canals constantly irrigated the land, waste was used as fertilizer, and the tremendously high yields were easily transported to markets. Observe how entire households worked: men, women, and children all had roles in Aztec agriculture.

other or found nuptial partners among the prominent families of other important cities. Not only did this concentrate power in the great city, it also ensured a pool of potential successors to the throne. In this fashion, a lineage emerged to create a corps of "natural" rulers. Priests legitimized the new emperor in rituals to convey for his subjects the image of a ruler close to the gods and to mark off the elite from the lower orders.

A hierarchy already present at the village level provided the bedrock for layers of increasingly centralized political authority. Local elders developed representative bodies and councils, which selected delegates to a committee responsible for electing the dominant civil authority, known as the chief speaker. As Aztec power spread, the chief speaker became a full-blown emperor. He was, however, not supreme, instead jockeying with rival religious and especially military power-wielders. At the top of the Aztec social pyramid thus stood a small but antagonistic nobility. This hierarchically organized society was held together by a shared understanding of the cosmos. The Aztecs believed that the universe was prone to unceasing cycles of disaster that would eventually end in an apocalypse. Such an unstable cosmos exposed mortals to repeated creations and destructions. The priesthood monitored the relationship between the people and their deities and balanced fatalism with a faith that the gods could be honored through rituals.

By the end of the fifteenth century, Aztec power had spread to much of Mesoamerica, but the empire's constant wars and conquests of neighboring territories deprived it of stability. In successive military campaigns, the Aztecs subjugated their neighbors, feeding off plunder and then forcing subject peoples to pay annual tribute of crops, gold, silver, textiles, and other goods that financed Aztec grandeur. Conquest of Aztec neighbors also provided imperial rulers with a constant supply of humans for sacrifice to the gods. Captives faced execution because the Aztecs believed that the great god of the sun required human hearts to keep on burning and blood to replace that given by the gods to moisten the earth through rain. Priests escorted captured warriors up the temple steps and tore out their hearts, offering their lives and blood as a sacrifice to the sun god. Allegedly, between 20,000 and 80,000 men, women, and children were slaughtered in a single ceremony in 1487, with the four-person-wide line of those who would be killed stretching for over two miles. In this marathon of bloodletting, knife-wielding priests collapsed from exhaustion and had to be replaced by fresh executioners.

The peoples the Aztecs sought to dominate did not submit peacefully. From 1440, the empire entered a state of constant turmoil as subject peoples rebelled against their oppressive Aztec overlords. Tlaxcalans and Tarascans along the Gulf of Mexico waged a relentless war for freedom, pinning down entire divisions of Aztec armies. To pacify the realm, the empire diverted more and more men and money into a mushrooming military. By the time the electoral committee chose Moctezuma II as emperor in 1502, divisions among elites and pressures from the periphery placed the Aztec Empire under stress.

CORTÉS AND CONQUEST Not long after Moctezuma became emperor, news arrived of strange sightings off the eastern coast of large floating mountains (ships) bearing pale, bearded men and monsters (horses and dogs). Moctezuma consulted with his ministers and soothsayers over the news, wondering if these men were the god Quetzalcóatl and his entourage. The people of Tenochtitlán saw omens of impending disaster. Moctezuma sank into despair, hesitating as

Aztec Sacrifice. This seventeenth-century illustration depicts the Aztec practice of sacrificing captives to the gods. Note the open chests: the hearts were cut out at the top of the temple steps before the victims were sent tumbling down.

to what course of action to take. He sent emissaries bearing jewels and prized feathers; later he sent sorcerers to confuse and bewitch the newcomers. But he did not prepare his city for any military engagement—Mesoamericans had no idea of the interlopers' destructive potential in weaponry and germs.

Aboard one of the ships was Hernán Cortés (1485–1547), a former law student from the Spanish province of Estremadura. Cortés was to become the model conquistador, just as Columbus was the model explorer. For a brief time, he was an *encomendero* in Hispaniola, but when news arrived of a potentially even more wealthy land to the west, he set sail with over 500 men, eleven ships, sixteen horses, and artillery.

When the expedition arrived near present-day Veracruz, Cortés acquired two translators, including the daughter of a local Indian noble family. The daughter, who became known

Cortés Meets Montezuma. This colonial image depicts the meeting of Cortés (second from right) and Moctezuma (seated to his left), with Doña Marina serving as an interpreter and informer for the Spanish conquistador. Notice at the bottom what are likely Aztec offerings for the newcomer.

as Doña Marina, was a "gift" from the ruler of the region of Tabasco, a rival to the Aztecs, to the triumphant Spaniards. Fluent in several languages, Doña Marina's linguistic skills and personal charms soon brought her to the attention of Cortés. She became his lover and was to reveal several clandestine Aztec plots to wipe out the tiny Spanish force. Doña Marina subsequently bore Cortés a son, who is considered one of the first mixed-blooded Mexicans (known as mestizos).

With the assistance of Doña Marina and other native allies, Cortés marched his troops to Tenochtitlán. Entering, he gasped in wonder that "this city is so big and so remarkable" that it was "almost unbelievable." One of his soldiers wrote, "It was all so wonderful that I do not know how to describe this first glimpse of things never heard of, seen or dreamed of before."

How was this tiny force to overcome an empire of many millions with an elaborate warring tradition? Crucial to Spanish conquest was their alliance, negotiated with the help of

the translators, with Moctezuma's enemies, especially the Tlaxcalans. After decades of yearning for release from the Aztec yoke, the Tlaxcalans and other Mesoamerican peoples embraced Cortés's promise of help. The Spaniards' second main advantage was their method of warfare. The Aztecs were seasoned fighters, but they fought to capture, not to kill. Nor were they familiar with gunpowder or sharp steel swords. Outnumbered, the Spaniards killed their foe with abandon, using their superior weaponry, horses, and war dogs. The Aztecs, still unsure who these strange men were, allowed Cortés to enter their city. With the aid of the Tlaxcalans and a handful of his own men, Cortés was able in 1519 to capture the Aztec ruler, Moctezuma, who became a puppet of his Spanish conqueror.

Within two years, the Aztecs realized that these newcomers were not gods and that Aztec warriors too could fight to kill. When Spanish troops massacred an unarmed crowd in Tenochtitlán's central square while Cortés was away, they provoked a massive uprising. The Spaniards led Moctezuma to one of the palace walls to plead with his people for a truce,

Cortés Meets the King of Tlaxcala. This detail from a twentieth-century Mexican mural depicts the meeting of Cortés and the king of Tlaxcala (enemy of the Aztecs). As Mexicans began to celebrate their mixed-blood heritage, Doña Marina (in the middle) became the symbolic mother of the first mestizos.

Primary Source

CORTÉS APPROACHES TENOCHTITLÁN

When the Spanish conquered the Aztec empire, they defeated a mighty power. The capital, Tenochtitlán, which was immensely rich, was probably the same size as Naples, Europe's biggest city at the time. Glimpsing the Aztec capital in 1521, Hernán Cortés marveled at the magnificence of the city. But to justify his acts, he claimed that he was bringing civilization and Christianity to the Aztecs. Note the contrast, however, between Cortés's admiration for Tenochtitlán and his condemnation of Indian beliefs and practices, as well as his claim that he abolished cannibalism, something the Aztecs did not practice (although they did sacrifice humans).

This great city of Tenochtitlán is built on the salt lake. . . . It has four approaches by means of artificial causeways. . . . The city is as large as Seville or Cordoba. Its streets . . . are very broad and straight, some of these, and all the others, are one half land, and the other half water on which they go about in canoes. . . . There are bridges, very large, strong, and well constructed, so that, over many, ten horsemen can ride abreast. . . . The city has many squares where markets are held. . . . There is one square, twice as large as that of Salamanca, all surrounded by arcades, where there are daily more than sixty thousand souls, buying and selling. . . . [I]n the service and manners of its people, their fashion of living was almost the same as in Spain, with just as much harmony and order; and considering that these people were barbarous, so cut off from the knowledge of God and other civilized peoples, it is admirable to see to what they attained in every respect. . . .

It happened . . . that a Spaniard saw an Indian . . . eating a piece of flesh taken from the body of an Indian who had been killed. . . . I had the culprit burned, explaining that the cause was his having killed that Indian and eaten him which was prohibited by Your Majesty, and by me in Your Royal name. I further made the chief understand that all the people . . . must abstain from this custom. . . . I came . . . to protect their lives as well as their property, and to teach them that they were to adore but one God . . . that they must turn from their idols, and the rites they had practised until then, for these were lies and deceptions which the devil . . . had invented. . . . I, likewise, had come to teach them that Your Majesty, by the will of Divine Providence, rules the universe, and that they also must submit themselves to the imperial yoke, and do all that we who are Your Majesty's ministers here might order them. . . .

→ *What does Cortés's report tell us about the city of Tenochtitlán?*

→ *Why does Cortés justify his actions to the degree he does?*

SOURCE: *Letters of Cortés*, translated by Francis A. MacNutt (New York: G. P. Putnam, 1908), pp. 244, 256–57.

but the Aztecs kept up their barrage of stones, spears, and arrows—striking and killing Moctezuma. Cortés returned to the city to reassert Spanish control, but realizing this was impossible, he gathered his loot and escaped. Left behind were hundreds of Spaniards, many of whom were dragged up the steps of the temple and sacrificed by Aztec priests.

With the help of the Tlaxcalans, Cortés regrouped. This time he chose to defeat the Aztecs completely. He ordered the building of boats to sail across Lake Texcoco to besiege the capital and bombard it with artillery. Even more devastating was the spread of smallpox, brought by the Spanish, which ran through the ranks of soldiers and commoners like wildfire. Still, led by a new ruler, Cuauhtémoc, the Aztecs rallied their forces and nearly drove the Spaniards from Tenochtitlán. But in the end starvation, disease, and lack of artillery ultimately vanquished the Aztec forces. More Aztecs died from disease than from fighting—the total number of casualties over two years of confrontation reached, it is said, 240,000. As Spanish troops retook the capital, they found it in ruins, with a population too weak to resist. Cuauhtémoc

The Conquest of the Aztecs. *(Left)* This is Diego Rivera's idealized account of the Spanish defeat of the Aztec warriors. It portrays Spanish soldiers with muskets and horses mowing down brave but technologically outgunned Indians. Of course, Rivera's efforts to accentuate Spanish brutality led him to exclude important factors in the fall of Tenochtitlán: Aztec rivals who joined with Spaniards, and diseases. In fact, guns and horses were important but not decisive in the Spanish conquest. *(Right)* This image of the conquest was drawn by a converted Indian later in the sixteenth century and relied on indigenous oral histories and familiar artistic forms. Observe the importance of Indians fighting Indians, and the conventional frontal images of bodies with profiles of heads.

himself was executed in 1524, thereby ending the royal Mexica lineage. The Aztecs lamented their defeat in verse: "We have pounded our hands in despair against the adobe walls, for our inheritance, our city, is lost and dead." In 1522, Cortés became the governor of the new Spanish colony which, by royal order, was renamed "New Spain." He quickly set about allocating *encomiendas* to his loyal followers and dispatching expeditions to conquer the more distant Mesoamerican provinces.

The Mexica experience taught the Spanish an important lesson: an effective conquest had to be swift—and it had to remove completely the symbols of legitimate authority. Their winning advantage, however, proved to be disease. The Spaniards unintentionally introduced germs that made their subsequent efforts at military conquests much easier.

THE INCAS

In addition to Cortés's victory over the Aztecs, the other great Spanish conquest was in the Andes, where Quechua-speaking rulers, called Incas, had established an impressive polity stretching from present-day Colombia to Argentina. From their base in the valley of Cuzco, the Incas governed an empire of 4 to 6 million. But the Incas were internally split.

Bereft of a clear inheritance system, the empire suffered repeated convulsions. In the early sixteenth century, the fight over who would succeed Huayna Capac, the Inca ruler, was especially fierce. Huascar, his "official" son, took Cuzco (the capital), while Atahualpa, his favored son, governed the province of present-day Ecuador. Open conflict might have been averted were it not for Huayna's premature death. His killer was probably smallpox, which along with other epidemics swept down the trade routes from Mesoamerica into the Andes (not unlike the bubonic plague's mid-fourteenth-century spread through the trade routes of Afro-Eurasia). With the father gone, Atahualpa declared war on his brother. After crushing his rival, Atahualpa forced him to witness the execution of all his supporters, then killed him and used his skull as a vessel for maize-beer.

When the Spaniards arrived in 1532, they ran into an empire that was already internally divided, a situation they quickly learned to exploit. Francisco Pizarro, who led the Spanish campaign, had spent time in Hispaniola and, inspired by Cortés's victory, yearned for his own glory. Pizarro commanded a force of about 600 men and invited Atahualpa to confer at the town of Cajamarca. There he laid a trap for the Inca ruler. As the columns of Inca warriors and servants covered with colorful plumage and plates of silver and gold marched into the main square of Cajamarca, the Spanish soldiers were awed. One recalled that "many of us urinated without noticing it, out of sheer terror." But Pizarro's plan worked. His guns and horses shocked the Inca forces. Atahualpa himself fell into Spanish hands, later to be decapitated. Pizarro's conquistadors overran Cuzco in 1533 and then went about mopping up the rest of the Inca forces, a process that took decades in some areas of the Andes.

In the intervening years, Spaniards began to arrive in droves, landing at the new coastal capital of Lima. They began to stake their own claims for *encomiendas,* outdoing each other with greed, and by 1538, they were at war with one another. In 1541, one armed faction managed to capture and assassinate Pizarro himself. Rival factions kept up a brutal war until the Spanish king dispatched a viceroy and issued a new set of laws in 1542 to prevent *encomiendas* from being heritable. This act was meant to prevent the establishment of a powerful aristocracy, to deter the outbreak of uncontrollable civil war, and to reinforce loyalty to Madrid, since once an *encomendero* died, his title would revert to the crown.

The defeat of the two great empires of the New World had enormous repercussions for world history. It meant first that Europeans had their way with the human and material wealth of the Americas. Second, it gave Europeans a market for their own products—goods that found little favor in Afro-Eurasia. Finally, it opened a vast new frontier, which could be colonized and made into staple-producing provinces. Now, following the Russian push into northern Asia (Siberia) and that of the Portuguese into Africa and southern Asia, the conquest of the New World introduced Europeans to a new scale of imperial expansion and enterprise—whose outcome would destabilize Europe itself.

"THE COLUMBIAN EXCHANGE"

The Spanish came to the Americas for its gold and silver, but the Indians offered Europeans a variety of hitherto unknown crops, especially potatoes and corn. Europeans also took away tomatoes, beans, cacao, peanuts, tobacco, and squash. These staples had the unexpected effect of transforming European diets and contributed to the explosion of population growth across Afro-Eurasia. In China, for example, corn could grow in areas too dry for rice and too wet for wheat.

What did the Indians get from this hemispheric transfer that historians have come to call "the Columbian exchange"? The Spanish brought wheat, grapevines, and sugarcane. But the most profound and destructive effect of the Columbian exchange was not immediately visible. For millennia, the isolated populations of the Americas had been cut off from Afro-Eurasian microbe migrations. Africans, Europeans, and Asians had long had at least some contact, even before the bubonic plague. Sharing disease pools, the peoples of Africa and Eurasia gained some immunities; in this sense, the Amerindians were indeed "worlds apart." As we saw in the last section, sickness spread from almost the moment the Spaniards arrived. One Spanish soldier noted, as he entered the Aztec capital after its fall, that "the streets were so filled with dead and sick people that our men walked over nothing but bodies." Native American accounts of the fall of Tenochtitlán recalled the epidemic of smallpox more vividly than the fighting. What made matters worse was that no sooner had smallpox done its work than Indians were visited by a second pandemic: measles. Then came pneumonic plague and influenza. As each wave retreated, it left behind a population more emaciated than before, even less prepared for the next

Disease and Decimation of Indians. The real conqueror of Native Americans was not so much guns as germs. Even before Spanish soldiers seized the Aztec capital, germs had begun decimating the population. The first big killer was in fact smallpox, recorded here by an Indian artist, covering the bodies of victims.

Global Connections & Disconnections

THE VOICE OF THE CONQUERED:
GUAMAN POMA DE AYALA

After defeating the Inca armies in the sixteenth century, the Spanish conquerors tightened their hold over the central Andes. They created new political authorities, invited victors to set up silver mines and trading networks using forced native Andean laborers, and licensed missionaries to go out into Andean communities to consolidate a more difficult "spiritual conquest." In reaction, Andean peoples resisted Spanish conquerors. They fled the mines, plundered trade routes, and kept fighting, now with the use of Spanish weaponry. The conquered Andeans also used techniques of the conquerors themselves, like the Spanish language and Spanish books, to resist Spanish control.

One of the most polemical voices of the conquered was a native Andean, Felipe Guaman Poma de Ayala (c. 1535–c. 1615). His illustrated history of the Inca kingdoms, *Primer nueva crónica y bien gobierno* (c. 1615), fiercely criticized colonial rule while urging the Spanish king, Philip III, to adopt a new model of "good government." The book itself, like the idea that Spain could govern the colonized peoples benevolently, disappeared and was only discovered in a library in Copenhagen in 1908. As a polemical testimony against European conquest, however, *Primer nueva crónica* offers readers a voice of colonized peoples.

The author's native tongue was Quechua, but he was schooled, possibly by missionaries, in Spanish language and culture. With his bilingual skills, he was drafted as an interpreter in the Christian campaigns to wipe out heresy and idol worship in the Andes. In this capacity, he read books belonging to missionaries and learned of the religious, political, and historical traditions of the Spaniards.

Guaman Poma also served as an interpreter for Andeans who challenged the land claims of the conquistadors, and in this capacity he eventually earned himself a reputation as a minor nuisance and was evicted from several jurisdictions. Frustrated that the Spanish conquerors refused to live by their spiritual and political proclamations, he grew increasingly bitter and delivered his illustrated text of 1,188 pages and 398 pen-and-ink drawings to the viceroy in Lima to defend the Andeans. Rebuffed, he wrote the king on February 14, 1615. Thereafter, Guaman Poma disappeared from the historical record.

Guaman Poma narrated the history of the Inca Empire, recounted the arrival and victory of the Spanish, and then described the misery of everyday life under colonial authority. Relying on his own firsthand experiences and centuries of oral culture, the author told an epic tale—very much in a Spanish mode—of the tragic fate of a non-Spanish people. Indeed, the book accepted in many ways the Andean destiny, while denouncing colonialism. He was pro-Andean, but he celebrated Catholicism and Spanish monarchical rule.

As a chronicler of the Andean peoples before the Spanish conquest, Guaman Poma argued that his people were innocents, a Christian people, well before the conquest. They lived, according to the author, by Christian principles and knew but one God, "though they were barbarous, knowing nothing." Indeed, his history of the Incas begins with biblical creation, the arrival in South America of one of Noah's sons, and ends with the rule of Inca Huayna Capac. While much of his historical account was his own fabrication, claiming Christian roots enabled the Andean

wave. The scale of death was and remains unprecedented. Imported pathogens wiped out up to 90 percent of the Native American population, which had stood at between 80 and 100 million in 1492. A century after smallpox arrived on Hispaniola in 1519, no more than 5 to 10 percent of the island's population was left alive. Diminished and weakened by disease, Amerindians could not forestall encroachment by European settlers. Thus were Europeans the unintended beneficiaries of a horrifying catastrophe.

Environmental effects were manifold. In addition to crops, Europeans also transported livestock such as cattle,

swine, and horses to the New World. In the highland regions lying to the north of the valley of central Mexico, where Native Americans had once lived in great numbers, employing irrigation systems to support highly productive agricultural estates, Spanish settlers opened up large herding ranches. An area that had once produced maize and squash for city dwellers living to the south now had herds of sheep and cattle, the sizes of which had never before been seen in the Americas. Without natural predators, these animals reproduced with lightning speed, destroying entire landscapes with their hooves and their foraging. On the islands of the West author to denounce the conquistadors as treasonous usurpers. They had killed the natural and legitimate Inca rulers and were thus eternally doomed.

Primer nueva crónica culminated in a detailed account of everyday life in the colony. It charted the system of forced labor in the mines, the burdens of Spanish taxes, and the hypocrisy of missionaries who seized Indian property and failed to defend Indian lives. Guaman Poma wrote that the colonists violated Christian precepts of justice and their own laws. He added that, given the origins of the Andean peoples and their colonial fates, the king of Spain had a moral as well as a political duty to protect his Christian subjects in the Andes: he should free them from sinful authorities and create a sovereign Andean state as a universal Christian kingdom ruled from Madrid. Guaman Poma simultaneously denounced colonialism, while affirming his loyalty to the king.

For all his skills at crossing the large cultural and political divide between Andeans and Spaniards, conquered and conquerors, Guaman Poma was not optimistic. Near the end of his work, he asked forlornly, "Where are you, our lord king Philip?" His prose invoked many of the conventions of Spanish treatises, and his strong visual representations were meant to stir the reader's Christian sentiments. But at the same time, his images portrayed the irreconcilable differences between Spaniards and Andeans. Isolation, and not understanding, was what characterized the colonial experience for Guaman Poma. As he doubted the potential for cross-cultural communication, he concluded that "there is no resolution in this world."

Pizarro and the Incas. This illustration is by the Andean native Guaman Poma, whose c. 1587 epic of the conquest of Peru depicted many of the barbarities of the Spanish. Here we see the conquistador Pizarro and a Catholic priest appealing to Atahualpa—before betraying and then killing him.

Indies, described by Columbus as "roses of the sea," the Spanish found lush tropical and semitropical forests. The Europeans cleared the abundant trees and other vegetation for sugar plantations. This undermined the habitat of most of the large-sized mammals and many birds. By the onset of the seventeenth century, nearly all of the islands' tall trees as well as many shrubs and ground plants were gone, and residents lamented the absence of bird song. Over the ensuing centuries, the flora and fauna of the Americas took on an increasingly European appearance—a process that the historian Alfred Crosby has called ecological imperialism.

SPAIN'S TRIBUTARY EMPIRE

Like the Europeans who sailed into the Indian Ocean to tap into existing commercial systems, the Spaniards sought to exploit the wealth of indigenous empires without fully dismantling them. In Mexico and Peru, where the Inca Empire suffered the same fate as the Aztecs, Spanish conquistadors decapitated native polities but left much of their structure intact. In both the valley of Mexico and the Andes, Spanish conquerors took over existing networks of tribute. But unlike the European penetration of the Indian Ocean, the occupation

Map legend:

Aztec Empire, 1519
Inca Empire, 1525
Spanish settlement
To 1640
To 1750
Frontier lands 1750
Portuguese settlement
To 1640
To 1750
Frontier lands, 1750

Map labels include: Silver, Precious stones, Gold, Tobacco, Sugar, Coffee, Mining; cities Monterrey 1579, Zacatecas 1547, Mexico City 1512, Acapulco 1550, Veracruz 1519, Puebla 1532, Santiago 1524, Merida 1542, Havana 1515, Santo Domingo 1496, Granada 1522, Portobelo, Cartagena 1532, Panama 1519, Caracas 1567, Quito 1534, Lima 1535, Cuzco 1534, Potosí 1545, Asunción 1537, Buenos Aires 1536, Recife 1535, Bahia 1549, Rio de Janeiro 1565; regions CHICHIMECS, AZTECS, ARAWAKS, INCAS, ANDES MOUNTAINS, AMAZON BASIN, BRAZIL, MATO GROSSO, MINAS GERAIS, PATAGONIA, VICEROYALTY OF SPAIN, VICEROYALTY OF PERU; Gulf of Mexico, Caribbean Sea, Atlantic Ocean, Pacific Ocean, Equator, Line of Treaty of Tordesillas 1494; islands CUBA 1511, JAMAICA 1509, HISPANIOLA 1492, PUERTO RICO 1512.

MAP 12-3   THE SPANISH AND PORTUGUESE EMPIRES IN THE AMERICAS, 1492–1750

This map examines the growth of Spanish and Portuguese empires in the Americas over two and half centuries. Why did Spaniards and Portuguese focus their empire building where they did? What were the major export commodities from these empires and how were they produced? How did the export of silver and sugar shape the labor systems that evolved in both empires?

of the New World was not restricted to control of commercial outposts. Instead, European colonialism in the Americas involved the control of large amounts of territory—and evolved into formal control over the entire landmass (see Map 12-3).

Across the heartlands of the new Spanish empire, villagers delivered goods and services to their new masters. But the Spanish authorities, as they had done in earlier conquests, also bestowed *encomiendas* on favored Spanish immigrants. Such rights enabled the *encomenderos* to demand labor from subject Indian inhabitants, for mines, landed estates, and public works. Aztec and Inca rulers had used labor conscription systems to build up their public domains; Spaniards did so for private gain.

Most Spanish migrants were men; only a few Spanish women accompanied the conquistadors and early settlers. One, Inés Suárez, reached the Indies to find her husband, who had traveled there earlier, dead. She then became the mistress of the conquistador Pedro de Valdivia, and the pair became a conquering team. Initially, she was given permission to join an expedition to conquer Chile as Valdivia's domestic servant, but she soon became much more—a nurse, caretaker, advisor, and a guard, having uncovered several plots to assassinate her lover. Suárez even served as a diplomat, shuttling between warring Indians and Spaniards in an effort to secure the conquest. Later, she helped to rule Chile as the wife of Rodrigo de Quiroga, governor of the province. Admittedly, hers was an exceptional story. More typical were female voyagers who foraged for food, tended wounded soldiers, and set up European-style settlements.

But there were always too few Spanish women to go around, and the sexual imbalance spurred Spanish men to consort with local women. Although the crown did not smile on the taking of concubines, the practice was widespread. From the onset of colonization, Spaniards also actively married into Indian families. After conquering the Incas, Francisco Pizarro wedded an Inca princess, thereby (or so he had hoped) inheriting the mantle of local dynastic rule. As a result of intermarriages, mestizos became the fastest-growing segment of the population of Spanish America.

Spanish migrants and their progeny preferred towns to the countryside. Ports (such as Veracruz, Havana, or Portobelo) excepted, the major cities of Spanish America were the former centers of Indian empires. Mexico City was built on the ruins of Tenochtitlán; Cuzco arose from the foundations of the razed Inca capital. In its architecture, its economy, and even its most intimate facets, the Spanish colonies adopted as much as they transformed the worlds they encountered.

SILVER

For the first European adventurers in the Americas, the foremost measure of wealth and power was the store of gold and silver that they could accumulate for themselves and the monarchs they served. On the surface, this seemed to benefit Spanish merchants and the Spanish crown. It was, after all, the Spanish who discovered, and then plundered, the vast

Silver. *(Left)* Silver was an important discovery for Spanish conquerors in Mesoamerica and the Andes. Conquerors expanded the customs of Inca and Aztec labor drafts to force the natives to work in mines, often in brutal conditions. *(Right)* By the middle of the sixteenth century, a vibrant trade had developed between the Americas and Asia, carrying silver, dyes, and foodstuffs. The conquest of the Americas helped give Europeans trade goods for sale in Asian markets. This image shows a fleet of Spanish galleons on the Pacific coast of Mexico as they are being loaded with the silver extracted from the mines.

Mission Sao Miguel. The Jesuits were avid missionaries in the Spanish and Portuguese empires and often tried to shelter native peoples from conquistadors and labor recruiters. Missions, like this one, in the borderlands between Brazil and Spanish colonies were targets of attack from both sides.

riches of the Aztecs and the Incas. In the twenty years after the fall of Tenochtitlán, the conquistadors took more precious metals from Mexico and the Andes than all the gold accumulated by Europeans over the previous centuries.

Having looted Indian coffers, the Spanish quickly entered the business of mining directly, opening the Andean Potosí mines in 1545. Between 1560 and 1685, Spanish America sent 25,000 to 35,000 tons of silver annually to Spain. From 1685 to 1810, this sum doubled. The two great mother lodes were Potosí in present-day Bolivia and Zacatecas in northern Mexico. Potosí was the greater fount in the sixteenth century, but the silver veins of Mexico proved the more lucrative over the centuries. Silver brought bounty not only to the crown, but also to a small coterie of families based in Spain's colonial capitals—private wealth that funded the formation of local aristocracies.

Colonial mines epitomized the new economy of the Atlantic world. They relied on an extensive network of Indian labor, at first enslaved, subsequently drafted. Here again, the Spanish adopted existing Inca and Aztec practices of requiring labor from subjugated villages. Each year, under the traditional system, village elders selected a stipulated number of men to toil in the shafts, refineries, and smelters. Under the Spanish, however, the burdens grew more onerous. The digging, hauling, and smelting of rocks taxed human limits to their capacity—and beyond. By one conservative estimate, 50,000 workers moved to Potosí each year; mortality rates were appalling. The system pumped so much silver into the networks of European commerce that it transformed Europe's relationship to all of its trading partners, especially those in China and India. It also shook up trade and politics within Europe itself.

PORTUGAL'S NEW WORLD COLONY

> → *What military and maritime technologies advanced Portuguese exploration?*

The Treaty of Tordesillas of 1494, drawn up by the pope, had foreseen that the non-European world—the Americas, Africa, and Asia—would be divided into spheres of interest between Spain and Portugal. Yet the treaty was unenforceable. No less interested in immediate riches than the Spanish, the Portuguese were disappointed by the absence of tributary populations and precious metals in the areas set aside for them. What they did find in Brazil, however, was abundant, fertile land on which favored persons received massive royal grants. These estate owners governed their plantations like fiefdoms.

COASTAL ENCLAVES

Hemmed in along the coast, the Portuguese created enclaves. By the end of the seventeenth century, Brazil's white population was 300,000. Unlike the Spanish, the Portuguese rarely intermarried with Indians, most of whom had fled or had died from imported diseases. Failing to find already established cities in Brazil, the colonists chose to remain in more dispersed settlements.

The problem for the settlers, though, was where to find the labor to work these rich lands. Unlike the Spanish in Mexico or the Andes, the Portuguese in Brazil did not encounter a centralized polity of Aztec or Inca dimensions to take over. Initially, the Portuguese tried to enlist the efforts of Brazil's fragmented and dispersed aboriginal population, but when recruitment became increasingly coercive, Indians turned on the interlopers. Some fought. Others fled to a vast interior rather than submit. Reluctant, indeed scared, to pursue the Indians inland, the Portuguese hugged their beachheads, extracting brazilwood (the source of a beautiful red dye) and sugar from their coastal enclaves.

African slaves became the solution to this labor problem. What had worked for the Portuguese on sugarcane plantations in the Azores and other Atlantic islands was now brought to their Brazilian plantations. Especially in the northeast, in the Bay of All Saints, the Atlantic world's first vast sugar emporium appeared.

SUGAR PLANTATIONS

Cultivation of sugarcane had originated in India, from where it spread to the Mediterranean region and then to the islands off the coast of West Africa. There, sugarcane plantations, tended by African slaves, flourished. This model was then transported by the Portuguese to Brazil and by other European powers to the Caribbean. By the beginning of the seventeenth century, sugar had become a major new export from the New World. By the eighteenth century, its value surpassed that of silver as an export from the Americas to Europe.

Most Brazilian sugar plantations were fairly small, employing between 60 and 100 slaves. But they were efficient enough to create an alternative model of empire, one that resulted in full-scale colonization and dislocation of the existing population. The slaves lived in wretched conditions. Their barracks were miserable, and their diets were insufficient to keep them alive under back-breaking work routines. Moreover, slaves working on Brazilian sugar plantations were disproportionately men. As the slaves rapidly died off, the only way to ensure a supply of labor for the Brazilian plantation complex was to import more Africans. This model of agrarian settlement, then, relied to a very high degree on the transatlantic flow of slaves.

BEGINNINGS OF THE TRANSATLANTIC SLAVE TRADE

The transatlantic slave trade began in a modest way in the late fifteenth century. It was inextricably linked to a single commodity, sugar. As the European demand for this commodity increased, so slavery and the slave trade expanded. From the time of Columbus until 1820, five times as many Africans as Europeans moved to the Americas. In that foundational period, approximately 2 million Europeans, voluntarily, and 10 million Africans, involuntarily, crossed the Atlantic.

First to master long-distance seafaring, the Portuguese also led the way in the taking of human cargo. The trade in slaves grew steadily through the rest of the fifteenth and sixteenth centuries, then expanded by leaps and bounds in the seventeenth and eighteenth centuries (see Chapter 13 for a map and further discussion). During the first two centuries of the slave trade, all European powers participated in the business—Portuguese, Spanish, Dutch, English, and French. Eventually, New World merchants in both North and South America also set up direct trade links with Africa.

Well before European merchants arrived off its west coast, Africa had been involved in long-distance slave trading. Owing to the long duration of this trade, the overall number of Africans sold into captivity in the Muslim world exceeded that of the Atlantic slave trade. Not only did Africans engage in long-distance slave trading, they also maintained slaves themselves. African slavery, like its American counterpart, was a response to labor scarcities. In many parts of Africa, however, slaves were not consigned to permanent servitude. Instead, slaves were assimilated into families, gradually losing their servile status and swelling the size and power of lineage groups.

With the additional European demand for slaves to work New World plantations alongside the ongoing Muslim slave trade, the pressure on the supply of African slaves intensified. Only a narrow band stretching down the spine of the African landmass in a north-south direction, from present-day Uganda and the highlands of Kenya to Zambia and Zimbabwe, escaped the impact of Asian and European slave traders.

Within Africa, the social and political consequences were not fully felt until the great age of the slave trade in the eighteenth century; but already some economic consequences were clear. The overwhelming trend was to further limit the population of Africa. African laborers fetched high enough prices to more than cover the costs of their capture and transportation across the Atlantic.

By the end of the sixteenth century, several important pieces had fallen into place to create a new Atlantic world, one that did not exist a century earlier and indeed could not have been imagined. This was a three-cornered system, with Africa supplying labor, the Americas land and minerals, and Europeans the technology and military power to keep the system together. Each part of the triangle emerged fundamentally transformed. Over the long haul, the wealth flows to Europe and the slave-based development of the Americas would alter the world balance of power.

THE TRANSFORMATION OF EUROPE

> → *How was Europe transformed politically and spiritually?*

Instead of uniting Europeans, the development of the new Atlantic system deepened the landmass's internal divisions. In particular, the growing wealth of the Spanish Empire tilted the weight of European power toward the Habsburg dynasty and toward the west. Europe was transformed by Atlantic rivalries, as well as by the Reformation, which resulted in religious divisions and led to warfare among states committed to different versions of the Christian faith.

THE HABSBURGS AND THE QUEST FOR UNIVERSAL EMPIRE IN EUROPE

The European dream of universal empire had persisted since the fall of ancient Rome and was almost realized by the Habsburg dynasts, heirs to the eastern half of Charlemagne's

Frankish empire. Here a loose confederation of principalities known as the Holy Roman Empire continued to be ruled by an emperor who was elected by an elite group of lower-level sovereigns (dukes, archbishops, and kings of individual states like Bavaria), but who, after 1273, usually came from the house of Habsburg. The emperor's dominions officially included territory now incorporated into the Netherlands, Germany, Austria, Belgium, Croatia and parts of Italy, Poland, and Switzerland; the realm was enormous, but power was never effectively centralized. Emperors were traditionally crowned by the pope in Rome, but there was persistent rivalry between the papacy and the empire, and resentment in many parts of the empire over southern Europe's hegemonic power in the church.

Charles V was the grandson of the Spanish monarchs Isabella and Ferdinand and of Maximilian I, who headed the Austrian Habsburg family and from 1493 to 1519 served as Holy Roman Emperor. In 1519, Charles was elected Holy Roman Emperor, largely because he had inherited the grandest imperial domain in European history. His realm encompassed Spain and Spain's new territories in the Americas, as well as the traditional central European holdings of the Habsburgs.

But even at its height, Charles V's loose-knit empire lacked a unified administrative structure, and religious and political divisions persisted. Moreover, Charles had to defend his eastern flank. The armies of the Ottoman Sultan Suleiman seized Habsburg Belgrade in Serbia in 1521 and Mohács in Hungary in 1526, and three years later they laid siege to Vienna but failed to capture it. Charles counterattacked in Hungary in 1531, and his successors ultimately regained Hungary from the Ottomans at the end of the seventeenth century.

Overstretched by the challenges of trying to keep such an ambitious empire intact, Charles abdicated in 1556 and formally divided his empire between his younger brother Ferdinand and his son Philip. Ferdinand (ruled 1556–1564) took the Austrian, German, and central European parts of the empire that straddled the Danube and was elected Holy Roman Emperor in 1556. The Austrian Habsburgs maintained dominance over central Europe.

Philip II (ruled Spain 1556–1598) received Spain, Belgium, the Netherlands, southern Italy, and the New World possessions. Moreover, in 1580, he inherited the Portuguese throne (his mother had been a Portuguese princess), adding Portugal and its colonial possessions to his empire; this gave him a virtual monopoly on Atlantic commerce. Yet, the Spanish Habsburgs had to defend their half of the empire against a series of Dutch revolts, beginning in 1566, as well as confront perpetual Ottoman harassment on land and at sea. Philip sent troops to subdue the Netherlands revolt—a move that ended with the massacre of civilians in the town of Antwerp—but the Spanish-Dutch war persisted. He also directed the Spanish fleet to set up defenses against the Ottomans and North African Muslim pirates in the Mediterranean Sea. In 1571, the Spanish fleet defeated the Ottoman fleet at Lepanto. But the size and wealth of Habsburg Spain continued to provoke enormous tension within Europe.

CONFLICT IN EUROPE AND THE DEMISE OF UNIVERSAL EMPIRE

French, English, and Dutch elites envied the riches of the Portuguese and Spanish colonial possessions. These rivals yearned for their own profitable colonies. But in their explorations of the New World, the French, English, and Dutch had not yet found their own mountains of gold and silver, nor had they discovered a new and easier route to Asia. Still, they were able to claim a share of the wealth of the Americas by stealing it on the high seas. Some of the plunderers were pirates, who raided for their own benefit; others were privateers, who did their stealing with official sanction and shared the profits of their thefts with their monarchs. Often the distinction between pirate and privateer was blurred.

The most famous of the raiders was Sir Francis Drake, who was commissioned by the English crown to plunder Spanish possessions. Circling the globe between 1577 and 1580, Drake plundered one Spanish port after another. His favorite hunting ground was the Caribbean, where Mesoamerican and Andean silver, loaded onto Spanish galleons (heavy, square-rigged ships used for war or commerce), made lucrative targets. Besides, the many islands provided natural shelter. While Drake's exploits were undertaken for personal gain, his monarch, Queen Elizabeth, approved of his assaults on the Spanish Empire, and rewarded him with a knighthood.

To retaliate, the Spanish sailed a mighty armada of 130 ships and almost 20,000 men into the English Channel in 1588, but England amassed 197 ships, 34 from its Royal Navy and the rest merchant vessels. The battle resulted in a devastating defeat for the Spanish fleet. In the retreat, the Spanish king lost many of his most prized battleships. The conflict between a rising England and Spain continued in other seas, and Drake returned to his career of privateering. When the news of Drake's death in the Caribbean (from yellow fever in 1596) arrived in Madrid, the Spanish court erupted in jubilation. The old, infirm King Philip declared that this news would allow him to recover quickly. Two months later, an English fleet of 40 warships and over 100 smaller vessels sailed into Spain's premier port of Cádiz and occupied the city for two weeks, burning 200 Spanish ships and seizing the massive treasure from the Indies. Spain, the powerhouse of the Atlantic world, had been severely humbled. Two years later, a despondent King Philip died. The dream of universal empire within Europe had failed, in large part because Christendom continued to be at war with itself.

→ *How was Europe transformed politically and spiritually?*

Defeat of the Spanish Armada. This engraving shows the defeat of the Spanish Armada off Plymouth, England, in May of 1588.

THE REFORMATION

The same internal political conflicts and pursuit of individual aims that characterized European activities in the New World also led to the Protestant Reformation in Europe. A growing number of Europeans, like the Dutch Brethren of the Common Life in the fourteenth century, despaired of the Catholic Church's ability to satisfy longings for deeper, more individualized religious experience. Movements such as the Brethren had inspired Christians to adopt devotional practices, like the Stations of the Cross, and to form reading groups among the laity. When sixteenth-century reformers took up the call for change, they were hopeful that an already reforming church would respond to their criticisms. They had no notion that their complaints would split Christendom for good.

What seemed to reformers to be constructive criticism was, in the eyes of church officials, heresy. The clergy were right to be worried about the claims of critics like the German monk Martin Luther (1483–1546), who in 1517 proclaimed "Salvation by faith alone" and pronounced the Bible as the sole source of Christian truth. Luther circulated ninety-five "theses" for disputation with his learned colleagues. In this declaration and in subsequent debates, Luther denounced the corruptions of the church and the repression of Germanic freedoms by faraway Latin authority. In *On the Freedom of the Christian Man* (1520), he upbraided "the Roman Church, which in past ages was the holiest of all" for having "become a den of murderers beyond all other dens of murderers, a thieves' castle beyond all other thieves' castles, the head and empire of every sin, as well as of death and damnation." His doctrine struck at both the spiritual and the social authority of the clergy over the laity, undermining the former's claims to control the channels for salvation and to determine Christian truth. He also translated the New Testament into German so that laypersons could have direct access, unmediated by the clergy, to the word of God.

Spread by printed books and ardent preachers in all the vernacular languages of Europe, Luther's doctrines won widespread support. Many of the German princes embraced the reformed faith as a means of asserting their independence from the Holy Roman Emperor. For many, the new ideas, known by 1529 as "Protestantism," promised not just the renewal of Christianity but attention to individual spiritual needs and a new moral foundation for community life. Across northern Europe, reformed ideas established a powerful presence, especially in the German states, France, Switzerland, the Low Countries, and England. The renewed Christian creed could and did appeal to commoners as well as elites. It found particular resonance among communities resentful of rule by Catholic "outsiders" (like Habsburg Philip II, who ruled the Netherlands from his palace in Spain).

Some zealous reformers, like Jean Calvin (1509–1564) in France, made their own modifications to Luther's ideas. To Luther's emphasis on the individual's relationship to God Calvin added an emphasis on moral regeneration through church discipline and the autonomy of religious communities. He laid out, and his successors underscored, the doctrine of predestination—the notion that each person was already "predestined" for damnation or salvation even before birth. The "elect," he thought, should also be free to govern themselves, a doctrine that ratified both radical political dissent (as in the case of the Puritans in England) and the rule of the clergy (as in the Swiss city-state of Geneva). Calvinism proved especially popular in Switzerland, the Netherlands, northeastern France, and Scotland (where it was called Presbyterianism).

In England, Henry VIII (ruled 1509–1547) and his daughter Elizabeth (ruled 1558–1603) crafted a moderate reformed religion—a "middle way"—called Anglicanism, which retained many Catholic practices and a hierarchy topped by bishops (hence its American followers would later call themselves Episcopalians, from the Latin word for bishop, *episcopus*). Although Anglican rule was imposed upon Ireland, most nonelite Irishmen continued to adhere to Catholicism. The Scots maintained a fierce devotion to their Presbyterian Church, ensuring a measure of religious diversity within the

British Isles. In England, as with the rest of Europe, more radical sects like the Anabaptists and the Quakers survived within mainstream Protestantism. While all Protestants were opposed to Catholicism and distrustful of the papal hierarchy, members of these different communities sometimes developed animosities toward one another as well (see Map 12-4).

The Catholic Church responded to the challenges of Luther and Calvin by embarking on its own renovation, which became known as the Counter-Reformation. At the Council of Trent (1545–1563), it reaffirmed its doctrines, sacraments, the importance of acts of charity, papal supremacy, and the distinctive role of its clergy. But it also enacted reforms to answer the Protestants' assaults on clerical corruption. In contrast to many of their predecessors, the popes who headed the Catholic Church during the second half of the sixteenth century became renowned for their piety and asceticism. These pontiffs also installed bishops and abbots who generally steered clear of the unscrupulous practices that had been so fervently attacked by Protestant critics. Taking on the Protestant theological challenge, Catholicism gave greater emphasis to individual spirituality. Like Protes-

The Reformation. Reformation images played an important role in the often violent polemics of the period. In this rather tame image, Luther preaches to Christ and the godly (*left*), while the pope (*right*) doles out indulgences to wealthy sinners.

MAP 12-4   RELIGIOUS DIVISIONS IN EUROPE AFTER THE REFORMATION, 1590

The Protestant Reformation divided Europe religiously and politically in the sixteenth century. Can you identify any geographic patterns in the distribution of Protestant communities? In what regions would you expect Protestant-Catholic tensions to be the most intense? Can you explain why Protestantism tended to triumph in the north but not in the south?

tants, reformed Catholics carried their message overseas, especially through the activities of an order established in 1534 by a former soldier named Ignatius Loyola (1491–1556). Loyola founded a brotherhood of priests, the Society of Jesus, or Jesuits, which was dedicated to the revival of the Catholic Church. From bases in Lisbon, Rome, Paris, and elsewhere in Europe, the Jesuits opened missions as far as South and North America, India, Japan, and China.

Despite these reforms, the Vatican continued to use repression and persecution to combat what it considered to be heretical beliefs. In sixteenth-century Augsburg, priests performed public exorcisms, seeking to free Protestant parishioners from the "demons" that supposedly possessed them. The Index of Prohibited Books (a list of books and theological treatises banned by the Catholic Church) and the Medieval Inquisition (from 1184) remained weapons to be used against those deemed the church's enemies. But the proliferation of printing presses and Protestantism's remarkable inroads made it impossible for the Catholic Counter-Reformation to turn back the tide leading toward increased autonomy from the papacy.

Both Catholics and Protestants persecuted witches. Between about 1500 and 1700, as many as 100,000 people, most of them women, were accused of being witches; many of them were tried, tortured, burned at the stake or hanged. Older women and widows, and women who worked as nurses were especially vulnerable to charges of having cursed or poisoned babies, causing them to become sick or die. But witches were also charged with killing livestock, causing hailstorms, or scotching marriage arrangements. The surrounding society was willing to believe that naturally weak and susceptible women might have sex with the devil or be tempted to do his bidding.

RELIGIOUS WARFARE IN EUROPE

The religious revival of the sixteenth century led Europe into another round of wars that were as disruptive and ferocious as those of the fourteenth century. Their ultimate effect was to weaken the Spanish and strengthen the English, French, and Dutch. The circulation of Luther's ideas—between 1518 and 1525, one-third of all books sold in the 300-odd German states were written by Martin Luther—precipitated a series of brutal peasant revolts across central Europe in 1524. These revolts often broke out when princes or town councils that had decided to accept or reject the Reformation tried to force religious uniformity on their subjects. Often this entailed burnings, beatings, and drownings to persuade those who were reluctant to change their beliefs. In contrast to the relatively small armies of earlier wars, in which one noble's retinue fought a rival's followers, the defense of the Catholic mass and the Protestant Bible brought a large number of simple folk to arms. In 1555, after nearly forty years of religious warfare, the Holy Roman Emperor Charles V was compelled to allow the German princes the right to choose whether Protestantism or Catholicism would be the official religion within their domains. This did not mean, however, that Europe's religious wars were over.

Religious conflicts both weakened European dynasties and made them all the more eager for conquest abroad. Spain, with its massive empire and its silver mines in the New World, spent much of its new fortune waging war in Europe. Most debilitating to Spain was its costly, and eventually futile, effort to subdue its recently acquired Dutch territories. After a series of wars that continued in fits and starts from 1566 to 1648, Catholic Spain finally conceded the Protestant Netherlands its independence.

Wars took their toll on the Spanish Empire, which was soon wallowing in debts; not even the riches of the American silver mines could bail out the court. In the late 1550s, Philip II had to renege on obligations to the empire's creditors. Within two decades, Spain was declared bankrupt three times. Spanish decline opened the way for the Dutch and the English to extend their trading networks into Asia and the New World. Competition between the latter two soon led to

St. Bartholomew's Day Massacre. An important wedding between French Catholic and Huguenot families in Paris was scheduled for August 24, 1572, St. Bartholomew's Day; but instead of reconciliation, that day saw a massacre, as Catholics tried to stamp out Protestantism in France's capital city.

trade wars, underscoring that religious differences were not the only sources of inter-European strife.

If religious conflicts drew Spain into costly struggles with the Netherlands and England, they also sparked civil wars. In France, the internal divide between Catholics and Protestants exploded in the St. Bartholomew's Day Massacre in 1572. Catholic crowds, shouting "Kill, kill, kill," rampaged through the streets of Paris murdering Huguenot (Protestant) men, women, and children and dumping their bodies into the Seine River; parades of rioters displayed the heads of Protestants on pikes. The number of dead reached 3,000 in Paris and at least 10,000 in provincial towns. Slaughter on this scale did not break the Huguenots' spirit, but it did bring more disrepute to the monarchy for failing to ensure peace. Indeed, this was the beginning of the end of the Valois dynasty. Another round of warfare exhausted the French and brought Henry of Navarre, a Protestant Bourbon prince, to the throne. To become king, Henry IV converted to Catholicism, and in 1598, he issued the Edict of Nantes. This proclamation declared France a Catholic country, but it at least temporarily diffused the tensions by tolerating some public Protestant worship.

Dynastic loyalties remained overarching, but religious ones came to the fore. As dynastic rulers sought to resolve religious questions within their own dominions—by peaceful or bloody means—and built up far larger armies than before, religious affiliations began to acquire a tinge of national identity. Religious strife propelled incipient nation formation and exacerbated still more ferocious rivalries for wealth and territory overseas. Thus, Europe entered its age of overseas exploration as a collection of increasingly powerful yet irreconcilably competitive rival states, whose differences stemmed not just from language but from the ways they worshipped the Christian God.

PROSPERITY IN ASIA

> → *Why did trade expand and wealth increase in sixteenth-century Asia?*

While Europe was beset by religious warfare, Asian empires were expanding and consolidating their power, and trade was flourishing.

MUGHAL INDIA AND COMMERCE

Illustrative of Asia's economic flourishing was the Mughal Empire, which became one of the world's wealthiest and most powerful at the very time when Europeans were establishing their first sustained connections with India. These connec-

tions, however, only touched the outer layer of Mughal India and were largely irrelevant to the emergence of one of Islam's greatest regimes. Established in 1526, the Mughal Empire was a vigorous, centralized state whose political authority extended over most of modern-day India. During the sixteenth century, its realm encompassed a population between 100 and 150 million.

The strength of the Mughals rested on their impressive military power (see Chapter 11). The dynasty's founder, Babur, brought horsemanship and, most notably, trained artillery men and field cannons from central Asia. Babur's gunpowder secured swift military victories and control over northern India. Not until the reign of his grandson, Akbar (ruled 1556–1605), however, did the empire experience a vast expansion and consolidation that would continue under Akbar's grandson Aurangzeb until the empire encompassed almost the whole of India (see Map 12-5). Known as the "Great Mughal," Akbar extended the military campaigns of his predecessors. These campaigns consolidated Akbar's control over much of the population. But the key to Akbar's success was not might alone. Akbar was a skilled practitioner of the art of alliance-making. Deals with Hindu chieftains through favors and intermarriage among notables also contributed to the growth and stability of Akbar's empire.

Mughal rulers were even more flexible in their dealings with the region's various peoples than their predecessors had been. This was especially true in spiritual affairs. Though its primary commitment to Islam was never in doubt, the imperial court patronized a variety of beliefs, earning it legitimacy in the eyes of diverse subjects. The contrast with sixteenth-century Europe, where religious differences created deep fractures within and between states, could not have been starker. Unlike European monarchs, who tried to enforce religious uniformity, whether out of their own piety or fear of instability, Akbar engaged in a systematic study and discussion of comparative religion. He hosted regular disputations in his famous *Din-i-Ilahi* (House of Worship), where Hindu, Muslim, Jain, Parsi, and Christian theologians debated the merits of different religions. Akbar had both a Hindu and a Christian wife (besides having a Muslim wife, as well as numerous concubines of many different nationalities and religions), and his palace boasted temples to each faith. Akbar's pragmatic tolerance did not always keep theologians happy—especially those who advocated orthodox beliefs—but it kept a sprawling and diverse spiritual kingdom under one political roof.

Akbar's court enjoyed the fruits of the commercial recovery and expansion in the Indian Ocean. The Mughals possessed no ocean navy, but merchants from Mughal lands used overland routes and rivers to exchange Indian cottons, tobacco, saffron, betel leaf, sugar, and indigo for Iranian melons, dried fruits, nuts, silks, carpets, and precious metals, or for Russian pelts, leathers, walrus tusks, saddles, and chainmail armor. Every year, Akbar ordered 1,000 new suits stitched of the most exquisite material. His harem was attired in fine silks dripping with gold, brocades, and pearls. Carpets,

MAP 12-5 EXPANSION OF THE MUGHAL EMPIRE, 1556–1707

Under Akbar and Aurangzeb the Mughal Empire expanded and dominated much of South Asia during this time. Yet, by looking at the trading ports along the Indian coast, one can see the growing influence of Portuguese, Dutch, French, and English interests. To what extent did these trading posts reflect a significant increase in European influence in the region? Did these European outposts play a role in shaping Mughal policies? Why did Mughal leaders tolerate this European presence?

mirrors, and precious metals decorated noble households and camps, while perfume and wine flowed freely. Retainers, even horses and elephants, were garbed in elaborate attire. The splendor of the realm was perhaps most evident in the field of fine arts. In architecture, for instance, Akbar's temporary capital at Fatehpur Sikri, near Agra, combined the fort's flat stone beams and sense of immensity from the Hindu tradition with the arches and the feathery lightness of Islamic art. Indian merchant diaspora communities took root in Bukhara and Astrakhan, Isfahan and Qandahar. India's Muslim and Hindu merchants learned Persian, the key language, and some knew Turkic languages.

New western European trading connections contributed to the flow of wealth to the Mughal polity, but the latter's strength limited European incursions. Although the Portuguese occupied Goa and Bombay on the Indian coast, they had little presence beyond these ports and, in fact, they did not dare to antagonize the Mughal emperor. In 1578, Akbar recognized the credentials of a Portuguese ambassador and allowed a Jesuit missionary to enter his court. In the ensuing years, the commercial ties between the Mughals and Portuguese intensified, but the latter's merchants were still effectively confined to a few ports on the fringes of the Mughal domain. More Portuguese ships entered those harbors, but many of these were manned by Indian seamen. In addition, the Mughals ended the Portuguese monopoly on the oceanic trade with Europe. In the 1580s and 1590s, to the chagrin of the Portuguese, Dutch and English merchantmen started to arrive in Indian ports.

Akbar seized on the commercial boom to overhaul his empire's revenue system. Until the 1560s, the Mughal state, unable itself to penetrate deeply into regional societies, relied on a vast network of decentralized tribute collectors called *zamindars*. These collectors possessed rights to claim a share of the harvest from the region's peasants, while earmarking part of their earnings for the emperor. But sharing the spoils between the emperor and cooperative local leaders created underlying problems, for the Mughals did not always see their agreed share, while the high levies did not always sit well with peasants. Local populations in the periphery mounted prolonged resistance to dynastic power. But as trade flourished, the supply of money rose. Akbar's officials, and especially the Hindu revenue minister Todar Mal, monetized the tax assessment system and curbed the political and fiscal power of the *zamindars* over the peasantry. The emperor undertook a variety of other reforms that further rationalized and centralized the revenue system. The result: imperial revenues began to rise markedly, and these helped cover the cost of Akbar's military expeditions and his extravagant spending on the beautification of his court.

These fiscal policies reinforced the commercialization of the empire. To generate the cash to pay taxes, peasants had to sell their produce in the market. Market towns and ports flourished. Dealers in grain and money became more promi-

Akbar Hears a Petition. In keeping with the multiethnic and multireligious character of Akbar's empire, the image reflects the diversity of peoples seeking to have their petitions heard by the Mughal emperor.

nent in the countryside as they helped peasants get their produce to market. Between one-fifth and one-third the value of all this burgeoning rural produce flowed into state coffers. The *zamindars* evolved from private tribute lords into servants of the state, though they continued to enjoy their share of the peasants' income.

Centered in northern India, Babur and Akbar's empire seized upon the wealth of the surrounding regions and channeled resources—military, architectural, and artistic—to glorify the court. At the same time, this enhanced wealth opened potential divisions between Indian regions, and even between merchants and rulers. So long as merchants relied upon rulers for their commercial gains, and so long as rulers carefully

Primary Source

COMMENTARY ON FOREIGNERS FROM A MING OFFICIAL

Although China had a long history of both overland and maritime trade with the outside world, Ming officials were often hostile toward contact with foreigners. Urging that the foreign presence must be brought under strict government control, the bureaucrat He Ao (Ho Ao) portrayed the Europeans (whom he called Feringis) as unruly, untrustworthy, and a threat to the security of the country in this commentary from around 1520. Such sentiments were also often found among Chinese officials in subsequent centuries, even as China thrived in the growing commercial exchanges of an increasingly connected world.

The Feringis are most cruel and crafty. Their arms are superior to those of other foreigners. Some years ago they came suddenly to the city of Canton, and the noise of their cannon shook the earth [these were cannon shots fired as a salute by the fleet of Fernão Peres]. Those who remained at the post-station [places where foreigners were lodged] disobeyed the law and had intercourse with others. Those who came to the Capital were proud and struggled [among themselves?] to become head. Now if we allow them to come and go and to carry on their trade, it will inevitably lead to fighting and bloodshed, and the misfortune of our South may be boundless. In the time of our ancestors, foreigners came to bring tribute only at fixed periods, and the law provided for precautionary measures, therefore the foreigners who could come were not many. But some time ago the Provincial Treasurer, Wu T'ing-chü, saying that he needed spice to be sent to the Court, took some of their goods no matter when they came. It was due to what he

did that foreigner ships have never ceased visiting our shores and that barbarians have lived scattered in our departmental cities. Prohibition and precaution having been neglected, the Feringis became more and more familiar with our fair ways. And thus availing themselves of the situation the Feringis came into our port. I pray that all the foreign junks in our bay and the foreigners who secretly live (in our territory) be driven away, that private intercourse be prohibited and that our strategical defence be close, so that that part of our country will have peace.

→ *What does this document tell us about the Chinese viewing of foreigners?*
→ *How does it compare to the earlier report from the European trader?*

SOURCE: T'ien-tse Chang, *Sino-Portuguese Trade, From 1514 to 1644: A Synthesis of Portuguese and Chinese Sources* (Leyden: E. J. Brill, 1934), pp. 51–52.

balanced local and imperial interests, however, the Mughal realm remained unified and kept Europeans on the outskirts of society.

PROSPERITY IN MING CHINA

In the late sixteenth century, China's Ming dynasty also prospered from increased commerce. As with the Mughals, the Ming seemed relatively unconcerned with the now more regular appearance of foreigners, including silver-bearing European traders. As in India, the Ming retained the power to confine Europeans to port cities, while the availability of silver facilitated the spread of market activities across the Ming realm. Employers paid their workers with money rather than with produce or goods. Agriculture and handicraft production soared. The injection of money eased the constraints of borrowing and lending. Rural industries also flourished. A cotton boom, for example, helped make spinning and weaving China's largest single industry.

A clear measure of the greater prosperity under the Ming—or "the Great Ming," as the dynasty was called—was its population surge. By the middle of the seventeenth century, the Chinese population probably accounted for a higher proportion of the total world population than at any other time in the history of the world—more than one-third, or approximately 250 million out of 750 million. Although fully 90 percent of the people lived in the countryside, large numbers swelled the ranks of the urban dwellers. Beijing, the Ming capital, saw its population grow to over 1 million, and Nanjing, the secondary capital, grew to nearly the same number of inhabitants. There were another half dozen cities with populations of 500,000, and another twenty or so with 100,000 or more residents. Cities allowed urbanites of means to find all manner of diversions, ranging from literary and theatrical societies to schools of learning, religious societies, and urban associations. Here, too, the diverse manufactures from all over the Ming Empire were available to satisfy the taste of the discerning consumer. The elegance and material prosperity of Chinese cities dazzled European visitors. Matteo Ricci, a Jesuit missionary, described Nanjing in 1600 as a city that surpassed all others in the world "in beauty and grandeur. . . . It is literally filled with palaces and temples and towers and bridges. . . . There is a gaiety of spirit among the people who are well mannered and nicely spoken."

Ming urban prosperity fostered entertainment districts, charcterized by anonymity and relative freedom. Some Ming women found a place here as refined entertainers and courtesans. Others were in demand as midwives, poets, sorcerers, and matchmakers. Female painters, occasionally wives or daughters of professional painters but mostly members of scholar-official families, emulated males who used the home and garden for creative pursuits. The growth of the book trade was also particularly important for women, who were writers as well as readers, not to mention literary characters and archetypes (especially of Confucian virtues). But Chinese women played their biggest roles, and made their greatest fortunes, inside the emperor's Forbidden City, as healers, consorts, and power brokers.

By the middle of the sixteenth century, Ming rule began to stumble owing to a variety of problems, from piracy along the coasts to ineptness in the state. Some Chinese were critical of the political corruption and social decay. One critic, Wang Yangming (1472–1529), a government official and a noted scholar of Neo-Confucian thought, urged commitment to social action. He argued for the unity of knowledge and action and claimed, most importantly, that the answers to problems lay within one's own mind. Taking Wang's emphasis on the individual further, some of his more radical later followers even suggested, against orthodox belief at the time, that women were equal to men intellectually and should be fully educated, a position that led to their banishment from the elite establishment. Even as new ideas and the state's weaknesses created internal discord, the commercial vibrancy of Ming society continued. China's economic vitality also survived the fall of the dynasty in 1644, laying the foundation and providing the resources for the population growth and subsequent territorial expansion of the seventeenth and eighteenth centuries.

ASIAN RELATIONS WITH EUROPE

Europe's overseas expansion had originally been directed toward Asia. The conquest and colonization of the New World gave Europeans the means to realize some of their dreams vis-à-vis Asia. The Portuguese led the way, profiting greatly from being the first Europeans to establish themselves in the Indian Ocean. They inserted themselves into the overseas trading networks bridging East Africa to China, and within a short while they became either important commercial intermediaries or collectors of customs duties from Asian traders. In 1557, the Portuguese arrival at Macao, a port city along the southern coast of China, enabled them to penetrate

Macao. This Chinese painting depicts the Portuguese enclave of Macao on the southern border of China around 1800.

China's expanding import-export trade. By 1563, the number of Portuguese in Macao neared 1,000.

To be sure, the Portuguese contingent in Macao was dwarfed by the far larger number of Melakans, Indians, and Africans enlivening the port. Moreover, while Ming authorities had finally permitted a Portuguese presence in Macao, the court in Beijing remained unwilling to establish an official relationship with European traders there. Like the Mughals, the Ming confined Portuguese merchants to a coastal enclave. Indeed, in 1574, the Chinese built a wall at the isthmus connecting Macao with the mainland. This barrier, and the soldiers who guarded it, served to restrict the movement of the Portuguese and their access to inland trade. Restricted though their presence was, however, the Portuguese did become important shippers of China's most prized manufactures, its porcelains and silks, throughout Asia and to Europe. They also took over much of the silver trade from Japan.

Seeing how much the Portuguese were earning on Asian trade, the Spanish, English, and Dutch adventured into Asian waters. With monopolistic access to American silver, Spain enjoyed a competitive advantage. In 1565, the first Spanish trading galleon reached the Philippines, and in 1571, after the Spanish captured the city of Manila and made it a colonial capital, they established a brisk trade with China. Each year, ships from the Spanish colonies in the Americas crossed the Pacific to Manila, bearing cargoes of silver. They returned carrying vast quantities of porcelain and silks for well-to-do European consumers. Merchants of Manila also procured silks, tapestries, and feathers from the China Seas for direct shipment to the Americas, where the mining potentates waited eagerly for their imports from China.

The year 1571, therefore, proved to be a decisive date in the history of the modern world, for in that year Spain inaugurated a trade circuit that made good on Magellan's achievement of a half-century prior. As Spanish ships circumnavigated the globe from the New World to China and from China eventually back to Europe, the world was commercially interconnected. It was silver that solidified the linkage, for silver was the only foreign commodity for which the Chinese had a constant and unquenchable demand. From the massive mother lodes of the Andes and Mesoamerica, silver made the commerce of the world go round.

Other Europeans, too, wanted their share of Asia's wealth. The English and the Dutch sailed into the South China Sea in the last decade of the sixteenth century. Captain James Lancaster made the first English voyage to the East Indies between 1591 and 1594. Five years later, in 1599, 101 English subscribers pooled their funds and formed a joint-stock company (an association in which each member owned shares of capital). With an initial capital of £30,000, the English East India Company was given a royal charter the following year. The charter granted the company exclusive rights to import East Indian goods. Rapidly, the company displaced the Portuguese in the Arabian Sea and the Persian Gulf. Doing a brisk trade in indigo, saltpetre, pepper, and cotton textiles, the English East India Company would eventually acquire control in villages on both coasts of India—Fort St. George (Madras; 1639), Bombay (1661), and Calcutta (1690).

Chronology

		1500	1510	1520	1530	15·
EUROPE		■ *Christians complete reconquest of Granada, 1492*		■ *Luther posts 95 theses, 1517* ■ *Magellan's ship circumnavigates the globe, 1519–1* ■ *Peasant wars in Holy Roman Empire,*		
AMERICAS		■ *Columbus discovers the New World, 1492*		■ *Magellan's ship circumnavigates the globe, 1519–1* ■ *Cortés conquers the Aztecs, 1519–1522* *Pizarro conquers the Incas, 1533* ■		
SOUTH ASIA		■ *Da Gama sails to the Indian Ocean, 1498* ■ *Portuguese establish Indian Ocean bases, 1508–1511*		■ *Magellan's ship circumnavigates the globe, 1519–1*		
EAST ASIA				■ *Magellan's ship circumnavigates the globe, 1519–1*		

It is tempting to see the arrival of Europeans in the waters of the South China Sea and the Indian Ocean as the beginning of the end of Asian autonomy. This was hardly the case, however. Through the sixteenth century, Europeans forged only very weak connections to Asian societies. For the moment, the increased presence of Europeans in Asia enhanced the wealth and might of Asian dynasties.

CONCLUSION

In the middle of the fifteenth century, the world had many different regional trading spheres. In this sense, it was multicentered. Islam occupied a kind of pivot. In an Indian Ocean system straddling Africa, the eastern Mediterranean, and South and East Asia, merchants plied their wares along overland and increasingly seaborne routes, while intermingling in multiethnic urban centers. To the extent that Asian empires expanded, they sought tribute and trade. Exchange, or better yet, tributary relations with subject peoples drove imperial agendas.

In this multicentered world of the fifteenth century, Europe was a poor cousin. A new spirit of adventure and achievement, however, animated European peoples, stirred up by the rediscovery of antiquity (the Renaissance), the ambitions of a rising mercantile elite, and later by the spiritual fervor of the Reformation and Counter-Reformation. Learning much from Arab seamen, European sailors perfected techniques for sailing into dangerous waters. Desiring Asian goods, especially for luxury consumption, European merchants and mariners were eager to exploit existing trade routes leading eastward. But far more consequentially, Europe's location gave its people another direction into which to expand, across the still largely unknown Atlantic Ocean. With the Ottoman conquest of Constantinople and control over the eastern Mediterranean, the Atlantic sea lanes offered an alternative route to Asia. As the Europeans searched for alternative routes around Islam, they first sailed down the coast of Africa and then across the Atlantic.

Encountering the "New World" was an accident of monumental significance. In the Americas, Europeans found riches. Mountains of silver and rivers of gold gave Europeans the currency they had lacked in dealing with Asian traders. In the Americas, Europeans also found opportunities for exchange and settlement. And here, unlike in Asian empires, European rivals were able to supplement their drive for commerce with conquest and colonization. Yet, establishing these transatlantic empires heightened tensions within Europe, as rivals fought over the spoils and as a religious schism turned into a political and spiritual struggle that divided Europe. For this reason two conquests in particular characterize this age of increasing world interconnections. The Islamic conquest of Constantinople drove Europeans to search for new links to Asia and demonstrated the centrality of Islam in the making of modern world history. In turn, the conquest of Tenochtitlán, some seventy years later, gave Europeans access to silver, which enabled them to increase their presence in Asian

1550	1560	1570	1580	1590	1600

▌ *Dutch revolt against Spanish rule, 1568*

▌ *Spanish fleet defeats Ottomans at Lepanto, 1571*

▌ *English defeat Spanish Armada, 1588*

▌ *Opening of Potosí mines, 1545*

▌ *Consolidation of Mughal Empire, 1556–1605*

▌ *Portuguese arrive at Macao (China); first permanent settlement established, 1557*

▌ *Spanish capture city of Manila, 1571*

▌ *Ming erect wall to Macao to restrict European movement, 1574* trading circuits. In this era of growing interconnectedness, these two conquests were decisive turning points in the making of the modern world.

American Indians also played an important role in the making of the modern world, as Europeans sought to conquer their lands, exploit their labor, and confiscate their gold and silver. Sometimes Indians worked with Europeans, sometimes they worked under Europeans, sometimes they worked against Europeans, and sometimes none were left to work at all. In this last all-too-common case, the Europeans made Africans do what Indians could not, thereby compounding the calamity of the encounter with the tragedy of slavery. Out of the catastrophe of contact, a new oceanic system arose, linking the peoples and products of Africa, America, and Europe. This was the Atlantic world, one that gave new meaning to the notion of oceanic systems. In contrast to the tributary and trading orders of the Indian Ocean and China Seas, the Atlantic Ocean became a system of formal imperial control and settlement of distant colonies.

STUDY QUESTIONS

 WWNORTON.COM/STUDYSPACE

1. Describe the new trade patterns in the Afro-Eurasian world during the fifteenth century. How similar and different were they from the Mongol period?
2. Describe the process through which Spain was able to create a vast empire in the Americas. How did the spread of lethal disease influence this outcome?
3. Explain the process involved in the "The Columbian Exchange." What consequences did this exchange (or exchanges) have on regions beyond the Atlantic world?
4. Compare and contrast Spain's "tributary empire" in the Americas with Portugal's "seaborne empire" in the Indian Ocean during the sixteenth century. Why did these empires pursue such different strategies?
5. Explain what conditions allowed for the strengthening of regional dynasties in Europe in the sixteenth century as opposed to the growth of one large European empire.
6. Explain the transformation of the African slave trade during this time period. What role did the growth of sugar plantations play in this process?
7. Analyze how the emergence of the Atlantic world in the sixteenth century transformed Europe, the Americas, and Africa. To what extent was each region transformed?
8. Compare and contrast political and commercial developments in the Mughal and Ming dynasties in Asia during the sixteenth century. How did the expansion of global commerce affect each region?
9. Evaluate to what extent an increased European presence altered the political balance of power in Asia during the sixteenth century. How did Asian dynasties react to increased European contacts?
10. Explain the role of silver in transforming global trade patterns during the sixteenth century. Which regions and dynasties benefited from the increased use of silver for monetary transactions?

FURTHER READINGS

Axtell, James, *Beyond 1492: Encounters in Colonial North America* (1992). A wonderfully informed speculation about Indian reactions to Europeans.

Brady, Thomas A., et al. (eds.), *Handbook of European History 1400–1600: Late Middle Ages, Renaissance, and Reformation, Structures and Assertions* (1996). A good synthetic survey of recent literature and historiographical debates.

Cass, Victoria, *Dangerous Women: Warriors, Grannies, and Geishas of the Ming* (1999). An original study of Chinese female archetypes in memoirs, miscellanies, short stories, and novels.

Chaudhuri, K. N., *Trade and Civilisation in the Indian Ocean: An Economic History from the Rise of Islam to 1750* (1985). An excellent, comprehensive work that deals with the Indian Ocean economy and the appearance of European merchants there from the sixteenth century onward.

Clendinnen, Inga, *Aztecs: An Interpretation* (1991). Brilliantly reconstructs the culture of Tenochtitlán in the years before its conquest.

Crosby, Alfred W., *The Columbian Exchange: Biological and Cultural Consequences of 1492* (1972). A provocative discussion of the ecological consequences that followed the European "discovery" of the Americas.

———, *Ecological Imperialism: The Biological Expansion of Europe, 900–1900* (1986). Another important work on the ecological consequences of European expansion.

Curtin, Philip, *Cross-Cultural Trade in World History* (1984). A work stressing the role of trade and commerce in establishing cross-cultural contacts.

Febvre, Lucien, *The Problem of Unbelief in the Sixteenth Century: The Religion of Rabelais* (1982). A tour de force of intellectual history by the man who moved the study of the Reformation away from great men to the broader question of religious revival and mentalities.

Flynn, Dennis, and Arturo Giráldez (eds.), *Metals and Monies in an Emerging Global Economy* (1997). Contains several articles relating to silver and the Asian trade.

Frank, Andre Gunder, *ReOrient: Global Economy in the Asian Age* (1998). A reassessment of the role of Asia in the economic development of the world from around 1400 onward.

Gruzinski, Serge, *The Conquest of Mexico* (1993). An important work on the conquest of Mexico.

Habib, Irfan, *The Agrarian System of Mughal India* (1963). One of the best studies on the subject.

Hall, Richard Seymour, *Empires of the Monsoon: A History of the Indian Ocean and Its Invaders* (1996). A very engaging journalistic account with fabulous details.

Hodgson, Marshall, *The Venture of Islam*, vols. 2 and 3 (1974). A magisterial work that includes the Indian subcontinent in its careful study of the political and cultural history of the whole Islamic world.

Hulme, Peter, *Colonial Encounters: Europe and the Native Caribbean, 1492–1797* (1986). Presents an interesting interpretation of the encounters of Europeans and Native Americans.

Lach, Donald F., *Asia in the Making of Europe*, 5 books in 3 vols. (1965–). Perhaps the single most comprehensive and innovative guide to the European voyages of discovery.

Lockhart, James, and Stuart Schwartz, *Early Latin America* (1983). One of the finest studies of European expansion in the late fifteenth century.

Melville, Elinor G. K., *A Plague of Sheep: Environmental Consequences of the Conquest of Mexico* (1994). A history of the transformation of a valley in Mexico from the Aztec period to the era of Spanish rule.

Mignolo, Walter D., *The Darker Side of the Renaissance: Literacy, Territoriality, and Colonization* (1995). Uses literary theory and literary images to present provocative interpretations of the encounter of Europeans and Native Americans.

Pagden, Anthony, *European Encounters with the New World* (1993). A complex look at the deep and lasting imprint of the New World on its conquerors.

Parker, Geoffrey, *The Military Revolution: Military Innovation and the Rise of the West, 1500–1800* (1996). Traces the changes in technology and tactics in the early modern period and discusses the political significance of this "revolution."

Pelikan, Jaroslav, *Reformation of Church and Dogma (1300–1700)* (1988). An important overview of major religious controversies.

Phillips, William D., and Carla Rahn Phillips, *The World of Christopher Columbus* (1992). One of the finest studies of European expansion in the late fifteenth century.

Russell-Wood, A. J. R., *The Portuguese Empire, 1415–1808* (1992). An important survey of early Portuguese exploration.

Von Glahn, Richard, *Fountain of Fortune: Money and Monetary Policy in China, 1000–1700* (1996). Includes an excellent analysis of the history of silver in Ming China.

Chapter

13

WORLDS ENTANGLED, 1600–1750

In 1720, a devastating financial panic swept across Europe, making rich men into paupers and ruining many political careers. The panic was rooted in a speculative mania surrounding anticipated high profits flowing from trade with the Americas. A group of British merchants set up the South Sea Trading Company to compete with French trading firms and obtained privileged trading rights with all of Spanish America. Most coveted of all was the exclusive right to sell African slaves to Spanish colonies. Enthusiasm for these and other less substantial companies soared, and investors rushed in, sending share prices skyrocketing. But rumors of fantastic spoils gave way to word that the original investors were dumping their shares and that many of the companies were worthless. The speculative bubble burst. Share prices plummeted, with nearly all the companies created at the time going bankrupt, and even many solid firms in Europe going under. The South Sea Bubble, as it came to be called, reflected the euphoria of overseas trading ventures and the greater interconnections across the world. But it also stood as a vivid example of the perils that could accompany global trade and investment.

From 1600 to 1750, the circuits of world trade expanded as commerce continued to flow across the world's oceans. Ships laden with sugar from Brazil, spices from Southeast Asia, cotton textiles from India, silks from China, and increasingly, silver from Mesoamerica and the Andes made their way from port to port. Global trading networks emerged, and global commodities made a decisive appearance. In these new interregional trading networks, New World silver played the major role. It gave Europeans a commodity to exchange with Asian partners and began to tilt the balance of wealth and power in a westerly direction across Afro-Eurasia.

During this period, increasing economic connection along with the territorial expansion of various empires produced dramatic, if sometimes unintended, effects around the world. In the Atlantic basin, European colonial powers consolidated their control over larger portions of the Americas. England and France joined Spain and Portugal in the full-scale colonization of American possessions. Populations moved around, as peoples of European and African descent took the place of Native Americans in the New World, creating the foundations for European and African diasporic communities in the Americas. The number of African slaves shipped to the Americas rose dramatically during the seventeenth and eighteenth centuries, drawing the peoples and products of Africa, Europe, and the Americas more closely together. Extreme gender imbalances occurred in those parts of Africa that were drawn into the Atlantic slave trade as well as within the enslaved populations in the Americas. By no means was this growing expansion of empires limited to the Atlantic world. European empires also established colonies in Southeast Asia and, with New World silver, sought to extend their trade with Asian societies. At the same time, rulers in India, China, and Japan enlarged the borders of their empires, while Russia's tsars incorporated vast Siberian territories into their domain.

Predictably, economic linkages and territorial expansion were tempestuous processes. Commercial, colonial, and religious rivalries provoked bitter and bloody conflicts between and within European states. In Asia, too, increasing global trade and political expansion produced political and economic instability. In particular, the increased flow of silver posed a stiff challenge to the centralized control of the Ottoman and Mughal empires and contributed to the toppling of the Ming dynasty.

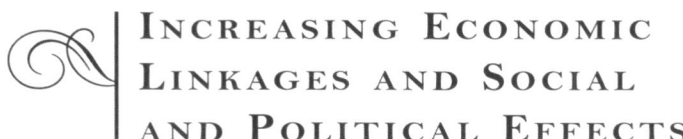

INCREASING ECONOMIC LINKAGES AND SOCIAL AND POLITICAL EFFECTS

> → *How did global economic integration affect political systems?*

Although transoceanic trade most directly affected mercantile groups and the nations who sponsored them, the deepening connections between the economies of distant places also affected both rulers and common people. Increasing economic ties brought new places and products into world markets: furs from French North America, sugar from the Caribbean, tobacco from the British mainland American colonies, and coffee from Southeast Asia and the Middle East. So important did the products of world trade become during the seventeenth and eighteenth centuries that interruptions in their availability sometimes destabilized regional economic and political systems. For example, the output of the new gold and silver mines of the Americas was vital to the commercial networks that linked the markets of the world. The supply of precious metals might fall because political disturbances brought work stoppages, or might increase greatly when new mines opened. The prices of commodities could soar or drop, bringing prosperity to some and poverty to others.

Focus Questions WORLDS ENTANGLED

- → *How did global economic integration affect political systems?*
- → *How did European mercantilism and colonialism transform the Americas?*
- → *How did the slave trade reshape African societies and polities?*
- → *How did global trade affect the Asian dynasties?*
- → *Why did the centers of European economic and political dynamism shift northward in the seventeenth century?*

 WWNORTON.COM/STUDYSPACE

STIMULANTS, SOCIABILITY, AND COFFEEHOUSES

As the world's trading networks expanded, the great merchants of Europe, Asia, Africa, and the Americas also globalized and popularized many new commodities. None were more enthusiastically received around the world than a group of stimulants—coffee, cocoa, sugar, tobacco, and tea—all of which, except for sugar, were slightly or highly addictive and had the added feature of producing a sense of well-being. Previously, many of these products had been grown in isolated parts of the world. Yemen had been the only location in the fifteenth century for the distribution of the coffee bean. Tobacco and cocoa were New World products, and sugar, while it originated in Bengal, did not become a product with a vast global market until it began to be cultivated on a large scale on American plantations. Yet, by the seventeenth century, in nearly every corner of the world, the well-to-do classes began to congregate in coffeehouses, consuming these new products and engaging in sociable activities.

Although sugar was probably consumed in larger amounts than any other product in this group, coffee and coffeehouses gained the greatest notoriety among the well-to-do. Coffeehouses everywhere served as locations for social exchange, political discussions, and business activities. Yet, they also varied from cultural area to cultural area, reflecting the values of the society in which they arose.

The coffeehouse first appeared in Islamic lands toward the end of the fifteenth century. As coffee's consumption caught on among the well-to-do and leisured classes in the Arabian Peninsula and the Ottoman Empire, local growers protected their advantage by monopolizing its cultivation and sale and refusing to allow any seeds or cuttings from the coffee tree to be taken abroad.

Despite some religious opposition, coffee spread into Egypt and throughout the Ottoman Empire in the sixteenth century. Ottoman bureaucrats, merchants, and artists assembled in coffeehouses to trade stories, to read, to listen to poetry, and to play chess and backgammon. Indeed, so deeply connected were the coffeehouses with the literary and artistic lives of

Turkish men drinking coffee at a banquet.

Drinking coffee in an English coffeehouse.

many people that they were referred to as schools of knowledge.

From the Ottoman territories, the culture of coffee drinking spread to western Europe. The first coffeehouse in London opened in 1652, and such establishments soon proliferated. By 1713, there were no fewer than 500 coffeehouses in London. The Fleet Street area of London was filled with so many of these establishments that the English essayist Charles Lamb commented "that the man must have a rare recipe for melancholy who can be dull in Fleet Street." Although the coffeehouses attracted people from all levels of society, they especially appealed to the new mercantile and professional classes as locations where stimulating beverages like coffee, cocoa, and tea easily led to lively conversations. Here, too, there were opponents, some of whom claimed that an excessive drinking of coffee destabilized the thinking processes and even resulted in conversions to Islam. But against such opposition, the pleasures of coffee, tea, and cocoa prevailed. These bitter beverages in turn required liberal doses of the sweetener, sugar. A smoke of tobacco topped off the experience. In this environment of pleasure, patrons of the coffeehouses indulged their addictions, engaged in gossip, conducted business, and talked politics.

The most ardent European exponents of coffee even suggested that its consumption would moderate another of the addictions that beset many people—the use of beer, wine, and spirits, often to excess. But this was destined not to be. Samuel Johnson, one of England's most astute observers, wryly observed that "a man is never happy in the present unless he is drunk."

MAP 13-1 TRADE IN SILVER AND OTHER COMMODITIES, 1650–1750

The seventeenth and eighteenth centuries were the first centuries of true global commerce. Silver was the one item that was traded all over the world. Can you trace the flows of silver from the Americas around the globe and identify the commodities that silver was exchanged for in different parts of the world? According to this map, how did increased trade shape European states' territorial ambitions? Does the map provide enough information for you to conclude which of these global empires was the wealthiest and most powerful?

ARCTIC OCEAN

SWEDEN

St. Petersburg

Danzig

POLAND
TRIA

RUSSIAN EMPIRE

OTTOMAN
EMPIRE

Aleppo

Baghdad
Basra

Alexandria Suez

Hormuz

Delhi

ARABIA

Muscat

Diu
Bombay
INDIA
Goa
Tellicherry
Pondicherry
Cochin

Calcutta

Rangoon

QING CHINA

Guangzhou

JAPAN

PACIFIC
OCEAN

ETHIOPIA

Madras

CEYLON

ANNAM
Da Nang

PHILIPPINES

Manila

NIN

Mogadishu

Malindi
Mombasa
ZANZIBAR

uanda

Kilwa

SUMATRA

Melaka

Banten

BORNEO

MALUKU

NEW GUINEA

Mozambique
Sofala

MADAGASCAR
MAURITIUS

RÉUNION

Batavia
JAVA

TIMOR

BANDA

Delagoa Bay

INDIAN
OCEAN

Cape Town
Cape of
Good Hope

← Spanish trade route	▮ Spanish territory	← Silver flow
← Portuguese trade route	▮ Portuguese territory	▮ Export
← English trade route	▮ English territory	▮ Import
← French trade route	▮ French territory	
← Dutch trade route	▮ Dutch territory	
	▮ Anglo-French contested area	

0   1000   2000 Miles
0   1000   2000 Kilometers

The benefits of closer economic contact enhanced the power of some states. Increased contact bolstered the legitimacy of the rising new states of England and France, and it also encouraged local power groups to throw their weight behind new rulers, as happened in Japan and in parts of sub-Saharan Africa. In England, France, Japan, and Russia and across Africa, the linkages of the seventeenth and eighteenth centuries were accompanied by civil wars and large-scale social unrest. For other regimes and economies, the impact of trade destabilized the existing systems of rule. The Ottoman state found outlying provinces slipping from central control. To the east of the Ottoman Empire's borders, the Safavid regime foundered in 1722, and it came to an end in 1773; the once mighty Ming dynasty gave way to a new dynasty, the Qing, in 1644. In India, internal rivalries among princes and powerful merchants whittled away at the central authority of the Mughals, compounding the instability caused by peasant uprisings.

EXTRACTING WEALTH: MERCANTILISM

Transformations in relations between different parts of the world began in the Atlantic, where the extraction and shipment of gold and silver siphoned wealth from the New World to the Old. Mined by Indian and African workers and delivered into the hands of merchants and monarchs, precious metals from the Andes and Mesoamerica accounted for a rising share of the world's supply of silver. Added to the output of these regions, a boom in gold production made Brazil the world's single largest producer of that metal in the eighteenth century.

So lucrative was American mining that other European powers wanted a share in the bounty that Spain and Portugal were reaping from mineral-rich possessions. Looking for their own areas in the Americas from which to take gold and silver, a number of European rivals launched colonizing ventures in the seventeenth century. In contrast to the first century of European colonialism, latecomers failed to find much in the way of minerals. But they devised other means to extract wealth. The New World had an abundance of resources and fertile lands on which to cultivate sugarcane, cotton, tobacco, indigo, and rice, as well as fur-bearing wildlife, whose pelts were much demanded in Europe (see Map 13-1). Better still from the perspective of new colonizers, New World crops and skins could be produced and transported easily and cheaply.

If silver quickened the pace of global trade, sugar transformed the European diet. First domesticated in Polynesia, sugar was not central to the European diets, for the most part, prior to the creation of New World plantations. Previously, Europeans had sweetened their diets with honey, but they soon became the world's great consumers of sugar. Be-

Tooth Decay. The influx of New World sugar sweetened European diets—but also led to the spread of a new affliction: tooth decay.

tween 1690 and 1790, Europe imported 12 million tons of sugar, or approximately one ton for every African captive who was enslaved in the Americas. Public tooth-pulling became a popular entertainment—for the spectators!—in cities like Paris, and tooth decay became a leading cause of death for Europeans.

Whether they supplied precious metals, cotton or sweeteners, colonies were supposed to provide wealth for "mother countries," or so held exponents of mercantilism, the economic theory that drove European empire-builders in this era. Coined by a French economist in 1763, *mercantilism* described a system that had developed over several centuries. Mercantilist doctrine presumed that the world's wealth was fixed and that one country's wealth came at the expense of other countries. The system's proponents assumed that overseas possessions existed solely to enrich European motherlands. In practice, this meant that colonies should ship more value to their mother country than they received in return. In addition to creating trade surpluses, colonies were supposed to be closed to competitors, lest foreign traders drain precious resources from an empire's exclusive domain. As the mother country's monopoly over the trade of its colonial ter-

Primary Source

THE PRINCIPLES OF MERCANTILISM

In 1757, a British commercial expert by the name of Malachy Postlewayt published a commercial dictionary, which he called The Universal Dictionary of Trade and Commerce. *Under the entry "trade," he set forth "some maxims relating to trade that should seem to be confirmed in the course of this work." The first five provide a succinct statement of the economic philosophy of mercantilism and the importance that countries attached to the acquisition of precious metals.*

I. That the lasting prosperity of the landed interest depends upon foreign commerce.

II. That the increase of the wealth, splendour, and power of Great Britain and Ireland depends upon exporting more in value of our native produce and manufactures than we import of commodities from other nations and bringing thereby money into the kingdom by means of freight by shipping.

III. That domestic and foreign trade, as they are the means of increasing national treasure, of breeding seamen, and of augmenting our mercantile and royal navies they necessarily become the means of our permanent prosperity and of the safety and preservation of our happy constitution.

IV. That the constant security of the public credit and the payment of interest and principal of the public creditors depend upon the prosperous state of our trade and navigation.

V. That gold and silver is the measure of trade, and that silver is a commodity and may be exported, especially in foreign coin as well as any other commodity.

→ *What are the key tenets of mercantilism?*
→ *Why is silver more important than gold in trade?*

SOURCE: Malachy Postlewayt, *The Universal Dictionary of Trade and Commerce*, vol. 2, p. 792.

ritories generated wealth for royal treasuries, European states acquired the wherewithal to wage almost unceasing wars against one another. Ultimately, mercantilists believed, as did Thomas Hobbes (1588–1679), that "wealth is power and power is wealth."

The mercantilist system rested on an alliance between the state and its merchants. Mercantilists believed economics and politics were interdependent, with the merchant needing the monarch to protect his interests, and the monarch relying on the merchant's trade to enrich the state's treasury. Chartered companies, such as the (English) Virginia Company or the Dutch East India Company (VOC), created by wealthy merchants and granted monopoly rights by European rulers, are ideal examples of this sort of alliance between merchants and the state.

NEW COLONIES IN THE AMERICAS

→ *How did European mercantilism and colonialism transform the Americas?*

One by one, rulers in England, France, and Holland granted monopolies to merchant companies, giving to them a monopoly over the trade and settlement of new colonies in the Americas (see Map 13-2). If old motives—finding precious metals or water routes to Asia—initiated many of these enterprises, the Dutch, French, and English learned that only

MAP 13-2   COLONIES IN NORTH AMERICA, 1607–1763

France, England, and Spain laid claim to much of North America in the seventeenth and eighteenth centuries. Where was each one of these colonial powers strongest before the outbreak of the Seven Years' War in 1756? Which empire gained the most North American territory and who lost the most at the end of the war in 1763? How do you imagine that Indian peoples reacted to the territorial arrangements agreed to by Spain, France, and England at the Peace of Paris, which ended the war?

by exploiting other resources could their claims in the Americas be made into profitable colonies. That the latecomers met with New World societies very different from those in Mesoamerica or the Andes also necessitated fresh thinking about the appropriate character of colonial regimes.

HOLLAND'S TRADING COLONIES

The Dutch first established a settlement in North America at the mouth of the Hudson River. The river was named for an Englishman, Henry Hudson, who had been hired by the

Dutch East India Company to explore the Atlantic coast of North America and find a "northwest passage" to Asia. Of particular promise was the broad river, which was given Hudson's name after he entered it in 1609. When his backers realized that the Hudson River did not lead to the Pacific Ocean, however, their interest in the area diminished. Still, Dutch merchants found that the waterway did provide access

Woodlands Indians. This late-sixteenth-century drawing by John White, a pioneer settler on Roanoke Island off the coast of North Carolina, depicts the Indian village of Secoton in eastern Virginia. In contrast to the great empires that the Spanish conquered in the valley of Mexico and in the Andes, the Indians whom English, French, and Dutch colonizers encountered in the woodlands of eastern North America generally lived in villages that were politically autonomous entities.

to a region filled with fur-bearing animals and with Indian peoples, notably the Iroquois, a confederation of "five nations," living in what is now upstate New York, able to trap and ready to trade. In 1624, thirty Dutch families settled on an island at the Hudson's mouth (Manhattan); many, however, soon abandoned the town for upriver locations where they could engage in exchanges with the Iroquois.

Trading furs with Indians was not the original idea behind Dutch colonization. In the sixteenth and seventeenth centuries, the Dutch happily used their vessels to transport the cargo of other nations to any corner of the world. Dutch merchants made considerable profits from handling the slaves, spices, textiles, and silver of other colonizers. They also coveted the riches that the Spanish and Portuguese took from their possessions. Especially tempting were some of the lesser Spanish island possessions in the Caribbean. In 1621, Amsterdam merchants founded the Dutch West India Company to regulate commerce, promote settlement, and maintain the flow of slaves to the Caribbean. The Dutch laid claim to St. Eustatius and two other islands in 1632, they captured Curaçao from Spain in 1634, and a few years later claimed Aruba and St. Martin (see Map 13-3). The Dutch successfully attacked and controlled the New World's main sugar zones in Brazil starting in 1620. By 1654, however, Brazilian settlers drove out the last of the company officials, and the firm was left with the puny outpost on the South American mainland, Surinam, where it tried to introduce plantation agriculture but with only meager results. Unfortunately for the company's backers, these colonies never yielded the profits that were expected of them. By 1674 the Dutch West India Company was bankrupt.

Although the Dutch efforts to establish colonies in the Americas were largely unsuccessful, their businessmen continued to profit from financing foreign merchants, lending vessels to other nations, and handling slaves, silver, and textiles. The Dutch were, in fact, often referred to as the world's "universal carriers." The most important Dutch colonial possessions were not in the Americas. More significant for the Dutch were their lucrative colony in the East Indies and a small colonial possession in South Africa (Cape Town), which was founded in 1652 as a refreshment station for ships going between the Atlantic and Indian Oceans.

FRANCE'S FUR-TRADING EMPIRE

The French also began their colonizing exploits in North America with a search for a northern water route to the Pacific that turned into a fur-trading enterprise. The initial French explorations were conducted by Jacques Cartier (1491–1557), and the chief French route into the interior of North America was the St. Lawrence River. Sailing up the St. Lawrence, Cartier and subsequent French explorers, most notably Samuel de Champlain (1567–1635), found not a

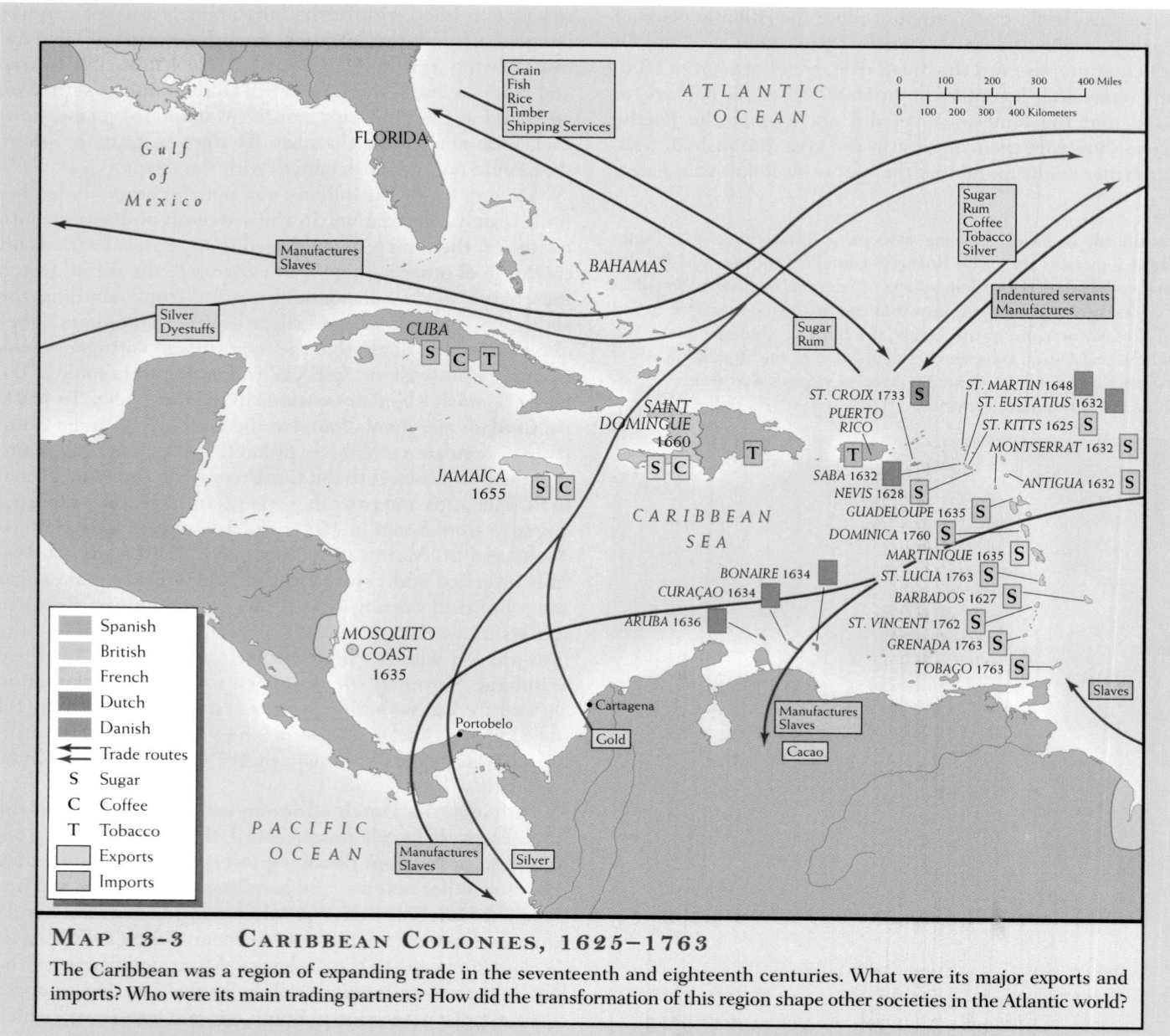

Grain
Fish
Rice
Timber
Shipping Services

ATLANTIC
OCEAN

FLORIDA

*Gulf
of
Mexico*

0 100 200 300 400 Miles
0 100 200 300 400 Kilometers

Sugar
Rum
Coffee
Tobacco
Silver

Manufactures
Slaves

BAHAMAS

Indentured servants
Manufactures

Silver
Dyestuffs

CUBA
S C T

*SAINT
DOMINGUE*
1660

*PUERTO
RICO*
T

ST. CROIX 1733 S

ST. MARTIN 1648
ST. EUSTATIUS 1632

ST. KITTS 1625 S

MONTSERRAT 1632 S

ANTIGUA 1632 S

Sugar
Rum

JAMAICA
1655
S C

S C

SABA 1632 S

NEVIS 1628 S

GUADELOUPE 1635 S

CARIBBEAN
SEA

DOMINICA 1760 S

MARTINIQUE 1635 S

BONAIRE 1634

CURAÇAO 1634

ARUBA 1636

ST. LUCIA 1763 S

BARBADOS 1627 S

ST. VINCENT 1762 S

GRENADA 1763 S

TOBAGO 1763 S

*MOSQUITO
COAST*
1635

Slaves

Spanish
British
French
Dutch
Danish
Trade routes
S   Sugar
C   Coffee
T   Tobacco
Exports
Imports

• Cartagena

Portobelo

Gold

Manufactures
Slaves

Cacao

*PACIFIC
OCEAN*

Manufactures
Slaves

Silver

MAP 13-3   CARIBBEAN COLONIES, 1625–1763

The Caribbean was a region of expanding trade in the seventeenth and eighteenth centuries. What were its major exports and imports? Who were its main trading partners? How did the transformation of this region shape other societies in the Atlantic world?

waterway to the Pacific but huge bodies of fresh water (the Great Lakes) in the midst of a massive continent. In the wake of this discovery, Champlain founded the colony of New France, with its base in Québec, in 1608. From Québec, French traders and missionaries penetrated deep into the interior of North America, eager to engage its Indian inhabitants in commercial exchange and to convert them to the Catholic faith.

At the center of the trade between the French and the Indians in northern North America was the beaver, an animal for which Indian peoples previously had little use. But Euro-peans coveted the barbed underfur of the beaver and were willing to give Indians a variety of goods in return. For the Indians, as one native hunter proclaimed, "the beaver does everything perfectly well; it makes kettles, hatchets, swords, knives, bread; in short it makes everything." As long as there were beavers to be trapped, trade between the French and their Indian partners flourished.

The distinctive aspect of the fur trade was the Europeans' utter dependence on Indian know-how. Trapping required close familiarity with the habits and habitats of the beaver—a form of knowledge that Europeans lacked. This reliance

The Fur Trade. For Europeans in northern North America, no commodity was as important as beaver skins. For the French especially, the fur trade determined the character of their colonial regime in North America. For Indians, it offered access to European goods, but overhunting depleted resources and provoked intertribal conflicts.

forced the French to adapt to Indian ways. Such accommodation is easily seen in the pattern of exchange. Although the French had wanted to make the export of beaver pelts a purely commercial venture, for their Indian partners exchange was governed by more than material concerns. Trade cemented familial bonds. For the most part, the French obeyed by giving gifts and partaking in Indian diplomatic rituals. To solidify their trade networks, Frenchmen often married into Indian families. As a result of these unions, *métis* (French-Indian offspring) played an important role in New France as interpreters, traders, and guides. Compared to all other empires, the French accomplished colonization without conquest, stretching their trading empire deep into North American forests.

ENGLAND'S LANDED EMPIRE

Part of the rationale for the French alliance with the Indians was strategic: the French and Indians shared a deep mistrust of the other major North American interlopers, the English. At the outset, the English, like the Spanish, sought colonies that would yield riches in the form of precious metals. But the settlements they established along the Atlantic coast of North America in the seventeenth century lacked such resources. Nor did these temperate lands boast beavers with the thick furs that French traders "mined" in lands to the north. What the English territories did have was land suitable for growing a variety of crops. And, as the population grew, English agrarian settlements expanded, encroaching

more and more on Indian lands. Accordingly, relations between English colonists and Indian inhabitants were generally far less cordial than relations between the French and their native trading partners.

Along the Atlantic seaboard, the English colonies differed from one another, but their settlers possessed a hunger for land that came at the expense of Indian inhabitants. Around Massachusetts Bay, one group of Protestant refugees (Puritans) founded a colony whose population rose substantially after 1630. As the colonial population of New England increased, so did the colonists' demand for fresh farmlands. The result was a souring of relations between natives and newcomers, which led to ferocious wars in the 1630s and 1670s.

A similar cycle unfolded farther south around Chesapeake Bay. In Virginia, the impulse for colonization was more commercial and less religious than among the Puritans of Massachusetts, but the pattern of intercultural relations was remarkably similar. The settlement at Jamestown was founded in 1607. The first disastrous winters wiped out large numbers of settlers, many of whom were gentlemen adventurers who had aimed to make money but had little interest in labor. Like the Puritans, Chesapeake colonists would not have survived their "starving times" had local Indians not provided them with food and other assistance. Within a few years, the colony began to thrive, especially once the colonists found a suitable staple that could be profitably exported. In Virginia the crop of choice was a weed that Indians cultivated called tobacco. The tobacco boom of the 1620s transformed a failing colony into a commercial phoenix. Prosperity induced thousands of English men and women to migrate to Virginia, compounding the pressures on Indian lands. As in Massachusetts, this hunger for plantations led to a series of wars and to the dispossession of Indians from their Chesapeake homelands. While the French intermixed freely with their trading partners and the Spanish married into Indian societies, English migrant communities in the New World included a larger number of women, and steered clear of marital-political alliances with natives. Instead of developing extensive trading networks, the English based their New World empire on land ownership—and did not hesitate to push the borders of European property ever deeper into Indian territory.

As Indians were evicted, European men and women, along with African slaves, occupied the Atlantic seaboard. By 1700, the European population of the English mainland colonies approached 250,000, with an additional 33,000 settled in the West Indies. At the same time, the African population of England's American possessions was close to 150,000, of whom three-quarters lived in the Caribbean islands.

THE PLANTATION COMPLEX
IN THE CARIBBEAN

As late as 1670, the most populous English colony was not on the North American mainland, but on the Caribbean island of Barbados. From the mid-seventeenth century onward, the sugarcane plantations of the Portuguese in Brazil were replicated on the English- and French-controlled islands of the Caribbean. All was not sweet in the Caribbean, however. Because no colonial power held a monopoly over the sugarcane-growing islands of the Caribbean, the competition to control the region—and to profit from the production of sugar—was especially fierce. The turbulence of the Caribbean was not simply a matter of imperial rivalry. It was also the result of the labor arrangements in the colonies. The indigenous populations of the Caribbean were decimated in Columbus's wake. Bereft of a local labor force, the owners of Caribbean estates looked to Africa to obtain workers for their plantations.

Sugar, whose cultivation employed the most slaves, was a killing crop. So deadly was the tropical environment in which sugarcane flourished—hot and humid climates were as fertile for disease as they were for tropical commodities—that many sugar barons spent little time on their plantations. Management fell to overseers who supervised crop production, and in short order they worked their slaves to death. Despite having immunities to yellow fever and malaria from being raised in a similar environment, Africans could not withstand the regimen. Poor food, atrocious living conditions, and filthy sanitation added to the miseries of life on Caribbean sugarcane plantations. Here, especially, Europeans treated their slaves as nonhumans. During the first day on the plantation, all recently bought slaves were branded with the planter's seal. In

Tobacco. The cultivation of tobacco saved the Virginia colony from ruin and brought prosperity to increasing numbers of planters. The spread of tobacco plantations also pushed Indians off their lands and led planters to turn to Africa for a labor force.

→ *How did European mercantilism and colonialism transform the Americas?*

Primary Source

SILVER, THE DEVIL, AND THE COCA LEAF IN THE ANDES

When the Spanish forced thousands of Andean Indians to work in the silver mines of Potosí, they also condoned the spreading habit of chewing coca leaves (which are now used to extract cocaine). Chewing the leaves gave Indians a mild "high," alleviated their hunger, and blunted the pain of hard work and deteriorating lungs. The habit also spread to some Spaniards. In this document, Bartolomé Arzáns de Orsúa y Vela, a Spaniard born in Potosí in 1676, expresses both how important coca was to Indian miners and how pernicious it was for Spaniards who fell under its spell.

I wish to declare the unhappiness and great evil that, among so many felicities, this kingdom of Peru experiences in possessing the coca herb. . . . No Indian will go into the mines or to any other labor, be it building houses or working in the fields, without taking it in his mouth, even if his life depends on it. . . .

Among the Indians (and even the Spaniards by now) the custom of not entering the mines without placing this herb in the mouth is so well established that there is a superstition that the richness of the metal will be lost if they do not do so. . . .

The Indians being accustomed to taking this herb into their mouths, there is no doubt that as long as they have it there they lose all desire to sleep, and since it is extremely warming, they say that when the weather is cold they do not feel it if they have the herb in their mouths. In addition, they also say that it increases their strength and that they feel neither hunger nor thirst; hence these Indians cannot work without it.

When the herb is ground and placed in boiling water and if a person then takes a few swallows, it opens the pores, warms the body, and shortens labor in women; and this coca herb has many other virtues besides. But human perversity has caused it to become a vice, so that the devil (that inventor of vices) has made a notable harvest of souls with it, for there are many women who have taken it—and still take it—for the sin of witchcraft, invoking the devil and using it to summon him for their evil deeds. . . .

With such ferocity has the devil seized on this coca herb that—there is no doubt about it—when it becomes an addiction it impairs or destroys the judgment of its users just as if they had drunk wine to excess and makes them see terrible visions; demons appear before their eyes in frightful forms. In this city of Potosí it is sold publicly by the Indians who work in the mines, and so the harm arising from its continued abundance cannot be corrected; but neither is that harm remediable in other large cities of this realm, where the use and sale of coca have been banned under penalties as severe as that of excommunication and yet it is secretly bought and sold and used for casting spells and other like evils.

Would that our lord the king had ordered this noxious herb pulled up by the roots wherever it is found. . . . Great good would follow were it to be extirpated from this realm: the devil would be bereft of the great harvest of souls he reaps, God would be done a great service, and vast numbers of men and women would not perish (I refer to Spaniards, for no harm comes to the Indians from it).

→ *Why would the Spaniards ban the sale of the coca herb everywhere except Potosí?*

→ *Why would Bartolomé believe that no harm would come to the Indians for taking the coca herb?*

SOURCE: Bartolomé Arzáns de Orsúa y Vela, *Tales of Potosí*, edited by R. C. Padden and translated by Frances M. López-Morillas (Providence: Brown University Press, 1975), pp. 117–20.

the words of one English gentleman, slaves were like cows, "as near as beasts may be, setting their souls aside."

More than disease and inadequate rations, the work process itself decimated the enslaved. The numbers are

ghoulish: average life expectancy on some sugarcane plantations in the Caribbean—no matter which European power controlled the territory—was a mere three years. Six days a week, slaves rose before dawn, labored continuously until

Slaves Cutting Cane. Sugar was the preeminent agricultural export from the New World for centuries. Owners of sugarcane plantations relied almost exclusively on African slaves to produce the sweetener. Labor in the fields was especially harsh, as slaves worked in the blistering sun from dawn until dusk. This image shows how women and men toiled side by side.

noon, ate a short lunch, and then worked until dusk. At harvest time, average days of sixteen hours saw hundreds of slaves—men, women, and children alike—doubled over to cut sugarcane and transport it to large factory-like refineries, sometimes seven days per week. Under this brutal schedule, slaves occasionally dropped dead from exhaustion in the fields. Moreover, this system of production lent itself to gang labor, depriving slaves of any control over their own work.

Amidst disease and toil, the enslaved resisted as they could. The most dramatic expression of slave resistance was violent insurrection. In the early sixteenth century, slave revolts were so frequent in Panama that the crown banned the slave trade to the region altogether. In the early seventeenth century, in parts of coastal Mexico, the viceroy had to negotiate an armistice with the slaves to pacify the region. Still, these instances of large-scale uprisings were sporadic. A more common form of resistance was flight. Thousands of slaves took to the hills to seek refuge from overseers. In the remote highlands of Caribbean islands, runaway slaves found sanctuary in "maroon" communities—named after the Spanish word *cimarron,* meaning people from the heights. But the largest of these refuge havens were in Brazil, where the vast interior sheltered communities of fugitive slaves. In the group of villages that made up Palmares, for instance, there were over 20,000 Africans in the late seventeenth century. Finally, for those who remained as slaves on the plantations, by far the most common, if least dramatic, form of resistance was the everyday pattern of foot dragging, pilfering, and sabotage, which slaves employed to soften the inhumanity of their condition.

The settlements and slaveholdings of Caribbean plantations were not restricted to any single European power. But it was the latecomers, the Dutch, the English, and especially the French, who concentrated on slave plantations in the Antilles. The English took Jamaica from the Spanish and made it the premier site of Caribbean sugar by the 1740s. When the French seized half of the island of Santo Domingo in the 1660s (renaming it Saint Domingue, which is present-day Haiti), they created one of the wealthiest societies based on slavery of all time. This single French colony's exports eclipsed those of all the Spanish and English Antilles' exports combined. The capital, Port au Prince, was one of the richest cities in the Atlantic world. The great merchants and planters of Saint Domingue, known as "big whites," built immense mansions worthy of the highest of European nobles. Thus the Atlantic system transformed the lives of elite Europeans who amassed new fortunes by exploiting the natural resources of the colonies and the labor of African slaves.

THE SLAVE TRADE AND AFRICA

→ *How did the slave trade reshape African societies and polities?*

Silver and sugar were the dominant commodities flowing from west to east across the Atlantic, and slaves filled the ships on their return. During the seventeenth and eighteenth centuries, far more Africans than Europeans crossed the Atlantic. Although the beginnings of the slave trade can be traced back to the mid-fifteenth century, only in the seventeenth and eighteenth centuries did the numbers of forced human exports from Africa begin to soar (see Map 13-4). By 1800, two slaves had crossed the Atlantic for every European. Those numbers were essential to the prosperity of Europe's American colonies. At the same time, the departure of so many inhabitants depopulated parts of Africa and destabilized many of its polities.

CAPTURING AND SHIPPING SLAVES

European slave traders grafted onto an existing system of slave commerce, much of it flowing north and east to the Red Sea and toward the Swahili coast of East Africa. From these destinations, merchants, most of them Muslim but also some Hindus, shipped slaves to ports around the Indian Ocean. Although the number of these slaves was significant, it could not match the volume destined for the Americas once extensive plantation agriculture began to spread. In the western flow, 12 million Africans survived forcible enslavement and shipment to Atlantic ports from the 1440s until 1867 (when the last ship carrying slaves reached Cuba). Far more slaves were in fact loaded onto the vessels in Africa and perished en route.

Merchant capitalists in Europe and the New World prospered as the slave trade soared, but their commercial fortunes depended on alliances with African trading and political networks. Indeed, European slavers in African ports knew little if anything about the happenings in the interior. They were not themselves involved in the lucrative capture of slaves in Africa. This was a business left to their African partners and their commercial networks, which linked money-lenders and traders on the coast with their allies in the African hinterland. In the West African Bight (bay) of Biafra, for instance, English merchants relied on traditional African practices of

"pawnship," the use of human "pawns" to secure European commodities in advance of the delivery of slaves. According to the custom of the region, a secret male society called Ekpe enforced payments of promised slave deliveries. If a trader failed to deliver on his promise, his pawns (quite often members of his kin group) were sold and shipped to the Americas. By the middle of the eighteenth century, Ekpe was a powerful institution with networks stretching deep into African hinterlands and supplying the expanding slave trade in the port of Old Calabar.

The slave ports along the African coast became vast, gruesome entrepôts. Indeed, the highest rates of slave mortality occurred on the African side of the shipping, with most slaves who perished doing so before ever losing sight of Africa. Stuck in vast holding camps, where disease and hunger ravaged the captives, the slaves were then forced aboard vessels in cramped and wretched conditions. These ships waited for weeks to fill their holds while their human cargoes wasted away below deck. Dead Africans were tossed overboard as other Africans were brought from the shore. When the cargo was finally complete, the ships weighed anchor and set sail. In their wake, crews continued to dump scores of dead Africans. Annual average losses on board reached 20 percent. Most died of gastrointestinal diseases, leading to dehydration. Smallpox and dysentery were also scourges. Either way, death was slow and agonizing. Because high mortality led to

Captured Africans. (*Left*) Africans were captured in the interior and then bound and marched to the coast. Note that there is only one woman among the men (and a couple of children), reflecting the gender imbalance among those captured. (*Right*) After reaching the coast, the captured Africans would be crammed into the holds of slave vessels, where they suffered grievously from overcrowding and unsanitary conditions. Long voyages were especially deadly. If the winds failed or ships had to travel longer distances than usual, many of the captives would die en route to the slave markets across the ocean.

MAP 13-4   THE AFRICAN SLAVE TRADE, 1440–1867

The Atlantic slave trade flourished in the seventeenth, eighteenth, and nineteenth centuries, linking many parts of Africa with the Americas. Where were the largest groups of African slaves found in the Americas, why were they taken to these areas, and what parts of Africa did they come from? What was the relationship between sugar cultivation in the Americas and the demand for African slave labor? How and where did the slave trade reshape African societies and polities?

NORTH AMERICA
400,000

New York

Charleston

New Orleans

Gulf of Mexico

Zacatecas

Havana

CUBA

SAINT DOMINGUE 860,000

ATLANTIC OCEAN

Mexico City

Veracruz

Acapulco

JAMAICA 750,000

ANTIGUA
GUADELOUPE 290,000
DOMINICA
MARTINIQUE 360,000
ST. VINCENT
BARBADOS 360,000

PACIFIC OCEAN

MEXICO AND SPANISH CARIBBEAN
c. 1,000,000

CARIBBEAN SEA

GRENADA 67,000

Cartagena

NEW GRANADA AND VENEZUELA c.320,000

GUIANA AND SURINAM 500,000

Recife

Lima

PERU 95,000

Potosí

BRAZIL 3,600,000

Bahia

SOUTH AMERICA

Rio de Janeiro
São Paulo

Buenos Aires

Main sources of African slaves
Main areas of slave importation in the New World
European slave trader routes
Muslim slave trader routes
Slave factory

OYO
Niger R.
YORUBA
Benue R.
ASANTE
Kumasi Accra
Winneba
Cape Coast Castle Keta
Commenda Whydah
Shama Ada
Axim Christiansborg Old Calabar
Dixcove Elmina SLAVE COAST
Butri GOLD COAST Bight of Benin

FERNANDO PO

Bight of Biafra

Gulf of Guinea

SÃO TOMÉ

0   100   200 Miles
0   100   200 Kilometers

British town
Dutch town
Danish town
Portuguese town

NORTH SEA

London • Amsterdam

E U R O P E
50,000

BLACK SEA

CASPIAN SEA

ARAL SEA

OTTOMAN EMPIRE

Lisbon
Seville

M E D I T E R R A N E A N   S E A

Algiers • Tunis

Tripoli

Alexandria
Cairo •

• Baghdad

P E R S I A

Tangiers

MOROCCO

EGYPT

Arguin

TRANS-SAHARAN
SLAVE TRADE
TO NORTH AFRICA
1,250,000

S A H A R A

TRANS-SAHARAN
SLAVE TRADE
TO OTTOMAN EMPIRE
AND OTHER PARTS
OF MIDDLE EAST
550,000

A R A B I A

RED SEA

St. Louis

Timbuktu

Gao

Aden •

ARABIAN
SEA

SIERRA
LEONE

DAHOMEY

Inset area

ARO

EAST
AFRICAN
SLAVE TRADE
700,000

ASANTE
Kumase

Whydah

OYO

A F R I C A

Elmina   Accra

• Old Calabar

ETHIOPIA

MIDDLE PASSAGE

FERNANDO PO

BOBANGI

Mogadishu •

SÃO TOMÉ

CONGO

Mombasa •

ZANZIBAR

ANGOLA
Luanda •

• Benguela

Mozambique •
MOZAMBIQUE

Sofala •

MADAGASCAR

MAURITIUS

I N D I A N
O C E A N

Cape Town •

0   500   1000   1500 Miles

0   500   1000   1500 Kilometers

African Trade with Europeans. (*Left*) People living along the Congo coast engaged in vigorous trade with European merchants. Portuguese slave traders are depicted on this late-sixteenth- or early-seventeenth-century plaque that decorated the doors of the Obas, or Kings, of Benin, one of the West African kingdoms deeply involved in the Atlantic slave trade. (*Right*) The kings and other high-ranking individuals in the Kongo kingdom in central Africa embraced Christianity as a result of their contacts with European traders. Here King Alvaro II, an active slave trader, is receiving a deputation of Dutch officials in 1642.

losses of profits, slavers learned to carry better food and more supplies of fresh water as the trade became more sophisticated in the eighteenth century. Mortality rates began to dip. Still, when slave ships finally reached New World ports, they reeked of disease and excrement.

SLAVERY'S GENDER IMBALANCE

The Atlantic slave trade not only moved vast numbers of Africans to the Americas; it also played havoc with sex ratios in both places. Most of the Atlantic slaves were adult men—only one-third were women and 10 percent were children. Although this reflected European preferences for male laborers, it also was the result of African slavers' desire to keep female slaves, primarily for household work. The imbalance of sex ratios made it difficult for slaves to reproduce in most places in the Americas. Accordingly, planters and slavers had to return to Africa to procure more captives, especially for the Caribbean sugar-growing islands, where the death rates of slaves were high.

Male slaves greatly outnumbered females in the New World, but in the slave-supplying regions of Africa the opposite was true—women outnumbered males in substantial numbers. African dynasties converted long-established patterns of domestic slavery (described in Chapter 10) into vast slave plantations; female captives were especially prized be-

cause of their traditional role in the production of grains, leather, and cotton. In this era Africa's female slaves served as cultivators and artisans and were more important contributors to the economy than they were on the male-dominated slave plantations in the Americas. The slave trade also reinforced the traditional practice of polygyny—allowing relatively scarce men to take several wives. But in some states, most notably the powerful slave-supplying kingdom of Dahomey on the West African coast, women were able to assert their power because of their large numbers and their heightened importance. Dahomean women became deeply involved in succession disputes, which were often violent and bloody. The intrigues of dynamic women made the difference between winning and losing political power.

Within the court the most powerful and wealthy woman was the queen mother, known as the *kpojito*. Each new ruler selected his queen mother from among the wives of his predecessors, though it is not known whether she was his actual birth mother. Because she was believed to have special powers of divination and to be in close communication with the supernatural, the King and his courtiers sought out her views before making important political decisions. The most dynamic of these queen mothers was Hwanjile (1740–1797), who was instrumental in placing king Tegbasa on the throne. Queen mothers were so influential that in reality the king and the kpojito were joint rulers.

AFRICA'S NEW SLAVE-SUPPLYING POLITIES

Africa's participation in the world economy through the slave trade profoundly reshaped its political and social structures. Africans did not stand on the sidelines, passively letting captives fall into the arms of European slave buyers. Instead, African political leaders and merchants played an active role in supplying slaves for transatlantic shipment. Their participation in the Atlantic slave trade contributed to the growth of centralized polities, particularly in the rain forest areas of West Africa. The trade also shifted control of wealth away from households that commanded large animal herds or land to those who profited from the capture and exchange of slaves—urban merchants and warrior elites. In Luanda and Benguela (in present-day Angola), where the Portuguese had established slave trading centers in 1575, African merchants erected impressive homes to emulate fashions in Lisbon.

In some parts of Africa, the booming slave trade wreaked only havoc. To get their share of the spoils, African leaders feuded over control of the traffic. In the Kongo kingdom, civil wars raged for over a century after 1665, and captured war-riors were sold as slaves. As members of the kingdom's royal family fought one another, entire provinces saw their populations vanish. Most important to the conduct of war and the control of trade were firearms and gunpowder. With this weaponry, capturing slaves became a highly efficient enterprise. Large numbers were also kidnapped. So prevalent was kidnapping in certain forest areas and among some of the stateless people that cultivators went out to their fields bearing weapons, leaving their children and wards behind in guarded stockades.

Some leaders of the kingdom of Kongo fought back against the ravages of the slave trade. The most impressive resister was Queen Nzinga (1583–1663), who was a masterful diplomat and a shrewd military planner. Converted to Christianity early in her life, she was able to keep the Portuguese slavers at bay during her long reign. Even after the Portuguese forces defeated her troops in open battle, she conducted effective guerrilla warfare, leading her troops in the field even into her sixties.

An equally powerful response to the political instability of the age was the Christian visionary Dona Beatriz Kimpa Vita, who was born in the Kingdom of Kongo in 1684 and

The Port of Loango. Partly as a result of the profits of the slave trade, African rulers and merchants were able to create large and prosperous port cities such as Loango, pictured here, which was on the west coast of south-central Africa.

baptized as a Christian. She experienced religious visions in her youth and in 1704, at the age of twenty, claimed to have received visions from St. Anthony of Padua, who then entered and took over her body. She believed that she died every Friday and was transported to heaven to converse with God, returning to earth on Monday to broadcast God's commands to the believers. Her message was directed to ending the Kongo civil wars and recreating a unified kingdom. Although she gained a large following, she failed to win the support of any of the leading political figures. In 1706 she was captured and burned at the stake.

As some African merchants and warlords became active vendors of other Africans, their commercial windfall enabled them to consolidate their political power. Through the taking and trading of slaves, West African kingdoms like the Oyo Empire in present-day Nigeria and the Asante state in present-day Ghana, as well as wealthy mercantile groups like the Aro peoples in southeastern Nigeria and the Bobangi canoemen in the Central Congo River, grew wealthy. That wealth enabled them to purchase additional weapons, with which they subdued their neighbors and extended their political control.

Three centuries of heavy involvement in the slave trade caused depopulation and disintegration in West Africa.

Among the most durable of the new polities was the Asante state, which arose in the West African tropical rain forest in 1701 and expanded through 1750. This state grew in power because of its access to gold, which its Akan speakers used to acquire firearms from European traders. They employed their arms to raid nearby communities for servile workers. At first, different village groups competed with one another for preeminence, but at the beginning of the eighteenth century, the Asante triumphed over their rivals. From its capital city at Kumasi, the state eventually encompassed almost the whole of present-day Ghana, an area of 250,000 square miles. A network of main roads spread out from the capital like spokes of a wheel, each of which was approximately twenty days' travel from the center. The empire thus acquired territorial definition, even clear boundary lines, which were established through the commonsense notion that the state could control territories within twenty days' march from the capital, but no more. Through the Asante trading networks, African traders bought, bartered, and sold slaves, who eventually wound up in the hands of European merchants waiting in coastal ports with vessels loaded with manufactures and weaponry.

Another regime that was active in the organization of the slave trade and enriched by it was the Yoruba-speaking Oyo Empire. The Oyo territory, which was strategically located astride the main trade routes, enjoyed easy transportation that linked tropical rain forests with interior markets of the savannah areas to the north. The king of the Oyo, called the *Alafin,* was in theory an absolute ruler, but he needed the support of powerful Yoruba families to remain in power. These families deposed or endorsed *Alafins* at will, which often led to turmoil during times of succession. The strength of the empire rested on its ability to field an impressive army bristling with weaponry secured from trade with Europeans. Straddling the boundary between the savannah and the rain forest, the Oyo used cavalry units in the savannah and infantry units in the rain forest. Military campaigns became annual incursions, only suspended so that the warriors could return for their agricultural duties. Every dry season, Oyo armies marched on their neighbors to capture entire villages.

African slavery and the emergence of new political organizations enriched and empowered some Africans, but they cost Africa dearly. For the princes, warriors, and merchants who organized the trade in Africa, their business, not unlike that of Amerindian fur suppliers, enabled them to obtain European goods, especially alcohol, tobacco, textiles, and guns. The Atlantic commercial system also tilted wealth away from rural dwellers and village elders and increasingly toward the port cities that handled the traffic in and out of Africa. Across the landmass, the slave trade thinned the population. True, Africa was spared a demographic catastrophe equal to the devastation of American Indians. The introduction of new American food crops, notably maize and cassava, capable of producing many more calories per acre than the old staples of millet and sorghum, blunted the depopulating aspects of the trade. Yet, some areas, such as Angola, suffered grievously. Three centuries of heavy involvement in the slave trade caused depopulation and disintegration in West Africa. The Atlantic slave trade enhanced the power of the warrior class, who were the vital element in carrying out raids for captives to be shipped to the Americas; the dislocations, internal power struggles, and economic hardships that followed precipitated the rise and fall of West African kingdoms.

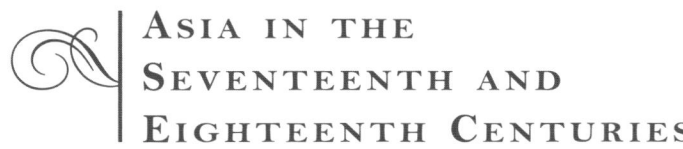

ASIA IN THE SEVENTEENTH AND EIGHTEENTH CENTURIES

> → *How did global trade affect the Asian dynasties?*

Long-distance trading networks blossomed as vigorously in Asia as they did in the Americas. In Asia, however, the Europeans were less dominant. With American silver, Europeans could open Asian markets, but they could not conquer powerful Asian empires or colonize vast portions of the region. Nor were Europeans able to enslave Asian peoples as they were enslaving Africans. The Mughals continued to expand their empire, and the Qing dynasty, which had wrested control of China from the Ming dynasty, initiated a vast expansion of the empire's borders. China remained the richest state in the world at the time. But in some places, the balance of power had begun to tilt in Europe's direction. The Ottomans experienced a contraction of their borders. Even more reflective of the tilt, by the end of the eighteenth century, Europeans had established economic and military dominance in parts of India and much of Southeast Asia.

THE DUTCH IN SOUTHEAST ASIA

In Southeast Asia the Dutch already enjoyed a dominant position by the seventeenth century. Although the Portuguese had seized the vibrant port city of Melaka in 1511 and the Spaniards had taken Manila in 1571, neither was able to monopolize the lucrative spice trade. To challenge the Portuguese and the Spaniards, the Dutch government took the initiative in persuading its merchants to charter the Dutch East India Company (abbreviated as VOC) in 1602. Making full use of Amsterdam's position as the most efficient money market with the lowest interest rates in the world, the VOC raised ten times the capital of its English counterpart—the royal chartered English East India Company, established two years earlier. The advantages of chartered companies could be seen in the VOC's scale of operation. At its peak in the 1660s, the company had 257 ships and employed 12,000 persons. In the two centuries of its existence, it sent ships manned by a

total of one million men to Asia, although the toll of the Asian trade was such that only a third of them ever returned to Europe.

Much of the impact of the VOC was felt in Southeast Asia, where spices, coffee, tea, and teak were grown and exported. The objective of the VOC was to secure a monopoly in trade wherever it could, to fix prices, and to replace the native population with Dutch planters. In 1619, under the militant leadership of Jan Pieterszoon Coen, who once said that trade could not be conducted without war nor war without trade, the Dutch swept into the Javanese port of Jakarta (renamed Batavia by the Dutch). In defiance of local rulers and English rivals, the Dutch burned all the houses, drove out the population, and proceeded to construct a fortress from which the VOC could control the Southeast Asian trade. Two years later, Coen and his fleet of twelve ships took over a cluster of five small nutmeg-producing islands known collectively as Banda. The traditional chiefs and almost the entire population of the islands, some 15,000 people, were killed outright, left to starve in isolation, or otherwise taken into slavery in Jakarta. Dutch planters and their slaves replaced the decimated local population and sent their produce to the VOC. The motive for such rapacious action was the huge profits that could be made by buying nutmeg at a small price in the Bandanese Islands and selling it at many times that price in Europe.

With their monopoly of nutmeg secured, the Dutch went after the market in cloves. The VOC's strategy was to control the clove-growing in one region and then destroy the rest, which entailed, once again, wars against both producers and traders in other areas. Portuguese Melaka fell to the Dutch in 1641 and became an outpost of the VOC. Resistance to

Batavia. At the beginning of the seventeenth century, Dutch traders established a base at the Javanese coastal settlement of Jakarta, which became Batavia, the capital of a Dutch Asian empire. The Batavian fortress projected Dutch power, as did the numerous warehouses for shipping the many riches coveted by Europeans.

THE CITTY OF BATAVIA

Attack on Bantam. This engraving depicts a Dutch attack on Bantam in the late seventeenth century as part of the VOC's effort to expand its empire in Southeast Asia.

this aggressive Dutch expansion was widespread among the local population, as well as among Muslim, Chinese, and other European merchants involved in the Southeast Asian trade. Nevertheless, with a combination of ruthlessness and ability in taking advantage of local political divisions, the Dutch had the whole of the lucrative Moluccan spice trade in their hands by 1670.

Next, the VOC set its sights on another of the important spices of Southeast Asia, pepper, which was a rather more difficult target to monopolize because its trade was scattered across a dozen major and minor ports. In this gambit, the VOC gained control of Bantam (present-day Banten), the largest pepper-exporting port, but the Dutch could not fully reserve the commerce in this spice to themselves. Chinese and English merchants continued to be competitors. Moreover, since there was virtually no demand for European products in Asia, the Dutch were forced to become more involved in inter-Asian trade as a way to reduce their payments in bullion. They purchased, for example, calicoes in India or copper in Japan for resale in Melaka and Java. They also diversified their trade to include silk, cotton, tea, and coffee, in addition to spices.

One of the significant side effects of the Dutch enterprise, however, was reducing old cosmopolitan cities such as Bantam, which had once served as centers of political power, economic life, and cultural creativity in Southeast Asia, to a subsidiary position eclipsed by newer European outposts such as Dutch Batavia or Spanish Manila. As Europeans penetrated and competed for supremacy in the borderlands of Southeast Asia, they harnessed local societies to their commercial ambitions and began replacing traditional Afro-Eurasian networks with Europe-serving trade routes.

TRANSFORMATIONS IN ISLAM

Compared with Southeast Asia, the Islamic empires were as yet not so directly affected by European intrusion. The Islamic empires did, however, face a variety of internal difficulties. While the Ottoman and Mughal empires continued to demonstrate resilience, the Safavid Empire by the mid-eighteenth century had entered a period of chaos.

THE SAFAVID EMPIRE   Challenged by neighboring powers, the Safavid Empire had always depended on a powerful, religiously inspired ruler, like the founding figure, Shah Ismail, and his most noteworthy successor, Abbas I. When such a figure was not present to enforce Shiite religious orthodoxy and to hold together the tribal, pastoral, mercantile, and agricultural factions, the state foundered. A series of weak successors to Abbas left the state in a chaotic condition. By 1722, it was under assault from within and without. Afghan clansmen, who had never been subdued by imperial armies, invaded Safavid territory. They overran the inept and divided armies and besieged Isfahan, the Safavid capital. The city's inhabitants began to perish from hunger and disease. Some survivors ate the corpses of the deceased. Finally the shah abdicated. The invading Afghan fighters executed thousands of Safavid officials and members of the royal household. The empire limped along until 1773, when a revolt toppled the last puppet ruler from the throne.

THE OTTOMAN EMPIRE   The threat to the Ottomans was not as great as the threat to the Safavids, but having attained a high point in the reign of Suleiman (ruled 1520–1566), the Ottoman Empire, too, entered a period of perceived decline. Some of the Ottoman Empire's subsequent difficulties stemmed from its successes. After Suleiman's reign, Ottoman armies and navies continued to try to expand the empire's borders but were defeated. On the empire's western flank, the European Habsburgs finally reversed Ottoman military expansion. Financing military campaigns strained the realm's limited resources, as did the needs of a growing population. Already at the end of the sixteenth century, Ottoman intellectuals were concerned that the empire's glory was ebbing, comparing the military triumphs and political expansion of early sultans to the difficulties of later rulers. During the seventeenth century, the sense of decline became a preoccupation of the Ottoman elite, whose essays were increasingly devoted to identifying causes of this supposed decline and proposing remedies for it.

A series of unimpressive successors to Suleiman allowed the Ottoman Empire's strength to wane. Suleiman the Great, for example, passed the crown to Selim, whom his detractors dubbed the Sot (ruled 1566–1574). He was succeeded by a string of incompetent sultans. Indeed, of the nine individuals who became sultans in the 1600s, only three were both adults and sane when they ascended to the throne. Such were the weaknesses of monarchy.

Competent or not, seventeenth-century sultans confronted the problems of a commercially more connected world. As silver flowed from the mines of Mesoamerica and the Andes, it entered Ottoman networks of commerce and money lending and eventually destabilized the empire. The early Ottoman rulers had endeavored to create an autonomous economy that did not depend for its well-being on trade with the outside world. The lure of silver broke through state regulations, however, drawing commodities like wheat, copper, wool, and other items in demand in Europe away from Ottoman areas. Merchants sidestepped imperial regulations by establishing black markets for commodities that were paid for in silver. Because these goods were illegally exported, their sale did not generate tax revenues, which led to a shortfall in money to pay administrative and military expenses. Ottoman rulers were then forced to rely on merchant loans of silver to sustain their civilian and especially military administration. Financial dependency meant that rulers could ill afford to impose their own official rules on those who bankrolled them.

More silver and budget deficits were a recipe for inflation. Indeed, prices doubled between 1550 and 1600 and then tripled in the first half of the seventeenth century. The surge in the price of goods hit the artisans and peasants living in Anatolia especially hard. Fed up with high food prices and shortages —and increasing taxes to pay off dynastic debts—they joined together in a series of popular uprisings, called the Celali revolts, which threatened the stability of the Ottoman state between 1595 and 1610. By the time of Sultan Ibrahim's reign (1640–1648), the cycle of spending, taxing, borrowing, and inflation was so bad that his own officials toppled and murdered him.

The Ottoman Empire also faced growing pressures for commercial and political autonomy from its outlying regions.

In 1517, Egypt became the Ottoman state's greatest conquest. As the wealthiest of the Ottoman territories, it was an imperial plum for any administrator. Egypt was also a great source of revenue, and its people shouldered heavy tax burdens. Moreover, trading routes continued to run through Egypt, and as commerce grew, many merchants began to resent Ottoman control. By the seventeenth century, the Ottoman administrator of Egypt had become a mere figurehead, funneling increasingly limited revenues to Istanbul but unable to control the military groups around him. When the sultan dispatched slaves who had converted to Islam from the Caucasus to extend military and administrative rule over Egypt, the newcomers forged alliances with Egyptian merchants and catered to the Egyptian *ulama*. These military groups were known as *Mamluks*. They were taken as youths from their Christian families in the Caucasus and brought to Egypt, where they converted to Islam and learned military and administrative skills. As a new provincial ruling elite, these men kept much of the fiscal wealth for themselves, at the expense not only of imperial coffers but also of the local peasantry.

Yet, there was great resilience in the Ottoman system. Decaying leadership provoked demands for reform from administrative elites. Toward the end of the seventeenth century, the Koprulu family took control of the powerful office of

Kara Mustafa Pasha. Kara Mustafa was a reformist-minded grand vizier of the Ottoman Empire. He led the second Turkish siege of Vienna in 1683.

grand vizier and spearheaded changes to revitalize the empire. Mehmed Koprulu, the first of the family to assume office, had been born into an obscure Albanian family. Taken as a slave in the *devshirme* (see Chapter 11), he slowly made his way up the bureaucratic ladder until he became grand vizier when he was eighty years old, in 1656. Pragmatic and incorruptible, Mehmed not only rooted out his venal peers but also balanced the budget and reversed the misfortunes of the Ottoman armies. His death in 1661 did not halt the reforms, for Mehmed had groomed his son, Fazil Ahmed Koprulu, to continue them. Indeed, Fazil Ahmed was, if anything, more successful than his father. Better educated and even more shrewd, the young grand vizier continued trimming the administration and strengthening the Ottoman armies until he died after fifteen years in charge.

Known as the "Koprulu reforms," the changes in public administration gave the state a new burst of energy and enabled the military to reacquire some of its lost possessions. Thanks to these reforms, revenues again began to rise and inflation abated, reviving expansionist ambitions. Emboldened by its new energy, Istanbul decided to renew its assault on Christianity. Fazil Ahmed's brother-in-law, Kara Mustafa Pasha, rekindled old plans to seize Vienna. Outside the Habsburg capital, the Ottomans gathered between 200,000 and 500,000 soldiers in July 1683. An all-out attack on September 12, 1683, inflicted heavy losses on both sides, after which

Kara Mustafa withdrew his forces, intending to renew his assault in the spring. The sultan, however, worried about disgracing the realm, ordered his followers to have Kara Mustafa strangled. Thereafter, the Ottomans halted their military advance, never again threatening Vienna. With the end of conquest, the Ottomans were deprived of the booty that had been theirs after taking over new regions. Worse still, the Treaty of Carlowitz (1699), the result of an Ottoman military defeat following the Austro-Ottoman war of 1683–1697, resulted in the Ottoman Empire's loss of major European territorial possessions, including Hungary, prompting further soul-searching for the causes of the empire's decline.

THE MUGHAL EMPIRE   In contrast to the Ottoman Empire's territorial setbacks, the Mughal Empire reached its height in the 1600s. By the end of the seventeenth century, Mughal rulers had extended their domain over almost all of India, and the Mughal Empire prospered from an increase in domestic and international trade. But as they expanded their empire, the Mughals eventually also faced the difficulties of governing dispersed and not always loyal provinces. Indeed, though nominally in control of wide areas, the Mughals had a limited impact on many villages, whose inhabitants retained their own religions and cultures.

Before the Mughals, India had never had a single political authority. Akbar conquered much territory, but expansion

Siege of Vienna. This seventeenth-century painting depicts the Turkish siege of Vienna, which began on July 14, 1683, and ended on September 12. The city might have fallen if the Polish king, John III, had not answered the pope's plea to defend Christendom and sent an army to assist German and Austrian troops in defeating the Turks.

did not stop after his death in 1605. Throughout the seventeenth century, Akbar's successors continued expanding the empire and extending administrative control over conquered territories (see Map 12-5, p. 544). With the north of India already under their jurisdiction, the Mughals turned to the south. Though the advances were slow and frustrating, the Mughals controlled most of the region by 1689. The new, outlying provinces of the empire provided the state with resources and local lords, warriors, and tributary chiefs, and the Mughal bureaucracy grew ever better at extracting services as well as taxes from the diverse inhabitants of this empire.

Mughal stability and prosperity did not depend on the revival and flourishing of the Indian Ocean trading system. Indeed, the Mughals showed little interest in becoming a naval power; they were willing to profit from seaborne trade, but they never undertook overseas expansion. The main source of their wealth remained land rents, which were increasing thanks to incentives offered to those who brought new land into cultivation; on these new farms peasants planted, in part, New World crops like maize and tobacco. But the empire's economy also benefited from the growing demand for Indian goods and services by Europeans. For example, the English East India Company's purchase of textiles rose from 4.2 million square meters in 1664 to 26.9 million square meters in 1684. Similar trends existed in the Dutch trade with India. As specie flowed in from Japan and the New World to finance this growing trade, the imperial mint struck increasing numbers of silver coins, which in turn contributed to the growth of trade and the use of specie as a medium of exchange.

To a considerable extent, the Mughals were victims of their own success. More than a century of imperial expansion, commercial prosperity, and agricultural development placed an increasing amount of resources in the hands of local and regional magnates. Using these resources, powerful local warrior elites, always looking for opportunities to evade imperial demands, became increasingly autonomous. By the late seventeenth century, many of these regional leaders were well positioned to resist Mughal authority.

As in the Ottoman Empire, then, distant provinces began to challenge central rulers. Under Aurangzeb (ruled 1658–1707), the Mughals had pushed the political frontier of the empire deep into southern India. There, however, the Mughals encountered fierce opposition from the powerful Marathas in the northwestern Deccan plateau. The military effort cost the imperial treasury a small fortune and pinned down Mughal armies. To finance these expansionist operations, Aurangzeb raised taxes on the empire's peasants. Resentment and alienation spread through the population, and even the Mughal elite grew restive at the continuing drain on imperial finances. In an effort to win the support of the orthodox *ulama*, the monarch abandoned the toleration of heterodoxy and of non-Muslims practiced by his predecessors. But ultimately only the strong hand of Aurangzeb kept order in the empire.

Indian Cotton. European traders were drawn to India by its famed cotton textiles. This image from c. 1800 shows a woman separating the cotton from the seeds; it captures the preindustrial technology of cotton production in India.

When Aurangzeb died in 1707, a war of succession broke out almost immediately. The revenue system eroded as local tax collectors kept more of the returns for themselves. Prosperous and powerful local elites used their growing fiscal autonomy to rally military forces of their own, annexing neighboring lands to their fiefdoms and chipping away at imperial authority.

Indian peasants, like their counterparts in Ming China, Safavid Persia, and the Ottoman Empire, capitalized on the breakdown in central authority to assert their independence from state authority. Many rose in rebellions; others took up banditry. Bonds of caste and religion were critical in the revolt of the Jat peasant caste in northern India in the late seventeenth century. Refusing to pay taxes, the Jat people killed a Mughal official and then seized lands and plundered the region. A half century later, peasant cultivators of the Punjab in northern India turned their closely knit community into a military power that was able to keep the Mughal forces off balance. Peasants were also critical in the rise of the Marathas of western India, whose charismatic leader, Shivaji (1627–1680), used the peasantry's hatred of imperial oppression to mount fierce resistance to Mughal hegemony.

The Mughal emperors had to reconcile themselves to their diminished power. The empire now existed as a loose

Aurangzeb. The last powerful Mughal emperor, Aurangzeb continued the conquest of the Indian subcontinent. Pictured in his old age, he is shown here with his courtiers.

unity of provincial "successor states." While the Marathas based in Poona and the Sikhs in the Punjab stood outside the imperial system, the successor states of Bengal, Awadh, and Hyderabad accepted Mughal paramountcy in name only. They administered semiautonomous regimes based on their access to local economic, political, and cultural resources.

Although local elites hollowed out the structure of the empire, India still flourished. Imperial expansion and the rising power of landed elites brought new territories into agrarian production. Cotton, for instance, became a major staple crop to supply a thriving textile industry. In many parts of India, peasant households complemented agrarian production with weaving and artisanal cloth production. Much of this industry was destined for export as the region deepened its integration into world trading systems.

The Mughals themselves paid scant attention to commercial matters, but local potentates, recognizing the benefits of exchange with foreign traders, encouraged the Europeans to establish posts at Indian ports. As more and more European ships arrived in Indian harbors, provincial magnates struck special deals with rival merchants from Portugal and increasingly from England and Holland. Some Indian merchants created trading companies of their own to control the sale of regional produce to competing Europeans; others set up vast trading networks that reached as far north as Russia, straddling west and east between Iraq and the South China Sea.

One of these companies was the house of Jagat Seths in eastern India. The Jagat Seths built a huge trading and banking empire, involving extensive shipments of Bengal cloth and commercial relations with Asian and European merchants. Increasingly, however, a large part of their business in the provinces of Bengal and Bihar was tax-farming, whereby the Jagat Seths took responsibility for collecting taxes for the imperial coffers. The Jagat Seths maintained their own retinue of agents to gather levies from farmers, while pocketing substantial profits for themselves. Thus did mercantile houses grow ever richer and gain greater political influence over financially strapped emperors. As a result, local economic and social prosperity undercut the Mughal dynasty.

FROM MING TO QING IN CHINA

China prospered enormously during the Ming period, but prosperity also led to a splintering of central control. As in Mughal India, local power holders in China often defied the authority of the Ming central government. Because Ming sovereigns turned inward and away from the possibilities of overseas commerce, forbidding the Chinese to travel abroad and prohibiting coastal shipping, the emperors did not reap the rewards of long-distance exchange. Rather, most of the profits went to traders and adventurers who successfully evaded imperial edicts. Together, the persistence of local autonomy and the challenge of defiant merchants weakened imperial structures until finally, in 1644, the Ming dynasty collapsed.

ADMINISTRATIVE PROBLEMS How did a dynasty that in the early seventeenth century governed perhaps a third of the world's population and was the most economically advanced society fall from power? As in the Ottoman Empire, bad rulers played a big role. Take, for example, the disastrous reign of Zhu Yijun, the Wanli Emperor (ruled 1573–1620). Reputedly a precocious young boy, Wanli ascended to the throne at age nine. Like his predecessors, he grew up within the confines of the Forbidden City (see Chapter 11). The emperor was secluded despite being surrounded by a staff of 20,000 eunuchs and 3,000 women. The "Son of Heaven" rarely ventured outside the palace compound in Ming times, and when he moved within it he was accompanied by a large retinue led by eunuchs clearing his path with whips. His day was filled with state functions, during which he had to change clothes to suit each occasion—including formal headgear with uncomfortable, curtain-like beads that forced the emperor to move solemnly and deliberately.

Ming emperors like Wanli quickly found out that while all the elaborate arrangements and ritual performances affirmed their position as the Son of Heaven, the rulers actually exercised little direct control over the vast bureaucracy. An emperor frustrated with his officials could do little more than punish them or refuse to cooperate. Unable to change or reshape the Ming administration, Wanli avoided any involvement with the administration of the realm, to the point that he refused to meet with his officials or preside over routine state ritual performances. A mountain of reports and petitions piled up in his study unattended, while some of his bureaucrats took advantage of his neglect to accumulate private wealth. During his long reign, Wanli's major claim to fame was his reputation for degrading the image of a wise and just emperor.

ECONOMIC PROBLEMS The timing of administrative breakdown in the Ming government was unfortunate. Expanding trade induced many to circumvent official regulations. From the mid-sixteenth century, bands of supposedly Japanese pirates, or *wokou,* ravaged the Chinese coast. Indeed, the Ming government had great difficulties regulating its official trade relations with Japan. Japanese missions, often armed and several hundred people strong, raided and looted Chinese coastal villages. Yet, while Ming officials labeled all pirates as Japanese, most of the *wokou* were in fact Chinese subjects.

Operating out of coastal towns of the empire, as well as from Japanese and Southeast Asian ports, these maritime adventurers deeply disturbed Ming authorities. In tough times, pirates became roving gangs, terrorizing sea lanes and harbors. In better times, some of them functioned much like mercantile groups; their leaders often mingled with gentry elites, foreign trade representatives, and imperial officials. What made these commercial predators so resilient—and their business so lucrative—was their ability to move among the mosaic of East Asian cultures.

The Chinese economy was further stimulated and commercialized by the influx of silver from the New World and from Japan. As noted in Chapter 12, Europeans used New World silver to pay for their purchases of Chinese goods. During the second half of the sixteenth century, silver imports contributed at least eight times more bullion to China's domestic stock of money; in the first half of the seventeenth century, silver imports exceeded domestic bullion production by some twentyfold. Increasing monetization of the economy bolstered market activity and state revenues at the same time.

As silver became the primary medium of exchange in the Chinese economy, peasants came under pressure to convert the copper coins that circulated widely in the local economy into silver. With this silver, they could pay off their taxes and purchase locally traded goods. But the need to acquire silver created hardships for the peasants. When silver supplies were abundant, peasants had to deal with price inflation. When silver supplies were interrupted, peasants faced problems discharging their obligations to state officials and merchants. Peasants thus often seethed with resentment, which quickly turned to rebellion.

Market fluctuations in trading centers as far off as Mexico now also affected the Chinese economy, introducing new sources of unpredictability and instability. After 1610, Dutch and English assaults on Spanish ships headed to Asia cut down silver flows into China. Then, in 1639, Japanese authorities clamped down on foreign traders, thereby curbing the outflow of Japanese specie to China. All these blows to the Asian trading system destabilized the supply of money in China and contributed to a downturn in the Chinese economy in the 1630s and 1640s.

THE COLLAPSE OF MING AUTHORITY By the seventeenth century, the administrative and economic difficulties of the Ming government had a visibly negative impact on the daily lives of its subjects. This became particularly evident when the regime failed to cope with the devastation caused by natural disasters in outlying regions such as the northwestern province of Shaanxi, once a center of the Chinese state and home to the capital (Chang'an) of earlier dynasties. By the late Ming, however, it had become a troubled province. Its once fertile soil lagged behind in productivity, and the center of economic activities and agrarian production gradually shifted over the centuries to the more hospitable environment and climatic conditions of the south. The decline of the region had been long in coming, but in the late 1620s the area was particularly hard hit by adverse weather conditions, resulting in protracted drought and a series of crop failures. Administrative and fiscal incompetence as well as failures to address the problems contributed to the crisis. The price of grain soared, and without relief from the government, the poor and the hungry fanned out to find food by whatever means they could muster. Officials wrote of abandoned babies and noted signs of cannibalism. Meanwhile, the financial problems of the government led to additional tax levies and cutbacks in the military budgets. A large contingent of young, mobile, and able-bodied males, including mutinous soldiers and demobilized government couriers, swelled the ranks of the desperate and the discontented. Many of them were instrumental in organizing the multitude of uprooted peasants into rebels, turning the late Ming world upside down in the process.

After 1600, increasingly large bands of dispossessed and marginalized peasants vented their anger at local tax collectors.

Primary Source

HUANG LIUHONG ON ELIMINATING AUTHORIZED SILVERSMITHS

The influx of silver into China had profound effects on its economy and government. In the seventeenth century, silver, for instance, gradually became the medium through which taxes were assessed. In his magistrate's manual from around 1694, Huang Liuhong (Huang Liu-hung) indicated the problems and abuses posed by the use of authorized silversmiths in the payment process, demonstrating clearly how silver had become an integral part of the lives of the Chinese people.

The purpose of using an authorized silversmith in the collection of tax money is twofold. First, the quality of the silver delivered by the taxpayers must be up to standard. The authorized silversmith is expected to reject any substandard silver. Second, when the silver is delivered to the provincial treasury, it should be melted and cast into ingots to avoid theft while in transit. But, to get his commission, the authorized silversmith has to pay a fee and arrange for a guarantor. In addition, he has to pay bribes to the clerks of the revenue section and to absorb the operating expenses of his shop—rent, food, coal, wages for his employees, and so on. If he does not impose a surcharge on the taxpayers, how can he maintain his business?

There are many ways for an authorized silversmith to defraud the taxpayers. First, he can declare that the quality of the silver is not up to standard and a larger amount is required. Second, he can insist that all small pieces of silver have to be melted and cast into ingots; hence there will be wastage in the process of melting. Third, he may demand that all ingots, no matter how small they are, be stamped with his seal, and of course charge a stamping fee. Fourth, he may require a fee for each melting as a legitimate charge for the service. Fifth, he can procrastinate until the taxpayer becomes impatient and is willing to double the melting fee. Last, if the taxpayer seems naive or simple minded, the smith can purposely upset the melting container and put the blame on the taxpayer. All these tricks are prevalent, and little can be done to thwart them.

When the silver ingots are delivered to the provincial treasury, few of them are up to standard. The authorized silversmith often blames the taxpayers for bringing in silver of inferior quality although it would be easy for him to reject them at the time of melting. Powerful official families and audacious licentiates often put poor quality silver in sealed envelopes, which the authorized silversmith is not empowered to examine. Therefore, the use of an authorized silversmith contributes very little to the business of tax collection; it only increases the burden of small taxpayers. . . .

→ *Why does the author suggest that the use of authorized silversmiths increases the burden of small taxpayers?*
→ *What reasons would the Chinese state have for maintaining such a "flawed" system?*

SOURCE: Huang Liu-hung, *A Complete Book Concerning Happiness and Benevolence: A Manual for Local Magistrates in Seventeenth Century China* (Tucson: University of Arizona Press, 1984), pp. 190–91.

At the core of these armed peasant bands, former soldiers and transport workers became leaders. Outlaw armies terrorized vast areas. Led by charismatic leaders whose appeals often contained messianic and religious overtones, half a dozen or so such large mobile armies—the so-called roving bandits—appeared in the 1620s. The most famous of these rebel leaders, the self-anointed "dashing prince" Li Zicheng, arrived at the outskirts of the capital, Beijing, on April 23, 1644. The capital's twenty-one miles of walls were defended by only a few companies of soldiers and a few thousand eunuchs, allowing Li Zicheng to take Beijing easily. Two days later, the emperor hanged himself. On the following day, the triumphant "dashing prince" rode into the capital and claimed the throne.

The news of the fall of the Ming capital sent shock waves around the empire. One hundred and seventy miles northeast of the capital, where northeast China meets Manchuria, the commander of the Ming army, Wu Sangui, received the news in late April of the death of the emperor and of Li Zicheng's triumph. Wu's task in the area was to defend the Ming against its increasingly menacing neighbor, a group who began to identify themselves as "Manchu" around 1635 but who were descendants of the Jurchens (see Chapter 10). In May 1644, Wu found himself in a very precarious position. Caught between an advancing rebel army on the one side, and the Manchus on the other, Wu made a fateful decision. He appealed for the cooperation of the Manchus to fight the "dashing prince," promising his newfound allies that "gold and treasure" awaited them in the capital. Thus, without shedding a drop of blood, the Manchus crossed the strategic pass and joined Wu's army. After years of coveting the Ming Empire, the Manchus were finally on their way to Beijing (see Map 13-5).

THE QING DYNASTY ASSERTS CONTROL At the time that they defeated Li Zicheng and seized power in Beijing, the Manchus numbered around 1 million. Assuming control of a domain that then included perhaps 250 million people, the conquerors were keenly aware of their minority status. Taking power, they understood, was one thing; keeping it was another. But keep it they did. In fact, in the eighteenth century, the Qing (which means "pure") dynasty (1644–1911) embarked on impressive economic expansion, incorporated new territories, and experienced substantial population growth. All this happened without provoking the kind of economic and political turmoil that rocked the societies of the Atlantic world.

The key to China's relatively stable economic and geographical expansion can be found in the shrewd and flexible policies of its rulers. The early Manchu emperors were able and diligent administrators. They also knew that to govern a sprawling and diverse population they had to adapt to local mores. To promote continuity with the earlier regime and draw upon the social and cultural practices of their predecessors, they respected Confucian ideas, codes, and ethics. The classic texts remained the basis of the prestigious civil service examinations. Social hierarchies of age, gender, and kin—indeed, the entire image of the family as the bedrock of social organization—endured. In some areas, like Taiwan, the Manchus consolidated new territories into existing provinces. Elsewhere, they gave newly acquired territories, like Mongolia, Tibet, and Xinjiang, their own distinct form of local administration. In these regions, imperial envoys presided, but they administered through staffs of locals and relied on indigenous institutions. Until the late nineteenth century, the Qing dynasty showed little interest in integrating those regions into "China proper."

At the same time, Qing rulers and their minions were determined to convey a clear sense of their own majesty and legitimacy. Rulers relentlessly promoted patriarchal values.

Widows who remained "chaste" were publicly praised, and women in general were exhorted to lead a "virtuous" life serving their male kin and family. To the majority Han, the Manchu emperor represented himself as the worthy upholder of familial values and classical Chinese civilization; to the Tibetan Buddhists, by contrast, the Manchu state offered plenty of imperial patronage. So, too, with otherwise disgruntled Islamic subjects. Although the Islamic Uighurs, as well as other Muslim subjects, might not have approved of the Manchus' easygoing religious attitude, they accepted the emperor's favors and generally endorsed his claim to rule.

But merely insinuating themselves into an existing order or simply appeasing subject peoples did not wholly satisfy the Manchu yearning to leave their imprint on the governed. They also introduced measures that extolled their authority, emphasized their distinctiveness, and ensured the submission of their mostly Han Chinese subjects. Qing officials composed or translated all important documents into Manchu and banned intermarriage between Manchu and Han (although this was difficult to enforce in practice). Other edicts imposed Manchu ways on Han subjects. The day after the Manchus entered Beijing in 1644, a decree required all Han Chinese males to follow the Manchu practice of shaving their foreheads and braiding their hair at the back in a queue. This met with immediate and vociferous protests from the Chinese and led to temporary shelving of the policy. A year later, however, feeling somewhat more secure, the new dynasty reissued the order and presented its subjects with the stark choice of cutting their hair or losing their heads. This time, the policy stuck. In a similar vein, the Qing also decreed that Han males adopt Manchu garb: instead of the loose Ming-style robes, they now had to wear high collars and tight jackets.

Although the Chinese people found ways to contest official Qing values, the Manchus sought to suppress dissent by assuming a role as guardians of moral rectitude, decrying the evidence of decadence and extravagance. Nothing earned the regime's opprobrium more than the urban elites' display of conspicuous consumption and indulgence in sensual pleasure. The Qing court regarded the "decadence" of the late Ming, symbolized by its famous actresses, as one of the latter's principal failings. In 1723, the Yongzheng emperor effectively banned female performers from the court, and the practice spread to commercial theaters, with young boys then assuming the role of females on stage. At the same time, mid-Qing prosperity created new wealth among the urban elites. They displayed their riches by becoming, for example, collectors—books, painting, calligraphy—and patrons of a vibrant public theater sector. The eighteenth century thus witnessed new dramatic forms. Merchants often traveled with their own troupes with distinctive regional styles, some of which were known for the robust sexuality of their performances. The popularity of female impersonators on stage even brought a new cachet to homosexual

MAP 13-5 FROM MING TO QING CHINA, 1644–1760

Qing China, as was the case with other dynasties during this era, expanded its territory significantly. Where did the Qing dynasty expand? How was the Qing expansion similar to and different from the expansion of European, including Russian, dynasties during this period? How did Qing expansionism reflect Qing concerns about foreign influence within the empire?

relationships, as the Qing government tried to regulate commercial theater still further by banning women from the audiences of public performances. But a gulf began to open between the government's aspirations and its ability to police society. For example, the urban public continued to flock to performances by female impersonators in defiance of Qing efforts to ban this and other sexually provocative forms of theater.

Manchu impositions fell mostly on the peasantry, for the Qing financed their administrative edifice by extracting surpluses from peasant households through taxation and surcharges. In response, the peasants spread out to border areas to find new lands to cultivate. Often they planted these newly occupied lands with New World crops that grew well in less fertile soils. This resulted in an important change in Chinese diets. While rice was the staple diet of wealthy Chinese, peasants increasingly relied on corn and sweet potatoes for their subsistence.

EXPANSION AND TRADE UNDER THE QING Despite the public's disregard for some imperial edicts, the Qing dynasty enjoyed something of a heyday during the eighteenth century. Territorial expansion extended the realm far beyond the frontiers of the Ming into central Asia, Tibet, and Mongolia. Tributary relations were established with Korea, Vietnam, Burma, and Nepal. While officials emphasized and redoubled their reliance on their agrarian base, trade and commerce flourished as they had done in the late Ming era. Chinese merchants continued to ply the waters stretching from Southeast Asia to Japan, exchanging textiles, ceramics, and medicine for spices and rice. In the early years of the dynasty, the Qing authorities vacillated about whether to permit trade with foreigners in China. Meanwhile, in 1720 in Canton, a group of merchants formed a monopolistic guild, known as the Cohong, to trade with European merchants, whose numbers rose as they vied for coveted Chinese goods and tried to peddle their wares to the vast Chinese market. Although the guild disbanded after a year in the face of opposition from foreign and other local merchants, it was revived after the Qing decided to restrict the Europeans to trading in Canton and ordered that Chinese merchants guarantee the good behavior and the payment of fees by the Europeans. This "Canton system," as it came to be known, would be formalized by decree of the emperor in 1759.

China, in sum, negotiated a century of upheaval without dismantling established ways of arranging politics or economics. For the peasantry, popular faiths continued to govern their belief systems, and most peasants continued to cultivate their crops and stay close to their fields and villages. Trading with the outside world was marginal to the overall commercial life of the Qing era; the Qing, like their Ming predecessors, cared more about the agrarian than the commercial health of the empire, believing the former to be the foundation of prosperity and social tranquility. As long as China's vast peasantry could keep the dynasty's coffers full, the government was content to squeeze the merchants when they needed funds. Some historians have labeled this China's

failure to adapt to a changing world order. In time, these historians assert, this left China vulnerable to outsiders, especially Europeans. But this view puts the historical cart before the horse. By the middle of the eighteenth century, it was still clear that Europe needed China more than the other way around. For the vast majority of Chinese, no superior model of belief, politics, or economics was conceivable. Indeed, although the Qing had taken over a crumbling empire in 1644, a century later China achieved a new level of prosperity.

TOKUGAWA JAPAN

Integration with the Asian trading system exposed Japan to new external pressures, even as the islands grappled with internal turmoil. But the Japanese dealt with these pressures far more successfully than did the four great mainland Asian empires (the Ottomans, the Safavid, the Mughal, and the Ming), where political fragmentation and even the overthrow of existing dynasties took place. In Japan, rivalry among powerful clans did not produce autonomous regimes. Instead, a single ruling family emerged, and this dynastic state, known as the Tokugawa Shogunate, managed to do something that eluded most of the regimes around the world at this time: regulate foreign intrusion into its islands. While Japan played a modest role in the expanding world economic system, it remained free of outside exploitation.

> *By the middle of the eighteenth century, it was still clear that Europe needed China more than the other way around.*

UNIFICATION OF JAPAN During the sixteenth century, Japan had suffered from chronic political instability, as rampant banditry and civil strife spread disorder across the countryside. Regional ruling households, called daimyos, had commanded private armies made up of skilled warriors known as samurai. The daimyos held sway over local populations and sometimes succeeded in bringing a measure of order to their domains. But no one daimyo family could establish its preeminence over others. Although Japan did have an emperor, who ruled from Kyoto, his authority did not extend beyond the court.

At the end of the sixteenth century, several military leaders attempted to unify Japan. One general loomed above his rivals: Toyotomi Hideyoshi (1535–1598). He not only conquered his rivals, but with the imprimatur of the Kyoto emperor, he became the supreme minister and proceeded to arrange marriages among the children of the local magnates to solidify political bonds. He also ordered that the wives and children of the daimyos be kept within reach as semihostages, thereby coaxing cooperation from powerful regional rulers.

Edo in the Rain. This facsimile of an *ukiyo-e* ("floating world") print by Hiroshige (1797–1858) depicts one of several bridges in the bustling city of Edo (later Tokyo), with Mount Fuji in the background.

After Hideyoshi died, one of the daimyos, Tokugawa Ieyasu (1542–1616), took power for himself. This was a decisive moment. In 1603, Ieyasu assumed the title of shogun (military ruler). He also solved the problem of succession, declaring that thereafter rulership was hereditary and that his family would be the ruling household. Ieyasu passed the shogunate to his son in 1605, though he continued to rule behind the scenes. This hereditary Tokugawa Shogunate lasted until 1867.

The source of administrative authority shifted from the imperial capital of Kyoto to the site of Ieyasu's new domain headquarters: the castle town called Edo (later renamed Tokyo). The Tokugawa built Edo out of a small earthen fortification that was in bad repair and clinging to a coastal bluff. Behind Edo lay a village in a swampy plain. In a monumental work of engineering, the rulers ordered the swamp drained, the forest cleared, many of the hills leveled, canals dredged, bridges built, the seashore extended by landfill, and a new stone castle completed. By the time Ieyasu died in 1616, Edo had a population of 150,000.

The Tokugawa shoguns ensured a flow of resources from the working population to rulers and from the provinces to the capital. Villages paid taxes to the daimyos, who in turn transferred resources to the seat of shogunate authority. No longer engaged in constant warfare, the samurai became administrators. Peace brought prosperity. Agriculture thrived. Improved farming techniques and land reclamation projects enabled the country's population to grow from 10 million in 1550 to 16 million in 1600 and 30 million by 1700.

FOREIGN AFFAIRS AND FOREIGNERS Having consolidated a national regime based on power sharing with the regions, Japanese rulers tackled foreign affairs. The most pressing concern for Hideyoshi's successors was what to do about the intrusion of foreigners, especially Christian missionaries and European traders, who had begun to arrive in Japan at the end of the sixteenth and beginning of the seventeenth centuries. Initially, Japanese officials welcomed trade and Christianity because of their eagerness to acquire muskets, gunpowder, and other new technology. But once the ranks of the converted had swelled into the hundreds of thousands, Japanese authorities came to see that Christians were intolerant of other faiths, believed Christ to be superior to any authority, and fought among themselves. Trying to stem the tide, the shoguns issued decrees to stop conversion to Christianity and attempted to ban its practice. After a 1637 rebellion, in which peasants in southwestern Japan who had converted to Christianity rose up in protest against high rents and taxes, the government cracked down, suppressing Christianity and driving European missionaries from the country.

Even more troublesome for the shogunate was how to handle the lure of trade with Europeans, whose record of conquest of Manila and Melaka was well known. The Tokugawa knew that trading at different ports in Japan threatened to pull the commercial regions in various directions, away from the capital. When it became clear that European traders preferred the ports of Kyūshū, the shogunate restricted Europeans to trade only in ports under Edo's direct rule. Then, one by one, Japanese authorities expelled all European

Legend:
- Outer daimyos
- Hereditary daimyos
- Tokugawa domains

0 50 100 Miles
0 50 100 Kilometers

RUSSIAN EMPIRE

SEA OF OKHOTSK

EZO (HOKKAIDŌ)

CHINA

KOREA

SEA OF JAPAN

JAPAN

Edo (Tokyo)

HONSHŪ

YELLOW SEA

Shimabara 1638: Uprising of Christian converts put down

Hirado 1609: Dutch trading post

Kyoto
Osaka

SHIKOKU

PACIFIC OCEAN

Nagasaki 1570: opened to European trade

KYŪSHŪ

EAST CHINA SEA

DESHIMA ISLAND: 1641 Dutch traders confined there

TANEGASHIMA: 1542 Portuguese trading post

MAP 13-6 TOKUGAWA JAPAN, 1603–1867

The Tokugawa Shoguns created a strong central state in Japan during the seventeenth and eighteenth centuries. According to this map, how extensive was their control? What other states challenged Tokugawa rule in this region? How did Tokugawa leaders attempt to manage relations with foreign states and entities?

Portuguese Arriving in Japan. In the 1540s, the Portuguese arrival on the islands of Japan sparked a fascination with the strange costumes and the great ships of these "southern barbarians" (so called because they had approached Japan from the south). Silk-screen paintings depicted Portuguese prowess in exaggerated form, such as in the impossible height of the fore and aft of the vessel pictured here.

competitors. Only the Protestant (and nonmissionizing) Dutch were permitted to remain in Japan, but they were confined to a small island near Nagasaki. The Dutch were allowed to unload just one ship each year, and only under strict supervision by Japanese authorities.

These measures did not close Tokugawa Japan to the outside world, however. Trade with the Chinese and Koreans flourished, and the shogun received Korean and Ryūkyū missions. Beyond these embassies, Edo gathered reports and publications about the outside world from the resident Dutch and Chinese (who included monks, physicians, and painters). A select few Japanese were permitted to learn Dutch and to learn about European technology, shipbuilding, and medicine (see Chapter 14). By setting the terms on which encounters with outsiders would occur, however, Japanese authorities ensured that foreigners would not threaten Japan's security.

Ruling over three islands, Tokugawa Japan was surrounded by "vassals" that were neither completely part of the realm nor entirely independent (see Map 13-6). The most important peripheral areas were the Ryūkyūs in the south and the island of Ezo to the north, neither of which the Japanese attempted to annex, preferring to maintain them as buffers. Establishing dependent buffer areas facilitated the strengthening of a distinct Japanese identity for all the peoples living "on the inside" and limited outside influence. When, beginning in 1697, the Russians approached Japan from the north, the Japanese rebuffed entreaties to open relations and instead sought to manage contacts with the Russians through their northern buffer zone. As the Russians became more aggressive in trying to "open" Japan to trade, the Japanese annexed and began to colonize Ezo. Ezo became Hokkaidō, the country's fourth main island, and a strong barrier to European penetration. In regulating outside contacts, Japanese rulers suppressed sources of upheaval and consolidated a dynasty that lasted well into the nineteenth century.

TRANSFORMATIONS OF EUROPE

> → *Why did the centers of European economic and political dynamism shift northward in the seventeenth century?*

Between 1600 and 1750, religious conflict, commercial expansion, and the consolidation of dynastic power transformed Europe. Commercial centers shifted northward, and Spain and Portugal lost ground to England and France. Waged chiefly over religion, the Thirty Years' War (1618–1648) changed the nature of warfare and political authority.

EXPANSION AND DYNASTIC CHANGE IN RUSSIA

Untouched by the devastation of the Thirty Years' War, the Russian Empire expanded in all directions to become the world's largest-ever state, gaining positions on Europe's Baltic Sea and the Pacific Ocean. Russia established political borders with the western-expanding Qing Empire and with Japan. These momentous shifts involved the elimination of the steppe nomads, who had roamed through Russia and China, as an independent force in world history and recast the problem of the Europe-Asia frontier. For China and Japan, Europe (in the form of predominantly Christian Russia) stretched right up to their states. By contrast, western Europeans placed the geographical boundary of Europe and Asia at the Ural Mountains. Culturally, Europeans as well as Russians debated whether Russia belonged more to Europe or to Asia. The answer was both.

→ *Why did the centers of European economic and political dynamism shift northward in the seventeenth century?*

Muscovy, like Japan and China, used territorial expansion and extended commercial networks to consolidate a powerful political order, the Russian Empire, the new name given to Muscovy by Tsar Peter the Great around 1700. But Russia was more internally heterogeneous than its Asian neighbors, both in its core and as a result of its annexation of adjacent lands. In the four centuries after 1480, the weak principality of Muscovy, a mixture of Slavs, Finnish tribes, Turkic speakers, and many others, expanded at the rate of about fifty square miles per day. Despite setbacks and long defensive periods, this new Russian Empire grew to occupy one-sixth of the earth's land surface, spanning parts of Europe, much of northern Asia, numerous islands in the North Pacific, and even a corner of North America. Territorial expansion, together with natural population growth, increased Russia's population from about 6 million in 1550 to 20 million by 1750.

Like Japan, Russia emerged out of turmoil. Muscovy's security concerns, the ambitions of private individuals, and religious conviction inspired the regime to seize territory. For the Muscovite grand prince Ivan III (ruled 1462–1505), expansion was inseparable from security. Because the steppe, which stretches deep into Asia, remained a highway for horse-riding peoples, especially descendants of the Mongols, Muscovy sought to dominate the areas south and east of Moscow.

By marrying the niece of the last Byzantine emperor, Ivan added a strong religious dimension to his expansionist claims. Now he could assert that Moscow was the center of the Byzantine faith and heir to the conquered city of Constantinople. Territorial expansion continued under Ivan III's successors, especially his grandson, Ivan IV (ruled 1533–1584), who adopted the title of tsar in 1547. To secure Muscovy's eastern borders, Ivan IV permitted private armies to extend the domain of the Russian state into Siberia. Beginning in the 1590s, Russian authorities built forts and trading posts along the great Siberian rivers for defensive purposes and to facilitate the taxation of aboriginal peoples. The rulers' efforts to control tribute and trans-Afro-Eurasian trade, however, could not prevent privateers, enticed by the large profits that could be made from the sale of furs, from pushing the Russian domain outward. In this fashion, Muscovy's frontier expanded eastward, reaching the Pacific, more than 5,000 miles from Moscow, in 1639. In just over a century, Moscow had created a landed empire straddling Eurasia from west to east, incorporating peoples of many languages and religions (see Map 13-7).

Much of this expansion occurred despite the dynastic chaos that followed the death of Ivan IV. Following what was known as the Time of Troubles, a group of prominent families gathered in 1613 to reestablish central authority and

Nenets Hunters. Hunters of the Nenets tribe in far North Asia's treeless tundra, showing off their warm animalskin clothing and self-fashioned weapons, as depicted in a 1620 engraving by Theodore de Bry, one of the first Europeans to come into contact with them.

MAP 13-7 RUSSIAN EXPANSION, 1462–1795

The state of Muscovy incorporated vast territories through overland expansion as it grew and became the Russian Empire. It did so in part because of its geographical position and its strategic needs. What were the strategic and geographical strengths and weaknesses of the state of Muscovy? What were the main directions and stages of its expansion? With what countries and cultures did the Russian Empire come into contact?

threw their weight behind a new family of potentates. These were the Romanovs, court barons who set about reviving the Kremlin's fortunes. Like the Ottoman and Qing dynasties, Romanov tsars and their aristocratic supporters would retain power into the twentieth century.

In the seventeenth and eighteenth centuries, the Romanovs created an absolutist system of government, clustering power in the hands of the ruling family. The right to make war, tax, judge, and coin money was limited to the tsar and his retinue. To transcend old sources of tension and friction, the Romanovs made the nobles serve as bureaucrats. Russia, following the Byzantine preference for a monarch, embraced a

despotic version of rulership. Moscow had no political assemblies for nobles or any other sectors of society. Powerful families at the court referred to themselves as "slaves of the tsar." Away from Moscow, local aristocrats exercised nearly unlimited authority in exchange for fealty and tribute to the tsar.

Russia's peasantry bore the burden of maintaining the wealth of the small nobility and the monarchy. Most of Muscovy's peasant families gathered into communes, enclosed rural worlds in which people helped each other to deal with the everyday strains of the harsh climate and the periodic travails of poor harvests and severe masters. Communes were

→ *Why did the centers of European economic and political dynamism shift northward in the seventeenth century?*

Celebration in Red Square. Russian nobles gathered to celebrate in Red Square, which originally meant "Beautiful Square" and was a processional and market space just outside the walls of the Kremlin fortress where the Muscovite tsars lived, ruled, and prayed. The Russian nobles wore long beards and caftans, or gowns, often lined with Siberian furs, which were much coveted both at home and abroad. Many Russian nobles were descended from Tatar (Turkish) Muslims, conquered peoples who converted to Christianity and loyally served the tsar.

not based on kinship, but they functioned like extended kin networks in that members reciprocated favors and chores for survival. Even with mutual support, the peasants lived poorly, their huts usually consisting of a single chamber heated by a wood-burning stove and no chimney. Livestock and humans often shared the same quarters. In 1649, peasants were legally bound as serfs to the nobles and the tsar, meaning they had to perform obligatory services and deliver part of their produce to their lords, who exercised almost complete command over the life and death of their minions. Serfdom grew directly out of the state's ever-increasing military ambitions and challenges.

Having consolidated an internal order, Russian leaders redoubled their pursuit of imperial expansion. Peter the Great (ruled 1682–1725) symbolized a westward push by founding, and building with forced labor, a new capital, St. Petersburg, in 1703. Under his successors, including the hard-nosed autocrat Catherine the Great (ruled 1762–1796), Russia added even more territory. In 1763, Catherine placed her former lover, Stanislaw Poniatowski, on the Polish throne, and three decades later, together with the Austrians and Prussians, carved up the great medieval state of Poland. Her armies' victories against the Ottoman Turks allowed Russia to annex the great "breadbasket" of central Europe, the Ukraine. By the late eighteenth century, Russian sovereignty stretched from the Baltic Sea through the heart of Europe, Ukraine, and the Crimea on the Black Sea and into the ancient lands of Ar-

menia and Georgia in the Caucasus Mountains bordering on the Ottoman Empire.

With a vast territorial empire secured, more people started to migrate eastward, some to escape being serfs and to settle their own land. At the beginning of the migration eastward, more than 90 percent of Siberia's approximately 200,000 inhabitants were indigenes (natives). By 1750, the number of Slavs in Siberia had almost caught up to the native population and soon surpassed it. Battling astoundingly harsh circumstances, temperatures falling to –40 degrees centigrade and freezing artic winds, peasant migrants traveled on horseback and foot to resettle in the east. Religious schismatics, known after 1667 as Old Believers because of their refusal to accept changes in the Eastern Orthodox liturgy, were deported to uninhabited areas. But the difficulties of clearing forested lands or planting crops in boggy Siberian soils, combined with extraordinarily harsh winters, made for very high attrition among settlers. To this was added the problem of isolation. There was no established land route back to Moscow until the 1770s, when the Great Siberian Post Road finally cut through the swamps and peat bogs of western Siberia. The writer Anton Chekhov called it "the longest and ugliest road in the whole world."

Russia's territorial acquisitions produced complex, mixed societies that bridged eastern and western ends of Eurasia, producing many children of mixed parentage. Perhaps half the inhabitants of Siberia in the 1750s were runaway serfs.

Catherine the Great. Catherine the Great styled herself an enlightened despot of the baroque epoch, furthering the Russian empire's adaptation of European high culture. Her dress is adorned with the Byzantine double-headed eagle.

Russian authorities also resettled in Siberia unwanted families and people banished by the tsar because they were considered politically dangerous or undesirable. These exiles, though they never approached in number the legions of hardy peasant settlers, would later make Siberia infamous as a land for prisoners, overshadowing its reputation as a destination of freedom. "The road to Siberia is wide," went the saying, "the way back, narrow."

ECONOMIC AND POLITICAL FLUCTUATIONS IN WESTERN EUROPE

During the seventeenth and eighteenth centuries, the commercial integration of different parts of the world shook up old regimes in Mughal India, Ming China, and the Ottoman Empire, while spawning new dynasties like the Tokugawa in Japan and the Romanovs in Russia. At the same time, European economies grew and became more commercialized, es-

pecially after the devastating Thirty Years' War (1618–1648). As in Asia, developments in distant parts of the world shaped upturns and downturns in European economies. Compounding the pressures of economic change in Europe was the continuation of dynastic rivalries and religious conflicts.

THE THIRTY YEARS' WAR Over the course of the century after Martin Luther broke with the Catholic Church, religious warfare continued to rage in Europe. To these tensions were added contests for territory, power, and, increasingly, trade wars. The Thirty Years' War (1618–1648) was all three of these—a war fought between the Protestant princes and the Habsburg Catholic emperor for religious predominance in central Europe; a struggle for regional control fought between Catholic powers (the Spanish and Austrian Habsburgs and the French); and a bid for independence (from Spain) by the Dutch, who wanted the freedom to trade and worship as they liked. It was a brutal conflict, which cost the lives of many civilians as well as mercenary soldiers. Just when it seemed as if Protestantism would be wiped off the central European map, the Swedish king, Gustavus Adolphus II (ruled 1611–1632), came to the rescue. Though he died from battle wounds, his intervention allowed the Protestant forces to survive. The most notorious battle in this conflict occurred in 1631 at Magdeburg, where Catholic forces sacked and destroyed the city of 40,000. Three-quarters of the civilian inhabitants died. In total, fighting, disease, and famine wiped out a third of the urban population and two-fifths of the rural population of the German states. The war also depopulated Sweden and Poland. Exhausted from the long conflict, the primary belligerents signed the Treaty of Westphalia in 1648, agreeing, in essence, that as there was a rough balance of power between Protestant and Catholic states, they would simply have to put up with each other. The Dutch got their independence, but the enormous costs of the war proved a major source of discontent in Spain, France, and England. Central Europe was so devastated that it did not recover in economic or demographic terms for more than a century.

The Thirty Years' War did not remake Europe's religious map, but it did transform European war-making, and with it, a series of other practices. Medieval struggles had been mainly sieges between nobles, and the belligerents had fielded relatively small armies. The Thirty Years' War enhanced the powers of larger centralized states. After 1648, with the increase in the size of standing armies, rulers had to wage decisive, grand-scale campaigns. The Thirty Years' War changed the nature of being a soldier, too; as the war ground on, enlisted men who had been recruited from among the local population to defend their king, country, and faith were replaced by criminals who were forced into service or mercenaries who were hired to fight. Even officers, previously granted their stripes by purchase or royal fiat, now earned them and became more professional. Gunpowder, cannons, and handguns became standardized and more efficient. By the eighteenth century, Europe's wars were being fought by

The Thirty Years' War. The mercenary armies of the Thirty Years' War were renowned for pillaging and tormenting the civilians of central Europe. Here, the townsfolk exact revenge on some of these soldiers, hanging, as the engraving's caption claims, "damned and infamous thieves, like bad fruit, from this tree."

huge standing armies boasting a professional officer corps and bristling with effective artillery. To keep these armies going, rulers had to organize and sustain long supply lines and make sure that food and ammunition got to the front. The costs—material and human—of war in Europe began to soar. In Holland, the public debt, mostly for supporting armies, soared from 140 million guilders in 1650 to over 400 million a century later.

WESTERN EUROPEAN ECONOMIES To finance their armies and balance the state's books, European rulers in this era, like the Mughals and Ottomans, depended chiefly on income from land—their own and that of their heavily taxed peasants. But commercial expansion had powerful effects on economic and social relations and spurred the growth of northern cities like Amsterdam and London. Here, powerful new merchant classes arose, able and willing to risk capital on new endeavors. In the meantime, some countries—especially those that had pioneered commercial connections in the fifteenth and sixteenth centuries—began to face new threats. In the seventeenth century, Spain, for example, began to lose ground to its rivals as the costs of defending the empire soared and north European merchants began to cut in on Spanish trading networks. The enormous costs of Spain's involvement in the Thirty Years' War dealt the Spanish economy a final, disastrous blow. But not only Spain felt the effects of new competition; many economies that had flourished in the sixteenth century now had difficulty adapting to the pressures of greater economic connection. The economy of Venice, which before the era of transoceanic shipping had been Europe's chief gateway to Asia, fell into decline.

During the seventeenth century, the centers of European dynamism shifted northward. The Dutch were at the forefront, creating new commercial practices and a new mercantile elite. They specialized in shipping and in financing regional and long-distance trade. Their famous *fluitschips* could carry heavy, bulky cargoes, like Baltic wood, with relatively small crews over long distances. The cost of shipping goods around the Atlantic world dropped significantly as Dutch ships transported their own goods as well as cargoes of other countries. Amsterdam's merchants founded an exchange bank in 1609 and even a rudimentary stock exchange in 1611—with a weekly publication of price quotations in 1613. They also pioneered systems of underwriting and insuring cargoes. Other mercantile centers in Europe followed suit and soon began to compete with Dutch merchants. The Dutch began to lose their share of the commercial activity and eventually fell behind the larger European commercial and military powers. But their pioneering ways set an early example for new trading and financing practices that helped integrate the Atlantic economies even further.

England and to some extent France also emerged as commercial powerhouses in the seventeenth century. Each was backed by aggressive state policies that aimed to promote national business and drive out competitors. The English Navigation Act of 1651, which stipulated that only English ships could carry goods between the mother country and its colonies, sought to protect English shipping and merchants, especially from the Dutch. The English subsequently launched a series of effective trade wars against Holland between 1652 and 1672. The French, too, especially under King Louis XIV's finance minister, Jean-Baptiste Colbert, aggressively applied mercantilist policies and joined forces with England to invade Holland in 1672. These European powers also perfected the use of official monopoly trading companies to organize commerce and drive away competitors.

Economic development was not limited to port towns. In the countryside, too, new techniques for organizing production led to breakthroughs. Most important was the expansion in the production of food. In northwestern Europe, especially, investments in water drainage, larger livestock herds, and the refinement of cultivation practices all helped farmers produce more and more food. A new four-field crop rotation, in which wheat, clover, barley, and turnips alternated, helped to keep nutrients in the soil and provided fodder for livestock year-round. This increased output supported a growing urban population. By contrast, in Spain and Italy, agricultural change came more slowly, and agrarian backwardness checked population growth.

Production rose most where farming underwent profound changes in the way rural property was organized. The sharpest transformation came in England. For generations, leading up to the end of the eighteenth century, landowners redefined their relations with their workforces. In a movement known as "enclosure," landowners took control of lands that local customs had treated as the common property of residents. Landowners now built fences, and claimed exclusive rights to these properties. They planted new crops or pastured sheep with the aim not of satisfying local needs, but of selling the products in distant markets—especially cities. At the same time, large landowners put their farms in the hands of tenants, who in turn hired wage laborers to till the land and col-

Amsterdam Stock Exchange. Buying and selling shares in the new joint-stock companies was daily business at the Stock Exchange in seventeenth-century Amsterdam. This image depicts gentlemanly negotiations between prosperous merchants and investors, but panics could also occur, as during the South Sea Bubble.

lect harvests. In England, peasant agriculture gave way increasingly to farms run by families who made their money from buying and selling what they needed (including labor) and what they produced in the marketplace. England was not alone in this practice; it simply was at the forefront of a European-wide process of commercializing the countryside.

DYNASTIC MONARCHIES: FRANCE AND ENGLAND
European monarchs had various degrees of success in their attempts to centralize state power. Louis XIII of France (ruled 1610–1643), and especially his chief minister Cardinal Richelieu, concentrated power in the hands of the king. By the time of Louis XIV's reign (ruled 1643–1715), the Bourbon family had established a monarchy in which succession passed strictly to the oldest male in the male line. After 1614, kings refused to convene the Estates-General, a medieval advisory body. Once composed of representatives of three groups—the clergy (the First Estate, those who pray), the nobility (the Second Estate, those who fight), and the unprivileged remainder of the population (the Third Estate, those who work)—the Estates-General was seen as an obstacle to the full empowerment of the king. Instead of sharing power, the king and his counselors sought to create a monarchy that was absolute. By this they did not mean tyrannical rule, but complete and thorough rule, free of bloody disorders such as the religious wars that shattered France during the sixteenth century. The king's rule was to be lawful, but it was he, not his jurists, who dictated the last legal word. If the king made a mistake, only God could call him to account. This was the "divine right of kings."

In absolutist France, privileges and state offices flowed from the king's grace. All patronage networks, even those headed by dukes and princes, ultimately were linked to the king's grants and treasury. The great palace Louis XIV built at Versailles teemed with noblemen and noblewomen from all over France, seeking favor, dressing according to the king's expensive fashion code, and attending the latest tragedies, comedies, and concerts. Just as the Japanese shogun monitored the daimyos by keeping them in Edo, so, too, did Louis XIV and his retainers keep a watchful eye on the French nobility at Versailles.

The French dynastic monarchy provided a model of absolute rule for other European dynasts, like the Habsburgs of the Holy Roman Empire, the Hohenzollerns of Prussia, and the Romanovs of Muscovy. Public power was clustered in the hands of the king and his ministers, while the various groups in society, from the nobility to the peasantry, were deprived of formal means to represent their interests. Nonetheless, French absolutist government was not as absolute as the king would have wished. Pockets of stalwart Protestants practiced their religion secretly in the plateau villages of central France. Peasant disturbances continued. Criticism of court life and of Louis's wars and religious policies flowed from pens in anonymous printed pamphlets, jurists' notebooks, and the private journals of courtiers. The nobility also grumbled

Versailles. Louis XIV's Versailles, just southwest of Paris, was a hunting lodge that was converted at colossal cost in the 1670s–1680s into a grand royal chateau with expansive grounds. Much envied and imitated across Europe, the palace became the epicenter of a luxurious court life that included entertainments such as plays and musical offerings, state receptions, royal hunts, boating, and gambling. Thousands of nobles at Versailles vied with each other for closer proximity to the king in the performance of court rituals.

about their political misfortunes, but since the king would not call the Estates-General, they had no formal way to express their political concerns.

England might also have evolved into an absolutist regime. Queen Elizabeth (ruled 1558–1603) and her successors in the early seventeenth century employed many of the same policies of the absolute monarchy in France, such as control of patronage and elaborate court festivities. Not wishing to share her power with a man, the "Virgin Queen" never married and exerted extensive control over the church, military, and aristocracy. But there were important differences. In England, the system of succession allowed women to rule as queens in their own right. In addition, in England, Parliament remained an important force. Importantly, while the French kings did not need the consent of the Estates-General to enact taxes, the English monarchs were required to call Parliament if they wanted to raise money.

Under Elizabeth's successors, fierce quarrels broke out over taxation, religion, and royal efforts to rule without parliamentary consent. Tensions ran high between the Puritans, with their relatively simple form of worship and more egalitarian church government, and the Anglicans, supporters of the Church of England, with its more ornate ceremonies and its hierarchy of bishops and archbishops headed by the king. Social and economic grievances aggravated the unrest. Civil war erupted in the 1640s, ending in a victory for the parliamentary army (which was largely Puritan) and the beheading of King Charles I (ruled 1625–1649). Twelve years of government as a commonwealth without a king ensued, during which the middle and lower classes enjoyed political and religious power, but the commonwealth became a military dictatorship.

In 1660, the monarchy was restored, but the issues of the king's relation to Parliament and of religious tolerance were

Queen Elizabeth of England. This portrait (c. 1600) depicts an idealized Queen Elizabeth near the end of her long reign. The queen is pictured riding in a procession in the midst of an admiring crowd composed of the most important nobles of the realm.

unresolved. Charles II (ruled 1660–1685) and his successor James II (ruled 1685–1688) aroused opposition by their autocracy and clandestine efforts to bring England back into the Catholic fold. The conflict between an aspiring absolutist throne and Parliament's insistence on shared sovereignty and Protestant succession culminated in the Glorious Revolution of 1688–1689. In a bloodless upheaval, James II fled to France and Parliament offered the crown to William of Orange and his wife Mary (a Protestant daughter of James II). The outcome of the conflict established the principle that monarchs must rule in conjunction with Parliament. The Church of England was reaffirmed as the official church, but Presbyterians and Jews, though saddled with many civic disabilities (they were not welcome at the universities, for instance), could at least practice their religions. Catholic worship was still officially forbidden but was in fact tolerated as long as the Catholics kept quiet. By 1700, then, England's powerful nobility and merchant classes were permanently guaranteed a say in public affairs and ensured that state activity would operate to the advantage of propertied classes and not just the ruler.

Events in France and England stimulated much political writing. In England, Thomas Hobbes published his *Leviathan* in 1651, a reasoned defense of the absolute power of the state over all competing forces as a necessary remedy against the natural "war of all against all." Nearly forty years later, John Locke published his *Two Treatises of Civil Government*, which laid out an argument based on the natural rights to liberty and property and on the rights of peoples to agree to form a government and to disband and reform it when it did not live up to its contract. French theorists, like Jean Bodin, also wrote about new forms of conducting politics and making law. More and more, writers began to discuss the costs of unchecked state power. What differed was the extent to which these elites could demand and win the right to check the king. As the eighteenth century unfolded, the question of where sovereignty lay grew ever more pressing.

MERCANTILIST WARS The ascendance of new powers in Europe, especially France and England, intensified commercial rivalries for control of the Atlantic system. In the eighteenth century, a new type of conflict replaced earlier religious and territorial struggles: mercantilist wars for control of commercial colonies and sea lanes. Commercial struggles, then, evolved into worldwide wars. Across the world, European empires engaged in constant skirmishing over control of trade and territory. The English and Dutch trading companies took aim at the Portuguese outposts in Asia and the Americas. Then they took aim at each other. Ports in India were the target for repeated assaults and counterassaults. In response, European powers built huge navies to protect their colonies and trade routes and to attack their rivals.

Smuggling across the mercantilist lines became rampant. English and French traders, sometimes with the open support of their political authorities, violated the sovereign claims of rival colonies. Curaçao, for instance, became an entrepôt for traders from England and the Low Countries to sell illegal goods in South America. French and English traders set up shop in southern Brazil to smuggle goods into the River Plate in return for Andean silver. All around the Gulf of Mexico and the Caribbean, merchants sought to introduce their goods into their enemies' colonies.

After 1715, mercantilist wars were mainly conducted outside Europe, as empires feuded over colonial possessions. They were especially bitter in border areas, where the lines between empires blurred. In the Caribbean and North America, in particular, mercantilist wars turned the borderlands into battlegrounds. Each round of peripheral warfare ratcheted up the scale and cost of fighting, culminating in the first world conflict, which was known as the French and Indian War in the United States but as the Seven Years' War (1756–1763) everywhere else. For the first time in history, a war was fought simultaneously across many hemispheric fronts: not just in Europe but also in India and across the Americas. American Indians, African slaves, and European settlers were all dragged into the conflict.

The Seven Years' War marked the triumph of the British Empire over its rivals, especially France and Spain. Britain captured one of Spain's prime Caribbean defensive bastions, Havana, as well as Florida and Manila, Spain's prize in Asia. Later, the British returned Havana and Manila, but they kept Florida, leaving little doubt that Spain's main rival in the New World was definitely Britain. France lost Canada and several outposts in India but hung onto its Caribbean possessions. While Britain emerged as the dominant overseas power in the world, the struggle left all the European empires in deep debt.

CONCLUSION

Between the beginning of the seventeenth century and the middle of the eighteenth century, the corners of the world went from being loosely connected to becoming more economically linked. Traders shipped ever more goods over longer distances. They exchanged a wider variety of commodities, from Baltic wood to Indian cotton. The world's commercial linkages could be seen in people wearing clothes manufactured elsewhere, consuming beverages made from products cultivated in far-off locations, and using imported guns to settle local conflicts. Colonization in the Americas provides an obvious example of this growing interdependence. European decisions to settle new colonies meant an increase in the Atlantic slave trade from Africa and the expulsion of Indians from their lands, clear cases of global connectedness—and glaring inequalities.

Economic integration had destabilizing and fragmenting political consequences for many of the great dynasties of Afro-Eurasia. The Mughals, the Ming, and the Ottomans all confronted rivals to their authority—both inside and out. Local magnates challenged the imperial centers, while European newcomers knocked with greater frequency at imperial doors, for royal favor, for rights to trade, and for permission to convert souls.

Politically, certain societies coped with increased commercial exchange more successfully than others, although everywhere greater linkages and new wealth shook up existing orders. The Safavid and Ming dynasties could not cope with these pressures; both collapsed. The Spanish and Mughal dynasts managed to survive, but they were harried by aggressive rivals. For the newcomers to the integrating world, the opportunity to trade helped create new dynasties. Japan, Russia, and England emerged on the world stage. But even in these newer regimes, competition and conflict created enormous internal pressures, some of which sparked domestic upheaval.

STUDY QUESTIONS

 WWNORTON.COM/STUDYSPACE

1. Define mercantilism and analyze how this philosophy shaped the Atlantic world during the period covered in this chapter. How did mercantilist practices affect all regions of the Atlantic world?
2. Describe the plantation complex in the Caribbean. Why was it so valued by Europeans relative to other regions of the Americas?
3. Analyze how the Atlantic slave trade reshaped sub-Saharan African societies and polities during this era. Which regions and groups benefited from Africa's growing entanglements in global commerce?
4. Analyze how global trade affected the history of the Ottoman and Mughal empires during this era. How did each regime respond to these growing entanglements?
5. List and describe major factors that caused the end of the Ming dynasty and the rise of the Qing dynasty in China during this era. How did global trade affect this outcome? How did Qing rulers react to global commerce?
6. Analyze to what extent the Tokugawa Shogunate succeeded in creating a strong central government in Japan during this time. How did it avoid the problems associated with expanding trade faced by many other dynasties during this time period?
7. Compare and contrast the expansionist policies of the Russian state with those pursued by the British and French regimes during this time period. How were they similar and how were they different?
8. Analyze how increased global trade shaped the history of Europe during this time period. Why did Britain (England) tend to be the largest beneficiary of these trends in terms of regional dynastic rivalries? What other social and political groups were strongly affected by Europe's increased global entanglements?
9. Compare and contrast the impact of global entanglements on European and Asian dynasties during this era. Did any dynasty hold an advantage over others in terms of controlling these entanglements and using them to enrich their societies?

FURTHER READINGS

Alam, Muzaffar, *The Crisis of Empire in Mughal North India* (1993). Represents the best of the new interpretations on the subject.

Bay, Edna, *Wives of the Leopard: Gender, Politics, and Culture in the Kingdom of Dahomey* (1998). A useful treatment of gender issues in Dahomey.

Blackburn, Robin, *The Making of New World Slavery: From the Baroque to the Modern, 1492–1800* (1997). A good place to begin when studying African slavery and the Atlantic slave trade, it compares the early expansion of the plantation systems across the Atlantic and throughout the Americas.

Crossley, Pamela, *A Translucent Mirror: History and Identity in Qing Imperial Ideology* (1999). The author historicizes the formation of identities such as "Manchu" and "Chinese" during the Qing period.

Dennis, Matthew, *Cultivating a Landscape of Peace: Iroquois-European Encounters in Seventeenth-Century America* (1993). An excellent discussion of the relations of the Iroquois and the European colonists.

De Vries, Jan, *The Economy of Europe in an Age of Crisis, 1600–1750* (1976). A useful discussion of the European economy.

Dvornik, Francis, *The Slavs in European History and Civilization* (1962). Thorough analysis of Muscovy as well as other Slavic dynasties that did not achieve the power of the Russian one.

Flynn, Dennis O., and Arturo Girladez (eds.), *Metals and Money in an Emerging World Economy* (1997). A collection of articles about the place of silver in the world economy.

Forsyth, James, *A History of the Peoples of Siberia: Russia's North Asian Colony 1581–1990* (1992). A narrative overview of a violent history reminiscent of the western expansion of the United States.

Glahn, Richard von, *Fountains of Fortune: Money and Monetary Policy in China, 1000–1700* (1996). A discussion of the place of silver in the Chinese economy.

Halperin, Charles J., *Russia and the Golden Horde: The Mongol Impact on Medieval Russian History* (1985). A book on the rise of Muscovy, forebear of the Russian Empire, from within the Mongol realm.

Hattox, Ralph S., *Coffee and Coffeehouses: The Origins of a Social Beverage in the Medieval Near East* (1985). This work shows how widespread and popular coffee consumption and coffeehouses were around the world.

Huang, Ray, *1587, A Year of No Significance: The Ming Dynasty in Decline* (1981). An insightful analysis of the problems confronting the late Ming.

Katz, Stanley N., John M. Murrin, and Douglas Greenberg (eds.), *Colonial America: Essays in Politics and Social Development* (5th ed., 2001). Brings together many of the most important interpretations of seventeenth- and eighteenth-century life in North America.

Klein, Herbert S., *The Atlantic Slave Trade* (1999). A recent study of the African slave trade.

Lensen, George, *The Russian Push Toward Japan: Russo-Japanese Relations 1697–1875* (1959). A discussion of why and how Japan established its first border with another state and how Russia pursued its ambitions in the Pacific.

Lockhart, James, *The Nahuas After the Conquest* (1992). A landmark study of the social reorganization of Mesoamerican societies under Spanish rule.

Lovejoy, Paul, *Transformations in Slavery: A History of Slavery in Africa* (1983). An excellent discussion of African slavery.

Nakane, Chie, and Shinzaburo Oishi (eds.), *Tokugawa Japan: The Social and Economic Antecedents of Modern Japan* (1990). First-

Chronology

1600

THE AMERICAS	English establish Jamestown colony, 1607 French establish colony of New France, 1608 Dutch settle New Amsterdam, 1624
SOUTH ASIA	Aurangzeb expands Mughal Empire, 1658–17
RUSSIA	Romanov dynasty established in Russia, 1613 Russian state's frontier reaches Pacific, 1639 Peter the Great rules Russia, 1682–1725
EAST ASIA	Political and economic problems in China, 1600–1640s Tokugawa Shogunate founded in Japan, 1603 Japanese expel European missionaries, 1637 Dutch seize Melaka from Portuguese, 1641 Ming dynasty falls to the Qing, 1644
EUROPE	English East India Company established, 1600 Dutch East India Company established, 1602 Thirty Years' War, 1618–1648 Dutch West India Company founded, 1621 English Civil War, 1642–1649 Reign of France's Louis XIV, 1643–1715 Glorious Revolution in England, 1688–1689
AFRICA	Massive expansion of the Atlantic slave trade, 1600–1800 Oyo Empire expands to coast of Africa, 1690s–1713
SOUTHWEST ASIA	Koprulu reforms revitalize Ottoman Empire, 1656–1676

rate essays on Japanese village society, urban life, literacy, and culture.

Pamuk, Sevket, *A Monetary History of the Ottoman Empire* (2000). A discussion of the place of silver in the Ottoman Empire.

Parker, Geoffrey (ed.), *The Thirty Years' War* (1997). The standard account of the conflict and its outcomes.

Perdue, Peter C., *China Marches West: The Qing Conquest of Central Asia* (2005). This volume chronicles the expansion of the Qing Empire to its northwest, drawing comparisons to other colonial empires and their legacies.

Platonov, S. F., *Ivan the Terrible* (1986). Covers the controversies over Russia's infamous tsar.

Rawski, Evelyn, *The Last Emperors: A Social History of Qing Imperial Institutions* (1998). This volume explores the mechanisms and processes through which the Qing court negotiated its Manchu identity.

Reid, Anthony, *Charting the Shape of Early Modern Southeast Asia* (1999). A collection of articles by a leading historian of Southeast Asia.

Richter, Daniel, *The Ordeal of the Longhouse: The Peoples of the Iroquois League in the Era of European Colonization* (1992). A superb analysis of the Iroquois and their relations with Dutch, English, and French colonists.

Spence, Jonathan, and John Wills (eds.), *From Ming to Ch'ing: Conquest, Region, and Continuity in Seventeenth-Century China* (1979). Covers the various aspects of a tumultuous period of dynastic transition.

Thornton, John, *Africa and Africans in the Making of the Atlantic World, 1400–1800* (1998). A wonderful discussion of how African slaves played a large role in the formation of the Atlantic world.

Thornton, John K., *The Kongolese Saint Anthony: Dona Beatriz Kimpa Vita and the Antonian Movement, 1684–1706* (1998). An excellent monograph on religious movements in the Kongo.

Toby, Ronald P., *State and Diplomacy in Early Modern Japan: Asia in the Development of the Tokugawa Bakufu* (1984). A demolition of the myth of Japanese isolationism with a subtle alternative view.

Vilar, Pierre, *A History of Gold and Money* (1991). An excellent study of the development of the early silver and gold economies.

1700   1800

■ *Seven Years' War, 1756–1763*

■ *Asante state expands in Africa, 1701–1750*

■ *Safavid Empire under assault, 1722–1773*

Cultures of Splendor and Power, 1500–1780

The flourishing of the Indian Ocean trade and the consolidation of empires made for considerable prosperity in Eurasia by 1500. In the seventeenth and eighteenth centuries, silver from the New World coursed through the arteries of world trade, creating new wealth, especially in western Europe. China, the Islamic empires, and Europe developed bureaucracies that could more effectively extract wealth from their lands and used their newfound prosperity to patronize the arts and sciences. Monarchs built architectural masterpieces often as a means to prove the legitimacy of their rule by displaying their taste and munificence. Book production and consumption soared, with some publications even finding their way across the world. Artists and writers in distant places reveled in their cultural attainments and celebrated the vitality of their ways of life. Experiments in religious toleration helped to foster cultural diversity, though these were often difficult to sustain.

World prosperity supported cultural splendors and fostered knowledge of foreign ways. This was an era of vastly increased cultural commerce. Europeans, the most avid observers and borrowers, invented what they believed to be universal principles. But intellectual developments still remained rooted in the cultural soil of each of the different regions of the world. In Africa, the slave trade enriched the rulers of some kingdoms, but the traditions of African sculpture and crafts developed as they had for centuries. So, too, Ottoman, Safavid, and Mughal architecture remained wedded to Islamic precepts, and Chinese writing and painting continued to be based on their particular beliefs and traditions. Muslim and Chinese scholars remained convinced that their forms of knowledge and art were superior to those of others. Even the indigenous peoples of the Americas, along with imported African slaves, tended to borrow European ideas selectively. Here, too, people ignored or rejected the universalist claims of Europeans and adhered instead to their own traditions of arts and sciences. Despite the increasing familiarity among peoples around the world, the real cultural battles of this period, like the struggles to achieve political autonomy, were waged inside polities, as centralized dynasties and new states struggled to dominate the cultural production of their intellectuals.

 TRADE AND CULTURE

> ⇥ *How did world trade begin changing world cultures?*

It is not surprising that in 1500 the world's most flourishing cultures were in Asia, in the areas profiting from the Indian Ocean and China Sea trades. It was in China and the Islamic world that the spice and luxury trades first flourished; here, too, rulers had been most successful in establishing political stability and consolidating centralized control of taxation, law-making, and military force. This often entailed recruiting talented individuals, some of whom came from different religious, ethnic, or class backgrounds than did the ruling elite. It also entailed the promotion of new kinds of secular education, which sometimes flew in the face of traditional, clerical learning. Though older ways of making sense of the world and giving pleasure to its inhabitants did not die out, both trade and empire-building contributed to the diversification of global cultural production.

Of course, some rulers and some polities were more eager for change than others, and some cultures—in the Americas and the South Pacific, for example—found that conquest and trade undermined many aspects of indigenous cultural life. Although Europeans and native peoples often borrowed ideas and practices from one another, these were not free and equal exchanges. Native Americans, for example, adapted to European missionizing efforts in resourceful ways, by creating mixed forms of religious worship, but they did so in response to external pressure. And as the Europeans grew richer and swallowed new territories, it was their culture, not that of the local populations, that spread and diversified, absorbing ideas and practices from Native Americans and African slaves but offering these contributors little share of either expanding sovereignty or increasing prosperity.

European cultural flourishing after the mid-seventeenth century resulted in part, too, from the consolidation of nation-states and the centralization of wealth, administration, and military power by rulers often described as "enlightened absolutists." Europe's internal religious and political rivalries and its commercial ambitions propelled it to develop new forms of information-gathering, at home and especially

Focus Questions CULTURES OF SPLENDOR AND POWER

⇥ *How did world trade begin changing world cultures?*
⇥ *How did the Islamic empires foster vibrant and syncretic cultures?*
⇥ *How and why did the Chinese and Japanese governments attempt to control culture and knowledge?*
⇥ *What were the major tenets of Enlightenment thought?*
⇥ *How did global entanglements, particularly involvement in the slave trade, reshape African cultures?*
⇥ *How did cultural developments in the Americas reflect new global entanglements?*
⇥ *What role did race play in how Europeans viewed others, especially those from Oceania?*

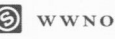 WWNORTON.COM/STUDYSPACE

abroad. By the eighteenth century's end, Europeans had collected information on everything from Sanskrit grammar to Polynesian wind currents. Based on the data they gathered, they created pragmatic principles for commercial and even colonial use, as well as a kind of empirical knowledge they felt could be extended to the rest of the world. In the eighteenth century, the decline of religious persecution and warfare made possible the notion that ideas and texts could and should circulate freely—though in many places, such as Tsarist Russia, this continued to be more dream than reality. The three scientific-colonizing voyages of Captain James Cook (1728–1779) in the South Pacific epitomized the search for knowledge about the unknown. In a few years, between 1768 and 1779, this virtually uncharted world suddenly became the subject of plays, poems, scientific treatises, and political rivalries. It is worth emphasizing how bizarre the desire to make this long, arduous trip would have seemed to Europeans just a few centuries earlier and how technically and fiscally impossible launching it would have been. Cook's voyages certainly signal, then, just how much Europe's wealth and aspirations had expanded.

The cultural flourishings of the sixteenth, seventeenth, and eighteenth centuries took place in a world much changed since the Mongol invasions and the Black Death. There were new dynasties. There were also many more people. By 1750, the world's population had doubled from its level in 1300. There was also a much greater volume of long-distance trade, which generated a level of prosperity that would have amazed even the wealthiest dynast 500 years earlier. Yet, despite the unifying aspects of world trade, each culture flourished in its own way and was shaped by local educational institutions and local artistic conventions. Ruling classes disseminated values that drew from their cherished classical texts, crafted their visions of the world on the basis of long-established moral and religious principles, mapped their geographies according to their traditional visions of the universe, and wrote their separate histories. They could still celebrate their achievements in politics, economics, and culture without worrying about threats from within or from without.

CULTURE IN THE ISLAMIC WORLD

> → *How did the Islamic empires foster vibrant and syncretic cultures?*

For centuries, Muslim elites had put significant resources into cultural development. As the Ottoman, the Safavid, and the Mughal empires extended their control, dominating territories from the Balkans to Bengal, new resources were available to fund cultural pursuits. Rulers used the vast agrarian and commercial wealth at their disposal to patronize new schools and building projects, and the elite produced and consumed new books, artworks, and luxury goods. Cultural life was clearly connected to the politics of empire-building, as emperors and elites sought to gain prestige from their patronage of intellectuals and artists.

Forged under contrasting imperial auspices, the cultural and intellectual life of the Islamic world was organized in three distinct, regional worlds. In place of an earlier Islamic cosmopolitanism, a specific pattern of cultural flourishing prevailed within the boundaries of each empire. Though the Ottomans, the Safavids, and the Mughals were united by a common faith, each developed a relatively autonomous form of Muslim culture.

THE OTTOMAN CULTURAL SYNTHESIS

By the sixteenth century, the Ottoman Empire had developed a remarkably rich and syncretic culture. Its blend of ethnic, religious, and linguistic elements, in fact, exceeded in diversity and depth those of previous empires of the Islamic world. The Ottomans' creative and flexible cultural synthesis accommodated both Sufis (mystics who stressed contemplation

Suleiman the Lawgiver. The most illustrious ruler of the Ottoman Empire was Suleiman, who began his reign in 1520 and brought the empire to its military and political height. This miniature painting shows Suleiman giving advice to the crown prince.

and ecstasy through poetry, music, and dancing) and ultra-orthodox *ulama* (Islamic jurists who stressed tradition and religious law). It also balanced the interests of military men and administrators with the desires of clerics. Finally, it allowed autonomy to the minority faiths of Christianity and Judaism.

The Ottomans permitted religious diversity, allowing *dhimmis* (followers of religions permitted by law: Armenian Christians, Greek Orthodox Christians, and Jews) to organize themselves into *millets* (minority religious communities) as long as they acknowledged the political superiority of the Sunni and Sufi Muslims. Drawing on Islamic law, the Ottomans allowed the *dhimmis* to worship as they pleased, to send their children to their own religious schools, and to cultivate the arts and sciences as they wished. For this cultural autonomy, the *dhimmis* paid a special tax (*jizya*) that applied to all non-Muslims.

The Ottoman world achieved its cultural unity, above all, by what many regarded as the supreme intellectual achievement of the Ottomans, its system of administrative law, known as *kanun*. As the sultans gained control over diverse cultures and territories, they realized that the *sharia* (Islamic holy law) by itself would not suffice; it was silent on many crucial secular matters. Moreover, the far-flung Ottoman state needed a comprehensive and well-understood set of laws to bridge differences between the many different social and legal systems that had come under Ottoman rule. Mehmed II, conqueror of Constantinople, began the process of administrative reform. Mehmed recruited young boys, rather than established noblemen, to be trained as professional bureaucrats or military men, accountable directly to the sultan. Mehmed's most illustrious successor, Suleiman the Magnificent and the Lawgiver, continued his work, overseeing the codification of a comprehensive legal code. The code included laws on the rights and duties of subjects, on what clothes they could wear, and on how Muslims were to

Islamic Scientists. This fifteenth-century Persian miniature shows a group of Islamic scholars working with sophisticated navigational and astronomical instruments and reflects the importance that the educated classes in the Islamic world attached to observing and recording the regularities in the natural world. Indeed, many of Europe's advances in sailing drew upon knowledge from the Muslim world.

Ottoman Court Women. This eighteenth-century watercolor found in Topkapi Palace in Istanbul shows various musical instruments being played by court women, who were often called upon to provide entertainment.

relate to non-Muslims. The code reconciled many differences between administrative and religious law.

A highly developed educational system was crucial for the religious and intellectual integration of the Ottoman Empire. Here, too, the Ottomans displayed a talent for flexibility and showed their tolerance of difference. They encouraged three distinct educational systems that produced three streams of talent—civil and military bureaucrats, *ulama*, and Sufi masters. The Ottoman administrative elite received its training at a hierarchically organized set of schools, culminating in the palace schools at Topkapi. The young men who passed through these institutions staffed the civil and military bureaucracy of the Ottoman state and accepted posts all across the empire. In the religious sphere, an equally elaborate series of schools took students from elementary schools, where they received basic instruction in reading, writing, and numbers, on to higher schools (*madrassas*), where they learned law, religious sciences, the *Quran*, and the regular sciences. Graduates became *ulama*. Some entered the court system as *qadis* (judges); others became *muftis* (experts in religious law) or teachers. Yet another set of schools (*tekkes*) taught the devotional strategies and the religious knowledge for students to enter Sufi orders and ultimately to become masters of these brotherhoods. Each of these sets of schools created linkages between members of the Ottoman ruling elite and the orthodox religious elite that lasted throughout their lifetimes. The *tekkes* were particularly effective in promoting empire-wide social and religious solidarity and creating frameworks of integration for the Muslim peoples living under Ottoman rule.

The Ottomans attached great prestige to education and scholarship. Scholars claimed that "an hour of learning was worth more than a year of prayer." Schools stressed training in law, language, religious commentary, rhetoric, logic, and theology over the natural and mathematical sciences. Yet, teachers did not ignore the sciences, and Ottoman scholars carried out important work in astronomy and physics, as well as in history, geography, and politics.

Under the patronage of a reformist-minded grand vizier, Damat Ibrahim Pasha, Ottoman intellectuals also took an interest in works of European science, some of which appeared in Turkish translation for the first time in the eighteenth century. The most impressive of these Ottoman efforts to disseminate European knowledge occurred when a Hungarian convert to Islam, Ibrahim Muteferrika (1674–1745), set up a printing press in Istanbul in 1729. Muteferrika published works on science, history, and geography. In one of his published essays, printed in 1731, he included sections on geometry, a discussion of the works of Copernicus, Galileo, and Descartes, and a plea to the Ottoman educated classes to learn from Europe. When his patron, the grand vizier Damat Ibrahim Pasha, was killed in 1730, however, the *ulama* moved vigorously to close off this promising avenue of contact with western learning.

The Ottomans combined inherited traditions with new elements in other ways as well. The Islamic world took up portraiture after the Italian painter Gentile Bellini visited Istanbul and composed a portrait of Mehmed II. Mehmed's pious successor, Bayezid II, disapproved and sold the portrait in the bazaar, but nonetheless, the genre spread.

In some areas the Ottomans kept their own styles. The magnificent architectural monuments of the sixteenth through eighteenth centuries, including mosques, gardens, tombs, forts, and palaces, were little touched by western influence. Nor did the Ottomans show much interest in western literature or music. For the most part, they still believed God had given the Islamic world a monopoly on truth and enlightenment; their military successes proved his favor for

The Ottomans and the Tulip. From the earliest times, the Ottomans admired the beauty of the tulip. (*Left*) Sultan Mehmed II smelling a tulip, symbol of the Ottoman sultans. (*Right*) The Ottomans used tulip motifs to decorate tiles in homes and mosques and pottery wares, as on the plate shown here.

their community and culture, over and against that of the infidel.

Despite being pushed back from the gates of Vienna in 1683, the Ottomans still enjoyed a sense of well-being and prosperity during the so-called Tulip Era that followed. The Ottoman elite had long been fascinated with the bold colors and delicate blooms of the tulip. For centuries, the flower served as the symbol of the Ottoman sultans. Mehmed the Conqueror and Suleiman the Lawgiver grew tulips in the most secluded and prestigious courtyards of the Topkapi Palace in Istanbul. Many Ottoman warriors wore undergarments embroidered with tulips into battle as a means to ensure victory. But the flower's great age was the early eighteenth century, which contemporaries dubbed "the tulip period." At this time, the Ottomans developed the same sort of infatuation that the Dutch had developed a century earlier. Interest in the flower spread from the sultan and his household to the wealthy classes, and estate owners began to specialize in growing tulips. They used tulip designs to decorate tiles and fabrics and to adorn public buildings, and they celebrated the beauty of the flower every spring by holding elaborate tulip festivals.

Fascination with the tulip was one manifestation of a widespread delight in the things of this world, encouraged by Grand Vizier Damat Ibrahim (ruled 1718–1730). As well as restoring order to the empire, Ibrahim loosened customary *ulama* controls over the social activities of the people, and he sanctioned elite consumption of luxury goods. The working classes, too, were drawn into this celebration of life's pleasures as coffeehouses and taverns became centers of popular entertainment. Indeed, eighteenth-century Ottoman demand for luxury goods was so extensive—including lemons, soap, pepper, metal tools, coffee, and wine—that a well-traveled diplomat looked askance at the supposed wealth of Europe. On the contrary, he wrote, "In most of the provinces [of Europe], poverty is widespread, as a punishment for being infidels. Anyone who travels in these areas must confess that goodness and abundance are reserved for the Ottoman realms."

SAFAVID CULTURE

The Safavid Empire in Persia was not as long-lived as the Ottoman Empire, but it was significant in the history of Southeast Asia for giving the Shiite version of Islam a home base. Previously, there had been Shiite governments, the most powerful being the Fatimid state in Egypt. But once the Mamluks overthrew the Fatimids in the thirteenth century, Shiism became overwhelmingly a religion of opposition and a faith embraced by those seeking to overthrow established rulers. This, of course, made for a great dilemma for Shiite groups; once they came to power they were likely to face opposition from other dissatisfied groups—who also drew on the tenets of Shiism. Rather like Protestant sectarianism, Shiism cre-

ated a culture of criticism with the potential to undermine dynastic stability.

The Safavids faced just such dilemmas, for they owed their rise to the support of Turkish-speaking tribesmen, the *kizilbash* ("red heads," so called because of the red color of their turbans), who espoused a populist and charismatic form of Islam. In power, the Safavid shahs endeavored to cultivate the more conservative elements of Iranian society: Persian-speaking landowners and orthodox *ulama*. They turned away from the Turkish-speaking Islamic brotherhoods with their mystical and Sufi qualities, in spite of the fact that these groups had facilitated their rise to power.

Just as the great achievement of the Ottomans was the ability to blend Sufism and clerical orthodoxy, so the Safavid triumph was to create a political-religious system based on Shiism and loyalty to the Safavid royal family. Also like the Ottomans, the Safavids used well-established institutions like the *madrassas* and brotherhood lodges (*takkiyas*) and the *ulama* to inculcate the new Shiite orthodoxy. Even after the Safavids were swept from power in the eighteenth century, Shiism remained the fundamental religion of the Iranian people.

Under the Safavids' most successful and energetic ruler, Shah Abbas I (ruled 1587–1629), Persia enjoyed a cultural revival stimulated by royal patronage and the great prosperity during his reign. Once Abbas had solidified his power, he

The King's Book of Kings. The Persian poet Firdawsi (934–1020) produced an epic poem, *The King's Book of Kings*, which celebrated the long history of Persia, glorifying its pre-Islamic past. This miniature illustration from a sixteenth-century version of the book portrays life at the royal palace.

Primary Source

ISLAMIC VIEWS OF THE WORLD

Although maps attempt to give the impression of objectivity and geographic precision, the way in which they arrange the world, the names that they give to locations, the areas that they place in the center or at the peripheries, and the text that accompanies them show the mapmakers' view of the world around them. Thus, in most cultures, official maps located their own major administrative and religious sites at the center of the universe and reflected local elites' speculations about how the world was organized. The two maps below, which are taken from the Islamic world, are interesting in this regard. The famous map of al-Idrisi, dating from the twelfth century, was a standard one of the period. It showed the world as it was known to peoples on the Afro-Eurasian landmass at that time and thus featured only three landmasses—Africa, Asia, and Europe. The second Islamic map, made in Iran around 1700, was unabashedly Islamic, for it offered a grid that measured the distances from any location in the Islamic world to the holy city of Mecca.

Al-Idrisi map, twelfth century.

Iranian map, seventeenth century.

→ *What does each map tell us about the worldview of these Islamic societies?*
→ *What main purposes do you think each map was used for?*

sought to make a grand gesture to display his power, wealth, and artistic sensibility. In 1598 he moved the capital of the state to Isfahan and hired elite artists and architects from all corners of Persia (as well as beyond) to design a city that would dwarf even Delhi and Istanbul, the other showplaces of the Islamic world. His centerpiece was the great plaza next to his palace and the royal mosque at the heart of the capital; when completed, the plaza, surrounded by elaborate public and religious buildings, was seven times as large as that of San Marco in Venice.

Other aspects of Safavid intellectual life also reflected a culture dominated by the ideals, aspirations, and wealth of the court and of its landed and commercial classes. Safavid artists perfected the design of the illustrated book, the outstanding example being *The King's Book of Kings*, which contained 250 miniature illustrations. They mastered the technique of three-dimensional representation and were skilled in harmonizing colors. Master weavers continued to produce the silks and carpets long traded throughout the world. Artisans painted tiles in vibrant colors and created tile mosaics that adorned mosques and other buildings. The Safavids also developed an elaborate calligraphy that was the envy of artists throughout the whole Islamic world.

POWER AND CULTURE UNDER THE MUGHALS

Like the Safavids and the Ottomans, the Mughals fostered a courtly and prosperous high culture. Because the Mughals, like the Ottomans and unlike the Safavids, ruled over a large non-Muslim population, the Islamic high culture that developed in South Asia was a broad and open one. This culture

Akbar Leading Religious Discussion. This miniature painting from 1604 shows Akbar receiving Muslim theologians and Jesuits. The Jesuits (in the black robes on the left) hold a page relating, in Persian, the birth of Christ. A lively debate will follow the Jesuits' claims on behalf of Christianity.

attached high value to works of art and learning, making it possible to overlook the religious identity of non-Muslim artists and to admit them into the world of the arts and learning. Thus, while Islamic traditions were structurally dominant, the Hindus shared with the Muslims the aristocratic culture of learning, music, painting, and architecture; the realm of high culture functioned as an arena in which religious differences could be bridged by aesthetic refinement and philosophical sophistication.

The promise of an open Islamic high culture found its greatest fulfillment under the Mughal emperor Akbar (ruled 1556–1605). In addition to being a very successful military leader, Akbar was a popular ruler who allowed common people as well as nobles from all ethnic groups to converse with him at court. His quest for universal truths outside the strict limits of the *sharia* led him to develop a religion of his own, which incorporated many aspects of Hindu belief and ritual practice. His trusted advisor Abulfazl (1551–1602) encouraged Akbar's eclectic pursuits and composed a grand-scale tribute to the ruler and his predecessors that is still a major source of our knowledge of early Mughal history. In the *Akbarnamah* (the Book of Akbar), written between 1587 and 1602, Abulfazl described Akbar as a philosopher-king, someone who had received kingship as a gift from God because he was a true philosopher and who was born a perfect person in the Sufi sense. Regrettably, Akbar's son Salim was jealous of Abulfazl and arranged for his murder.

In architecture, too, the Mughals produced eclectic masterpieces. This was already evident in the combination of Persian, Indian, and Ottoman elements in the tombs and mosques built by Akbar's predecessors. But Akbar enhanced this syncretic tendency in the elaborate new city he built at Fatehpur Sikri, beginning in 1571. The buildings included residences for the nobility (whose loyalty Akbar wanted to secure), gardens, a drinking and gambling zone, and even an experimental school devoted to studying language acquisition in children. The huge complex was completed in about a decade, a much shorter time than it took for Louis XIV to build the comparable royal residence—a century later—at Versailles.

Akbar's descendant Shah Jahan (ruled 1628–1658) was also a lavish patron of architecture and the arts. In 1630, Shah Jahan ordered the building in Agra of a magnificent tomb of white marble for his beloved wife, Mumtaz Mahal, who had been—like many other women in the Mughal court—an important political counselor. Designed by an Indian architect of Persian origin, this structure, known as the Taj Mahal, took twenty years and 20,000 workers to build. The forty-two-acre complex included a main gateway, garden, minarets, and a mosque; the mausoleum for Mumtaz Mahal was built of translucent white marble and lay squarely in the middle of the structure, enclosed by four identical facades and crowned by a majestic central dome rising to 240 feet. The stone inlays of different types and hues, organized in geometrical and floral patterns, and Quranic verses inscribed in

The Taj Mahal. A symbol of Mughal splendor, the Taj Mahal was a mausoleum that was built of white marble. Often described as poetry in stone, it was constructed under Shah Jahan as an homage to his deceased wife, Mumtaz Mahal (*below*).

Arabic calligraphy gave the white marble surface an appearance of delicacy and lightness. Blending Persian and Islamic design with Indian materials and motifs, this poetry in stone represented the most splendid example of Mughal cultural efflorescence and the combining of cultural traditions. Like Shah Abbas's great plaza, the Taj Mahal lent a sense of refined grandeur to this Islamic empire's formidable political, military, and economic power.

Though the brilliance of Akbar, Abulfazl, and Shah Jahan was not equaled under later emperors, Mughal culture remained vibrant. François Bernier, a seventeenth-century French traveler to the Mughal Empire, wrote admiringly of the broad philosophical interests of Danishmand Khan, a prominent intellectual whom the Emperor Aurangzeb had appointed as the governor of Delhi. According to Bernier, Khan avidly read the works of the French philosophers Gassendi and Descartes and studied Sanskrit treatises to understand different philosophical traditions. But Aurangzeb, a very pious Muslim, heavily favored Islamic arts and sciences. He dismissed many of the court's painters and musicians, and in 1669 ordered that all recently built non-Islamic places of worship be torn down. In his court, intellectuals debated whether metaphysics, astronomy, medicine, mathematics, and ethics were of any use in the practice of Islam. Clearly women, at least at court, were not discouraged from pursuing the arts; two of Aurangzeb's daughters, Zebunissa and Zinat-um-nissa, were accomplished poets.

Well into the eighteenth century, the Mughal nobility exuded confidence and lived in unrivaled luxury. The presence of foreign scholars and artists only added to the luster of courtly culture, and the elite eagerly consumed foreign luxuries. Traders who carried goods from China or Europe were welcome. Besides, foreign trade brought increasing supplies of silver to India, helping to advance the money economy and support the sumptuous urban lifestyles of the nobility. The Mughals were also quick to assimilate European military technology and resources. They hired the Europeans as gunners and sappers in their armies, employed them to forge guns, and bought guns and cannons from them. Their appreciation for European knowledge and technology, however, was limited. Thus, when Thomas Roe, the representative of the English East India Company, presented an edition of Mercator's *Maps of the World* to Emperor Jahangir in 1617, the emperor returned it a fortnight later with the remark that no one could read or understand it. Supremely confident of their own cultural world, the Mughals saw limited use for European knowledge and culture.

The cultural life of the Islamic world was centered in Istanbul, Cairo, Isfahan, and Delhi and thus drew on intellectual currents that spanned the Eurasian–North African landmass.

Global Connections & Disconnections

ROYAL ARCHITECTURE IN THE AGE OF SPLENDOR AND POWER

By the seventeenth century, all of the great imperial monarchies of the Afro-Eurasian landmass had elaborate architectural structures that projected the power and the values of their individual states. All were ornate and splendid. All were expensive to construct and involved the best craftsmen and artists available to the monarchs. While they seem not to have consciously borrowed from one another, they all arose or were elaborated on in an age when imperial and monarchical power was at a high point. In the case of the Ottoman, Safavid, and Mughal royal structures, the emperors brought in skilled artisans and craftsmen from outside their empires, and through the work of these skilled people they indirectly borrowed from the achievements of other cultures. Yet, each structure reflected unique elements of its own culture as well as the vision of the ruler or rulers who paid for its construction.

We start with the Forbidden City of Beijing, which was the earliest of these sites of royal power and, because of its worldwide reputation, an inspiration to other powerful monarchs and emperors. Beijing became the capital of a unified Chinese empire for the first time under the Mongols in the thirteenth century, although the city had enjoyed some prominence in earlier times. Chinggis Khan had razed the old city to the ground, but his successor, Kubilai Khan, restored the city and made it the capital of his empire. Kubilai Khan did more than that, however. He rebuilt the city, calling it Khanbaliq, along the lines of early imperial Chinese capitals. Following the classical ideal of a capital city, Khanbaliq was laid out on strict north-south and east-west axes. It was surrounded by high walls, and the inner part of the city housed the emperor and his court. The Ming successors, who overthrew the Mongols, first made Nanjing their capital, but the Yongle Emperor reinstated Beijing as the imperial capital. The inner areas of the city, known as the Imperial City and the Forbidden City, were aligned on a firm north-south axis and were thought to be the very center of the Chinese state and indeed of the whole universe. Here, government took place, and it was to here that those who sought the favor of the emperor journeyed. Indeed, only those who had business with the state were permitted to enter the imperial domain. They entered bowing and scraping ("kowtowing") as indications of the great respect they felt for the awesome power of the emperor. As befit a powerful figure, the ruler was expected to stay within the confines of the imperial quarters (although Qing emperors—who succeeded the Ming in the seventeenth century—did travel with more regularity) and had to rely on envoys and chief ministers for information about the rest of his kingdom and the outside world. So effective were these arrangements that the Qing rulers retained Beijing as their capital, and, despite changes and renovations, the Qing kept the Ming structures mostly in place.

The center of Safavid power in the seventeenth century was the great plaza at Isfahan, the inspiration of Shah Abbas, who ruled from 1587 to 1629. It reflected Shah Abbas's notion that trade, government, and religion should be brought together under the authority of the supreme political leader. A great public mosque, called the Shah Abbas Mosque, dominated one end of the plaza, which measured 1,667 feet by 517 feet. At the other end were the trading stalls and markets, which made Iran wealthy. On one side of the rectangular mosque were the offices of the government, and on the other side was an exquisite mosque, called the Mosque of Shaykh Lutfollah, set aside for the shah's personal use. Many of Shah Abbas's most proficient craftsmen came from India and were familiar with the architecture of the Mughal Empire.

The Palace of Versailles, which Louis XIV built in the 1660s, has many similarities with the Isfahan plaza, although the French builders had no knowledge of Isfahan. Here, too, the great royal palace opens outward onto a large courtyard. The buildings adjoining the central palace housed the great notables and clergy, whom the French monarchs wanted to keep an eye on.

The Topkapi Palace was in Istanbul, the capital of the Ottoman Empire. Topkapi began to take shape in 1458 under Mehmed II and was steadily added to over the years. As described in detail in Chapter 11, Topkapi projected royal authority in much the same way as the Forbidden City emphasized the power of the Chinese emperors. Here, too, the governing officials worked enclosed within massive walls, and the monarchs rarely went outside their inner domain. By isolating the rulers from the rest of society the Ottomans and the Chinese made even more awesome the power of their monarchs.

Yet another advocate of royal architecture was the Mughal emperor Shah Jahan, who ruled from 1628 until 1658. He is best known for his peacock throne; for the Taj Mahal, which he built as a magnificent tomb for his wife, Mumtaz Mahal; and for his building program for the state's capital at Delhi.

But from Islam's founding, Muslims had looked eastward, to India and China, not to Europe, for external inspiration. While the crusades had proved that Europeans could be worthy military rivals, most Muslims continued to regard Europeans as rude barbarians, who had little to teach Islamic scholars. Thus, the world histories that Muslim intellectuals had composed in the fourteenth century had said little about Europe, and the Islamic elites in Persia, India, and the Ottoman Empire in the seventeenth and eighteenth centuries continued to view Europeans as less than their cultural and political equals.

CULTURE AND POLITICS IN EAST ASIA

> → *How and why did the Chinese and Japanese governments attempt to control culture and knowledge?*

Like the Ottomans, Safavids, and Mughals, the Chinese did not need to prove to anyone the richness of their scholarly and artistic traditions. China had long been a venerable and renowned center of learning, its emperors and elites serving as patrons to a large number of artists, poets, musicians, scientists, and teachers. But the cultural flourishing that characterized late Ming and early Qing China owed less to imperial leadership than to a robust internal market. A growing population and extensive mercantile networks proved instrumental in enhancing the circulation and exchange of ideas as well as goods. As a result, China's cultural sphere underwent significant diversification and expansion, predating similar changes elsewhere. For the dynasty to remain at the center of this expanding cultural sphere, it had to exert increased control over new consumers and producers.

In Japan, too, economic prosperity created favorable conditions for cultural dynamism in this period. The looming presence of its giant neighbor across the sea had rendered the Japanese historically amenable to recognizing outside influences. Like the Chinese dynastic government, the ruling Tokugawa Shogunate tried to disseminate a cultural orthodoxy based on Confucian notions of order and hierarchy and to shield the country from potentially subversive ideas. But the forces that worked to undermine the government's control of knowledge in China proved stronger still in Japan. Japan's decentralized political structure facilitated the spread of different cultural currents, including European ideas and practices. By the eighteenth century, in struggling to define its own identity through these different contending currents, the cultural scene in Japan was rather more lively, open, and varied than its counterpart in China.

CHINA: THE CHALLENGE OF EXPANSION AND DIVERSITY

TRANSMISSION OF IDEAS   In the sixteenth and seventeenth centuries, China witnessed significant expansion in the publication and circulation of books and ideas. The phenomenon had less to do with technological innovations—both woodblock and moveable type printing had been known in China for centuries—than with the gradual decentralization of cultural production. At the outset, the state provided the initiative for book production—sponsoring and printing editions of Confucian texts—but as the years passed, the increasing commercialization of the economy eroded governmental controls.

Schools acquired books not officially sanctioned by the state as early as the fifteenth century. As an observer proudly remarked when a school in Shanghai built a library in 1484, its collection included "the six classics, the imperially produced books issued by the Ming court, plus the philosophers of the hundred schools and the histories; there isn't a title they don't have!" The holdings, in other words, clearly exceeded the corpus of official publications. Although local magistrates still backed library expansion, seeing this as part of a government effort to control the production of knowledge, the state could not dictate the way in which all books were produced and consumed. While officials could and did clamp down on unorthodox texts, the empire had no centralized system of censorship, and many unauthorized opinions circulated freely.

By the late Ming era, a burgeoning commercial publishing sector had emerged, catering to the diverse social, cultural,

Ming Publication. A typical late Ming publication with illustrations of the lives of emperors. These images refer to the First Emperor (r. 221–210 BCE), who was said to have buried scholars alive and burned books deemed threatening to his rule.

and religious needs of the educated elites and the growing urban population. European visitors were struck by the vast collections of printed materials housed in Chinese libraries, describing them as "magnificently built" and "finely adorn'd." In fact, the latter part of the Ming was an age of collections of other sorts as well. Many members of the elite in this increasingly affluent society cultivated a passion for acquiring physical objects for display as a sign of their status, refinement, and taste. Connoisseurship of all the arts reached unprecedented levels. Consumers could build their collections by purchasing artworks from multiple sources, from roadside peddlers to monasteries to gentlemen dealers whose proclaimed love of art masked the commercial orientation of their passions.

Perhaps more importantly, books and other luxury goods were now more affordable. A low-quality commentary on the Confucian classics—the Four Books—published in Nanjing in 1615 cost only half a tael of silver (a unit of measurement based on the silver's weight). Even a low-level private tutor could earn more than forty taels from tuition in a year. Increasingly, publishers offered diverse wares: readers could purchase guidebooks for patrons of the arts, travelers, or merchants; handbooks for those performing rituals; manuals on how to choose dates for ceremonies or on how to write proper letters. Other book choices included almanacs, encyclopedias, morality books, and medical manuals. Demand was especially high for study aids for the civil service examination. By the late fifteenth century, examinees were required to submit their answers in the so-called eight-legged style, a highly structured form of essay in eight parts. Model essays, written by either examiners or successful candidates, flooded the market. In 1595, a scandal broke out in Beijing as the second-place graduate at the metropolitan examination reproduced verbatim a series of model essays published by commercial printers. Just over twenty years later, the top graduate was found to have plagiarized a winning essay submitted years earlier. Ironically, then, the increased circulation of knowledge led critics to bemoan a decline in real learning; instead of mastering the classics, they charged, the candidates were simply memorizing the work of others.

Examination hopefuls were not the only beneficiaries of the booming book trade. Elite women also took advantage of widening access to China's literary culture. As readers, writers, and editors, educated women now assumed a limited but visible presence in what was hitherto an exclusively male domain. Anthologies of poetry produced by women were particularly popular. Besides producing for the market, some collected works of individual women were issued by their families for limited circulation to celebrate the refinement of the family. Men of letters were quick to recognize the market potential of women's writings; some also saw the less regularized style of women—who usually acquired their skills through family channels rather than through state-sponsored schools—as a means to challenge what was perceived as the stifling stylistic conformity of the sixteenth century. The promotion of new styles opened up opportunities for women writers. On rare occasions, women even served as publishers themselves.

If in this era some elite women enjoyed success in the cultural sphere, the period also brought increasing restrictions on their lives. Widow remarriage and premarital sex might have been discouraged in earlier times, but in the sixteenth, seventeenth, and eighteenth centuries they had become unthinkable for women from "good" families. The practice of footbinding, meanwhile, continued to spread among the common people; small, delicate feet signified femininity and respectability for a larger share of the population. Ironically, the thriving publishing sector produced plays and novels that helped the government's effort to promote a stricter morality for women, underscoring the fact that increasing cultural production has not always served the cause of human liberation.

POPULAR CULTURE AND RELIGION   Important as the development of the book trade was, its impact on the majority of men and women in late Ming China was indirect. To those excluded from the literary culture because they could not read or could not read well, the transmission of cultural norms and values occurred through oral communication, ritual performance, and daily practices. The Ming government tried to control these channels, too. It appointed village elders as guardians of local society and instituted a system of "village compacts" to ensure communal social responsibility for proper conduct and observation of the laws.

Still, the everyday life of rural and small-town dwellers existed mostly outside these official networks. Apart from toiling in the field, the villagers' social milieu was typically shaped

Chinese Civil Service Exam. Lining the sides of this Chinese examination compound were cells in which candidates sat for the examination. Other than three long boards—the highest served as a shelf, the middle one as a desk, and the lowest as a seat—the cell had neither furniture nor a door. Indeed, the cells were little more than spaces partitioned on three sides by brick walls and covered by a roof; the floors were packed dirt. Generations of candidates spent three days and two nights in succession in these cells as they strove to enter officialdom.

Foot Binding. Two images of bound feet: (*left*) as an emblem of feminine respectability when wrapped and concealed, as on this well-to-do Chinese woman; (*right*) as an object of curiosity and condemnation when exposed for the world to see.

by a variety of popular cultural and religious practices. Most villages had shrines honoring the guardian spirits of the locality as well as Buddhist and Daoist temples, not all of which were officially approved.

Villagers often undertook group pilgrimages to religious sites. They might attend periodic markets in adjacent towns, which during good times would be filled with restaurants, brothels, and other venues of entertainment. Otherwise, their links to the outside world were forged by gathering news and gossip in the teahouses or marketplaces, listening to the tales of itinerant storytellers and traveling monks, or by watching performances by touring theater groups on portable stages or in the courtyards of temples. Despite official vigilance, the open-ended nature of such a process of cultural transmission meant that village audiences were quite capable of appropriating and reinterpreting official norms and values to serve their own purposes and to challenge the dictates of the government.

The popular religions of the late Ming period were syncretic, and religious practices remained diffuse and decentralized. Sectarian lines were usually of minimal significance; at the grassroots level there was often little distinction between Buddhist, Daoist, and local cults. Thus, China avoided the sectarian or religious warfare of post-Reformation Europe. This was largely because the Chinese believed in cosmic unity and, although they recognized and venerated spiritual forces, they did not consider any of them a Supreme Being who favored one faction over another. It was the emperor, rather than any religious group, who was supposed to have the Mandate of Heaven. The enforcement of orthodox norms and values and the suppression of popular resistance to them were more a matter of political than of religious control. Unless sects posed an obvious threat, the emperor had no real reason to regulate their spiritual practices. This situation made for a unique kind of religious tolerance.

TECHNOLOGY AND CARTOGRAPHY Belief in cosmic unity did not prevent members of the Chinese elite from devising technologies to master and control nature's operations in this world, however. The magnetic compass, gunpowder, and the printing press were invented in China. Chinese technicians had mastered iron casting and produced mechanical clocks centuries before Europeans managed such feats. Chinese astronomers were historically the most accurate observers of celestial phenomena in the premodern period, and they had compiled records of eclipses, comets, novae, and meteors. Their interest in astronomy and calendrical science was driven in part by the needs of the emperor—it was his job as the Son of Heaven, and thus mediator between heaven and earth, to determine the dates for the beginning of the agrarian seasons, festivities, mourning periods, and judicial assizes (periodic court sessions). The Chinese believed that the very stability of the empire depended on correct calculation of these dates. Even by modern standards, the Chinese were quite precise.

European missionaries and traders who arrived in China were greatly impressed by Chinese technological expertise, eloquence, and artistic refinement. Nonetheless, convinced of the superiority of their sciences, Christian missionaries sought to impress the Chinese with their knowledge in areas such as astronomy and cartography. Possessing sophisticated sciences of their own, the Chinese were selective in their appropriation of these novel European practices. To be sure, members of the Jesuit order served in the astronomy bureau within the imperial bureaucracy. In the early eighteenth century, they also undertook a series of monumental surveys of the Qing Empire for the emperor. Taken as a whole, however, the cultural impact of the Europeans in China in this period was decidedly limited.

Nowhere was this more evident than in the realm of cartography. Here, the Chinese demonstrated most clearly their understanding of the world. Significantly, Chinese maps were meant to encompass elements of history, literature, and art, not simply to offer technical detail. It was not that the necessary "scientific" techniques were lacking; a map made as early as 1136 reveals that Chinese cartographers were fully capable of producing maps drawn to scale. Yet, operating within a cultural context in which the written text was often privileged over visual and other forms of representation, Chinese elites did not always treat geometric and mathematical precision as the principal objective of cartography. Rather, these maps offered vivid testimony to the worldview of the Chinese elites. The realm of the Chinese emperor, as the ruler of "all under Heaven," typically occupied the very center of the map surrounded by foreign countries. As such, the physical scale of China and the actual size and distances to other lands were generally distorted. Still, some of the maps do manage to cover a vast expanse of territory. One fourteenth-century map includes an area stretching from Japan to the Atlantic, encompassing Europe and Africa.

Although Europeans might understand resistance to Christianization—they had, after all, long experience with heretics, infidels, and sectarian intransigence at home—they were puzzled by the Chinese resistance to the adoption of European science. In 1583, the Jesuit missionary Matteo Ricci brought European maps to China, hoping to impress the local elite with European learning. Ricci challenged the conventional wisdom of the Chinese elites, who held that the world was flat. His maps demonstrated the spherical shape of the earth—and that China was just one country among many other similar ones. Chinese critics complained that he treated the Ming Empire as just "a small unimportant country." As a concession, Ricci modified his projection and placed China closer to the center of the maps. He also followed the practice of Chinese cartographers in providing additional textual information. Still, the long-term impact of Ricci's maps was negligible. The makers of "Complete Maps of All under Heaven," who provided Qing China's images of the world until the mid-nineteenth century, did not consider the earth's shape or precise mathematical scale particularly important.

Jesuit Missionary. Shown in the garb of a Qing official, Father Johann Adam Schall von Bell was in Beijing when the Ming fell in 1644. Recognizing his scientific expertise, the new Qing government appointed him the director of the Imperial Bureau of Astronomy. Schall von Bell was close to the young Shunzhi Emperor, who called the Jesuit "Grandpa" and regularly discussed religion and politics with him.

CHINESE VIEWS OF THE WORLD

The Chinese developed cartographical skills at an early stage in their history. A third-century map, no longer extant, was designed to enable the emperors to "comprehend the four corners of the world without ever having to leave their imperial quarters." *The Huayi tu* map from 1136 depicted the whole world on stone stele and included 500 place names and textual information on foreign lands. The Jesuit missionary Matteo Ricci modified his original map of the world in response to Chinese concerns and placed China more in the center. Chinese maps devoted more attention to textual explanations that carried moral and political messages than to locating places. One such map is a Chinese wheel map, which is from the 1760s and is full of textual explanations.

The *Huayi tu* map, 1136.

Chinese wheel map, 1760s.

→ *Why do you think Chinese maps included textual messages that focused on moral and political themes?*

→ *How are these maps similar to and different from the Islamic maps?*

The European regime of spatial ordering, as represented through its cartography, was rejected as mostly irrelevant.

In China, prior to the nineteenth century, knowledge regarding foreign lands, despite a long history of contacts, remained rather partial. Like many other cultures, the Chinese empire cultivated an image of its own superiority and tended to see others through its own prism. From antiquity onward,

Chinese elites glorified their own "white" complexions against the dark skin of the peasants, the black, wavy-haired "devils" of Southeast Asia, and the "ash-white" pallor of the Europeans. Chinese writers often identified groups of people as oddities, to be scrutinized with a mixture of curiosity and revulsion. A Ming geographical publication, for example, portrayed the Portuguese as "seven feet tall, having eyes like a cat, a mouth like an oriole, an ash-white face, thick and curly beards like black gauze, and almost red hair." In a ten-volume compendium put together as late as the mid-eighteenth century, the authors vaguely described the "Great Western Ocean Country" as somewhere in the Atlantic region. They did not distinguish European countries from their Asian counterparts. They confused France with the Portugal known during Ming times, and they characterized England and Sweden as dependencies of Holland. During this period of cultural flourishing, in short, the Qing Empire did not yet feel any compelling reason to revise its view of the world.

CULTURAL IDENTITY AND TOKUGAWA JAPAN

Chinese cultural influence had long crossed the Sea of Japan. But during the Tokugawa Shogunate, there was also a renewed interest in a competing cultural model from Europe. Japanese interest in Europe grew via the Dutch presence in Japan and more limited contacts with Russians. In addition to such foreign influences, however, there was also a surge in "native learning," or the study of Japanese traditions and culture in the late seventeenth and especially eighteenth centuries. Thus, Tokugawa Japan found itself engaged in a three-cornered conversation among time-honored Chinese ways (transmitted via Korea), distinctly Japanese traditions, and European teachings. Increased trade, new prosperity in the land, and a long period of domestic and international peace were, in turn, accompanied by a remarkable cultural flowering that provided the background for debates over competing cultural models.

Until the sixteenth and seventeenth centuries, cultural patronage remained the preserve of the imperial court in Kyoto (which did not rule), the hereditary shogunate, religious institutions, and the upper class, about 5 percent of the population. Samurai (former warriors turned bureaucrats) and daimyo (the regional lords) favored a masked theater, called Nō, and an elegant ritual for making tea and engaging in contemplation. In their gardens, the lords built teahouses with stages for Nō drama. There arose hereditary schools of actors, tea masters, and cultivated flower arrangers. The upper classes also used the services of commoner-painters, who decorated tea utensils and other articles made of lacquer (dried sap of the sumac tree) and painted the brilliant interiors and standing screens in grand stone castles. Some upper-class men did their own painting, called literati painting, which was supposed to convey philosophical thoughts. Calligraphy was also proof of cultivation.

Alongside this elegant elite culture of theater and stylized painting arose a new, rougher urban culture, one that was patronized by artisans and especially merchants. Urban dwellers, consisting of 10 percent of the population by 1800, delighted in an array of popular entertainment; consumers could purchase works of fiction and colorful prints made

from carved wood blocks—also used to make books—that were often risqué. A new class of female entertainers appeared who were known as geisha because they were artistically skilled (*gei*) in the three-stringed instrument (*shamisen*), storytelling, and performing, though some were also prostitutes. Geisha could be found in officially approved pleasure quarters of the big cities, which were famous for their geisha houses, public baths, brothels, and theaters. Kabuki, a type of theater that combined song, dance, and skillful staging to dramatize conflicts between duty and passion, became a wildly popular diversion and art form characterized by bravura acting, brilliant makeup, and sumptuous costumes. In 1629, the shogunate, concerned for public order, banned female actors, and so men began to play women's roles. These male actors sometimes maintained their impersonations of females offstage, and they inspired trends in fashion for urban women.

Much Japanese popular entertainment chronicled the world of the common people rather than politics or high society. The pleasure-oriented culture of urbanites was known

Artist and Geisha at Tea. The erotic, luxuriant atmosphere of Japan's urban pleasure quarters was captured in a new art form, the *ukiyo-e*, or "pictures from a floating world." In this image set in Tokyo's celebrated Yoshiwara district, several geisha flutter about a male artist.

→ *How and why did the Chinese and Japanese governments attempt to control culture and knowledge?*

Kabuki Theater. Kabuki originated among dance troupes in the environs of temples and shrines in Kyoto in the late sixteenth and early seventeenth centuries. The characters used to denote *kabuki* mean "song, dance, and skill," though some scholars believe the term derives from a related word (*kabuku*) meaning eccentric, rakish, deviant, outlandish, or erotic. As kabuki spread to the urban centers of Japan, the theater designs enabled the actors to enter and exit from many directions and to step out into the audience, lending the skillful, raucous shows great intimacy.

as "the floating world" (*ukiyo*), and the woodblock prints depicting it as *ukiyo-e* (*e* meaning picture). Here, the normal order of society was temporarily turned upside down. The wealth of the socially low-ranked merchant trumped the official highly ranked samurai. Those who were otherwise looked down upon—actors, musicians, courtesans, and rakes—became idols and objects of dedicated imitation. To a degree, upper-class samurai partook of this "lower" culture. But to enter the pleasure quarters, samurai had to leave behind their swords, a prime mark of rank, since commoners were not allowed to carry such weapons.

Literacy in Japan approached a remarkable one-third of the population (it was far higher for men). The most popular novels sold 10,000 to 12,000 copies. In the late eighteenth century, Edo had some sixty booksellers and also had hundreds of book lenders, who provided an alternative to the relatively high cost of buying books and thereby spread them to a wider public. By the late eighteenth century, as books proliferated and some criticized the government, officials made arrests and sought to exercise control over publications.

THE INFLUENCE OF CHINA AND EUROPE ON JAPAN
In the realm of higher culture, China, the largest and wealthiest of Japan's neighbors, loomed large in the Tokugawa world. Japanese scholars wrote imperial histories of Japan in the Chinese style. Chinese law codes and other books at-

tracted a significant readership, and many Japanese wrote exclusively in Chinese. Some Japanese traveled south to Nagasaki just to meet Zen Buddhist masters and Chinese residents of cosmopolitan Nagasaki. Some Chinese monks were even allowed to found monasteries outside Nagasaki and to travel to Kyoto and occasionally to Edo to give lectures and construct temples.

Chinese Confucianism offered the Tokugawa Shogunate a set of politically useful teachings. Initially, Zen Buddhists and monks had nurtured the study of Confucian teachings, but in the seventeenth century, some devotees of Confucianism, encouraged by the political authorities, brought Buddhism outside monasteries and developed the doctrines into a lay school of thought. After 1640, all Japanese were required to register at a Buddhist temple.

Buddhist temples grew in number, but they did not displace the indigenous Japanese practice of ancestor veneration and worshipping gods in nature, later called Shintō (the way of the gods), which boasted an extensive network of shrines throughout the country. In Japan, the religious practices that were eventually called Shintō developed through adaptation of time-honored beliefs in spirits (*kami*) who were present in or closely associated with places (mountains, rivers, waterfalls, rocks, the moon) and activities (harvest, fertility). These spirits in nature and daily life had to be addressed for healing or other assistance. Some women under

Shintō served as *mikos*, a kind of shamaness who possessed special divinatory powers. These rituals competed with a powerful strain of neo-Confucianism that set down a set of moral and behavioral precepts. In 1762, someone compiled a "Greater Learning for Females" (*onna daigaku*), which has been attributed to the earlier writings of the botanist and thinker Kaibara Ekiken or Ekken (1630–1714) or to the record of his ideas by his wife, Kaibara Token (1652–1713), who was also a scholar. This influential text rendered the precepts of Confucianism accessible to nonscholars, while, in particular, explicitly outlining for the first time societal roles that stressed hierarchy based on age and gender as a way to ensure order. At the same time, any person's place in the social hierarchy, including a woman's, was also determined by merit, such as one's record of doing the right thing (propriety) and one's virtue.

By the early eighteenth century, neo-Confucian teachings of filial piety and loyalty to superiors had become the de facto official credo of the state. The new philosophy legitimated the social hierarchy and the absolutism of the political order, but it also instructed the shogun and the upper class to provide "benevolent administration" (*jinsei*) for the people's benefit.

In partial reaction to the official credo that adapted Chinese traditions to Japanese circumstances, but also out of a desire to venerate the greatness of Japan, some creative Japanese thinkers promoted nativist intellectual traditions drawn from Japan's past. After 1728, for example, Kada Azumamaro (1668–1736), a Shintō priest, initiated a movement stressing "native learning" and the celebration of Japanese texts. Subsequent proponents of native learning, such as Motoori Norinaga (1730–1801), emphasized Japanese uniqueness, helped codify the elements of a Japanese religious and cultural tradition, and denounced Confucianism and Buddhism as foreign contaminants from a country of disorder and deceit. A few also looked to the nonruling but uninterrupted imperial line in Kyoto for validation of Japan's intellectual lineage and cultural superiority. While some who called for the revival of rule by the dormant Japanese emperor were arrested, others went on to develop Japanese poetry, one of the art forms popular with both upper and lower social groups.

Not only did Chinese intellectual authority in Japan have to compete with a new native learning, but by the late seventeenth century, Japan was also tapping other imported sources of knowledge. In East Asia in the late seventeenth

Japanese Map of the World. Japanese maps underwent a shift in connection with their encounters with the Dutch. Here, in a map dated 1671, much information is incorporated about distant lands, both cartographically on the globe and pictorially, to the left, in two-person images representing various peoples of the world in their purported typical costumes.

century, Portuguese was the *lingua franca* (common language), and even the Dutch used it in communicating with the Japanese. By 1670, however, there was a guild of Japanese interpreters in Nagasaki who could speak and read Dutch and who accompanied Dutch merchants on trips to Edo. European knowledge also spread to high circles in Edo in 1709. In 1720, the shogunate lifted its ban on foreign books. Thereafter, European ideas, called "Dutch learning," circulated more openly. Scientific, geographical, and medical texts, such as *The New Book of Dissection,* were translated into Japanese and in some cases displaced Chinese texts, particularly for the calculation of important celestial phenomena. A Japanese-Dutch dictionary appeared in 1745, and the first official school of Dutch learning followed. Students of Dutch or European teachings remained a limited, if enthusiastic, segment of Japanese society, but the demand for translations rose appreciably.

One of the strong proponents of a European orientation was Honda Toshiaki (1744–1821), who traveled to Ezo to examine the frontier, studied European texts, and set his thoughts down in late-eighteenth-century unpublished manuscripts. Toshiaki believed that Japan should learn about and adapt European advances in science, especially geography and astronomy, which helped in ocean trade. He also praised European economic progress, while extolling the vastness and might of Japan's new neighbor to the north, the Russian Empire. For Toshiaki, the greatness of Japan depended on its ability to modernize. Nonetheless, despite his admiration for European advances, Toshiaki did not reject Confucianism, nor did he repudiate Japan's system of social ranks, based on Confucianism, and he showed Confucian contempt for unethical businessmen. What comes across most clearly in his celebrations of European prowess are his pragmatism about adaptation and his aspirations for Japan.

Japanese deliberations about what and how to borrow from the Europeans and the Chinese illustrate the vast changes that the world had undergone in the previous several centuries. A few hundred years earlier, products and ideas did travel, but they usually did not travel very far or make significant inroads into local cultural practices. By the eighteenth century, new networks of exchange and communication and new prosperity made the integration of foreign ideas into local cultures feasible and sometimes desirable. The Japanese were especially eager to choose among useful new ideas and practices and often to transform them. This selective openness to the ideas of foreigners stemmed from Japan's long historical relationship to outside influences, particularly its receptivity to Chinese thought and institutions. The Japanese did not consider embracing learning from overseas as a mark of inferiority or subordination, particularly when they knew that they could put new ideas to good use at home. This was not the case for the great Asian land-based empires, which were eager lenders but hesitant borrowers.

THE ENLIGHTENMENT IN EUROPE

> → *What were the major tenets of Enlightenment thought?*

An extraordinary cultural flourishing, often defined in intellectual terms as the Enlightenment but in fact a much broader series of developments, took place in Europe in the seventeenth and eighteenth centuries. This era was unique in the history of thought, in that the individuals who championed the new ideas sought not simply to sell them to the elite but to diffuse them widely. They wanted not only to change their contemporaries' worldviews but also to transform political and social institutions. Crucial for the success of their endeavor were widening patronage networks that extended beyond the traditional ecclesiastical and monarchical supporters of arts and sciences to the lower aristocracy and members of the bureaucratic and commercial elites. Equally important was an expansion in the methods and networks of communication that now included cafes and intellectual salons, newspapers, extensive exchanges of correspondence, public theaters, and book publishing. The men and women of letters of this period, although their ideas frequently clashed, nonetheless shared a desire to "spread light" and to change the way their societies were governed.

Abandoning traditional Christian belief in original sin and God's mysterious tamperings with natural forces and human events, Enlightenment thinkers aspired to know the world in new ways. They sought universal and objective knowledge, knowledge that would not depend on the knower's religion, political views, class, or gender. Recognizing no territorial boundaries, scholars sought to formulate natural laws, which they presumed applied everywhere and to all peoples. Most of these thinkers were quite unaware of the extent to which their "objective" knowledge was colored by European, upper-class, male perspectives.

ORIGINS OF THE ENLIGHTENMENT

Well into the seventeenth century, European culture continued to be defined by two major institutions: the Catholic and Protestant churches and the dynastic court system. After the Reformation, Europeans were more divided than ever into hostile states. While the sixteenth century brought new prosperity, the seventeenth century produced grand-scale disasters: civil and religious wars, dynastic conflicts, and famine. These crises devastated central Europe and bankrupted the Spanish; they resulted in five years of chaos in France (the "Fronde"), the execution of Charles I of England, and the

EUROPEAN VIEWS OF THE WORLD

As the Europeans became world travelers and traders, they needed accurate information on places and distances that they had reached so that they could get home as well as return to these sites. This meant forsaking their own tradition of placing Jerusalem at the world's core. Europe's first printed map to show the New World, the Waldseemüller map, was produced in 1507 and portrayed the Americas as a long and narrow strip of land, its unexplored landmass dwarfed by Asia and Africa. By the mid-seventeenth century, maps were seemingly more objective, yet European maps invariably grouped the rest of the world around the European countries. Moreover, the effort to make world maps that could actually be used for navigational purposes led to certain distortions (like the stretching of the polar zones in the popular 1569 Mercator projection) that made Europe seem disproportionately large and central. Had Europeans had a map, like the Peterson projection, only developed much later, in which the landmasses of the world were in correct geographical proportion to one another, Europe would have seemed quite small. Moreover, the mapmaker decided which territories appeared at the center of the map and which appeared on the edges. Maps made in Europe invariably grouped the rest of the world around the European countries.

Waldseemüller map, 1507.

Mercator projection, 1569.

→ *What are the most striking differences between the two maps?*

→ *How are these European maps similar to and different from the Islamic and Chinese ones?*

securing of Dutch independence from Spanish control. They contributed as well to the spread of Protestantism in Europe. But they also resulted in a general revulsion toward religious strife, a widespread desire among monarchs to centralize and regularize their powers, and a longing for impersonal, useful knowledge of the world.

By 1750, the sons and daughters of the lower clergy, of the provincial nobility, of the commercial classes, and even of skilled craftsmen had begun to participate in the production and consumption of the arts and sciences. A new set of cultural ambitions emerged as this group of literate, middle-class men and women gained confidence in their own worthiness —to create art, to write books, to observe the world accurately, and perhaps even to rule their states.

To understand the development of this confidence, and of Enlightenment knowledge as a whole, it is necessary to understand the powerful effects of the Reformation and Counter-Reformation in increasing literacy and the diffusion of the new science and its premises. But it is also important to take stock of the increasing contacts between Europeans and the wider world that had taken place since the fourteenth century. Europeans had been consumers of the cultural goods of other peoples. From the trapping methods of Native Americans to the crop cultivation techniques of African slaves, from Chinese porcelain to New World tobacco and chocolate, Europe in the seventeenth and eighteenth centuries continued to be shaped by its contact with others. Yet, European intellectuals became more and more critical of other cultures —and more confident that their culture was unique and su-

perior and that it should be the standard against which other cultures were judged.

THE NEW SCIENCE

The search for objective knowledge is most apparent in the seventeenth-century flourishing of natural science. Scientific visions of astronomers like Nicolaus Copernicus (1473–1542) and Galileo Galilei (1564–1642), once reviled by the church, now began to gain acceptance. Galileo's findings in mathematics, physics, and astronomy contradicted age-old assumptions. His belief that the earth revolved around the sun led to his publication of *Dialogue on the Two Chief Systems of the World* (1632) and to his subsequent trial (1633) for heresy. But this was a late, and much criticized, attempt to put the genie back in the bottle. By this time, a small but influential group of new scientists increasingly expected that theories were to be built on experiment and observation. The skepticism of the philosopher Sir Francis Bacon (1561–1626) became these scientists' unwritten code of conduct. According to Bacon, in such works as *The Advancement of Learning* (1605) and the *Novum Organum* (1620), the duty of the scientist was to observe and to test nature himself following the inductive method. By means of carefully controlled, empirical testing, Bacon believed that modern man could gradually comprehend the general principles of nature's manifold operations and thus bend nature to man's will. Bacon believed experiments should be conducted, samples collected,

Galileo. The Catholic Church was initially worried that the new science would undermine Christian faith. In 1633, the Italian scientist Galileo was put on trial for espousing heretical beliefs and was condemned to house arrest.

variables isolated; traditional authorities should not be trusted. Of course, Bacon was chiefly concerned that classical and medieval authorities be distrusted, but the principle would be the same when European scientists confronted traditional knowledge in the rest of the world. Confident of their own calculations, scientists like Isaac Newton (1642–1727) defined what they believed were the universal laws that applied to all matter and motion, and they disparaged all older conceptions of nature—from Aristotelian ideas to folkloric and foreign ones—as absurd and obsolete. Thus, in his *Principia Mathematica* (1687), Newton set forth the laws of motion, including the famous law of gravitation, which explained falling bodies on earth and planetary motion.

It is no longer fashionable to speak about the changing views of sixteenth- and seventeenth-century Europeans regarding nature and the universe as a scientific revolution. European thinking about nature and the universe did not change overnight. Only gradually and fitfully did a group of European thinkers come to see the natural world as operating according to inviolable laws that experimenters could fathom. But by the late seventeenth century monarchs and oligarchs, particularly in Protestant countries, had developed a new interest in science's discoveries, and many established royal academies of science to encourage local endeavors. This patronage, of course, was not purely disinterested; in incorporating the British Royal Society in 1662, for example, Charles II hoped to show not only that the crown backed scientific progress but also that England's great minds backed the crown. Similar reasoning was shown in the founding of the French Royal Academy of Sciences in 1666. Support for artistic monuments had a similar political function. In France, Louis XIV's erection of the fabulously expensive new palace complex at Versailles beginning in 1661 was meant to show not only that he had taste but also that he had power. The nobility, he meant to say, needed to look to him for both cultural and political guidance.

Gradually, science began to expand beyond court circles around 1700. By the early eighteenth century, the new science was becoming popular in elite circles; the upper-crust Marquise de Châtelet (1706–1749) built a scientific laboratory in her home and translated Newton's *Principia* into French. Groups of well-to-do landowners formed societies, like the Society for the Improvement of Knowledge in Agriculture—founded in Edinburgh in 1723—to discuss the latest methods of successful animal breeding. Military schools increasingly stressed engineering methods and thus produced graduates with refined technical skills. By about 1750, even artisans and journalists, especially in England, could be found applying Newtonian mechanics to their practical problems and inventions. In Italy, a number of female natural philosophers emerged, and the genre of scientific literature for "ladies" became popular. In 1763, the mathematician Diamante Medaglia Faini delivered an oration recommending that all women

Marquise de Chatelet-Lomont. Gabrielle-Emilie Le Tonnelier de Breteuil, Marquise de Chatelet-Lomont (1706–1749), was one of the few in her day to understand Newtonian physics. Her French translation of Newton's *Principia Mathematica* included extensive explanations of the science that informed Newton's thinking. Her lover and admirer Voltaire wrote of her, "She was a great man whose only fault was in being a woman."

seek to increase their knowledge of science. A consensus emerged among European proponents of the new science that useful knowledge came from collecting data and organizing it into universally valid systems, rather than from revered classical texts.

By no means, however, was the scientific worldview the only one held by Europeans; most still understood their relationships with God, nature, and fellow humans by reference to Christian doctrines on the one hand and local customs on the other. Although literacy was increasing, especially in northern Europe, it was by no means universal; schools remained church-governed or elite, male institutions. All governments employed censors and punished, often severely, radical thinkers; peasants still suffered under arbitrary systems of taxation, and judicial regimes had hardly improved since medieval times. It certainly cannot be said that science and rationality pervaded all spheres of European life by 1700.

Indeed, if it had been so, there would have been no need for the movement we now call the Enlightenment.

ENLIGHTENMENT THINKERS

Enlightenment thinkers like Voltaire (1694–1778), Denis Diderot (1713–1784), and Adam Smith (1723–1790) believed in the power of human reason and the perfectibility of humankind; they rejected the medieval belief in man's helplessness and God's remoteness. But while these writers affirmed the ultimate rationality of the universe, they also observed with unprecedented acuity the evils and flaws of human society in their day. Voltaire wrote scathing critiques of the torture of criminals; Diderot denounced the despotic tendencies of Louis XIV and Louis XV; Smith detailed the inefficiency of mercantile economics.

In general, Enlightenment thinkers trusted nature and individual human reason and distrusted institutions and traditions. "Man is born good," Jean-Jacques Rousseau (1712–1778) wrote in *Émile* (1762); "it is society that corrupts him." In *The Social Contract* (1762) Rousseau wrote about government as the expression of the general will and how the people could withdraw their support if the government violated this social contract. Moreover, in *Candide* (1759), Voltaire warned against undue optimism in a world suffused with stupidity, greed, and injustice. Like Rousseau and Voltaire, other Enlightenment thinkers believed that improvements could be made to human society but that there

was a great deal that needed to be altered. Their critiques of tradition, of religious and secular customs and authorities, and of barriers to social mobility were largely directed at contemporary European conditions, and they were often imprisoned or exiled as punishment for writing about what they considered to be superstitious beliefs and corrupt political structures.

The Enlightenment can be described as a pan-European movement, but the extent of its reach varied in different countries: in France and Britain, enlightened learning spread rather widely; in other places, like Spain, Poland, and Scandinavia, enlightened circles were small and had little influence either on the rulers or on the population at large. Enlightened thought flourished in commercial centers like Amsterdam and Edinburgh, and it also spread to colonial ports like Philadelphia and Boston. As education and literacy became more widespread in these commercial cities, book sales and newspaper circulation expanded. By 1770, approximately 3,500 different books and pamphlets were being produced each year in France alone, as compared to 1,000 in 1720. By 1776, about 12 million copies of newspapers were being issued in Britain.

POPULAR CULTURE In the emerging marketplace for new books, new ideas, and new visions, some of the most popular works were not from the high intellectuals of the period. Pamphlets alleging rampant corruption circulated widely wherever reading publics flourished; charges of fraudulent stock speculation and insider trading provided raw material

Salon of Madame Geoffrin. Much of the important work—and wit—of the Enlightenment was the product of private gatherings known as salons. Often hosted, like the one depicted here, by aristocratic women, these salons also welcomed down-at-the-heels writers and artists, offering everyone, at least in theory, the opportunity to discuss the sciences, the arts, politics, and the idiocies of their fellow humans on an equal basis.

for popular literary slander. Sex, too, sold well. While the works of Voltaire, for instance, enjoyed a respectable readership among France's increasingly literate population, some of the real best-sellers of the age came from the pens of cruder and more sensationalist essayists. Works like *Venus in the Cloister or the Nun in a Nightgown* (anonymous, with at least twenty-two editions between 1682 and 1782) sold as well as many of the now-classical works of the Enlightenment and were full of bawdy and irreligious material. These vulgar best-sellers took advantage of consumer demand—but they also seized the opportunity to mock icons of authority. In many of these works, nuns often came across as lascivious, priests as fornicators. Some were daring enough to go after the royal family, portraying Louis XV as a king fond of being spanked or Marie Antoinette copulating with her court confessor. In these cases, pornography—some of it even philosophical—spilled into the literary marketplace for political satire. These works display the seamier side of the Enlightenment. But they too spoke of the willingness of intellectuals—high and low alike—to explore new and iconoclastic modes of thought.

Those who were part of the growing reading public also participated in the creation of a whole new set of cultural institutions and practices. In Britain and Germany, book clubs proliferated and coffeehouses sprang up to cater to sober men of business and learning; here, aristocrats and well-to-do commoners could read some of the first news sheets or discuss stock prices, political affairs, or technological novelties. The same sort of noncourtly socializing was available in Parisian salons, over which female aristocrats often presided. Able to speak their minds more openly in these private settings than at court or at public assemblies, women here exchanged ideas quite freely with men. The most successful salons were the ones renowned for witty gossip, but would-be philosophers and writers also attended in order to secure jobs as secretaries or to obtain commissions for their projects. Libraries began to open their doors to the public. It must be understood, however, that aristocratic, royal, and even ecclesiastical patronage remained the major source of funding for intellectuals in this age; in the German states, Enlightenment thinkers were chiefly university professors, bureaucrats, and pastors. Art collecting boomed—primarily because local aristocrats found it a means to display their good taste, wealth, and distance from the rabble.

CHALLENGES TO AUTHORITY AND TRADITION   While they took the aristocracy's money, many Enlightenment thinkers nonetheless sought to overturn the status distinc-

tions that defined the worth of individuals in Europe at this time. They emphasized merit rather than birth as the basis for status. John Locke (1632–1704) claimed that man was born with a mind that was a clean slate (*tabula rasa*) and acquired all his ideas as a result of experience. Locke's *Essay Concerning Human Understanding* (1690) stressed that cultural differences were the result not of unequal natural endowments, but rather of unequal opportunities to develop men's faculties. Similarly, in *The Wealth of Nations* (1776), Adam Smith remarked that there was little difference (other than education) between a philosopher and a street porter. Both had been endowed with reason, and were (or should be) free to rise in society according to their talents. Yet, Locke and Smith still believed that a mixed set of social and political institutions would be needed to regulate relationships between ever-imperfect humans. Moreover, they did not believe that women could act as independent, rational individuals in the same way that all men, presumably, could. Although educated women like Mary Wollstonecraft and Olympe de Gouges took up the pen to protest these inequities, the Enlightenment actually did little to change the subordinate status of women in European society.

Inspired by the new science, many Enlightenment thinkers sought to discover the "laws" of human behavior, an endeavor closely bound up with criticism of existing governments. Explaining the laws of economic relations was chiefly the work of Adam Smith. His *The Wealth of Nations*, in which he described universal economic laws, was one of the most influential and long-lived of enlightened treatises. Smith claimed that unregulated markets in a laissez-faire economy best suited mankind because they allowed our "trucking and bartering" nature full expression. In Smith's view, the "invisible hand" of the market, rather than the regulations of government, would lead to general prosperity and social peace. Interestingly, Smith was quite conscious of growing economic gaps between the "civilized and thriving" and the "savage" nations, which remained so miserably poor, that in Smith's view, they were reduced to infanticide, starvation, and euthanasia. Yet, he believed that until these nations learned to play by what he called nature's laws, they could not expect a happy fate. Smith was just one of many Enlightenment thinkers to paint a picture of what they believed to be universal laws that offered non-Europeans no other solution but that of imitation.

One of the most controversial realms for the application of universal laws was that of religion. Although few Enlightenment thinkers were actually atheists, most advocated some kind of religious toleration, insisting that reason, not force,

> *Inspired by the new science, many Enlightenment thinkers sought to discover the "laws" of human behavior, an endeavor closely bound up with criticism of existing governments.*

was the means to create a community of believers and moral actors. For European audiences, these critiques of church authorities and practices were highly controversial. States often reacted to radical critiques by censoring books or exiling writers, but some princes were convinced by these arguments. In response, acts of toleration were passed in the late eighteenth century by governments from Denmark to Austria offering religious minorities some freedom of worship. Toleration did not mean, however, that full civil rights were bestowed on, for example, Catholics in England or Jews anywhere in Europe. Toleration simply meant a loosening of religious uniformity, and the population as a whole often resented even this. The "No Popery" riots in Edinburgh and Glasgow in 1779, for example, compelled the British government to withdraw its proposed moderation of restrictions on Catholics.

The Enlightenment produced numerous works that purported to encompass universal knowledge, the most important of which was the French *Encyclopedia,* which began to be published in 1751 and would run to twenty-eight volumes by 1772. Nearly 200 intellectuals, including Voltaire and Rousseau, contributed essays; it was extremely popular among the elite, despite its political, religious, and intellectual radicalism. Its purpose, claimed Diderot, its editor and energizing force, was "to collect all the knowledge scattered over the face of the earth" and to make it useful to men and women in the present and future. Indeed, the *Encyclopedia* offered a wealth of information about the rest of the world, including more than 2,300 articles (constituting 4 percent of the total word space) that treated Islam. Here, quite typically, the authors praised Arab culture for preserving and even extending Greek and Roman science, and in doing so, preparing the way for scientific advances in Europe. But predictably, too, the *Encyclopedia* writers portrayed Islam with the same malevolence that they applied to all other organized religions, condemning Muhammad as the apostle of a bloodthirsty religion and Muslim culture in general for its inability to renounce superstition.

Enlightenment thinkers also championed a new cultural hierarchy that extolled commerce and rationality and placed those regions of the world that lacked these ingredients at the bottom of the world's cultures. While praising some of the world's cultures like the Chinese for having achieved much in these areas, Enlightenment thinkers were confident that Europe was advancing over the rest of the world in its acquisition of goods and universal knowledge.

Absolutist governments were not entirely hostile to enlightened ideas, recognizing the virtues of universality (as in a universally applicable system of taxation) and precision (as in a well-drilled army). After all, social mobility allowed more skilled bureaucrats to rise through the ranks, while commerce provided the state with new riches. Knowledge collection, too, appealed to states that had begun to exert greater and greater dominion over their subjects; Louis XIV was persuaded to establish a census, though he never carried it out, so that he could "know with certitude in what consists his grandeur, his wealth, and his strength." Some enlightened princes, like Frederick II of Prussia and Joseph II of Austria, even instituted impressive legal reforms and backed innovations in the arts and agriculture and were accordingly idolized by Enlightenment thinkers, who liked their "top down" approach

ENCYCLOPEDIE,

O U

DICTIONNAIRE RAISONNÉ

DES SCIENCES,

DES ARTS ET DES MÉTIERS,

PAR UNE SOCIÉTÉ DE GENS DE LETTRES.

Mis en ordre & publié par M. *DIDEROT*, de l'Académie Royale des Sciences & des Belles-Lettres de Pruſſe; & quant à la PARTIE MATHÉMATIQUE, par M. *D'ALEMBERT*, de l'Académie Royale des Sciences de Paris, de celle de Pruſſe, & de la Société Royale de Londres.

Tantùm ſeries juncturaque pollet,
Tantùm de medio ſumptis accedit honoris! HORAT.

TOME PREMIER.

A PARIS,

Chez { BRIASSON, *rue Saint Jacques, à la Science.*
DAVID l'aîné, *rue Saint Jacques, à la Plume d'or.*
LE BRETON, Imprimeur ordinaire du Roy, *rue de la Harpe.*
DURAND, *rue Saint Jacques, à Saint Landry, & au Griffon.*

M. DCC. LI.

AVEC APPROBATION ET PRIVILÈGE DU ROY.

Title Page of the *Encyclopedia*. Originally published in 1751, the *Encyclopedia* was the most comprehensive work of learning of the French Enlightenment. The title page features an image of light and reason being dispersed throughout the land. The title itself identifies the work as a dictionary, based on reason, that deals not just with the sciences but also with the arts and occupations. It identifies two of the leading men of letters (*gens de lettres*), Denis Diderot and Jean le Rond d'Alembert, as the primary authors of the work.

The *Encyclopedia* on Pin Making. Contributors to the *Encyclopedia* included craftsmen as well as intellectuals. This detailed illustration of a pin factory and the processes and machinery employed in pin making is from a plate in the fourth volume of the *Encyclopedia* and demonstrates its emphasis on practical information.

to reform. The Enlightenment was responsible for spreading the idea of liberty far and wide, even to the women, lower-class men, and enslaved peoples whom European elites were less sure deserved it. But many eighteenth-century male thinkers, like their absolutist sovereigns, were quite uncomfortable with the idea of offering liberty and equality (not to mention sovereignty) to *all* the people.

AFRICAN CULTURAL FLOURISHING

> → *How did global entanglements, particularly involvement in the slave trade, reshape African cultures?*

Unbeknownst to much of the rest of the world, kingdoms throughout Africa had strong artisanal and artistic traditions dating back centuries. But as in Europe, new wealth from the slave trade gave the upper classes the ability to fund new cultural achievements. Africa was more like East Asia, however, in that it maintained local forms of cultural production, such as wood carving, weaving, and metal-working.

Cultural traditions in Africa varied by the different kingdoms, but there were patterns among them. West African ruling classes encouraged local artisans to produce carvings, statues, masks, and other objects that would extol the power and achievements of rulers, as royal patrons in Europe, Asia, and the Islamic world would do with architecture and painting. Also widespread in West African kingdoms was a belief that rulers had the blessing of the gods, and if they were not themselves descendants of the divinities, their families were thought to enjoy spiritual sanction. Arts and crafts not only glorified royal power, they were also thought to capture the energy of a universe that was believed to be suffused with spiritual beings. Starting in the 1500s and culminating in the 1700s when the slave trade reached its zenith, African rulers had even more reason—and means—to support cultural pursuits, because as destructive and debilitating as the slave trade was for the peoples of Africa, it made the most successful slave-trading states wealthy and powerful.

THE ASANTE, OYO, AND BENIN CULTURAL TRADITIONS

The kingdom of Asante, which became prominent in the slave trade in the seventeenth and eighteenth centuries, was also well known because of its access to gold. It used its gold

Asante Gold Discs. Gold discs like these were hung on chains and worn around the necks of kings' servants and often by kings themselves.

mines to celebrate its royal tradition, crafting magnificent seats or stools coated with gold as the symbols of the authority of the chiefs. The most ornate of the golden royal stools was reserved for the titular head of the Asante federation, the Asantehene, who ruled his far-flung empire from the capital city of Kumasi and who ventured out from his secluded royal palace rarely except on ceremonial and feast days. When he would emerge, he would be clad in sumptuous garments, the famed Kente cloth woven by the artisans of his state, and hold aloft maces, spears, staffs, and other symbols of power fashioned from the abundant gold supplies in the kingdom. These articles were intended to reveal his connection to the gods.

Equally resplendent were the rulers of the Oyo Empire and Benin located in the territory that now constitutes Nigeria. The bronzes of Ife, capital city of the Yoruba Oyo Empire, are among the most elegant and sophisticated pieces of art to be found anywhere in the world. According to one commentator, they were so impressive that "little that Italy or Greece or Egypt ever produced could be finer and the appeal of their beauty is immediate and universal." Although the Ife heads were not discovered until just before World War II, they mark the high point of Yoruba craft and artistic tradition that dated back to the first millennium CE. Their elegance, refinement, and repose reflected the esteem in which the Yoruba peoples held their rulers. The best known of these works were fashioned before the slave trade era in the thirteenth century, but the tradition was maintained and elaborated in the seventeenth and eighteenth centuries.

Benin has come down through the historical records as one of the most fearsome and brutal slave-trading regimes in Africa. Whether this reputation was deserved or rather part of Europe's later desire to label African rulers as "savage" in order to justify their conquest of the landmass cannot detract from the originality and beauty of the famed Benin bronzes. Many of the terra-cotta and bronze heads did not become known outside Benin until the kingdom had been conquered by a British expeditionary force in 1897. Among the finds was a remarkable brass head dating from 1515, which was worn by a ruler (the Ata of Idah) whom the Benin forces subdued at the beginning of the sixteenth century. Benin craftsmen did not confine themselves to heads. They were also expert at presenting the whole body of the ruling classes, which they clothed in the most elaborate fighting attire.

In those parts of Africa little affected by Islam entering from the north and the east and European influences operating along the slaving coasts of west, central, and east Africa, African cultural traditions developed relatively uninfluenced by outside elements throughout the seventeenth and eighteenth centuries. The magnificent artistic achievements of the tropical rainforest peoples of west and central Africa became known to the rest of the world only as a result of

Brass Oba Head. The brass head of an Oba, or king, of Benin. The kingdom's brass and bronze work was among the finest in all of Africa.

European colonial conquests in the late nineteenth and early twentieth centuries. By contrast, where the slave trade flourished, those traditions were more deeply affected, often by the transfer of craftsmen across the Atlantic as slaves. Though some African crafts would be transferred to the Americas, African artistic skills were not valued by the Europeanized elite. The colonizers in the Americas had their own aesthetic tastes, which they tended to impose on others.

HYBRID CULTURES IN THE AMERICAS

> → *How did cultural developments in the Americas reflect new global entanglements?*

In the Americas, mingling between European colonizers and native peoples (as well as African slaves) produced new, hybrid cultures. But this syncretism, or mixing, of cultures grew increasingly unbalanced as Europeans imposed their political and cultural authority over more and more of the Americas. For Native Americans, the pressure to adapt their cultures to those of the European colonists began with their first encounters (indeed, in some places, such as North America's Great Plains, where horses spread ahead of European colonizers, borrowing and cultural adaptations preceded human contacts). Over time, Indians faced mounting pressure to accept the ways of Europeans, who insisted that their conquests and colonizations were not simply military endeavors but also spiritual errands. In addition to their guns and germs, all of Europe's colonizers brought their bibles, prayerbooks, and crucifixes. With these, they set out to Christianize and "civilize" the Indian and African populations in the Americas. Still, even with the imbalance of military power, the efforts of Christian missionaries to convert Indians and slaves produced uneven and often unpredictable outcomes. Indian and African converts adopted Christian beliefs and practices, but they also often retained older religious practices.

European colonists, too, adapted to their new cultural environments, borrowing from the peoples they subjugated and enslaved. This was especially true in the sixteenth and seventeenth centuries, when the survival of Europeans in the New World often depended on such adaptations. By the middle of the eighteenth century, however, many American settlements had achieved a level of stability and prosperity, and colonists became less and less likely to admit their past dependency on others. New sorts of hierarchies emerged, and elites in Latin and North America began increasingly to set their cultural standards according to the tastes and fashions of European aristocrats. Yet, even as they imitated Old World

ways, these colonials also forged identities that separated them from Europe.

SPIRITUAL ENCOUNTERS

In the New World, unlike in other European colonial outposts, settlers possessed the military and economic power to impose their culture and especially their religion on indigenous peoples on an unprecedented scale. Although the Jesuits had relatively little impact in China and the Islamic world, Christian missionaries in the Americas had armies and officials to support their insistence that indigenous peoples and African slaves abandon their own deities and spirits for Christ.

European missionaries, especially Catholics, employed a vast range of techniques to bring and keep Indians within the Christian fold. Smashing idols, razing temples, and whipping backsliders all belonged to the missionaries' arsenal. Dominicans, Jesuits, and Franciscans also learned what they could about Indian beliefs and rituals and used their knowledge in their efforts to make conversions to Christianity. Many of the missionaries found it useful to demonize native gods, subvert indigenous spiritual leaders, and transform In-

Indians Becoming Christians. This image is from a colonial chronicle, illustrated and narrated by indigenous scribes who had converted to Christianity. The picture of Indians before the conquest entering a house of prayer is intended to represent the Indians as proto-Christians.

dian iconography into Christian symbols. But historians have reason to be grateful to these missionaries, for they are responsible for preserving much of the linguistic and ethnographic information about these communities that survives. In sixteenth-century Mexico, the Dominican friar Bernardino de Sahagún compiled an immense ethnography of Mexican ways and beliefs. In seventeenth-century Canada, French Jesuits prepared dictionaries and grammars of the Iroquoian and Algonquian languages and translated Christian hymns into Amerindian tongues.

Neither gentle persuasion nor violent coercion produced the results that missionaries desired. When conversions did occur, the Christianity practiced was usually a hybrid form in which indigenous deities and rituals merged with newly adopted Christian ones. Among Andean mountain people, for example, priestesses of native cults were given the name of Maria to mask their secret worship of the traditional deities of local kinship groups. In other cases, indigenous communities made no secret of their disdain for missionaries. They simply turned their backs on Christianity and accused missionaries of bringing plague and death. New converts tended to see Christian spiritual power as an addition to, not as a replacement for, their own religions.

More distressing to missionaries than evidence of syncretic beliefs and outright defiance were the successes of Indians in converting colonists. Many Indian groups had long practiced adoption of captives. Such adoptions were a common means to replenish numbers and replace lost kin. That many colonists adjusted to their captivity and accepted their adoptions, refusing to return to colonial society even when given

the chance, was deeply troubling to missionaries. So were those Europeans who chose to live among the Indians. Comparing the records of cultural conversion, one eighteenth-century colonist in British America suggested that "thousands of Europeans are Indians," yet, "we have no examples of even one of those Aborigines having from choice become European." While this calculation exaggerated the imbalance in rates of intercultural borrowing, it points to the fact that Europeans who adopted Indian culture, like Christianized Indians, lived in a mixed cultural world. Indeed, their familiarity with both Indian and European ways made them ideal cultural brokers, intermediaries who facilitated diplomatic arrangements and economic exchanges.

Beyond the attractions of Indian cultures, Europeans were inclined to mix with Indians because of the demography of colonization. Almost all of the early European traders, missionaries, and settlers were men, and the preponderance of male colonists remained true in all but the British North American settlements. In response to the scarcity of women and as a means to acculturate native peoples, the Portuguese crown authorized intermarriage between Portuguese men and local women. In truth, colonizing men needed no official encouragement to consort with native women; indeed, these relations often amounted to little more than rape. But in those places where Indians retained their independence, longer-lasting relationships were common, as among French fur traders and Indian women in Canada, the Great Lakes region, and the Mississippi Valley. Whether by coercion or consent, sexual relations between European men and native women created

Racial Mixing. (*Left*) This image shows racial mixing in colonial Mexico—the father is Spanish, the mother Indian, and the child a mestizo. This is a well-to-do family, illustrating how Europeans married into the native aristocracy. (*Right*) Here too we see a racially mixed family. The father is Spanish, the mother black or African, and the child a mulatto. Observe, however, the less aristocratic and markedly less peaceful nature of this family.

new, hybrid peoples—the mestizos of Spanish colonies and the métis of French outposts, who soon outnumbered settlers of wholly European ancestry.

The increasing numbers of Africans who were forcibly transported to the Americas added to and complicated the mix of New World cultures. In contrast with the marriages between fur traders and Indian women, in which the latter held considerable power thanks to the connections they offered to Indian trading partners, the sexual intercourse between European slaveholding men and enslaved African women almost always rested on coercion. The children who were born from such unions swelled the ranks of mixed ancestry people in the colonial population. Europeans initiated campaigns to Christianize slaves, though many slave owners expressed doubts about the wisdom of converting persons they regarded as mere property. Protestants had more difficulty than Catholics in reconciling the belief that Africans could be both slaves and Christians, and they were less aggressive than Catholics in mounting missionary efforts.

Sent forth with papal blessing, Catholic priests went to work among the slave populations of the American colonies of Portugal, Spain, and France. Employing many of the same techniques that had been used with Indian "heathens," missionaries produced similarly syncretic results. Often converts blended Islamic or indigenous African religions with Catholicism. Converted slaves wove remembered practices and beliefs into their American Christianity, transforming both along the way. In the northeast of Brazil, for example, slaves combined the Yoruba faiths of their ancestors with Catholic beliefs, and they frequently attributed powers of African deities to Christian saints. Sometimes Christian and African faiths were practiced side by side, as in the case of *candomblé*, a Yoruba-based religion in northern Brazil, where slaves from the Oyo and Dahomey kingdoms were shipped in large numbers. In Saint Domingue, slaves and free blacks practiced *vodun* (meaning "spirit" in the Dahomey tongue) and in Cuba, *santería*, a faith of similar origins.

Just as slaveholders feared, Christianity, especially in its syncretic forms, could inspire resistance, even revolt, among slaves. A major maroon (runaway slave) leader in mid-eighteenth-century Surinam was a Christian. In the English colonies, those held in bondage drew inspiration from Christian hymns that promised deliverance and embraced as their own the Old Testament's story of Moses leading the Israelites out of Egypt. By the end of the eighteenth century, freed slaves like the Methodist Olaudah Equiano were saying in their own voices that slavery was unjust and incompatible with Christian brotherhood.

THE MAKING OF COLONIAL CULTURES

In Spanish America, widespread ethnic and cultural mixing led to the emergence of a powerful new class, the creoles, persons of European descent who were born in the Americas. By the latter part of the eighteenth century, creoles had become increasingly restive about the control that "peninsulars"—men and women born in Spain or Portugal—had over colonial society. Mercantilist restrictions, which gave peninsular merchants exclusive privileges and forbade creoles from trading with other colonial ports, fired local resentments. So, too, did the practice of royal ministers who dished out most official posts to peninsulars. While the Spanish and Portuguese rulers did occasionally soften the discriminatory blows for fear of angering the creoles, their reforms often aggravated tensions with peninsulars.

The growing sense of creole identity also stemmed from the dissemination of new ideas in the colonies, especially many of the notions circulating in the rest of the Atlantic world under the umbrella of the Enlightenment. Abbé Raynal's *History of the Settlements and Trade of the Europeans in the East and West Indies* (1770), for example, was one of the favorite texts among the colonial reading circles in Buenos Aires and Rio de Janeiro. As a history of colonization in the New World, it was unkind to Iberian emperors and conquerors—and often helped creoles justify their dissatisfaction. Other French works were also popular, especially those of Rousseau. So were some English texts, like Adam Smith's *The Wealth of Nations*. Although Smith's treatise was not translated into Spanish until the 1790s (the Portuguese translation came even later), educated creoles read it with ease in English. Smith's reformist spirit contributed to creole impressions that mercantilist Iberian authorities were political and economic laggards.

In many of the cities of the Spanish and Portuguese empires, reading clubs and salons provided environments where fresh ideas and concepts could be deliberated. Even among Catholic circles, Rousseau was made to fit a Christian critique of Spanish exploitation of the natives. In one university in Upper Peru, Catholic scholars taught their students that Spanish labor drafts and taxes on Andean natives were more than a violation of divine justice; they offended the natural rights of free men. The Spanish crown, recognizing the importance of printing presses in the spread of insidious ideas, strictly controlled the number and location of printers in the colonies; in Brazil, the royal authorities banned them altogether. In spite of these controls, books, pamphlets, and

> *By the latter part of the eighteenth century, creoles had become increasingly restive about the control that "peninsulars" had over colonial society.*

simple gossip allowed new notions of science, history, and politics to circulate widely among literate creoles.

Wealthy colonists in British America were similar to the creole elites in Spanish and Portuguese America. They, too, strove to emulate European ways, using their profits to construct "big houses" in Virginia modeled on the country estates of English gentlemen, to import opulent furnishings and fashions from the finest British stores, and to exercise more control over colonial assemblies. Becoming like the English also involved a solidification of patriarchal authority at all levels, but especially among the colonial elite. In seventeenth-century Virginia, men had vastly outnumbered women, which gave women a measure of power, with widows in particular gaining hold of substantial property. During the eighteenth century, however, sex ratios became more equal, and women's property rights diminished as they reverted to English norms. Symbolically, the new order was displayed in countless family portraits, where husband-patriarchs were customarily pictured above their wives and children.

Intellectually, too, British Americans were linked to Europe, importing enormous numbers of books and journals. Indeed, Americans played a significant role in the Enlightenment, serving as both producers and consumers of political pamphlets, scientific treatises, and social critiques. Drawing on the words of Montesquieu (1689–1755), Locke, and Rousseau, genteel American intellectuals created the most famous of enlightened documents, the Declaration of Independence (1776), which announced that all men were endowed with equal rights and created to pursue this worldly happiness. Here, Anglicized Americans showed themselves, like the creole elites of Latin America, to be both European and products of New World encounters.

Chronometer. In the 1760s, the English clockmaker John Harrison perfected the chronometer, a timepiece mariners could use to reckon longitude while at sea. Although the Royal Scientific Society initially refused to believe that Harrison had solved this long-standing problem, Harrison's instrument made navigation so much safer and more predictable that it became standard equipment on European ships.

IMPERIALISM IN OCEANIA

> → *What role did race play in how Europeans viewed others, especially those from Oceania?*

Not only in Europe and the Americas, but also in the South Pacific, especially in Australia, a new, enlightened form of cultural aggrandizement was under way in the eighteenth century. Though in centuries past Hindu, Buddhist, Islamic, and Chinese missionaries and traders had brought their cultures to Malaysia and nearby islands, they had not ventured beyond Timor. Europeans began to do so in the years after 1770. Using their new wealth—public and private—to fund voyages that were both scientific and political, Europeans invaded these remaining aboriginal areas. The results were

mixed: while some islands maintained their autonomy, through resistance or European disinterest, the biggest prize, Australia, underwent thorough Anglicization.

Until Europeans colonized it in the late eighteenth century, Australia was truly a world apart. Separated by water and sheer distance from other regions, it was characterized primarily by its generally harsh natural conditions and sparse population. At the time of the European colonization, the island was home to around 300,000 people, mostly hunter-gatherers. While seafarers from Java, Timor, and particularly the port of Makassar were likely to have ventured into the area in the past, there was little evidence that either Chinese or Muslim merchants ever strayed that far south despite their active involvement in the Southeast Asian trade.

Europeans had visited Oceania before the eighteenth century. Spices drew the Portuguese and Dutch into the South Pacific (see Chapter 13). The Spanish had regularly plied the Pacific waters on their travels between Manila and Acapulco, but they had made habitual stops only in Guam and the Mariana Islands. In the 1670s and 1680s, they attempted to conquer these islands, and despite considerable resistance, finally succeeded in doing so by 1700. The Dutch visited Easter Island in 1722, and the French arrived in Tahiti in 1767. The Portuguese (in the sixteenth century) and the Dutch (in the seventeenth century) had seen the northern and western

MAP 14-1 SOUTHEAST ASIA

Captain Cook's voyages throughout the Pacific Ocean symbolized a new era in European exploration of other societies. Where did Cook explore and what peoples did he encounter? How did Cook's endeavors symbolize "scientific" imperialism? How are his explorations similar to those of Christopher Columbus three centuries earlier? How are they different?

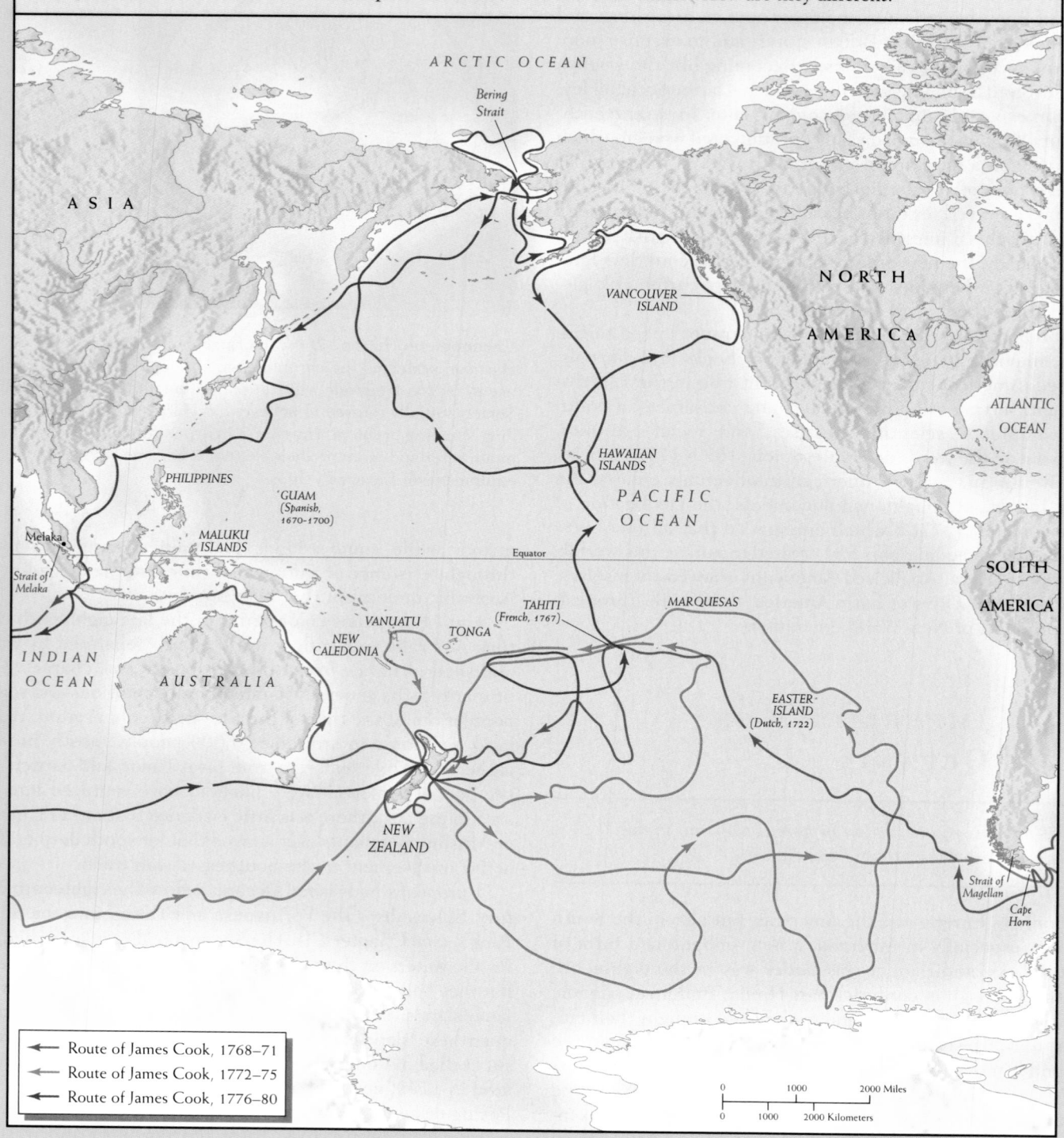

- ←—— Route of James Cook, 1768–71
- ←—— Route of James Cook, 1772–75
- ←—— Route of James Cook, 1776–80

coasts of Australia, but they had found only sand, flies, and Aborigines. Not until the late eighteenth century did Europeans see Australia's verdant eastern coast or find grounds for serious interest in colonization.

THE SCIENTIFIC VOYAGES OF CAPTAIN COOK

In Oceania and the South Pacific, Europeans experimented with a scientific form of imperialism. The story of the region's most famous explorer, Captain James Cook, shows how intimately related science and imperialist ventures could be and how cultural exchange became unequal even before the onset of the industrial age. As Columbus was a man of a mystical age, Cook was a man of an enlightened one—but both served the cause of European expansion. Cook's voyages and his encounter with the South Sea Islanders opened up the Pacific, and particularly Australia, to European colonizers. Captain Cook has become a legendary figure in European cultural history, portrayed as one of the saintly scientists of enlightened progress. Charged by the Royal Society with the scholarly task of observing the transit of the planet Venus from the Southern Hemisphere and by the British government with the more pragmatic, if secret, mission of finding and claiming "the southern continent" for Britain, Cook set sail for the Pacific in 1768. This voyage proved so fruitful that Cook was sent back on two more scientific-imperial adventures. The extremely popular accounts of his discoveries, and the engravings that accompanied them, opened up the exotic worlds of Tahiti, New Zealand, Australia, and Hawaii to European scrutiny. They also prepared the way for a new, more intensive sort of cultural colonization.

Cook was chosen to head the first expedition because he, like many of his British contemporaries, was scientifically inclined. Although he had little schooling, Cook had gone to sea early and, through long experience in navigating the uncharted waters of Newfoundland, had developed excellent surveying skills. Besides Cook, the Royal Society sent on the expedition one of its members, Joseph Banks, a gentlemanly but serious botanist; Daniel Solander, a doctor and student of the renowned Swedish botanist Linnaeus; and a number of artists and scientists. The crew also took along sophisticated instruments, and they were asked to keep extensive, detailed diaries. This was to be a grand data-collecting odyssey, a heroic, scientific response to recent French expeditions to the same regions.

Cook's voyages surpassed even the Royal Society's hopes. It is said that on his three voyages to the South Pacific between 1768 and 1779, the scientists made about 3,000 drawings of Pacific plants, birds, landscapes, and peoples never seen before in Europe. Naturally, the flora and fauna were described according to the new Linnaean classificatory system, and the geographical features were given English desig-

Captain James Cook. During his celebrated voyages to the South Pacific, Cook kept meticulous maps and diaries. Although he had little formal education, he became one of the great exemplars of enlightened learning through experience and experiment.

nations, like the Bay of Good Success, where Cook's ship the *Endeavour* anchored in 1769. Cook and his crew kept meticulous diaries and records, which fascinated scholars, travelers, missionaries, and government officials across Europe. Just as many poems and plays were written in celebration of the great navigator, Cook's expeditions were also considered state-of-the-art scientific practice.

More than a mere trading area, Australia was intended to supply Britain with raw materials. But the Aborigines of Australia, like the Indians of the Americas, succumbed in great numbers to new imported diseases, and survivors generally fled to escape dependency on British masters. Thus, to secure a labor force, plans were developed for grand-scale conquest and resettlement by and for British colonists. On his third voyage, Cook took with him a veritable Noah's ark of animals and plants with which to turn the South Pacific into a European-style garden. Cook's lieutenant, William Bligh, later brought apples, quinces, strawberries, and rosemary to Australia; the seventy sheep imported in 1788 laid the foundations for the region's wool-growing economy. The domestication of Australia was born from certainty about Europeans' superior know-how and a desire to make the landmass as a whole serve British interests.

In 1788, a British military expedition took official possession of the whole eastern half of Australia. The intent was, in part, to set up a prison colony far from home. This plan, too, belonged to the realm of enlightened dreams: that of ridding "civilized" society of all evils by resettling the lawbreakers among the "uncivilized" (previously convicts had been sent to Georgia in North America). Australia, too, was to be exploited for its timber and flax and used as a strategic base against Dutch and French expansion. In the next decades, immigration —free and forced—increased the Anglo-Australian population from an original 1,000 to about 1.2 million by 1860. Importing their customs and their capital, British settlers turned Australia into a frontier version of home, just as they had done in British America. Yet, as in the Americas, such large-scale immigration had disastrous consequences for the Aborigines. Like the Native Americans, the original inhabitants of Australia were decimated by diseases and increasingly forced westward by European settlement.

In one important way Cook had not departed so decisively from the practices of the past. Earlier travelers had developed an efficient means of studying foreign peoples and their languages: taking certain of them to Europe, by kidnapping if necessary. On his first voyage to the New World, Columbus captured six Amerindians and took them back to Spain, to show off these exotic people and so that they could learn Spanish and thus serve as intermediaries between the two cultures. Other explorers did the same, seizing local people, taking them to Europe, and even putting them on display. This was not the way that Europeans learned the languages of peoples they considered to be civilized, for example, the Chinese and Arabs; texts stood in for living bodies of "civilized" peoples. But exhibiting live individuals continued to be a crude means of ethnography for peoples the Europeans

Omai. Omai, the South Sea Islander brought to England by Captain Cook, was the object of much curiosity in London in the 1780s.

considered uncivilized. Through the nineteenth century, exhibitions of Laplanders, Africans, and Polynesians traveled, circus-like, from town to town through Europe. Cook himself captured and transported to England a highly skilled Polynesian navigator, Omai. Arriving in 1774, Omai quickly became the talk of London society and symbolized for some people the innocence and beauty that was being lost as Europe developed complicated machines and stock exchanges. Cook's return of Omai to his home on his third voyage was a sensation of equal proportions, seen as a colossally generous act by the revered British explorer.

Engraving from Cook's *Voyage Round the World in the Years 1768–1771*. Kangaroos were unknown in the West until Cook and his colleagues encountered (and ate) them on their first visit to Australia. This engraving of the animal (which unlike most animals, plants, and geographical features actually kept the name the Aborigines had given it) from Cook's 1773 travelogue lovingly depicts the kangaroo's environs and even emotions.

→ *What role did race play in how Europeans viewed others, especially those from Oceania?*

CLASSIFICATION AND "RACE"

Cook's description of the South Sea Islanders underscores the place that race had come to occupy in eighteenth-century Europeans' views of themselves and others. Previously, the word *race* referred to a swift current in a stream or a trial of speed, and on occasion meant a lineage, mainly that of a royal or noble family. By the end of the seventeenth century, a few writers were beginning to expand the definition of race to designate a European ethnic lineage, identifying, for example, the indomitable spirit and freedom-loving ethos of the Anglo-Saxon race. François Bernier, who had traveled in Asia, may have been the first European to attempt a racial division of the globe in his 1684 *New Division of the Earth by the Different Groups or Races Who Inhabit It.* Carolus Linnaeus (1707–1778); Georges Louis LeClerc, the comte de Buffon (1707–1788); and Johann Friedrich Blumenbach (1752–1840) would be the first to use racial principles to classify humankind.

Europe's most accomplished naturalist, Carolus Linnaeus, took his passion for classifying and naming all the plants and animals in the world to identify several species within the genus *Homo—Homo sapiens, Homo caudatus* (tailed man), and *Homo troglodytes*—in his *Systema Naturae* (1735). The latter two species—the tailed man and troglodyte man—were groups Linnaeus defined on the basis of classical texts, travelers' accounts, rumors, freak show exhibits, and misunderstandings. Within *Homo sapiens,* he identified five groups, or races, using a combination of physical characteristics, including skin pigmentation and social qualities. Linnaeus characterized the Europeans as light-skinned and governed by laws. In contrast with Chinese conceptions of color, by which they were of white skin, Linnaeus's scheme described the peoples of Asia as "sooty" and deemed them regulated by opinion. He said that copper-skinned, indigenous American peoples were governed by custom. He wrote that Africans, whom he consigned to the lowest rung of the human ladder, were ruled by little other than personal whim. Later eighteenth-century natural historians dismissed Linnaeus's troglodyte and tailed men, but the habit of ranking races and lumping together physical and cultural characteristics persisted. In time, some would even question the unity of the human species.

In inventorying the peoples of the world and assigning each group a place on the ladder of human achievement, the long-standing idealization of classical sculpture played a role: those who most resembled Greek nudes were believed to be the most beautiful, as well as the most civilized and suited for world power. In his *Natural History* (1750), a noted French scientist, the comte de Buffon, insisted that proper proportion for the human form had been established by classical sculptures. Having divided the human genus into distinct races, he determined white peoples to be the most admirable, and Africans the most contemptible.

The father of physical anthropology, Johann Friedrich Blumenbach, crystallized much of Enlightenment thought about race in his authoritative book *De Generis Humani Natura,* published in 1775. He divided humanity into four races: Europeans, Asians, Africans, and Americans, with these classifications based largely, although not exclusively, on physical characteristics, like skin color, cranial size, hair, and the like. Blumenbach introduced the word *Caucasian* to denote Europeans, but he believed Caucasians and "Ethiopians" (his word for Africans) belonged to the same species because they had the same physical characteristics. Blumenbach, in fact, asserted a rough racial equality, maintaining that there were beautiful Ethiopians just as there were ugly Caucasians.

Linnaeus and Classification. Linnaeus's famous system of plant and animal classifications, which depended on sexual forms (such as the stamen and pistil in plants), was in wide use by the end of the eighteenth century.

South Sea Islanders, like Omai, fell somewhere between the Caucasians and the Ethiopians. They retained an aura of mythical similarity to the Greek gods, but in succeeding decades Europeans would cease to view them as "noble savages," a phrase coined by Rousseau to describe the virtues of the uncivilized. The waning of appreciation for their innocence and simplicity may indeed have begun with the final act in the Cook legend: his killing by the Hawaiians in 1779.

In their first encounters, Cook had greatly impressed the Hawaiians; some commentators believe the Hawaiians recognized in him the embodiment of their god Lono; others simply think they treated him as an important chief. He had, in any event, deeply offended them by destroying one of their sacred shrines, ostensibly for firewood but possibly because he wished to destroy symbols of their religion. When he then tried to take several chiefs hostage in order to force the return of a boat, tensions rose. In unclear circumstances, his men killed several important Hawaiians, and the islanders, incensed and frightened by the violence, closed in on the captain, stabbing him repeatedly. The news, of course, scandalized Cook's homeland; the king himself, it is said, shed tears. Europeans began to expound upon the "darker side" of South Pacific cultures. *Ode to the Memory of the Late Captain James Cook* (1780) depicted the sullen, vengeful savage "Whose darken'd mind in mercy found no joy." A French traveler, who had seen the explorer Marion de Fresne killed by Maoris on New Zealand's coast, similarly denounced "the passions of rapacity, violence, and treachery" common to the South Pacific "Children of Nature."

CONCLUSION

New wealth produced by increasing commerce and the consolidation of polities created the conditions for a kind of global cultural renaissance in the period between 1500 and 1780, beginning in the Chinese and Islamic empires but stretching into Europe and Africa and extending into previous worlds apart in the Americas and Oceania. Experiments in religious toleration encouraged cultural exchange; book production and consumption soared; grand new monuments arose; luxury goods became available for wider enjoyment.

Perhaps the most striking thing about this cultural renaissance was its unevenness. While elites and sometimes the middle classes benefited, the poor did not. They remained illiterate, undernourished, and often subjected to brutal treatment by rulers and landowners. In Europe and China, elite women increasingly joined literate society, writing, reading, and publishing books, acting as patrons and translators, but they gained no new rights. Urban areas also profited much more from the new wealth than rural ones, and those seeking refinement flocked to the cities. Some regions, which had once been cultural meccas, like the Italian peninsula, lost their luster as new, more commercially and culturally dynamic centers took their place.

Between states, too, cultural inequalities were now glaring. Although the Islamic and Chinese worlds confidently retained their own systems of knowing, believing, and representing, the Americas and Oceania were increasingly sub-

Chronology

		1600		
THE ISLAMIC WORLD		▌ *Abulfazl's* Akbarnamah *in Mughal India, 1587–1602*		
		▌ *Building of palace and plaza in Isfahan, Iran, 1598–1629*		
		▌ *Building of Taj Mahal in Agra, India, 1630–165(*	
EUROPE	*Galileo Galilei's* Dialogue on the Two Chief Systems of the World, *1632* ▌			
		Building of Versailles begins outside Paris, 1661 ▌	
		Incorporation of British Royal Society, 1662 ▌	
AMERICAS		▌ *Hybrid cultures emerge in Americas, 1600s*		
AFRICA		▌ *Oyo and Asante kingdoms produce vibrant artistic work, 1600s*		
EAST ASIA	▌ *Jesuit missionary Matteo Ricci brings European cartography to China, 1583*			
		▌ *Growing circulation of books and ideas in China, 1600s*		
		▌ Kabuki *theater appears in Japan, 1600s*		

jected to European cultural pressures. Here, while syncretic practices were widespread by the later eighteenth century, clearly European ideas, beliefs, and habits had become the standards by which degrees of "civilization" were judged. African cultures were the exception in that they largely managed to escape this influence, though because of the slave trade, the peoples of that landmass certainly felt the impact of European expansionism.

As the Oceania example shows, by the late eighteenth century, Europeans had an expansive view of the world and their place in it. They were gleefully classifying the plants, animals, and peoples of the world and seeking ways to make new worlds more and more useful and comfortable for themselves. It is important to recognize, however, that Europe's categories and descriptions did not win easy acceptance beyond Europe's self-created borders. The Chinese, Ottomans, Safavids, Mughals, and Africans remained largely unaware of or unimpressed by European endeavors, and resistance from Native Americans as from South Sea Islanders remained stiff.

From a commercial standpoint, the world in the seventeenth and eighteenth centuries was more tightly integrated than ever before. Populations moved around with increasing ease and frequency, and mercantile dealings involving distant groups became more common. In general, well-established cultural groups and traditional institutions dealt effectively with these interactions and transactions.

In some respects, borrowing and exposure only reconfirmed established ways. The Chinese, for instance, still believed in the superiority of Chinese knowledge and customs

and regarded those who had not mastered their ways as lesser peoples. Islamic rulers, too, claimed universality on behalf of Islam as a body of revealed, not objective, knowledge. Confident of the superiority of Islam, the dynasts allowed others to form their own—though clearly subordinate—cultural communities. At the elite level, they accommodated non-Muslim subjects and knowledge by constructing a realm of courtly culture and philosophy, where the superiority of Islam was not in question but where other systems of knowledge could be discussed and debated. Within these imperial Islamic cultures, the Europeans were useful, decorative pieces, and their knowledge, to the extent considered helpful for imperial purposes, was taken into account.

Only the Europeans were constructing knowledge that they believed was both universal and objective, a kind of knowledge that could be used to master nature and all its inhabitants. This approach to cultural differences was to prove consequential as well as controversial, in the centuries to come.

STUDY QUESTIONS

 WWNORTON.COM/STUDYSPACE

1. Explain the processes that brought forth new syncretic cultural syntheses in the three Islamic dynasties during this era. To what extent did European ideas and culture influence each empire?

1700		1800

■ *Tulip Period in Ottoman Empire, 1720s*

■ *Isaac Newton's* Principia Mathematica, *1687*   ■ *Carolus Linnaeus's* Systema Naturae, *1735*

  ■ *John Locke's* Essay Concerning Human Understanding, *1690*   ■ *Denis Diderot's* Encyclopedia, *1751–1772*

              ■ *Voyages of Captain James Cook, 1768–1779*

                ■ *Adam Smith's* The Wealth of Nations, *1776*

  ■ *Enlightenment philosophy introduces elite thought in American colonies, 1700s*

        ■ *Shogun lifts ban on foreign books, 1720*

          ■ *Movement for "native learning" begins in Japan, 1728*

2. List and describe Chinese and Japanese cultural achievements during this time period. How did foreign influences shape ideas and beliefs in each dynasty?

3. Define the term *Enlightenment* as it pertained to Europe during this time period. How did Enlightenment ideas shape European attitudes toward other cultures?

4. Explain the various factors that contributed to the growth of hybrid cultures in the Americas during this era. How similar and different were these new societies across the Americas?

5. Analyze the impact of Enlightenment ideas in the Americas. Did the spread of this new philosophy bring communities across the Atlantic together or did it drive them apart?

6. Compare and contrast European exploration of Oceania in the eighteenth century to European exploration of the Americas in the sixteenth century. How did European exploration of Oceania transform European attitudes toward non-European groups around the world?

7. Analyze how world trade changed world cultures during this time period. To what extent did a universal culture emerge?

8. Analyze to what extent dynastic rulers around the world were able to control cultural developments during this era. How did new cultural manifestations potentially undermine local governments?

FURTHER READINGS

Axtell, James, *The Invasion of America: The Contest of Cultures in Colonial North America* (1985). Discusses the strategies of Christian missionaries in converting the Indians, as well as the success of Indians in converting Europeans.

Berlin, Ira, *Many Thousands Gone: The First Two Centuries of Slavery in North America* (1998). Surveys the development of African-American culture in colonial North America.

Brook, Timothy, *The Confusions of Pleasure: Commerce and Culture in Ming China* (1999). An insightful survey of Ming society.

Clunas, Craig, *Superfluous Things: Material Culture and Social Status in Early Modern China* (1991). A good account of the late Ming elite's growing passion for material things.

Collcutt, Martin, Marius Jansen, and Isao Kumakura, *A Cultural Atlas of Japan* (1988). A sweeping look at the many different forms of Japanese cultural expression over the centuries, including the flourishing urban culture of Edo.

Darnton, Robert, *The Business of the Enlightenment: A Publishing History of the Encyclopédie, 1775–1800* (1979). The classic study of Europe's first great compendium of knowledge.

Dash, Mike, *Tulipomania: The Story of the World's Most Coveted Flower and the Extraordinary Passions It Aroused* (1999). A global perspective on and lively account of the spread of the tulip around the world as a flower signifying both beauty and status.

Elman, Benjamin A., *On Their Own Terms: Science in China, 1550–1900* (2005). A study of the development of "native" Chinese science and how the process interacted with the introduction of western science to China over the course of three and a half centuries.

Eze, Emmanuel Chukwudi (ed.), *Race and the Enlightenment: A Reader* (1997). Readings examining the idea of race in the context of the Enlightenment.

Fleischer, Cornell, *Bureaucrat and Intellectual in the Ottoman Empire: The Historian Mustafa Ali (1540–1600)* (1986). Offers good insight into the world of culture and intellectual vitality in the Ottoman Empire.

Grafton, Anthony, April Shelford, and Nancy Siraisi, *New Worlds, Ancient Texts: The Power of Tradition and the Shock of Discovery* (1995). A concise discussion of the impact of the New World on European thought.

Gutierrez, Ramon, *When Jesus Came, the Corn Mothers Went Away: Marriage, Sexuality, and Power in New Mexico, 1500–1846* (1991). A provocative dissection of the spiritual dimensions of European colonialism in the Americas.

Hannaford, Ivan, *Race: The History of an Idea in the West* (1996). A study of how race began to take on critical importance in western thinking in the seventeenth and eighteenth centuries.

Harley, J. B., and David Woodward (eds.), *The History of Cartography.* Vol. 2, Book 2: *Cartography in the Traditional East and Southeast Asian Societies* (1994). An authoritative treatment of the subject.

Horton, Robin, *Patterns of Thought in Africa and the West: Essays on Magic, Religion, and Science* (1993). Reflections on African patterns of thought and attitudes toward nature, which can help us to understand African-American religious beliefs and resistance movements.

Keene, Donald, *The Japanese Discovery of Europe: Honda Toshiaki and Other Discoverers, 1720–1798* (1952). A study of the ways Japan managed to incorporate knowledge from the outside world with the development of national traditions.

Ko, Dorothy, *Teachers of the Inner Chambers: Women and Culture in Seventeenth-Century China* (1994). Explores the lives of elite women in late Ming and early Qing China.

Lewis, Bernard, *Race and Color in Islam* (1979). Examines the Islamic attitude toward race and color.

Morgan, Philip D., *Slave Counterpoint: Black Culture in the Eighteenth-Century Chesapeake and Lowcountry* (1998). Describes the development of African-American culture in colonial North America.

Munck, Thomas, *The Enlightenment: A Comparative Social History, 1721–1794* (2000). A wonderful survey, with unusual examples from the periphery, especially from Scandinavia and the Habsburg Empire.

Necipoglu, Gulru, *Architecture, Ceremonial and Power: The Topkapi Palace in the Fifteenth and Sixteenth Centuries* (1991). A magnificently illustrated book that shows the enormous artistic talent that the Ottoman rulers poured into their imperial structure.

Publishing and the Print Culture in Late Imperial China (Special Issue). *Late Imperial China*, Vol. 17:1 (June 1996). Contains a collection of important articles with a foreword by the French cultural historian Roger Chartier.

Qaisar, Ahsan Jan, *The Indian Response to European Technology, AD 1498–1707* (1998). A meticulous, scholarly work on this little-studied subject.

Rizvi, Athar Abbas, *The Wonder That Was India.* Vol. 2: *A Survey of the History and Culture of the Indian Sub-continent from the Coming of the Muslims to the British Conquest, 1200–1700* (1987). A deeply learned work in intellectual history.

Shapin, Stephen, *The Scientific Revolution* (1998). An overview that is informed by innovative new thinking on the subject.

Smith, Bernard, *European Vision and the South Pacific* (1985). An excellent cultural history of Cook's voyages.

Smith, Richard J., *Chinese Maps: Images of "All under Heaven"* (1996). Provides a good introduction to the history of cartography in China.

Welch, Anthony, *Shah Abbas and the Arts of Isfahan* (1973). Describes the astonishing architectural and artistic renaissance of the city of Isfahan under the Safavid ruler, Shah Abbas.

Whitfield, Peter, *The Image of the World: Twenty Centuries of World Maps* (1994). A good introduction to the history of cartography in different parts of the world.

Zilfi, Madeline C., *The Politics of Piety: The Ottoman Ulema in the Post-Classical Age (1600–1800)* (1988). Explores the cultural flourishing that took place within the Islamic world in this period.

Chapter 15

REORDERING THE WORLD, 1750–1850

A t the end of the eighteenth century, the commander of a French army, Napoleon Bonaparte, led an expedition to Egypt. For many Europeans, Egypt was an exalted territory—the cradle of a once-great culture, the setting for many a Biblical story, a land bridge to the Red Sea and trade with Asia, and a provincial outpost of an old rival, the Ottoman Empire. Introducing the principles of the recent French Revolution (liberty, equality, and fraternity) to distant lands would bring glory to France. Occupying the country would also represent a strategic victory over Great Britain for the control of trade routes to Asia. Most important to Napoleon, however, defeat of the Ottomans would catapult him to historic greatness.

But the revolutionary crusade of 1798 did not go as Napoleon planned. After defeating the Mamluk army of Egypt beneath the pyramids just outside Cairo, his troops bogged down in the country and faced the wrath of the local population. Eager to play a larger role in Europe, Napoleon returned to France a little more than one year after he had stepped on Egyptian soil, leaving his troops vulnerable to inevitable counterattacks. But the invasion of Egypt did shake up Ottoman rule and played a role in altering the

European balance of power. Indeed, Napoleon's actions in Africa, the Americas, and Europe combined with the principles of the French Revolution laid the foundations for the era of the nation-state. What gave these political events added impact were a number of equally disruptive changes in social and economic arrangements around the world.

The period 1750–1850 witnessed a fundamental reordering of the balance of power in the world. The reordering began in the Atlantic world, where political upheavals destroyed the colonial domains of Spain, Portugal, Britain, and France in the Americas and established a number of new nations. To these political events were added far-reaching economic changes that propelled western Europe to global preeminence. These reorderings, in turn, forced Asian and African governments to come to terms with the new economic and political might of Europe. In Egypt and the Ottoman Empire, reform-minded leaders undertook desperate modernizing efforts to deal with Europe's threatening power. In China, too, by the 1830s the ruling Manchus were faced with European gunboats insisting that the Chinese permit expanded trade with the Europeans.

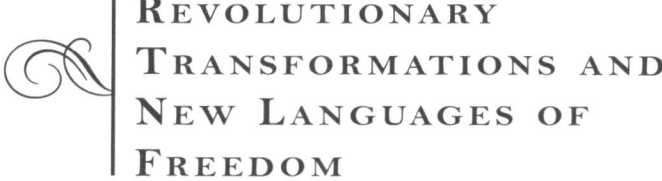

REVOLUTIONARY TRANSFORMATIONS AND NEW LANGUAGES OF FREEDOM

> → *How did Enlightenment ideas transform the world?*

In the eighteenth century, the increasing circulation of goods, people, and ideas created new pressures for reform around the Atlantic world. As economies expanded, many men and women felt that the restrictions of the mercantilist system stood in the way of their aspirations. They clamored for changes that would enable them to partake of this wealth and power. Similarly, as enlightened ideas spread through an increasingly literate public, new voices called for their states to adopt rational, humane, and just practices, including the abolition of torture and the accountability of the governors to the people they governed. Demanding more freedom to trade and more influence in governing institutions, these reformers ran up against the resistance of aristocratic elites. It is a testimony to the weakness of these elites, as well as to the power of these new forces, that those in power could not stamp out these demands before they became—in a number of places—full-scale revolutions. Reformers began to advance concepts of popular sovereignty (of power residing in the people themselves) and to argue that unregulated economies would produce more rapid economic growth. In denouncing commercial privileges and monopolies, as well as arbitrary rulers, reformers employed a rhetoric of freedom, which would alter the course of world history. They argued that free trade, free markets, and free labor would yield more just and more efficient societies. With time, proponents of the new order argued that this new social order would benefit everyone everywhere in the world.

The struggle to create new political and economic relationships offered people the opportunity to think differently about the way the world should be ordered. In this era languages of nationalism (the idea that the people who belonged to a shared community called a "nation" should enjoy sovereignty within the borders of their state) and democracy (that these people, by virtue of their membership in the nation, enjoyed public rights to representation) appealed to so many that it would be difficult afterward to restore absolute sovereignty to monarchs or lasting stability to multiethnic empires. The first expression of this new thinking occurred in thirteen of Britain's North American colonies and in France, where in the late eighteenth century the "nation" and the "people" mobilized sufficient opposition to topple old rulers.

Focus Questions REORDERING THE WORLD

→ *How did Enlightenment ideas transform the world?*

→ *What major changes in government and society grew out of the Atlantic revolutions?*

→ *Why did the abolition of the slave trade have unintended effects on African society?*

→ *How did the industrial and commercial revolutions reorder society?*

→ *How did the Atlantic revolutions affect Afro-Eurasian societies?*

WWNORTON.COM/STUDYSPACE

As democratic and nationalist ideas emerged in the American and French revolutions, the question arose as to how far freedom should be extended, even within the Atlantic world. Should women, Native Americans, and slaves be given the rights of citizens? Should people without property be given the vote? Moreover, should freedom be extended to non-Europeans? By and large, European and Euro-American elite groups answered no to these questions, and often they backed their answer with violence. The very same elites who championed a freer world often exploited slaves and those in the lower orders, denied women equal treatment, restricted colonial economies, and were prepared to use force to expand further the markets of Asia and Africa to European trade and investment. In Africa, the third corner of the Atlantic world, idealistic upheavals resulted not in the emergence of free and sovereign peoples but in intensified enslavement.

POLITICAL REORDERINGS

> ➔ *What major changes in government and society grew out of the Atlantic revolutions?*

The second half of the eighteenth century witnessed the spread of revolutionary ideas across the Atlantic world (see Map 15-1). In part, this spread followed the trail of Enlightenment ideas about freedom and reason. By the late eighteenth century, the number of newspapers, pamphlets, and books in circulation had soared, drawing readers in European countries and American colonies into a discussion of their society's problems—and how to fix them. Many more people began to believe that they had the right to participate in governance. Gradually and unevenly, on both sides of the Atlantic, politics became a noisier activity, involving a wider group (though chiefly of middle- and upper-class males), rather than a matter reserved for kings, court advisers, and landed magnates. Increasingly, too, those who made or wished to make political revolutions claimed that they were acting for the good of "the people."

The slogans of the era—independence, freedom, liberty, and equality—were especially powerful terms that seemed to promise an end to oppression, hardship, and inequities of all kinds. Fired by these new ideas, political revolts spread throughout the Atlantic world, starting first in Britain's North American colonies and spreading to France's absolute monarchy. In both, revolutions ultimately caused monarchies to be replaced with republics. The examples of the United States and France soon encouraged others in the Caribbean and Central and South America to seek king-less polities. In all of these revolutionary environments, new representative institutions such as permanent parliaments, enshrined in written consti-

tutions, came into being. The rhetoric of revolution, once unleashed, proved difficult to contain in later generations.

THE NORTH AMERICAN WAR OF INDEPENDENCE, 1776–1783

By the mid-eighteenth century, Britain's mainland colonies swelled with people and prosperity. Through bustling port cities like Charleston, Philadelphia, New York, and Boston, African slaves, European migrants, and manufactured goods flowed in, while agrarian staples flowed out. A colonial "genteel" class, composed of merchants and landowning planters, came to dominate the affairs of these colonies and aspired to the status of English gentlemen. But with settlers arriving from Europe and slaves from Africa, land was a constant source of dispute. Planters collided with independent farmers (yeomen). Sons and daughters of farmers, unable to inherit or acquire real estate near their parents, spilled into the landmass's interior, and their land-seeking put them in conflict with Indian peoples. To defend their lands, many Indians allied with Britain's rival, France, but after losing the Seven Years' War (1756–1763), France ceded its Canadian colony to Britain. Without French support and overwhelmed by settlers, many Indians continued to mount a spirited resistance, but they often died in battle or of disease. A large number of survivors fled west.

By the mid-1760s, the British Empire stood supreme in eastern North America. A political revolution seemed unimaginable. And yet, a decade later, that is precisely what occurred. Why did colonists sever their ties with England? They acted, paradoxically, in defense of their rights as "freeborn Englishmen." The spark was provided by King George III, who proposed to end the policy of benign neglect of the colonies and to make the colonists pay for Britain's war with France and for the benefits of being subjects of the empire. Colonial merchants, particularly in New England, protested the Revenue Act of 1764, which sought to end lucrative smuggling by many colonists. Even more vexing to the colonists was taxation without representation, for no colonists sat in the British House of Commons, Great Britain's governing legislative body. Agitation for freedom turned to open warfare between a colonial militia and British troops at Lexington and Concord, Massachusetts, in the spring of 1775. One firebrand, Thomas Paine, a recent immigrant from England, captured the mood in a pamphlet published in January 1776, in which he argued to an increasingly literate public that it was "common sense" for people to govern themselves. Paine's pamphlet had sold more than 100,000 copies by July 1776, when the Continental Congress adapted part of it for the Declaration of Independence.

The declaration—written primarily by the Virginia tobacco planter Thomas Jefferson—drew on themes of the European Enlightenment. It championed the "natural rights"

RUSSIA

BRITISH NORTH AMERICA

Hudson

Bay

OREGON
(Claimed by Spain,
Russia and Britain)

LOUISIANA

Quebec •

Boston •
New York •
Philadelphia •
UNITED
STATES
✳ 1776
(independence recognized
by Great Britain 1783)
Charleston •

Washington, D.C. •

• Santa Fe

MEXICO
✳ 1821

FLORIDA

Gulf
of
Mexico

A T L A N T I C

O C E A N

Mexico City •

CUBA

PUERTO RICO

BELIZE

JAMAICA *REPUBLIC*
OF HAITI
✳ 1804

GUADELOUPE (Fr.)

MARTINIQUE (Fr.)

UNITED PROVINCES
OF CENTRAL AMERICA
✳ 1823   Cartagena •

• Caracas

TRINIDAD (Br.)

P A C I F I C

REPUBLIC OF
COLOMBIA
✳ 1819

G U I A N A

O C E A N

• Quito

PERU
✳ 1821
Lima •

B R A Z I L
✳ 1822

BOLIVIA
✳ 1825

PARAGUAY
✳ 1811

• Rio de Janeiro

CHILE
✳ 1818

PROVINCES
OF LA PLATA
✳ 1816

URUGUAY
✳ 1828

Buenos Aires •
• Montevideo

British possessions
Spanish possessions
French possessions
Portuguese possessions
Dutch possessions
✳ 1776 Date of political independence
from European (or Ottoman)
colonial rule

0   1000   2000 Miles

0   1000   2000 Kilometers

MAP 15-1   REVOLUTIONS OF NATIONAL INDEPENDENCE IN THE ATLANTIC WORLD, 1776–1829

Colonies gained independence from European powers (and in the case of Greece from the Ottoman Empire) in the late eighteenth and early nineteenth centuries under the influence of Enlightenment thinkers and the French Revolution. What were the first two American colonial territories to gain independence? Why was the United States reluctant to recognize the political independence of the second independent American republic? Why did colonies in Spanish and Portuguese America obtain their political independence decades after the United States gained its independence?

The Boston Massacre. Paul Revere's idealized view of the Boston Massacre of March 5, 1770. In the years after the Seven Years' War, Bostonians grew increasingly disenchanted with British efforts to enforce imperial regulations. When British troops fired on and killed several members of an angry mob in what came to be called the "Boston Massacre," the resulting frenzy stirred revolutionary sentiments among the populace.

of people to govern themselves and the idea, drawn from John Locke's political writings, that governments should be based on a social contract, according to which both the sovereign and the people are bound by the law. Locke also stipulated that the people had the right to rebel against their government if it did not obey the contract and tried to infringe on the rights of the people. "We hold these truths to be self-evident," the declaration proclaimed, "that all men are created equal, that they are endowed by their Creator with certain inalienable Rights, that among these are Life, Liberty and the Pursuit of Happiness. That to secure these rights, Governments are instituted among Men, deriving their just powers from the consent of the governed. That whenever any Form of Government becomes destructive of these ends, it is the Right of the People to alter or abolish it." Thus the Americans announced their right to rid themselves of the English king and form their own independent polity, but neither the Declaration of Independence nor *Common Sense* provided a blueprint for how a nonmonarchical government might be organized or how thirteen tenuously connected states might win a war against the world's most powerful empire.

During the War of Independence, Americans began to work out new political arrangements. Much of that work occurred in the individual states, where elections were held to select delegates to constitutional conventions. These elec-

tions were unprecedented, as was the decision to put the constitutions in writing. Constitution-writers exhibited a revolutionary faith in representative government. Dispensing with royal authority, all the new state constitutions assigned sweeping powers to legislative bodies, whose members were to be elected by "the people." But who constituted the people? No women qualified as voters. Property qualifications also continued to limit the franchise (the right to vote) to a percentage of adult white men, though the constitutions generally reduced the landholding requirements that had prevailed during the colonial era.

The notion that all men were created equal flew in the face of established hierarchies in which people supposedly knew—and kept—their place. Taking this rhetoric to heart, common men no longer automatically deferred to gentlemen of higher rank. Many women, too, claimed that their contributions to the patriots' cause, managing farms and shops in the absence of husbands, merited greater respect and equality in marital relations, including property rights. In letters to her husband, John Adams, Abigail Adams stopped referring to the family farm as "yours." In a telling substitution of pronouns, she started writing of the farm as "ours." Most revolutionary of all, tens of thousands of slaves from the Carolinas to Maryland fled plantations to join the war effort, though these runaways usually sided with the British, believing that loyalty to the crown would win them freedom from their masters.

The prospect of a social revolution of artisans, women, and slaves, rather than a narrower liberal revolution, generated a reaction against what American elites called the "excesses of democracy." Their fears grew after farmers in western Massachusetts, led by Daniel Shays, interrupted court proceedings in which the state sought to foreclose on properties for nonpayment of taxes. The farmers who joined in Shays rebellion in the fall of 1786 also denounced illegitimate taxation, this time by the American government. Massachusetts militiamen easily defeated the ragtag rebel army, but to save the nation from falling into "anarchy," propertied men convened the Constitutional Convention in Philadelphia in the summer of 1787.

Amid fierce debate among the assembled merchants, planters, physicians, governors, military officers, and lawyers (common farmers were not in attendance), the Constitutional Convention drafted a charter for a republican government. The convention looked back to the ancient Roman Republic for a model of a state ruled by representatives of the people rather than by a king. It adopted some aspects of the Roman system but also added some of its own innovations, such as the institution of a single, elected head of state: the president. The new Constitution substantially enlarged the power of the federal government and, compared to the state constitutions of a decade earlier, reduced the stature of the legislature, the branch of government most responsive to popular will. The Constitution also included a system of checks and

Abigail Adams. Abigail Adams was the wife of John Adams, a leader in the movement for American independence and later the second president of the United States. Abigail's letters to her husband testified to the ways in which revolutionary enthusiasm for liberty and equality began to reach into women's minds. While the Continental Congress was debating whether to declare independence in the spring of 1776, Abigail wrote to implore that the men in the Congress "remember the ladies, and be more generous and favorable to them than your ancestors. Do not put such unlimited power into the hands of the Husbands. Remember all Men would be tyrants if they could. If particular care and attention is not paid to the Ladies we are determined to foment a Rebellion, and will not hold ourselves bound by any Laws in which we have no voice, or Representation."

balances. These included the legislature's right to impeach the head of the executive branch (the president) and the judiciary's right to test the constitutionality of laws passed by the legislature. Thus was the Constitution designed to prevent any of the three branches of government from becoming too powerful and to deter majorities from trampling on the rights and property of a wealthier minority. Submitted to the states for approval, the Constitution proved controversial. Its critics, known as Anti-Federalists, echoing Shays, claimed to be defending the people against the growth of a potentially tyrannical federal government. Anti-Federalists also insisted

on the inclusion of the Bill of Rights to protect individual liberties from abusive government intrusions. After a series of closely contested campaigns, the Constitution won ratification, though the Bill of Rights was soon amended to it.

From the 1780s onward, the Federalists and Anti-Federalists disagreed fervently over the new design of the United States, as the new country was called, but they confined their jousting to the constitutional arena. In an uneasy truce, property owners agreed not to convert the debate over whether to abolish slavery, brewing since the 1770s, into a cause for disunion. As the frontier expanded westward, the question of which new states would allow slavery and which would not led to a series of contentious compromises. For the moment, the existence of ample land postponed a confrontation, but with ideas of the dignity and rights of free labor gaining currency in the northern states (and across the North Atlantic world), it became impossible to remove slavery, as southern slaveholders sought, from the realm of national politics. In 1800, the election of Thomas Jefferson as the third president of the United States signaled the triumph of a model of sending pioneers out to new lands to defuse conflict on old lands. In the same year, however, a Virginia slave named Gabriel Prosser hatched a plan to raise an army of slaves to seize the state capital at Richmond and win support from white artisans and laborers for a more inclusive republic. Gabriel's dream of an egalitarian revolution fell victim to white terror and black betrayal. Twenty-seven slaves, including Gabriel, went to the gallows. With them, for the moment, died the dream of a multiracial republic in which all men were truly created equal.

THE FRENCH REVOLUTION, 1789–1799

The rhetoric of freedom and rights also shook up social and political hierarchies in Europe's capitals. Partly inspired by the American Revolution, French men and women soon began to issue their own calls for liberty—and the result was a series of events that, even more than the American Revolution, shook Europe's established dynasties and social hierarchies. In France, the revolution changed its course so suddenly, involved so many participants, and was so extensively reported in books, pamphlets, journals, and songs across the globe that it had a riveting effect on all who heard of it. The revolution's powerful ideas and its violent course inspired so many other rebels around the world, and terrified so many members of the ruling classes, that it must be considered an event not only of European but also of global importance.

ORIGINS AND OUTBREAK For decades before the outbreak of the revolution, enlightened thinkers had attacked the inefficiencies, inequalities, and cruelties of France's old regime. In widely read pamphlets and books, satirists poked fun at the corruptions and prejudices of the church, the court, and the aristocracy and offered suggestions on how the system might be reformed. Their criticisms often resulted in their imprisonment or exile, but by the mid-eighteenth century, discontent with France's ruling elite had spread beyond the educated few. In the countryside, peasants grumbled about paying taxes and tithes to the church and, despite generally improved health and nutrition, suffered periods of deprivation (while the nobility and clergy paid almost no taxes). But revolutions do not occur simply because people are oppressed, hungry, and angry—as had been the case for the European peasantry for centuries—or even because some begin to imagine alternatives to the order of things. It took a unique combination of these pressures, and the opportunity provided by a fiscal crisis, to unleash the French Revolution of 1789.

Interestingly, it was the king himself who opened the door to revolution. Eager to weaken his arch-rival, England, Louis XVI (ruled 1774–1793) spent huge sums in support of the American rebels; by doing so, he greatly increased France's state debt, which consumed some 50 percent of France's national budget by 1788. In and of itself, this was not disastrous —the Dutch and the English at the time had even larger debts. But in France, the king could not raise taxes on the privileged classes without calling a meeting of the Estates-General, a medieval advisory body that had last met in 1614. Like American colonists, French nobles argued that taxation gave them the right of representation. When the king reluctantly agreed to summon the Estates-General in 1788, he still believed that his will would prevail: the delegates of the clergy (the First Estate) and the aristocracy (the Second Estate) could overrule the delegates who represented everybody else (the Third Estate) because each estate voted as one body rather than as individuals, which meant that the Third Estate could be outvoted.

When the delegates finally assembled in the spring of 1789, the Third Estate refused to be outvoted by the other two, insisted that those who worked and paid the taxes *were* the nation, and demanded that the delegates sit together in one chamber and vote as individuals. The privileged few, some began to say, were simply parasites. As arguments raged and pamphlets poured out of Paris in the spring and early summer of 1789, peasants in the countryside began to sack castles—yet another indication that "the people" now believed the time had come to throw off the old system of inequalities. In June 1789, the delegates of the Third Estate simply declared themselves to be the "National" Assembly, the body fit to determine France's future.

On July 14, 1789, a Parisian crowd, angered at the king's dismissal of a favorite minister, attacked a medieval armory in search of weapons. Not only did this armory, the Bastille, hold gunpowder, it was also an infamous prison for political prisoners—though in 1789 it held only five forgers and two lunatics. Enraged at the commanding officer's refusal to open the doors, the crowd stormed the prison and murdered the officer, then cut off his head and paraded it through the streets of Paris, stuck on a pike. On this day, subsequently celebrated as Bastille Day, the king made the fateful decision not to call out the army, and the capital city belonged to the crowd. The news from Paris quickly spread to the countryside, emboldening peasants to burn down manor houses and destroy municipal archives, where the records of the hated feudal dues were kept. Reformist sentiment ran so high that on August 4, 1789, the deputies of the French National Assembly declared

The "Tennis Court Oath." Locked out of the chambers of the Estates General, the deputies of the Third Estates reconvened at a nearby indoor tennis court in June 1789; there they swore an oath not to disband until the king recognized the sovereignty of a National Assembly.

→ *What major changes in government and society grew out of the Atlantic revolutions?*

Women March on Versailles. On October 5, 1789, a group of market women, many of them fishwives (traditionally regarded as leaders of the poor), marched on the Paris city hall to demand bread. Quickly, their numbers grew, and they redirected their march to Versailles, some twelve miles away and the symbol of the entire political order. In response to the women, the king finally appeared on the balcony and agreed to sign the revolutionary decree and return with the women to Paris.

the abolition of the feudal privileges of the nobility and the clergy and the opening of a new era of liberty, equality, and fraternity.

REVOLUTIONARY TRANSFORMATIONS The "Declaration of the Rights of Man and Citizen" followed on August 26. Its seventeen articles echoed Jefferson's Declaration of Independence—but the grander promises of the French document and its different context made it a more radical statement. It endowed all citizens of the French nation with inviolable liberties and gave all men equality under the law. The French document also proclaimed in Article 3 that "the principle of all sovereignty rests essentially in the nation." Thus, the French Revolution not only trumpeted individual rights and the principle of equality but also connected more closely the concept of a people with a nation. Both the rhetorical and real war against feudal privileges marked the beginning of the end of dynastic and aristocratic rule in Europe.

Altering social hierarchies affected the relations among men and women. Some women felt that the new principles of citizenship should also include the rights of women. Radical republican ideology spawned an early feminist movement. In 1791, a group of women circulated a petition demanding the right to bear arms to defend the revolution, but they stopped short of demanding equal rights for both sexes. Women would become citizens by being good revolutionary wives and mothers, not by virtue of enjoying their own natural rights. In that same year, Olympe de Gouges (1748–1793) composed the "Declaration of the Rights of Woman and Citizen," in which she repeated the seventeen articles of the Rights of Man, adding to each one the word "woman," and proposed female rights to divorce, to hold property in marriage, to be educated, and to have public careers. The all-male assembly did not

take up these proposals, despite the claims that "liberty and equality" were universal rights. For them, it was self-evident that a "fraternity" of free *men* composed the nation.

As the revolution gained momentum between the fall of 1789 and the winter of 1792, the radicals gained greater power, and more and more nobles and clergy fled the country. In late 1790, all clergy were forced to take an oath of loyalty to the new state. This action created enormous opposition among pious Catholics and spurred a major counter-revolutionary movement. Meanwhile, the revolutionary ranks began to splinter, as men and women discussed the proper aims and ends of the revolution. In September 1792, a new National Convention was elected by universal manhood suffrage (the first such election in Europe), and the first French Republic was proclaimed. By early 1793, Louis XVI had been tried, found guilty of treason, and guillotined, and France was at war with many of its neighbors. The events in France, especially the execution of the king, shocked Europeans accustomed to fixed social hierarchies and a world in which the king was presumed to rule as God's representative on earth, answering to no one.

THE TERROR In the wake of the king's execution, radicals known as Jacobins, who had sought to extend the revolution beyond France's borders, launched a campaign known as the Reign of Terror to purge the nation of its enemies. Jacobin leaders, such as the lawyer Maximilien Robespierre (1758–1794), oversaw the execution of as many as 40,000 people who were judged enemies of the state—most of whom were peasants and urban laborers. The institution of universal conscription allowed radicals to create an army large enough to spread the revolution to Europe. By the spring of 1794, France's army numbered some 800,000 soldiers,

THE RIGHTS OF WOMEN

In the late eighteenth century, revolutionaries extolled the rights of "man" across the Atlantic world. But what about women? Mary Wollstonecraft (1759–1797), an English writer, teacher, editor, and proponent of spreading education, grew exasperated at her male colleagues' celebration of newfound liberties for men. In 1792, she published A Vindication of the Rights of Woman, *one of the founding works of modern feminism. In this work, she argued that the superiority of men was as arbitrary as the divine right of kings. For this, she won the opprobrium of male progressives. The author is a "hyena in petticoats," noted one critic. In fact, she was arguing that women had the same rights to be reasonable creatures as men, and that especially education should be available equally to both sexes.*

I love man as my fellow; but his sceptre, real or usurped, extends not to me, unless the reason of an individual demands my homage; and even then the submission is to reason, and not to man. In fact, the conduct of an accountable being must be regulated by the operations of its own reason; or on what foundation rests the throne of God?

It appears to me necessary to dwell on these obvious truths, because females have been insulated, as it were; and while they have been stripped of the virtues that should clothe humanity, they have been decked with artificial graces that enable them to exercise a short-lived tyranny. Love, in their bosoms, taking the place of every nobler passion, their sole ambition is to be fair, to raise emotion instead of inspiring respect; and this ignoble desire, like the servility in absolute monarchies, destroys all strength of character. Liberty is the mother of virtue, and if women be, by their very constitution, slaves, and not allowed to breathe the sharp invigorating air of freedom, they must ever languish like exotics, and be reckoned beautiful flaws in nature. Let it also be remembered, that they are the only flaw.

As to the argument respecting the subjection in which the sex has ever been held, it retorts on man. The many have always been enthralled by the few; and monsters, who scarcely have shown any discernment of human excellence, have tyrannized over thousands of their fellow-creatures. Why have men of superior endowments submitted to such degradation? For, is it not universally acknowledged that kings, viewed collectively, have ever been inferior, in abilities and virtue, to the same number of men taken from the common mass of mankind—yet have they not, and are they not still treated with a degree of reverence that is an insult to reason? China is not the only country where a living man has been made a God. *Men* have submitted to superior strength to enjoy with impunity the pleasure of the moment; *women* have only done the same, and therefore till it is proved that the courtier, who servilely resigns the birthright of a man, is not a moral agent, it cannot be demonstrated that woman is essentially inferior to man because she has always been subjugated.

Brutal force has hitherto governed the world, and that the science of politics is in its infancy, is evident from philosophers scrupling to give the knowledge most useful to man that determinate distinction.

→ *In what ways are Mary Wollstonecraft's ideas an outgrowth of Enlightenment thinking?*
→ *Do you find Wollstonecraft's arguments compelling?*

SOURCE: Mary Wollstonecraft, *A Vindication of the Rights of Woman*, edited by Miriam Brody (New York: Penguin Books, 1792/1993), pp. 122–23.

making it the world's largest. In a startling departure from older practice, most of the French officers came from the middle classes, and some even had lower-class origins; foot soldiers identified with the French *patrie,* or fatherland, and demonstrated their solidarity with revolutionary songs like "The Marseillaise," which soon became the French national anthem. This enormous conscript army also was a major means by which ordinary Frenchmen learned to identify themselves with the goals of the nation as a whole.

The revolutionaries understood that to change society fundamentally they would have to do away with the symbols and rituals of the old regime. They changed street names and took down monuments to the royal family, substituting for religious and dynastic names the names of revolutionary heroes. They adopted a new flag, eliminated titles, and insisted that everyone be addressed as "Citizen." The revolutionaries' passion for rationalizing the world and the prospect of creating a new world should not be forgotten or underestimated. Indeed, they were so exhilarated by the new world they were creating that they changed time itself. Time was now reckoned not from the birth of Christ but from the moment that the French Republic was proclaimed: September 22, 1792, became day 1 of year 1 of the new age. The new calendar boasted only ten months, which were named after natural phenomena; one of the hottest summer months, for example, was called Thermidor and the often foggy late fall month was called Brumaire (*brume* in French means mist or fog). The radicals also attempted to supplant the Catholic faith, since they believed it smacked of corruption and inequality, with a religion of Reason. The French people could, they were told, worship a rational Supreme Being on days prescribed by the state. This did not go over very well, however. In 1794, in the town of Saint Vincent, the unveiling of a statue of the Supreme Being invited characteristic derision from townspeople. The occasion was interrupted by an old woman who motioned to all the women in the crowd to rise, turn their backs to the secular altar, raise their skirts, and expose their buttocks to the Supreme Being.

By mid-1794, enthusiasm for Robespierre's measures had lost popular support, as had the perpetrators of the Terror, many of whom would lose their heads. Robespierre himself went to the guillotine on 9 Thermidor (July 28, 1794), an event that marked the end of the Terror. In 1799, following more political turmoil, a coup d'état unexpectedly resulted in the rise to power of a thirty-year-old general from the recently annexed Mediterranean island of Corsica, Napoleon Bonaparte (1769–1821).

Napoleon checked the excesses and chaos of radical rule, while letting some revolutionary changes continue. Retreating from the anti-Catholicism of the Jacobins, Napoleon signed a concordat with the Vatican in 1801, which allowed religion to be freely practiced again in France. Determined to reform France as well as win the ongoing wars with her enemies, he retreated more and more from republican principles. Napoleon first was a member of a three-man consulate, then became first consul, and in 1804 proclaimed himself emperor. But he took the title Emperor of the French, not Emperor of France, and he prepared a constitution, which he submitted to a vote of approval known as a plebiscite. Maintaining the revolution's enthusiasm for a more rational order, he centralized government administration (appointing local prefects who reported to the central government) and revamped finances by eliminating tax exemptions and centralizing tax collection. Most important, he codified the nation's laws, including those for property and contracts, thereby providing a legal framework for business and commerce. The new "Code Napoleon" eliminated a baroque system of old laws and privileges and created a uniform civil law code for all of France. By emphasizing the equality of all men and the protection of individual property across France, Napoleon's reforms revolutionized European legal history.

NAPOLEON'S EMPIRE, 1799–1815

Napoleon shared with the radicals a determination to extend the geographic reach of the French Revolution. He dreamed of reinventing the Roman Empire on new foundations. Everywhere that French armies advanced, they claimed to be introducing the principles of liberty, equality, and fraternity, and in many places local populations embraced the French, regarding them as liberators from the old order. Napoleon believed that the entire world would greet his cause with open arms. But such was not always the case, as he learned in Egypt. After defeating Ottoman troops at the Battle of the Pyramids in 1798, Napoleon soon found himself faced with uprisings by the local Egyptian population.

In Portugal, Spain, and Russia, French troops also faced fierce national resistance. Portuguese and Spanish soldiers and peasants formed bands of resisters called guerrillas (after the French word *guerre*), and they were joined by British troops to fight the French in what became known as the Peninsular War (1808–1813). In Germany and in Italy, French occupiers quickly wore out their welcome, as they plundered resources, imposed taxes, and conscripted young men. As the locals in these areas tired of being told that French ways were better in all spheres of life, many looked

Battle of the Pyramids. The French army invaded Egypt with grand ambitions and high hopes. Napoleon brought a large cadre of scholars along with his 36,000-man army, intending to win Egyptians to the cause of the French Revolution and to establish a French imperial presence on the banks of the Nile. This idealized portrait of the famous Battle of the Pyramids, fought on July 21, 1798, shows Napoleon and his forces crushing the Mamluk military forces.

backward to their past for comfort and for inspiration to oppose the French. In so doing, they discovered something that had only barely been visible before: *national* traditions, borders, and character types. It is one of the great ironies of Napoleon's attempt to bring all of Europe under French rule that it did not create a unified landmass, but rather laid the foundations for nineteenth-century nationalist strife.

The revolutionary conflicts of the 1790s became, after 1800, a world war, with armies inspired by the revolutionary message fighting in Africa, across Europe, and throughout the Americas. In Europe, Napoleon extended his empire from the Iberian Peninsula in southwestern Europe all the way to the

Austrian and Prussian borders (see Map 15-2). By 1812, when he invaded Russia, however, his forces were overstretched and lacked food supplies to survive the harsh winter. Napoleon had been aided by divisions among his enemies; only Great Britain had been continuously at war with France (except for 1803–1804). But in 1813, after Napoleon's attack on Russia, all the major European powers (Austria, Prussia, Russia, and Great Britain) united against the French. Forced to retreat from Russia and now confronted by a united force of all his enemies, Napoleon and his army were finally vanquished in Paris in 1814. Exiled to the island of Elba, Napoleon escaped to lead his troops one last time. At the Battle of Waterloo in

MAP 15-2   NAPOLEON'S EMPIRE, 1812

During the first decade of the nineteenth century, Napoleon controlled almost the whole of Europe. How did Napoleon redraw the map of Europe? How did he administer regions directly under his control? What long-term impact would his reforms have on these regions?

Belgium in 1815, however, a coalition of armies from Prussia, Austria, Russia, and Britain decisively crushed Napoleon and his troops as they made their last stand.

At the Congress of Vienna (1814–1815), convened to restore peace, the victorious European monarchies agreed to respect each other's borders and to cooperate in guarding against future revolutions and war. Delegates to the congress understood that the world had changed, but they were determined to manage those changes as best they could. France became a monarchy once more, under Louis XVIII (the Bourbon brother of executed Louis XVI). Great Britain and Russia—one a constitutional monarchy (ruled primarily by a prime minister and legislative body but with monarchical oversight), the other an autocracy in which the ruler was not bound to share power with anyone—cooperated to prevent a revival of French or other attempts to assert hegemony over the continent.

The impact of the French Revolution and Napoleon's conquests, however, proved to be far reaching. In many of the smaller German principalities (states) between Prussia and France—which Napoleon reduced from roughly 300 to around 30—the changes introduced under French revolutionary occupation, such as the abolition of serfdom, remained in place after Napoleon's defeat. Napoleon's occupation of the Italian peninsula also sparked a number of underground movements for liberty and for Italian unification, much to the chagrin of Austrian and French monarchs. These upheavals also had decisive effects on Spain and Portugal's links to their colonies in the Americas.

REVOLUTIONS IN THE CARIBBEAN AND IBERIAN AMERICA

From North America and France, revolutionary enthusiasm spread through the Caribbean and Spanish and Portuguese America. But while men of property directed the war of independence that gave birth to the United States, the political upheaval in the rest of the Americas started from the bottom up, with uprisings by subordinated people of color, whose desire for freedom from exploitation predated the French Revolution's insistence on liberty.

Even before the French Revolution, Andean Indians had risen against Spanish colonial authority to protest onerous taxes and labor obligations. In a spectacular uprising in the 1780s, Andean Indians called for freedom from the forced labor draft and compulsory consumption of Spanish wares. Led by a local political chieftain who took the name of an early anti-Spanish rebel, Tupac Amarú, an Indian army of 40,000 to 60,000 besieged the ancient capital of Cuzco and nearly vanquished Spanish armies. It took the Spanish many years to eliminate the insurgents.

This uprising shook the confidence of Iberian-American colonial elites whose fear of their Indian or slave majorities caused them to renew their loyalty to the Spanish or Portuguese crown. For a time, these elites hesitated to follow the example of independence-seeking Anglo-American colonists, lest the struggle for political power unleash a more radical and uncontrollable social revolution. Ultimately, however, the French Revolution and Napoleonic wars shattered the ties between Spain and Portugal and their colonies in the Americas. Like their counterparts in the United States, Iberian-American elites severed colonial ties, but they sought to minimize the power of lower orders by establishing regimes that interpreted the principle of liberty to mean freedom for the property-owning classes. Only in the French colony of Saint Domingue (modern-day Haiti) did slaves carry out a successful insurrection. This sent shivers down the spine of white elites throughout the Americas and made them even more determined to secure property and order.

REVOLUTION IN SAINT DOMINGUE (HAITI) The French Revolution had its most immediate reverberation in the most highly prized of all French colonies, Saint Domingue. There, it led to the loss of the colony and the emancipation of its slaves, though the road to independence and emancipation was a bloody one. The island's black slave population numbered 500,000, compared with 40,000 white French settlers and about 30,000 free "people of color" (free mulattoes, who were of mixed black and white ancestry, as well as freed black slaves). After the events of 1789 in France, white settlers in Saint Domingue campaigned for self-government, while slaves borrowed the revolutionary language to denounce their masters. As whites clashed with people of color and slaves in 1791, the island descended into civil war. Dominican slaves fought French forces dispatched

Toussaint L'Ouverture. In the 1790s, Toussaint L'Ouverture led the slaves of the French colony of Saint Domingue in the world's largest and most successful slave insurrection. Toussaint embraced the principles of the French Revolution and demanded that universal rights be applied to people of African descent.

Revolution in Saint Domingue. In 1791, slaves and people of color rose up against the white planters. This engraving was based on a contemporary German report on the uprising and depicted the fears of the whites in the face of slave rebellion as much as the actual events themselves.

in 1792 to restore order. Finally, in 1793, the National Convention in France abolished slavery. Championed by highly influential figures like Robespierre and the Marquis de Lafayette, the argument that the principles of the revolution—liberty, fraternity, and equality—should apply to the French colonies as well as to the metropole briefly won out over claims that abolition would mean economic disaster. Once liberated, the former slaves took control of the island but had to fight British and Spanish forces sent to Saint Domingue to stir up trouble. When Napoleon took power, he decided to reassert French authority on the island, and he restored slavery in 1802. Napoleon sent an army of 58,000 under his brother-in-law, General Victor-Emmanuel Leclerc, to quash the forces led by Toussaint L'Ouverture (1743–1803), a former slave. Leclerc's army, perhaps the most fearsome in Europe, was decimated by guerrilla fighters and yellow fever. After eighteen months, the French surrendered and left, having lost over 50,000 of their finest soldiers. Toussaint L'Ouverture died in a French jail, after treachery led to his capture while he was trying to negotiate a settlement. Nonetheless, in January 1804, General Jean-Jacques Dessalines declared "Haiti" independent.

The scale of the revolt had serious environmental consequences. Not only did the canefields become battlefields, with extensive burnings and destruction that left the land smoldering in ashes, but freed slaves rushed to stake out independent plots of land for their subsistence. In some cases, old sugar plantations became peasant plots; in other cases the slaves fled to wooded hinterlands. In both places the new peasant class began to clear the land with great energy. The small country soon found itself increasingly deforested, and the intensive cultivation of small farms initiated a gradual process of erosion and soil depletion, which locked independent Haiti into a vicious cycle of environmental degradation and poverty.

Nor did independence bring the victorious Haitians international recognition from fellow revolutionaries. France's commitment to empire ultimately overrode its commitment to the ideals of republican citizenship. Toussaint (the "black Jacobin") and the slaves of Saint Domingue had shown a greater fidelity to ideals of liberty than the French themselves. Yet, Thomas Jefferson, the author of the Declaration of Independence and the U.S. president at the time, refused to recognize Haiti. Like many other American slave owners, Jefferson worried that the example of a successful slave insurrection might inspire slave revolts in the United States.

BRAZIL AND CONSTITUTIONAL MONARCHY   Brazil offers an example of a colonial society whose path to independent statehood minimized political turmoil and avoided social revolution. In late 1807, French troops stormed Lisbon, but they were too late to capture the royal Braganza family. The royal family and their extensive retinue fled to Rio de Janeiro, the capital of Portugal's prize colony, Brazil. Upon arrival, they instituted reforms in administration, agriculture, and manufacturing, and established schools, hospitals, and a library. The migration of the royal family to Brazil preempted colonial claims for autonomy, for Brazil was now the center of the Portuguese empire. Further dampening revolutionary enthusiasm was the royal family's willingness to share power with the local planter aristocracy. Over the ensuing years, the economy prospered, and slavery expanded.

In 1821, the exiled Portuguese king agreed to return to Lisbon, leaving instructions to his son Pedro to preserve the family lineage in Rio de Janeiro. It did not take long, however, before Brazilian elites rejected Portugal altogether. Faced with the threat that colonists might topple the dynasty in Rio de Janeiro and concerned that such upheaval might cascade into regional disputes and rivalries, Pedro declared Brazil an independent empire that was free from Portugal in 1822. Shortly thereafter, he signed a charter establishing a constitutional monarchy that would last until the late nineteenth century.

Brazilian business elites and bureaucrats collaborated to minimize their conflicts, lest an insurrection of slaves erupt. Regional insurrections, like the creation of the fledgling Republic of the Equator in 1817, were crushed. In the south, a campaign by cowboys, known as gauchos, who wanted a

INSPIRATIONS FOR SLAVE REBELLION ON HAITI

The ideals of the French Revolution spread rapidly beyond France through the rest of Europe and even overseas. In few places did they produce a more radical effect than on the island of Saint Domingue, renamed Haiti after it acquired independence. By the 1780s, Saint Domingue was France's richest colony and its most valuable overseas trading possession. Its wealth came from sugar plantations that depended on a vast, highly coerced slave population. About 40,000 whites ruled over and ruthlessly exploited 500,000 enslaved Africans, approximately two-thirds of whom had recently arrived from Africa. The lives of the slaves were short and brutal, lasting on average only fifteen years; hence the need for the wealthy planter class to replenish their labor supplies from Africa at frequent intervals. White planters from the island had the reputation of great wealth. People who dressed ostentatiously as they strode the streets of Paris in the late eighteenth century were said to be as wealthy as a "creole," meaning a Caribbean planter. But the white planters also knew their privileges were vulnerable, which made them eager to amass quick fortunes so that they could sell out and return to France. These men and women were vastly outnumbered by the enslaved, who were seething with resentment, at a time when abolitionist sentiments were gaining ground in Europe and even circulating among the slaves in the Americas.

Yet, the planters greeted the onset of the French Revolution in 1789 with enthusiasm. They saw an opportunity to gain internal political power and to engage in wider trading contacts with North America and the rest of the world. They ignored, at their peril, the fact that the ideals of the French Revolution, and especially its slogan of liberty, equality, and fraternity, could inspire the island's free blacks, free mulattoes, and slaves. Indeed, no sooner had the white planters thrown in their lot with the Third Estate in France than a slave rebellion broke out in their midst in Saint Domingue. From its inception in August 1791, it led, after great loss of life to African slave dissidents and French soldiers, to the proclamation of an independent state in Haiti in 1804, ruled by African-Americans. Haiti became, in fact, the Americas' second independent republican government.

The revolution had many sources of inspiration. It was both French and African. According to a later West Indian scholar, a group of black Jacobins, determined to carry the ideals of the French Revolution to their logical end point—the abolition of slavery—made up the revolutionary cadre. Their undisputed leader was a freed black by the name of Toussaint L'Ouverture, who had learned about the French abolitionist writings of the age. But it is hardly surprising, given how recently most of the slaves had arrived from Africa, that African cultural and political ideals also fomented slave resistance. At a secret forest meeting held on August 14, 1791, the persons who were to lead the initial stage of the revolution gathered to affirm their commitment to one another at a voodoo ritual, presided over by a tall, black priestess, "with strange eyes and bristly hair." Voodoo was a mixture of African and New World religious beliefs that existed among slave communities in many parts of the Americas (see Chapter 14). According to one description of the forest ceremony, the priestess arrived "armed with a long pointed knife that she waved above her head [as] she performed a sinister dance singing an African song, which the others, face down against the ground, repeated as a chorus. A black pig was then dragged in front of her, and she split it open with her knife. The animal's blood was collected in a wooden bowl and served still foaming to each delegate. At a signal from the priestess, everyone threw themselves on their knees and swore blindly to obey the orders of Boukman, who had been proclaimed supreme chief of the rebellion." Boukman was a voodoo chief himself, and he initiated the revolution against the planters, though it was Toussaint L'Ouverture who later assumed leadership of the revolt.

Inspired by both voodoo and the French Revolution, the rebellion in Saint Domingue resulted in a series of dramatic ruptures. European slavery came to an end. White planters yielded to a black political elite. Hundreds of thousands of slaves and French soldiers perished or were maimed, and the old sugar export economy could no longer be sustained. No slave shipments arrived, and no sugar was exported.

decentralized federation with a great deal of autonomy, also proved to be no match for the central government's powerful army and navy. Even the largest urban slave revolt in the Americas, led by African Muslims in the Brazilian state of Bahia in 1835, was put down in a matter of days. By the 1840s, Brazil had achieved a political stability unmatched in the Americas. Indeed, Brazil's socially controlled transition from colony to nation proved to be the exception in Latin America.

The strength of the Brazilian state and its ruling elite gave tremendous impetus to the expansion of the agrarian frontier and eventually led to profound environmental degradation. Especially in the new coffee belts, landowners oversaw the clearing of old Atlantic hardwood forests, pushing the frontier inward and opening swaths of land for slaves and squatters to plant coffee trees in lieu of ancient woodlands. This was a process that had begun with coastal sugarcane but accelerated with coffee plantings, which drove the frontier into the hilly regions of São Paulo (which eventually became the world's largest single regional supplier of coffee). Coffee was a more intense threat to Brazil's great forests than any other invader in the previous 300 years. But it also created problems. Coffee trees thrived on soils that were neither soggy nor parched. But this fertile soil was also quickly depleted by the monocrop as planters razed the "virgin" balanced forest, leading within a generation to infertile soils and extensive erosion. This propelled coffee planters further into the frontier to clearcut or burn the old forest and plant coffee groves. The scale of the environmental change was monumental: between 1788 and 1888 (when slavery was abolished), Brazil produced about 10 million tons of coffee, which required the clearing or burning of 300 million tons of ancient forest biomass.

MEXICO'S INDEPENDENCE When Napoleon occupied Spain, he sparked a crisis in the Spanish empire. Unlike the Portuguese Braganza family, which managed to elude French troops, the Spanish Bourbons fell captive to Napoleon in 1807 and spent many years under comfortable house arrest. Colonial elites in Buenos Aires, Caracas, and Mexico City, grappling with the problem of self-rule without an emperor, came to enjoy autonomy from Madrid. Creoles (American-born Spaniards) resented it when the mother country reinstated peninsulars (officials from Spain) once the Spanish Bourbons returned to power in 1814. The creoles disliked the economic regulations and taxation of the mother country and chafed under the rule of the peninsulars. Inspired by Enlightenment thinkers and revolution in North America, the creoles wished to retain their elite privileges and to rid their lands of the peninsulars.

In Mexico, the royal army prevailed as long as there was any hope that the emperor in Madrid could keep a firm grip on political authority. But from 1810 to 1813, two rural priests, Father Miguel Hidalgo (1753–1811) and Father José María Morelos (1765–1815), galvanized an insurrection that

Miguel Hidalgo y Costilla. At the center of this mural by Juan O'Gorman is the revolutionary Mexican priest Miguel Hidalgo y Costilla, who led the first uprising against Spanish rulers. This painting suggests the rebellion was a multiclass and multiethnic movement.

incorporated a broad alliance of peasants, Indians, and artisans. They advocated an end to elite abuses, denounced bad government, and called for redistribution of wealth, return of land to the Indians, and respect for the Virgin of Guadalupe (who would become Mexico's patron saint). The rebels sent shock waves across the viceroyalty and nearly encircled Mexico City itself, the capital of Spain's richest colony. This horrified peninsulars and creoles alike, who overcame internal disputes to plead with Spanish armies to rescue them from the rebels. It took years, but the royal armies eventually crushed the uprising.

Despite the military victory, the Spanish crown's hold on its colony gave way. In these years of conflict, colonists started to enjoy measures of autonomy and even began electing representatives to local assemblies. Moreover, like the creoles of South America, those of Mexico were beginning to identify themselves more as Mexicans and less as Spanish Americans. So, when Ferdinand VII, the Spanish king, appeared unable to handle affairs, not only abroad but within Spain itself, the colonists began considering home rule. The critical factor was the army, which remained faithful to the crown. When anarchy seemed to spread through Spain in 1820, however, Mexican generals, with the support of the creoles, cut their losses, proclaiming Mexican independence in 1821.

OTHER SOUTH AMERICAN REVOLUTIONS Most political independence movements in Spanish America evolved into noisy social revolutions or civil wars. The process of uncoupling Spain's grip on mainland America was far more prolonged and militarized than was Britain's separation from its American colonies. The struggle for independence from Spain completely refashioned the nature of political leadership in South America. Venezuela's Simón Bolívar (1783–1830), the son of a wealthy merchant-planter family who was weaned on European Enlightenment texts, dreamed of a land governed by reason. In Napoleonic France, he found a compelling model of a new state, one forged by military heroism and constitutional proclamations. The same held true for the less aristocratic Argentine leader, General José de San Martín (1778–1850). Men like Bolívar, San Martín, and their many generals waged extended wars between 1810 and 1824. In some areas, like present-day Uruguay and Venezuela, the carnage depopulated entire provinces.

What in South America started as a political revolution against Bourbon authority escalated into a social struggle among Indians, mestizos, slaves, and whites. The militarized populace threatened the fortunes of planters and great merchants. Rural folk from the grasslands rode into battle against aristocratic creoles. Andean Indians fled the mines and occupied great estates. Provinces fought their neighbors. Popular armies, having defeated Spain by the 1820s, engaged in civil wars over the new postcolonial order in South America. By the 1840s and 1850s, the old viceroyalties had broken up.

Simón Bolívar. The son of a wealthy creole family, Simón Bolívar fought Spanish armies from Venezuela to Bolivia, securing the independence of five countries. Bolívar wanted to transform the former colonies into modern republics and used many of the icons of revolution from the rest of the Atlantic world—among his favorite models were George Washington and Napoleon Bonaparte. Notice how this image portrays Bolívar in a quintessential Napoleonic pose on horseback.

In Latin America, new states, common myths of sacrifice, and collective identities of nationhood emerged, but the people active in these political communities made up a narrow social elite, and the myths were contradictory. Simón Bolívar, for instance, repeatedly urged his followers to become "American," to identify with a larger, pan-creole ideal. He tried to get the liberated countries to unite into a Latin American confederation, urging Peru and Bolivia to join Venezuela, Ecuador, and Colombia in the "Gran Colombia." But the confederation quickly fell apart as local identities continued to take precedence over Spanish-American unity. Bolívar's dream of a United States of South America, possibly even governed by a hereditary king or dictator, gave way to unstable national republics. Bolívar met his end surrounded and hounded by his enemies; San Martín died in exile. The real heirs to independence were not slaves, Indians, or even republican national leaders, but local military chieftains called *caudillos,* who often forged alliances with landowners. The contradictory legacy of the revolutions of Spanish America was the triumph of wealthy and powerful elites under a banner of liberty yet often at the expense of poorer, ethnic, and mixed populations.

CHANGE AND TRADE IN AFRICA

> → *Why did the abolition of the slave trade have unintended effects on African society?*

Along with Europe and the Americas, Africa, the third corner of the Atlantic world, was also swept up in revolutionary tides. Increased domestic and world trade, particularly but not exclusively in African slaves, shifted the terms of state-building across the landmass. Around the edges of Lake Victoria, in the highlands of present-day Rwanda and Burundi, and in southern Africa, new, more powerful kingdoms emerged in the first half of the nineteenth century. Burgeoning commerce created new sources of wealth for ruling groups, who began to assert their power over other peoples. Some regimes, however, fell apart as a result of internal rivalries. The main commercial catalyst for Africa's political shake-up was the rapid growth and then the demise of the Atlantic slave trade.

ABOLITION OF THE SLAVE TRADE

Even as it enriched and empowered some Africans and many Europeans, the slave trade became a subject of fierce debate in the late eighteenth century. Some European and American revolutionaries wanted trade and production to be governed not by the laws of compulsion, but by the laws of supply and demand. Alongside these advocates of free trade emerged a small but committed group of abolitionists who insisted that traffic in slaves was immoral. In London, they created committees, often led by Quakers, to lobby Parliament for an end to the slave trade. Quakers in Philadelphia followed suit. Pamphlets, reports, and personal narratives denounced the traffic in people.

In response to abolitionist campaigns, North Atlantic powers moved to prohibit the international slave trade. Denmark acted first in 1803, Great Britain followed in 1807, and the United States banned it in 1808. Over time, the British persuaded the French and other European governments of the rightness of this position, with France abolishing the slave trade in 1814, the Netherlands in 1817, and Spain in 1845. To enforce the ban, Britain posted an anti-slave-trade naval squadron off the coast of West Africa to cut off traders operating above the equator and compelled the emperor of Brazil

to respect earlier promises to end slave imports. After 1850, Atlantic slave-shipping dropped sharply. In 1867, the last slave vessel entered a New World harbor, Havana.

But until the 1860s, slavers continued to ply the waters of the West African coast to buy captives and illegally transport them as slaves. The British naval squadrons stopped as many smugglers as they could and took the captives they freed to the British base at Sierra Leone, where they were resettled. Liberia, first settled in 1821 by free black Americans, also became a refuge for freed captives and for former slaves returning to Africa from the Americas.

NEW TRADE WITH AFRICA

While eventually choking off the Atlantic slave trade, Europeans endeavored to promote new forms of commerce with Africa. European traders, who had previously thought of Africa only as a source of human captives, now wanted Africans to supply Europe with raw materials and for them to purchase European manufactures. European publicists dubbed the new trade "legitimate" commerce to distinguish it from the "illegitimate" trade in human beings. It was intended to raise the standards of living of Africans by substituting trade in produce for trade in slaves. West African cultivators responded by beginning a brisk export in palm kernels and peanuts. The real bonanza was in vegetable oils to lubricate machinery and to be made into candles, and especially palm oil to produce soap. European merchants argued that by becoming vibrant export societies, Africans would earn the wealth to become potentially profitable importers of European wares.

Arising in the age of legitimate commerce, the new palm and peanut plantations of Africa were less devastating to the environment than their predecessors in the West Indies. There forests were felled to make way for sugar estates (Chapter 12). In West Africa, where palm products became crucial exports, the palm tree had always grown wild and though some areas of intensive cultivation witnessed a degree of deforestation, the results were not comparable to the Caribbean. Especially in northwest Africa (present-day Senegal) peanuts thrive in sandy soils and their cultivation often leads to tree removal. But the great period of deforestation did not occur until the twentieth century when cultivators moved into the more arid regions. There removal of trees altered the environment and the climate, and led quickly to a process of desertification.

The gradual abolition of the slave trade and the emergence of legitimate commerce gave rise to a new generation of West African merchants. Inserting themselves between African producers in the interior or plantations on the coast, and the European export-import firms, they amassed fortunes. There were many rags-to-riches stories, like that of King Jaja of Opobo (1821–1891), who was kidnapped and

→ *Why did the abolition of the slave trade have unintended effects on African society?*

Chasing Slave Dhows. From being the major proponents of the Atlantic slave trade the British became its chief opponents, using their naval forces to suppress those European and African slave traders who attempted to subvert the injunction against slave trading. Here a British vessel chases an East African slaving dhow trying to run slaves from the island of Zanzibar.

sold into slavery as a youngster. Jaja was initially one of the many slaves who paddled the canoes that carried palm oil from inland markets to coastal ports. He rose to become the head of a coastal canoe house. As a powerful merchant-prince and chief, he founded the new port of Opobo and could summon a flotilla of war canoes on command. Another freed slave, a Yoruba, William Lewis, made his way back to Africa and settled in Sierra Leone in 1828. Starting with only a few utensils and a small plot of land, Lewis became a successful merchant who was able to send his son Samuel to England for his education. There, Samuel studied law, attended University College in London, and eventually became an important political leader in Sierra Leone. Queen Victoria recognized him with a knighthood.

Just as the slave trade shaped the rhythms of African political communities, its demise forced African polities to adjust. For some, it was a boon because it ended the constant drainage of people from an already underpopulated region. For others, especially if they had positioned themselves as the commercial brokers between African slave supply and Euro-American demand, the demise of the traffic was a disaster, cutting off income necessary to buy European arms and luxury goods. The Asante state, however, endured even as the slave trade declined and despite British military efforts to de-

King Jaja of Opobo. Among the merchant-princes who came to prominence along the West African coast in the nineteenth century was King Jaja of Opobo, who rose out of slavery to become the head of a canoe house that transported and traded palm oil. In 1869, Jaja established an independent trading state based around the city of Opobo.

stroy it. Other West African regimes, like the Yoruba kingdom, collapsed. There, civil strife broke out once chieftains could no longer use the spoils of the slave trade to support retinues and armies.

The rise of free labor in the Atlantic world and the dwindling of the foreign slave trade had another unintended and even perverse effect in Africa: it strengthened slavery in Africa

Primary Source

FREDERICK DOUGLASS ASKS, "WHAT TO THE SLAVE IS THE FOURTH OF JULY?"

Born in 1818, Frederick Douglass spent the first twenty years of his life as a slave. After running away in 1838, Douglass toured the northern United States delivering speeches that attacked the institution of slavery. The publication of Douglass's autobiography in 1845 cemented his standing as a leading abolitionist. In the excerpt below, taken from an address delivered on July 5, 1852, Douglass contrasts the freedom and natural rights extolled in the American Declaration of Independence and celebrated on the Fourth of July with the dehumanizing condition—and lack of freedom—of African-American slaves.

Fellow-Citizens—pardon me, and allow me to ask, why am I called upon to speak here to-day? What have I, or those I represent, to do with your national independence? Are the great principles of political freedom and of natural justice, embodied in that Declaration of Independence, extended to us? and am I, therefore, called upon to bring our humble offering to the national altar, and to confess the benefits, and express devout gratitude for the blessings, resulting from your independence to us? . . .

But, such is not the state of the case. I say it with a sad sense of the disparity between us. I am not included within the pale of this glorious anniversary! Your high independence only reveals the immeasurable distance between us. The blessings in which you this day rejoice, are not enjoyed in common. The rich inheritance of justice, liberty, prosperity, and independence, bequeathed by your fathers, is shared by you, not by me. The sunlight that brought life and healing to you, has brought stripes and death to me. This Fourth of July is *yours*, not *mine*. *You* may rejoice, *I* must mourn. . . .

. . . Must I undertake to prove that the slave is a man? That point is conceded already. Nobody doubts it. The slaveholders themselves acknowledge it in the enactment of laws for their government. They acknowledge it when they punish disobedience on the part of the slave. There

are seventy-two crimes in the state of Virginia, which, if committed by a black man (no matter how ignorant he be) subject him to the punishment of death; while only two of these same crimes will subject a white man to the like punishment. What is this but the acknowledgment that the slave is a moral, intellectual, and responsible being. The manhood of the slave is conceded. It is admitted in the fact that southern statute books are covered with enactments forbidding, under severe fines and penalties, the teaching of the slave to read or write. When you can point to any such laws, in reference to the beasts of the field, then I may consent to argue the manhood of the slave. When the dogs in your streets, when the fowls of the air, when the cattle on your hills, when the fish of the sea, and the reptiles that crawl, shall be unable to distinguish the slave from a brute, then will I argue with you that the slave is a man!

➔ *How does Douglass suggest that slaves are indeed human beings?*
➔ *What is the significance of the last sentence of Douglass's speech?*

SOURCE: David W. Blight (ed.), *Narrative of the Life of Frederick Douglass: An American Slave, Written by Himself* (Boston: Bedford Books, 1993), pp. 141–45.

itself. In some African locales by the mid-nineteenth century, slaves accounted for more than half of the population. No longer were slaves mainly to be found in domestic employment, sharing the same table with their masters, eating the

same foods, and likely to be assimilated into that society. Instead, slaves worked on palm oil plantations or, in East Africa (especially in Zanzibar), on clove plantations owned by Arabs or Swahilis. They also served in the military forces, carried palm oil and ivory to markets as porters, or served as the oars-men on the canoes that plied the rivers leading to the coast. In 1850, the Fulani emirates of northern Nigeria had as many as 2.5 million slaves, more than the slaves in independent Brazil and second only to the number of slaves in the United States. No longer the supplier of slaves, Africa, in the wake of Atlantic world revolutions, had turned into the largest slaveholding region.

ECONOMIC REORDERING

> → *How did the industrial and commercial revolutions reorder society?*

The political upheavals in the Atlantic world shattered the old mercantilist system and encouraged economic transfor-mations that placed western Europe at the hub of an in-creasingly interconnected world economy. These economic transformations are often referred to collectively as the in-dustrial revolution. They also marked the opening of what many scholars regard as "the great divide" in world history between the economically developed areas of the world and less developed areas. Certainly by 1850 people living in west-ern Europe and North America were wealthier and healthier than their counterparts elsewhere—a statement that proba-bly could not have been made about the world's population a century earlier. In addition, the western Europeans, notably

the British, were able to translate their economic prowess into political power and were in the process of altering the global balance of power.

BRITAIN'S ECONOMIC LEADERSHIP

The presence of a variety of institutional and economic fac-tors enabled the British to pioneer the innovations that have ever since characterized economic modernity. To begin with, Britain had large and accessible supplies of coal and iron, two of the most important raw materials used to produce the goods of what has conventionally been called the industrial revolution. This term has usually been employed to designate developments in Britain beginning in the second half of the eighteenth century—though historians now know that there were similar phases of development earlier, during the Song dynasty in China (960–1127 CE), for example, and that fur-ther "industrial revolutions" would later ensue in Europe and elsewhere. In addition, Britain's manufacturers benefited from a cascade of technological innovations, notably in steam power and textile production, which they put to practical use to produce cheaper goods in larger quantities. But none of these physical or technological factors alone propelled an economic revolution. What was crucial also was that politi-cal and social conditions enabled merchants and industri-alists to mobilize capital for investment while expanding internal and international markets for their commodities. Finally, Britain's agrarian colonies provided it with sources of financial investment, raw materials, and markets for manu-factured goods. And after the independence of most New

A Model Textile Mill. In the nineteenth century, the English industrialist and reformer Robert Owen tried to create humane factories. Worried about the terrible conditions in most textile mills, Owen created clean and orderly working environments in his mills and had the work rules posted on the walls. Owen still shared most of his contemporaries' employment of children, as can be seen in this image.

New Farming Technologies. Although new technologies only gradually transformed agriculture, the spread of more intensive cultivation led to increased yields.

World colonies in the late eighteenth and early nineteenth centuries, the commitment to free trade enabled British consumers to import cheap foodstuffs from the Americas. It is important to note that these factors were present individually elsewhere in Europe; but in Britain they converged, driving the British economy into continuous and self-sustaining economic growth and constituting a "revolution" that would transform social relations across most of the country.

A crucial aspect of economic progress also involved a remarkable expansion in agricultural production for the market, and here, too, British farmers led the way. By exploiting new lands and making existing lands more productive (through enclosing fields and pastures and draining swamp land), farmers in western Europe and North America could feed more mouths and support a large increase in population. In Great Britain, for example, the population rose from about 5 million in the early 1700s to 9 million by 1800 and to 18 million by 1851. Population growth, in turn, generated pressure on the land and forced many people to migrate to the cities, creating a supply of urban laborers for the new manufacturing industries. Also adding to the growth of the labor force was the appropriation of common lands as private property by English landowners in the eighteenth century. This threw a large number of small farmers off the land, compelling them to earn their livelihood as wage workers.

As Britain outdistanced its European rivals in manufacturing, claiming for itself the designation "the workshop of the world," a new economic world order began to emerge (see Map 15-3). Britain's industrial capitalists increased productivity by drawing on labor from around the world. British wage laborers turned the raw cotton grown by peasants in India and slaves in North America into cloth, which was then sold in the home market or exported abroad in exchange for agricultural products from India and Argentina. Thus emerged a new organization of labor, whereby colonies and dependencies would export raw materials to industrializing states, which would then export manufactures to colonies and dependencies, all under the banner of free trade and free (wage) labor.

TRADING AND FINANCING

Economic reordering involved dramatic expansions and alterations in patterns of commerce and consumption. By the eighteenth century, sugar and silver, the pioneering commercial commodities of world trade, were joined by other products. Tea became a beverage of international commerce. Its leaves came from China, the sugar to cut its bitterness from the Caribbean, the slaves to harvest the sweetener from Africa, and the ceramics from which to drink a proper cup from the English Midlands. Soap was another truly international commodity. In the 1840s, the American entrepreneur William Colgate was importing palm oil from the slave states of West Africa, coconut oil from Malabar and Ceylon, and poppy seed oil from colonial South Asia, all to make aromatic bars of soap, which were then sold around the world.

So widespread was the economic reordering that ordinary people were able to purchase imported goods with their earnings. Thus, even the poor expanded their diets to include coffee, tea, and sugar—all tropical goods, and all goods that had to be purchased on the market with cash. European artisans as well as farmers purchased tools, furnishings, and home decorations on the market. Slaves and colonial laborers also used their meager earnings to buy imported cotton cloth made in Europe from the raw cotton they picked.

Merchants reaped the greatest rewards of international trade, earning more money than previous traders ever had and enjoying higher social status than they had under dynastic regimes. To be sure, merchants faced great risks. Bad weather, unexpected price fluctuations, and inept handling turned many promising deals into bankrupting disasters. But successful merchants accumulated immense fortunes. Also profiting were accountants and lawyers, who assisted with insurance, bookkeeping, and the recording of legal documents. The new class of commercial men and women, known as the "bourgeoisie," took up residence in thriving ports and other centers of trade. The bourgeoisie formed a new elite, not of birth and titles, but of property and capital. They increasingly assumed positions of authority to match their growing wealth. Indeed, if the bourgeoisie sometimes strove to marry their sons and daughters into old aristocratic families as a way to establish legitimacy for their new wealth, aristocrats just as often sought such marriages for the money and property they brought.

→ *How did the industrial and commercial revolutions reorder society?*

MAP 15-3   INDUSTRIAL EUROPE AROUND 1850
Why were the effects of the Industrial Revolution more rapidly apparent in Great Britain and in north-central Europe? How did the presence of an extensive railroad system help to accelerate industrialization? What effects did the Industrial Revolution have on urban population densities?

The greatest fortunes—and considerable political power—flowed to those who bankrolled world trade. Some financiers, like many merchants, emerged not from long-established noble families but from the common people. Consider, for example, Mayer Amschel Rothschild (1744–1812). Born the son of a money changer in the Jewish ghetto of Frankfurt, Rothschild expanded his activities from coin dealing to money changing, from trading textiles to lending funds to kings and governments, especially to those at war. By the time of his death, he owned the world's biggest banking operation, and his five sons were running powerful branches in London, Paris, Vienna, and Naples, as well as in Frankfurt.

By extending credit for a fee, families like the Rothschilds also enabled traders to ship goods across long distances without having to worry about immediate payment. All these financial changes eased the way for world integration through the flow of goods as well as the flow of money. In the 1820s, sizeable funds amassed in London flowed out to Egypt, Mexico, and New York to support trade, public investment, and even speculation. Some eager British financiers, for example, jumped at the promise of untold fortunes in the silver mines of La Rioja in South America. They invested some of their own capital and, even more, the capital of others in the mines, but they never saw a return.

Merchants and financiers soon recognized that a new commercial order was emerging and wanted new laws to support it. Through the eighteenth century, and especially with the political shake-up of old regimes, these emerging urban elites gained more political power. By the early nineteenth century, they began to press for free trade, the right to trade freely across borders. This idea dated back to the sixteenth century and had been extensively elaborated in the writings of Adam Smith in the eighteenth century. But it took decades for the doctrine to become practice, partly because so many domestic interests benefited from special tariff protections and exclusive access to certain markets. For example, Europe's landed interests ensured that laws obstructed the entry of cheaper foodstuffs; in Great Britain, the Corn Laws imposed a tariff on imported grain and thereby kept the price of bread artificially high. Old mercantilist laws likewise protected national shipping interests. As long as more businesses profited from commercial protection, free trade was a pipe dream.

The first region to embrace free trade practices and policies was the Americas. Merchants in the former colonies wanted access to obstructed markets. Especially in Iberian America, merchants wanted to export raw materials and import needed European, and especially British, manufactured goods—all with a minimum of hurdles and taxes. After 1810, Latin American countries abolished most tariffs protecting local producers and removed all special laws covering Spanish and Portuguese commerce. The United States also sought to promote its raw materials, but never went as far as Latin America in dismantling protection of local producers against competitive imports. Rather, in the United States, local industries clamored for laws to stop cheap British goods from entering the domestic market.

The rise of free trade in the Americas offered European consumers access to cheap foodstuffs and other primary staples, like timber, cotton, leather, and minerals. The British were the first to seize on the opportunity of free trade with New World societies. Indeed, with fewer formal ties, restricted only to a handful of Caribbean islands and Canada, free trade became the de facto guiding principle of Atlantic commerce between Britain and the Americas. In the 1840s, old protectionist laws gave way to open markets. Under the Conservative British prime minister Robert Peel (1788–1850), new budgets slashed the duties on all kinds of imported staples. Moreover, when the potato famine hit Ireland in the mid-1840s, the British government repealed the Corn Laws (in 1846) to allow grains to enter duty free from around the world. Finally, the succeeding Liberal government abolished many of the remaining obstacles and pref-

Irish Potato Famine. Victims of the Irish potato famine, winter 1849–50. By this time, hundreds of thousands of men, women, and children had already died or left Ireland for the Americas.

→ *How did the industrial and commercial revolutions reorder society?*

Primary Source

THE OTHER REVOLUTION OF 1776

The year 1776 is mainly known as the year American colonists declared their independence from the British Empire, but it also was the year of the publication of Adam Smith's An Inquiry into the Nature and Causes of the Wealth of Nations, *the most important book in the history of economic thought. Smith, a Scottish philosopher, felt that constraints on trade, by governments or private monopolies, deprived people of their ability to realize their full potential and as such impoverished nations. Although he was not opposed to colonies* per se, *in this short selection, he warns British authorities that the exclusions placed on their colonies, which bear the brunt of mercantilist controls, are not only unjust, they are counterproductive. Thus, "free trade" is tied up with the fate of Europe's colonies.*

The exclusive trade of the mother countries tends to diminish, or, at least, to keep down below what they would otherwise rise to, both the enjoyments and industry of all those nations in general, and of the American colonies in particular. It is a dead weight upon the action of one of the great springs which puts into motion a great part of the business of mankind. By rendering the colony produce dearer in all other countries, it lessens its consumption, and thereby cramps the industry of the colonies, and both the enjoyments and the industry of all other countries, which both enjoy less when they pay more for what they enjoy, and produce less when they get less for what they produce. By rendering the produce of all other countries dearer in the colonies, it cramps, in the same manner, the industry of all other countries, and both the enjoyments and the industry of the colonies. It is a clog which, for the supposed benefit of some particular countries, embarrasses the pleasures, and encumbers the industry of all other countries; but of the colonies more than of any other. It not only excludes, as much as possible, all other countries from one particular market; but it confines, as much as possible, the colonies to one particular market: and the difference is very great between being excluded from one particular market, when all others are open, and being confined to one particular market, when all others are shut up. The surplus produce of the colonies, however, is the original source of all that increase of enjoyments and industry which Europe derives from the discovery and colonization of America; and the exclusive trade of the mother countries tends to render this source much less abundant than it otherwise would be.

→ *According to Smith, how does exclusive trade between the north country and the colonists diminish the development of the colonies?*
→ *What historical developments in this period contributed to the growth of free trade?*

SOURCE: Adam Smith, *An Inquiry into the Nature and Causes of the Wealth of Nations,* Book 4, edited by Edwin Cannan (Chicago: The University of Chicago Press, 1776/1977), pp. 105–106.

erences, especially the Navigation Acts, which had been originally designed to prevent Dutch merchants from taking over English trade routes. Free trade then became the guiding commercial policy of Great Britain as it embraced the idea that domestic wealth depended on imports of basic goods and exports of new industrial commodities to the world's consumers.

MANUFACTURING

Bankers and merchants facilitated the development not only of trade but also of industries. Industrial development was due to several interlocking changes, however. The accumulation and diffusion of technical knowledge necessary for manufacturing began in the countryside, where handicraft operations were gradually enlarged and mechanized. Often it was small- and medium-sized producers, and the occasional crackpot in a barn, who were the inventors and innovators. Numerous little inventions, applied and diffused across the Atlantic world, gradually built up a stock of technical knowledge and practice that was widely available.

Most famous of these inventors was James Watt (1736–1819) of Scotland, who succeeded in making steam engines more efficient. Steam engines burned coal to boil water, and the resulting steam drove mechanized devices. Watt devised a way to separate steam condensers from piston cylinders so that pistons could be kept hot and therefore running constantly. This set the stage for a fuel-efficient engine. Early prototypes of Watt's engine were used to pump water out of mines. After moving to Birmingham in 1774, Watt joined forces with the industrialist Matthew Boulton (1728–1809), who marketed the steam engine, won an extension of the patent for another twenty-five years, and set up a special laboratory for Watt so that he could refine his device. Collaboration between inventors and entrepreneurs was a sign of the new times. Moreover, perhaps the most important aspect of Watt's engineering feat was that it was subject to a stream of improvement and adaptation, not just from Boulton and company, but from its competitors as well.

The steam engine, driven by burning coal, provided vastly increased power and catalyzed a revolution in transportation. Steam-powered ships and railroads, built once inventors were able to construct lighter engines that required less coal to run, slashed the time and cost of long-distance travel. Steam power's diffusion accelerated when iron-making improved, allowing for the production of railroad track and cables used to hang suspension bridges. The first public rail line opened in 1830 in England between Manchester and Liverpool. Dur-

ing the next twenty years, railway mileage increased from less than 100 to almost 25,000 in England, France, Russia, and the German-speaking countries. Steamships appeared in the 1780s in France, Britain, and the United States, and in 1807 Robert Fulton inaugurated the first commercially successful route between New York City and Albany on the Hudson River. A century of toying with boilers and pistons culminated in the radical reduction of distances. Steam-powered engines also improved sugar refining, pottery making, and many other industrial processes. Mechanizing processes that would have taken much longer and been subject to human error if done by hand enabled manufacturers to make more products at cheaper cost.

Textile production was one of the areas that benefited from both technical changes and the consolidation of different stages of the work in a factory. With new machinery, a single textile operator could handle many looms and spindles at once and could produce bolts of cloth with stunning efficiency. Gone were the hand tools, the family traditions, and the loosely organized and dispersed systems of households producing cloth in their homes for local merchants to carry to markets. The new material was also stronger, finer, and more uniform. Thanks to such innovations, British cotton output increased tenfold between 1770 and 1790, leading to a 90 percent decline in the price of cloth between 1782 and 1812.

Most raw cotton for the British cloth industry had come from colonial India until 1793, when the American inventor Eli Whitney (1765–1825) patented a device called a "cotton gin" that separated cotton seeds from fiber. Cotton farming quickly spread from South Carolina into Georgia, Alabama, Mississippi, and Louisiana, as the United States came to produce more than 80 percent of the world cotton supply by the

Steam Locomotive. A woodcut of a steam locomotive in Syracuse New York, c. 1850.

A Cotton Textile Mill in the 1830s. The region of Lancashire became one of the major industrial hubs for textile production in the world. By the 1830s, mills had made the shift from artisanal work to highly mechanical mass production. Among the great breakthroughs was the discovery that cloth could be printed with designs, such as paisley or calico (as in this image), and marketed to middle-class consumers.

1850s. Thus, the American South became a supplier of raw cotton to Britain. In turn, every black slave in the Americas and many Indians in British India could be consumers of cheap, British-produced cotton shirts. Between 1816 and 1848, cotton goods amounted to 40 percent of British exports.

Manufacturing was not only developing in England, however; it had a place in other western European economies as well. Coal mining and textile and iron industries could also be found in various parts of northern Europe in the middle of the nineteenth century, although only England at this time had half its labor force employed in manufacturing. In the rest of Europe, manufacturing accounted for between 5 and 10 percent of employment, most of it still in rural domestic workshops. Except for Great Britain, the quantity and quality of the agrarian harvest remained by far the primary economic concern for most people throughout the world.

WORKING AND LIVING

While the industrial revolution did not mean a wholesale shift to factory labor, industrialization did alter where people worked and how they worked. People had to work harder and had more demanding work routines. This was true in the industrializing economies of western Europe and North America and on the farms and plantations of Asia and Africa. The European side of the story is better known and more fully documented, but it had its counterpart in intensified agrarian routines throughout the rest of the world.

Increasingly, Europe's workers dwelled and made their livings in cities. London, already Europe's largest city in 1700, saw its population nearly double over the next century to almost 1 million. By the 1820s, the rate of population growth was even greater in the industrial hubs of Leeds, Glasgow, Birmingham, Liverpool, and Manchester. By contrast, in the Low Countries and France, where the pace of industrializa-tion was more gradual and small-scale rural-based manufacturing flourished, the shift to cities was less marked.

For most urban dwellers, cities were not healthy places. No European city in the early nineteenth century had as clean a water supply as the largest towns of the ancient Roman Empire once had. Water that was used to power the mills along with chemicals used in the dyeing process were poured directly back into waterways, like Manchester's filthy Irk River, which also served as the source of drinking water for thousands of residents. Overcrowded tenements shared a very small number of outhouses; in most European cities, as late as 1850, there was no running water or garbage pickup, and underground sewers were virtually unknown. Disease, not surprisingly, was widespread.

As families moved to cities and found jobs in small and large factories, they earned wages, which they brought home and added to the family's revenues. Children, wives, and husbands, who ordinarily had worked at home and sold the goods they produced, increasingly worked outside the home for cash (though many members of most families continued to work at least part of the time at making handicrafts inside the home). Urban employers experimented with various ways of paying workers according to tasks performed or the number of goods produced per day (piece rates). To earn subsistence wages, men, women, and children frequently remained on the job for twelve or more hours. In 1851 in England, in the cotton and woolen industries, the most mechanized industries, there were 811,000 workers, about two-thirds of whom were women and children. England also had 1 million domestic servants, the large majority of whom were women, and 1.8 million agricultural laborers.

Changes in work affected the understanding of time. Whereas most farmers had adapted tasks and workloads to seasonal demands and constraints, employers and master artisans had always asked workers to obey some form of schedule. After about 1800, a more rigid concept of work discipline began to spread in industrial settings. To keep new machinery operating, factory and mill owners fastened huge clocks at the top of towers over work sites, using bells or horns to signify the beginning or end of the workday. Employers also used clocks to measure output per hour and to compare one worker's performance to that of others. Josiah Wedgwood (1730–1795), a maker of teacups and other porcelain, installed a Boulton & Watt steam engine in his manufacturing plant, and saw to it that his workers used it efficiently. He rang a bell at 5:45 in the morning so that employees could get to work as day broke. At 8:30 the bell rang for breakfast, 9:00 to call them back, and 12:00 for a half-hour lunch, and it last tolled when darkness put an end to the workday. Sometimes, however, the clocks at factories were put back in the morning and forward at night, falsely extending the workday and cheating workers. In response, some workers smashed the timekeeping instruments.

> *Periodic downturns in the economy put wageworkers, most of whom had no savings, at risk and many responded to involuntary unemployment by organizing protests.*

Industrialization meant greater levels of production, but it established numbing work routines and provided paltry wages. Real wages did not begin to rise for most workers until after 1850. Worse than the drudgery or low pay, however, was having no work at all. As families moved off farmland and became dependent on wages, being idle meant having no source of income. Periodic downturns in the economy put wageworkers, most of whom had no savings, at risk and many responded to involuntary unemployment by organizing protests. The spectacle of riotous crowds and strikers haunted Europe's propertied sectors. In 1834, the British Parliament centralized the administration of all poor relief under a national board and deprived able-bodied workers of any relief unless they joined a workhouse, where working conditions resembled those of a prison. Work routines in these houses were intended to be more heinous than working for an employer.

Even as much new literature celebrated "entrepreneurs" who accumulated private wealth through diligence and enterprise, the effects of the industrial revolution on working-class families became a cause of widespread concern. In the 1810s in England, groups of jobless craftsmen, who called themselves Luddites, smashed the machines that had rendered them unemployed. In 1849, the English novelist Charlotte Brontë published a novel, *Shirley,* which depicted the misfortunes wrought by the power loom. Yorkshire weavers lost their jobs, leading to, in Brontë's words, a moral earthquake and forcing the poor to drink the waters of affliction. Charles Dickens described a mythic Coketown to evoke pity for the proletariat in his 1854 classic, *Hard Times.* Both Elizabeth Gaskell, in England, and Emile Zola, in France, described the hardships suffered by women whose children were perpetually malnourished and forced into the workforce too early; the novels written by these two reformers also highlighted the miseries of prostitutes and widows, whose lives, like their real-life counterparts, were characterized by hunger, loneliness, and illness. These social advocates added to the pressures to promulgate protective legislation for workers, including curbing child labor, limiting the work day, and even, in some countries, legalizing prostitution so that the courtesans' health could be monitored.

Capital and Labor. By the 1840s, many people in Europe were growing worried about the effects of industrialization. This English cartoon from 1843 depicts the terrible laboring conditions for coal miners and satirizes the lazy and idle owners of mining capital. Around this time, writers invented the term *capitalist* to deride this class.

Some, however, preferred to vote with their feet rather than wait for legislative reform. The period of European industrialization was also one of the greatest periods of emigration, as unemployed workers or peasants whose lands were exhausted or enclosed abandoned their homes to seek their fortunes, especially in America, Canada, and Australia. During the Irish Potato Famine of 1845–1849, at least one million Irish men, women, and children left their country—a further million or so died (estimates range between 500,000 and two million) when fungi attacked their single subsistence crop. Irish immigrants desperate to escape starvation at home sold their belongings and booked cheap passage to North America from Liverpool. The ships they sailed on were so deadly that they were called "Coffin Ships"; often the death-rate onboard, from disease and malnutrition, exceeded one-third of the number of passengers. Those who did survive would face discrimination—many Americans feared that the mostly unskilled and Catholic Irish would drive down wages and/or create social unrest—at least until the 1880s, when a wave of new emigrants, this time chiefly from southern Europe, took their place at the bottom of the social and economic ladder.

The economic reordering of the late eighteenth and early nineteenth centuries transformed virtually all aspects of the lives of people who were caught up in it. It required people to alter the way they traded with one another and what they consumed. It also required new methods for mobilizing capital, as well as changes in the rhythms and work routines of merchants, wage laborers, and farmers. Furthermore, changes affected where people worked, where they lived, whom they married, how many children they had, and how they regarded people whose lives were different from their own. And, for many Europeans, it even meant starting life over in a different region of the world, far away from the places their parents had inhabited.

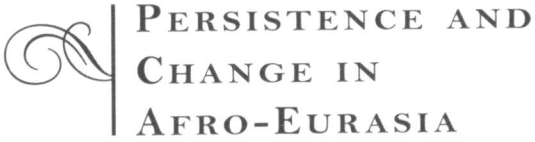

PERSISTENCE AND CHANGE IN AFRO-EURASIA

> → *How did the Atlantic revolutions affect Afro-Eurasian societies?*

While the ideas that originated in the Enlightenment and stimulated the American and French revolutions spread across the Afro-Eurasian landmass, western Europe's military might, its technological achievements, and its economic strength represented the clearest threat to the well-being of the remaining Afro-Eurasian empires. Everywhere on the Afro-Eurasian landmass, western European merchants and industrialists, often backed by military power, sought to forge tighter economic and sometimes even political ties. They did so in the name of securing "free" access to Asian markets and products. In response, ruling elites in the Russian and the Ottoman empires moved rapidly to modernize their military organizations and to emulate Europe's economic accomplishments. At the same time, they distanced themselves from the liberal, egalitarian, and democratic principles of the French Revolution. The Chinese empire, at a long distance from the revolutionary epicenter in the Atlantic world, remained largely unaffected by Europe and America's revolutionary transformations, until the first Opium War of the early 1840s forced the Chinese to face up to their military weaknesses. Thus, changes in the Atlantic world unleashed new political and economic pressures around the world, though with varying degrees of intensity.

REVAMPING THE RUSSIAN MONARCHY

Some eastern European dynasties responded to western European economic and political pressures by bolstering the strength of traditional rulers—enacting modest reforms combined with the suppression of domestic opposition. This was how Russian rulers reacted in the nineteenth century. Tsar Alexander I (ruled 1801–1825) was fortunate that Napoleon committed a number of blunders and lost the world's most modern army in the Russian snows. Yet, even though Russia was among the victors at the Congress of Vienna in 1815, the French Revolution and the massive French armies motivated by patriotism struck at the heart of Russian political institutions, which were based upon the enserfment of the peasantry. The autocratic tsars could no longer justify their absolutism by claiming that enlightened despotism was the most advanced form of government, since a new model, rooted in popular sovereignty and the concept of the nation, had taken its place. One response was to make much of the heroic resistance of the Russian people that culminated in the great victory over the French. Tsar Alexander glorified patriots who had either fought in the war or grown up hearing about it, but he offered few concessions for any new political order.

In December 1825, when Alexander died unexpectedly and childless, there was a question as to which of his brothers would be the next tsar. In the confusion, some members of the Russian officer corps launched a patriotic revolt, hoping to convince one of Alexander's brothers, Constantine, to take the throne (and to guarantee a constitution) in place of another, more conservative brother, Nicholas. The Decembrists, as they were called, came primarily from elite families. Many had first-hand knowledge of western European life and institutions, some from the campaigns against Napoleon.

Decembrists in St. Petersburg. Russians energetically participated in the coalition that defeated Napoleon, but the ideas of the French Revolution exerted great appeal to the educated upper classes, including aristocrats of the officer corps. In December 1825, at the death of Tsar Alexander I, some regimental officers staged an uprising of about 3,000 men, demanding a constitution and the end of serfdom. But Nicholas I, the new tsar, called in loyal troops and brutally dispersed the "Decembrists," executing or exiling their leaders.

A few Decembrists called for a constitutional monarchy to replace Russia's despotism; others favored a tsar-less republic and the abolition of serfdom. But they failed to win over the peasantry, who continued to believe in the divine right of the tsar to rule without constraints. Constantine supported Nicholas's claim to power. Nicholas (ruled 1825–1855) became tsar and brutally suppressed the insurrectionists. For the time being, the influence of the French Revolution was quashed.

Still, Alexander's successors had to meet the challenges of a world in which powerful European states had constitutions and national armies of citizens, not subjects. One way Russian tsars tried to reinvigorate absolute rule was by idealizing the monarch's family as the historical embodiment of the nation with direct ties to the people. But in addition to cultivating this image, Nicholas sought to keep thoughts and acts of rebellion under control by expanding the Third Section (a political police force), enforcing censorship, having his army engage in military exercises, and maintaining serfdom.

Not all subjects were susceptible to Russian national feeling or could be kept under control by the secret police, however. It took the government more than a year to suppress a revolt that began in November 1830 in the empire's Polish provinces. The special constitution granted in 1815 for Russian Poland was abolished, and Nicholas sought a closer alliance with the conservative monarchies of Austria and Prussia. In the 1830s, Nicholas introduced a conservative ideology with the slogan of "Orthodoxy, Autocracy, and Folk Nationality," which stressed religious faith, hierarchy, and

obedience, and idealized but did not enfranchise the people. And while some reformers continued to call for more far-reaching changes, these as yet led nowhere.

REFORMING EGYPT AND THE OTTOMAN EMPIRE

Unlike in Russia, where Napoleon's army had reached Moscow, the Ottoman capital in Istanbul was never threatened by French troops. Still, the Napoleonic invasion of Egypt shook the Ottoman Empire and led European merchants to press Ottoman rulers for increased commercial concessions. Even before this trauma, imperial authorities faced the challenge that increased trade with Europe—and the increased presence of European merchants and missionaries—posed. Many of the non-Muslim religious communities in the sultan's empire openly looked to the European powers to advance their interests. In the wake of Napoleon, who had promised to remake Egyptian society, reformist energies swept from Egypt to the center of the Ottoman domain.

In Egypt, far-reaching changes came with Muhammad Ali (ruled 1805–1848), the most adept of the area's modernizing rulers. After the French withdrawal in 1801, Muhammad Ali emerged victorious in a chaotic struggle for supreme power in Egypt, defying Ottoman superiors and aligning himself with influential Egyptian merchant and scholarly families. Yet he looked to revolutionary France for a model of modern state-building. As with Napoleon and Simón Bolívar, the key to his rise and hold on power was the army. With the

Primary Source

AN EGYPTIAN INTELLECTUAL'S REACTION TO THE FRENCH OCCUPATION OF EGYPT

In the invasion of Egypt in 1798, the French commander, Napoleon Bonaparte, attempted to win rank-and-file Egyptian support against the country's Mamluk Turkish rulers by portraying himself as a liberator and by invoking the ideals of the French Revolution as he had done with great success all over Europe. His campaign did not succeed, and the French met with bitter local opposition. The Egyptian chronicler Abd al-Rahman al-Jabarti has left one of the most perceptive accounts of these years.

On Monday news arrived that the French had reached Damanhur and Rosetta [in the Nile delta]. . . . They printed a large proclamation in Arabic, calling on the people to obey them. . . . In this proclamation were inducements, warnings, all manner of wiliness and stipulations. Some copies were sent from the provinces to Cairo and its text is:

In the name of God, the Merciful, the Compassionate. There is no God but God. He has no son nor has He an associate in His Dominion.

On behalf of the French Republic which is based upon the foundation of liberty and equality, General Bonaparte, Commander-in-Chief of the French armies makes known to all the Egyptian people that for a long time the Sanjaqs [its Mamluk rulers] who lorded it over Egypt have treated the French community basely and contemptuously and have persecuted its merchants with all manner of extortion and violence. Therefore the hour of punishment has now come.

Unfortunately, this group of Mamluks, imported from the mountains of Circassia and Georgia, have acted corruptly for ages in the fairest land that is to be found upon the face of the globe. However, the Lord of the Universe, the Almighty, has decreed the end of their power.

O ye Egyptians . . . I have not come to you except for the purpose of restoring your rights from the hands of the oppressors and that I more than the Mamluks serve God. . . .

And tell them also that all people are equal in the eyes of God and the only circumstances which distinguish one from the other are reason, virtue, and knowledge. . . . Formerly, in the lands of Egypt there were great cities, and wide canals and extensive commerce and nothing ruined all this but the avarice and the tyranny of the Mamluks.

[Jabarti then undertook to challenge the arguments in the French proclamation and to portray the French as godless invaders, inspired by false ideals.] They follow this rule: great and small, high and low, male and female are all equal. Sometimes they break this rule according to their whims and inclinations or reasoning. Their women do not veil themselves and have no modesty. They do not care whether they uncover their private parts. Whenever a Frenchman has to perform an act of nature he does so where he happens to be, even in full view of people, and he goes away as he is, without washing his private parts after defecation. . . . They have intercourse with any woman who pleases them and vice versa. . . .

His saying "[all people] are equal in the eyes of God" the Almighty is a lie and stupidity. How can this be when God has made some superior to others as is testified by the dwellers in the Heavens and on Earth? . . .

So those people are opposed to both Christians and Muslims, and do not hold fast to any religion. You see that they are materialists, who deny all God's attributes. . . . May God hurry misfortune and punishment upon them, may He strike their tongues with dumbness, may He scatter their hosts, and disperse them.

→ *Why do you think Napoleon's appeals to the ideals of the French Revolution failed with Egyptians?*

→ *Why does al-Jabarti claim that the invaders are godless even though the proclamation clearly suggests otherwise?*

SOURCE: Abd al-Rahman al-Jabarti, *Napoleon in Egypt: al-Jabarti's Chronicle of the French Occupation, 1798,* translated by Shmuel Moreh (Princeton: Markus Wiener Publishing, 1993), pp. 24–29.

Muhammad Ali. The Middle Eastern ruler who most successfully assimilated the educational, technological, and economic advances of nineteenth-century Europe was Muhammad Ali, ruler of Egypt from 1805 until 1848.

help of French advisors, including one who had served with Napoleon but converted to Islam and took the name Suleiman Pasha, the Egyptian army became the most powerful fighting force in the Middle East.

Along with modernizing the military, Muhammad Ali pushed for reforms in education and agriculture. He established a school of engineering, and he opened the first modern medical school in Cairo under the supervision of a French military doctor, A. B. Clot. During an autopsy, an enraged student attacked the French doctor, claiming that the dissection of human cadavers violated Islamic norms. With time Clot accustomed his students to anatomical lessons, but he still conducted his classes in secret. In the countryside, Muhammad Ali made Egypt one of the world's leading cotton exporters and the primary region for the cultivation of the highly prized long-staple cotton. A summer crop, cotton required steady watering during the low Nile season when irrigation waters were in short supply. To meet those needs, Muhammad Ali's Public Works Department, acting under the advice of European engineers, deepened the irrigation canals and began to construct a series of dams across the Nile.

Muhammad Ali's modernizing reforms, however, disrupted the habits of the local peasantry. Incorporation into the new industrial world economy, whether as wage laborers in English factories or peasants on Egyptian cotton estates, entailed harder and more demanding work, often with little additional compensation. Because irrigation improvements permitted year-round cultivation, peasants now had to plant and harvest three crops instead of one or two. Moreover, the Egyptian state controlled the prices at which cultivators sold their products, so peasants saw little profit from their added exertions. Young men also now faced conscription into the state's enlarged army, while whole families had to engage in unpaid public works projects. Those who had to work on Egypt's irrigation canals often contracted *bilharzia,* a waterborne illness that debilitated its hosts. Egypt's ruler also designed a state-sponsored program of industrialization that would put Egypt on a par with Europe. Within the short span of a decade and a half, the state had set up textile and munitions factories that employed 200,000 workers. But Egypt had few skilled laborers or cheap sources of energy. By the time of Muhammad Ali's death in 1849, few of the factories still survived.

External forces also checked Muhammad Ali's ambitious plans. At first, his new army enjoyed spectacular success. At the bidding of the Ottoman sultan, the Egyptian military fought credibly against Greek nationalists, although Egyptian forces were unable to prevent the Greeks from acquiring independence in 1829. Egyptian soldiers also carried out conquests in the Sudan. Muhammad Ali overplayed his hand, however, when he sent his forces into Syria in the early 1830s and later in the decade when he threatened to launch expeditions into Anatolia, the heart of the Ottoman state. The prospect that an Egyptian ruler might march into Istanbul and supplant the Ottoman sultan alarmed the European powers. Led by the British foreign minister Lord Palmerston, European diplomats compelled Egypt to withdraw from Anatolia and in 1841 to reduce its army to 18,000 soldiers. In the name of free trade, European merchants pressed for unobstructed access to Egyptian markets, just as they did in Latin America and Africa.

Under political and economic pressures that were similar to those facing Muhammad Ali in Egypt, Ottoman rulers also began to change their ways. Already in the eighteenth century, the more forward-looking sultans were well aware of the rising power of Europe. Military defeats and humiliating treaties with Europe provided ample reminders of the Ottoman rulers' vulnerability. This vulnerability deepened as Europe's economic and military might increased. Stunned by Napoleon's defeat of the Egyptian Mamluks and disenchanted with conservative and privileged janissaries who resisted efforts to impose discipline and reforms, in 1805 Sultan Selim III tried to create a new and effective source of military strength. He founded the New Order infantry, trained by western European officers. But before he could bring this new force up to fighting strength, the janissaries rose in revolt, storming the palace, killing New Order officers and sticking their heads on poles outside the palace. They overturned the New Order army and deposed Selim in 1807. Over the next decades, janissary military men and clerical scholars (*ulama*) cobbled together an alliance that continuously thwarted reformers.

Why did reform falter in the Ottoman state even before it had a chance to be implemented? After all, in France and Spain, the old regimes were also inefficient and saddled with accumulated debts and military losses. But reform or revolution was only feasible if the forces of restraint—especially in the military—were weak and the reformers strong; in France, a domestic coalition toppled the ruling bloc; in Spain, colonists allied to reject absolutism and mercantilism. In the Ottoman Empire, the janissary class had grown powerful, providing the bulwark of resistance to change. Also, Ottoman authority aligned with and depended upon clerical support, and the clergy also resisted change. Blocked at the top, Ottoman rulers were loath to appeal for popular support in a struggle against anti-reformers. Such an appeal, in the new age of popular sovereignty and national feeling, was always dangerous for an unelected dynast in a multiethnic and multireligious realm.

The political deadlock was broken by Mahmud II (ruled 1808–1839), who spoke no European languages but was painfully aware of the need to deal with Europe's rising power. He was also a shrewd tactician, able to manipulate his conservative opponents. Convincing some clerics that the janissaries neglected old laws and customs of discipline and piety and promising that a new corps would pray fervently, the sultan won the support of the *ulama* and in 1826 established a new European-style army corps. When the janissaries plotted their inevitable mutiny, Mahmud rallied clerics, students, and his subjects. The schemers retreated to their barracks, only to be shelled by the sultan's artillery and then destroyed in flames. Thousands of janissaries were rounded up and executed.

The sultan was now freer to follow the example of Muhammad Ali in Egypt and pursue reform within an autocratic framework. Like Muhammad Ali, Mahmud brought in a group of European officers (in 1835) to advise his forces. Here, too, military reform spilled over into nonmilitary areas. The Ottoman modernizers created a medical college, then a school of military sciences. To understand Europe better and to create a first-rate diplomatic corps, the Ottomans schooled their officials in European languages and encouraged the translation of European classics into Turkish. Mahmud's successors kept up the reforms and extended them into civilian life. This era, referred to as the *Tanzimat*, or Reorganization period, saw legislation that guaranteed equality for all Ottoman subjects, regardless of religion.

The reforms, however, stopped well short of revolutionary change. For one thing, reform relied too much on the personal whim of rulers. The bureaucratic and religious infrastructure of the Ottoman Empire remained wedded to old ways. Moreover, any effort to reform the rural sector encountered the resistance of the landed interests. Finally, the merchant classes profited from business with a debt-ridden sultan. By staving off the fiscal collapse of the empire, the bankers alleviated the pressure for reform and removed the spark that had fired the revolutions in Europe. Together, these factors impaired the cause of reform in the Ottoman Empire. Yet, by failing to make greater reforms, the empire lost economic and military ground to its European neighbors. For centuries, European traders had needed Islam's goods and services more than the other way around. By the nineteenth century, however, the ties of trade and financial dependency bound the Ottomans to Europe on terms that the Europeans controlled.

> By the nineteenth century, the ties of trade and financial dependency bound the Ottomans to Europe on terms that the Europeans controlled.

COLONIAL REORDERING IN INDIA

The largest and most important of Europe's Asian colonial possessions between 1750 and 1850 was British India. Unlike in North America, the changes that the British fostered in Asia at this time did not lead to political independence. Quite the contrary, India was increasingly dominated by the East India Company, a private company that had been chartered by the crown in 1600. The company's increasing control over India's imports and exports in the eighteenth and nineteenth centuries, however, flew in the face of British professions about their allegiance to a world economic system based on "free trade."

Initially, the British, through the East India Company, sought to control the commerce of India by establishing trading posts along the coast but without taking complete political control. After conquering the princely state of Bengal in 1757 and placing a puppet on Bengal's throne, the East India Company began to fill its coffers, and company officials began to amass personal fortunes. In 1760, several senior officials were making the astonishing sum of £500,000 a year through illicit and predatory business ventures. Robert Clive, the governor of Bengal, accrued a huge private fortune by forcing the ruler to cede him a portion of the tax revenues. The unbridled abuse of power caused the Bengal ruler to initiate hostilities against the company. In 1764, the forces of the Mughal emperor and the ruler of Awadh joined with his army to battle against British troops. They were defeated, but instead of decapitating the empire, British officials elected to leave the emperor and most provincial leaders in place—at least as nominal rulers. Nonetheless, in 1765, the British extracted a proclamation from the Mughal emperor that granted the East India Company the right to collect the tax revenues in Bengal as well as in Bihar and Orissa. In addition, the company secured the right to trade free of duties throughout the Mughal territory. In return, the company agreed to pay the emperor an annual pension of £260,000. The company went on to annex other territories, bringing much of South Asia and its estimated 200 million inhabitants under company rule by the early 1800s (see Map 15-4).

To carry out its responsibilities, the East India Company needed to establish a civil administration. Rather than place Britons in these positions, the company preferred to enlist Hindu kings and Muslim princes. The company allowed them to retain their royal symbols and privileges while depriving them of their autonomy. Though the Mughal emperor proclaimed in 1765 that the East India Company was his "servant," the roles were in fact reversed. Previously weakened by the rise of provincial rulers, the emperor was now permanently under the thumb of the company's administrators. Still,

the company did not depend entirely on local leaders to enforce its dictates, for it also maintained a large standing army. By 1805, this army included 155,000 soldiers, more than a third of whom were native recruits or sepoys (a corruption of the Urdu term *sipahi* for soldier). It employed a centralized bureaucracy that by the 1780s was trained to rule colonial subjects. Together, the military force, bureaucracy, and an array of local rulers enabled the company state to maintain security and assure the stability of revenue collection.

To rule with a minimum of interference and cost, however, required knowing the conquered society. This provided the impetus for what became known as "Orientalist" scholarship. English scholar-officials wrote the first modern histories of South Asia, translated and published Sanskrit and Persian texts, identified philosophical writings, and compiled Hindu and Muslim law books. The most famous of these scholars was William Jones who, while serving as a judge in Calcutta between 1783 and 1794, founded the Asiatic Society. While Jones and like-minded Orientalists admired Sanskrit language and literature, they still approved of English colonial rule. Thanks to their efforts, the company state presented itself as a force for revitalizing authentic Hinduism and recovering India's literary and cultural treasures. Nonetheless, the views of Orientalist scholars did not always ac-

MAP 15-4 THE BRITISH IN INDIA, 1767–1857

Starting from locations in eastern and northeastern India, the British East India Company extended its authority over much of South Asia prior to the outbreak of the Indian Rebellion of 1857. Why did this process take several centuries to unfold? How did the company administer these possessions? Why did it choose a strategy of direct and indirect rule over different areas within the larger region?

Indian Resistance to Company Rule. Tipu Sultan, the Mysore ruler, put up a determined resistance against the British. This painting by Robert Home shows Cornwallis, the East India Company's governor, receiving Tipu's two sons as hostages after defeating him in the 1792 war. The boys remained in British custody for two years. Tipu returned to fighting the British and was killed in the war of 1799.

cord with the actual Indian village beliefs in local deities and the importance of local vernacular tongues.

Maintaining a sizeable military and civilian bureaucracy compelled the East India Company to intrude on the lives of Indians in many ways, especially through taxation. Landholding arrangements were of vital importance to the company because taxes on land were its largest source of revenue. From 1793 onward, a series of land settlements bolstered state revenues and undercut the autonomy of villagers. These policies made large and small landowners responsible for paying taxes to the company—in so doing, tax policies helped spread private property at the expense of traditional landowning rights. In particular, large estate owners gained more power and joined with the company in determining who could own property. The old flexible tax system gave way to one in which all landholders had to pay, irrespective of means. When proprietors defaulted on their taxes, the company put their properties up for auction, with the firm's own employees and large estate owners often obtaining title. Some took out loans to save their property or to make rental payments, exposing themselves to rural moneylenders.

Company rule altered India's urban geography as well. By the early nineteenth century, colonial cities, like Calcutta, Madras, and Bombay, became the new and growing centers at the expense of older Mughal cities like Agra, Delhi, Murshidabad, and Hyderabad. As trade boomed, colonial cities attracted British merchants and Indian clerks, artisans, and laborers. Calcutta's population reached 350,000 in 1820, and

Bombay's jumped to 200,000 by 1825. In these cities, Europeans lived in enclaves around the company's fort and trading stations, while migrants from the Indian countryside clustered in crowded quarters called "black towns."

Back in Britain, the debts of rural Indians and the conditions of black towns generated little concern. Instead, calls for reform focused on the East India Company's monopoly. Criticism of colonial methods, but not of colonialism, mounted as the company's arbitrary rule in India became better known in London. British critics of the company objected to its monopoly over access to Indian wealth, and British industrialists resented the protection afforded to the company's shareholders and investors. In 1813, the British Parliament, responding to the wishes of merchants and traders to participate in the Indian economy, abolished the East India Company's monopoly over trade with India.

No longer the preserve of a single company, India was now expected to serve the interests of an industrializing Britain. In pursuit of this goal, India became an important market for British textiles, as well as an exporter of raw cotton. This was a new trading arrangement, entailing a reversal of India's traditional trade. In the past, even under early company rule, India had been an important textile manufacturer, exporting fine cotton goods throughout the Indian Ocean and to Europe. But the Indian business elites had difficulty resisting the import of cheap British textiles. As a result, a long-term partial deindustrialization took place in the region. In addition, Indian imports of British manufactures

Primary Source

JAMES MILL ON INDIAN TRADITION

James Mill was a Scottish political economist and philosopher and a follower of Jeremy Bentham, the Utilitarian thinker. In line with Utilitarianism, Mill believed that law and government were of central importance in maximizing utility and happiness. With this idea in mind, he penned the multivolume History of British India *in 1818. He criticized India's Hindu and Muslim cultures and traditions and attributed their so-called backwardness to the absence of a strong and systematic form of law. His trenchant critique of India's traditions was also an attack on earlier British Orientalists who stressed the study of indigenous texts and noninterference in traditional practices. A year after the publication of the book, he was appointed as an official by the East India Company.*

The condition of the women is one of the most remarkable circumstances in the manners of nations. Among rude people, the women are generally degraded; among civilized people they are exalted.

————————

Nothing can exceed the habitual contempt which the Hindus entertain for their women. Hardly are they ever mentioned in their laws, or other books, but as wretches of the most base and vicious inclinations, on whose natures no virtuous or useful qualities can be engrafted. "Their husbands," says the sacred code, "should be diligently careful in guarding them: though they well know the disposition with which the lord of creation formed them; Manu allotted to such women a love of their bed, of their seat, and of ornament, impure appetites, wrath, weak flexibility, desire of mischief, and bad conduct."

————————

They are held, accordingly, in extreme degradation. They are not accounted worthy to partake of religious rites but in conjunction with their husbands. They are entirely excluded from the sacred books. . . .

————————

It is not surprising, that grossness, in ideas and language, respecting the intercourse of the sexes, is a uniform concomitant of the degraded state of the women. . . . Inquiry discovers, that grossness in this respect is a regular ingredient in the manners of a rude age; and that society, as it refines, deposits this, among its other impurities. The ancient inhabitants of our own country were as indelicate as those of the hottest regions of Asia. All European witnesses have been struck with the indelicacy of the Hindus. The gross emblems and practices of their religion are already known. To the indecent passages in the books of law, and the practices which they describe, exceedingly numerous, and exceedingly gross, we can here only allude. Both the writings and conversation of the Hindus abound with passages which are shocking to European ears.

————————

led to unfavorable trade balances that changed India from a net importer of gold and silver to an exporter of these precious metals.

Nor were the British content simply to alter the Indian economy. The colonial rulers also advocated far-reaching changes in traditional Indian society and culture so that its people would place a high value on British goods and culture. In 1817, James Mill, a philosopher and an employee of the East India Company, condemned the backwardness of indigenous social practices and cultural traditions. He and his son, John Stuart Mill, who was also employed by the company, argued that only dictatorial, illiberal rule could bring good government and economic progress to Indians, who were deemed unfit for autonomy, self-rule, or liberalism.

Evangelicals and liberal reformers also agitated for a thorough transformation of Hindu and Muslim social practices through legislation and the introduction of European education. For example, they sought to stop the practice of *sati*, wherein a woman was burned to death on the funeral pyre of her dead husband. The mood swung away from the Orientalists' respect for India's classical languages, philosophies, cultures, and texts. In 1835, Lord Macaulay, entrusted with the task of making recommendations on educational policies, declared that a single shelf in any decent western library con-

They are remarkably prone to flattery; the most prevailing mode of address from the weak to the strong, while men are still ignorant and unreflecting. The Hindus are full of dissimulation and falsehood, the universal concomitants of oppression. The vices of falsehood, indeed, they carry to a height almost unexampled among other races of men. Judicial perjury is more than common; it is almost universal.

———————————

This religion has produced a practice, which has strongly engaged the curiosity of Europeans; a superstitious care of the life of the inferior animals. A Hindu lives in perpetual terror of killing even an insect; and hardly any crime can equal that of being unintentionally the cause of death to any animal of the more sacred species. This feeble circumstance, however, is counteracted by so many gloomy and malignant principles, that their religion, instead of humanizing the character, must have had no inconsiderable effect in fostering that disposition to revenge, that insensibility to the sufferings of others, and often that active cruelty, which lurks under the smiling exterior of the Hindu.

———————————

Few nations are surpassed by the Hindus, in the total want of physical purity, in their streets, houses, and persons. Mr. Forster, whose long residence in India, and knowledge of the country, render him an excellent witness, says of the narrow streets of Benares; "In addition to the pernicious effect which must proceed from a confined atmosphere, there is, in the hot season, an intolerable stench arising from the many pieces of stagnated water dispersed in different quarters of the town. The filth also which is indiscriminately thrown into the streets, and there left exposed, (for the Hindus possess but a small portion of general cleanliness) add to the compound of ill smells so offensive to the European inhabitants of this city."

———————————

The attachment with which the Hindus, in common with all ignorant nations, bear to astrology, is a part of their manners exerting a strong influence upon the train of their actions. "The Hindus of the present age," says a partial observer, "do not undertake any affair of consequence without consulting their astrologers, who are always Brahmans." The belief of witchcraft and sorcery continues universally prevalent; and is everyday the cause of the greater enormities.

→ *What did James Mill hold to be the chief indicator of a civilization's accomplishment?*
→ *Did Mill's views on India imply a wholesale transformation of society and government?*

SOURCE: James Mill, *The History of British India* (New Delhi: Atlantic Publishers & Distributors, 1990), pp. 279, 281–82, 286–87, 288, 289, 297, 299.

tained more valuable knowledge than all the accumulated Sanskrit and Persian texts. English was to replace Persian as the language of administration, and European education was to displace training in Oriental learning. The result, reformers hoped, would be the raising of a class that was Indian in blood and color, but English in tastes and culture.

Packing Cotton Bales. This 1864 engraving of the packing of cotton bales registers the shift in cotton trade between India and Britain: from being an exporter of cotton manufactures up to the eighteenth century, India became a source of raw cotton in the nineteenth century.

This was a new colonial order, but it was not a stable one. While some European-educated Indians thanked the British rulers for their benevolent reforms, most landed magnates, facing dispossession and loss of their authority, grumbled with disaffection. Peasants, thrown to the mercy of the market, moneylenders, and landlords were in turmoil. The so-called tribals, or non-Hindu forest dwellers and shifting cultivators, faced with the hated combination of the colonial state and moneylenders, revolted. Dispossessed artisans brought unrest to towns and cities. Merchants and industrialists resented the fact that they could now make money only by working as subordinates in a British-dominated economy. Undeterred, the British persevered in extending and refining the reach of the colonial state, combining reform with autocracy, advancing free trade with colonial dictates. India participated in an increasingly interconnected world and contributed to Europe's industrialization, but it did so as a colony. Expanding freedom in Europe was paralleled by exploitation in India.

PERSISTENCE OF THE QING EMPIRE

In contrast to the declining fortunes of the other dynasts, the Qing dynasty, which had taken power in China in 1644, was still enjoying considerable economic prosperity and territorial expansion as the nineteenth century dawned. The Chinese were largely unaware of the revolutionary events taking place in North America, France, and Britain, and they felt no great compulsion to alter the fundamentals of their society. Their sense of imperial splendor continued to rest upon the political structure and social order inherited from the Ming. Although some Chinese felt that the Manchu Qing were foreign occupiers, the Qing carefully adapted Chinese institutions and philosophies. Thus, Chinese elites at court did not challenge the prerogatives of the dynasty—unlike the delegates to the Estates-General in France in 1788–1789.

EXPANSION OF THE EMPIRE The Qing demonstrated a special talent for extending the boundaries of the empire and fostering settlement in frontier lands. Before 1750, they conquered Taiwan (the stronghold of remaining Ming forces), pushed westward into central Asia, and annexed Tibet. In the 1750s, the Qianlong Emperor (ruled 1736–1796) marched a quarter million men against the powerful West Mongol Oirats, who were utterly decimated. The Qing victory ended Russian efforts to take southern Siberia. Subsequent treaties with Russia established the limits of Chinese westward expansion into Turkic- and Mongol-speaking lands. To secure these territorial gains, the Qing encouraged settlement of western frontier lands like Xinjiang. New crops from the Americas aided this spread of China's population into recently acquired lands. Corn and sweet potatoes, which could grow well in less fertile soils, became more prominent. Crops were seeded methodically in neat rows, unlike in Europe, where the broadcast method of seeding caused much wastage.

Thanks to rising agricultural productivity and population growth, rural life became more commercialized and state revenues increased. In the eighteenth century, rural markets multiplied, increasing the volume of interregional trade in grain, cotton, tea, and silk. Rural industries also proliferated. As in Europe, peasant households became the backbone of early manufactures, especially in textiles. The Chinese espoused an ideal in which women stayed home while men worked in the field, but in China as in Europe, relatively few rural households could afford to exclude women from fieldwork.

Like their European counterparts, Chinese peasants were on the move. Migration to frontier regions occurred in Qing China for different reasons. In the case of the westward move into Xinjiang, or "New Borderlands," the movement was state-sponsored and initiated to secure a recently pacified frontier region through military colonization, followed by civilians—peasants enticed by the offer of at least 4.5 acres of land, a set of tools, twelve pecks of seed, and a loan of two taels of silver and a horse valued at eight taels—with the objective of producing enough food grain to supply the troops as well as to relieve the pressure on the poor and arid northwestern part of the country. Perhaps as many as half a million

Rice Paddies. Farmers working in neatly planted rice paddy fields in late imperial China. The process was labor intensive, but it reduced wastage.

acres of land were brought under cultivation by 1840, fundamentally transforming the ecological and social landscape of the region.

Other migrants were on the move by their own initiative. Pushed by the ever-growing competition for land in the core areas of the country—by 1850 the Qing population had increased by 200 to 250 million since the dynasty's founding in the mid-seventeenth century—they even found themselves in areas that the Qing regime tried to restrict them from going, such as Manchuria and Taiwan. The migrants brought their agricultural techniques and settlements to those areas, reshaping the environment through their land reclamation and irrigation projects. The migrant population in Taiwan grew from around a hundred thousand in the late seventeenth century to close to a million a century later, while over two million made their way to Manchuria in the same period, with the amount of taxable land there increasing from about 9,700 acres in 1661 to over a million acres by 1820.

> *Even as Qing rulers recognized the problems, their ability to tackle them was limited.*

PROBLEMS OF THE EMPIRE Despite their success in expanding the boundaries of the empire, the Qing faced a number of obvious problems. As a ruling minority among the vast Han Chinese majority, the Manchu Qing tended to take a conservative approach to internal innovation. Only toward the end of the eighteenth century did they grapple with problems of rapid growth in population. On the one hand, the tripling of China's population since 1300 attested to the strength and prosperity of the realm. On the other, a population that had surpassed 300 million put severe pressure on various resources, especially soil for growing crops and wood for fuel.

Even as Qing rulers recognized the problems, their ability to tackle them was limited. The taxes they levied, in comparison with those levied by European monarchs, were light. Chinese bureaucrats, who were supposed to hire and pay their underlings out of their own salaries, found themselves understaffed. As local bureaucrats introduced many ad hoc taxes, the people came to see the bureaucrats as corrupt. The Qing, however, proved unable to rationalize the taxation system or to regularize the administrative apparatus at the grass-roots level. In fact, the Qing rulers could not even put an end to the corruption of their court officials. In the late eighteenth and early nineteenth centuries, the White Lotus Rebellion, a series of uprisings inspired by mystical beliefs in folk Buddhism (especially the belief that the Maitreya Buddha would appear to rescue the people from their suffering) and at times by the idea of restoring the Ming, engulfed much of northern China.

Some historians have suggested that the Qing fell into deep crisis and "failed" to seek new technologies and new systems of knowledge and rule. In time, these historians assert, that failure left China vulnerable to outsiders, especially Europeans. Yet, throughout the eighteenth century, European rulers and upper classes remained avid consumers of Chinese silks, teas, carved jade, tableware, jewelry, paper for covering walls, ceramics, and other artifacts of what the French called *chinoiserie*. The Chinese, for their part, felt little need to acquire European manufactures. In 1793, Emperor Qianlong wrote in response to a request for trade by Britain's George III that "as your ambassador can see for himself, we possess all things," adding, "I have no use for your country's manufactures."

By the mid-nineteenth century, however, the Qing had lost their ability to dismiss the Europeans and their manufactures. This resulted from the extraordinary and unforeseen changes that had made western European powers far stronger than they had ever been. The first unambiguous evidence of an altered balance of power was not the rise of Napoleon, about whom the Chinese knew little, but a British-Chinese war over a narcotic, opium. The Opium War exposed China's vulnerability in a new era of European ascendancy.

THE OPIUM WAR AND THE "OPENING" OF CHINA Europeans had been selling staples and intoxicants in China for a long time. Tobacco, a New World crop, had become a ubiquitous sight in China by the seventeenth century. Stores offered a variety of brands. While ordinary people smoked with a water pipe, members of the elite learned to use snuff. The significance of these imports was not immediately apparent. Few would have predicted that tobacco smoking would prepare the ground for the widespread use of opium, previously consumed as a medicine or an aphrodisiac. At first, crude opium was mixed with tobacco and smoked by Chinese in Southeast Asia, Taiwan, and along the southern coast of China in the seventeenth century. But the practice spread from these centers of the maritime trade to the north and the interior of the region. By the late eighteenth century, opium smokers with their long-stemmed pipes were conspicuous in every stratum of Chinese society.

The Qing banned opium imports in 1729, yet the Chinese continued to smoke the drug and illegally to import it through Portuguese and other merchants. Sensing its economic potential, the East India Company created an opium monopoly in India in 1773. The reason was a rapid growth in the company's purchase of tea. Because the Chinese showed little taste for British goods, the British had financed their tea imports with exports of silver to China. By the end of the eighteenth century, however, the quantity of its tea purchases had become too large to finance with shipments of silver. Fortunately for the company, the Chinese showed an eagerness

Opium Dens. A common sight in late Qing China were establishments catering specifically to opium smoking. Taken from a volume condemning the practice, this picture shows opium smokers idling their day away.

for Indian goods—first cotton and opium, and subsequently mostly opium—permitting the British to export very little or no silver after 1804. Given the importance of opium, the company extended its cultivation by offering loans to Indian peasants who, in return, agreed to grow opium and sell it to the company's agents at a predetermined price.

The illegal opium traffic could not have flourished without the connivance of corrupt Chinese bureaucrats and a network of local brokers and distributors. Yet, a Qing decree of 1799 reiterated the official ban. Until 1821, no more than 5,000 chests of opium per year found their way into China,

but the number increased to 16,500 chests in 1831–1832 and 40,000 in 1838–1839. The import explosion resulted primarily from an influx of private British merchants in 1834, when the British government revoked the East India Company's monopoly over trade with China, which meant that anyone could now enter the trade.

The impact of opium on the Qing's trade balance was devastating. In a clear reversal from earlier trends, silver began to flow out of instead of into China. About 2 million taels of silver left the country each year in the 1820s. The figure jumped to 9 million taels a decade later. China experienced

Opium Warehouse in India. Having established a monopoly in the 1770s over opium cultivation in India, the British greatly expanded their manufacture and export of opium to China to balance their rapidly growing import of Chinese tea and silk. This picture from the 1880s shows an opium warehouse in India where the commodity was stored before being transported to China.

→ *How did the Atlantic revolutions affect Afro-Eurasian societies?*

Trade in Canton. In this painting, titled *A View of the Hongs*, we can see the hongs, the buildings that made up the factories, or establishments, where foreign merchants conducted their business in Canton. From the mid-eighteenth century to 1842, Canton was the only Chinese port open to European trade.

silver shortages, and ordinary peasants saw their tax burden surge (remember that taxes had to be paid in silver; see Chapter 13). Unrest in the countryside, on the rise since the 1790s, spread and gained momentum. At the Qing court, some officials wanted to legalize the opium trade to stamp out corruption and to channel revenues into the treasury (as long as it remained officially an illegal substance, the government could not tax the traffic). Others wanted stiffer prohibitions, though they did not specify how they would be enforced. The emperor followed the latter tack, and in 1838 sent a specially appointed commissioner, Lin Zexu, to the main entrepôt, Canton (now called Guangzhou, it was the only port, besides the Portuguese settlement of Macao, where foreigners could trade with the Chinese), to eradicate the influx of opium. In a letter to Queen Victoria of Britain, Lin claimed that China exported its goods such as tea and silk for no other reason than "to share the benefit with the people of the whole world," asking why the British inflicted harm on the Chinese people through opium imports.

Lin demanded that foreigners surrender their opium stocks to the Chinese government for destruction and stop the trade in opium. When British merchants in Canton balked at Lin's instructions, he ordered the arrest of Lancelot Dent, head of the second largest foreign firm in Canton and president of the British Chamber of Commerce, in March 1839. Dent refused to comply with the arrest order, and 350 foreigners were blockaded inside their own quarters. Lin scored an apparent victory when the foreign community in Canton, after forty-seven days of blockade, gave up 20,283 chests of opium, with an estimated value of $9 million, an enormous sum in those days. But merchants had overstocked their supplies in anticipation of the legalization of the trade, and the British government representative in Canton promised to compensate the merchants for their losses. For Lin, the surrendering of the opium, which the Chinese flushed out to sea, was proof that foreigners accepted submission. The Chinese victory, however, was short-lived. As a member of the British Parliament put it, the opium merchants in Canton "belonged to a country unaccustomed to defeat, to submission or to shame."

A British fleet, including four newly armed steamers, entered Chinese waters in June 1840. For the Chinese, a steam-powered battleship was a new sight. British warships bombarded Chinese coastal regions near Canton and even sailed in shallow water upriver for a short way. On land, Qing soldiers commanded by hereditary bannermen—the Chinese equivalent to the equally out-of-date Ottoman janissaries—used spears and clubs, and a few imported matchlock muskets, against the modern artillery of British troops, many of whom were Indians supplied with percussion cap rifles. Still,

Steamer *Nemesis* Destroying Junks. The Opium War was fought between a newly industrialized power and an established landed empire. One of the major disparities between the two sides was military technology. Here is a scene of a British steam-powered warship, the *Nemesis*, sailing up the Pearl River toward the city of Canton, bombarding areas along the river at will and destroying Chinese ships that attempted to block its way.

along the Yangzi River, outgunned Chinese forces fought fiercely. Rather than surrender, many Qing soldiers killed their own wives and children before committing suicide.

The British prevailed, as the Qing preferred to sue for peace rather than risk all-out war. The British seized the tiny island of Hong Kong, and with the 1842 Treaty of Nanjing they received the right to trade in five treaty ports and forced the Chinese to pay an "indemnity" for the war and compensation for the opium destroyed by Lin. British traders were now given the right to trade directly with the Chinese (and not only through the Cohong; see Chapter 13) and to reside in the treaty ports.

That the British government would go to such lengths merely to force trade struck many Chinese as barbaric. In addition, subsequent treaties guaranteed the principle of extraterritoriality, which meant that the British and other foreign nationals would be tried in their own courts for crimes, rather than in Chinese courts, and would be exempt from Chinese law. Of further threat to Chinese autonomy, the British insisted that any privileges granted to future treaty signatories would also apply to them. Accordingly, if one European country acquired special rights, others would, too, which ensured all Europeans and North Americans a privileged position in China.

Still, China did not suffer India's fate and become a formal colony. To the contrary, in the mid-nineteenth century Europeans and North Americans were trading only on the outskirts of China and restricted their presence to a few coastal cities. Most Chinese did not encounter the Euro-

Chronology

	1700					
THE AMERICAS					*American Revolution, 1776–1783* ▮	
						Haitian Rebellion, 1791–180
						Eli Whitney invents the cotton gin, 1
EUROPE					*James Watt invents steam engine, 1769* ▮	
						French Revolution, 1789–1799 ▮
RUSSIA AND OTTOMAN EMPIRE						
AFRICA						
SOUTH ASIA					*British establish company rule in India, 1765* ▮	
EAST ASIA				▮ *Chinese expansion under Qianlong emperor, 1736–1796*		

peans, and daily life for the majority of the Chinese went on as it had before the Opium War and the Treaty of Nanjing. Only the political leaders and urban dwellers were beginning directly to feel the foreign presence and to ponder what steps, if any, China might take to acquire European technologies, goods, and learning.

CONCLUSION

During the second half of the eighteenth century and into the early nineteenth century, changes wrought by politics and ideas, on the one hand, and commerce, industry, and technology, on the other, resulted in unprecedented upheaval in the Atlantic world. The reordering of the Atlantic world occurred against the background of several centuries of trade and imperial conquests, and it reverberated, to varying degrees, elsewhere around the world. By 1850, the world was more integrated economically, with Europe more than ever before at the center of global affairs.

The political crises and the economic and social revolutions in western Europe and the Americas disrupted polities around the world, though less so in China than anywhere else. In the Americas, colonial ties were severed; in France, the people toppled the monarchy, and dissidents threatened the same in Russia. Political upheavals did not rewrite the rules of state completely, but they did introduce a new public vocabulary that would enjoy increasing power as the nine-

teenth century unfolded: the language of the nation. Equally important, they made the idea of revolution—that societies could be changed in radical ways—empowering. In the Americas and parts of Europe, nation-states, with new symbols of authority, national armies, and a mystique of self-governing communities took shape around redefined social hierarchies of class, gender, and color. Western Europe, particularly Britain and France, emerged from the political crises of the late eighteenth century with determination to expand their influence beyond their borders. Their drive forced older empires such as Russia and the Ottoman state to undertake state-led reforms.

Commerce and industrialization played a decisive role in the reshuffling of economic and political power. Through the end of the seventeenth century, commerce bridged distant cultures; thereafter, as trade deepened and diversified, it began to transform those cultures. European governments and their armies compelled various countries—including Egypt, India, and China—to expand their trade with European merchants. Ultimately this meant that these and other countries were not free to pursue whatever economic policies they wished. Rather, they were expected to participate in a European-centered economy as exporters of raw materials and importers of European manufactures.

By the 1850s, the density and strength of trading ties had helped create a more interconnected world order. More of the world's peoples produced less for themselves and more for distant markets. Thanks to changes in the organization and technology of manufacturing, some areas of the world

800							1900

■ *Robert Fulton launches first commercial steamship, 1807*

■ *Revolutions in South America, 1810–1824*

■ *Brazil declares independence, 1822*

■ *Napoleon's empire, 1804–1815*   ■ *First railway launched in England, 1830*

■ *Reign of Mahmud II, Ottoman Empire, 1808–1839*

■ *Decembrist Revolt in Russia, 1825*

■ *Greek independence, 1829*

ch invasion of Egypt, 1798–1801

■ *Abolition of Atlantic slave trade, 1803–1867*

■ *Reign of Muhammad Ali, Egypt, 1805–1848*

■ *Abolition of company trade monopoly in India, 1813*

Lotus Rebellion, China, 1796–1804   ■ *Opium War, China, 1839–1842* also made more goods than ever before. Although the world remained multicentered, economic power in the early nineteenth century was shifting to the western end of the Afro-Eurasian landmass. With manufactures to sell in Asia and a new ideology of free trade, Europe began to force open new markets, even to the point of colonizing them. Gold and silver, which had poured into China and India in the sixteenth and seventeenth centuries, were now flowing out to pay for European-dominated products like opium and textiles.

Nonetheless, the reordering of the world did not mean that Europe's rulers had uncontested control over other people, or even over their own people. Nor did it mean that the institutions and cultures of Asia and Africa ceased to be dynamic. Some countries became informal dependencies, like the Ottomans; others, like India, became outright European colonies. China escaped colonial rule but was forced into unfavorable trade relations with the Europeans. In sum, changes in commerce, manufacturing, technology, politics, and ideas combined to unsettle systems of rulership and to alter the economic and military balance between western Europe and the rest of the world.

STUDY QUESTIONS

 WWNORTON.COM/STUDYSPACE

1. Describe the political and social revolutions that occurred in the Atlantic world between 1750 and 1850. What ideas inspired these changes? How far did revolutionaries extend these changes?

2. Compare and contrast how Latin American peoples achieved independence to the similar process in the United States. How similar were their goals? How well did they achieve these goals?

3. Explain the role of Napoleon in spreading the ideas of the Atlantic world's political and social revolution. How did Napoleon's armies spread the concept of nationalism? How did Napoleon's military pursuits affect political and social ferment in the Americas?

4. Explain how the Atlantic world's political and social revolution led to the end of the Atlantic slave trade. What economic, social, and political consequences did this development have on sub-Saharan Africa?

5. Define industrialization. Where did it begin? What other parts of the Atlantic world did it spread to during this time?

6. Explore how industrialization altered the societies that began to industrialize during this time. What impact did this process have on the environment? How were gender roles and familial relationships altered?

7. Analyze how the two intertwined Atlantic revolutions (political and industrial) altered the global balance of power. How did the Russian, Mughal, Ottoman, and Qing dynasties respond to this change?

8. To what extent did Great Britain emerge as the leading global power between 1750 and 1850. How did the British state shape political and economic developments around the world during this era?

FURTHER READINGS

Anderson, Fred, *Crucible of War: The Seven Years' War and the Fate of Empire in British North America, 1754–1766* (2000). The best synthesis of the "great war for empire" that set the stage for the American Revolution.

Bayly, C. A., *Indian Society and the Making of the British Empire* (1998). A useful work on the early history of the British conquest of India.

Blackburn, Robin, *The Overthrow of Colonial Slavery, 1776–1848* (1988). Places the abolition of the Atlantic slave trade and colonial slavery in a large historical context.

Brook, Timothy, and Bob Tadashi Wakabayashi (eds.), *Opium Regimes: China, Britain, and Japan, 1839–1952* (2000). Examines the role of opium in the various aspects of modern Chinese history.

Cambridge History of Egypt: Modern Egypt from 1517 to the End of the Twentieth Century, Vol. 2 (1998). Volume 2 contains authoritative essays on all aspects of modern Egyptian history, including the impact of the French invasion and the rule of Muhammad Ali.

Chaudhuri, K. N., *The Trading World of Asia and the East India Company, 1660–1760* (1978). An authoritative economic history of the East India Company's operations.

Crafts, N. F. R., *British Economic Growth During the Industrial Revolution* (1985). A pioneering study that emphasizes a long-term, more gradual process of adaptation to new institutional and social circumstances.

Doyle, William, *The Oxford History of the French Revolution* (1990). A highly detailed discussion of the course of events.

Elvin, Mark, *The Retreat of the Elephants: An Environmental History of China* (2004). A study of the different ways in which China's natural environment was shaped.

Fick, Carolyn E., *The Making of Haiti: The Saint Domingue Revolution from Below* (1990). Provides a detailed account of the factors that led to the great slave rebellion on the island of Haiti at the end of the eighteenth century.

Findley, Carter, *Bureaucratic Reform in the Ottoman Empire: The Sublime Porte, 1789–1922* (1980). A useful guide to Ottoman reform efforts in the nineteenth century.

Hevia, James, *Cherishing Men from Afar: Qing Guest Ritual and the Macartney Embassy of 1793* (1995). Offers a new interpretation of the nature of Sino-British conflict in the Qing period.

Hobsbawm, Eric, *Nations and Nationalism since 1780* (1990). Charts how the French Revolution generated a tradition of imagined realities of nationhood.

Hunt, Lynn, *Politics, Culture and Class in the French Revolution* (1984). Examines the influence of sociocultural shifts as causes and consequences of the French Revolution, emphasizing the symbols and practice of politics invented during the Revolution.

Jones, E. L., *Growth Recurring* (1988). Discusses the controversy over why the industrial revolution took place in Europe, stressing the unique ecological setting that encouraged long-term investment.

Kinsbruner, Jay, *Independence in Spanish America* (1994). A fine study of the Latin American revolutions for independence that argues that the struggle was as much a civil war as a fight for national independence.

Mokyr, Joel, *The Lever of Riches* (1990). An important study of the causes of the industrial revolution that emphasizes the role of small technological and organizational breakthroughs.

Naquin, Susan, and Evelyn Rawski, *Chinese Society in the Eighteenth Century* (1987). A survey of mid-Qing society.

Neal, Larry, *The Rise of Financial Capitalism* (1990). An important study of the making of financial markets.

Nikitenko, Aleksandr, *Up from Serfdom: My Childhood and Youth in Russia, 1804–1824* (2001). One of the very few recorded life stories of a Russian serf.

Pomeranz, Kenneth, *The Great Divergence: Europe, China, and the Making of the Modern World Economy* (2000). Offers explanations of why Europe and not some other place in the world, like parts of China or India, forged ahead economically in the nineteenth century.

Rudé, George, *Europe in the Eighteenth Century* (1972). Emphasizes the rise of a new class, the bourgeoisie, against the old aristocracy, as a cause of the French Revolution.

Wakeman, Frederic, Jr., "The Canton Trade and the Opium War," in John K. Fairbank (ed.), *The Cambridge History of China*, Vol. 10 (1978), pp. 163–212. The standard account of the episode.

Wong, R. Bin, *China Transformed: Historical Change and the Limits of European Experience* (2000). Draws attention to the relative autonomy of merchant capitalists in relation to dynastic states in Europe compared to China.

Wood, Gordon, *The Radicalism of the American Revolution* (1991). Makes a persuasive case for the revolutionary consequences of American independence and nationhood.

Wortman, Richard, *Scenarios of Power: Myth and Ceremony in Russian Monarchy*, 2 vols. (1995–2000). Examines how dynastic Russia confronted the challenges of the revolutionary epoch.

16

ALTERNATIVE VISIONS OF THE NINETEENTH CENTURY

By the last decades of the nineteenth century, the territorial expansion of the United States left almost all Indians confined to reservations. Across the American West during the 1880s, many on the reservations fell into despair. Among the downtrodden was a Paiute Indian named Wovoka. But on January 1, 1889, Wovoka had a vision that proposed an alternative, and much brighter, future. In his dream, the "Supreme Being" told Wovoka that if Indians lived harmoniously, shunned white ways (especially alcohol), and performed the cleansing Ghost Dance, the buffalo would return and multiply to their former numbers, and all Indians, including the dead, would be reborn to live in eternal bliss. As word spread of Wovoka's vision, Indians from hundreds of miles around made pilgrimages to the lodge of this new prophet. Many came away proclaiming him the Indians' messiah or the "Red Man's Christ," an impression fostered by the scars on Wovoka's hands, which he maintained had resulted from his centuries-old crucifixion. Especially among the Shoshone, Arapaho, Cheyenne, and Sioux peoples of the northern Plains, Wovoka's message inspired new hope. In the fall of 1890, increasing numbers joined in the ritual Ghost Dance hoping that it would restore, as Wovoka claimed, the good life that colonialism had seemed to extinguish. Among those given hope by the Ghost Dance was Sitting Bull, the revered

Sioux chief, who was himself famous for his visions. Yet, less than two years after Wovoka's initial vision, Sitting Bull was killed by police forces on a Sioux reservation. A few days later, on December 29, 1890, Sioux Ghost Dancers were massacred at a South Dakota creek called Wounded Knee. With them died the dream of the retreat of white people and the return of the buffalo.

Though it failed, this movement was connected to a much longer and larger history of prophetic crusades that challenged an emerging nineteenth-century order based on the ideals of the French and American revolutions, the worldwide spread of laissez-faire capitalism, the nation-state organization, new technologies, and industrial organizations. This emerging new order provided a set of answers to the questions of who should govern and what beliefs should prevail. But it did not stamp out other answers, which were equally important, if less influential, during this period. A diverse assortment of political radicals, charismatic prophets, peasant rebels, and anticolonial insurgents, animated by a sense of the impending loss of their existing worlds and energized by visions of utopian futures, put forward striking counterproposals to those that capitalists, colonial modernizers, and nation-state builders had developed.

REACTIONS TO SOCIAL AND POLITICAL CHANGE

> → *What did radical alternative movements have in common?*

The transformations of the late eighteenth and early nineteenth centuries had upset polities and economies around the globe. In Europe, the old order had been either swept aside or severely battered by the tide of political and eco-nomic revolutions. In North America, the newly independent United States began an expansion across the landmass. Territorial growth led to the dispossession of hundreds of Indian tribes and the acquisition of nearly half of Mexico by conquest. In Latin America, fledgling nation-states, which had replaced the Spanish Empire at the beginning of the nineteenth century, struggled to maintain control over their subject populations. And in Asia and Africa, rulers and people confronted the growing might of western military and industrial power. At stake were how territories were to be defined and ruled and what social and cultural visions they were to embody.

The alternatives to the dominant political, economic, and cultural trends varied considerably. Some called for the revitalization of traditional religions; others sought to strengthen village and communal bonds; still others imagined a society where there was no private property and where goods were shared equally. The actions of these rebels and dissidents depended on their local traditions and the degree of contact with the emergent power of industrial capitalism, European colonialism, and centralizing nation-states.

In this era of flux and rapid social change, when differing visions of power and justice vied with each other, we have unique opportunities to hear the voices of the lower orders—the peasants and workers, whose perspectives the elites so often ignored or suppressed. While there are few written records that capture the views of the illiterate and the marginalized, folklore, dreams, rumors, and prophecies, spread and handed down from generation to generation through oral tradition, illuminate the visions of common folk.

In this chapter, we highlight the emergence of three distinct alternative visions. The first comprised movements in regions not colonized by Europeans, but where European ideas and European commerce had disrupted the existing order: the Islamic Middle East and Islamic Africa, non-Islamic Africa, and China. Some of these areas were quite distant from industrial capitalism and European colonialism but were feeling the effects of these forces in more indirect

Focus Questions ALTERNATIVE VISIONS OF THE NINETEENTH CENTURY

→ *What did radical alternative movements have in common?*

→ *How did prophets and big men tap into Islamic and African traditions?*

→ *Why did the Taiping Rebellion arise in the 1850s in China?*

→ *What forces fueled European radicalism?*

→ *How were the alternative movements in the Americas and India similar and different?*

 WWNORTON.COM/STUDYSPACE

ways. Others, like China, were being drawn rapidly into a European commercial world but had managed to stay free of outright colonization. Here, population growth, new patterns of world trade, and the growing power of Europe disrupted the old order. Accordingly, during the first half of the nineteenth century, these regions witnessed the rise of leaders who believed that their traditions required rejuvenation. Dynamic religious prophets and charismatic military leaders seized the historical stage and set out to reorganize their communities into powerful polities.

A second pattern appeared in Europe and the Americas, in what were the heartlands of industrial capitalism, colonialism, and the new nation-states. Here, there was no turning back, especially following the collapse of old regimes under the onslaught of revolutions, wars, and the rising power of the bourgeoisie in the first half of the nineteenth century. Yet, here, too, utopians, romantics, and radicals dreamed of new, more far-reaching changes to the order that economic and political revolutions had created. The most thoroughgoing radical conceptions envisioned an end to private property and a socialist alternative to capitalism.

The third pattern of alternative visions took shape in the fierce struggle to defend traditional worlds under attack from imperialist nation-states in areas where European colonizers and settlers already dominated. Under this pattern, we find Indian prophets in North America who produced compelling visions to mobilize their people against the westward expansion of the United States. So, too, the Mayans in the Yucatan, confronted with the domineering power of the Mexican state, fought wars until the end of the nineteenth century to defend their cultural and political autonomy. Also within this pattern, peasants and old elites in British India advanced their conceptions of a just order that led to a fierce revolt to replace colonial rule in 1857.

Much separated one movement from another in the three patterns identified above, but together they offered radical alternatives to a world that was being structured by industrial capitalism and centralized modern states—national and colonial. Although these movements happened in different places and times, they shared four characteristics. First, whether presented by secular intellectuals or religious prophets, by ordinary peasant rebels or charismatic elite leaders, all of them opposed some form of established authority. Second, in giving voice to these visions, they steeped themselves in their own historical and cultural traditions, regarding their local communities as the source of political and cultural legitimacy. Third, and paradoxically, these movements authorized new social and political arrangements. Fourth, the movements in favor of alternatives either took

> *Dynamic religious prophets and charismatic military leaders seized the historical stage and set out to reorganize their communities into powerful polities.*

place in regions far from the center of the developing world or were led by men and women who were themselves on the margins of political and social power.

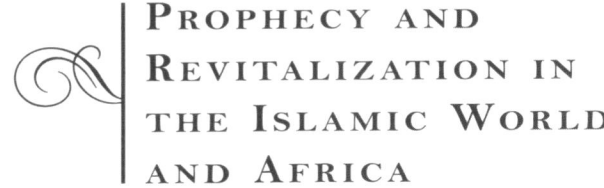

PROPHECY AND REVITALIZATION IN THE ISLAMIC WORLD AND AFRICA

↠ *How did prophets and big men tap into Islamic and African traditions?*

Our first category of alternative visions appeared in the parts of the world that had felt the effects of European and American commercial and cultural influence but that had not fallen under direct colonial rule. In such regions, alternative perspectives took on their most forceful expression in areas distant from the main trade and cultural routes and were led by persons who were outside the emerging capitalist world order. In the Islamic world, the margins played an especially important role in articulating these views because, in the Islamic heartland (the Ottoman Empire) and the most western-influenced regions of sub-Saharan Africa (the west coast and the southern tip of the landmass), reformers were trying to adapt to Europe—that is, to reform their societies along European lines.

Even though much of the Islamic world and non-Islamic Africa had not been colonized and were only partially integrated into a European-dominated set of trading networks, these regions had reached turning points at the end of the eighteenth century. By then, the era of Islamic expansion and the flowering under the Ottomans, Safavids, and Mughals was over. The dominance of these empires had extended Muslim trading orbits, facilitated cross-cultural communication, and led to the formation of common knowledge over vast territories. Their political and military decline, however, confronted the faithful with new challenges. The sense of alarm grew as the power of Christian Europe spread from the edges of the Islamic world to its centers. While this perception of danger motivated military men in Egypt and the Ottoman sultans to modernize their states (see Chapter 15), it also fomented the emergence of religious revitalization movements throughout the Islamic world. Led by prophets who were convinced that the Islamic faith was in trouble, these movements spoke the language of revival and restoration as they sought to establish new theocratic governments across the Islamic lands.

Prophecy also surfaced and exerted a powerful influence in non-Islamic Africa as it, too, experienced social change brought about by long-distance trade and population growth. Just as Muslim clerics and political leaders sought solutions to destabilizing changes in their world by re-reading Islamic classics, so, too, African communities, caught up in a world of changing trade relations and new ideas, looked to charismatic leaders. Drawing strength from the spiritual and magical traditions of African communities, the new leaders often succeeded in uniting previously disparate and dispersed communities behind their dynamic visions. Prophetic leaders and other "big men" rose to power because they were able to resolve local community crises—often related to a drought, a shortage of arable land, or another issue that sprang from the harsh environment.

ISLAMIC REVITALIZATION

Movements to revitalize Islam took place on the peripheries—in areas that seemed more distant and thus immune from the intense and potentially threatening repercussions of the world economy. In the peripheral zones, religious leaders rejected westernizing influences (see Map 16-1). Instead, the leaders of Islamic revitalization movements looked back to Islamic traditions and modeled their revolts on the life of Muhammad. But even as they looked to the past, they strove to establish something new: full-scale theocratic polities. The new generation of Islamic reformers conceived of the state as the primary instrument of God's will and as the vehicle for purifying Islamic culture.

WAHHABISM One of the most powerful of these purifying reformist movements arose on the Arabian Peninsula, the birthplace of the Muslim faith. In the Najd region of the peninsula, an area surrounded by mountains and deserts, and located just north of one of the most barren places in the world—the Empty Quarter—a religious cleric, Muhammad Ibn abd al-Wahhab (1703–1792), galvanized the local population by attacking what he regarded as lax religious practices. His message found a ready response among the local inhabitants, who felt threatened by the new commercial activities and fresh intellectual currents stirring around them. Abd al-Wahhab demanded a return to the pure Islam of Muhammad and the early caliphs. Although Najd was as far removed from the currents of the expanding world economy as an area could be, Abd al-Wahhab himself was not. Educated in Iraq, Iran, and the Hijaz (a region on the western end of what is currently Saudi Arabia, on the Red Sea) before returning to his home region, he believed that Islam had fallen into a degraded state, particularly in its birthplace. He railed against

the polytheistic beliefs that had taken hold of the people, complaining that men and women in defiance of the tenets of Muhammad, were worshipping trees, stones, and tombs and making sacrifices to false images. Abd al-Wahhab's movement stressed the absolute oneness of Allah (hence his followers were referred to as *Muwahhidin*, or Unitarians) and directed its most severe criticism against Sufi sects for extolling the lives of saints over the worship of God.

As Wahhabism swept across the Arabian Peninsula, the movement posed less of a threat to European power than it did to the Ottomans' hold on the region. Wahhabism gained a powerful political ally in the Najdian House of Saud, whose followers, inspired by the religious zeal of the Wahhabis, went on a militant religious campaign. They sacked the Shiite shrines of Karbala in southern Iraq, and in 1803 they overran the holy cities of Mecca and Medina, where they damaged the tombs of the saints. Frightened by the Wahhabi challenge, the Ottoman sultan persuaded the breakaway provincial ruler of Egypt, Muhammad Ali, to send troops to the Arabian Peninsula to suppress the movement. The Egyptians defeated the Saudis, but Wahhabism and the House of Saud continued to represent a pure Islamic faith that attracted clerics and common folk throughout the Muslim world.

DAN FODIO AND THE FULANI In West Africa, as in the Arabian Peninsula, Muslim revolts erupted from Senegal to Nigeria in the late eighteenth and early nineteenth centuries, responding in part to western inroads. In this region, the Fulani people played the decisive role in religious uprisings that sought, like the Wahhabi movement, to re-create a supposedly purer Islamic past. Although the Fulani originated in the eastern part of present-day Senegal (and retain a powerful presence there today), they moved eastward to escape drought in their home territory. Over time, the Fulani set down roots in strategic locations across the savannah lands of West Africa. The majority were cattle-keepers, practicing a pastoral and nomadic way of life. But some were sedentary, and people in this group converted to Islam, read the Islamic classics, and put themselves in touch with holy men of North Africa, Egypt, and the Arabian Peninsula. They concluded that the peoples of West Africa were violating Islamic beliefs and were engaging in irreligious practices.

The most powerful of these Islamic reform movements flourished in what is today northern Nigeria. It was led by a Fulani Muslim cleric, Usman dan Fodio (1754–1817), who succeeded in creating a vast Islamic empire. Dan Fodio's movement had all the trappings of the Islamic revolts of this period. It sought inspiration in the life of Muhammad and demanded a return to early Islamic practices. It attacked false belief and heathenism and called upon its followers to wage holy war (*jihad*) against unbelievers. Usman dan Fodio's adversaries were the old Hausa rulers, whose commitment to Islam, in his view, was less than absolute. To register his aversion to leaders who were not sufficiently faithful to Islamic beliefs and practices, dan Fodio withdrew from his original

MAP 16-1   MUSLIM REVITALIZATION MOVEMENTS IN THE MIDDLE EAST AND AFRICA AND THE *MFECANE* MOVEMENT IN SOUTHERN AFRICA

The nineteenth century saw a series of Muslim revitalization movements take place throughout the Middle East and North Africa. Why do you think these movements occurred on the peripheries of the Islamic world? How did forces in the global economy and changes in the global political balance of power affect these regions? Were any of the same factors that led to Islamic revitalization involved in the *Mfecane* developments in southern Africa?

ISLAMIC REBELS: ABI AL-QASIM AND ZAYNAB

Reformist ideas swirled through the Islamic world throughout the nineteenth century, producing new visions and powerful new communities across the Middle East and Africa. In no part of the Islamic world was opposition to European colonial and capitalist encroachment more strongly articulated than in Algeria, over which France claimed jurisdiction beginning in 1830. Algerians rose in bold and bloody revolts. The most violent of these uprisings were the rebellion of Abd al-Qadir in the 1830s and the revolt of 1849. The French repressed these movements ruthlessly, resulting in heavy losses to combatants and to many civilians. The military lessons took hold. Algerian Muslims, living on the edges of French authority, learned to use more subtle means to preserve their autonomy, fearing to challenge the French authorities openly.

A master in the art of protecting his community's religious and political autonomy in the face of France's constantly encroaching power was Shaykh Muhammad ibn Abi al-Qasim (1823–1897), a religious notable who lived in southern Algeria at the foothills of the Saharan Atlas Mountains. He gained a large circle of religious devotees because his Sufi brotherhood served as a safe haven for those who did not want to live under direct French rule. When, however, al-Qasim's health deteriorated, in the late 1870s, the French became embroiled in an internal struggle over his succession. Accepting the conventional wisdom that Islam was a patriarchal religion, the French supported the candidacy of the shaykh's male cousin over his daughter, Zaynab (1850–1904). Unfortunately, their calculations proved utterly wrong, having failed to account for Zaynab's

powerful personality and her religious legitimacy. When al-Qasim passed away in 1897, the French found themselves in a situation for which their traditional dealings with Islamic leaders had not prepared them. They stood in opposition to a dynamic female religious personage.

Zaynab laid claim to her father's legacy because of her exemplary piety, her understanding of her father's teachings, her vow of celibacy, and her independence from the French. Her descent from the family of the prophet Muhammad and the many miracles attributed to her soon elevated her to the status of a religious holy person and gave her a legitimacy that women did not frequently attain in Islamic religious affairs. But as we have seen in other settings (see the box on Joan of Arc in Chapter 11), at times when communal values are under great pressure, as they were because of the French advance into southern Algeria and France's interference in local religious succession, people were prepared to turn to a woman. Indeed, Zaynab was willing to contest French power more vigorously and directly than her father would have considered prudent because she realized that the French had never faced a woman leader before. Zaynab's actions revealed how vulnerable and uncertain the French were in their response to opposition from women. Colonial authorities claimed they were protecting women from male exploitation; nonetheless, the French turned against Zaynab, describing her as "passionate to the point of hatred and bold to the point of insolence and impudence." But their opposition only heightened her appeal and her legitimacy among her followers.

habitation in Konni. He then set up a new community of believers at Gudu, citing the precedent of Muhammad, who had withdrawn from Mecca to establish a community of true believers at Medina. The practice of withdrawal, called *hijra* in Muhammad's time, was yet another of the prophet's inspirations invoked by the religious reformers.

Dan Fodio was a member of a Sufi brotherhood, the Qadiriyya, one of the many Sufi orders that, from the sixteenth century onward, had facilitated the spread of Islam into West Africa. Sufism, the mystical and popular form of Islam, sought an emotional connection with God through a strict regimen of prayers, fasting, and religious exercises to obtain mystical states. Like Wovoka and Sitting Bull in North

America, dan Fodio's visions led him to challenge the ruling classes of West Africa. In one of his visions, the founder of the Qadiriyya order came to him and ordered him to unsheathe the sword of truth against the enemies of Islam.

Dan Fodio won the support of devout Muslims in the area, who agreed with his message that Islam was not being properly practiced. He also gained the backing of his Fulani tribes and many of the Hausa peasantry, who had suffered under the rule of the Hausa landlord class. The revolt, initiated in 1804, resulted in the overthrow of the Hausa rulers and the creation of a confederation of Islamic emirates, almost all of which were in the hands of the Fulani allies of dan Fodio.

Fulani women of northern Nigeria made critical contributions to the success of the religious revolt that took place there. Although dan Fodio and the other male leaders of the purification movement expected women to live their lives in accordance with the *sharia* (Islamic law), being modest in their dress and their association with men folk outside the family, they also expected women to support the community's military and religious endeavors, citing the important role that women had played in the first days of Islam. The best known of these Muslim women leaders was Nana Asma'u, daughter of dan Fodio. In Fulani society women of the upper ranks acquired an Islamic education, and Asma'u was as astute a reader of Islamic texts as any of the learned men in her society. Like many of the other Muslim Fulani devotees, she accompanied the warriors on their campaigns, encamping with them. The women prepared food for the soldiers, bound up their wounds, and provided daily encouragement. According to many Fulani accounts, Asma'u inspired the warriors at their most crucial battle, hurling a burning spear into the midst of the enemy army. Her poem "Song of the Circular Journey" celebrates the triumphs of the military forces who trekked thousands of miles to bring a reformed Islam to the area.

Usman dan Fodio considered himself a cleric first and a political and military man second. Although his political leadership was decisive in the success of the revolt, once military success was assured, dan Fodio retired to a life of scholarship and writing. He delegated the political and administrative functions of the new empire to his brother, Abdullahi, and his son, Muhammad Bello. An enduring decentralized state structure, which became known as the Sokoto Caliphate in 1809, became a solid and stable empire that fostered the spread of Islam through the region. In 1800, on the eve of dan Fodio's revolt, Islam was the faith of only a minority of people living in northern Nigeria; a century later, it had become the religion of the vast majority.

CHARISMATIC MILITARY MEN IN NON-ISLAMIC AFRICA

In non-Islamic Africa, revolts, new states, and prophetic movements arose from the same combination of factors that were at work in the rest of the world, particularly long-distance trade and population increase. Local communities here also looked to religious traditions and new political leaders. In southern Africa, during the first three decades of the nineteenth century, a group of political revolts, called in Zulu the *Mfecane* ("the crushing"), reordered the political map. Its epicenter was a large tract of land lying east of the Drakensberg Mountains, an area where growing populations and land resources existed in a precarious balance (see Map 16-1). Compounding this pressure, trade with the Portuguese in Mozambique and with other Europeans at Delagoa Bay had

disrupted the traditional social order. This set the stage for a political crisis for the northern Nguni (Bantu-speaking) peoples.

Many different branches of the Bantu-speaking peoples had inhabited the southern part of the African landmass for centuries. At the end of the eighteenth century, however, their political organizations still operated on a small scale, revolving around families and clans and modest chieftaincies. These tiny polities could not cope with the problems of overpopulation and competition for land that had become prevalent in southern Africa at that time. A branch of the Nguni, the Zulus, produced a fierce war leader, Shaka (1787–1828), who created a ruthless warrior state that drove other populations out of the region and forced a shift from small clan communities to large, centralized monarchies throughout southern and central Africa.

Shaka was the son of a minor chief who managed to emerge as the victor in the struggle for cattle-grazing and farming lands that arose during a severe drought. A

Shaka, King of the Zulus. This illustration, the only one from the time, may be an exaggeration, but it does not exaggerate the view that many had of the awesome strength and power of Shaka, the leader who united the Zulu peoples into an invincible warrior state.

Primary Source

A FEMALE MUSLIM VOICE IN AFRICA

The Islamic scholar and writer Nana Asma'u was the daughter of Usman dan Fodio, the leader of the Fulani revolt in northern Nigeria at the turn of the nineteenth century. She was a prolific writer and a fine poet who wrote in the Fulani language (Fulfude) using the Arabic script. Many of her poems were full of religious inspiration and sought to demonstrate how much her father's revolt was inspired by the life and message of the Prophet Muhammad. She was also deeply attached to her brother, Muhammad Bello, who succeeded their father as head of the Sokoto Caliphate. Muhammad Bello looked to Nana Ama'u, his sister, to promote Muslim orthodoxy among the female population in his empire, and she worked to extend education to rural women, encouraging them to come to her and to learn at her side. Following is a poem she wrote in praise of her brother, underlining his commitment to an Islamic way of life.

1 I give thanks to the King of Heaven, the One God. I invoke blessings on the Prophet and set down my poem.

2 The Lord made Heaven and earth and created all things, sent prophets to enlighten mankind.

3 Believe in them for your own sake, learn from them and be saved, believe in and act upon their sayings.

4 I invoke blessings on the Prophet who brought the Book, the Qur'an: he brought the *hadith* to complete the enlightenment.

5 Muslim scholars have explained knowledge and used it, following in the footsteps of the Prophet.

6 It is my intention to set down Bello's characteristics and explain his ways.

7 For I wish to assuage my loneliness, requite my love, find peace of mind through my religion.

8 These are his characteristics: he was learned in all branches of knowledge and feared God in public and in private.

9 He obeyed religious injunctions and distanced himself from forbidden things: this is what is known about him.

10 He concentrated on understanding what is right to know about the Oneness of God.

11 He preached to people and instructed them about God: he caused them to long for Paradise.

12 He set an example in his focus on eternal values: he strove to end oppression and sin.

13 He upheld the *shari'a,* honored it, implemented it aright, that was his way, everyone knows.

14 And he made his views known to those who visited him: he said to them "Follow the *shari'a,* which is sacred."

15 He eschewed worldly things and discriminated against anything of ill repute; he was modest and a repository of useful knowledge.

16 He was exceedingly level-headed and generous, he enjoyed periods of quietude: but was energetic when he put his hand to things.

17 He was thoughtful, calm, a confident statesman, and quick-witted.

18 He honored people's status: he could sort out difficulties and advise those who sought his help.

---

muscular and physically imposing figure, Shaka was also a violent man who did not hesitate to use terror to intimidate his subjects or to overawe his adversaries. His enemies knew that the price of opposition would be a massacre, which would include the killing of women and children. Nor was he much kinder to his own people. Following the death of his beloved mother, Shaka took out his feelings of grief by executing those who were not properly contrite and who did not weep profusely. Reportedly, it took 7,000 lives to assuage his grief.

Shaka built his new state around his own military and organizational skills and the fear that his personal ferocity produced. He drilled his men relentlessly in the use of short stabbing spears and in discipline under pressure. Like the Mongols, he had a remarkable ability to incorporate defeated communities into the state and to absorb young men into his ultra-dedicated warrior forces. His army numbered 40,000 men and was organized into regiments that lived, studied, and fought together. Forbidden from marrying until discharged from the army, Shaka's warriors developed an intense

19 He had nothing to do with worldly concerns, but tried to restore to a healthy state things which he could. These were his characteristics.

20 He never broke promises, but faithfully kept them: he sought out righteous things. Ask and you will hear.

21 He divorced himself entirely from bribery and was totally scrupulous: He flung back at the givers money offered for titles.

22 One day Garange [chief of Mafora] sent him a splendid gift, but Bello told the messenger Zitaro to take it back.

23 He said to the envoy who had brought the bribe, "Have nothing to do with forbidden things."

24 And furthermore he said, "Tell him that the gift was sent for unlawful purposes; it is wrong to respond to evil intent."

25 He was able to expedite matters: he facilitated learning, commerce, and defense, and encouraged everything good.

26 He propagated good relationships between different tribes and between kinsmen. He afforded protection; everyone knows this.

27 When strangers came he met them, and taught about religious matters, explaining things: he tried to enlighten them.

28 He lived in a state of preparedness, he had his affairs in order and had an excellent intelligence service.

29 He had nothing to do with double agents and said it was better to ignore them, for they pervert Islamic principles.

30 He was a very pleasant companion to friends and acquaintances: he was intelligent, with a lively mind.

31 He fulfilled promises and took care of affairs, but he did not act hastily.

32 He shouldered responsibilities and patiently endured adversities.

33 He was watchful and capable of restoring to good order matters which had gone wrong.

34 He was resourceful and could undo mischief, no matter how serious, because he was a man of ideas.

35 He was gracious to important people and was hospitable to all visitors, including non-Muslims.

36 He drew good people close to him and distanced himself from people of ill repute.

37 Those are his characteristics. I have recounted a few examples that are sufficient to provide a model for emulation and benefit.

38 May God forgive him and have mercy on him: May we be united with him in Paradise, the place we aspire to.

39 For the sake of the Prophet, the Compassionate, who was sent with mercy to mankind.

40 May God pour blessings on the Prophet and his kinsmen and all other followers.

41 May God accept this poem. I have concluded it in the year 1254.

→ *Why would Nana Asma'u feel compelled to write a poem in praise of her brother?*

→ *What two basic categories does Nana Asma'u's praise fall into? How are they interrelated?*

SOURCE: Beverly B. Mack and Jean Boyd, *One Woman's Jihad: Nana Asma'u, Scholar and Scribe* (Bloomington: Indiana University Press, 2000), pp. 97–99.

esprit de corps and regarded no sacrifice as too great in the service of the state. So overpowering were Shaka's forces that other peoples of the region fled from their home areas, and Shaka laid claim to their estates for himself and his followers.

Thus did the Zulus under Shaka create a ruthless warrior state that conquered much territory in southern and central Africa, assimilating some peoples and forcing others to fashion their own similarly centralized polities. Shaka's defeated foes themselves adopted many of the Zulu state's military innovations. They did so first to defend themselves and then to take over new land as they were driven away from their old areas. The new states of the Ndebele in what later became Zimbabwe and of the Sotho of South Africa came into existence in the middle of the nineteenth century in this way and proved long-lasting.

In turning southern Africa from a region of smaller polities into an area with larger and more powerful ones, Shaka seemed very much a man of the modern, nineteenth-century world. Yet he was in his own unique way a familiar kind of African leader. He shared a charismatic and prophetic style

Zulu Regiments. Shaka's Zulu state owed its political and military successes to its young warriors, who were deeply loyal to their ruler and whose training and discipline were exemplary. Shown here is a regimental camp in which the warriors slept in huts massed in a circular pattern and trained in military drill and close combat in the inside circle.

with others who emerged during periods of acute social change. He was, in this sense, one of many big men to seek dominance.

PROPHECY AND REBELLION IN CHINA

> → *Why did the Taiping Rebellion arise in the 1850s in China?*

The prophetic and charismatic movements in the Islamic world and Africa appeared in areas relatively distant from western influences. By contrast, China, which had seen its trade surplus with Europe turned into a deficit in the first half of the nineteenth century through a brisk trade in opium, was no longer isolated. Until 1842, the Chinese had confined trade with Europeans to the port city of Canton. After the Opium War, westerners forced Qing rulers to open up a number of other ports to trade. To be sure, the dynasty retained its authority over almost the whole realm, and western influence remained confined to a small minority of merchants and missionaries. Nevertheless, foreign gunboats and extraterritorial rights reminded the Chinese of the power of the West.

As in the Islamic world and other parts of sub-Saharan Africa, population increases in China—from 250 million in 1644 to around 450 million by the 1850s—had put considerable pressure on land and other resources. Moreover, the rising consumption of opium, grown in India and brought to China in increasing quantities by English traders, had produced further social instability and financial crisis. As social dislocation spread, banditry and rebellions became frequent. The ruling Qing dynasty turned to the gentry to maintain order in the countryside. But as the gentry raised its militia to put down secret societies and bandits, it whittled away at the authority of the Qing Manchu rulers. Faced with these changes, the Qing dynasty, already weakened by the humiliating Treaty of Nanjing (1842) imposed by Britain following the Opium War, struggled to maintain control and legitimacy in the eyes of many subjects. Searching for an alternative present and future, beginning in 1850 hundreds of thousands of disillusioned and impoverished peasants joined in what became known as the Taiping Rebellion.

The uprising drew upon China's long history of peasant revolts. Traditionally, these rebellions were rooted in popular religious sects. These sects frequently espoused visions that were egalitarian or millenarian (convinced of the imminent coming of a just and ideal society). Inspired by Daoists, who looked to a past golden age before the world was corrupted by human conventions, or Buddhist sources, these popular religious sects posed threats to the established order. In contrast to orthodox institutions, here women played important roles. In times of political breakdown, millenarian sects provided the organizational networks for transforming local revolts into large-scale rebellions. Thus did the Taiping Rebellion, which began as a local movement in southern China, tap into this millenarian tradition and spread rapidly.

THE DREAM

The story of the Taiping Rebellion begins with a complex and convoluted dream that inspired its founding prophet, Hong Xiuquan (1813–1864). A native of Guangdong province in the southernmost part of the country, Hong first encountered Christian missionaries in the 1830s. He was then trying, unsuccessfully, to pass the civil service examination, which would have afforded him entry into the elite stratum and a potential career in the Qing bureaucracy. Disappointed by his poor showing, Hong began to have visions, including a dream in 1837 that led him to form the Society of God Worshippers in the 1840s and subsequently to establish the Taiping Heavenly Kingdom in 1851.

In this dream, a ceremonial retinue of heavenly guards escorted Hong to heaven. The group included a cock-like figure, which he later identified as Leigong, the Duke of Thunder, a familiar figure in indigenous mythology. When Hong reached heaven, his belly was slit open, and his internal or-

Taiping Rebellion. A painting depicting the Taiping rebels attacking a town. Had the Taiping succeeded in overthrowing the Qing, it would have changed the course of Chinese history and profoundly affected the rest of the world.

gans were removed and replaced with new ones. As the operation for his renewal was completed, heavenly texts were unrolled for him to read and absorb. The "Heavenly Mother" then met and thoroughly cleansed him. She addressed him as "Son" before bringing him in front of the "Old Father." Although not part of the heavenly bureaucracy, Confucius and women generals from the Song dynasty were also present. Upon meeting Hong, the "Old Father" complained that human beings had been led astray by demons, as demonstrated by the vanity of their shaven heads (a practice imposed by the Qing regime), their consumption of opium, and other forms of debauchery. The "Old Father" even denounced Confucius, who, after being flogged and begging for mercy before Hong's heavenly "Elder Brother," was allowed to stay in heaven but forbidden to preach his teachings again. But the world was not yet free of demons. Thus the "Old Father" instructed Hong to leave his heavenly family behind and return to earth to rescue human beings from demons.

How much of this account of Hong's dream has been embellished with hindsight we will probably never know. What we do know is that Hong, after he failed the civil service examination for the third time in 1837, was afflicted with a strange "illness" in which he had visions of combating demons. He also took to proclaiming himself the Heavenly King. Relatives and neighbors thought he might have gone mad. Yet, after a burst of apparently outlandish behavior, Hong gradually returned to his normal state. In 1843, after failing the examination for the fourth time, Hong immersed himself in a Christian tract entitled *Good Words for Exhorting the Age*. Reportedly, reading this tract enabled Hong to realize the full significance of his earlier dream. All the pieces suddenly fell into place. The "Old Father" in his dream, he came to understand, was the Lord Ye-huo-hua (a Chinese rendering of Jehovah), the creator of heaven and earth. Accordingly, the cleansing ritual foretold his baptism. The "Elder Brother" was, in turn, Jesus the Savior, son of God. He, Hong Xiuquan, was the younger brother of Jesus—God's other son. Just as Jesus had previously descended to save mankind, Hong was now being sent by God to rid the world of evil and demons. What was once a dream was now a prophetic vision.

THE REBELLION

Unlike earlier sectarian leaders whose rebellions tended to operate in secrecy before exploding onto the public arena, Hong chose a more audacious path. Once convinced of his vision, he began to preach his doctrines openly, baptizing converts and destroying Confucian idols and ancestral shrines. Such frontal assaults on the establishment testified to his conviction that he was carrying out God's will rather than engaging in heterodox activities. Hong's message of revitalization of a troubled land and "restoration" of the "heavenly kingdom," imagined as a just and egalitarian order, appealed to the subordinate classes caught in the flux of social change. Drawing on a largely rural social base and asserting allegiance to Christianity, the Taiping ("Great Peace") Rebellion claimed to herald a new era of economic and social justice.

Many of Hong's early followers came from the marginal sectors of local society, those whose anger at social and economic dislocations caused by the Opium War was directed not at the Europeans but at the Qing government. The Taiping identified the Manchus as the "demons" and as the chief obstacle to the realization of God's kingdom on earth. Taiping policies were demanding and strict: the rules prohibited the consumption of alcohol, smoking of opium, or indulgence in sensual pleasure. Men and women were segregated for administrative and residential purposes. At the same time, in a most drastic departure from the dynastic practice, women joined the army in segregated units. These female military units were comprised mostly of Hakka women. Hakka is an ethnic sub-group within the Han (to which Hong Xiuquan,

Primary Source

THE TAIPING ON THE PRINCIPLES OF THE HEAVENLY NATURE

In this excerpt from 1854, the Taiping leaders envisage a radically new community based on values that challenge the conventional modes of social organization of Chinese society. Inspired by their understanding of Christianity, the Taiping leadership confronted the central role of the family and ancestral worship in Chinese social life by urging all its followers to regard themselves as belonging to a single family. It also advocated the segregation of the sexes, despite its efforts to improve the lives of women in some of its other policy proclamations.

We brothers and sisters, enjoying today the greatest mercy of our Heavenly Father, have become as one family and are able to enjoy true blessings; each of us must always be thankful. Speaking in terms of our ordinary human feelings, it is true that each has his own parents and there must be a distinction in family names; it is also true that as each has his own household, there must be a distinction between this boundary and that boundary. Yet we must know that the ten thousand names derive from the one name, and the one name from one ancestor. Thus our origins are not different. Since our Heavenly Father gave us birth and nourishment, we are of one form though of separate bodies, and we breathe the same air though in different places. This is why we say, "All are brothers within the four seas." Now, basking in the profound mercy of Heaven, we are of one family. . . .

We brothers, our minds having been awakened by our Heavenly Father, joined the camp in the earlier days to support our Sovereign, many bringing parents, wives, uncles, brothers, and whole families. It is a matter of course that we should attend to our parents and look after our wives and children, but when one first creates a new rule, the state must come first and the family last, public interests first and private interests last. Moreover, as it is advisable to avoid suspicion [of improper conduct] between the inner [female] and the outer [male] and to distinguish between male and female, so men must have male quarters and women must have female quarters; only thus can we be dignified and avoid confusion. There must be no common mixing of the male and female groups, which would cause debauchery and violation of Heaven's commandments. Although to pay respects to parents and to visit wives and children occasionally are in keeping with human nature and not prohibited, yet it is only proper to converse before the door, stand a few steps apart and speak in a loud voice; one must not enter the sisters' camp or permit the mixing of men and women. Only thus, by complying with rules and commands, can we become sons and daughters of Heaven.

At the present time, the remaining demons have not yet been completely exterminated and the time for the reunion of families has not yet arrived. We younger brothers and sisters must be firm and patient to the end, and with united strength and a single heart we must uphold God's principles and wipe out the demons immediately. With peace and unity achieved, then our Heavenly Father, displaying his mercy, will reward us according to our merits. Wealth, nobility, and renown will then enable us brothers to celebrate the reunion of our families and enjoy the harmonious relations of husband and wife.

→ *How would you characterize the view of the Taiping toward the sexes?*

→ *How do their views on these matters compare and contrast with other alternative visions described in this chapter?*

SOURCE: *The Principles of the Heavenly Nature*, in *Sources of Chinese Tradition*, 2nd ed., Vol. 2, compiled by Wm. Theodore de Bary and Richard Lufrano (New York: Columbia University Press, 2000), pp. 229–30.

the founder of the Taiping, belonged) with a strong sense of its own distinct identity, an important part of which was that Hakka women did not bind their feet.

Women could also serve in the Taiping bureaucracy. Examinations were based on a translated version of the Bible and assorted religious and literary compositions by Hong. Finally, all land was to be divided among the families according to family size, with men and women receiving equal shares. Once each family's own need for sustenance could be met, the communities shared the remaining surplus. These were all radical departures from Chinese traditions. But the Taiping opposition to the Manchus did not entail the formation of a modern nation-state. The rebellion remained caught between the modern and the traditional.

By 1850, Hong's movement had amassed a following of over 20,000, giving Qing rulers cause for concern. They sent troops to arrest Hong and other rebel leaders. But they were repelled by Taiping forces, who then began to spread their rebellion beyond Hong's original base in the southwestern part of the country. In 1851, Hong declared himself the Heavenly King of the "Taiping Heavenly Kingdom" (or "Heavenly Kingdom of Great Peace"). By 1853, the Taiping rebels had captured major cities, swelling their ranks (see Map 16-2). Upon capturing Nanjing, the Taiping cleansed the city of "demons," systematically killing all the Manchus—men, women, and children—they found, and established their own "heavenly" capital in the city.

But the rebels could not sustain their vision. Deadly struggles within the leadership, uncompromising codes of conduct, and the rallying of Manchu and Han elites around the dynasty all contributed to the fall of the Heavenly Kingdom. Disturbed by the Taiping's repudiation of Confucianism and wanting to protect their property, local landowning gentry led militias against the Taiping. Moreover, western governments also opposed the rebellion. Despite the constant reiteration of the "brotherhood" of Christians, western governments claimed that the Taiping's doctrines represented a perversion of Christianity. Although the rebellion's inception had much to do with the disruptive forces unleashed by an expansive West, a foreign-officered mercenary army eventually took part in its suppression. Hong

himself perished as his heavenly capital fell in 1864. With the Qing victory imminent, few of the perhaps 100,000 rebels in Nanjing surrendered. The slaughter of the Taiping rebels prepared the stage for a concerted attempt by imperial bureaucrats and elite intellectuals to rejuvenate the Qing state. Although the Taiping's millenarian vision vanished, the desire to reconstitute Chinese society and government did not. The rebellion, in that sense, continued to inspire reformers as well as future peasant mobilizations.

MAP 16-2   THE TAIPING REBELLION IN CHINA, 1851–1864

Note that the Taiping Rebellion started in the southwestern part of the country. The rebels, however, went on to control much of the lower Yangzi region and part of the coastal area. Why do you think the Taiping rebels were so successful in southern China and not in northern regions? How did western powers react to the Taiping Rebellion? Would they have been as concerned if the rebellion took place farther to the north or west?

Like their counterparts in the Islamic world and Africa, the Taiping based their critique of the old order on a promise to restore lost harmony. For all the differences of cultural and historical location, what Abd al-Wahhab, dan Fodio, Shaka, and Hong had in common was the perception that the present world was unjust. Thus, they set out to reorganize their respective communities. Characteristically, these communities were caught up in the flux of change, and their reorganization into new polities involved confrontations with the established authorities. In this regard, the language of revitalization used by religious prophets in Islamic areas and China proved crucial, for it provided an alternative vocabulary of political and spiritual legitimacy. Although in non-Islamic Africa it was not religious revitalization that powered the creation of new polities, it still was an appeal to tradition—to communal solidarity and to the widespread tradition of big men in stateless societies. By mobilizing those eager to return to an imagined golden age, these prophets and charismatic leaders gave voice to those dispossessed by global change, while producing new, alternative ways of organizing society and politics.

UTOPIANS, SOCIALISTS, AND RADICALS IN EUROPE

> → *What forces fueled European radicalism?*

Europe and North America were the core areas of capitalist activity, nation-state building, and colonialism. But there, too, divergent conceptions of the political and social order challenged the main currents of thought and activity. Prophets of all stripes—political, social, cultural, and religious—propounded antiestablishment values and dreamed of alternative arrangements. Radicals, liberals, utopians, romantics, nationalists, abolitionists, and religious mavericks made plans for better worlds to come. They did so in the face of a new era of monarchical-conservative dominance after the Congress of Vienna in 1815. This conservative turn was especially pronounced in central Europe, where reestablished kings and aristocrats revived many of their privileges and much of their power. The restoration of old regimes, arranged by Austrian diplomat Clemens von Metternich (1773–1859), succeeded in turning back the clock only by ceaselessly tinkering with the gears. But opposition to the restored regimes was widespread, and radical voices confidently predicted the coming of a new day.

RESTORATION AND RESISTANCE

The social and political ferment of the Restoration period (1815–1848) owed a great deal to the ambiguous legacies of the French Revolution and the Napoleonic wars. As a result of the innovations of the revolutionaries and the Napoleonic regime, there were now many different state forms and ideologies from which to choose. In the 1820s, 1830s, and 1840s, Europeans could also draw on a long tradition of religious radicalism. Like the purification movements in the Islamic World and religious sects in China, fundamentalist beliefs fueled social and political rebellion. The sixteenth- and seventeenth-century English Puritans and German Anabaptists sought to remake communities from the ground up. Predicting an apocalyptic end for those who lived under sinful and oppressive rulers, these radical dissenters had established principles of both violent and passive resistance that would be employed again and again in centuries to come. Europeans of the Restoration era also had utopian ideals at their beck and call; they could invoke the early egalitarian image of "Pansophia," an ideal republic of inquisitive Christians, united in the search for knowledge of nature as a means of loving God. Or they could refer to the utopian Enlightenment thinkers like William Godwin and the Marquis de Condorcet, men confident that mankind was already well on its way to scientific, political, and even biological perfection. Critics of the old regime in the Restoration period appeared in many stripes, but all of them were shaped, in one way or another, by a combination of recent experience and older traditions.

Self-conscious "reactionaries" emerged at this time; their crusade was not just to restore privileges to kings and nobles, but also to reverse all the secularizing and democratizing concessions sovereigns had accorded their subjects during the revolutionary and Napoleonic periods. In Russia, for example, the Slavophiles touted what they regarded as "native" traditions and institutions against the excessively "westernizing" reforms introduced by Peter the Great and continued by his self-styled "enlightened despot" successors. Many Slavophiles were ardent monarchists. Their desire for a strong yet "traditional" Russia brought them into conflict with the conservative, but modernizing, tsarist state.

The liberals, on the other hand, wanted their states to carry through the legal and political reforms envisioned in 1789 but not to attempt economic equalizing in the manner of the radical Jacobins. Liberals were eager to curb the states' restrictions on trade, destroy the churches' stranglehold on education, and enlarge the franchise, all the while preserving the free market, the Christian churches, and the rule of law. Proponents of liberalism, like John Stuart Mill, insisted on the individual's right to think, speak, act, and vote as he or she pleased, so long as no harm was done to people or property. Liberals feared the corruptibility of powerful states and held that the proper role of government was to foster civil liberties and promote legal equality.

In sum, the reactionaries wished for a return to privilege, the liberals for reforms that would not endanger order. Both could find elements to their taste in all the nations of the post-Napoleonic world. Indeed, it was the rivalry between

Congress of Vienna. At the Congress of Vienna in 1815, the Austrian prime minister Clemens von Metternich took the lead in drafting a peace settlement that would balance power between the states of Europe.

these two groups that defined much of the political landscape of the era before 1848.

RADICAL VISIONS

Reactionaries and liberals did not form the only alternative groups of importance at this time. Most discontented of all—and most determined to bring about grand-scale change—were the radicals. The term *radicals* refers to those who favored the total reconfiguration of the old regime's state system: radicalism meant going to the root of the problem, continuing the revolution, not reversing it or stopping reform. In general, radicals shared a bitter hatred for the status quo and an insistence on popular sovereignty, but beyond this consensus, there was much dissension in their ranks. If some radicals demanded the equalization, or even abolition, of private property, others, like Serbian, Greek, Polish, and Italian nationalists, were primarily interested in throwing off the oppressive overlordship of the Ottoman and Austrian empires and creating their own nation-states. It was the radicals' threat of reopening the age of revolution that ultimately reconciled both liberals and reactionaries to preserving the status quo.

NATIONALISTS   The least terrifying of the radicals, in the long run, proved to be the nationalists, though for those in power, nationalist uprisings like those of the Poles, Serbs, Greeks, and Italians were unsettling enough (see Map 16-3). The Poles rose twice, once in 1830 and again in 1846; both times, Prussian, Austrian, and Russian oppressors bloodily

put down their nationalist revolts. By contrast, the Greeks, inspired by religious revivalism as well as by enlightened ideas, managed to wrest independence from the Ottoman Turks after a long series of skirmishes (1821–1829). Invoking both the classical tradition and their membership in the community of Christians, Greek patriots won support among Europeans in their fight against the Muslim Ottoman Empire. Interestingly, however, most of this support had to come in the form of private donations or volunteer soldiers. European rulers feared that sympathy for the oppressed Greeks would fan the flames of revolution at home. Still, to counter the power of the Ottomans, the Europeans sent their ships to the Mediterranean and defeated the Ottomans at Navarino in 1827. The Ottomans finally recognized Greek independence in 1829. In the new state, the Greeks could not resolve differences between those who wanted a small, essentially secular republic and those who wanted to reclaim Istanbul for Greek Orthodoxy, and they ended up inviting Otto, a Bavarian prince, to be the new king of Greece in 1832. The new Greek state had won its independence from the Ottomans, but it was neither the resurrected Athens nor the revivified Byzantium that the revolutionaries had envisioned.

Other nationalist movements were suppressed or at least slowed down with little bloodshed, and they gradually developed a more conservative character. In places like the German principalities, the Italian states, and the Hungarian parts of the Habsburg Empire, secret societies composed of young men—students and intellectuals—gathered to plan bright, republican futures. Regrettably for these patriots, however, organizations like "Young Italy," founded in 1832 by Giuseppe

MAP 16-3   CIVIL UNREST AND REVOLUTIONS IN EUROPE, 1819–1848
Civil unrest and revolution were endemic to Europe after the Congress of Vienna, with conservative governments fighting off liberal rebellions and demands for change. On the basis of this map, what parts of Europe would appear to have been politically stable and conservative and what parts rebellious? Can you explain the reasons for the stability of some parts of Europe and the instability of others? What states were most heavily involved in suppressing civil unrest and revolutionary activity, and why did they do so?

Mazzini (1805–1872) to bring about national unification and renewal, had little popular or foreign support. Censorship and a few strategic executions suppressed them. In this way, German, Hungarian, and Italian campaigns for national recognition were prevented from reaching the revolutionary stage. Nonetheless, all of these movements would ultimately succeed in the century's second half, when conservatives and liberals in western Europe recognized the advantages of permitting a tamer sort of nationalist fervor. Nationalism remained, however, a perilous force in central Europe, where minority groups like the Czechs, Serbs, and Poles would continue to campaign for states of their own.

SOCIALISTS AND COMMUNISTS   Much more threatening to the ruling elite were the radicals who believed that the French Revolution had not gone far enough. They longed for a new, grander revolution that would sweep away the Restoration's political *and* economic order. Early socialists and communists (the terms were more or less interchangeable at the time) insisted that political reforms offered no effective answer to the more pressing "social question": what was to be done about the inequalities being introduced by industrial capitalism? The socialists worried in particular about the deleterious effects of the division of labor on the human personality and the growing gap between impoverished workers and newly wealthy employers. They believed that the whole free market economy, not just the state, had to be transformed to save the human race from self-destruction. Liberty and equality, they insisted, could not be separated; aristocratic privilege along with capitalism ought to be thrown on history's ash heap.

No more than a handful of radical prophets hatched revolutionary plans in the years after 1815. Yet by no means were they the only participants in the many strikes, riots, peasant uprisings, and protest meetings of the era. Ordinary workers, artisans, women employed in textile manufacturing, and domestic servants all participated in attempts to answer "the social question" to their satisfaction. A few socialists and feminists campaigned for the social and political equality of the sexes. In Britain in 1819, Manchester workers at St. Peter's Field demonstrated peacefully for political reform—specifically, increased representation in Parliament—but were fired on by panicking guardsmen, who left 11 dead and 460 injured in an incident later dubbed the Peterloo Massacre. In 1839 and 1842, more than 3 million people, or nearly half the adult population of Britain, signed the People's Charter, which called for universal suffrage for all adult males, the secret ballot, equal electoral districts, and annual parliamentary elections. This mass movement, known as Chartism, like most such endeavors, ended in defeat. Parliament rejected the charter in 1839, 1842, and 1848.

FOURIER AND UTOPIAN SOCIALISM Despite their many defeats, the radicals kept trying. Some sense of this age of revolutionary aspirations reveals itself in one European visionary who had big grievances and even bigger plans, the "utopian socialist" Charles Fourier (1772–1837). Utopian socialism was the most visionary of all Restoration-era alternative movements, though not the most radical in either political or social terms. Utopians introduced planning,

where the revolutionaries invoked violence, and they generally rejected the equalizing of conditions, fearing the suppression of diversity. Still, they dreamed of transforming states, workplaces, and human relations in a much more thorough way than their religious or political predecessors. Fourier, in particular, deserves to be classed among the most influential of Europe's prophet-visionaries.

Fired by the egalitarian hopes and the cataclysmic failings of the French Revolution, Charles Fourier believed himself to be the scientific prophet of the new world to come. He was a highly imaginative, self-taught man who earned his keep in the cloth trade, an occupation that gave him an intense hatred for merchants and middlemen. Convinced that the division of labor and repressive moral conventions destroyed mankind's natural talents and passions, Fourier concluded that a revolution grander than that of 1789 was needed. But this utopian transformation of economic, social, and political conditions, he thought, could be accomplished by organization, not by bloodshed. Indeed, Fourier, by 1808, believed that the thoroughly corrupt world was already on the brink of giving way to a new and harmonious age, of which he was, of course, the oracle.

First formulated in 1808, his "system" envisioned the reorganization of human communities into what he called phalanxes: in these harmonious collectives of about 1,500 to 1,600 people and 810 personality types, diversity would be preserved, but efficiency maintained; best of all, work would become enjoyable. All members of the phalanx, rich and poor, would work, if not necessarily at the same tasks. All, however, would work only in short spurts of no more than two hours, so as to make labor more interesting and sleep, idleness, and profligacy less attractive. A typical rich man's day would begin at 3:30 A.M.; the first two hours would be spent eating breakfast, reviewing the previous day, and participating in an industrial parade. At 5:30, he would hunt; at 7:00

The Phalanx. The Phalanx, as one of Fourier's German followers envisioned it. In this rendering, the idealized home for the residents of the cooperative social system is represented as a building architecturally similar to the home of the French kings, the Louvre.

THE COMMUNIST MANIFESTO

In January 1848, Karl Marx and Friedrich Engels prepared a party program for the Communist League, a German workingman's association. Published in French as The Communist Manifesto *on the eve of the June 1848 uprisings, the document foretold the inevitable overthrow of bourgeois-dominated capitalism by the working classes and the transition to socialism and ultimately to communism. The following excerpt gives the reader a sense of their certainty that history, driven by economic factors and class conflict, was moving inexorably toward the revolution of the proletariat. Marx and Engels defined the bourgeoisie as capitalists, owners of the means of production and employers of wage laborers, and they defined proletariats as wage laborers who had to sell their labor to live.*

A spectre is haunting Europe—the spectre of Communism. . . .

The history of all hitherto existing society is the history of class struggles. . . .

The modern bourgeois society that has sprouted from the ruins of feudal society has not done away with class antagonisms. It has but established new classes, new conditions of oppression, new forms of struggle in place of the old ones.

Our epoch, the epoch of the bourgeoisie, possesses, however, this distinctive feature: it has simplified the class antagonisms: Society as a whole is more and more splitting up into two great hostile camps, into two great classes directly facing each other: Bourgeoisie and Proletariat. . . .

The bourgeoisie . . . has put an end to all feudal, patriarchal, idyllic relations. It has pitilessly torn asunder the motley feudal ties that bound man to his "natural superiors," and has left remaining no other nexus between man and man than naked self-interest, than callous "cash payment.". . .

The need of a constantly expanding market for its products chases the bourgeoisie over the whole surface of the globe. It must nestle everywhere, settle everywhere, establish connexions everywhere. . . .

The bourgeoisie, by the rapid improvement of all instruments of production, by the immensely facilitated means of communication, draws all, even the most barbarian, nations into civilisation. The cheap prices of its commodities are the heavy artillery with which it batters down all Chinese walls, with which it forces the barbarians' intensely obstinate hatred of foreigners to capitulate. . . .

The weapons with which the bourgeoisie felled feudalism to the ground are now turned against the bourgeoisie itself.

But not only has the bourgeoisie forged the weapons

---

he would turn to fishing. At 8:00, he would have lunch and read the newspapers (though what news there might be in this world is hard to fathom). At 9:00, he would meet with horticulturists, and at 10:00 he would go to mass. At 10:30, he would meet with a pheasant breeder; later he would tend exotic plants, herd sheep, and attend a concert. Each man would cultivate what he wanted to eat and learn about what he wanted to know—as long, that is, as he could find fellows who shared this particular passion. As for unpleasant tasks, they would become less so because they would now be done in more comfortable settings, in warmed barns and spotless factories. Truly undesirable jobs, like sweeping out the stables or cleaning the latrines, would be done by hordes of young

adolescents, who, Fourier argued, actually liked mucking about in filth. This was by no means an Eden in which humankind lived without knowing what it was like to sweat; rather it was a workers' paradise in which comforts and rewards made working enjoyable. Importantly, however, this would be a system of production and distribution run without merchants. Fourier intentionally excluded middlemen like himself from his plan for paradise. He believed that they corrupted civilization and introduced unnaturalness into the division of labor.

Fourier's writings finally gained popularity in the 1830s, appealing to radicals devoted to a variety of causes. In France, women were particularly active in spreading his ideas. Long-that bring death to itself; it has also called into existence the men who are to wield those weapons—the modern working class—the proletarians. . . . These labourers, who must sell themselves piece-meal, are a commodity, like every other article of commerce, and are consequently exposed to all the vicissitudes of competition, to all the fluctuations of the market. . . .

But with the development of industry the proletariat not only increases in number; it becomes concentrated in greater masses, its strength grows, and it feels that strength more. . . . Thereupon the workers begin to form combinations (Trades Unions) against the bourgeois; they club together in order to keep up the rate of wages; they found permanent associations in order to make provision beforehand for these occasional revolts. Here and there the contest breaks out into riots.

Now and then the workers are victorious, but only for a time. The real fruit of their battles lies, not in the immediate result, but in the ever-expanding union of the workers. . . .

. . . What the bourgeoisie, therefore, produces, above all, is its own grave-diggers. Its fall and the victory of the proletariat are equally inevitable.

. . . The first step in the revolution by the working class is to raise the proletariat to the position of ruling class, to win the battle of democracy.

These measures . . . will be pretty generally applicable.

1. Abolition of property in land. . . .
2. A heavy progressive or graduated income tax.
3. Abolition of all right of inheritance. . . .
6. Centralisation of the means of communication and transport in the hands of the State. . . .

If the proletariat during its contest with the bourgeoisie is compelled, by the force of circumstances, to organise itself as a class, if, by means of a revolution, it makes itself the ruling class, and, as such, sweeps away by force the old conditions of production, then it will, along with these conditions, have swept away the conditions for the existence of class antagonisms and of classes generally. . . .

Let the ruling classes tremble at a Communistic revolution. The proletarians have nothing to lose but their chains. They have a world to win.

→ *Why do Marx and Engels think that capitalism is so dynamic and productive?*

→ *If capitalism is as productive as they say, why are they against it? Are they in fact against it?*

→ *Is the new social system supposed to arise automatically, or is human action required to bring it about?*

SOURCE: Karl Marx and Friedrich Engels, *The Communist Manifesto*, in *The Marx-Engels Reader*, 2nd ed., edited by Robert C. Tucker (New York: W. W. Norton & Co., 1978), pp. 473–83, 490–91, 500.

ing for social and moral reforms that would address problems such as prostitution, poverty, illegitimacy, and the exploitation of workers (including women and children), some women saw in Fourierism a higher form of Christian communalism. By reshaping the phalanx to accommodate monogamous families and Christian values, women helped to make his work more respectable to middle-class readers. In Russia, Fourier's works fired the imaginations of the young writer Fyodor Dostoevsky (1821–1881). Dostoevsky and fourteen others in the radical circle to which he belonged were sentenced to death for their views, though their executions were called off at the last minute. In 1835–1836, both the young Italian nationalist Giuseppe Mazzini and the Spanish republican Joaquin Abreu

published important articles on Fourier's thought. Karl Marx (1818–1883) read Fourier with great care, and there are many remnants of utopian thought in Marx's work. In *The German Ideology* Marx describes life in an ideal communist society; in a post-revolutionary world, he predicts "nobody has one exclusive sphere of activity but each can become accomplished in any branch he wishes, society regulates the general production and thus makes it possible for me to do one thing today and another tomorrow, to hunt in the morning, fish in the afternoon, rear cattle in the evening, [and] criticize after dinner."

MARXISM Marx, indeed, proved to be the most consequential of Restoration-era radicals. University educated and philosophically radical, Marx took up a career in journalism. Required to cover legislative debates over property rights and taxation, he was forced to deal with economics. His understanding of *capitalism*, a term he was instrumental in popularizing, was greatly enhanced by his collaboration after 1845 with Friedrich Engels (1820–1895). Like Marx, Engels was a German-born radical, who in 1844, after spending two years observing conditions in the factories owned by his wealthy father in Manchester, England, published a hair-raising indictment of industrial wage-labor entitled *The Condition of the Working Class in England.*

Together, Marx and Engels developed a materialist theory of history. What mattered in history, they argued, were the production of goods and the ways in which society was organized into classes of producers and exploiters. History consisted of successive forms of exploitative production and rebellions against them. Capitalist exploitation of the wage worker was only the latest, and worst, version of endemic class conflict. In industrialized societies, capitalists owned the means of production (the factories and machinery) and exploited the wage workers. Marx and Engels were confident that the clashes between industrial wage workers—or "proletarians"—and capitalists would end in a colossal transformation of human society and would usher in a brave new world of true liberty, equality, and fraternity.

Marx and Engels issued a comprehensive critique of post-1815 Europe. They identified a whole class of the exploited—the working class. They believed that more and more people would fall into this class as industrialization proceeded and that the masses would not share in the rising prosperity that capitalists monopolized. They predicted that there would be overproduction and underconsumption, which would lead to lower profits for capitalists and consequently to lower wages or unemployment for workers and that this would ultimately lead to a proletarian revolution. This revolution would result in a "dictatorship of the proletariat" and the end of private property. With the destruction of capitalism, exploitation would cease, and the state would wither away.

In 1848 revolutionary fervor resulted in uprisings in France, Austria, Russia, Italy, Hungary, and the German states. In February of that year, after hearing that revolution had broken out in France, Marx and Engels published *The Communist Manifesto,* calling on the workers of all nations to unite in overthrowing capitalism. They would be sorely disappointed, not to mention exiled, by the reactionary crackdowns that followed the 1848 revolutions. After 1850, Marx and Engels took up permanent residence in England, where they tried to organize an international workers' movement. In the doldrums of midcentury, they turned to science and organization, but they never abandoned the romantic dream of total social reconfiguration, nor would their many admirers and heirs. The failure of the 1848 revolutions did not doom prophecy itself or diminish commitment to alternative social landscapes.

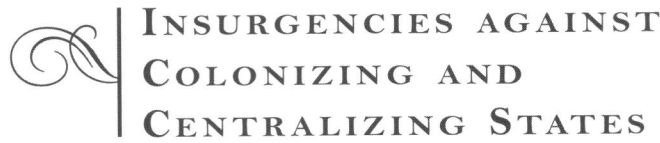

INSURGENCIES AGAINST COLONIZING AND CENTRALIZING STATES

> → *How were the alternative movements in the Americas and India similar and different?*

Outside Europe, for Native Americans and Britain's colonial subjects it was not industrial capitalism and centralizing states that were seen as the greatest threat to traditional worlds, but the colonizing process itself. While European radicals looked back to revolutionary legacies in imagining a transformed society, Native American insurgents and rebels in British India drew upon their traditional cultural and political resources to imagine new, local alternatives to alien impositions. Like the peoples of China, Africa, and the Middle East, the indigenous groups in the Americas and India met challenges to their political and cultural worlds with rebellion, prophecy, and charismatic leadership. Everywhere the insurgents spoke in the languages of the past, but the new worlds they envisioned nonetheless bore unmistakable marks of the present as well.

ALTERNATIVE TO THE EXPANDING UNITED STATES: NATIVE AMERICAN PROPHETS

Like other native peoples threatened by an expansionist imperial power, the Indians of North America's Ohio Valley dreamed of a world in which intrusive colonizers disappeared. Taking such dreams as prophecies, many Indians flocked in the spring of 1805 to hear the revelations of a Shawnee Indian named Tenskwatawa (1768–1834). Facing a dark present and a darker future, they enthusiastically embraced the Shawnee Prophet's visions, which, like that of the Paiute prophet Wovoka nearly a century later, foretold how invaders would vanish if Indians returned to their customary ways and traditional rites.

Tenskwatawa's visions—and the anticolonial uprising they inspired—drew on a long tradition of visionary leaders. From the first encounters with Europeans, Indian seers had periodically emerged to encourage native peoples to purge their worlds of colonial influences and to revitalize indigenous traditions. Often these prophets had aroused their adherents not only to engage in cleansing ceremonies but also to cooperate in violent, anticolonial uprisings. In 1680, for example, previously divided Pueblo villagers in New Mexico had united behind the prophet Popé to chase Spanish missionaries,

Primary Source

TENSKWATAWA'S VISION

In the first decade of the nineteenth century, the Shawnee Indian leader Tenskwatawa recalled an earlier, happier time for the Indian peoples of the Great Lakes and Ohio Valley before the coming of the Europeans. In this oration, Tenskwatawa recounts how Indians were contaminated and corrupted by contact with the "white men's goods" and urges them to spurn the ways of white Americans and return to the pure ways of a precolonial past. Nonetheless, Tenskwatawa's message itself reflects certain colonial influences.

Our Creator put us on this wide, rich land, and told us we were free to go where the game was, where the soil was good for planting. That was our state of true happiness. We did not have to beg for anything. Our Creator had taught us how to find and make everything we needed, from trees and plants and animals and stone. We lived in bark, and we wore only the skins of animals. . . .

Thus were we created. Thus we lived for a long time, proud and happy. We had never eaten pig meat, nor tasted the poison called whiskey, nor worn wool from sheep, nor struck fire or dug earth with steel, nor cooked in iron, nor hunted and fought with loud guns, nor ever had diseases which soured our blood or rotted our organs. We were pure, so we were strong and happy. . . .

For many years we traded furs to the English or the French, for wool blankets and guns and iron things, for steel awls and needles and axes, for mirrors, for pretty things made of beads and silver. And for liquor. This was foolish, but we did not know it. We shut our ears to the Great Good Spirit. We did not want to hear that we were being foolish.

But now those things of the white men have corrupted us, and made us weak and needful. Our men forgot how to hunt without noisy guns. Our women don't want to make fire without steel, or cook without iron, or sew without metal awls and needles, or fish without steel hooks. Some look in those mirrors all the time, and no longer teach their daughters to make leather or render bear oil. We learned to need the white men's goods, and so now a People who never had to beg for anything must beg for everything! . . .

And that is why Our Creator purified me and sent me down to you, to make you what you were before! As you sit before me I will tell you the many rules Our Creator gave me for you.

No red man must ever drink liquor, or he will go and have the hot lead poured in his mouth! . . .

Do not eat any food that is raised or cooked by a white person. It is not good for us. Eat not their bread made of wheat, for Our Creator gave us corn for our bread. . . .

The Great Good Spirit wants our men to hunt and kill game as in the ancient days, with the silent arrow and the lance and the snare, and no longer with guns.

If we hunt in the old ways, we will not have to depend upon white men, for new guns and powder and lead, or go to them to have broken guns repaired. Remember it is the wish of the Great Good Spirit that we have no more commerce with white men! . . .

Our Creator told me that all red men who refuse to obey these laws are bad people, or witches, and must be put to death. . . .

The Great Good Spirit will appoint a place to be our holy town, and at that place I will call all red men to come and share this shining power. For the People in all tribes are corrupt and miserable! In that holy town we will pray every morning and every night for the earth to be fruitful, and the game and fish to be plentiful again.

→ *What does Tenskwatawa's message share with other "alternative visions" discussed in this chapter?*

→ *How is it different?*

SOURCE: http:courses.smsu.edu/ftm922f/Documents/Prophet&Tecumseh. htm. Words of Tenskwatawa, in *Messages and Letters of William Henry Harrison*, edited by Logan Esarey (Indianapolis: Indiana Historical Commission, 1922).

Tenskwatawa. A portrait of Tenskwatawa, the "Shawnee Prophet," whose visions stirred thousands of Indians in the Ohio Valley and Great Lakes to renounce dependence on colonial imports and resist the expansion of the United States. Tenskwatawa's message raised hopes for a restoration of an older, better world. But his ability to rally Indians behind his vision faded after an American army destroyed his village.

soldiers, and settlers out of that colony. In the wake of their military victory, Popé's followers destroyed all things European: wheat fields and fruit orchards were torched, livestock was slaughtered, and Catholic churches were ransacked. For a dozen years, the Indians of New Mexico reclaimed control over their lands, but divisions within native ranks soon returned and prepared the way for Spanish reconquest in 1692.

Seventy years later and half a landmass away, the preachings of the Delaware shaman Neolin encouraged Indians of the Ohio Valley and Great Lakes to take up arms against the British, leading to the capture of several British military posts. Although the British were able to put down the uprising, imperial officials learned a lesson from this expensive conflict. They assumed a less arrogant posture toward Ohio Valley and Great Lakes Indians, and to preserve peace, they issued a proclamation that forbade colonists from trespassing on lands

west of the Appalachian Mountains. The British, however, proved incapable of restraining the flow of settlers across the mountains, and the problem became much worse for the Indians once the American Revolution ended. With the Ohio Valley transferred to the new United States, American settlers crossed the Appalachians and flooded into Kentucky and Tennessee. Still, despite this considerable migration, much of the territory between the Appalachians and the Mississippi, which Americans referred to as the "western country," remained an Indian country. North and south of Kentucky and Tennessee, Indian warriors more than held their own against American forces. As in previous anticolonial campaigns, the visions of various prophets bolstered the confidence and unity of Indian warriors, who in 1790 and again in 1791 joined together to rout invading American armies. But the confederation of Indian warriors was defeated in a third encounter, in 1794, and their leaders were forced to surrender lands in what is now the state of Ohio to the United States.

The Shawnee, who had lost most of their holdings, were among the most bitter—and bitterly divided—of the Indian peoples living in the Ohio Valley. Some Shawnee leaders concluded that their people's survival now required that they cooperate with American officials and Christian missionaries. This strategy, they realized, entailed wrenching changes in Shawnee culture. European reformers, after all, insisted that Indian men give up hunting and take up farming, an occupation that the Shawnee and their neighbors had always considered "women's work." What is more, the Shawnee were pushed to abandon communal traditions in favor of private property rights. Of course, missionaries prodded Indians to quit their "heathen" beliefs and practices and become faithful, "civilized" Christians. For many Shawnee, these demands went too far, and worse, they promised no immediate relief from the dispossession and impoverishment that now marked their daily lives. Young men especially grew angry and frustrated.

Among the demoralized was a Shawnee Indian named Tenskwatawa, whose story of overcoming personal failures through religious visions and embracing a strict moral code has uncanny parallels with that of Hong Xiuquan, the Taiping leader. In his first thirty years, Tenskwatawa could claim few accomplishments. He had failed as a hunter and as a medicine man, had blinded himself in one eye, and had earned a reputation as an obnoxious braggart. All this changed in the spring of 1805, however, after he fell into a trance and experienced a vision, which he vividly recounted to one and all. In this dream, Tenskwatawa encountered a heaven where the virtuous enjoyed the traditional Shawnee way of life and a hell where evildoers were punished. Additional revelations followed, and Tenskwatawa soon stitched these together into a new social gospel that urged disciples to abstain from alcohol and return to traditional customs.

Like other prophets, Tenskwatawa exhorted Indians to reduce their dependence on European trade goods and to sever their connections to Christian missionaries. To these ends,

→ *How were the alternative movements in the Americas and India similar and different?*

MAP 16-4   INDIAN REVOLTS IN THE UNITED STATES AND MEXICO

The new world order of expanding centralized nation states and industrial markets strongly affected the lives of indigenous peoples in North America. According to this map, where did the alternative visions and resistance to centralizing states and global market forces occur? How similar were these movements? To what extent, if any, did they manage to create or preserve an alternative to the new emerging order?

Tenskwatawa urged his audiences to replace imported cloth and metal tools with animal skins and implements fashioned from wood, stone, and bone. So, too, livestock was to be banished, as Indian men again gathered meat by hunting wild animals, with bows and arrows instead of guns and powder. If Indians obeyed these dictates, Tenskwatawa promised, the deer, which "were half a tree's length under the ground," would come back in abundant numbers to the earth's surface. Likewise, Indians killed in conflict with colonial intruders would be resurrected, while evil Americans would depart from the country west of the Appalachians.

Like the Qing's response to Hong's visions, American officials initially dismissed Tenskwatawa as deluded but harmless; their concerns grew, however, as the Shawnee Prophet

gathered more and more adherents during the summer and fall of 1805. These converts came not only from among the Shawnee, but also from Delaware, Ottawa, Wyandot, Kickapoo, and Seneca villages. The spread of Tenskwatawa's message raised anew the specter of a pan-Indian confederacy. Hoping to undermine the Shawnee Prophet's claims to supernatural power, territorial governor William Henry Harrison (1773–1841) challenged Tenskwatawa to make the sun stand still. But Tenskwatawa one-upped Harrison. Having learned of an impending eclipse from white astronomers, Tenskwatawa assembled his followers on June 16, 1806. On schedule, and as if on command, the sky darkened. Claiming credit for the eclipse, Tenskwatawa's standing soared, as did the ranks of his disciples. Now aware of the growing threat,

American officials tried to bribe Tenskwatawa, hoping that cash payments might dim his vision and quiet his voice. Failing that, they wondered if one of the prophet's Indian adversaries might be encouraged to assassinate him.

In fact, Tenskwatawa had made plenty of enemies among his fellow Indians. His visions, after all, consigned drinkers to hell where they would be forced to swallow molten metal and singled out those who cooperated with colonial authorities for punishment in this world and the next. Indeed, Tenskwatawa condemned as witches those Indians who rejected his preaching and stuck instead to the teachings of Christian missionaries and American authorities. To be sure, Tenskwatawa's damnation of Christianized Indians was somewhat paradoxical, for missionary doctrines obviously influenced his vision of a burning hell for sinners and his crusade against alcohol.

Although Tenskwatawa's accusations alienated some Indians, his prophecies gave heart to many more, particularly once his brother, Tecumseh (1768–1813), helped circulate the message of Indian renaissance among Indian villages from the Great Lakes to the Gulf Coast. On his journeys after

Tecumseh. A portrait, supposedly of Tecumseh, by an unknown artist. To spread the vision of his brother, Tenskwatawa, Tecumseh traveled from the Great Lakes to the Gulf of Mexico, urging Indians to join together to combat the expansion of the United States. Tecumseh succeeded in building a significant pan-Indian confederation, which unraveled following his death at the Battle of Thames in 1813 and the end of warfare between the United States and Britain the following year.

1805, Tecumseh did more than spread his brother's visions; he also wed them to the idea of a resurgent and enlarged Indian confederation. Moving around the Great Lakes and traveling across the southern half of the western country as well, Tecumseh preached the need for Indian unity. Always, he insisted that Indians resist any American attempts to get them to sell more land. Thousands of followers renounced their ties to colonial ways and prepared to combat the expansion of the United States.

By 1810, Tecumseh had emerged, at least in the eyes of American officials, as even more dangerous than his brother. Impressed by Tecumseh's charismatic organizational talents, William Harrison warned that this new "Indian menace" was forming "an Empire that would rival in glory" that of the Aztecs and the Incas. In 1811, while Tecumseh was traveling among southern tribes, Harrison attacked Tenskwatawa's village, Prophet's Town, on the Tippecanoe River in what is now the state of Indiana. The resulting battle was evenly fought, but the Indians eventually gave ground and American forces burned Prophet's Town. That defeat discredited Tenskwatawa, who had promised that his followers would be protected from destruction at American hands. Spurned by his former disciples, including even his brother, Tenskwatawa fled to Canada.

Tecumseh soldiered on. Although he mistrusted the British, Tecumseh recognized that only a British victory over the Americans in the War of 1812 could check further American expansion. Commissioned as a brigadier general in the British army, Tecumseh recruited many Indians to the British cause, though his real aim remained the building of a pan-Indian union. But, on October 5, 1813, with the war's outcome in doubt and the pan-Indian confederacy still fragile, Tecumseh was killed at the Battle of the Thames.

The discrediting of Tenskwatawa and the death of Tecumseh damaged the cause of Indian unity; British betrayal dealt it a fatal blow. Following the end of the war in 1814, the British withdrew their support and left the Indians south of the Great Lakes to fend for themselves against land-hungry American settlers and the armies of the United States. By 1815, American citizens outnumbered Indians in the western country by a seven-to-one margin, and this gap dramatically widened in the next few years. Recognizing the hopelessness of military resistance, Indians south of the Great Lakes resigned themselves to relocation. During the 1820s, most of the peoples north of the Ohio River were removed to lands west of the Mississippi River. During the 1830s, the southern tribes were cleared out, completing what amounted to an ethnic cleansing of Indian peoples from the region between the Appalachians and the Mississippi. In the midst of these final removals, Tenskwatawa died, though his dream of an alternative to American expansion had faded for his people years earlier. Through the rest of the nineteenth century, however, other Indian prophets emerged, and their visions continued to inspire their followers with the hope of an alternative to life under the colonial rule of the United States. But like Wovoka and the Ghost Dancers in 1890, these dreams failed to halt the expansion of the United States and the contraction of Indian lands.

ALTERNATIVE TO THE CENTRAL STATE: THE CASTE WAR OF THE YUCATAN

As in North America, the Spanish establishment of an expansionist nation-state in Mexico sparked widespread revolts by indigenous peoples. The most protracted—and militarily the most successful of all rebellions in the modern history of the New World—was the Mayan revolt in the Yucatan. The revolt started in 1847, and its flames were not finally doused until the full occupation of the Yucatan by Mexican national troops in 1901.

The strength and endurance of the Mayan revolt stemmed in large measure from the unusual features of the Spanish conquest in southern Mesoamerica. Because this area was not a repository of precious metals or fertile lands, Spain and its rivals focused on central and northern Mexico and the Caribbean islands. As a result, the Mayan Indians escaped forced recruitment for silver mines or sugar plantations. This does not mean that global processes sidestepped the Indians. Production of dyes and foodstuffs for shipment to other regions drew the Yucatan into long-distance trading networks. Nonetheless, cultivation and commerce were much less disruptive to indigenous lives in the Yucatan than elsewhere in the New World.

The strength and endurance of the Mayan revolt stemmed in large measure from the unusual features of the Spanish conquest in southern Mesoamerica.

The dismantling of the Spanish empire in the first decades of the nineteenth century gave way to almost a century of political turmoil in Latin America. In the Yucatan, civil strife gave the region autonomy by default, allowing Mayan ways to survive without much upheaval. Their villages remained the chief political domain, ruled by elders; their land was held collectively, the property of families and not individuals. Corn, a mere staple to white consumers, continued to enjoy sacred status in Mayan culture.

Local developments, however, encroached on the Mayan world. First, regional elites—mainly white, but often with the support of mestizo populations—bickered for supremacy so long as the central authority of Mexico City remained weak. Weaponry flowed freely through the peninsula, and some belligerents even appealed for Mayan support. At the same time, regional and international trade spurred the spread of sugar estates. This threatened traditional corn cultivation. Over the decades, plantations encroached on Mayan properties. Planters used several devices to lure independent Mayans to work, especially in the harvest. The most important, debt peonage, gave small cash advances to Indian families, which obligated fathers and sons to work for meager wages to pay off these debts. In addition, Mexico's costly wars, culminating in the showdown with the United States in 1846, drove tax collectors and army recruiters into villages in search of revenues and soldiers.

The combination of spiritual, material, and physical threats was explosive. When a small band of Mayans, fed up with rising taxes and ebbing autonomy, used firearms to drive back white interlopers in 1847, they sparked a war that took a half-century to complete. The rebels were primarily free Mayans who had not yet been absorbed into the sugar economy. They wanted to dismantle old definitions of Indians as a caste—a status that deprived Indians of rights to defend their sovereignty on equal legal footing with whites and that also subjected the Indians to special taxes. Thus, local Mayan leaders, like Jacinto Pat and Cecilio Chi, upheld a republican model in the name of formal equality of all political subjects and devotion to a spiritual order that did not distinguish between Christians and non-Christians. "If the Indians revolt," one Mayan rebel explained, "it is because the whites gave them reason; because the whites say they do not believe in Jesus Christ, because they have burned the cornfield."

Horrified, the local white elites reacted to the uprising with vicious repression, and dubbed the ensuing conflict a "Caste War." In their view, the bloody conflict was a struggle between forward-looking liberals and backward-looking Indians. At first, whites and mestizos were no match for determined Mayans. Mayan forces took town after town. They especially targeted the emblems of their subservience. With relish they demolished the whipping posts that had previously been used for public humiliation and punishment of Indians. By July 1848, Indian armies controlled three-quarters of the peninsula and were poised to take the Yucatan's largest city, Mérida. Fear seized the embattled whites, who appealed for U.S. and British help, offering the peninsula for foreign annexation in return for military rescue from the Mayans.

In the end, fortune, not political savvy, saved the Yucatan's whites. The farmers, who had picked up arms to defend their world, went back to being farmers. The planting season called. When rain clouds appeared, related the son of the Mayan leader Crecencio Poot, the Indians saw "that the time has come for us to make our planting, for if we do not we shall have no Grace of God to fill the bellies of our children." But by putting down their weapons and returning to their fields, Mayan farmers became vulnerable to military reconquest by Mexican armies. Furthermore, they were unaware of international changes: settlement of the war with the United States in 1848 enabled Mexico City to rescue local elites. With the help of a $15 million payment from Washington for giving up its northern provinces, Mexico could spend freely to build up its southern armies. The Mexican government soon fielded an army of 17,000 reinforced soldiers and waged a scorched earth campaign to drive back the depleted Mayan forces.

By 1849, the confrontation had entered a new phase in which Mexican troops engaged in mass repression of the Mayans. Mexican armies set Indian fields and villages ablaze. Slaughtering Indians became a blood sport of barbaric proportion. Between 30 and 40 percent of the Mayan population perished in the war and its repressive aftermath. The white governor even sold captured Indians into slavery to Cuban sugar planters. The white formulation of the caste nature of the war eventually became a self-fulfilling prophecy. Entire Mayan cities pulled up stakes and withdrew to more isolated districts protected by fortified villages. War between armies degenerated into guerrilla warfare between an occupying Mexican army and mobile bands of Mayan squadrons, inflicting a gruesome toll on the invaders. As years passed, the war ground to a stalemate, especially once the U.S. indemnity ran out and Mexican soldiers began deserting in droves.

Warfare prompted a spiritual transformation that reinforced a purely Mayan identity against the invaders' "national" project. Thus, a struggle that began by demanding legal equality and relative cultural autonomy became a crusade for spiritual salvation and the complete cultural separation of the Mayan Indians. A particularly influential group under José María Barrera retreated to a hamlet called Chan Santa Cruz (Little Holy Cross). There, at the site where he found a cross carved into a mahogany tree, Barrera had a vision of a divine encounter. A swath of Yucatan villages refashioned themselves as moral communities orbiting around Chan Santa Cruz. Leaders created a polity, with soldiers, priests, and tax collectors pledging their fealty to the Speaking Cross. As with the followers of Hong in China's Taiping Rebellion, Indian rebels forged a syncretic religion, blending Christian rituals, faiths, and icons with Mayan legends and beliefs. At the center was a stone temple, Balam Na (House of God), 100 feet long and 60 feet wide. Through pious pilgrimages to Balam Na and the secular justice of Indian judges, the Mayans soon governed their autonomous domain in the Yucatan, almost completely cut off from the rest of Mexico.

This alternative to Latin American state formation, however, faced formidable hurdles. Disease ravaged the people of the Speaking Cross. Once counting 40,000 inhabitants, the villages dwindled to 10,000 by 1900. Also a new crop, henequen, used to bind bales for North American farms and to stuff the seats of new automobiles, began to spread across the Yucatan. In place of the mixed agrarian societies of the peninsula, it became a dessicated region producing a single crop, driving the people to seek refuge further into the interior. As profits from henequen production rose, white landowners began turning the Yucatan into a giant plantation. But Mayan villagers refused to give up their autonomy and rejected labor recruiters. Finally, the Mexican oligarchy, having resolved its internal disputes, threw its weight behind the strong-arm ruler, General Porfirio Díaz (ruled 1876–1911). The general sent one of his veteran commanders, Ignacio Bravo, to do what no other Mexican could accomplish: vanquish Chan Santa Cruz and drive Mayans into the henequen cash economy. When General Bravo finally entered the town, he found the once-imposing temple Balam Na covered in vegetation. Nature was reclaiming the territories of the Speaking Cross. Hunger and arms finally drove Mayans to work on white Mexican plantations; the alternative vision was vanquished.

THE REBELLION OF 1857 IN INDIA

Like Native Americans, the peoples of nineteenth-century India could point to a long history of opposition to colonial domination. Armed revolts had been endemic since the onset of rule by the English East India Company. Nonetheless, the uprising of 1857 was unprecedented in its scale, and it posed a greater threat than had any previous rebellion. Marx, with the hope for revolution dashed in Europe, cast his eyes on the revolt in British India, eagerly following the events and commenting on them in daily columns for the New York *Daily Tribune*. Though led primarily by the old nobility and petty landlords, it was a popular insurrection with strong support from the lower orders of Indian society. The rebels appealed to bonds of local and communal solidarity, invoked religious sentiments, and reimagined traditional hierarchies in egalitarian terms. They did this to pose alternatives to British rule and the deepening involvement of India in a network of capitalist relationships.

When the revolt broke out in 1857, the East India Company's rule in India was a century old. During that time, the company had become an increasingly autocratic power, its reach extending across the whole region. Mughal rule still existed in name, but the emperor lived in Delhi, all but forgotten and without any effective power. For a while, the existence of several princely states with which the British had entered into alliances prevented the British from exercising complete control over all of India. These princely domains enjoyed a measure of fiscal and judicial authority within the British Empire. They also contained landed aristocrats who enjoyed the right to shares in the produce and maintained their own militias. By the 1840s, however, the company had come to see the princely powers and landed aristocracies as anachronisms. Lord Dalhousie, upon his appointment as the governor-general in 1848, immediately set about annexing what had been independent princely domains and stripping native aris-

→ *How were the alternative movements in the Americas and India similar and different?*

tocrats of their privileges. Swallowing one princely state after another, the British removed their erstwhile allies. The government also decided to collect taxes directly from peasants, displacing the landed nobles as intermediaries. In disarming the landed nobility, the British threw the retainers and militia of the notables into unemployment. Moreover, the company's new systems of land settlement not only dispossessed the old gentry; they also eroded peasant rights and enhanced the power of moneylenders. Meanwhile, the company transferred judicial authority to an administration insulated from the indigenous social hierarchy.

The most prized object for annexation was the kingdom of Awadh in northern India (see Map 16-5). Founded in 1722 by an Iranian adventurer, it was one of the first successor states to have extracted a measure of independence from the Mughal ruler in Delhi. With access to the fertile resources of the Gangetic plain, its opulent court in Lucknow was known to be one place where Mughal splendor still survived. In 1765, the company imposed a treaty on Awadh under which the ruler paid an annual tribute for the British troops stationed in his territory to "protect" his kingdom from internal and external enemies. The British constantly ratcheted up their demands for tribute and abused their position to monopolize the lucrative trade in commodities. But the more successful they were in exploiting Awadh, the more they longed to annex it

MAP 16-5   INDIAN REBELLION OF 1857

The Indian Rebellion of 1857 broke out first among the Indian soldiers of the British army. Other groups soon joined the struggle. Can you speculate on why the rebellion was centered in the interior of the subcontinent rather than along the coasts? Referring to the map of the British East Indian Company's possessions in India in Chapter 15 (Map 15-4, p. 672), especially the map that shows the company's holdings in 1805, locate the primary areas of rebellion in relationship to the heart of the company's territory and those territories that enjoyed some degree of autonomy at that time. Do you think that the company's expansion into once autonomous princely states was a factor in the rebellion?

completely. Thus, Dalhousie declared in 1851 that Awadh was "a cherry which will drop into our mouths some day."

In 1856, citing misgovernment and deterioration in law and order, the East India Company violated its treaty obligations and sent its troops to Lucknow to assume control of the province. Nawab Wajid Ali Shah, the poet-king of Awadh, whom the British saw as effete and debauched, refused to sign the treaty of abdication. Instead, he came dressed in his mourning robes to meet with the British official charged to take over the province. After pleading unsuccessfully for his legal rights under the treaty, he handed over his turban to the official and then left for Calcutta to argue his case before Dalhousie. There was widespread distress at the treatment meted out to the nawab. Dirges were recited, and religious men rushed to Lucknow to denounce the annexation.

The annexation of princely domains and the abolition of feudal privileges formed part of the developing philosophy and practices of European imperialism. To the policy of annexation, Dalhousie added an ambitious program of building railroads, telegraph lines, and a postal network to unify the disjointed territory into a single "network of iron sinew" controlled by the British. Dalhousie saw these infrastructures as key to developing India into a productive colony, a supplier of raw materials for British industry and a market for its manufactures.

A year after Dalhousie's departure in 1856, India went up in flames. The spark that ignited the simmering discontent into a furious rebellion was the famous "greased cartridge" controversy. At the end of 1856, the British army, which consisted of many Hindu and Muslim recruits (sepoys), commanded by British officers, introduced the new Enfield rifle to replace the old-style musket. To load the rifle, the soldiers were required to bite the cartridge open. Though manufacturing instructions stated that linseed oil and beeswax were to be used to grease the cartridge, a rumor circulated that cow and pig fat had been used. To bite into cartridges greased with cow and pig fat meant the violation of the religious

taboos of Hindu and Muslim sepoys. They became convinced that there was a plot afoot to defile them and to compel their conversion to Christianity. A wave of rebellion spread among the 270,000 Indian soldiers, who greatly outnumbered the 40,000 British soldiers employed to rule over 200 million Indians.

The mutiny broke out on May 10, 1857, at the military barracks in Meerut. The previous day the native soldiers had witnessed eighty-five of their comrades being manacled and shackled in irons and marched off to the prison for refusing to load their rifles. The next day, all three regiments at Meerut mutinied, killed their British officers, and marched thirty miles south to Delhi, where they were welcomed by their comrades in regiments stationed there. Together, they "restored" the aging Bahadur Shah as the Mughal emperor, which lent legitimacy to the uprising. The revolt then spread rapidly to other garrisons and soon turned from a limited military mutiny into a widespread civil rebellion that involved peasants, artisans, day laborers, and religious leaders. While the insurgents did not eliminate the power of the East India Company, which managed to retain the loyalty of princes and landed aristocrats in some places, they did throw the company into a crisis. The mutineers in Delhi issued a proclamation in August, declaring that, because the British were bent upon destroying the religion of both Hindus and Muslims, it was the duty of the wealthy and the privileged to support the rebellion. To promote Hindu-Muslim unity, rebel leaders asked Muslims to refrain from killing cows in deference to Hindu sentiments.

Triumphant in Delhi, the rebellion spread to other parts of India. In Awadh, proclamations in Hindi, Urdu, and Persian called on Hindus and Muslims to rise. On May 30, troops at the garrison in Lucknow, Awadh's capital, did just that. Seizing control of the town, rebels crowned a ten-year-old putative son of the deposed king as the new ruler, but his mother, the Begum (queen mother) Hazrat Mahal, emerged as the real force. The queen mother, however, accepted the

The Indian Sepoys. Pictured here are Indian soldiers, or sepoys, who were armed, drilled, and commanded by British officers. The sepoys were drawn from indigenous groups that the British considered to be "martial races." This illustration shows the Sikhs, designated as one such "race."

→ *How were the alternative movements in the Americas and India similar and different?*

The Indian Rebellion of 1857. The 1857 rebellion was sparked by the mutiny of Indian sepoys in the British army. The rebellion left a deep impression on the British. This British engraving depicts a cavalry attack by the rebel soldiers.

condition laid down by the rebel army that the king be subordinate to the Mughal emperor in Delhi. The rebels then called upon all classes to unite in expelling the British and succeeded in compelling the colonial forces to retreat from Lucknow.

Though the dispossessed aristocracy and petty landholders led the rebellion, leaders also appeared from below. Bakht Khan, who had been a junior noncommissioned officer in the British army, became the commander-in-chief of the rebel forces in Delhi, replacing one of the Mughal emperor's sons who had been discredited in the eyes of the ordinary rebels. Devi Singh, a wealthy peasant, set himself up as a peasant king. Dressed in yellow, the insignia of royalty in the Hindu idiom, he constituted a government of his own, modeling it on the British administration. While his imitation of company rule showed his respect for the British bureaucracy, he defied British authority by leading an armed peasantry against the hated local moneylenders. The call to popular forces also marked the rebel career of Maulavi Ahmadullah Shah, a Muslim theologian. He stood at the head of the rebel forces in Lucknow, leading an army composed primarily of ordinary soldiers and people from the lower orders. Claiming to be an "Incarnation of the Deity," and thus inspired by the divine will, he emerged as a prophetic leader of the common people. He voiced his undying enmity to the British in religious terms, calling upon Hindus and Muslims to destroy British rule and warning his followers against betrayal by landed magnates.

The presence of popular leadership points to the role of lower classes as historical actors. Though feudal chieftains often brought them into the rebellion, they made the insurrection their own. The organizing principle of their insurgency was the common experience of oppression. Thus, they destroyed anything that represented the authority of the company: prisons, factories, police posts, railway stations, European bungalows, and law courts. Equally significant, the peasantry attacked indigenous moneylenders and local magnates who had purchased land at government auctions and were seen as benefiting from company rule.

Vigorous and militant as the popular rebellion was, it was limited in its territorial and ideological horizons. To begin with, the uprisings were local in scale and vision. Peasant rebels attacked the closest seats of administration and sought to settle scores with their most immediate and visible oppressors. They did not carry their action beyond the village or collection of villages. Their loyalties remained intensely local, based on village attachments and religious, caste, and clan ties. Nor did popular militants seek to undo traditional hierarchies of caste and religion.

Convinced that the rebellion was the result of the plotting of a few, the British carried out their counterinsurgency with brutal vengeance. Villages were torched, and rebels were tied to cannons and blown to bits to teach Indians a lesson in power. Delhi fell in September 1857, and Lucknow was captured in March 1858. The British exiled the unfortunate Mughal emperor, Bahadur Shah, to Burma, where he died. The emperor's sons were murdered in cold blood. Most of the other rebel leaders were either killed in battle or captured and executed. When, at the same time, the British also moved to annex the state of Jhansi in northern India, its female leader, Lakshmi Bai, mounted a counterattack. After a two-week siege, Jhansi fell to the British; but Lakshmi Bai escaped on horseback, only to die in the fighting for control of the fortress of Gwalior. Her intelligence, bravery, and youth (she was only twenty-eight at the time of the rebellion) made her the subject of many popular Indian ballads in the decades to follow.

By July 1858, the vicious pacification campaign had achieved its object. Yet, in August, the British Parliament abolished company rule and the company itself and transferred

Primary Source

THE INDIAN REBELLION OF 1857

The Indian leaders of the Rebellion of 1857 issued numerous proclamations. The Azamgarb Proclamation, excerpted below, is representative of these petitions. It was issued in August 1857 by the Emperor Bahadur Shah on behalf of the mutineers who had seized the garrison town of Azamgarb, sixty miles north of Benares. Like other proclamations, it attacks the British for subverting Indian traditions and calls on its followers to restore the pre-British order, in this case the Mughal Empire.

It is well known to all, that in this age the people of Hindoostan, both Hindoos and Mohammedans, are being ruined under the tyranny and oppression of the infidel and treacherous English. It is therefore the bounden duty of all the wealthy people of India, especially of those who have any sort of connection with any of the Mohammedan royal families, and are considered the pastors and masters of their people, to stake their lives and property for the well being of the public. . . .

Several of the Hindoo and Mussalman chiefs, who have long since quitted their homes for the preservation of their religion, and have been trying their best to root out the English in India, have presented themselves to me, and taken part in the reigning Indian crusade. . . . Parties anxious to participate in the common cause, but having no means to provide for themselves, shall receive their daily subsistence from me; and be it known to all, that the ancient works, both of the Hindoos and the Mohammedans, the writings of the miracle-workers and the calculations of the astrologers, pundits, and rammals, all agree in asserting that the English will no longer have any footing in India or elsewhere. . . .

Section I—Regarding Zemindars. It is evident, that the British Government in making zemindary settlements have imposed exorbitant *Jumas,* and have disgraced and ruined several zemindars. . . . Such extortions will have no manner of existence in the Badshahi Government; but on the contrary, the *Jumas* will be light, the dignity and honour of the zemindars safe, and every zemindar will have absolute rule in his own zemindary. . . .

Section II—Regarding Merchants. It is plain that the infidel and treacherous British Government have monopolized the trade of all the fine and valuable merchandise, such as indigo, cloth, and other articles of shipping, leaving only the trade of trifles to the people, and even in this they are not without their share of the profits, which they secure by means of customs and stamp fees, &c. in money suits, so that the people have merely a trade in name. . . . When the Badshahi Government is established, all these aforesaid fraudulent practices shall be dispensed with, and the trade of every article, without exception, both by land and water, shall be open to the native merchants of India. . . .

Section IV—Regarding Artisans. It is evident that the Europeans, by the introduction of English articles into India, have thrown the weavers, the cotton dressers, the carpenters, the blacksmiths, and the shoemakers, &c., out of employ, and have engrossed their occupations, so that every description of native artisan has been reduced to beggary. But under the Badshahi Government the native artisan will exclusively be employed in the services of the kings, the rajahs, and the rich. . . .

Section V—Regarding Pundits, Fakirs and other learned persons. The pundits and fakirs being the guardians of the Hindoo and Mohammedan religions respectively, and the Europeans being the enemies of both the religions, and as at present a war is raging against the English on account of religion, the pundits and fakirs are bound to present themselves to me, and take their share in the holy war.

→ *What are the main grievances against the English in India?*

→ *What was the role of religion in the 1857 rebellion?*

SOURCE: "Proclamation of Emperor Bahadur Shah," in *India in 1857: The Revolt against Foreign Rule,* edited by Ainslie T. Embree (Delhi: Chanakya Publications, 1987), pp. 3–6.

CONCLUSION

The nineteenth century was a time of turmoil and transformation. As powerful forces reconfigured the world as a place for capitalism, colonialism, and nation-states, so too did prophets, charismatic leaders, radicals, peasant rebels, and anticolonial insurgents arise to offer alternatives. Responding to specific circumstances and drawing upon particular traditions, the struggles of these men and women for a different political and cultural future opened up spaces for the ideas and activities of subordinate classes. Conventional historical accounts either neglect these struggles or fail to view them as a whole. These individuals were not just romantic, last-ditch resisters, as some have argued. Even after defeat, their messages remained alive within their communities. Nor were their actions isolated and aberrant events, for when viewed on a global scale, they bring to light a world that looks very different from the one that became dominant. To see the Wahhabi movement in the Arabian Peninsula together with the Shawnee Prophet in North America, utopians and radicals in Europe with the peasant insurgents in British India, and the Taiping rebels with the Mayans in the Yucatan is to glimpse a world of marginalized regions and groups, a world that the more powerful endeavored to suppress but could not erase.

In this world, the prophets and rebel leaders usually cultivated power and prestige locally; the emergence of an alternative polity in one region did not impinge on communities and political organizations in others. As much as these radicals, prophets, charismatic leaders, and anticolonial insurgents had in common, they envisioned widely different kinds of futures rooted in their particular contexts. Even Marx, who called the workers of the world to unite, was acutely aware that the call for a proletarian revolution applied only to the industrialized countries of Europe. Others had even more localized horizons. A world fashioned by movements for alternatives meant a world with multiple centers and divergent historical trajectories.

What gave force to a different mapping of the world was that common people were at the center of these alternative visions, and their voices, however muted, gained a place on the historical stage. Egalitarianism in different shapes and forms defined efforts to reconstitute alternative worlds. In Islamic regions, the egalitarianism practiced by revitalization movements was evident in their mobilization of all Muslims, not just the elites. Even charismatic military leaders in Africa, such as Shaka, for all their use of raw power, utilized the framework of community to build new polities. The Taiping Rebellion distinguished itself by seeking to establish an equal society of men and women in service of the Heavenly Kingdom. Operating under very different conditions, the European radicals imagined a society free from the hierarchical order of both aristocratic privileges and bourgeois property. Anticolonial rebels and insurgents depended upon local solidarities and advanced alternative imagined moral communities. In so

The Rani of Jhansi. The Rani of Jhansi, who was deposed by the British, rose up during the revolt of 1857. In subsequent nationalist iconography, as this twentieth-century watercolor illustrates, she is remembered as a heroic rebel, all the more so because of her gender.

responsibility for the governing of India to the crown. In November, Queen Victoria issued a proclamation guaranteeing religious toleration, promising improvements, and allowing Indians to serve in the government. She promised to honor the treaties and agreements with princes and chiefs and to refrain from interfering in religious matters. The insurgents rose up, not as a nation, but as a multitude of communities acting independently and often without coordination, and their determination to find a new order shocked the British and threw them into a panic. Having crushed the uprising, the British resumed the work of transforming India into a modern colonial state and economy. But the desire for radical alternatives and traditions of popular agency, though vanquished, did not vanish.

doing, these movements compelled ruling elites to adjust the way they governed. This challenge is discussed in the next chapter.

STUDY QUESTIONS

WWNORTON.COM/STUDYSPACE

1. Define the new global order emerging in the nineteenth century in light of the revolutions in the Atlantic world studied in Chapter 15. How did it challenge other modes of social organization?
2. Explain the goals and ideas surrounding Islamic revitalization movements such as Wahhabism in the Arabian Peninsula and dan Fodio's movement in West Africa. How were these regions affected by the newly emerging world order? What kind of alternative to the newly emerging world order did Islamic revitalization propose?
3. Describe Hong Xiuquan's vision for China during the Taiping Rebellion. How did he propose reordering Chinese society?
4. Describe the various alternative visions to the status quo that European radicals proposed in the nineteenth century. What traditions and beliefs did they reflect?
5. Compare and contrast the Shawnee rebellion in the United States and the Caste War in Mexico. How did they reflect tensions between Native Americans and European Americans?
6. Analyze to what extent the Indian Rebellion of 1857 encouraged a new identity among its followers. What goals did participants in the rebellion share?
7. Explore the role of women in shaping and advocating alternative visions around the world in the nineteenth century. Which alternative vision movements proposed new roles for women in society?
8. List major similarities among all the alternative visions explored in this chapter to the newly emerging world order. Why did they all ultimately fail to achieve their objectives? Did they have any important legacies?

FURTHER READINGS

Anderson, David M., *Revealing Prophets: Prophets in Eastern African History* (1995). Good discussion of the prophets in eastern Africa.

Beecher, Jonathan, *The Utopian Vision of Charles Fourier* (1983). A fine biography of this important thinker.

Boyd, Jean. *The Caliph's Sister: Nana Asma'u, 1793–1865, Teacher, Poet, and Islamic Leader* (1988). A study of the most powerful female Muslim leader in the Fulani religious revolt.

Clancy-Smith, Julia, *Rebel and Saint: Muslim Notables, Populist Protest, Colonial Encounter (Algeria and Tunisia, 1800–1904)* (1994). Examines Islamic protest movements against western encroachments in North Africa.

Chronology

	1800				
THE AMERICAS		*Preaching of Tenskwatawa (North America), 1805–1811*	*American Indians moved west of Mississippi River, 1820s–1830s*	*Yucatan Caste War (Mexico), 1847*	
SOUTH ASIA					
EAST ASIA					
EUROPE		*Congress of Vienna, 1814–1815* / *Peterloo Massacre (England), 1819* / *Greek war for independence, 1821–1829* / *Revolutions in France, Belgium, Rhineland, Italy, 1830* / *Mazzini founds "Young Italy" movement, 1832*	*Revolutions in Poland and Italy, 1831* / *Chartism in England, 1839–1848*		
AFRICA AND THE MIDDLE EAST	*Dan Fodio leads revolt in West Africa, 1804–1809* / *Wahhabis wage militant religious campaign, 1813–1815* / *Shaka creates Zulu empire, 1818–1828*				

Clogg, Richard, *A Concise History of Greece* (1997). A good introduction to the history of Greece in its European context.

Dowd, Gregory E., *A Spirited Resistance: The North American Indian Struggle for Unity, 1745–1815* (1992). Emphasizes the importance of prophets like Tenskwatawa in the building of pan-Indian confederations in the era between the Seven Years' War and the War of 1812.

Guha, Ranajit, *Elementary Aspects of Peasant Insurgency in Colonial India* (1983). Not specifically on the Indian Rebellion of 1857 but includes it in its pioneering "subalternist" interpretation of South Asian history.

Hamilton, Carolyn (ed.), *The Mfecane Aftermath: Reconstructive Debates in Southern African History* (1995). Debates on Shaka's *Mfecane* movement and its impact on southern Africa.

Hiskett, Mervyn, *The Sword of Truth: The Life and Times of the Shehu Usman dan Fodio* (1994). A recent and authoritative study of the Fulani revolt in northern Nigeria.

Johnson, Douglas H., *Nuer Prophets: A History of Prophecy from the Upper Nile in the Nineteenth and Twentieth Centuries* (1994). Deals with African prophetic and charismatic movements in eastern Africa.

Michael, Franz, and Chung-li Chang, *The Taiping Rebellion: History and Documents*, 3 vols. (1966–1971). The basic source for the history of the Taiping.

Mukherjee, Rudrangshu, *Awadh in Revolt 1857–58* (1984). A careful case study of the Indian Rebellion.

Omer-Cooper, J. D., *The Zulu Aftermath: A Nineteenth-Century Revolution in Bantu Africa* (1966). A good place to start in studying Shaka's *Mfecane* movement, which greatly rearranged the political and ethnic makeup of southern Africa.

Peires, J. B. (ed.), *Before and After Shaka* (1981). Discusses new elements in the debate over Shaka's *Mfecane* movement.

Pilbeam, Pamela. *French Socialists Before Marx: Workers, Women and the Social Question in France* (2001). Describes the development of a variety of socialist ideas in early nineteenth-century France.

Reed, Nelson, *The Caste War of Yucatan* (1964). A classic narrative of the Caste War of the Yucatan.

Restall, Matthew, *The Maya World* (1997). Describes in economic and social terms the origins of the Yucatan upheaval in southern Mexico.

Rugeley, Terry, *Yucatán's Peasantry and the Origins of the Caste War* (1996). Explains the combination of economic and cultural pressures that drove the Mayans in the Yucatan to revolt in the Caste War.

Spence, Jonathan, *God's Chinese Son: The Taiping Heavenly Kingdom of Hong Xiuquan* (1996). A fascinating portrayal of the Taiping through the prism of its founder.

Wagner, Rudolf, *Reenacting the Heavenly Vision: The Role of Religion in the Taiping Rebellion* (1982). A brief but insightful analysis of the religious elements in the Taiping's doctrines.

White, Richard, *The Middle Ground: Indians, Empires, and Republics in the Great Lakes Region, 1650–1815* (1991). A pathbreaking exploration of intercultural relations in North America that offers a provocative interpretation of the visions of Tenskwatawa and the efforts of Tecumseh to resist the expansion of the United States.

1900

■ *Ghost Dance movement (North America), 1889–1890*

■ *British take over Lucknow in India, 1856*
■ *Indian Rebellion, 1857–1858*

■ *Taiping Rebellion (China), 1851–1864*

utions in France, Austria, Prussia, Italy, 1848

Chapter

17

NATIONS AND EMPIRES, 1850–1914

In 1895, the Cuban patriot José Martí launched a rebellion against the last Spanish holdings in the Americas. The anti-Spanish struggle continued until 1898, when Spain withdrew its last forces from Cuba and Puerto Rico. Martí hoped to bring freedom to a new Cuban nation and republican equality to all Cubans regardless of race or class. But if Martí's efforts helped secure freedom from the declining Spanish empire, he could not prevent Cuba's military occupation and political domination by the world's newest imperial power, the United States.

Martí's hopes and frustrations found parallels around the world. After 1850, nation-state building and imperial expansion changed the map of the world. This remapping stemmed, in the first place, from the great political and economic upheavals of the late eighteenth and early nineteenth centuries that had battered the old regimes. American revolutionaries, Haitian slaves, and Napoleon's armies had embraced the concept of popular sovereignty (of power residing in the people themselves) and challenged the legitimacy of kings and conservative elites. Simultaneously, new forms of production were bringing to the fore persons of wealth and merit to rival older aristocratic groups whose high status rested on the ownership of land. Close on the heels of these transformations came the upsurge of charismatic leaders, radicals, peasant rebels, and anticolonial insurgents who put forth alternative visions of power and community. These developments prepared the way for the rise, in the second half of the nineteenth century, of new rulers and elites who embraced the nation-state organization at home and fostered territorial empires overseas.

NATION BUILDING AND EXPANSION

> → *What was the relationship between nationalism and imperialism?*

During the second half of the nineteenth century, the ideology of nation-state building spread across the globe. Already a century earlier, Enlightenment thinkers had emphasized the importance of nations, defined as peoples who shared a common past, territory, culture, and traditions; Adam Smith had described the wealth of each nation as equivalent to the combined output of all its producers, and not the same as the sum in the king's treasury. The German thinker J. G. Herder had emphasized the need for nations to retain their own independent cultures and to cultivate their own unique institutions. To many in the nineteenth century, touched by revolutionary rhetoric and desiring liberty and prosperity for their regions, it seemed natural that once absolutist rulers had been toppled, the nation should become one and the same with the state, the body of institutions that governed each territory. The world's population should be divided up into nation-states, freed from external overlords, and each in its own way able to pursue national well-being. This seemed

such a natural process that little thought was given to how nation-states arose—they were simply supposed to well up from the people's longing for liberty and togetherness.

In practice, however, in many instances, the state created the nation rather than the other way around. It did so by compelling diverse communities and regions to accept a unified network of laws, administration, time zones, national markets, and a single regional dialect as the "national" language. To overcome strong regional identities, the state broadened public education in this national language and imposed universal military service to build a national army. In this fashion, the state nurtured the notion that there was a one-to-one correspondence between a "people" and a nation-state. Those who spoke different languages became national minorities, often compelled to assimilate or face discrimination.

The new nation-state took on its clearest expression in the Americas, Japan, and parts of Europe. In the latter, two new polities—Germany and Italy—forced nations into existence through strategic conquests. Central European, Balkan, Polish, and Ukrainian intellectuals also began to envision consolidated national communities as autonomous regions within the multiethnic Habsburg, Ottoman, and Russian empires, or even as breakaway nation-states. In response, imperial rulers tried to promote identities that crossed ethnic and cultural borders—with varying degrees of success. In the Russian Empire, the ruling Romanovs tried to forge their religiously and linguistically diverse realm into a nation-state through heavy-handed, if nonsystematic, Russification. This could only be a stopgap measure, however, for as Russia expanded farther into central Asia, its land empire became even more diverse and more difficult to characterize as a single nation-state.

Whereas highly developed nation-states could readily acquire overseas territories without upsetting their national agendas at home—indeed, the popularity of overseas acqui-

Focus Questions NATIONS AND EMPIRES

→ *What was the relationship between nationalism and imperialism?*

→ *How did nation-building patterns compare among the United States, Canada, and Brazil?*

→ *How did European nation-states forge national identities?*

→ *How did new materials and technologies transform industry and the global economy?*

→ *What were the motives for imperialism and the practices of colonial rulers?*

→ *How did expansionism affect Japan, Russia, and China?*

 WWNORTON.COM/STUDYSPACE

sitions helped nation-states domestically—the expansion of landed empires greatly complicated the challenge of creating a single "people" out of many ethnic and national groups. In those countries that could successfully forge a nation-state, state-led nation building, territorial expansion, and imperialism went hand in hand. The rulers believed that national strength was measured not only by the unity and loyalty of the people but also by the conquest of new territories and the possession of the most modern forms of production. Thus did a large number of great powers—Germany, France, the United States, Russia, and Japan—seek to rival Britain by expanding and modernizing their internal industries (thereby kicking off a second industrial revolution in the nineteenth century's final decades) and by seizing adjacent or far-off colonies. By the century's end, conquest of new territory had become so important to the prestige of these states that they engaged in a veritable "scramble" to colonize peoples from Africa to the Amazon, from California to Korea.

Never before had there been such a rapid reshuffling of peoples and resources as in these decades. As transportation costs declined, workers left their homes in search of better opportunities across the world. In large numbers, Japanese moved to Brazil, Indians to South Africa and the Caribbean, Chinese to California, and Italians to New York and Buenos Aires. At the same time, American capitalists began to invest outside the United States, and British investors reaped handsome profits by financing the construction of railroads in China and India. Raw materials from Africa and Southeast Asia flowed to the manufacturing nations of Europe and the Americas.

Imperial umbrellas facilitated this movement of labor, capital, and commodities. As mapmakers filled in the "empty spaces," labeling territory that had not been measured, mapped, or owned by Europeans, scholars and officials carried out studies of tribes and races. New schools taught the colonized the languages, religions, scientific practices, and cultural traditions of the colonizers, while publications and artifacts from the "mother country" circulated more widely, at least among the indigenous elites. Yet, empire builders were not willing to extend to nonwhite inhabitants of their colonies the same rights as they conferred on inhabitants of their own nations; here, nation and empire were incompatible. Not only were the colonized prohibited from participating in government—as were the working classes and women in Europe itself—colonial subjects were not considered members of the nation at all.

We begin the story of nation and empire with the Americas, where the quest for national self-rule had enjoyed its first successes and generated the desire for territorial aggrandizement. From the New World, we turn to the Old World, where

nationalism and nation building emerged as a more immediate response to the popular upheavals of the 1840s. In contrast to the American model, in which frontier territories were incorporated into the nation, often by force, the expansion of western European nations into Africa and Asia involved the erection of colonial systems. Nation building and imperial expansion, however, were not confined to Europe and the Americas; to the East, a similar rise in nationalist fervor and scramble for possessions took place. Thus, a series of events drew three other states—Russia, China, and Japan—into rivalry and warfare over colonial domains in Asia.

> *Not only were the colonized prohibited from participating in government, colonial subjects were not considered members of the nation at all.*

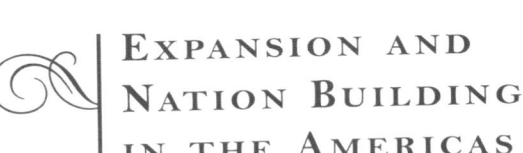

EXPANSION AND NATION BUILDING IN THE AMERICAS

→ *How did nation-building patterns compare among the United States, Canada, and Brazil?*

Freed from European control in the late eighteenth and early nineteenth centuries, the elites of the Americas set about creating political communities of their own. By the 1850s, they shared a desire to establish—at least nominally—inclusive political systems and expand territorial domains. This required that they refine the tools of government to induct the people into public life with national laws and court systems, standardized money, and national political parties. It also meant devising ways to occupy and settle hinterlands that previously belonged to the hemisphere's aboriginal populations. Once themselves European colonies, New World territories emerged as vibrant nation-states, based on growing material prosperity and industrialization.

While the decades after 1850 saw general expansion and development of nation-states throughout the world, the Americas witnessed the most thoroughgoing and complete assimilation of new possessions into old domains. Instead of treating peripheral areas merely as colonial outposts, American nation-state builders turned their conquered territories into new provinces. With the help of rifles, railroads, schools, and land surveys, frontiers became lucrative and strategic possessions, central to the very fabric of North and South American societies. For the indigenous peoples of these newly colonized territories, however, national expansion meant the loss of land on a vast scale.

Not all conquests, colonizations, and national consolidations in the Americas were the same, however. The United States, Canada, and Brazil, to cite three examples, experienced differing processes of nation building, territorial expansion, and economic development. Each of these three successfully incorporated frontier regions into national polities and economies, though they employed varying techniques for subjugating Indian peoples and administering new holdings. While Brazil and Canada did not rival the economic power of the United States, by century's end they, too, had become durable nation-states.

THE UNITED STATES

Military might, fortuitous diplomacy, and the power of numbers enabled the United States to lay claim to a trans land-mass territory. By the middle of the nineteenth century, hundreds of thousands of American citizens occupied the Pacific slope (see Map 17-1). The territorial expansion and economic development of the United States appears even more impressive given the deep cleavages of race and geography that beset the republic. From the American Revolution, the new nation had emerged as a barely united confederation of states. Indian resistance and Spanish and British rivalry hemmed in "Americans" (as they came to call themselves). At the same time, these disunited states also threatened to fracture into separate northern and southern polities, as questions of slavery versus free labor intruded into national politics.

President Thomas Jefferson (1743–1826) had boldly predicted the independence of America's family farmers for a thousand years soon after he had procured the vast French Louisiana Territory from Napoleon (for a mere $15 million) in 1803. But expansion required the violent dispossession of Indian peoples and the invasion of Mexican territory. Not long after Jefferson concluded the Louisiana Purchase, ardent expansionists began to fix their attention on lands even farther to the west of this area. Rallying to the rhetoric of Manifest Destiny, which maintained that it was God's will for the United States to "overspread" North America, the most aggressive expansionists sought control of British lands in the northwest (in the Oregon country) and of the lands south and west of the Louisiana Territory (in the northern provinces of Mexico). A peaceful compromise was reached with Britain, but the United States went to war against Mexico in 1846, which resulted in the former's acquisition of almost half of Mexico's land. In a treaty with Mexico, the United States guaranteed the Mexican nationals who remained within the territory it had acquired equal rights with American citizens. In practice, however, Mexicans who became American citizens often lost their landholdings and suffered other forms of discrimination.

Even before the United States reached its compromise with Britain and gained by war the territory from Mexico, its citizens were making their presence felt in the Oregon country and in the provinces of northern Mexico. Beginning in the 1820s, Americans started to move into Texas. Initially, the migration was at the invitation of the Mexican government, which was desperate to attract colonists to Texas in hopes that their settlements would secure Mexico's northern territories from hostile Indians. Surging westward, Americans soon far outnumbered Mexicans in Texas. This demographic imbalance alarmed Mexican officials, but they were unable to stop the migration or to keep Texans from declaring and winning independence in 1836. Although American migrations into other parts of northern Mexico were as yet on a much smaller scale, American merchants were capturing an increasingly large share of the commerce of New Mexico and California. In the early 1840s, California saw a rise in American immigration. But, prior to the Mexican War, the vast majority of overland migrants from the United States chose the Oregon country as their destination.

The distance migrants would travel to Pacific shores was unprecedented in the history of the United States. Prior to the 1840s, the westward moves of Americans generally involved relocations into contiguous districts. In the 1840s, however, Americans in the Mississippi Valley skipped over the adjacent grass lands of the Great Plains, which they deemed unfit for family farms of the kind that Jefferson idealized. Instead, thousands of migrants made the daring trek across fifteen hundred miles of inhospitable plains, mountains, and deserts to take up lands near the west coast of North America.

The scale of this migration and the primary destination of migrants shifted decisively following the discovery of gold in California in 1848. As news of the find spread, hopeful prospectors raced to stake their claims. In the next few years, well over one hundred thousand Americans took to the overland trails and to the seas in quest of California's riches.

The California gold rush, however, was not only a great American migration; it also inspired a massive global immigration as tens of thousands of individuals from Latin America, Australia, Asia, and Europe poured into California. What had just a few years earlier been a relatively remote and sparsely populated corner of northwestern Mexico had almost overnight been transformed into the most cosmopolitan place on earth. In the 1850s, California was truly where worlds came together.

And yet California and the territories that the United States took from Mexico also precipitated the coming apart of the American nation. Whether these newly acquired lands

> *Mexicans who became American citizens often lost their landholdings and suffered other forms of discrimination.*

Canadian Westward Expansion
- Settled before 1825
- Settled between 1825 and 1871
- Settled between 1871 and 1891
- Settled between 1891 and 1911
- Boundary of original Confederation, 1867
- Rupert's Land territories added to provinces, 1912

United States Westward Expansion
- United States, 1783
- Louisiana Purchase, 1803
- West Florida annexation, 1810, 1813
- East Florida ceded by Spain, 1819
- Acquired from Britain, 1818, 1842
- Texas annexation, 1845
- Oregon Country, 1846
- Ceded by Mexico, 1848
- Gadsden Purchase, 1853
- Acquired from Russia, 1867
- Annexed, 1894
- Railroad

MAP 17-1   U.S. AND CANADIAN WESTWARD EXPANSION, 1803–1912

The Americans and the Canadians expanded westward rapidly in the second half of the nineteenth century, aided greatly by railways. What role did railroad construction play in this process? How did territorial expansion strengthen Canadian and American nationalism? According to the map, what other states and peoples were involved in this process of territorial expansion?

Primary Source

"MANIFEST DESTINY"

In July 1845, the New York newspaper editor John L. O'Sullivan (1813–1895) coined the phrase Manifest Destiny *to explain how the "design of Providence" supported the territorial expansion of the United States. In this excerpt, O'Sullivan outlines the reasons why the United States was justified in annexing Texas and why it must soon do the same in supplanting Mexican rule in California. Cries of* Manifest Destiny *often accompanied American conquest and colonization of new territories.*

. . . Texas has been absorbed into the Union in the inevitable fulfilment of the general law which is rolling our population westward; the connexion of which with that ratio of growth in population which is destined within a hundred years to swell our numbers to the enormous population of *two hundred and fifty millions* (if not more), is too evident to leave us in doubt of the manifest design of Providence in regard to the occupation of this continent. It was disintegrated from Mexico in the natural course of events, by a process perfectly legitimate on its own part, blameless on ours; and in which all the censures due to wrong, perfidy and folly, rest on Mexico alone. And possessed as it was by a population which was in truth but a colonial detachment from our own, and which was still bound by myriad ties of the very heart strings to its old relations, domestic and political, their incorporation into the Union was not only inevitable, but the most natural, right and proper thing in the world—and it is only astonishing that there should be any among ourselves to say it nay. . . .

California will, probably, next fall away from the loose adhesion which, in such a country as Mexico, holds a remote province in a slight equivocal kind of dependence on the metropolis. Imbecile and distracted, Mexico never can exert any real governmental authority over such a country. The impotence of the one and the distance of the other, must make the relation one of virtual independence; unless, by stunting the province of all natural growth, and

forbidding that immigration which can alone develop its capabilities and fulfil the purposes of its creation, tyranny may retain a military dominion which is no government in the legitimate sense of the term. In the case of California this is now impossible. The Anglo-Saxon foot is already on its borders. Already the advance guard of the irresistible army of Anglo-Saxon emigration has begun to pour down upon it, armed with the plough and the rifle, and marking its trail with schools and colleges, courts and representative halls, mills and meeting-houses. A population will soon be in actual occupation of California, over which it will be idle for Mexico to dream of dominion. They will necessarily become independent. All this without agency of our government, without responsibility of our people—in the natural flow of events, the spontaneous working of principles, and the adaptation of the tendencies and wants of the human race to the elemental circumstances in the midst of which they find themselves placed.

→ *What is the main reason O'Sullivan gives for why the United States must expand westward?*
→ *Why does O'Sullivan think that the people of Texas and California will want to join the United States?*

SOURCE: John L. O'Sullivan, "Manifest Destiny," *Democratic Review* (July 1845), pp. 7–10, in Clark C. Spence, ed., *The American West: A Source Book* (New York: Thomas Y. Crowell Company, 1966), pp. 108–9.

would be open to slavery or restricted to free labor sparked an increasingly fierce debate during the late 1840s and through the 1850s. Following the 1860 election of Abraham Lincoln, who had pledged to halt the expansion of slavery, the United States divided between North and South and plunged into a gruesome Civil War (1861–65).

The bloody conflict led to the abolition of slavery, and the struggle to extend voting and citizenship rights to the freed

African American Gains and Losses. In the immediate aftermath of the American Civil War, "Radical Republicans" asserted political control by passing laws and constitutional amendments ending slavery, guaranteeing equal rights, and enfranchising freedmen. One result was the election of African Americans (*above*) to the United States Congress. During the 1870s, however, white leaders retreated from the commitment to black rights, allowing ex-Confederates to re-assert control over southern politics. (*Right*) Hooded members of the Ku Klux Klan terrorized African Americans in the post-Civil War South. The violence of the Klan reversed many of the legal and political gains made by freedmen and helped restore planters to power in the South.

slaves qualified the Civil War as a second American Revolution. It gave the nation a new generation of heroes and martyrs such as the assassinated president, Abraham Lincoln. Lincoln had promised a new model of freedom for a nation reborn out of bloodshed. Its cornerstone would be the incorporation of the freed slaves as citizens of the United States. Alas, the experiments in biracial democracy during the Reconstruction period of 1867–1877 were short-lived. In the decades after the Civil War, counterrevolutionary pressure, spearheaded by the terrorism of the Ku Klux Klan, led to the denial of voting rights to African-Americans and the restoration of (white) planter rule in the southern states.

Nonetheless, the war brought enduring changes across the United States. The defeat of the South vanquished the chief proponents of states' rights and established the preeminence of the national government. After the Civil War, Americans learned to speak of their nation in the singular ("the United States is" in contrast to "the United States are"). With an invigorated nationalism came an enlarged national government. Even more dizzying were the social and economic changes that flowed from the Civil War. Within ten years of the Civil War's end, the industrial output of the United States had climbed by 75 percent from its already high wartime levels. Symbolizing and stimulating this growth was the expansion of railroad lines. In 1865, the United States boasted

35,000 miles of track. By 1900, nearly 200,000 miles of track connected the Atlantic to the Pacific and crisscrossed the American territory in between. Increasingly, steam-powered machines supplanted human muscle as the engine of production, bringing dramatic improvements in output. Before the Civil War, it took sixty-one hours of labor to produce an acre of wheat; by 1900, new machinery cut the time to a little over three hours. On farms and in factories, mechanization boosted production, and rapid railroad transportation permitted the shipment of more goods at lower prices across greater distances. Wheat production, with the help of new technologies, jumped 250 percent in the last quarter of the nineteenth century.

Americans also made impressive industrial gains, so much so that the United States joined Britain and Germany atop the list of economic giants. The Americans innovated in nearly all of the areas necessary for industrial success—technical education, inventions, factory routines, marketing, and above all, the mobilization of capital. In the United States (as in Germany), a potent instrument of capital accumulation appeared at this time—the limited-liability joint-stock company. Firms such as Standard Oil and U.S. Steel mobilized capital from shareholders, who left the running of these enterprises to paid managers. Intermediaries, like J. Pierpont Morgan, the New York financial titan who became the world's wealthiest man, loaned money and brokered big deals on the New York Stock Exchange. So great were the fortunes amassed by leading financiers and corporate magnates that by 1890 the richest 1 percent of Americans owned nearly 90 percent of the nation's wealth.

As mechanized production churned out ever more goods, the threat of overproduction became a pressing concern. Farms and factories produced more than Americans needed or could afford to purchase. In the 1890s, the problem of overproduction plunged the American economy into a harsh depression. Millions of urban workers were thrown out of work, while those who kept their jobs suffered sharp cuts in their wages. Radical labor leaders called for the dismantling of the industrial capitalist order, and strikes proliferated. Discontent spread to the countryside as well, where declining prices and unfair railroad freight charges pushed countless farmers toward bankruptcy.

In the decades after the Civil War, Americans had continued their migrations west, but instead of jumping over the Great Plains, many began to settle the grasslands. These migrants, along with tens of thousands of immigrants from Europe, were attracted by generous homestead acts, which promised nearly free acreage to settlers, and by the assurances of the railroad's real estate promoters. (Railroad corporations had been given enormous land grants as a subsidy for building transcontinental lines, and they sold those lands with promises that "rain would follow the plow" and that the release of steam into the air would also permanently moisten the climate of the Great Plains.) The movement of so many settlers onto the plains sparked yet another round of wars with Indians and culminated in 1889 in the opening of Oklahoma, which had been the reserve of Indians who had been removed from the southeastern United States. A year after the Oklahoma land rush, the U.S. Census Bureau pronounced the "American frontier" closed.

During the 1890s, anxieties about the fate of post-frontier American society combined with economic hard times to provoke political challenges to the dominant industrial capitalist order. The spread of the agrarian opposition of "Populists" and "Greenbacks" (political parties advancing the interests of farmers) reinforced the Jeffersonian image of a virtuous agrarian republic going sour. Ex-homesteaders and those for whom there were no good lands left to homestead were becoming disillusioned.

One solution to the problem of overproduction and the threat of class unrest was to increase exports and create new frontiers abroad. Exports of agricultural and industrial commodities had, in fact, already more than tripled in value since the Civil War. Yet, even this increase did not absorb the surplus of goods, leading farmers and industrialists to demand greater access to foreign markets.

By the end of the nineteenth century, the United States had become a major world power. It boasted an expanding economy, an ever more integrated nation after the Civil War, and a constitution that claimed to uphold equality of all members of the American nation. But there was no full agreement on what that equality should entail or how the country would adjust to a new century in which the nation's "destiny" had already been fulfilled.

CANADA

Canadians also built a new nation, enjoyed economic success, and followed an expansionist course. Like the United States, Canada had access to a frontier, a vast western prairie

Agricultural Technology. During the last decades of the nineteenth century, the introduction of new technology, such as the steam harvester, which combined the work of both reaper and thresher, led to dramatic increases in agricultural output in the United States. Thanks to new machinery and the opening of new farmlands on the Great Plains, wheat production more than tripled between 1875 and 1900.

Oklahoma Land Rush. This photograph captures the rush of homesteaders to claim lands on the "Cherokee Strip" on September 16, 1893. The opening of land that had previously been restricted to Indians set off several similar rushes in the Oklahoma Territory.

for growing agricultural exports. These lands also became the homes and farms of increasing numbers of European immigrants. Canada's path to nationhood was, however, different from that of its southern neighbor. While the United States had to fight and win a war to gain independence, Canada's separation from Britain was a peaceful process. From the 1830s to the 1860s, the mother country gradually passed authority to the colony, leaving Canadians to grapple with the task of creating a shared national community.

That task was made more difficult by sharp internal divisions. The French population left behind after the British took the northern colony from France in 1763 wanted to keep their villages, their culture, their religion, and their language intact. They did not feel completely integrated into the new Canadian national entity. Nor were they eager to join the English-speaking Canadian population in expanding into new areas, for such migration threatened to dilute the French-Canadian presence. The English speakers were no more enthusiastic about creating an independent nation. Fear of being absorbed into the American republic reinforced Canadian loyalty to the British crown and made Canadians content with colonial status. Indeed, when Canada finally gained its independence in 1867, it was by an Act of Parliament in London and not by revolution. But even with nationhood granted, Canadians, including some prominent French speakers like George Etienne Cartier and Hector-Louis Langevin, promised to retain their loyalty to the British crown and declared themselves a "dominion" within the British Commonwealth.

Without cultural or linguistic unity and bereft of an imperial overlord, the Canadians also used territorial expansion to fashion an integrated state for a "people." But they did in a different way than had their neighbor to the south. In response to the U.S. purchase of Alaska from Russia in 1867 and the movement of settlers onto the American plains, Canadian leaders realized that they had to incorporate their own western territories, lest these, too, fall into American hands (see Map 17-1). Pioneers seemed unwilling to venture to these prairies of their own accord—it was far, it was cold, and the growing season was so short that farmers had only a hundred days between sowing their crops and harvesting them. As a result, the Canadian state became actively involved in promoting expansion. It lured emigrant farmers from Europe and the United States with subsidized railway rates and the promise of fortunes to be made. It also offered attractive terms to railway companies to connect dispersed agrarian hinterlands with Montreal and Toronto and not with commercial cities in the United States.

Governments also played an important role in handling the inevitable friction with Indians. Frontier warfare threatened to drive away investors and settlers—who always had access to property south of the border. To prevent the kind of bloodletting among settlers and Indians that characterized the westward expansion of the United States, the Canadian government signed treaties with Indians to ensure strict separation between natives and newcomers. To keep settlers off Indian lands, the government created a special police force, the Royal Canadian Mounted Police (the "Mounties"), to patrol the territories.

Canadian expansion was hardly bloodless, however. Many Indians and mixed-blood peoples (métis) resented the treaties. Moreover, the government was often less than honest in its dealings. As in the United States, the government's Indian policy sought to turn Indians into farmers and then to incorporate them into Canadian society. And as in the United States, the Canadian government paid little heed to whether Indians or métis wished to become farmers or join the nation.

The combination of defensive expansionism, the need to accommodate French speakers, and the respect for at least some minimal degree of legality in dealings with Indians meant that the Canadian government emerged with fuller powers to intervene, regulate, and mediate than did the U.S. government. But if the state was relatively strong, the nation was comparatively weak. Expansionism helped Canada remain an autonomous state, but it did not solve the internal question of what it meant to belong to a Canadian nation.

LATIN AMERICA

Latin America also engaged in nation-state building and joined the expansionist fervor. But unlike in the United States and Canada, expansion and the creation of new provinces did not always create homesteader frontiers. In Spanish America, countries were fractured and wracked by civil war, while in Brazil, the country remained united. Yet despite these political differences, much of Latin America shared a common social history: far more than in North America, the richest lands in Latin America

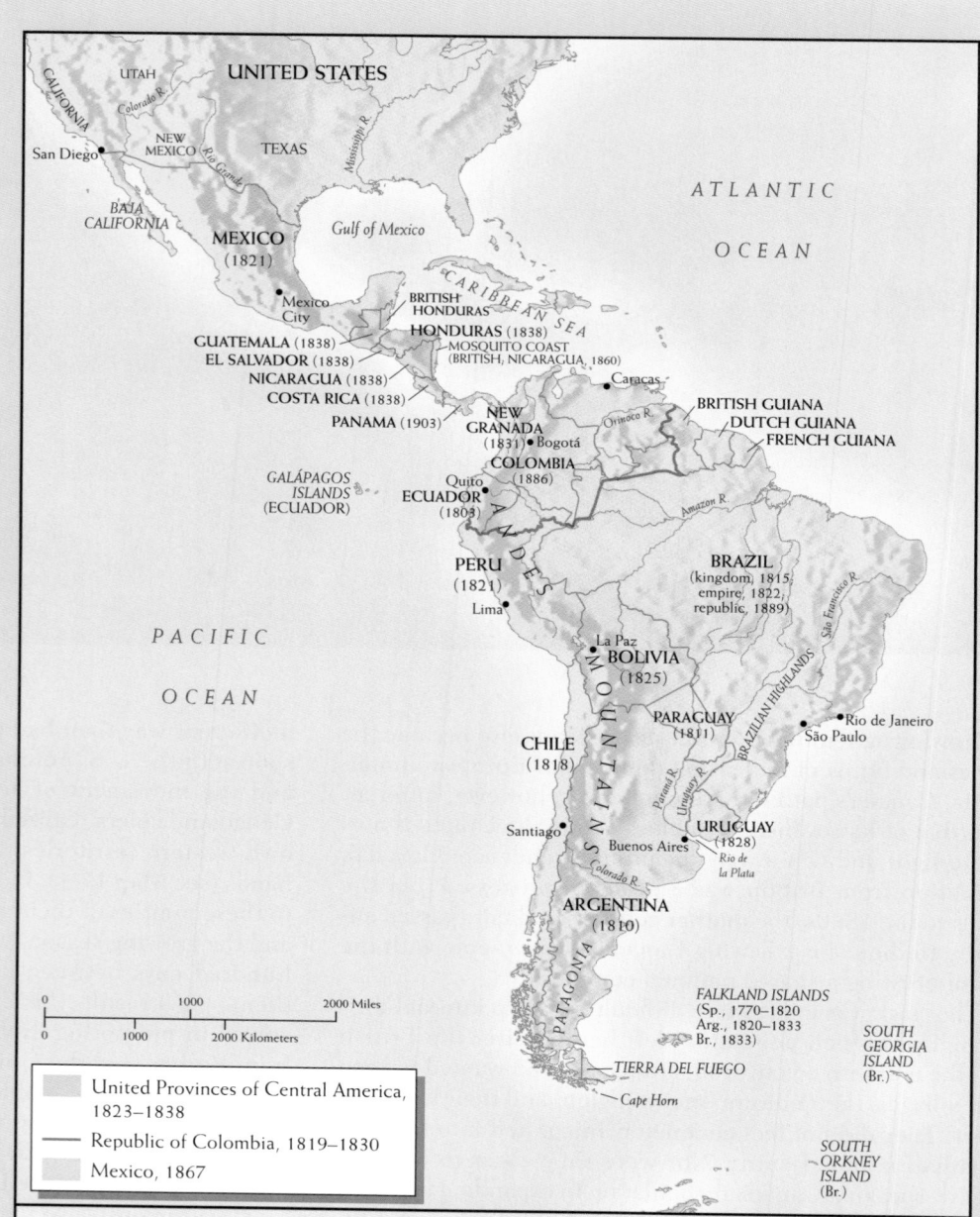

Map 17-2 LATIN AMERICAN NATION BUILDING

Creating strong, unified nation states proved difficult in Latin America. The map highlights this experience in Mexico, the United Provinces of Central America, and the Republic of Columbia. In each case, the territorial and nation-building ambitions of the government failed to some degree. What factors contributed to the fragmentation of these experiments? Why did each effort fragment into smaller territories than originally conceived? What role did foreign imperialism play in this fragmentation?

went not to small farmers, but to large estate holders producing exports such as sugar, coffee, or beef. In addition, privileged elites monopolized political power more effectively than in North America's fledgling democracies. While territorial expansion and high rates of economic growth were Latin American hallmarks, these processes sidelined the poor, Indians, and blacks from participating fully in market or political life.

Indian and peasant uprisings were a major worry in new Latin American republics. Fearing insurrections, elites devised governing systems that protected private property and investments while enabling the state and privileged individuals to curb the political rights of the poor and the propertyless. Likewise, the specter of slave revolts, driven home not just by events in Haiti between 1791 and 1804 but also by the constant daily rumors of rebellions, kept elites in a state of alarm. The Argentine liberal writer Domingo Faustino Sarmiento (1811–1888) captured the sentiment of many of his Latin American peers when he described the challenge of nation-state building as a struggle between elitist "civilization" and popular "barbarism."

Latin American statesmen, then, sought to build nation-states that excluded large swathes of the population from both the "nation" and the "state." Brazil provides a stark example of this process. Through the nineteenth century, rulers in Rio de Janeiro defused political conflict and allowed planters to retain the reins of power. Although the Brazilian government officially abolished the slave trade in 1830, it allowed illegal slave imports to continue for another two decades. Finally, British pressure compelled Brazil to enforce the ban. The end of the slave trade, coupled with slave resistance, began to choke the planters' system by driving up the price of slaves. Sensing that the system of chattel labor was unraveling, slaves began to flee the sugar and coffee plantations en masse. Many in the army no longer supported the system and refused to hunt down runaway slaves. In the 1880s, even while laws upheld bonded labor, country roads in the state of São Paulo were filled with fugitive slaves looking for relatives or access to land. Finally, in 1888, the Brazilian emperor, with the support of some planters, abolished slavery. Brazil was the last American country to put an end to slavery. But, as in the United States, in addition to retaining ex-slaves as gang-workers or sharecroppers, Brazilian elites created a new labor force for their estates by importing workers, especially from Italy, Spain, and Portugal. These European laborers often came as seasonal migrant workers or poor, indentured tenant farmers. Indeed, European and even Japanese migration to Brazil helped planters adjust to the post-slavery era and preserve their holdings. In all, 2 million Europeans moved to Brazil (less than the larger wave of 4 million to Argentina, but enough to be Latin America's second largest destination); in addition some 70,000 Japanese moved to Brazil.

The Brazilian state was deliberately exclusive. The new constitution of 1891, establishing a federal system and proclaiming Brazil a republic, separated those who could be trusted with power from the rest. Previously, the political system had been remarkably open. Elections were contested, if often bloody, affairs. But with the abolition of slavery, the sudden enfranchisement of millions of freedmen threatened to flood the electoral lists with propertyless, potentially uncontrollable voters—many of them black. Politicians responded by slapping severe restrictions on suffrage and rigging rules to reduce political competition.

Like Canada and the United States, the Brazilian state expanded its control over distant areas and incorporated them as provinces of the republic. The largest land-grab occurred in the Amazon river basin, the world's largest drainage watershed—indeed this was also the world's largest tropical forest, built up over millennia around the relatively flat and meandering tributaries that conveyed runoffs from the eastern slopes of the Andean mountains all the way to the Atlantic ocean. It was a massive if delicate habitat of carefully balanced biomass suspended by towering trees with a canopy of leaves and vines that kept the basin ecologically diverse. Here, the Brazilian state allocated giant concessions to capitalists to extract the rubber latex from the region. Rubber, when combined with sulfur, was the raw material for tire manufacturing for European and North American bicycle and automobile industries. As Brazil became the world's exclusive exporter of rubber, its planters, merchants, and workers prospered. Rich merchants became the lenders and financiers, not only to workers, but also to the landowners themselves. The mercantile upper crust of Manaus, the capital of the Amazon region, designed and decorated their city to reflect the bounty of their new fortunes. While the streets were still paved with mud, the town's potentates built a replica of the Paris Opera House, and Manaus was, for a time at least, a regular stopover for European opera singers on the New

Opera House in Manaus. The turn-of-the-century rubber boom brought immense wealth to the Amazon jungle. As in many boom-and-bust cycles in Latin America, the proceeds from rubber flowed to a small elite and soon diminished when the rubber supply outstripped the demand. But the wealth produced was sufficient to prompt the local elite to build temples of modernity in the midst of the jungle. Pictured here is the Opera House built in the rubber capital of Manaus. Typical of other works built by Latin American elites of the period, this one emulated the original in Paris.

Rubber Plantation Workers. (*Left*) Workers on rubber plantations draw latex from rubber plants by using taps that have been sunk into the plant. (*Right*) The workers collect the latex in buckets and then take it to central collection points.

World circuit between Buenos Aires and New York. The rubber workers, called *tappers* because they drew the oozing latex from taps sunk into the rubber plant, also benefited from the boom. Mostly either Indians or mixed-blood people, they remitted their wages to families living elsewhere in the Amazon jungle or on the northeastern coast of Brazil.

But the Brazilian rubber boom soon went bust. Part of the problem was rooted in the ecosystem: such a diversified biomass could not tolerate a regimented, agrarian form of production, which emphasized the cultivation of rubber trees at the expense of other vegetation and made the forest prone to assault by nonhuman predators. Leaf blight and ferocious ants destroyed all experiments at creating more sustainable rubber plantations. In addition, it was expensive to haul the rubber latex out of the jungle to the coast along the slow-moving Amazon River. Brazilian rubber also faced severe competition from other rubber-producing regions of the world once a British scientist named Henry Wickham had smuggled rubber plant seeds out of Brazil in 1876. Following many years of experimenting with the plant at Kew Gardens in London, British patrons transplanted a new blight-resistant hybrid to the British colony of Ceylon (present-day Sri Lanka). Competition increased supplies and reduced prices, bankrupting Brazilian producers. In the Amazon, merchants called in their loans, landowners forfeited their titles, and tappers returned to their subsistence economies. The Manaus Opera House fell into disrepair.

Throughout the Americas, nineteenth-century societies worked to adapt obsolete elite models of politics and to sat-

isfy popular demands for inclusion. While the ideal was to construct nation-states that could reconcile underlying differences among their citizens and pave the way for economic prosperity, in fact, political autonomy did not bring prosperity, or even the right to vote, to all. As each nation-state gave in to the urge to expand its territorial boundaries, many new inhabitants of the nation were left out of the political realm.

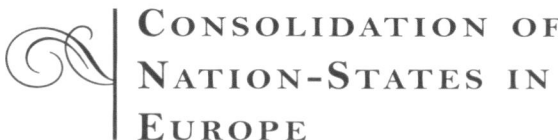

CONSOLIDATION OF NATION-STATES IN EUROPE

> → *How did European nation-states forge national identities?*

The sources of nineteenth-century nationalism are many and can be traced backward into the medieval period. But the most powerful and persistent forms were born in the revolutionary era and came of age in the popular upheavals of the 1830s and 1840s. The political revolutions of 1848, in particular, mark a pivotal moment in European politics. Everywhere, in the spring of 1848, the rebels declared that the state belonged to the people; as in France in 1789, there was a general consensus among those who made the revolution,

Primary Source

WHAT IS A NATION?

The French linguist and historian of religion Ernest Renan (1823–1892) frequently embroiled himself in controversy. The piece below, from an 1882 essay entitled "What Is a Nation?" offers an explicitly republican model of nationhood (note that he is arguing with racial, religious, and dynastic interpretations of nationhood).

. . . The principle of nations is our principle. But what, then, is a nation? . . . Why is Switzerland, with its three languages, its two religions, and three or four races, a nation, when Tuscany, for example, which is so homogeneous, is not? Why is Austria a state and not a nation? In what does the principle of nations differ from that of races? . . .

Ethnographic considerations have . . . played no part in the formation of modern nations. France is Celtic, Iberic, and Germanic. Germany is Germanic, Celtic, and Slav. Italy is the country in which ethnography finds its greatest difficulties. Here Gauls, Etruscans, Pelasgians, and Greeks are crossed in an unintelligible medley. The British Isles, taken as a whole, exhibit a mixture of Celtic and Germanic blood, the proportions of which are particularly difficult to define.

The truth is that no race is pure, and that to base politics on ethnographic analysis is tantamount to basing it on a chimera. . . .

What we have said about race, applies also to language. Language invites union, without, however, compelling it. The United States and England, as also Spanish America and Spain, speak the same language without forming a single nation. Switzerland, on the contrary, whose foundations are solid because they are based on the assent of the various parties, contains three or four languages. There exists in man a something which is above language: and that is his will. The will of Switzerland to be united, in spite of the variety of these forms of speech, is a much more important fact than a similarity of language, often attained by vexatious measures. . . .

Nor can religion provide a satisfactory basis for a modern nationality. . . . Nowadays . . . everyone believes and practices religion in his own way according to his capacities and wishes. State religion has ceased to exist; and a man can be a Frenchman, an Englishman, or a German, and at the same time a Catholic, a Protestant, or a Jew, or practice no form of worship at all.

A nation is a soul, a spiritual principle. Two things, which are really only one, go to make up this soul or spiritual principle. One of these things lies in the past, the other in the present. The one is the possession in common of a rich heritage of memories; and the other is actual agreement, the desire to live together, and the will to continue to make the most of the joint inheritance. . . . The nation, like the individual, is the fruit of a long past spent in toil, sacrifice, and devotion. . . . To share the glories of the past, and a common will in the present; to have done great deeds together, and to desire to do more— . . . these are things of greater value than identity of custom-houses and frontiers in accordance with strategic notions. These are things which are understood, in spite of differences in race and language.

. . . The existence of a nation is . . . a daily plebiscite. . . . A province means to us its inhabitants; and if anyone has a right to be consulted in the matter, it is the inhabitant. It is never to the true interest of a nation to annex or keep a country against its will. The people's wish is after all the only justifiable criterion, to which we must always come back.

→ *According to Renan, what are the key ingredients needed to create a nation-state?*

→ *Do you agree that these elements are more important than a common race, religion, or language?*

SOURCE: Ernest Renan, "What Is a Nation?" in *The Nationalism Reader,* edited by Omar Dahbour and Micheline R. Ishay (Atlantic Highlands, NJ: Humanities Press, 1995), pp. 143–55.

the liberals and radicals, that the nation should be sovereign. But who were "the people" and what was "the nation"? The revolutions themselves turned out to be short-lived, and by 1851, the monarchies had been reinstated. But these questions continued to plague Europe for many years to come.

In his famous pamphlet of early 1789, the left-leaning clergyman Emmanuel Joseph Sieyès had argued that the nation consisted of all of those who worked to enrich it; those who were merely "parasites" on the nation's body (here Sieyès meant the clergy and the aristocracy) did not belong. For many liberals who followed Sieyès, the nation was composed of all those subject to its laws, which were presumed to be rational and to apply equally to all residing in its borders. This liberal definition of the nation made it stand out against older, still feudal forms, where kings, clergymen, and nobles enjoyed special privileges above and outside the law. But it did not help decide which people belonged inside which nation-state, for belonging to a nation had also long been associated with the sharing of cultural or religious traditions. For some, the nation was a collection of all those who spoke one language (for example, the Czechs). This did not work for the Irish, who spoke English but who were predominately Catholics and wanted to be free from Anglican rule. As the century wore on, writers increasingly began to suggest that communities were, or ought to be, defined by race, a term that sometimes referred to physical and biological features such as skin color and head shape but usually meant something more like our term *ethnicity*, which refers to the sociocultural as well as biological circumstances from which a person comes. Confused and complicated as nationalism might appear, and despite the fact that most existing states contained minority ethnic, linguistic, and religious groups, the longing for unified, homogeneous states spread throughout the region. In time, nationalism would both inspire the creation of new states, including Belgium, Italy, and Germany, and contribute to the collapse of older ones, most importantly the Austro-Hungarian and Ottoman empires.

Answering the question, who are "the people"—and who should rule on their behalf—was equally controversial and divisive. The radicals had claimed the right for all to participate in ruling Europe's states (though even this all very rarely included women, and often excluded religious minorities as well); some had even claimed that all had a right, too, to a share of the nation's wealth. This had terrified not only the backward-looking conservatives but also the middle-class liberals, men who supported the expansion of the franchise but not full-on popular sovereignty and certainly not economic equality. After 1848, the two groups frequently made common cause against the threat from below. In some cases, too,

> *In time, nationalism would both inspire the creation of new states and contribute to the collapse of older ones.*

reforms were instituted in order to placate the lower classes and to remedy some of capitalism's worst abuses, like child labor.

In a final blow to the hopes of many revolutionaries, Louis Napoleon (nephew of Napoleon) staged a coup against the French republic in December 1851. With the help of lower-middle-class conservatives and the army, he declared himself Emperor Napoleon III and ruled until 1870. Thus, in much of Europe, nationalism assumed a conservative quality by the second half of the nineteenth century, as middle-class liberals sided increasingly with conservatives rather than radicals. In many ways, Louis Napoleon provided an example for other European nation-builders: popular (male) suffrage and nationalism could blunt radicalism. After 1850, Italian and German nationalists took the lessons to heart.

UNIFICATION IN GERMANY AND IN ITALY

Two of Europe's fledgling nation-states came into being when the dynastic states of Prussia and Piedmont-Sardinia swallowed their smaller, linguistically related neighbors, creating the new German and Italian nation-states (see Map 17-3). In both regions, astute conservative prime ministers, Count Otto von Bismarck (1815–1898) of Prussia and Count Camillo di Cavour (1810–1861) of Piedmont, exploited radical, and especially liberal, nationalist sentiment to rearrange the map of Europe.

Clever strategists, Bismarck and Cavour used nationalist feelings and small-scale, limited wars to enlarge their states. To these ends, they appealed to shared literary traditions and languages to paper over social, economic, political, and religious fault lines. They also used force to obtain their aims. In a famous address in 1862, Bismarck bellowed: "Not through speeches and majority decisions are the great questions of the day decided—that was the great mistake of 1848 and 1849—but through blood and iron." Taking his own advice, he accomplished the unification of the northern German states in the 1860s by war: with Denmark in 1864, Austria in 1866, and France (over the western provinces of Alsace and Lorraine) in 1870–1871. Italy also was united by means of a series of small conflicts, many of them engineered to head off the establishment of more radical republics.

These new, "unified" states were economically and militarily able to compete with Britain, France, and the United States, but they rejected democracy. In the new Italy, which was a constitutional monarchy, not a republic, less than 5 percent of the 25 million people could vote. The new German

→ *How did European nation-states forge national identities?*

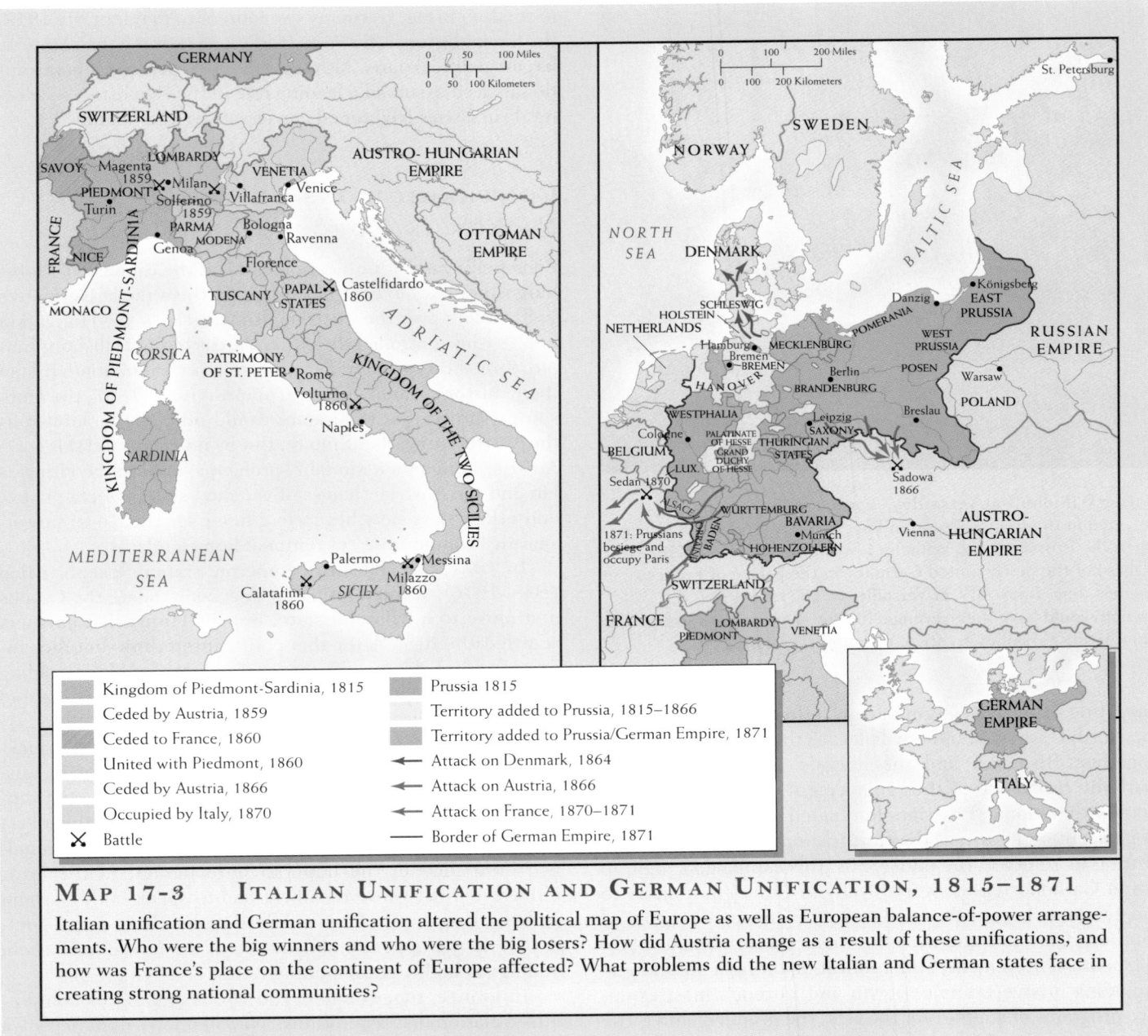

MAP 17-3   ITALIAN UNIFICATION AND GERMAN UNIFICATION, 1815–1871

Italian unification and German unification altered the political map of Europe as well as European balance-of-power arrangements. Who were the big winners and who were the big losers? How did Austria change as a result of these unifications, and how was France's place on the continent of Europe affected? What problems did the new Italian and German states face in creating strong national communities?

empire (the Reich) was ruled by a combination of aristocrats and efficient bureaucrats. Liberals dominated in many localities, but only the emperor (the kaiser) could depose the prime minister, and Bismarck continued to dominate Prussian politics for twenty-eight years, displaced only in 1890 by the new sovereign, Kaiser Wilhelm II (ruled 1888–1918), who proved to be even more authoritarian and bellicose than the Iron Chancellor.

The new German and Italian nation-states had many internal problems. In Italy, Piedmontese liberals had hoped that centralized rule would transform southern Italy, making

it a prosperous, commercial, and industrial region like their own. But southern notables, owing their wealth mainly to their large agricultural estates, had little interest in conforming to northern standards and customs. Germany contained many non-Germans—Poles in Silesia, French in Alsace and Lorraine, Danes in the provinces of Schleswig-Holstein—who became "national minorities" and whose rights remained in question. In addition, many non-Prussian Germans—Bavarians, Hanoverians, Saxons, and others—remained wary of a united Germany, believing that it signified Prussian Protestant rule. State authorities countered by

Kaiser Wilhelm I at Versailles. For the French, recently defeated in the Franco-Prussian War, insult was added to injury when the Prussian king, Wilhelm I, was proclaimed emperor (kaiser) of the newly united Germany in the palace of France's greatest king, Louis XIV, at Versailles in 1871. In 1919, the French would have their revenge, forcing the Germans to sign the humiliating Versailles Treaty in the same location.

mounting extensive "Germanizing" efforts, including using the North German Hamburg dialect as the national language. Together, Bismarck and the liberals sought to root out Catholic resistance to the replacement of regional institutions with national, Prussian-dominated ones, in a campaign of persecution known as the *Kulturkampf* (fight for culture). Hitting its zenith in the mid-1880s, this campaign sought to brand Catholics (who swore loyalty to Rome) as traitors to the new state but resulted simply in the further alienation of southern Germans and the formation of a formidable Catholic political movement. Still, unification brought advantages, including brisk economic growth and Europe's most extensive programs of support for the sick, the disabled, and those injured at work—programs enacted by Bismarck to diminish socialism's appeal.

Berlin, the capital of Prussia, became the capital of the German Reich. Kaiser Wilhelm II remarked in 1892 that "the glory of Paris robs Berliners of their sleep." But Berlin was on the rise. Its population of 1 million people in 1875 doubled by 1910. The German population more generally boomed; and the French, whose birthrates were dropping, had their own nightmares, involving swelling battalions of well-drilled German soldiers, to contend with.

The new Germany, with its great might, was divided along class as well as regional and religious lines. In the 1890 elections, the Social Democratic Party garnered thirty-five seats in the Reichstag, Germany's version of parliament. By 1912, the Social Democratic Party (SPD) had become the country's largest political party. Although the SPD became less revolutionary as it assumed a leading role in the Reichstag, its electoral successes frightened conservatives and liberals.

CONTRADICTIONS OF THE NATION IN EUROPE

Bismarck's wars of unification came at the expense of Habsburg supremacy in central Europe. In the wake of Germany's swift victory over the Austrian army in 1866, the Hungarian nobles who controlled the eastern areas of the Habsburg Empire forced the weakened dynasts to grant them home rule in their "historic" lands. In the Compromise of 1867, the Habsburgs agreed that their state would officially be known as the Austro-Hungarian Empire. But by no means did this solve Austria-Hungary's nationality problems; in both the Hungarian and the Austrian halves of the dual state, Czechs, Poles, and other Slavs now began to clamor for their own power-sharing "compromise" or national homelands.

In 1871, the Habsburg emperor, Francis Joseph (ruled 1848–1916), seemed prepared to accommodate the Czechs and move to a trilateral state, but his Hungarian partners scuttled the deal. After this point, interethnic conflict increased as inhabitants fought over language and land-holding rights, and as separate charitable organizations were created to cater exclusively to Czechs or Poles, Slovaks or Slavs. By the 1880s, a new wave of Eastern European Jews was making its way into Austria-Hungary, fleeing persecution in Russia; these mostly rural and poor emigrants were greeted with an upsurge of anti-Semitic feeling and the organization of reactive, racist political pressure groups. Still, multinationalism flourished in the imperial bureaucracy, in the army officers' corps (whose members had to speak both German and the languages of the soldiers under their direct command), in the upper administration of the Catholic Church, and in the highly cosmopolitan cities.

In France, too, events of the 1860s and 1870s compromised nationalist aspirations. Napoleon III dreamed of a France with restored grandeur—only to run headlong into expansionist Prussians. In the Franco-Prussian War of 1870–1871, Prussian troops delivered a swift and sound drubbing: in early September 1870, the German army broke through French defenses, captured the French emperor, and besieged Paris. Unprepared, Parisians had no food stocks and were compelled to eat all sorts of things, including two zoo elephants. Under terrible conditions and without effective leadership, the French capital resisted until January 1871, when the government signed a humiliating peace treaty. The Germans left in power an impotent provisional French government under the right-wing liberal Adolphe Thiers. Furious Parisians vented their rage and established a socialist commune proclaiming the city a utopia for workers. The popular regime lasted until May 21, 1871, when Thiers's army stormed Paris. At least 25,000 Parisians died in the bloody mop-up that followed.

Even the British Isles suffered from national divisions. Its leaders wrestled with lower-class agitation and demands for independence from Irish nationalists. More rapidly and thoroughly than elsewhere (except France), however, England responded to these pressures by gradually extending political rights to all men but not women. Free trade and progress became the dogmas of a middle class flush with new wealth generated by industry and empire. The long reign of Queen Victoria (ruled 1837–1901), as well as England's prosperity, overseas conquests, and world power, increasingly bound both workers and owners to the nation. Yet, Ireland remained England's Achilles' heel. Although Catholic emancipation in 1836 finally made Irish Catholics nominally equal to Protestants before the law, the political and economic conditions of the two communities remained very uneven. The English were widely condemned for their failure to relieve Irish suffering during the potato famine of 1846–1849 (see chapter 15); even though millions of poor Irish and Scottish workers made their way to England, seeking either passage to North America or work in the English mill towns, they did not assimilate easily and were often given the lowliest jobs. All of this, on top of three hundred years of repressive English domination, lay behind the birth of a mass movement for Irish home rule.

INDUSTRY, SCIENCE, AND TECHNOLOGY

> → *How did new materials and technologies transform industry and the global economy?*

A powerful combination of industry, science, and technology shaped the establishment of nation-states in North America and western Europe and reordered the relationships between different parts of the world. The industrial sector of the world economy expanded and became more advanced after 1850 as western Europe and North America underwent a new phase of industrial development, which came to be called the second industrial revolution. After the 1880s, Japan, too, joined the ranks of industrializing nations as its state-led program of industrial development started to pay dividends. These changes transformed the global economy and intensified rivalries among industrial societies. Although Britain had been the leader of the earlier phase of industrial expansion, it now had to contend with competition from the United States and Germany. Between 1870 and 1913, Germany's

share of world industrial output rose from 13 percent to 16 percent. U.S. output soared from 23 percent to 36 percent and surpassed Britain's, which fell from 32 percent to 14 percent.

NEW MATERIALS, TECHNOLOGIES, AND BUSINESS PRACTICES

New materials and new technologies were vital in late-nineteenth-century economic development. For example, steel, which was more malleable and stronger than iron, became an essential ingredient for industries like shipbuilding and railways. The world output of steel shot up from half a million tons in 1870 to 28 million tons in 1900. The miracle of steel was celebrated through the construction of the Eiffel Tower (completed in 1889) in Paris, an aggressively modern monument that loomed over Paris's picturesque cityscape and was double the height of any other building in the world at the time. Steel was part of a bundle of innovations that included chemicals, oil, pharmaceuticals, and mass transportation vehicles like trolleys and automobiles.

A new source of cheap energy—electricity—was also developed over the course of the nineteenth century; as its use was perfected, manufacturers found they no longer had to be close to their energy source (previously, factories needed

Eiffel Tower. Gustave Eiffel, a French engineer known for his innovative iron bridges, built this tower for the 1889 Universal Exhibition in Paris.

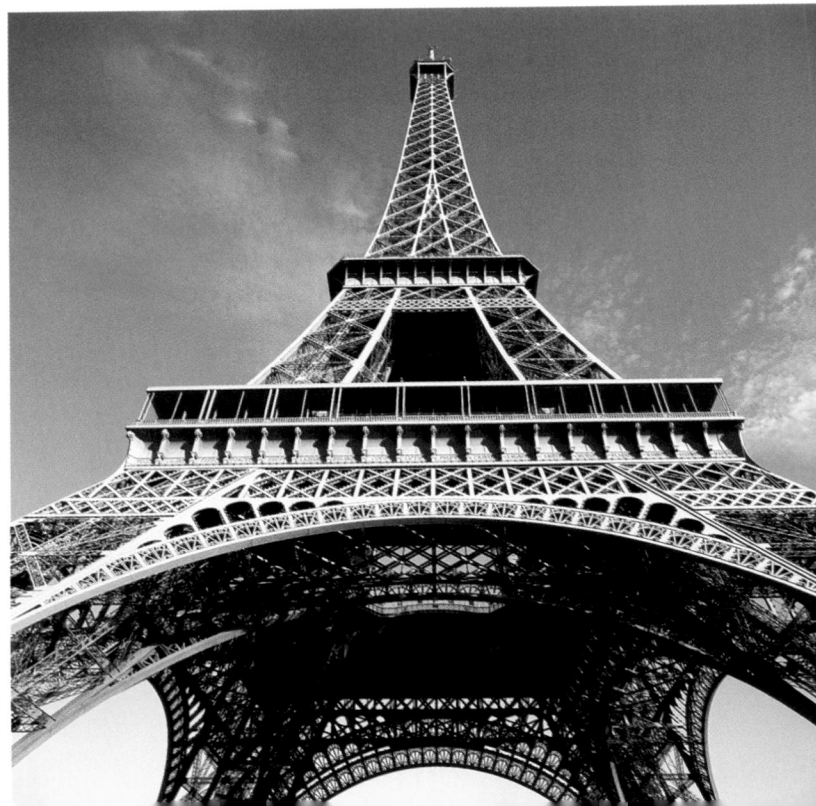

to be near coal deposits or running water) and were able to slash their production costs. Scientific research also became important to industrial development. German companies led the way in creating laboratories where university-trained chemists and physicists conducted research to serve industrial production. The United States followed the German example in consummating a profitable marriage between scientific research and capitalist enterprise. Universities and in-house corporate laboratories produced swelling ranks of engineers and scientists, as well as patents.

The breakthroughs of the second industrial revolution ushered in new business practices, most importantly mass production and the creation of the giant integrated firm. No longer would relatively modest investments suffice, as they had in Britain a century earlier when a wealthy family or a few partners were able to accumulate enough capital to establish new firms and support industrial schemes. Now large banks were major providers of funds. In Europe and the United States, limited-liability joint-stock firms provided even more powerful means of raising capital on stock markets. Companies like Standard Oil, U.S. Steel, and Siemens mobilized capital from a large number of investors, called *shareholders*, who because of the new limited-liability laws were no longer personally responsible for the debts of their firms. The scale of these firms was awesome. U.S. Steel alone produced over half the world's steel ingots, castings, rails, and heavy structural shapes—and nearly half of all its steel plates and sheets.

INTEGRATION OF THE WORLD ECONOMY

Not only did industrial change concentrate power within North Atlantic societies, it also reinforced their power on the world economic stage. The development of new products en-

abled Europe and the United States to increase their exports. At the same time, the new industrial wave intensified Europe's and North America's desires to control the importing of tropical commodities such as cocoa and coffee. While the North Atlantic societies were still largely self-sufficient in coal, iron, cotton, wool, and wheat—the major commodities of the first industrial revolution—the second industrial revolution rendered European and North American factories reliant on rubber, copper, oil, and bauxite, which were not available domestically. Equally important, large pools of money became available for investing overseas. London may have lost its industrial leadership, but it retained its dominance over the world's financial operations. By 1913, the British had the huge sum of £4 billion overseas—funds that generated an annual income of £200 million, or one-tenth of Britain's national income.

Finally, the enlarged and more integrated world economy needed workers for the fields, factories, and mines. This led to vast movements of the laboring population seeking new opportunities and an escape from poverty. Indians moved thousands of miles to work on sugar plantations in the Caribbean, Mauritius, and Fiji, to labor in South African mines, and to build East African railroads. Chinese laborers constructed railroads in the western United States and worked on sugar plantations in Cuba. The Irish, Poles, Jews, Italians, and Greeks flocked to North America to fill its burgeoning factories. Italians in great numbers also moved to Argentina to harvest wheat and corn.

New technologies of warfare, transportation, and communication eased global economic integration—and buttressed European domination. With steam-powered gunboats and breech-loading rifles, Europeans opened new territories for trade and conquest. At home and in their colonial possessions, imperial powers constructed networks of railroads that facilitated the movement of people and goods from the hinterland to the coasts. From there, steamships carried them

Railroad Workers. The construction of railroad lines across the United States was dangerous work, much of it done by immigrant laborers, including large numbers of Chinese, such as those in this photograph taken in Utah c. 1869.

Suez Canal. The Suez Canal opened to world shipping in 1869 and reduced the time it took to sail between Europe and Asian ports. Although the French and the Egyptians supplied most of the money and the construction plans and Egyptians were the main workforce, British shipping dominated canal traffic from the outset.

across the seas. The completion of the Suez Canal in 1869 shortened ship voyages between Europe and Asia and lowered the costs of interregional trade. Information moved even faster than cargoes, thanks to the laying of telegraph cables under the oceans, supplemented by overland telegraph lines.

The integration of the world economy also produced a bumper crop of scientific and technological innovations. Although machines were the most visible new manifestations of Euro-American confidence that the universe could be mastered, perhaps the most momentous shift in the nineteenth-

century conception of nature was the product of the travels of one scientist: Charles Darwin (1809–1882). Longing to see exotic fauna, Darwin abandoned his pursuit of a clerical career. In 1831, he signed on for a four-year voyage on the *Beagle,* a surveying vessel bound for Latin America and the South Seas—a voyage made possible by Europe's imperial expansion and mastery of the sea. As the ship's naturalist, Darwin collected large quantities of specimens and recorded observations daily. After his return to England in 1836, he became ever more convinced that the species of organic life

Charles Darwin. Darwin testing the speed of a tortoise in the Galapagos Islands. It was during his visit to these islands that Darwin developed many of the ideas that he would put forth in his 1859 *Origin of Species.*

THE ORIGIN OF SPECIES

Charles Darwin's Origin of Species *(1859) was the product of the British naturalist's many years of studying animals and plants. In offering Darwin's solution to the longstanding question "How and why are new species created?" the book described the process of natural selection, according to which nature itself creates overabundance and struggle in order that the "fittest" individuals survive to reproduce. Although Darwin said nothing in the book about human beings, his contemporaries immediately began to speculate on the implications of his theory for the evolution of humankind and of human "races."*

Again, it may be asked, how is it that varieties, which I have called incipient species, become ultimately converted into good and distinct species, which in most cases obviously differ from each other far more than do the varieties of the same species? How do those groups of species, which constitute what are called distinct genera, and which differ from each other more than do the species of the same genus, arise? All these results, as we shall more fully see in the next chapter, follow inevitably from the struggle for life. Owing to this struggle for life, any variation, however slight and from whatever cause proceeding, if it be in any degree profitable to an individual of any species, in its infinitely complex relations to other organic beings and to external nature, will tend to the preservation of that individual, and will generally be inherited by its offspring. The offspring, also, will thus have a better chance of surviving, for, of the many individuals of any species which are periodically born, but a small number can survive. I have called this principle, by which each slight variation, if useful, is preserved, by the term of Natural Selection, in order to mark its relation to man's power of selection. We have seen that man by selection can certainly produce great results, and can adapt organic beings to his own uses, through the accumulation of slight but useful variations, given to him by the hand of Nature. But Natural Selection, as we shall hereafter see, is a power incessantly ready for action, and is as immeasurably superior to man's feeble efforts, as the works of Nature are to those of Art.

We will now discuss in a little more detail the struggle for existence. . . . I should premise that I use the term Struggle for Existence in a large and metaphorical sense, including dependence of one being on another, and including (which is more important) not only the life of the individual, but success in leaving progeny. Two canine animals in a time of dearth, may be truly said to struggle with each other which shall get food and live. But a plant on the edge of a desert is said to struggle for life against the drought, though more properly it should be said to be dependent on the moisture. . . .

A struggle for existence inevitably follows from the high rate at which all organic beings tend to increase. Every being, which during its natural lifetime produces several eggs or seeds, must suffer destruction during some period of its life, and during some season or occasional year, otherwise, on the principle of geometrical increase, its numbers would quickly become so inordinately great that no country could support the product. Hence, as more individuals are produced than can possibly survive, there must in every case be a struggle for existence, either one individual with another of the same species, or with the individuals of distinct species, or with the physical conditions of life. It is the doctrine of Malthus applied with manifold force to the whole animal and vegetable kingdoms; for in this case there can be no artificial increase of food, and no prudential restraint from marriage. Although some species may be now increasing, more or less rapidly, in numbers, all cannot do so, for the world would not hold them.

———

It may be said that natural selection is daily and hourly scrutinising, throughout the world, every variation, even the slightest; rejecting that which is bad, preserving and adding up all that is good; silently and insensibly working, whenever and wherever opportunity offers, at the improvement of each organic being in relation to its organic and inorganic conditions of life. We see nothing of these slow changes in progress, until the hand of time has marked the long lapses of ages, and then so imperfect is our view into long past geological ages, that we only see that the forms of life are now different from what they formerly were.

→ *How does Darwin explain the divergence of species?*
→ *Why does Darwin think struggle is inevitable for all living beings?*

SOUCE: Charles Darwin, *The Origin of Species*, Chapters 3 and 4, www.talkorigins.org/faqs/origin/.

were not fixed but had instead evolved under the uniform pressure of natural laws, not by means of a special, one-time creation as described in the Bible.

Darwin's theory, finally articulated in his epoch-making *Origin of Species* in 1859, laid out the principles of natural selection. Inevitably, he claimed, populations grew faster than the food supply; this condition created an equally inevitable "struggle for existence" among members of a species, the outcome of which was that the "fittest" survived to reproduce, while the less adaptable or healthy did not. The "economy of nature" was, Darwin readily confessed, a rather painful reality; people would rather behold "nature's face bright with gladness" than recognize that some animals must be others' prey and that shortages are, ultimately, necessary to prevent disastrous overpopulation. But in the end, nature's selections were, in his words, "infinitely better adapted to the most complex conditions of life" than humans could appreciate, and the miraculous efficiency with which nature chose the fittest to survive strongly suggested a process which, again in his words, ought to "plainly bear the stamp of far higher workmanship." Although Darwin's *Origin of Species* dealt exclusively with animals (and mostly with birds), his readers immediately realized what his theory implied for humans.

Although Darwin's Origin of Species *dealt exclusively with animals, his readers immediately realized what his theory implied for humans.*

A widespread and passionate debate began among scientists and laymen, clerics and anthropologists. Some read the doctrine of the "survival of the fittest" to mean that it was natural for the strong nations to dominate the weak. In the years that followed the publication of Darwin's treatise, Europeans would repeatedly suggest that they had evolved more than Africans and Asians, and that hence nature itself gave them the right to rule others. Some asserted that Darwinian doctrines justified the right of the ruling classes to dominate the rest. A whole set of beliefs known as Social Darwinism ratified the suffering of the underclasses in industrial society: it was unnatural, Social Darwinists claimed, to tamper with natural selection.

IMPERIALISM

> → *What were the motives for imperialism and the practices of colonial rulers?*

One of the reasons upper-crust Europeans believed themselves "the fittest" in the contest for "survival of the fittest" was their success in bringing others—including enslaved

Africans and impecunious European workers—under their rule. Expansion affirmed national greatness. It also lined some people's pockets—though whether or not imperialism was more lucrative for the global economy than was free trade was a matter of much dispute. Increasing rivalries among nations and increasing social tensions within them produced an expansionist wave in the last half of the nineteenth century. Although Africa became the primary focus of interest, a frenzy of territorial conquest overtook Asia as well. The period between the 1860s and the 1890s witnessed the French occupation of Vietnam, Cambodia, and Laos, and the British expansion in Malaya (present-day Malaysia) in the 1870s and 1880s. The competition to establish spheres of influence, whereby foreign powers carved up China's territories into various regions, with each claiming a specific region as its exclusive domain of interest, heated up in the 1890s. Real and perceived threats to India provoked the British to conquer Burma (present-day Myanmar) in the 1880s. Moreover, Britain and Russia competed for imperial preeminence from their respective outposts in Afghanistan and central Asia. In the Americas, expansion usually involved the incorporation of new territories into enlarged nations as provinces, meaning that they became integral parts of the nation and that their inhabitants were generally recognized as citizens of the state. But European imperialism in Asia and Africa turned far-flung territories into colonial possessions, territories considered extraneous to the core of the nation. Here, the inhabitants were usually designated as subjects of the empire without the rights and privileges of citizens. Britain's imperial regime in India provided lessons to a generation of European colonial officials in Africa and other parts of Asia on how to build this kind of empire.

INDIA AND THE IMPERIAL MODEL

Britain's successful implementation of colonial rule in India would provide a much-envied model for others, but British methods of rule also were responses to popular discontent. Having suppressed the Indian Rebellion of 1857 (see Chapter 16), authorities revamped the colonial administration. Indians were not to be appeased—and certainly not brought into British public life. But they did have to be governed, and the economy revived. So, immediately after suppressing the rebellion and replacing East India Company rule by crown government in 1858, the British set out to make India into a more secure and productive colony, vesting authority in Her Majesty's viceroy, who was responsible to the secretary of state for India, a member of the British Cabinet. This period of British sovereignty was known as the Raj (rule).

The most urgent task facing the British in India was that of modernizing her transportation and communication systems and transforming the country into an integrated colonial state. These changes had begun under Lord Dalhousie, the governor-general of the East India Company. During his eight-year tenure, Dalhousie oversaw the development of India's modern infrastructure. When he left office in 1856, he boasted that he had harnessed India to the "great engines of social improvement—I mean Railways, uniform Postage, and the Electric Telegraph." A year later, northern India exploded in the 1857 rebellion. But the rebellion also demonstrated the military value of railroads and telegraphs. After the British suppressed the revolt, they took up the construction of public works with renewed vigor. The railways formed a key element in this project, attracting approximately £150 million of British capital during the nineteenth century. Though the capital came from British investors, Indian taxpayers paid off the debt through their taxes. The first railway line opened in 1853, and by 1910 India had 30,627 miles of railway track in operation, making the Indian railways the fourth largest railway system in the world.

The construction of other public works followed. Military engineers built dams across rivers to tame their force and to channel the water to irrigate lands; workers installed a grid of telegraph lines that made communication possible between distant parts of the region. These public works served imperial and economic purposes. India was to become a consumer of British manufactures and a supplier of primary staples like cotton, tea, wheat, vegetable oil seeds, and jute, used for making rope or burlap sacking. The control of India's massive rivers allowed farmers to cultivate the rich floodplains, converting large areas into lucrative cotton-producing provinces. On the hillsides of the island of Ceylon and the northeastern plains of India, the British established vast plantations to grow tea, which was then marketed in England, especially by the firm Lipton's, as a healthier alternative to Chinese green tea. India also became an important consumer of British manufactures, especially textiles, which was ironic given India's centuries-old tradition of producing and exporting cotton and silk textiles.

India recorded a consistent surplus in its foreign trade through the export of agricultural goods and raw materials.

The Mem Sahib. This late-eighteenth-century painting shows a British woman surrounded by her Indian servants. European women were addressed as *Mem sahib*—combining *Mem*, a corruption of madam, and the Hindi honorific title *sahib*. The decor of the room, including both European and Indian elements, and the scene itself present an image of imperial power in an exotic setting.

Sinews of the Raj. (*Top*) During the second half of the nineteenth century, the British built an extensive system of railroads to develop India as a profitable colony and to maintain military security. This engraving shows the East India Railway around 1863. (*Bottom*) The British allowed several native princes to remain as long as they accepted imperial paramountcy. This photograph shows a road-building project in one such princely state. Officials of the Muslim princely ruler and British advisers supervise the workers.

But what India gained from its trade to the world it lost to Britain, its colonial master. India was forced to use its export surplus to pay for "home charges," such as interest on railroad loans, salaries to colonial officers on furlough in Britain, and the maintenance of imperial troops outside India. Home charges meant that India ended up balancing Britain's huge trade deficits with the rest of the world, especially the Americas. Favorable trade with India helped Britain retain its financial might and sustain the international gold standard, a mechanism devised by the Bank of England to preserve stability of the British currency (the pound) by making it "convertible" to gold.

Nonetheless, administrative programs made India into a unified territory and enabled its inhabitants to regard themselves as "Indians." India had taken the first steps to becoming a "nation"—like Italy and the United States. There were, of course, profound differences: Indians lacked a single national language, and they were not citizens of their political community able to enjoy a semblance of sovereignty. Rather, they were colonial subjects ruled by outsiders.

DUTCH COLONIAL RULE IN INDONESIA

The Dutch, like the British, joined the parade of governments trying to modernize and integrate their colonies economically without integrating colonial peoples into the life of the nation at home. Decades before the British had taken control of India away from the East India Company, Holland had put an end to the rule of the Dutch East India Company over the archipelago of islands we now call Indonesia. Beginning in the 1830s, the Dutch government assumed direct administrative responsibility over Indonesian affairs. Holland's new colonial officials envisioned an even more completely regulated colonial economy than that of their British counterparts in India. For example, they ordered villagers to allocate one-third of their land for coffee bean cultivation. In return, the colonial government paid a set price (well below world market prices) and placed a ceiling on rents owed to landowners.

These policies—the rhetoric of "free trade" notwithstanding—had dreadful local consequences. Increased production of coffee beans, sugar, and tobacco led to a reduction of food production. By the 1840s and 1850s, famine spread across Java. In 1849–1850, over 300,000 Indonesians, like the Irish, perished from mass starvation. Surviving villagers voiced growing discontent, prompting harsh crackdowns by colonial forces. Back in Holland, the spectacle of colonial oppression proved embarrassing and prompted calls for reform. This led the Dutch government to introduce in the 1860s what it called an ethical policy for governing Asian colonies. This policy reduced governmental exploitation and encouraged Dutch settlement of the islands and more private enterprise. For Indonesians, the replacement of government agents with private merchants meant little difference, however. In some areas, islanders put up fierce resistance. On the sprawling island of Sumatra, for instance, villagers armed themselves and fought off Dutch invaders. After decades of warfare, costing the lives of 4,000 Dutch soldiers, Sumatra was finally subdued in 1904, and the shipping of Indonesian staples, like sugar, tobacco, rice, tin, oil, and eventually rubber, continued to bring large profits to the Dutch.

COLONIZING AFRICA

No region felt the impact of European colonialism more powerfully than Africa. In 1880, the only two large European colonial possessions on the African landmass were French

Algeria and the two British-ruled South African states, the Cape Colony and Natal. By 1914, seven European states (Britain, France, Germany, Spain, Italy, Portugal, and Belgium) had carved almost all of Africa into colonial possessions (see Map 17-4). Only two corners remained independent: Liberia, thanks to American protection for this home for freed American slaves, and Ethiopia, because Emperor Menelik II (ruled 1889–1913) had harnessed a budding sense of Ethiopian national identity to a strong, well-disciplined army.

British and French forces occupied toeholds in Africa from earlier in the nineteenth century—the British in the south, the French in the north. The French had conquered Algeria in 1830 and then proceeded to expand their influence in Morocco, Tunisia, Senegal, and Egypt, where they built the Suez Canal (1854–1869). When the British invaded and occupied Egypt in 1882, they angered the French, who had regarded Egypt as a special sphere of French cultural influence ever since the Napoleonic invasion of that country in 1798, thus intensifying the rivalry between the British and French for additional colonial territories in Africa. The British took the former Dutch colony of Cape Town after the Peace of 1815 ended the Napoleonic wars. They immediately ran into trouble not just with Africans, but with fundamentalist Protestant Afrikaans speakers, who had begun to settle in the region. Over time the Afrikaners established a powerful historical tradition of their pioneering days, celebrating the colony's founder, Jan van Riebeeck, who built a fort at the Cape in 1652 and planted fruits and vegetables there, thus enabling the Cape to serve as a resupply and resting station for Dutch East India ships sailing to and from Asia. Conflicts between the British and the Afrikaners (often referred to as the Boers) festered until the latter led the Great Trek to the interior in the 1830s to escape British rule, displacing the Bantu-speaking peoples who had previously occupied much of the area. Subsequent discoveries of diamonds and gold in the 1860s and 1880s only spurred the British to penetrate farther into the interior of southern Africa, leading to more friction with Africans and Afrikaners.

With the example of French and British colonization of Africa, other Europeans rushed to the region. As European powers joined the scramble for Africa, Portugal called for an international conference to discuss claims to Africa. Promoted by Germany's Bismarck, this conference met in Berlin between 1884 and 1885, with delegates from Germany, Portugal, Britain, France, Belgium, Spain, Italy, the United States, and the Ottoman Empire in attendance. They agreed to carve up Africa and to recognize the acquisitions of any European power that had achieved occupation on the ground.

The consequences for Africa of the European partition were devastating. Nearly 70 percent of the newly drawn borders failed to correspond to older demarcations of ethnicity, language, culture, and commerce, as Europeans knew little of the landmass beyond its coast and rivers. They based colonial boundaries on European trading centers rather than on the location of the African populations. In West Africa, the Yoruba were split between the French in Dahomey and the British in southwestern Nigeria. Nigeria became an administrative nightmare, as the British endeavored to integrate the politically centralized Muslim populations of the north (Hausa, Fulani, and Kanuri) with the city-state Yoruba dwellers and small tribes of the Ibos of the south.

Several motives led the European powers into their frenzied partition of Africa. In general, European business magnates were not excited about Africa, except for Egypt and South Africa, where European investment was substantial and lucrative. But smaller-scale European traders and investors were intrigued by the economic prospects on the western and eastern coasts of Africa. These capitalist adventurers had some knowledge of the coastal areas, and they harbored fantasies of great treasures locked in the vast uncharted interior of Africa. Politicians, publicists, and the reading public also took an interest in Africa. The writings of explorers like David Livingstone (1813–1873), a Scottish doctor and missionary, and Henry Morton Stanley (1841–1904), an adventurer in the pay of *The New York Herald*, excited readers with accounts of Africa as a continent of unlimited economic potential.

There was, of course, also the lure of building personal fortunes and reputations. In eastern Africa, Carl Peters (1856–1918) aspired to be the maker of a vast German colony, and he brought German East Africa into existence. In southern Africa, the British champion of imperialism Cecil Rhodes (1853–1902) exclaimed that he would annex the planets if he could. Instead, he contented himself with bringing the Rhodesias, Nyasaland, Bechuanaland, the Transvaal, and the Orange Free State into the British Empire. He was delighted that the Rhodesias bore his name, and in his later years, as his heart condition worsened, he worried about his legacy. "They can't change the name of a country, can they?" he anxiously wondered.

Even more committed to the imperialist project was Leopold II (ruled 1865–1909), king of the Belgians. Chafing at the prospect of being a minor monarch of a small European state with a population of 5 million, Leopold saw in empire a way to be a player on the world stage. He seized for himself a colonial state ten times the size of Belgium, dubbing his possession the Congo Independent State. Leopold's agent in the Congo was Henry Stanley, known to his adversaries

> *The consequences for Africa of the European partition were devastating. Nearly 70 percent of the newly drawn borders failed to correspond to older demarcations of ethnicity, language, culture, and commerce.*

MAP 17-4   PARTITION OF AFRICA, 1880–1939

The partition of Africa took place between the early 1880s and the outbreak of World War I. Which of the European powers gained the most territory in Africa? Did territorial acquisition translate into profound economic and political gain for these European states? Did any of the European states realize their ambitions in Africa?

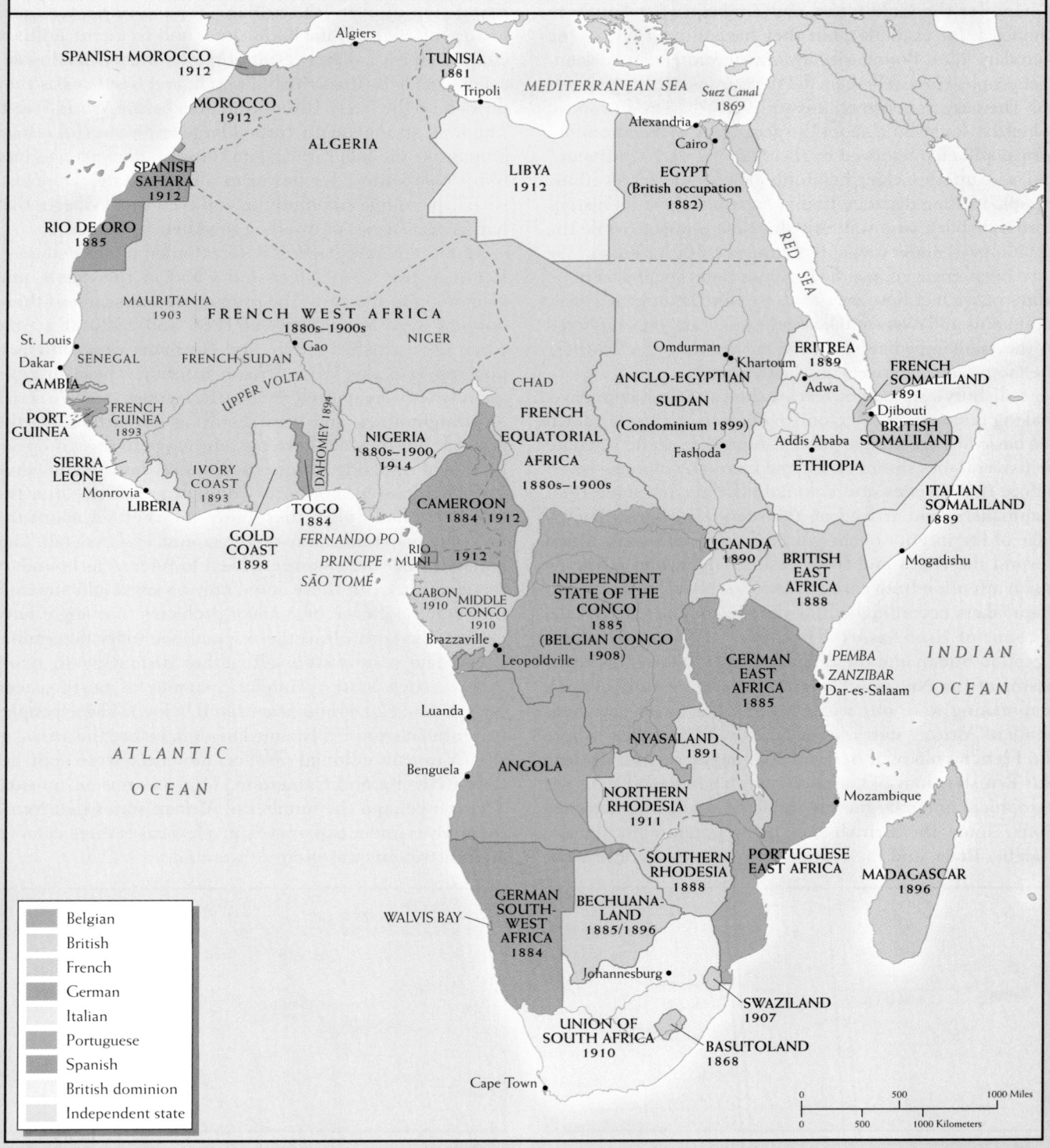

SPANISH MOROCCO
1912

Algiers

TUNISIA
1881

MEDITERRANEAN SEA

Suez Canal
1869

MOROCCO
1912

Tripoli

Alexandria

SPANISH
SAHARA
1912

ALGERIA

LIBYA
1912

EGYPT
(British occupation
1882)

Cairo

RIO DE ORO
1885

RED SEA

MAURITANIA
1903

FRENCH WEST AFRICA
1880s–1900s

St. Louis
Dakar
SENEGAL

FRENCH SUDAN

Gao

NIGER

Omdurman
Khartoum

ERITREA
1889

FRENCH
SOMALILAND
1891

GAMBIA

UPPER VOLTA

CHAD

ANGLO-EGYPTIAN
SUDAN

Adwa

Addis Ababa

Djibouti

BRITISH
SOMALILAND

PORT.
GUINEA

FRENCH
GUINEA
1893

DAHOMEY 1894

NIGERIA
1880s–1900,
1914

FRENCH
EQUATORIAL
AFRICA
1880s–1900s

(Condominium 1899)

Fashoda

ETHIOPIA

SIERRA
LEONE

IVORY
COAST
1893

Monrovia

LIBERIA

TOGO
1884

GOLD
COAST
1898

FERNANDO PO

PRINCIPE

SÃO TOMÉ

RIO
MUNI

1912

CAMEROON
1884 1912

ITALIAN
SOMALILAND
1889

Mogadishu

GABON
1910

MIDDLE
CONGO
1910

Brazzaville

Leopoldville

INDEPENDENT
STATE OF THE
CONGO
1885
(BELGIAN CONGO
1908)

UGANDA
1890

BRITISH
EAST
AFRICA
1888

GERMAN
EAST
AFRICA
1885

PEMBA

ZANZIBAR

Dar-es-Salaam

INDIAN

OCEAN

Luanda

ATLANTIC

OCEAN

ANGOLA

Benguela

NYASALAND
1891

NORTHERN
RHODESIA
1911

Mozambique

PORTUGUESE
EAST AFRICA

SOUTHERN
RHODESIA
1888

MADAGASCAR
1896

WALVIS BAY

GERMAN
SOUTH-
WEST
AFRICA
1884

BECHUANA-
LAND
1885/1896

SWAZILAND
1907

Johannesburg

UNION OF
SOUTH AFRICA
1910

BASUTOLAND
1868

Cape Town

▉	Belgian
▉	British
▉	French
▉	German
▉	Italian
▉	Portuguese
▉	Spanish
▉	British dominion
▉	Independent state

0   500   1000 Miles

0   500   1000 Kilometers

DRAWING THE BOUNDARIES OF AFRICA

The political boundaries of contemporary Africa are largely those drawn by European colonizers. So far, the new African leaders have elected to change the names of their countries (Ghana for the Gold Coast and Zimbabwe for Southern Rhodesia, for example), but they have altered few of the boundary lines. Boundaries invariably connect and disconnect people. How well, then, did the European cartographers do? The easy, yet correct, answer is poorly. The European colonizers knew little about the geography of the interior of Africa, still characterized by them as "the dark continent," and were utterly lacking in information about Africa's ethnic groups, its long-distance trading networks, and its history. Lord Salisbury, who was British prime minister while the partition was under way, aptly summed up the problem: "We have been engaged in drawing lines upon maps where no white man's feet have ever trod; we have been giving away mountains and rivers and lakes to each other, only hindered by the small impediment that we never knew exactly where the mountains and rivers and lakes were."

Salisbury's statement reveals the European boundary-making dilemma. The colonizing powers had to lay down the basic lines of the partition—those that would separate British colonies from French and German colonies—even before their armies and colonial officials, let alone their mapmakers, had arrived on the scene. European knowledge of the interior of the continent did not extend much beyond the rivers and their basins, which had attracted much attention from earlier European travelers. European mapmakers accordingly drew the new boundaries to take account of river basins. Thus, for example, the Anglo-Egyptian Sudan and the Belgian Congo followed the river basins of the Nile and Congo rivers. The results of such mapmaking were often catastrophic for latter-day independent African states, as is clear in West Africa, where the French colony of Senegal completely surrounded the tiny British colony of Gambia (see Map A below). This geographical anomaly merely reflected prepartition conditions, since the British had been preeminent on the Gambia River, and the French everywhere else. But what

a dilemma it has made for the modern leaders of Senegal and Gambia!

Nigeria is Africa's most populous state today, with a population of over 100 million. Its tangled postcolonial history of civil war, civil violence, and frequent military coups d'état is a direct result of the boundary-making decisions made by the British, French, and Germans as they divided up the Niger River basin area before World War I. The final arrangements turned large and powerful ethnic groups like the Ibo, Yoruba, and Hausa-Fulani peoples into bitter competitors for power in a single state. They also sliced apart large communities and even small villages that had long histories of dwelling together.

Contemporary Nigeria is surrounded by four states—Benin in the west, Niger and Chad in the north, and Cameroon in the east. The primary decisions about these borders were made between 1880 and 1900 at a time when the British, French, and Germans were only just pushing into the West African interior. These original boundaries were entirely geometrical, consisting of a series of straight lines and arcs, ignoring conditions on the ground. But they did have the advantage to the European powers of resolving the question of how far the individual European powers' authority would extend. Only after the colonizers had drawn these lines did they set about the task of demarcating them on the ground and in detail. This entailed what the colonizers liked to refer to as boundary rectifications. But these could only be small adjustments; they could not overcome major problems that might have occurred as a result of the original boundary determinations. The results were altogether dismaying to many groups, such as the Mandara peoples of northeastern Nigeria and Cameroon (see Map B below). These peoples had formed a unified Islamic kingdom before the arrival of the European colonial powers; now they were split between Nigeria and Cameroon. This was not an unusual occurrence, and the number of African states that found themselves under two or even in a few cases three colonial administrations was quite substantial.

Map A

Map B

Europeans in Africa. (*Left*) Henry Morton Stanley was one of the most famous of the nineteenth-century explorers in Africa. He first made his reputation when he located the British missionary-explorer David Livingstone, feared dead, in the interior of Africa, uttering the famous words, "Dr. Livingstone, I presume." Stanley worked on behalf of King Leopold, establishing the Belgian king's claims to territories in the Congo and often using superior weaponry to cow African opponents. (*Right*) The ardent British imperialist Cecil Rhodes endeavored to bring as much of Africa as he could under British colonial rule. He had an ambition to create a swath of British-controlled territory that would stretch from the Cape in South Africa to Cairo in Egypt, as this cartoon shows.

locally as *bula matari,* the breaker of rocks. Stanley did not shrink from using overwhelming firepower to subdue local populations. The Congo Independent State was unique in that it belonged to a single individual, the Belgian king. It remained Leopold's personal fiefdom until 1908, when gruesome news of the enslavement and slaughter of innocent Congolese began to leak out. Belgians were horrified, and international criticism mounted. Finally, the Belgian parliament took away Leopold's African property and made the Congo a Belgian colony.

While longing for national grandeur and personal fortunes drove many Europeans to Africa, others saw the region as a grand opportunity for converting souls to Christianity. Europe's civilizing mission was an important motive in the scramble for African territory. In Uganda, northern Nigeria,

and central Africa, missionaries went ahead of European armies, imploring the European statesmen to follow their lead.

Contrary to European assumptions, Africans did not welcome or wait for European "civilization" to arrive; resistance, however, with few exceptions, proved futile. Africans faced two unattractive options. They could capitulate to the Europeans and seek through negotiations to limit the loss of their autonomy. Or they could fight. Only a few chose the course of moderation. For the most part, African leaders opted to fight to preserve their sovereignty. Lat Dior, a Muslim warlord in Senegal, refused to let the French build a railway through his kingdom. "As long as I live, be well assured," he wrote the French commandant, "I shall oppose with all my might the construction of this railway. I will always answer no, no, and

I will never make you any other reply. Even were I to go to rest, my horse, *Malay*, would give you the same answer." Conflict was inevitable, and Lat Dior lost his life in a battle with the French in 1886.

In fact, only Menelik II of Ethiopia repulsed the Europeans, for he knew how to play European rivals off against each other. By doing so, he procured weapons from the French, British, Russians, and Italians. He also had a united and powerful army that was reasonably well-equipped and dedicated to the Ethiopian cause. In 1896, his troops routed Italian forces at the Battle of Adwa, in which many Italians lost their lives or were captured and the rest of the Italians scattered. Hereafter, Adwa became a celebrated moment in African history and its memory inspired many of Africa's later nationalist leaders.

Most resisters were not so fortunate, however. They misjudged the strength and determination of their adversaries and were ignorant of the disparity in the military technology of the Africans and the Europeans, especially the killing power of European breech-loading weapons and the Maxim machine gun. In addition to superior weaponry, the European armies had better tactics and a more sustained appetite for battle. Africa's armies fought during the non-agricultural season, engaging in open battles so that the warriors could achieve quick and decisive results and then return to their farms. African military traditions were effective in fighting neighbors, but not when it came to fighting well-equipped invaders.

Some African forces did succeed in adapting their military techniques to the European challenge. Samori Touré

Missionary School. Throughout colonial Africa, European missionary organizations dominated African education. Here, a missionary teacher oversees a class in Swahili in German East Africa just before the outbreak of World War I. Portraits of the German kaiser, Wilhelm II, and his wife are prominently displayed in the front of the classroom.

(1830–1900) proved a stubborn foe for the French, employing guerrilla warfare and avoiding full-scale battles in the savannah lands of West Africa. From 1882 until 1898, Touré eluded the French. Dividing his 35,000-man army, Touré had one part take over territories not yet conquered by the French and there reestablish a fully autonomous domain. A smaller contingent of Touré's army conducted a scorched-earth campaign in the regions from which it was retreating, leaving the French with parched and wasted new possessions. But these tactics only delayed the inevitable. The French finally defeated and captured Touré and sent him into exile in Gabon, where he died in 1900.

COLONIAL ADMINISTRATIONS

With so much African opposition and so many European adventurers staking out their fiefdoms, how did imperial states establish colonial governments? The new colonial states continued to rely on superior firepower. Toward the end of Joseph Conrad's novel *Heart of Darkness,* first published in a magazine in 1899, the rapacious ivory trader Kurtz utters the words "the horror, the horror" just before dying. Conrad's novel called attention to the butchery of Leopold's regime in the Congo and fueled a debate about the practice of administration in Africa. The Congo, with its large loss of African life, may have been extreme, but it was not unique. The early years of European rule in Africa were full of pillage and plunder.

Once the euphoria of partition and conquest had worn off, power devolved to "men on the spot"—military adventurers, settlers, and avaricious entrepreneurs. Their main goal was to enrich themselves as fast as possible. Strong-willed individuals established near-fiefdoms in some areas. Africans, like Native Americans, found themselves confined to territories where they could barely provide for themselves. To keep the colonized in their place and uphold such an invasive system, Europeans had to create permanent standing armies. They did not want to spend the money, however, on more European soldiers and administrators. Instead, the new governors armed their African supporters, who were bribed or compelled to join the side of the victors. They created the new African armies, like the *Force Publique* in the Congo, which bullied local communities into doing the bidding of the colonial authorities.

Having suppressed African revolts and subdued the civilian population, rulers had to create lasting administrations. As in India, the colonial powers in Africa laid the foundations for future nation-state organizations. By then, information trickling out of Africa left little doubt that the imperial governments were not realizing their goal of bringing "civilization" to the "uncivilized." To correct these failings, each European power implemented a new rationalized form of colonial rule, stripping the strongman conquerors of their absolute powers. Various terms described the policy: the Germans called their reformed system scientific colonization, the

Battle of Adwa. Portrait of King Menelik, who defeated the Italian forces at the battle of Adwa in 1896, thus saving his country from European colonization.

Belgians *dominer pour servir* (dominate to serve), the French *mission civilisatrice* (civilizing mission), and the British "native paramountcy."

However much the colonial administrative systems of the European states differed from each other, colonial rule, for all of them, was meant to satisfy three goals. First, the colony was to pay for its own administration. Second, administrators on the spot had to preserve the peace; nothing brought swifter criticism or more rapid censure from the mother country than a colonial rebellion. Third, colonial rule was also to attract other European groups—missionaries, settlers, and merchants. Missionaries came to Africa to convert "heathens" to Christianity, convinced that they were locked in a great battle with Islam for the soul of the continent. Settlers went only to those parts of Africa that had climatic conditions similar to Europe. They poured into Algeria and South Africa but came in much smaller numbers to Kenya, Southern Rhodesia, Angola, and Mozambique. Often they were attracted by advertising campaigns at home that stressed the comfortable living conditions and promised that these areas over time would become white man's territories. Already before the partition Africa had attracted European investment and merchants. The prospect of European colonial rule and promises on the part of colonial governments to construct

railroads, roads, and deep water facilities persuaded even more of the merchants to take out bigger commercial stakes in Africa. The three goals were, of course, often incompatible and would eventually undermine colonial polities in Africa.

Eventually, stabilized, rationalized colonies did begin to deliver on their economic promise. Early imperialism in Africa had been based on the export of ivory and wild rubber. When overexploitation depleted these resources at the turn of the century, the colonies in Africa turned to a new range of exports. From the tropical rain forests came cocoa, coffee, palm oil, and palm kernels, cultivated mainly by small-scale African farmers, who responded quickly to the prospects of growing these new products. In the highlands of East Africa, tea, coffee, sisal (used in cord and twine), and pyrethrum (a flower used to make insecticide) became the major exports, though these tended to be cultivated on European settler farms. Another important commodity was long-staple, high-quality cotton, grown in abundance in Egypt and the Anglo-Egyptian Sudan. From across Africa, as from India and Latin America, tropical commodities flowed to industrializing societies. Unable to contest the disadvantageous terms of trade enforced by public policy and private monopolies of export-import houses, African peasant producers benefited even less than European workers from the new scale and scope of world trade.

Thus, European colonial administrators saw Africa, like India, as fitting into the world economy in the comfortable niche of exporter of raw materials and importer of manufactures. They expected Africa to profit from its incorporation into the world economy. But, in truth, the African workers gained little from participating in colonial commerce, while the price they paid in disruption to traditional social and economic patterns was substantial. Women took care of domestic needs, while men worked for wages or sold cash crops such as peanuts and cocoa at markets. Traditional African age and gender roles were dramatically disrupted in many regions. In the mining areas of southern Africa, most of the able-bodied males worked in the mines. Subsistence farming had to be handled entirely by women and those men too old to go to the mines. In big cash-cropping regions, like West Africa with its cocoa farms, men took control of the cash crops, leaving women responsible for domestic production. Men's incomes rose disproportionately to women's incomes.

The disruptions to traditional life were particularly acute in southern Africa, where mining operations lured African men thousands of miles from their homes. Katanga and parts of South Africa were, in the opinion of one mining expert, "a geological scandal," so abundant were the deposits of gold, diamonds, and copper. With cash advances, European companies lured African workers from their villages to the mines, but indebted laborers often had difficulty paying off these loans. Meanwhile, it fell to women to take care of subsistence and cash crop production in the home villages. By the turn of the century, the gold mines of Witwatersrand in South Africa required a workforce of 100,000. Miners had to be drawn

Diamond Mine. The discovery of diamonds and gold in South Africa in the late nineteenth century led to the investment of large amounts of overseas capital, the mobilization of poorly paid and severely exploited African mine workers, and the Boer War of 1899 to 1902, which resulted in the incorporation of the Afrikaner states of the Transvaal and the Orange Free State into the Union of South Africa.

from as far away as Mozambique, the Rhodesias, and Nyasaland, as well as from South Africa itself. Work below ground was hazardous, and the health services were inadequate. Once aware of these conditions, workers often tried to flee. But their debts, as well as armed guards and barbed-wired compounds, kept them in the mines. In the diamond mines, workers were strip-searched before being discharged to prevent diamond smuggling. The companies made enormous profits for their European shareholders, while the workers toiled in dangerous conditions and barely eked out a living wage.

To the outside observer, the European empires of the late nineteenth century were solid and durable institutions, but in fact, European colonial rule was fragile. The staffing of imperial armies and administrations required the recruitment of many Africans. For all of British Africa, the only all-British force was 5,000 men, garrisoned in Egypt. Elsewhere in colonial territories, European officers commanded African military and police forces. The colonial civil services were equally thin on the ground and profoundly dependent on the participation of the colonized. Prior to 1914, the number of British administrative officers available for the whole of northern Nigeria was less than 500. These were hardly powerful—never mind permanent—foundations for statehood. It would not take much to destabilize the European order in Africa.

THE AMERICAN EMPIRE

Imperial adventurism was not limited to European powers. In the United States, too, overseas expansion offered a means to create new frontiers and to restore prosperity to the Amer-

ican economy during the economic doldrums of the 1890s. Echoing the rhetoric of Manifest Destiny from the 1840s, the expansionists of the 1890s claimed that Americans still had a divine mission to spread their superior civilization and their Christian faith around the globe. In the 1890s, however, America's new imperialists chose to emulate the European model of colonialism in Asia and Africa: colonies were to provide harbors for American vessels, supply raw materials to American industries, and buy the surplus production of American farms and factories. America's new territorial acquisitions were not intended for American settlement or destined for American statehood. Nor were their inhabitants to become American citizens, for nonwhite foreigners were deemed unfit for incorporation into the American nation.

The pressure to expand came to a head in the late 1890s, when the United States declared war on Spain and invaded the Philippines, Puerto Rico, and Cuba. From 1895, Cuban patriots had slowly pushed back Spanish troops and had begun to occupy sugar plantations—some of which belonged to American planters. Concerned about the specter of social revolution off the shores of Florida, the American expansionists presented themselves as the saviors of Spanish colonials yearning for freedom, while at the same time safeguarding property for foreign interests in the Spanish-American War (1898). After easily defeating Spanish regulars in Cuba, American forces began disarming Cuban rebels and returning lands to their owners.

Although the Americans had claimed that they were intervening to promote freedom in Spain's colonies, they quickly forgot their promises. The United States quietly annexed Puerto Rico after minimal resistance. Cubans and Filipinos met American plans to make them into colonial subjects with insurrection. Bitterness ran particularly high among Filipinos, who had been promised independence by American leaders if they joined in the war against Spain. Betrayed, Filipino rebels launched a war for independence in the name of a Filipino nation. In two years of fighting, over 5,000 Americans and perhaps 200,000 Filipinos perished.

Colonies in the Philippines and Cuba laid the foundations for a revised model of twentieth-century U.S. expansionism. The earlier pattern had been to turn Indian lands into privately owned farmsteads and to expand the reach of the Atlantic market across the continent. This now yielded to a new era in which the nation's largest corporations, supported by the enlarged power of the American national government, aggressively intervened in the affairs of near and distant neighbors. Following the Spanish-American War, the United States repeatedly sent troops to many Caribbean and Central American countries. The Americans preferred to make these regimes into dependent client states, however, rather than making them part of the United States itself, as was done

Uncle Sam Leading Cuba. In the years before the Spanish-American War, cartoonists who wished to see the United States intervene on behalf of Cuba in the islanders' struggle for independence from Spain typically depicted Cuba as a white woman in distress. By contrast, in this and other cartoons following the Spanish-American War, Cubans were drawn as black, and usually as infants or boys unable to care for themselves and in need of the benevolent paternal rule of the United States.

"That wicked man is going to gobble you up, my child!"

with Alaska and Hawaii, or converting them into formal colonies, as the Europeans had done in Africa and Asia.

IMPERIALISM AND CULTURE

There has been a vigorous debate, of late, about the extent to which overseas empires transformed European and North American culture as a whole. Some historians believe that empire redefined the identities of westerners; others argue that while the ruling of empires changed the lives of those most directly involved (colonial officials, merchants, and soldiers, for example), its effects on the wider population were not so great. Both sides agree that imperialism did change European consumption patterns and introduced new content into familiar media. In literature and painting, for example, a genre known as *Orientalism* flourished, in which nonwestern peoples were portrayed as exotic, sensuous, and economically backward with respect to Europeans. It is quite clear that imperialism gave new legitimacy to ideas of European and American racial superiority—and such ideas, in turn, also helped make imperialism seem natural and even just. But empire did not affect, or interest, all Europeans equally. Many Britons were probably proud to see Queen Victoria crowned Empress of India in 1877; but it was only in 1916 that "Empire Day" was officially declared a British holiday. Before the Great War broke out in 1914, there were many who opposed the idea of celebrating empire as jingoistic (that is, blindly patriotic). In general, we might say that the extension and upkeep of colonies directly involved only a small minority of Europeans, which made the impact of those few all the more remarkable.

At least since the Crusades, Europeans had regularly written and thought about others. These images and ideas had been used to inform, entertain, flatter, and criticize European culture and practices, and they continued to have a diverse set of motivations and functions right through the nineteenth century. What was novel in this period was the brute fact that these "others" had now been brought under European control; somehow this seemed to solidify their status as "lower" races. Europe's relationship to them might be one of condescending sympathy or of hard-nosed, Darwinian exploitation but in no sense were the two parties equal. The strong sense that a cultural gradient ran from west to east and from north to south allowed Europeans to put Africans in native costumes on display at the Paris World's Fair of 1889, alongside the "gallery of machines" which represented European cultural progress. Working on the same assumption, European scholars worked hard to refine their expertise in "oriental" languages, believing indigenous peoples could not do justice to their own great texts. Some of these Europeans were probably too wrapped up in their own lives and career prospects to think much about the actual conquering of peoples, and some people—including free-traders and socialists—actively

The Women of Algiers in Their Apartment. An oil painting by Eugene Delacroix (1798–1863) of Algerian women being attended by a black servant. European painters in the nineteenth century often used images of women to portray Arab Muslim society.

to fill the sparsely settled regions around the globe, the population of other nations would. Population was power, and the number of children provided an accurate measure of global influence. But the concern was not just for children, but particularly for healthy children. Wars in the colonies exemplified the need for an abundant and healthy soldiery. "Empire cannot be built on rickety and flat-chested citizens," warned a British member of Parliament in 1905. Another British ideologue touted the German example of patriotic mothers nurturing "a land devoted to the three Ks—*Kinder, Küche, Kirche* [Children, Kitchen, and Church]." Thus did the desire for healthy bodies also entail the idealization of domesticity as women's destiny and duty. Those who wrote for more popular, and especially juvenile, audiences often invoked colonial settings and themes. Where girls' literature stressed domestic service, childrearing, and nurturing, boys' readings described exotic locales, depicted devious Orientals and savage Africans, and extolled daring colonial exploits. No one evoked this notion of empire as boyish adventure better than Rudyard Kipling (1865–1936) in his immensely popular novels and short stories. Born in India, Kipling was dispatched to an English boarding school at a young age. Compared with his carefree childhood in India, the public school provided a dreary, regimented experience, and it furnished him with an enduring subject matter—the interaction

opposed new conquests. But for many, European dominance was simply a fact.

Especially in middle- and upper-class circles, Europeans did celebrate imperial triumphs. Once the invention of photographic film and the appearance of the Eastman Kodak camera in 1888 revolutionized the visual media, imperial images surfaced routinely in popular forms such as postcards and advertisements. Europeans abroad used their cameras to record imperial achievements in transport, engineering, and architecture, to portray as if typical contented colonial subjects, and to commemorate visits by royal figures. Imperial themes and myths were widely used in packaging materials, and tins of coffee, tea, tobacco, and chocolates featured pictures that highlighted the colonial origins of these commodities. Cigarettes often had names like "Admiral," "Royal Navy," "Fighter," and "Grand Fleet." Of course, some of this was in one way or another propaganda, produced by investors in imperial commodities or by colonial pressure groups like the British Empire League or the Deutsche Kolonial Gesellschaft.

Propaganda touted imperialism abroad but was also tied to changes taking place at home. Champions of empire argued that if the British population did not grow fast enough

The first step towards lightening

The White Man's Burden

is through teaching the virtues of cleanliness.

Pears' Soap

is a potent factor in brightening the dark corners of the earth as civilization advances, while amongst the cultured of all nations it holds th[e]

The Civilizing Mission. This advertisement for Pears' Soap shamelessly tapped into the idea of Europeans bringing civilization to the people of their colonies. It said that use of Pears' Soap would teach the virtues of cleanliness to the "natives" and implied that it would even lighten their skin.

between youth and unpleasant authority. His most popular novel, *Kim* (1901), described the life of a thirteen-year-old Irish boy, Kim, who goes "native" and then participates in a wondrous "Great Game," a spy adventure pitting the British against the Russians over central Asia.

JAPAN, RUSSIA, AND CHINA

> → *How did expansionism affect Japan, Russia, and China?*

The challenge of integrating political communities and extending territorial borders was a problem not just for the nations of western Europe and the United States. Other societies also aimed to overcome domestic dissent and to extend their command over larger domains. Japan, Russia, and China provide three contrasting models of expansionism; their differing forms of expansion led these societies to converge on—and eventually fight over—East Asian possessions.

JAPANESE TRANSFORMATION AND EXPANSION

Starting in the 1860s, Japanese rulers sought to recast their country to look less like an old dynasty and more like a modern nation-state. Since the early seventeenth century, the Tokugawa Shogunate had kept outsiders within strict limits and thwarted internal unrest. But an American officer, Com-

modore Matthew Perry (1794–1858), entered Edo Bay in 1853, leading a fleet of steam-powered ships. Other Americans, Russians, Dutch, and British followed and forced the Tokugawa rulers to sign humiliating treaties, which opened Japanese ports, slapped limits on Japanese tariffs, and exempted foreigners from Japanese laws. Younger Japanese, especially among the military (samurai) elites, felt that Japan should respond by adopting, not rejecting, western practices. In 1868, a group of these reformers toppled the Tokugawa Shogunate and promised to return Japan to its mythic greatness. When they forced the shogun to resign, Emperor Mutsuhito, known as the Meiji Emperor ("Enlightened Rule"), became the symbol of a new Japan. His reign, from 1868 to 1912, was referred to as the Meiji Restoration. By founding schools, initiating an active propaganda campaign, and revamping the army to create a single "national" fighting force, the new government put forward a new model of political community. The new nationalists stressed linguistic and ethnic homogeneity—as well as superiority compared to others. In this fashion, the Meiji leaders overcame age-old regional divisions, subdued local political magnates, and mobilized the country to face the threat of the powerful Europeans.

One of the Meiji period's remarkable achievements was the economic transformation of the island. In 1871, the government banned the feudal system and allowed peasants to become small landowners. Farmers subsequently improved their agrarian techniques and saw their standard of living rise. Some business practices that underlay the economic transformation had taken shape under the shogunate, but the new government was far more activist. Under the slogan "rich country, strong army," it unified the currency around the yen, created a postal system, introduced tax reforms, laid telegraph lines, formed compulsory foreign trade associations, launched savings and export campaigns, established an advanced civil

Perry Arrives in Japan. A Japanese woodblock print portraying the uninvited arrival into Edo (Tokyo) Bay on August 7, 1853, of a tall American ship, which was commanded by Matthew Perry. This arrival marked the end of Japan's ability to fully control the terms of its interactions with foreigners.

Economic Transformation of Japan. During the Meiji period, the government transformed the economy by building railroads, laying telegraph lines, founding a postal system, and encouraging the formation of giant firms known as *zaibatsu*, which were family organizations consisting of factories, import-export businesses, and banks. Here we see a raw-silk reeling factory that was run by one of the *zaibatsu*.

service system, began to build railroads, and hired thousands of foreign consultants. In 1889, the Meiji oligarchs introduced a constitution, based largely on the German model. The following year, 450,000 people—about 1 percent of the population—elected Japan's first parliament, the Imperial Diet.

The government sold valuable enterprises to the people it knew best, creating private economic dynasties. Of the country's powerhouse family-holding companies such as Sumitomo, Yasuda, Mitsubishi, and Mitsui, only the last pre-dated 1868. The new giant firms were family organizations. Fathers, sons, cousins, and uncles participated, running different parts of large integrated corporations—some in charge of banks, some running the trade wing, and others overseeing factories. Women played a crucial role—not just as custodians of the home, but as cultivators of important family alliances, especially among potential marriage partners. In contrast to American limited-liability firms, which issued shares on stock markets to anonymous buyers, Japan's version of managerial capitalism was a personal and family affair.

As in many other emerging nation-states, expansion in Japan was a tempting prospect. It offered markets in which to sell goods and procure staples and offered a means to burnish the image of national superiority and greatness. Japanese ventures abroad were initially spectacularly successful. The Meiji moved first to take over the kingdom of the Ryūkyūs, located southwest of Japan (see Map 17-5). A small

show of force, only 160 Japanese soldiers, was enough to establish the new Okinawa Prefecture in 1879. The Japanese regarded the people of the Ryūkyūs as an ethnic minority and refused to incorporate them into the nation-state on equal terms. In contrast with the British in India or the Americans in Puerto Rico, the Japanese conquerors refused to train a native governing class. Meiji intellectuals insisted that the "backward" Okinawans were unfit for local self-rule and representation.

In 1876, the Japanese turned to the Asian mainland and fixed upon Korea, which put Meiji plans on a collision course with what the Chinese considered their sphere of influence. In a formal treaty, the Japanese recognized Korea as an independent state, opened Korea to trade, and were given extra-territorial rights, which allowed them to operate abroad under the laws of their home countries. The Chinese worried that soon the Japanese would try to take over Korea. These fears were well founded, for nationalist Japanese leaders regarded the peninsula, in the words of one of their German advisers, as "a dagger pointed at the heart of Japan." Japanese designs on Korea eventually brought on the Sino-Japanese War of 1894–1895 in which the Chinese suffered a humiliating defeat.

The Sino-Japanese War accelerated Japan's rapid transformation to a nation-state and colonial power with no peer in Asia. China lost the war and was forced to cede the province of Taiwan to the Japanese. Japan also annexed Korea

Japanese Empire, 1870

Japanese acquisition, 1874–1895

← Japanese attacks in Sino-Japanese War, 1894–1895

← Japanese attacks in Russo-Japanese War, 1904–1905

Japanese acquisition, 1905–1910

MAP 17-5 JAPANESE EXPANSION, 1870–1910

Under the Meiji Restoration, the Japanese state aimed to forge a strong national identity and compete with foreign powers for imperial advantage in East Asia. According to the map, was there a "logic" to the process of Japanese expansionism, and at whose expense was it directed? What were the new Japanese state's objectives? How were they similar to or different from European expansionism of the same period?

in 1910 and converted Taiwan and Korea into the twin jewels of its nascent empire. The colonial administration built transportation networks and created educational and health institutions to develop its colonies—while still keeping the colonized from top managerial and technical positions. Like the British in India, the Japanese regarded the peoples they had colonized as racially inferior and unworthy of the privileges of citizenship. Like other imperial powers of the day, the Japanese expected their possessions to serve the economic interests of the metropolitan center. Japan, densely populated and short of land, wished these colonies to become granaries, sending rice to the mother country. Moreover, the Meiji regime further exploited Taiwanese sugar exports, which provided relief for a Japanese economy heavily dependent on imports. Indeed, Korean and Taiwanese farmers exported their produce to the rest of Asia, especially China. These staple-exporting regions thereby provided Japan with a source of foreign exchange to help defray its trade deficits, incurred as a result of massive imports to build up new industries.

RUSSIAN TRANSFORMATION AND EXPANSION

Russia embarked as well on expansion in the late nineteenth century, out of a sense of mission and as a defensive response to the expansion of countries along its immense border. An emerging Germany, British presence in the Middle East and Persia, a consolidating China, and an ascendant Japan meant that Russia, too, would have to enlarge its domain. What is remarkable is how many expansionist fronts Russia opened simultaneously. Russians went southwest to the Black Sea, south into the Caucasus and Turkestan, and east into Manchuria (see Map 17-6). Success depended on adopting techniques akin to those used on the American frontier: annexing territories as provinces and establishing protectorates over the vulnerable peoples it conquered.

Looking to expand to the west and the south, Russia invaded the Ottoman territories of Moldavia (present-day Moldova) and Walachia (present-day Romania) in 1853. The invasion provoked opposition from Britain and France, who joined with the Ottomans to defeat Russia in the Crimean War (1853–1856). The defeat exposed Russia's military weaknesses, including a lack of modern weapons and problems supplying troops over long distances without a railway system.

Russia's defeat in the Crimean War had a similar, yet even more immediate, effect than that of Commodore Perry's 1853 intrusion into Japan: it spurred the authorities on a course of aggressive modernization and expansion. In the 1860s, Tsar Alexander II (ruled 1855–1881) launched a wave of "Great Reforms." These were designed to make Russia more competitive without going too far politically. Autocratic rule remained, but officials revamped and reintegrated the society they oversaw. In 1861, a decree emancipated peasants from serfdom. Landowners kept the most fertile land, however, and the peasants had to pay large redemption taxes for the poor-quality land they received. Other changes included a reduction in military service from twenty-five years to six, education for the conscripts, and the beginnings of a mass school system to teach children reading, writing, and Russian culture. Beginning in the 1890s, railroads spread and factories expanded, as did the steel, coal, and petroleum industries. Peasants who could not make ends meet often wound up working in the newly built factories or in the mines.

The reforms revealed a fundamental problem: officials were more interested in reforming society than in reforming government. This caused many—liberals, conservatives, and malcontents alike—to question the state-led modernizing mission. In the press, courtrooms, and streets, men and women denounced the regime. Revolutionaries, forbidden from forming legal political parties, engaged in terror and assassination. In 1881, a terrorist bomb blew the tsar to pieces. In the 1890s, following yet another period of famine, the radical doctrines of Marxism gained popularity in Russia. Even aristocratic intellectuals, such as the author of *War and Peace* Count Leo Tolstoy, lamented their despotic government.

Yet, the shortcomings of internal reform did not interfere with the ambitions—and achievements—of Russian expansionists. The Russian expansionists believed that they had to take over certain lands to prevent them from falling into the hands of rivals. Thus, for example, they conquered the highland people of the Caucasus Mountains to prevent the Ottomans and Persians from taking over this area on Russia's southern flank. They butted heads with the British over the areas between Turkestan and British India, such as Persia (Iran) and Afghanistan, in a competition known as "The Great Game." While Russians moved to the lands they had conquered, however, they never made up the majority there. The new provinces still consisted of multiethnic and multireligious communities that were only partially integrated into the Russian state.

Perhaps the most impressive Russian expansion transpired in East Asia. Here Russian ambitions came into conflict with the Chinese, who had also sought to occupy and colonize the vast, underpopulated area of the Amur River basin (just north of Manchuria, with rich lands, mineral deposits, and access to the Pacific Ocean). After wrestling with the Chinese between 1840 and 1860, the Russians eventually acquired land north and south of the Amur River and in 1860 founded Vladivostok, a port on the Pacific Ocean. Deciding to put its money and efforts into exploiting these areas in Asia, the Russian government sold Alaska, its only overseas possession, to the United States (for $7.2 million) in 1867 and thus no longer had to overextend itself to govern and defend this territory in North America. To link the capital (Moscow) and the western part of the country to its East Asian spoils, it began construction of the Trans-Siberian Rail-

MAP 17-6   RUSSIAN EXPANSION, 1801–1914

The Russian state continued to expand territorially in the nineteenth century. Compare this map on Russian expansion with Map 13-7 (p. 588). Did the direction of territorial acquisition of the expanded Russian empire change in the nineteenth century? How did the Russian state treat the people of newly acquired territories? Who did Russian expansionism resemble more in this era, western European states (such as Great Britain) or American states (such as the United States)?

road. When it was completed in 1903, after thirteen years of hard labor, the new railroad created an overland bridge between the east and the west. Russia then began to eye the Korean peninsula, on which Japan, too, had set its sights.

Russia was a huge empire—one-sixth of the world's landmass—and its rulers were only partially effective at integrating its disparate parts into a political community. In 1897, the Russian government took its first complete population census. Ethnographers and political authorities struggled to figure out what to call and how to classify all of the peoples inhabiting the empire. Should they be considered as nations or tribes? In the end, the census opted for the term *nationalities*, recognizing 104 of them, speaking 146 languages and dialects. Ethnic Russians accounted for slightly more than half the population.

Counting and categorizing peoples formed part of the state's attempts to figure out how to govern this diverse realm. Russia did not follow Britain's policy in India, that is, creating a small but efficient bureaucracy and imposing law through a trained native elite. Rather, as in the United States, conquered regions were made full parts of the empire. But unlike the United States, Russia was suspicious of decentralized federalism, fearing that this would lead to secession. Moreover, Russia's tsars were terrified by the idea of popular sovereignty. They preferred the tried-and-true method of centralized autocracy. With the exceptions of two protectorates, Bukhara and Khiva, and the Grand Duchy of Finland, no province enjoyed self-rule. The rest of the empire was divided into governorships ruled by appointed civilian or military governors who had varying powers.

The Trans-Siberian Railroad. Russia's decision to build a railway across Siberia to the Pacific Ocean derived from a desire to expand the empire's power in East Asia and to forestall British advances in Asia. The colossal undertaking, which claimed the lives of thousands of workers, reached completion just as Russia clashed militarily with Japan. The new railroad ferried Russian troops over long distances to battles, such as the one at Mukden, in Manchuria, which was then the largest land battle in the history of warfare and observed by military attachés from all the great powers.

Unlike the other transcontinental nation-empire, the United States, which displaced or slaughtered native populations during expansion, Russia faced a more daunting task of assimilating new peoples. State treatment of the empire's peoples was inconsistent, ranging from outright repression (Poles, Jews) to favoritism (Baltic Germans, Finns). In the western regions, linguistic Russification programs provoked opposition from those upon whom it was applied. In the south and east, Russians built cities and garrisons alongside the indigenous towns, leaving the local elites in place and coaxing them to cooperate with the central state. But this, too, had its limitations. Further, unlike the United States, which managed to pacify its borders with its weaker neighbors, Russia faced the constant suspicions of Persians and Ottomans and the menace of British troops in Afghanistan that were sent to prevent Russia from cutting off the overland route to India. In East Asia, a clash with expansionist Japan loomed on the horizon. Russia's expansionism meant that defending its borders was a constant fiscal drain and a heavy burden on the population. To promote the image of a great Russian Empire, rulers had to lean more heavily on the rural poor and to pursue more intensive modernization strategies, but all that generated instability. For the time being, however, the main threat, as far as Moscow was concerned, did not come from within Russia's borders. It came from the outside.

CHINA UNDER PRESSURE

While the Russians and Japanese scrambled to emulate European models of industrialism and imperialism, the Qing, in the wake of China's territorial expansion in the eighteenth century (see Chapter 15), were slower to mobilize against threats from the west. For a long time, the Chinese were not inclined to see the Europeans as serious threats. Historically, they were much more worried about internal revolts and overland threats from the dynasty's northern borders. This is why the Treaty of Nanjing's stipulations (following the Opium War of 1839–1842) calling for indemnities, the opening of a few extra ports, including Shanghai, and the cession of the sparsely populated island of Hong Kong to the British seemed a small price to pay to satisfy the demands of these lesser aggressors. Into the 1850s and 1860s, the dynasts continued to be more concerned with dissenters from within, such as the Taiping Rebellion (1851–1864; see Chapter 16). Many Qing officials still considered foreigners a minor—if noisy—nuisance.

A growing number of officials, however, recognized the superior armaments and technology of rival powers. Starting in the 1860s, reformist Chinese bureaucrats sought to adopt elements of western learning and technological skills but with the intention of keeping the core of Chinese culture intact. Collectively known as the Self-Strengthening movement, these measures included a variety of new ventures: arsenals, shipyards, coal mines, a steamship company to contest the foreign domination of coastal shipping, and schools for learning foreign ways and languages. The most interesting was the dispatch abroad of about 120 schoolboys under the charge of Yung Wing. Yung, having graduated from Yale University in 1854, was the first Chinese graduate of an American college and believed that western education would greatly benefit Chinese students. Yung took his charges to Hartford, Connecticut, in the 1870s to attend school and live with American families. In 1881, after the U.S. government refused to admit the boys into military academies, conservatives at the Qing court, dismayed by the travelers' liking for Christianity and aptitude for baseball, summoned the students home.

Yung Wing's abortive educational mission was not the only setback for the Self-Strengthening movement. Skepticism

TWO FACES OF EMPIRE

Russification (forced assimilation) became one of the Russian Empire's responses to the challenge of the nation-state idea. In 1863, the tsar prohibited publication of the Bible in the Little Russian (Ukrainian) language, alienating many otherwise loyal Slavic subjects. By contrast, most non-Christians, such as the Muslim peoples of newly annexed Turkestan (central Asia), were exempted from Russification as they were considered "aliens" who should be ruled separately. Here, the bureaucracy prohibits use of Ukrainian in an 1876 Russification edict, while G. P. Fedorov of the Russian governor-general's office in Turkestan celebrates colonialism.

Russification in Ukraine

In order to halt what is, from the state's point of view, the dangerous activity of the Ukrainophiles, it is appropriate to take the following measures immediately: 1. To prohibit the import into the empire of any books published abroad in the Little Russian dialect [Ukrainian], without the special permission of the Chief Press Administration. 2. To prohibit the printing inside of the empire of any original works or translations in this dialect, with the exception of historical documents. . . . 3. Equally to prohibit any dramatic productions, musical lyrics and public lectures (which at present have the charter of Ukrainophile demonstrations) in this dialect. 4. To support the publication in Galicia of the newspaper *Slovo*, hostile to Ukrainophilism, assigning it a small but permanent subsidy. . . . 6. To strengthen supervision by the local educational administration so as not to allow any subjects in primary schools be taught in the Little Russian dialect. . . . 7. To clear the libraries of all primary and secondary schools in the Little Russian provinces of books and pamphlets prohibited by paragraph 2. . . . 8. . . . To demand from the heads of these districts a list of teachers with a note as to their reliability in relation to Ukrainophile tendencies. Those noted as unreliable or doubtful should be transferred to Great Russian provinces. . . .

Colonialism in Turkestan

Our battalion arrived in Tashkent four years after Turkestan had been annexed to the empire. Tashkent at that time looked more like a military settlement than the chief city of the region, that is the capital of Russian Central Asia. The majority of the inhabitants were soldiers, either resting after some campaign or else about to go out on a new expedition. Civilians and women were a rarity. Now, thirty-six years later, looking proudly at the path we have followed, I can see the colossal results achieved by the Russian government, always humane to the vanquished, but insistently pursuing its civilising mission. Of course, there have been many mistakes, there have been abuses, but this has not halted the rational and expedient intentions of the government. We went into a region which had a population alien to us. . . . They had for many centuries been accustomed to submitting humbly to the barbaric and cruel despotism of their rulers, but they nevertheless came to terms with their position because their rulers were of their own faith. . . . The fanatical mullahs began rumours amongst the mass of the population that, instead of true believer khans, they were to be ruled by heathens who would convert them to Christianity, put crosses around their necks, send them to be soldiers, introduce their own laws, revoke the Sharia [the fundamental law of Islam] and make their wives and daughters uncover their faces.

. . . Frequent outbursts, uprisings and disorders took place and repression followed. But at the same time the natives saw that the very first steps of the first Governor-General proved the complete falseness of the mullahs. . . . It was announced solemnly everywhere to the local population, that as subjects of the Russian monarch, the population would keep its faith, its national customs, its courts and its judges, that all taxes demanded by the previous collectors were illegal and burdensome in the extreme and would be revoked, and that instead just taxes would be imposed, and that the position of women would remain inviolable. All this of course soon calmed the population and an industrious people settled down to a peaceful life.

→ *Of which document and which country do the arguments of the Muslim mullahs remind you?*

→ *Why do you think Russification was not imposed on the aliens?*

SOURCE: Martin McCauley and Peter Waldron, *The Emergence of the Modern Russian State, 1855–1881* (Totowa, NJ: Barnes and Noble Books, 1988), pp. 209, 211–12.

about the wisdom of appropriating western technology was rife among conservative officials. Some insisted that the introduction of machinery would lead to unemployment. Even more adamant was the opposition to the construction of railways. Detractors maintained railways would simply facilitate western military maneuvers and lead to an invasion of the country. Others complained that the crisscrossing tracks were an affront to aesthetic sensibilities and disturbed the harmony between humans and nature. The first short railway track ever laid in China was torn up in 1877 shortly after it was built. Indeed, there were a mere 288 kilometers of track in China prior to 1895, less than a tenth of the total boasted by the small island nation of Japan.

Even without the railways, however, the Chinese were on the move. The population explosion of the previous centuries and the increasing shortage of arable land forced many to head to the frontier areas, such as Manchuria or Southeast Asia and beyond. In some cases these migrations facilitated the further consolidation of the polity. For example, the northwestern region of Xinjiang, which had been incorporated into the Qing Empire in the eighteenth century, became a full-fledged province in 1884. Similarly, Taiwan, soon to be lost to Japan, earned provincial status the following year.

Although they did not acknowledge the usefulness of the railroad, the Chinese did take advantage of other new technologies to gain access to a wider range of information more quickly than ever before. That was particularly true for those residing in the coastal cities. By the early 1890s, there were about a dozen Chinese-language newspapers (as distinct from the foreign-language press) published in the major cities, with the largest ones based in Shanghai and having a circulation of 10,000 to 15,000 each. To avoid government intervention, these papers were careful to sidestep political controversy. Instead, they emphasized commercial news and often accepted literary contributions. In 1882, *Shenbao*, the newspaper with perhaps the largest circulation, made use of a new telegraph line to publish dispatches within China.

China's defeat by Japan in the Sino-Japanese War (1894–1895), sparked by quarreling over Korea, provided the impetus for the first serious attempt at comprehensive reform by the Qing. Known as the Hundred Days' Reform, the episode lasted only from June to September 1898. The force behind it was a thirty-seven-year-old scholar named Kang Youwei (1858–1927) and his twenty-two-year-old student Liang Qichao (1873–1929). The reformers argued that the Qing needed to go much beyond the Self-Strengthening movement. Citing rulers such as Peter the Great of Russia and the Meiji Emperor of Japan as their inspiration, the reformers urged Chinese leaders to develop a railway network, a state banking system, a modern postal service, and institutions to foster the development of agriculture, industry, and commerce.

Chronology

	1830		
THE AMERICAS			▮ *U.S. Civil War, 1861–1865* *Canada gains self-rule, 1867* ▮ *Russia sells Alaska to the U.S., 1867* ▮
EUROPE			▮ *Publication of Darwin's* Origin of Specie *Franco-Prussian War, 1870–1871* ▮
RUSSIA			▮ *Crimean War, 1853–1856* ▮ *"Great Reforms" to modernize Russia,*
EAST AND SOUTHEAST ASIA			▮ *Commodore Perry "opens" Japan, 1853* *Self-Strengthening movement (China), 1860s–1890s* ▮ *Meiji Era in Japan, 1868–1912* ▮ *French occupation of Vietnam, Cambodia, and Laos, 1860s–1890s* ▮ *Japan takes over Ryūkyūs, 1872* ▮ *British expansion in Southeast Asia, 1870s–1880s* ▮
AFRICA			*Opening of Suez Canal, 1869* ▮
SOUTH ASIA			▮ *"The Raj" begins in India, 1858*

If reformers wanted to accelerate change, their opportunity came in the summer of 1898 when the twenty-seven-year-old Guangxu Emperor decided to put into practice many of their ideas, including changes in the venerable civil service examination system. But the effort was short-lived. Conservative officials rallied behind Guangxu's aunt, the Empress Dowager Cixi, who emerged from retirement to overturn the reforms. The young emperor was put under house arrest. Kang and Liang fled for their lives and went into exile.

The reforms of the Self-Strengthening movement were too modest, and they were poorly implemented. Very few Chinese acquired new skills. Despite talk of modernizing, the civil service examination was still based on the Confucian classics and still opened the only doors to governmental service. The official governing elites were not yet ready to reinvent the principles of their political community, and they adhered instead to the traditional dynastic structure.

CONCLUSION

Between 1850 and 1914, the majority of the world's people lived not in nation-states but in landed empires—the Ottoman, Habsburg, Russian, and Chinese—or in the colonies of nation-states, as in Africa, the Middle East, and South and Southeast Asia. But as many rulers and reformers around the world sought a new political framework to meet the crises of authority created by popular upheavals and economic transformations, the nation-state became an increasingly desirable form of governance. Strengthening state power went hand in hand with widening sovereignty and reordering the polity around the "nation."

The new ideal of "a people" united by territory, history, and culture was a fiction (an "imagined" reality) that was becoming increasingly powerful and popular around the world. Deepening and extending this imagined reality was a difficult matter. Official histories, national heroes, novels, poetry, and music helped, but central to the process of nation formation were the actions of bureaucrats. Asserting sovereignty over what it claimed as national territory, the state sought to "nationalize" diverse populations by creating a unified system of law, education, military service, and government. Toward the end of the nineteenth century, such projects of nation building created strong states with greater capacities to act upon their subjects and to seize new territories.

Colonization beyond borders was an integral part of nation building in many societies. States sought to establish the nation by undertaking territorial conquests, which they touted as nationalist endeavors. In Europe, the Americas, Japan, and, to some extent, Russia, the intertwined processes of nation building and territorial aggrandizement were most

1900

▪ *Brazil abolishes slavery, 1888*

▪ *Spanish-American War, 1898*

▪ *Construction of the Eiffel Tower, 1887–1889*

▪ *Russia constructs Trans-Siberian Railroad, 1891–1903*

▪ *Sino-Japanese War, 1894–1895*   ▪ *Japan annexes Korea, 1910*

▪ *British occupy Egypt, 1882*
▪ *Berlin Conference on Africa, 1884–1885*

▪ *Victoria crowned empress of India, 1877*

effective. The Amazon, Okinawa, and most especially the North American West became important provinces of integrated nation-states, populated with settlers and producing for national and international markets. By the end of the nineteenth century, the world saw the emergence of three great states, which a century earlier had played only bit parts on the world stage: the United States, Germany, and Japan. Russia, too, emerged as a world power—if standing on a less firm foundation.

It should be said, however, that these emerging nations did not wipe out local differences. Provincial differences in the new Germany remained marked, so much so that the state nearly splintered again after the Great War. Nor were class antagonisms or gender inequalities wiped away by nationalist propagandists. The identities of the colonizers, like those of the colonized, were undergoing transformation, as economic and political power was concentrated more and more in the hands of the former. All too often, Europeans and Americans came to see themselves as chosen, collectively, by God or by natural selection, to rule the rest. But there were also deep divisions within America—between northerners and southerners, for example—and within Europe as well, and it is very likely that the essential self-conceptions of most inhabitants of these regions remained local (Philadelphians; Parisians) or linked to employment (peasant; professor). Not everyone identified with the nation-state or the empire—or shared the same definition of what it meant to belong or to conquer. But by the century's end, a rapidly expanding cadre of racist ideologues and colonial lobbyists seems to have convinced many that their interests and their destinies were bound up with their nations' unity, prosperity, and global clout.

The drive to found nation-states and subordinate colonies provided an effective catalyst for integrating the global economy. More regions of the world became industrialized, and capital, labor, and commodities moved across the world more rapidly and in greater numbers than ever before. Nonetheless, capital, labor, and commodities were described in national terms—British capital, Chinese labor, German goods—and the system of imperial nation-states structured their movement. Thus, Indian laborers migrated to British possessions in Africa and the Caribbean; Britain used colonial control to fend off Japanese and German competition; and colonized and semicolonized territories became suppliers of raw materials for the North Atlantic imperial nation-states. The political division of the world into imperial nation-states and colonial outposts shaped the economic division of the world into industrialized and nonindustrialized societies.

One of the great ironies of this age was the unintended consequence of nation building for societies that were also embarking on external expansion. The purported new openness and opportunities of national and even colonial cultures bred discontents. Self-determination could also apply to racial or ethnic minorities both at home and in the colonies.

Armed with the rhetoric of progress and uplift, colonial authorities sought to subjugate distant people. But as the gap between rhetoric and rule yawned ever wider, colonial subjects embraced the language of the nation and accused imperial overlords of betraying their own lofty principles. As the twentieth century opened, Filipino and Cuban rebels used Thomas Jefferson's Declaration of Independence to oppose American invaders, Koreans defined themselves as a nation crushed under Japanese heels, and Indian nationalists made colonial governors feel shame for violating their own conceits about English "fair play."

STUDY QUESTIONS

 WWNORTON.COM/STUDYSPACE

1. Explain the process of nation building that occurred in the nineteenth century. Who initiated these efforts and what strategies were involved?
2. Locate where strong nation-states emerged during the nineteenth century. How did the nation-state idea challenge certain polities and other organized groups during this era?
3. Define imperialism. Why did state-directed efforts at nation building often lead to imperialism efforts and other forms of territorial expansion?
4. List and explain several major sources of the new wave of imperialism that occurred in the second half of the nineteenth century. To what extent were these ideas supported among the population of imperialist states?
5. Analyze to what extent colonized societies around the world resisted imperialist efforts. How successful were their actions?
6. Describe the policies that imperial powers used to govern overseas colonies during this era. What were the goals of imperial administrations and how successful were they in achieving them?
7. Analyze the cultural impact of imperialist ambitions on imperialist nations. How did colonization and territorial expansion shape notions of race, ethnicity, and gender?
8. Analyze how the spread of nationalism and imperialism shaped state behavior in China, Russia, and Japan. To what extent did each state adapt to these new patterns?
9. Explain how nation-state building, territorial expansion, and imperialism reshaped the global economy. How would you describe the relationship between industrial regions and the rest of the world's societies?

FURTHER READINGS

Cain, P. A., and A. G. Hopkins, *British Imperialism: Innovation and Expansion, 1688–1914* (1993). An excellent discussion of British imperialism, especially British expansion into Africa.

Cronon, William, *Nature's Metropolis: Chicago and the Great West* (1991). Makes connections among territorial expansion, industrialization, and urban development.

Davis, John, *Conflict and Control: Law and Order in Nineteenth-Century Italy* (1988). A superb study of the north-south and other rifts after Italian political unification.

Friesen, Gerald, *The Canadian Prairies* (1984). The most comprehensive account of Canadian westward expansion.

Gluck, Carol, *Japan's Modern Myths: Ideology in the Late Meiji Period* (1985). A study of how states fashion useful historical traditions to consolidate and legitimize their rule.

Headrick, Daniel R., *The Tools of Empire: Technology and European Imperialism in the Nineteenth Century* (1981). A useful general study of the relationship between imperialism and technology.

Hine, Robert V., and John Mack Faragher, *The American West: A New Interpretive History* (2000). Presents an excellent synthesis of the conquests by which the United States expanded from the Atlantic to the Pacific.

Hobsbawm, Eric J., *Nations and Nationalism since 1780: Programme, Myth, Reality* (1993). The most insightful recent survey of the origins and development of nationalist thought throughout Europe.

Lee, Leo Ou-fan, and Andrew Nathan, "The Beginnings of Mass Culture: Journalism and Fiction in the Late Ch'ing and Beyond," in David Johnson, Andrew Nathan, and Evelyn Rawski (eds.), *Popular Culture in Late Imperial China* (1985), pp. 360–95. An important article on the emergence of a mass-media market in late-nineteenth- and early-twentieth-century China.

Lieven, Dominic, *Empire: The Russian Empire and Its Rivals* (2000). A comparison of the British, Ottoman, Habsburg, and Russian empires.

Mackenzie, John M., *Propaganda and Empire* (1984). Contains a series of useful chapters showing the importance of the empire to Britain.

McClintock, Anne, *Imperial Leather: Race, Gender and Sexuality in the Colonial Contest* (1995). A study of the imperial relationship between Victorian Britain and South Africa from the point of view of cultural studies.

McNeil, William, *Europe's Steppe Frontier: 1500–1800* (1964). An excellent study of the definitive victory of Russia's agricultural empire over grazing nomads and independent frontier people.

Montgomery, David, *The Fall of the House of Labor: The Workplace, the State, and American Labor Activism, 1865–1925* (1987). An excellent discussion of changes in work in the late nineteenth century.

Myers, Ramon, and Mark Peattie (eds.), *The Japanese Colonial Empire, 1895–1945* (1984). A collection of essays exploring different aspects of Japanese colonialism.

Needell, Jeffrey, *A Tropical Belle Epoque: Elite Culture and Society in Turn of the Century Rio de Janeiro* (1987). Shows the strength of the Brazilian elites at the turn of the century.

Pan, Lynn (ed.), *The Encyclopedia of Chinese Overseas* (1999). A comprehensive coverage of the history of the Chinese diaspora.

Porter, Bernard, *The Absent-Minded Imperialists: What the British Really Thought about Empire* (2004). A careful dissection of the ways in which empire changed the British—and did not.

Sperber, Jonathan, *The European Revolutions, 1848–1851* (1994). A survey of the movements that led to revolutions between 1848 and 1851, and the course of events that ensued across Europe.

Topik, Steven, *The Political Economy of the Brazilian State, 1889–1930* (1987). An excellent discussion of the Brazilian state, and especially of its elites.

Walker, Mack, *German Home Towns: Community, State, and the General State, 1648–1871* (1971, 1998). A brilliant, street-level analysis of the Holy Roman Empire (the First Reich) and the run-up to the German unification of 1871 (the Second Reich).

Wasserman, Mark, *Everyday Life and Politics in Nineteenth-Century Mexico* (2000). Wonderfully captures the way in which people coped with social and economic dislocation in late-nineteenth-century Mexico.

Weeks, Theodore R., *Nation and State in Late Imperial Russia: Nationalism and Russification on the Western Frontier, 1863–1914* (1996). A good discussion of the Russian Empire's responses to the concept of the nation-state.

Yung Wing, *My Life in China and America* (1909). The autobiography of the first Chinese graduate of an American university.

Chapter

18

An Unsettled World, 1890–1914

In 1905 a young African man, Kinjikitile Ngwale, began to move among the different ethnic groups in the newly founded colony of German East Africa, inspiring his followers with a message of opposition to the German colonial authorities. In the tradition of visionary prophets (see Chapter 16), Kinjikitile claimed that by anointing adherents with specially blessed water (*maji* in Swahili), he could protect them from European bullets and drive the unwanted Germans from East Africa. Kinjikitile's reputation quickly spread, drawing followers to him and other like-minded prophets across 100,000 square miles of territory. Although the Germans executed Kinjikitile in 1905, they could not prevent his followers from taking part in a broad insurrection, called the Maji-Maji Revolt. The Germans brutally suppressed the uprising, killing between 200,000 and 300,000 Africans.

The Maji-Maji Revolt and its brutal suppression revealed an intensity of opposition to the world of nations and empires (described in Chapter 17). Pressures against the dominant system, which had been building since the early nineteenth century (see Chapter 16), now came from two distinct directions. In Europe and North America, cultural and social changes prompted a diverse group of critics who felt left out of the emerging nation-states, especially women, proletarians (wage workers), and frustrated nationalists, to demand far-reaching reforms. In Asia, Africa, and Latin America, anticolonial critics and exploited classes also expressed their opposition to European domination. The alternative social and political visions of the early nineteenth century had developed into formal groups that survived outside the mainstream, and by the early twentieth century those groups had amassed the strength and numbers to gain the notice of nations and empires.

European elites for the most part remained confident of their ability and right to dominate the rest of the world's population. Events like the Maji-Maji Revolt and other insurrections that swept through Africa in the wake of Europe's scramble for colonies, however, suggested that colonial rule required more than promises of progress to colonial peoples. Progress, in the colonizer's view, required order—and sometimes order demanded the application of brute force. Yet, resistance to European coercion led to doubts about Europe's imperial mission and the nature of "European civilization." Making matters worse, back home the social and economic dislocations of the last decades of the nineteenth century also produced discontent and social unrest. The rule of European elites now depended upon the dynamic forces of industrialization, global commerce, nation building, science, and the ideals (if not practices) of freedom and equality. Would it last?

That this question arose at the turn of the nineteenth century was surprising, because people of European descent then occupied a commanding position in the world. Their share of the world's population stood at an all-time high of nearly 30 percent. Their proportion of the world's wealth was still greater. They had become the primary decision makers throughout the world. Looking to the future, they envisioned the twentieth century as a "European century." Yet, despite these hopeful prospects, European confidence and Europe's preeminence were hardly secure. Even as statesmen and artists extolled the achievements of European civilization, new developments at home and abroad unsettled their faith in the persistence of a Euro-centered world order. At the end of the nineteenth century and beginning of the twentieth,

economic, cultural, and political changes reverberated around the globe as never before, with varying results. People reacted to these changes with a mixture of faith in progress and distress about it, a reaction that would become a defining characteristic of the tumultuous era.

PROGRESS, UPHEAVAL, AND MOVEMENT

> → *How did an unsettled world produce new anxieties?*

The decades leading up to 1914 were a time of unprecedented possibility for some, and social disruption and economic frustration for others. They were also years of anxiety throughout the world. Rapid economic progress and opportunity led to challenges to the established order and the people in power. In Europe and the United States, left-wing radicals and middle-class reformers agitated for political and social change. Their reforming efforts resulted in a larger number of men participating in choosing their rulers and in programs to assist the poor, the unemployed, the sick, and the aged. In areas colonized by European countries and the United States, resentment was sometimes directed at colonial rulers and sometimes at indigenous elites, whose authority had already been eroded by imperial incursions. Even in nations such as China, which had not been formally colonized but whose state's autonomy had been compromised by less direct foreign intrusions, popular discontent fastened on the domination of Europeans. In China, Mexico, and Russia, angry peasants and workers, allied with frustrated reformers, toppled autocratic regimes.

In the late nineteenth century, whole new industries fueled high levels of economic growth, especially in the industrial countries and in those territories that exported vital raw

Focus Questions AN UNSETTLED WORLD

→ *How did an unsettled world produce new anxieties?*

→ *How did Africans and Chinese show their opposition to imperialism?*

→ *What were the sources of unease around the world?*

→ *How was cultural modernism manifested in different fields?*

→ *How did conceptions about race and nation change in this era?*

 WWNORTON.COM/STUDYSPACE

materials to Europe and the United States. But the flowering of industrial capitalism also ushered in growing inequalities within industrial countries and especially between the industrial and nonindustrial regions of the world. Industrialization also enforced unwelcome changes in how and where people worked and lived. Rural peoples flocked into the cities, hoping to expand their economic opportunities and to escape widespread rural poverty. Urbanization tore at communal solidarities, though it also offered some individuals new freedoms. In cities, grand-scale public building projects produced new amenities like sewer systems, museums, parks, and libraries. But the poor, crowded together in unhealthy slums, often had little access to them. The anxieties of the poor—as well as the not-so-poor—became particularly acute when economic downturns threw thousands into the ranks of the unemployed. This led to increased disillusionment, and in some cases, to organized opposition to authoritarian regimes or to the free market system.

This disillusionment took shape in the shadow of developments in the arts and sciences. Scientific and technological progress enabled men and women to accomplish feats unimaginable a generation earlier. This facilitated the circulation of ideas around the world that paralleled the dispersion of goods and people. The uneven spread of scientific breakthroughs and economic advances and the use of knowledge and wealth to conquer and regulate lives led intellectuals to worry about the downside of progress. European and North American intellectuals began to worry that the world was less rational and the future much bleaker than Enlightenment thinkers had believed. Their writings were labeled modernism. Modernist ideas also circulated in areas that were subjected to colonial rule, as well in those where imperial domination was not complete or formalized, but for the western-trained intelligentsia in these areas achieving political independence and understanding the challenge of the West had the highest priority.

The uneven spread of scientific breakthroughs and economic advances and the use of knowledge and wealth to conquer and regulate lives led intellectuals to worry about the downside of progress.

PEOPLES IN MOTION

If the world was being *unsettled* by political and economic changes at the fin de siecle (that is, "end of the century"), it was also being *resettled* by mass emigration. (See Map 18-1.) Most well-known is what historian Alfred Crosby called a "Caucasian tsunami": the emigration of enormous numbers of Europeans to North America and Australia, but also to Argentina, Africa, and Cuba. The "tsunami" began slowly after the Napoleonic Wars and gathered momentum in the 1840s, when the Irish poured out of their starving communities to

seek better lives in North America. Indeed, it was this Irish exodus that finally meant the number of European migrants moving across the Atlantic eclipsed the traffic in slaves. After 1870, the flow of Europeans became a torrent. Never in human history had so many relocated and in such a brief amount of time. From 1904 to 1914 alone, more people moved to the Americas than all the migrants from Europe and Africa for the entire colonial period combined. This, in short, was nothing less than a demographic revolution.

But the Europeans were not the only peoples on the move; between the 1840s and 1940s, 29 million Indians flowed into the Malay Peninsula and Burma (British colonies), the Dutch Indies (Indonesia), East Africa, and the Caribbean. Most Indian migrants were recruited to work as laborers on plantations, railways, and mines and went typically to the territories controlled by the British Empire. Their reasons for migration varied, but generally they were poor peasants and laborers from the countryside who were pushed out by increasing pressure on land. Recruiters, responding to the demand for labor in the empire, signed them up often as indentured servants and transported them overseas. Merchants followed laborers, and soon the Indian migrant populations became more diverse. During these same years, the Chinese also emigrated in significant numbers. Between 1845 and 1900, population pressure, a shortage of cultivable land, and the social turmoil of the mid-nineteenth century forced an estimated 800,000 Chinese to seek new homes in North and South America, New Zealand, Hawaii, and the West Indies. Close to four times as many settled in Southeast Asia.

In addition, industrial transformation induced millions to migrate *within* their own countries or to adjacent countries, some heading for employment in the burgeoning cities and others seeking opportunities in frontier regions. In North America, hundreds of thousands "went west" across the Mississippi River until they hit the Pacific Ocean. In Asia, about 10 million Russians went east to Siberia and central Asia, and 2 million Koreans moved northwest to Manchuria. In Africa, small numbers of South Africans moved north into Northern and Southern Rhodesia in search of arable land and precious metals.

Across the world, gold rushes, silver rushes, copper rushes, and a diamond rush took people across landmasses and across oceans. These entailed rapid migrations, mostly of men, hell-bent on profit and often willing to destroy the land in order to extract precious commodities as quickly as possible.

People traveled with different portfolios and different aspirations. Some went as colonial officials and soldiers, some as missionaries or big-game hunters—though most of these

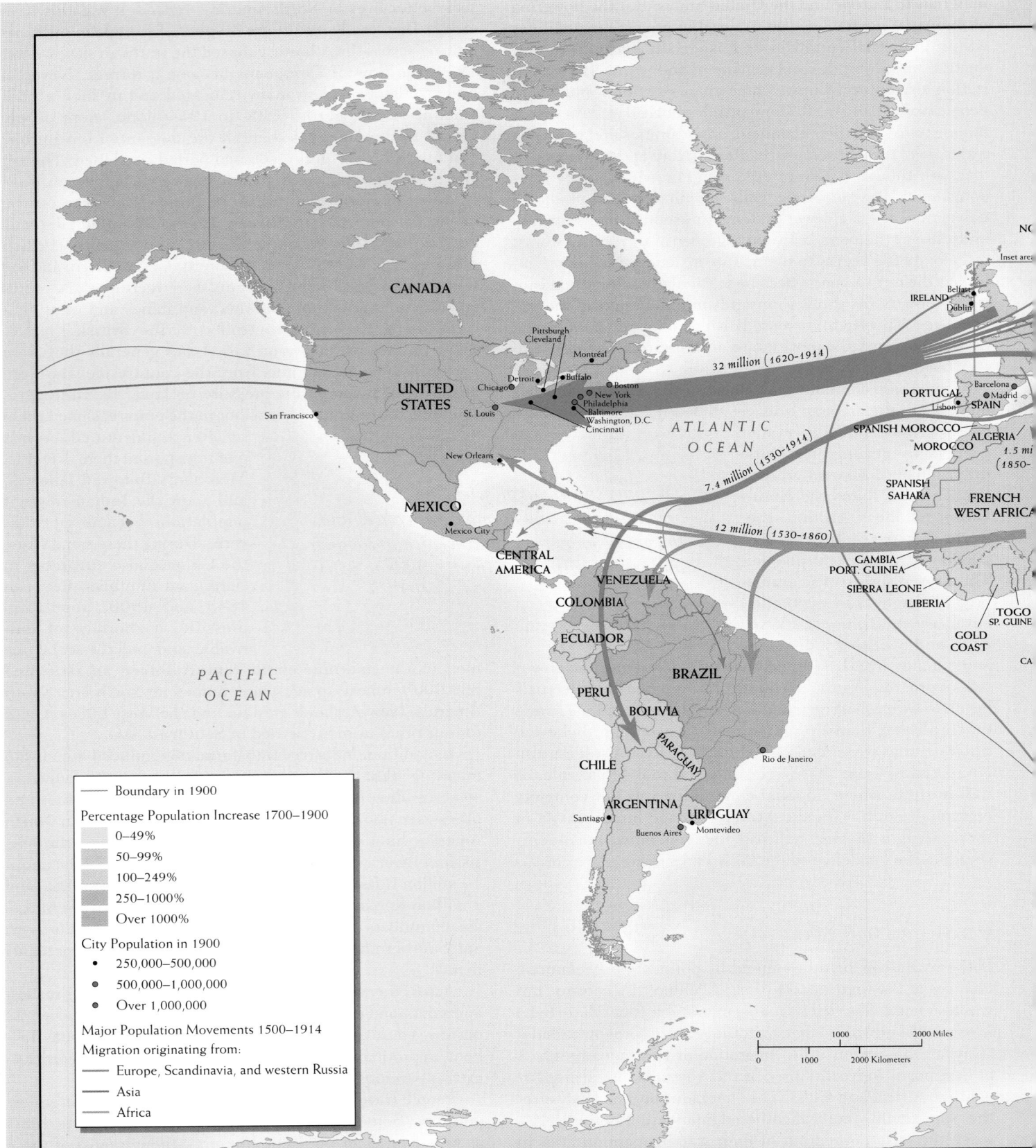

CANADA

Pittsburgh
Cleveland
Montréal
Detroit
Buffalo
Chicago
UNITED
STATES
Boston
New York
Philadelphia
Baltimore
St. Louis
Washington, D.C.
Cincinnati
San Francisco

32 million (1620–1914)

ATLANTIC
OCEAN

New Orleans

7.4 million (1530–1914)

MEXICO

Mexico City

12 million (1530–1860)

CENTRAL
AMERICA

VENEZUELA

COLOMBIA

ECUADOR

BRAZIL

PERU

BOLIVIA

PARAGUAY

Rio de Janeiro

CHILE

PACIFIC
OCEAN

ARGENTINA

Santiago

URUGUAY

Buenos Aires
Montevideo

NO

Inset area

IRELAND
Belfast
Dublin

PORTUGAL
Barcelona
Madrid
Lisbon
SPAIN

SPANISH MOROCCO
ALGERIA
MOROCCO

1.5 mi
(1850–

SPANISH
SAHARA

FRENCH
WEST AFRICA

GAMBIA
PORT. GUINEA

SIERRA LEONE

LIBERIA

TOGO
SP. GUINE

GOLD
COAST

CA

Legend:

— Boundary in 1900

Percentage Population Increase 1700–1900

- 0–49%
- 50–99%
- 100–249%
- 250–1000%
- Over 1000%

City Population in 1900

- 250,000–500,000
- 500,000–1,000,000
- Over 1,000,000

Major Population Movements 1500–1914
Migration originating from:

— Europe, Scandinavia, and western Russia
— Asia
— Africa

0   1000   2000 Miles
0   1000   2000 Kilometers

MAP 18-1 NINETEENTH-CENTURY MIGRATION

The nineteenth century witnessed a demographic revolution in terms of migration and urbanization patterns. Based on your study of population flows in previous chapters, which nineteenth-century migration patterns reflected older trends, and which were new? What factors contributed to these new trends? How were migration flows and urbanization connected?

ARCTIC OCEAN

Stockholm
St. Petersburg
Riga
Moscow
10 million (1880-1914)
RUSSIAN EMPIRE
Warsaw
Łódz
2.2 million (1880-1914)
AUSTRO-HUNGARIAN EMPIRE
Odessa
Budapest
Bucharest
Istanbul
OTTOMAN EMPIRE

MONGOLIA

Beijing
Tianjin
KOREA
Kyoto
JAPAN
Kobe
Tokyo
Yokohama
Osaka
Nagoya
1 million (1880-1914)

CHINA
Wuhan
Chongqing
Shanghai

ISIA
Alexandria
Cairo
EGYPT
PERSIA
AFGHANISTAN
NEPAL
BHUTAN
Lucknow
INDIA
Calcutta
BURMA
Guangzhou
22 million (1820-1914)
8 million (1900-1914)
PHILIPPINES

PACIFIC OCEAN

IPOLI
OMAN
Bombay
Hyderabad
Madras
SIAM
Bangkok
FRENCH INDOCHINA

ANGLO-EGYPTIAN SUDAN
ERITREA
FRENCH SOMALILAND
BRITISH SOMALILAND
ITALIAN SOMALILAND
ETHIOPIA
ENCH QUA-RIAL RICA ROON
UGANDA
BELGIAN CONGO
GERMAN EAST AFRICA
4.3 million (1500-1900)
3 million (1850-1914)

MALAYA
BRUNEI
SARAWAK
N. BORNEO
DUTCH EAST INDIES

KAISER WILHELMSLAND
PAPUA
EAST TIMOR

GOLA
RHODESIA
MADAGASCAR
MOZAMBIQUE
BECHUANALAND
CAPE COLONY
AN H T A

INDIAN OCEAN

3 million (1790-1914)

AUSTRALIA

Sydney
Melbourne
NEW ZEALAND

0   100   200   300 Miles
0 100 200 300 Kilometers

NORTH SEA
DENMARK
Copenhagen
Glasgow
BRITAIN
Bradford
Leeds
Manchester and Liverpool
Sheffield
Birmingham
London
Bristol
NETHERLANDS
Amsterdam
Rotterdam
Antwerp
BELGIUM
Brussels
Hamburg
Berlin
GERMANY
Wuppertal
Cologne
Leipzig
Dresden
Frankfurt
Nuremberg
Munich
LUX.
Paris
FRANCE
SWITZ.
AUSTRIA-HUNGARY
Bordeaux
Lyons
Turin
Milan
ITALY
Marseilles

DEN

folks did not plan to stay. Merchants and traders were more likely to settle in for the long-term—and there were hundreds of thousands of them. Several million from East Asia, mostly Chinese on labor contracts, went to the Philippines and South Africa, California and Cuba, British Columbia and Singapore, Guyana, and Trinidad, replacing freed slaves on plantations or doing construction. Japanese laborers migrated to Peru to mine guano for fertilizer and to Hawaii to harvest sugar. This stood in stark contrast to the forced migration of approximately 20 million Africans shipped to North America, Brazil, the Caribbean, and the Persian Gulf from 1500 to the 1800s.

Migrants took big risks. Transit itself was often hard and hazardous. Leaving behind native cultures and kin groups was often painful, and homesickness common. Many experienced conflicts or misunderstandings with resident populations, as did, for example, Chinese migrants who ventured into the relatively sparsely populated regions of the southwest and Taiwan. In the cities, social tensions were heightened as migrant workers confronted the reality of low wages, poor working and living conditions, and barriers to their entry into higher-paying positions. Strikes were increasingly common. Women from the provinces without male relatives to protect them were sometimes abused or exploited. And yet, conditions back home were desperate enough, and hopes were high enough, that the risks seemed worth taking.

Until 1914, governments imposed almost no controls on immigration to their borders or emigration from their borders. The Qing government tried to restrict emigration into the northeastern homelands of the Manchus, but its attempts failed. The United States allowed entry to anybody who was not a prostitute, a convict, or a "lunatic," but in 1882, racist reactions resulted in legislation that refused entry to almost all Chinese. Travel within Europe was largely uncontrolled—no passports or work permits were required. Foreign-born criminals could expect to be deported, but that was the extent of immigration policy. There was really no reason to have an imigration policy, because imigration was doubly good: emigrants allowed large productivity gains in the countries they *left* (because low-productivity populations departed), and immigrants fueled economic growth in the countries they *entered*. This was especially true in North America, thanks to parallel capital flows for building railroads and other infrastructure and thanks to the creation of very large markets. Overall, immigration expanded the New World labor force by as much as 40 percent, opening the way for enormous leaps in productivity in the century to follow.

Cities boomed. The population of Tokyo climbed from 500,000 in 1863 to 1,750,000 in 1908, and by this time London had passed 6.5 million. There were housing shortages in most major cities, even though many states were undertaking

Urban Transportation. (*Left*) Streetcars in Tokyo, Japan's capital, are watched over by sword-bearing patrolmen in 1905, during the Russo-Japanese War. The first electric streetcar began running in Japan in 1895. Note the elevated electricity lines, which dated from the 1880s. (*Right*) Heavy traffic in London, about 1910, points to an urban population on the move. Note the many kinds of transportation—motor buses as well as horse-drawn wagons; the railings in the foreground mark the entrance to the Underground, or subway.

massive rebuilding and beautification projects. This was the era in which city planning came into its own, to widen and regularize thoroughfares for new train and streetcar traffic and to make crowded city life attractive to the new inhabitants. City governments in New York, Cairo, Buenos Aires, and Brussels spent lavishly on new public facilities such as opera houses, libraries, sewers, and parks, hoping to ward off disease and crime and to impress others with their modernity.

Life in the metropolis at the turn of the century *was* different from city living in the mid-1800s; workplaces were often farther away from residences, and the different social classes lived in separate districts with leafy suburbs or plush townhouses for the middle and upper classes and crowded tenements for the working classes. Women's lives in particular were transformed. Women had long been employed outside the home, as domestic servants, textile workers, or tea-plantation employees. In the late nineteenth century some were able to take on positions a bit more removed from family control—as shop girls, secretaries, or, thanks to new educational opportunities, teachers. Increasing female literacy and the falling price of books and magazines gave women access to new models and ideas of acceptable female behavior. In the new cities it became respectable, even fashionable, for women to be seen on the boulevards. The availability in some places of ready-made clothes and packaged goods offered some relief from household drudgery—provided, of course, one could afford them. Yet, for most women, leisure time and luxury consumption belonged more to the realm of dreams than to that of realities.

In response to political upheavals, economic uncertainties, social disruptions, massive migrations, and modern ideas, personal and national identities came under scrutiny. Race became a central part of new identities and a justification for inequalities. In the effort to reimagine and revitalize nations, writers, artists, and political leaders created mythic histories to complete the internal unification of states. Such inventions would prove crucial in the twentieth century's work of nation building. But they also contributed to conflict between nations that in 1914 erupted in the Great War, an event that would generate another huge wave of emigration, this time much of it involuntary.

DISCONTENT WITH IMPERIALISM

> → *How did Africans and Chinese show their opposition to imperialism?*

In the decades before the Great War, opposition to European colonial rule in Asia and Africa gathered strength. During the nineteenth century, Europeans had commenced colonial ex-

pansion quite sure of their "civilizing mission." True, a number of prophetic leaders had presented "alternative visions" that contested the supremacy of Europeans (see Chapter 16). Although these localist movements were quashed, opposition to European influence and dominance did not abate, and in some cases that opposition drew inspiration from these earlier movements. While European imperialists consolidated their hold over their colonial possessions, they found themselves suppressing unrest and uprisings in their colonies with more force and more bloodshed. As the cycle of resistance and repression escalated, many Europeans back home grew increasingly distressed and questioned the harsh means that were being used to control the colonies. By 1914, these questions were intensifying as colonial subjects challenged imperial domination across Asia and Africa. In China, too, where Europeans were scrambling for new trading opportunities without formally seizing the reins of power, local populations were rising up against foreign control.

UNREST IN AFRICA

Last to be colonized, Africa witnessed many anticolonial uprisings and scandals in the first decades of colonial rule (see Map 18-2). Violent conflicts embroiled not only the Belgians and the Germans, who ruled autocratically, but also the British, who often boasted that their colonial system was superior because it left traditional African rulers in place. These uprisings made thoughtful Europeans uneasy: why were Africans trying to overthrow regimes that had huge technological advantages in firepower and mechanical transport and that were supposed to be bringing medical skills, literacy, and the fruits of European civilization? Some concluded that the Africans simply were too stubborn or too unsophisticated to appreciate Europe's generosity and would have to be forced along the path to progress. Others, shocked by colonial cruelty, called for reform. A few radicals even called for an end to imperialism.

African opposition to European conquest and colonial rule was too spirited to ignore. Across the region, organized African armies and unorganized African villagers rose up to challenge the European conquest. The resistance of African villagers in the central highlands of British East Africa (Kenya) was so intense that the British had to mount savage punitive expeditions to bring the area under their control. But even after European powers had put down this early resistance, Africans continued to revolt against imperial authority. Uprisings were particularly common in areas where colonial rulers enacted programs that resulted in forced labor, increased taxation, and land appropriation. In northern Nigeria, in 1906, a mere three years after the British had conquered the area, an Islamic leader claiming to be the *mahdi*, or the chosen one, rallied people anew in opposition to the British and their African collaborators. Similar rebellions erupted in other colonies.

The South African War. Between 1899 and 1902, the Afrikaner states of the Transvaal and the Orange Free State fought a bitter struggle against British troops based in South Africa in an unsuccessful effort to maintain their political independence.

The most devastating of all of the wars and uprisings in colonial Africa occurred in South Africa. Unlike other conflicts in Africa, this struggle pitted two white communities against each other: the British in the Cape Colony and Natal against the Afrikaners, descendants of the original Dutch settlers, who lived in the Transvaal and the Orange Free State. Although fought between two white regimes, the South African War (often called the Boer War; 1899–1902) involved the 4 million black inhabitants as fully as the area's 1 million whites. Its horrors particularly traumatized the British, who had come to see themselves as Europe's most enlightened and efficient colonial rulers.

The war's origins lay in the discovery of gold in the Transvaal in the mid-1880s. With exports amounting to £24 million per year during the 1890s, the Transvaal had become the richest state in Africa. The prospect that the mineral-rich Afrikaner republics might become the powerhouse in southern Africa was more than British imperialists like Joseph Chamberlain, colonial secretary in London, and Cecil Rhodes, the leading politician in the Cape Colony, could accept. They found ready allies in the non-Afrikaner, British population living in the Afrikaner republics. Denied voting rights and subject to other forms of discrimination, these outsiders (*uit-landers*) protested the Afrikaner governments' policies and pressed the British to intervene. For their part, Afrikaner leaders initiated a campaign of anticolonial rhetoric that emphasized the rights of a free people to resist.

Fearing that war was inevitable, the president of the Transvaal, Paul Kruger, launched a preemptive strike against the British. In late 1899, Afrikaner forces crossed into South Africa. British glee at what they considered a fateful political blunder soon turned to frustration, even despair, as the fast-moving Afrikaner forces won early victories. Recruiting nearly every able-bodied man and fighting a guerrilla campaign that broke all the rules of military manuals, the Afrikaners waged a war that would last three years and cost Britain 20,000 soldiers and £200 million. Britain's frustrated attempts to respond to Afrikaner hit-and-run tactics and contain the local civilian population led the British to institute a terrifying innovation: the concentration camp. At one moment in the war, no fewer than 155,000 captured men, women, and children were being held in camps surrounded by barbed wire. Nor were the camps restricted to Afrikaners. The British also rounded up Africans whom they feared would side with the "anticolonial" Dutch descendants. The suffering and loss in these camps were appalling; by war's end, 28,000 Afrikaner women and children, as well as 14,000 black Africans, had perished in these camps. These atrocities did not go unnoticed, however, as new means of mass communication, newspaper reports, and photographs brought the misery of the South African War back to Europe.

Ultimately, the British won the war, bringing the Transvaal and the Orange Free State—with their vast gold reserves—into their empire. But the chill of revulsion that the South African War sent through western public opinion deepened after Germany's African adventures also went brutally wrong. Germany had established colonies in Southwest Africa (present-day Namibia), Cameroon, and Togo in 1884 and in East Africa in 1885. In German Southwest Africa, the Herero and San people resisted the Germans, and in German East Africa (modern-day Tanzania), the Muslim Arab peoples rebelled. Between 1904 and 1906, the fighting in German Southwest Africa escalated into a no-holds-barred conflict, during which the German commander General von Trotha issued a genocidal extermination order against the Herero population. Equally troubling was the Maji-Maji Revolt in German East Africa of 1905–1906, already described at the beginning of this chapter. (See Map 18-2.)

Numerous apologists for imperial violence tried to dampen public outcries. Journalists portrayed the Maji-Maji rebels as fanatics in the thrall of a demonic African witch doctor, Kinjikitile Ngwale, and the Afrikaners as uncouth ruffians who deserved what they got. The best-selling German novel by Gustav Frenssen, *Peter Moor's Trip to the Southwest* (1906), glorified the small-town Aryan hero who gives his all to defend noble German settlers against the barbarism of the Hereros. According to defenders, the unjustifiable horrors of

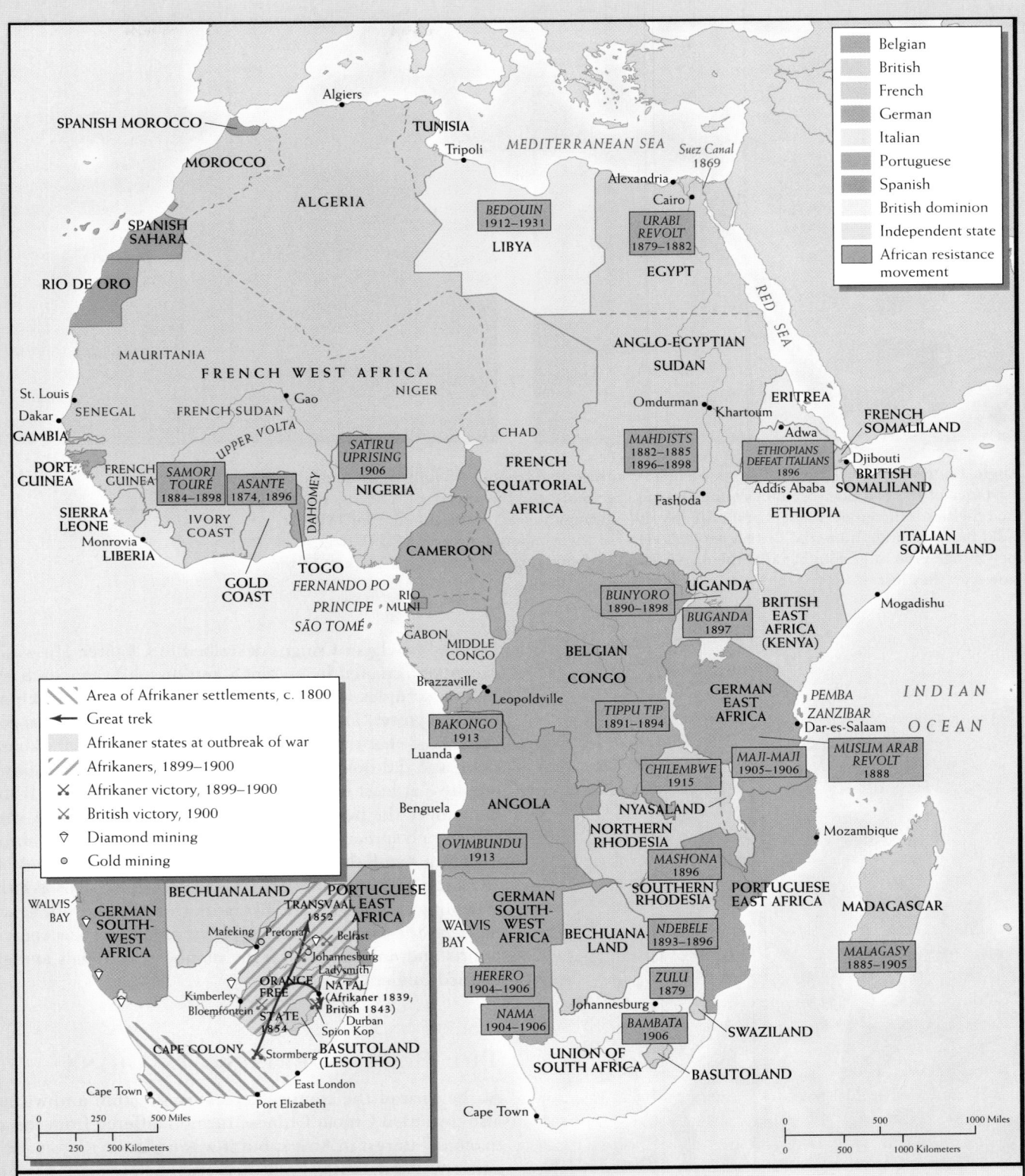

Legend (main map)

- Belgian
- British
- French
- German
- Italian
- Portuguese
- Spanish
- British dominion
- Independent state
- African resistance movement

Legend (inset map)

- Area of Afrikaner settlements, c. 1800
- Great trek
- Afrikaner states at outbreak of war
- Afrikaners, 1899–1900
- Afrikaner victory, 1899–1900
- British victory, 1900
- Diamond mining
- Gold mining

Main map labels

SPANISH MOROCCO — Algiers — TUNISIA — Tripoli — MEDITERRANEAN SEA — Suez Canal 1869

MOROCCO — ALGERIA — LIBYA — Alexandria — Cairo — RED SEA

SPANISH SAHARA — BEDOUIN 1912–1931 — URABI REVOLT 1879–1882 — EGYPT

RIO DE ORO — ANGLO-EGYPTIAN SUDAN — ERITREA — FRENCH SOMALILAND

MAURITANIA — FRENCH WEST AFRICA — NIGER — Omdurman — Khartoum — Adwa — Djibouti — BRITISH SOMALILAND

St. Louis — Dakar — SENEGAL — FRENCH SUDAN — Gao — CHAD — MAHDISTS 1882–1885 1896–1898 — ETHIOPIANS DEFEAT ITALIANS 1896 — Addis Ababa — Fashoda

GAMBIA — UPPER VOLTA — SATIRU UPRISING 1906 — FRENCH EQUATORIAL AFRICA — ETHIOPIA

PORT. GUINEA — FRENCH GUINEA — SAMORI TOURÉ 1884–1898 — ASANTE 1874, 1896 — NIGERIA — ITALIAN SOMALILAND

SIERRA LEONE — IVORY COAST — DAHOMEY — Monrovia — LIBERIA — GOLD COAST — TOGO — FERNANDO PO — PRINCIPE — SÃO TOMÉ — RIO MUNI — CAMEROON — BUNYORO 1890–1898 — UGANDA — BRITISH EAST AFRICA (KENYA) — Mogadishu

GABON — MIDDLE CONGO — BELGIAN CONGO — BUGANDA 1897 — GERMAN EAST AFRICA — PEMBA — ZANZIBAR — INDIAN OCEAN

Brazzaville — Leopoldville — TIPPU TIP 1891–1894 — Dar-es-Salaam

BAKONGO 1913 — MAJI-MAJI 1905–1906 — MUSLIM ARAB REVOLT 1888 — Luanda — CHILEMBWE 1915

ANGOLA — NYASALAND — NORTHERN RHODESIA — Benguela — Mozambique

OVIMBUNDU 1913 — MASHONA 1896 — SOUTHERN RHODESIA — PORTUGUESE EAST AFRICA — MADAGASCAR

GERMAN SOUTH-WEST AFRICA — BECHUANA LAND — NDEBELE 1893–1896 — MALAGASY 1885–1905

WALVIS BAY — HERERO 1904–1906 — ZULU 1879 — Johannesburg — SWAZILAND

NAMA 1904–1906 — BAMBATA 1906 — UNION OF SOUTH AFRICA — BASUTOLAND — Cape Town

Inset map labels

WALVIS BAY — GERMAN SOUTH-WEST AFRICA — BECHUANALAND — PORTUGUESE EAST AFRICA — TRANSVAAL 1852

Mafeking — Pretoria — Belfast — Johannesburg — Ladysmith — NATAL (Afrikaner 1839; British 1843) — Durban — Spion Kop

Kimberley — ORANGE FREE STATE 1854 — Bloemfontein — Stormberg — BASUTOLAND (LESOTHO)

CAPE COLONY — East London — Cape Town — Port Elizabeth

0 250 500 Miles
0 250 500 Kilometers

0 500 1000 Miles
0 500 1000 Kilometers

MAP 18-2   UPRISINGS AND WARS IN AFRICA

The European partition and conquest of Africa were violent affairs. Referring to the map, can you determine in which parts of Africa conquest took the longest? Where was resistance the most prolonged? Why were Ethiopians, who sustained their autonomy, able to do what other African opponents of European armies were not? How and with whom did British expansion in southern Africa precipitate military conflict?

The Anglo-Boer War. (*Left*) The British sent a large contingent of troops to South Africa to deal with the resistance of the two Boer republics—the Orange Free State and the Transvaal. The loss of life and the cruelties inflicted on soldiers and civilians alike during the war, which lasted from 1899 to 1902, did much to undermine the British people's views of their imperial mission. (*Right*) Transvaal and the Orange Free State fought valiantly to keep from becoming part of the British Empire. In the end, however, they lost.

Leopold's Belgian Congo (described in Chapter 17) was an exception, created by an aging and dissolute monarch who had no scruples when it came to enhancing his wealth and political power. The rationalizers from all the European powers argued that these incidents reflected unpleasant aberrations and did not represent the real purpose and reality of empire—at least not *their* nation's empire. Thus, the British denounced the Belgians to tout their own benevolence, while the French spread gory images of German repression abroad to contrast with their own success at uplifting Africans. What all European rationalizers did was to portray Africans as either accepting subjects or childlike primitives. For Europe's rationalizers, the message was simply to redouble their coercive efforts and, in many cases, the number of officials and garrisoned soldiers.

THE BOXER UPRISING IN CHINA

At the turn of the century, forces from within and without also unsettled China. Chinese turmoil differed from the anticolonial unrest in Africa, but it was no less symptomatic of concern about European intrusions. The population, which

Extermination of the Herero. The Germans carried out a campaign of near extermination against the Herero population in German South-West Africa in 1904–05. Nearly 90 percent of the Herero were killed.

→ *How did Africans and Chinese show their opposition to imperialism?*

exceeded half a billion, was outstripping the country's resources. Landlessness, poverty, and peasant discontent, constants in China's modern history, led many to mourn the decay of political authority. In response, Guangxu, the Qing Emperor, had tried to enact reforms in the summer of 1898 to deal with accumulating social problems. The reforms were intended to modernize industry, agriculture, commerce, education, and the military. But opponents blocked the emperor's designs. By September, Guangxu found himself under house arrest in the palace, while the Empress Dowager Cixi, around whom the conservatives rallied, actually ruled.

The breakdown of dynastic authority can be traced in large part to foreign pressure. China's defeat at the hands of Japan in the Sino-Japanese War of 1894–1895 (see Chapter 17) deeply humiliated the Chinese. That defeat also upset the tacit agreement among foreign powers to keep China open to trade with all. Although Japan, which acquired Taiwan as its first major colony, was the immediate beneficiary of the war, Britain, France, Germany, and Russia quickly scrambled for additional concessions from China. These European powers demanded that the Qing government grant them specific areas within China as their respective "spheres of influence" (see Map 18-3). The United States, prompted by a combination of ideology and self-interest, argued instead for maintaining an "open door" policy in which access would remain available to all traders. But the Americans also wished to force the Qing regime to assent to western norms of political and economic exchange and to convince the Chinese of the truth and superiority of Christian civilization. In response, some Chinese political and intellectual leaders developed an anti-European stance while advocating the use of European ideas and technology to strengthen China itself.

The most explosive reaction to these internal and external problems originated within the peasantry and was known as the Boxer Uprising. Like colonial peoples in Africa, the Boxers employed violence against the unwelcome meddling of Europeans in their communities. As in the case of the Taiping Rebellion decades earlier (described in Chapter 16), the story of the Boxers was tied to missionary activities. In earlier centuries, Jesuit missionaries had sought chiefly to convert the court and the elites. By the mid-nineteenth century, evangelical revivals in Europe had made converting Chinese commoners seem a critical goal. In the decades after the Taiping Rebellion, Christian missionaries had streamed into China, impatient to make new converts in the hinterlands and confident of the backing of their governments. With the dynasty in a weakened state, Christian missionaries became more aggressive, often challenging local officials and the customary practices of Chinese communities.

An incident in 1897, in which Chinese residents killed two German missionaries, brought tensions to a boil. The missionaries had been attempting to "open" the city of Yanzhou (located in the northern province of Shandong, long a hotbed of unrest and rebellion) for Catholic proselytizing. In retribution for the deaths, the German government demanded the right to construct three cathedrals, to remove hostile local officials, and to seize the port of Jiaozhou. As tensions mounted between the Chinese and western missionaries, martial arts groups in the region became increasingly politicized and began to attack the missionaries and converts, calling for an end to specific privileges for the Christians. In early 1899, several of these groups joined together under the rubric "Boxers United in Righteousness" and adopted the slogan "Support the Qing, destroy the foreign."

Cixi's Allies. The Empress Dowager Cixi emerged as the most powerful figure in the Qing court in the last decades of the dynasty, from the 1860s until her death in 1908. Highly able, she approved many of the early reforms of the Self-Strengthening movement, but her commitment to the preservation of the Manchu Qing dynasty made her suspicious of more fundamental and wide-ranging changes. Here she is shown surrounded by court eunuchs. Early Qing rulers were very conscious of the danger of the meddling of eunuchs in court affairs. Yet, as a woman whose power relationships with orthodox officials were often ambivalent, Cixi was perhaps particularly compelled to ally herself closely with the eunuchs as a counterweight to the other official factions.

Spheres of Influence
- British
- French
- German
- Japanese
- Russian

Colonies
- British
- French
- Japanese
- • Treaty port, 1842
- • Treaty port, 1858–1889
- • Treaty port, 1890–1907

MAP 18-3   FOREIGN SPHERES OF INFLUENCE IN CHINA, 1842–1907

While technically independent, the Qing dynasty could not prevent foreign penetration and domination of its economy during the nineteenth century. Note the location of the different spheres of influence claimed by the foreign powers in China. What did western and Japanese powers hope to achieve within these spheres of influence? Did this competition for spheres of influence produce conflict between these states? What kinds of opposition did it inspire among local populations?

Rather like the African followers of Kinjikitile, the Boxers believed that their divine protection rendered them immune to all earthly weapons. As a Boxer put it, "We requested the gods to attach themselves to our bodies. When they had done so, we became Spirit Boxers, after which we were invulnerable to swords and spears, our courage was enhanced, and in fighting we were unafraid to die and dared to charge straight ahead."

The Boxer movement flourished especially where natural disasters and harsh economic conditions spread suffering. In Shandong, where the movement began, there had been floods throughout much of the decade, followed by a prolonged drought in the winter of 1898. Idle, restless, and often hungry, peasants, boatmen, and peddlers turned to the Boxers for support. They were also receptive to the Boxers' message that the gods were angry because of the foreign presence in general and Christian activities in particular.

These indigent activists, many of them young men, swelled the ranks of the Boxers, and women also found a place in the movement. The so-called Red Lanterns were mostly teenage girls and unmarried women, who announced their loyalty by dressing entirely in red garments. Though the Red Lanterns were segregated from the male Boxers— they worshipped at their own altars and practiced their martial arts at separate boxing grounds—they were important to the movement as a way to counteract the influence of Christian women. Indeed, one of the Boxers' greatest fears was that cunning Christian women would use their guile to weaken their spirits. The Boxers believed that their invulnerability came from spirit possession, and the threat to their "magic" came from the inherent polluting power of women. They accused, for example, Christian—not necessarily western, as the Boxers were equally hostile to converts—women of exposing themselves and waving "dirty things" at them to drive out their spirits. Such a threat, however, could be countered by the "purity" of the Red Lanterns. The Red Lanterns, too, were believed to be able to carry out incredible feats: they could walk on water or fly through the air. Their magical power was said to provide critical assistance for the uprising.

As the movement gained momentum, the Qing vacillated between viewing the Boxers as a threat to order and embracing them as a potential force to check increasingly brazen foreign encroachment. In the early part of 1900, Qing troops on occasion clashed with the Boxers in an escalating cycle of violence. By spring, however, it was clear that the Qing could not control the Boxers, tens of thousands of whom roamed the vicinities of Beijing and Tianjin. Embracing the Boxers' cause, the empress dowager declared war against the foreign powers in June 1900.

Acting without any discernible plan or leadership, the Boxers went after Christian and foreign symbols and persons. In addition to harassing and sometimes killing Chinese Christians in various parts of northern China, the Boxers attacked owners of foreign objects such as lamps and clocks. Railroad tracks and telegraph lines also became targets of destruction. In Beijing, the Boxers besieged the foreign embassy compounds within which were the foreign diplomats and their families. The Boxers also reduced the Southern Cathedral to ruins, then besieged the Northern Cathedral, where more than 3,000 Catholics and 40 French and Italian marines had sought refuge. Those inside were rescued only with the arrival of a foreign expeditionary force.

The Boxer Uprising in China. The Boxer Uprising was eventually suppressed by a foreign army made up of Japanese, European, and American troops that arrived in Beijing in August 1900. The picture here shows fighting between the foreign troops and the combined forces of Qing soldiers and the Boxers. After a period of vacillation, the Qing court, against the advice of some of its officials, finally threw its support behind the quixotic struggle of the Boxers against the foreign presence, laying the ground for the military intervention of the imperialist powers.

In August 1900, a foreign army of 20,000 men crushed the Boxers. About half of the troops came from Japan; the rest came primarily from Russia, Britain, Germany, France, and the United States. Following the suppression of the uprising, the victors forced the Chinese to sign the punitive Boxer Protocol in September 1901. Among other punishments, it required the regime to pay an exorbitant indemnity in gold for damages to foreign life and property. The cost was about twice the annual income of the empire. The Boxer Protocol also authorized western powers to station troops in Beijing.

The humiliating terms prompted the Qing to make a last-ditch effort to reform. The post-Boxer "New Policy" included the reorganization of the ministries and the army, an attempt to recentralize the government, the abolition of the old civil service examination system, and the promise of constitutional reform. But by then the Qing regime was so crippled that these abrupt reforms merely snapped the ties between the rulers and their subjects.

Even in defeat, the Boxers' antiwestern uprising showed how much had changed in China since the Taiping Rebellion. Although primarily peasants from a relatively remote part of what was still an agrarian empire, the Boxers shared in the unsettledness generated by European inroads into China. The commercial and spiritual reach of Europeans, once confined to elites and port cities, had extended across much of China. While the Taiping Rebellion had mobilized millions against the Qing, the Boxers remained loyal to the dynasty and focused their wrath on foreigners and Chinese Christians. In the process, they demonstrated the possibility for mass political opposition to westernization.

WORLDWIDE INSECURITIES

> → *What were the sources of unease around the world?*

The protests against European intrusion in Africa and China were distant movements that most Europeans could in the end disregard. News of unrest in the colonies and in China did not lead many Europeans to lose faith in the superiority of European ways. Quite the contrary, it reinforced their belief in the inferiority of the other cultures. The imperial powers overcame their differences to join together to put down the Boxers in China. In Africa, unrest in a rival's empire was taken as a sign of poor management with the accompanying belief that colonial administration was better done in one's own empire. Anxiety here was primarily generated by the difficulty and costs of the "civilizing mission" though a few did begin to worry about its ethics. At the same time, however, conflicts closer to home tore at European and North American confidence. These included political and military rivalries among the western powers, the booms and busts of the expanding industrial economies, and the problems that developed as a result of uncontrolled urbanization (see Map 18-4).

IMPERIAL RIVALRIES COME HOME

Many internal factors fostered conflict among the western powers, including France's smoldering resentment at its defeat in the Franco-Prussian War of 1870–1871. But political and military tension increased among the European states as they competed for raw materials and colonial footholds. The western powers built up their supply of weapons as well as ships and railroads to transport troops where needed. Yet, not everyone supported the military buildup. Many decried the money spent on massive new steam-powered warships. Others, especially the socialists, warned that the arms race would culminate in a devastating war.

In the main, the creation of a European-centered world deepened rivalries within Europe and promoted instability across the region. Competition accentuated the position of two powers in particular: Germany and Russia. The unifications of Germany and Italy at the expense of France and the

Austrian Empire had smashed the old balance of power in Europe. New alliances began to crystallize after 1890, as German-French hostility persisted and German-Russian friendship broke down. This left Germany surrounded by foes: Britain and France to the west, Russia to the east. Adding to the instability among reigning great powers was the weakening of Europe's old empires, the Ottoman and the Habsburg. On the flanks of these empires were the Balkans, where a series of small wars and the rise of Slavic nationalism destabilized the area in the years between 1909 and 1913. Sensing conflict on the horizon, Britain, Germany, France, Austria-Hungary, and Russia entered into a massive arms race, investing much of their newfound prosperity in the very weapons that would destroy millions of their subjects after 1914.

FINANCIAL, INDUSTRIAL, AND TECHNOLOGICAL INSECURITIES

Economic developments helped make powers "great," but the same industrial and commercial dynamism upset the arrangements that had held societies together. Certainly those at the apex of the capitalist system had reason to celebrate the wealth that industrialism had brought to Europe and the United States in the nineteenth century. Living standards had never been higher in the West. But pride about wealth and growth coincided with laments about changes in national and international economies. To begin with, Americans and Europeans recognized that the small-scale, laissez-faire capitalism that Adam Smith had championed had given way by the close of the nineteenth century to an economic order dominated by huge, heavily capitalized firms. Gone, it seemed, was Smith's vision of a capitalist system of many small producers in vigorous competition with one another, all benefiting from efficient, but not exploitative, divisions of labor.

Instead of smooth progress, the economy of the West in the nineteenth century bounced between booms and busts. Thus, the industrial system was characterized by long-term business cycles of rapid growth, followed by counter-cycles of stagnation. In the last quarter of the century, the pace of economic change accelerated. Large-scale steel production, railroad building, and textile manufacturing expanded at breakneck speed, while waves of bank closures, bankruptcies, and agricultural crises ruined many small-holders. By century's end, European and North American economies were dominated as never before by a few large-scale firms that were, however, more efficient for the production of commodities like steel.

During this era, the power of the industrial magnate was matched by the power of the financier. These were years of heady international financial integration. More and more countries joined a world system of borrowing and lending; more and more countries embraced a set of economic rules governed by the gold standard. The hub of this world system was composed of the banks of London, which since the Napoleonic wars had been a major source of capital for international borrowers.

The rise of giant banks and huge industrial corporations caused much alarm, for it seemed to signal an end to the age of free markets and competitive capitalism. In the United States, an entire generation of journalists cut their teeth exposing the skullduggery of financial titans and industrial magnates. These "muckrakers" portrayed the captains of finance like J. P. Morgan and John D. Rockefeller as plutocrats bent on amassing ever greater private power at the expense of working families and public authorities. In Europe, too, critics decried a similar trend toward economic monopolies or oligopolies in which lack of competition generated profiteering and created greater disparities of wealth between the owners of firms and the workforce.

Rather than longing for the return of truly free markets, many critics argued for reforms and regulations that would

protect people from economic instability. Indeed, starting in the 1890s, the reaction against economic competition gathered steam. Producers, big and small, grew disenchanted with supply and demand mechanisms and sought to circumvent them. To cope with an unruly market, farmers created cooperatives, while big industrialists attempted to create their own monopolies, or cartels, in the name of improving "efficiency," correcting failures in the market, and heightening profits. At the same time, government officials, along with a new class of academic specialists, worried openly that modern economies were inherently unstable, often prone to produce too much, and thus liable to bankruptcy and crisis. The solution, according to many turn-of-the-century economists, was for the state to step in and manage the market's inefficiencies.

Banking especially seemed in need of closer government supervision. In many industrial societies, central banks already existed and, in London, the Bank of England had long since taken on the supervision of local and international money markets. But public institutions did not yet have the

Labor Disputes. The late nineteenth century witnessed a surge in industrial strife, worker strikes, and violent suppression of labor movements. (*Left*) One of the deadliest confrontations in the United States occurred in May 1892, when a strike against the Carnegie Steel Company escalated into a gunfight, which left ten dead and many more wounded. Here, a group of striking workers keeps watch over the steel mill in Homestead, Pennsylvania. (*Right*) Striking dock workers rally in London's Trafalgar Square, 1911. By this time, residents of European cities were used to seeing crowds of protesters pressing for improved working conditions or political reform.

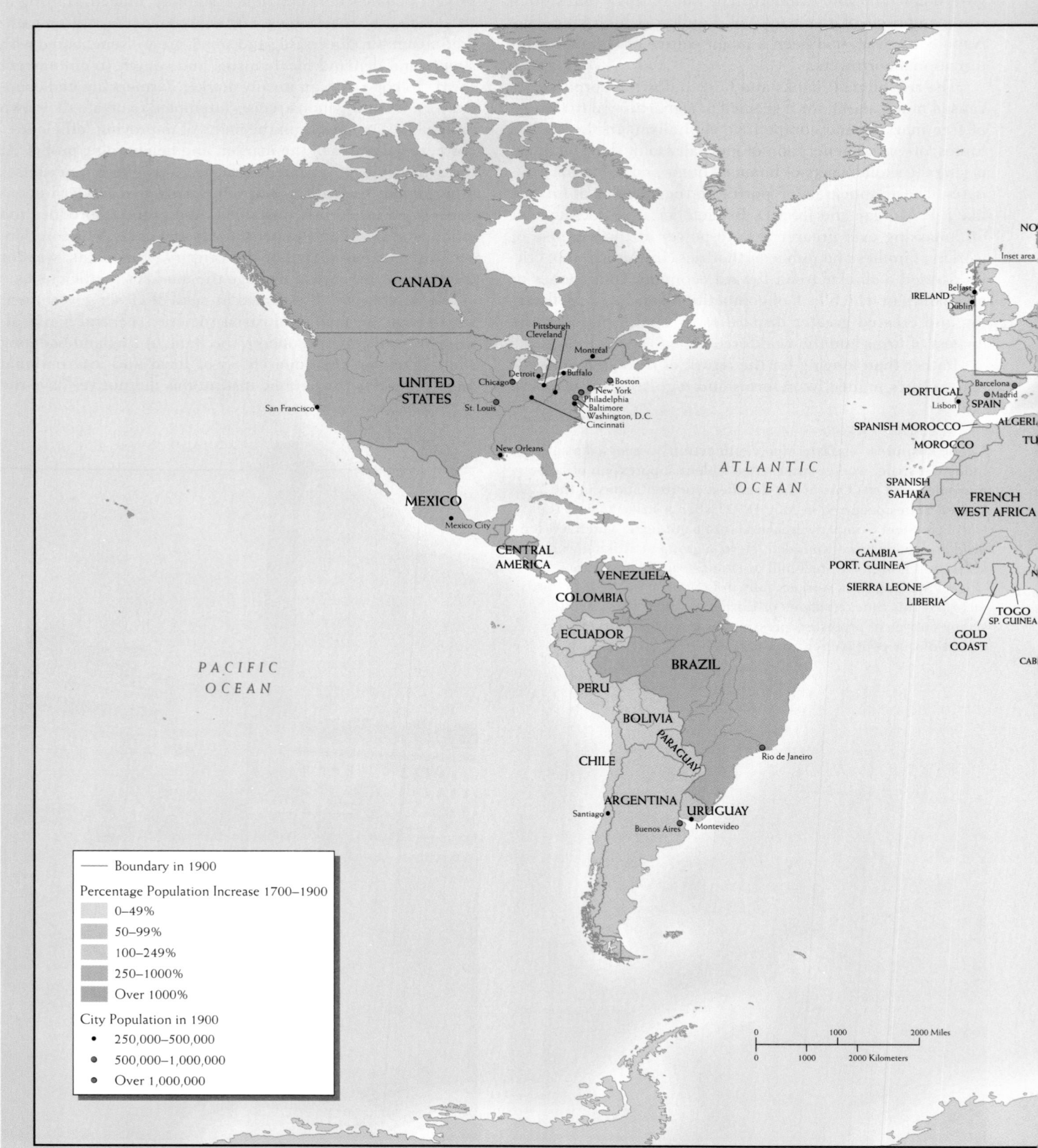

Boundary in 1900

Percentage Population Increase 1700–1900
- 0–49%
- 50–99%
- 100–249%
- 250–1000%
- Over 1000%

City Population in 1900
- • 250,000–500,000
- • 500,000–1,000,000
- • Over 1,000,000

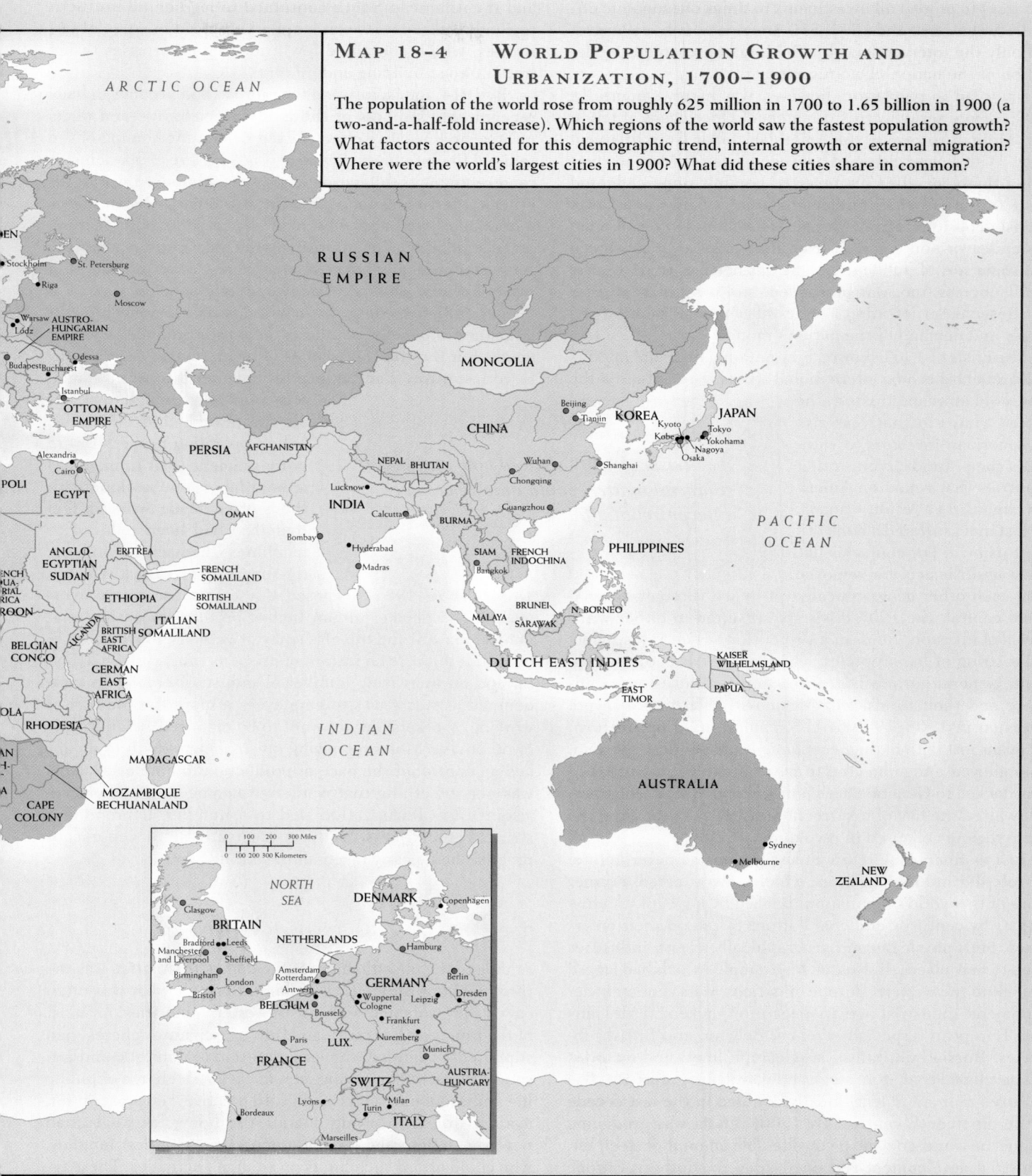

MAP 18-4 WORLD POPULATION GROWTH AND URBANIZATION, 1700–1900

The population of the world rose from roughly 625 million in 1700 to 1.65 billion in 1900 (a two-and-a-half-fold increase). Which regions of the world saw the fastest population growth? What factors accounted for this demographic trend, internal growth or external migration? Where were the world's largest cities in 1900? What did these cities share in common?

resources to protect all investments in times of economic crisis. Between 1890 and 1893, 550 American banks collapsed, and only the intervention of J. P. Morgan prevented the depletion of the nation's gold reserves.

The road to regulation, however, was hardly smooth. In 1907, a more serious crisis threatened. Once again, it fell to J. P. Morgan to rescue the American dollar from financial panic. With a cigar clenched between his teeth, Morgan compelled financier after financier to commit unprecedented funds (eventually $35 million) to protect banks and trusts against depositors' panic. Morgan himself lost $21 million in this endeavor and emerged from the bank panic convinced that some sort of public oversight was needed. By 1913, the U.S. Congress, too, was persuaded, and it ratified the Federal Reserve Act, creating a series of boards to monitor the supply and demand of the nation's money.

The crisis of 1907 showed how national financial matters could quickly become international affairs. The sell-off of the shares of banks and trusts in the United States in that year also led American investors to withdraw their funds from other countries that relied on American capital. As a result, Canada, for instance, suffered a bank crisis of its own. For countries like Egypt and Mexico, far removed from each other geographically yet linked through international capital, the 1907 crisis also resulted in either withdrawal of investors' funds or a suspension of new investments and a string of bankruptcies. The head of Mexico's government, General Porfirio Díaz, tried to regain investors' confidence and their funds. But Mexico still fell into a severe recession in 1908–1909 as U.S. capital dried up. In turn, Mexicans lost faith in their economic—and political—system. Unemployed and subjected to new hardships, many Mexicans flocked to General Díaz's political opponents, who eventually lifted the flag of insurrection in 1910. A year later, the entire regime collapsed in revolution.

Just as financial circuits linked nations as never before, so, too, did industrialization, which now affected a larger share of the world's population. Backed by big banks, industrialists by century's end could afford to extend their enterprises, both physically and geographically. Heavy industries came to new places. In Russia, for example, which had lagged far behind the western European nations in its economic development, industrial activity began to quicken. With loans from European (especially French, Belgian, and British) investors, Russia built railways, telegraph lines, and factories and developed coal, iron, steel, and petroleum industries. The country's railroad mileage nearly doubled in the last decade of the nineteenth century. By 1900, Russia was producing half of the world's oil and a considerable amount of steel. Yet, industrial development remained uneven: southern Europe and the American South continued to lag behind northern regions. The gap was even more pronounced in colonial territories, which contained few industrial enterprises (aside from railroad building and mining).

By 1914, the factory and the railroad had become globally recognizable symbols of the modern economy—and of its positive and negative effects. Everywhere, the coming of the railroad to one's town or village was a big event: for some, it represented an exhilarating leap into the modern world; for others, a terrifying abandonment of the past. Ocean liners, automobiles, and airplanes, likewise, could be both dazzling and disorienting. Not surprisingly, the older conservative elite found technological development more worrying than did urban liberals, who increasingly set state policies.

For ordinary people, the new, industrial economy brought a mixture of benefits and costs. Factories produced cheaper goods, but they belched clouds of black smoke. Railways offered faster travel and transport, but they also ruined small towns unlucky enough to be left off the branch line. Machines (when operating properly) were more efficient than human and animal labor, but working with them often made workers feel that they had been reduced to machines themselves. Indeed, the American Frederick Winslow Taylor (1856–1915) proposed a system of "scientific management" to make human bodies perform more like machines, maximizing the efficiency of workers' movements in order not to waste an instant of precious time. But what Taylor and an increasing number of industrial employers condemned as waste was to employees a more flexible way of working. Workers did not want to be managed, scientifically or otherwise. Moreover, giving up customary rhythms meant ceding control of the pace of production to employers. This was not something that workers welcomed, and labor's resistance to "Taylorization" led to a number of prominent strikes. For strikers, as for conservatives, the course of progress had clearly taken an unsettling turn.

The crisis of 1907 showed how national financial matters could quickly become international affairs.

THE "WOMAN QUESTION"

Adding to the unsettledness of the domestic situation was the turmoil about the politics of domesticity, or what was often called the "woman question." In western countries, for most of the nineteenth century, an ethos of "separate spheres" had supposedly confined women's attention to domestic and private matters, while leaving men in exclusive charge of public life and economic undertakings. In practice, the proscription against women working outside the home for wages had never been enforced, except among the wealthiest families, who could afford such limits on women's activities. These re-

Primary Source

VIRAGOES OR TEMPLE COURTESANS?

The German avant-garde novelist Franziska von Reventlow occupied one of the more radical positions in the fragmented European women's movement. In the 1899 essay excerpted below, Reventlow attacked the feminist "viragoes" (aggressive women) who failed to understand that freedom for women did not mean making them into men. Instead of pressing for political and economic rights, Reventlow—who was herself notorious for her many affairs—advocated a return to the promiscuity permitted to special temple courtesans in Ancient Greece and the freeing of women from oppressive work and the sensuality-killing conventions of middle-class Christian culture.

The most fanatical members of the women's movement have put forward the claim: women can do everything men can do. . . . We don't want to deny that there are many achievements of which both sexes are equally capable. . . . But when it comes to heavy physical labor, that is a different question. One has only to look at these hard-working women of the lower classes, who, in addition to their jobs: bring a child into the world every year, to see that the female body is not made for this, and that it in this way loses its form and gradually is ruined. . . .

The man has the role that he has been given by nature, he is everywhere the dominant, the attacker, in all areas of life, in all professions. . . . The woman is not made for the harder things of this world, but for ease, for joy, for beauty. . . .

But perhaps a women's movement will arise in this sense, one that frees the woman as a sexual being, and which teaches her to demand what it is proper to demand, full sexual freedom, that is, full control over her body, which publicly sanctioned promiscuity will bring back. Please, no cries of indignation! The temple courtesans of antiquity were free, highly cultivated, and respected women, and no one took offense when they gave their love and their bodies to whom and as often as they like and at the same time took part in the intellectual life enjoyed by men. Instead of this, Christianity created monogamy—and prostitution. The latter is a proof that marriage is a flawed institution. While, by means of Christian moral education, there is an attempt to kill the sexual feelings of one part of womankind . . . at the same time, prostitution is institutionalized, and thereby another part of womankind is compelled to be polygamous in order to service men for whom marriage is unsatisfying. . . .

To return to the women's movement: it is the declared enemy of all erotic culture, because it wants to make women into men. . . .

Darwin tells us that the English sheep breeders weed out the sexual mutants from their herds because they don't produce either beautiful wool or good mutton chops. Nature has already done the same among humans; the newest textbooks on anatomical pathologies show that hermaphrodites are dying out. The viragoes, who want to do away with our men, are for the most part just hermaphroditic ghosts who will soon be banished by the healthy erotic spirit of the new paganism whose triumph we await in the next century.

→ *How does Reventlow define a woman's freedom?*
→ *How does Reventlow's vision for a woman's freedom compare to "lipstick" feminism today?*

SOURCE: Franziska von Reventlow, "Viragines oder Hetaeren," in *Autobiographisches: Novellen, Schriften, Selbstzeugnisse,* edited by Else Reventlow (translated by S. Marchand) (Frankfurt: Ullstein Verlag, 1986), pp. 236–49.

strictions were further breached as economic developments created new paid jobs for women. At century's end, women were increasingly employed as teachers, secretaries, typists, department store clerks, social workers, and telephone operators. These jobs offered women a greater degree of economic and social independence. They also required some education, which was increasingly open to women. Some of these educated women became involved in public life, spearheading efforts to improve the conditions of the urban poor and to expand the role of government in the regulation of economic affairs. A large portion of the population, however, continued to think that higher education and public activism were not suitable for women.

Probably the most important change in women's lives was the control that many began to assert over reproduction. Although many countries had made it a crime to advocate the use of contraceptive devices, women still found ways to limit the number of children they bore. At the opening of the twentieth century, the birthrate in America was half of what it had been at the beginning of the nineteenth century. By having fewer children, families could devote more income to education, food, housing, and leisure activities. Naturally, too, declining birthrates, on top of improved medicine, meant that fewer women died in childbirth and more could expect to see their children reach adulthood.

Still, these changes in women's social status did not translate readily into electoral reform at the national level. At midcentury, several women's suffrage movements had been founded, but these campaigns bore little immediate fruit. In 1868, women received the right to vote in local elections in Britain. Within a few years, Finland, Sweden, and some American states allowed single, property-owning women the

Woman Suffrage in Finland. The British and then the French introduced the concept of citizenship with universal rhetoric, but in practice the category of citizen was generally restricted to property-holding males. Only gradually were all men, and then women, recognized as citizens, with the right to own property, associate in public, and vote. Finland granted its women the right to vote in 1906, earlier than most countries. In the photo, the Finnish woman casts her ballot in the election of 1906.

right to cast their ballots, again only in local elections. Women obtained the right to vote in national elections in New Zealand in 1893, in Australia in 1902, in Finland in 1906, and in Norway in 1913. Despite these gains, male alarmists frequently portrayed women's suffrage and women's rights as the beginning of civilization's end.

To be sure, most middle-class women were not seeking to make women equal to men. Many bourgeois women recoiled from the symbiotic relationships that existed in many countries between socialism and feminism. In Latin America, for example, anarchists championed a version of feminism, arguing that the abolition of private property would liberate women from their misery and that the traditional family was a bourgeois convention. Other women feared becoming too "mannish," and a few feared equality would destroy female sensuality. Most, probably, looked to reform less in the shape of suffrage than simply in the form of better treatment and more autonomy within families and local communities (see primary source boxes).

Radicalized women, like radicalized men, met stiff repression wherever they challenged the established order. In 1903, China's Qiu Jin (1875–1907) left her husband and headed to Japan to study. There she was drawn to other radicals and made a name for herself by dressing in men's clothing, carrying a sword, and trying her hand at bombmaking. Returning to China in 1906, she founded the *Chinese Women's Journal* (*Zhongguo nübao*) and wrote articles urging women to fight for their rights and to leave home if necessary. She remained a radical and was executed by the Qing after she participated in a failed attempt to topple the dynasty in 1907.

In the colonial world, the woman question was a hotly debated issue, but there it was mainly argued among males. European authorities liked to boast that colonial rule improved the status of women. They cited examples of traditional societies' subordination of women in Africa and Asia and insisted that women fared better under European rule. They criticized the practices of veiling women in Islamic societies, binding women's feet in China, widow burning (*sati*) in India, and female genital mutilation in Africa as evidence of barbarism. Europeans believed that prohibiting such acts was a justification for colonial intervention.

And yet, women in Africa, the Middle East, and India found colonialism added to their burdens. As male workers were drawn into the export economy, formerly shared agricultural work fell exclusively on women's shoulders. In Africa, for example, the opening of vast new gold and diamond mines induced thousands of men to go to work in the mines, leaving women to fend for themselves. Similarly, the rise of large European-owned agricultural estates in Kenya and southern Rhodesia depleted surrounding villages of male family members, who went to work on the estates. In these circumstances, women kept the local, food-producing economy afloat. Nor did colonial "civilizing" rhetoric improve women's

Primary Source

A CHINESE FEMINIST CONDEMNS INJUSTICES TO WOMEN

Although a small minority, the Chinese feminists of the early twentieth century were vocal in their condemnation of the injustices inflicted upon women in China. In this famous essay from 1904 titled "An Address to Two Hundred Million Fellow Countrywomen," Qiu Jin compares the treatment of Chinese women to slavery. Typical of her generation, Qiu's feminism also bears a strong nationalistic streak as she ties the future of Chinese women to the fate of the Chinese nation.

Alas! The greatest injustice in this world must be the injustice suffered by our female population of two hundred million. If a girl is lucky enough to have a good father, then her childhood is at least tolerable. But if by chance her father is an ill-tempered and unreasonable man, he may curse her birth: "What rotten luck: another useless thing." Some men go as far as killing baby girls while most hold the opinion that "girls are eventually someone else's property" and treat them with coldness and disdain. In a few years, without thinking about whether it is right or wrong, he forcibly binds his daughter's soft, white feet with white cloth so that even in her sleep she cannot find comfort and relief until the flesh becomes rotten and the bones broken. What is all this misery for? Is it just so that on the girl's wedding day friends and neighbors will compliment him, saying, "Your daughter's feet are really small"? Is that what the pain is for?

But that is not the worst of it. When the time for marriage comes, a girl's future life is placed in the hands of a couple of shameless matchmakers and a family seeking rich and powerful in-laws. A match can be made without anyone ever inquiring whether the prospective bridegroom is honest, kind, or educated. On the day of the marriage the girl is forced into a red and green bridal sedan chair, and all this time she is not allowed to breathe one word about her future. . . .

When Heaven created people it never intended such injustice because if the world is without women, how can men be born? Why is there no justice for women? We constantly hear men say, "The human mind is just and we must treat people with fairness and equality." Then why do they greet women like black slaves from Africa?

How did inequality and injustice reach this state? . . .

I hope that we all shall put aside the past and work hard for the future. Let us all put aside our former selves and be resurrected as complete human beings. Those of you who are old, do not call yourselves old and useless. If your husbands want to open schools, don't stop them; if your good sons want to study abroad, don't hold them back. Those among us who are middle-aged, don't hold back your husbands lest they lose their ambition and spirit and fail in their work. After your sons are born, send them to schools. You must do the same for your daughters and, whatever you do, don't bind their feet. As for you young girls among us, go to school if you can. If not, read and study at home. Those of you who are rich, persuade your husbands to open schools, build factories, and contribute to charitable organizations. Those of you who are poor, work hard and help your husbands. Don't be lazy, don't eat idle rice. These are what I hope for you. You must know that when a country is near destruction, women cannot rely on the men any more because they aren't even able to protect themselves. If we don't take heart now and shape up, it will be too late when China is destroyed.

Sisters, we must follow through on these ideas!

➢ *Why does Qiu Jin compare the plight of Chinese women to slavery?*
➢ *Why is nationalism an important part of her message?*

Source: Qiu Jin, "An Address to Two Hundred Million Fellow Countrywomen," in *Chinese Civilization: A Sourcebook* (2nd ed., revised and expanded), edited by Patricia Buckley Ebrey (New York: The Free Press, 1993), pp. 342–44.

Primary Source

INDUSTRIALIZATION AND WOMEN'S FREEDOM IN EGYPT

In this selection, taken from a 1909 lecture in Cairo open only to women, Bahithat al-Badiya (1886–1918) insists that female confinement is unnatural and absurd, and demands a place for women in the workplace. Here, the writer, an educated upper-class Egyptian woman, deplores the effect of traditional religious practices on women's freedom, but she also urges her countrywomen not to follow blindly in the path of the West.

Men say when we become educated we shall push them out of work and abandon the role for which God created us. But isn't it rather men who have pushed women out of work? Before, women used to spin and to weave cloth for clothes for themselves and their children, but men invented machines for spinning and weaving and put women out of work. . . . Since male inventors and workers have taken away a lot of our work should we waste our time in idleness or seek other work to occupy us? Of course, we should do the latter. . . . Obviously, I am not urging women to neglect their home and children to go out and become lawyers or judges or railway engineers. But if any of us wish to work in such professions our personal freedom should not be infringed. . . .

Men say to us categorically, "You women have been created for the house and we have been created to be bread-winners." Is this a God-given dictate? How are we to know this since no holy book has spelled it out? Political economy calls for a division of labor but if women enter the learned professions it does not upset the system. The division of labor is merely a human creation. . . . If men say to us that we have been created weak we say to them, "No it is you who made us weak through the path you made us

follow." After long centuries of enslavement by men, our minds rusted and our bodies weakened. . . .

Men criticize the way we dress in the street. They have a point because we have exceeded the bounds of custom and propriety. . . . [But:] veiling should not prevent us from breathing fresh air or going out to buy what we need if no one can buy it for us. It must not prevent us from gaining an education nor cause our health to deteriorate. When we have finished our work and feel restless and if our house does not have a spacious garden why shouldn't we go to the outskirts of the city and take the fresh air that God has created for everyone and not just put in boxes exclusively for men.

→ *How has al-Badiya's Muslim faith influenced her views on the role of women in society?*

→ *How have western influences affected her views on the role of women in society?*

SOURCE: Bahithat al-Badiya, "A Public Lecture for Women Only in the Club of the Umma Party," in *Opening the Gates: A Century of Arab Feminist Writing*, edited by Margot Badran and Miriam Cooke (translated by Ali Badran and Margot Badran) (Indianapolis: Indiana University Press, 1990), pp. 228–38.

political or cultural circumstances. European missionaries preached a cult of domesticity to Asian and African families, emphasizing that a woman's place was in the home raising children and that women's education should be different from that of men. Thus males overwhelmingly dominated the new schools that Europeans built. Customary law in colonial Africa, as interpreted by chiefs who collaborated with the colonial powers, favored men, and women were often deprived of landholding and other rights that they had enjoyed before the arrival of Europeans.

CLASS CONFLICT IN A NEW KEY

Capitalism's new dynamism, and especially its volatility, as we have seen, shook confidence in free market economies.

Although living conditions for European and North American workers improved over time, increasing inequalities in income led to sharper conflicts between the classes. While most of these workers remained committed to peaceful agitation, some radicals gave up on capitalism and on the political process and turned to violence to achieve their aims. Often, especially in eastern Europe and Russia, the conservative and closed character of political systems contributed to the growth of frustration—and of radicalism. This was also the case in Latin America, where economic development was not accompanied by political democratization. Here, the middle classes, too, were largely shut out of politics until the rise of new parties offered fresh opportunities for political expression. In Argentina, for example, workers found syndicalism (the organization of workplace associations for even the unskilled laborers), socialism, and anarchism appealing banners for urban protest.

In the Americas and in Europe, radicals of various persuasions adopted numerous new tactics for asserting the interests of the working class. In Europe, the franchise was gradually expanded in the hopes that the lower orders would prefer voting to revolution—and indeed, most of the new political parties that catered to workers had no desire to overthrow the state. Conservatives feared them nonetheless, especially as they began to achieve real electoral clout. The Labour Party, which was founded in Britain in 1900, quickly gained a large share of the vote. By 1912, the German Social Democratic Party had become the largest party in the Reichstag. But it was not the legally sanctioned parties that sparked the violent street protests and strikes, which grew exponentially in the last decades of the century. A whole array of syndicalists, anarchists, radical royalists, and revolutionary socialists sprang up in this period, making work stoppages, particularly in big cities like Paris, everyday affairs.

Although the United States did not see the emergence of similarly radical factions or successful labor parties, American workers were also organizing in larger numbers. The new power of the labor movement burst forth dramatically in 1894 when the newly organized American Railway Union launched a strike that spread across the nation. Spawned by wage cuts and firings in the wake of an economic downturn, the Pullman Strike (directed against the maker of railway sleeping cars, George Pullman) involved approximately 3 million workers. The strike's conclusion was, however, indicative of the enduring power of the status quo. After hiring replacement workers to break the strike, Pullman requested the intervention of federal troops to protect his operation. The troops arrived, infuriating strikers and precipitating violence, which led to a further crackdown by the government against the union. When its leaders were jailed, the strike by the American Railway Union against the Pullman Company collapsed.

A few upheavals from below did succeed—at least briefly. In 1905, in the wake of the Russo-Japanese War, in which the Russians were defeated by the Japanese, revolt briefly shook the tsarist state, forcing Nicholas II (ruled 1894–1917) to establish a fledgling form of representative government. The revolutionaries tried some new forms, most notably workers' soviets, which were groups of delegates representing particular industries. A wave of peasant uprisings ensued.

Latin American Labor Organizing. The upsurge in social agitation in Buenos Aires, one of the world's biggest cities in 1914, led to a wave of labor organizing. This photograph shows the leader of the Cart-Drivers' Union talking with rank-and-file-members.

Ultimately, however, the army put down both urban and rural unrest, and autocracy was reestablished; the liberals, not to mention the radicals, were excluded from power.

Perhaps the most successful turn-of-the-century revolution occurred in Mexico. This was the century's first great peasant revolution, and it thoroughly transformed Mexico. Long in gestation and fueled by the unequal distribution of land and by disgruntled workers, the Mexican Revolution erupted in 1910 when political elites openly split over the succession of General Porfirio Díaz after decades of his strong-arm rule. Dissidents balked when Díaz refused to step down, and peasants and workers rallied to the call to arms. What destroyed the Díaz regime and its powerful army were the swelling armies of peasants, farmers, cattlemen, and rural workers desperate for a change in the social order. From the north—led by the charismatic, if mercurial, Pancho Villa—to the south—under the helm of the legendary Emiliano Zapata —rural folk helped topple the Díaz regime. In the name of providing land for the farmers and ending oligarchic rule, peasant armies defeated General Díaz's troops; they then proceeded to destroy many of Mexico's large estates. The fighting lasted for ten brutal years, at the cost of 1 million Mexicans, almost 10 percent of the country's population. But popular forces succeeded, forcing new political leaders to accept their demands for democracy, respect for the sovereignty of peasant communities, and land reform. The Constitution of 1917 incorporated widespread reform. By 1920, as the revolution was winding down, an emerging generation of politicians recognized the power of a mobilized and militarized peasantry and began to implement deep-seated changes in Mexico's social structure. These leaders also realized that they needed to make their new regime ideologically appealing to popular folk. The revolution thus spawned a set of new national myths, based on the heroism of rural peoples, Mexican nationalism, and a celebration of the Aztec past.

Although the Mexican Revolution succeeded in toppling the old elite, elsewhere in Latin America the ruling establishment remained united and withstood assaults from below. Already in 1897, the Brazilian army had mercilessly suppressed a millenarian peasant movement in the northeastern part of the country. Moreover, in Cuba, the Spanish and then the American armies crushed organized tenant farmers' efforts to reclaim land from sugar estates. In Guatemala, Mayan Indians lost land to coffee barons and their private troops.

The preservation of established orders did not rest on repression alone. By the century's end, left-wing agitators, muckraking reporters, and middle-class reformers began to achieve their goal of meaningful social improvements. Elites, unwilling to rely purely on force to stay in power, grudgingly agreed to gradual change. Unable to suppress the socialist movement, Otto von Bismarck, the German chancellor, defused the appeal of socialism by enacting social welfare measures in 1883–1884 (as did France in 1904 and England in 1906). He pushed through legislation insuring workers against

The Pullman Strike. In 1894, in response to wage cuts and layoffs by the Pullman Company, the American Railway Union organized a nationwide strike that brought 3 million workers onto the picket lines. That year's labor unrest often turned violent, as in the incident pictured here, showing strikers setting fire to several hundred freight cars.

The Mexican Revolution. (*Left*) By 1915, Mexican peasants, workers, and farmers had destroyed much of the old elitist system. This was the first popular, peasant revolution of the twentieth century. Among the most famous leaders were Pancho Villa and Emiliano Zapata. They are pictured here in the presidential office in the capital. Villa took the president's chair jokingly. Zapata, carrying the broad hat typical of his people, refused to wear military gear and glowered at the camera suspiciously. (*Right*) By the 1920s, Mexican artists and writers were putting recent events into images and words. Pictured here is one of the muralist Diego Rivera's paintings of the Mexican Revolution. Notice the nationalist interpretation: Porfirio Díaz's troops defend foreign oil companies and white aristocrats against middle-class and peasant (and darker-skinned) reformers who call for a "social revolution." Observe also the absence of women in this epic mural.

illness, accidents, and old age and establishing maximum working hours. In the United States, it took lurid journalistic accounts of unsanitary practices in Chicago slaughterhouses —including tales of workers falling into lard vats and being rendered into cooking fat—to spur the federal government into action. In 1906, President Theodore Roosevelt signed a Meat Inspection Act that provided for government supervision of meatpacking operations. Ironically, this measure, though opposed vigorously by meatpackers, ultimately helped to restore the public's confidence in a much tarnished industry; in numerous other cases (banking, steel production, railroads), the enhancement of the federal government's supervisory authority served corporate interests as well.

These consumer and family protection measures were part of a broader reform movement, in the United States especially but also elsewhere, dedicated to creating a more efficient society and correcting the unsavory consequences of urbanization and industrialization. At local and state levels, self-styled progressive reformers attacked corrupt city governments that had, in the eyes of mostly native-born reformers, fallen into the hands of immigrant-dominated "political machines." Other vices, such as gambling, drinking, and prostitution, all associated in reformers' minds with industrialized, urban settings, were also targeted by progressives. The creation of city parks became an obsession for urban planners, who hoped their greenery would serve as the "lungs" of

the city and offer healthier (and less dangerous) forms of entertainment than houses of prostitution, gambling dens, and bars. In Europe and the United States, thousands of associations were formed in the hopes of tempering capitalism's excesses. From Scandinavia to California, the backers of old-age pensions and the proponents of public ownership of utilities put pressure on lawmakers, and they occasionally succeeded in changing state policies. Intervening in the market and attending to the needs of the poor, the aged, the unemployed, and the sick in ways never dreamed of in classical liberal philosophy, reform movements laid the foundations for the modern welfare state.

CULTURAL MODERNISM

→ *How was cultural modernism manifested in different fields?*

As revolutionaries and reformers wrestled with the problems of progress, intellectuals, artists, and scientists also revealed the age's insecurities and uncertainties. What we call "modernism," the self-conscious sense of having broken with tradition, came to prominence in many fields, from physics to architecture, from painting to the social sciences. The movement largely originated from the experimental thinking shaped by turn-of-the-century anxieties. Emblematic of innovative conceptions was the work of Sigmund Freud (1856–1939), the Jewish physician in Vienna who emphasized the power of sexual drives in the formation of individual character. Modernist movements were also notably international as traffic in ideas and forms now passed in multiple directions. Egyptian social scientists read the works of European thinkers, while French and German painters flocked to museums to inspect artifacts from Egypt, as well as artworks collected from other parts of Africa, Asia, and Oceania. These museums, as well as numerous international exhibitions that were held in the second half of the century, reflected a change in the meaning of "culture," which was gradually becoming less elitist and more democratic.

The European elites did not give up their opera houses and paintings, however, in favor of arts and entertainments that were popular among urban workers or colonized peoples. To the contrary, elite culture became even more elitist as modern musicians abandoned the comfort of harmonic and diatonic sound (the eight-tone scale standard in classical western music at the time) and left representational art behind. Contemptuous of the popular press and of what they considered to be middle-brow forms of beauty, many artists sought to demonstrate their avant-garde, or cutting-edge,

Sigmund Freud, at Work in His Study in Vienna. Freud surrounded himself not only with books but also with Egyptian figurines and African masks, expressions of universal artistic prowess—and irrational psychological drives.

originality, spurning sales figures for loftier ambitions. "Art for art's sake" became the motto of some of these artists; their aim was to speak to posterity, not to the undiscriminating bourgeois public of the present.

Above all, modernism in arts and sciences replaced the certainties of the Enlightenment with the unsettledness of the new age. No longer confident about civilizing missions or urban and industrial "progress," artists and scientists struggled to make sense of a world in which older beliefs and traditional faiths had given way. What would come next, however, was unknown.

POPULAR CULTURE COMES OF AGE

By the late nineteenth century, the production and consumption of the arts, books, music, and sports were much different from what they had been a century earlier, thanks chiefly to new urban settings, technological innovations, and increased leisure time. As education, especially in America and Europe, became nearly universal, there were many more readers and museum-goers. At the same time, there were also new forms of cultural activity that were created by and for non-elite members of society. Lithographs and mass-produced engravings were bought by middle-class art lovers who could not afford original paintings; dance halls and vaudeville (a form of entertainment that included popular singers, dancers, and comedians) pleased millions who could not attend operas and formal dress balls. For the first time, sports began to attract mass followings, making soccer in Europe, baseball in the United States, and cricket in India highly popular games that had middle- and working-class fans.

At the century's close, the press had emerged as a major form of popular entertainment and information. This was partly because publishers had begun to cater to specialized markets, offering different wares to different classes of readers —and because there were now many more who could read among the world's inhabitants, especially in Europe and the Americas. The "yellow press" was full of stories of murder and sensationalism that appealed to the urban masses. By the turn of the century, the English *Daily Mail* and the French *Petit Parisien* boasted circulations over 1 million. In the United States, urban dwellers, many of whom were immigrants, avidly read newspapers, some in English, others in their native languages. Here, too, newspapers like Joseph Pulitzer's *New York World* and William Randolph Hearst's *New York Journal* employed banner headlines, sensational stories, and simple language to reach out to readers with little education— or rudimentary English. Books, too, increased in number— and fell in price; penny novels about cowboys, murder, and romance became the rage. The Mexican printmaker and artist José Guadalupe Posada became a favorite source of what might be considered a forerunner of comics. In fliers, new songs, cooking recipes, and especially gory sensational news

Díaz and the Liberal Party. In this 1910 print, the Mexican satirist José Guadalupe Posada portrays the leaders of the popular Liberal Party as being literally under the feet of the elitist followers of General Porfirio Díaz.

stories, Posada criticized the Díaz regime and revolutionary excess and parodied Mexican life in the country's popular penny press. His allegorical skeleton drawings, known as *calaveras*, issued for Mexico's celebration of the Day of the Dead, dwelled on popular themes of betrayal, death, and festivity.

By the turn of the century, the kind of culture one consumed had become a reflection of one's real (or desired) status in society, a central part of one's identity. For many Latin American workers, for example, reading one's own newspaper or comic strip was part of the business of being a worker. Argentina's socialist newspaper, *La Vanguardia*, was one of Buenos Aires's most prominent periodicals, read and debated at work and in the popular cafés of the city's working-class neighborhoods. Anyone seen reading the bourgeois paper, *La Prensa*, was heckled and ridiculed by proletarian peers.

The community of cultural consumers was now much enlarged from that of previous centuries, and writers, artists, and scholars were now subject to a much wider range of influences than ever before. As new forms and ideas trickled in, regions with rich cultural traditions and an elite class of producers, as in Europe and China, tried to adapt to the social, political, and economic changes all around them. Their attempts to confront the brave new world in the making resulted in a series of remarkable innovations, which have usually been described as "modernism."

EUROPE'S CULTURAL MODERNISM

In intellectual and artistic terms, Europe at the turn of the twentieth century experienced perhaps its richest age since the Renaissance. A desire to understand social and imperial maladies laid the foundations for the twentieth century's social sciences; the French scholar Emile Durkheim (1858–1917), for example, pioneered the field of sociology by studying what he took to be a characteristic affliction of his age, suicide. In 1895, the popular writer Gustave Le Bon (1841–1931) wrote a treatise on crowd behavior that became a classic in Europe and beyond; he equated the unconscious volatility of crowds with the irrationality of women and "primitives." Le Bon's work, a true product of the century's end, gained great popularity, appealing to, among others, Benito Mussolini in Italy and Vladimir Lenin in Russia.

The work of artists reflected their ambivalence about the modern, as represented by the railroad, the big city, and the factory. While the left-leaning impressionists and realists of the mid-nineteenth century had largely celebrated progress, the painters and novelists of the century's end almost universally took a darker view. They turned away from enlightened clarity and descriptive prose in search of new, more mysterious and instinctual truths. In this epoch, the primitive came to symbolize both the romance of lost innocence and the terrors of the prerational mind. The term *primitivism* accurately reflects the ambivalence of this new appreciation for nonwestern art. The painter who led the way in incorporating these themes into modern art was Pablo Picasso (1881–1973). The son of an impressionist painter, Picasso found in African art forms, notably masks and wood carvings, a shocking new way of expressing interior human sentiments. Against considerable conservative criticism, Picasso and his contemporaries claimed that African and Oceanic forms were both beautiful and more instinctual than overly refined western forms.

Europeans began to see the world in a fundamentally different way, aided by the experience of nonwestern visual arts. A way of seeing that was structured by classical and Christian images and forms, pervasive since the Renaissance, now began to seem at best banal, at worst lifeless and passé. The experience of seeing the artwork of other peoples was essential to this revolutionary change. But there were many other sources of this new vision, from anti-bourgeois attitudes

Pablo Picasso. The Franco-Spanish artist Pablo Picasso was one of the first to incorporate "primitive" artistic forms into his work. Here he is pictured with some of his ceramic work outside his studio at Vallauris, France. Picasso's revolutionary painting *Les Demoiselles d'Avignon* (The Courtesans of Avignon), completed in 1907, was inspired by the artist's study of African sculpture and masks.

among Bohemian (unconventional) artists, to a new machine aesthetic, to the desire to convey the content of dreams. And painting was certainly not the only art form in which contemporary observers registered the arrival of a modern style. Arnold Schönberg (1874–1951) composed the first piece of music with no reference to a key and began to explore the limits of western tonality. World-famous dancers like Isadora Duncan (1877–1927) pioneered the expressive, free-form movements that laid the foundations for modern dance.

But the arts alone did not undermine older Christian, classical, and comfortable views of the world. Even science, in which the Enlightenment had placed so much faith, worked a disenchanting magic on the liberal, Victorian worldview. Darwinism claimed that progress could not be achieved without a "struggle for existence." James Clerk Maxwell (1831–1879), the Scottish physicist, described the law of entropy, which indicated that our universe was destined to die. Matter, Maxwell argued, is moved by heat, but as heat over time increasingly loses its ability to move particles, and as the universe has a fixed supply of energy, sooner or later, entropy —the inability of heat to do work—will set in, and an exhausted, chaotic universe will emerge. In Maxwell's wake, the pioneering physicists and mathematicians of the turn of the century took apart the Enlightenment's conviction that man could achieve full knowledge of, and control over, nature.

Probabilities took the place of certainties in physics. Although most scientists continued to collect data with the conviction that they could and would plumb nature's depths, some of their prescient colleagues began to question the arrogance expressed in this view.

From the time of the Enlightenment, Europeans had prided themselves on their "reason"; to be rational was to be civilized, and respectable, middle-class nineteenth-century men were thought to be exemplars of both of these high virtues. But in the late nineteenth century, faith in rationality began to falter; perhaps reason was *not* man's highest attainment, said some; perhaps reason was too hard for man to sustain, said others. Friedrich Nietzsche (1844–1900) demonstrated that behind many a bourgeois truism lay not reason, but what he called the "will to power." Sigmund Freud began to excavate the layers of the human subconscious, where all sorts of irrational desires and fears lay buried. For Freud, human nature was not as simple as it had seemed to the thinkers of the Enlightenment—humans were driven by sexual longings and childhood traumas, some of these so thoroughly repressed that they were revealed only as neuroses, in dreams, or in the course of extensive psychoanalysis (a therapy Freud invented). Neither Nietzsche (who went mad in 1889) nor Freud (who lived almost long enough to become respectable) was well loved, certainly not among the nineteenth-century liberal elites. But in the new century, Nietzsche would be made the prophet for a wide range of antiliberal, antirational causes, from nudism to Nazism, and Freud's dark vision, more than that of any other intellectual, would become central to the twentieth century's understanding of the self.

CULTURAL MODERNISM IN CHINA

What it meant to be modern was a question that was debated beyond the borders of western Europe and North America. In other parts of the world, too, the debate did not yield to a particular meaning. The Europeans provided one set of answers; intellectuals elsewhere, drawing on separate cultural traditions and confronted with different problems, often offered quite different answers. For example, the Chinese literati also became caught up in the debate about what it meant to be modern, and they articulated their own perspectives. As in Europe, Chinese artists and scientists at the turn of the century engaged in considerable experimentation and innovation, including selectively importing western ideas and cultural forms. In the realm of literature, for instance, late Qing writers strove to produce narrative strategies that were recognizably new; their works explored the self, technology, and sexuality. As in the West, Chinese writers could now write for a wider and more diverse readership. By the end of the nineteenth century, there were more than 170 presses in China serving a potential readership of 2 to 4 million. Indeed, some have argued that the late Qing period should be described as a time of competing cultural *modernities*, in contrast to the post-Qing era, characterized by the self-conscious pursuit of a single, western-oriented *modernity*. These forms of modernity were characterized by both critical reflection on Chinese traditions and ambivalent reactions to western culture.

Consumers of late Qing literature were most likely to be urbanites, particularly in the treaty ports, the coastal cities that had been designated as centers of trade and residence for the growing foreign community. These cities typically boasted an environment that was more economically vibrant and culturally fluid than the hinterlands. Not only was there an expanding body of readers, but the *nouveaux riches*, beneficiaries of the newly reconfigured treaty-port economy, now formed a group of patrons for the arts. In the latter half of the nineteenth century, for example, painters from different parts of the lower Yangzi region congregated in Shanghai to practice their craft. Collectively known as the Shanghai School, they symbolized the vitality of the artistic scene. The Shanghai painters adopted elements from both indigenous and foreign sources for their innovations in compositional structure, coloring, figural rendering, and spatial conception. Classically trained, they appropriated western technical novelties into their artistic practice. One of the most famous ear-

lier examples was the self-portrait of the artist Ren Xiong (1820–1857), an arresting image of the artist himself, bareheaded and legs apart, standing upright and staring straight at the viewer. Ren Xiong was not the only Chinese artist whose work embraced photography, although the effect of this new visual medium was usually most popular among professional effigy painters rather than scholarly artists.

Similarly, the fantasy novels of the late Qing period drew both on the authors' knowledge of western science and on indigenous supernatural beliefs. Experimental writers turned out titles such as *The End of the World*, *Moon Colony*, and *The Future of New China*, some of which explicitly treated the question of Chinese-western relations. The 1908 novel *New Era*, for example, put its opening scenes in the year 1999, by which time China had become a supreme world power and a constitutional monarchy. Depicting China at war with western powers, *New Era* celebrated conventional military ventures and heroism, but it also introduced the readers to new inventions such as electricity-repellent clothing and bulletproof satin. More visionary still was the novel *The Stone of Goddess Nüwa*, published in 1905. Here the male author imagined a technologically advanced feminist utopia in which the female residents studied subjects ranging from the arts to physics, drove electric cars, and were nourished by purified liquid extracts of food from a breast-shaped device. Their mission was to save China by getting rid of corrupt male officials. As the authors of these fantasy novels combined the fanciful with the critical, their works sought to resolve the very real cultural tensions of their era and offered a new and provocative vision of China.

Ren Xiong, Self-Portrait. This famous self-portrait of Ren Xiong was most likely produced in the 1850s. Ren Xiong was probably familiar with the new practice of portrait photography in the treaty ports. Although his self-portrait reproduced some old conventions of Chinese scholarly art, such as the unity of the visual image with a lengthy self-composed inscription, it is also clear that, through its rather unconventional pose and image, Ren Xiong had pointed to the establishment of a new kind of subject position characteristic of the trend of cultural modernism in China during this period.

Yet, if western science proved to be an inspiration for late Qing writers, its integration into Chinese culture was an intellectual challenge. Did being modern entail forsaking China's scholarly traditions, or could western science exist alongside Chinese values? The nineteenth century had seen Christian missionaries, following in the footsteps of the Jesuits, use their scientific knowledge to attract followers. For example, John Fryer, an English missionary and translator, founded *The Science Journal* (*Gezhi huibian*) in 1876. Other publications in the same period included *The Universal Gazette* (*Wanguo gongbao*). Recognizing its utilitarian value, many Chinese scholars assisted missionaries in their efforts to promote western science, although they continued to regard it mostly as a means of acquiring national wealth and power rather than as a means of understanding the world. It is not surprising that they took this stance; western visitors to China also tended to present science as little more than a means to material ends. The result was that while steamships, telegraphs, and railroads captured public attention, there was little interest in changing fundamental Chinese beliefs. Indeed, even as Chinese intellectuals lamented how traditional learning had fallen victim to empty and superfluous studies and even as they recognized the need to incorporate new modes of knowledge into their repertoire, many members of the elite insisted that traditional Chinese learning remain the principal source of all knowledge. What kind of balance should exist between western thought and Chinese learning, or indeed whether the ancient classics should retain their fundamental role, remained an issue that would haunt generations to come.

> *Nationalist and racial ideas had different configurations in different portions of the world.*

RETHINKING RACE AND REIMAGINING NATIONS

> → *How did conceptions about race and nation change in this era?*

Ironically, in this world of huge population transfers and increasingly shared technological modernization, individuals and nations became passionate defenders of the idea that identities were deeply rooted and unchangeable. Although physical characteristics had always played *some* role in identifying persons, by the late nineteenth century, the Linnaean classifications developed in the eighteenth century had become the means for ranking the worth of whole nations. As we saw in Chapter 17, race now defined who could belong to the nation and share in its rights and privileges; by the century's close, racial roots had also become a crucial part of cultural identity. This was the era, par excellence, of ethnographic museums, folkloric collectors, national essence movements, and racial genealogies; people wanted to know who they (and their neighbors) were—and, increasingly, this was defined by one's *biological* ancestry. Just as traditional ways of life and family ties were being disrupted by imperialism and extensive industrialization, inheritance took on new weight, both in cultural and in biological forms. Doctors, officials, and novelists described the genetic inheritance of madness, alcoholism, criminality, and even homosexuality; nationalists spoke of the uniqueness of the Slavic soul, the German mind, Hindu spirituality, the Hispanic race. The preoccupation with race testified to a worldwide longing for new, fixed roots—and unshakable hierarchies—in an age that seemed to be burning all its bridges to the past.

Nationalist and racial ideas had different configurations in different portions of the world. In Europe and America, debates about race and national purity evolved from a combination of fears about the loss of individuality and vitality in a technological world, rising tensions between states, and fear of being defeated or overrun by the brown, black, and yellow peoples beyond the borders of "civilization." By contrast, in India, these ideas evolved as part of an anticolonial discourse, and they were involved in the beginnings of popular political mobilization, particularly among the urban elite. This was also the case in China, Latin America, and the Islamic world, where discussions of identity were wrapped up with opposition to western domination and to corrupt indigenous elites. Especially in the colonial and semicolonial world, the question of racial identity was very much a question about the coherence and endurance of the community, not about the races of man in general.

These new voices and new fears produced a variety of new national movements, from China's anti-Qing campaign to India's Swadeshi movement. At the same time, panethnic movements attempted to go beyond the nation-state, proposing the creation of communities based on ethnicity. Although these projects were not realized then, the notion that political communities should be built on racial purity or draw on unsullied indigenous traditions did not die. These new national and panethnic movements inspired later leaders, especially in the years between the two world wars. They also offered further evidence of just how unsettled the world was by the century's end and how urgent the questions of identity and belonging had become.

NATION AND RACE IN NORTH AMERICA AND EUROPE

In the United States, where belief in progress had been strongest, the changing temper was particularly striking. Americans greeted the end of the century with a combination of chest-beating pride and shoulder-slumping pessimism. In the early 1890s, for example, Americans flocked to scores of extravagant commemorations of the four hundredth anniversary of Christopher Columbus's discovery. The largest of these was the Columbian Exposition in Chicago. At that world's fair and at smaller gatherings, Americans saw displays of the most modern machinery and celebrated the nation's marvelous destiny. Yet, even as Americans glorified the progress of their times, they worried about the present and future of their nation. Foremost among their anxieties was the fear that America had exhausted what had once been thought an infinite supply of new land and resources. The disappearance of the buffalo, the erosion of soils, and the depletion of once abundant timber stands by aggressive logging companies had worried some early conservationists, and that alarm became more intense with the 1890 announcement by the Census Bureau that the American frontier had "closed."

With the succession of Theodore Roosevelt (1858–1919) to the presidency in 1901, the concerns about conserving natural resources were translated into government policy. Fearing a world without conquerable frontiers, Roosevelt, like a growing number of his generation, agonized about the fate of market economies and the decline of America's pioneering ethos. The market, insisted Roosevelt and like-minded conservationists, could not be trusted to protect "nature." Instead, federal regulation, on a scale far beyond nineteenth-century imaginations, was necessary, leading to the creation in 1905 of the National Forest Service, with its cadre of scientifically trained officials to manage the development of millions of acres of permanent public lands. Roosevelt also feared that a nation dominated by impersonal corporations and populated primarily by urban-dwelling factory workers would lose its spirit of pioneer individualism. He worried in particular that modern comforts in post-frontier America would deprive men of the tests of rough-and-ready manhood that generations of pioneers had found in conquering Indians and taming wilderness. To give Americans a chance to play pioneer, Roosevelt pushed for lands to be set aside as wildlife reserves and national parks, where he hoped that future generations would continue to experience what he extolled as "the strenuous life."

What white Americans did not, in general, agonize about was what the African-American intellectual W. E. B. Du Bois (1868–1963) predicted would be "the problem of the twentieth century," that is, "the problem of the color line." Rather, white Americans were busily drawing color lines, initiating new forms of racial discrimination where old forms (like slavery) had broken down. In the American West, virulent animosity toward Chinese workers culminated in the 1882 Exclusion Act, which prohibited almost all immigration from China. In the

The Columbian Exposition. More than 27 million people attended the Columbian Exposition in Chicago in 1893. Like many of the era's world's fairs, the Columbian Exposition celebrated technological progress, including the spread of electricity, as evidenced by the General Electric Tower of Light, pictured on the left.

The Conservation Movement. Recognizing that certain vital resources were being rapidly depleted and concerned that urban men were losing the vitality of their pioneer forebears, a conservation movement gathered political strength in the United States in the last decades of the nineteenth century. Among the notable early victories for conservationists was the setting aside of California's Yosemite Valley as a national park.

American South, where most of the nation's 7 million African Americans resided, a system of "Jim Crow" laws codified racial segregation and inequality.

The anxieties of white Americans intensified as more and more "swarthy" immigrants entered the United States. These people were primarily from southern and eastern Europe, but to the champions of "Anglo-Saxonism" these Europeans were not "white." Even more threatening were the darker peoples over whom the United States now ruled as colonial subjects in the Philippines, Puerto Rico, and Cuba. Talk of the demise of white America permeated elite conversations, and these fears built support for more restrictive immigration policies.

These conversations about race and national identities were not limited to North America. Across the North Atlantic, European elites engaged in similar discussions. For European elites, the final divvying up of Africa was in many respects equivalent to the closing of the American frontier. The Germans and Italians, in particular, complained bitterly about the lack of new territories on which to plant their flags. The French and British began to worry more about how their empires were to be preserved, especially as they became more aware of the anticolonial sentiments that were seething in their domains.

Like Americans, Europeans also expressed concerns about trends at home. Intellectuals in Europe, as in the United States, suggested that mechanization deprived men of their vitality. At the same time, the spread of Darwinist theory provoked new anxieties about inherited diseases, racial mixing, and the dying out of white "civilizers." Sexual relations between European colonizers and indigenous women and the resulting mixed offspring had almost always been part of European expansionism, but as racial identities hardened, the consorting of white men with native women now seemed to threaten the moral fiber of the whole nation. A new discourse of virility arose, in part provoked by the increased involvement of doctors and scientists in the treatment of social problems. In the century's last decades, English and American schoolboys were encouraged to play sports, if not to be like pioneers, then at least to avoid becoming weak degenerates unable to defend the nation should the need arise. In addition, new medical attention was given to homosexuality, which was viewed as a disease and a threat to the future of Anglo-Saxon civilization. In France, the falling birthrate, especially after the loss of Alsace-Lorraine to Germany at the end of the Franco-Prussian War, convinced many officials, social scientists, and artists that their nation had entered a period of decadence, characterized by weak, sickly men and irrational women.

Some tied decadence to debates about whether or not Jews—defined by religious practice or, increasingly, simply by ethnicity—could be fully assimilated into European society. Even though Jews had been officially offered rights as citizens in most European nations by the nineteenth century's end, powerful prejudices against a group traditionally seen as dangerous outsiders persisted. In the Russian "Pale of Settlement," where most Jews lived, violent pogroms in the 1880s and 1890s pushed the persecuted to flee westward; the presence of these new emigrants stirred up fear and resentment, especially in Austria, Germany, and France. Reactionaries began to talk about the "pollution" of the European races by their mixture with Semites and to circulate rumors about the conspiratorial powers of Jewish bankers. Perhaps because nothing else seemed stable and enduring, white, well-to-do male Europeans, like their American counterparts, looked to racial purity to shore up the civilizations they saw coming apart at the seams.

RACE-MIXING AND THE PROBLEM OF NATIONHOOD IN LATIN AMERICA

Latin American debates about identity were chiefly defined by the question of ethnic intermixing and the legacy of a system of government that, unlike much of the North Atlantic world, excluded rather than included the populace. Social hierarchies reaching back to the sixteenth century ranked white Iberians at the top, creole elites in the middle, and indigenous and African populations at the bottom. According to this formulation, the higher on the social ladder, the more likely the people were to be white. In fact, however, the "racial" order did not stick, since some Iberians occupied the lower ranks, while a few people of color did manage to ascend the ladder. Moreover, starting in the 1880s, the racial hierarchy was further disrupted by the deluge of poor European migrants to prospering Latin American countrysides or to booming cities like Buenos Aires in Argentina or São Paulo in Brazil. Latin American societies, then, did not easily become homogeneous "nations." Indeed, many Latin American observers began to wonder whether national identities could survive these transformations at all.

In an age of acute nationalism, the mixed racial composition of Latin Americans generated special anxieties. In the 1870s in Mexico, it was common to view Indians as obstacles to change. The demographer Antonio García Cubas, for example, stressed what he considered to be "the decadence and degeneration in general of the indigenous race and the few elements of vitality and vigor that it offers for the republic's

progress." In Cuba and Brazil, observers made the same claims about blacks. Latin America, according to many modernizers, was being held back by its own people. The solution, argued some writers, was to attract white immigrants and to implement educational programs that would uplift Indians, blacks, and people of mixed descent. Thus, many intellectuals joined the crusade to modernize and westernize their populations.

For their part, Latin American leaders began to exalt a mythic past and to celebrate bygone glories as a way to promote a strong sense of national selfhood. In Mexico, General Díaz placed the bell that Father Hidalgo had tolled on September 16, 1810, to mark the beginning of the war against Spain (see Chapter 15) in the National Palace in Mexico City. In the month of that centennial in 1910, a series of grand processions wound through the capital. Many of these parades celebrated Aztec grandeur, thereby creating a mythic arc from the greatness of the Aztec past to the triumphal story of Mexican independence—and thence to the benevolence and progress of the Díaz regime. As the government glorified

Diego Rivera's History of Mexico. This is one of the most famous works of Mexican art, a portrait of the history of Mexico by the radical nationalist painter Diego Rivera. In this chapter and in previous chapters, we have illustrated parts of this mural. In stepping back to view the whole work, which is in the National Palace in Mexico City, we can see how Rivera envisioned the history of his people generally. Completed in 1935, this work seeks to show a people fighting constantly against outside aggressors, from their glorious preconquest days (lower center), winding like a grand epic through the conquest, colonial exploitation, the revolution for independence, nineteenth-century invasions from France and the United States, to the popular 1910 Revolution. It culminates in an image of Karl Marx, framed by a "scientific sun"—pointing to a future of progress and prosperity for all, as if restoring a modern Tenochtitlán of the Aztecs. This work captured many Mexicans' efforts to return to the indigenous roots of the nation and to fuse them with modern scientific ideas.

the Aztecs with pageants, statues, and pavilions, however, it continued to ignore modern Aztec descendants, who lived in squalor.

In these years, some thinkers began to celebrate a premodern basis of national identities. For some, especially in Mexico and eventually in the Andes, the pre-Spanish past became a crucial foundation stone of the nation-state. The young Mexican writer José Vasconcelos (1882–1959) grew disenchanted with the brutal rule of Díaz and his westernizing ambitions. Nonetheless, he endorsed Díaz's celebration of the Indian past—for his own purposes. Mexicans, he believed, were capable of a superior form of civilization. He insisted that if they were less driven by material concerns, their combined Aztec and Spanish Catholic origins could create a spiritual domain of even higher achievement. Mexico's greatness flowed not in spite of, but because of, its mixture. Vasconcelos's inspiration was itself mixed. He drew on European spiritualism to expose the false illusions of material freedoms. At the same time, Indian philosophy inspired him to believe that what he described as the Anglo civilization was bound to give way to a moral and aesthetic successor. He argued that this new civilization would eventually be governed by a "Cosmic Race." It is telling that Vasconcelos, who would soon emerge as one of Latin America's leading writers and the founder of Mexico's modern school system, still clung to biological explanations of culture and national identity.

> *In these years, some thinkers began to celebrate a premodern basis of national identities.*

SUN YAT-SEN AND THE MAKING OF A CHINESE NATION

The turn to an authentic and usable past that characterized Latin American thought at the end of the century paralleled the development in China of a literature that emphasized the power and depth of Chinese culture—in obvious contrast to the Qing Empire's failing political power and social instability. Here, writers invoked race to emphasize the superiority of the Han Chinese. Here, too, the increasing pace of change generated the desire to trace one's roots back to secure foundations. And here, as well, traditions were reinvented in the hope of saving the Chinese soul threatened by modernity.

In China, as elsewhere, the reformulation of identities was a matter for scholars and political mobilizers. By the century's end, prominent members of both groups had abandoned their commitment to the preservation of the old order. Yet, most were not prepared to seek a solution in the wholesale adoption of western norms and practices. In these attempts at salvaging and selective borrowing, combining traditions and values from home and abroad, the modern Chinese intelligentsia and modern Chinese nationalism were born.

The challenge of nation-building was symbolized, most spectacularly, by the endeavors of one man, Sun Yat-sen (1866–1925), though he was part of an emerging generation of critics of the old regime. Like his European counterparts, Sun dreamed of a reconstituted political community along national lines. Born into a modest rural household in the Canton region in southern China, Sun studied medicine in the British colony of Hong Kong in the late 1880s. A man of forceful personality and grand ambitions, he turned to politics at the time of the Sino-Japanese War of 1894–1895. The Qing government spurned his offer of service to the Chinese cause, an act that not only embittered Sun but also convinced him of the decrepitude of China's rulers. Shortly thereafter, he set up an organization based in Hawaii to advocate the Qing downfall and the cause of republicanism. The cornerstone of his message was Chinese, or more specifically, Han, nationalism.

Sun blasted the feeble rule by outsiders, the Manchus, and trumpeted the image of a virile, sovereign political community of "true" Chinese. No ruler, he argued, could enjoy legitimacy without the nation's consent. Accordingly, Sun articulated a vision of a new China free of Manchu rule, moving gradually toward a democratic form of government and an economic system based on vaguely defined processes for equalizing land rights. In this fashion, China would join the world community of nation-states and have the will and power to defend its borders against aggressors.

Sun's nationalism did not catch on immediately in China itself, in part because the Qing regime persecuted all dissenters, executing them or forcing them into exile. This persecution prevented the organization of popular protest in China. But his ideas fared much better among the hundreds of thousands of Chinese, almost all of whom were men, who, because of scarcity of land and social turmoil, had left southern and southeastern China for points foreign in the second half of the nineteenth century. Often victims of discrimination in their adopted homelands, members of these overseas communities applauded Sun's brand of racial nationalism and democratic ideas. In addition, Chinese students who were studying abroad, including a growing number of young women, found inspiration in Sun's message.

Sun's nationalist and republican call resonated more powerfully as the Qing Empire grew weaker in the first decade of the twentieth century. Defeat at the hands of the Japanese was especially humiliating, coming as it did from those whom the Chinese had historically considered a "lowly" folk. The Manchu court realized that reforms were necessary and set about overhauling the administrative system and the military and enacting constitutional reforms. Yet, these changes came much too late and satisfied no one. The old elites grumbled.

Sun Yat-sen. Through the medium of clothing, these two images of Sun Yat-sen, the man generally known as the "father of the Chinese nation," epitomize the changes and the evolving cultural ambiguities of China in the late nineteenth and early twentieth centuries. *(Left)* As a young man studying medicine in the British colony of Hong Kong in the late 1880s, Sun and his friends are seen here in the conventional Qing garb of Chinese gentlemen. *(Right)* Two decades later in early 1912, Sun and the officials of the new republic appeared in public donning full Western-style jackets and ties. Clothing, like so many other parts of the cultural arena in China during this period, had become a contested ground in the battle to forge a new nation's identity.

The new stratum of urban merchants, entrepreneurs, and professionals, who were benefiting from the recent socioeconomic changes and the opportunities of doing business with westerners, regarded the government as outmoded. Peasants and laborers resented the high cost of the reforms, which seemed to help only the rulers and not the ruled. A mutiny, sparked in part by the government's nationalization of China's railroads and low compensation to native Chinese investors, that broke out in the city of Wuchang in central China in October 1911 quickly spread to other parts of the country. Sun Yat-sen wrapped up his travels in the United States and hurried home. Few people rallied to the emperor's cause, and the Qing dynasty collapsed. The emperor, who was a six-year-old child, abdicated in February 1912. A dynastic tradition of more than two thousand years had come to an abrupt end. In the provinces, coalitions of gentry, merchants, and military leaders ran the government.

China would soon be reconstituted, and Sun's ideas, in particular those regarding race, would play a central role in the configuration of the new state. The original flag of the republic, for example, consisted of five colors. These were meant to represent the five major racial groups that made up the citizenry: red for the Han, yellow for the Manchus, blue for the Mongols, white for the Tibetans, and black for the Muslims. But Sun was never really comfortable with this multiracial flag, believing that there should be only one Chinese race. The existence of the different groups in China, he argued, was simply the result of incomplete assimilation, a

Soldiers Cutting Manchu Queues. The queue was initially the hairstyle of the Manchus. It was forcibly imposed upon the Han Chinese after the establishment of the Qing regime in the seventeenth century. With the founding of the republic in 1912, the new government regarded cutting the queue as an important symbolic gesture for its citizens, both as a final defiance of the authority of the old regime and as an embrace of modernity. The irony was that, over the centuries, many Chinese had come to accept the queue as an integral part of their own cultural identity, and its often involuntary cutting, as shown in this picture, turned out to be a traumatic event for many in the early republic.

problem that the modern nation, having replaced an outmoded imperial dynasty, now had to confront.

NATIONALISM AND INVENTED TRADITIONS IN INDIA

British imperial rule persisted in India, but the turn of the century saw cracks widen in the colonial edifice. The consolidation of colonial administration, the establishment of railways and telegraphs, the growth of western education and ideas, and the development of colonial capitalism had transformed and unified the territory, not only for the purposes of commerce and transportation, but also in people's minds. Now it was possible to speak of India as a single unit, which also made it possible for anticolonial thinkers to imagine seizing and ruling India by themselves. A new form of anticolonial resistance emerged, one that differed from the peasant rebellions of the past. Unlike earlier visionaries and local opposition movements, the proponents of resistance at the beginning of the twentieth century talked of Indians as "a people" who had a national past as well as national traditions.

The leaders of the nationalist opposition were western-educated intellectuals from colonial cities and towns. The origin of this group went back to the early nineteenth century when western education was first introduced. By 1900, nearly half a million Indians had some form of western education.

Though they formed less than 1 percent of the Indian population, they came to occupy the center stage in colonial India because they enjoyed access to the official world and were familiar with European knowledge and history. This elite intellectual group, or intelligentsia, used this knowledge to develop characteristically modern cultural forms. It turned colloquial languages into standardized, literary forms for writing novels and dramas. Hindi, Urdu, Bengali, Tamil, Malayalam, and other languages developed as modern vernaculars, with the aid of a lively print culture in different Indian languages. The publication of journals, magazines, newspapers, pamphlets, novels, and dramas increased rapidly. The development of this print culture created networks of exchange and communication throughout the territorial boundaries of British India.

The development of print culture went hand in hand with the growth of a new public sphere where the intelligentsia discussed and debated social and political matters. By the 1860s and the 1870s, voluntary associations had begun to proliferate in big cities. The urban professionals who ran these associations coordinated their efforts and eventually established a political party in 1885, the Indian National Congress. Lawyers, prominent merchants, and local notables dominated the early leadership of the congress. Deeply committed to constitutional methods, the congress leadership composed long, well-reasoned petitions demanding greater representation of Indians in administrative and legislative

Symbols of Imperial Power. George V, king of England and emperor of India, with his wife, Queen Mary, at a *durbar* (ceremony) in Delhi, the capital city of India, in 1911. Using the symbols of imperial power to show the pomp and splendor of the British Raj, the British rulers receive homage from their imperial subjects and thereby cement the ties between England and India.

Primary Source

A MUSLIM WOMAN DREAMS OF SECLUDING MEN FROM THE WORLD

Though international in its breadth, the women's movement took on very different concerns and causes in different national contexts. In the Muslim world, many women demanded the end to their seclusion and the right to appear in public without being fully veiled. In this selection, Rokeya Sakhawat Hossain (1880–1932), a Muslim Bengali woman, uses satire to underline the injustices and inefficiencies of confining women to the zenana *(the harem). In Hossain's story, originally published in 1905 in* The Indian Ladies Magazine, *an English journal in Madras, India, the heroine dreams of the perfections of a world turned upside down, in which women, not men, fill the streets and lock away the men.*

One evening I was lounging in an easy chair in my bedroom and thinking lazily of the condition of Indian womanhood. I am not sure whether I dozed off or not. But, as far as I remember, I was wide awake. I saw the moonlit sky sparkling with thousands of diamondlike stars, very distinctly.

All of a sudden a lady stood before me; how she came in, I do not know. I took her for my friend, Sister Sara. . . .

I used to have my walks with Sister Sara, when we were at Darjeeling. Many a time did we walk hand in hand and talk lightheartedly in the botanical gardens there. I fancied Sister Sara had probably come to take me to some such garden, and I readily accepted her offer and went out with her.

When walking I found to my surprise that it was a fine morning. The town was fully awake and the streets alive with bustling crowds. I was feeling very shy, thinking I was walking in the street in broad daylight, but there was not a single man visible.

Some of the passersby made jokes at me. Though I could not understand their language, yet I felt sure they were joking. I asked my friend, "What do they say?"

"The women say you look very mannish."

"Mannish?" said I. "What do they mean by that?"

"They mean that you are shy and timid like men."

"Shy and timid like men?" It was really a joke. . . .

"I feel somewhat awkward," I said, in a rather apologizing tone, "as being a *purdahnishin* woman I am not accustomed to walking about unveiled."

"You need not be afraid of coming across a man here. This is Ladyland, free from sin and harm. Virtue herself reigns here.". . .

I became curious to know where the men were. I met more than a hundred women while walking there, but not a single man.

"Where are the men?" I asked her.

"In their proper places, where they ought to be."

"Pray let me know what you mean by 'their proper places.'"

"Oh, I see my mistake, you cannot know our customs, as you were never here before. We shut our men indoors."

"Just as we are kept in the *zenana*?"

"Exactly so."

"How funny." I burst into a laugh. Sister Sara laughed too.

"But, dear Sultana, how unfair it is to shut in the harmless women and let loose the men. . . . Why do you allow yourselves to be shut up?"

"Because it cannot be helped as they are stronger than women."

"A lion is stronger than a man, but it does not enable him to dominate the human race. You have neglected the duty you owe to yourselves, and you have lost your natural rights by shutting your eyes to your own interests."

"But my dear Sister Sara, if we do everything by ourselves, what will the men do then?"

"They should not do anything, excuse me; they are fit for nothing. Only catch them and put them into the *zenana*."

→ *What does Hossain believe to be the fundamental difference between men and women?*

→ *How would you compare Hossain's view of the role of Muslim women with al-Badiya's?*

SOURCE: Rokeya Sakhawat Hossain, *Sultana's Dream and Selections from The Secluded Ones*, edited and translated by Roushan Jahan (New York: The Feminist Press at the City University of New York, 1988), pp. 7–9.

Rabindranath Tagore. The Bengali writer, philosopher, and teacher Rabindranath Tagore became the poet laureate of the Swadeshi Movement in Bengal in 1903–1908. The first Asian Nobel laureate, he became disenchanted with nationalism, viewing it as narrow-visioned and not universalistic. The photo shows Tagore reading to a group of his students in 1929.

bodies. They penned sharp critiques of the government's economic policies and wrote essays proposing policies to encourage India's industrialization.

Underlying political nationalism, expressed in the formation of the Indian National Congress, was cultural nationalism. The nationalists claimed that Indians might not be a single race but were at least a unified people because they possessed a unique culture and a common colonial history. Of course, such a claim was not peculiar to India; everywhere nations were imagined in a similar fashion, forging new national identities for societies in the midst of economic and political transformations. But nationalism in India, unlike in Europe, developed with an acute awareness of Indians as colonial subjects. The nationalists criticized the West in order to differentiate their movement from western visions of a modern world. The critical question for nationalists was: could India be both a modern nation *and* retain its Indian identity? How could India be distinguished from the West and at the same time be modern?

Like their Latin American counterparts, Indian intellectuals delved into the past and rewrote the histories of the ancient empires and kingdoms. The recovery of traditions became the intelligentsia's consuming concern, its means to establish a modern Indian identity without adopting the subordinate role assigned to Indians by British colonizers. In this way, they disseminated the idea of the nation-state, which had not had an integrated, national history prior to coloniza-

tion. To press the claims of Indians as a people with a unifying religious creed, intellectuals reconfigured Hinduism so that it resembled western religion. While traditional Hinduism did not possess a singular textual authority, a monotheistic God, an organized church, or an established creed, nationalist Hindu intellectuals combined the diverse range of philosophical texts, cultural beliefs, social practices, and Hindu historical traditions into a synthetic creation that they then identified as the authentic Hindu religion. In this formulation, Indianness was revived, not invented. Similarly, other late-nineteenth-century Indian revivalists explored the roots of a national culture in the subcontinent's past. Some delved into ancient manuscripts to discover Indian contributions to astronomy, mathematics, algebra, chemistry, and medicine and advocated the development of a national science. In the fine arts, intellectuals constructed an imaginary line of continuity to the glorious past to formulate a vivid notion of a specifically Indian art and aesthetics.

Reviving the past opened the way for creative accommodations of indigenous and modern cultures, but in the process of fashioning these hybrid forms, revivalists also produced a narrowed definition of Indian traditions. As the Hindu intelligentsia looked back, it identified Hindu traditions and the pre-Islamic past as *the* sources of India's culture. Other contributors to the Indian mosaic's cultural past were forgotten. Indeed, the history of India was increasingly identified with the history of Hinduism; the Muslim past, in particular, enjoyed no prominent role in this movement. There were, however, also attempts by other religious, ethnic, and linguistic groups to mobilize their communities for modern, secular purposes. The Indian National Muslim League, for example, formed in 1906, dedicated itself to advancing the *political* interests of Muslims, not to spreading the Islamic religion.

Hindu revivalism became a powerful political force during the closing years of the nineteenth century, when the nationalist challenge to the colonial regime took a decidedly militant turn. New leaders arose who disdained constitutionalism and called for militant methods of agitation. The British decision to partition Bengal in 1905 into two provinces—one predominantly Muslim, and the other with a Hindu majority—prompted militants to take to the streets in protest and to urge the boycott of British goods. Rabindranath Tagore (1861–1941), the famous Bengali poet and future Nobel laureate, was inspired to compose stirring nationalist poetry. To promote self-reliance, the activists formed voluntary organizations, called Swadeshi (meaning "one's own country") Samitis. These organizations championed the creation of indigenous enterprises for the manufacture of soap, cloth, medicine, iron, and paper, as well as the establishment of schools to impart nationalist education. Few of these experiments were successful, but the efforts nonetheless reflected the nationalist desire to assert the autonomy of Indians as a people.

GERMAN AND EGYPTIAN UNIVERSITIES

In the late eighteenth and early nineteenth centuries, sweeping reforms transformed the universities of German-speaking Europe. No longer polishing schools for aristocrats, these centers for higher learning became the preeminent institutions for the collection and dissemination of knowledge. Taking the place of salons, courts, and royal societies (see Chapter 16), the universities now determined which subjects were worthy of study and which were not. The ideal of the German universities was to combine research with teaching in such a way that each complemented the other; and both would be protected from the interference of the state or the market. The new German universities were so successful in producing pathbreaking scholarship that other Europeans and Americans looked to them as models for organizing higher learning and promoting scholarship.

These new institutions were places where researchers, students, and teachers exchanged ideas and information, supposedly on an equal basis (though in practice, one still had to be male, and middle class or above, to be able to attend courses there). For most of the nineteenth century, they were dominated by humanists, those who studied languages (especially classical languages), history, philosophy, and religion. Proficiency in Latin and ancient Greek was particularly prized, for educated Europeans still looked to classical antiquity for the origins of their advanced "civilization," as opposed to what was seen as the non-culture of the Americas and Africa and the decadent culture of Asia. This focus on the classics produced a wealth of important studies and insights—but it was extremely narrow. And by the century's end, these institutions were under siege, both from within and from without.

From within, the natural scientists and specialists in modern subjects (such as the social sciences, modern European history and languages) claimed a greater share of the university's budget and curriculum. Their demands suited Germany's modernizing aims, and by the end of the century a recognizably "modern" set of laboratories, lecture courses, and scholarly institutes had become central to the mission of the university. The universities were more reluctant to attend to the demands of women and workers, who insisted that they, too, should be allowed to attend courses. Ultimately, some accommodations were made, but not until the 1920s did these outsiders really make their presence felt. Increasingly, too, it was argued that the universities should increase their attention to non-European subjects, especially in order to prepare businessmen and state officials for service in the colonies. In 1910, the Hamburgisches Kolonialinstitut was founded for this purpose, which it should be noted, departed radically from the universities' aim to exclude the state and the marketplace from the domain of pure knowledge. In 1919, when Germany was forced to give up its colonies, the Kolonialinstitut was closed, to be replaced by a new institution on the old model: the University of Hamburg.

As the university became the hallmark of modern learning, the colonial and semi-colonial areas of the world struggled to adapt their traditional scholarly institutions to it. In Egypt the approach to higher learning followed two pathways. On the one hand, a group of Egyptian reformers sought to create afresh a university that replicated the institutions of higher learning in Europe. They agitated in favor of a purely secular and modern Egyptian university, finally overcoming the opposition of British officials, who had argued that Egypt was not yet ready for a full-scale university. In 1908, the Egyptian University came into being. It proved an immediate success, attracting the cream of Egypt's student population, and it was staffed in its early days by top European academics. Its curriculum was hardly different from the curriculum found in the European and North American universities, on which it was so carefully modeled.

The second pathway proved more difficult. Egypt's religiously trained elite, not wishing to be left behind, adapted Egypt's, and indeed the Islamic world's, leading center of higher religious learning, al-Azhar, to modern purposes. Founded in the tenth century during the Fatimid conquest of Egypt, the mosque of al-Azhar had become by the Ottoman era in the sixteenth century the leading center of learning throughout the Islamic world as well as a venerable place of worship, attracting Islamic scholars from all over the world. But the secular and westernizing tendencies that swept through Egypt in the nineteenth century threatened to render it irrelevant. In response, its advocates sought to bring it up to date. Al-Azhar's most energetic reformer, the noted Islamic modernist Muhammad Abduh, who had studied there as a youth, introduced modern and secular subjects alongside traditional religious subjects. The reformers altered the curriculum, improved the training of the faculty, regularized the course work, instituted regular examination procedures, and expanded the library. In short, they introduced many of the features of the modern Western university while retaining the traditional training in Islamic learning. Indeed, they gave al-Azhar a new breath of life, enabling it to retain an important place in the hierarchy of Egyptian schools in the twentieth century.

Marshaling cultural resources, reconfiguring society, and inspiring popular participation in the antipartition agitation, the Swadeshi movement swept aside the old moderate leadership of the Indian National Congress and installed a new, radical leadership. The leadership achieved notable successes in broadening the nationalist agitation. No longer was nationalism just an ideology for the few: by century's end, it had become a broad-based movement. Though the people did not topple the colonial regime, the experience of Indian mass mobilization was enough to shake the confidence of the British rulers, who found themselves having to resort to coercive measures to keep the colony intact. When the movement slipped into a campaign of terrorism in 1908, the government responded by imprisoning militant leaders. But the colonial administrators also annulled the partition of Bengal in 1911. Late-nineteenth-century Indian nationalism posed a different kind of challenge to the British than the suppressed 1857 rebellion. The insurgents of 1857, too, had spoken in the idiom of religion, but they had proclaimed an alternative order; they had wanted to preserve local identities against the encroachment of the modern state and the colonial economy. Millennialism had fired the rebels as they strove to build a social and political order based on bonds of kinship, locality, religion, and traditional authority. Nationalist leaders, by contrast, drew on traditional forms but imagined a modern national community. Invoking religious and ethnic symbols and idioms, they formed modern political associations and intended to operate as rational political actors in a national public arena. Unlike the insurgents of 1857, they did not seek a radical alternative to the colonial order; rather, they fought for the political rights of Indians as a secular, national community. In these new nationalists, British rulers discovered an enemy not so different from themselves.

THE PAN MOVEMENTS

India and China were not the only places where activists dreamed of founding new states. Indeed, across the globe, groups had begun to imagine new communities based on ethnicity. Some of these transcended a single ethnicity, looking to religion as a basis for unity. Pan movements sought to link people across state boundaries and included such diverse movements as pan-Asianism, pan-Islamism, pan-Africanism, pan-Slavism, pan-Turkism, pan-Arabism, pan-Germanism, and Zionism. The grand aspiration of all these groups, however, was the rearrangement of borders so that dispersed communities would be united. But such remappings posed a threat to existing states, which made these movements extremely dangerous in the eyes of the rulers of the Russian, Austrian, and Ottoman empires, as well as of the overseers of the British and the French colonial empires.

Within the Muslim world, intellectuals and political leaders begged their co-religionists to put aside sectarian and political differences so that they could unite under the banner of Islam in opposition to European incursions. The leading spokesman for pan-Islamism was the well-traveled and intellectually nimble Jamal al-Din al-Afghani (1839–1897). Born in Iran and given a Shiite upbringing, he nonetheless called on Muslims around the world to overcome their Sunni and Shiite differences so that they could make common cause against the West. Afghani called for unity and action, for an end to corruption and stagnation, and for the acceptance of the true principles of Islam. During a sojourn in Egypt, in the 1870s, Afghani joined with a young Egyptian reformer, Muhammad Abduh (1849–1905), to inspire a proto-nationalist and Islamic protest against Europe. Later, in 1884, Afghani and Abduh, then living in exile in Paris following the British occupation of Egypt in 1882, published a pan-Islamic newspaper, *al-Urwah al-Wuthqa* (*The Indissoluble Bond*) that popularized Afghani's call for a union of all Islamic countries. In the latter years of his life, Afghani made his way to Istanbul, where he supported the pan-Islamic ambitions of Sultan Abdul Hamid II, who made the defense of Islam one of the devices to thwart European schemes to divide up the Ottoman Empire.

> *The pan-Islamic appeal only added to the confusion of Muslims as they confronted the West.*

The pan-Islamic appeal only added to the confusion of Muslims as they confronted the West. Arab Muslims living as Ottoman subjects had multiple identities and many calls on their loyalties. Should they support the Ottoman Empire as a means to defend themselves from European encroachments? Or should they embrace the Islamism of Afghani? At this stage, most opted to work within the embryonic nation-states that were arising in the Islamic world, looking to a Syrian or Lebanese identity as the way to deal with the West and gain autonomy. But Afghani and his disciples had struck a chord in Muslim culture, and their Islamic message has long retained a powerful appeal.

Pan-Germanism, to cite another example of a movement that crossed national boundaries, found followers across central Europe, where it often competed with a pan-Slavic movement that threatened to unite all the Slavs against their Austrian, German, and Ottoman overlords. This area had traditionally been ruled by German-speaking elites, who owned the land farmed by Poles, Czechs, Russians, and other Slavs. German elites began to feel increasingly uneasy as Slavic nationalisms, spurred by the midcentury revivals of traditional Czech, Polish, Serbian, and Ukrainian languages and cultures, became more popular. Even more threatening to the

German elites was the fact that the Slavic populations were growing faster than the German. As pogroms, or organized massacres, in the Russian Empire's borderlands in the 1880s drove a large number of eastern European Jews westward, German resentment toward these newcomers also increased.

What made pan-Germanism a movement and an ideology, however, was the intervention at this point of a former liberal, Georg von Schönerer (1842–1921). In 1882, Schönerer, outraged by the Habsburg Empire's failure to favor Germans, founded the League of German Nationalists, a group composed of several hundred students, artisans, teachers, and small businessmen. Schönerer detested the Jews, defining them by their "racial characteristics" rather than by their religious practices. When he was elected to the Austrian upper house, he attempted to pass anti-Jewish legislation modeled on the American Chinese Exclusion Act of 1882. Schönerer's subsequent campaigns in the 1890s to promote the interests of Germans within the Habsburg Empire were designed to break what he believed to be Austria's anti-German dependency on the pope. Ultimately, he aimed for German Austria to unite with the Germans in Bismarck's empire, thus forming a huge, racially unified state to dominate central Europe. Although Schönerer's plans were too radical for the majority of German Austrians (most of whom were Catholic), his anti-Semitism was revived in a milder form by Viennese mayor Karl Lueger in the late 1890s, and a more virulent form by Adolf Hitler after 1933.

> The rhetoric of pan-Germanism accustomed central Europeans to thinking of themselves as members of a German race, *their identities fixed by blood rather than defined by state boundaries.*

The rhetoric of pan-Germanism accustomed central Europeans to thinking of themselves as members of a German *race*, their identities fixed by blood rather than defined by state boundaries. This, too, was very much the lesson of pan-Slavism. Both led fanatics to take actions that were dangerous to existing states; the organization of networks of radical southern Slavs, for example, unsettled Serbia and Herzegovina (annexed by the Austrians in 1908). Indeed, it was a Serbian proponent of plans to carve an independent Slav state out of Austrian territory in the Balkans who assassinated the heir to the Habsburg throne, Archduke Francis Ferdinand, in June 1914. By August, the whole of Europe had descended into mass warfare, bringing much of the rest of the world directly or indirectly into the conflict as well. Eventually, the war would realize the pan-Slav, pan-German, and anti-Ottoman Muslim nationalist longing to tear down the Ottoman and Habsburg empires. The irony was that the post-1918 situation, in which these multinational empires were divided into polities based essentially on race, would prove to be far more unstable and unsettled even than the world at the turn of the century.

CONCLUSION

Ever since the Enlightenment, Europeans had put their faith in "progress." Through the nineteenth century, educated elites took pride in their improvements—as evidenced in booming industries, bustling cities, and burgeoning colonial empires. Yet, by century's end, many came to question that faith. Urbanization and industrialization, the signatures of the age, seemed more disrupting than uplifting, more disorienting than reassuring. Moreover, the burdens of colonial rule, especially the resistance of colonial people to what was termed the "civilizing mission," only fueled doubts about the course of progress.

Perhaps nothing was so unsettling to the ruling elite as the realization that "the people" not only were against them, but also were developing the means to unseat them. In colonial settings, nationalists learned how to mobilize large populations. In Europe, charismatic socialist and right-wing leaders found the means to challenge liberal political power. By contrast, old elites, whose politics relied on closed-door negotiations between "rational" gentlemen, were unprepared to deal with modern popular ideas and identities.

Nor were they able to control the pace and scope of change. The expansion of empires had drawn more people into an unbalanced global economy, one that enriched many landowners, financiers, and industrialists. Everywhere, new disparities in wealth appeared—especially in Africa, Asia, and Latin America, where traditional peasant economies had to conform to an integrated world market. Moreover, the increased scale of enterprise produced its own dangers within Europe and North America. The size and power of industrial operations threatened small firms and made individuals seem insignificant. So, too, cities seemed too big and too dangerous. All these social and economic challenges stretched the capacities of gentlemanly politics.

Yet, the anxieties of the age also stimulated a burst of creative energy. Western artists borrowed nonwestern images and vocabularies. At the same time, nonwestern intellectuals and artists looked to the West for inspiration, even as they formulated antiwestern ideas. The process of exchange, and the dislocations of modern experience, propelled writers and scholars to look more deeply into the past, as well as to fabricate utopian visions of the future. As some explored the darker, mysterious sides of human character, others developed new means of escaping convention and tradition.

We have seen in this chapter how revivals and dislocations, as well as cultural and political movements, participated in this process of reformulating identities; in concluding it, we should reiterate the incomplete nature of this process. For, while economic, social, and cultural changes unsettled the European-centered world, they also intensified the struggles among European powers. Thus, this order was most unstable at its own center—Europe itself. And in the massive conflict that brought a definitive end to the late-nineteenth-century faith in progress, Europe would ravage itself. The Great War would give rise to an age of even more rapid change—and even more violent consequences.

STUDY QUESTIONS

Ⓢ WWNORTON.COM/STUDYSPACE

1. Explain why westerners used the term *progress* to describe the world at the end of the nineteenth and beginning of the twentieth centuries. What did they believe were the sources of this progress?
2. List and explain various examples of worldwide anxieties that challenged the idea of progress during this time. Which groups protested against the status quo?
3. Describe the armed insurrections against western imperialism in Africa and China during this era. How similar were these movements to other alternative visions to the new world order explored in Chapter 16?
4. Compare and contrast revolutionary and reform movements around the world during this era. How were their goals and methods similar and different?
5. Analyze how anxieties about progress shaped cultural developments around the world during this time. How did cultural modernism challenge traditional assumptions about art and science?
6. Define the term *popular culture*. Why did it become so powerful during this time and how did it shape individuals' identity?
7. Analyze to what extent new conceptions of race and nation created tension within and between states during this era. What new forms of nationalism emerged?

FURTHER READINGS

Bayly, C. A., *The Birth of the Modern World, 1780–1914: Global Connections and Comparisons* (2004). A general study of the key

Chronology

	1870	1880	1890
THE AMERICAS		▌ *Chinese Exclusion Act (United States), 1882* ▌ *Labor unrest, 1880s–1910s*	
EUROPE		*Social welfare laws (Germany), 1883–1884* ▌ ▌ *Labor unrest, 1880s–1910s*	
SOUTH ASIA		*Indian National Congress established, 1885* ▌	
EAST ASIA			*Sino-Japanese War, 1894–*
RUSSIA			
AFRICA			▌ *Discovery of gold in the Transvaal, 18*
MIDDLE EAST			

political, economic, social, and cultural features of the modern era in world history.

Chatterjee, Partha, *The Nation and Its Fragments* (1993). One of the most important recent works on Indian nationalism by a leading scholar of "Subaltern Studies."

Cohen, Paul, *History in Three Keys: The Boxers as Event, Experience, and Myth* (1997). An exploration of the various problems regarding the historical reconstruction of the Boxer episode.

Conrad, Joseph, *Heart of Darkness* (1899). First published in a magazine in 1899, this novella contained a searing critique of King Leopold's oppressive and exploitative policies in the Congo and was part of a growing concern for the effects that European empires were having around the world, especially in Africa.

Dikötter, Frank, *The Discourse of Race in Modern China* (1992). Traces the lineage of racial thought in Chinese history.

Esherick, Joseph, *The Origins of the Boxer Uprising* (1987). The definitive account of the episode.

Everdell, William R., *The First Moderns: Profiles in the Origins of Twentieth-Century Thought* (1997). A rich account of the many faces of modernism, focusing particularly on science and art.

Gay, Peter, *The Cultivation of Hatred* (1994). A provocative discussion of the violent passions of the immediate pre–Great War era.

Gilmartin, Christina, Gail Hershatter, Lisa Rofel, and Tyrene White (eds.), *Engendering China: Women, Culture, and the State* (1994). Analyzes politics and society in modern China from the perspective of gender.

Hevia, James L., *English Lessons: The Pedagogy of Imperialism in Nineteenth-Century China* (2003). A cultural history of British imperialism in late Qing China, emphasizing the pedagogical aspect of the imperialist project that was itself a form of colonization.

Hochschild, Adam, *King Leopold's Ghost: A Story of Greed, Terror, and Heroism in Colonial Africa* (1998). A well-written account of the violent colonial history of the Belgian Congo under King Leopold in the late nineteenth century.

Katz, Friedrich, *The Life and Times of Pancho Villa* (1998). A recent work on the Mexican Revolution that shows how Villa's armies destroyed the forces of Díaz and his followers.

Kern, Stephen, *The Culture of Time and Space 1880–1918* (1986). A useful study of the enormous changes in the experience of time and space in the age of late industrialism in Europe and America.

McKeown, Adam, *Chinese Migrant Networks and Cultural Change: Peru, Chicago, Hawaii, 1900–1936* (2001). An examination of the layers of networks and institutions that connected Chinese migrant enterprises and families across national borders.

———, "Global Migration, 1846–1940," *Journal of World History* (2004). A good overview of migration patterns.

1900	1910	1920

■ *Mexican Revolution, 1910–1920*

■ *Paris Exhibition, 1900*
■ *British Labour Party founded, 1900*
　　■ *Social welfare laws (France), 1904*
　　　■ *Social welfare laws (Great Britain), 1906*
　　　■ *Women vote in national elections in Finland, 1906*

　　■ *British partition of Bengal, 1905*
　　　■ *Indian National Muslim League founded, 1906*

■ *Boxer Uprising (China), 1899–1900*
　　■ *Russo-Japanese War, 1904–1905*　　■ *Chinese Republican Revolution, 1911*

　　■ *Russo-Japanese War, 1904–1905*
　　　■ *Revolt in Russian Empire, 1905*

■ *South African (Boer) War, 1899–1902*
　　■ *Herero Revolt, 1904–1906*
　　　■ *Maji-Maji Revolt, 1905–1906*

Meade, Teresa, *"Civilizing" Rio: Reform and Resistance in a Brazilian City, 1889–1930* (1997). A wonderful study of cultural and class conflict in Brazil.

Pick, Daniel, *Faces of Degeneration: A European Disorder, c. 1848–c. 1918* (1993). A study of Europe's fear of social and biological decline, particularly focusing on France and Italy.

Sarkar, Sumit, *The Swadeshi Movement in Bengal* (1973). A comprehensive study of an early militant movement against British rule.

Schorske, Carl E. *Fin-de-Siècle Vienna: Politics and Culture* (1980) The classic treatment of the birth of modern ideas and political movements in turn-of-the-century Austria.

Slotkin, Richard, *Gunfighter Nation: The Myth of the Frontier in Twentieth-Century America* (1992). Probes the unsettled character of American culture at the turn of the century in ways that illuminate the beginnings of American imperialism.

Trachtenberg, Alan, *The Incorporation of America: Culture and Society in the Gilded Age* (1982). A provocative synthesis of changes in the American economy, society, and culture in the last decades of the nineteenth century.

Wang, David Der-wei, *Fin-de-Siècle Splendor: Repressed Modernities of Late Qing Fiction, 1849–1911* (1997). A fine work that attempts to locate the "modern" within the writings of the late Qing period.

Womack, John, Jr., *Zapata and the Mexican Revolution* (1968). A major work on the Mexican Revolution that discusses peasant struggles in the state of Morelos in great detail.

Chapter

19

OF MASSES AND VISIONS OF THE MODERN, 1910–1939

The last guns of the Great War (later dubbed World War I) fell silent not on the bloody battlefields of Europe but in a remote corner of East Africa. It took a full day for news that the powers had signed an armistice on November 11, 1918, to reach that part of East Africa where African soldiers, under British and German officers, were locked in a deadly struggle for the possession of German East Africa. It was altogether fitting that this war, which had begun as a European balance-of-power struggle but had rapidly become a world conflagration, came to a close outside Europe. The East African campaigns were particularly lethal. Here, the German general Paul von Lettow-Vorbeck, with never more than 10,000 African soldiers, used hit-and-run guerrilla tactics to thwart the efforts of more than 300,000 British-led African soldiers. Thousands of African soldiers died in these East African battles, or from disease and inadequate medical attention, though they did so beyond the spotlight of international opinion. But while the African theater shared in the destruction of the Great War, the conflict and its aftermath fostered here, as well as elsewhere in the colonized world, universalistic notions of freedom and self-determination and a growing disillusionment with European rule.

Raging from August 1914 to November 1918, World War I shook the foundations of the nineteenth-century European-centered world. Although most of the major battles were fought on European soil, the conflict involved large numbers of American, African, and Asian soldiers who were ferried across the oceans to join European soldiers for the killing and maiming that occurred on European battlefields. Significant military campaigns also took place in Turkey, Egypt, Syria, and sub-Saharan Africa. This war was the first modern war involving whole societies. The scale and spread of the war accelerated mass production and consumption and inflamed disputes over how to manage mass societies. After the war, leaders and masses grappled with how to deal with the new forms of production, consumption, culture, and politics that had come into being during the war and that engaged not just elite individuals but entire societies.

In politics especially, the emergence of mass society put liberal regimes on the defensive as workers, peasants, women, and colonial subjects of all classes and ethnicities demanded more rights and better lives. The challenge to liberal governance became even more pressing once economic depression spread during the 1930s. In that decade, the success of autocratic regimes threw into doubt the future of liberalism, capitalism, and democracy. At the end of the 1930s, when World War II erupted, the nineteenth-century liberal credo extolling limited government and individual initiative seemed to many to be a thing of the past. Certainly, it did not seem a system upon which to build a viable, much less desirable, modern society.

ECONOMIC AND POLITICAL MODERNITIES

> → *What were the different forms of political modernity?*

When people spoke of "modernity," of "being or becoming modern" in the 1920s and 1930s, they disagreed on what it

meant and on how to achieve or manage it. Most did agree, however, that in economic terms modernity entailed the development of mass production and mass consumption. Here, the automobile, especially Henry Ford's Model T, exemplified the potential of economic modernism—in theory at least, an efficient and accessible mode of mass transportation. In the realm of culture, a variety of new technologies for communication and entertainment also stood for modernity. Available to the many, as opposed to an elite few, at least in the United States and parts of Europe, the gramophone (a record player), the cinema, and the radio carried the promises of modern mass culture.

When it came to political issues there was much dispute. Many favored a strong hand to reinvigorate their societies; others wanted more democracy to fill the vacuum opened by the war's discrediting of monarchical and colonial rule. Then, when the Great Depression hit in the 1930s, it became undeniable that U.S.- and Europe-centered markets failed to provide prosperity for *all*, and there arose an even more intense debate over the organization of modern mass society. By the 1930s, three competing visions for how to be modern had emerged in various parts of the world: liberal, authoritarian, and anticolonial.

The first political vision of modernism reworked a form of old nineteenth-century liberalism, confronting the economic failings of the interwar years without sacrificing capitalism or parliamentary democracy. The United States was the leading example of the enduring liberal perspective. As the pacesetter in the mass production and consumption of automobiles and the leader in new forms of popular entertainment, the United States had emerged in the 1920s as the great international symbol of being modern. Here, as in several European countries, women were given the vote, and rural dwellers flocked to the swelling cities in search of new opportunities. But the Great Depression of the 1930s undermined faith in American-style institutions. As hard times and unemployment spread across the United States, the American model based on linking capitalism and democracy no longer seemed to be working for the people. Around the world, and even in the United States, citizens looked to al-

Focus Questions OF MASSES AND VISIONS OF THE MODERN

→ *What were the different forms of political modernity?*

→ *In what ways did the Great War change the world?*

→ *How was mass culture utilized by different political systems?*

→ *How are mass production and consumption related?*

→ *How did different political systems respond to economic, political, and social disorder?*

 WWNORTON.COM/STUDYSPACE

ternative systems that they hoped would better deliver the benefits and promises of modernity. Although many repudiated the liberal perspective, the system survived in the United States, parts of western Europe, and several Latin American nations. It did so, however, only thanks to far-reaching reforms that widened participation in governance and tempered some of liberal capitalism's ills, but also dramatically expanded the power of state bureaucracies.

For many contemporaries, liberal reforms fell short of matching the astonishing dynamism of the second political vision for becoming modern, that of the authoritarian regimes. Formed in the crucible of World War I and furthered during the Great Depression of the 1930s, authoritarian regimes subordinated the individual to the state, managed and often owned most aspects of the production process, used censorship and terror to enforce loyalty, and exalted an all-powerful leader. Appealing to radicals at opposite ends of the conventional political spectrum, authoritarianism was manifested in both right-wing dictatorships (Fascist Italy, Nazi Germany, and militaristic Japan) and a left-wing dictatorship (the Soviet Union). Needless to say, these regimes differed radically. In common, however, they shared in the rejection of parliamentary rule, believing instead that forceful authoritarian rule more effectively delivered the benefits and promises of modernity.

The third variant, anticolonialism, also rejected the liberal order, primarily because of its connection to colonialism, though its exponents did not usually repudiate parliaments or private enterprise. Resentful of European rulers who preached democracy but practiced despotism, anticolonial leaders looked first to oust their colonial rulers and then to find their own path to modernity. Their views of the modern advocated political independence from the West but favored some mixing of western ideas and institutions with indigenous traditions. Yet, in working to create unified polities out of disparate colonial subjects, nationalists in India, China, the Middle East, and Africa had to confront their own internal conflicts, as well as the hostility of the colonial powers.

THE GREAT WAR

> → *In what ways did the Great War change the world?*

Few events were more decisive in drawing men and women all over the world into national and international politics than the Great War. For over four years, millions of soldiers from Europe, as well as from its dominions and colonies, killed and mutilated one another. Such carnage damaged European claims to civilized superiority and encouraged colonial subjects to break from imperial masters. Among Europeans, too,

Trenches in World War I. The anticipated war of mobility turned out to be an illusion; instead, armies dug trenches and filled them with foot soldiers and machine guns. To advance entailed walking into a hail of machine-gun fire. Life in the trenches meant cold, dampness, rats, disease, and boredom.

the unsettling effects of World War I shook the hierarchies that defined prewar society. Above all, the war made clear how much the power of the state now depended on the support of the people.

The causes of the war were complex. Disputes over colonial territories heightened tensions in the prewar period, to which were added disputes about the southeastern corner of Europe. As the Ottoman Empire was slowly evicted from the Balkans, the rival ambitions of Austria-Hungary and Russia came to the fore. Combustible too was the rivalry between Great Britain and Germany. Through most of the nineteenth century, Britain had been the preeminent power. In 1871, the year of German unification, Britain accounted for almost one-third of world economic output. By the end of the century, however, German industrial output had surpassed Britain's, and Germany had begun building a navy. For the British, who controlled the world's seas, a German navy seemed an impermissible affront; for the Germans, it was a logical step in their expanding ambitions.

International insecurity and rivalry led the great powers to construct political and military alliances. Germany joined Austria-Hungary to form the Central Powers; Britain affiliated itself with France and Russia in the Triple Entente (later called the Allies after Italy joined in 1915). The alliance of the French and Russians with the British meant that Germany needed to prepare for and fight a two-front war. Well armed and secretly pledged to defend their partners, the rivals lacked only a spark to set off open hostilities. That came in August 1914, when Archduke Francis Ferdinand, the heir to the Habsburg throne, was assassinated in Sarajevo, the capital of

MAP 19-1   WORLD WAR I: THE EUROPEAN AND MIDDLE EASTERN THEATERS

Most of the fighting in World War I, despite its designation as a world war, occurred in Europe. Although millions of soldiers fought on both sides, the actual territorial advances were relatively small. Did the armies of the Central Powers or the Allies gain the most territory during the war? Which countries had to fight a two-front war? How did this factor affect the outcome of the war?

Austrian Bosnia. In murdering the archduke, the assassin hoped to trigger an independence movement that would detach South-Slav territories from the Austro-Hungarian Empire (see Chapter 18). This led to a cascade of diplomatic events over the next six weeks, culminating in intensified preparations for war by every major power in Europe. The world war that followed did, in fact, lead to the dismemberment of Austria-Hungary, at the cost of millions of lives.

THE FIGHTING

The declarations of war were greeted with jubilation by those who anticipated a short conflict culminating in a swift triumph for their side. Dreams of glory inspired tens of thousands of men to rush to enlist. But the fighting did not go as expected. The initial German offensive intended to thrust through neutral Belgium in a grand "wheeling motion" stalled thirty miles outside Paris (see Map 19-1). The Germans had hoped to encircle Paris and defeat France with a single blow, but they were stopped by the Allies at the Battle of the Marne in September 1914 and forced to retreat. A stalemate ensued. Instead of a quick war, vast land armies, employing defensive techniques, dug trenches along the Western Front—from the English Channel through Belgium and France to the Alps—installing barbed wire and setting up machine-gun posts. The troops became immobilized. Anything but glorious, life in the trenches mixed boredom, dampness, dirt, vermin, and disease, punctuated by the terror of being ordered to "go over the top" to attack the enemy's entrenched position. Doing so meant running across a "no man's land" in which machine guns mowed down all but a few attackers.

On the other side of Europe, Russian troops advanced into East Prussia and Austria-Hungary along the Eastern Front. Although the Russians managed to defeat Austro-Hungarian troops in Galicia (a region between present-day Poland and the Ukraine) and to score some initial victories in eastern Germany, they suffered a terrible defeat at Tannenberg in East Prussia once the Germans threw in well-trained divisions that were better armed and better provisioned than the Russian troops.

By 1915, the war had ground to a gruesome standstill. Along the Western Front, neither the Allies nor the Central Powers were able to advance. On the Eastern Front, the Russians had been driven back and had lost much of Poland. At Ypres in 1915, the Germans tried to break the stalemate by introducing poison gas, which at first caused panic, but the advantage was nullified by equipping soldiers with gas masks. On July 1, 1916, the British launched an offensive along the Somme River. By November, when the futile attack was halted, approximately 600,000 British and French and 500,000 Germans had perished. For all of these casualties, the battle lines had hardly budged. Attempts to win by open-

ing other fronts, like the Allied invasion of Turkey at Gallipoli in 1915 and fronts in the Middle East and in Africa, failed and added to the war's carnage (see Map 19-2).

The death toll forced governments to call up more men than ever before. Nearly 70 million men worldwide fought in the war, including almost the whole of Europe's young adult male population. From 1914 to 1918, 13 million served in the German army, almost one-fifth of Germany's total population in 1914. In Russia, more than 15 million men, mostly peasants, took up arms. The British mobilized 5.25 million troops, almost half the prewar population of men aged fifteen to forty-nine, and in France, around 8 million served, nearly 80 percent of the prewar fifteen- to forty-nine-year-old population.

Mass mobilization made visible a gathering breach in gender boundaries as well. Tens of thousands of women served in auxiliary units at or near the front as doctors, nurses, and technicians. Even more women were mobilized on the "home front"—a new concept. In Britain more than 1 million women replaced men in a variety of previously male occupations. In France, nearly 700,000 women worked in munitions plants, while German women made up more than one-third of the workforce at the great Krupp Armament works.

But women could also turn against the state, particularly in central Europe and Russia, where the demand for soldiers left farms untended and the demand from armies caused food shortages on the home front by 1915. The bread riots and peaceful protests instigated by women, traumatized by loss and desperate to feed their children, put states on notice that

Gallipoli. In April 1915 the British and the French landed a huge force of 450,000 troops on the Gallipoli peninsula, a daring operation intended to protect colonial possessions, reestablish direct communications with Russia, and knock Germany's ally, the Ottomans, out of the war. After a year of battle and about 150,000 killed, the French and British gave up and left in January 1916.

Women's War Effort. With armies conscripting nearly every able-bodied man, women filled their places in factories, especially in those that manufactured war materials, such as the French plant pictured here in 1916.

their citizens expected compensation for their sacrifices to the nation. In many places, civilian pressure forced states to make promises they would have to fulfill after the war, in the form of welfare provisions, expanded suffrage, and pensions for widows and the wounded.

In the four full years of the war, military deaths exceeded 8 million. Another 20 million soldiers were wounded. Vast numbers of survivors bore artificial limbs. Naval blockades and aerial bombardments had extended combat to civilian areas, exacerbating food shortages and leaving people susceptible to epidemics, like influenza. Demobilizing soldiers spread the diseases into their communities. Influenza claimed no fewer than 50 million people worldwide, including 18.5 million in India and 2.3 million in Europe.

EMPIRE AND WAR The horrors of the war reached across the world's regions (see Map 19-2). The sprawling Ottoman Empire sided with the Central Powers, battling British- and Russian-led forces in Egypt, Iraq, and the Caucasus. In 1915–1916, Ottoman forces massacred or deported between 800,000 and 1.3 million Armenians, who were said to be collaborating with the Russians. In East Asia, Japan declared war on Germany and seized German possessions in China. To increase their military forces, the British and French conscripted colonial subjects. India provided 1 million soldiers to the Allies. More than 1 million Africans fought in Africa and Europe for their colonial masters, and another 3 million were

made to transport war supplies. Around 60,000 Indians and 150,000 Africans lost their lives, and a greater number were wounded. Even the scantily populated British dominions of Australia, New Zealand, and Canada dispatched over a million loyal young men to fight for the empire.

Despair and disillusionment at the bloody war turned into revolt and revolution. In British-ruled Nyasaland, a mission-educated African, John Chilembwe, directed his compatriots to refuse British military demands and to stand up for the new ideal, "Africa for the Africans." The British, who received 40 percent of their wartime human and material resources from colonies and dominions, suppressed the insurrection and executed the rebel leader. Yet, Chilembwe's death did not stop the growing desire of the colonized to undo their bonds to the mother country.

Controlling the mobilized masses proved even more difficult in Europe. In 1916, after the second winter of deprivation, antiwar demonstrations broke out in Europe. The next year, strikes roiled Germany, France, Britain, Italy, and Russia. Meanwhile, in an effort to break the stalemate on the battlefield, Allied commanders introduced new weapons such as the tank to counteract the omnipresent machine guns, which took a huge toll on the soldiers. Neither civilian protest nor new armaments could stop the war's devastation. As a result, Europe's postwar leaders would reap a bitter harvest of anger, sorrow, and despair.

THE RUSSIAN REVOLUTION The war destroyed entire empires. The first to go was Romanov Russia. In February 1917, Tsar Nicholas II was induced to abdicate by his generals, who wanted to quash the mass unrest in the capital which, they believed, was threatening the war effort along the Eastern Front. Some members of the Duma, the restricted Russian parliament, formed a provisional government; at the same time, in factories, garrisons, and towns, grassroots councils (soviets) were established. The irony of Russia's February Revolution was that the military and civilian elites, acting to restore order, seemed to sanction and encourage revolution. With the removal of the tsar, millions of peasants seized land, soldiers and sailors mutinied at the front and departed for home, and the borderland nationalities declared autonomy or independence from the crumbling Russian Empire.

In October 1917, with the tsar gone but the war still going on, left-wing Socialists calling themselves Bolsheviks decided the time was right to seize power. Led by Vladimir Lenin (1870–1924) and Leon Trotsky (1879–1940), the Bolsheviks took advantage of the political vacuum following the dynasty's fall and drew support among radicalized soldiers, sailors, and factory workers organized in the soviets. Arresting the members of the provisional government and claiming power in the name of the soviets, the Bolsheviks proclaimed a Socialist revolution to overtake the February "bourgeois" revolution.

Petrograd Workers. The July 1917 demonstrations were among the largest in the Russian Empire during that turbulent year of war and revolution. In the photo, marchers carry banners, "Down with the Ministers-Capitalists" and "All Power to the Soviets of Worker, Soldier and Peasant Deputies."

In March 1918, Soviet Russia signed the Treaty of Brest-Litovsk, a separate peace acknowledging German victory on the Eastern Front as the Russian army collapsed and gave way to German occupation. For protection, the Bolshevik leadership relocated the capital from Petrograd to Moscow and set up what they called a dictatorship of the proletariat, whose fortunes, for the moment, remained unclear. Lenin insisted upon accepting the peace treaty and loss of vast territories to safeguard the Socialist revolution at all costs. A child of modest privilege and a law-school dropout, he had spent most of the years prior to 1917 in foreign exile, participating in small revolutionary discussion circles and writing voluminously. After the abdication of Nicholas II, Lenin had snuck back into Russia, thanks to the Germans, who sent him on a special train across front lines to foment further chaos against their military foe. Neither the Germans nor Lenin's comrades foresaw how he would spearhead the creation of a new state out of the Russian Empire's ruins.

THE FALL OF THE CENTRAL POWERS With the withdrawal of Russia from the war, the Germans were able to concentrate their forces on the Western Front. In March 1918, after signing the peace treaty with the Russians, German troops began several offensives to break through Allied lines, but they could not capture Paris because of logistical problems and a lack of reserves. They now also found themselves faced by the United States, which had declared war on Germany in 1917 after German submarines sank several American merchant ships and after the discovery of a secret telegram in which German officials sought to win Mexican support by promising to help Mexico regain the territories it had lost to the United States in 1848. With fresh U.S. troops added to the fray, the Allies were able to turn the tide at the Second Battle of the Marne in July 1918 and to force the Germans to retreat into Belgium. German troops began to surrender en masse, and some announced a soldiers' strike against the war, as hunger and influenza became too much for them to bear. By the fall of 1918, Germany tottered on the edge of civil war as the Allied blockade led to food shortages. Many Germans feared—and some prayed—that the Russian Revolution would spread westward. Faced with defeat and civil strife, the Central Powers fell in succession. Bulgaria withdrew from the war in September; Turkey surrendered in October; nationalist unrest in Austria-Hungary diverted some of its troops, though most remained at the war front. But German generals, threatened by a massive strike wave, agreed to an armistice in November 1918. Kaiser Wilhelm II (ruled 1888–1918) slipped into exile in the Netherlands; the German empire became a republic. The last Habsburg emperor, Charles I (ruled 1916–1918), also abdicated, and Austria-Hungary dissolved into several new states. With the collapse of the Ottoman Empire, the war added a fourth dynasty to its list of casualties.

THE PEACE SETTLEMENT AND THE IMPACT OF THE WAR

To decide the fate of vanquished empires and the future of the modern world, the victors convened a peace conference at Versailles, France, in January 1919. Thirty-seven delegations devised a punitive treaty, largely dictated by the leaders of Britain and France. It assigned Germany sole blame for the war and forced it to pay reparations. In addition, the victorious states took over Germany's colonies. Arab lands of the dissolved Ottoman Empire fell under French (Lebanon and Syria) or British (Iraq and Palestine) "mandates," that is, the League of Nations gave France and Britain permission to establish governments over the former German colonies in Africa and the Arab provinces of the Ottoman Empire. The Russians, once part of the Allies, by then under the Bolsheviks, were not invited to the talks.

The American president, Woodrow Wilson, had originally hoped to make a "peace without victory," but he, too, accepted the punitive treaty. Still, Wilson hoped that the postwar world might be a more harmonious one in which a newly organized League of Nations would bring the blessings of liberal freedom to all mankind. Realizing the ideal of self-determination that Wilson as well as Lenin had proclaimed during the war, 60 million people in central and eastern Europe emerged after the Treaty of Versailles as inhabitants of new nation-states. But such idealism had its limits. Suddenly

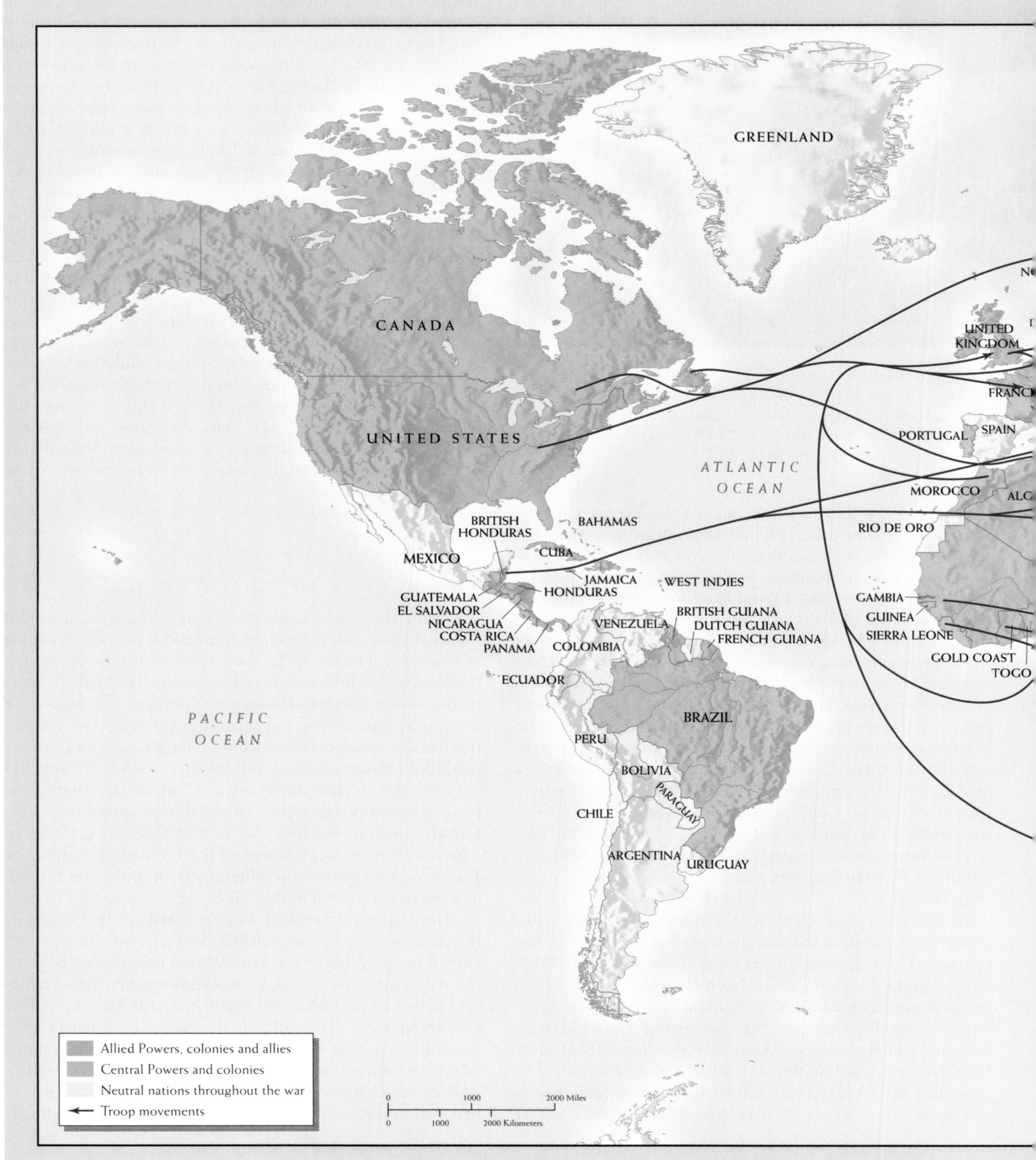

GREENLAND

CANADA

UNITED STATES

ATLANTIC OCEAN

BRITISH HONDURAS

BAHAMAS

MEXICO

CUBA

JAMAICA
HONDURAS

WEST INDIES

GUATEMALA
EL SALVADOR
NICARAGUA
COSTA RICA
PANAMA

VENEZUELA

COLOMBIA

BRITISH GUIANA
DUTCH GUIANA
FRENCH GUIANA

ECUADOR

PACIFIC OCEAN

BRAZIL

PERU

BOLIVIA

PARAGUAY

CHILE

ARGENTINA

URUGUAY

NO

UNITED KINGDOM

FRANC

PORTUGAL SPAIN

MOROCCO ALG

RIO DE ORO

GAMBIA
GUINEA
SIERRA LEONE

GOLD COAST
TOGO

Allied Powers, colonies and allies
Central Powers and colonies
Neutral nations throughout the war
→ Troop movements

0   1000   2000 Miles
0   1000   2000 Kilometers

ARCTIC OCEAN

FINLAND

EDEN

RUSSIA

Y   POLAND

STRIA-
NGARY

ROMANIA
BULGARIA

SERBIA

GREECE   OTTOMAN
EMPIRE

PERSIA   AFGHANISTAN

CHINA

JAPAN

IBYA   EGYPT

TIBET

ARABIA

INDIA

BURMA

ANGLO-
EGYPTIAN
SUDAN

SIAM

ETHIOPIA

ROON

BRITISH
EAST
AFRICA

UGANDA

GERMAN
EAST
AFRICA

PACIFIC
OCEAN

GERMAN
PACIFIC
POSSESSIONS
(lost 1914)

NORTHERN
RHODESIA

AN

SOUTHERN
RHODESIA

H-
A

INDIAN
OCEAN

SOUTH
AFRICA

AUSTRALIA

NEW
ZEALAND

MAP 19-2   WORLD WAR I: THE GLOBAL THEATER

This map helps us to understand the ways in which World War I was a world conflict.
Which states outside Europe became involved in the war and why? How did hostilities affect colonial societies of European empires? What long-run impact did the massive mobilization of troops around the world have on global political developments?

MAP 19-3   OUTCOMES OF WORLD WAR I IN EUROPE, NORTH AFRICA, AND SOME OF THE MIDDLE EAST

The political map of Europe and the Middle East changed greatly after the peace treaty of 1919. Comparing this map with Map 19-1, the European and Middle Eastern theaters of war, identify the new European countries that came into existence after the war. How accurately did these territorial boundaries reflect national aspirations? What happened to the Ottoman Empire and what powers gained control over many of the territories of the Ottoman state? Why did Allied statesmen recognize political independence for various European groups but not for Arab subjects of the Ottoman Empire?

more than 25 million central and eastern Europeans found themselves as ethnic minorities or completely stateless (see Map 19-3). The limits were even more telling when it came to establishing the rights of non-Europeans, for the peace-makers at Versailles were not prepared to extend self-determination beyond Europe.

What idealism survived the peacemaking process absorbed another blow when the U.S. Senate, reflecting a resurgence of isolationism among Americans, turned down the Treaty of Versailles and kept the United States out of the League of Nations. Russia, too, was outside the league. For Britain, France, Japan, and the United States, the isolation of "Red" Russia became a postwar priority.

The war also ushered in many changes invisible on the world map. It loosened relations between classes, contributed to the making of mass societies, and shook up gender relations. Demobilization hit working women hard; when soldiers hobbled home, women were laid off from many of the jobs they had assumed during the war. Still, women did not retreat entirely back into their homes. In Russia, women gained the vote in 1917. The following year, the struggles of suffragists, who were campaigning for the right of women to vote, bore some fruit as women thirty years and older were enfranchised in Britain. In Germany, women won the vote in 1919; in the United States, they gained it in 1920. France, however, held out against this trend until 1944, in part because many members of the left feared that French women were under the thumb of the Catholic Church. Nonetheless, in France, as in these other nations, women came out of the war claiming new privileges. Increasingly, young, unmarried women went out in public unescorted, dressed as they saw fit, and maintained their own apartments. Such behavior shocked cultural conservatives, but their sermons did not impress young women—or men—critical of established authority and determined to enjoy the new, modern world.

 MASS CULTURE

> → *How was mass culture utilized by different political systems?*

Indicative of the new, modern world were new forms of mass communication and entertainment. These, too, were at least partially wartime products. To mobilize populations for total war, leaders disseminated propaganda as never before. Through public lectures, theatrical productions, musical compositions, and (censored) newspapers, they attempted to unify and energize the masses. Thus did the war politicize cultural activities while broadening the audience for nationally oriented information and entertainment. Together with the expanding impact of the new media, the war was instrumental in fostering "mass culture."

Postwar mass culture was distinctive in several ways. First, it differed from elite culture (opera, classical music, paintings, literature; see Chapter 14). Thanks to rising incomes and leisure time, non-elites, lumped together as "the masses," now had more time and money to spend on entertainment. To be sure, elite culture did not disappear after World War I, and the masses (beneficiaries of expanded education) proved increasingly interested in elite culture, but high culture had to compete with the tastes of the working class and middle class. Second, mass culture relied on new technologies, of which film and radio were the most important. These new media allowed images and ideas to spread much more widely than had the penny press or lithographs of the nineteenth century. This meant that cultural products could now reach the population of an entire nation—indeed, mass culture could consolidate people's sense of being a single nation. Accordingly, during the 1920s and 1930s, politicians as well as advertisers recognized the power of mass culture and strove to manipulate the new media to their own ends.

RADIO

Radio entered its golden age after World War I. Invented at the beginning of the twentieth century, radio made little impact until the 1920s, when powerful transmitters permitted stations to reach much larger audiences, often with nationally syndicated entertainment programs. Radio "broadcasts," as they were called, entered right into the home, giving listeners a sense of intimacy with newscasters and stars, despite the fact that the programs were being heard by millions simultaneously. Consumers were addressed as personal friends and drawn into the lives of serial heroes. Special programs targeted children and women, making radio listening something for the whole family. Even the illiterate could enjoy the programs, such as *The Lone Ranger*. Already by the end of the 1920s, nearly two-thirds of the homes in the United States had at least one radio. Britain achieved similar radio saturation a decade later.

Radio offered a means to mobilize the masses for political purposes. Authoritarian regimes especially depended on radio to get their message out. The Italian dictator Benito Mussolini pioneered the radio address to the nation. Later, Nazi propagandist Joseph Goebbels used this format with great regularity and effect. In Japan, too, radio became a tool to promote the right-wing government's goals. But even dictatorships could not exert total control over mass culture. Though the Nazis believed jazz to be racially inferior music, they could not prevent young Germans from tuning in to foreign radio broadcasts or smuggling gramophone records over the borders.

FILM AND ADVERTISING

Like radio, film had deep, if unpredictable, effects on societies and politics. For traditionalists, Hollywood, California, which had emerged by the 1920s as the movie-making capital of the world, became synonymous with vulgarity and decadence. Indeed, modern sexual mores were on display on the silver screen—and often also in the back rows of darkened theaters. Like radio, film was also put to political ends. Here, again, antiliberal governments took the lead. German filmmaker Leni Riefenstahl's movie of the Nazi Nuremberg rally of 1934, *Triumph of the Will*, is the most notable example of propagandistic cinema. Riefenstahl's film was an artistic, as well as propagandistic, triumph. Almost half of the approximately 1,100 original Nazi-era films were comedies and musicals; hundreds more were melodramas, detective films, and adventure epics, sometimes framed by racial stereotypes and political goals, but almost always light entertainment. In the Soviet Union, film studios also produced Hollywood-style musicals alongside didactic pictures about Socialist triumphs.

In market economies, radio and film grew into big businesses, and with the expansion of product advertising, they promoted other enterprises as well. Especially in the United States, advertising emerged as a major industry, with commercials on radio becoming the preferred means for shaping national consumer tastes. Increasingly, too, American-produced entertainment, radio programs, and cinematic epics reached an international audience. Thanks to new media, America and the world began to share mass-produced images and fantasies.

Triumph of the Will. The shooting of *Triumph of the Will*, perhaps the greatest propaganda film ever, directed by Leni Riefenstahl. The film, later denounced, won gold medals in Venice in 1935 and at the World's Fair in 1937.

Charlie Chaplin in *Modern Times*. In 1936, Charlie Chaplin directed and starred in *Modern Times*. In the film, originally titled *The Masses*, Chaplin played a factory worker whose travails on and off the assembly line offered a darkly comic view of mass production and modern politics in the 1930s. In this still photo from the film, Chaplin is shown caught in the immense machinery and wending his way through the gears like film through a projector.

MASS PRODUCTION AND MASS CONSUMPTION

> → *How are mass production and consumption related?*

The same factors that contributed to the emergence of mass culture played a crucial role in enhancing production and consumption on a mass scale. Even more than its role in stimulating mass culture, World War I paid perverse tribute to the power of industry. Machine technologies were used to make war materials with abundant and devastating effect. Never before had armies had so much firepower at their disposal. In 1809, at the Battle of Wagram, Napoleon won the largest battle ever waged in Europe at that point, using to devastating effect his artillery, which discharged 90,000 shells over the two days of the battle. By way of contrast, at the bloody Battle of Verdun in 1916, 1,400 German guns fired off 100,000 rounds of shells per hour over the full twelve hours of the battle. To sustain the military production that supplied such large amounts of ammunition to the soldiers in the field, millions of men and women went to work in factories at home and in the colonies. Producing huge quantities of identical guns, gas masks, bandage rolls, and boots, these factories gave a broad cross-section of the world's population a feel for the modern world's demands for greater volume, faster speed, reduced cost, and standardized output.

The war reshuffled the world's economic balance of power, destroying much of Europe's wealth, while playing a significant role in the rise of the United States as the world's economic powerhouse. As the American share of world industrial production climbed above one-third in 1929, roughly equal to that of Britain, Germany, and Russia *combined,* people around the globe came to look to the United States as a "working vision of modernity," in which not only production but also consumption boomed. During the 1920s, mean household income rose by 25 percent in the United States, so that average Americans enjoyed an unprecedented prosperity. This was a modern condition quite unlike the nineteenth century's liberal vision: assembly-line workers were joining the middle class and devoting their leisure hours not to quiet edification but to jazz and motoring.

MASS PRODUCTION OF THE AUTOMOBILE

The most outstanding example of the relationship between mass production and consumption in the United States was the motor car, which more than any other product came to symbolize the machine age—and the American road to modernization. Before World War I, the automobile had been a rich man's recreational toy. Around the turn of the century, dozens of small companies manufactured automobiles, yet total annual production did not reach 200,000 cars. Then came Henry Ford, who founded the Ford Motor Company in 1903. Five years later, he began production of the Model T, a car that at $850 considerably reduced the price at which comparably powerful vehicles were selling. Soon popular demand far outstripped supply. Seeking to make more cars faster and cheaper, Ford used mechanized conveyors to send the auto frame along a track or line. In this assembly line, each worker was assigned one simplified, repetitive task to perform. By standardizing the manufacturing process, subdividing work, and substituting machinery for manual labor, Ford's assembly line brought a new efficiency to the mass production of automobiles.

By the 1920s, at Ford's River Rouge factory near Detroit, a finished car rolled off the assembly line every ten seconds. Although many of Ford's workers complained about speedups and being turned into "cogs" in a depersonalized labor process, managers properly credited the system with boosting output and reducing costs. The effects reverberated across the nation and throughout the economy. River Rouge alone

Car Assembly Line. Mass production was made possible by the invention of the electric motor in the 1880s, and it enacted three principles: the standardization of core aspects of products, the subdivision of work on assembly lines, and the replacement of manual labor by machinery as well as by reorganizing flow among shops. The greatest successes occurred in the auto plants of Henry Ford, shown here in 1930. With each worker along the line assigned a single task, millions of automobiles rolled off the Ford assembly line, and millions of Americans became owners of automobiles.

employed 68,000 workers, making it the largest factory in the world. In addition, millions of cars required millions of tons of steel alloys, as well as vast amounts of glass, rubber, textiles, and petroleum. Cars also needed roads to drive on and service stations to keep them running. Altogether, nearly 4 million jobs were connected directly or indirectly to the automobile, an impressive total in a labor force of 45 million workers.

After World War I, the ownership of automobiles became more affordable and more common among Americans. By the 1920s, assembly-line mass production had dropped the price of the Model T from $850 to $290. Ford further expanded the market for cars by paying his own workers $5 per day—approximately twice the average manufacturing wage in the United States. He understood that without mass consumption there could be no mass production. Whereas in 1920 Americans owned 8 million motor cars, a decade later, ownership nearly tripled to 23 million. The spread of the automobile in the 1920s seemed to demonstrate that mass production worked.

THE GREAT DEPRESSION

Not all was easy listening or smooth motoring in the United States or in other countries where mass societies were taking

Primary Source

BRUCE BARTON'S GOSPEL OF MASS PRODUCTION

In 1925, the journalist (and, later, advertising executive) Bruce Barton published The Man Nobody Knows, *which became a best-seller. In the book, Barton interpreted the life and teachings of Jesus as a gospel for success in modern business. In the excerpt below, Barton uses Henry Ford, whose Model T automobile reigned as the era's marvel of mass production, to show the profitable connections between religion and commerce.*

"If you're forever thinking about saving your life," Jesus said, "you'll lose it; but the man who loses his life shall find it."

Because he said it and he was a religious teacher, because it's printed in the Bible, the world has dismissed it as high minded ethics but not hard headed sense. But look again! . . .

What did Henry Ford mean, one spring morning, when he tipped a kitchen chair back against the whitewashed wall of his tractor plant and talked about his career?

"Have you ever noticed that the man who starts out in life with a determination to make money, never makes very much?" he asked. It was rather a startling question; and without waiting for my comment he went on to answer it: "He may gather together a competence, of course, a few tens of thousands or even hundreds of thousands, but he'll never amass a really great fortune. But let a man start out in life to build something better and sell it cheaper than it has ever been built or sold before—let him have *that* determination, and, give his whole self to it—and the money will roll in so fast that it will bury him if he doesn't look out.

"When we were building our original model, do you suppose that it was money we were thinking about? Of course we expected that it would be profitable, if it succeeded, but that wasn't in the front of our minds. We wanted to make a car so cheap that every family in the United States could afford to have one. So we worked morning, noon and night, until our muscles ached and our nerves were so ragged that it seemed as if we just couldn't stand it to hear anyone mention the word automobile again. One night, when we were almost at the breaking point I said to the boys, 'Well, there's one consolation,' I said, 'Nobody can take this business away from us unless he's willing to work harder than we've worked.' And so far," he concluded with a whimsical smile, "nobody has been willing to do that."

➢   *How do the lessons from the Bible and Henry Ford relate to each other?*

➢   *What are the key ingredients to success according to Ford?*

SOURCE: Bruce Barton, *The Man Nobody Knows: A Discovery of the Real Jesus,* in Loren Baritz, ed., *The Culture of the Twenties* (Indianapolis: Bobbs-Merrill, 1925), pp. 241–42.

root in the 1920s. During that decade, many primary producers of foodstuffs, coal, and ores faced sagging prices because of overproduction. By the late 1920s, staple prices were declining in proportion to manufactured goods, and farmers throughout the United States, Canada, Australia, and Latin America were complaining bitterly about their dwindling fortunes compared to their urban cousins. The world economy was on a downward spiral that was much worse than previous panics because of the scale and interconnectedness of postwar economies.

On Black Tuesday, October 24, 1929, the American stock market collapsed, plunging not only the American economy but also international financial and trading systems into crisis and leading the world into the Great Depression. The causes of the Great Depression went back to the Great War, which had left European nations in deep debt as they struggled to rebuild their economies and to pay off war debts. To restore stability after the war, Europeans borrowed heavily from the United States, the world's largest lender of capital. When wobbly governments and small investors defaulted on

Stock Traders after the Crash. On October 24, 1929, the American stock market crashed. Here traders are pictured congregating in the financial district of New York City, on what came to be known as "Black Tuesday." As stock values plummeted, panic gripped Wall Street and soon spread across the nation. The market crash was followed by even more devastating bank runs as the Great Depression overtook the world.

their loans, the U.S. Federal Reserve managers reacted by raising interest rates. One by one, financial institutions, starting with banks in central Europe, began to collapse. As banks fell, other lenders scrambled to call in their loans. Companies, governments, and private borrowers were soon floating in a sea of debt. The panic then spread to the world's stock markets, where investors had been purchasing stocks for much more than they were worth and investing in risky speculative ventures. This led to the Wall Street crash of 1929, which was followed by a wave of bank closures.

Financial turmoil produced a major contraction of world trade. Striving to protect workers and investors at home from the influx of cheap foreign goods, governments raised tariff barriers against foreign inputs. After the United States enacted the first protective tariffs, other governments around the world, one by one, abandoned free trade in favor of protectionism. Manufacturers cut back production, laid off millions of workers, and often went out of business. By 1935, world trade had shrunk to one-third of its 1929 level. Primary producers felt the harshest effects. Their international markets shut down almost completely. The world prices for Argentine beef, Chilean nitrates, and Indonesian sugar all dropped sharply. The combination of shrinking markets and drastic shortages of credit forced industries and farms across the world to the brink of bankruptcy—or in many cases, over it.

The Great Depression soon spawned some rethinking of the tenet that markets should govern themselves, the core of laissez-faire liberalism. By the late 1930s, the exuberant embrace of private mass production as the means to modern happiness had given way to a new conviction that state intervention to regulate the economy was critical to prevent

disaster. Many governments launched make-work projects, such as building highways and dams. Some even found militarization a way to prime the market with demand for manufactures. In 1936, the Cambridge University economist John Maynard Keynes published one of the landmark treatises in economic thought, *The General Theory of Employment, Interest, and Money*. In it, Keynes argued that the market could not always adjust to its own failures and that sometimes the state had to step in to manage the economy and to stimulate it by increasing the money supply and creating jobs for those in need. While the "Keynesian Revolution" took years to transform economic policy and to produce what became known as the welfare state, many governments were determining that capitalism had to be saved from itself, which called into question political liberalism.

MASS POLITICS: COMPETING VISIONS OF BECOMING MODERN

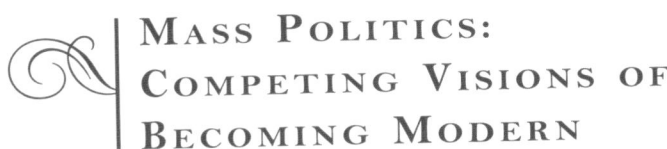

➔ *How did different political systems respond to economic, political, and social disorder?*

World War I heightened the prewar unsettling of class, gender, and colonial relations, further challenging the liberal vision of technological progress, free markets, and societies guided by the educated few. On battlefronts and homefronts, workers, peasants, women, and colonial subjects had sacrificed and expected to share in the fruits of peace; many, even in the victorious nations, had lost confidence in the traditional authorities who had failed to prevent the cataclysm and allowed it to go on so long. Politics could no longer be contained in genteel chambers and often shifted to the street. Everywhere except in the United States, variants of Socialism gained enormous numbers of new adherents. In the Soviet Union, the Bolsheviks began to construct a new society whose rules defied capitalist principles. On the right, too, mass movements sought to replace imperiled liberal orders, as in Germany, Italy, and Spain. Liberal empires such as Britain and France faced new challenges to square their rule over colonial subjects with their rhetoric of freedom. The Great Depression further undermined capitalism and parliaments.

Authoritarian solutions to problems like mass unemployment grew more and more popular, especially as the Communist Soviet Union, Nazi Germany, Fascist Italy, and militaristic Japan projected images of national strength and pride. Outside Europe, anticolonial movements gathered steam; here, too, it was clear that liberal models could not cope with the scale and diversity of the new politics. Thus, by the late 1930s, the states that retained democracy and capitalism in some form appeared weak and vulnerable; dictators seemed to be riding the wave of the future, and the colonies threatened to go their own separate ways. Whereas in 1920, briefly, almost all of Europe's states were parliamentary democracies, by the end of the 1930s only a few of those democracies remained.

LIBERAL CAPITALISM UNDER PRESSURE

In Europe of the 1920s, anxiety about modernization, already a feature of the pre-1914 years, spread. The slaughter of millions during the war added to the disenchantment with the course of modernity. A primitivist aesthetic flourished during the 1920s and 1930s, as elite Europeans looked longingly for supposedly pristine worlds that their own corrupting civilization had not destroyed. Josephine Baker, the African-American dancer who performed nude, wild dances on the Parisian stage, enjoyed colossal popularity. So, too, did Oswald Spengler's *The Decline of the West* (1919), a best-seller whose title seemed to capture the trajectory of liberal modernity.

The demands of fighting a total war had offered European states the opportunity to experiment with illiberal policies. The war brought both the suspension of parliamentary rule and government efforts to manage industry and distribution. States on both sides of the conflict jailed many who opposed the war. Governments regulated and organized both production and, through rationing, consumption. Wartime organization of the economy went furthest in Germany, where it

Josephine Baker. The African-American entertainer Josephine Baker was a sensation on the stage in interwar Paris. Many of her shows exoticized or even caricatured her African descent.

was dubbed "war Socialism" (and became an inspiration to the Soviet Union). Above all, the war revolutionized the size and scope of the state. The British established a wartime Munitions Ministry that grew from 20,000 to 65,000 bureaucrats. State budgets in prewar France had peaked at around 5 billion francs, but in 1918, the French budget was 190 billion francs.

BRITISH AND FRENCH RESPONSES TO ECONOMIC CRISES Liberal elites, especially in Britain, wished to return to free-market policies at the end of the war. But women, veterans, and workers insisted that the states for which they had fought respond to their needs—for jobs, for housing, and for compensation for war wounds. Many responded to the promises for such benefits by Socialists, Communists, or radical right-wing movements. Recurrent economic crises, especially the Great Depression, swelled the ranks of antiliberalism and forced all but the most die-hard liberals to rethink their ideas. By 1930, even Britain had given up on free trade, and other countries were avidly seeking economic self-sufficiency.

Britain and France were the two major powers to retain their parliamentary systems, but even here, old-fashioned liberalism was on the run. Strife rippled across the British Empire, and in the home isles Britain gave independence to what became the Republic of Ireland in 1922. Britain's working-class Labour Party first came to power briefly in 1923, and then again from 1929 to 1931, but either alone or in coalition with Liberals and Conservatives, Labour, too, proved unable to lift the country out of the economic crisis. In 1926, 162 million working days were lost to strikes. Still, despite hard times, the British retained their commitment to parliamentarianism and capitalism.

Disorder was even more pronounced in France, which suffered the deaths of 10 percent of its young men and the destruction of vast territory during the war. French government coalitions changed often. In 1932–1933, six cabinets came and went over the course of just nineteen months. Against the threat of a rightist coup, a broad coalition of the moderate and radical left, including the French Communist Party, formed the Popular Front government (1936–1939). It introduced the right of collective bargaining, a forty-hour workweek, two-week paid vacations, and minimum wages.

THE AMERICAN NEW DEAL In the United States as well, markets and liberalism faced challenges from those who found them threatening to traditional values. When the Great Depression shattered the nation's fortunes, the fears grew more widespread, as did the pressure to create a more secure political and economic system.

In contrast to postwar Europe, where labor parties and Socialist movements were on the upswing, the 1920s saw a conservative tide sweep across American politics. Calling for a "return to normalcy," by which he meant a retreat from the government activism that had characterized the presidencies of Theodore Roosevelt and Woodrow Wilson, Warren Harding won the presidency in 1920 with a resounding 60 percent of the popular vote. Four years later, Calvin Coolidge, whose remark that the "business of America is business" reflected his antipathy for government interference with the workings of free enterprise, scored an even greater landslide. With the election of Herbert Hoover in 1928, Republicans continued their string of presidential triumphs.

Left behind for the most part was the nation's African-American population. In the rural American South, where most blacks lived, "Jim Crow" laws enforced social segregation, economic inequality, and political disenfranchisement. Like rural whites, millions of blacks quit the countryside and moved to northern cities in the years after World War I. In New York, Chicago, and other metropolises, the migrants found some relief from the legal barriers that had restricted their opportunities and reduced their rights. But social and economic discrimination continued to hold African-Americans down and to restrict their residences to emerging urban ghettos. Still, within black neighborhoods,

"Jim Crow." "Jim Crow" laws mandated the segregation of races in the American South, with African Americans forced to use separate, and usually unequal, facilities, including schools, hotels, and theaters, such as this one in Mississippi.

most famously New York City's Harlem, a vibrant cultural scene emerged. The New Negro Movement, or Harlem Renaissance, as it was variously called, showcased black novelists, poets, painters, and musicians, many of whom used their art to protest racial subordination.

With the beginning of the Great Depression came broader and deeper challenges to liberal modernity. By the end of 1930, more than 4 million American workers had lost their jobs. As President Hoover insisted that individual thrift and self-reliance, not government handouts, would restore prosperity, the economic situation steadily worsened. By 1933, industrial production had dropped a staggering 50 percent since 1929. One in four workers was unemployed, and those who remained on the job suffered drastic wage and salary cuts. Across the country, joblessness and bankruptcies swelled the ranks of the hungry and the homeless. The hard times were even more severe in the countryside, where farm income plummeted by an additional two-thirds between 1929 and 1932.

In the 1932 presidential election, a Democrat, Franklin Delano Roosevelt (1882–1945), defeated the discredited Republican, Hoover, in a landslide. The new president certainly fulfilled his promise of "bold, persistent experimentation." Indeed, in his first hundred days in office, Roosevelt pushed through Congress legislation to provide relief for the jobless and to rebuild the shattered economy. Among the experiments were the Federal Deposit Insurance Corporation to guarantee bank deposits up to $5,000, the Securities and Exchange Commission to monitor the stock market, and the Federal Emergency Relief Administration to help states and local governments assist the needy. Taking state intervention a step further, the National Recovery Administration for in-

dustrial planning was also established, though this was declared unconstitutional by the Supreme Court. These early efforts were followed in 1935 by the Works Progress Administration, which put nearly 3 million people to work building roads, bridges, airports, and post offices. That same year, the Social Security Act inaugurated old-age pensions supported by the federal government.

Never before had the federal government of the United States expended so much on social welfare programs or intervened so directly in the workings of the national economy. Yet, despite these varied efforts, the Depression lingered. Two years into Roosevelt's administration, his wide-ranging agenda, collectively referred to as the New Deal, had reduced unemployment only to around 20 percent. The next two years offered signs of recovery, but, just as Roosevelt began his second term, another contraction shrank the economy. Unemployment again climbed—from 7 million in 1937 to 11 million in 1938.

The persistence of hard times opened the New Deal to acidic attacks from both the left and right. Emboldened labor leaders, resurgent radicals, and populist demagogues claimed that the New Deal was not addressing the problems of the poor and the unemployed. But Roosevelt continued to plot a moderate course. The New Deal did not substantially redistribute national income. Likewise, while the Roosevelt administration established public agencies to build dams and to oversee the irrigation of arid lands and the electrification of rural districts, these were the exceptions to the rule. Privately owned enterprises continued to dominate American society. Roosevelt's aim was not to destroy capitalism but to save it. In this regard, the New Deal succeeded. Although the United States was hit hardest among industrial powers by the worldwide economic collapse, the New Deal staved off authoritarian solutions to modern problems.

AUTHORITARIANISM AND MASS MOBILIZATION

Like the liberal systems they challenged, authoritarian regimes came in various stripes. On the right arose dictatorships in Italy, Germany, and Japan. These differed from one another in important respects, though all shared an antipathy to the left-wing dictatorship of the Soviet Union. The Soviets had no liking for the Fascists. Yet, all the postwar dictatorships, on both the right and left, were forged principally in opposition to the liberal democracies, whose "decadence" they claimed to have transcended. In place of liberal inertia, these regimes professed their success in mobilizing the masses to create dynamic yet orderly societies. All also had charismatic leaders, who personified the power and unity of the societies over which they ruled.

Although dismissive of liberal democracy, postwar dictators insisted that they had the support of the people. True,

Bread Lines. In the early 1930s, the Great Depression left millions of American workers unemployed, making the prosperity of the "roaring twenties" a distant memory and leading not only to widespread suffering but also to a crisis of confidence and legitimacy in capitalism and its institutions. Prior to the establishment of government relief programs under the "New Deal," many of the unemployed had no choice but to depend on private charities for handouts and to spend long hours waiting for food on bread lines, such as this one in lower Manhattan.

they demanded much of the people, treating society as a mass conscript army that needed to be commanded if new societies were to be built. But their demands, the leaders maintained, would result in robust economies, restored order, and renewed pride. In addition, dictators gained support by embracing, to varying degrees, public welfare programs. Thus, in the short run, authoritarians claimed to protect the people's well-being better than did liberal regimes and vowed to deliver on all of modernity's promises—prosperity, national pride, technology—without having to endure any of modernity's costs—class divisions, unemployment, urban-industrial squalor, and the breakdown of morals. For a time, a large number of the globe's inhabitants believed them.

THE SOVIET UNION The most dramatic blow against liberal capitalism was struck in Russia, where liberalism had never had deep roots. In October 1917, with World War I still going on and the empire strained, the most radical of Russia's political parties, the Bolshevik Party, seized power in the capital. Their coup d'état aroused opposition inside and outside the country. Fearing the spread of Socialist revolution, Britain, France, Japan, and the United States sent armies to Russia to subvert or at least contain Bolshevism. After the Bolsheviks executed the tsar and his family in July 1918, they rallied support for their cause by defending the homeland against its invaders. They also mobilized to fight a civil war (1918–1921) in the name of defending the revolution. The conflict pitted an array of disunified forces (former supporters of the tsar but also some social democrats and large independent peasant armies) against the Bolsheviks and their supporters (many soldiers, sailors, workers, and state functionaries). Their armed opponents came close but failed to dislodge the Bolsheviks from the Muscovite core of the former Russian Empire.

It was precisely in the all-out mobilization against those whom they labeled the Whites, or counterrevolutionaries, that the Bolsheviks, calling themselves the Reds, began to rebuild state institutions. The civil war also provided an impetus for Bolshevik-led armies to reconquer, in the name of revolution, many of the former tsarist lands that had seceded from the empire. The need to requisition grain from the peasantry as well as the military operations that covered much of the country weighed heavily on the population and interfered with the harvest. From 1921 until 1923, Russia suffered a severe famine, whose immediate cause was severe drought, but whose deeper roots traced to the impact that world war and civil war had on Russian society. Some 7 to 10 million people died from hunger and disease. To revive the economy in the early 1920s, the Bolsheviks enacted dozens of decrees (collectively known as the New Economic Policy) that grudgingly sanctioned private trade and private property. In 1924, with the country still recovering from the civil war, the undisputed leader of the revolution, Lenin, died. Lenin had suffered a series of strokes in 1922, but until that time no one

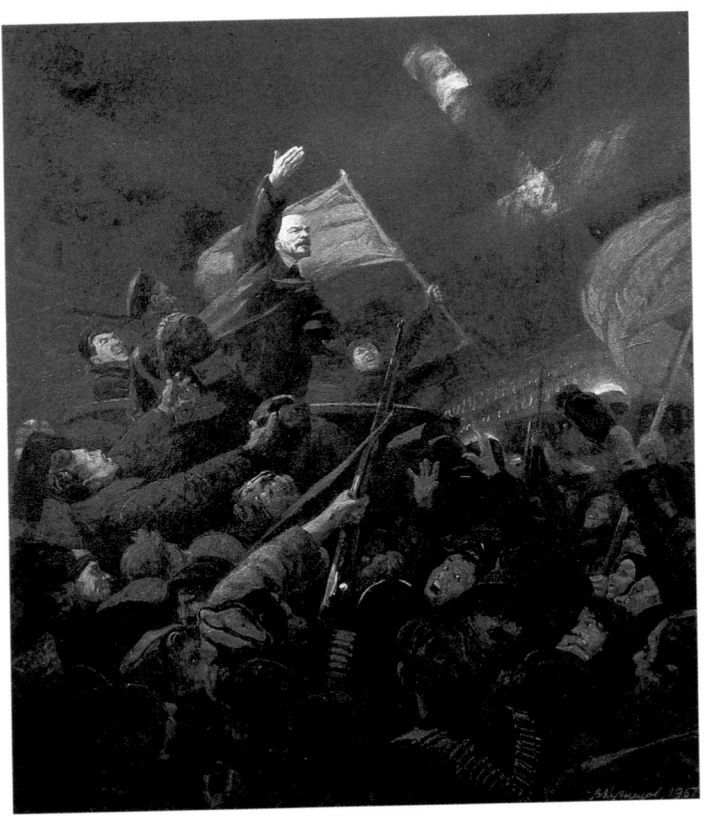

Lenin. Vladimir Lenin died just six years and three months after the October 1917 revolution, but he lived on in his writings and images, such as in this painting by Pavel Kuznetsov. Artists and propagandists helped make Lenin a ubiquitous icon of the new Soviet order.

had done more to shape the institutions of the revolutionary regime, including creating expectations for a single ruler. After skillfully eliminating his rivals, especially Leon Trotsky, Joseph Stalin (1878–1953) emerged as the new leader of the Communist Party and the country, which in 1922 became the Union of Soviet Socialist Republics (U.S.S.R.) or Soviet Union.

Stalin and the Soviet leadership understood history as moving in stages, defined by Karl Marx, from feudalism to capitalism to socialism to communism, the final stage in which there would be a classless society and a withering away of the state. First, though, the Communists would have to build Socialism. Yet, since Socialism as a fully developed social and political order did not exist anywhere in the 1920s, no one was quite sure how it would work in practice. From the late 1920s, Stalin moved aggressively to resolve this dilemma by defining Soviet or revolutionary Socialism in opposition to capitalism. Since capitalism had "bourgeois" parliaments serving the interests of the rich, Socialism, as elaborated by the Stalinist leaders, would have soviets (councils) of worker and peasant deputies. Since capitalism had

Stalin. Joseph Stalin posing at the Allies "Big Three" conference in Yalta, on Soviet soil, February 1945. Much had changed since Stalin became leader of the Communist Party of the Soviet Union in 1922.

run by regime loyalists. Tens of thousands of enthusiastic urban activists and Red Army soldiers led a drive to establish these new collective farms and to compel the farmers working on them to sell all of their grain and livestock at state-run collection points for whatever price the state was willing to pay, often nothing.

In protest, many peasants burned their crops, killed their livestock, and destroyed their farm machinery. These protesters, derided as *kulaks* (supposedly better-off peasants even if they were dirt poor), along with many bystanders, were deported to remote areas of the country. Villages were given quotas for deportation, and often those selected were the people who had slept with someone's wife or whose cows produced the most milk; thus, "class warfare" was likely to be based on personal animosities, greed, ambition, and vengeance. In the midst of this turmoil, harvests again declined, and a second famine between 1931 and 1933 claimed another 3 to 5 million lives. Grudgingly, the regime conceded to the collectivized peasants household plots, on which they could grow their own food. The peasants were even allowed to take some of their produce to legally sanctioned markets. But few escaped the collectives, which in turn became dependent on the state for seed, fertilizers, and farm equipment.

In the late 1920s, the leadership announced the beginning of a frenzied Five-Year Plan to "catch and overtake" the leading capitalist countries. In cities and at construction sites, millions of enthusiasts as well as deported peasants set about building a new Socialist urban utopia, founded upon advanced technology, almost all of it purchased from the Depression-mired capitalist countries. In just a few years, more than 10 million people moved to cities, where they helped build or rebuild hundreds of giant factories, as well as hospitals and schools. A number of the Soviet projects were intended to demonstrate the audacity of the new regime: huge hydroelectric dams, automobile and tractor factories, or heavy machine-building plants. These stood as symbols of the promise of Soviet-style modernity, which eliminated unemployment during the capitalist Great Depression.

The Soviet authorities also embarked upon what they called building Socialism in the borderlands. In 1922, the U.S.S.R. joined the independent states of Ukraine, Belorussia (Belarus), and the Transcaucasian Federation with Soviet Russia to form a single nominal federal state. The U.S.S.R. also soon included a number of completely new republics, such as those in central Asia; eventually there would be fifteen (see Map 19-4), all of which acquired borders and their own institutions, though they were subject to centralized rule from Moscow. A policy of "nativization" of the union republics fostered native-language schools and the development of local elites. In the 1930s, the collectivization and mass arrests devastated the peasants and nomads as well as the officials of the republics, but industrialization and urbanization helped to consolidate the power of local elites who advanced the cause of the Soviet Union and Socialism.

unregulated markets, which led to inefficiency and unemployment, Socialism would have economic planning and full employment. Because capitalism permitted the "exploitation" of private ownership, Socialism would outlaw private trade and private property. In short, Socialism would eradicate capitalism and then attempt to invent Socialist forms in housing, culture, values, dress, and even modes of reasoning.

The efforts to build a noncapitalist society were by design violent—class war—and they began in the countryside, where the majority of the population lived. Peasants had long been organized in village communes, leasing the land together while working it individually (as households). Stalin wanted to combine the farms into larger units, called collectives, that would be owned and worked collectively and that would be

MAP 19-4   THE SOVIET UNION

The Union of Soviet Socialist Republics (U.S.S.R.) came into being after World War I. How did the territorial boundaries of the U.S.S.R. compare with the older Russian Empire of the nineteenth century as shown in Map 17-6 (p. 755)? How did Soviet leaders govern non-Russian minorities within the new state? What kind of tensions did the multinational character of the state create for Soviet leaders?

The Soviet political system grew more despotic as the state bureaucracy expanded its size and reach. Political police power grew the most, partly as a result of its role in forcing peasants into collectives and organizing mass deportations. During the early 1930s, as the ranks of the party grew, ongoing loyalty verifications also led to the removal or purge of members from the rolls, even when they professed absolute loyalty. Initially most former party members were not arrested. All that began to change in the mid-1930s. From 1936 to 1938, both public and closed trials of supposedly treasonous "enemies of the people" resulted in the execution of around 750,000 people and the arrest or deportation of several million more. They were sent to forced labor camps, collectively known as the Gulag, which spread across the country. Such purges decimated the loyal Soviet elite—party officials, state officials, intelligentsia, army officers, and even-

tually even members of the police who had enforced the terror.

Behind this mass terror stood fear, a sense of omnipresent conspiracies, and the Soviet leader, Joseph Stalin, who relentlessly built up a personal dictatorship. Although Stalin initiated the mass terror against the elite, his motives remain unclear. Neither he nor the regime were threatened, and the loyalty of the leaders was not in doubt. What is clear is that the political police, given sizeable arrest quotas, often exceeded them. In addition, millions of ordinary people helped to implement the terror. Some reluctantly turned in neighbors; some did so to try to save themselves; many showed fanatical zeal in fingering "enemies." In the end, the terror, like the regime's grandiose rule more generally, was actualized by the pettiest of motives, to avenge wrongs, assuage hunger, and satisfy greed, but also by a desire to play one's part in the

Collectivized Agriculture. Soviet plans for the socialist village envisioned the formation of large collectives supplied with advanced machinery, thereby transforming peasant labor into an industrial process. The realities behind the images of smiling farmers—such as in this poster, exhorting "Let's Achieve a Victorious Harvest"—were low productivity, enormous waste, and often broken-down machinery.

violent crusade of building Socialism in a hostile world. Indeed, it appears that most inhabitants of the Soviet Union accepted the upheaval and mass arrests as a response to internal and external opposition and as a method for creating a new world.

ITALIAN FASCISM Long before the Soviets could boast any accomplishments, disillusionment with the costs of the Great War, along with lessons drawn from the Bolshevik takeover in Russia, had begun to alter the political situation in capitalist societies. In Italy, for example, mass strikes, occupations of factories, and peasant land seizures swept the country in 1919 and 1920. In response to this disorder, rightists, under the leadership of Benito Mussolini (1883–1945), a former Socialist journalist, seized power.

In 1919, Mussolini sought to organize disaffected veterans into a mass political movement that he called Fascism. His early programs mixed nationalism with social radicalism and revealed a yearning to sweep away all the institutions discredited by the war. Fascist supporters demanded the annexation of "Italian" lands in the Alps and on the Dalmatian coast and called for female suffrage, an eight-hour workday, a share of factory control for workers, a tax on capital, land redistribution, and a constituent assembly—in short, a populist program. Fascists believed in the value of direct action and attracted numerous followers. Their violence-prone shock troops wore black shirts and loose trousers tucked into high black leather boots and saluted with a dagger thrust into the air. In 1920, the squads received money from landowners and factory owners to beat up Socialist leaders, and at this point Italian Fascism became fully identified with the right. Still, the Fascists saw themselves as champions of the little guy, of peasants and workers, as well as of war veterans, students, and white-collar types. By 1921, the squads numbered 200,000.

In 1922, Mussolini announced a march on Rome. The march was a colossal bluff, an exercise in psychological warfare, but it worked—intimidating King Victor Emmanuel III (1900–1946), who opposed Fascist ruffians but feared bloodshed and thus withheld use of the well-equipped army against the lightly armed marchers. When the Italian government resigned in protest, the monarch invited Mussolini to become prime minister, despite the fact that the Fascists had won only 35 seats out of 500 in the 1921 elections.

The 1924 elections, in which the Fascists won 65 percent of the vote, were conducted in an atmosphere of intimidation and fraud. Mussolini dealt with other challenges by mobilizing the squads and police for crackdowns on the liberal and Socialist opposition. A series of decrees transformed Italy from a constitutional monarchy into a dictatorship. By the end of 1926, all parties except that of the Fascists were dissolved.

Mussolini's dictatorship came to terms with big business and the church, thus falling short of the social revolution that the Fascist rank and file desired. Nonetheless, it was skilled at using parades, films, the radio, and visions of recapturing Roman imperial grandeur to boost support during the troubled times of the Depression. The cult of the leader, *Il Duce*,

Mussolini. Benito Mussolini liked to puff out his chest, particularly when appearing in public. *Il Duce* pioneered the leader's radio address to the people, and he encouraged Fascist versions of the mass spectacles that also became common in Soviet Russia.

Hitler. Adolf Hitler and his advisors mastered the staging of mass rallies. These rallies and marches projected an image of dynamism and collective will, which Hitler claimed to embody.

also provided cohesion and uplift. As the first antiliberal, anti-Socialist alternative, Italian Fascism served as a model for other countries.

GERMAN NAZISM In Germany, too, fear of Bolshevism and anger over the peace imposed after the war helped to propel the right to power. Here, the dictator was Adolf Hitler (1889–1945), whose rise to power, like Mussolini's, was anything but inevitable. Throughout 1918, and for several years thereafter, Germany was in political ferment, marked by the appearance of many political groups. In Munich in January 1918, a small nationalist workers' organization was formed, dedicated to winning workers over from Socialism. In 1920, a young demobilized corporal was ordered by the army high command to infiltrate and observe this new nationalist group. That corporal, Adolf Hitler, the son of an Austrian customs official, soon dominated the nationalist workers' movement, whose name he changed to the National Socialist German Workers' Party (*National-Sozialisten,* or Nazis). Unlike Mussolini, the young Hitler was never a Socialist. The first Nazi party platform, set forth in 1920, combined nationalism with anticapitalism and anti-Semitism. The program also called for the renunciation of the Treaty of Versailles. It was an assertion of Germany's grievances against the world and of the small man's grievances against the rich.

The Nazis came to public attention with the Beer Hall Putsch in 1923. That year, the French occupied the industrial Ruhr Valley to obtain German reparation payments that had not been forthcoming, and German Communists attempted to seize power in the provinces of Saxony and Thuringia. Making their own grab for power, Hitler and his associates invaded a meeting of Bavarian leaders in a Munich beer hall to force them to support the Nazis. The army, however, fired on the Nazis and arrested Hitler. He was sentenced to five years in prison for treason, though he served less than a year. While in prison, he wrote an autobiography, *Mein Kampf* (*My Struggle*) (1925), which laid out in deranged detail his racist worldview.

In the 1928 elections, the Nazi Party received only 2.6 percent of the vote, but it started to build support when it broadened its appeal to small farmers, shopkeepers, and clerks. As Germany's economy sagged, Nazi fortunes rose. More and more people, out of work and seeing their savings wiped out by hyperinflation, lost faith in Germany's Weimar Republic and looked to radical alternatives. Fearing the growing popular support of both the Communist and Socialist parties and convinced that he could control Hitler, Germany's eighty-five-year-old president, Field Marshal Paul von Hindenburg (1847–1934), appointed Hitler chancellor (prime minister) in January 1933. Initially, Hitler pledged that the government would be dominated by traditional conservatives. Thus, like Mussolini, Hitler came to power peacefully and legally. Troops of young men (the "brown shirts," who grew from 100,000 in 1930 to 1 million in 1933) kept up the pressure in the streets with marches, rallies, confrontations, and beatings, but Hitler was invited to become chancellor by the existing elites, who feared a Russian-style revolution.

Once in power, Hitler's first step was to heighten the impression that there was a Communist conspiracy to take power. The burning of the Reichstag building in Berlin on February 27, 1933, provided the opportunity. The Nazis

Primary Source

CULT OF THE DYNAMIC LEADER

Nazi political theorists offered no apologies for dictatorship. On the contrary, like their Soviet, Italian, and Japanese counterparts, they bragged about it as the most efficacious form of mobilizing the energies of the masses and directing the state. The Führer, or Leader, stood above the Nazi Party and all government institutions and embodied the supposed will of the German nation. The Führer also decided who belonged, or did not belong, to the nation. Even though Nazi administration proved to be chaotic, the Führer and the idea of dictatorship were popular. The following excerpt, taken from the writings of Ernst Rudolf Huber, Germany's major constitutional expert of the 1930s, elaborated on the awesome powers that were being conferred on Hitler as Führer.

The office of Führer has developed out of the National Socialist movement. In its origins it is not a State office. This fact must never be forgotten if one wishes to understand the current political and legal position of the Führer. The office of Führer has grown out of the movement into the Reich, firstly through the Führer taking over the authority of the Reich Chancellor and then through his taking over the position of Head of State. Primary importance must be accorded to the position of "Führer of the movement"; it has absorbed the two highest functions of the political leadership of the Reich and thereby created the new office of "Führer of the Nation and of the Reich." . . .

The position of Führer combines in itself all sovereign power of the Reich; all public power in the State as in the movement is derived from the Führer power. If we wish to define political power in the Third Reich correctly, we must not speak of "State power" but of "Führer power." For it is not the State as an impersonal entity which is the source of political power but rather political power is given to the Führer as the executor of the nation's common will. Führer power is comprehensive and total; it unites within itself all means of creative political activity; it embraces all spheres of national life; it includes all national comrades who are bound to the Führer in loyalty and obedience. Führer power is not restricted by safeguards and controls, by autonomous protected spheres, and by vested individual rights, but rather it is free and independent, exclusive and unlimited.

→ *How would you best characterize the power of the Führer according to Huber?*

→ *What is the source of "Führer power" according to Huber?*

SOURCE: Ernst Rudolf Huber, *Führergewalt*, in *Nazism 1919–1945: A History in Documents and Eyewitness Accounts*, edited by J. Noakes and G. Pridham (Exeter, England: University of Exeter Press, 1984), pp. 198–99.

blamed the fire on the Communists, and arrested a young, deranged Dutch Communist. A decree on February 28 suspended civil liberties "as a defensive measure against the Communists"; the left-wing press was immediately forced out of business, robbing opponents of the ability to criticize the regime publicly. Hitler then proposed the Enabling Act so that he could promulgate laws on his authority as chancellor without the parliament.

The Enabling Act passed on March 23, 1933 and freed Hitler from the parliament and from the traditional conservative elites who had agreed to make him chancellor. In May, the offices, banks, and newspapers of trade unions were seized, and their leaders were arrested. The Socialist and Communist parties were outlawed; other parties of the center were dissolved. By July 1933, the Nazis were the only legal party. Hitler, who had become a German citizen only in 1932, was dictator of Germany. He aggressively curbed dissent and banned strikes, jailing political opponents and building the first concentration camps (initially to house political prisoners) when the jails overflowed.

He also unleashed a campaign of persecution against the Jews. As a young man in Vienna, Hitler had already despised

Jews, believing, like many of the Habsburg Empire's ultranationalists, that assimilated Jews controlled the banks and that Eastern Jewish emigrants carried disease. Like too many other right-wing Germans, he also believed that a Jewish-socialist conspiracy had stabbed the German army in the back, causing its surrender in World War I, and that the supposed purity and power of the Aryan race (which included northern, white, Europeans) were being destroyed by intermarriage with Jews. Unlike earlier Christian anti-Semites, Hitler and the Nazis did not believe Jewishness could be defined by religious practice; instead, they held that it was transmitted, biologically, from parents to children. Once in power, Hitler unleashed a campaign of persecution against the Jews excluding them from the civil service and the professions, forcing them to sell their property, depriving them of citizenship, and forbidding them to marry or have sex with Aryans (so-called "pure Germans"). In addition to these legal measures, Hitler also encouraged the use of terror against Jews to destroy their businesses, homes, and marriages with non-Jews, to frighten them into leaving Germany, and ultimately to eliminate all traces of Jewish life and culture in Nazi-dominated central Europe.

> *Although some in Germany opposed Hitler's illiberal activism, the Nazis won popular support for restoring order and reviving the economy.*

Although some in Germany opposed Hitler's illiberal activism, the Nazis won popular support for restoring order and reviving the economy. In 1935, Hitler repudiated certain provisions of the Treaty of Versailles and began a vast rearmament program, which absorbed the unemployed. The Nazis transformed economic despair and national disgrace into fierce pride and impressive national power. Ownership of the economy remained in private hands, but the state coordinated it. The state also financed public works like reforestation and swamp drainage projects, organized leisure, entertainment, travel, and vacations, and built highways and public housing. Anti-Semitism mixed with full employment and social welfare programs that privileged racially approved groups.

Germany reemerged as a great power with expansionist aspirations. Hitler called his state the Third Reich (the first being the Holy Roman Empire, or Reich, and the second the Reich created by Bismarck in 1871) and claimed that, like the Holy Roman Empire, his empire would last 1,000 years. Hitler also harbored grand aspirations to impose racial purity and German power in Europe and perhaps beyond. As the popular song went, "Today Germany, tomorrow the whole world."

MILITARIST JAPAN Unlike in other authoritarian regimes, power and pride in Japan were not wounded during World War I. To the contrary, because wartime disruptions greatly reduced European and American competition, Japanese products found new markets in Asia. Japan managed to expand production, exporting munitions, textiles, and consumer goods to Asian and western markets. During the war, the Japanese gross national product (GNP) grew 40 percent, and the country built the world's third largest navy. Like the United States, Japan had been a debtor nation in 1913, but it became a creditor by 1920. Japan also experienced a twelvefold increase in manufacturing and a threefold increase in the production of raw materials between 1910 and the 1930s. After a devastating earthquake and fire in 1923, Tokyo was rebuilt with steel and reinforced concrete, symbolizing the new, modern Japan.

Initially, post–World War I Japan seemed headed down the liberal road. When Japan's Meiji Emperor, symbol of national power and prosperity, died in 1912, his third son took over and ruled from 1912 to 1926, overseeing the rise of mass political parties. These eclipsed the oligarchic rule of the Meiji era. Suffrage was expanded in 1925 to all males over twenty-five, increasing the electorate from around 3 million to 12.5 million. But democratization was accompanied by new repressive measures. Although the Meiji Constitution remained in effect, the Peace Preservation Law, passed the same year as expanded male suffrage, specified up to ten years' hard labor for any member of an organization advocating a basic change in the political system or abolition of private property. The law served as a club against the mass leftist parties, such as the Japanese Communist Party, which was founded in 1922.

Japan veered still further from the liberal road after Emperor Hirohito succeeded his enfeebled father in 1926. In Japan, as in Germany, a major catalyst in the eventual shift to dictatorship was the Great Depression. Japan's trade with the outside world had more than tripled in value between 1913 and 1929, but after 1929 China and the United States imposed barriers on Japanese exports in preference for domestic products. The demand for silk and cotton goods also dropped precipitously. These measures contributed to a 50 percent decline in Japanese exports. Unemployment surged.

Such turmoil invited calls for stronger leadership, which military commanders were eager to provide. Already the leaders of Japan's armed forces were beyond civilian control. In 1927 and 1928, the army flexed its muscles by twice forcing prime ministers out of office. New "patriotic societies" echoed the calls for order. Professing dedication to the emperor and nation, these squads used violence to intimidate political opponents. Violence culminated in the assassination of Japan's prime minister in 1932, accompanied by an uprising of young naval officers and army cadets. Their coup

Hirohito. A portrait of Crown Prince Hirohito of Japan in 1925, the year before he ascended the Japanese throne. Hirohito presided over Japan's war in Asia, beginning with the 1931 seizure of Manchuria and culminating in the 1945 surrender, but he remained emperor for another four decades. When he died in 1989, his wartime responsibility was still a difficult subject for many.

failed, but it further eclipsed the power of the political parties.

It was in the Japanese Empire that the course of militarism and expansionism received a boost. In 1931, a group of army officers arranged an explosion on the Japanese-owned South Manchurian Railroad, using this as a pretext for taking over Manchuria. The following year, adding Manchuria to its Korean and Taiwanese colonies (see Map 19-5), Japan oversaw the proclamation of the puppet state of Manchukuo. At home, "patriots" continued their campaign of terror against uncooperative businessmen and critics of the mili-

tary. As in Italy and Germany, the state in Japan took on a sacred aura. This was done through promotion of an official religion, Shinto, "the way of the gods," and of the emperor's divinity. By 1940, the clique at the top dissolved all political parties into the Imperial Rule Assistance Association, ending even the semblance of parliamentary rule.

COMMON FEATURES Important differences aside, Communist Soviet Union, Fascist Italy, Nazi Germany, and militarist Japan shared many traits and, to some extent, imitated each other. All four rejected parliamentary rule as ineffective and sought to revive their countries' power through authoritarianism, violence, and the cult of the leader.

In the economic sphere, all were convinced that modern economies required state direction. In Japan, the government fostered the emergence of huge business conglomerates, known as *zaibatsu*. The two largest *zaibatsu*, Mitsui and Mitsubishi, were probably the biggest private economic empires in the world. The Italians encouraged big business to form cartels. In Germany, the state also looked to the private sector as the vehicle of economic growth, but it expected entrepreneurs to support the Nazis' racial, antidemocratic, and expansionist aims. The most thorough form of economic coordination took place in the Soviet Union, which enthusiastically adopted American-style mass production while eliminating private enterprise. Instead, the Soviet state owned and managed all the country's industry, with separate government ministries overseeing the manufacture of different products. Here, as elsewhere, state-organized labor forces replaced independent labor unions.

Employing mass organizations for state purposes was a second common feature of the four authoritarian regimes. Russia, Italy, and Germany had single mass parties; the Japanese had various rightist groups until a merger occurred in 1940. All sought to rally the young, often with dynamic youth movements, such as the Hitler Youth and the Union of German Girls, the Soviet Communist Youth League, and the Italian squads marching to their anthem "Giovinezza" (Youth).

Three of the four states adopted large-scale social welfare policies for members of the national community. Only the Japanese failed to enact innovative social welfare legislation, but the Home Affairs Ministry eagerly enlisted helpmates among civic groups, seeking to co-opt the new middle classes to raise savings rates and improve childrearing. The Nazis emphasized full employment, built public housing, and provided assistance to families in need as long as they were racially Aryans. The Italian National Agency for Maternity and Infancy, created in 1925, provided services for unwed mothers and infant care. The Soviet authorities proclaimed social welfare as one of the fundamental tenets of the Socialist revolution. Unemployment benefits ended when the government announced the end of unemployment in 1930. Still, the state created or extended programs to deal with

RUSSIA

AMUR
PROVINCE

SAKHALIN

SEA OF
OKHOTSK

KURILE ISLANDS

MANCHURIA
(MANCHUKUO, 1932)

OUTER
MONGOLIA

INNER
MONGOLIA

JEHOL

Vladivostok

EZO
(HOKKAIDŌ)

Mukden

SEA OF
JAPAN

JAPAN

Beijing

Dalian

Tianjin

Lüshun
(Port Arthur)

Weihaiwei

Seoul

KOREA

Pusan

HONSHŪ

Tokyo

Kyoto

Qingdao

SHIKOKU

CHINA

YELLOW
SEA

Nagasaki

KYŪSHŪ

PACIFIC
OCEAN

BONIN
ISLANDS

Nanjing

Shanghai

RUSSIAN BALTIC FLEET

EAST
CHINA
SEA

VOLCANO
ISLANDS

OKINAWA

RYŪKYŪ ISLANDS

Fuzhou

Japanese acquisitions as of 1895

Japanese acquisitions, 1905–1910

Japanese area of influence before 1914

Xiamen
(Amoy)

TAIWAN

Japanese attack, 1914

Occupied by Japan after 1918

Guangzhou (Canton)

PESCADORES

Occupied by Japan, 1920–1925

Japan forms puppet state of Manchukuo, 1932

Macao

Hong Kong

Occupied by Japan, 1933

0   100   200   300 Miles

0   100   200   300 Kilometers

MAP 19-5   THE JAPANESE EMPIRE IN ASIA

Japan aspired to become a great imperial power like the European states and succeeded in creating a far-flung set of colonies and spheres of influence before the outbreak of World War II. What were the main territorial components of the Japanese Empire? How far did the Japanese succeed in extending their political influence throughout East Asia? What problems did the desire to extend Japanese influence in China present Japanese leaders?

Hitler Youth. Like the Communists in the Soviet Union, the Nazis organized and indoctrinated boys and girls in the hopes of making them strong supporters of the regime. Pictured here are members of the Hitler Youth, about 1939.

disability, sickness, old age, death, maternity, and retirement. Unencumbered by private property interests, the Soviet state had ceased to think of welfare assistance as a stopgap in cases of social breakdown; instead, it was viewed as an ongoing, comprehensive program that distinguished Socialism from capitalism.

A fourth common feature of the dictatorships was ambivalence about women in public roles—the Soviet Union excepted. But the Soviet state along with the other dictatorships eventually targeted women in campaigns aimed at higher rates of reproduction, rewarding mothers who had many children and restricting abortion. State officials were eager to honor new mothers as a way to repair the loss of so many young men during the Great War. Yet, women were also entering professional careers in greater numbers. Monetary losses that middle-class families had suffered during the war, coupled with a rise in the number of single women, compelled many women to become primary wage earners. In Italy, the Fascist authorities were forced to accept the existence of *la maschietta*—the new woman, or flapper, who wore short skirts, bobbed her hair, smoked cigarettes, and engaged in freer sex. In Japan, she was called the *moga* or *modan gāru* (modern girl), and though her presence provoked considerable negative comment, the authorities could not suppress the phenomenon. The Soviets offered the most glaring case of contradictory behavior. In 1918, they declared men and women equal, legalized (and subsidized) abortion, and eased divorce laws. The state changed its mind, however, and in 1935–1936, new laws made divorce nearly impossible, drove

abortion underground, and rewarded "hero mothers" of multiple children. But the rapidly industrializing Soviets had by far the highest percentage of women in the paid workforce.

Finally, the four dictatorships used violence and terror against their own citizens, colonial subjects, and "foreigners" living within their state borders. Violence was not an external element but was viewed as an essential lever for remaking the sociopolitical order. To be sure, the extent of that violence varied greatly. The Italians and the Japanese were not shy about arresting political opponents, particularly in their colonies, but it was the Nazis and especially the Soviets who filled concentration and labor camps with those deemed to be enemies of the state, whether Jews or supposed counterrevolutionaries.

Still, brutal as all these regimes were, they were founded on mobilizing popular support for their schemes. Their successes in mastering the masses were apparent enough and drew envious glances even from those still trying to stay on the liberal road. Given the power projected by dictatorships, above all, by Nazi Germany and the Soviet Union, it is not surprising that they attracted imitators. British and French Fascists and Communists, though they never came to power, formed national parties and proclaimed their support for foreign models. Admirers of Hitler, Lenin, and Stalin could also be found among politicians, intellectuals, and labor organizers in South and North America. Often, admirers saw what they wanted to see rather than the realities of the political and economic systems of Germany and the Soviet Union. Many also admired the methods of mass mobilization and mass violence, which they hoped to use for their own ends. This was particularly true of anticolonial movements.

THE HYBRID NATURE OF LATIN AMERICAN CORPORATISM

Latin American nations were subject to the same pressures that produced liberal and authoritarian responses to modern problems in Europe, Russia, and Japan. But here leaders devised solutions to their problems that had elements of both democracy and authoritarianism. The Latin American countries had stayed out of the fighting in World War I, but their export economies had suffered. As trade plummeted, popular confidence in oligarchic political regimes fell, and radical agitation surged. During the war years, trade unionists in the port of Buenos Aires took control of the city's docks, and the women of São Paulo's needle trades inspired Brazil's first general strike. Bolivian tin miners, inspired by events in Russia, proclaimed a full-blown Socialist revolution.

The Great Depression of the 1930s brought even more severe challenges to the status quo from workers' groups. More than in any other region of the world, the Depression hammered at the trading and financial systems of Latin America because it was most dependent on the exports of basic staples, from sugar to nitrates, and had to face stiff protection or evaporating demand for its commodities. The region, in fact, suffered a double whammy, because it had borrowed so much money. Unlike Europe, which had borrowed to pay for old war debts, Latin American borrowers needed extensive funds to invest in infrastructure and the expansion of their own countries. When the world money markets went belly-up, creditors called in their loans from Latin America. And as happened in Europe, this drove borrowers to default. What made Latin America so unique was the combination of pressures. Responding to the Depression's destruction, Latin American governments, with the enthusiastic backing of people from the middle classes, nationalist intellectuals, and urban workers, created an economic model that looked toward domestic rather than foreign markets as an engine of growth. The state, as in the United States and much of Europe, was called upon to play a more interventionist role in market activity.

In Latin America after the war, elites had to confront the mass age. The solution they devised was to establish new mass parties and encourage interest groups to associate with them. Collective bodies like chambers of commerce, trade unions, peasant associations, and organizations for minorities like blacks and Indians all operated with state sponsorship. This form of modern politics, often labeled corporatist, used social groups to bridge the ruling elites and the rank and file of the population.

Consider, for example, Brazil, where the old republic collapsed in 1930. In its place, a new coalition, led by a skilled civilian politician, Getúlio Vargas (1883–1954), sought to create a strong political following by enacting socially popular reforms. Vargas dubbed himself the "father of the poor" and encouraged workers to organize. The government began to build schools across Brazil. Vargas made special efforts to appeal to Brazilian blacks, who had been left out of public life since the abolition of slavery. To reinforce his paternalistic image, he legalized many proscribed Afro-Brazilian practices, lifting proscriptions on the ritual performance of the Afro-Brazilian dance "candomblé," which had frightened many white elites because of its African and martial overtones and gestures. Vargas also pledged support for samba schools (organizations that taught popular dances like the samba but that also raised funds to help with public works). Being a good patriarch also meant providing for Brazilian women and families. Accordingly, Vargas tinkered with maternity and housing policies. His Constitution of 1934 made Brazil one of the first Latin American countries to enfranchise women (although they had to be able to read, just as did male voters).

Getúlio Vargas. This cartoon of Vargas, governor of the southern state of Rio Grande do Sul, portrays him as a country bumpkin even as he leads the overthrowing of Brazil's Old Republic.

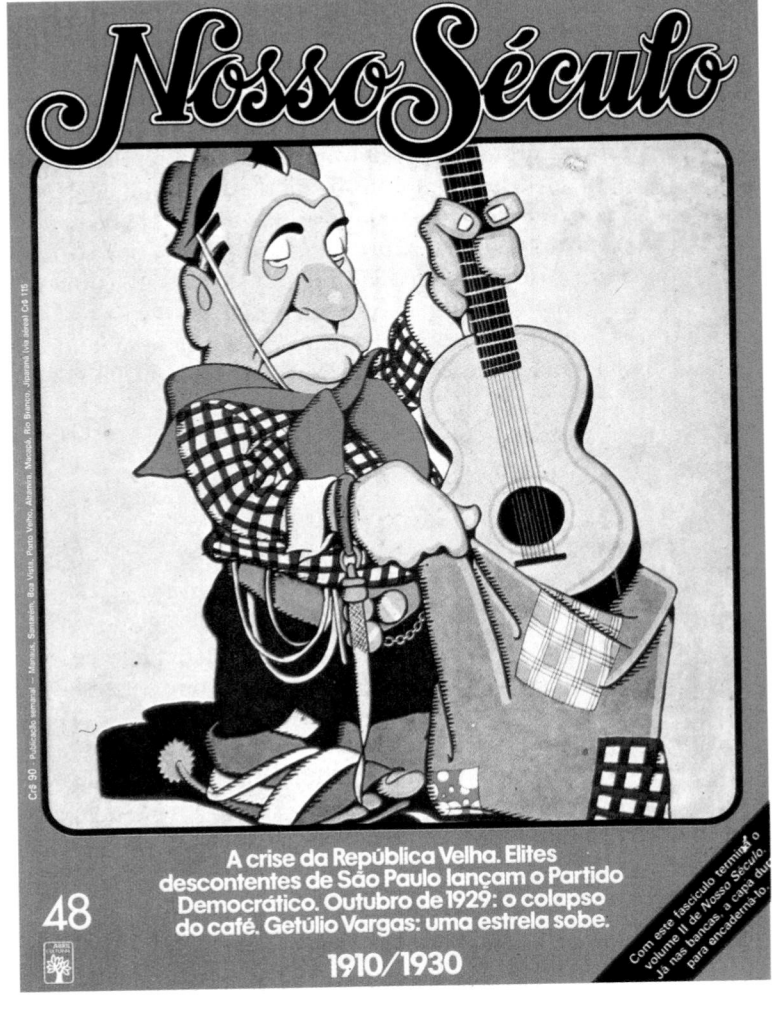

A crise da República Velha. Elites descontentes de São Paulo lançam o Partido Democrático. Outubro de 1929: o colapso do café. Getúlio Vargas: uma estrela sobe.

48

1910/1930

SAMBA: MASS CULTURE FROM THE BOTTOM UP

Although the instruments of the new mass media originated in Europe and North America and were more widely dispersed in these societies, African, Asian, and Latin American audiences also gained access to them. Radio especially helped to diffuse distinctly regional cultural products throughout Latin America. The evolution and dissemination of the musical and dance form known as samba in Brazil illustrates the ways in which mass culture could emerge in poorer societies and then spread upward to elite consumers and outward across national borders. Samba originated in Rio de Janeiro's shantytowns as a mixture of popular Spanish fandangos and the 2/4 meter of slave songs. Samba's lyrics extolled the freeing of the slaves in 1888 and the benevolence of the old monarchs. But mostly samba celebrated the idea that life was not all squalor, despite the dreadful conditions of the shantytowns. Samba was not high culture (though many in the elite had joined the audiences and even the dance troupes by the 1920s), and it was not the culture of any race or ethnic group (though it had African roots). Nor was it simply popular culture. Rather, it became a mass culture uniting the people of Rio de Janeiro and soon thereafter other parts of Brazil, and eventually it found an international audience as well.

What transformed the samba musical form from a local into a national and then international mass cultural phenomenon was the invention of the phonograph and long-playing records. These allowed samba to be broadcast on the new medium, radio. In Brazil, the phenomenally popular *Casé Program* on radio was exclusively dedicated to broadcasting popular music. In 1936, the national *Hour of Brazil* radio program featured the songs of the greatest samba school, Mangueira, in a special broadcast to Germany. The movie house, too, aided in the dissemination of samba. Brazilian samba musical films brought fame to a

Portuguese-born dancer, Carmen Miranda, whose fruit-decorated hats made her a household symbol of the tropics in the United States. Records and radio also spread the tango of Argentina, boleros of Mexico, and salsa, the New York musical creation of Cuban and Puerto Rican emigrés that became a mass phenomenon in the Spanish Caribbean by the 1930s.

The content and influence of musical mass culture were internationalized, but music and dance were also instrumental in fostering "national" cultures in Latin America. Songs and artists transcended physical barriers and regional accents, and as such, they did the work of nation building, creating cultural links between disparate people. Samba took on new political implications during the 1920s when dance organizations began to create "schools" to instruct neighbors and to raise funds to help with public works in the face of the Brazilian state's neglect. By the 1930s, samba schools were often the largest benefactors of schools, roads, and utilities in Rio de Janeiro. They also became patronage machines for local political bosses competing for the support of clienteles. For many years, the Brazilian government banned these organizations as potentially subversive, although they continued to operate illegally. But President Getúlio Vargas, aware that prohibition was politically costly and eager to induct the schools into his own political network, legalized the schools in 1935 and allowed them to occupy an ever more prominent place in the capital's cultural landscape. Thereafter, the annual festival of Mardi Gras evolved from a boisterous parade and religious celebration to an occasion for Rio's proliferating samba schools to strut their colorful and highly choreographed stuff. The belated efforts by the authorities to harness samba for their own purposes demonstrated its power as a mass culture from and for the people.

He paved roads, erected monuments to national heroes, and invoked a nationalist discourse to legitimize himself and condemn the old elites who had betrayed the country to serve the interests of foreign consumers and investors. Although Vargas also arranged foreign funding and technical transfers to build steel mills and factories, he did it to create domestic industry so that Brazil would not be so dependent on imports.

Ruling as a patriarch allowed Vargas to squelch rivals and dissent and build new lines of obedience. When he revamped

the constitution in 1937, Vargas banned competitive political parties and created forms of national representation along corporatist lines. Each social sector or class would be represented by its function in society (for example, as workers, industrialists, or educators), and each one would pledge allegiance to the all-powerful state. Although his opponents complained vociferously about losing their democratic rights, Vargas also created rights for hitherto excluded groups like trade unions, who now could use their corporatist representatives to press for their collective demands. To bolster the system, he employed a small army of modern propagandists who used billboards, loudspeakers, and the radio to broadcast the benevolence of "Father" Vargas.

ANTICOLONIAL VISIONS OF MODERN LIFE

The debates that engulfed Europe and the Americas over liberal democratic versus authoritarian solutions to modern problems engaged peoples in the colonial and semicolonial regions of the world as well. But here there was a larger concern: What was to be done about colonial authority? Throughout Asia, the goal of most of the educated members of these communities was to roll back the European and American imperial presence. Some Asians even accepted Japanese imperialism as an antidote, under the slogan "Asia for the Asians." In Africa, however, where the European colonial presence was more recent, most intellectuals were still trying to discern the real meaning of colonial rule: Were the British and the French sincerely committed to African improvement, as they claimed to be? Or were they obstacles to the well-being of the peoples of the continent?

World War I crippled Europe but gave it more colonies than ever before. Ottoman territories, in particular, wound up in Allied hands. Great Britain emerged from the war with an empire that now straddled one-quarter of the earth—some 450 million people. The spoils of war included vast oil fields in the Middle East, which had formerly been held by the Ottoman Empire, and mineral-rich possessions in what had been German Africa. Rechristened as the British Commonwealth of Nations in 1926, the British conferred dominion status on white-settler colonies in Canada, Australia, and New Zealand. This meant independence in internal and external affairs in exchange for continuing loyalty to the crown. But no such privileges were extended to possessions in Africa and India, where nonwhite peoples made up the vast majority. To justify the discriminatory practices applied to nonwhite colonial subjects, the British fell back on an old line: nonwhite peoples were not yet ready for self-government.

In Africa as well as Asia, then, the search for the modern came to encompass demands for power sharing or even outright full political independence. Otherwise divided, the intelligentsias of different countries agreed that the only sure path to the future required an end to their colonial or quasi-colonial status. Thus, anticolonialism served as the preeminent vision of educated and literate Asians and Africans during the years between World War I and World War II. To

overcome the contradictions of European liberalism, they proposed various incarnations of nationalism.

Not far beneath the surface of the Asian and African nationalist movements were profound disagreements about how nations should be governed once they gained independence and about how citizenship should be defined. For many of the educated elite, the democratic ethos of the imperial powers had great attraction. For others, the radical authoritarianism of Fascism and Communism, with their promises of rapid and guided change and a quick transit to the modern world, had much appeal. Whatever their political preferences, the majority of literate colonials, including those with secular, western educations, also looked to their own religious and cultural traditions as sources for political mobilization and organization. Muslim, Hindu, Chinese, and African values became vehicles for galvanizing the rank and file around the nation. The colonial figures involved in political and intellectual movements, whose visions for modern change derived in part from western modernity, still insisted that their views were different from those that existed in Europe; the new societies they sought to establish were going to be modern *and* at the same time retain their indigenous characteristics.

> *In Africa as well as Asia, the search for the modern came to encompass demands for power sharing or even outright full political independence.*

The diversity of nationalist and anticolonial movements depended on a variety of factors. Whether an area had been formally colonized (India and Africa), or was a semicolonial territory (China), or was an area threatened by colonization (Turkey) was important. Equally relevant was the duration of the colonial experience.

AFRICAN STIRRINGS Africa contained the most recent territories to come under the control of the European powers, and as such, anticolonial nationalist movements were just getting under way. The fate of the region remained very much in the hands of Europeans. After 1918, however, African peoples probed more deeply for the meaning of Europe's imperial presence.

In some parts of Africa, environmental degradation contributed to resentment against European colonial rule. In the peanut belt of Senegal, African cultivators pushed into more arid regions, cutting down trees and eventually wearing out the soil. The problem of desertification that became so severe after the end of colonial rule was already appearing in the western area of Senegal. Across the landmass, in Kenya, where African peoples were confined to specific locations, called reserves, so as to make land available to European settlers, Africans began to overgraze and overcultivate their lands. A severe problem occurred among the Kamba people living close to Nairobi. Their herds had become so large that the government attempted to implement a forcible campaign of culling. The Kamba responded by refusing to cooperate with the colonial officials and joined the growing chorus of African protesters against British authority.

There was some room, albeit very confined, for voicing African interests under colonialism. The French—the world's second largest colonial power, which, like Britain, had emerged from the war with an expanded empire—had long held to a vision of assimilation, that is, the incorporation, of its colonial peoples, whatever their race and religion, into French culture. In France's primary West African colony, Senegal, four coastal cities had elected one delegate to the French National Assembly. In this long-standing tradition, voters sent delegates of mixed African and European ancestry. That practice lasted until 1914, when Blaise Diagne (1872–1934), an African candidate, ran for office and won, invoking his African origins and garnering the African vote. The electorate was small, no more than 5,000 in all, and Diagne's presence in the French Assembly posed no serious challenge to the French empire. But his election signaled the potential for political change. So did his bold, if quickly rebuffed, call in 1918 for granting all Africans the vote. Yet, Diagne's example of the incorporation of the African population into the French polity did not spread elsewhere in French colonial Africa. The British were no more accommodating to demands for local elections and fully desegregated schooling. Assimilation remained a policy without practice.

Excluded from representative bodies, Africans began to experiment with various forms of protest. For example, in southeastern Nigeria in 1929, Ibo and Ibibio women responded to a new tax by refusing to have contact with the local colonial chiefs, a form of action they referred to as "sitting on a man." Moving beyond boycotts of local officials, women burned down chiefs' huts, as well as European and Lebanese trading establishments, to protest their exploitation.

Opposition was still not massive in Africa. Such protests ran up against not only colonial administrators but also urban-based and western-educated African elites, who often embraced European products and manners, built western-style homes, drove automobiles, wore western clothing, and consumed western foods. Yet, even this relatively privileged group began to reconsider its relationship to colonial authorities. In Kenya, immediately after World War I, a small contingent of mission-educated Africans, mainly Kikuyu speakers living in or near Nairobi, demanded that the British correct what they regarded as clear violations of Britain's obligations to them. Led by Harry Thuku, they called on the British to provide more and better schools and to return lands they claimed European settlers had stolen from them. Although they enlisted the support of liberal missionaries in drafting their petitions, their pleas for change fell on deaf ears. In 1922, Thuku was arrested and placed in detention. Although defeated in this instance, the young, educated nationalists drew important lessons from their confrontation with the authorities. They now viewed colonialism in a more combative light. Their new spokesperson, Jomo Kenyatta (1898–1978), turned away from missionary and colonial sources and invoked precolonial Kikuyu traditions as a basis for resisting colonialism. In Kenyatta's ethnographical description of the precolonial Kikuyu peoples, entitled *Facing Mount Kenya*, published in 1937, Kenyatta invoked African traditional ways as an antidote to Europeanization.

IMAGINING AN INDIAN NATION As Africans began to explore the use of modern politics against Europeans, in India opposition was taking on a still more advanced form. The war and its aftermath led to full-blown challenges to British rule. Indeed, the Indian nationalist challenge to the British provided inspiration and methods for other anticolonial movements.

For over a century, Indians had heard British authorities extol the virtues of parliamentary government, yet they, like other colonial peoples, were excluded from participation. In 1919, the British did enlarge the franchise in India, but the reforms brought voting rights to only 3 percent of the population. They also granted more power to Indians in local self-government. Again, however, giving Indians limited responsibility for local taxation and administration did not satisfy nationalist strivings. During the 1920s and 1930s, the nationalists, led by Mohandas Karamchand (Mahatma) Gandhi (1869–1948), laid the foundations for an alternative, anticolonial movement.

Gandhi had studied law in England and had worked in South Africa on behalf of Indian immigrants before returning to India in 1915. Upon his return, he assumed leadership in what were then local struggles. He also spelled out the moral and political philosophy of *satyagraha,* or nonviolent resistance, which he first developed while he was in South Africa.

Blaise Diagne. Diagne was the first African elected to the French National Assembly. He won the election to the French Parliament in 1914, beating white and mixed-race candidates by appealing to the majority black African population that lived in the four communes of Senegal.

Primary Source

FACING MOUNT KENYA

Jomo Kenyatta, one of Kenya's leading nationalists, wrote a moving account of his own Kikuyu community in Facing Mount Kenya, *published in 1937. The book went to great lengths to show the cohesion and strong tribal bonds of precolonial Kikuyu society and the destructive elements of the colonial assault of African traditions. The excerpt below is from the conclusion.*

And it is the culture which he inherits that gives a man his human dignity as well as his material prosperity. It teaches him his mental and moral values and makes him feel it worth while to work and fight for liberty.

But a culture has no meaning apart from the social organisation of life on which it is built. When the European comes to the Gikuyu country and robs the people of their land, he is taking away not only their livelihood, but the material symbol that holds family and tribe together. In doing this he gives one blow which cuts away the foundations from the whole of Gikuyu life, social, moral, and economic. When he explains, to his own satisfaction and after the most superficial glance at the issues involved, that he is doing this for the sake of the Africans, to "civilise" them, "teach them the disciplinary value of regular work," and "give them the benefit of European progressive ideas," he is adding insult to injury, and need expect to convince no one but himself.

There certainly are some progressive ideas among the Europeans. They include the ideas of material prosperity, of medicine, and hygiene, and literacy which enables people to take part in world culture. But so far the Europeans who visit Africa have not been conspicuously zealous in imparting these parts of their inheritance to the Africans, and seem to think that the only way to do it is by police discipline and armed force. They speak as if it was somehow beneficial to an African to work for them instead of for himself, and to make sure that he will receive this benefit they do their best to take away his land and leave him with no alternative. Along with his land they rob him of his government, condemn his religious ideas, and ignore his fundamental conceptions of justice and morals, all in the name of civilisation and progress.

If Africans were left in peace on their own lands, Europeans would have to offer them the benefits of white civilisation in real earnest before they could obtain the African labour which they want so much. They would have to offer the African a way of life which was really superior to the one his fathers lived before him, and a share in the prosperity given them by their command of science. They would have to let the African choose what parts of European culture would be beneficially transplanted, and how they could be adapted. He would probably not choose the gas bomb or the armed police force, but he might ask for some other things of which he does not get so much to-day. As it is, by driving him off his ancestral lands, the Europeans have robbed him of the material foundations of his culture, and reduced him to a state of serfdom incompatible with human happiness. The African is conditioned, by the cultural and social institutions of centuries, to a freedom of which Europe has little conception, and it is not in his nature to accept serfdom for ever. He realises that he must fight unceasingly for his own complete emancipation; for without this he is doomed to remain the prey of rival imperialisms, which in every successive year will drive their fangs more deeply into his vitality and strength.

→ *Why do you think the Europeans were not zealous in imparting "progressive ideas" to the Africans?*

→ *Why does Kenyatta think the Africans would not choose "the gas bomb or the armed police force" as a part of what they would adopt from European culture?*

SOURCE: Jomo Kenyatta, *Facing Mount Kenya: The Tribal Life of the Gikuyu* (New York: Vintage Books, 1937), pp. 304–06.

His message to Indians was simple: Develop your own resources and inner strength and control the instincts and activities that encourage participation in colonial economy and government, and you shall achieve *swaraj* (self-rule). Faced with Indian self-reliance and self-control pursued nonviolently, eventually the British would have to leave.

A crucial event in rising Indian opposition to British rule was a massacre on April 13, 1919, of Indian civilians who

Gandhi and the Road to Independence. *(Left)* Gandhi launched a civil disobedience movement in 1930 by violating the British government's tax on salt. Calling it "the most inhuman poll tax the ingenuity of man can devise," Gandhi, accompanied by his followers, set out on a month-long march on foot covering 240 miles to Dandi on the Gujarat coast. The picture shows Gandhi arriving at the sea, where he and his followers broke the law by scooping up handfuls of salt. *(Right)* Gandhi believed that India had been colonized by becoming enslaved to modern industrial civilization. Indians would achieve independence, he argued, when they became self-reliant. Thus, he made the spinning wheel a symbol of *swaraj* and handspun cloth the virtual uniform of the nation.

were protesting British policies at Amritsar in the Punjab. The incident, in which British general Reginald Dyer ordered soldiers to fire on the protesters, left 379 Indian civilians dead and more than 1,200 wounded. As news of the Amritsar massacre spread, many Indians were infuriated and were more so when they learned that British authorities were unwilling to punish General Dyer.

This and other conflicts with state officials spurred the nationalists to oppose cooperation with government officials, to boycott the purchase of goods made in Britain, to refuse to send their children to British schools, and to withhold their taxes. Gandhi added his voice to the protest movement, calling for an all-India *satyagraha*. He also formed an alliance with Muslim leaders and began turning the Indian National Congress from an elite organization of wealthy lawyers and merchants into a mass organization open to anyone who paid dues, even the illiterate and poor.

When the Depression struck India in 1930, Gandhi singled out a seemingly harmless commodity, salt, as a testing ground for his ideas on civil disobedience. Every Indian used salt, whose production remained a heavily taxed government monopoly. Thus, salt symbolized the Indians' subjugation to an alien government. To break the colonial government's monopoly, Gandhi began a march from his *ashram* (commune) in western India to the coast to gather sea salt for free. Accompanied by seventy-one followers chosen to represent different regions and religions of India, Gandhi walked 240 miles to the sea. News wire services and mass circulation

newspapers in India and around the world reported on the drama of the Salt March. Photographs of Gandhi walking determinedly to the sea circulated widely at the time. The picture of the sixty-one-year-old Gandhi, with his wooden staff in hand, dressed in coarse homespun garments, and leading the march of volunteers, reminded European journalists of a modern-day Moses. Indeed, a religious aura enveloped the march as Gandhi and his followers conducted themselves as disciplined and Spartan pilgrims. Thousands of people who had gathered en route were moved by the sight of the frail apostle of nonviolence encouraging them to embrace independence from colonial rule. The air thickened with tension as observers speculated on the British reaction to Gandhi's arrival at the sea. After nearly three weeks of walking, Gandhi finally waded into the surf, picked up a lump of natural salt, held it high, confessed that he had broken the salt law, and invited every Indian to do the same.

Inspired by Gandhi's example, millions of Indians found ways to violate the salt monopoly and to further challenge British rule by joining strikes, boycotting foreign goods, and substituting indigenous handwoven cloth for imported textiles. Many Indian officials in the colonial administration resigned from their jobs to demonstrate solidarity with Gandhi's vision. The colonizers were taken aback by the mass mobilization. Yet, British denunciations of Gandhi only added to his personal aura and to the anticolonial crusade that he embodied. By insisting that Indians follow the dictates of their conscience, though always in nonviolent forms of protest, by

INDIA AND SELF-GOVERNMENT

The following excerpt is from Mohandas (Mahatma) Gandhi's Hind Swaraj, *a widely read pamphlet that he wrote in 1909 to explain his views on why India needed self-government. Gandhi wrote it as a dialogue between a newspaper editor and a reader. He assumed the role of the editor and criticized modernity as represented by modern western civilization, which was based on industry and materialism. Set against modernity was his imagined civilization of India—one that derived from religion and that drew on harmonious village life. According to him, India demanded modern nationhood so that it could return to its age-old civilization.*

READER: . . . I would now like to know your views on Swaraj. . . .

EDITOR [GANDHI]: It is quite possible that we do not attach the same meaning to the term. You and I and all Indians are impatient to obtain Swaraj, but we are certainly not decided as to what it is. . . .

Why do we want to drive away the English?

READER: Because India has become impoverished by their Government. They take away our money from year to year. The most important posts are reserved for themselves. We are kept in a state of slavery. They behave insolently towards us, and disregard our feelings.

EDITOR: Supposing we get self-government similar to what the Canadians and the South Africans have, will it be good enough?

READER: . . . We must own our navy, our army, and we must have our own splendour, and then will India's voice ring through the world.

EDITOR: . . . In effect it means this: that we want English rule without the Englishman. You want the tiger's nature, but not the tiger; that is to say, you would make India English, and, when it becomes English, it will be called not Hindustan but Englistan. This is not the Swaraj that I want.

READER: Then from your statement I deduce that the Government of England is not desirable and not worth copying by us.

EDITOR: . . . If India copies England, it is my firm conviction that she will be ruined.

READER: To what do you ascribe this state of England?

EDITOR: It is not due to any peculiar fault of the English people, but the condition is due to modern civilisation. It is a civilisation only in name. Under it the nations of Europe are becoming degraded and ruined day by day.

READER: . . . I should like to know your views about the condition of our country.

EDITOR: . . . India is being ground down not under the English heel but under that of modern civilisation. It is groaning under the monster's terrible weight. . . . India is becoming irreligious. Here I am not thinking of the Hindu, the Mahomedan, or the Zoroastrian religion, but of that religion which underlies all religions. We are turning away from God.

READER: You have denounced railways, lawyers and doctors. I can see that you will discard all machinery. What, then, is civilisation?

READER: . . . The tendency of Indian civilisation is to elevate the moral being, that of the Western civilisation is to propagate immorality. The latter is godless, the former is based on a belief in God. So understanding and so believing, it behooves every lover of India to cling to the old Indian civilisation even as a child clings to its mother's breast.

READER: . . . What, then, . . . would you suggest for freeing India?

EDITOR: . . . Those alone who have been affected by Western civilisation have become enslaved. . . . If we become free, India is free. And in this thought you have a definition of Swaraj. It is Swaraj when we learn to rule ourselves. . . . Passive resistance is a method of securing rights by personal suffering; it is the reverse of resistance by arms. When I refuse to do a thing that is repugnant to my conscience, I use soul-force. For instance, the government of the day has passed a law which is applicable to me. I do not like it. If, by using violence, I force the government to repeal the law, I am employing what may be termed body-force. If I do not obey the law, and accept the penalty for its breach, I use soul-force. It involves sacrifice of self.

→   *Why does Gandhi reject modern civilization?*
→   *According to Gandhi, how will India achieve its freedom?*

SOURCE: M. K. Gandhi, *Hind Swaraj and Other Writings*, edited by Anthony J. Parel (Cambridge: Cambridge University Press, 1997), pp. 26–91.

Gandhi and Nehru Sharing a Light Moment. Despite their divergent views on modernity, Gandhi was personally close to Nehru, who was his chosen political heir.

exciting the masses through his defiance of colonial power, and by using symbols like homespun cloth to counter foreign, machine-spun textiles, Gandhi strengthened Indian national awareness and instilled in the people a sense of pride and resourcefulness.

Unlike the charismatic authoritarians who came to power in Italy, Germany, and Russia, Gandhi did not aspire to dictatorial power, and his program met opposition from within the anticolonial movement itself. Many in the Indian National Congress Party did not share Gandhi's communitarian vision, which opposed individualism and advocated community as the founding source of public life. Cambridge-educated Jawaharlal Nehru (1889–1964), for example, believed that only by embracing science and technology could India develop as a cosmopolitan, modern nation. Still, Gandhi's idea of forming the nation through self-reliance and sacrifice enthralled Nehru.

Less enamored were radical activists who wanted a revolution, not peaceful protest. In the countryside, these radicals scorned Gandhi's appeals to use nonviolence, and they sought to organize peasants to overthrow colonial domination. Other activists sought to bring the growing industrial proletariat into mass politics by organizing trade unions. Their stress on class conflict ran against Gandhi's ideals of national unity.

Religion, too, threatened to fracture Gandhi's hope for anticolonial unity. The Hindu-Muslim alliance crafted by nationalists in the early 1920s began to splinter. Differences arose not over the religious rights of the Muslims but over who represented them and what political arrangements were necessary to assure them of their political rights. The gulf widened after the elections held under the Government of India Act of 1935, which conceded substantial provincial au-

tonomy and enlarged the franchise to encompass 10 percent of the population. The Indian National Congress Party swept the elections in most provinces, except the two Muslim-majority states of Bengal and the Punjab. But because the Muslim votes went to provincial parties rather than to the national Muslim party (the Muslim League), the Congress Party rebuffed overtures from the league's leader, Muhammad Ali Jinnah (1876–1948). In response, Jinnah set about making the Muslim League the sole representative of the Muslims. In 1940, the Muslim League passed a resolution demanding independent Muslim states in provinces where they constituted a majority, on the grounds that Muslims were not a religious minority of the Indian nation, but a nation themselves.

Hindus also sought to claim a political role on the basis of religious identity. Movements to revitalize Hinduism, which in the nineteenth century had focused on theological and philosophical matters, began organizing Hindus as a religious nation. The most extreme expression of this trend was the formation of the Rashtriya Swayamsevak Sangh (RSS)—the National Volunteer Organization—in 1925. Openly admiring the Nazis' antiliberal nationalism, the RSS campaigned to organize Hindus as a militant, modern community. Instead of reviling Jews, the RSS spewed hatred at Muslims. Although the RSS remained a fringe group, the influence of Hindu culture on Indian nationalism was broad. Hindu symbols and a Hindu ethos colored the fabric of Indian nationalism woven by Gandhi and the Indian National Congress Party.

A further challenge came from women. Long-standing nineteenth-century efforts to "uplift" women escalated during the interwar period into a demand for women's rights. The demand for women's suffrage appeared as early as 1917, and the formation of the All India Women's Conference (AIWC) in 1927 completed the shift from social reform to political rights. The AIWC activists took up issues relating to women workers, health, employment, education, and literacy and demanded that legislative seats be reserved for women. The Indian National Congress Party, however, elevated its nationalist agenda above women's demand for a change in male-female power relations, just as it had done in dealing with the lower castes and the relations between Hindus and Muslims.

In 1937, the British belatedly granted India provincial assemblies, a bicameral (that is, having two chambers or bodies) national legislature, and a self-governing executive. By then, however, the people of India were deeply politicized. The Congress Party, which helped bring the masses onto the political stage to overthrow British rule, struggled to contain the different ideologies and new political institutions, such as labor unions, peasant associations, religious parties, and communal organizations. Confronted with the economic power of property owners, the party searched, too, for a path to economic modernization that suited Indian conditions and values. On one side, Gandhi looked back to the supposed harmony of self-sufficient village communities, envisioning independent India as an updated collection of village republics organized around the benevolent authority of patriarchal households. On the other side, his fellow nationalist, Nehru, hoped for a far-reaching socioeconomic transformation powered by science and planning. Both, however, believed that India's traditions of collective welfare and humane religious and philosophical practices set it apart from the modern West.

CHINESE NATIONALISM Unlike India and Africa, China was never formally colonized. But its sovereignty was compromised by substantial "concession areas" established by various foreign powers on Chinese soil. Foreign nationals who lived in China enjoyed many privileges, including the right to be tried by their own consuls and to be immune from Chinese law. Furthermore, huge indemnities imposed upon the Qing government had robbed China of its customs and tariff autonomy. Thus, the Chinese nationalists' vision of a modern alternative echoed that of the Indian nationalists. They, too, saw ridding the nation of foreign domination as the initial condition of national fulfillment. To many, the 1911 Revolution, as the fall of the Qing dynasty came to be known, symbolized the first step toward transforming a large and crumbling agrarian empire into a modern nation.

Despite high hopes for the new government run by a loose alliance of gentry, merchants, and military leaders and influenced by the ideas of the nationalist leader Sun Yat-sen (1866–1925), the new republic could not establish its legitimacy. For the most part, the government was hobbled by factional and regional conflicts. In March 1912, shortly after the abdication of the Qing Emperor, a military strongman, Yuan Shikai (1859–1916), forced Sun Yat-sen to concede the presidency to him. While Sun had organized his followers into a political party, called the Guomindang, Yuan dismissed all efforts to further democracy and halted China's first electoral experiment by dissolving the parliament in 1913. Only Yuan's death in 1916 ended his attempt to establish a new personal dynasty.

The republic endured another blow when the Treaty of Versailles awarded Germany's old concession rights in the Shandong peninsula to Japan. On May 4, 1919, thousands of Chinese students demonstrated in Beijing. The protests quickly spread to other cities, with students for the first time openly appealing to workers and merchants to join their ranks. In what became known as the May Fourth movement, workers went on strike, and merchants closed shops. Across the country, the Chinese boycotted Japanese goods.

As the Guomindang, still led by Sun Yat-sen, tried to rejuvenate itself, it looked to the new waves of social agitation by students and workers as well as the Russian Revolution for inspiration. In 1923, Sun reached agreement with

Chiang. Riding the current of anti-imperialism, Chiang Kaishek, shown here in military garb in a picture taken in 1924, led the Guomindang on a military campaign in 1926–1928 and seized power, establishing a new national government based in Nanjing.

the Russians and admitted Chinese Communists to the Guomindang as individual members. Under the banner of anti-imperialism, the newly reorganized party sponsored mass organizations of workers' unions, peasant leagues, and women's associations.

In 1926, one year after the death of Sun, amid a renewed tide of antiforeign agitation, Chiang Kai-shek (1887–1975) seized control of the party following Sun's death. Chiang launched a military campaign, the Northern Expedition, to reunify the country under the Guomindang. Although Chiang's success was only partial, he was able to establish a new national government with its capital in Nanjing. In April 1927, however, Chiang broke with the Soviets and the Chinese Communists, whom he viewed as more threat than ally. Furthermore, his regime, despite its anti-imperialist platform, was generally careful to honor the treaty rights and concessions gained by the foreigners in the late Qing.

Still, Chiang acknowledged that China needed to change in order to succeed as a modern nation. He believed that the Chinese masses had to be mobilized behind the nation. The New Life movement, launched with a torchlight street parade in early 1934, best exemplified his aspiration for a new Chinese national consciousness. Drawing on diverse ideas—from Confucian precepts to Social Darwinism—and Fascist practices such as the militarization of everyday life in the name of sacrificing for the nation, the New Life movement was supposed to instill discipline and moral purpose into a unified citizenry. Among the measures were dress codes for women, condemnation of casual sexual liaisons, and campaigns against spitting, urinating, or smoking in public.

PEASANT POPULISM IN CHINA: WHITE WOLF To many of the Guomindang leaders, the vast majority of the peasant population represented a backward class. Thus, the Guomindang leadership failed to see the revolutionary potential of the countryside, a failure that the Chinese Communists would later exploit. Nonetheless, the countryside was alive with grassroots movements, such as that of "White Wolf."

From late 1913 to 1914, Chinese newspapers were filled with reports about a roving band of armed men, led by a mysterious figure known as White Wolf, who, in a large part of northern and central China, terrified many members of the elite with his almost magical power. It is unlikely that the band, rumored to have close to a million followers, had more than 20,000 members even at its height. But the mythology surrounding White Wolf was so widespread that the movement's impact was felt well beyond its physical presence.

Popular myth depicted White Wolf as a Chinese Robin Hood with the mission to restore order. The band's proclaimed objective was to rid the country of the injustices of Yuan Shikai's government. Raiding major trade routes and market towns, White Wolf's followers quickly gained a reputation for robbing the rich and aiding the poor. It was said that once the band captured a town, "cash and notes were flung out to the poor." Such stories won the White Wolf army followers in rural China, where local peasants joined temporarily as fighters and then returned home when the band moved on.

> *The Guomindang leadership failed to see the revolutionary potential of the countryside, a failure that the Chinese Communists would later exploit.*

Although the White Wolf army lacked the power to restore order to the Chinese countryside, its presence reflected the changes that had come to China and suggested those still to come. The White Wolf army struck areas where inhabitants were feeling the effects of the new market forces. In the northwestern province of Shaanxi (Shensi), for example, where the band made its most famous march, markets that were once alive with trade in Chinese cotton now awaited camels carrying cotton bales shipped from Fall River, Massachusetts. That the Guomindang never managed to bridge the differences between themselves and a rural-based movement such as the White Wolf army showed the limits of their nationalist vision. It was left to the Chinese Communists, who had fled to the countryside to escape Chiang's persecution, to take up the challenge. The Communists learned that the passivity and vulnerability of the peasants were illusions and that the rural population could be turned into a mass political force, a lesson that served them well during the subsequent war and Japanese occupation in the 1930s and 1940s.

A POST-IMPERIAL TURKISH NATION Of all the anticolonial nationalist and modernizing movements of the 1920s

and 1930s, none were more politically successful or more thoroughly committed to European models than that of Mustafa Kemal Ataturk (1881–1938), who helped forge the modern Turkish nation-state. Until 1914, the Ottoman Empire was a colonial power in its own right. But having fought on the losing German side, it collapsed. The 1920 Treaty of Sèvres, which ended the war between the Allies and the Ottoman Empire, reduced the empire's realm to a part of Anatolia. Some of its former territories, such as those in southern Europe, became independent states; others, such as those in the Middle East, became British and French mandates. Elites in the former Ottoman military feared that the rest of the empire would be colonized. Although as Ottoman loyalists many of these military men had resisted Turkish nationalism, they now embraced the cause. What made modern Turkish nationalism so successful was its ability to convert the mainstay of the old regime, the army, to the goal of creating a Turkish nation-state. These men, in turn, sought to mobilize the Turkish masses and to launch a state-led drive for modernity.

In the wake of the Ottoman Empire's resounding defeat in World War I, survival of even a truncated Turkey had not been assured. But harnessing a groundswell of popular opposition to Greek troops, who had been sent to enforce the peace treaty and were trying to extend their own influence, Mustafa Kemal, an Ottoman army officer and military hero, organized a military offensive in the summer of 1920. Rallying troops to defend the fledgling Turkish nation, Kemal reconquered most of Anatolia and the area around Istanbul. The French and Italians decided to come to terms. The British, too, unable to convince their dominions to lend troops for more fighting, negotiated. Thus, in 1923, Turkish leaders signed a new treaty, the Peace of Lausanne, abrogating punitive reparations and expanding the original borders inscribed in the Treaty of Sèvres. Turkish negotiators relinquished claims to Arab lands and several Aegean islands. A vast, forcible exchange of populations took place. Approximately 1.2 million Greek Christians left Turkey to settle in Greece, and 400,000 Muslims relocated from Greece to Turkey.

With the Ottoman Empire gone, Kemal and his followers moved to build a state based upon Turkish national consciousness. That meant first deposing the sultan in 1922. Two years later, the new leaders abolished the office of the Ottoman caliphate and proclaimed Turkey a republic, whose supreme authority would be lodged in an elected House of Assembly. Later, after Kemal insisted that the people should adopt European-style surnames, the assembly conferred on Kemal the mythic name "Ataturk," father of the Turks.

Ataturk. In the 1920s, Mustafa Kemal, known as Ataturk, introduced the Latin alphabet for the Turkish language as part of his campaign to modernize and secularize Turkey. He underscored his commitment to change by being photographed while giving instruction.

In forging a Turkish nation, Kemal looked to construct a European-like secular state and to eliminate Islam's hold over civil and political affairs. The Turkish elite replaced Muslim religious law with the Swiss civil code, instituted the western (Christian) calendar, and abolished the once-powerful dervish religious orders. They also suppressed Arabic and Persian words from Turkish and substituted the Roman script for Arabic letters. Polygamy was proscribed. Wearing the fez (a brimless cap) was criminalized, and Turks were instructed to wear European-style hats. The veil, though not outlawed, was denounced as a relic. In 1934, the government enfranchised Turkish women, granted them property rights in marriage and inheritance, and allowed them to enter the professions. Schools, too, were taken out of the hands of Muslim clerics, placed under the control of the state, and, along with military service, became the chief instrument for making the masses conscious of belonging to a Turkish nation. Yet, many villagers did not accept Ataturk's non-Islamic nationalism, remaining devoted to Islam and resentful of the prohibitions against dervish dancing.

In emulating Europe, Kemal borrowed Europe's antiliberal models. Inspired by the Soviets, he inaugurated a five-year plan for the economy, though the emphasis on centralized coordination was not tied to the abolition of private property. During the 1930s, Turkish nationalists also drew on Nazi examples by advocating racial theories that posited central Asian Turks as the founders of all civilization. In another move characteristic of authoritarian dictators, Kemal occasionally rigged parliamentary elections, while using the police and judiciary to silence his critics.

THE MUSLIM BROTHERHOOD IN EGYPT Elsewhere in the Middle East, where France and Britain expanded their holdings at the Ottomans' expense, anticolonial movements borrowed from European models while putting their own stamp on nation-making and modernization campaigns. In Egypt, for example, British occupation predated the fall of the Ottoman Empire by several decades, but here, too, World War I energized the forces of anticolonial nationalism. When the war ended, Sa'd Zaghlul (1857–1927), an educated, upper-crust Egyptian patriot, pressed for an Egyptian delegation to be invited to the peace conference at Versailles. There, he hoped to present Egypt's case for national independence. Instead, British officials arrested and exiled him and his most vocal supporters to Malta. When news of this action came out, the country burst into revolt. Rural rebels broke away from the central government, proclaiming local republics. Villagers tore up railway lines and telegraph wires, the symbols of British authority.

After defusing the conflict, British authorities tried to mollify Egyptian sensibilities. Their half-hearted efforts helped at first but then aggravated tensions. In 1922, Britain proclaimed Egypt independent, though it retained the right to station British troops on Egyptian soil. Ostensibly, this provision was adopted to protect traffic through the Suez Canal and foreign populations residing in Egypt, but it also enabled the British to continue to influence Egyptian politics. Two years later, elections took place, and Zaghlul's new nationalist party, the Wafd, took office. But the British prevented the Wafd from exercising real power.

This subversion of independence and democracy in Egypt provided an opening for antiliberal variants of anticolonialism to arise. During the Depression years, a Fascist group, called Young Egypt, garnered wide appeal. So did an Islamic group established in 1928, the Muslim Brotherhood, which attacked liberal democracy as a facade for middle-class, business, and landowning interests. The Muslim Brotherhood was anticolonial and anti-British, but its members considered mere political independence insufficient. Egyptians, they argued, must also renounce the blandishments of the West, whether they be those of liberal capitalism or godless Communism, and return to a purified form of Islam. For the ideologues of the Muslim Brotherhood, Islam offered a complete way of life. A "return to Islam" through the nation-state created yet another model of modernity for colonial and semicolonial peoples.

CONCLUSION

The Great War and its aftermath accelerated the trend toward mass society and the debate over how to organize it. Mass society meant production and consumption on a staggering scale. Politics and culture were no longer the exclusive province of a small number of elite men and women. For rulers around the globe, satisfying the populace became a pressing concern. Indeed, it became the central problem of the postwar decades, with competing programs vying for ascendancy in the new, broader, public domain.

Most of the programs fell into three categories: liberal, authoritarian, and anticolonial. The first, liberalism, was a holdover from the nineteenth century—and to varying extents, it defined the political and economic systems in western Europe and the Americas. Resting on faith in free enterprise and representative democracy (with a restricted franchise), liberal regimes had already been unsettled before the Great War. Turn-of-the-century reforms had broadened electorates and brought government oversight and regulation into private economic activity. But during the Great Depression, dissatisfaction again deepened. Only far-reaching reforms, introducing greater regulation and more aggressive government intervention to provide for the welfare of the citizenry, saved capitalist economies and the democratic political systems to which they were attached from collapse.

Still, through the 1930s, liberalism was in retreat. Authoritarianism seemed better positioned to satisfy the masses while claiming to represent the dynamism of modernity. Dictatorial regimes challenged liberalism from both the left (in the Soviet Union) and right (in Italy, Germany, and Japan) of the political spectrum. While authoritarians differed about the faults of capitalism, they joined in the condemnation of electoral democracy. Authoritarians mobilized the masses to put the interests of the nation above the individual. That mobilization often entailed brutal repression of large portions of the population, and yet the grand crusade seemed also to restore pride and purpose to the masses.

In the colonial and semicolonial world, the tribulations of liberalism and the triumphs of authoritarianism, especially those of Soviet Communism and German Nazism, were closely watched by those searching to escape from the domination of European empires. In Asia and Africa, anticolonial leaders confronted diverse situations. In common, however, they faced the challenge of how to eliminate foreign rule while turning colonies into nations and subjects into citizens. Some anticolonial intellectuals and leaders looked to the liberal West for models of nation building. But for some in Asia and Africa, liberalism was discredited because it was associated with colonial rule. Instead, Socialism, Fascism, and a return to religious traditions offered more compelling models for the anticolonial crusade.

The competition among democratized liberalism, radical authoritarianism, and anticolonial nationalism was not purely

Chronology

	1910	1920
AMERICAS		▌ *United States enters World War I, 1917*
EUROPE	*The Great War begins, 1914* ▌	▌ *Dissolution of German and Austro-Hungarian Empir* ▌ *Treaty of Versailles ends World War I, 19* *Mussolini and Fascists march on Rome, 1922* ▌
RUSSIA (SOVIET UNION)		▌ *Bolshevik Revolution, 1917* ▌ *Russian Civil War, 1918–1921*
EAST ASIA		▌ *May Fourth movement (China), 1919*
SOUTH ASIA		▌ *Massacre at Amritsar, 1919*
MIDDLE EAST		▌ *Dissolution of Ottoman Empire, 1918* *Ottoman sultan deposed, 1922* ▌ *Mustafa Kemal leads Turkey to nationhood,*

intellectual. It entailed geopolitical rivalry among the great powers, and it involved the fate of their existing empires. Yet, while the age of mass production and mass politics was marked by political upheavals and economic dislocations, it was tame compared to what was about to erupt in 1939—World War II.

STUDY QUESTIONS

 WWNORTON.COM/STUDYSPACE

1. List and explain numerous ways in which World War I changed the world. How did it usher in a new age for diverse societies?
2. Define the terms *mass culture*, *mass production*, and *mass consumption*. How did World War I help to diffuse these concepts across the world's cultures?
3. Analyze how the Great Depression challenged political establishments across the world barely a decade after World War I. How were the two events linked? What values and assumptions did the Great Depression challenge?
4. Explain new competing visions of modernity that emerged around the world during the era covered in this chapter. How were they similar and how were they different?
5. Compare and contrast the liberal and authoritarian visions of modernity as epitomized by various states in the 1930s. What did they share in common?

6. List and explain various anticolonial visions of modern life that emerged in the first half of the twentieth century. To what extent did they reflect developments borrowed versus native traditions and ideas?
7. Describe how Latin American societies adjusted to modern ideas during this era. How did visions of modernity affect states and societies in that region of the world?

FURTHER READINGS

Bergère, Marie-Claire, *Sun Yat-sen* (1998). Originally published in French in 1994, this is a judicious and most recent biography of the man generally known as the father of the modern Chinese nation.

Brown, Judith, *Gandhi: Prisoner of Hope* (1990). A biography of Gandhi as a political activist.

De Grazia, Victoria, and Ellen Furlough (eds.), *The Sex of Things: Gender and Consumption in Historical Perspective* (1996). Pathbreaking essays on how gender affects consumption.

Dumenil, Lynn, *The Modern Temper: America in the 1920s* (1995). A general discussion of American culture in the decade after World War I.

Fainsod, Merle, *Smolensk under Soviet Rule* (1989). The most accessible and sophisticated interpretation of the Stalin revolution in the village.

	1930	1940
	▌ *Great Depression begins, 1929*	
	▌ *Getúlio Vargas becomes leader of Brazil, 1930*	
	▌ *American "New Deal," 1933–1941*	
	▌ *Great Depression begins, 1929*	
	▌ *Hitler becomes dictator of Germany, 1933*	
	▌ *Popular Front rules France, 1936–1939*	
	▌ *Collectivization in Russia, 1929–1935*	▌ *Great Purge in the Soviet Union, 1936–1938*
▌ *Chiang Kai-shek becomes leader of China, 1928*	▌ *Japan annexes Manchuria, 1932*	
	▌ *Gandhi's March to the Sea, 1930*	
▌ *Muslim Brotherhood established (Egypt), 1928*		

Friedman, Edward, *Backward toward Revolution: The Chinese Revolutionary Party* (1974). An insightful look at the failure of liberalism in early republican China through the prism of the short-lived Chinese Revolutionary Party.

Gelvin, James, *Divided Loyalties: Nationalism and Mass Politics in Syria at the Close of Empire* (1998). Offers important new insights into the development of nationalism in the Arab world.

Horne, John (ed.), *State, Society, and Mobilization during the First World War* (1997). Essays on what it took to wage total war among all the belligerents.

Johnson, G. Wesley, *The Emergence of Black Politics in Senegal* (1971). A useful examination of the stirrings of African nationalism in Senegal.

Kennedy, David M., *Freedom from Fear: The American People in Depression and War, 1929–1945* (1999). A wonderful narrative of turbulent years.

Kershaw, Ian, *Hitler*, 2 vols. (1998–2000). A masterpiece combining biography and context.

Kimble, David, *A Political History of Ghana* (1963). An excellent discussion of the beginnings of African nationalism in Ghana.

Kotkin, Stephen, *Magnetic Mountain: Stalinism as a Civilization* (1995). Recaptures the atmosphere of a time when everything seemed possible, even creating a new world.

LeMahieu, D. L., *A Culture for Democracy: Mass Communication and the Cultivated Mind in Britain between the Wars* (1988). One of the great works on mass culture.

Lyttelton, Adrian, *The Seizure of Power: Fascism in Italy, 1919–1929* (1961). Still the classic account.

Marchand, Roland, *Advertising the American Dream: Making Way for Modernity, 1920–1945* (1985). An excellent discussion of the force of mass production and mass consumption.

Mazower, Mark, *Dark Continent: Europe's Twentieth Century* (1999). A wide-ranging overview of Europe's tempestuous twentieth century.

Nottingham, John, and Carl Rosberg, *The Myth of "Mau Mau": Nationalism in Kenya* (1966). Dispells the myths in describing the roots of nationalism in Kenya.

Strachan, Hew (ed.), *World War I: A History* (1998). Cutting-edge essays that dispel many myths.

Thorp, Rosemary (ed.), *Latin America in the 1930s* (1984). An important collection of essays on Latin America's response to the shakeup of the interwar years.

Tsin, Michael, *Nation, Governance, and Modernity in China: Canton, 1900–1927* (1999). An analysis of the vision and social dynamics behind the Guomindang-led revolution of the 1920s.

Vianna, Hermano, *The Mystery of Samba* (1999). Discusses the history of samba, emphasizing its African heritage as well as its persistent popular content.

Wakeman, Frederic, Jr., *Policing Shanghai, 1927–1937* (1995). An excellent account of Guomindang rule in China's largest city during the Nanjing decade.

Winter, J. M., *The Experience of World War* (1988). A comprehensive presentation of the many sides of the twentieth century.

Young, Louise, *Japan's Total Empire: Manchuria and the Culture of Wartime Imperialism* (1998). An innovative case study of Japanese imperialism and mass culture with broad implications.

THE THREE-WORLD
ORDER, 1940–1975

*I*n February 1945, the three leaders of the World War II Allies—President Franklin Delano Roosevelt of the United States, Prime Minister Winston Churchill of Great Britain, and Premier Joseph Stalin of the Soviet Union—met in the Black Sea resort city of Yalta in the Russian Crimea to make preparations for the postwar order. By then, Germany, Italy, and Japan were losing the war. The three men had different visions of how a war-torn world should be reconstructed. Roosevelt anticipated a world of independent nation-states, kept at peace by an international body. He had no interest in restoring the old European empires, which he believed had been ruled selfishly with little commitment to a civilizing mission. But Britain's Churchill had no intention, as he so aptly put it after the war, of presiding over the liquidation of the British Empire. Just what Stalin wanted was not clear, though the Soviet leader's negotiations at Yalta left no doubt that he intended to secure influence in eastern Europe and Asia and to weaken Germany so that it could never again menace the Soviet Union. In short, as the end of the war approached, these contrasting visions of the postwar world order threatened to usher in a contentious era.

If World War I shocked the Europe-centered world, World War II destroyed it. When the fighting finally stopped in August

1945, empires had been destroyed or were set for dismantling by colonial independence movements. The nation-state more than ever had emerged as the prevailing political organization. Moreover, the reach of the state had been expanded as it took on new functions related to postwar reconstruction. Meanwhile, with the end of the war and the weakening of the former great powers—Great Britain, France, and Germany—a new three-world order began to emerge. Heading the "First World" was the United States. Leading the "Second World" was the Soviet Union. Allies during World War II, the United States and the Soviet Union became postwar enemies. Their rival blocs—Capitalist and Communist—were locked in a "cold war." Caught in between were formerly colonized and semicolonized people lumped together as the "Third World."

COMPETING BLOCS

> → *What challenges did each world bloc face?*

The roots of the division of the world into three blocs lay in the breakup of Europe's empires and the demise of European world leadership. The destruction of Europe and the defeat of Japan left a power vacuum, which the United States and the Soviet Union rushed to fill. The United States and the Soviet Union both believed that their respective ideologies—liberal capitalism and Communism—had universal application. In the new world order, they were superpowers—so called because of their size, their possession of the atomic bomb, and the fact that each embodied a model of civilization applicable to the whole world. As both nations expanded their spheres of influence, they engaged in an arms race that threatened world peace. Bitter rivalry dominated world politics for several decades.

While the capitalist and Communist blocs embarked on a cold war, in which no direct war was fought between the two, in the Third World the conflicts got very hot indeed. In Asia and Africa, anticolonial leaders capitalized on European weakness and Japanese defeat to intensify their campaigns for independence. Winning popular support by mobilizing deep-seated desires for justice and autonomy, they were able to sweep away foreign rulers and assert their claims for national independence. Latin American countries, too, joined this effort to achieve progress and nationhood. But newfound political freedom did not easily translate into economic development or social equity. Moreover, as the two superpowers looked for allies and client states that would serve their interests, they militarized rival states and factions within the Third World. Still, the Third World continued to nurture powerful movements for national liberation and social transformation.

While each superpower touted its own achievements, each also had to confront internal problems. The United States maintained that its booming industrial economy, abundant consumer goods, liberal democracy, and entertaining popular culture were proof of the superiority of capitalism. The United States also wrestled with deep-rooted racism that diminished the appeal of the American way of life for non-white peoples. And it became involved in unpopular wars to stop the spread of Communism, most notably in Vietnam. The Soviet Union celebrated its own economic prowess and social welfare policies. But its continued authoritarianism, its millions of political prisoners, and its use of military force to crush reform efforts within the Soviet bloc undermined Communism's allure.

By the 1960s and the early 1970s, tensions were beginning to appear in the three-world order. The United States and the Soviet Union faced discontent within their societies and opposition within their respective blocs. At the same time, the rising economic might of Japan and the other Pacific economies, the emerging clout of oil-rich states, and the specter of radical revolution in Africa, Asia, and Latin Amer-

Focus Questions THE THREE-WORLD ORDER

- → *What challenges did each world bloc face?*
- → *In what ways was World War II a global conflict?*
- → *How did the United States try to contain the spread of Communism?*
- → *To what extent did decolonization involve large-scale violence?*
- → *What were the successes and failures of each world bloc?*
- → *What were the major fissures that developed in the three-world order?*

 WWNORTON.COM/STUDYSPACE

→ *In what ways was World War II a global conflict?*

ica suggested a shift in the balance of wealth and power away from the First and Second worlds, if not toward the Third.

WORLD WAR II AND ITS AFTERMATH

→ *In what ways was World War II a global conflict?*

The seeds for World War II grew out of unresolved problems connected to the Great War. World War I had not been, as many had prophesied, "the war to end all wars." It became instead merely the *First* World War after the *Second* World War began in 1939. Especially influential were the resentments bred by the harsh provisions and controversial new state boundaries set out in the treaties signed at the war's end. Germany sought to end reparations payments imposed after World War I and demanded the right to rearm itself.

World War II, however, was also an outgrowth of the aggressive ambitions and racial theories of Germany and Japan, which sought to impose their theories of racial hierarchy (master/dominant and inferior races) through conquest and coerced labor. By the late 1930s, German and Japanese ambitions to expand and to become colonial powers, like Britain, France, and the United States, brought these conservative dictatorships (which along with Italy constituted the Axis powers) into conflict with France, Britain, the Soviet Union, and eventually the United States (the Allied powers).

Even more than its predecessor, World War II was truly a world conflict and was devastatingly total. Fighting took place in Europe, Africa, and Asia, the Atlantic and the Pacific, and the Northern and Southern hemispheres. Warring nations mobilized millions of people into armed forces and placed enormous demands on civilian populations. Noncombatants had to produce far more to support the war effort, and they had to consume far less. Moreover, as aerial bombardment of cities resulted in colossal numbers of civilian casualties, the new total war erased the old distinction between soldiers and civilians. Women—as victims and as collaborators, as volunteers and as forced laborers, as workers behind the scenes and as witnesses to the conflict—were involved as never before; they, together with children, the infirm, and the elderly would also make up the lion's share of the enormous population of refugees, seeking desperately for safety in the midst of worldwide chaos.

In addition to refashioning the nature of modern war, World War II completed the decline of European world dom-

> *World War II completed the decline of European world dominance that World War I had set in motion.*

inance that World War I had set in motion. The unspeakable acts of barbarism perpetrated during the war, including the Nazi genocides directed against Jews and others, robbed Europe of its lingering claims as a superior civilization. In the war's wake, anticolonial movements demanded national self-determination from exhausted and battered European powers.

THE WAR IN EUROPE

Although Hitler had annexed Austria and parts of Czechoslovakia in 1938, World War II officially began in Europe in September 1939, with Germany's invasion of Poland and the British and French decision to oppose it. Hitler's early success in the air and on the battlefield was staggering. He overran Poland, France, Norway, Denmark, Luxembourg, Belgium, and Holland. In 1940 he signed the Tripartite Pact with Italy, a fellow Fascist state, and with Japan, formally creating an alliance between the Axis powers. Within less than two years, the Germans controlled virtually all of western Europe (see Map 20-1). Only Britain escaped Axis control, though Nazi airplanes pulverized British cities with bombs. In the east, Germany had a non-aggression pact with the Soviet Union, but in June 1941, the German army invaded the Soviet Union with 170 divisions, 3,000 tanks, and up to 4 million men—an unprecedented invasion force. Here, as elsewhere, the Germans fought what was called a *blitzkrieg*, or lightning war, of tank-led assaults followed by motorized infantrymen (and then foot soldiers). Already by October 1941, the Germans had conquered Romania, Hungary, Bulgaria, Yugoslavia, and the western portion of the Soviet Union and had reached the outskirts of Moscow. The Soviet Union seemed on the verge of a monumental defeat.

One response to the intensification of the war, on both sides, was to draft more laborers. Before World War II, Soviet women already made up 40 percent of the workforce outside the home. But after 1941, millions more women workers, and schoolchildren (ages fifteen or younger) as well as pensioners, were recruited to work for the war effort. Prewar Nazi Germany had near full employment, too, but when wartime labor demand exceeded supply, the Nazis, by contrast, refused to mobilize more women to work outside the home and instead reluctantly began to press-gang workers from Poland, then France, and finally the Soviet Union to the Reich, despite fears of racial contamination. Altogether, more than 12 million foreign laborers (including 2 million prisoners of war) were forcibly imported to Germany. These workers were not allowed to leave, received low wages (or none at all), and lived in conditions inferior to those

MAP 20-1 WORLD WAR II: THE EUROPEAN THEATER

The Axis armies enjoyed great success during the early stages of World War II. What were the territorial boundaries when the Axis powers reached their greatest extent? When did the military balance begin to turn against Germany and Italy? Where do you think the outcome of the conflict was decided, eastern Europe or western Europe?

of the German population. Resettling the migrants who survived the war would prove impossible, leaving some former residents of eastern Europe permanently displaced.

The Nazi war was not just a grab for land; it was also a crusade to create a new order based on race. Nazi occupation policies were monstrous and created massive social, economic, and political upheavals throughout Europe. To enforce his policies, Hitler established puppet governments, which complied with deportation orders against Jews and dissidents. Hitler's police and the puppet states turned Europe into a giant police state and spawned both collaborators and resistance fighters. Even within the resistance movements, however, there were many different points of view—from nationalists, who opposed German domination, to Communists, who wanted to defeat both Fascism and capitalism; here, the seeds for many postwar enmities were sown.

→ *In what ways was World War II a global conflict?*

The Devastation of War. (*Left*) In the Battle of Britain, Nazi warplanes strafed British cities in an effort to break British morale. But the devastating bombing raids, such as this one in Coventry in November 1940, helped rally the British, who refused to give in. (*Right*) In November 1942 Nazi troops entered Stalingrad, some 2,000 miles from Berlin. Hitler wanted to capture the city not only to exploit the surrounding wheat fields and the oil of the Caucasus, but also for its very name. With handheld flamethrowers and sometimes just their fists, Soviet troops drove out the Germans in February 1943.

In the east, the tide turned against the Germans and their collaborators after the ferocious battles of Stalingrad in 1942–1943 and Kursk in 1943. Once the Soviet army blunted the initial German assault, it launched a massive counteroffensive. This was the beginning of the end of the German war effort on the Eastern Front, but the full retreat would take another two years as the Soviets drove Hitler's army slowly westward. Before 1944, the Soviets bore the brunt of the fighting, although the British attacked the Nazis in the air and on the sea and, along with American troops, they stopped a German advance across North Africa into Egypt. The D-Day landing of western Allied forces in Normandy on June 6, 1944, however, brought the Germans face to face with American and British troops determined to fight their way to Germany itself. On April 30, 1945, as Soviet and Anglo-American forces converged on Berlin, Hitler committed suicide in his concrete bunker. On May 7, 1945, Germany surrendered unconditionally. Still, the question of what the postwar European map would look like was unresolved.

The war in Europe had devastating human and material costs. This was particularly the case in eastern Europe, where the Germans had plundered and murdered the local populations. Fighting on the Eastern Front leveled more than 70,000 Soviet villages and obliterated one-third of the Soviet Union's wealth. Soviet military deaths numbered 7 million, about half the total of all combatants (by contrast, the Germans lost 3.5 million men). Estimates of Soviet civilian deaths range from 17 to 20 million. Bombing of British cities, such as London, by the German *Luftwaffe* (air force) inflicted a heavy toll on civilians and buildings, as did Allied bombing

of war plants and Axis cities like Dresden and Toyko. But urban casualties were perhaps greatest in Leningrad, a city that was surrounded and besieged for nine hundred days; 900,000 people lost their lives in the course of this struggle. By the end of the war, Poland had lost 6 million people, and Great Britain had lost 400,000. Tens of millions in the east and west were left homeless.

Europe's Jews paid an especially high price. Hitler had long talked of "freeing" Europe of all Jews. At the outset of the war, the Nazis herded Jews into ghettos and labor camps, seizing their property. But as the army moved eastward, more and more Jews came under German control. At first, the Nazi bureaucrats contemplated deportation, perhaps to the island of Madagascar. But transporting "subhumans" was ruled out as too costly and complicated, and already by 1940, special troops in the east had begun mass shootings of Communists and Jews. This, however, was seen as a waste of ammunition. Accordingly, shootings gave way to the use of mobile gas vans. By the fall of 1941, Hitler and the S.S. (the *Schutzstaffel*, a security police force) began to plan a series of killing centers. The largest of these concentration camps was a complex known as Auschwitz-Birkenau in Poland. Cattle cars shipped Jews from all over Europe to the new extermination sites, where the latest technology was used to kill men, women, and children. Around 6 million—two-thirds of all European Jews—died, many from gassing, others from starvation or exhaustion. The Nazis also turned their mass killing apparatus against gypsies, homosexuals, Communists, and Slavs, with deportations to the death camps continuing to the very end of the war.

THE PACIFIC WAR

Like the war in Europe, the conflict in the Pacific transformed the military and political landscape (see Map 20-2). The war broke out when Japan's ambitions to obtain access to vital Southeast Asian oil and rubber supplies and to become a major colonial power in the area ran squarely into American opposition. Japan's expansionist aims became clear in 1931 when its forces invaded and occupied Manchuria in northern China and intensified when it launched an offensive against the rest of China in 1937. Although the Japanese captured a large amount of Chinese territory, they were not able to force China's complete submission. But the invaders exacted a terrible toll on the Chinese population. The most infamous of Japanese atrocities was the "rape of Nanjing," in which the aggressors indiscriminately slaughtered at least 100,000 civilians and raped thousands of women in the Chinese city between December 1937 and February 1938.

Events in Europe opened opportunities for further Japanese expansion in Asia. Germany's swift occupation of western Europe left the colonies of defeated nations at the mercy of Japanese forces. After concluding a pact with Germany in 1940, the Japanese proceeded to occupy French Indochina in 1941 and made demands on the Dutch East Indies for oil and rubber. Now the chief obstacle to further expansion in the Pacific was the United States, which had demonstrated its own imperial interest in East Asia in the first half of the twentieth century in places like the Philippines and China, as well as other Pacific islands. Hoping to strike the United States before it was prepared for war and before the Americans could prevent Japan from seizing resource-rich territories in Southeast Asia, the Japanese launched a full-scale surprise air attack on the American naval base at Pearl Harbor in Hawaii on December 7, 1941. As the United States entered the war, Germany and Italy, under the terms of the Tripartite Pact of 1940, also declared war on America.

In the months after Pearl Harbor, Japan's expansion shifted into high gear. During 1942, the Japanese military achieved spectacular successes, racking up victory after victory over the tottering western armies. With French Indochina already under their control, the Japanese turned against the American colony of the Philippines and against

Japanese Aggression. (*Left*) The brutal Battle of Shanghai (August–November 1937) marked the beginning of what turned out to be World War II in Asia. Claiming to be "protecting" China from European imperialists and expecting a relatively easy victory, the Japanese instead met with stiff resistance from the Chinese troops under Chiang Kai-shek. Here we see Japanese marines parading through the streets of the city after they finally broke through Chinese defenses. About a quarter of a million Chinese soldiers, close to 60 percent of Chiang's best troops, were killed or wounded in the campaign, a blow from which Chiang's regime never recovered. The Japanese sustained over 40,000 casualties. (*Right*) Japanese troops celebrate a victory over the Americans on Bataan in April 1942. Only the stalemate of the Battle of the Coral Sea (south of New Guinea) halted the run of Japanese victories. With the defeat of the Japanese at the Battle of Midway in June 1942, the United States began to turn the tide of the Pacific War.

Japanese Empire, 1 Dec. 1941

Ally of Japan

· · · · · Furthest line of Japanese advance, July 1942

Date Japanese attack or capture

Date Allied attack or capture

← Allied offensive

← Japanese offensive

← British offensive

←- Chinese-U.S. offensive

← Chinese offensive

← Soviet offensive

⬅ Japanese naval victory

⬅ U.S. naval victory

✹ Conventional bombing

✹ Nuclear bombing

✳ Japanese battle victory

✳ U.S. battle victory

MAP 20-2   WORLD WAR II: THE PACIFIC THEATER

Like Germany and Italy, Japan experienced stunning military successes in the early years of the war. Can you explain why the Japanese military was so successful at this time? How well did the European empires in Asia fare during the war in the Pacific? How did the Allied strategies to defeat the Japanese Empire shape postwar relations in the region?

The Aftermath of the Atomic Bomb. (*Left*) A view of Nagasaki less than half a mile from "ground zero" after the atomic bomb was dropped in August 1945. A few reinforced concrete buildings still stand. (*Right*) Thousands of people were immediately crushed or burned to death in the blast. Many died later from horrendous burns and radiation poisoning.

the Dutch East Indies, both of which fell in 1942. By coordinating their army, naval, and air force units and using tactical surprise, the Japanese were able to seize a huge swath of Asian territory that included British-ruled Hong Kong, Singapore, Malaya, and Burma, while threatening the British Empire's hold on India as well.

Japan christened its new empire the Greater East Asia Co–Prosperity Sphere, dressing its aggression in the garb of anticolonial pan-Asianism. In practice, however, the Japanese made huge demands on Asians for resources, developed their own myth of Japanese racial purity and supremacy, and treated Chinese and Koreans with brutality. Asians under Japanese dominion soon discovered that "Asia for Asians" was an empty slogan. During the war, Japan put up to 4 million Koreans to work for its empire, while forcibly importing another 700,000 Korean men as laborers. Up to 200,000 young women, most but not all from Korea, were pressed into service as prostitutes, euphemistically referred to as "comfort women," for Japanese soldiers.

Like the Germans in their war against Russia, the Japanese could not sustain their military successes against the United States. By the middle of 1943, U.S. forces had thrown the Japanese on the defensive. Fighting from island to island, American troops under General Douglas MacArthur (1880–1964) recaptured the Philippines, and a combined force of British, American, and Chinese troops returned Burma to Britain. The Allies then moved toward the Japanese mainland. By the summer of 1945, American bombers had all but devastated the major cities of Japan. Japan did not surrender. Anticipating that an invasion of Japan would cost hundreds

of thousands of American lives, Harry Truman (1884–1972), recently elevated to the American presidency following the death of Franklin Roosevelt, decided to unleash the Americans' secret weapon, which had been developed by a team of scientists predominantly made up of European refugees. On August 6, 1945, an American plane dropped an atomic bomb on the city of Hiroshima, killing or maiming over 100,000 people. Three days later, the Americans dropped a second atomic bomb on Nagasaki. Five days after this second attack, Emperor Hirohito announced Japan's surrender; but the bombs' work was not over. Air, soil, and groundwater were irradiated, poisoning the sources of sustenance. This was not the first time, nor would it be the last, that human-made technologies not only clinched victory for one army, but also altered the chemical composition of the land itself.

THE BEGINNING OF THE COLD WAR

> → *How did the United States try to contain the spread of Communism?*

World War II left much of Europe in ruins. Charred embers lay where great cities had once stood. Major bridges lay crumbled at the bottom of rivers; railway lines were twisted scrap; sunken ships blocked harbors. Industrial and agricultural production plummeted, leading to widespread scarcity and hunger. Millions had died; tens of millions more were wounded, displaced, widowed, and orphaned. Soviet soldiers fighting their way across Germany engaged in systematic rape as a form of retribution, victimizing millions of German women and girls. "What is Europe now?" mused British prime minister Winston Churchill at the war's end. "A rubble heap, a charnel house, a breeding ground of pestilence and hate."

REBUILDING EUROPE

The task of political rebuilding was daunting. The old order, which had either collaborated with Fascists or crumpled before their armies, was discredited. By contrast, Communism gained new appeal—many underground resisters were Communists, and their credo promised a clean slate. Some eastern Europeans, knowing little of Stalin's crimes, wanted Soviet help to create proletarian paradises. After the horrors of Fascism, some form of Socialism seemed to offer the potential to create powerful, modern, egalitarian societies in Europe.

Europe's leftward tilt alarmed U.S. policymakers. They feared that the Soviets would use their ideological influence and the territory conquered by the Red Army to establish a Communist bloc and that Stalin might lay claim to Europe's possessions overseas, thereby creating Communist regimes outside Europe. American and British governments had mistrusted Stalin during the war, but they had depended on the Soviet Union's strength against Germany. With a common enemy gone, however, misgivings quickly evolved into a decision to hold the line against further Soviet influence. An American journalist coined and popularized the term "cold war" in 1946 to describe the new struggle.

President Truman advocated a policy of containing Soviet Communism. America's policy soon faced a test in Germany, which had been partitioned into British, French, American, and Soviet zones of occupation after the war. Although Berlin, the capital city, was technically in the Soviet occupation zone, postwar agreements stipulated that it was to be jointly administered by all four powers. In 1948, the Soviets attempted to seize Berlin for themselves by blocking all routes to the capital. The Allies responded by launching a massive effort, the Berlin Airlift, which transported supplies in planes to the western zone of Berlin to keep the population from capitulating to the Soviets. This crisis lasted for almost a year, until Stalin allowed trucks to roll through the eastern zone in May 1949.

Stalin and his successors did not, however, relax their hold on eastern Germany, and in 1949, a line drawn through occupied Germany split the territory into two hostile states: the democratic Federal Republic of Germany in the west, and the Communist German Democratic Republic in the east. In 1961, the easterners built a wall around West Berlin to insu-

Postwar Planning at Yalta. The "Big Three" allies confer about the end of the war at the Black Sea resort of Yalta in February 1945. On the left is British prime minister Winston Churchill, at the center is American president Franklin Roosevelt, and on the right is Soviet premier Joseph Stalin.

late the east from capitalist propaganda and halt a flood of emigrés fleeing Communism. The Berlin Wall emerged as the symbol of a divided Europe and the cold war.

U.S. policymakers wanted to shore up democratic governments in Europe. Hoping to prevent western European voters from electing Communist governments, Truman proclaimed the Truman Doctrine, which promised American military and economic aid where needed. Containing the spread of Communism meant securing a capitalist future for western Europe, a job that fell to Truman's Secretary of State, General George C. Marshall. He launched the Marshall Plan, an ambitious program through which, between 1948 and 1952, the United States provided over $13 billion in grants and credits to reconstruct Europe. Earmarked for the purchase of technology and capital goods, the money facilitated an economic revival. U.S. policymakers hoped the aid would dim Communism's appeal by fostering economic prosperity, muting class tensions, and integrating western European nations into an alliance of capitalist democracies.

Stalin saw the Marshall Plan, along with the formation in 1949 of the North Atlantic Treaty Organization (NATO), a military alliance between countries in western Europe and North America, as direct threats to the Soviet Union. He believed that the Soviet Union, having sacrificed millions of its people to the war against Fascism, deserved to be the dominant influence in eastern Europe. Soviet troops had occupied the eastern European nations at the end of the war, and both Communists and leftist members of other parties formed Soviet-backed coalition governments. By tricking their moderate

The Berlin Airlift. In summer 1948, a new currency was issued for the united occupation zones of West Germany. It began to circulate in Berlin at more favorable exchange rates than the eastern zone's currency, and Berlin seemed poised to become an outpost of the West inside the Soviet occupation zone. The Soviets responded by blocking western traffic into Berlin; the West countered with an airlift, forcing the Soviets to back down in May 1949, but hastening the division of Germany into two countries.

leftist allies and repressing their critics and opponents, the Communists established dictatorships in Bulgaria, Romania, Hungary, and Czechoslovakia in 1948. It was with these Communist nations that the Soviets, responding to NATO, formed the Warsaw Pact, a military alliance of their own, in 1955. As the Warsaw Pact nations of eastern Europe faced off against NATO's forces in western Europe (see Map 20-3), the 1950s and 1960s witnessed a series of tense confrontations, which brought the world to the brink of an atomic World War III.

THE NUCLEAR AGE

The cold war changed military affairs forever. When the Americans dropped atomic bombs on Japan, they had a decisive technological edge. In 1949, however, the Soviets tested their first nuclear bomb—to the dismay of the West. Thereafter, each side rushed to stockpile nuclear weapons and to update its military technologies. In so doing, they shifted from explosives using nuclear fission to those using nuclear fusion. The weapon that destroyed Hiroshima, a fission bomb, was calculated in kilotons (each kiloton was the equivalent of 1,000 tons of TNT). Fusion, or hydrogen, bombs became calculated in megatons (one *million* tons of TNT, or 1,000 kilotons). Moreover, the bombs on both sides became physically smaller, could be launched and propelled independently on missiles, and could be carried in mobile units either on land or at sea—or even under the sea, as the Americans demonstrated in deploying their nuclear-powered Polaris submarine. Thus, more devastating weapons became almost impossible to detect. By 1960, it was possible that an all-out nuclear war might lead to the destruction of the world—without a soldier firing a single shot. This changed the rules of the game. Each side possessed the power to infllict total destruction on the other, a circumstance that caused great anxiety but also inhibited direct confrontations. Proxy wars, such as the Korean War, became the norm.

The confrontation between capitalist and Communist blocs turned into open military struggle in Asia where, in contrast to Europe after World War II, no well-defined Soviet and American spheres of influence came into being. In East and Southeast Asia, the postwar settlement was murky. After the war, the French wanted to restore their Indochinese empire, but they met fierce resistance from Vietnamese nationalists. China descended into a civil war that was won by the Communists, forcing remnants of the American-backed regime to flee to Taiwan. Korea was divided at the thirty-eighth parallel, having been liberated from the Japanese by the Americans from the south and the Soviets from the north.

In June 1950, Soviet-backed troops from North Korea invaded U.S.-backed South Korea, setting off the Korean War (see Map 20-4). Claiming this violated the Charter of the

> *The cold war changed military affairs forever.*

ATLANTIC OCEAN

ICELAND

U.S. and Canada are also part of NATO

NORTH SEA

BALTIC SEA

FINLAND

NORWAY
$236 million

SWEDEN
$107 million

SOVIET UNION

IRELAND
$148 million

GREAT BRITAIN
$3190 million

DENMARK
$273 million

NETHERLANDS
$1084 million

BELGIUM

Luxembourg and Belgium together receive $546 million

LUXEMBOURG

EAST GERMANY

POLAND

WEST GERMANY
1955
$1391 million

CZECHOSLOVAKIA

FRANCE
$2714 million

SWITZERLAND

AUSTRIA
$678 million

HUNGARY

ROMANIA

PORTUGAL
$51 million

SPAIN
1982

YUGOSLAVIA

BLACK SEA

BULGARIA

CORSICA

ITALY
$1509 million

ADRIATIC SEA

BALEARIC ISLANDS

SARDINIA

ALBANIA
until 1968

TURKEY
1952
$225 million

GREECE
1952
$707 million

AEGEAN SEA

M E D I T E R R A N E A N

SICILY

CRETE

RHODES

S E A

NATO
Warsaw Pact
Neutral
U.S. $ Marshall aid recipient

MAP 20-3   NATO AND WARSAW PACT COUNTRIES

The cold war divided Europe into two competing blocs: those joined with the United States in the North Atlantic Treaty Organization (NATO) and those linked to the Soviet Union under the Warsaw Pact. How did combat patterns in World War II shape the dividing line between these two blocs? How did the Marshall Plan contribute to this postwar division? According to the map, where would you expect cold war tensions to be the most intense?

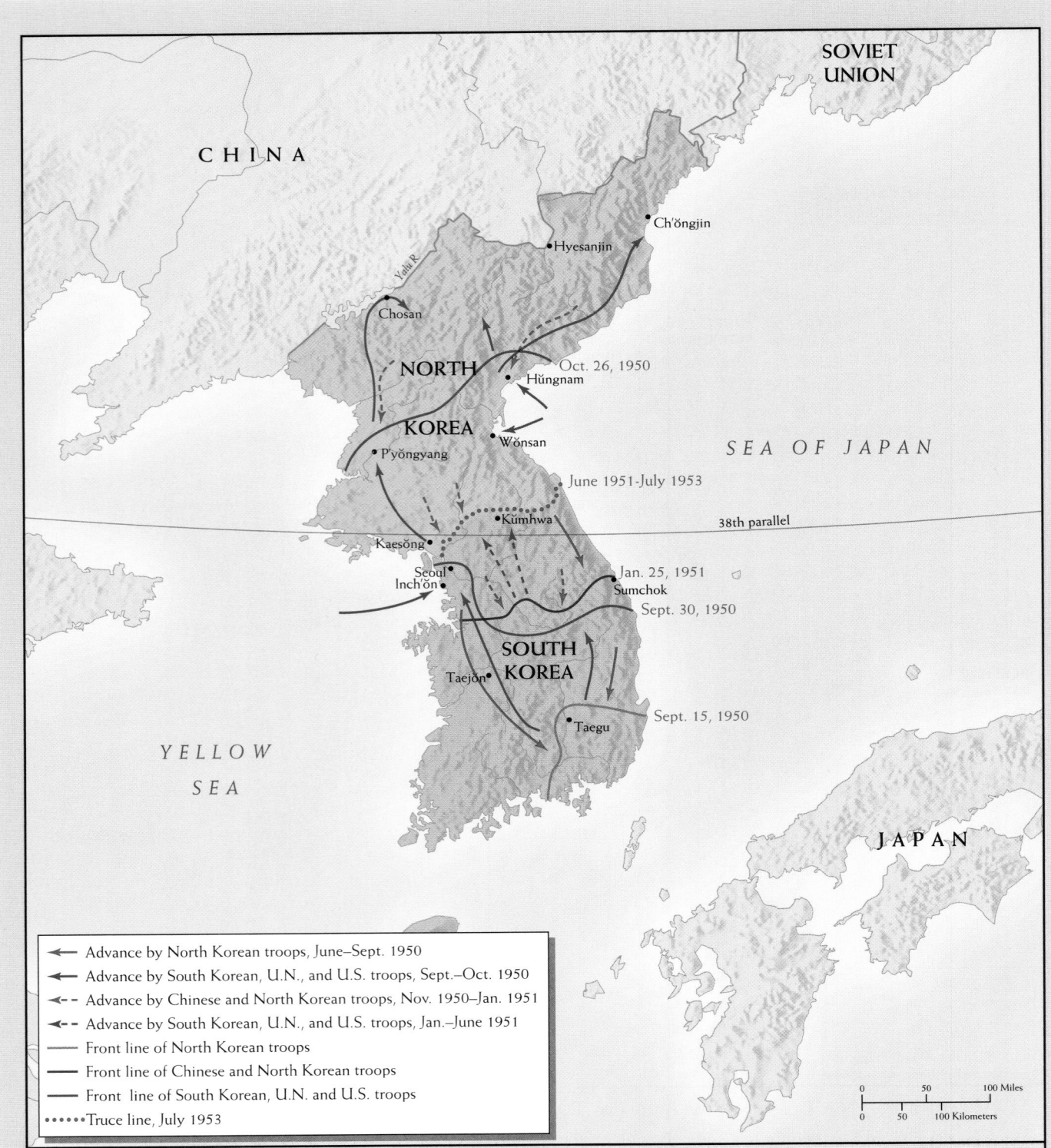

SOVIET UNION

CHINA

Ch'ŏngjin

Hyesanjin

Yalu R.

Chosan

NORTH

Oct. 26, 1950

KOREA

Hŭngnam

P'yŏngyang

Wŏnsan

SEA OF JAPAN

June 1951–July 1953

38th parallel

Kŭmhwa

Kaesŏng

Seoul

Jan. 25, 1951

Inch'ŏn

Sumchok

Sept. 30, 1950

SOUTH

KOREA

Taejŏn

Sept. 15, 1950

Taegu

YELLOW

SEA

JAPAN

- ← Advance by North Korean troops, June–Sept. 1950
- ← Advance by South Korean, U.N., and U.S. troops, Sept.–Oct. 1950
- ◄- - Advance by Chinese and North Korean troops, Nov. 1950–Jan. 1951
- ◄- - Advance by South Korean, U.N., and U.S. troops, Jan.–June 1951
- — Front line of North Korean troops
- — Front line of Chinese and North Korean troops
- — Front line of South Korean, U.N. and U.S. troops
- •••••Truce line, July 1953

0   50   100 Miles
0 50 100 Kilometers

MAP 20-4   THE KOREAN WAR

The Korean War was an early confrontation between the capitalist and Communist blocs during the cold war era. Why was this peninsula strategically important? Besides the Koreans themselves, which other powers were directly involved in the standoff? How did the outcome of the war shape political affairs in East Asia for the next several decades?

Atom Bomb Anxiety. Schoolchildren taking shelter under their desks during an A bomb drill in Brooklyn, New York, 1951. The Soviets had exploded their first test bomb in 1949. Underground bomb shelters were built in many American urban areas as places in which to survive a possible doomsday attack.

United Nations, which had been established in 1945 to safeguard world peace and protect human rights, President Truman ordered American troops to drive back the North Koreans. The U.N. Security Council declared North Korea the aggressor and sent troops from fifteen nations to restore peace. Within a year, the invaders had been routed and were near collapse. When U.N. troops advanced to the Chinese border, Stalin maneuvered his Communist Chinese allies into rushing to the rescue of the Communist regime in North Korea and driving the South Koreans and the U.N. forces back to the old boundary. Across the Korean isthmus, Communist and American-led U.N. troops waged a seesaw war. The fighting continued until July 1953, when an armistice divided the country at roughly the same spot as at the start of the war. Nothing had been gained. Losses, however, included 33,000 Americans, at least 250,000 Chinese, and up to 3 million Koreans.

The Korean War energized America's anti-Communist commitments. No longer did elected officials hesitate about the need to contain Soviet Communism at any cost. NATO forces were rapidly increased, reaching 7 million by 1953. While Japan was demilitarized at the end of World War II, and some militarists and ultranationalists were purged, U.S. policy shifted as Japan was seen as a bulwark against Communism. Although Japan renounced war in its new postwar constitution, a 1951 treaty with the United States stipulated that the Japanese could rearm for self-defense and that American troops could be stationed in Japan. Moreover, the United States resolved to rebuild Japanese economic power. Like West Germany, Japan went from being the enemy in World War II to being a valued ally. American aid and investment—though never matching the scale of the Marshall Plan—helped blunt any leftist drift in war-torn Japan.

DECOLONIZATION

> → *To what extent did decolonization involve large-scale violence?*

The unsettling of all empires during the war inspired colonial peoples to reconsider their political futures. Rid of the Japanese, the peoples of liberated Asian territories had no desire to restore colonial or even quasi-colonial rule. In Africa, too, the years after World War II brought increasing pressure for decolonization. As it became apparent that the European-centered world was no more, anticolonial nationalism surged after 1945. Drawing on the lessons in mass politicization and mass mobilization of the 1920s and 1930s, anticolonial leaders set about dismantling the European order and creating a world of their own.

The process of decolonization and nation building followed three broad patterns: civil war, negotiated independence, and incomplete decolonization. The first can be identified principally in China, where the ousting of the Japanese occupiers led to a civil war, culminating in a Communist triumph. Here, national independence was associated with a Socialist revolution. The second pattern was negotiated independence, as in the case of India and much of Africa. Algeria and South Africa exemplify the third pattern, in which the presence of sizeable European settler populations complicated the path from colony to nation.

THE CHINESE REVOLUTION

Although the Japanese defeat left China politically independent, some of China's leaders, notably the Chinese Communists, looked askance at any restoration of the prewar regime. Their campaign formed part of a more general worldwide movement to achieve autonomy from the western powers. Painfully aware of China's long semicolonial subordination, the Communists vowed to free themselves from colonialism.

The triumph of the Chinese Communists in 1949 had been in the making for decades. Back in 1927, the Nationalist regime of Chiang Kai-shek had driven outgunned Communist forces from China's cities into remote, mountainous

Primary Source

MAO ZEDONG "ON NEW DEMOCRACY"

Many twentieth-century Chinese political and intellectual leaders, including the Communists, believed that the rejuvenation of China would necessitate a change of its culture. The key question, then, was what to embrace and what to discard. Here we find Mao in 1940 explicating the New-Democratic culture—nationalistic, scientific, and mass-based—that he regarded as a transitional stage to Communism. He cautions against the uncritical wholesale importation of western values and practices, including Marxism, and emphasizes instead the specific conditions of the Chinese revolution.

New-Democratic culture is national. It opposes imperialist oppression and upholds the dignity and independence of the Chinese nation. . . . China should absorb on a large scale the progressive cultures of foreign countries as an ingredient for her own culture; in the past we did not do enough work of this kind. We must absorb whatever we today find useful, not only from the present socialist or New-Democratic cultures of other nations, but also from the older cultures of foreign countries, such as those of the various capitalist countries in the age of enlightenment. However, we must treat these foreign materials as we do our food, which should be chewed in the mouth, submitted to the working of the stomach and intestines, mixed with saliva, gastric juice, and intestinal secretions, and then separated into essence to be absorbed and waste matter to be discarded—only thus can food benefit our body; we should never swallow anything raw or absorb it uncritically. So-called wholesale Westernization is a mistaken viewpoint. China has suffered a great deal in the past from the formalist absorption of foreign things. Likewise, in applying Marxism to China, Chinese Communists must fully and properly unite the universal truth of Marxism with the specific practice of the Chinese revolution; that is to say, the truth of Marxism must be integrated with

the characteristics of the nation and given a definite national form before it can be useful; it must not be applied subjectively as a mere formula. . . .

Communists may form an anti-imperialist and anti-feudal united front for political action with certain idealists and even with religious followers, but we can never approve of their idealism or religious doctrines. A splendid ancient culture was created during the long period of China's feudal society. To clarify the process of development of this ancient culture, to throw away its feudal dross, and to absorb its democratic essence is a necessary condition for the development of our new national culture and for the increase of our national self confidence; but we should never absorb anything and everything uncritically.

→ *How did Mao integrate Marxism with the characteristics of China?*
→ *How does Mao differ from the rulers of China who came before him?*

SOURCE: Mao Zedong, *Selected Works*, in *Sources of Chinese Tradition*, 2nd ed., vol. 2, edited by Wm. Theodore de Bary and Richard Lufrano (New York: Columbia University Press, 2000), pp. 422–23.

refuges. There, the Communists had established so-called red bases, or soviets, and there Mao Zedong (1893–1976) had emerged as the leader of the largest soviet. In late 1934, under attack by Chiang's Nationalist forces, Mao and his associates abandoned their base and embarked on an arduous, year-long 6,000-mile journey through some of the world's most rugged terrain. Often covering more than twenty miles per day, they

finally retreated to the distant northwest of the country (see Map 20-5). This great escape, subsequently glorified in Communist lore as the Long March, was costly. Of the approximately 80,000 people who started the journey, fewer than 10,000 made it to their destination. Fortunately for the Communists, the Japanese invasion diverted Nationalist troops and offered Mao and the survivors a chance to regroup.

Legend:

- Early Soviets (self-governing Communist areas) 1927–1935
- ← Route of the main Chinese Communist forces from Ruijin after Guomindang assaults on Jinagxi Soviet area
- ← Route of Communist forces from other areas
- Main Communist base area, governed from Yan'an 1935–1945
- "Liberated areas" dominated by local Communist groups by 1945

MAP 20-5   THE LONG MARCH, 1934–1935

During the Long March, which took place during the struggle for power between the Guomindang (Nationalists) and the Communists within China, Communist forces traveled all the way from the southeastern part of the country to the northwestern. Why did the Communists take this particular route? How would you describe political and economic conditions in China during this time? How did this movement affect the outcome of this internal struggle in the long run?

The Long March. In China, the Long March of 1934–1935 has been commemorated by the ruling Communists as one of the most heroic episodes in the party's history. This picture shows Communist partisans crossing the snow-covered mountains in the western province of Sichuan in 1935. Despite their efforts, the ranks of the party were decimated by the end of the 6,000-mile journey from the southeastern to the northwestern part of the country—less than one in eight reached their destination.

When the Japanese seized China's major cities but were unable fully to control the countryside, the Communists were able to expand their support among the peasantry, whom they had been organizing for years. In contrast to other Marxist theorists who thought that waging a successful "class struggle" required primarily the allegiance of the industrial proletariat, Mao urged his followers to recruit China's vast rural populace. They moved in behind Japanese lines and established their own governing apparatuses, particularly in the northern part of the country. To foster anti-Japanese unity, the Communists deemphasized land redistribution. Instead, they used rent reduction, carefully designed electoral systems, graduated taxes, mutual aid, cooperative farming, and anti-Japanese propaganda to gain popular support. Mao's emphasis on a peasant revolution proved immensely effective, and his success served as inspiration to many later revolutionaries in largely agrarian societies, notably Ho Chi Minh (1890–1969) in Vietnam and Fidel Castro (1926–) in Cuba.

The Founding of the People's Republic of China. (*Left*) Mao Zedong standing atop the reviewing stand at Tiananmen Square declares the founding of the People's Republic of China on October 1, 1949. Although most Chinese knew little about the Communist Party, many had high hopes for a new, independent, and liberated China. (*Right*) With flags flying, the crowd celebrates the dawn of a new era.

As part of their critique of the oppressiveness of traditional China, the Communists promised women that liberation would apply to them, too. Like many anticolonial reformers and revolutionaries, Mao regarded women's emancipation as a key component in the building of a new nation, since he considered oppression of women to be both unjust and an obstacle to economic and social progress. As early as 1931, Mao's rural base had promulgated a new marital law forbidding arranged marriages and allowing either partner to initiate divorce proceedings. The Communists also promised improvements in health care and access to education. These measures helped to mobilize support for Communist plans. Indeed, the growth of the Communist Party during the war years was spectacular. Party membership swelled from a mere 40,000 in 1937 to over a million in 1945, at which time about 100 million people, or between a fifth and a sixth of the total population, lived under the jurisdiction of the Communists.

After Japan surrendered to end World War II in August 1945, the civil war between the Nationalists and the Communists resumed. But the Communist forces now had the numbers, the guns, and the popular support to launch assaults on Nationalist strongholds. By contrast, although the Nationalist government had weapons and financing from the United States and control of the cities, it had never fully recovered from its demoralizing defeat at the hands of the Japanese. The Nationalists proved no match for the invigorated Communists and fled to set up a rival Chinese state on the island of Taiwan.

In 1949, Mao proclaimed that China had "stood up" to the world and had experienced a "great people's revolution." In subsequent years, many of Mao's ventures proved disastrous failures, but the Chinese model of an ongoing people's revolution provided much hope in the Third World.

NEGOTIATED INDEPENDENCE IN INDIA AND AFRICA

In India and much of colonial Africa, independence came with little bloodshed. The British, realizing that they would be unable to rule India after World War II without strong doses of coercion, bowed to the inevitable and withdrew. Much the same happened in Africa, even though the British and French colonial officials were aware that there were few educated Africans and that African territories were much less ready for independence than India.

INDIA Unlike China, where the path out of semicolonial domination involved first a war against Japan and then a prolonged civil war ending in a "people's revolution," India achieved political independence without an insurrection. But after that mostly nonviolent achievement, India veered dangerously close to civil war. In British India, anticolonial elites in the Indian National Congress Party negotiated a peaceful transfer of power from British to indigenous rule. Within the congress leadership, however, there was much disagreement about what kind of state an independent India should have. Should it, as Gandhi wished, be constructed as a nonmodern utopia of self-governing village communities, or should it emulate western and Soviet models with the goal of establishing a modern nation-state? Even more pressing was the question of relations between a Hindu majority and the Muslim minority.

As negotiations for independence moved forward, Hindu-Muslim unity deteriorated. Whose culture would define the new nation?

For the most part, the congress leadership continued to exercise tight control over the mass movement that it had mobilized in the 1920s and 1930s. Even Gandhi remained skeptical of leaving the initiative to the common people, believing that they had not assimilated the doctrine of nonviolence. Accordingly, Gandhi and the congress leadership worked hard to convince the British that they, the middle-class leaders, spoke for the nation. At the same time, the threat of a mass peasant uprising with more radical aims (as was occurring in China) encouraged the British to hasten negotiations for a transfer of power.

As negotiations for independence moved forward, Hindu-Muslim unity deteriorated. Whose culture would define the new nation? Insofar as an Indian nationalism existed in the later nineteenth century, it was based on the culture and symbols of the Hindu majority. Yet, this movement masked the multiplicity of regional, linguistic, caste, and class differences *within* the Hindu community, just as Muslim movements overlooked divisions within their ranks. Now, however, the real prospect of defining "India" created a grand contest between newly self-conscious communities. Riots broke out between Hindus and Muslims in 1946, which increased the mutual distrust between congress and Muslim League leaders. With the British playing their usual divide-and-rule role, Muhammad Ali Jinnah, the leader of the Muslim League, demanded that British India be partitioned into separate Hindu and Muslim states if there were no constitutional guarantees for Muslims. The specter of civil war haunted the proceedings, as outgoing colonial rulers decided to divide the subcontinent into two states, India and Pakistan.

On August 14, 1947, Pakistan gained independence from Britain; a day later, India did the same. The euphoria of decolonization, however, was drowned in a frenzy of brutality. In the days after independence, perhaps as many as 1 million Hindus and Muslims killed one another. Fearing further violence, 12 million Hindus and Muslims left their homes to

Primary Source

NEHRU ON BUILDING A MODERN NATION

The following excerpt was written by Jawaharlal Nehru in 1940 and documents the centrality that planning occupied in the desire to build a modern nation. Although the idea of planning was derived from the Soviet experience, Nehru did not wish India to adopt Communism; he saw planned development as a scientific instrument for achieving rapid economic growth and fundamental social changes. Planning would avoid the excesses and inequalities of capitalism and provide a "third way"—equally distanced from both Communism and capitalism.

The octopus of war grips and strangles the world and the energy of mankind is more and more directed to destroying what man has built up with infinite patience and labour. Yet it is clear that war by itself cannot solve any problem. It is by conscious, constructive and planned effort alone that national and international problems can be solved. In India many people thought, with reason, that it was premature to plan, so long as we did not have the power to give effect to our planning. The political and economic freedom of India was a prerequisite to any planning, and till this was achieved our national and international policy would continue to be governed, as heretofore, in the interests of the City of London and other vested interests. And yet we started, wisely I think, a National Planning Committee and we are trying, even in these days of world conflict and war, to draw up a picture of planned society in the free India of the future.

Our immediate problem is to attack the appalling poverty and unemployment of India and to raise the standards of our people. That means vastly greater production which must be allied to juster and more equitable distribution, so that the increased wealth may spread out among the people. That means a rapid growth of industry, scientific agriculture and the social services, all co-ordinated together, under more or less state control, and directed towards the betterment of the people as a whole. The resources of India are vast and if wisely used should yield rich results in the near future.

We do not believe in a rigid autarchy, but we do want to make India self-sufficient in regard to her needs as far as this is possible. We want to develop international trade, importing articles which we cannot easily produce and exporting such articles as the rest of the world wants from us. We do not propose to submit to the economic imperialism of any other country or to impose our own on others. We believe that nations of the world can co-operate together in building a world economy which is advantageous for all and in this work we shall gladly co-operate. But this economy cannot be based on the individual profit motive, nor can it subsist within the framework of an imperialist system. It means a new world order, both politically and economically, and free nations cooperating together for their own as well as the larger good.

→ *According to Nehru, what are the key problems that India faces?*

→ *How does Nehru's vision of India compare to Gandhi's?*

SOURCE: Jawaharlal Nehru, "A Note to the Members of the National Planning Committee," May 1, 1940, in *Jawaharlal Nehru: An Anthology*, edited by Sarvepalli Gopal (Delhi: Oxford University Press, 1980), pp. 306–7.

relocate in the new country where they would be in the majority. Distraught by the violent rampage, Gandhi fasted, refusing sustenance until the killings stopped. The violence abated. This was perhaps Gandhi's finest hour. But while his actions prevented the violence from turning into all-out war, animosity and fanaticism remained. Less than six months later, on January 30, 1948, a Hindu zealot shot Gandhi dead as he walked to a prayer meeting.

Had Gandhi lived, he would not have approved of the direction independent India took. Already before his death, he

Jawaharlal Nehru. Nehru, the leader of independent India, sought to combine a "mixed economy" of private and public sectors with democracy to chart an independent path for India. The photo shows him at a public meeting in 1952.

had begun to voice his disapproval of industrialization and equipping the Indian state with army and police forces. But India's first prime minister and leader of the Indian National Congress Party, Jawaharlal Nehru, and other congress leaders were committed to the goal of state-directed modernization. Inspired by Soviet-style planned development, on the one hand, and by western democratic institutions, on the other, Nehru strove to establish a "socialistic pattern of society" based on a mixed economy of public and private sectors. Declaring that he wanted to give India the "garb of modernity," he asked Indians to consider hydroelectric dams and steel plants the temples of modern India. His watchwords were education and economic development, believing that these would loosen the hold of religion on Muslims and encourage them to join the national mainstream. He also hoped that the diminished role of religious traditions would improve women's condition and permit them to function as modern citizens. Such a vision allowed Nehru, until his death in 1964, to guide Indian modernization along a third path.

> *The postwar years saw large numbers of Africans flock to the cities in search of a better life.*

AFRICA FOR AFRICANS Within a decade and a half of Indian independence, most of the African states also gained their sovereignty. Except for the southern part of Africa, where minority white rule persisted, the old colonial states disappeared, replaced by indigenous rulers. One reason for this rapid decolonization was the power gained by the nationalist movements during the interwar period. These years had taught a generation of nationalist critics of colonial rule to rely upon themselves and to seek mass support for their political parties. World War II, then, swelled the ranks of anticolonial political parties, as many African soldiers came to expect tangible rewards for serving in imperial armies.

The postwar years also saw large numbers of Africans flock to the cities in search of a better life. Expanding educational systems produced a wave of primary and secondary school graduates. Like the new urban dwellers, these educated young people became disgruntled when attractive employment opportunities were not forthcoming. These three groups—the ex-servicemen, the urban unemployed or underemployed, and the educated—became the leaders of the nationalist agitation that began in the late 1940s and early 1950s (see Map 20-6).

Faced with rising nationalist demands, European powers agreed to decolonize. The new world powers, the Soviet Union and the United States, for their own reasons, also favored decolonization. Given this background, decolonization in most of Africa was a rapid and relatively sedate affair. In 1957, the Gold Coast (renamed Ghana) under Prime Minister Kwame Nkrumah (1909–1972) became tropical Africa's first independent state. Other British colonial territories followed in rapid succession, so that by 1963 all of British-ruled Africa except for southern Rhodesia was independent.

In each of these colonial possessions, charismatic nationalist leaders took charge of populist political parties and became the authorities to whom the British turned over power. Many of the new rulers of Africa had obtained western educations but were committed to returning Africa to the Africans. Nkrumah had studied in American universities before returning to Africa. The Nigerian nationalist, Nnamdi Azikiwe (1904–1996), was also a graduate of American colleges and universities as well as a newspaper editor and businessman. Others, too, returned from western schools, organizing new political parties, establishing nationalist newspapers, and appealing to the masses, especially the youth who had flocked to the cities after the war.

Decolonization in much of French-ruled Africa followed a similarly smooth path, though the French were initially more resistant than the British. Immediately after World War II, the French planned to respond to growing anticolonial sentiments, not by giving states more autonomy, as the British had, but by drawing protesting territories closer to France. Believing their empire to be eternal and their culture

MAP 20-6 DECOLONIZATION IN AFRICA

African decolonization, like such developments elsewhere, occurred after World War II, largely in the 1950s, 1960s, and 1970s. What areas gained independence early in this process? What areas took longer? What problems and tensions contributed to this uneven process across the region?

Kwame Nkrumah. West Africa's leading nationalist, Kwame Nkrumah mobilized the peoples of the Gold Coast and, through electoral successes, convinced the British to confer independence on the Gold Coast, which was renamed Ghana in 1957.

unrivaled, the French treated decolonization as assimilation. Instead of negotiating independence, the French tried first to accord fuller voting rights to their colonial subjects, even allowing Africans and Asians to send delegates to the French National Assembly. In the end, however, the French electorate had no desire to share their assemblies and the privileges of French citizenship with overseas populations. Thus,

Léopold Sédar Senghor. Senghor combined sharp intellect with political savvy. An accomplished poet and essayist and one of the founders of the Negritude movement among Francophone intellectuals, he became Senegal's first president when the country gained full independence in 1960.

under the leadership of Charles de Gaulle (1890–1970), France dissolved its political ties with French West Africa and French Equatorial Africa in 1960, having already given the protectorates in Morocco and Tunisia their independence in 1956. Algeria, always regarded as an integral part of France overseas, was a different matter. Its independence did not come quickly or easily.

Among the leaders of African independence, the sense of creating something new—different from the existing patterns in the world—was strong. For men like Nkrumah of Ghana, Azikiwe in Nigeria, and Julius Nyerere (1922–1999) in Tanzania, Africa's precolonial traditions would enable the region to move from colonialism right into a special African form of Socialism, escaping the depredations of capitalism. Without rejecting western culture completely, they argued that the so-called African personality, exemplified by the idea of "Negritude" developed by Senegal's first president Léopold Sédar Senghor (1906–2001) and his circle, was steeped in communal solidarities and able to embrace the values of social justice and equality, while rejecting the naked individualism that Africans felt lay at the core of European culture.

VIOLENT AND INCOMPLETE DECOLONIZATIONS

Although decolonization in most of Africa and Asia ultimately occurred through peaceful transfers of power, there were notable exceptions. In Palestine, Algeria, and southern Africa, the presence of European immigrant groups impeded negotiations and created violent conflicts that aborted any peaceful transfer of power—or left the process incomplete. In Vietnam, the process was also violent and delayed, though the problem was not the intransigence of European colonists. Instead, it stemmed first from France's desire to reimpose its colonial control, and then from the power politics of cold war competition. In this last respect, Vietnam's struggle foreshadowed the fate of much of the Third World: newly independent nations finding their pursuit of a "third way" thwarted by superpower demands that client states stay close to the capitalist or Communist line.

PALESTINE, ISRAEL, EGYPT In Palestine, Arabs and Jews had been on a collision course from the moment that the British promulgated the Balfour Declaration in 1917. Before World War I, a group of European Jews, known as Zionists, had argued that only an exodus from existing states to their place of origin in Palestine could lead to Jewish self-determination. Championed by Jewish intellectuals like Hungarian-born Theodore Herzl (1860–1904), Zionism combined a yearning to realize the ancient biblical injunction to return to the holy lands with a fear of European anti-Semitism and anguish over increasing Jewish assimilation. Zionists advocated the creation of a Jewish state, and they

Primary Source

SENGHOR'S VIEW OF POLITICAL INDEPENDENCE

One of the most striking visions of African independence as a "third way" separate from western capitalism and Soviet Communism came from the pen of Léopold Sédar Senghor, a Senegalese nationalist leader, who became the first president of Senegal. The first excerpt, drawn from his essay "African Socialism," published in 1959, differentiates the Socialism of Africa from Marxism, while the second document, taken from a speech that Senghor delivered at Oxford University in 1961, develops the idea of "Negritude," or black civilization, as a way of thinking and acting that was markedly different from but not inferior to European cultural forms.

African Socialism

In the respective programs of our former parties, all of us used to proclaim our attachment to socialism. This was a good thing, but it was not enough. Most of the time, we were satisfied with stereotyped formulas and vague aspirations, which we called scientific socialism—as if socialism did not mean a return to original sources. Above all, we need to make an effort to rethink the basic texts in the light of Negro African realities. . . .

Can we integrate Negro African cultural values, especially religious values, into socialism? We must answer that question once and for all with an unequivocal "Yes." . . .

We are not Communists for a practical reason. The anxiety for human dignity, the need for freedom—man's freedom, the freedoms of collectivities—which animate Marx's thought and provide its revolutionary ferment—this anxiety and this need are unknown to Communism, whose major deviation is Stalinism. The "dictatorship of the proletariat," which was to be only temporary, becomes the dictatorship of the party and state by perpetuating itself. . . .

The paradox of socialistic construction in Communist countries—in the Soviet Union at least—is that it increasingly resembles capitalistic construction in the United States, the American way of life, with high salaries, refrigerators, washing machines, and television sets. And it has less art and freedom of thought. Nevertheless, we shall not be won over by a regime of liberal capitalism and free enterprise. We cannot close our eyes to segregation, although the government combats it; nor can we accept the elevation of material success to a way of life.

We stand for a middle course, for a *democratic socialism* which goes so far as to integrate spiritual values, a socialism which ties in with the old ethical current of the French socialists. . . . In so far as they are idealists, they fulfill the requirements of the Negro African soul, the requirements of men of all races and countries. . . .

A third revolution is taking place, as a reaction against capitalistic and Communistic materialism—one that will integrate moral, if not religious, values with the political and economic contributions of the two great revolutions. In this revolution, the colored peoples, including the Negro African, must play their part; they must bring their contribution to the construction of the new planetary civilization.

"What Is Negritude?"

Assimilation was a failure; we could assimilate mathematics or the French language, but we could never strip off our black skins or root out black souls. And so we set out on a fervent quest for the "holy grail": our collective soul. And we came upon it. . . .

Negritude is the *whole complex of civilized values—cultural, economic, social, and political—which characterize the black peoples,* or, more precisely, the Negro-African world. All these values are essentially informed by intuitive reason, because this sentient reason, the reason which comes to grips, expresses itself emotionally, through that self-surrender, that coalescence of subject and object; through myths, by which I mean the archetypal images of the collective soul; and, above all, through primordial rhythms, synchronized with those of the cosmos. In other words, the sense of communion, the gift of mythmaking, the gift of rhythm, such are the essential elements of Negritude, which you will find indelibly stamped on all the works and activities of the black man.

→ *What is African socialism for Senghor?*
→ *How are Senghor's views of Marxism similar to and different from Mao's?*

SOURCE: Léopold Sédar Senghor, "African Socialism" and "What Is Negritude?" in *The Ideologies of the Developing Nations,* edited by Paul Sigmund (New York: Frederick A. Praeger, Publisher, 1959), pp. 240–44, 248–49.

won a crucial victory during World War I when the British government, under the Balfour Declaration, promised a homeland for the Jews in Palestine. This encouraged the immigration of Jewish settlers into the country. At the same time, however, it also guaranteed the rights of indigenous Palestinians.

The immigration of Jews to Palestine set the stage for a conflict between fledgling Jewish and Arab nations. Contrary to Zionist assertions, a substantial Arab population already lived in Palestine, and the Palestinian Arabs joined with their Arab neighbors to oppose a Jewish political entity. In due course, they proclaimed their own right to self-determination as Palestinians. When Hitler came to power in Germany, European Jews looked to Palestine as a haven, but the British, increasingly mindful of Arab opposition and the strategic oil wealth of the Arab states, vacillated over supporting Zionist demands for greater immigration. How the conflicting aspirations of Jewish settlers and indigenous Palestinians were to be reconciled was not clear to anyone. Moreover, the pressure to allow more immigration increased after World War II as hundreds of thousands of survivors of the Nazi concentration camps clamored for entry into Palestine. The Arabs resented the presence of the Jews, who continued to buy land and to displace farmers who had lived on the land for generations.

In 1947, the British announced that they would end their role administering Palestine as a mandate (first of the League of Nations, then of the United Nations) in one year's time and leave negotiations over the fate of the area to the United Nations. The United Nations tried to resolve the conflict by voting in November 1947 to partition Palestine into Arab and Jewish territories. When the British withdrew their troops on May 15, 1948, a Jewish provisional government proclaimed the establishment of the state of Israel. Although the Jews were delighted to have an independent state, they were dismayed by the small size of their country, its indefensible borders, and the fact that it did not include all of the lands that had belonged to ancient Israel. For their part, the Palestinians were shocked at the partition, and they looked to their better-armed Arab neighbors to take back Israeli territories.

The ensuing Arab-Israeli War of 1948–1949, the first of many such conflicts, shattered the legitimacy of Arab ruling elites. Arab states entered the war poorly prepared to take on the newly established but well-run and enthusiastically supported Israeli Defense Force. When the United Nations finally negotiated a truce between the combatants, Israel had extended its boundaries, and more than 1 million Palestinians had become refugees, living in makeshift camps in surrounding Arab countries.

Embittered by this defeat, a group of young officers in the Egyptian army plotted to overthrow a regime that they felt had not yet shed its colonial subordination. Though Egypt had acquired its legal independence from Britain in 1936, the plotters believed that the nation's sovereignty was being

The Creation of the State of Israel. Standing beneath a portrait of Theodore Herzl, the founder of the Zionist movement, David Ben Gurion, the first Israeli prime minister, proclaimed independence for the state of Israel in May 1948.

squandered by incompetent leaders like King Faruq (ruled 1936–1952), whom they condemned as corrupt and decadent. Among the disaffected officers, Gamal Abdel Nasser (1918–1970) had distinguished himself in battle, and he became the head of a secret organization of junior military officers that called itself the Free Officers Movement. Nasser and his like-minded colleagues debated the maladies of Egyptian society and devised a program to transform it. The Free Officers had ties with Communists and numerous other dissident groups, including the Muslim Brotherhood, which favored a return to Islamic rule.

Fearing that King Faruq would strike before they had a chance, the young officers launched a successful coup d'état in the early hours of July 26, 1952. Within a week, they forced Faruq to abdicate and to leave the country. Within three months, they enacted a far-reaching land reform scheme that deprived the large estate owners of lands in excess of 200 acres. They expropriated all of the lands belonging to the royal family, some 180,000 acres, and redistributed these estates to the landless and small-holders, who instantly became ardent supporters of the new regime. The Revolutionary Command Council, the executive body of the new regime, consolidated its power through such reforms but also through political changes like dissolving the parliament, banning political parties, and enacting a new constitution. It turned against its rivals for power, banning the Communists and the Muslim Brotherhood and stripping the old elite of most of its wealth.

Israel viewed Egypt's resurgence with suspicion, fearing that a strengthened Egypt would become the focal point of

The Anglo-Egyptian Treaty. The photo shows Egyptian president Nasser signing the Anglo-Egyptian Treaty with the British minister of state in 1954. The agreement ended the stationing of British troops on Egyptian soil and called for the withdrawal of British troops stationed at the Suez Canal military base. Shortly after the last British soldiers left Egypt in early 1956, however, Britain invaded the country in a vain effort to block Nasser's nationalization of the Suez Canal Company and to remove the Egyptian leader from power.

Arab opposition to the Zionist state. In 1956, shortly after Nasser nationalized the Suez Canal Company—an Egyptian company, mainly run by French businessmen and experts, the Israelis as well as the British and the French invaded Egypt. The invaders seized territory along the Suez Canal, but they had to agree to a ceasefire before they were able to control all of it. Opposition by the United States and the Soviet Union forced the invaders to withdraw, providing Nasser with a spectacular diplomatic triumph. As Egyptian forces reclaimed the canal, Nasser's reputation as leader of the Arab world soared. He became the chief symbol of a pan-Arab nationalism that swept across the Middle East and North Africa and especially through the camps of Palestinian refugees.

THE ALGERIAN WAR OF INDEPENDENCE

Arab nationalism's appeal was particularly strong in Algeria, where a sizeable French settler population (the *colons*) also stood in the way of a complete and peaceful decolonization. Even as decolonization proceeded in many French colonies, French leaders claimed that Algeria was an integral part of metropolitan France, an overseas department that was juridically no different from Brittany or Normandy. With nearly 1 million European inhabitants, Algeria's *colon* population ranked second in Africa only to the 4 million Europeans in South Africa. Although the *colons* constituted a minority to the

nearly 9 million indigenous Arab and Berber peoples, they held the best land and lived in wealthy residential quarters in the major cities. In addition, although all of Algeria was supposed to be a part of France and entitled to the rights and privileges of the French citizenry, in fact the *colons* reserved these advantages to themselves.

As elsewhere, anticolonial nationalism in Algeria gathered force after World War II. When French settlers refused to share their privileges and when the French military responded to anticolonial demands with harsh countermeasures, the movement for independence gained strength. The Front de Libération Nationale (FLN), as the leading nationalist party called itself, used violence to provoke its opponents and to force the local population to decide whether to support the nationalist cause or to rally to the side of the *colons*. The full-fledged revolt that erupted in 1954 pitted the FLN troops and guerrillas against thousands of French troops. Atrocities and terrorist acts were perpetrated on both sides.

Algerian Protests. When the new French Premier, Guy Mollet, visited Algiers in February 8, 1956, his presence led to rioting against French rule. This picture shows an injured demonstrator being carried away from the scene.

The war dragged on for eight years (1954–1962), at a cost of as many as 300,000 lives. At home, French society was torn asunder; many French citizens had come to accept the myth that Algeria was not a colonial territory but part of France itself. The *colons* ceaselessly reiterated this point, insisting that they had emigrated to Algeria in response to government promises and that yielding power to the nationalists would be a betrayal. In fact, the migration from France and other parts of the European side of the Mediterranean had been steady from the early days of French rule. Some immigrants had come from wealthy families, and some from poor, but all claimed a superior place for themselves and were, not surprisingly, bitterly opposed to giving up their many privileges to the local population. The negotiations to end the war began only after an insurrection led by *colons* and army officers had caused the Fourth Republic to fall in 1958 and brought Charles de Gaulle to power. Concluding that France could not continue to squander resources on colonial wars, De Gaulle negotiated a peace accord with the Algerian nationalists.

Although the final agreement, signed at Evian on March 18, 1962, contained elaborate protections for the European settlers of Algeria, these proved unnecessary. In June, shortly after handing over power to the Algerian nationalists of the FLN, more than 300,000 *colons* left. By the end of 1962, over nine-tenths of the European population had departed. At independence, then, Algeria had a population mix no different from that of the other countries of North Africa.

EASTERN AND SOUTHERN AFRICA   The bloody conflict in Algeria highlights one of the harsh realities of African decolonization. The presence of European settlers prevented the smooth transfer of power. Even in British-ruled Kenya, where the European settler population had never exceeded 20,000, a violent war of independence broke out between European settlers and African nationalists. Employing secrecy and intimidation, the Kikuyu peoples, Kenya's largest ethnic group, organized a revolt against British colonial rule and in favor of independence. This uprising, known as the Mau Mau Revolt, which began in 1952, forced the British to fly in troops to suppress it, but the rebellion ultimately persuaded the British government to concede independence to a black majority in Kenya in 1963. Jomo Kenyatta (1898–1978), a nationalist leader who had been jailed by the British, became its first president. Decolonization proved even more difficult in the southern third of the African continent, where the political independence of Portuguese Angola, Portuguese Mozambique, and British Southern Rhodesia (present-day Zimbabwe) had to wait until the 1970s.

Women played vital roles in the decolonization struggles, especially when the disputes turned violent. In Egypt, for example, the leading nationalists were all men, but they gained crucial support from educated and modernizing women, many of whom organized impressive demonstrations on their

Mau Mau Rebellion. A large segment of the Kikuyu population rose up against the British colonial occupation of their country. This revolt, which began in 1952, was finally suppressed by British arms and Kikuyu "loyalists." Nonetheless, the Mau Mau Revolt led to Kenya's independence from British rule.

behalf. The wife of Sa'd Zaghlul, Egypt's most dynamic nationalist figure after World War I, gained a large following and was called the mother of the nation. Elsewhere, too, women became deeply involved. During the Mau Mau fighting in Kenya against British colonial rule, women served as part of the passive wing of the movement, supplying the fighters in the forest with food, medical resources, and information about the British. Those who were caught suffered grievously. They were interned in concentration camps and treated brutally by their prison guards. Yet, in most cases, once the fighting was over and independence achieved, women reverted to their traditional subordinate status in society.

South Africa defied the "wind of change" and black majority rule longer than other African states. The largest and wealthiest settler population in Africa resided in South Africa, where more than 4 million white residents fervently resisted the stirrings of black power. After winning the elections of 1948, the Afrikaner-dominated National Party enacted an extreme form of racial segregation known as apartheid.

Apartheid Protest. In Johannesburg, South Africans march in the street to protest the new restrictions on African citizens, soon to be known worldwide as apartheid, implemented by the white minority government of Daniel Malan. During the Malan administration (1948–1954), informal discrimination was systematically made law, and all electoral, housing, civil, and employment rights of African citizens were dismantled.

Apartheid laws stripped Africans, Indians, and colored persons (those of mixed descent) of their few political rights. Racial mixing of any kind, including mixed marriage, was forbidden, and schools were strictly segregated. The Group Areas Act, passed in 1950, divided the country into separate racial and tribal areas and required Africans to live in their own racial areas, called homelands. Pass laws prohibited Africans from traveling outside their homelands without special work or travel passes.

The ruling party tolerated no protest. Nelson Mandela (1918–), one of the leaders of the African National Congress (ANC), campaigned for an end to discriminatory legislation and was harassed, detained, and tried by the government on numerous occasions, even though he urged peaceful resistance. After the Sharpeville massacre in 1960, in which the police killed demonstrators who were peacefully protesting the pass laws, Mandela and the ANC decided to oppose the apartheid regime with violence. Responding to Sharpeville, the government announced a state of emergency, banned the ANC, and arrested those of its leaders who had not fled the country or gone underground. A South African court sentenced Mandela to life imprisonment and sent him to the most notorious of the South African prisons, Robben Island, in 1962. Other black leaders were tortured, and some were beaten to death. Despite such human rights violations, the whites still retained external support. Through the 1950s and 1960s, western powers, especially the United States, saw South Africa as a bulwark against the spread of communism in Africa. The same concern to contain communism also drew the United States into support—and eventually into war—for another unpopular regime in Vietnam.

VIETNAM Vietnam had come under French rule in the 1880s. After putting down all armed resistance, the French proceeded to establish a highly centralized administration. By the 1920s, approximately 40,000 Europeans lived among and ruled over roughly 19 million Vietnamese. To promote an export economy of rice, mining, and rubber, the colonial rulers granted vast land concessions to French companies and local collaborators, while leaving large numbers of landless peasants.

The colonial system also gave rise to a new intelligentsia. Primarily schooled in French and Franco-Vietnamese schools, educated Vietnamese worked as clerks, shopkeepers, teachers, and petty officials. Yet, their educational achievements did not open many opportunities for advancement in the French-dominated colonial system. Discontented, the educated turned from the traditional ideology of Confucianism to modern nationalism. The Vietnamese intellectuals overseas, most notably Ho Chi Minh, took the lead in imagining a new Vietnamese nation-state.

Ho had left Vietnam at an early age and found his way to London and Paris. In Paris in the interwar period, he became acquainted with the writings of Marx, Engels, and Lenin, and he discovered not only an ideology for opposing French injustice and exploitation, but also a vision for turning the common people into a political force. He was a founding member of the French Communist Party and went to the Soviet Union, where he extended his knowledge of classical Marxism and Leninism. Returning to Vietnam, he founded the Indochinese Communist Party. After the Japanese occupied Indochina, he traveled to China, where he embraced the idea of an agrarian revolution and established the Viet Minh, a liberation force, in 1941. Back in Vietnam, the Communist-led Viet Minh became a powerful nationalist organization as it mobilized the peasantry.

When the French tried to restore their rule after Japan's defeat in 1945, Ho appealed to the United States (for whom he had been an intelligence agent during the war) for diplomatic and moral support, citing the American Declaration of Independence as an inspiration for Vietnam. His appeals fell on deaf ears, but the Viet Minh declared independence anyway. War with France followed (1946–1954). In the ensuing combat, Ho and the Viet Minh relied on guerrilla tactics to

Ho Chi Minh. Ho Chi Minh's formation of the League for the Independence of Vietnam, or Viet Minh, in 1941 set the stage for his rise at the end of World War II. Here he attends a youth rally in October 1955, just over a year after the victory of his forces at Dien Bien Phu, which resulted in the ousting of the French from Vietnam.

undermine French positions. They were most successful in the north, but even in the south their campaign bled the French. Finally, in 1954, the Battle of Dien Bien Phu resulted in a decisive victory for the anticolonial forces. At the Geneva Peace Conference in April 1954, Vietnam (like Korea) was divided into two zones, north and south. Ho controlled the north, while a government with French and American support was installed in the south—with a promise of popular elections for future reunification that was not fulfilled because of American opposition.

Though the French had departed, decolonization in Vietnam was incomplete. North Vietnam supported the Viet Cong—Communist guerrillas—who were determined to overthrow the non-Communist government in South Vietnam and to unite the north and south. Determined to contain the spread of Communism in Southeast Asia, the United States began smuggling arms to the regime in the south. During the early 1960s, U.S. involvement steadily escalated beyond that of an advisory role. In 1965, large numbers of American troops entered the country to fight on behalf of South Vietnam, while Communist North Vietnam turned to the Soviet Union for supplies. Over the next several years, the United States sent more and more soldiers. Yet, even the deployment of 500,000 troops in Vietnam could not prevent the spread of Communism in Southeast Asia.

Combining anti-imperialist nationalism with a radical land reform program, the Communists won the support of the peasantry. Drawing on this support, the Viet Cong insurgents carried out a fierce guerilla war against the United

States and its South Vietnamese puppet regime. The Americans tried in vain to shore up their South Vietnamese allies with the carpet bombing of villages and counterinsurgency operations but found themselves ever more deeply mired in an unwinnable war. Faced with antiwar opposition at home and ferocious resistance from the Vietnamese, the United States decided to cut its losses. It adopted the policy of "Vietnamizing" the war, that is, placing the responsibility of fighting the Communists on the South Vietnamese puppet government. Vietnamization was a convenient fiction spun to enable the United States to withdraw without losing face. In 1975, just two years after the signing of the Paris Peace Accords and the withdrawal of American troops, the South Vietnamese government collapsed.

THREE WORLDS

World War II made the Soviet Union and the United States into superpowers. Possessing nuclear weapons, superior armies, and industrial might that gave them the clout to dominate other nations, they vied for influence around the globe. As decolonization spread, the two cold war belligerents offered new leaders their models for economic and political modernization. On one side, the United States, together with its western European allies and Japan, had developed democratic forms of governance and a dynamic capitalist economy capable of producing an immense quantity of ever-cheaper consumer goods. The Soviet Union, on the other side, was ruled by the Communist Party, which trumpeted its egalitarian ideology and its remarkably rapid transition from a "backward" to a highly industrialized nation as worthy of emulation. Both the First World and the Second World expected other nations, including those in the decolonized Third World, to adopt their models wholesale.

The decolonized, however, often had ideas of their own. With the Communist takeover in 1949, China had freed itself from semicolonial status, but Mao soon broke from Soviet direction. Other newly decolonized nations in Asia and Africa had inherited underdeveloped economies and could not leap into capitalist or Communist industrial development. Moreover, in various corners of the globe, decolonization remained incomplete. Most problematic for Third World nations was the widening scope of the cold war. In Europe, First and Second worlds coexisted uneasily alongside one another, but in the Third World, the conflict often turned hot—and bloody. And even at peace, Third World nations found their search for alternative models of development confined by the strings that the superpowers attached to their support.

THE FIRST WORLD

As the cold war spread in the early 1950s, western Europe and North America became grouped together as the First World, or what its champions referred to as "the free world." Later on, Japan joined this group. Building on the principles of liberal modernism, which had been salvaged by the New Deal and by victory in World War II, the First World sought to organize and administer the world on the basis of capitalism and democracy. Yet, in its struggle against Communism, the free world sometimes aligned itself with Third World dictators, thereby sacrificing its commitment to freedom and democracy to political expediency.

WESTERN EUROPE The reconstruction of western Europe after World War II was by most measures a spectacular success. By the late 1950s, the economies of most nations in western Europe were thriving, thanks in part to massive postwar American economic assistance through the Marshall Plan. Improvements in agriculture were particularly impressive. With increased mechanization and the use of pesticides, fewer farmers fed more people. In 1950, for example, each French farmer produced enough food for seven people; in 1962, one farmer could feed forty. Industrial production also boomed, doubling between 1948 and 1951 and again by 1960. As real wages rose, consumer goods that had been luxuries before World War II—refrigerators, telephones, automobiles, and indoor plumbing—became commonplace. Prosperity also allowed governments in western Europe to expand social welfare systems. By the end of the 1950s, western European nations had brought education and health care within the reach of virtually all citizens.

Western Europe's economic recovery blunted the appeal of Socialist and Communist political programs. Moreover, the cold war tempered anti-Fascist reckonings, putting stability first. Although the victors convened war crimes trials that resulted in the conviction of a number of prominent Nazis, the fear was that a thorough de-Nazification would deprive Germany of political and economic leaders, leaving it more susceptible to Communist subversion.

THE UNITED STATES While Europe lay in ruins after World War II, the United States entered a period of prolonged economic expansion that raised the standard of living of virtually every segment of the population. Thanks to steadily rising incomes, Americans could afford more consumer goods than ever before. These were almost always items manufactured within the United States. Home ownership became more common, especially in the burgeoning suburbs to which millions of Americans moved in the decades after World

War II. Stimulating this suburban development was a baby boom that reversed more than a century of declining birthrates. Indeed, in contrast to the gloomy outlook of the 1930s, in the 1950s Americans enjoyed unprecedented prosperity and broadcast their faith in capitalism's future.

Yet, even as suburbanites basked in the unparalleled affluence that they credited to free enterprise, anxieties about the future of the free world abounded. In the wake of the Soviet Union's explosion of an atomic bomb, the Communist Revolution in China, and the outbreak of the Korean War, fear of the Communist threat prompted increasingly strident rhetoric. No individual exploited the anti-Communist hysteria more effectively than the Republican senator from Wisconsin, Joseph McCarthy. In 1950, he commenced a campaign to uncover closet Communists in the State Department and in Hollywood. Televised congressional hearings gave the Wisconsin senator a forum to broadcast his views to the entire nation. Though by the end of 1954 the tide had turned decisively against him, McCarthyism persisted in American foreign policy, where almost all elected officials, not wanting to risk being labeled "soft" on Communism, voted to spend more money on American armies and armaments.

Postwar American prosperity did not benefit all citizens equally. During the prosperous 1950s, nearly a quarter of the American population lived in what the government designated as poverty. But progress emboldened those living on the margins to demand more. Many African-Americans, a group disproportionately trapped below the poverty line, par-

Levittown. In the decades after World War II, the American population shifted from the cities to the suburbs. To satisfy the demand for single-family homes, private developers, assisted by government policies, built thousands of new communities on the outskirts of urban centers. Places like Long Island's Levittown (pictured here), made affordable by the use of standard designs and construction, enabled many middle-class Americans to own their own homes.

Anti-Communist Hysteria. As the cold war heated up, anti-Communist fervor swept the United States. Leading the charge against the "Communist conspiracy" was the Wisconsin senator Joseph McCarthy, pictured here with his aide, the attorney Roy Cohn.

ticipated in an increasingly powerful movement for equal rights and the end of racial segregation. In the courts, the National Association for the Advancement of Colored People (NAACP) won a series of victories that mandated the desegregation of schools with "all deliberate speed." Boycotts, too, became a weapon of a growing civil rights movement, with Martin Luther King, Jr. (1929–1968) rising to prominence after leading a successful strike against injustices in the bus system of Montgomery, Alabama. Here and in subsequent campaigns to overturn white supremacy, King borrowed his most effective weapon, the commitment to nonviolent protest and the appeal to conscience, from Gandhi. As the civil rights movement grew, officials in the federal government gradually came to support programs for racial equality. Eager not to destabilize the existing order, however, President Dwight D. Eisenhower (1890–1969) used federal power to enforce court-ordered desegregation only with great reluctance.

THE JAPANESE "MIRACLE"   Unquestionably, one of the most impressive triumphs for the western liberal capitalist vision was the emergence of Japan, America's enemy during World War II, as an economic powerhouse after the war. The war had ended with Japan's unconditional surrender in 1945, its dreams of dominating East Asia dashed, and its homeland devastated. As in war-devastated Europe, Socialism and Com-

munism were enticing options for rebuilding the country and meeting basic needs. Yet, by the middle of the 1970s, Japan (like West Germany), once a dictatorship, had emerged as a politically stable civilian regime with a dynamic, thriving economy. As in the case of Germany, Japan owed some of this momentous change to American military protection, investment, and transfers of technology. Japan, therefore, exemplified the benefits of being incorporated into the First World.

American military protection, especially from any Communist threat, spared the Japanese from the rising military expenditures of western nations and of Soviet-bloc states. Even more important was economic support. To facilitate recovery, the United States opened its enormous domestic market to Japanese goods. Initially, Japanese goods were rather rudimentary, but over time, thanks to a skilled labor force and design expertise, they became more and more sophisticated. Japanese women left the traditional family farms and businesses in droves to enter the salaried workforce. Moreover, to replace the country's physical plant, which had been largely destroyed during the war, the Americans transferred considerable technology to Japan. These transfers helped Japan rebuild its industries from top to bottom with a greater percentage of up-to-date equipment than any other country except perhaps West Germany. To enhance the rebuilding effort, the Japanese government guided much of the country's economic development through directed investment, working partnerships with private firms, and protectionist policies. To promote an export-driven economy, the government encouraged its citizens to save, not spend. At the same time, it erected import barriers that allowed specially targeted industries to take off without foreign competition. Together, these factors resulted in, if not a miracle, then at least an unprecedented boom from the 1950s into the 1970s.

Japanese Women in the Workforce. Japan was the most reluctant of the developed countries to accept widespread female participation in the workforce, but World War II forced the issue. Here, women make castings at a Toyota Motors plant in 1952, during Japan's postwar economic boom, which was set off by the stimulus of the Korean War.

THE SECOND WORLD

The scourge of World War II and the shadow of the cold war fell even more decisively—and gloomily—on the Soviet Union, which with its satellites in eastern and central Europe constituted the Second World. Having suffered more deaths and more damage than any other industrialized nation during the war, the Soviet Union was determined to insulate itself from future aggression from the West. That meant turning eastern Europe into a bloc of Communist buffer states. Just as American leaders had warned of Communist plots to undermine the free world, so, too, Soviet leaders were suspicious of American actions, seeing them as part of a concerted effort to destroy Socialism. Under siege, or so they thought, the Soviets used coercion at home and in eastern Europe to enforce their conception of state socialism.

THE APPEAL OF THE SOVIET MODEL   For many who had seen capitalism and democracy flounder in the 1920s and 1930s and experienced the devastation wrought by Fas-

Soviet Propaganda. Amid the brick-by-brick reconstruction efforts following World War II, a 1949 Soviet poster depicts a youth in red scarf with a fatherly Stalin and the slogan "May Our Motherland Live Long and Flourish."

ПУСТЬ ЗДРАВСТВУЕТ И ПРОЦВЕТАЕТ НАША РОДИНА!

cist militarism, the Soviet model had appeal. Its egalitarian ideology and success in achieving rapid industrialization made it seem a worthy alternative to capitalism. Here, there was no private property and thus, in Marxist terms, no exploitation. Workers "owned" the factories and worked for themselves. The Soviet state claimed to assure full employment, and Soviet ideologues boasted that a state-run economy would be immune from upturns and downturns in business cycles. Freedom from exploitation, combined with security, was contrasted with the capitalist model of owners hoarding profits and suddenly firing loyal workers when they were not needed.

Enthusiasts of the Soviet system pointed to the protections afforded workers. The state gave a high priority to inexpensive mass transit. In addition, the state granted women paid maternity leave and guaranteed them their jobs when they returned. Health care was technically free, and education, with particular emphasis on the sciences, was made universally available. Under the tsarist regime, less than half of the Russian population was literate; by the 1950s, the literacy rate soared above 80 percent, and it would eventually reach nearly 100 percent—the highest in the world. True, these policies did not provide material abundance of the sort that First World nations were enjoying. But if consumer goods were often scarce, they were cheap. Likewise, while it sometimes took ten years or more to obtain a small apartment through waiting lists at work, when one's turn finally came, the apartment carried only a nominal annual rent and could be passed on to one's children.

Critical to the attractiveness of the Soviet system was its victory in World War II and the fact that few ordinary people in the Soviet Union knew how their counterparts lived in the capitalist world. Government censors skewed news about the First World to present a negative picture. At the same time, they suppressed unfavorable information about the Soviet Union and the Communist bloc. Yet, even when people in the Soviet Union learned about the prosperity of western Europe and the United States, usually from western films and radio, they often clung to the idea that the Soviet Union remained the more just society. Theirs, they believed, was a land without a gulf between rich and poor, indeed, with no racial or class divisions at all. If members of the Soviet elite lived in privileged circumstances, evidence of their luxurious lifestyles was concealed from the public. Indeed, socialism's internal critics did not typically seek to overthrow the system and restore capitalism. Rather, they wanted the Soviet regime to live up to its promises and introduce reforms that would create what was termed "socialism with a human face."

REPRESSION OF DISSENT   Few outside the Soviet sphere knew just how inhuman the face of Soviet Communism was, and few within knew the extent of the brutality. In the wake of the war, rather than a hoped-for relaxation of political controls and a rumored de-collectivization (that is, the restoration of private peasant ownership in impoverished vil-

The Gulag. The Soviet labor camp system was an integral part of the Soviet economy. At any given time, around three million prisoners labored in camps, like this one in Perm, Siberia, felling timber, building railroads, or digging for gold. Several million more were forced into exile in isolated locales. During World War II, the Gulag population fell drastically, as inmates were sent to certain death at the front or perished from starvation. Between the war's end and Khrushchev's destalinization in the 1950s, the Gulag system reached its peak, with German and Japanese POWs, the deportation of entire nations, and the Soviet internment of their own returnees from German camps.

lages), the Kremlin leadership tightened its grip. Surviving soldiers who had been prisoners of war in Germany and civilians who had been slave laborers for the Germans and had somehow managed to survive captivity were sent to special screening camps, simply because they had been abroad; many disappeared. By the time of Stalin's death in 1953, the vast Gulag (or labor camp complex) confined several million people behind barbed wire.

Stalin's successors had to face the questions: What was to be done with so many prisoners? How could the existence of the labor camp system as a whole be explained? This problem became acute when a series of strikes rocked the camps, often led by veterans from World War II. In February 1956, the new party leader, Nikita Khrushchev (1894–1971), delivered a speech in which he attempted to separate Stalin's crimes from true Communism. Given at the final, closed session of the Communist Party's Twentieth Congress, this "secret" speech was never published in the Soviet Union, but it was widely discussed among party members and distributed to party organizations abroad. The crimes that Khrushchev revealed came as a terrible shock.

The repercussions, especially in eastern Europe, were immediate and far-reaching. Eastern European leaders interpreted Khrushchev's speech as an endorsement for political liberation and economic experimentation. Right away, Polish intellectuals began a drive to revive prewar institutions and break free from the Communist ideological straitjacket. In June 1956, Polish workers joined the intellectuals, and a general strike occurred in Poznan, first over bread and wages, then in protest against Soviet occupation. Emboldened by the events in Poland, Hungarian intellectuals and students held demonstrations demanding an uncensored press, free elections with genuine alternative parties, and the withdrawal of Soviet troops. The Hungarian Party leader, Imre Nagy (1896–1958), joined with the rebels.

But the seeming liberalization promised by Khrushchev's speech proved short-lived. Rather than let eastern Europeans stray too far or allow the Soviet people to call for changes, the Soviet leadership crushed dissent. In Poland, the security police massacred strikers. In Hungary, on the morning of November 4, 1956, tanks from the Soviet Union and other Warsaw Pact members invaded the country, overthrew Nagy, and installed a new government that was expected to smash all "counterrevolutionary" activities. After these revolts, Hungary and Poland did win some economic and cultural autonomy—in Poland, for example, the collectivization of agriculture ended, and the Catholic Church resumed its spiritual and educational role, while in Hungary a small private sector emerged—but unquestionably, the Second World remained very much the dominion of the Soviet Union.

The crackdown in 1956 did not stamp out the tensions within eastern Europe or the Soviet Union. Intellectuals, when given some freedom, demanded more, eliciting new repression. Many Soviet youths evinced what the authorities considered to be dangerous apolitical attitudes and a taste for unorthodox dress and behavior. In the republics of the

Hungarian Revolt. Khrushchev's secret 1956 speech denouncing Stalin's crimes unintentionally destabilized the Communist bloc. Tanks of the Soviet-led Warsaw Pact crossed into Hungary to put down a revolt that year, restoring the Soviet-style system but damaging Soviet prestige. Some American officials and especially American-supported radio had encouraged the Hungarians to rise up, but then did nothing to support them, damaging U.S. prestige. The upshot was a turn to "national communism" in the Soviet satellites as a way to promote stability and loyalty.

Soviet Union, nationalists clamored for greater rights and more liberal language policies to combat the central government's efforts to spread the Russian language and Russian culture. Sporadic worker strikes over living conditions and price rises were ruthlessly suppressed.

Despite its repressive policies, the Soviet Union was undeniably a superpower. Its status was further enhanced by the launching of Sputnik, the first satellite, into space in 1957. Students from Third World countries flocked to the Soviets' excellent education system to be trained as engineers, scientists, army commanders, and revolutionaries. The updated 1961 Communist Party program predicted euphorically that within twenty years the Soviet Union would surpass the United States and eclipse the First World.

THE THIRD WORLD

In the 1950s, French intellectuals coined the term Third World (*tiers monde* in French) to describe those countries seeking a "third way" between Soviet Communism and west-

ern capitalism. By the early 1960s, the term had come to identify a large bloc of countries from Asia, Africa, and Latin America. What they shared was that all, at one time or another, had been subjected to European or North American domination and now believed that they could create more just and humane societies than those that existed in the First and Second Worlds. This search for anticolonial forms of modernity had been under way at least since the end of World War I. After World War II, the time had come, many thought, to realize long-thwarted dreams. The exuberant hopes were eloquently captured by the African-American writer Richard Wright, who attended a meeting of the leaders of decolonized nations in 1955. "Only brown, black, and yellow men who had long been made agonizingly self-conscious, under the rigors of colonial rule, of their race and their religion could have felt the need for such a meeting. There was something extra-political, extra-social, almost extra-human about it."

Flush with their recently gained freedom, the leaders of the newly independent nations believed that they could build strong democratic polities, like those in the West, and also promote rapid economic development, as the Soviet Union had done. All of this could be achieved without experiencing the empty materialism that they believed characterized western capitalism or the state oppression of Communist regimes. The early 1960s were years of heady optimism in the Third World. Ghanaian prime minister Kwame Nkrumah trumpeted pan-Africanism as a way for the region to place itself on a par with the rest of the world. Egyptian president Gamal Abdel Nasser boasted that his democratic Socialism was neither western nor Soviet-inspired and that Egypt would retain its neutrality in the cold war struggle. Indian prime minister Jawaharlal Nehru blended democratic politics and vigorous state planning to promote India's quest for political independence and economic autonomy.

LIMITS TO AUTONOMY   Charting a "third way" between the West and the Soviet Union proved difficult, both economically and politically. Both the Soviets and the Americans saw the Third World as "underdeveloped," and Americans especially sought to ensure that market structures and private property established the girders for modernization. The western powers looked to two new instruments of global capitalism, the World Bank and the International Monetary Fund (IMF), both created in 1944 at Bretton Woods, New Hampshire, to provide crucial economic guidance in the Third World. Originally designed to help restore order in Europe, these institutions quickly turned their attention to promoting economic development in the Third World. The World Bank funded loans for projects to lift poor societies out of poverty, while the IMF supported the monetary systems of these new governments when they experienced economic woes. Yet, while World Bank money financed programs to provide electricity to Indians and roads in Indonesia, and the IMF propped up the economies of Ghana, Nigeria, and

Egypt, to mention only a few of its clients, they also intruded on the autonomy of these states.

Another force that threatened Third World economic autonomy was the multinational corporation. In the rush to transfer advanced technology from the First to the Third World, Africans, Asians, and Latin Americans struck deals with multinationals to import their know-how. Owned primarily by American, European, and Japanese entrepreneurs, firms such as United Fruit, Firestone, and Volkswagen expanded cash cropping and plantation activities and established manufacturing branches around the globe. But large foreign corporations impeded the growth of indigenous business firms in developing countries. To critics, multinationals merely remitted the profits from their overseas ventures to stockholders in the United States, western Europe, and Japan. Although the world's nations were more economically interdependent than ever before, it was still clear that the West made the decisions —and reaped most of the profits.

> One of the major consequences of the proliferation of military alliances was the militarization of many Third World countries.

Whether dealing with the West or the Soviet Union, Third World leaders found their options limited. During the cold war, neither the United States nor the Soviet Union welcomed neutral parties. To create more client states, the Soviet Union backed Communist insurgencies around the globe, while the United States supported almost any leaders who declared their anti-Communism. To contain Communist expansion, the United States formed military alliances. Following the 1949 creation of NATO, similar regional arrangements were made in Southeast Asia (SEATO) in 1954 and in the Middle East (the Baghdad Pact) in 1955. These organizations brought many Third World nations into American-led alliances and allowed the United States to establish military bases in foreign territories. For its part, the Soviet Union countered by positioning its forces in friendly Third World countries.

One of the major consequences of the proliferation of military alliances was the militarization of many Third World countries. Nowhere was this development more apparent or more threatening to economic development than in Africa. In the colonial era, African states had spent little on their military forces. All of this came to an abrupt halt when they became independent and were swept up in the cold war. Civil wars, like the one that tore apart Nigeria between 1967 and 1970, yielded opportunities for the great powers to wield influence. When the West refused to sell weapons to the Nigerian government so it could suppress the breakaway eastern province of Biafra, the Soviets supplied MIG aircraft and other vital weapons. A similar situation occurred in Egypt, which was Africa's most strategic region to both the West and the Soviets. After the founding of Israel, the new military rulers in Egypt insisted that their country never again be caught militarily unprepared. Keenly aware of the West's support for Israel, the Egyptians turned to the Soviet bloc. The arms race between Egypt and Israel left the region bristling with the most modern weaponry, including surface-to-air missiles and the most expensive military jets, some of which were even flown by Soviet pilots.

Thus, the Third World nations discovered that, having shrugged off the colonial yoke, they now confronted a new series of "neocolonial" problems. How were they to apply liberal or Socialist models within the context of their specific national conditions? How were they to deal with economic relations that seemed to reduce their autonomy and limit their development? And how, finally, might they escape being puppets of the West or the Soviet Union? Facing these difficult questions, Third World nations grew frustrated and disenchanted about the prospects for an alternative way to modernity.

By the middle of the 1960s, as the euphoria of decolonization evaporated and new states found themselves mired in debt and dependency, many Third World nations fell into dictatorship and authoritarian rule. Although some of these dictators continued to speak about forging a "third way," they did so mainly to justify their corrupt regimes. They had forgotten the democratic commitments that the term had initially implied. For the most part, they also had allowed themselves to be drawn into the cold war, the better to extract arms and assistance from one or the other superpower.

THIRD WORLD REVOLUTIONARIES AND RADICALS
Against this background of blasted expectations, Third World radicalism emerged as a powerful force. Recalling the attempts of the early leaders of new nations to find a "third way," revolutionary movements in the late 1950s and the 1960s sought to transform their societies. But while some Third World radicals seized power, they, too, had trouble cracking the existing world order.

For inspiration, Third World revolutionaries drew especially on the pioneering writings of Frantz Fanon (1925–1961). While serving as a psychiatrist in French Algeria, Fanon, who was born in the French Caribbean colony of Martinique, became deeply aware of the psychological damage of European racism and published a powerful book, *Peau Noire, Masques Blancs* (*Black Skin, White Masks*), in 1952. He subsequently joined the Algerian Revolution and became a radical theorist of liberation. His 1961 book *The Wretched of the Earth* urged Third World peoples to achieve a collective catharsis through violence against their European oppressors. *The Wretched of the Earth* also offered a scathing critique of those Third World nationalists who wished merely to replace

European masters without undertaking radical social transformations. Fanon's books became popular among radicals in the Third World who were inspired by his vision for decolonizing the mind as well as society.

THE MAOIST MODEL While Fanon moved people with his writings, others did so by organizing radical political organizations and undertaking revolutionary social experiments. One model was Mao Zedong. In 1958, Mao introduced a program that he called the Great Leap Forward. True to his vision of an ongoing people's revolution, the Great Leap Forward was an audacious attempt to unleash the people's energy. It organized China into 24,000 basic social and economic units, called communes, of roughly 30,000 persons. Peasants left their fields and took up industrial production in their own backyards. The campaign was supposed to catapult China past the developed countries. But the experiment was a dismal failure. The communes failed to feed the people, and the industrial goods were of inferior quality. China took an economic leap backward. Some 20 million perished from famine and malnutrition, forcing the government to abandon the experiment. After the Great Leap Forward, Mao retreated from the day-to-day administration of the government.

Fearing that China's revolution was losing spirit, Mao reasserted his authority in 1966 and launched the Great Proletarian Cultural Revolution. To break the opposition that had grown up during the Great Leap Forward, Mao turned against his longtime associates in the Communist Party, appealing to China's young people to reinvigorate the revolution. Brought up to revere Mao, these young people enthusiastically responded to his call to action. Organized into "Red Guards," over 10 million of them journeyed to Beijing to participate in eight huge rallies in Tiananmen Square between August and November 1966. Chanting, crying, screaming, and waving the little red book of Mao's quotations, they pledged to cleanse the party of its corrupt elements and to carry out Mao's will by thoroughly remaking Chinese society from top to bottom.

With the collusion of the army, the young revolutionary warriors set out to rid society of the "four olds"—old customs, old habits, old culture, and old ideas. They ransacked homes, libraries, museums, and temples. Classical texts, artworks, and monuments were declared to be feudal poison and were destroyed. With its rhetoric of struggle against American imperialism and Soviet revisionism, the Cultural Revolution also took on a xenophobic cast. Knowledge of a foreign language was enough to compromise a person's revolutionary credentials. The Red Guards attacked government officials, party cadres, or just plain strangers on the streets in an escalating cycle of violence. As the process intensified, family members and friends were pressured to denounce each other, and all were required to demonstrate purity and prove themselves faithful followers of Chairman Mao. With the chaos mounting, the army asserted itself in late 1967, moving in to quell the disorder and to reestablish control. To forestall further political disruption in the urban areas, the government cre-

The Cultural Revolution in China. (*Left*) Young women were an important part of the Red Guards during the Cultural Revolution. Here female Red Guards, armed with their "little red books," march in the front row of a parade in the capital city of Beijing under a sign that reads "Rise." (*Right*) In their campaign to cleanse the country of undesirable elements, the Red Guards often turned to public denunciation as a way to rally the crowd. Here a senior provincial party official is made to stand on a chair wearing a dunce's cap, while the young detractors chant slogans and wave their fists in the air.

ated an entire "lost generation" when, between 1967 and 1976, it deprived some 17 million Red Guards and students of their formal education and relocated them to the countryside "to learn from the peasants."

Given the costs of the Great Leap Forward and the Cultural Revolution, many of Mao's revolutionary policies were hard to celebrate; but radicals in much of the Third World were unaware of these costs and found the style of rapid and massive—if deeply undemocratic—uplift of the populace attractive. At least rhetorically, such policies aimed to transform poor countries within a generation.

LATIN AMERICAN REVOLUTION   Most Third World radicals did not go as far as Mao, but they still dreamed of overturning the social order. In Latin America, such dreams excited those who wished to free their nations from the influence of U.S.-owned multinational corporations and from the power of local elites. Within the Americas, the United States had long flexed its political and economic muscle. Into the 1950s, no European state, the Soviet Union included, dared infringe on this sphere of American influence. Within Latin America, however, discontent bred calls for reform and, when these were repressed or went unheeded, for revolution.

Reform programs in Latin America addressed a variety of concerns. Seeking to free Latin American economies from U.S. domination, economic nationalists urged greater protection for domestic industries and sought to curb the might of multinationals. Liberal reformers emphasized the need to democratize political systems and to redistribute land, lest discontent blossom into full-blown revolutions like China's. But when liberals and nationalists joined forces, as in Guatemala in the early 1950s, their reforms met resistance from local conservatives and from the United States. In Guatemala, the banana-producing American multinational United Fruit Company, which was the largest landowner and controlled the country's railroads and its major port, opposed land reform. Still, the progressive and nationalist regime of Jacobo Arbenz (1913–1971) persevered with its plans for agrarian reform and proposed taking over uncultivated land owned by the United Fruit Company. Despite Arbenz's intention of compensating the company for its land, the U.S. Central Intelligence Agency (CIA) plotted with sectors of the Guatemalan army to put an end to reform, culminating in a coup d'état in 1954.

In the midst of the cold war, the United States effectively warned other wayward governments that Washington would not brook assaults on its national and security interests. Across Latin America, foreign—mainly American—power was synonymous with the impossibility of gradual reform. In

In the midst of the cold war, the United States effectively warned other wayward governments that Washington would not brook assaults on its national and security interests.

1954, the year of the Guatemalan coup, the Brazilian populist president Getúlio Vargas killed himself after writing to his people that he could not protect Brazilians against "domination and looting by international economic and financial groups."

In Cuba, as reformers predicted and feared, the failure to address political, social, and economic concerns brought on a revolution. Ironically, this rebellion occurred in the country most tied to the United States. Since the Spanish-American War of 1898, Cuba had been ruled by governments better known for their compliance with U.S. interests than with popular sentiment. In 1933, during the crisis resulting from the Great Depression, Sergeant Fulgencio Batista (1901–1973) emerged as a strongman, and in 1952 he led a military coup that deposed a corrupt civilian government and made him dictator. The Batista dictatorship did little to clean up public affairs, while continuing to bend to the wishes of North American investors. Although sugar planters and casino operators prospered, middle- and working-class Cubans did not. The latter demanded a voice in politics and a new moral bond between the people and their government. Especially at the University of Havana, students became exponents of revolution. In 1953, a group of young men and women launched a botched assault on a military garrison. One of the leaders, a young law student named Fidel Castro, gave a stirring speech at the rebels' trial, which made him a national hero. After he was freed from prison in 1955, he fled to Mexico. Several years later, he returned with a small band of armed comrades and started organizing guerrilla raids.

Batista's fortunes nose-dived when, to his great surprise, the majority Democratic U.S. Congress suspended military supplies and aid in response to newspaper reports about Batista's physical thuggery. Deprived of American support, his regime crumbled in 1958. Entire regiments of his army defected to the rebels. On New Year's Day 1959, at a party at one of Havana's sumptuous hotels, Batista announced that he was leaving Cuba. He and his entourage fled to the airport to escape, and within days, young guerrillas took control of the capital.

As Castro began to consolidate his hold on power, his regime grew increasingly more radical. He elbowed aside rivals and seized control of the economy from the wealthy elite, who fled in droves to exile in southern Florida and elsewhere. Even before Castro's full intentions were apparent, American leaders began to plot his demise. Castro replied by announcing a massive redistribution of land and eventually the nationalization of foreign oil refineries. Outraged, the United States ended all aid and sealed off the American market to

Fidel Castro and Cuba's National Liberation. (*Left*) The Cuban Revolution of 1958–1959 was a powerful model for many national liberation movements elsewhere in the world. Pictured here are the icons, Che Guevara and Fidel Castro, discussing guerilla strategy in the Cuban highlands. (*Right*) No sooner did Cuban rebels force a break with the United States in 1959 than they discovered that they needed outside support to survive. The Soviet Union, eager to lay a toehold for communism so close to the United States, began to provide economic and military subsidies to their Caribbean ally. Here Castro grasps the hand of Nikita Khrushchev (bedecked with three Order of Lenin medals) atop the Lenin Mausoleum for the May Day parade in 1963.

Cuban sugar. Then, in April 1961, the CIA mounted an invasion by Cuban exiles, landing at the Bay of Pigs. A fiasco from the start, the invasion not only failed to overthrow Castro, it also further radicalized Castro's ambitions for Cuba. At this point, Castro declared himself a Socialist and openly courted the support of the Soviet Union. Within two years of coming to power, Cuban revolutionaries had consolidated a regime that openly defied the United States and aligned itself with the Soviet Union.

It was over Cuba and its radicalizing revolution that the world came closest to nuclear Armageddon in the Cuban Missile Crisis of 1962. To deter any further U.S. attacks, Castro appealed to the Soviet Union to install nuclear weapons in Cuba—ninety miles off the coast of Florida. When U.S. intelligence detected the weapons in October 1962, President John F. Kennedy ordered a blockade of Cuba, just as a flotilla of weapons-bearing Soviet ships was heading toward Havana. For several weeks, the world was paralyzed with anxiety as Kennedy, Khrushchev, and Castro matched threats. In the end, Kennedy succeeded in getting the Soviets to withdraw their nuclear missiles from Cuba.

If radicals could make a revolution ninety miles off the coast of the United States, what did this spell for the rest of the hemisphere? In Washington, many feared that revolution might become infectious. To combat the germ of revolution, the Kennedy administration unveiled the Alliance for Progress in 1961. Under this program, American advisers fanned out across Latin America to dole out aid and offer blueprints on how to reform local land systems and how to teach the populace the benefits of liberal capitalism.

To most Latin American radicals, these were inadequate band-aids. Instead, inspired by the Cuban Revolution, many citizens wanted to take matters into their own hands. In Colombia and Venezuela, peasants seized estates; in Argentina, workers occupied factories. And in Chile, a leftist alliance led by President Salvador Allende (1908–1973) showed increasing strength at the ballot box, finally triumphing in 1970.

Reacting to the rising tide of revolutionary insurgency, the United States and its allies in the region bolstered their own counterinsurgency program. Under the guidance of American advisers, Latin American militaries were trained to root

Latin American Human Rights. By the early 1980s, human rights movements were gaining strength all over Latin America, even in Chile under the repressive General Pinochet. Here, a crowd of 400,000 demonstrates against his rule in November 1983.

RADICALIZING THE THIRD WORLD:
CHE GUEVARA

The Cuban Revolution was a turning point in the making of the Third World. After 1959, the Castro regime championed liberation for the Third World from the First World and embraced Socialism as a radical solution to underdevelopment. By rejecting the power of capitalist industrial societies, Castro and his followers thereby promoted revolution, and not reform, as a way to achieve Third World liberation. The symbol of this new spirit of revolution was Castro's closest lieutenant, Ernesto "Che" Guevara (1928–1967). Che wanted to unite the Third World as a Socialist, postcolonial bloc and thereby to undermine the capitalist world led by the United States.

"El Che," as he was known, grew up in Argentina and traveled widely around Latin America as a student. Shortly after receiving his medical degree in 1953, he set off once again, arriving in Guatemala in time to witness the CIA-backed overthrow of the progressive Jacobo Arbenz government in 1954. Thereafter, Guevara became increasingly bitter about American influences in Latin America. He joined Castro's forces and helped topple the pro-American regime of Fulgencio Batista in Cuba in 1958. After 1959, he held several posts in the Cuban government, but he grew increasingly restive for more action. Latin America, according to Guevara, should become the source of "many Vietnams" and should challenge the world power of the United States. Soon his casual military uniform, his patchy beard, his cigar, and his moral energy became legendary symbols of revolt.

The image of the guerrilla fighter as savior appealed to young people around the world. Che Guevara published a manual in 1960, *Guerrilla Warfare,* to instruct radicals on how to mount a successful revolution. Although Mao Zedong and North Vietnamese general Vo Nguyen Giap had also published blueprints for peasant-based revolutions, Che was able to draw on the more recent and successful experiences of the Cuban struggle. If Cuba could radicalize the Third World, any underdeveloped society could. Che told his radical readers to blend in with the urban and especially the rural poor to create a "people's army" and to strike blows at the weakest points in the established order. He enjoined men in particular to lead the crusade to show the poor that their misery could be reversed through heroic violence. Women, too, had a role to play in revolution. According to Guevara, they could cook for, nurse, and serve as helpmates for fighters. For all of Guevara's radicalism, he did not transcend conventional models of relations between the sexes. Not surprisingly, the image of the armed freedom fighter for Third World liberation appealed mainly to young men.

The idea of revolution as a way to overcome underdevelopment and free Third World societies spread beyond Latin America. Che became Castro's envoy to world meetings and summits of Third World state leaders, where he celebrated the Cuban road to freedom. The Soviet premier Nikita Khrushchev recognized the power of Che's message and in 1961 proclaimed his support for all "wars of national liberation." Che himself exported his model to Africa, seeking to link Africa and Latin America in a common front against American and European capitalism. Che led a group of Cuban guerrillas to join Congolese rebels under Laurent Kabila to fight the CIA- and South African–backed regimes in south-central Africa. The expedition failed, presaging the difficulties of throwing badly prepared rebels against armies trained in counterinsurgency techniques. Che, disgusted at Kabila's ineptitude and cowardice, withdrew, though Cuban forces remained involved in African struggles into the 1980s.

Che relocated to Latin America, where he believed that "many Vietnams" might be created. He set up his center of operations in highland Bolivia in 1966, among South America's poorest and most downtrodden Indians. "We have to create another Vietnam in the Americas with its center in Bolivia," he proclaimed. Guevara did not, however, know the local Indian language, and he had little logistical support. He and his two dozen fighters launched their region-wide war in absolute isolation. It took little time for the Bolivian army and CIA operators to surround and capture the small band of exhausted rebels. After a brief interrogation, Bolivian officers ordered that the guerrilla commander be killed on the spot. The executioner first shot the fighter's arms and legs; with Che agonizing on the ground, biting his fist to stifle his cries, another bullet penetrated his thorax. As Che's lungs filled with blood, he died.

Third World governments blocked radical options just as they had done with Che Guevara's movement. Only in Nicaragua—twenty years after Castro's victory—would rebels ever take control, and this exception had more to do with the degree of despotism exercised by the ruling Somoza family than with the appeal of radicalism. In Africa and Asia, too, Third World revolution became a rarity. Militaries in Latin America, Asia, and Africa learned to fight guerrillas with new technology and new counterinsurgency techniques. And all too often, poor people found guerrilla commanders as despotic as their governments.

out radicalism. They learned that gaining the support of civilians, usually the most indigent, was the key to defeating the guerrillas; by targeting civilians, rather than the armed combatants, counterinsurgent forces were able to isolate and destroy guerrilla campaigns. Even Salvador Allende's democratically elected Socialist government in Chile was not spared; the CIA and U.S. policymakers aided General Augusto Pinochet's military coup (in which Allende died) against the regime in 1973 and looked the other way while the junta butchered political opponents. By 1975, rebel forces had been liquidated in Argentina, Uruguay, Brazil, Mexico, Bolivia, and Venezuela. Elsewhere, they hunkered down in isolated hamlets. Where civilian governments failed to keep stability, militaries took over, not just to topple weak governments, but to rule directly.

TENSIONS IN THE THREE-WORLD ORDER

> → *What were the major fissures that developed in the three-world order?*

Third World radicalism raised hopes, but it did not alter the existing balance of global wealth and power. Still, through the 1960s and into the early 1970s, it exposed vulnerabilities in the three-world order. So did the continuation of the Vietnam War, which revealed the limits of American power and opened fissures within the First World. As antiwar and civil rights movements mushroomed, the United States experienced social unrest on a scale not seen since the Great Depression of the 1930s. In the Second World, too, division and dissent challenged the Soviet Union's hold on world Communism. In eastern Europe, satellite states sought more flexible orbits, while Mao's China charted a course at odds with Soviet designs. Finally, in the 1970s, the rising fortunes of oil-producing nations and of Japan introduced new problems in the relations within and between worlds.

TENSIONS IN THE FIRST WORLD

In western Europe, internal social tensions were softened in the wake of World War II by the creation of expanded welfare states that preserved free enterprise while protecting citizens from the excesses of capitalism. That the United States proved slower in developing such a state, and also moved haltingly to deal with its legacy of racial discrimination, made U.S. social tension after 1945 especially acute. But all across the First World, there was one common source of social dissension: the still unanswered "woman question." After World War II, in Italy, France, and Belgium, women finally obtained the right to vote. In postwar Europe, more and more jobs were opening up in the service sector, and women were filling them. Of course, women had long been prominent in a number of occupations (textiles, domestic servants). But more and more the female workforce comprised not single servant or factory girls but mature women in offices, stores, hospitals, and, with the headlong expansion of education systems, in teaching. Already by 1961, fully a third of the workforce consisted of women. Even in mostly Catholic Italy, where attitudes about women in public changed more slowly, women made strong gains in employment outside the home, but waited mostly in vain for a corresponding decrease in their domestic responsibilities. This major faultline would create long-lasting conflict and debate in western societies, while the incorporation of women into the economy would also increase western prosperity over time.

But there were other sources, too, of tension in the West. During the 1960s, American society lost some of the confidence and much of the contentment that had characterized it in the previous decade. Although the economy continued to grow impressively until the early 1970s, prosperity no longer translated into complacency. First, there was the assassination of President Kennedy in 1963, and then there was the violence that accompanied African-American struggles for equality. In 1964, resistance to the civil rights movement turned lethal. In Mississippi that year, three civil rights workers were murdered, and two dozen African-American churches were bombed and burned. In response, some

Sit-in at Woolworth's Lunch Counter. Borrowing the tactics of nonviolent civil disobedience championed by Gandhi, civil rights protestors staged "sit-ins" across the southern United States in the early 1960s, as in this photograph of black and white students seated together at a segregated lunch counter in Jackson, Mississippi. Protestors peacefully defied laws that prohibited African-Americans from being served at "white" establishments.

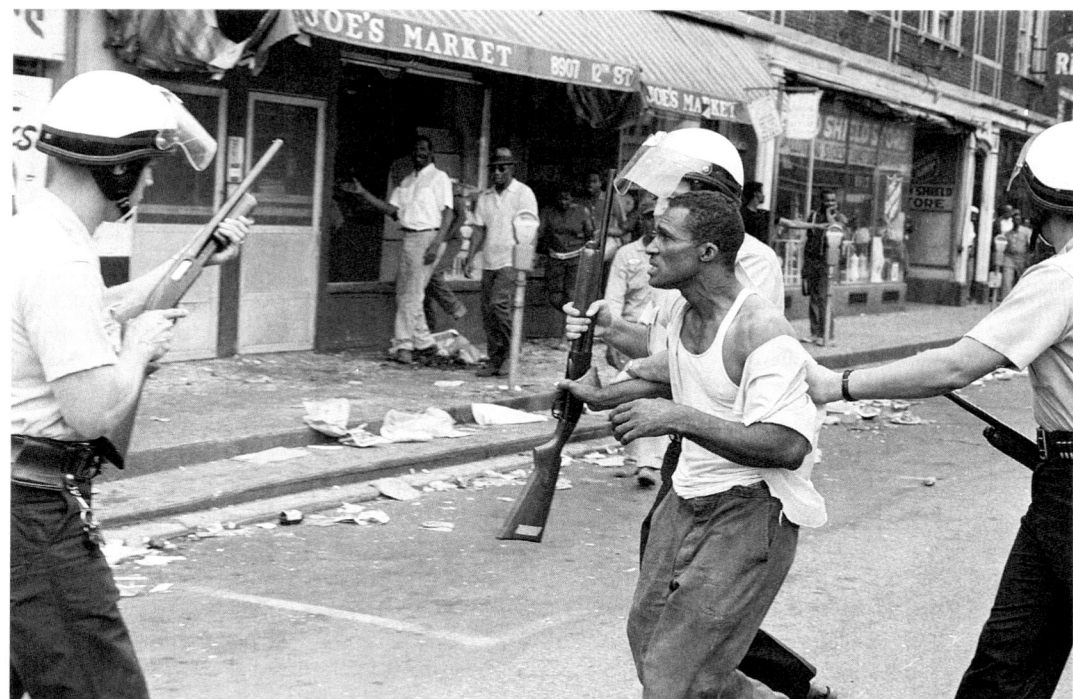

Urban Riots. Racial tensions boiled over in a number of American cities during the 1960s. This photograph of a man being taken into custody was snapped on July 23, 1967, the first day of what turned out to be five days of rioting in Detroit. The unrest left 43 people dead, 467 injured, and more than 2,000 buildings burned down.

African-Americans turned away from the goal of integration and abandoned the commitment to nonviolent civil disobedience. Race riots rocked American cities and radicalized black nationalists. The 1960s also brought increasingly angry resistance to the war in Vietnam. College campuses became the staging grounds for massive antiwar protests that ruptured the cold war consensus.

Ironically, these protests occurred even as prosperity continued and government actions ameliorated legal and economic inequalities. In the wake of Kennedy's assassination, the new president, Lyndon Johnson, forwarded a bold plan to ensure civil rights and end poverty. The passage of the Civil Rights Act of 1964, banning segregation in public facilities and outlawing racial discrimination in employment, marked an important step in correcting legal inequality. The following year, the Voting Rights Act afforded millions of previously disenfranchised African-Americans an opportunity to exercise equal political rights. Addressing economic inequities, the Johnson administration secured significant increases for a range of social programs. Between 1965 and 1970, federal spending on social security, health, education, and assistance to the poor doubled. Aided by impressive economic growth, Johnson's War on Poverty made considerable strides. In the second half of the 1960s, the poverty rate in the United States was nearly halved.

Legacies of racism and inequality were not easily overcome, however. In spite of Supreme Court decisions, most schools remained racially homogeneous. This was true not only in the South but across the United States, as "white flight" to the suburbs left inner-city neighborhoods and schools to racial minorities. The migration of whites from cities to suburbs occurred across the country and was particularly pronounced in Atlanta, Philadelphia, Detroit, Miami, and St. Louis, where the exoduses reduced the number of white residents by more than half. Within these cities, frustration over discrimination and lack of economic opportunity led to violence. Riots in Los Angeles, Newark, and Detroit killed scores of people and destroyed significant portions of these cities. Within the African-American community, militant voices, like those of Malcolm X (1925–1965) and the Black Panthers, became more prominent. Instead of integration into white society, these radicals advocated black separatism, and instead of Americanism, they espoused pan-Africanism. Although black division and white backlash derailed the momentum of the civil rights movement, these developments did not reverse the gains made in erasing legal discrimination and political inequality.

African-American struggles against segregation and injustice inspired Native Americans, Mexican-Americans, homosexuals, and women to initiate their own campaigns for equality and empowerment. Women came to question a life built around taking care of home and family. Historians often point to the introduction of the birth control pill in 1960 and the 1963 publication of Betty Friedan's *The Feminine Mystique* as watershed moments in American women's history. Within a year of the pill's arrival on the market, 1 million women in the United States were using this contraceptive. The availability of oral contraception allowed women to

THE FEMININE MYSTIQUE

In 1963, Betty Friedan published The Feminine Mystique, *which challenged the idea that women found fulfillment solely by getting married, keeping house, and raising children. Friedan's book contributed to the rise of the women's movement in the United States. In this excerpt from the first chapter of* The Feminine Mystique, *Friedan writes about "the problem" that afflicted suburban housewives—a problem that, she suggested, was widely shared, but as yet had "no name."*

The problem lay buried, unspoken, for many years in the minds of American women. It was a strange stirring, a sense of dissatisfaction, a yearning that women suffered in the middle of the twentieth century in the United States. Each suburban wife struggled with it alone. As she made the beds, shopped for groceries, matched slipcover material, ate peanut butter sandwiches with her children, chauffeured Cub Scouts and Brownies, lay beside her husband at night—she was afraid to ask even of herself the silent question—"Is this all?"

For over fifteen years there was no word of this yearning in the millions of words written about women, for women, in all the columns, books and articles by experts telling women their role was to seek fulfillment as wives and mothers. Over and over women heard in voices of tradition and of Freudian sophistication that they could desire no greater destiny than to glory in their own femininity. Experts told them how to catch a man and keep him, how to breastfeed children and handle their toilet training, how to cope with sibling rivalry and adolescent rebellion; how to buy a dishwasher, bake bread, cook gourmet snails, and build a swimming pool with their own hands; how to dress, look, and act more feminine and make marriage more exciting; how to keep their husbands from dying young and their sons from growing into delinquents. They were taught to pity the neurotic, unfeminine, unhappy women who wanted to be poets or physicists or presidents. They learned that truly feminine women do not want careers, higher education, political rights—the independence and the opportunities that the old-fashioned feminists fought for. Some women, in their forties and fifties, still remembered painfully giving up those dreams, but most of the younger women no longer even thought about them. A thousand expert voices applauded their femininity, their adjustment, their new maturity. All they had to do was devote their lives from earliest girlhood to finding a husband and bearing children.

By the end of the nineteen-fifties, the average marriage age of women in America dropped to 20, and was still dropping, into the teens. Fourteen million girls were engaged by 17. The proportion of women attending college in comparison with men dropped from 47 per cent in 1920 to 35 per cent in 1958. A century earlier, women had fought for higher education; now girls went to college to get a husband. By the mid-fifties, 60 per cent dropped out of college to marry, or because they were afraid too much education would be a marriage bar. Colleges built dormitories for "married students," but the students were almost always the husbands. A new degree was instituted for the wives—"Ph.T." (Putting Husband Through). . . .

The suburban housewife—she was the dream image of the young American women and the envy, it was said, of women all over the world. The American housewife—freed by science and labor-saving appliances from the drudgery, the dangers of childbirth and the illnesses of her grandmother. She was healthy, beautiful, educated, concerned only about her husband, her children, her home. She had found true feminine fulfillment. As a housewife and mother, she was respected as a full and equal partner to man in his world. She was free to choose automobiles, clothes, appliances, supermarkets; she had everything that women ever dreamed of. . . .

If a woman had a problem in the 1950's and 1960's, she knew that something must be wrong with her marriage, or with herself. Other women were satisfied with their lives, she thought. What kind of a woman was she if she did not feel this mysterious fulfillment waxing the kitchen floor? She was so ashamed to admit her dissatisfaction that she never knew how many other women shared it. If she tried to tell her husband, he didn't understand what she was talking about. She did not really understand it herself. . . .

If I am right, the problem that has no name stirring in the minds of so many American women today is not a matter of loss of femininity or too much education, or the demands of domesticity. It is far more important than anyone recognizes. It is the key to these other new and old problems which have been torturing women and their husbands and children, and puzzling their doctors and educators for years. It may well be the key to our future as a nation and a culture. We can no longer ignore that voice within women that says: "I want something more than my husband and my children and my home."

→ *What criticisms do you think were leveled at Friedan's book when it appeared in 1963?*

→ *What criticisms have emerged in subsequent decades?*

SOURCE: Betty Friedan, Chapter 1, "The Problem That Has No Name," *The Feminine Mystique* (New York: Norton, 1963, 1974).

⇢ *What were the major fissures that developed in the three-world order?*

Feminism. Betty Friedan, author of *The Feminine Mystique* (see Primary Source excerpt), leads a 1970 march in New York City on the fiftieth anniversary of the passing of the Nineteenth Amendment, which granted American women the right to vote.

delay and limit childbearing and to have sex with less fear of pregnancy. This freedom helped unleash a sexual revolution. The pill alone, however, did not liberate women. Friedan's best-seller blasted the myth of middle-class domestic contentment, describing the idealized 1950s suburban home as a "comfortable concentration camp" from which women must escape. In fact, the number of married women in the paid workforce was slowly rising, as was the number of college-educated women. Despite these educational attainments, working women discovered that their compensation and opportunity for advancement lagged far behind those of men.

The civil rights and women's movements of the early 1960s led many white college students to question the ideals of American society, but what turned this questioning into massive resistance was the escalation of the war in Vietnam. As the United States increased the number of its troops in Vietnam in the 1960s, it started to conscript more and more men into the armed services. Tens of thousands of young

Americans fled the country to escape the draft. Upwards of 250,000 simply did not register for conscription, while another 100,000 burned their draft cards. As the decade progressed, protesters took to the streets of college towns around the country, and they descended upon Washington, D.C., as well. In April 1965, 25,000 people gathered for an antiwar protest in front of the White House, and two years later, a march on the Pentagon drew four times that number. After President Richard Nixon (1913–1994) sent American troops into Cambodia in 1970 to root out North Vietnamese soldiers who were hiding there, students at over 500 campuses rose in protest. Across the country, protesters occupied buildings and closed down universities. At Kent State University in Ohio, National Guardsmen, who had been called out to stop the protests, killed four students. The United States finally agreed to withdraw its troops from Vietnam in 1973, and Saigon (present-day Ho Chi Minh City) and South Vietnam fell to the Communists in 1975, but not before the divisions created by the war had put a great strain on the First World.

TENSIONS IN WORLD COMMUNISM

The unity of the Communist world also came under increasing pressure. As early as 1948, Yugoslavia had broken free of the Soviet embrace and embarked on its own road to building Socialism. Other satellites within the Soviet bloc had more trouble freeing themselves. In 1956, Poland and Hungary were forced back in line. Twelve years later, Czechoslovakia experienced the Prague Spring, in which Communist authorities experimented with policies to create a democratic and pluralist "Socialism with a human face." Workers and students rallied behind the reformist government of Alexander Dubček (1921–1992), calling for more freedom of expression, more autonomy for workers and consumers, and more debate within the ruling party. Once again, Soviet tanks crushed this "counterrevolutionary" movement. As the Russian tanks rolled into Prague, the Czech capital, one desperate student doused himself with gasoline and lit a match—his public suicide a gesture of defiance against Communist rule. Thereafter, the Prague Spring served as a symbol for dissenters. Underground reading groups proliferated in cities across eastern Europe; many Russians renewed their faith in Orthodox Christianity, returning to their prerevolutionary religion. Many dissidents were exiled from the Soviet Union. The most famous by the early 1970s was the great Russian novelist Alexander Solzhenitsyn (1918–). His masterwork, *The Gulag Archipelago,* became a best-seller in the West and repudiated the notion that Socialism could be reformed by a turn away from Stalin's policies. Yet, very few people in the Soviet Union were able to obtain copies of Solzhenitsyn's exposé, which had been published abroad.

Still, there were important changes within the Second World. During the 1950s and 1960s, "national Communism" became the rule throughout eastern Europe, even in countries that suffered from Soviet invasions. National variations were also observable within the Soviet Union, where Moscow conceded some autonomy to the Communist Party machines of its fifteen republics—in exchange for fundamental loyalty. Cracks in the Soviet model, particularly in eastern Europe, became points of tension and unease. The possibility of rupture became a reality in China. After the Chinese Revolution of 1949, Marxist ideology as well as a shared antipathy toward the United States had helped cement the Sino-Soviet alliance. By the late 1950s, the Soviet Union had contributed large amounts of military and economic aid to China. But the Chinese increasingly sought to define their own brand of Marxism, which the Soviets would not tolerate. And whereas the Soviets became interested in a lessening of tensions with the United States, the Chinese preferred to accentuate confrontation and to build their own nuclear weapons. Another key factor in the split was personal. At the beginning of China's Communist Revolution, Mao Zedong had had little choice but to defer to Stalin, who even pushed for and received extraterritoriality rights in China for Soviet advisers. But after Stalin died in 1953, Mao had little interest in deferring to Nikita Khrushchev.

During the 1960s, the Chinese aggressively presented themselves as a peasant-Socialist alternative to the Soviet model of development, especially for Third World countries. The fissure raised China's profile throughout Asia and even reverberated into eastern Europe. In the 1960s, Romania achieved a measure of autonomy in foreign policy by playing off China and the Soviet Union. Albania declared its allegiance to China. African nations, interested in Soviet aid, increased their demands with subtle hints that they might consider deepening ties with China. It was clear that the Second World, too, was no monolith.

TENSIONS IN THE THIRD WORLD

In contrast to the First and Second Worlds, the Third World was never unified by economic, military, or political alliances. While the common history of domination and the shared search for a "third way" provided some basis for cooperation, the cold war polarized Third World nations, pushing states to choose between alignment with the First World or the Second. Nonetheless, the rise of radicalism nourished new hopes for unifying and empowering the Third World.

Chronology

	1935	1940	1945	1950
AMERICAS		U.S. enters World War II, 1941 ∎	∎ World War II ends, 1945	∎ American civil rig movement, 1950.
EUROPE		∎ Britain and France declare war on Germany after Germany's invasion of Poland, 1939	∎ World War II ends, 1945 ∎ Marshall Plan, 1948–1952 ∎ Berlin blockade and airlift, 194∎ ∎ NATO formed, 1949	
SOVIET UNION			∎ World War II ends, 1945	Stalin dies, 19
AFRICA			∎ Apartheid begins in South Afric African countries gain independence, 1950s–1960s ∎	
SOUTH ASIA			∎ India and Pakistan gain independence,	
MIDDLE EAST			∎ Arab-Israeli War, 1948–1949	
EAST AND SOUTHEAST ASIA	∎ Japan invades China, 1937		∎ World War II ends, 1945 ∎ Nationalists fight Communists in China, 1945–1949 ∎ Korean War, 195	

⤳ *What were the major fissures that developed in the three-world order?*

One effort at collaboration among Third World countries was the formation in 1960 of a cartel of oil exporters. The Organization of Petroleum Exporting Countries (OPEC), which included Algeria, Ecuador, Gabon, Indonesia, Iran, Iraq, Kuwait, Libya, Nigeria, Qatar, Saudi Arabia, the United Arab Emirates, and Venezuela, had little impact in raising oil revenues through the 1960s, even though several members did nationalize their oil fields. But after the fourth major Arab-Israeli war broke out, in the fall of 1973, OPEC's Arab members decided to pressure Israel's First World allies by halting oil exports to them. Overnight, the embargo lifted oil prices from $3 to $10 per barrel, a bonanza that enriched all oil producers and led to an oil crisis in the West. To many, the bulging treasuries of OPEC nations seemed like the Third World's revenge. Here were Saudi Arabian princes, Venezuelan magnates, and Indonesian ministers dictating world prices to industrial consumers. American secretary of state Henry Kissinger later wrote that the oil embargo "altered irrevocably the world as it had grown up in the postwar period." Kissinger meant that the oil embargo confounded the cold war's balance of power by introducing a new set of powerful, nonallied players onto the stage.

But the realignment was not as thorough as Kissinger feared. Third World producers of other raw materials such as coffee and rubber tried to duplicate OPEC's model, but these associations failed to control the market as effectively as the oil nations. OPEC's members also had trouble maintaining their control. During the 1970s, new discoveries in the North Sea, Mexico, and Canada reduced the pressures on the large oil-consuming states to be more fuel efficient as new supplies began to flood the oil market. With supply up, prices fell. To make up for lost revenue, various OPEC states raised their own production, putting further downward pressure on prices.

Nor did oil revenues do much to overcome the poverty and dependency of the Third World as a whole. To the contrary, most revenue surpluses from OPEC simply flowed back to First World banks or were plowed into real-estate holdings in Europe and the United States. Some of it was in turn re-loaned to the world's poorest countries in Africa, Asia, and Latin America, at high interest rates, to pay for more expensive imports—including oil! Moreover, the biggest bonanza from rising oil prices went to multinational petroleum firms whose control over production, refining, and distribution allowed them to reap enormous profits.

For all the talk in the mid-1970s of changing the balance of international economic relations between the world's rich and poor countries, fundamental inequalities were not redressed. For those nations that appeared to break out of the

1955	**1960**	**1965**	**1970**	**1975**

erthrow of Guatemalan government, 1954
▌ *Cuban Revolution, 1958–1959*
▌ *Cuban Missile Crisis, 1962*

Warsaw Pact formed, 1955
▌ *Soviet crackdown in Hungary, 1956*　　　　　　　▌ *Prague Spring, 1968*

▌ *Soviets launch* Sputnik, *1957*

n War, 1954–1962

▌ *Arab oil embargo, 1973*

nese defeat French, 1954
▌ *China's Great Leap Forward, 1958–1961*

▌ *China's Cultural Revolution, 1966*
Fall of Saigon and end of Vietnam War, 1975 ▌

cycle of poverty, like South Korea and Taiwan, their successes did not result from the workings of international markets. Rather, the states regulated markets, nurtured new industries, educated the populace, and required multinationals to work more collaboratively with native firms. These were exceptions that proved the general rule: the international economy reinforced existing structures.

 CONCLUSION

The three-world order arose on the ruins of European empires and their Japanese counterpart. First, the Soviet Union and the United States emerged as superpowers. Second, World War II affirmed the nation-state rather than the empire as the primary form for organizing communities; the formation of new nations completed this process. Third, in spite of the rhetoric of individualism and the free market, the war and the postwar reconstruction greatly enhanced the reach and functions of the modern state. Never before had the state enjoyed as great a role as in the postwar economies and societies of the Soviet Union and its eastern European satellites, and of western Europe and the United States. In the Third World, too, the leaders of new nations saw the state as the primary instrument for promoting economic development and creating nations.

The organization of the world into three blocs lasted into the mid-1970s. This arrangement fostered the economic recovery of western Europe and Japan from the political and economic wounds inflicted by the war. Recovery was linked to a cold war alliance with the United States, where an economic boom was accompanied by anti-Communist hysteria. The cold war also cast a shadow over the citizens of the Soviet Union and eastern Europe. Gulags and political surveillance became the lot of the people, while the Soviets and their satellite regimes mobilized resources for military purposes. The Third World, squeezed by its inability to reduce poverty, on the one hand, and superpower rivalry, on the other, struggled to pursue a "third way." While some states managed to maintain democratic institutions and promote economic development, many tumbled into dictatorships and authoritarian regimes. In this context Third World revolutionaries took to radical programs of social and political transformation, seeking paths different from both western capitalism and Soviet Communism. Though not successful, they brought to the surface the considerable tensions in the three-world order. These tensions intensified in the late 1960s and the early 1970s as the Vietnamese Communists defeated the United States, the oil crisis struck the West, and protests against the existing order escalated in the First and Second Worlds. Thirty years after the war's end, the world order forged after 1945 was beginning to give way.

STUDY QUESTIONS

 WWNORTON.COM/STUDYSPACE

1. Analyze how, World War II even more than World War I, was a truly global war and why it led to the end of a European-dominated world. How did the war challenge the ideological justifications for imperialism?

2. Define the term *cold war*. How did the task of rebuilding Europe and Asia after World War II lead to this intense global rivalry between the Soviet Union and the United States?

3. Describe the other global process that also dominated world affairs during the period covered in this chapter—decolonization. What various forms did this process take?

4. Compare and contrast the three worlds of the postwar order. What was each world attempting to achieve? How successful was each in achieving these goals?

5. List and explain various tensions that existed between the three worlds of the postwar era. How did cold war rivalries affect the Third World?

6. List and explain various successes and failures in the three competing worlds between 1945 and 1975 as they struggled to create "modern societies." What problems did the Third World face?

7. Evaluate the impact of Third World revolutionaries and radicals in transforming their societies. How successful were Mao and Castro in reforming their societies and challenging the international status quo?

8. Assess the impact of nuclear weapons on state rivalries and relations after World War II. How did the proliferation of these weapons affect Soviet-American relations?

9. Explain new tensions that emerged between 1945 and 1975 to challenge the three-world order. What challenges did they present for various states?

FURTHER READINGS

Anderson, Jon Lee, *Che Guevara: A Revolutionary Life* (1997). A sweeping study of the radicalization of Latin American nationalism.

Chatterjee, Partha, *Nationalist Thought and the Colonial World: A Derivative Discourse?* (1986). An influential interpretation of the ideological and political nature of Indian nationalism and the struggle for a postcolonial nation-state.

Crampton, R. J., *Eastern Europe in the Twentieth Century and After* (2nd ed., 1997). Comprehensive overview covering all Soviet-bloc countries

Dower, John W., *Embracing Defeat: Japan in the Wake of World War II* (1999). A prize-winning study of the transformation of one of the war's vanquished.

Gao Yuan, *Born Red: A Chronicle of the Cultural Revolution* (1987). A gripping personal account of the Cultural Revolution by a former Red Guard.

Gordon, Andrew (ed.), *Postwar Japan as History* (1993). Essays covering a wide range of topics on postwar Japan.

Hargreaves, John D., *Decolonization in Africa* (1996). A good place to start when exploring the history of African decolonization.

Hasan, Mushirul (ed.), *India's Partition: Process, Strategy and Mobilization* (1993). A useful anthology of scholarly articles, short stories, and primary documents on the partition of India.

Iriye, Akira, *Power and Culture: The Japanese-American War, 1941–1945* (1981). A discussion that goes beyond the military confrontation in Asia.

Jackson, Kenneth T., *Crabgrass Frontier: The Suburbanization of the United States* (1985). An insightful and influential consideration of the movement of the American population from cities to suburbs.

Jalal, Ayesha, *The Sole Spokesman: Jinnah, the Muslim League and the Demand for Pakistan* (1985). A study of the high politics leading to the partition of British India.

Keep, John L. H., *Last of the Empires: A History of the Soviet Union 1945–1991* (1995). A detailed overview of the core of the "Second World."

Morris, Benny, *Righteous Victims: A History of the Zionist-Arab Conflict, 1881–1999* (2000). On the Arab-Israeli War of 1948.

Overy, Richard, *Russia's War: Blood Upon the Snow* (1997). An up-to-date narrative about World War II's decisive Eastern Front.

Patterson, James T., *Grand Expectations: The United States, 1945–1974* (1996). Synthesizes the American experience in the postwar decades.

Patterson, Thomas, *Contesting Castro* (1994). The best study of the tension between the United States and Cuba. Culminating in the Cuban Revolution, it explores the deep American misunderstanding of Cuban national aspirations.

Ruedy, John, *Modern Algeria: The Origins and Development of a Nation* (1992). Gives the history of the Algerian nationalist movements and provides an overview of the Algerian war for independence.

Saich, Tony, and Hans van de Ven (eds.), *New Perspectives on the Chinese Communist Revolution* (1995). A collection of essays reexamining different aspects of the Chinese Communist movement.

Schram, Stuart, *The Thought of Mao Tse-tung* (1989). Standard work on the subject.

Wright, Gordon, *The Ordeal of Total War, 1939–1945* (1968). A superb treatment of the many dimensions of the war in Europe.

Zubkova, Elena, *Russia after the War: Hopes, Illusions, and Disappointments, 1945–1957* (1998). Uses formerly secret archives to catalogue the devastation and difficult reconstruction of one of the war's victors.

21

GLOBALIZATION, 1970–2000

$\mathcal{I}$n the thirteenth century, few ordinary people could comprehend moving beyond their local kingdoms and regions. Venetian explorer Marco Polo, who traveled through China, and Arab scholar Ibn Battuta, whose voyages covered the known Islamic world from West Africa to Southeast Asia, were the rare exceptions (see Chapter 10). But even their scope was limited—it wasn't until the sixteenth century that Ferdinand Magellan became the first to circumnavigate the globe, though he perished in the attempt (as we saw in Chapter 12). In contrast, at the end of the twentieth century, many people were able to move around the world with ease and speed, spanning in a matter of hours the distances that it took Marco Polo and Ibn Battuta years to cover. Even those who do not travel still have the wider world brought into their homes via the Internet, computers, books, newspapers, and televisions.

Consider two very different, contemporary, settings: a fishing village in the Amazon River basin and the cosmopolitan sprawl of Los Angeles. Picture a sixty-four-year-old fisherman in an Amazonian village trying to teach his eleven children their parents' tongue, Cocama-Cocamilla, but to no avail. All his children speak Spanish instead. "I tried to teach them," he notes. "It's like paddling against the current." Seven centuries ago, over 500 languages were spoken in the Amazon River basin. As of 2000, only 57 languages survived there, and probably around half were doomed to extinction. Evidently, one effect of globalization, the development of integrated worldwide cultural and economic structures, is to reduce diversity. But globalization can also lead to increasing local diversity. For example, Los Angeles, once the emblem of white, suburban America, became a cacophonous city in which over 100 languages are spoken by pupils in its public schools.

Whole families, even whole groups, as well as goods and ideas, crossed over the boundaries that once divided religious, ethnic, and national communities. This is one aspect of globalization. The forces of globalization include new technologies, cultures, economic exchanges, and political movements. While not entirely new, these forces have had greater significance since the 1970s, crossing national borders with greater ease than ever before.

Yet, while this flow of capital, goods, people, and ideas across national boundaries wove the world's population more tightly together, it also produced different effects and experiences around the world. Most people do not travel in airplanes. Many move in response to local conflicts, political chaos, or religious persecution or simply in hopes of escaping poverty. In contrast to jet-setting global adventurers, these migrants often slip across borders in the dark of night, travel literally as human cargo inside containers, or use their own feet for locomotion. Billions of others continue to live in worlds set apart from the technological wonders—and economic opportunities—of the global age. Many are deprived of the benefits of the new integration. Thus, while globalization created possibilities for some, it also led to a deepening of income and power disparities between and within different regions of the world.

> *From the end of the three-world order emerged a new architecture of power that organized the world into a unified marketplace with virtually unhindered flows of capital, commerce, culture, and labor across borders.*

GLOBAL INTEGRATION

> → *How has globalization changed the nation-state?*

The full impact and final consequences of our era's globalization remain unknown to us. What was clear by the end of the twentieth century was that the new forces driving global integration—and inequality—were no longer the large political empires that dominated the preceding centuries. Already by the middle of the twentieth century, the European empires that had ruled so much of the world during the nineteenth century had lost their sway. The cold war and decolonization movements that had dominated so many events immediately after World War II and had given rise to the three-world order had ceased to matter. The structures of power in the First World, under such stress in the 1970s, did not crack. But those in the Second World did. The cold war ended with the implosion of the Soviet bloc. The Third World also splintered, with some areas and regions becoming highly advanced, while others became mired in deeper poverty; the phrase now commonly used to refer to them, "the developing world," obscured these differences. From the end of the three-world order emerged a new architecture of power that organized the world into a unified marketplace with virtually unhindered flows of capital, commerce, culture, and labor across borders. By 2000, most of the world's societies had endorsed electoral systems and adopted some form of market economy.

The United States promoted these changes, and globalization has looked to some like "Americanization." The

Focus Questions GLOBALIZATION

- → *How has globalization changed the nation-state?*
- → *What were the major obstacles to globalization?*
- → *What are the agents of globalization?*
- → *What are the characteristics of the new global order?*
- → *How did citizenship in the global world create new problems and responses?*

 WWNORTON.COM/STUDYSPACE

United States unquestionably emerged as the most influential society in the world, with its music, food, principles of representative government, and free markets spreading to most corners of the globe. Yet, the process has not run one way. The world also came to America and shaped the texture of American society: the people living in the United States, their patented inventions, sports stars, and musical inspirations have been increasingly imported from elsewhere.

Nor was the United States immune from the transnational forces that have challenged the power of the nation-state itself. In the United States, as elsewhere, globalization increasingly functioned through networks of investment, trade, and migration that operated relatively independently of nation-states. In the process, globalization shook deep-rooted forms of political and social identifi-cation, from ecclesiastical to military authority. Nation-states have faced great difficulty commanding the imaginations of political communities: members of societies often identify more strongly with local, subnational, or even international movements or cultures.To be sure, nation-states remained essential for establishing democratic institutions and protecting human rights, but supranational institutions like the European Union and the International Monetary Fund (IMF) have often impinged on their autonomy.

REMOVING OBSTACLES TO GLOBALIZATION

> → *What were the major obstacles to globalization?*

In the mid-1970s, a set of political practices and institutions associated with the three-world order started to deteriorate. By the end of the 1980s, the Communist Second World had begun to disintegrate. The collapse of the Soviet Union brought the cold war to an end. At the same time, the capitalist First World gave up the last of its colonial possessions, and the remnants of white settler supremacy disintegrated. But as this occurred, the formerly colonized Third World's dream of a "third way" also vanished. As empires withdrew from the world historical stage, they revealed a world integrated by ties other than forced loyalties to imperial masters.

ENDING THE COLD WAR

A world divided between two hostile factions after World War II limited the prospects for the global exchange of peoples, ideas, and resources. The many regional conflicts of the cold war era (Vietnam, Afghanistan, Nicaragua) were costly for the countries caught in the ideological crossfire. Vietnam became a battleground for Russian, Chinese, and American ambitions. This war spilled over into Laos and Cambodia, dragging these countries to ruin along with Vietnam. China attracted several client states in the struggle for influence in the Third World and within the Communist bloc. In Afghanistan, Moscow propped up a puppet regime, only to get drawn into a bloody war against Islamic guerrillas financed and armed by the United States. In Central America, U.S. president Ronald Reagan and his advisers opposed the victory of the left-leaning Nicaraguan Sandinista coalition in 1979. In the 1980s, the United States pumped millions of dollars to the Contras (opponents of the Sandinistas) and also lent military and monetary assistance to other Central American anti-Communist forces (although many Americans opposed such actions and even brought those involved to trial for overstretching their authority). Thus, for much of the world, the cold war was a real confrontation with tremendously high costs for local powers.

But the struggle was costly to the superpowers as well. The 1970s and 1980s saw the largest peacetime accumulation of arms in world history. Despite efforts to halt the arms buildups with endless rounds of treaties and summits, the United States and the Soviet Union stockpiled their nuclear and conventional weaponry. To top things off and to add yet more to American military expenditures, in 1983 Reagan unveiled the Strategic Defense Initiative ("Star Wars," as some called it), a master plan to use satellites and space missiles to insulate the United States from incoming nuclear bombs. For both sides, though, military spending sprees brought economic troubles. The U.S. national debt increased; in the Soviet Union, the civilian infrastructure decayed, and life expectancies declined.

The cracks on either side of the Iron Curtain appeared in the 1970s. The KGB and, to a lesser extent, the CIA, produced secret memos questioning whether the Soviet bloc could sustain its global position. Stalemate in Afghanistan, a war that Soviet censors acknowledged only obliquely, destroyed the myth of the mighty Soviet armed forces. Mothers of Soviet soldiers protested the Kremlin's adventures abroad. The eastern European satellites became dependent on western European loans and consumer goods. At the same time, the western alliance also faced internal tensions. In Europe and North America, the antinuclear movement rallied millions to the streets. Western industrialists worried about Japanese competition, as Japan had made great economic strides since it plowed its money into rapid industrialization rather than arms. Political leaders also grappled with distressingly high unemployment rates. Thus, both sides shared a common crisis: fatigue from the strains and costs of the cold war and an economic challenge from East Asia.

In the end, the Soviet bloc buckled—and then, with startling rapidity, collapsed (see Map 21-1). Moscow capitulated, ending the cold war, because it could no longer compete. Planned economies employed the entire population, but they failed to fill department stores with consumer goods for the masses. Socialist health care and benefits lagged behind

NORTH SEA

DENMARK

1989: Mass demonstrations, fall of the Berlin Wall
1990: Reunited with West Germany

BALTIC SEA

Gdansk

1980 onward: Solidarity leads opposition
1981: Crackdown against Solidarity, driving it underground
1989: Solidarity wins 99 of the 100 seats in parliament that it is permitted to contest

S O V I E T U N I O N

NETHERLANDS

POLAND

EAST GERMANY

Berlin

Warsaw

1989: Mass demonstrations
1990: Multiparty elections
1993: Czechoslovakia splits into Czech Republic and Slovak Republic

BELGIUM

Leipzig

LUX.

WEST GERMANY

Prague

CZECHOSLOVAKIA

CZECH REPUBLIC

1989: Removal of barbed wire on border with Austria allows East German tourists to cross westward
1990: Multiparty elections

FRANCE

SLOVAKIA

Bratislava

1989: National uprising against Ceausescu
1992: First multiparty general election
1996: First non-Communist government

SWITZERLAND

AUSTRIA

Budapest

HUNGARY

1990: Multiparty elections

SLOVENIA

ROMANIA

1990: Multiparty elections
1991–1992: War between Croats and Serbs

CROATIA

Timisoara

1992: Fighting begins between Serbs and Bosnian Muslims
1995: Divided in two

BOSNIA-HERZOGOVINA

Belgrade

Bucharest

BLACK SEA

YUGOSLAVIA

SERBIA

Danube R.

ITALY

MONTE-NEGRO

BULGARIA

1990: Multiparty elections
1991: Dissolved into warring states

KOSOVO

Sofia

MACEDONIA

1989: Demonstrations
1990: Multiparty elections

Tirana

1989: Loses autonomy from Serbia
1998–1999: Fighting between Serbs and ethnic Albanians
2000: First free elections

ALBANIA

GREECE

1990: Multiparty elections
2001: Fighting erupts between Macedonians and ethnic Albanians

TURKEY

1990: Demonstrations, civil war
1991: Multiparty elections

✳ Civil unrest

MEDITERRANEAN SEA

MAP 21-1   COLLAPSE OF THE COMMUNIST BLOC IN EUROPE

The Soviet Union's domination of eastern Europe began to falter in the 1980s and ended in the 1990s. The political map of eastern and central Europe took on a different shape. Identify the new states that came into being in the 1990s. In what part of eastern and central Europe did the collapse of the Communist bloc produce the most political instability and conflict? Why did the end of Communist rule precipitate the reshuffling of political boundaries in the region?

those of the capitalist welfare states, especially of neighboring western Europe. Authoritarian political structures were based on deception and coercion rather than on elections and civic activism.

The catalyst in Socialism's defeat proved to be Poland. A critical turning point was the naming of the Polish archbishop of Cracow as Pope John Paul II (1920–2005) in late 1978. The first non-Italian pope in 455 years, John Paul opposed Soviet Socialism. In 1979, he made a pilgrimage to his native Poland, holding enormous outdoor masses; in 1980 he helped inspire and supported a series of mass strikes at the Gdansk shipyard, which led to the formation of the Soviet bloc's first independent trade union, Solidarity, led by the electrician Lech Walesa (1943–). As Communist Party members defected to its side, the union became a society-wide movement calling itself "civil society"; it aimed not to reform Socialism (as in Czechoslovakia in 1968) but to abolish it. A crackdown by the Polish military and police in December 1981 put most of Solidarity's leadership in prison and drove the movement underground, but the KGB secretly reported that Solidarity would eventually triumph.

In 1985, instability mounted when Mikhail Gorbachev (1931–) became general secretary of the Soviet Communist Party and launched an effort to reform the Soviet system (which he described as *perestroika*, or reconstruction) along the lines of the 1968 Prague Spring. He permitted contested elections for Communist Party posts, relaxed censorship, sanctioned civic associations, legalized small nonstate businesses, granted state firms autonomy, and encouraged the republics to be responsible for their affairs within the Soviet Union. Gorbachev's attempts to create "Socialism with a human face" were combined with dramatic arms control initiatives to ease the superpower burden on the Soviet Union.

Lech Walesa. A Polish electrician from the Lenin Shipyard in the Baltic port city of Gdansk, Walesa spearheaded the formation of Solidarity, a mass independent trade union of workers who opposed the Communist regime that ruled in their name. He later was elected president of post-Communist Poland.

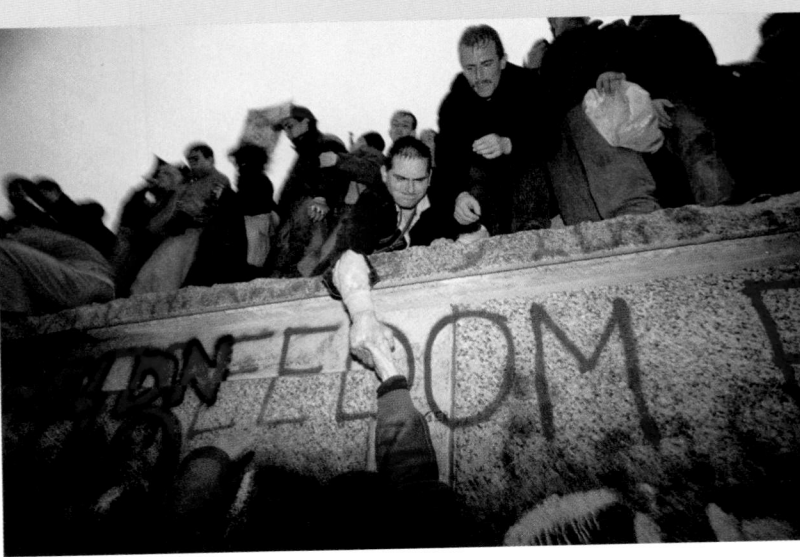

The Berlin Wall. The breaching of the Berlin Wall in late 1989 spelled the end of the Soviet bloc. Decades of debate over whether Communism could be reformed turned out to be moot. In the face of competition from the richer, consumer-oriented West, Communism collapsed.

Gorbachev began a withdrawal from Afghanistan in 1989 and informed eastern European leaders that they could not count on Moscow's armed intervention to prop up their regimes.

Having set out to improve Socialism, however, Gorbachev instead destabilized it. Civic groups called not for reform of the system but for its liquidation. Eastern Europe declared its intention to leave the Soviet orbit, and the leaders of the many union republics pushed for independence. Some factions within the Communist Party and the Soviet military objected to Gorbachev's initiatives and tried to restore the old order. A gang of hard-liners, including the chiefs of the KGB, military, and some top party officials, belatedly tried to preserve what was left of the crumbling system. They staged a disorganized coup in August 1991. The former Communist Party boss of Moscow and president of the Russian republic, Boris Yeltsin (1931–2007), however, rallied the opposition and faced down the hard-liners. Under Yeltsin, Russia, like Ukraine and the other republics of the Soviet Union, became a refuge for the beleaguered Soviet elites, who abandoned the cause of the Soviet Union and Socialism and became preoccupied with dividing up state property among themselves.

When Communist regimes collapsed, the European and Asian political maps changed dramatically. Old states disappeared, and many more were born. In Asia, although division between North and South Korea remained, Vietnam was united and, along with China, opened its country to western capitalism. In Europe, however, East Germany ceased to exist; its remnants were folded into West Germany in 1990, shortly after the Berlin Wall came down in 1989. Gone was the original dividing line that froze the antagonisms between East and West. Soon followed the voluntary dissolution of the Soviet empire into independent states (see Map 21-2).

Primary Source

TIDAL PULL OF THE WEST: EAST GERMANY DISAPPEARS

After Soviet premier Mikhail Gorbachev instituted a series of reforms to save Socialism, dissenters in eastern Europe saw their chance to throw off Russian dominance. The Berlin Wall was the most visible symbol of Soviet oppression. Here journalist Ann Tusa recalls the November 1989 press conference that accidentally led to the opening of the Berlin Wall (first erected in 1961). As both the wall and East Germany fell, Russia kept its nearly 400,000 troops that were on East German soil confined to their barracks.

At about 7 o'clock on the evening of November 9, 1989, some 300 journalists from all over the world are crammed into a room in East Berlin for a routine press conference. . . . For the first time since the foundation of a separate Communist East German state in 1946, the German Democratic Republic, there have been massive demonstrations against the regime. . . . The Communist Party's only response so far has been to shuffle the men at the top. . . .

East Germans, who have not known a free election since 1933, have been voting with their feet. From January to October 1989, some 200,000 people had left their country. By early November the figure was up to 250,000—and that was out of a total population of 16.7 million. At first, many East Germans went out on "holiday visas" to Iron Curtain countries, then claimed asylum in West German embassies in Warsaw, Budapest or Prague. Thousands more have driven or walked round the East German frontiers looking for an undefended crossing or a guard with a blind eye, wriggled across, then headed for Austria and a refugee camp. . . .

The November 9 press conference is handled by Günter Schabowski. . . . This evening he feeds the press a startling hint that there might soon be free elections. Good story. Everyone wants to go out and file it. But then Schabowski turns up a sheet from the bottom of the pile of papers on his table. "This will be interesting for you." And in a style that suggests it is all news to him, slowly reads aloud: "Today the decision was taken to make it possible for all citizens to leave the country through the official border crossing points. All citizens of the GDR can now be issued with visas for the purposes of travel or visiting relatives in the West. This order is to take effect at once. . . ."

The news is broadcast on an East German television bulletin at 7:30 P.M. The station's switchboard is immediately jammed with callers. "Is it true? I can't believe it." They always believed West German television, though, and it is soon flashing the announcement. A few East and West Berliners go to the Wall to see what is happening. . . . Then at 10:30 a discussion program on Sender Freies Berlin, the West Berlin television station, is interrupted by a live broadcast from the Wall. No preamble, just shots of a small crowd milling round a checkpoint, then a man runs toward the camera: "They've opened the crossing at Bornholmer Strasse." After that the news spreads like wildfire, by radio, television, telephone, shouts in the street. The trickle across the Wall swells to a flood. That weekend 2 million East Germans are reckoned to have stood in West Berlin. One reaction is common to them all: "We've seen the West on TV, of course. But this is real."

. . . The fatal piece of paper had been hurriedly swept up as he left for the press conference. It had never been intended for publication. It was a draft based on a recent Politburo decision: unable to control the tide of refugees, thrashing around for ways to quiet the demonstrators on the streets, they had decided that in their own good time they would ease travel restrictions, having first made arrangements for a limited issue of visas under carefully controlled circumstances.

→ *Why didn't Russian troops intervene during the collapse of the Berlin Wall?*
→ *What does this piece tell us about the state of mind of the East German government at this time?*

SOURCE: Ann Tusa, "A Fatal Error," in *Media Studies Journal*, Fall 1999, pp. 26–29.

MAP 21-2   THE BREAKUP OF THE SOVIET UNION

The Soviet Union broke apart in the 1990s. Compare this map with Map 17-6 (see p. 755), which explores Russian expansion in the nineteenth century. Which parts of the old Russian Empire remained under Russian rule, and which territories established their own states? Can you explain the large population migrations that accompanied the breakup? How did the breakup of the Soviet Union change the position of Russia in Europe and Asia?

But the end of Soviet-style Socialism and of the Soviet Union was not entirely peaceful. The worst carnage took place in the former Yugoslavia, where the collapse of Communism took the form of a violent tug of war between manipulative leaders playing to ethnic fears. Serbs and Croats, in particular, engaged in savage struggles over territories in the Balkans.

By historical standards, the cold war had been relatively brief, spanning four decades. But Communism had played a major role in the military conflicts and unprecedented modernization of two of Afro-Eurasia's largest societies, Russia and China, and it exercised an important influence on a third, India. Communism was, as one historian observed, a heavy-metal ideology. For the lighter stuff, it was ill-suited; it could not keep up the cold war fight *and* deliver the good life to its citizenry *and* survive in a more competitive world economy.

> *Communism was a heavy-metal ideology. For the lighter stuff, it was ill suited; it could not keep up the cold war fight and deliver the good life to its citizenry and survive in a more competitive world economy.*

AFRICA AND THE END OF WHITE RULE

Although the two decades that followed the end of World War II saw the dismantling of most of Europe's formal empires, remnants of colonial rule remained in the southern part of Africa (see Map 20-6 on p. 872). Here, whites held firmly to the centuries-old notions of innate white racial superiority over non-European peoples. Final decolonization meant that self-rule would return to all of Africa.

The last fortresses under direct European control were the Portuguese colonies of southern and western Africa, which, dating to the fifteenth century, had been the first European colonies in the region. But, by the mid-1970s, efforts to suppress African nationalist movements had exhausted Portugal's resources. Demoralized and fed up, Portuguese officers pushed aside the dictatorship founded by Antonio Salazar (1889–1970) and began the Portuguese experiment with democracy in 1974–1975. The African nationalist demands for freedom led to a hurried Portuguese withdrawal from Guinea-Bissau, Angola, and Mozambique. Thus did formal European colonialism in Africa come to an end.

But white rule still prevailed elsewhere in Africa. In Rhodesia, a tiny white minority clung to power and resisted all international pressure to give way to black rule. In the end, independent African neighbors helped support a liberation guerrilla movement under Robert Mugabe. Surrounded, Rhodesian whites finally capitulated. Mugabe swept to power with massive electoral support in 1979. The new constitutional government renamed the country Zimbabwe, erasing the name of the long-deceased British expansionist Cecil Rhodes from Africa's map.

The final outpost of white rule was South Africa, where a European minority was much larger, richer, and more entrenched than elsewhere in the region. In other countries international firms had played important roles in overthrowing regimes, as British Petroleum did in Iran in 1953. Here, BP helped the CIA oust Mohammed Mossadegh, who had just nationalized the Anglo-Iranian Oil Company, and restored to power the pro-Western Shah of Iran. But in South Africa such international firms were reluctant to enforce any boycott on the racist regime. For the United States, South Africa's large army was a useful tool to fight Soviet allies in other parts of southern Africa. The Afrikaner-led National Party seemed invulnerable to international economic and cultural pressures, and it used ruthless tactics in dealing with its internal critics. Yet, in the countryside and cities, defiance of white rule was growing. Africans lobbed rocks and crude bombs called Molotov cocktails at tanks, and organized mass strikes in the country's multinational-owned mines. At the same time, pressures from abroad were mounting. South African athletes were banned from the Olympics starting in 1970. American students insisted that their universities divest themselves of companies that had investments in South Africa. As international pressures increased, foreign governments, including the United States, applied economic sanctions against South Africa. Around the world, a swelling chorus demanded that Nelson Mandela, the imprisoned leader of the African National Congress (ANC), be freed. The white political elite eventually realized that it could not maintain apartheid without becoming a pariah police state and that it was better to negotiate new arrangements than to endure years of internal warfare against a majority population and international ostracism. In 1990, President F. W. de Klerk (of the National Party) released Mandela from prison and legalized the ANC and the Communist Party of South Africa. The ensuing negotiations between the ANC and the National Party produced South Africa's first free, mass elections in April 1994. These resulted in an overwhelming victory for the ANC, with Nelson Mandela elected as president. Majority rule had finally come to South Africa, and for the first time in many centuries, Africans ruled over all of Africa.

In Nelson Mandela, South Africa's white rulers found a man of exceptional integrity and political savvy. He had spent more than two decades in prison, much of it at hard labor. But he looked beyond past injustices to ease the transition to full democracy. Besides, he was aware that, with the country veering toward civil war, only a negotiated change would preserve South Africa's industries, wealth, and educational system.

Still, the leaders of politically independent Africa did not deliver on many of their promises. Decolonized Africa was

The End of Apartheid. *(Left)* Nelson Mandela, running for president in 1994 as the candidate of the African National Congress, here casts a ballot in the first all-races election in South Africa. This election ended apartheid and saw the African National Congress take control of the Republic of South Africa. *(Right)* After the overwhelming electoral triumph of Mandela, F. W. de Klerk, leader of the once-powerful Afrikaner-dominated National Party, shakes hands with his successor.

beset by immense problems. New political rulers faced the arduous task of building coherent and stable political communities where artificial colonies had previously existed. In their effort to do so, Africans set out to destroy the vestiges of colonial political structures and to erect new African-based public institutions. Turning colonial subjects into citizens of nation-states was not easy, however, for it often created local contests for political power. Ethnic and religious rivalries, held in check to a degree in the colonial period, burst forth at independence. Civil wars erupted in many countries, most violently in Nigeria, Sudan, and Zaire, and military leaders were drawn into politics. Coups d'état were so common that the few countries not to experience at least one, such as Kenya and Senegal, stand out as exceptions. Nigeria, for instance, had no fewer than 6 military coups between 1966 and 1999. The ruling elements increasingly kept themselves in power by using the resources of the state to reward their clients and to punish their enemies. By the 1990s, the continent was aflame with civil strife—armed conflicts that started with the cold war and lasted well after it ended.

UNLEASHING GLOBALIZATION

→ *What are the agents of globalization?*

With many of the political and ideological obstacles to international integration dissolving, capital, commodities, people, and culture crossed borders with ever-greater freedom. Most

states of the world moderated restraints on the flow of resources, ideas, and individuals across borders, changing, for example, tariff and immigration laws. While trade, foreign investment, migration, and cultural borrowing have long been hallmarks of modern history, the global age has changed the sheer scale of these activities. Nonetheless, as we shall also see, never have there been so many inequities in access to and distribution of the fruits of globalization.

FINANCE AND TRADE

The increased flow of goods and capital across national boundaries was already well underway in the 1970s, but the end of the cold war removed many impediments to globalization. During the 1990s, even the strongest of nation-states, such as the United States, were affected by economic globalization.

Major transformations occurred in the world's financial system in the 1970s. America's budget and trade deficits prompted President Richard Nixon to take the dollar off the gold standard in 1971, an action that facilitated global financial transfers. One by one, the yen, the lira, the pound, the franc, and other national currencies cut their ties to the American dollar. Gone were centuries of "hard" money, anchored to silver or gold or fixed to a solid reserve currency, like the British pound or American dollar. With the end of any fixed standard for money, international financiers enjoyed greater freedom from national regulators and found fresh business opportunities. A new system of informal management of money across borders replaced an older system of formal management within borders. Where formal management of world financial relations existed, it was exercised

World Tourism. One of the signs of increasing globalization is the importance of world tourism. By the thousands, travelers have ventured to remote corners of the world, bringing with them many of the components of world consumerism. This image of the ancient Inca capital (Cuzco) in the Andes conveys how old colonial architecture has been combined with the latest of modern financial services (such as the Visa card).

increasingly by international authorities such as the Bank for International Settlements and the IMF.

The primary agents of this heightened global financial activity were some old actors: banks. Based mainly in London, New York, and, increasingly, in Tokyo, commercial banks became conduits for large amounts of mobile capital looking for lucrative ventures. The revenues from oil producers provided a large injection of cash into the global economy in the 1970s. At the same time, banks joined forces to issue mammoth loans to developing nations.

The banks found important academic allies whose treatises laid out the economic rules of financial and fiscal sobriety for a global economic environment. These intellectuals were primarily North American–trained economists who were schooled in a new framework of economic thinking, one that minimized the welfare concerns that had been so fundamental to the Keynesian approach. This younger generation of economists emphasized the power of unfettered markets and profit motivations as the cornerstone of capitalist economic development. Employed in banks and ministries around the world, they argued that the old regulatory and interventionist policies of nation-states prevented rather than promoted economic growth. Working as advisers in many gov-

ernments, but especially under Margaret Thatcher in Britain and Ronald Reagan in the United States, these economists effectively guided public policy to deregulate market life.

No international financial organization, however, played a more decisive role than the IMF. As the 1980s unfolded, the IMF emerged as a central player, especially in response to what was called the debt crisis in Third World and eastern-bloc countries. Throughout the 1970s, European, Japanese, and North American banks had loaned money on very easy terms to cash-strapped Third World and eastern-bloc borrowers. But what was once good business soon turned sour. In 1982, a wave of defaults threatened to overrun Latin America in particular. Through the 1980s, international banks and the IMF kept heavily indebted customers solvent. The IMF offered short-term loans to governments on condition that recipients adopt new fiscal and financial ways and compel civilian populations to tighten their belts. Latin Americans pioneered the process of merging their domestic markets with international ones. Trade barriers crumbled; state enterprises became private firms; and foreign investors called the former debtors "emerging markets." Eastern Europe and Asia followed suit in the 1990s, and emerging market mania buoyed a boom in international finance.

New technologies and institutions enabled many more financial investors and traders to participate in these integrated networks of world finance. The Internet and online trading accelerated the mobility—and volatility—of capital across borders. For instance, in the United States, the amount of American investment abroad in bonds and equities soared nearly tenfold between 1980 and 1990 and expanded even more in the following decade. Volatility soon created problems, however. In the 1990s, currency devaluations in Mexico, in Russia, and across East Asia shocked financiers. When the Mexican economy went into paralysis in late 1994, the crisis was so large that not even the IMF could bail it out; it took the U.S. Treasury to issue the largest international loan in history to pull the southern neighbor out of its economic tailspin. Despite acting as the lender in that instance, the United States emerged in this new financial world order as the world's largest borrower. Early in the new millennium, its net foreign debt soared past $2 trillion (nearly a quarter of its Gross Domestic Product, or GDP), which represented a 700 percent increase since the early 1990s. Much of this debt was owed to Asian, especially Chinese, bankers.

Globalization increased commercial, as well as financial, interdependence. The total value of world trade increased nearly tenfold between 1973 and 1998, and trade in Asia grew even faster than that. In 1960, trade accounted for 24 percent of the world's GDP; by 1995, that share had climbed to 42 percent. Where an American would once have worn American-made clothes (Levi's), driven an American car (a Ford), and watched an American television (Zenith), such was rarely the case by century's end. More and more, consumers bought goods and services provided by foreigners and sold a greater share of their own output abroad. This pattern had always been true of smaller countries and regions like Central America or southern Africa. But in the 1980s, it intensified, with Hong Kong and Singapore prospering thanks to expanding world trade.

International trade not only made people more interdependent; it also shifted the international division of labor. After World War II, Europeans and North Americans dominated manufacturing, while Third World countries supplied raw materials. By the 1990s, this was no longer the case. Brazil became a major airplane maker, South Korea exported millions of automobiles, and China emerged as the world's largest source of textiles, footwear, and, increasingly, electronics.

The most remarkable global shift involved the rise of East Asian industry and commerce. Manufactured goods, including high-technology products, were now built on the eastern fringe of Afro-Eurasia as often as on its western fringe. Building on its postwar "miracle" (see Chapter 20), Japan blazed the Asian trail. Between 1965 and 1990, Japan's share of world trade doubled to almost 10 percent. China, too, began to flex its economic muscle. When Deng Xiaoping (1905–1997) took power in 1978, China was already a growing economy. Under Deng, China started to become an economic powerhouse for Asia. For the next two decades, China chalked up astounding 10 percent annual growth rates, swelling its share of world GDP from 5 percent to 12 percent.

For East Asia as a whole, the share of world exports also doubled in the same period, to 22 percent, with smaller countries like Singapore, Taiwan, South Korea, and Hong Kong becoming mini-powerhouses. By the early 1990s, these countries and Japan also became major investors abroad. Japan was the world's largest foreign investor. Overall, East Asia's share of world production rose from 13.6 percent to 25.3 percent between 1965 and 1989. By contrast, over the same period, the U.S. share shrank from 38.6 percent to 35.4 percent, and Europe's share decreased from 33.5 percent to 30.6 percent.

Industrialization of previously less developed countries, combined with lower trade barriers, increased the pressures of world competition on national economies. Some areas responded to global competition by creating regional blocs. In North America, a great deal of trade and finance flowed back and forth across the U.S.-Canadian border. By the 1980s, fearing competition from inexpensive Asian manufactures, the two North American countries decided to admit Mexico into the trading bloc, to encourage plants to locate within the region. They negotiated a North American Free Trade Agreement (NAFTA) in 1992. The most complete process of regional integration took place in Europe. Europeans slashed

trade barriers and harmonized their commercial policies toward the rest of the world. In December 1991, the Maastricht Treaty won the approval of most European states, which paved the way for creating a single European currency, the euro. Maastricht became, in effect, the constitution for the European Union, which was to be a fully integrated trading and financial bloc with its own bureaucracy and elected representatives.

Trade integration and interdependence coincided with a transformation in what was traded. Pharmaceuticals, computers, software, and services from insurance to banking have become ever more important exports and imports. High technology, in particular, occupies an ever greater share of the manufacturing and exports of the world's richest countries.

Competition and the shift to the production of sophisticated goods have had enormous effects on world incomes. For the "rich" countries as a whole, about half of total GDP is based on the production and distribution of these goods and services, giving those countries a competitive advantage over others. In general, where global incomes are lower and people are less educated, the share of knowledge as a contributor to wealth is also lower. Poor nations remain, with few exceptions, locked in the production of low-tech goods and the export of raw materials. Between 1976 and 1996, as the share of high-tech goods in total world trade doubled from 11 percent to 22 percent, the share of primary products shrank from 45 percent to under 25 percent. Increasingly, technology and knowledge now divide the world into affluent, technically sophisticated countries and poor, technically underdeveloped regions.

> *Competition and the shift to the production of sophisticated goods have had enormous effects on world incomes.*

MIGRATION

Not only do capital and products flow across borders, but the migration of peoples also knits the world closer together. Migration has been a constant feature of world history. But in the twentieth century, and especially after the 1970s, the movement of peoples within and across national boundaries became more widespread (see Map 21-3). True, the relative numbers did not reach the scale of demographic reshuffling of Europeans to the Americas from 1880 to 1914. Although after 1970 fewer Europeans were on the move, more Asians, Africans, and Latin Americans had become mobile. Indeed, one of the important destinations was Europe. By 2000, there were 120 million migrants scattered across 152 countries, up from 75 million in 1965. The vast majority of these migrants left poorer countries for richer destinations.

Who went where and why? To a large extent, migratory flows conformed to the contours of existing political relations.

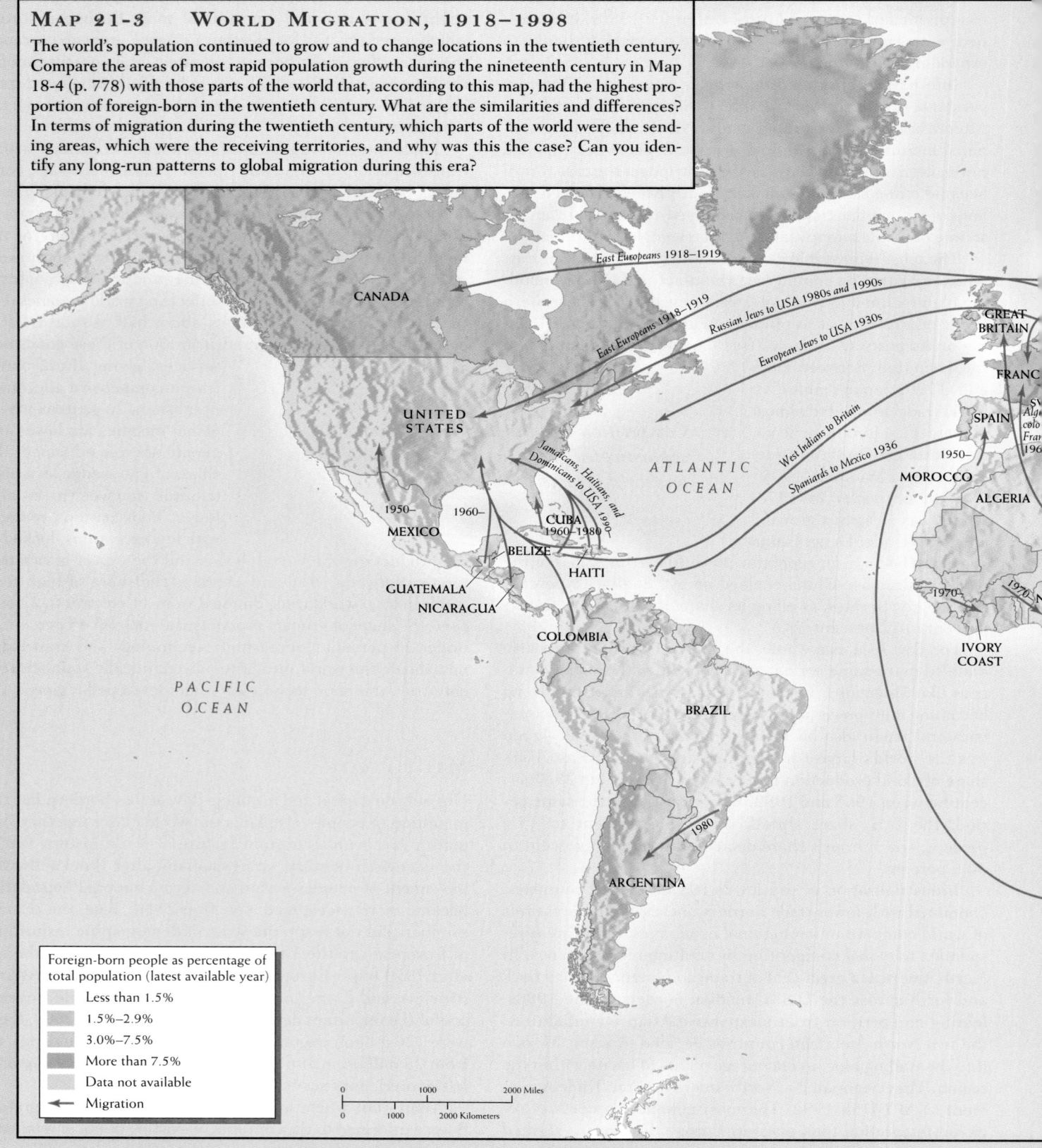

MAP 21-3   WORLD MIGRATION, 1918–1998

The world's population continued to grow and to change locations in the twentieth century. Compare the areas of most rapid population growth during the nineteenth century in Map 18-4 (p. 778) with those parts of the world that, according to this map, had the highest proportion of foreign-born in the twentieth century. What are the similarities and differences? In terms of migration during the twentieth century, which parts of the world were the sending areas, which were the receiving territories, and why was this the case? Can you identify any long-run patterns to global migration during this era?

East Europeans 1918–1919

East Europeans 1918–1919

Russian Jews to USA 1980s and 1990s

European Jews to USA 1930s

West Indians to Britain

Spaniards to Mexico 1936

Jamaicans, Haitians and Dominicans to USA 1990s

CANADA

UNITED STATES

MEXICO   1950–

1960–

BELIZE

GUATEMALA

NICARAGUA

CUBA 1960–1980

HAITI

COLOMBIA

BRAZIL

ARGENTINA   1980

PACIFIC OCEAN

ATLANTIC OCEAN

GREAT BRITAIN

FRANCE

SPAIN   1950–

MOROCCO

ALGERIA

IVORY COAST   1970

1970

Foreign-born people as percentage of total population (latest available year)

Less than 1.5%

1.5%–2.9%

3.0%–7.5%

More than 7.5%

Data not available

← Migration

0   1000   2000 Miles

0   1000   2000 Kilometers

ARCTIC OCEAN

Poles and Baltic peoples to Siberia 1939–1940

RUSSIA

1930s and 1940s

POLAND

1918–1922

UKRAINE

Russian Jews to Israel 1980s and 1990s

1945

GEORGIA 1922

1922

TURKEY

SYRIA 2003

1945– 2003

ISRAEL IRAQ 1947–

JORDAN

EGYPT

BYA 1947–

1980

Falashas to Israel 1991

SAUDI ARABIA

1970–

SUDAN mid 1980s

ETHIOPIA 1980s

CONGO

RWANDA 1994

TANZANIA

BOTSWANA 1960–

MOZAMBIQUE 1960–

SOUTH AFRICA

INDIAN OCEAN

AFGHANISTAN 1979

PAKISTAN

1970

1947

INDIA 1972

BANGLADESH

1947

CHINA

HONG KONG

to UK

THAILAND

VIETNAM

1975

1975

MALAYSIA

1975

INDONESIA

to Western Europe and USA

to France

Southeast Asians to Australia 1970s

NORTH KOREA

1950–1954

SOUTH KOREA

JAPAN

to Canada and USA 1980–

PACIFIC OCEAN

to USA

to USA 1990–

AUSTRALIA

Europeans to Australia/New Zealand 1918–

NEW ZEALAND

Lagos, Nigeria. Lagos is one of the fastest-growing and most crowded cities in Africa. This picture shows the new buildings and the streets; notice the mosque on the left.

Where North America and Europe had colonies or dependencies, their political withdrawal left tracks for migrants to follow. Indians and Pakistanis moved to Britain. Dominicans, Haitians, and Mexicans went to the United States. Algerians and Vietnamese moved to France. And where emerging rich societies cultivated close diplomatic ties, these relations opened migratory gates. This was the case, for instance, of Germany's relationship with Turkey, Japan's with South Korea, and Canada's with Hong Kong. In most cases, economic factors were what propelled migrants across national borders.

International migration was often an extension of regional and national migration from poorer, rural areas to urban centers. In Nigeria, for example, rural-urban migration intensified after 1970. In 1900, Nigeria's capital, Lagos, had a population of 41,847. At the century's end, Lagos had more than 10 million people, with predictions that it would grow to 20 million by 2025. The key to Lagos's boom in the 1970s was its black gold: oil. When the Organization of Petroleum Exporting Countries (OPEC) sent oil prices soaring after 1973, money poured into Nigeria. The government kept most of it in the capital. That, in turn, encouraged people from the countryside to move to Lagos. This rural-urban migration increased Lagos's population by 14 percent per year in the 1970s and 1980s. No government, least of all a new, weakly supported one like Nigeria's, could cope with such a huge population influx. Electricity supplies failed regularly. There were never enough schools, teachers, or textbooks. But the city burst with the vitality of the new arrivals, prompting one new immigrant to exclaim: "It's a terrible place; I want to go there."

The search for opportunities that sent people from the countryside to the cities also pushed them across national borders. Just as money and jobs in cities stimulated movement from rural areas to urban areas, so, too, did global inequities stimulate mass movements from less developed to more developed nations. Although many corporations relocated their manufacturing plants in poorer countries, where unskilled labor was abundant and government regulations were few, these jobs remained less attractive than even the lowest wage positions available in richer nations. Thus, the possibility for better wages—and the hope for better lives—inspired millions to leave their homelands.

As in earlier times, some internal and international migrants moved for only temporary sojourns. At least that was the original intent. In the 1950s and 1960s, southern Europeans moved northward, but when Spain, Portugal, Greece, and Italy also became wealthy societies, not only did the exodus decline, but these countries became magnets for Middle Eastern, North African, and more recently eastern European migrants. Europeans' strong identification with their nations did not permit the easy integration of foreigners. Nor did European states support the permanent settlement of immigrants. Most of the migrants from Asia and Africa went initially to Europe in search of temporary jobs and were known as guest workers. With time they settled in their host countries, and migrants found themselves living in urban squalor: Pakistanis in Britain's city of Leeds and Algerians in impoverished suburbs of Paris. In Japan, too, immigrants were not easily incorporated into public life. Tokyo's policy in the 1970s resembled the European guest worker program in Europe. Discouraging permanent settlement and immigration, Japan encouraged mainly itinerant workers to move to the country, yet its economy required increasing numbers of these sojourners. Indeed, Japan's deep reluctance to integrate migrants has led to dire labor shortages—as late as 1998, only 1.1 million foreigners had registered as residents in Japan.

After Japan, the economic boomers of Hong Kong, Taiwan, and Malaysia all became hosts for temporary migrants. The result was that millions of guest workers moved to these destinations, but after years of living in prosperous Asian and European cities, migrants sank ever deeper roots, especially once their children entered schools. This created a new challenge in host societies that were accustomed to thinking of national communities as ethnically homogeneous. At times, the discrimination and exclusion ran high and led to violent backlashes. Governments also grappled with the challenge of extending citizenship rights to newcomers.

One society that had far fewer problems integrating migrants and that attracted the lion's share of international migrants was the United States. For a long time a magnet for Europeans, the United States enacted an immigration reform in 1965 that threw open its gates to the world's migrants.

Japanese Market in Los Angeles. After the enactment of a new immigration law in 1965, millions of immigrants from Latin America and Asia profoundly altered the ethnic composition of the United States. Nowhere was the change more evident than in Los Angeles, where by the year 2000 the foreign-born accounted for 40 percent of the population. Immigrants brought a new cosmopolitanism to cities like Los Angeles, where the foods of the world were readily available at diverse restaurants and markets.

Latin Americans, especially Mexicans, accounted for the largest single source of migrants to the United States. By 2000, 27 million immigrants lived in the United States, accounting for almost 10 percent of the population—double the share in 1970. The profile of migration also changed dramatically. In 1970, there were more Canadians or Germans living in the United States than Mexicans. In the ensuing thirty years, the Mexican influx rose tenfold and by 2000 accounted for almost one-third of the immigrants in the United States. The numbers migrating from Asia also surged, accounting for over 40 percent of all immigrants to the United States in the 1990s. But it was above all from south of the Rio Grande that the American demographic landscape changed.

As the world came to the United States, it transformed American cities. Nowhere was the changing ethnic composition of American cities more vivid than in Los Angeles, which had been the "whitest" of major American cities until it became the destination for millions of migrants after the 1965 Immigration Act. By the end of the twentieth century, two out of five Los Angelenos were foreign-born, and more than 40 percent of residents were Latino. Likewise, the proportion of Asians jumped fivefold. The percent of African-Americans showed a similar rise beginning in 1930, though much of this expansion took place before 1965.

In the wake of this surge in immigration Americans grappled with the challenge of bridging the widening gap between where one lives and one's nationality, between residence and citizenship. This issue has been fraught with tensions, as some longtime residents of the southwestern states, in particu-lar, objected to spending tax dollars on non-English-speaking immigrants.

The arguments in Los Angeles over schools and health care for resident noncitizens have been part of a global debate. In Argentina, 500,000 undocumented Peruvians, Bolivians, and Paraguayans also live without rights as citizens. Even more staggering, between 3 and 8 million migrants have moved from Mozambique, Zimbabwe, and Lesotho to South Africa. In some Middle Eastern countries, like Saudi Arabia and Kuwait, the share of foreign-born workers tops 70 percent of the workforce. In general, migrants have been only partially accommodated, while many have been fully excluded from the mainstream of host societies. Thus, even though population movements have flowed across political, kinship, and market networks, the great demographic reshuffling resulting from globalization has heightened national concerns about the ethnic makeup of political communities.

Finally, forced migrations have remained a hallmark of the modern world. But rather than migration of slaves from Africa, the more recent involuntary flows have been of refugees fleeing civil war and torture. Many have not been able to migrate far, and they have been left to suffer for weeks, months, or years in refugee camps on the periphery of the violence. It is hardly surprising that the greatest concentration of refugees has occurred in the poorest region of the world—Africa. Those Africans who have not been able to make their way to the wealthier areas of the world have often been caught up in ethnic and religious conflicts that have resulted in vast refugee camps, where people survive through the generosity of host governments and international contributions.

African Refugees. Africa has become a continent of displaced persons and refugee camps. Pictured here is a camp in Chad for Sudanese driven out of the Darfur region by government-sponsored raids.

CULTURE

Migrations and new technologies have contributed to the creation of a more global entertainment culture as well. In this domain above all, globalization has often been equated with Americanization. Yet, the American entertainments that have spread around the world have themselves been shaped by artistic practices from diverse parts of the globe, as one mass culture meets another. On the global scale, there was less diversity in 2000 than in 1300; but on the level of the individual's everyday experience, the potential for experiencing cultural diversity—if one could afford the technology to do so—was greatly increased.

NEW MEDIA Technology has played an important part in the diffusion of entertainment. In the 1970s, cassette tapes became the dominant circulating medium for popular music, sidelining the long-playing record and the short-lived eight-track tape. Cassette tapes could be illegally mass reproduced at home by bootleggers who disregarded copyright laws and sold them cheaply to young consumers. Television was another globalizing force. American producers bundled old dramas and situation comedies to stations around the world. Finally, films created global cultural linkages. American movie distributors sent movies to theaters around the world and made videocassettes of movies that were distributed (and also illegally copied) worldwide. But Americans were not the only entertainment exporters. Brazilian soap operas began to penetrate Spanish-language American TV markets in the 1980s, often inducing Mexican viewers to rush home from work to catch the latest episode. Latin American television shows and music were distributed in the United States in areas that had large Spanish-speaking populations. Bombay also produced its fair share of programs for viewers of British television. Movies and actors from New Zealand, Australia, France, Italy, China, India, and Iran found audiences in Europe and the United States.

In the early 1980s, a new form of television programming was developed and spread rapidly: cable. Once again, the United States pioneered the medium, but the innovation soon caught on elsewhere. Increasingly, viewers had access to dozens, even hundreds, of specialized channels, challenging the dominance of the traditional national networks. Cable TV networks like MTV were devoted to pop music and introduced music videos, which popularized performers who had learned that a music video was both a musical and a visual product.

Television's globalizing effects were especially evident in sports. In many parts of the globe, American sports made particularly deep inroads. Increasing numbers of foreigners participated in American sports, and more important, television time increasingly was devoted to broadcasting American games in other countries. The National Basketball Association (and the athletic footwear firm Nike) was particularly successful in its international marketing and in the process made Michael Jordan the world's best-known athlete, and perhaps the world's best-known person, at the end of the twentieth century. Soccer (known as football outside the

Bollywood. By the 1990s, Bombay cinema had an increasing global presence and had acquired the name "Bollywood." This image is from *Lagaan* (Land Revenue), a four-hour film that was a huge hit in India in 2001 and gained commercial success internationally—even a nomination in the best foreign film category at the Oscars.

BOMBAY/MUMBAI

Bombay, more than any other Indian city, has always been connected to the world economy. Acquired by the Portuguese in the sixteenth century, who then transferred its control to the East India Company, Bombay developed as a colonial creation. Composed of seven islands joined by lands taken back from the sea, Bombay developed as a port city for colonial commerce, becoming an economic powerhouse during the nineteenth century. It profited from the cotton trade, developed a vibrant textile industry, attracted migrants, and took on a cosmopolitan image. The twentieth century brought it unprecedented growth as Indian-owned economic institutions achieved dominance and nationalist politics won popular support. After India's independence in 1947, Bombay came to epitomize the modern face of the nation, and its heterogeneous population became the ur (prototypical) symbol of the Indian melting pot.

Beginning with the 1980s, however, the nature and effects of integration into the world economy started to change. The cotton textile industry, which had served as Bombay's economic backbone since the late nineteenth century, went into a steep decline. Industrial employment fell sharply, the era of the trade unions ended, and the share of the informal sector of household enterprises, small shops, petty subcontractors, and casual laborers, along with the financial services sector of banking and insurance, rose. Economic liberalization transformed Bombay further, removing hurdles against the entry of foreign businesses and integrating the city into the global economy.

Even as Bombay continues to be a part of the nation, it now occupies, as do other global cities, a strategic place in transnational geography. It serves as a center for the servicing and financing of international trade, investment, and corporate office functions. The global constitution of Bombay is evident in the increasing presence in the city of financial institutions, trading organizations, insurance companies, telecommunications corporations, and information technology enterprises with worldwide operations. Forces of change can be observed even in its vibrant film industry, which produces roughly 120 films a year. Its trademark is spectacular melodramatic fantasies. But since the 1980s, Bombay films are increasingly addressed to a global, not only national, audience of Indians. In addition, many of the most successful and glossy productions can be characterized as "placeless"; that is, the narrative is not pinned down to a definable place but situated in a global locale. Reflecting its increasingly global location, Bombay cinema has acquired the moniker "Bollywood" in recent years.

A striking effect of the concentration of global economic operations in the city is the high economic value that these activities command. Finance, banking, telecommunications, the software industry, and corporate headquarters operations generate profits and offer remunerations to employees on a much richer scale than other sectors of the economy. On the other hand, low-skilled and unskilled workers, lacking union organization, receive low wages. The city still attracts a large number of poor migrants who live in slums, where they are lucky to have a roof over their heads, or call the pavements their home. The gap between the rich and the poor, which has always been legendary in Bombay, has grown alarmingly. A tiny, rich elite connected to the global economy is dwarfed by millions who eke out a miserable living. This inequality also affects governance. The government is asked to protect global capital from the encroachment of squatters and pavement dwellers, and municipal services have been increasingly deployed to clear illegally constructed slums.

Globalization has also affected the very name of the city and sparked a contest over the identity of its residents. In January 1996, Mumbai became the official name of Bombay, which serves as the capital of the Maharashtra province. The government represented the renaming as an act of indigenizing the colonial name. The political party then in power in Maharashtra was the Shiv Sena, a nativist regional party named after the seventeenth-century Maratha chieftain Shivaji, who was an adversary of the Mughal Empire. Since its inception in 1966, the Shiv Sena has campaigned militantly for the reservation of jobs and economic opportunities for Marathi speakers, who constitute a little over 40 percent of the city's heterogeneous population of 15 million. It was only in the 1980s, however, that the Shiv Sena grew rapidly. The timing is significant because it was then that the city's economy and society began to change dramatically. As the industrial economy and trade unions gave way to the service sector and unorganized labor, and as globalization uprooted identities located in the framework of the secular nation-state, a space opened for alternative mobilizations. It was in this context that the Shiv Sena emerged triumphant. It did so, not by opposing economic globalization, but by utilizing the social and political fluidity produced by deindustrialization and globalization to win support for its nativist and Hindu chauvinist ideology. Bombay's cosmopolitan image went up in smoke in 1992–1993, when the Shiv Sena directed and led pogroms against the city's Muslim residents.

Bombay/Mumbai today manifests the contradictory, conflictual, and uneven effects of globalization. The society is sharply divided, economic disparities are great, and its politics is a cauldron of conflicting identities. These are the local forms in which globalization is experienced in this vast and influential city.

United States) became an international passion, with devoted national followings for national teams. Indeed, by the 1980s, soccer was becoming *the* world sport, and its schedule is now decided increasingly by television ratings. The organizers of the 1986 World Cup in Mexico insisted that big soccer matches be held at midday so that games could be televised live at prime time in Europe, despite players' grumbling about having to play under the scorching sun.

GLOBAL CULTURE Technology was not the only driving force of world cultures. Migration and exchange were also important. As people moved around, they brought with them their musical tastes, and they borrowed from other cultures they encountered. Reggae, born in the 1960s among Jamaica's Rastafarians, became a hit sensation in London and Toronto, where large West Indian communities had moved in the 1960s and 1970s. Reggae lyrics and realist imagery invoked a black countercultural sensibility and a redemptive call for a return to African roots. Soon, Bob Marley and the Wailers, reggae's flagship band, played to audiences around the world. In northeast Brazil, where African culture emerged from decades of official and unofficial disdain, Bob Marley became a folk hero. In Soweto, South Africa, populated by black workers, he was also a symbol of resistance. Reggae propelled a major shift in black American music. In broadcasting reggae, DJs merged sounds and chant lyrics over a beat, a "talkover" form of music that also would be used in rap music. This was a disruptive concept in the late 1970s, but by the late 1980s, rap became a club favorite—and a non-conventional provocation. Rap lyrics emulated reggae realism by focusing on black problems, but they also pushed the countercultural messages into a new domain of controversies involving gang worldviews. On the world stage, Latino rappers used lyrical interventions to stress multicultural themes,

Bob Marley. In the 1970s, young Europeans and North Americans began to listen to music from the Third World. Among the most popular was Jamaican-based reggae, and its most renowned artist, Bob Marley. Marley's music combined rock and roll with African rhythms and lyrics about freedom and redemption for the downtrodden of the world.

often in "Spanglish." Asian rap dispensed with the notion that the genre was the property of any ethnicity or race at all and stressed that rap was a new musical form that enabled cross-cultural sharing.

The effects of migration on global music are also evident in Latin American transformations of North American genres. Latin music came into its own thanks to Latin-American migrants to the United States. In New York and New Jersey, Puerto Ricans and Dominicans made boogaloo, salsa, and merengue popular. In Los Angeles, Mexican *corridos* (ballads) became pop hits. In the 1980s, East Los Angeles produced its own local rock sensation, Los Lobos, a Chicano band that fused Mexican popular tunes with Californian themes. Their best-selling albums often had bilingual lyrics.

What reinforced cross-cultural borrowing was not just the medium of production and distribution of entertainment across borders, but also the message. Increasingly, world popular culture was youth culture. Often, what was appealing about television and music was its generational opposition. In Egypt, one of the most popular TV serials, *The School of Troublemakers*, carried a resolutely antiestablishment message. It showed schoolboys challenging the authority of their teachers and reveling in the chaos that they created. In Argentina, rock and roll was crucial to the counterculture during the military dictatorship of the 1970s and 1980s. Charlie García urged his Buenos Aires audiences to defy authorities by daring to dream of a different order. Indeed, in countries where public cultures were squashed underfoot by repressive regimes, pop culture was very often counterculture. In East Germany, before the fall of the Berlin Wall, rappers denounced the ruler Eric Honecker and his generation as a bunch of senile plutocrats.

The same globalizing effects could also be seen in sports. Consider the staple of American identity: baseball. Compared with basketball, baseball lagged in its global marketing, but rosters of major league teams took on a more global cast. Beginning in the 1960s, the number of Latin Americans playing in North American professional leagues grew steadily. Most notable in the 1980s, perhaps, was the Mexican pitcher Fernando Valenzuela, whose exploits as a member of the Los Angeles Dodgers made him a hero to that city's Mexican population and to people in his native land as well. The Dodgers also took the lead in reaching for Asian talent. In the 1990s, as Los Angeles became home to a growing Asian immigrant population, the Dodgers added the Japanese pitcher Hideo Nomo to the team. In many respects, "Nomo-mania" repeated the "Fernando-mania" of the previous decade, the difference being that Nomo's greatest acclaim came among Asian-Americans in Los Angeles and among his countrymen in Japan. In the Dominican Republic, baseball fans were riveted on their favorite players in the big leagues, slugger Sammy Sosa and ace pitcher Pedro Martínez.

LOCAL CULTURE World cultures may have become more integrated and homogeneous, but they did not completely ef-

Baseball Goes International. The 1980s and 1990s saw an influx of ballplayers from Latin America and quite a few from Asia as well. (*Left*) Boston Red Sox slugger David Ortiz hails from the Dominican Republic. (*Right*) Seattle Mariner superstar Ichiro Suzuki is from Japan.

face national and local cultures. Indeed, technology and migration often reinforced the appeal of "national" cultural icons, as national celebrities gained popularity among immigrant groups abroad. New technology that was cheaply available allowed these stars to be known to more and more people. In Egypt, the most popular singer of the Nasser years was Umm Kalthum, who in 1975 was given a state funeral, the likes of which had rarely been seen. She was the favorite of the middle classes of her era—and radio was her main medium. Egypt's more liberal economic and cultural policies under Nasser's successor, President Anwar al-Sadat, created new national pop stars. Some, like Muhammad Abd al-Wahhab, artfully blended western and eastern musical themes. Educated in *Quranic* schools, where he developed a talent for chanting the *Quran*, he caught on with a local touring group as a youngster and eventually became a big singing attraction. When he fused his *Quranic* vocals and chants with western synthesizers and beats, he went from attraction to sensation.

The market for world cultures was increasingly competitive, and competition created more room for acceptable per-formance. Since the 1970s, competition in the world cultural markets registered some breakthroughs. Without a doubt, the most important was the triumph of black performers (Bob Marley, Whitney Houston), black athletes (Pelé, Michael Jordan), and black writers (Toni Morrison, Chinua Achebe), not just among white consumers, but among world consumers. Competition also shattered some sexual biases. Female performers like Madonna became popular icons. So did gay performers, starting with the Village People, whose campy multicultural anthem "YMCA" disturbed fundamentalists but created a place for a new generation of homosexual or bisexual artists. Of course, beyond Europe and North America, flirting with sexual conventions had its limits. In the Middle East, female video artists continued to wear veils—but they still swung their hips.

The globalization of culture since the 1970s introduced world consumers to a set of common icons—athletic, musical, and performing. In this sense, globalization created an increasingly homogeneous world culture. Mass culture from the United States became an especially important purveyor of products to the rest of the world. At the same time, however, local cultures became increasingly diverse. Relatively homogeneous national cultures, often dominated by mature men representing the ethnic majority, gave way to a wide variety of entertainers and expressions. Artists and entertainers crossed gender, racial, generational, and international boundaries with unprecedented ease and broke loose of often confining local cultures.

COMMUNICATIONS

Migration, markets, and mass entertainment are not the only forms in which global networks have been created; a technological revolution in communications played an even more important role. By the 1970s, satellites relayed telecommunications into living rooms around the world. Television brought the world home—but it was still a one-way technology. It was not interactive. Starting in the 1970s and early 1980s, however, engineers based primarily in California's Santa Clara Valley between San Francisco and San Jose, in what became known as the Silicon Valley, tinkered with the idea of computers (which had been used in government and corporations since the 1940s) for personal use. At first, these were big, underpowered machines with little memory. But with the invention of the silicon chip, the computer weighed less and gained enormous memory power. On the heels of this hardware revolution, a software revolution enabled people to process words, run businesses, play games, and eventually communicate with each other from computer terminal to computer terminal.

Computer technology helped create new networks of interactive communications. In the late 1980s, while working in Switzerland, a British physicist named Tim Berners-Lee devised a means to pool the data he had stored on various computers. Hitherto, electronic links existed only between major universities and research stations. Berners-Lee figured out how to make data more accessible by creating the World Wide Web. With each use and each connection, and as people entered more data, however, the Web grew more and more crowded. Pretty soon it was clear that users could get lost and tangled in unfamiliar electronic syntax. In the early 1990s, the first commercial browsers were developed to aid in navigating the so-called Internet. Within just a few years, the computer revolution moved from hardware to software to a fully interactive form of communications and storage with the clarity and resolution of a television. By the mid-1990s, people were communicating across global networks more easily than with neighbors and more inexpensively than with local phone calls.

The change created a whole new generation of wealth. Old stalwart CEOs from the top industries, like General Motors, Royal Dutch Shell, or Merck, were soon dwarfed monetarily by Michael Dell (a hardware maker), Bill Gates (a software maker), and Jeff Bezos (creator of Amazon.com). Ac-

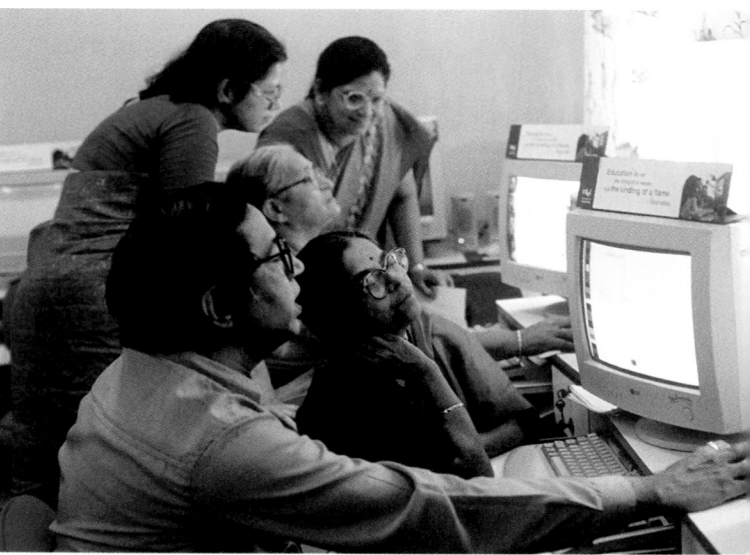

Computers and India. Programmers trained by Indian educational institutions became commonplace in the computer industry worldwide, and many became successful as entrepreneurs in Silicon Valley.

cordingly, a boom in shares of Internet firms, known as dot-coms, swept the world's stock markets. In 2000, Gates's Microsoft had a market capitalization that was the size of Spain's robust GDP (around $600 billion). Money from these companies flowed globally as these businesses established offices around the world. Software and Internet technologies developed enormous economies of scale and thus became prone to monopolization. Monoliths emerged by taking over smaller companies.

Hardware, software, and the Internet were by no means purely American innovations. Within a few years of their invention, personal computers were made in Mexico, and computer chips were mass-produced in Taiwan. The brains behind the Internet were less likely to be Ivy League graduates than students from Indian institutes of technology, especially the one located in Bombay. Originally devised as engineering schools to create the knowledge needed to modernize India, these institutes trained a whole generation of pioneering computing engineers, many of whom resettled in the Silicon Valley in the United States. By 1996, Indians had taken half of the 55,000 temporary work visas issued by the U.S. government for high-tech employees. Roughly half of the Silicon Valley start-up companies in the late 1990s were the brainchildren of Indian entrepreneurs.

While this revolution gave people new means to communicate, share, and sell information, it also reinforced hierarchies between the haves and the have-nots. Great swathes of the world's population living outside the big cities were left beyond the reach of the Internet. According to World Bank calculations, in the late 1990s, countries with low-income economies had, on average, 26 phone lines per 1,000 people; countries with high-income economies had 550 per 1,000 people. In 1996, the ratio of Internet users in countries with rich economies versus countries with poor economies was over 10,000 to 1. The real losers were the billions living in rural areas or towns neglected by state and private communications providers. The have-nots were poor not just because they had no capital but because they had no access to knowledge or to the new communications media. The result was a widening gap between rich and poor. In 1870, the average American made nine times what the average African earned; by 1990, an American earned forty-five times the income of someone in Chad or Ethiopia. From 1990, as the forces of globalization intensified, world inequities became massive. The haves never had it so good; the have-nots never were more miserable. Thus, globalization paradoxically integrated the world's peoples ever more tightly and at the same time intensified the disparities among them.

CHARACTERISTICS OF THE NEW GLOBAL ORDER

→ *What are the characteristics of the new global order?*

By 2000, population migrations, international banking, expanded international trade, and technical breakthroughs in communications had contributed to increasing integration and to the creation of new power arrangements within and between societies. Around the world, globalization developed a number of clearly recognizable social and economic characteristics. The world's population expanded dramatically, requiring greater industrial and agricultural output that came from all parts of the world. Families changed dramatically, and people's lifespans increased. Decent education and good health determined one's status in society as never before. In general, while giving people access to an unimaginable array of goods, services, and culture, globalization also deepened world inequalities, widening age-old divisions between the rich and the poor, the haves and the have-nots.

THE DEMOGRAPHY OF GLOBALIZATION

It took 160 years (1800–1960) for the world's population to increase from 1 billion to 3 billion; in the next 40 years (1960–2000), it jumped from 3 billion to over 6 billion. Behind this steepening curve were two important developments: the decline in mortality, especially among children, and a rise in life expectancy.

Population growth was hardly equal across the globe (see Map 21-4). In Europe, population growth peaked around 1900, and it moved upward only gradually from 400 million to 730 million during the twentieth century, with little growth after the 1970s. In North America, population quadrupled over the same century but rose mainly because of immigration. The population booms in the twentieth century occurred in Asia (400 percent), Africa (550 percent), and Latin America (700 percent). China and India each passed the billion-person mark. Increases were greatest in the cities. By the 1980s, the world's largest cities were no longer European and North American, but Asian, African, and Latin American. Greater Tokyo-Yokohama had 30 million inhabitants, while Mexico City had 20 million, São Paulo 17 million, Calcutta 15 million, Cairo 16 million, and Jakarta 12 million.

Population growth slowed the most in richer societies. For some, like Italy, the growth rate declined to zero. More recently enriched societies like Korea, Taiwan, and Hong Kong also had fewer births. The societies that did not see their birthrates decline by the same rate—much of Africa, southern Asia, and impoverished parts of Latin America—had great difficulty raising income levels. But even among the poor nations, birthrates have declined since the 1970s.

The most remarkable turnaround in fertility rates occurred in China, the world's most populous country. In the 1950s and 1960s, the annual growth rate of the Chinese population was in excess of 2 percent. In the 1980s, it was down, according to the official count, to just above 1.4 percent.

Family Planning in China. To control China's burgeoning population, the government tried to enforce a "one-child family" policy after 1979. While the policy has generally been effective, its impact varies in different places and times, and disparity can often be found between urban and rural areas. Recent market reforms, moreover, have further eroded government control. Shown on this giant billboard from the city of Wuhan in 1996 is a propaganda slogan that says "Family planning is the need of mankind." Beneath the slogan is the image of an ideal family, with its single child being, significantly, a girl.

MAP 21-4 WORLD POPULATION INCREASES, 1950–1997

The population of the world more than doubled between 1950 and 1997, rising from approximately 2.5 billion to nearly 6 billion. Which countries exhibited the largest population increases over these five decades? Can you speculate on why these countries experienced such high population increases? Why did western Europe and Russia have the lowest population increases?

The demographic shift did not occur by choice. After 1979, China tried to enforce a "one-child family" policy, with rewards for compliance and penalties for transgression. Cash subsidies, preferential access to nurseries and kindergartens, priority in medical care, and the promise of favored treatment in the allocation of housing, education, and employment were used as inducements in the one-child campaign. The policy also contributed to the increasing imbalance in sex ratio at birth, which currently stands at about 117–120 boys to 100 girls. The bias in favor of sons, long regarded as vital in the patrilineal system (descent through the male line) in China, together with the availability of inexpensive and portable ultrasound scanners since the 1980s, has been responsible for the widespread, albeit illegal, practice of prenatal sex selection.

In general, however, the decline in family size resulted from choice, not coercion. In rich countries, more and more women chose to defer having children. Education, career prospects, and birth control devices—the contraceptive "pill" in particular—created incentives for women to pursue other ways of life before starting a family. One important part of

this change was to make love a precondition to marriage and family formation. While this had been a romantic ideal for centuries, reality now conformed more completely to the ideal.

FAMILIES The legal definition of families became more fluid in this period than at any time in modern history. Here again, the change reflected women's choices and the relationship between love and marriage. First, couples chose to end their marriages at historically unprecedented rates. In the United States, for example, the divorce rate doubled between 1970 and 1998—at the end of the twentieth century, one in two marriages ended in divorce. In Belgium and Britain in the last decades of the twentieth century, fewer than half of all marriages survived. So, too, in China the divorce rate soared. In a large city such as Beijing, at the century's end it was reportedly close to 25 percent, double the 1990 rate. Notably, as of 2000, more than 70 percent of the divorces were initiated by women.

As marriages became shorter-lived, new forms of child-rearing proliferated. In the United States, out-of-wedlock

Wedding Ceremonies. (*Left*) At this Hindu ceremony in northern India, the union of bride and groom is symbolized by the knot between their clothes. (*Right*) South Korean Kim Jong-bok hugs his bride, Song Hee-jung, during their wedding ceremony on the Tokto islets off the Korean peninsula in 2005. Traditional martial arts performer Kim and stage actress Song held their wedding on Tokto to protest Japan's claim over the islets.

childbirths accounted for one-third of all births in the late 1990s, with only about half of American children living in households with both parents (compared with nearly three-quarters of children in the early 1970s). Europeans, too, including the supposedly more traditional Italians and Greeks, also abandoned nuclear family conventions. In those European countries where divorce remained difficult, more and more couples opted to live together without getting married.

AGING Longer lifespans also affected family fortunes. More infants survived childhood and lived to be old—in some areas very old. Along with other industrialized nations, the population of the United States "grayed" considerably. Fewer children and longer-living adults resulted in a marked increase in the median age of the American population. In 1970, half of

all Americans were twenty-eight or under. By 1990, the median age had risen to thirty-four. Likewise, the percentage of Americans over the age of sixty-five grew from 8 percent in 1950 to 13 percent in 1990. In western Europe and Japan, graying rates were even more marked. In Japan, the birthrate plummeted, and the citizenry aged at such a rate that the country began to depopulate. From a population of 127 million in 2000, estimates forecast a decline to 105 million by 2050.

The aging of the world's population presented new challenges for families. For centuries, being a parent meant providing for children until they could be self-sufficient. Old age, the years of relatively unproductive labor, was brief. Communities and households absorbed the cost of caring for the elderly. Household savings, if any, became family bequests to future, not older, generations. But as societies aged, retirees turned to society's savings to survive. Public and private pension funds swelled to accommodate the need for future pools of money for the retired. In Germany, over 30 percent of the government's social policy spending was earmarked for the state pension fund. Chinese demographers warned that the one-child family threatened to create an unbalanced population structure. In a society in which the safety net was still largely assumed by the family, many worried that each able-bodied person may potentially have to support two parents and four grandparents.

In Africa, where publicly supported pension funds were rare, the aged faced more dire futures. In an earlier age the elderly, especially men, were thought to be the fount of wisdom. Colonial rule and the postcolonial world, however, elevated the position of the young, especially those who had acquired western educations and were able to earn western-style livings. Then, in the 1970s, as birthrates began to soar, the demand on family resources to care for infants and children rose, at the very moment in which society's resource base began to shrink. The elderly could no longer work, but neither could they rely on the household's support.

HEALTH The distribution of contagious diseases also exemplified the inequities of the globalized world. On the surface, the spread of diseases would suggest that historically little had changed. After all, the Black Death of the fourteenth century was a pan–Afro-Eurasian epidemic, while after 1492 the spread of European maladies catastrophically reduced Native American populations across the Americas. It remains true that microbes have no respect for national,

linguistic, or religious borders. Still, the incidence of world diseases reveals a great deal about how human lives changed. Public health regulations, antibiotics, and vaccination campaigns reduced the spread of contagions. By the late twentieth century, not only did nutrition and healthy habits count, as they always had, but so did access to medicines. What used to be universal afflictions in 1300, 1500, and 1850 were becoming more peculiar to particular peoples. Water treatment and proper sewerage, for example, had banished cholera from most urban centers by the middle of the twentieth century. In more recent decades, however, its deadly impact again reached across Asia and into the eastern Mediterranean, parts of Latin America, and much of sub-Saharan Africa. From the 1970s, Africa suffered widespread and frequent outbreaks of the disease. The crucial cause of the re-spread of cholera was the failure of urban developers to keep sanitation systems growing apace with the demand for water. Thus, diseases proliferated where urban squalor was most acute—in cities with the greatest post-1970s population growth.

The global redistribution of sickness became more than a matter of combating old diseases. In the 1970s, entirely new diseases appeared and began to devastate the world's population. This is best exemplified by a disease called Acquired Immunodeficiency Syndrome (AIDS), which can be transmitted through contact with the semen or blood of an infected person. AIDS, in time, compromises the ability of the infected person's immune system to ward off disease. First detected by a drug technician at Atlanta's Centers for Disease Control and Prevention in early 1981, AIDS was initially stigmatized as a "gay cancer" (at the outset appearing primarily in homosexual men) and received little attention. As the

AIDS Treatment and Education. *(Left)* At the Thirteenth International AIDS Conference in Durban, South Africa, in July 2000, AIDS activists express their displeasure at the high prices and unavailability of life-saving drugs for most of those in the Third World who are affected by AIDS. *(Right)* African governments have not tackled the problem of AIDS in their severely affected continent with the energy that it warrants. Pictured here, however, a doctor seeks to impress on the youth of a local community how they should conduct their social and sexual lives in light of the AIDS crisis.

disease spread to heterosexuals and public awareness about it increased, a new campaign urged the practice of safe sex, control of blood stocks, and restrictions on sharing hypodermic needles. In Europe and North America, where the campaigns intensified in the late 1980s and new drugs were developed to keep the virus under control, AIDS rates began to stabilize, though in its first two decades AIDS killed 12 million people, 2.6 million in 1999 alone.

Although doctors developed new treatments, these were very expensive, leaving the poor and disadvantaged still vulnerable to infection. For the poor, therefore, most treatments remained out of reach. By 2000, 33 million people had AIDS, the vast majority in poor countries, and even more were infected with HIV, the human immunodeficiency virus that causes AIDS (see Map 21-5). No fewer than two-thirds of those with AIDS lived in Africa below the Sahara. In Botswana, a quarter of the adult population was infected. In India, 7 million carried the virus; in China, the figure topped 1 million.

The expense of medical care was not the only factor in explaining the geographical and demographic prevalence of AIDS. Schooling and literacy played an important role in health promotion, especially in AIDS prevention. Better education led to safer sexual practices. Around the world, more educated men and women showed higher use of condoms. One Tanzanian survey showed that 20 percent of women with four to five years of education insisted that their sexual partners used condoms, whereas only 6 percent of women with no education insisted on the use of condoms during sex with a casual partner.

EDUCATION Access to decent education increasingly separated the haves from the have-nots. Moreover, because educational opportunities often tilted in favor of men, schooling shaped differences between males and females. In sub-Saharan Africa and in India, for example, where men typically receive more formal education than women, literacy rates in these two regions were 63 and 64 percent for men

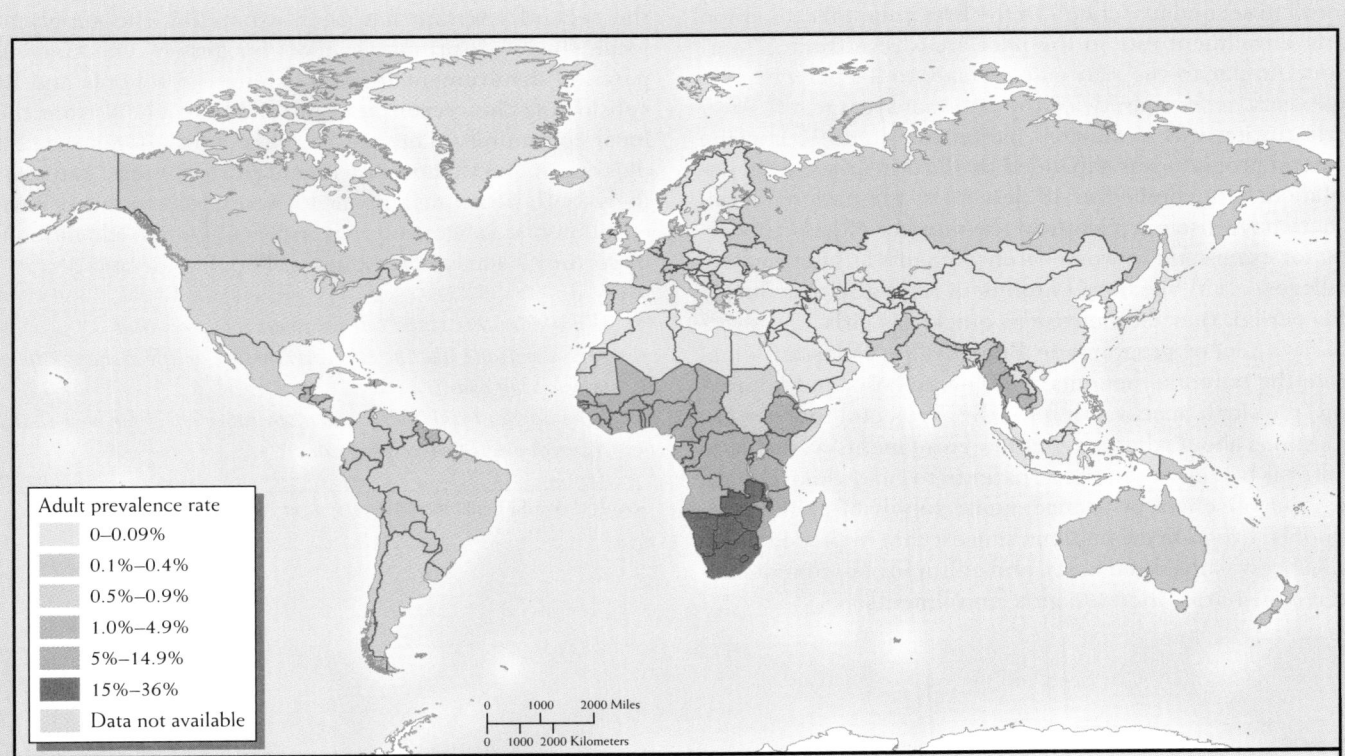

Adult prevalence rate
- 0–0.09%
- 0.1%–0.4%
- 0.5%–0.9%
- 1.0%–4.9%
- 5%–14.9%
- 15%–36%
- Data not available

0   1000   2000 Miles
0   1000   2000 Kilometers

MAP 21-5   HIV INFECTION ACROSS THE WORLD, 1999

HIV, which leads to AIDS, spread across the whole world, further evidence of global interconnectedness in the late twentieth century. The outbreak of HIV began in Africa. Which countries outside the African continent have had the highest rates of infection, and why is this so? Why have the highest infection rates occurred in Africa south of the Sahara? Why have Egypt, North Africa, and much of the rest of the Islamic world, despite their close connections with Africa below the Sahara, thus far been little affected?

Primary Source

EDUCATION AND INEQUALITY: WHY GENDER MATTERS

In the 1970s, aid agencies recognized that reducing world poverty means improving educational opportunities. International organizations urged national governments to plow resources into schools. The results were stunning. But a disparity appeared: the beneficiaries were mainly boys. So, beginning in the 1980s, aid organizations, influenced by the growing strength of world feminism, became especially active in trying to channel educational opportunities to girls. In this World Bank study, researchers found that development among the poor improves not just with better education, but especially with better education for girls.

Evaluations of recent initiatives that subsidize the costs of schooling indicate that demand-side interventions can increase girls' enrollments and close gender gaps in education. A school stipend program established in Bangladesh in 1982 subsidizes various school expenses for girls who enroll in secondary school. In the first program evaluation girls' enrollment rate in the pilot areas rose from 27 percent, similar to the national average, to 44 percent over five years, more than twice the national average. . . . After girls' tuition was eliminated nationwide in 1992 and the stipend program was expanded to all rural areas, girls' enrollment rate climbed to 48 percent at the national level. There have also been gains in the number of girls appearing for exams and in women's enrollments at intermediate colleges. . . . While boys' enrollment rates also rose during this period, they did not rise as quickly as girls'.

Two recent programs in Balochistan, Pakistan, illustrate the potential benefits of reducing costs and improving physical access. Before the projects there were questions about whether girls' low enrollments were due to cultural barriers that cause parents to hold their daughters out of school or to inadequate supply of appropriate schools. Program evaluations suggest that improved physical access, subsidized costs, and culturally appropriate design can sharply increase girls' enrollments.

The first program, in Quetta, the capital of Balochistan, uses a subsidy tied to girls' enrollment to support the creation of schools in poor urban neighborhoods by local NGOs. The schools admit boys as long as they make up less than half of total enrollments. In rural Balochistan the second program has been expanding the supply of local, single-sex primary schools for girls by encouraging parental involvement in establishing the schools and by subsidizing the recruitment of female teachers from the local community. The results: girls' enrollments rose 33 percent in Quetta and 22 percent in rural areas. Interestingly, both programs appear to have also expanded boys' enrollments, suggesting that increasing girls' educational opportunities may have spillover benefits for boys.

> → *What does this study tell us about the ways that organizations like the World Bank try to affect change in developing countries?*
> → *Why do you think there was a spillover effect for boys that coincided with these programs?*

SOURCE: World Bank, *World Development Report*, 2000–2001.

and only 39 and 40 percent for women as of 2000. In the Arab world, the literacy gap between men and women has decreased in recent years. Still, in most Arab countries adult male literacy is between 15 and 20 percent greater than female literacy.

The generally low levels of literacy overall and the depressed levels for women in particular continued to be major impediments to each region's efforts to combat poverty. Gender bias also remained present in rich societies. For decades, however, women and girls pressed for equal access, with some astounding results. In the United States, women spent more time in school as well as more time in the workforce in this period than they did in the past. By the late 1980s, more than half of all college degrees were granted to women (up from 38 percent in 1960). Even more dramatic was the rise in proportion of women among those earning postgraduate degrees (up from 3 percent to 35 percent). In China, women made even more enormous strides, although they also continued to hit roadblocks. Ironically, with the recent market reforms, women's access to basic education regressed, as families, particularly in the rural areas, reverted to the practice of spending their limited resources educating sons rather than daughters. Thus, in 2000, as many as 70 percent of China's 140 million illiterates were female.

WORK Although women were holding jobs outside the home in increasing numbers, they faced obstacles to full equity at work. Limited by job discrimination and by burdens of child-rearing, women's participation in the workforce reached a fairly stable level by the 1980s. Roughly one-quarter to one-half of adult women across the world worked for a cash income. In Russia and Mexico, middle-class women opted for professional careers. Like their cousins elsewhere, they often encountered informal obstacles to many careers and found themselves channeled into feminized professions, such as nursing, teaching, and marketing. The percentage of women at the top of the corporate pyramid was considerably smaller than their overall participation in the labor force or even than their college graduation rates. In 1995, the Chinese government claimed that Chinese women had made better advances than their U.S. counterparts—it stated that there were more Chinese women (10 percent) than American women (3 percent) in senior managerial posts, defined as directors of enterprises or institutes. Still, Chinese women graduates consistently complained of discrimination in the job market. In 2000, some 60 percent of China's unemployed were women, and the number was growing. Women around the world faced difficulties breaking through the "glass ceiling"—a seemingly invisible barrier to advancement. Consequently, while income disparities between men and women narrowed, a significant gap persisted.

Working outside the home created problems for handling work inside the home. Who would take care of the children? Jamaican and Filipino women migrated by the thousands in the 1970s and 1980s to Canada and Australia to work as nannies to raise money to send back home, where they had often left their own children. In South Africa and Brazil, domestic servants and nannies came from local sources. They were doing the jobs that once belonged to middle- and upper-class homemaking women, women who now wanted the same rights as men: to parent *and* to work.

FEMINISM The deeply ingrained inequality between men and women prompted calls for change. Feminist movements

African Women and Education. Though women's education has lagged behind that of men in Africa, a number of women, like Stella Kenyi, pictured above, have graduated from African high schools and attended universities at home or abroad. Kenyi is teaching business skills to men and women in Sudan after completing an undergraduate degree at Davidson College in North Carolina.

arose mainly in Europe and in North America in the 1960s to call attention to the unequal treatment of men and women. The movement started to become global in the 1970s. In 1975, the first truly international women's forum was held in Mexico City. But becoming global did not necessarily imply running roughshod over local customs. Across the world, what feminists called for was not the abolition of gender differences, but equal treatment—equal pay and equal opportunities for obtaining jobs and advancement.

Women took increasingly active stances against discrimination. Across the world, countries passed laws to combat discrimination in government and in the workplace. Indeed, as economic integration across borders intensified with regional trade pacts, usually negotiated by men in the interest of male-owned and male-run firms, women struggled to ensure that economic globalization did not cut them out of new opportunities. For instance, after Argentina, Uruguay, Paraguay, and Brazil negotiated the Mercosur free trade pact, the traffic across South American borders soared. But as trade grew, so did the governments' efforts to monitor the illegal commerce and foster licit trade along new highways and across new bridges. One kind of illicit commerce was conducted by women, who for generations had transported goods back and forth across the river separating Argentina and Paraguay. At the Argentine-Paraguayan border, customs officers tried to stop this transport. In response, in the mid-1990s, Argentine and Paraguayan women locked arms to occupy the new bridge that male truckers used to ship Mercosur products, protesting the increasing restrictions on their age-old enterprise.

This rising tide of global feminism culminated in a conference in Beijing in September 1995. More than 4,000 government delegates from more than 180 countries met there for the Fourth World Conference on Women, the largest gathering of its kind, to produce "a platform for action" on policies regarding women's rights in politics, business, education, and health. More impressive, alongside the official conference, there was a parallel conference for close to 30,000 representatives at the Non-Governmental Organizations (NGOs) Forum for Women. These grassroots activists represented 2,000 NGOs from literally every corner of the globe. Despite the persistent harassment of the Chinese security apparatus, which was suspicious of any discussions that touched on issues of human rights, the representatives were able to exchange ideas, plan strategies, and coordinate programs on how to improve the living and working conditions of women. What emerged from the conference were associations and groups that were ready and determined to lobby for the rights of women and girls around the world.

PRODUCTION AND CONSUMPTION IN THE GLOBAL ECONOMY

The growth of the world's population, the desire for more education and better health, the entry of women into paid employment, and the promise of rising standards of living resulted in the accelerated production and consumption of the world's resources at an astonishing rate. The most immediate challenge was how to feed all these people (roughly 90 million additional people per year by the end of the 1990s) while developing sustainable practices that do not use up limited natural resources.

AGRICULTURAL PRODUCTION Changing agrarian practices made a huge difference in increasing food production. Starting in the 1950s, chemistry increased outputs dramatically. The "green revolution," largely involving the use of nonfarm inputs such as chemical fertilizers, herbicides, and pesticides, produced dramatically larger harvests. Then, in the 1970s, biologists took over, offering genetically engineered crops that multiplied yields at an even faster rate.

But these agrarian breakthroughs were far from evenly distributed across the globe. American farmers were the biggest innovators, and hence the greatest beneficiaries. American farms, for example, by century's end produced approximately one-ninth of the world's wheat and two-fifths of its corn. From this output, American exports accounted for about one-third of the world's international wheat trade and four-fifths of all corn exports. At the heart of the innovation was political power—farmers had the clout to force officials to maintain roads, to subsidize credit and prices, and to mop up surplus supply. Asian rice farmers made impressive innovations, too. In Taiwan and Korea, chemical and biological breakthroughs allowed rice yields to jump by 53 and 132 percent respectively between 1965 and 1985. Indian wheat farmers also deployed chemical fertilizers and new seed varieties and built irrigation systems to double their output. The Ganges River basin became able to feed an ever larger urban population. The most miraculous transformation occurred in China in the wake of the reforms of Deng Xiaoping. Beginning in the late 1970s, the Chinese government broke up some of the old collective farms and restored the primacy of the individual household as the basic economic unit in rural areas. In the wake of the reforms, the value of agricultural output surged by an average rate of 9 percent per year between 1978 and 1986.

Other agricultural producers also replied to world demand, but in some areas their added production was disruptive. While biology and chemistry allowed some farmers to get more out of their land, other farmers simply opened up new lands to cultivation. This pattern of extensive land use was, in many respects, cheaper and involved less reliance on nonfarm inputs. Moreover, it reflected the relative weakness of small farmers who, bereft of access to credit, seed, and especially land, had to go where land was cheap to make their living. In Java, farmers cleared the sloping forest land to make way for coffee. In southern Colombia, peasants moved into semitropical woodlands to cultivate coca bushes (the source of cocaine) at profits that other cultivators could not expect to realize. The most notorious frontier expansion took place in the Amazon River basin. Populations flocked to the Amazon frontier, largely from impoverished areas in northeastern Brazil. They cleared (by fire) cheap land, staked their claims,

Forum on Women. Women representing different cultures of the world hold a "peace torch" during the opening ceremony of the Non-Governmental Organizations Forum for Women in Beijing in 1995.

and, like nineteenth-century American homesteaders, tried to move up the social ladder by cultivating crops and raising livestock. But the promise of bounty failed: the soils were poor and easily eroded, and their land titles provided little security, especially once large speculators moved into the area. So the frontiersmen pulled up their stakes and moved farther inland to repeat the cycle. By the 1980s, the migrants to the Amazon River basin had burned away much of the jungle in clearing the area, contaminated the biosphere (the environment in which life exists), reduced the world's stock of diverse plant and animal life, and fostered social conflict in the Brazilian hinterland between the haves and the have-nots.

Nor were breadbaskets always able to feed exploding populations. This was especially true in Africa from the 1970s onward, when the region became a major importer of foodstuffs because domestic food production could not keep pace with population growth (see Map 21-6). Food shortages, rare in Africa before the 1970s, thereafter increased in frequency and duration, wiping out large numbers of sub-Saharan peoples. The protruding ribs on African children became a

clichéd image of the region as the first and second generations of the "green revolution" largely bypassed Africa. What explained Africa's famines? As the Indian Nobel Prize–winning economist Amartya Sen observed, famines—and their increasing frequency—are not natural disasters; they are man-made. Food shortages in Africa stemmed in large measure from governments that ignored the rural sector and its politically unorganized farmers. Unable to persuade the government to raise the prices that were paid for their crops, the farmers lacked incentives to expand their production. Food shortages were also by-products of global inequities. African countries, compelled to earmark hefty chunks of their economies to agrarian exports to pay for debts incurred in the 1970s, were unable to produce enough foodstuffs domestically and became food importers.

NATURAL RESOURCES While American farmers in this period produced a large share of the world's food, Americans also consumed a high proportion of the globe's natural resources. By 2000, Americans were using water at a per-capita

MAP 21-6   FOOD CONSUMPTION AND FAMINE SINCE THE 1940S

There is perhaps no better indicator of the division of the world into rich and poor, haves and have-nots, than this map on food consumption and famine. Which parts of the world have had the most difficulty in feeding their populations? What have been the causes of famine and malnourishment in these regions? How much have they been due to human agency, and how much to climate and other matters over which human beings have little control?

Saving the Amazon. The rise of an international environmental movement in the 1970s led to alliances with local indigenous and environmental leaders, especially in the Amazon. (*Left*) One of the most prominent figures advocating the rights of indigenous people and the need to protect imperiled jungles was the British musician Sting. Here he is pictured alongside one of the Amazon's foremost Indian leaders, Bep Koroti Paiakan. (*Right*) Farmers and ranchers cut and burn the Amazon at a ferocious rate in pursuit of frontier lands. In these remote regions, it is hard for local authorities to enforce conservation laws.

rate three times the world's average. Indeed, extensive water consumption for irrigation was crucial to the growth of California's agricultural sector, the most productive and profitable in the world. Gathering more water also allowed a desert metropolis like Los Angeles to grow; only rarely have the city's residents questioned the environmental costs of their water use.

Energy consumption presents a similar story, though America's enormous appetite for fossil fuels generated a domestic debate about reliance on foreign sources and the pollution of the environment. In the United States and Canada, attempts to curb energy consumption met with little success, and the United States grew more dependent on imported oil. In the late 1990s, North American demand for fuel-guzzling Sport Utility Vehicles (SUVs) took off, intensifying oil imports. Dependence on foreign sources of precious fuel locked oil importers into recurring clashes with oil exporters. In the 1970s, OPEC established an effective cartel to raise the price of crude oil (see Chapter 20). The cartel weakened in the 1980s, in part because new oil fields emerged elsewhere in the world, increasing supply, and because internal struggles divided the exporters. The most bitter conflict was the savage war fought in the mid-1980s between Iran and Iraq, followed by the Iraqi invasion under Saddam Hussein of neighboring Kuwait in 1990 to seize its vast oil fields. Iraq was poised to assume a dominant status in the area and thus to have considerable control over oil policies. The conquest of Kuwait would have given Iraq control over about 7 percent of world oil supplies and nearly 20 percent of the world's known re-

serves. Only Iraq's neighbors Saudi Arabia and Iran would have been larger oil exporters, and Iraq would have been in a position to menace both of them. The Americans quickly responded to restore the regional balance of oil power. Rallying a large coalition of other nations, the Americans and their allies built up a substantial military force to participate in Operation Desert Storm. The 1991 Gulf War, which ended with Iraq's expulsion from Kuwait, restored an order in which the global distribution of power favored oil consumers over producers and preserved a regional balance of power.

ENVIRONMENT The consumption of water, oil, and other natural resources increasingly became matters of international concern in the last decades of the twentieth century. So did problems associated with pollution control and the disposal of waste products. Part of this internationalization resulted from the recognition that environmental issues could not be handled by separate national exertions. Air and water, after all, do not stop flowing at political boundaries.

As Canadians saw their northern lakes fill up with "acid rain" (precipitation laced with heavy doses of sulfur, mainly from coal-fired plants), they urged their southern neighbor to curb emissions. Reciprocal agreements between Canada and the United States were signed in the 1980s. Europeans, beset by their own acidification, also negotiated regional environmental treaties. But some polluters simply moved overseas, to poorer and less politically powerful nations. As the West cleaned up its environment, the rest of the world ended up paying the price.

Likewise, the problems associated with the greenhouse effect and global warming (the release into the air of human-made carbons that contribute to the rising temperatures worldwide), as well as ocean pollution and the decline in biological diversity, crossed all man-made borders. Successive rounds of international meetings addressed these threats inconclusively. It was difficult to enforce an international solution on all national authorities when the forces of globalization compelled some of them to rely on energy-intensive industries, which generate massive emissions, in order to produce exports to pay off their debts. In 1992, the world's governments flocked to the first Earth Summit in Rio de Janeiro. But much eco-friendly fanfare yielded only ineffective accords. Several years later, world leaders again met, this time in Kyoto, Japan, to draft a plan with teeth to enforce compliance. Even the grumblers agreed that something had to be done to reverse the emission of gases that led to global warming. When the new administration of George W. Bush came to power in Washington in early 2001, one of its first decisions was to revoke the U.S. support for the Kyoto Treaty, which led others to defect as well. As a result, global climate change did not gain a global accord to reverse it.

The relationship between power and resources during this time was especially stark in dealing with contaminants. Increasing numbers of automobiles, and the attendant carbon fumes, presented serious air pollution problems in the world's cities like Los Angeles, Tokyo, Mexico City, and Jakarta. But where environmentalists acquired political power, they forced regulators to curb emissions. Starting in the late 1960s, Japanese local governments slapped pollution controls on filthy coal plants. Japan pioneered what one historian has called an "environmental miracle," spreading its regulations to many contaminating activities. By 1978, Japanese cars discharged only 10 percent as much pollution as in 1968. In 1987, Japan banned leaded gas altogether. But controls on fossil fuel emissions were dependent on power and wealth. It was much harder to impose restrictions in societies for whom high energy use was deemed a necessity of economic life. Even the Japanese pioneers of clean fuel were polluters in other spheres. With increasing controls at home, Japanese industrialists went abroad to unload Japanese hazardous waste. U.S. industrialists did the same, sending hazardous waste to Mexico. Argentina and Canada sent their nuclear detritus not abroad but to poor provinces desperate for jobs.

Environmental problems took on a new urgency after Soviet authorities revealed the meltdown of a nuclear reactor in Chernobyl in 1986. Initially, Communist authorities tried to cover up the mess, but when the fallout reached Sweden, they had to accept responsibility for the debacle. The delayed response was disastrous for Ukraine and Belarussia (present-day Belarus), which, relatively powerless under a centralized authoritarian regime, had no political voice to cry out for help from the contamination.

Chernobyl and Protest. *(Left)* Among the victims of the 1986 explosion at the Chernobyl power plant, history's worst nuclear meltdown, were firefighters, such as the man pictured here, sent in to put out the blaze. *(Right)* Chernobyl turned Mikhail Gorbachev's *glasnost,* or openness, into more than a slogan, and it became a rallying cry for the populace, which hoped for political change and improvements in daily life.

CITIZENSHIP IN THE GLOBAL WORLD

> ➔ *How did citizenship in the global world create new problems and responses?*

Globalization distributed its benefits unequally. In general, those with access to better education and more opportunities embraced the new order with enthusiasm and profited from the border-crossing freedoms it permitted. For the majority of the world's population, however, the new power structure was not so kind. Finding little opportunity in the globalized world, the disadvantaged often expressed their discontent by invoking older religious and nationalist ideals. As globalization fostered human rights, environmental and labor standards, and women's rights across the globe, critics claimed that the language of international rights and standards promotes neocolonial power in the form of a new "civilizing mission."

In particular, globalization posed massive problems for the political organization that many had expected to emerge triumphant once empires had dissolved—the nation-state. Since the nineteenth century, nation-states were supposed to play the primary role in defining the rights of citizens. The rapid movement of ideas, goods, capital, and people across national boundaries undercut the authority and legitimacy of even the most powerful and long-standing nations. Accordingly, other political spheres emerged to define and defend citizens. After the 1970s, people came to understand that international organizations often had more influence over their lives than did their own national governments. Supranational organizations became increasingly important in shaping the meaning of citizenship. This is true especially in the Third World, where nation-states struggled hardest to come to terms with globalization. In the end, however, local and regional forces made an enormous difference. Globalization implied greater integration of the world's societies, but it has not meant that all societies look the same. The world may have become increasingly together, but in decisive ways, it still remained apart.

SUPRANATIONAL ORGANIZATIONS

A variety of international bodies came into existence following the end of World War II for the purpose of facilitating

After the 1970s, people came to understand that international organizations often had more influence over their lives than did their own national governments.

global activities. Although these organizations often successfully dealt with crisis situations, they also impinged on the autonomy of all but the most powerful states. Most prominent and powerful of the financial organizations are the World Bank and the IMF. They provided vital economic assistance to poorer nations, financing and providing essential technical information for some of the largest development programs in the Third World, as well as handling financial crises that could have brought on a new world depression. The World Bank provided funds for the large Volta River Project in Ghana to create an electrical power grid, as well as a system of national parks in the Philippines to help indigenous people manage rain forests, coral reefs, and other threatened ecological zones. Nonetheless, the World Bank tied its financial assistance to demands that recipient governments implement far-reaching economic reform packages, which were often resented. Not infrequently, World Bank and IMF-imposed programs required local governments to abolish subsidies for essential foodstuffs, leading to riots and demands to defy these international groups as agents of a new kind of imperialism.

Another set of supranational bodies, called nongovernmental organizations (NGOs), also stepped forward in the last several decades of the twentieth century. Many sought to champion human rights around the world or to call attention to environmental problems that cross national boundaries. Others, like the International Committee of the Red Cross, an older organization once dedicated mainly to war relief, became more active in peacetime, sheltering the homeless or providing food for famine victims. What united NGOs was not so much their goals but how they pursued them: autonomously from state power. NGOs created a layer of international forces that rivaled the political power of nation-states. They joined other international organizations, like the United Nations or the IMF, to make up a set of actors operating on a worldwide scale.

International NGOs reached a new level of influence in the 1970s because most of the world's nation-states at that time were still not democracies. Of the 121 countries in the world in 1980, only 37 were democracies, accounting for only 35 percent of the world population. People found it difficult to rely on authoritarians to uphold their rights as citizens. So much of the lofty language of the United Nations—like the 1948 Universal Declaration of Human Rights, "the Magna Carta for Mankind," in Eleanor Roosevelt's words—rang hollow. Indeed, the United Nations itself was a latecomer to enforcing human rights provisions, largely because its own members were the self-same authoritarians.

NGOs, then, took the lead in trying to make the language of human rights stick. The brutality of the military regimes in

Latin America inspired the emerging network of international human rights organizations to take action. After the overthrow of Chile's Salvador Allende in 1973, solidarity groups proliferated to protest the new military junta's harsh repression. When the Argentine military began killing tens of thousands of innocent civilians in 1976 and news of their refined torture techniques began to leak out, human rights movements again took action. Prominent among them was a relatively small organization called Amnesty International. Formed in 1961 by a British lawyer, Peter Benenson, to defend the cause of prisoners of conscience (detained for their beliefs, color, sex, ethnic origin, language, or religion), Amnesty International catalogued these human rights violations across the world. From these efforts, it went on to become one of the most influential and largest human rights organizations in the world. Moreover, even American foundations saw the importance of NGOs. The biggest of them all, the Ford Foundation, initiated support for human rights groups and research. By 2000, there was an extensive network of associations informing the public, lobbying governments, and pressuring the United Nations, and its member nations, to live up to commitments to respect the rights of citizens.

Bosnia in the Midst of War. Despite extensive destruction and perpetual sniper fire, the multiethnic population of Sarajevo refused to abandon their city. With the help of U.N. soldiers and aid workers, they kept alive the hope for the peaceful coexistence of Muslims, Serbs, and Croats in Bosnia.

VIOLENCE

International organizations and NGOs could play only a limited role in preserving peace and strengthening human rights. The end of the cold war left entire regions in such political turmoil that even the most effective humanitarian agencies could not prevent mass killings, as became terrifyingly apparent in the Balkans in the 1990s. In the territorial remains of Yugoslavia, Serbs, Croats, Bosnians, ethnic Albanians, and others fought for control. Former neighbors, fueled by the heated rhetoric of opportunistic leaders, no longer saw themselves as citizens of pluralistic political communities. Instead, demagogues trumpeted the superiority of ethnically-defined states. Serbians took up arms against their Croat neighbors, and vice versa. International agencies moved in to try to bolster public authority. They, too, failed as Yugoslavia's ethnic mosaic imploded into an ugly civil war. The Dayton Accords of 1995 ended the bloodshed by partitioning Bosnia and assigning a number of international organizations to maintain peace, but in 1999 Serbia president Slobodan Milosevic sent troops in to suppress unrest in the province of Kosovo; only NATO airstrikes on Serbia's capital, Belgrade, convinced Milosevic to back down. The International Court in the Hague charged Milosevic of war crimes and crimes against humanity; he died while defending himself in 2006.

The Balkan tragedy was not an exception. Indeed, by the late twentieth century, with the end of the cold war and increasing economic integration among nations, most warfare was conducted not between states, but within them, with devastating consequences for innocent civilians. Between 1989

and 1992, eighty-three armed conflicts erupted. All but three were civil wars, and 90 percent of the casualties were civilian. By 1995, the world had 42 million displaced people; another 160 million were victims of disasters; and 2 billion lived in conditions of abject poverty.

The most gruesome political violence in the global age occurred in Africa—where nation-states capable of upholding stability and the rule of law for all citizens were weakest. In Africa, the tension was often expressed as a conflict between ethnic groups. The crisis of African agriculture, its inability to sustain growing populations, and conflicts over unequal access to important resources like education exacerbated underlying ethnic rivalries. Droughts, famine, and corruption led the rivalries to explode into riots and killings, or even to bitter civil war and the breakdown of centralized authority. In Rwanda, for example, friction grew between the majority Hutus (agrarian people, often very poor) and the minority Tutsis (herders, often with better education and more wealth), after the two peoples had intermarried and lived side by side for many generations. Some resentful Hutus blamed the Tutsis for all their woes. As tensions mounted, the United Nations dispatched 2,500 peacekeeping troops. Moderate Hutus urged peaceful coexistence, only to be shouted down by government forces in command of radio stations and a mass propaganda machine. Alerted to the impending problem, the Clinton administration blocked the U.N. Security Council in 1993 and 1994 from taking emergency actions. The international forces, fearing a clash, withdrew their troops, leaving a rump force. International involvement was

Rwandan Refugees. Perhaps as many as 800,000 Tutsis were killed in 1994 as the Hutus turned against the local Tutsi population while Rwanda was being invaded by a Tutsi-led army from Uganda. Not surprisingly, the massacre led to an enormous refugee crisis.

thus downright destructive; the decision first to get involved, then to disengage, gave the Hutu government a green light to wipe out opponents. In one hundred days of carnage in 1994, Hutu militias massacred 800,000 Tutsis and moderate Hutus. This was not, as many proclaimed, the militarization of ancient ethnic rivalries: many Hutus were butchered as they tried to defend friends, relatives, and neighbors. Meanwhile, the refugee crisis that ensued, first of terrorized Tutsis, then of fleeing armed Hutus, destabilized a dozen African neighbors and heightened tensions in Burundi and the Congo. The civil war in Rwanda sent riptides across eastern and central Africa, creating a whole new generation of conflicts.

Some societies, however, endeavored to put political violence behind them. In some of the most heinous cases of human rights abuse, in Argentina, El Salvador, Guatemala, and South Africa, the transition to democracy compelled elected rulers to establish inquiries to look into past violations. These "truth" commissions were vital instruments for creating a new aura of legitimacy for democracies and for promising to uphold the rights of individuals to live free from arbitrary authority. In South Africa, many blacks backed the new president Nelson Mandela, but they also demanded a reckoning with the punitive experience of the apartheid past. To avoid a backlash against the former white rulers, the South African leadership opted to record the events of the past rather than avenge them. Truth, the new leaders argued, would be powerful enough to heal old wounds. The Truth and Reconciliation Commission, under the chairmanship of Nobel Peace Prize winner Bishop Desmond Tutu, called on all who had been involved in political crimes, whites as well

as blacks, to come before its tribunal and speak the truth. Although the truth alone did not fully settle old scores in South Africa, a more open discussion of the importance of basic liberties helped create new legitimate bonds between public authority and citizens.

RELIGIOUS FOUNDATIONS OF POLITICS

Secular concerns for human rights and international peace were not the only foundations for politics after the cold war. In many regions, people sought to give a new role to religion to define the moral fabric of political communities. Indeed, very often, religion provided a way to reimagine the nation-state, just as globalization undermined national autonomy.

In India, Hindu nationalism offered a communal identity for a country rapidly transformed by the forces of globalization. In the 1980s, India freed market forces, privatized state firms, and withdrew from its role as welfare provider. Economic reforms under the ruling Congress Party sparked economic growth, creating in the process Asia's largest, best-educated, and most affluent middle class. But these changes also widened the gap between the rich and the poor. Lower classes and castes formed political parties to challenge the dominant position of traditional elites. With established hierarchies and loyalties eroding under the pressure of economic change, right-wing Hindu nationalists argued that religion could now fill the role once occupied by a secular state. Arguing that the ideology of Hindutva (Hinduness) would bring the help that secular nationalism had failed to give, Hindu militants aggressively promoted the idea of India as a nation of Hindus (the majority), with minorities relegated to a lesser status in the political community.

The chief political beneficiary of the politics established by economic liberalization was a Hindu nationalist party, the Bhartiya Janata Party (BJP), or Indian People's Party. The BJP was the political arm of an alliance of Hindu organizations devoted to establishing the Indian nation-state as a Hindu state. Until the mid-1980s, the BJP and other like-minded parties were influential, though not dominant, players in Indian politics. By the late 1980s, however, they rose to dominance, relentlessly advancing an antiminority (chiefly anti-Muslim) ideology. Claiming that the state had consistently and systematically appeased the minorities and trampled on the rights of the majority, they called upon Hindus to overthrow "pseudo secularism." This communal ideology proved to be a winning formula in competitive electoral politics, and by 1998, a BJP coalition came to power under the leadership of A. B. Vajpayee, reducing the century-old Congress Party to an ineffectual opposition party. Hindu nationalists sought to transform the secular nation-state into a moral community but without challenging the economic forces of globalization.

In some cases, religion provided a way to resist what has been seen as American-dominated globalization. One of the most spirited challenges to globalism arose in the Islamic Middle East. Significant segments of the people of that region believed that the modernizing and westernizing programs being enacted in their region were leading their societies toward rampant materialism and unchecked individualism. The critics included traditional clerics and young western-educated elites whose job prospects seemed bleak and those who had become convinced that the promise of modernization had failed. Having criticized modernizing processes since the nineteenth century, Islamic conservatives flourished once more in the 1970s, as global markets and social dislocations undermined the moral foundations of secular leadership.

The most explosive and revolutionary of the Islamic movements took place in Iran, where clerics organized opposition against the shah and forced him from power in 1979. The revolt seemed to pit unequal forces against each other: a cadre of religious officials possessing only pamphlets, tracts, and tapes against the military arsenal and the vast intelligence apparatus that served the Iranian state. Shah Mohammad Reza Pahlavi had enjoyed unstinting U.S. technical and military support since the Americans had helped to place him on the throne of Iran in 1953. His bloated army and police force, as well as brutally effective intelligence service, had crushed all challenges to his authority. The shah also had benefited from infusions of oil revenues after 1973. Yet, the maldistribution of income, the oppression of a police state, and the public ostentation of the royal family fueled widespread discontent. As the discontent rose, so did the levels of repression. And as repression intensified, so did the impression that the government had abandoned the people. The most vociferous critique of the shah's rule came from Islamic quarters, mullahs (Muslim scholars or religious teachers) who found in the Ayatollah Ruhollah Khomeini a courageous and ob-durate leader. Khomeini used his traditional Islamic education and his training in Muslim ethics to attack the shah and to accuse his

American Hostage Crisis in Iran. The United States was stunned in 1979 by Iran's Islamic Revolution, which overthrew the shah and brought the exiled cleric Ayatollah Ruhollah Khomeini to power. After radical students captured the U.S. embassy, as well as fifty-three hostages, an American rescue raid failed, leading to celebration by Iranians, as shown here.

government of gross violations of Islamic norms. He also identified the shah's ally, America, as the great Satan. With opposition mounting, the shah fled the country in January 1979. In the shah's wake, Khomeini returned from exile and established a theocratic state ruled by a council of Islamic clerics. Although some Iranians grumbled about many aspects of this return to Islam—the reduced status of women, the arbitrariness of the leaders, the rupture in relations with the West, and the failure to institute democratic procedures— they prided themselves on having inspired a revolution based on principles other than those drawn from the West.

The search for moral foundations of politics in the global age was not restricted to nonwestern societies. Indeed, in the United States, religion became an even more powerful force in politics after the 1970s. Organized religion had long loomed large in the United States, especially compared with its relatively less important place in other developed nations. A poll taken in the mid-1970s, for example, found that 56 percent of Americans rated religious faith as "very important" to them. By contrast, only 27 percent of Europeans made the same claim. From the 1970s on, the membership and activism of conservative, fundamentalist Protestant churches eclipsed more liberal mainline denominations. Insisting on the literal interpretation of the Bible, Protestant fundamentalists railed against secularizing trends in American society. This traditionalist crusade grew more fervent and took up a broad range of cultural and political issues. Religious conservatives, predominantly evangelical Protestants but including some Catholics and Orthodox Jews, attacked many of the social changes that emerged from liberation movements of the 1960s. Shifting sexual and familial relations were sore points for these religious conservatives, but the real diatribe was reserved for public leaders who, by legalizing abortion and supporting secular values, in the religious conservatives' view had abandoned the moral purpose of authority.

ACCEPTANCE OF AND RESISTANCE TO DEMOCRACY

New sources of power and new social movements drastically changed politics in the global age. Increasingly, international organizations played a decisive role in defining the conditions of democratic citizenship.

Perhaps most remarkable was how much democracy spread in the last decades of the twentieth century. In South Africa, Russia, and Guatemala, elections decided the fate of politicians. In this sense, the world's societies embraced the idea that people have a right to choose their own representatives. Nevertheless, democracy did not triumph everywhere. An important holdout was China. Mao died in 1976, and within a few years, his successor, Deng Xiaoping, opened the nation's economy to market forces. But Deng and other leaders in the Chinese Communist Party resisted opening the po-

litical system to multiparty competition. Instead of capitalism and western-style democracy, Chinese officials maintained that China should follow its own path to modernity.

By the late 1980s, economic reforms had produced spectacular increases in production and rising standards of living for most of China's people. But the widening gap between rich and poor, together with increasing public awareness of corruption within the party and the government, triggered popular discontent. Worker strikes and slowdowns, peasant unrest, and student activism spread. On April 22, 1989, some 100,000 people gathered in Tiananmen Square at the heart of Beijing, in silent defiance of a government ban on assembling, under the pretext of honoring the recent death of a reformist official. The following month brought an even greater show of defiance. Television cameras and journalists of the world converged on China to cover the historic official visit

Tiananmen Square. This white plaster and styrofoam statue, inspired in part by the Statue of Liberty and dubbed the Goddess of Democracy, was created by students in Beijing in the spring of 1989. It was brought to Tiananmen Square and unveiled at the end of May in an attempt to reinvigorate the democracy movement and the spirits of the protesters. For five days it captured the attention of viewers around the world, until it was toppled by a tank on the morning of June 4 and crushed as the Chinese People's Liberation Army cleared the square of its democracy advocates.

Primary Source

INDIGENOUS PEOPLE IN MEXICO SPEAK OUT

In late 1993, peasants of Chiapas, a southern state of Mexico, rejected the false promises of the national government. Mostly Indians living in the Lacandon jungle region, they had seen their land rights taken away and had tired of living under the boot of oppressive authorities. On January 1, 1994, they finally took up arms against the government, protesting official abuses and calling for a restoration of the principles of the Mexican Revolution: land for the hungry, democracy, and an end to centuries of neglect and oppression of Indians across the Americas. They formed an organization, the Zapatista Army for National Liberation (EZLN—known familiarly as the Zapatistas, recalling the name of the hero of the 1910 Revolution). Vastly out-armed, the EZLN mounted a brilliant public relations campaign and enlisted massive international support. Here is an excerpt from their official declaration of war against the Mexican government.

We are a product of 500 years of struggle: first against slavery, during the War of Independence against Spain led by the insurgents; afterward to avoid being absorbed by American imperialism; then to promulgate our constitution and expel the French Empire from our soil; and later the Porfirista dictatorship denied us just application of the Reform laws, and the people rebelled, forming their own leaders; Villa and Zapata emerged, poor men like us, who have been denied the most elemental preparation so as to be able to use us as cannon fodder and pillage the wealth of our country, without it mattering to them that we have nothing, absolutely nothing, not even a decent roof over our heads, no land, no work, no health care, no food, or education; without the right to freely and democratically elect our authorities; without independence from foreigners, without peace or justice for ourselves and our children.

But TODAY WE SAY, ENOUGH! We are the heirs of those who truly forged our nationality. We the dispossessed are millions, and we call on our brothers to join in this call as the only path in order not to die of hunger in the face of the insatiable ambition of a dictatorship for more than 70 years led by a clique of traitors who represent the most conservative and sell-out groups in the country. They are the same as those who opposed Hidalgo and Morelos, who betrayed Vicente Guerrero, the same as those who sold over half our territory to the foreign invader, the same as those who brought a European prince to rule us, the same as those who formed the dictatorship of the Porfirista "scientists," the same as those who opposed the Oil Expropriation, the same as those who massacred the railroad workers in 1958 and the students in 1968, the same as those who today take everything from us, absolutely everything.

To prevent this, and as our last hope, after having tried everything to put into practice the legality based on our Magna Carta, we resort to it, to our Constitution, to apply Constitutional Article 39, which says:

"National sovereignty resides essentially and originally in the people. All public power emanates from the people and is instituted for the people's benefit. The people have, at all times, the unalienable right to alter or modify the form of their government."

Therefore, according to our Constitution, we issue this statement to the Mexican federal army, the basic pillar of the Mexican dictatorship that we suffer, monopolized as it is by the party in power and led by the federal executive that is presently held by its highest and illegitimate chief, Carlos Salinas de Gortari.

In conformity with this Declaration of War, we ask the other branches of the Nation's government to meet to restore the legality and the stability of the Nation by deposing the dictator. . . .

PEOPLE OF MEXICO: We, upright and free men and women, are conscious that the war we declare is a last resort, but it is just. The dictators have been applying an undeclared genocidal war against our people for many years. Therefore we ask for your decided participation in support of this plan of the Mexican people in their struggle for work, land, housing, food, health care, education, independence, liberty, democracy, justice, and peace.

→ *In what other periods in this book have we encountered the ancestors of the Chiapas peasants?*
→ *What does this declaration of war suggest about the current and past Mexican governments?*

SOURCE: General Council of the EZLN, *Declaración de la Selva Lacandona*, 1993 (www.ezln.org, January 1, 1994).

of Soviet leader Mikhail Gorbachev. Several hundred students, flanked by thousands of their supporters, began a hunger strike at the foot of the Monument to the Heroes of the Revolution at the center of the square. They demanded the opening up of the political system to demo-cratic reform. Tiananmen Square was now their stage and the world their audience. Within days, the strike spread to other cities. In Beijing, well over a million people filled the city center in what was perhaps the largest mass rally since the founding of the People's Republic in 1949. Even as dehydrated strikers were rushed to hospitals, a carnivalesque atmosphere pervaded the square as the students sang and danced to rock songs and folk ballads.

The regime responded by declaring martial law on May 19. Two huge protest demonstrations of over a million participants each followed, and residents erected barricades to defend the city against the troops that had descended upon the capital. As the momentum of the protest waned, a twenty-eight-foot icon, in part inspired by the Statue of Liberty, was unveiled at the square on May 30, capturing the imagination of the crowd and the attention of the cameras. But by then the government had assembled its loyal troops to crush the movement. In a night of terror that began at dusk on June 3, the People's Liberation Army turned their guns against the people. Most students in the square were able to negotiate a safe passage; those who lost their lives—estimates vary from about 2,000 to 7,000—were the nameless people who picked up Molotov cocktails, sticks, or bricks in a heroic, if futile, attempt to repel the occupying troops.

The Chinese government, unlike its eastern European counterparts, weathered the storm. The government continued to suppress unofficial social organizations, to control access to information, including that obtained over the Internet, and to crack down on dissidents. But the Chinese government could not completely control the forces of globalization. Some organizations, like the quasi-religious group Falun Gong, managed to elude authorities and even to use the Internet to enlist international support and membership. At the dawn of the twenty-first century, signs of change were also apparent. A visible urban entrepreneurial class emerged, whose top echelon conducted its global businesses over near ubiquitous cellular phones. Rural dwellers, particularly from the southeastern coast, paid what little they had to be smuggled abroad, at great risk and often with lethal consequences, so that they could make a better living in America or Europe. Within China, tens of millions of people lived a transient existence, with tens of thousands daily leaving the countryside for the cities. There they often became the victims of economic and social exploitation, to say nothing of police and other government abuse. Existing at the margins of the new

Protests in Mexico. *(Left)* After generations of oppression and exclusion, peasants of Chiapas, in southern Mexico, called for democracy and respect for their right to land. When Mexican authorities refused to bend, peasants took up arms. While they knew that they posed no military threat to the Mexican army, the Zapatista rebels used the world media and international organizations to embarrass the national political establishment into allowing reforms. *(Right)* Among the great Mexican muralists of the twentieth century, David Alfaro Siqueiros most advocated class struggle. In this 1957 mural image, *The People in Arms,* Siqueiros portrays Mexican peasants as they pick up arms in 1910 to fight for a new order. Paintings such as these provided inspiration for movements such as the Chiapas Rebellion.

prosperity, they, too, served as reminders of the uneven and unsettling effects of globalization.

In Mexico, democracy finally triumphed, as the single party that dominated the country for seventy-one years was defeated with the election of Vicente Fox in July 2000. Until that time, Mexican rulers had combined patronage and rigged elections to stay in office. By the 1980s, corruption and widespread abuse permeated the system. The abuse of democratic rights fell hardest on poor communities, especially hitting provinces where there were large numbers of indigenous people, as in the state of Chiapas in the south. Chiapas, an impoverished area with a significant population of Mayan descendants, encountered great difficulties coping with the challenges of social and economic change in the 1980s. From Mexico City, the president stripped Indians of their right to communal land and let the ruling party run Chiapas like a fiefdom. By the early 1990s, Chiapas was seething with discontent and demanding material betterment, cultural recognition of Indian rights, and local democracy. One group of rebels, called the Zapatistas in honor of the hero of the Mexican Revolution, rose up against Mexico City on January 1, 1994. In response, the government prepared to crush the insurgents. What no one anticipated was how supranational forces would play a role in helping local democracy. Cable News Network (CNN) set up a caravan to broadcast the clash to living rooms around the world; rebel leader Subcommander Marcos, meanwhile, set up a website, whose humor and wit immediately attracted thousands of "hits." Thereafter, international news media flooded Chiapas, filming parading Indians waving flags and pronouncing victory. Mexico City, deeply embarrassed, asked local church authorities to help negotiate peace and to lead a special commission to hear the concerns of the villagers. In 2000, national elections toppled the ruling party, including its representatives in the state of Chiapas, and Mexico dismantled its one-party ruling system.

 CONCLUSION

In the thirteenth century (as long before), people ventured over long distances, to trade, to explore, and to convert souls; yet, communications technology was rudimentary, making long-distance mobility and exchange expensive, rare, and often perilous. The vast majority organized their livelihoods and identified themselves with local places. The world was much more a series of communities set apart than a world bound together by culture, capital, and communication networks.

By the end of the twentieth century, that balance had changed. Food, entertainment, clothing, and even family life appeared more and more similar around the world than ever before. To be sure, local differences were not obliterated. In 2000, the local lived on, and in some cases was revived,

thanks to the challenges to the authority of nation-states. No longer did the nation-state or any single level of community life define collective identities. At the same time, worldwide purveyors of cultural and commercial resources offered local communities the same kinds of products, from aspirin to Nike shoes. Exchanges across local and national boundaries became easier. For the first time many of the world's peoples felt themselves part of a global culture.

New technologies, new methods of production and investment, and, above all, the greater importance of personal health and education for human betterment created new possibilities and greater inequalities. Indeed, in contrast to the world in 1300, or in 1800, the degrees of disparity between the haves and the have-nots in 2000 could scarcely have been imagined. For, as humanity learned to harness new technologies to accelerate and intensify exchanges across and within cultures, a larger and larger gulf separated those who participated in the networks of globalization and enjoyed its fruits from those who languished on the margins. This disparity produced divergent and different political and cultural forms, despite the collapse of the three-world order. Thus, as the world became more integrated and grew more together, it also grew apart along new, ever-deeper lines.

STUDY QUESTIONS

 WWNORTON.COM/STUDYSPACE

1. Analyze to what extent the three-world order discussed in Chapter 20 no longer existed by 1975. What new architecture of power was replacing it?

2. Explain the events and processes that led to the end of the cold war. How did U.S. containment policies contribute to the Soviet Union's demise?

3. Describe the process through which apartheid was dismantled in South Africa. Why was the process relatively nonviolent?

4. List and define the agents of globalization. How did they change the world in the late twentieth century?

5. Analyze how globalization transformed popular culture worldwide. To what extent does global popular culture reflect American culture and values?

6. Analyze how globalization transformed world demography. What patterns emerged in terms of international migration?

7. Analyze how globalization affected women. Have new patterns in trade, production, and finance helped or hindered opportunities for women around the world?

8. Explain large trends in agricultural production and natural resource consumption in the world over the last several decades. Who has produced the goods, and who has consumed them?

9. Analyze how globalization shaped the world's environment. How effectively has the global community addressed new concerns and issues?

10. Explain how globalization altered people's sense of identity around the world in the last few decades. How has globalization challenged national identity and the idea of the nation-state?

FURTHER READINGS

Bakhash, Shaul, *The Reign of the Ayatollahs: Iran and the Islamic Revolution* (1984). Provides good historical background on the events that resulted in the overthrow of the shah.

Davis, Deborah (ed.), *The Consumer Revolution in Urban China* (2000). A look at the different aspects of the recent, profound social transformation of urban China.

Davis, Mike, *City of Quartz: Excavating the Future in Los Angeles* (1990). Offers sometimes prescient, sometimes polemical, and always provocative reflections on the recent history, current condition, and possible future of Los Angeles.

———, *Ecology of Fear: Los Angeles and the Imagination of Disaster* (1998). More on Los Angeles, with special attention to the connections between environmental problems and social inequities.

Dutton, Michael, *Streetlife China* (1999). A fascinating portrayal of the survival tactics of those inhabiting the margins of society in today's China.

Eichengreen, Barry, *Globalizing Capital: A History of the International Monetary System* (1996). An insightful analysis of how international capital markets changed in the period from 1945 to 1980.

Guillermoprieto, Alma, *Looking for History: Dispatches from Latin America* (2001). A collection of articles by the most important journalist reporting on Latin American affairs.

Han Minzhu (ed.), *Cries for Democracy: Writings and Speeches from the 1989 Chinese Democracy Movement* (1990). A collection of documents from the events leading up to the incident in Tiananmen Square on June 4, 1989.

Hancock, Graham, *Lords of Poverty: The Power, Prestige, and Corruption of the International Aid Business* (1989). An exposé of the many downsides of humanitarianism in the age of globalization.

Herbst, Jeffrey, *States and Power in Africa: Comparative Lessons in Authority and Control* (2000). Explores the political dilemmas facing modern African polities.

Honig, Emily, and Gail Hershatter, *Personal Voices: Chinese Women in the 1980's* (1988). A record of Chinese women during a period of rapid social change.

Chronology

	1975	1980	1985
THE AMERICAS		Nicaraguan Revolution, 1979 ▌ ▌ AIDS first detected, 1981 Strategic Defense Initiative authorized (U.S.), 1983 ▌	
EUROPE			
THE SOVIET UNION	Soviet war in Afghanistan, 1979–1989 ▌	Chernobyl nuclear accident (Soviet Union), 1986 ▌ Gorbachev becomes general secretary of Communist Party (Soviet Union), 1985 ▌	
AFRICA			
THE MIDDLE EAST		▌ American hostage crisis in Iran, 1979–1980 ▌ Khomeini establishes theocratic state in Iran, 1979–1980 ▌ Iran-Iraq War, 1980–1988	
SOUTH ASIA			
EAST ASIA			

Keddie, Nikki R., *Roots of Revolution: An Interpretive History of Modern Iran* (1981). Provides good historical background on the Iranian Revolution.

Klitgaard, Robert, *Tropical Gangsters* (1990). On the contemporary world's symbiosis between corrupt native elites and international agencies.

Kotkin, Stephen, *Armageddon Averted: The Soviet Collapse, 1970–2000* (2001). Places the surprise dissolution of the Soviet Union firmly in the context of shifts in the post–World War II world.

Mamdani, Mahmood, *Citizen and Subject: Contemporary Africa and the Legacy of Late Colonialism* (1996). Discusses the political problems of modern Africa in light of the legacy of colonialism.

Patel, Sujata, and Alice Thorner (eds.), *Bombay: Metaphor for Modern India* (1997). Articles on the politics and economy of the city of Bombay.

Portes, Alejandro, and Rubén G. Rumbaut, *Immigrant America* (2nd ed., 1996). A good comparative study of how immigration has transformed the United States.

Van Der Wee, Hermann, *Prosperity and Upheaval: The World Economy, 1945–1980* (1986). Describes very well the transformation and problems of the world economy, particularly from the 1960s onward.

Winn, Peter, *Americas: The Changing Face of Latin America and the Caribbean* (1992). A useful portrayal of Latin America since the 1970s.

1990	1995	2000
	▮ *North American Free Trade Agreement (NAFTA) negotiated, 1992*	
	▮ *Earth Summit (Rio de Janeiro), 1992*	
	▮ *Chiapas Revolt begins (Mexico), 1994*	
▮ *Berlin Wall falls, 1989*		
▮ *Eastern European Communist regimes topple, 1989*		
▮ *Secession wars in former Yugoslavia, 1989–1995*		
▮ *Germany reunited, 1990*		
▮ *Maastricht Treaty (Europe), 1991*		
▮ *Dissolution of Soviet Union, 1991*		
▮ *Mandela released from prison, 1990*		
▮ *Civil war in Rwanda (Africa), 1990–1998* ▮ *Free elections in South Africa, 1994*		
▮ *Gulf War (Middle East), 1991*		
		▮ *BJP Party becomes majority in ruling coalition in India, 1998*
▮ *Tiananmen Square demonstrations (China), 1989*	▮ *Fourth World Conference on Women (Beijing), 1995*	

Epilogue

2001 – THE PRESENT

On December 31, 1999, people across the world celebrated the beginning of a new millennium. It did not matter to most of the celebrants that the twentieth century did not technically end for another year. Largely forgotten as well were the fears that circulated in the months and weeks leading up to the big night about a possible terrorist attack or about how the world's computer systems would handle (or fail to handle) the turn from 1999 to 2000 (what was called the Y2K problem). Instead, revelers greeted the turn from 1999 to 2000 in a spirit of exultation and expectation. Thanks to satellite television coverage, viewers in Australia, Asia, Africa, Europe, and the Americas watched midnight come to each time zone and saw fireworks light up the night again and again. (See the fireworks over the Thames in London, at left.) With the cold war now over, optimists, especially in the West, expressed hope for an end to the history of ideological conflict that had bloodied the twentieth century and looked forward to an era of peace and prosperity. But when the new century and the new millennium actually arrived, it became painfully clear that history had not ended, that there would be prosperity for some but poverty for more, and that while technologies had brought the world together as never before, divergent ideals could still blow things apart.

The United States, the European Union, and Japan

Barely nine months into what really was the start of the twenty-first century, terrorist violence shattered the exuberance with which so many people had welcomed the new millennium. On the morning of September 11, 2001, nineteen hijackers commandeered four airplanes. The hijackers slammed two of the planes into the World Trade Center in New York City and a third into the Pentagon Building (home of the U.S. Department of Defense) in Washington, D.C. The fourth hijacked plane was deterred from its intended target—the White House or the Capitol—by the courageous actions of its passengers and crashed in a field in southwestern Pennsylvania. As on the millennium eve, television captured the event live for global viewers, glued to the horrifying, yet almost surreal, images of the Trade Center's twin towers engulfed in flames, then crumbling one after the other into a heap of ash and twisted metal.

Across the United States, grief unified the nation. Anger focused on Osama bin Laden and al-Qaeda (the base), the militant Islamic group that had organized the terrorist attack. Many Americans likened "9/11" to the Japanese bombing of Pearl Harbor sixty years earlier. George W. Bush, who had ascended to the presidency after a close and disputed election the year before, gained broad public support for his tough talk about bringing terrorists to justice and for his insistence that the events of September 11 had introduced a new divide between the "pre-9/11 world" and the "post-9/11" one. Domestically, President Bush pushed for security measures, which he insisted were needed to curb future terrorist violence, protect freedom, and secure the American homeland. In the face of overwhelming popular backing, little attention was given to those critics who contended that the policies threatened American civil liberties.

Internationally, President Bush declared a "global war on terrorism" and promised to "get" bin Laden "dead or alive." With the nearly unanimous backing of the American people, as well as strong support from many nations, Bush sent American forces to Afghanistan to hunt down bin Laden, destroy al-Qaeda training camps, and topple the Taliban government that had provided a haven to the terrorists. Although the United States achieved this last goal, it failed to capture bin Laden. Expanding the battlefront of the war on terror, in 2003, Bush ordered an invasion of Iraq, whose brutal dictator, Saddam Hussein, reputedly had abetted terrorists and was thought to have developed weapons of mass destruction. As in Afghanistan, the initial offensive went well for the United States and its military coalition made up of Britain, Spain, Italy, and several eastern European nations, quickly achieving its goal of overthrowing Hussein's regime. But defeating the Iraqi army and finding and imprisoning Hussein proved easier than restoring order to the country, improving living standards, and persuading the population to rally around the American vision of a new democratic polity. Moreover, the failure to find weapons of mass destruction or uncover indisputable links between Hussein and al-Qaeda, together with mounting American losses from an ongoing insurgency, left many in the United States questioning the wisdom of this war. President Bush did win re-election in 2004, but the national unity so evident in the weeks and months after September 11 seemed increasingly distant, as was the sense that the new century would be one of peace and prosperity under an American-led world order.

In Afghanistan, the situation began to shift noticeably with the U.S.-led coalition forces starting to find themselves in a situation that soon took on the look and feel of the quagmire that the Soviets found themselves in there two decades earlier. Early successes to maintain order and stability in Afghanistan became more challenging as local warlords continued to exercise their personal power toward achieving their own goals and in the form of the revitalized Taliban, who had received support from warlords in neighboring Pakistan.

The American invasion of Iraq also created fractures in the alliance between the United States and western Europe. During the 1990s, the collapse of the Soviet Union and the development of the European Union (EU) had caused some rumblings about the future of NATO, but disagreements remained relatively muted prior to the American military's entrance into Iraq. In fact, in the immediate wake of September 11, European allies rallied behind the United States. But before and after the invasion of Iraq, leaders in France and Germany sharply criticized the foreign policy of the United States, leading Donald Rumsfeld, the American secretary of defense, to disparage these countries as representatives of the "old Europe."

Although Rumsfeld suggested that a twenty-first-century split between "old" and "new" had supplanted the cold war division between west and east in Europe, more striking from a historical standpoint was the continuing integration of the region. By 2005, the European Union had widened its membership to twenty-five, including nine nations that had been behind the Iron Curtain. True, this unification faced some reversals, most notably when voters in France and the Netherlands rejected the EU constitution. Still, viewed against the backdrop of twentieth-century total wars and attempts at ethnic cleansing, it is remarkable that member states were able to bind themselves together in a union to which each relinquished significant degrees of sovereignty.

Looking forward, the greater threat to European integration—and to Europe's future peace and prosperity—remains the interlocking issues of aging and immigration. Roughly speaking, to maintain its existing population of 450 million people, each female in Europe is expected to bear a mean of 2 children, but women in the European Union now average only 1.5 offspring. Adding to the demographic and labor pressures is

9/11. (*Left*) The North Tower already aflame, this photograph captures a second hijacked jet, an instant before it crashes into the South Tower of New York's World Trade Center on the morning of September 11, 2001. (*Right*) Firefighters search for survivors in the smoldering ruins.

the aging of the European population. With the percentage of elderly Europeans rising rapidly, sustaining the present workers-to-retirees ratio and paying for the region's bulging number of pensioners will require the European Union to attract something on the order of 15 million immigrants annually.

Although these numbers have not been reached, European populations have been boosted by millions of immigrants, many of them Muslims. As of 2005, Europe was home to some 50 million Muslims, of whom approximately 15 million resided within member states of the European Union. This represented a little over 3 percent of the European Union's population, though in France the figure topped 10 percent. These immigrants often live in impoverished circumstances, and in many countries, their status as guest workers denies them the full benefits of citizenship. Their presence in virtually all of Europe's larger cities continues to threaten those who still equated Europe with Christendom and challenges those who believe that European integration requires complete assimilation of all inhabitants.

Europe is not alone in confronting the problems of an aging population and the integration of immigrants. As its baby boom generation ages, the United States faces a similar imbalance between retirees and workers that endangers its social security system. So, too, the flood of immigrants, particularly from Asia and Latin America, continues to shift the nation's ethnic composition. By 2005, people of Latin American descent in the United States numbered more than 37 million (or about 12 percent of the population). The presence of so many Spanish-speakers troubles those who thought the United States should remain an English-only country, and the degree to which immigrants should be required to assimilate remains a contentious issue. More heated still are ongoing debates about illegal immigration, which have led some in the government and the media to call for the construction of a barrier between the United States and Mexico.

In many respects, the twin dilemmas of aging and immigration press hardest today on Japan. Like Europeans and North Americans, the Japanese are marrying later and having fewer children. Japan's female population now averages barely 1.2 children, compared with nearly 3.7 in 1950. At the same time, Japanese life expectancy has now reached eighty-five, the highest in the world, which further tilts the nation's age pyramid. In 1970 the elderly comprised around 7 percent of the population; their proportion reached 20 percent in 2005, and it is expected to hit 30 percent by 2025. Already by the end of the 1990s, Japan's population over sixty-five eclipsed that below fifteen. Analysts surmise that Japan's population peaked at around 128 million and will decline to perhaps 90 million by 2050. Such a downturn bodes ill for Japan's dynamic economy, which retains its position as the world's second largest, despite having staggered through the first years of the twenty-first century in a protracted recession.

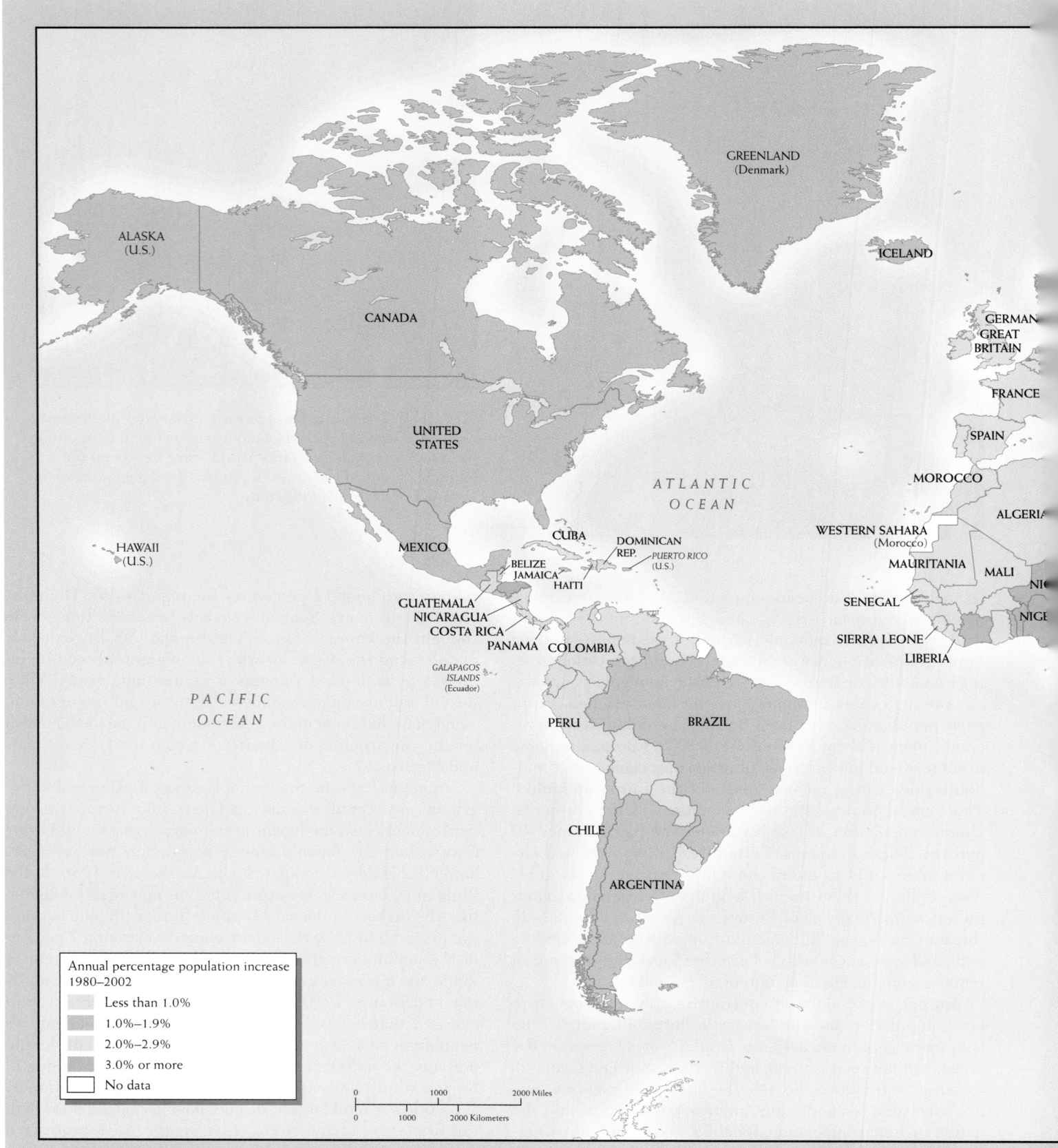

GREENLAND
(Denmark)

ICELAND

ALASKA
(U.S.)

CANADA

GERMAN
GREAT
BRITAIN

FRANCE

SPAIN

UNITED
STATES

ATLANTIC
OCEAN

MOROCCO

ALGERIA

HAWAII
(U.S.)

MEXICO

CUBA

DOMINICAN
REP.

PUERTO RICO
(U.S.)

WESTERN SAHARA
(Morocco)

MAURITANIA

MALI

NI

BELIZE
JAMAICA

HAITI

GUATEMALA
NICARAGUA
COSTA RICA
PANAMA

COLOMBIA

SENEGAL

SIERRA LEONE

LIBERIA

NIGE

GALAPAGOS
ISLANDS
(Ecuador)

PACIFIC
OCEAN

PERU

BRAZIL

CHILE

ARGENTINA

Annual percentage population increase
1980–2002

Less than 1.0%

1.0%–1.9%

2.0%–2.9%

3.0% or more

No data

0	1000	2000 Miles
0	1000	2000 Kilometers

MAP E-1   POPULATION GROWTH, 1980–2002

Strong demographic patterns at the beginning of the twenty-first century pose major problems for the industrialized societies of western Europe, North America, and Japan. As life expectancy increases and population growth slows, these region's economies face labor shortages that have fueled immigration. According to this map and Map E-2, Life Expectancies in Global Perspective, 2002, which regions of the world are prime candidates for sending migrants to the industrialized world? What cultural and political dilemmas does this phenomenon create? Which states within the industrialized world do you think have created the best environment for immigrant residents?

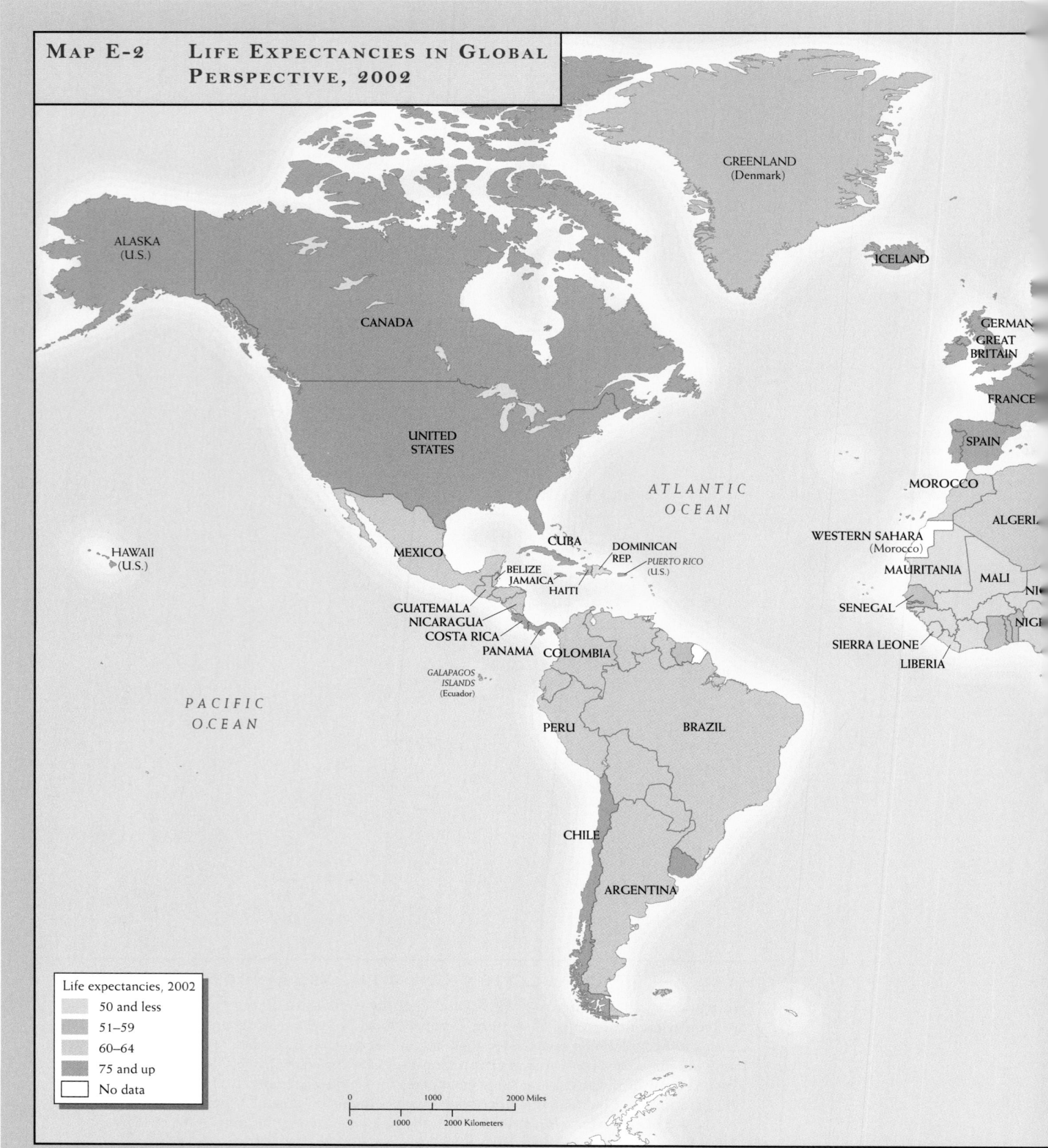

MAP E-2 LIFE EXPECTANCIES IN GLOBAL PERSPECTIVE, 2002

Life expectancies, 2002
- 50 and less
- 51–59
- 60–64
- 75 and up
- No data

São Paulo, Brazil. An aerial view of one of São Paulo's biggest slums, Favela Morumbi; Favela Morumbi borders one of the city's richest neighborhoods, also called Morumbi.

As in Europe and North America, Japan has come to rely on immigrants to fill out its labor force. In the 1960s, the booming Japanese economy experienced labor shortages, but neither the government nor major corporations elected then to invite foreign laborers, preferring automation or recruitment of workers of Japanese descent from abroad. By the 1980s, however, deepening labor shortages and the rise in the yen's value led to an expanded dependence on immigrant workers. Recent estimates put the number of foreign nationals in Japan (registered and unregistered) at nearly 2 million, or around 1.5 percent of the total population. Most of them hail from the Korean peninsula, the Philippines, Indochina, Brazil, and Iran.

In Europe, where unemployment rates remain higher than in Japan or North America, the political reaction against immigration has been sharpest. Far right groups support xenophobic platforms, demanding immigration be halted or "foreigners" expelled; their electoral resurgence in the late 1990s and early 2000s, however, may now be abating. Support levels vary in each country, but across Europe the far right's electoral base appeared to be around 15 percent; in some countries, it is above 25 percent. The Freedom Party in Austria and the Northern League and National Alliance in Italy regularly place cabinet representatives in coalition governments. Ultra-right forces such as France's National Front, Denmark's People's Party, and the League of Polish Families sometimes induce governing coalitions to slow EU integration and immigration, especially from Muslim countries.

In recent years, anti-immigrant sentiments in general and anti-Muslim ones in particular have risen in the wake of several violent episodes. In Holland, the precipitant was the grisly murder of filmmaker Theo Van Gogh by Mohammed Bouyeri in November 2004. Bouyeri claimed he was fulfilling his duty as a Muslim by killing Van Gogh, who had made a film about the abuse of Muslim women. In the wake of the assassination, many in Holland questioned the nation's traditional tolerance of diversity and expressed concern that Muslims were too alien in their values to ever fit in Dutch society. Such questions about the assimilation (and assimilability) of Muslims were raised once more in 2006 after the publication of anti-Islamic cartoons in a Dutch newspaper generated violent demonstrations across Europe and throughout the Muslim world. During these same years, France confronted similar dilemmas after rioting rocked the mostly Muslim suburbs of Paris in 2005. This unrest alerted many French officials to the desperate plight of unemployed and alienated immigrants, but it also fed fears about the loyalties of Muslims and led some politicians to take a harder line against foreigners. Interior Minister Nicolas Sarkozy ordered the deportation of immigrants convicted of rioting, while Jean-Marie Le Pen, leader of the far right National Front, went further, demanding that even naturalized rioters be stripped of their citizenship. In the May 2007 race for the French presidency, Sarkozy defeated Le Pen as well as the first French woman to run for the seat, Ségolène Royal. Sarkozy has promised to serve all of France's citizens but has also promised to set up a new office of immigration and French nationality.

Still more alarming to Europeans' sense of well-being after the millennium were several deadly terrorist bombings. In March 2004, a series of bombings of commuter trains in

Madrid killed 191 people and wounded more than 2,000; in July 2005, terrorists struck London's subways, leaving 52 dead and 700 injured. In both cases, authorities pinned responsibility on al-Qaeda. But investigators also alleged that the operations were carried out by Muslims who had resided in Spain or Britain for some time, which sparked doubts about the integration of all immigrants into European society.

In just a few years, then, the mood of the world's most advanced industrial societies has shifted decisively. The triumphant atmosphere that had ushered in the new millennium has given way to a far more pessimistic outlook. Whereas in 2000 talk of the blessings of global integration dominated the political and economic scene, by the middle of the first decade of the twenty-first century, prognosticators more often warned about the dangers that emanate from the disaffected within their societies and from radicals, especially Islamic radicals, willing and able to unleash terror anywhere in the world.

Russia, China, and India

Fueling anti-immigrant fires in Europe, Japan, and North America are the increasing number of jobs being "outsourced." In the past, businesses had turned to immigrants to fill low-wage positions (and to keep all wages down). But at the end of the twentieth and the beginning of the twenty-first centuries, it has become easier and more economical to relocate manufacturing in places where cheap labor is already available. To compete successfully in the global market, businesses need to be agile, to take advantage of differences in prevailing wages. "Ideally," acknowledges Jack Welch, the longtime chief executive of General Electric, "you'd have every plant you own on a barge." In the new millennium, such mobility is not limited to low-skilled and low-wage jobs. As the *New York Times* columnist Thomas Friedman observed in a best-selling book, "the world" had become "flat." By this, he meant that technological advances, particularly in computers and communication, have truly brought the world together by virtually erasing distances and effectively enabling all sorts of enterprises to be conducted from almost any point on the globe. No longer do educated workers have to leave India and China for employment in Europe or North America, because it has become more cost-effective for more and more corporations to shift some of their operations to those countries. The playing field has been essentially leveled in the new globalized market economy, though countries with vast labor resources such as China, India, and even Russia still have to surmount their cultural and political histories to compete with older capitalist societies like the United States, Europe, and Japan.

Certainly, Russia, China, and India each boasted healthy economic growth in the first years of the new century. With the price of oil topping $60 per barrel, Russia enjoys windfall energy revenues that contribute to hefty budget and trade surpluses and expanding personal incomes. Between 2001 and 2005, Russia's gross domestic product climbed at an average of more than 7 percent per year, which was all the more impressive coming as it did after the years of steep economic decline that followed the dissolution of the Soviet Union in 1991.

At the same time that Russia's economy is opening to the world, however, its political system seems to be closing in on itself. In addressing the anarchy of the Yeltsin era (see Chapter 21), President Vladimir Putin has presided over the seizing of billionaires and the reassignment of their private properties to the state or to his cronies from the former KGB. He has also eliminated elections for regional executives, tightened control over the media, and restricted NGOs receiving foreign financing. In short, Russia's economy is now more firmly connected to the capitalist world, but its political system remains totally dominated by the executive branch, dashing hopes for the eventual consolidation of a real legislature and an independent judiciary that were raised during the Gorbachev-Yeltsin era.

The Chinese have followed an inverse path, permitting capitalist economic reforms first, while quashing the possibilities for political liberalization. From an economic standpoint, in any event, their strategies seem to be successful. Over the last two decades, China's economy has grown at a breathtaking rate of over 9 percent annually, and this spectacular ascent shows no sign of abating. Consumer goods made in China so dominate many markets that it is virtually impossible, as several newspaper reporters found, to supply an American family's needs on a "China-free" diet. At the close of 2005, China's economy was already the sixth largest

Child Labor. Girls in a Javanese village work in a factory transferring bundles of cotton yarn to bobbins to be used in handlooms.

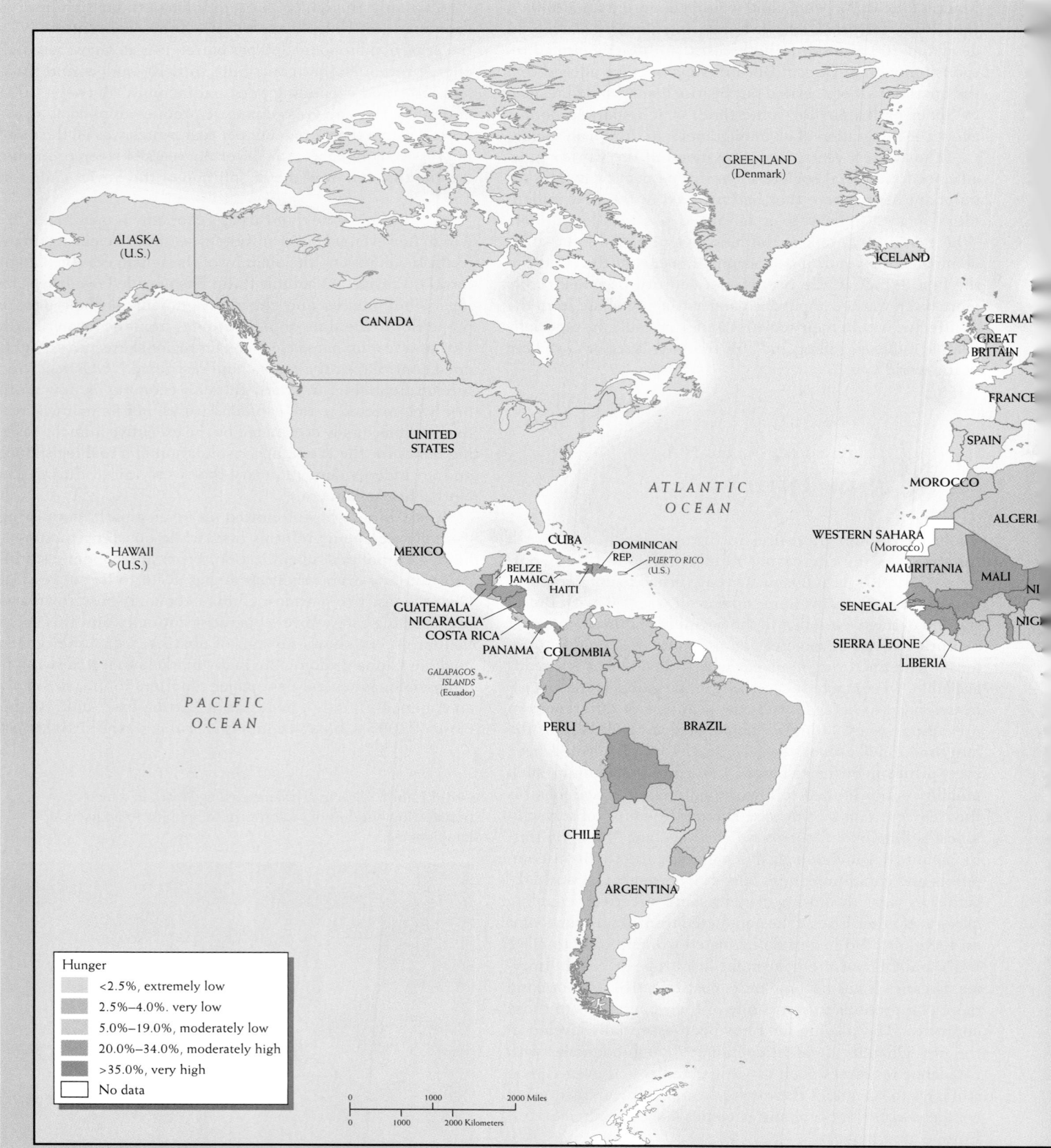

Hunger

<2.5%, extremely low
2.5%–4.0%. very low
5.0%–19.0%, moderately low
20.0%–34.0%, moderately high
>35.0%, very high
No data

MAP E-3   HUNGER IS A GLOBAL PROBLEM

Despite much optimism, globalization has not yet shown the ability to meet the basic human needs of the entire world population. According to this map, in which regions is hunger extremely high? What characteristics do these regions share? What do these statistics reveal about income disparity within and between countries?

ARCTIC OCEAN

RUSSIA

KAZAKHSTAN

MONGOLIA

NORTH KOREA

BANIA

TURKEY

CYPRUS
LEBANON
ISRAEL

SYRIA

IRAQ

JORDAN

IRAN

AFGHANISTAN

PEOPLE'S REPUBLIC OF CHINA

SOUTH KOREA

JAPAN

LIBYA

EGYPT

KUWAIT

SAUDI ARABIA

U.A.E.

PAKISTAN

NEPAL

BANGLADESH

TAIWAN

HONG KONG

PACIFIC OCEAN

CHAD

SUDAN

ERITREA

OMAN

YEMEN

INDIA

LAOS

MARIANA ISLANDS (U.S.)

DJIBOUTI

ETHIOPIA

SOMALIA

SRI LANKA

THAILAND

CAMBODIA

VIETNAM

PHILIPPINES

GUAM

MARSHALL ISLANDS

ONGO

UGANDA

RWANDA

KENYA

DEMOCRATIC REP. OF CONGO

BURUNDI

TANZANIA

INDIAN OCEAN

BRUNEI

MALAYSIA

SINGAPORE

INDONESIA

PAPUA NEW GUINEA

SAMOA

ANGOLA

MOZAMBIQUE

MADAGASCAR

EAST TIMOR

FIJI

ZIMBABWE

BOTSWANA

AUSTRALIA

SOUTH AFRICA

NEW ZEALAND

Chinese Environmental Concerns. Despite its prosperity, Hong Kong, like other major Chinese cities, suffers from severe air pollution, which threatens its future as a hub of international commerce. This picture shows part of the city's waterfront shrouded in smog.

in the world, and projections suggest that China will have the world's largest economy by midcentury (though its per capita income will still lag behind that of the United States).

In many ways, China's fortunes exemplify both the promises and the pitfalls of the economic reforms undertaken by many developing countries—what used to be called the Third World—in the era of globalization. On the one hand, despite the continued monopoly of political power by the Chinese Communist Party at home, China's entry into the World Trade Organization (WTO) in 2001 signified its full integration into the global capitalist economy. On the other hand, the reforms have resulted in a number of political, social, and environmental problems that defy easy solutions. The disparity between the relatively prosperous coastal areas and the poor interior of the country—a problem that was supposedly redressed by the Communist government after it came to power in 1949—has once again become a glaring challenge. At the same time, the gap between the rich and the poor in the more economically developed urban areas has widened at an alarming rate, with the government's own statistics indicating that the richest 10 percent of households own 45 percent of private urban wealth, while the poorest tenth command less than 1.4 percent of the wealth in the cities. At home and abroad, concerns have also been raised about the environmental impact of China's economic development. China's homes and factories, for instance, use 40 percent more coal than those in the United States, and Chinese city dwellers now suffer from some of the world's worst smog and least healthy air quality.

As China's consumption of energy has soared along with its wealth and military might, commentators have predicted that China will soon join the United States as a superpower. Two decades ago, Americans fretted about how Japan's "economic miracle" threatened the place of the United States as the world's preeminent power; now China has become the chief focus of such fears. The Chinese government appears ready for the coming competition. As the host nation for the 2008 Summer Olympics to be held in Beijing, the Chinese government has made it an official goal to win more medals than the United States or any other nation.

Like China, India seems one of the success stories of economic globalization, yet here, too, the old divisions in South Asia between Hindus and Muslims threaten to undo any benefits. After coming to power in 1998, a coalition led by the BJP, the Hindu nationalist party, embraced market liberalization. Over the next five years, the government opened India to the global market economy with spectacular economic results. Growth rates consistently topped 7 percent annually, and its stock market boomed. India has emerged as one of the favorite destinations for the flow of international capital, particularly in the information technology sector. Bangalore, Hyderabad, Mumbai, and Delhi have prospered as hot spots in the global economy.

At the same time that the BJP-led government promoted market reforms, it also championed *Hindutva* (Hinduness) as the bedrock of Indian identity. Nowhere were the effects of this twin strategy of economic liberalism and Hindu nationalism more visible than in the western state of Gujarat. Home to merchant communities for centuries, Gujarat has been in the forefront of capitalist manufactures and commerce. While aggressively participating in the global economy, the state has also served as a fertile ground for Hindu nationalism. The dark side of that nationalism erupted in February 2002 after sixty Hindus perished in a fire that consumed a train compartment. Although the exact circumstances of the fire remain disputed, a rumor immediately spread, authenticated by the BJP government in Gujarat, that Muslims and a "foreign hand" were responsible. For the next few months, Hindu mobs went on a rampage, burning Muslim homes and hacking the residents to death. Newspapers widely reported that the government leaders and the police force assisted in this carnage or looked the other way as over 2,000 Muslims lost their lives. Faced with the widespread condemnation of the violence against the Muslims, the BJP leaders justified it as an understandable Hindu response to Muslim provocation. In the provincial elections of December 2002, the BJP aggressively projected itself as a Hindu nationalist and pro-business party. This strategy paid rich dividends, and the BJP was re-elected to power with a commanding majority.

Still more dangerous was the ongoing tension between India and Pakistan. Flexing its nationalist muscles, the Indian government exploded a nuclear device in 1998. Pakistan, then, built its own bomb, casting an ominous shadow over the two nations' unresolved conflict over Kashmir. In that contested province, terrorist violence repeatedly disturbed

Hindu-Muslim Tensions. In 2002, Gujarat was consumed by sectarian riots, set off by a train fire that killed fifty-nine Hindu pilgrims. Though an Indian government investigation concluded that the fire was accidental, the incident sparked an orgy of violence by Hindu mobs against Muslims. This image shows an angry right-wing Hindu party activist against a background of the carnage.

THE MIDDLE EAST, AFRICA, AND LATIN AMERICA

Although anxieties about terrorism and immigration add to the worries of the West, North American, European, and Japanese societies still boast the world's largest economies and longest life expectancies. Likewise, Russia, China, and India, for all the problems that they face, have clearly benefited from the bulging trade surpluses and rising per capita incomes that their economies generated in the first years of the twenty-first century. Elsewhere, however, it is harder to find signs of enduring peace or general prosperity.

Today, the Middle East remains a particularly volatile region, with dysfunctional civil societies and undemocratic political regimes feeding militant Islamicist fury. The appeal of radical and religious solutions was manifested in various elections in 2005 and 2006. In Iraq, under American occupation since 2003, the December 2005 elections resulted in a triumph for sectarian and regionalist parties. The major Shiite religious party won heavily in Shiite areas while the Kurdish party swept the northern, predominantly Kurdish region of Iraq.

Iraqi Elections. Iraqis voted on December 15, 2005, while the country was under American and allied military occupation. Voters had their fingers stained after voting so that they could not vote twice; many walked away from the polling booths showing their stained fingers with pride.

the peace and brought nuclear-armed neighbors closer to a potentially devastating war.

Presently, India and Pakistan appear to have taken a step away from that brink, in part because national elections in 2004 returned a coalition headed by the Congress Party to power in India. Led by the Italian-born Sonia Gandhi, the wife of the deceased Rajiv Gandhi, Nehru's grandson, the coalition included diverse caste, regional, and ideological interests. Its victory represented a setback to the Hindu nationalist effort to define India's identity in singular terms—at least for the time being.

Projecting recent trends into the future, many pundits forecast a rearrangement of the world's economic order, with China and India especially moving to the fore during the twenty-first century. China, India, and Russia, like other parts of the world, have not escaped from the past. These societies, too, struggle with widening internal divisions and potentially devastating external rivalries. Here as well, the impulse toward greater global integration conflicts with the desire to preserve local, regional, and national autonomy.

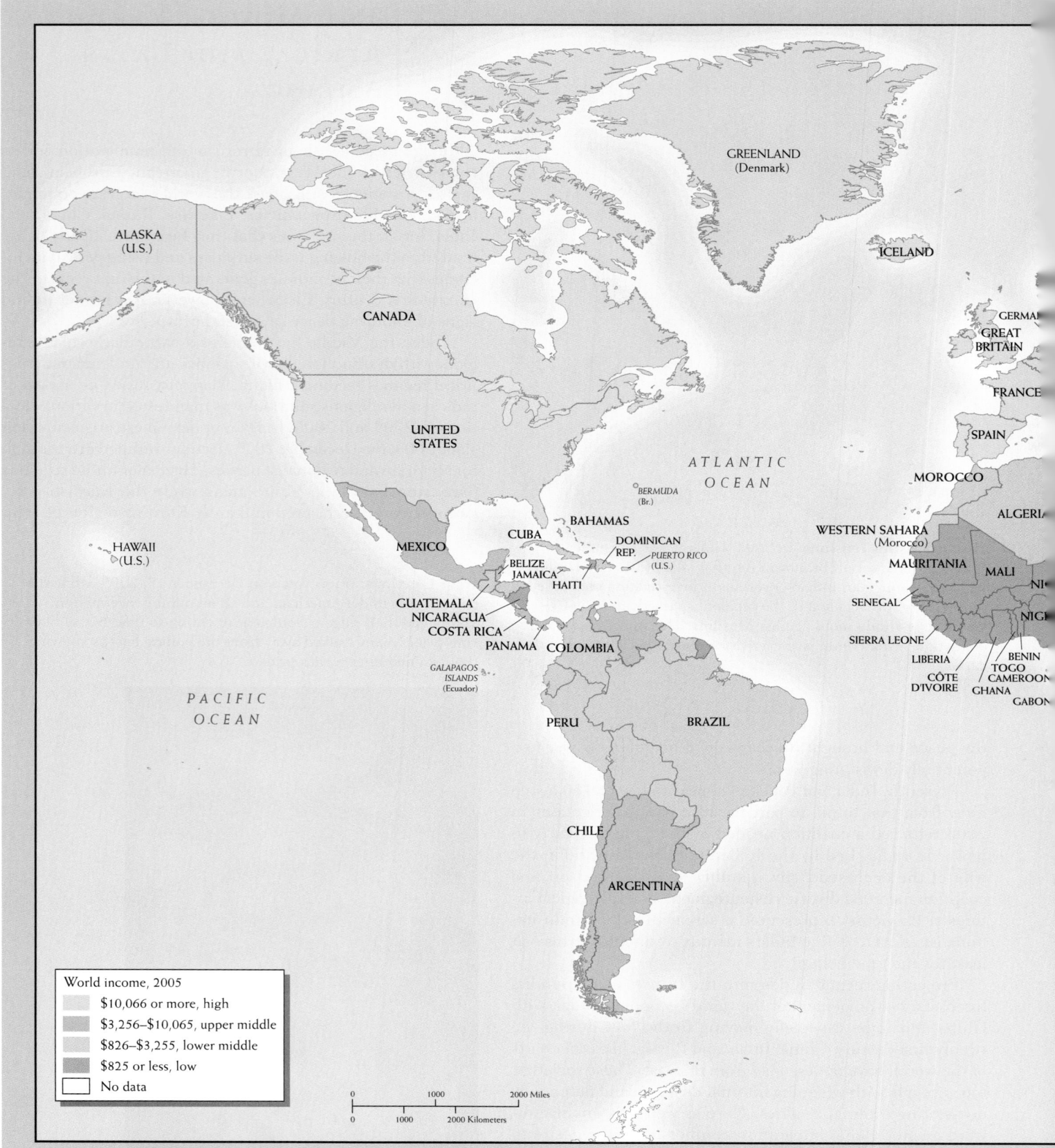

GREENLAND
(Denmark)

ICELAND

ALASKA
(U.S.)

CANADA

GERMA
GREAT
BRITAIN

FRANCE

SPAIN

UNITED
STATES

ATLANTIC
OCEAN

MOROCCO

BERMUDA
(Br.)

BAHAMAS

ALGERIA

HAWAII
(U.S.)

CUBA

DOMINICAN
REP.

PUERTO RICO
(U.S.)

WESTERN SAHARA
(Morocco)

MEXICO

BELIZE
JAMAICA

HAITI

MAURITANIA

MALI

NI

GUATEMALA
NICARAGUA
COSTA RICA
PANAMA

SENEGAL

NIGE

COLOMBIA

SIERRA LEONE

*GALAPAGOS
ISLANDS*
(Ecuador)

LIBERIA

BENIN
TOGO
CAMEROON

CÔTE
D'IVOIRE

GHANA

GABON

PACIFIC
OCEAN

PERU

BRAZIL

CHILE

ARGENTINA

World income, 2005

	$10,066 or more, high
	$3,256–$10,065, upper middle
	$826–$3,255, lower middle
	$825 or less, low
	No data

0   1000   2000 Miles

0   1000   2000 Kilometers

MAP E-4   RICH AND POOR COUNTRIES: THE WORLD
BY INCOME, 2005

Wealth and income derived from globalization have not been shared equally among the
world population. Using this map, identify the regions with the largest per capita income
and those with the smallest. What factors do you think account for this disparity? What historical antecedents helped to create this disparity? Why have India and China, despite impressive economic growth over the last decade, failed to catch up with the United States,
western European countries, and Japan in terms of per capita income?

Secular parties had no success at all, and the Sunni population, living in the center of the country, supported its own religious party, but its representation in parliament was no more than a small majority. Similarly, in elections in Palestine in late January 2006, Hamas, the radical Islamicist party and avowed foe of the state of Israel, triumphed over Fatah, the party of the once-dominant Palestine Liberation Organization. Even in rigidly controlled Egypt, Hosni Mubarak's National Democratic Party, while winning a majority in parliament in the 2005 elections, saw independent candidates gain far more seats than they had ever held. Most observers of the Egyptian political scene believe that in a free and open election Mubarak's party would lose to the Muslim Brotherhood, who, however, are still outlawed as a political party.

The reasons for the turn to radical Islam are not hard to discern. With the exception of oil-rich Persian Gulf states that are awash in petroleum-dollars, the Arab world remains deeply mired in poverty. Across the Middle East, oppressive and dictatorial regimes dominate. Although Americans insisted that the invasion of Iraq was intended to free Iraqis from the tyrannical rule of Saddam Hussein and bring democratic governance to the region, the occupation has created new resentments against the United States and failed to bring with it real political reform.

Perhaps the most chilling recent development in the Middle East is Iran's declared intention to develop its own nuclear program. Iran's new president, Mahmoud Ahmadinejad, maintains that Iran seeks nuclear power for only peaceful purposes. But Ahmadinejad's fiery diatribes against Israel and the West suggest more belligerent motives, as did the Iranian regime's defiance of efforts to monitor the program.

The power of a revivified Islam reaches far beyond the Middle East. Across the Islamic world, pressures to institute reforms based on Muslim law (the *sharia*) and Muslim principles of social justice have intensified. Among the many Muslim communities of northern Nigeria, for instance, one state after another has embraced the *sharia* as its legal guide and moral compass. As in the Middle East, the failure of the

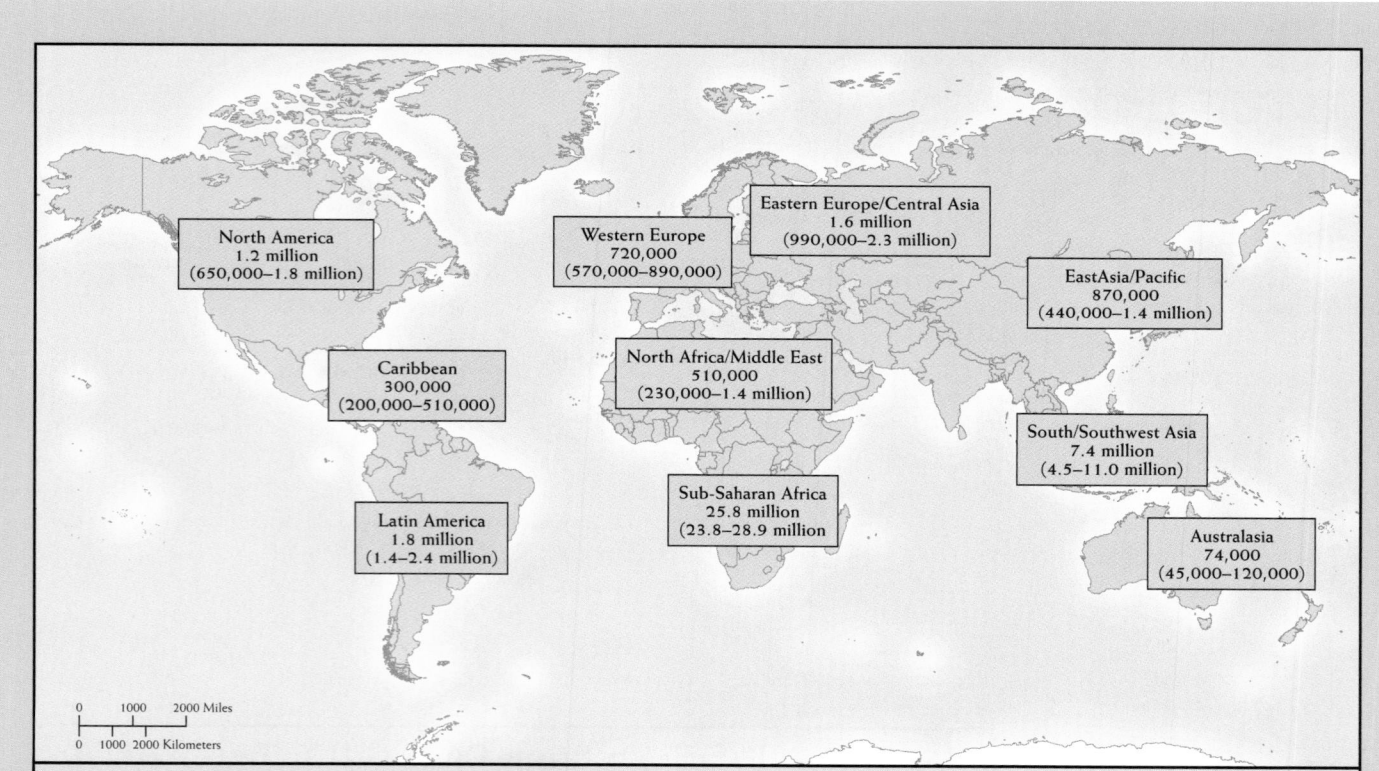

North America
1.2 million
(650,000–1.8 million)

Eastern Europe/Central Asia
1.6 million
(990,000–2.3 million)

Western Europe
720,000
(570,000–890,000)

EastAsia/Pacific
870,000
(440,000–1.4 million)

Caribbean
300,000
(200,000–510,000)

North Africa/Middle East
510,000
(230,000–1.4 million)

Latin America
1.8 million
(1.4–2.4 million)

Sub-Saharan Africa
25.8 million
(23.8–28.9 million

South/Southwest Asia
7.4 million
(4.5–11.0 million)

Australasia
74,000
(45,000–120,000)

0   1000   2000 Miles

0   1000   2000 Kilometers

MAP E-5   THE NUMBER OF HIV-POSITIVE PEOPLE AROUND THE WORLD
The spread of the HIV virus threatens the development of human capital in the twenty-first century. According to this map, which region has the highest amount of HIV infection? Using Maps E-3 and E-4 as reference, do you see any connection between poverty and HIV prevalence? How does the spread of HIV compromise economic development in poorer regions of the world?

AIDS Awareness. (*Left*) A Gambian health worker offers AIDS awareness literature. (*Right*) Protestors, many of them prostitutes and health care workers, march in New Delhi's red light district, calling for job opportunities and medical facilities on World AIDS Day 1997.

Nigerian government, despite the wealth generated by oil production, to provide adequately for most people helps to explain the Islamicist turn.

Indeed, the new millennium did not begin auspiciously for the peoples of Africa. The region remained the poorest region in the world and was afflicted by the virtually uncontrolled and uncontrollable spread of HIV/AIDS. Of the thirty-four sub-Saharan African countries surveyed in the World Bank *Annual Development Report* for 2005, all but three were low-income countries. The poorest of the poor, Burundi, the Democratic Republic of the Congo, and Ethiopia, reported per capita incomes of $100 or less. Botswana, which enjoyed the highest per capita income level at $3,430, was so devastated by HIV/AIDS that life expectancy, once the highest in Africa at close to seventy years, had tumbled to thirty-eight years in 2002.

To be sure, there are a few promising signs. Ghana embraced parliamentary and presidential elections. Civil strife ended in Mozambique and Angola. South Africa used a Truth and Reconciliation Commission to put the trauma of apartheid behind it and to stay on the course of parliamentary democracy while addressing the gross disparities of income between the white and black populations that were legacies of the twentieth century.

But these have been exceptions to the rule in which political instability wrought misery and devastation. Three of West Africa's most important countries—Liberia, Sierra Leone, and the Ivory Coast—were recently torn asunder because of ethnic and personal rivalries and required foreign interventions. Nigeria finally rid itself of unwanted military dictatorial control and moved to a civil, parliamentary sys-

tem, holding elections in 1999 and again in 2004. But the country's new president, Olusegun Obasanjo, is now barely able to hold the country together. The northern, mostly Muslim territories continue to fear and resent the southern, mainly Christian communities. In 2003, just when Africa's longest-running civil war, pitting the animist and Christian southern Sudanese against the northern Muslim peoples, had been resolved, a new dispute broke out in the western Sudan. In the region of Darfur the state allowed local horse-riding, nomadic tribesmen to carry out ethnic cleansing campaigns against settled agriculturalists. This has led to perhaps the worst case of displaced peoples in the early twenty-first century, with over two million refugees having fled government terror and civil war to huddle in vast, miserable camps. As in Rwanda in the 1990s (see Chapter 21), genocide has once more visited Africa, and at this writing, the killing has not been stopped. But there is some hope. In the West African country of Liberia, after years of pitiless civil war, belligerents agreed to put down their guns in 2004; in 2005, remarkable elections swept Ellen Johnson-Sirleaf into office to be Africa's first woman president.

Compared with sub-Saharan Africa, Latin America's situation is not so bleak. Across the region, globalization has had profound effects on Latin America, but it has not created an entirely new age. In some areas, globalization has changed

Liberia's President. Ellen Johnson-Sirleaf after her inauguration at the Capitol Building in Monrovia, on January 16, 2006. Johnson-Sirleaf is Africa's first elected woman president; she enjoys strong U.S. support and has vowed to fight graft and rebuild her country after years of war.

the way Latin Americans see their worlds and their place in the wider world. In other domains, globalization has deepened underlying features of the social and political landscape.

Across the region, the divide between haves and have-nots has widened what already had been historically the world's most unequal region. The very rich in Buenos Aires live like the very rich in Boston; magnates of Mexico City drive the same cars, eat the same food, read the same books, and vacation in the same spots as their social cousins from Moscow. They send their children to private schools in the United States and the United Kingdom to join a cosmopolitan worldwide elite class. To Latin-American elites, globalization has been a boon to their wealth and has facilitated increasing integration into international circulation of goods, ideas, and people. Many, in fact, identify less and less with a particular place in the world.

Some of the same features hold for the social bottom. For them, too, being disadvantaged and poor in southern Mexico

looks a lot like being on the losing end in southern Africa, clinging to tiny parcels of land, migrating long distances for seasonal jobs, and fighting against insensitive authorities for basic needs to be met. Globalization has offered few opportunities to make it at home. Old factories have had to close in Rosario, Argentina, when faced with Japanese competition; maize farmers in Mexico have had to contend with imports from Iowa. In many cases, thanks to globalization, the main solution to the problem is to leave—move to the city or cross borders in search of opportunities elsewhere.

To these challenges Latin-Americans have responded in many ways. One sweeping trend is for Latin-American voters to elect left-wing governments. Most of these are not like the rebel firebrands of the 1960s. Instead, in Brazil, Chile, Argentina, and Uruguay, where left-wing governments have established control, leaders offer policies designed to soften the blows of globalization and meet basic needs for land, schools, and decent housing. Here, the same pressures of globalization that contribute to leftist electoral triumphs limit what these fledgling governments can do. Elsewhere, in a few places, a more nationalist and populist brand of politics has emerged—

decrying globalization altogether. Rather than softening its effects, leaders here promise to reverse them. In Venezuela, Ecuador, and Bolivia, much to the consternation of onlookers in Washington, presidents lambaste imperialism and challenge American influence. Their message is that Latin America is better off being a world apart; being together, especially if it means cozying up to the United States, implies a future of subservience and impoverishment. But many of these leaders are also stifling criticism at home; being apart does not ensure empowerment and prosperity for all, either.

The appeal of antiglobalist politics is not limited to Latin America, or even to the underdeveloped world. In the most advanced industrial societies, as well as in fast-rising nations like China and India, programs to check globalization or buffer people from its destabilizing effects have found receptive audiences. Still, opposition to deeper global integration continues to be greatest in the poorest parts of the world, where globalization's benefits are least apparent and its costs often so lethal.

CONCLUSION

Protests against globalization were on display at the thirty-third meeting of the Group of Eight (G8), a forum of leaders from Canada, France, Germany, Italy, Japan, Russia, the

Latin American Inequality. (*Left*) Latin America's wealthy are in many ways hard to distinguish from the rich of North America. This picture is of a suburb of Santagio, Chile, called Providencia, where the well-heeled live and shop just as they do in Beverly Hills. (*Below*) Since the 1960s, millions of Latin Americans have moved from rural provinces to booming cities. But the promised jobs and services were very often not to be found. The result has been sprawling shantytowns, like this one in Rio de Janeiro, Brazil.

Anti-Globalization. Anti-globalization activists target annual summits of the leaders of the eight most industrialized countries. This one, in Germany in June 2007, saw riot police drive back protesters. Notice the New York baseball cap on one of the protestors.

United Kingdom, and the United States, held in June 2007. The summit was hosted by German chancellor Angela Merkel, one of a new generation of women to try their hand at leadership on the world stage. A key topic of the summit was global warming, which, along with fear of Islamic fundamentalism and concerns over the U.S. armed involvements in other regions, has emerged as one of the primary concerns of this new millennium. Scientific researchers continue to confirm that mankind is contributing to, if not causing, the increase in temperatures and that climate change, if not curbed, will bring catastrophic storms, severe droughts, famine, and flooding. Natural disasters at an extreme scale have already appeared, such as a monster earthquake in the Indian Ocean that caused tsunamis that consumed hundreds of thousands of people in 2004 and Hurricane Katrina that destroyed much of the city of New Orleans and the Mississippi Gulf Coast in 2005. Both of these events left behind large numbers of refugees who struggled to find homes elsewhere. As always, the impact of these changes may be unevenly felt, but global warming, if the warnings are correct, will reshape the lives of everyone on the planet. Indeed, global warming affirms just how integrated the world has become.

Global warming is just one of a number of environmental issues that have gained prominence in the new millennium. As world population continues to grow and as more areas industrialize, the pressure on vital natural resources — most obviously oil and water—has inspired calls for greater conservation and more environmental sustainable economic development. But the resistance of the United States to global regulations and the rising demand for resources, especially by the surging economies of China and India, have left the future of the earth's environment uncertain.

Historians, it must be said, are better at interpreting the past than forecasting the future. What seems certain, though, is that economic, cultural, political, and environmental developments will continue in the new millennium to encourage exchange and interaction, fostering the integration of peoples and cultures. But cultural and religious diversity, local political institutions and prerogatives, economic competition and environmental particularities will also persist. And so will the dynamic tensions that both link our worlds together and keep our worlds apart.

Abd al-Rahman III Islamic ruler in Spain who held a countercaliphate and reigned from 912 to 961 CE.

Absolutism Form of government where one body, usually the monarch, controls the right to make war, tax, judge, and coin money. The term was often used to refer to state monarchies in seventeenth- and eighteenth-century Europe.

Acid rain Precipitation containing heavy doses of sulfur, mainly from coal-fired plants.

African National Congress (ANC) Multiracial organization founded in 1912 in an effort to end racial discrimination in South Africa.

Afrikaners Descendants of the original Dutch settlers of South Africa; formerly referred to as Boers.

Agones Athletic contests in ancient Greece.

Ahmosis An Egyptian ruler in the southern part of the country who ruled from 1550 to 1525 BCE; Ahmosis used Hyksos weaponry—horse chariots in particular—to defeat the Hyksos themselves.

Ahura Mazda The Supreme God of the Persians believed to have created the world and all that is good and to have appointed earthly kings.

Akbarnamah Mughal intellectual Abulfazl's *Book of Akbar*, which attempted to reconcile the traditional Sufi interest in the inner life within the worldly context of a great empire.

Alaric II Visigothic king who issued a simplified code of innovative imperial law.

Alexander the Great Alexander came from the frontier state of Macedonia, to the north of Greece. He was a path-breaking conqueror who transformed the Mediterranean world. In the fourth decade of the fourth century BCE, Alexander brought under the rule of his Greek-speaking forces all the lands that had comprised the Persian Empire that extended from Egypt and the shores of the Mediterranean to the interior of what is now Afghanistan and as far as the Indus River valley.

Alexandria A port city in Egypt named after Alexander the Great. Alexandria was a model city in the Hellenistic world. It was built up by a multiethnic population from around the Mediterranean world.

Al-Khwarizmi A scientist and mathematician who lived from 780 to 850 CE and is known for having modified Indian digits into Arabic numerals.

Allies Term used to identify those states that fought against Germany in World War I and World War II.

Allomothering A system by which mothers relied on other women, including their own mothers, daughters, sisters, and friends, to help in the nurturing and protecting of children.

American Railway Union Workers' union that initiated the Pullman Strike of 1894, which led to violence and ended in the leaders' arrest.

Amnesty International Nongovernmental organization formed to defend "prisoners of conscience"—those detained for their beliefs, race, sex, ethnic origin, language, or religion.

Amorites A name that Mesopotamian urbanites called the transhumant herders from the Arabian desert. Around 2300 BCE, the Amorites, along with the Elamites, were at the center of newly formed dynasties in southern Mesopotamia.

Amun A once insignificant Egyptian god elevated to higher status by Amenemhet (1991–1962 BCE). Amun means "hidden" in Ancient Egyptian; the name was meant to convey the god's omnipresence.

Analects Texts that included the teachings and cultural ideals of Confucius.

Anarchism Political belief that society should be a free association of its members, not bound by government, laws, or the police.

Anatolia Now mainly the area known as modern Turkey; in the sixth millennium BCE, people from Anatolia, Greece, and the Levant took to boats and populated the Aegean. Their small villages endured almost unchanged for two millennia.

Angkor Wat A magnificent Khmer Vaishnavite temple that crowned the royal palace in Angkor. It had statues representing the Hindu pantheon of gods.

Animal domestication A gradual process that occurred simultaneously with or just before the domestication of plants, depending on the region.

Annals Historical records. Notable annals are the cuneiform inscriptions that record successful Assyrian military campaigns.

Anti-Federalists Critics of the U.S. Constitution who sought to defend the people against the power of the federal government and insisted on a bill of rights to protect individual liberties from government intrusion.

Apartheid Racial segregation policy of the Afrikaner-dominated South African government. Legislated in 1948 by the Afrikaner National Party, it had existed in South Africa for many years.

Aramaic A dialect of a Semitic language spoken in Southwest Asia; it became the lingua franca of the Persian Empire.

Aristotle Philosopher who lived from 384 to 322 BCE; he was a pupil of Plato's but came to different conclusions about nature and politics. Aristotle believed in collecting observations about nature and discerning patterns to ascertain how things worked.

Aryans Nomadic charioteers who spoke Indo-European languages and entered South Asia in 1500 BCE. The early Aryan settlers were herders.

Asante state Located in present-day Ghana, this state was founded by the Asantes at the end of the seventeenth century. It grew in power in the next century because of its access to gold and its involvement in the slave trade.

Ashur One of two cities on the upper reaches of the Tigris River that were the heart of Assyria proper (the other was Nineveh).

Asiatic Society Cultural organization founded by British Orientalists who supported native culture but still believed in colonial rule.

Aśoka Emperor of the Mauryan dynasty from 268 to 231 BCE, he was a great conqueror and unifier of India. He is said to have embraced Buddhism toward the end of his life.

Aśvaghosa The first known Sanskrit writer. He may have lived from 80 to 150 CE and may have composed a biography of the Buddha.

Atlantic system New system of trade and expansion that linked Europe, Africa, and the Americas. It emerged in the wake of European voyages across the Atlantic Ocean.

Atma Vedic term signifying the eternal self, represented by the trinity of deities.

Atman In the Upanishads, an eternal being who exists everywhere. The atman never perishes but is reborn or transmigrates into another life.

Attila From 433 to 453, Attila was the sole ruler of all Hunnish tribes. Harsh and much feared, he formed the first empire to oppose Rome in northern Europe.

Augustus In 27 BCE, Octavian (63–14 BCE) assumed the title Augustus, "Revered One." This was one of many titles he assumed; others included *imperator*, *princeps*, and *Caesar*.

Australopithecus africanus A hominid species that appeared 3 million years ago. It had a brain capacity of approximately one pint, or a little less than one-third of the brain size of a modern human and about the same size as modern-day African apes. These beings were different from other animals because they walked on two legs.

Austro-Hungarian empire Dual monarchy established by the Habsburg family in 1867; it collapsed at the end of World War I.

Authoritarianism Centralized and dictatorial form of government, proclaimed by its adherents to be superior to parliamentary democracy and especially effective at mobilizing the masses. This idea was widely accepted in parts of the world during the 1930s.

Avesta A compilation of holy works transmitted orally by priests for millennia and eventually recorded in the sixth century BCE.

Baby boom Post–World War II upswing in U.S. birth rates; it reversed a century of decline.

Bactrian camel Domesticated in Central Asia around 2500 BCE, the two-humped camel was heartier than the one-humped dromedary and became the animal of choice for the harsh and varied climates typical of Silk Road trade.

Baghdad Founded in 762 CE, Baghdad (in modern-day Iraq) was the capital of the Islamic Empire under the Abbasid dynasty. In the medieval period, it was a center of administration, scholarship, and cultural growth for what came to be known as the Golden Age of Islamic science.

Baghdad Pact (1955) Middle Eastern military alliance between countries friendly with America who were also willing to align themselves with the western countries against the Soviet Union.

Balam Na Stone temple and place of pilgrimage for the Mayan people of Mexico's Yucatan peninsula.

Balfour Declaration Letter (November 2, 1917) by Lord Arthur J. Balfour, British Foreign Secretary, that promised a homeland for the Jews in Palestine.

Bamboo Annals Shang stories and foundation myths that were written on bamboo strips and later collected.

Banana plant For the Bantu of the equatorial rain forests of central Africa, known as the Western Bantu, the introduction of the banana plant around 525 CE was a major development.

Bantu Language first spoken by people who lived in the southeastern area of modern Nigeria around 1000 CE.

Barbarian A derogatory term used to describe pastoral nomads, painting them as enemies of civilization; the term "barbarian" used to have a more neutral meaning than it does today.

Barbarian invasions A violent migration of people in the late fourth and fifth centuries into Roman territory. These migrants had long been used as non-Roman soldiers.

Basilicas Early church buildings, based on old royal audience halls.

Battle of Adwa (1896) Battle in which the Ethiopians defeated Italian colonial forces; it inspired many of Africa's later national leaders.

Battle of Wounded Knee (1890) Bloody massacre of Sioux Ghost Dancers by U.S. armed forces.

Bay of Pigs (1961) Unsuccessful invasion of Cuba by Cuban exiles supported by the U.S. government. The invaders intended to incite an insurrection in Cuba and overthrow the Communist regime of Fidel Castro.

Bedouins Nomadic pastoralists in the deserts of the Middle East.

Beer Hall Putsch (1923) Nazi intrusion into a meeting of Bavarian leaders in a Munich beer hall; the Nazis were attempting to force support for their cause; Adolf Hitler was imprisoned for a year after the incident.

Beghards (1500s) Eccentric European group whose members claimed to be in a state of grace that allowed them to do as they pleased—from adultery, free love, and nudity to murder; also called Brethren of Free Speech.

Bell beaker An artifact from Europe, this ancient drinking vessel was so named because its shape resembles an inverted bell.

Berenice of Egypt An Egyptian "queen," she helped rule over the Kingdom of the Nile from 320 to 280 BCE.

Beringia A prehistoric thousand-mile-long land bridge that linked Siberia and North America (which had not been populated by hominids). About 18,000 years ago, *Homo sapiens* edged into this landmass.

Berlin Airlift (1948) Supply of vital necessities to West Berlin by air transport primarily under U.S. auspices. It was initiated in response to a land and water blockade of the city instituted by the Soviet Union in the hope that the Allies would be forced to abandon West Berlin.

Berlin Wall Wall built by the Communists in Berlin in 1961 to prevent citizens of East Germany from fleeing to West Germany; torn down in 1989.

Bhakti A religious practice that grew out of Hinduism and emphasizes personal devotion to gods.

Bhakti Hinduism Popular form of Hinduism that emerged in the seventh century. The religion stresses devotion (*bhakti*) to God and uses vernacular languages (not Sanskrit) spoken by the common people.

Big man Leader of the extended household communities that formed village settlements in African rain forests.

Big whites French plantation owners in Saint Domingue (present-day Haiti) who created one of the wealthiest slave societies.

Bilad al-Sudan Arabic for "the land of the blacks"; it consisted of the land lying south of the Sahara.

Bilharzia Debilitating water-borne illness. It was widespread in Egypt, where it infected peasants who worked in the irrigation canals.

Bill of Rights The first ten amendments to the U.S. Constitution; ratified in 1791.

Bipedalism Walking on two legs, thereby freeing hands and arms to carry objects such as weapons and tools; one of several traits that distinguished hominids.

Black Death Great epidemic of the bubonic plague that ravaged Europe, East Asia, and North Africa in the fourteenth century, killing large numbers, including perhaps as many as one-third of the European population.

Black Jacobins Nickname for the rebels in Saint Domingue, including Toussaint L'Ouverture, a former slave who led the slaves of this French colony in the world's largest and most successful slave insurrection.

Black Panthers Radical African-American group in the 1960s and 1970s; they advocated black separatism and pan-Africanism.

Black shirts Fascist troops of Mussolini's regime; the squads received money from Italian landowners to attack socialist leaders.

Black Tuesday (October 24, 1929) Historic day when the U.S. stock market crashed, plunging the United States and international trading systems into crisis and leading the world into the "Great Depression."

Blitzkrieg "Lightning war"; type of warfare in which the Germans, during World War II, used coordinated aerial bombing campaigns along with tanks and infantryman in motorized vehicles.

Bodhisattvas In Mahayan Buddhism, enlightened demigods who were ready to reach *nirvana* but delayed so that they might help others attain it.

Bolsheviks Former members of the Russian Social Democratic Party who advocated the destruction of capitalist political and economic institutions and started the Russian Revolution. In 1918 the Bolsheviks changed their name to the Russian Communist Party.

Book of the Dead An Ancient Egyptian funerary text that contains drawings and paintings as well as spells describing how to prepare the jewelry and amulets that were buried with a person in preparation for the afterlife.

Bourgeoisie The middle class. In Europe, they sought to be recognized not by birth or title, but by capital and property.

Boxer Protocol Written agreement between the victors of the Boxer Uprising and the Qing Empire in 1901 that placed western troops in Beijing and required the regime to pay exorbitant damages for foreign life and property.

Boxer Uprising (1899–1900) Chinese peasant movement that opposed foreign influence, especially that of Christian missionaries; it was put down after the Boxers were defeated by an army composed mostly of Japanese, Russians, British, French, and Americans.

Brahma One of three major deities that form a trinity in Vedic religion. Brahma signifies birth. *See also* Vishnu *and* Siva.

Brahmans Vedic priests who performed rituals and communicated with the gods. Brahmans provided guidance on how to live in balance with the forces of nature as represented by the various deities. The codification of Vedic principles into codes of law took place at the hands of the Brahmans. They memorized Vedic works and compiled commentaries on them. They also developed their own set of rules and rituals, which developed into a full-scale theology. Originally memorized and passed on orally, these may have been written down sometime after the beginning of the Common Era. Brahmanism was reborn as Hinduism sometime during the first half of the first millennium CE.

British Commonwealth of Nations Formed in 1926, the Commonwealth conferred "dominion status" on Britain's white settler colonies in Canada, Australia, and New Zealand.

Bronze An alloy of copper and tin brought into Europe from Anatolia; used to make hard-edged weapons.

Brown shirts Troops of German men who advanced the Nazi cause by holding street marches, mass rallies, and confrontations and by beating Jews and anyone who opposed the Nazis.

Bubonic plague Acute infectious disease caused by a bacterium that is transmitted to humans by fleas from infected rats. It ravaged Europe and parts of Asia in the fourteenth century. Sometimes referred to as the "black death."

Buddhism One of China's major religions, it extolled the life and teachings of the Indian ascetic Siddhartha Gautama (563–483 BCE).

Cahokia A commercial center for regional and long-distance trade in North America. Its hinterlands produced staples for urban consumers. In return, its crafts were exported inland by porters and to North American markets in canoes.

Calaveras Allegorical skeleton drawings by the Mexican printmaker and artist José Guadalupe Posada. The works drew on popular themes of betrayal, death, and festivity.

Caliphs The spiritual and political leaders of the Islamic community.

Candomblé Yoruba-based religion in northern Brazil; it interwove African practices and beliefs with Christianity.

Caravan cities A set of networks at long-distance trade locations where groups of merchants could assemble during their journeys. Several of these developed into full-fledged cities, especially in the deserts of Arabia.

Caravans Companies of men who transported and traded goods along overland routes in North Africa and central Asia; large caravans consisted of 600–1,000 camels and as many as 400 men.

Caravansarais Inns along major trade routes that accommodated large numbers of traders, their animals, and their wares.

Caravel Sailing vessel suited for nosing in and out of estuaries and navigating in waters with unpredictable currents and winds.

Carrack Ship used on open bodies of water, such as the Mediterranean.

Carthage A city in what is modern-day Tunisia; emblematic of the trading aspirations and activities of merchants in the Mediterranean. Pottery and other archaeological remains demonstrate that trading contacts with Carthage were as far-flung as Italy, Greece, France, Iberia, and West Africa.

Caste system Hierarchical system of organizing people and distributing labor.

Caste War of Yucatan (1847–1901) Conflict between Mayan Indians and the Mexican state over Indian autonomy and legal equality, which resulted in the Mexican takeover of the Yucatan peninsula.

Çatal Hüyük A site in Anatolia discovered in 1958. It was a dense honeycomb of settlements filled with rooms whose walls were covered with paintings of wild bulls, hunters, and pregnant women. Çatal Hüyük symbolizes an early transition into urban dwelling and dates to the eighth millennium BCE.

Cathedra A bishop's seat, or throne, in a church.

Catholicism Religion headed by the pope in Vatican City (Rome); worship is centered in the gospel of Jesus Christ and the sacraments.

Cato the Elder Often seen as emblematic of the transition from a Greek to a Roman world, Cato the Elder wrote a manual for the new economy of slave plantation agriculture, invested in shipping and trading, learned Greek rhetoric, and added the genre of history to Latin literature. He lived from 234 to 149 BCE.

Caudillos South American local military chieftains.

Cave drawings Images on cave walls. The subjects are most often large game, although a few are images of humans. Other elements are impressions made by hands dipped in paint and pressed on a wall or abstract symbols and shapes.

Celali revolts (1595–1610) Peasant and artisan uprisings against the Ottoman state.

Central Powers Defined in World War I as Germany and Austria-Hungary.

Chan Chan Between 850 and 900, the Moche people founded the city of Chan Chan in what is now modern-day Peru, with a core population of 30,000 inhabitants.

Chan Santa Cruz Separate Mayan community formed as part of a crusade for spiritual salvation and the complete cultural separation of the Mayan Indians; means "little holy cross."

Chandra Gupta II In South Asia, this king, who reigned from 320 to 335 CE, shared his name with Chandragupta, the founder of the Mauryan Empire.

Chandravamsha One of two main lineages (the lunar one) of Vedic society, each wth its own creation myth, ancestors, language, and rituals. Each lineage included many clans. *See* Suryavamsha.

Chapatis Flat, unleavened Indian bread.

Chariots Horse-driven carriages brought by the pastoral nomadic warriors from the steppes that became the favored mode of transportation for an urban aristocratic warrior class and for other men of power in agriculture-based societies. Control of chariot forces was the foundation of the new balance of power across Afro-Eurasia during the second millennium BCE.

Charlemagne Emperor of the West and heir to Rome from 764 to 814 CE.

Chartism (1834–1848) Mass democratic movement to pass the Peoples' Charter in Britain, granting male suffrage, secret ballot, equal electoral districts, and annual Parliaments, and absolving the requirement of property ownership for members of the Parliament.

Chattel slavery Form of slavery that sold people as property, the rise of which coincided with the expansion of city-states. Chattel slavery was eschewed by the Spartans, who also rejected the innovation of coin money.

Chavín A people who lived in what is now northern Peru in the period from 1400 to 200 BCE. They were united more by culture and faith than by a unified political system.

Chernobyl (1986) Site in the Soviet Union (in Ukraine) of the meltdown of a nuclear reactor.

Chimu Empire South America's first empire, it developed during the first century of the second millennium in the Moche Valley on the Pacific Ocean.

Chinampas Floating gardens used by Aztecs in the 1300s and 1400s to grow crops.

China's Sorrow Name for the Yellow River, which, when it changed course or flooded, could cause mass death and waves of migration.

Chinoiserie Chinese silks, teas, tableware, jewelry, and paper; popular among Europeans in the seventeenth and eighteenth centuries.

Church of England The established form of Christianity in England dating from the sixteenth century.

City-states Small self-governing polities across the Mediterranean; they integrated an otherwise geographically dispersed region. The Greek city-states produced generations of thinkers and philosophers who influenced Western politics and philosophy.

Civil Rights Act (1964) U.S. legislation that banned segregation in public facilities, outlawed racial discrimination in employment, and marked an important step in correcting legal inequality.

Civil service examination system The world's first written civil service examination system instituted by the Tang. These exams helped to unite the Chinese state by making knowledge of a specific language and Confucian classics the only route to power.

Civil War, American (1861–1865) Conflict between the northern and southern states of America; this struggle led to the abolition of slavery in the United States.

Clandestine presses Small printing operations that published banned texts in the early modern era, especially in Switzerland and the Netherlands.

Clovis people Early humans in America who used basic chipped blades and pointed spears in pursuing prey. They extended the hunting traditions they had learned in Afro-Eurasia, such as establishing campsites and moving with their herds. They were known as "Clovis people" because the arrowhead point that they used was first found by archaeologists at a site near Clovis, New Mexico.

Codex An early form of book, with separate pages bound together; it replaced the scroll as the main medium for written texts. The codex emerged around 300 CE.

Cohong Chinese merchant guild that traded with Europeans under the Qing dynasty.

Coins This form of money replaced goods, which previously had been bartered for services and other products. Originally used mainly to hire mercenary soldiers, coins became the commonplace method of payment linking buyers and producers throughout the Mediterranean.

Cold war (1945–1990) Ideological conflict in which the Soviet Union and Eastern Europe opposed the United States and Western Europe.

Colons French settler population in Algeria.

Colosseum A huge amphitheater completed by Titus and dedicated in 80 CE. Originally begun by Flavian, the structure is named after a colossal statue of Nero that formerly stood beside it.

Communist Manifesto Pamphlet published by Karl Marx and Friedrich Engels in 1848 at a time when political revolutions were sweeping Europe. It called on the workers of all nations to unite in overthrowing capitalism.

Compromise of 1867 Agreement between the Habsburgs and the peoples living in Hungarian parts of the empire that the Habsburg state would be officially known as the Austro-Hungarian empire.

Concession areas Territories, usually ports, where Chinese emperors allowed European merchants to trade and European people to settle.

Confucian ideals By 50 BCE, the Han dynasty had made the Confucian ideals of honoring tradition, emphasizing the responsibility of the emperor, and respect for the lessons of history the official doctrine of the empire.

Confucianism The ethics, beliefs, and practices stipulated by the Chinese philosopher Kong Qiu, or Confucius (551–479 BCE).

Confucius Influential teacher, thinker, and leader in China from 551 to 479 BCE.

Cong tubes A ritual object crafted by the Liangzhu. A cong tube was made of jade and was used in divination practices.

Congo Independent State Large colonial state in Africa created by Leopold II, king of Belgium, during the 1880s, and ruled by him alone. After rumors of mass slaughter and enslavement, the Belgian parliament took the land and formed a Belgian colony.

Congress of Vienna (1814–1815) International conference to reorganize Europe after the downfall of Napoleon. European monarchies agreed to respect each other's borders and to cooperate in guarding against future revolutions and war.

Conquistadors Spanish military leaders who led the conquest of the New World in the sixteenth century.

Constantine Roman emperor who converted to Christianity in 312 CE. In 313, he issued a proclamation that gave Christians new freedoms in the empire. He also founded Constantinople (at first called "New Rome").

Constantinople Capital city, formerly known as Byzantium, which was founded as the New Rome by Constantine the Great.

Constitutional Convention (1787) Meeting to formulate the Constitution of the United States of America.

Contra rebels Opponents of the Sandinistas in Nicaragua; they were armed and financed by the United States and other anti-Communist countries (1980).

Conversos Jewish and Muslim converts to Christianity in the Iberian peninsula and the New World.

Coptic A form of Christianity practiced in Egypt. It was doctrinally different from Christianity elsewhere, and Coptic Christians had their own views of Christology, or the nature of Christ.

Corn Laws Laws that imposed tariffs on grain imported to Great Britain, intended to protect British farming interests. The Corn Laws were abolished in 1846 as part of a British movement in favor of free trade.

Council of Nicaea A church council convened in 325 CE by Constantine and presided over by him as well. At this council, a Christian creed was articulated and made into a formula that expressed the philosophical and technical elements of Christian belief.

Counter-Reformation Movement to counter the spread of the Reformation; initiated by the Catholic Church at the Council of Trent in 1545.

Coup d'état Overthrow of established state by a group of conspirators, usually from the military.

Creed A formal statement of faith or expression of a belief system. A Christian "creed" or "credo" was formulated by the Council of Nicaea in 325 CE.

Creoles Persons of full-blooded European descent who were born in the Americas.

Crimean War (1853–1856) War waged by Russia against Great Britain and France. Spurred by Russia's encroachment on Ottoman territories, the conflict revealed Russia's military weakness when Russian forces fell to British and French troops.

Crossbow Innovative weapon used at the end of the Warring States period that allowed archers to shoot their enemies with accuracy, even from a distance.

Crusades In the late eleventh century, western Europeans launched the wave of attacks called the Crusades. The First Crusade began in 1095, when Pope Urban II appealed to the warrior nobility of France to free Jerusalem from Muslim rule. Four subsequent Crusades were fought over the next two centuries.

Cuban Missile Crisis (1962) Diplomatic standoff between the United States and the Soviet Union that was provoked by the Soviet Union's attempt to base nuclear missiles in Cuba; it brought the world close to a nuclear war.

Cultigen An organism that has diverged from its ancestors through domestication or cultivation.

Cuneiform As people combined rebus symbols with other visual marks that contained meaning, they became able to record and transmit messages over long distances by using abstract symbols or signs to denote concepts; such signs later came to represent syllables, which could be joined into words. By impressing these signs into wet clay with the cut end of a reed, scribes engaged in a form of wedge-shaped writing that we call *cuneiform*.

Cyrus the Great Founder of the Persian Empire, this sixth-century ruler (559–529 BCE), conquered the Medes and unified the Iranian kingdoms.

Daimyo Ruling lords who commanded private armies in pre-Meiji Japan.

Daoism A school of thought contemporary with others at the end of the Warring States period, but with a great emphasis on the Dao, or the natural way of the cosmos. It did not have the same emphasis on ritual as Confucianism.

Dar al-Islam Arabic for "the House of Islam," it describes a sense of common identity.

Darius I After Cyrus's death, Darius I (521–486 BCE) put the emerging unified Persian Empire onto solid footing.

D-Day (June 6, 1944) Day of the Allied invasion of Normandy under General Dwight Eisenhower to liberate western Europe from German occupation.

Dear Boy The nickname of an early human remain discovered in 1931 by a team of archaeologists named the Leakeys. They discovered an almost totally intact skull. Other objects discovered with Dear Boy demonstrated that by the time of Dear Boy, early humans had begun to fashion tools and to use them for butchering animals and also, possibly, for hunting and killing smaller animals.

Decembrists Russian army officers who were influenced by events in revolutionary France and formed secret societies that espoused liberal governance. They were put down by Nicholas I in December 1825.

Declaration of Independence U.S. document stating the theory of government on which America was founded.

Declaration of the Rights of Man and Citizen (1789) French charter of liberties formulated by the National Assembly that marked the end of dynastic and aristocratic rule. The seventeen articles later became the preamble to the new constitution, which the Assembly finished in 1791.

Delhi sultanate The Turkish regime of northern India, which lasted from 1206 to 1526.

Democritus Thinker in ancient Greece who lived from 470 to 360 BCE; he deduced the existence of the atom and postulated that there was such a thing as an indivisible particle.

Demotic writing The second of two basic forms of ancient Egyptian writing. Demotic was a cursive script written with ink on papyrus, on pottery, or on other absorbent objects. It was the most common and practical form of writing in Egypt and was used for administrative record keeping and in private or pseudo-private forms like letters and works of literature. *See also* Hieroglyphs.

Devshirme System of taking non-Muslim children in place of taxes in order to educate them in Ottoman Muslim ways and prepare them for service in the sultan's bureaucracy.

Dhamma A moral code espoused by Aśoka in the Kalinga edict, which was meant to apply to all—Buddhists, Brahmans, and Greeks alike.

Dhimmis Followers of religions, other than Islam, that were permitted by Ottoman law: Armenian Christians, Greek Orthodox Christians, and Jews.

Dhows Ships used by Arab seafarers; the dhow's large sails were rigged to maximize the capture of wind.

Dien Bien Phu (1954) Defining battle in the war between French colonialists and the Viet Minh that secured North Vietnam for Ho Chi Minh and his army and left the south to form its own government to be supported by France and the United States.

Din-I-Ilahi "House of worship" in which the Mughal emperor Akbar engaged in religious debate with Hindu, Muslim, Jain, Parsi, and Christian theologians.

Diogenes A Greek philosopher who lived from 412 to 323 BCE and who espoused a doctrine of self-sufficiency and freedom from social laws and customs. He rejected cultural norms as out of tune with nature and therefore false.

Directory Temporary military committee that took over the affairs of the state of France in 1795 from the radicals and held control until the coup of Napoleon Bonaparte.

Djoser This ancient Egyptian king reigned from 2630 to 2611 BCE. He was the second king of the Third Dynasty and celebrated the Sed festival in his tomb complex at Saqqara.

Dominion in the British Commonwealth Canadian promise to keep up the country's fealty to the British crown, even after its independence in 1867. Later applied to Australia and New Zealand.

Dong Zhongshu Emperor Wu's chief minister, who advocated a more powerful view of Confucius by promoting texts that focused on Confucius as a man who possessed aspects of divinity.

Double-outrigger canoes Vessels used by early Austronesians to cross the Taiwan Straits and colonize islands in the Pacific. These sturdy canoes could cover over 120 miles per day.

Duma The Russian parliament.

Dutch East India Company (1600–1858) British charter company created to outperform Portuguese and Spanish traders in the Far East; in the eighteenth century the company became, in effect, the ruler of a large part of India.

Dutch learning Broad term for European teachings that were strictly regulated by the shoguns inside Japan.

Earth Summit (1992) Meeting in Rio de Janeiro between many of the world's governments in an effort to address international environmental problems.

Eastern Front Battlefront between Berlin and Moscow during World War I and World War II.

Edict of Nantes (1598) Edict issued by Henry IV to end the French Wars of Religion. The edict declared France a Catholic country, but tolerated some Protestant worship.

Eiffel Tower Completed in 1889 for the Paris Exposition, this steel monument was twice the height of any other building at the time.

Eight-legged essay Highly structured essay form with eight parts, required on Chinese civil service examinations.

Egyptian Middle Kingdom Lasting from about 2040 to 1640 BCE, this period of Egyptian history was characterized by a consolidation of power and building activity in Upper Egypt.

Ekklesia A church or an early gathering committed to leaders chosen by God and fellow believers.

Ekpe Powerful slave trade institution that organized the supply and purchase of slaves inland from the Gulf of Guinea in West Africa.

Elamites A people with their capital in the upland valley of modern Fars who became a cohesive polity that incorporated transhumant people of the Zagros Mountains. A group of Elamites who migrated south and west into Mesopotamia helped conquer the Third Dynasty of Ur in 2400 BCE.

Enabling Act (1933) Emergency act passed by the Reichstag (German parliament) that helped transform Hitler from Germany's chancellor, or prime minister, into a dictator following the suspicious burning of the Reichstag building and a suspension of civil liberties.

Encomenderos Commanders of the labor services of the colonized peoples in Spanish America.

Encomiendas Grants from European Spanish governors to control the labor services of colonized people.

Endeavor Ship of Captain James Cook, whose celebrated voyages to the South Pacific in the late eighteenth century supplied Europe with information about the plants, birds, landscapes, and people of this uncharted territory.

Engels, Friedrich (1820–1895) German social and political philosopher who collaborated with Karl Marx on many publications, including *The Communist Manifesto*.

English Navigation Act of 1651 Act stipulating that only English ships could carry goods between the mother country and its colonies.

Enlightenment Intellectual movement in eighteenth-century Europe stressing natural laws and reason as the basis of authority.

Entrepôts Trading stations at the borders between communities, which made change possible among many different partners. Long-distance traders could also replenish their supplies at these stations.

Epicurus A Greek philosopher who espoused emphasis on the self. He lived from 341 to 279 BCE and founded a school in Athens called The Garden. He stressed the importance of sensation, teaching that pleasurable sensations were good and painful sensations bad. Members of his school sought to find peace and relaxation by avoiding unpleasantness or suffering.

Estates-General French quasi-parliamentary body called in 1789 to deal with the financial problems that afflicted France. It had not met since 1614.

Etruscans Until the fourth century BCE, the Etruscan states were dominant on the Italian peninsula. They were part of the foundation of the Roman Empire.

Eurasia The combined area of Europe and Asia.

European Union (EU) International body organized after World War II as an attempt at reconciliation between Germany and the rest of Europe. It initially aimed to forge closer industrial cooperation. Eventually, through various treaties, many European states relinquished some of their sovereignty, and the cooperation became a full-fledged union with a single currency, the euro, and with a somewhat less powerful common European parliament.

Eunuchs Both Abbasid and Tang rulers relied for protection on a cadre of loyal and well-paid men who were surgically castrated as youths and remained in service to the caliph or emperor.

Examination system Examinations that were open to most males and used to recruit officials and bureaucrats in imperial China.

Exclusion Act of 1882 U.S. congressional act prohibiting nearly all immigration from China to the United States; fueled by animosity toward Chinese workers in the American West.

Ezo Present-day Hokkaido, Japan's fourth main island.

Fascists Radical right-wing group of the disaffected that formed around Mussolini in 1919 and a few years later came to power in Rome.

Fatehpur Sikri Mughal emperor Akbar's temporary capital near Agra.

Fatimids The Shiite dynasty that ruled parts of the Islamic Empire beginning in the tenth century CE. They were based in Egypt and founded the city of Cairo.

February Revolution (1917) The first of two uprisings of the Russian Revolution, which led to the end of the Romanov dynasty.

Federal Deposit Insurance Corporation (FDIC) Created in 1933 to guarantee all bank deposits up to $5,000 as part of the New Deal in the United States.

Federal Republic of Germany (1949–1990) Country formed of the areas occupied by the Allies after World War II. Also known as West Germany, this country experienced rapid demilitarization, democratization, and integration into the world economy.

Federal Reserve Act (1913) U.S. legislation that created a series of boards to monitor the supply and demand of the nation's money.

Federalists Supporters of the ratification of the U.S. Constitution, which was written to replace the Articles of Confederation.

Ferangi An Arabic word meaning "Frank" that was used to describe Crusaders.

Fertile Crescent The site of the world's first agricultural revolution, this area is in Southwest Asia, bounded by the Mediterranean Sea in the west and the Zagros Mountains in the east.

Feudalism A system instituted in medieval Europe after the collapse of the Carolingian Empire (814 CE) whereby each peasant was under the authority of a lord.

Fiefdoms Medieval economic and political units.

First World War A total war from August 1914 to November 1918, involving the armies of Britain, France, and Russia (the Allies) against those of Germany, Austria-Hungary, and the Ottoman Empire (the Central Powers). Italy joined the Allies in 1915, and the United States joined them in 1917, helping tip the balance in favor of the Allies, who also drew upon the populations and material of their colonial possessions. Also known as the Great War and World War I.

Five Pillars of Islam The five tenets, or main aspects, of Islamic practice are the testification or bearing witness that there is no God other than God (Allah, in Arabic) and that Muhammad is the messenger of God; praying five times a day; fasting from sunup to sundown every day during Ramadan (a month on the Islamic calendar); giving alms; and making a pilgrimage to Mecca.

Five-Year Plan Soviet effort launched under Stalin in 1928 to replace the market with a state-owned and state-managed economy, to promote rapid economic development over a five-year period of time and thereby "catch and overtake" the leading capitalist countries. The First Five-Year Plan was followed by the Second Five-Year Plan (1933–1937), and so on, until the collapse of the Soviet Union in 1991.

Flagellants European social group that came into existence during the bubonic plague in the fourteenth century; they believed that the plague was the wrath of God.

Floating population Poor migrant workers in China who supplied labor under Emperor Wu.

Fluitschips Dutch shipping vessels that could carry heavy bulky cargo with relatively small crews.

Flying cash Letters of exchange—early predecessors of paper cash instead of coins—first developed by guilds in the northwestern Shanxi. By the thirteenth century, paper money had eclipsed coins.

Fondûqs Complexes in caravan cities that included hostels, storage houses, offices, and temples.

Forbidden City The palace city of the Ming and Qing dynasties.

Force Publique Colonial army used to maintain order in the Belgian Congo; during the early stages of King Leopold's rule, it was responsible for bullying local communities.

Free Officers Movement Secret organization of Egyptian junior military officers who came to power in a coup d'état in 1952, forced King Faruq to abdicate, and consolidated their own control through dissolving the parliament, banning opposing parties, and rewriting the constitution.

Front de Libération Nationale (FLN) Algerian anti-colonial, nationalist party that waged an eight-year war against French troops, beginning in 1854, that forced nearly all of the 1,000,000 colonists to leave.

Fulani Muslim group in West Africa that carried out religious revolts at the end of the eighteenth and the beginning of the nineteenth centuries in an effort to return to the pure Islam of the past.

Fur trade The trading of animal pelts (especially beaver skins) by Indians for European goods in North America.

Gandhi, Mohandhas (1869–1948) Indian leader who led a nonviolent struggle for India's independence from Britain.

Garrisons Military bases inside cities; often used for political purposes, such as protecting rulers and putting down domestic revolts or enforcing colonial rule.

Gauchos Argentine, Brazilian, and Uruguayan cowboys who wanted a decentralized federation, with autonomy for their provinces and respect for their way of life.

Gdansk shipyard Site of mass strikes in Poland that led in 1980 to the formation of the first independent trade union, Solidarity, in the Communist bloc.

Gendered relations A relatively recent development, these imply roles that emerged only with the appearance of modern humans and perhaps Neanderthals. When humans began to think imaginatively and in complex symbolic ways and give voice to their insights, perhaps around 150,000 years ago, gender categories began to crystallize.

Geneva Peace Conference (1954) International conference to restore peace in Korea and Indochina. The chief participants were the United States, the Soviet Union, Great

Britain, France, the People's Republic of China, North Korea, South Korea, Vietnam, the Viet Minh party, Laos, and Cambodia. The conference resulted in the division of North and South Vietnam.

Genoa In 1300 CE, Genoa and Venice were two nodes of commerce linking Europe, Africa, and Asia. Genoese ships linked the Mediterranean to the coast of Flanders through consistent routes along the Atlantic coasts of Spain, Portugal, and France.

German Democratic Republic Nation founded from the Soviet zone of occupation of Germany after World War II; also known as East Germany.

German Social Democratic Party Founded in 1875, it was the most powerful Socialist party in Europe before 1917.

Ghana The most celebrated medieval political kingdom in West Africa.

Ghost Dance American Indian ritual performed in the nineteenth century in the hope of restoring the world to precolonial conditions.

Gilgamesh A heroic narrative written in the Babylonian dialect of Semitic Akkadian. This story and others like it were meant to circulate and unify the kingdom.

Girondins Liberal revolutionary group that supported the creation of a constitutional monarchy during the early stages of the French Revolution.

Gold Coast Name that European mariners and merchants gave to that part of West Africa from which gold was exported. This area was conquered by the British in the nineteenth century and became a British colony; upon independence, it became Ghana.

Goths One of the groups of "barbarian" migrants into Roman territory in the fourth century.

Government schools Schools founded by the Han dynasty to provide an adequate number of officials to fill positions in the administrative bureaucracy. The Imperial University had 30,000 members by the second century BCE.

Gracchus brothers In 133 and 123–21 BCE, two Tribunes, the brothers Tiberius and Gaius Gracchus, attempted to institute land reforms that would guarantee all Rome's poor citizens a basic amount of land that would qualify them for army service. Both men were assassinated.

Grand Canal Created in 486 BCE, this was a thousand-mile-long connector between the Yellow and Yangzi rivers, linking the north and south, respectively.

Grand unity A guiding political idea embraced by Qin rulers and ministers, with an eye toward joining the states of the Central Plain into one empire and centralizing administration.

"Greased cartridge" controversy Controversy spawned by the rumor that cow and pig fat had been used to grease the shotguns of the sepoys in the British army in India. Believing that this was a British attempt to defile their religion and speed their conversion to Christianity, the sepoys mutinied against the British officers.

Great Depression Worldwide depression following the U.S. stock market crash on October 29, 1929.

Great divide The division between economically developed nations and less developed nations.

Great East Asia Co-Prosperity Sphere Term used by the Japanese during the 1930s and 1940s to refer to Hong Kong, Singapore, Malaya, Burma, and other states that they seized during their run for expansion.

Great Flood The Sumerian King List refers to an event known as the Great Flood, one of many traditional Mesopotamian stories that were transmitted orally from one generation to another before being recorded. The Great Flood, a crucial event in Sumerian memory and identity, assigned responsibility for Uruk's demise to the gods.

Great Game Competition over areas such as Turkistan, Persia (present-day Iran), and Afghanistan. The British (in India) and the Russians believed that controlling these areas was crucial to preventing their enemies' expansion.

Great League of Peace and Power Iroquois Indian alliance that united previously warring communities.

Great Leap Forward (1958–1961) Plan devised by Mao Zedong to achieve rapid agricultural and industrial growth in China. The plan failed miserably and more than 20 million people died.

Great Proletarian Cultural Revolution (1966–1976) Mass mobilization of urban Chinese youth inaugurated by Mao Zedong in an attempt to reinvigorate the Chinese revolution and to prevent the development of a bureaucratized Soviet style of communism; with this movement, Mao turned against his longtime associates in the Communist Party.

Great Trek Afrikaner migration to the interiors of Africa after the British abolished slavery in the empire in 1833.

Great War (1914–1918) World War I.

Greenbacks Members of the American political party of the late nineteenth century that worked to advance the interest of farmers by promoting cheap money.

Griots Counselors and other officials to the royal family in African kingships. They were also responsible for the preservation and transmission of oral histories and repositories of knowledge.

Group Areas Act (1950) This act divided South Africa into separate racial and tribal areas and required Africans to live in their own separate communities, including the "homelands."

Guerillas Portuguese and Spanish peasant bands who resisted the revolutionary and expansionist efforts of Napoleon; after the French word *guerre*.

Guest workers Migrants looking for temporary employment abroad.

Gulag Administrative name for the vast system of forced labor camps under the Soviet regime; it originated in a small monastery near the Arctic Circle and spread throughout the Soviet Union and to other Soviet-style socialist countries. Penal labor was required of both ordinary criminals (rapists, murderers, thieves) and those accused of political crimes (counterrevolution, anti-Soviet agitation).

Gulf War (1991) Armed conflict between Iraq and a coalition of thirty-two nations, including the United States, Britain, Egypt, France, and Saudi Arabia. It was started by Iraq's invasion of Kuwait, which it had long claimed, on August 2, 1990.

Gunpowder By 1040, the first gunpowder recipes were being written down. Over the next 200 years, Song entrepreneurs invented several incendiary devices and techniques for controlling explosions.

Gunpowder empires Muslim empires of the Ottomans, Safavids, and the Mughals that used cannonry and gunpowder to advance their military causes.

Guomindang Nationalist party of China, founded just before World War I by Sun Yat-sen and later led by Chiang Kai-shek.

Habsburg Empire Ruling house of Austria, which once ruled both Spain and Central Europe but came to settle in lands along the Danube River; it played a prominent role in European affairs for many centuries. In 1867, the Habsburg Empire was reorganized into the Austro-Hungarian Dual Monarchy, and in 1918 it collapsed.

Hadith Sayings attributed to the Prophet Muhammad and his early converts. Used to guide the behavior of Muslim peoples.

Hagia Sophia An enormous and impressive church sponsored by Justinian and built starting in 532 CE. At the time, it was the largest church in the world.

Hajj The pilgrimage to Mecca; an obligation for Muslims.

Hammurapi and his code Hammurapi, the most famous of the Mesopotamian rulers, reigned from 1792 to 1750 BCE. He sought to create social order by centralizing state authority and creating a new legal code, a grand legal structure that embodied paternal justice. The code was quite stratified, dividing society into three classes: free men, dependent men, and slaves, each with distinct rights and responsibilities.

Han agrarian ideal A guiding principle for the free peasantry that made up the base of Han society, this was a system in which peasants were honored for their labors, while merchants were subjected to a range of controls, including regulations on luxury consumption, and were belittled for not engaging in physical labor.

Han Chinese Inhabitants of China proper who considered others to be outsiders. They felt that they were the only authentic Chinese.

Han Fei A Chinese state minister who lived from 280 to 223 BCE; he was a proponent and follower of Xunzi.

Han military Like its Roman counterpart, the Han military was a ruthless military machine that expanded the empire and created stable conditions that permitted the safe transit of goods by caravans. Emperor Wu heavily influenced the transformation of the military forces and reinstituted a policy that made military service compulsory.

Hangzhou This city and former provincial seaport became the political center of the Chinese people in their ongoing struggles with northern steppe nomads. It was also one of China's gateways to the rest of the world by way of the South China Sea.

Hannibal A great Roman general from Carthage whose campaigns in the third century BCE swept from Spain toward the Italian peninsula. He crossed the Pyrenees and the Alps mountain ranges with war elephants. He was unable, however, to defeat the Romans in 217 BCE.

Harappa One of two cities that, by 2500 BCE, began to take the place of villages throughout the Indus River valley. The other was Mohenjo Daro. Each covered an area of about 250 acres and probably housed 35,000 residents.

Harem Secluded women's quarters in Muslim households.

Harlem Renaissance Cultural movement in the 1920s that was based in Harlem, a part of New York City with a large African-American population. The movement gave voice to black novelists, poets, painters, and musicians, many of whom used their art to protest racism; also referred to as the "New Negro Movement."

Harnesses Tools made from wood, bone, bronze, and iron for steering and controlling chariot horses. Harnesses discovered by archaeologists reveal the evolution of headgear from simple mouth bits to full bridles with headpiece, mouthpiece, and reins.

Hatshepsut Known as Ancient Egypt's most powerful woman ruler, Hatshepsut served as regent for her young son, Thutmosis III, whose reign began in 1479 BCE. She remained co-regent until her death.

Haussmannization The redevelopment and beautification of urban centers; named after the city planner who "modernized" mid-nineteenth-century Paris.

Hegira The "emigration" of Muhammad and his followers out of a hostile Mecca to Yathrib, a city that was later called Medina. The year in which this journey took place, 622 CE, is also year 1 of the Islamic calendar.

Heian period The period from 794 to 1185, during which began the pattern of regents ruling Japan in the name of the sacred emperor.

Hellenism The process by which the individuality of the cultures of the earlier Greek city-states gave way to a uniform culture that stressed the common identity of all who embraced Greek ways. This culture emphasized the common denominators of language, style, and politics to which anyone, anywhere in the Afro-Eurasian world, could have access.

Hieroglyphs One of two basic forms of Egyptian writing that were used in conjunction throughout antiquity. Hieroglyphs are pictorial symbols; the term derives from a Greek word meaning "sacred carving"—they were employed exclusively in temple, royal, and divine contexts. *See also* Demotic writing.

Hijra Tradition of Islam, whereby one withdraws from one's community to create another, more holy, one. The practice is based on the Prophet Muhammad's withdrawal from the city of Mecca to Medina in 622 CE.

Hinayana Buddhism A form of Buddhism that accepted the divinity of Buddha himself but not of demigods, or bodhisattvas.

Hindu revivalism Movement to reconfigure traditional Hinduism to be less diverse and more amenable to producing a narrowed version of Indian tradition.

Hiroshima Japanese port devastated by an atomic bomb on August 6, 1945.

Hittites One of the five great territorial states. The Hittites campaigned throughout Anatolia, then went east to northern Syria, though they eventually faced weaknesses in their own homeland. Their heyday was marked by the reign of the king Supiliulimua (1380 to 1345 BCE), who preserved the Hittites' influence on the balance of power in the region between Mesopotamia and the Nile.

Holy Russia Name applied to Muscovy and then to the Russian empire by Slavic Eastern Orthodox clerics who were appalled by the Muslim conquest in 1453 of Constantinople (the capital of Byzantium and of Eastern Christianity) and who were hopeful that Russia would become the new protector of the faith.

Home charges Fees India was forced to pay to Britain as its colonial master; these fees included interest on railroad loans, salaries to colonial officers, and the maintenance of imperial troops outside India.

Hominids Humanlike beings who walked erect and preceded modern humans.

Homo A word used by scientists to differentiate between pre-human and "true human" species.

Homo caudatus "Tailed man," believed by some European Enlightenment thinkers to be an early species of humankind.

Homo erectus A species that emerged about 1.5 million years ago and had a large brain and walked truly upright. *Homo erectus* means "Standing man."

Homo habilis The scientific term for "Skillful man." Toolmaking ability truly made *Homo habilis* the forerunners, though very distant, of modern humans.

Homo sapiens The first humans; they emerged in a small region of Africa about 200,000 years ago and migrated out of Africa about 100,000 years ago.

Homogeneity Uniformity of the languages, customs, and religion of a particular people or place. It can also be demonstrated by a consistent calendar, set of laws, administrative practices, and rituals.

Horses By the second millennium BCE, full-scale nomadic communities dominated the steppe lands in western Afro-Eurasia. Horse-riding nomads moved their large herds across immense tracts of land within zones defined by rivers, mountains, and other natural geographical features. In the arid zones of central Eurasia, the nomadic economies made horses a crucial component of survival.

Huguenots French Protestants who endured severe persecution in the sixteenth and seventeenth centuries.

Hundred Days' Reform (1898) Abortive modernizing reform program of the Qing government of China.

Hyksos A western Semitic-speaking people whose name means "Rulers of Foreign Lands"; they overthrew the unstable Thirteenth Dynasty in Egypt around 1640 BCE. The Hyksos had mastered the art of horse chariots, and with those chariots and their superior bronze axes and composite bows (made of wood, horn, and sinew), they were able to defeat the pharaoh's foot soldiers.

Ibn Sina Philosopher and physican who lived from 980 to 1037 CE. He was also schooled in the Quran, geometry, literature, and Indian and Euclidian mathematics.

Iliad An epic Greek poem about the Trojan War, composed several centuries after the events it describes. It was based on oral tales passed down for generations.

Il Duce Term designating the fascist Italian leader, Benito Mussolini.

Il-khanate Mongol-founded dynasty in thirteenth-century Persia.

Imam Muslim religious leader and also a politico-religious descendant of Ali; believed by some to have a special relationship with Allah.

Imperium A Latin word used to express Romans' power and command over their subjects. It is the basis of the English words "empire" and "imperialism."

Indian Institutes of Technology (ITT) Originally designed as engineering schools to expand knowledge and to modernize India, ITTs produced a whole generation of pioneering computer engineers, many of whom moved to the United States.

Indian National Congress Formed in 1885, this political party was deeply committed to constitutional methods, industrialization, and cultural nationalism.

Indian National Muslim League Founded in 1906, the league was dedicated to advancing the political interests of Muslims in India.

Indo-Greek The fusion of Indian and Greek culture in the area under the control of the Bactrians, in the northwestern region of India, around 200 BCE.

Indu What we would today call India. Called "Indu" by Xuanzang, a Chinese Buddhist pilgrim who visited the area in the 630s and 640s CE.

Indulgences Church-sponsored fund-raising mechanism that gave certification that one's sins had been forgiven in return for money.

Internal and external alchemy In Daoist ritual, this refers to the use of trance and meditation or chemicals and drugs, respectively, to cause transformations in the self.

Inquisition Tribunal of the Roman Catholic Church that enforced religious orthodoxy during the Protestant Reformation.

International Monetary Fund (IMF) Agency founded in 1944 to help restore financial order in Europe and the rest of the world, to revive international trade, and to support the financial concerns of Third World governments.

Invisible hand As described in Adam Smith's *The Wealth of Nations,* the idea that the operations of a free market produce economic efficiency and economic benefits for all.

Iron A cheap and highly durable metal, harder than tin or copper; iron went into the creation of tools and weapons that were instruments of major change in the first millennium BCE. The advent and use of iron affected warfare and agrarian culture across cultures.

Iron Curtain Term popularized by Winston Churchill after World War II to refer to a rift, or an iron curtain, that divided western Europe, under American influence, from eastern Europe, under the domination of the Soviet Union.

Irrigation Technological advance whereby water delivery systems and water sluices in floodplains or riverine areas were channeled or redirected and used to nourish soil.

Jacobins Radical French political group that came into existence during the French Revolution and executed the French king and sought to remake French culture.

Jacquerie (1358) French peasant revolt in defiance of feudal restrictions.

Jade The most important precious substance in East Asia. Jade was associated with goodness, purity, luck, and virtue, and was carved into such items as ceremonial knives, blade handles, religious objects, and elaborate jewelry.

Jagat Seths Enormous trading and banking empire in eastern India.

Jainism Along with Buddhism, one of the two systems of thought developed in the seventh century BCE that set themselves up against Brahmanism.

Janissaries Corps of infantry soldiers recruited as children from the Christian provinces of the Ottoman Empire and brought up with intense loyalty to the Ottoman state and its sultan. The Ottoman sultan used these forces to clip local autonomy and to serve as his personal bodyguards.

Jati Social groups as defined by Hinduism's caste system.

Jesuit Religious order founded by Ignatius Loyola to counter the inroads of the Protestant Reformation; the Jesuits were active in politics, education, and missionary work.

Jihad Literally, "striving or struggle," this word also connotes military efforts or "striving in the way of God." It also came to mean spiritual struggles against temptation or inner demons, especially in Sufi, or mystical, usage.

Jih-pen Chinese for "Japan."

Jim Crow laws Laws that codified racial segregation and inequality in the southern part of the United States after the Civil War.

Jizya Special tax that non-Muslims were forced to pay to their Islamic rulers in return for which they were given security and property and granted cultural autonomy.

Jong Large ocean-going vessels, built by Southeast Asians, which plied the regional trade routes from the fifteenth century to the early sixteenth century.

Judah The southern kingdom of David, which had been an Assyrian vassal until 612 BCE, when it became a vassal of Assyria's successor, Babylon, against whom the people of Judah rebelled, resulting in the destruction of Jerusalem in the sixth century BCE.

Julius Caesar A formidable Roman general who lived from 100 to 44 BCE. He was also a man of letters, a great orator, and a ruthless military man who boasted that his campaigns had led to the deaths of over a million people.

Junks Trusty seafaring vessels used in the South China Seas after 1000 CE. These helped make shipping by sea less dangerous.

Justinian Roman or Byzantine emperor who ascended to the throne in 527 CE. In addition to his many building projects and military expeditions, he issued a new law code.

Kabuki Theater performance that combined song, dance, and skillful staging to dramatize conflicts between duty and passion in Tokogawa, Japan.

Kamikaze Japanese for "divine winds" or typhoons; such a storm saved Japan from a Mongol attack.

Kanun Highly detailed system of Ottoman administrative law that jurists developed to deal with matters not treated in the religious law of Islam.

Karma Literally "fate" or "action," in Confucian thought; this is a universal principle of cause and effect.

Kassite Nomads who entered Mesopotamia from the eastern Zagros Mountains and the Iranian plateau as early as 2000 BCE. They gradually integrated into Babylonian society by officiating at temples. By 1745 BCE, they had asserted order over the region, and they controlled southern Mesopotamia for the next 350 years, creating one of the territorial states.

Keynesian Revolution Post-Depression economic ideas developed by the British economist John Maynard Keynes, wherein the state took a greater role in managing the economy, stimulating it by increasing the money supply and creating jobs.

KGB Soviet political police and spy agency, formed as the Cheka not long after the Bolshevik coup in October 1917. Grew to more than 750,000 operatives with military rank by the 1980s.

Khanate Major political unit of the vast Mongol empire. There were four Khanates, including the Yuan empire in China, forged by Chinggis Khan's grandson Kubilai.

Kharijites A radical sect from the early days of Islam, the Kharijites seceded from the "party of Ali" (who themselves came to be known as the Shiites) because of disagreements over succession to the role of the caliph. They were known for their strict militant piety.

Khmers In what is modern-day Cambodia, the Khmers created the most powerful empire in Southwest Asia between the tenth and thirteenth centuries.

Khufu This pyramid, among those put up in the Fourth Dynasty in ancient Egypt (2575–2465 BCE), is the largest stone structure in the world. It is in an area called Giza, just outside of modern-day Cairo.

Khusro I Anoshirwan Sasanian emperor who reigned from 530 to 579 CE. He was a model ruler and was seen as the personification of justice.

Kiev After the eleventh century, Kiev became one of the greatest cities of Europe. It was built to be a small-scale Constantinople on the Dnieper.

Kikuyu Kenya's largest ethnic group; organizers of a revolt against the British in the 1950s.

Kingdom of Awadh One of the most prized lands for annexation, the Kingdom of Awadh was the fertile, opulent, and traditional vestige of Mughal rule in India.

Kingdom of Jerusalem What Crusaders set out to liberate when they launched their attack.

Kizilbash Mystical, Turkish-speaking tribesmen who facilitated the Safavid rise to power.

Knossos Area in Crete where, during the second millennium BCE, a primary palace town existed.

Koine Greek A common form of Greek that became the international spoken and written language in the Hellenistic world. This was a simpler everyday form of the Ancient Greek language.

Koprulu reforms Named after two grand viziers who revitalized the Ottoman Empire in the seventeenth century through administrative and budget trimming as well as by rebuilding the military.

Koryo dynasty Leading dynasty of the northern-based Koryo kingdom in Korea. It is from this dynasty that the name "Korea" derives.

Kremlin Once synonymous with the Soviet government, it refers to Moscow's walled city center.

Kshatriyas Originally the warrior caste in Vedic society, they were dominant clan members and a ruling caste who controlled the land.

Ku Klux Klan Racist organization that first emerged in the U.S. South after the Civil War and then gained national strength as a radically traditionalist movement during the 1920s.

Kulaks Originally a pejorative word used to designate better-off peasants, it was used in the late 1920s and early 1930s to refer to any peasant, rich or poor, perceived as an opponent of the Soviet regime. Russian for "fist."

Kumarajiva A renowned Buddhist scholar and missionary who lived from 344 to 413 CE. He was brought to China by Chinese regional forces from Kucha, modern-day Xinjiang.

Kushans A northern nomadic group that migrated into South Asia in 50 CE. They unified the tribes of the region and set up the Kushan dynasty. The Kushans' empire embraced a large and diverse territory and played a critical role in the formation of the Silk Road.

Labour Party Founded in Britain in 1900, this party represented workers and was based on socialist principles.

"Land under the Yoke of Ashur" Lands not in Assyria proper, but under its authority; they had to pay the Assyrian Empire exorbitant amounts of tribute.

Language A system of communication reflecting cognitive abilities. Natural language is generally defined as words arranged in particular sequences to convey meaning and is unique to modern humans.

Language families Related tongues with a common ancestral origin; language families contain languages that diverged from one another but share grammatical features and root vocabularies. More than a hundred language families exist.

Laozi Also known as Master Lao; perhaps a contemporary of Confucius and the person after whom Daoism is named. His thought was elaborated upon by generations of thinkers.

Latifundia Broad estates that produced goods for big urban markets, including wheat, grapes, olives, cattle, and sheep.

Law Book of Manu Part of the handiwork of Brahman priests, this was a representative code of law that incorporated social sanctions and practices.

League of Nations Organization founded after World War I to solve international disputes through arbitration; it was dissolved in 1946 and its assets were transferred to the United Nations.

Legalism Also called Statism, a system of thought about how to live an ordered life. It was developed by Master Xun, or Xunzi (310–237 BCE). It is based on the principle that people, being inherently inclined toward evil, require authoritarian control to regulate their behavior.

Lenin, Nikolai (1870–1924) Leader of the Bolshevik Revolution in Russia and the first leader of the Soviet Union.

Liangzh Spanning centuries from the fourth to the third millennium BCE, the Liangzhu represented the last new Stone Age culture in the Yangzi River delta. The culture, one of the Ten Thousand States, was highly stratified and is known for its jade objects.

Liberalism Political and social theory that advocates representative government, free trade, and freedom of speech and religion.

Linear A and B On the island of Crete and on the mainland areas of Greece, documents of the palace-centered societies were written on clay tablets in two scripts that were linear. These were first discovered on Crete in 1900. Linear A script, apparently written in Minoan, has not yet been deciphered. Linear B was first deciphered in the early 1950s.

"Little Europes" Between 1100 and 1200 CE, these were urban landscapes comprised of castles, churches, and towns in what are today Poland, the Czech Republic, Hungary, and the Baltic States.

Liu Bang Reigned from 206 to 195 BCE; after declaring himself the prince of his home area of Han, in 202 BCE, Liu declared himself the first Han emperor.

Llamas Similar in utility and function to camels in Afro-Eurasia, llamas could carry heavy loads for long distances.

Long March (1934–1935) Trek of over 10,000 kilometers by Mao Zedong and his Communist followers to establish a new base of operations in northwestern China.

Longshan peoples The Longshan peoples lived in small agricultural and riverine villages in East Asia at the end of the third millennium BCE. They set the stage for the Shang in terms of a centralized state, urban life, and a cohesive culture.

Lord Privileged landowner who exercised authority over the people who lived on his land.

Lost generation Refers to the 17 million former members of the Red Guard and other Chinese youth who were denied education from the late 1960s to the mid-1970s as part of the Chinese government's attempt to prevent political disruptions.

Louisiana Purchase (1803) American purchase of French territory from Napoleon, including much of the present-day United States between the Mississippi River and the Rocky Mountains.

Lucy In 1974, an archaeological team working at a site in present-day Hadar, Ethiopia, unearthed a relatively intact skeleton of a young adult female australopithecine in the valley of the Awash River. The researchers nicknamed the skeleton Lucy. She stood just over three feet tall and walked upright at least some of the time. Her skull contained a brain within the ape size range. Also, her jaw and teeth were humanlike. Lucy's skeleton was relatively complete and was the oldest hominid skeleton ever discovered.

Luftwaffe German air force.

Maastricht Treaty (1991) Treaty that formed the European Union, a fully integrated trading and financial bloc with its own bureaucracy and elected representatives.

Ma'at In ancient Egypt, this term referred to stability or order, the achievement of which was the primary task of Egypt's ruling kings, the Pharaos.

Maccabees Leaders of a riot in Jerusalem in 166 BCE; the riot was a response to a Roman edict outlawing the practice of Judaism.

Madrassas Higher schools of Muslim education that taught law, the Quran, religious sciences, and the regular sciences.

Mahayana Buddhism A school of Buddhist theology that believed that the Buddha was a deity, unlike previous groups that had considered him a wise human being.

Mahdi The "chosen one" in Islam whose appearance was supposed to foretell the end of the world and the final day of reckoning for all people.

Maize Grains, the crops that the settled agrarian communities across the Americas cultivated, along with legumes (beans) and tubers (potatoes).

Maji-Maji Revolt (early 1900s) Swahili insurrection against German colonialists; inspired by the belief that those who were anointed with specially blessed water (*maji*) would be immune to bullets. It resulted in 200,000–300,000 African deaths.

Manaus Opera House Opera house built in the interior of Brazil in a lucrative rubber-growing area at the turn of the twentieth century.

Manchukuo Japanese puppet state in Manchuria in the 1930s.

Mandate of heaven Ideology established by Zhou dynasts to communicate the moral transfer of power. Originally a pact between the Zhou people and their supreme god, it evolved in the first century BCE into Chinese political doctrine.

Mande The Mande or Mandinka people lived in the area between the bend in the Senegal River and the bend in the Niger River east to west and from the Senegal River and Bandama River north to south. Their civilization emerged around 1100 CE.

Manifest Destiny Belief that it was God's will for the American people to expand their territory and political processes across the North American continent.

Maroon community Sanctuary for runaway slaves in the Americas.

Marshall Plan Economic aid package given by the United States to Europe after World War II in hopes of a rapid period of reconstruction and economic gain, thereby securing the countries who received the aid from a Communist takeover.

Martyrs People executed by the Roman authorities for persisting in their Christian beliefs and refusing to submit to pagan ritual or belief.

Marx, Karl (1818–1883) German philosopher and economist who created Marxism and believed that a revolution of the working classes would overthrow the capitalist order and create a classless society.

Mastaba This word means "bench" in Arabic; it refers to a huge flat structure identical to earlier royal tombs of ancient Egypt.

Mau-Mau Revolt (1952–1957) Uprising orchestrated by a Kenyan guerilla movement; this conflict forced the British to grant independence to the black majority in Kenya.

Mauryan Empire From 321 to 184 BCE, from the Indus Valley to the northwest areas of south Asia, in a region previously controlled by Persia, the Mauryans extended their dynasty. It was the first large-scale empire in South Asia and was to become the model for future Indian empires.

Mawali Non-Arab "clients" to Arab tribes in the early Islamic Empire. Because tribal patronage was so much a part of the Arabian cultural system, non-Arabs who converted to Islam affiliated themselves with a tribe and became clients of that tribe.

Maxim gun European weaponry that was capable of firing many bullets per second; it was used against Africans in the conquest of the continent.

Mayans The civilization that ruled over large stretches of Mesoamerica; it was composed of a series of kingdoms, each built around ritual centers rather than cities. The Mayans engaged neighboring peoples in warfare and trade and expanded borders through tributary relationships. They were not defined by a great ruler or one capital city, but by their shared religious beliefs.

McCarthyism Campaign by Republican senator Joseph McCarthy in the late 1940s and early 1950s to uncover closet Communists, particularly in the State Department and in Hollywood.

Meat Inspection Act (1906) Provided for government supervision of meat-packing operations; it was part of a broader "Progressive" reform movement dedicated to correcting the negative consequences of urbanization and industrialization in the United States.

Mecca Arabian city in which Muhammad was born. Mecca was a trading center and pilgrimage destination in the pre-Islamic and Islamic period. Exiled in 622 CE because of resistance to his message, Muhammad returned to Mecca in 630 CE and claimed the city for Islam.

Medes Rivals of the Assyrians and the Persians, the Medes inhabited the area from the Zagros Mountains to the modern city of Tehran; known as expert horsemen and archers, they were eventually defeated by the Persians.

Megaliths Literally, "great stone"; the word *megalith* is used when describing structures such as Stonehenge. These massive structures are the result of cooperative planning and work.

Megarons Large buildings found in Troy (level II) that are the predecessors of the classic Greek temple.

Meiji Empire Empire created under the leadership of Mutsuhito, emperor of Japan from 1868 until 1912. During the Meiji period Japan became a world industrial and naval power.

Meiji Restoration The reign of the Meiji emperor, which was characterized by a new nationalist identity, economic advances, and political transformation.

Mencius A disciple of Confucius who lived from 372 to 289 BCE.

Mercantilism Belief that a country's wealth and power were based on a favorable balance of trade (more exports and imports) and the accumulation of precious metals.

Mercosur Free-trade pact between the governments of Argentina, Brazil, Paraguay, and Uruguay.

Meroe Ancient kingdom in what is today Sudan. It flourished for nearly a thousand years, from the fifth century BCE to the fifth century CE.

Mestizos Mixed-blood offspring of Spanish settlers and native Indians.

Métis Mixed-blood offspring of French settlers and native Indians.

Mexican Revolution (1910) Conflict fueled by the unequal distribution of land and by disgruntled workers; it erupted when political elites split over the succession of General Porfirio Díaz after decades of his rule. The fight lasted over ten years and cost one million lives, but resulted in a widespread reform and a new constitution.

Mfecane African political revolts in the first half of the nineteenth century that were caused by the expansionist methods of King Shaka of the Zulu people.

Millets Minority religious communities of the Ottoman Empire.

Minaret Slender tower within a mosque from which Muslims are called to prayer.

Minbar Pulpit inside a mosque from which Muslim religious speakers broadcast their message to the faithful.

Minoans Around 2000 BCE, a large number of independent palace centers began to emerge on Crete, at Knossos, and elsewhere. The people who built these elaborate centers are called the Minoans, after the legendary King Minos, said to have ruled Crete at the time. They sailed throughout the Mediterranean and by 1600 BCE had planted colonies on many Aegean islands, which in turn became trading and mining centers.

Mission civilisatrice Term French colonizers used to refer to France's form of "rationalized" colonial rule, which attempted to bring "civilization" to the "uncivilized."

Mitochondrial DNA A form of DNA found outside the nucleus of cells, where it serves as cells' microscopic power packs. Examining mitochondrial DNA enables researchers to measure the genetic variation among living objects, including human beings.

Moche At the height of the Chimu Empire, the Moche people extended their power over several valleys in what is now modern-day Peru, and their wealth grew as well.

Model T First automobile, manufactured by the Ford Motor Company of Henry Ford, to be priced reasonably enough to be sold to the masses.

Mohism A school of thought in ancient China, named after Mo Di, or Mozi, who lived from 479 to 438 BCE. It emphasized one's obligation to society as a whole, not just to one's immediate family or social circle.

Monasticism A Christian way of life that originated in Egypt and was practiced as early as 300 CE in the Mediterranean. The word itself contains the meaning of a person "living alone" without marriage or family.

Mosque Place of worship for the people of Islam.

"Mound people" A name for the people of Cahokia, since its landscape was dominated by earthen monuments in the shapes of mounds. The mounds were carefully maintained and were the loci from which Cahokians paid respect to spiritual forces.

Mu Chinese ruler (956–918 BCE) who put forth a formal bureaucratic system of governance, appointing officials, supervisors and military captains to whom he was not related. He also instituted a formal legal code.

Muckrakers Journalists who aimed to expose political and commercial corruption in late-nineteenth- and early-twentieth-century America.

Muftis Experts on Muslim religious law.

Muhammad Born in 570 CE in Mecca in Saudi Arabia, Muhammad was the prophet and founder of the Islamic faith. Orphaned when young, Muhammad lived under the protection of his uncle. His career as a prophet began around 610 CE, with his first experience of scriptural revelation.

Muhammad Ali Ruler of Egypt between 1805 and 1848, he initiated a set of modernizing reforms that sought to make Egypt competitive with the great powers.

Mullahs Religious leaders in Iran who in the 1970s led a movement opposing Shah Reza Pahlavi and denounced American materialism and secularism.

Multinational corporations Corporations based in many different countries that have global investment, trading, and distribution goals.

Mutiny of 1857 Indian rebellion against the English East India Company to bring religious purification, an egalitarian society, and local and communal solidarity without the interference of British rule.

Muslim Brotherhood Egyptian organization founded in 1938 by Hassan al-Banna. It attacked liberal democracy as a cover for middle-class, business, and land-owning interests and fought for a return to a purified Islam.

Muslim League National Muslim party of India.

Mussolini, Benito (1883–1945) Italian dictator and founder of the fascist movement in Italy.

Muwahhidin A term meaning "unitarians"; these were followers of the Wahhabi Movement that emerged in the Arabian peninsula in the eighteenth century.

Mycenaeans The mainland competitors of the Minoans; they took over Crete around 1400 BCE. Migrating to Greece from central Europe, they brought their Indo-European language, horse chariots, and metalworking skills, which they used to dominate until 1200 BCE.

Nagasaki Second Japanese city to be hit by an atomic bomb near the end of World War II.

Napoleonic Code Legal code drafted by Napoleon in 1804, it distilled different legal traditions to create one uniform law. The code confirmed the abolition of feudal privileges of all kinds and set the conditions for exercising property rights.

National Assembly of France Governing body of France that succeeded the Estates-General in 1789 during the French Revolution. It was composed of, and defined by, the delegates of the Third Estate.

National Association for the Advancement of Colored People (NAACP) Founded in 1910, this U.S. civil rights organization was dedicated to ending inequality and segregation for black Americans.

National Recovery Administration (NRA) New Deal agency created in 1933 to prepare codes of fair administration and to plan for public works. It was later declared unconstitutional.

National Socialist German Workers Party (Nazi Party) German organization dedicated to winning workers over from socialism to nationalism; the first Nazi Party platform combined nationalism with anticapitalism and anti-Semitism.

Native learning Japanese movement to promote nativist intellectual traditions and the celebration of Japanese texts.

Native paramountcy British form of "rationalized" colonial rule, which attempted to bring "civilization" to the "uncivilized" by proclaiming

that when the interests of European settlers in Africa clashed with those of the African population, the latter should take precedence.

Natural rights Belief that emerged in eighteenth-century western Europe and North America that rights fundamental to human nature were discernible to reason and should be affirmed in human-made law.

Neanderthals Members of an early wave of hominids from Africa who settled in western Afro-Eurasia, in an area reaching from present-day Uzbekistan and Iraq to Spain, approximately 150,000 years ago.

Needle compass A crucial instrument made available to navigators after 1000 CE that helped guide sailors on the high seas. It was a Chinese invention.

Negritos Hunter-gatherer inhabitants of the East Asian coastal islands who migrated there around 28,000 BCE but by 2000 BCE had been replaced by new migrants.

Negritude Statement of the virtues of the black identity and the validation of African culture and the African past, even in a westernizing world. This idea was shaped by African and African-American intellectuals like Senegal's first president, Léopold Sédar Senghor.

Nehemiah A Jewish eunuch of the Persian court who was given permission to rebuild the fortification walls around the city of Jerusalem from 440 to 437 BCE.

Neo-Assyrian empire In around 950 BCE, the Neo-Assyrians came to dominate. They were Afro-Eurasia's empire, extending their control over resources and people beyond their own borders. The empire lasted for three centuries.

Nestorian Christians A denomination of Christians whose beliefs about Christ differed from those of the official Byzantine church. Named after Nestorius, former bishop of Constantinople, they emphasized the human aspects of Jesus.

New Deal President Franklin Delano Roosevelt's package of government reforms that were enacted during the 1930s to provide jobs for the unemployed, social welfare programs for the poor, and security to the financial markets.

New Economic Policy Enacted decrees of the Bolsheviks between 1921 and 1927 that grudgingly sanctioned private trade and private property.

New Negro Movement Cultural movement in the 1920s that gave voice to black novelists, poets, painters, and musicians, many of whom used their art to protest racism; also referred to as the "Harlem Renaissance."

Nirvana Literally, nonexistence; nirvana is the state of complete liberation from the concerns of worldly life, as in Buddhist thought.

Nō drama Masked theater favored by Japanese bureaucrats and regional lords during the Tokogawa period.

Noble Eightfold Path Buddhist concept of a way of life by which people may rid themselves of individual desire to achieve Nirvana. The

path consists of wisdom, ethical behavior, and mental discipline.

Nok culture Spectacular culture that arose in what is today Nigeria, in the sixth century BCE. Iron smelting occurred there around 600 BCE. Thus the Nok people made the transition from stone to iron materials.

Nomads People who move across vast distances without settling permanently in a particular place. Often pastoralists, nomads and transhumant herders introduced new forms of chariot-based warfare that transformed the Afro-Eurasian world.

Nongovernmental organizations (NGOs) Term used to refer to private organizations like the Red Cross that play a large role in international affairs.

North American Free Trade Agreement (NAFTA) Treaty negotiated in the early 1990s to promote free trade between Canada, the United States, and Mexico.

North Atlantic Treaty Organization (NATO) International organization set up in 1949 to provide for the defense of western European countries and the United States from the perceived Soviet threat.

Northwest passage Long-sought marine passageway between the Atlantic and Pacific oceans.

Oceania Collective name for the lands of the Central and Southern Pacific Ocean.

Odyssey Composed in the eighth century BCE, this is the epic tale of the journey of Odysseus, who traveled the Mediterranean back to his home in Ithaca after the siege of Troy.

Oikos The word for "small family unit" in ancient Greece, similar to the *familia* in Rome. Its structure, with men as heads of household over women and children, embodied the fundamental power structure in Greek city-states.

Olmecs Emerging around 1500 BCE, the Olmecs lived in Mesoamerica. The name means those who "lived in the land of the rubber." Olmec society was comprised of decentralized villages. Its members spoke the same language and worshipped the same gods.

Open Door Policy As European imperial powers carved out spheres of trade in late-nineteenth-century China, American leaders worried that the United States would be excluded from trade with China. To prevent this, American Secretary of State John Hay proposed a policy that would give all foreign nations equal access to trade with China.

Opium War (1839–1842) War fought between the British and Qing China over British trade in opium; resulted in the ceding of Hong Kong to the British.

Oracle bones Shang diviners applied intense heat to the shoulder bones of cattle or to turtle shells, which caused them to crack. Diviners would then interpret the cracks as signs from the ancestors regarding royal plans and actions.

Organization of Petroleum Exporting Countries (OPEC) International association established in 1960 to coordinate price and supply policies of oil-producing states.

Orientalists Western scholars who specialized in the study of the East.

Orrorin tugenensis A predecessor to hominids that first appeared 6 million years ago.

Pacific War (1879–1883) War between Chile and the alliance of Bolivia and Peru.

Pagani A pejorative word used by Christians to designate pagans.

Palace The palace, both as an institution and as a set of buildings, appeared around 2500 BCE, about a millennium later than the Mesopotamian temple. The palace quickly joined the temple as a defining landmark of city life. Eventually, it became a source of power rivaling the temple, and palace and temple life often blurred, as did the boundary between the sacred and the secular.

Palmyra A Roman trading depot in modern-day Syria; part of a network of trading cities that connected various regions of Afro-Eurasia.

Pan-Germanism Movement to encourage German-speaking peoples to think of themselves as members of a German race, with their identities fixed by blood and "race" rather than defined by state boundaries.

Pan-Islamism Movement to overcome political and religious differences within the Islamic world, including the divide between Sunni and Shiite Muslims, in order to make a common cause against the West.

Pan-Slavism Movement to unite all Slavs (Czech, Polish, Serbian, and Ukrainian) against their Austrian, German, and Ottoman overlords.

Pansophia Ideal republic of inquisitive Christians united in the search for knowledge of nature as a means of loving God.

Papacy The institution of the pope; the Catholic spiritual leader in Rome.

Papal Of, relating to, or issued by a pope.

Parthians A horse-riding people who pushed southward around the middle of the second century BCE and wiped out the Greek kingdoms in Iran. They then extended their power all the way to the Mediterranean, where they ran up against the Roman Empire in Anatolia and Mesopotamia.

Pastoral nomadic communities Around 3500 BCE, western Afro-Eurasia witnessed the growth and spread of pastoral nomadic communities that herded domesticated animals with demanding grazing requirements.

Pastoralism The herding and breeding of sheep and goats or other animals as a primary means of subsistence.

Paterfamilias The father of the family, which itself was the foundation of the Roman social order.

Patria French, meaning "fatherland."

Patrons In the Roman system of patronage, men and women of wealth and high social status acted as "patrons," protecting dependents or "clients" of a lower class.

Pax Mongolica Term that refers to the political and especially the commercial stability that the vast Mongol Empire provided for the travelers and merchants of Eurasia during the thirteenth and fourteenth centuries.

Pax Romana Latin for "Roman Peace," this term refers to the period between 27 BCE and 180 CE during which conditions in the Roman Empire were settled and peaceful.

Pax Sinica A period of peace (the first century BCE) during which agriculture, commerce, and industry flourished in East Asia under the rule of the Han.

Peace Preservation Act (1925) Act instituted in Japan that specified up to ten years hard labor for any member of an organization advocating a basic change in the political system or the abolition of private property.

Pearl Harbor American naval base in Hawaii on which the Japanese launched a surprise attack on December 7, 1941, bringing the United States into World War II.

Peloponnesian War A war fought between 431 and 404 BCE between two of Greece's most powerful city-states, Athens and Sparta.

Peninsular War (1808–1814) Conflict in which the Portuguese and Spanish populations, supported by the British, resisted the French invasion under Napoleon of the Iberian peninsula.

Peninsulars Spaniards who, although born in Spain, resided in the Spanish colonial territories. They regarded themselves as superior to Spaniards born in the colonies (Creoles).

Peoples' Charter Between 1839 and 1842 over 3 million British signed this document calling for universal suffrage for adult males, the secret ballot, electoral districts, and annual parliamentary elections.

Periplus A book that reflected sailing knowledge; in such books captains would record landing spots and ports. The word *periplus* literally means "sailing around."

Persepolis Darius I's capital city in the highlands of Fars; a ceremonial center and expression of imperial identity as well as an important administrative hub.

Peterloo Massacre (1819) The killing of 11 and wounding of 460 following a peaceful demonstration for political reform by workers in Manchester, England.

Petra City in modern-day Jordan that was the Nabataean capital. It profited greatly by supplying provisions and water to travelers and traders. Many of its houses and shrines were cut into the rocky mountains. Petra means "rock."

Phalanx The military formation used by Philip II of Macedonia, whereby heavily armored infantry were closely arrayed in battle formation.

Philip II of Macedonia The father of Alexander the Great, under the rule of whom Macedonia developed into a large ethnic and territorial state. After unifying Macedonia, Philip went on to conquer neighboring states.

Philosophia Literally "love of wisdom"; this system of thought originally included speculation on the nature of the cosmos, the environment, and human existence. It eventually came to include thought about the nature of humans and life in society.

Phoenicians Known as the Canaanites in the Bible, they were an ethnic group in the Levant under Assyrian rule in the seventh century BCE; they provided ships and sailors for battles in the Mediterranean. The word *Phoenician* refers to the purple dye they manufactured and widely traded, along with other commercial goods and services, throughout the Mediterranean. While part of wider Mesopotamian culture, their major contribution was the alphabet, first introduced in the second millennium BCE, which made far-reaching communication possible.

Phonemes Primary and distinctive sounds that are characteristic of human language.

Plant domestication Plant domestication occurred as far back as 5000 BCE, when plants began to naturally retain their seeds. With the domesticated plant, seeds could be harvested. Most were used for food, but some were saved for planting in subsequent growing cycles, resulting in a steady food supply. This process happened first in the southern Levant and spread from there into the rest of Southwest Asia.

Plato A disciple of the great philosopher Socrates, Plato lived from 427 to 347 BCE; his works are the only record we have of Socrates' teaching. He was also the author of formative philosophical works on ethics and politics.

Plebs In Rome, this term referred to the "common people." Their interests were protected by officials called Tribunes.

Pochteca Archaic term for merchants of the Mexicos.

Polyglot communities Societies composed of diverse linguistic and ethnic groups.

Populists Members of a political movement that supported U.S. farmers in late-nineteenth-century America. The term is often used generically to refer to political groups who appeal to the majority of the population.

Potassium-argon dating A major dating technique based on the changing chemical structure of objects over time, since over time potassium decays into argon. This method makes possible the dating of objects up to a million years old.

Potato famine (1840s) Severe famine in Ireland that led to the rise of radical political movements and the migration of large numbers of Irish to the United States.

Potter's wheel An advance made at the city of Uruk, where potters made significant technical breakthroughs using a fast wheel that enabled them to mass-produce vessels in many different shapes.

Pottery Vessels made of mud and later clay that were used for storing and transporting food. The development of pottery was a major breakthrough.

Prague Spring (1968) Program of liberalization under a new Communist party in Czechoslovakia that strove to create a democratic and pluralist socialism.

Predestinarian Belief of many sixteenth- and seventeenth-century Protestant groups that God had foreordained the lives of individuals, including their bad and good deeds.

Primitivism Western art movement of the late-nineteenth and early-twentieth centuries that drew upon the so-called primitive art forms of Africa, Oceania, and pre-Columbian America.

Progressive movement U.S. reform movement in the early twentieth century that aimed to eliminate political corruption, improve working conditions, and regulate the power of large industrial and financial enterprises.

Prophet's Town Indian village that was burned down by American forces in the early nineteenth century.

Protestantism Division of Christianity that emerged in sixteenth-century western Europe at the time of the Reformation. It focused on individual spiritual needs and rejected the authority of the papacy and the Catholic clergy.

Proto-Indo-European The parent of all the languages in the Indo-European family, which includes, among many others, English, German, Norwegian, Portuguese, French, Russian, Persian, Hindi, and Bengali.

Pullman Strike (1894) American Railway Union strike in response to wage cuts and firings.

Puppet states Governments with little power in the international arena that follow the dictates of their more powerful neighbors or patrons.

Puritans Seventeenth-century reform group of the Church of England; also known as dissenters or nonconformists.

Qadiriyya Sufi order that facilitated the spread of Islam into West Africa.

Qadis Judges in the Ottoman Empire.

Qanats Underground water channels, vital for irrigation, which were used in Persia. Little evaporation occurred when water was being moved through qanats.

Questions of King Milanda (Milindapunha) The name of a second-century BCE text espousing the teachings of Buddhism as set forth by Menander, a Yavana king. It featured a discussion between the king and a sophisticated Buddhist sage named Nagasena.

Quetzalcoatl Ancient deity and legendary ruler of Native American peoples living in Mexico.

Quran The scripture of the Islamic faith. Originally a verbal recitation, the Quran was eventually compiled into a book in the order in which we have it today. According to traditional Islamic interpretation, the Quran was revealed to Muhammad by the angel Gabriel over a period of twenty-three years.

Radicals Widely used term in nineteenth-century Europe that referred to those individuals and political organizations that favored the total reconfiguration of Europe's old state system.

Radiocarbon isotope C^{14} All living things contain the radiocarbon isotope C^{14}, which plants acquire directly from the atmosphere and animals acquire indirectly when they consume plants or other animals. When living things die, the C^{14} isotope they contain begins to decay into a stable nonradioactive element, C^{12}. The rate of decay is regular and measurable, making it possible to ascertain the date of fossils that leave organic remains for ages of up to 40,000 years.

Raj Referred to the British crown's administration of India following the end of the East India Company's rule after the Mutiny of 1857.

Raja "King" in the Kshatriya period in South Asia; could also refer to the head of a family, but indicated the person who had control of land and resources in South Asian city-states.

Rajanya Meaning "group of brilliant ones," a senior clan of a Vedic lineage.

Ramadan Ninth month of the Muslim year, during which all Muslims must fast during daylight hours.

Rape of Nanjing Attack against the Chinese in which the Japanese slaughtered at least 100,000 civilians and raped thousands of women between December 1937 and February 1938.

Rashtriya Swayamsevak Sangh (RSS) (1925) Campaign to organize Hindus as a militant, modern community in India; translated in English as "National Volunteer Organization."

Rebus Probably originating in Uruk, a rebus is a representation that transfers meaning from the name of a thing to the sound of that name. For example, a picture of a bee can represent the sound "b." Such pictures opened the door to writing: a technology of symbols that uses marks to represent specific discrete sounds.

Reconquista The Spanish reconquest of territories lost to the Islamic Empire, beginning with Toledo in 1061.

Red Guards Chinese students who were the shock troopers in the early phases of Mao's Cultural Revolution in 1966–1968.

Red Lanterns Female supporters of the Chinese Boxers who rebelled against foreign intrusions in China at the turn of the twentieth century. Most were teenage girls and unmarried women and dressed in red garments.

Red Turbans Diverse religious movement in China during the fourteenth century that spread the belief that the world was drawing to an end as Mongol rule was collapsing.

Reds The Bolsheviks.

Reformation Religious and political movement in sixteenth-century Europe that led to the breakaway of Protestant groups from the Catholic Church.

Reich German empire composed of Denmark, Austria, and parts of western France.

Reichstag The German parliament.

Reign of Terror Campaign at the height of the French Revolution in the early 1790s that used violence, including systematic execution of opponents of the Revolution, to purge France of its enemies and to extend the Revolution beyond its borders; radicals executed as many as 40,000 persons who were judged enemies of the state.

Renaissance Term meaning "rebirth" that historians use to characterize the expanded cultural production of European nations between 1430 and 1550. Emphasized a break from the church-centered medieval world and a new concept of humankind as the center of the world.

Res publica Literally "public thing"; this referred to the Roman republic, in which policy and rules of behavior were determined by the Senate and by popular assemblies of the citizens.

Restoration period (1815–1848) European movement after the defeat of Napoleon to restore Europe to its pre-French revolutionary status and to quash radical movements.

Rift Valley An area of northeastern Africa where some of the most important early human archaeological discoveries of fossils were found, especially one of an intact skull that is 1.8 million years old.

Riverine Denoting an area whose inhabitants depended on irrigation for their well-being and whose populations are settled near great rivers. Egypt was, in a sense, the most riverine of all these cultures, in that it had no lowland plains as did Mesopotamia and the Indus valley. Away from the banks of the Nile, there is only largely uninhabitable desert.

Roman army The Romans devised a military draft that could draw manpower from a huge population. In their encounter with Hannibal, they lost up to 80,000 men in three separate encounters and still won the war.

Roman law Under the Roman legal system, disputes were brought to the public courts, and decisions were made by judges and sometimes by large juries. Rome's legal system featured written law and institutions for settling legal disputes.

Roving bandits Large bands of dispossessed and marginalized peasants who vented their anger at tax collectors in the waning years of the Ming dynasty.

Royal Road A 1,600-mile road from Sardis in Anatolia to Susa in Iran; used by messengers, traders, the army, and those taking tribute to the king.

Russification Programs to assimilate people of over 146 dialects into the Russian empire.

S.S. (*Schutzstaffel*) Hitler's security police force.

Sack of Constantinople In 1204 Frankish armies went on a rampage and sacked the capital city of Constantinople.

Sacred kingships Institutions that marked the centralized politics of West Africa. The inhabitants of these kingships believed that their kings were descendants of the gods.

Sahel region Area of sub-Saharan Africa with wetter and more temperate locations, especially in the upland massifs and their foothills, villages, and towns.

Saint Patrick A former slave brought to Ireland from Briton who later became a missionary, or the "Apostle of Ireland." He died in 470 CE.

Salt March (1930) A 240-mile trek to the sea in India, led by Mohandas Gandhi, to gather salt for free, thus breaking the British colonial monopoly on salt.

Samurai Japanese warriors who made up the private armies of Japanese daimyos.

Sandinista coalition Left-leaning Nicaraguan coalition of the 1970s and 1980s.

Santería African-based religion, blended with Christian influences, that was first practiced by slaves in Cuba.

Sargon the Great Reigning from 2334 to 2279 BCE, Sargon was the king of Akkad, a city-state near modern Baghdad; he helped bring the competitive era of city-states to an end and sponsored monumental works of architecture, art, and literature.

Sasanians An empire that succeeded the Parthians in the mid 220s CE in Inner Eurasia.

Sati Hindu practice whereby a woman was burned to death on the pyre of her dead husband.

Satrap The governor of a province in the Persian Empire. Each *satrap* was a relative or intimate associate of the king.

Satyagraha Moral and political philosophy of nonviolent resistance developed by Indian National Congress leader Mohandas Gandhi.

Scramble for Africa European rush to colonize parts of Africa at the end of the nineteenth century.

Scythian ethos In part the result of the constant struggle between settlers, hunter-gatherers, and nomads on the northern frontier of Europe, this was a warrior ethos that embodied the extremes of aggressive mounted-horse culture, c. 1000 BCE.

Sea Peoples Migrants from north of the Mediterranean who invaded the cities of Egypt and the Levant in the second millennium BCE. Once settled along the coast of the Levant, they became known as the Philistines and considerably disrupted the settlements of the Canaanites.

SEATO (Southeast Asia Treaty Organization) Military alliance of pro-American, anti-Communist states in Southeast Asia in 1954.

Second World Term invented during the cold war to refer to the Communist countries, as opposed to the West (or First World) and the former colonies (or Third World).

Second World War Worldwide war that began in September 1939 in Europe, and even earlier in Asia, and pitted Britain, the United States, and the Soviet Union (the Allies) against Nazi Germany, Japan, and Italy (the Axis).

Second-generation cultures Societies that expanded old ideas and methods by incorporating new aspects of culture and grafting them onto, or using them in combination with, established norms.

Seleucus Nikator A successor of Alexander the Great who lived from 358 to 281 BCE. He controlled Mesopotamia, Syria, Persia, and parts of the Punjab.

Self-Strengthening Movement Movement in which reformist Chinese bureaucrats attempted to adopt western elements of learning and technological skill in the latter half of the nineteenth century.

Semu This term referred to "outsiders" or non-Chinese people—Mongols, Tanguts, Khitan, Jurchen, Muslims, Tibetans, Persians, Turks, Nestorians, Jews, and Armenians—who became a new ruling elite over a Han majority population in the late thirteenth century.

Sepoys Hindu and Muslim recruits of the East India Company's military force.

Serfs Peasants who farmed the land and paid fees to be protected and governed by lords under a system of rule called feudalism.

Seven Years' War (1756–1763) Worldwide war that ended when Prussia defeated Austria, establishing itself as a European power, and when Britain gained control of India and many of France's colonies through the Treaty of Paris.

Shah Traditional title of Persian rulers.

Shamisen Three-stringed instrument, often played by Japanese geisha.

Shandingdong Man A *Homo sapiens* whose fossil remains and relics can be dated to about 18,000 years ago. His physical characteristics were closer to those of modern humans, and he had a similar brain size.

Shang State Dynasty in northeastern China that ruled from 1600 to 1045 BCE. Though not as well defined by borders as the territorial states in the southwest of Asia, it did have a ruling lineage. Four fundamental elements of the Shang state were a metal industry based on copper, pottery making, standardized architectural forms and walled towns, and divination using animal bones.

Shanghai School Style of painting characterized by an emphasis on spontaneous brushwork, feeling, and the incorporation of western influences into classical Chinese pieces.

Sharecropping A system of farming in which tenant farmers rented land and gave over a share of their crops to the land's owners. Sometimes seen as a cheap way for the state to conduct agricultural affairs, sharecropping often resulted in the impoverishment and marginalization of the underclass.

Sharia Literally, "the way"; now used to indicate the philosophy and rulings of Islamic law.

Sharpeville Massacre (1960) Massacre of sixty-nine black Africans when police fired upon a rally against the recently passed laws requiring non-white South Africans to carry identity papers.

Shawnees Native American tribe that inhabited the Ohio valley during the eighteenth century.

Shays's Rebellion (1786) Uprising of armed farmers when the Massachusetts state government refused to offer them economic relief.

Shiism One of the two main branches of Islam. Shiites recognize Ali, the fourth caliph, and his descendants as rightful rulers of the Islamic world; practiced in the Safavid empire.

Shiites The group of supporters of Ali, Muhammad's cousin and son-in-law, who wanted him to be the first caliph and believed that members of the Prophet's family deserved to rule. Although always a minority sect in the Islamic world, Shiism itself contains several subsects, each of which has slightly different interpretations of theology and politics. The leaders of the Shiite community are known as "Imam," which means "leaders."

Shinto Japan's official religion; it promoted the state and the emperor's divinity; meaning "the way of the gods."

Shoguns From 1192 to 1333, the Kamakura shoguns were generalissimos who served as military "protectors" of the ruler in the city of Heian.

Shotoku Prince in the early Japanese Yamoto state (574–622 BCE) who is credited with having introduced Buddhism to Japan.

Shudras Literally "small ones," these people were workers and slaves from outside the Vedic lineage.

Siddhartha Gautama Another name for the Buddha; the most prominent opponent of the Brahman way of life; he lived from 563 to 483 BCE.

Silicon Valley Valley between the California cities of San Francisco and San Jose, known for its innovative computer and high-technology industries.

Silk A luxury textile that became a vastly popular export from China (via the Silk Road) to the cities of the Roman world.

Silk Road Trade route linking China with Central Asia and the Mediterranean; it extended over 5,000 miles, land and sea included, and was so named because of the quantities of silk that were traded along it. The Silk Road was a major factor in the development of civilizations in China, Egypt, Persia, India, and even Europe.

Silla One of three independent Korean states that may have emerged as early as the third century BCE. These states lasted until 668 CE, when Silla took control over the entire peninsula.

Silver Islands Term used by European merchants in the sixteenth century to refer to Japan, because of its substantial trade in silver with China.

Sino-Japanese War (1894–1895) Conflict over the control of Korea in which China was forced to cede the province of Taiwan to Japan.

Sipahi Urdu for soldier.

Siva The third of three Vedic deities, signifying destruction. *See also* Brahma *and* Vishnu.

Slave plantations A system whereby labor was used for the cultivation of crops wholly for the sake of producing surplus that was then used for profit; slave plantations were a crucial part of the growth of the Mediterranean economy.

Small seal script A unified script that was used to the exclusion of other scripts under the Qin, with the aim of centralizing administration; its use led to a less complicated style of clerical writing than had been in use under the Han.

Social Darwinism Belief that Charles Darwin's theory of evolution was applicable to humans and justified the right of the ruling classes or countries to dominate the weak.

Social Security Act (1935) New Deal act that instituted old-age pensions and insurance for the unemployed.

Socialism Political ideology that calls for a classless society with collective ownership of all property.

Sogdians A people who lived in central Asia's commercial centers and maintained the stability and accessibility of the Silk Road. They were crucial to the interconnectedness of the Afro-Eurasian landmass.

Solidarity The Communist bloc's first independent trade union, it was established in Poland at the Gdansk shipyard.

Song dynasty This dynasty took over the mandate of heaven for three centuries starting in 976 CE. It was an era of many economic and political successes, but they eventually lost northern China to nomadic tribes.

Song porcelain A type of porcelain perfected during the Song period that was light, durable, and quite beautiful.

South African War (1899–1902) Often called the Boer War, this conflict between the British and Dutch colonists of South Africa resulted in bringing two Afrikaner republics under the control of the British.

Soviet bloc International alliance that included the East European countries of the Warsaw Pact as well as the Soviet Union, but also came to include Cuba.

Spanish-American War (1898) War between the United States and Spain in Cuba, Puerto Rico, and the Philippines. It ended with a treaty in which the United States took over the Philippines, Guam, and Puerto Rico; Cuba won partial independence.

Speciation The formation of different species.

Spiritual ferment After 300 CE religion touched more areas of society and culture than before and touched them in different, more demanding ways.

Spring and Autumn period Period between the eighth and fifth centuries BCE, during which China was ruled by the feudal system. Considered an anarchic and turbulent time, there were 148 different tributary states in this period.

St. Bartholomew's Day Massacre Massacre in Paris of French Protestants by Catholics in 1572.

Stalin, Joseph (1879–1953) Leader of the Communist Party and the Soviet Union; sought to create "socialism in one country."

Stoicism A widespread philosophical movement initiated by Zeno (334–262 BCE). Zeno and his followers sought to understand the role of people in relation to the cosmos. For the Stoics, everything was grounded in nature. Being in love with nature and living a good life required being in control of one's passions and thus indifferent to pleasure or pain.

Strait of Malacca The seagoing gateway to Southeast and East Asia.

Strategic Defense Initiative ("Stars Wars") Master plan, championed by U.S. president Ronald Reagan in the 1980s, that envisions the deployment of satellites and space missiles to protect the United States from incoming nuclear bombs.

Suez Canal Built in 1869 across the Isthmus of Suez to connect the Mediterranean Sea with the Red Sea and to lower the costs of international trade.

Sufi brotherhoods Mystics within Islam who were responsible for the expansion of Islam into many regions of the world.

Sufism Emotional and mystical form of Islam that appealed to the common people.

Sultan An Islamic political leader. In the Ottoman Empire, the sultan combined a warrior ethos with an unwavering devotion to Islam.

Sumerian King List The Sumerian King List is among the texts that recount the making of political dynasties and depict great periodic floods. Recorded around 2000 BCE, it organizes the reigns of kings by dynasty, one city at a time.

Sumerian pantheon The Sumerian gods, each of whom had a home in a particular floodplain city. In the Sumerian belief system, both gods and the natural forces they controlled had to be revered.

Sumerian temples Temples were thought of as homes of the gods and symbols of Sumerian imperial identity. They also represented the ability of the gods to hoard wealth at sites where people exchanged goods and services. In addition, temples distinguished the urban from the rural world.

Sun Yat-sen (1866–1925) Chinese revolutionary and founder of the Nationalist Party in China.

Sunni Orthodox Islam, as opposed to the Shiite Islam.

Sunnis The majority sect of Muslims, who originally supported the succession of Abu Bakr over Ali, and supported the rule of consensus rather than family lineage for the succession to the Islamic caliphate.

Superior man In the Confucian view, a person of perfected moral character, fit to be a leader.

Supranational organizations International organizations such as NGOs, the World Bank, and the IMF.

Survival of the fittest Charles Darwin's belief that as animal populations grew and resources became scarce, a struggle for existence arose, the outcome of which was that only the "fittest" survived.

Suryavamsha The second lineage of two (the solar) in Vedic society. *See* Chandravamsha.

Swadeshi Movement Voluntary organizations in India that championed the creation of indigenous manufacturing enterprises and schools of nationalist thought, in order to gain autonomy from Britain.

Syndicalism Organization of workplace associations that included unskilled labor.

Tabula rasa Term used by John Locke to describe the human mind before it begins to acquire ideas from experience; French for "clean slate."

Taiping Heavenly Kingdom (Heavenly Kingdom of Great Peace) Religious sect established by the Chinese prophet Hong Xiuquan in the mid-nineteenth century. The group struggled to "restore" the heavenly kingdom, imagined as a just and egalitarian order.

Taiping Rebellion Chinese rebellion against the Manchu leaders, led by Hong Xiuquan.

Taj Mahal Royal palace of the Mughal empire, built by Shah Jahan in the seventeenth century in homage to his wife.

Tale of Genji Written by Lady Murasaki, a Japanese work that gives vivid accounts of Heian court life; Japan's first novel (early eleventh century).

Talking cures Psychological practice developed by Sigmund Freud whereby the symptoms of neurotic and traumatized patients would decrease after regular periods of thoughtful discussion.

Talmud Huge volumes of oral commentary on Jewish law eventually compiled in two versions, the Palestinian and the Babylonian, in the fifth and sixth centuries BCE.

Talmud of Jerusalem The codified written volumes of the traditions of Judaism; produced by the rabbis of Galilee around 400 CE.

Tanzimat The reorganization period of the Ottoman Empire in the mid-nineteenth century; modernizing reforms affected the military, trade, foreign relations, and civilian life.

Tappers Rubber workers in Brazil, mostly either Indian or mixed-blood people.

Tarascans Mesoamerican society of the 1400s; rivals to and sometimes subjects of the Aztecs.

Tatish Ruler of Chan Santa Cruz during the Mexican Caste War; meaning "father."

Tekkes Schools that taught devotional strategies and the religious knowledge for students to enter Sufi orders and become masters of the brotherhood.

Teotihuacán A city-state in a large, mountainous valley in present-day Mexico; the first major community to emerge after the Olmecs.

Territorial state A political form that emerged in the riverine cities of Mesopotamia, which was overwhelmed by the displacement of nomadic peoples. These states were kingdoms organized around charismatic rulers who headed large households; each had a defined physical border.

Third Estate The French people minus the clergy and the aristocracy; this term was popularized in the late eighteenth century and used to exalt the power of the bourgeoisie during the French Revolution.

Third Reich The German state from 1933 to 1945 under Adolf Hitler.

Third World Nations of the world, mostly in Asia, Latin America, and Africa, that were not highly industrialized like First World nations or tied to the Soviet Bloc (the Second World).

Thirty Years' War (1618–1648) Begun as a conflict between Protestants and Catholics in Germany, it escalated into a general European war fought against the unity and power of the Holy Roman Empire.

Tiananmen Square Largest public square in the world and site of the pro-democracy movement in 1989 that resulted in the killing of as many as a thousand protesters by the Chinese army.

Tiers monde French intellectuals coined this term meaning "Third World" to describe countries seeking a "third way" between Soviet communism and western capitalism.

Tiglath Pileser III Ruling the Assyrians from 745 to 728 BCE, this leader instituted reforms that changed the administrative and social structure of the empire to make it more efficient and also introduced a standing army.

Tiwanaku Another name for Tihuanaco, the first great Andean polity, on the shores of Lake Titicaca.

Tlaxcalans A Mesoamerican society of the 1400s; these people were enemies of the powerful Aztec empire.

Tokugawa Shogunate Founded in 1603, this hereditary military administration ruled Japan while keeping the emperor as a figurehead; it was toppled in 1868 by reformers who felt that Japan should adopt, not reject, Western influences.

Toltecs By 1000, the Toltecs had filled the political vacuum created by the decline of the city of Teotihuacán.

Tomb culture In the middle of the third century CE, a warlike group from northeast Asia arrived by sea and imposed their military and social power on southern Japan. These conquerors are known today as the "Tomb culture" because of their elevated necropolises near present-day Osaka.

Topkapi Palace Political headquarters of the Ottoman Empire, it was located in Istanbul.

Total war All-out war involving civilian populations as well as military forces, often used in reference to World War II.

Transhumant migrants Nomads who entered settled territories in the second millennium BCE and moved their herds seasonally when resources became scarce.

Trans-Siberian Railroad Railroad built over very difficult terrain between 1891 and 1903, and subsequently expanded; it created an overland bridge for troops, peasant settlers, and commodities to move between Europe and the Pacific.

Treaty of Brest-Litovsk (1918) Separate peace between imperial Germany and the new Bolshevik regime in Russia. The treaty acknowledged the German victory on the Eastern Front and withdrew Russia from the war.

Treaty of Nanjing (1842) Treaty between China and Britain following the Opium War; it called for indemnities, the opening of new ports, and the cession of Hong Kong to the British.

Treaty of Tordesillas (1494) Treaty in which the pope decreed that the non-European world would be divided into spheres of trade and missionary responsibility between Spain and Portugal.

Trickle trade Also called "down the line trade," this is a method by which a good is passed from one village to another, as in the case of obsidian among farming villages; the practice began around 7000 BCE.

Tripartite Pact (1940) A pact that stated that Germany, Italy, and Japan would act together in all future military ventures.

Triple Entente Alliance developed before World War I that eventually included Britain, France, and Russia.

Troy Founded around 3000 BCE, Troy was an important third millennium BCE site in Anatolia, to the far west. Troy is legendary as the site of the war that was launched by the Greeks (the Achaeans) and that was recounted by Homer in the *Iliad*.

Truman Doctrine (1947) Declaration promising U.S. economic and military intervention, whenever and wherever needed, for the sake of preventing Communist expansion.

Truth and Reconciliation Commission Quasi-judicial body established after the overthrow of the apartheid system in South Africa and the election of Nelson Mandela as the country's first black president in 1994. The commission was to gather evidence about crimes committed during the apartheid years. Those who showed remorse for their actions could appeal for clemency. The South African leaders believed that an airing of the grievances from this period would promote racial harmony and reconciliation.

Tsar/czar Russian word derived from the Latin "Caesar" to refer to the Russian ruler of Kiev, and eventually to all rulers in Russia.

Tula The Toltec capital city; a commercial hub and political and ceremonial center.

Uitlanders British populations living in Afrikaner republics; they were denied voting rights and subject to other forms of discrimination in the late nineteenth century; meaning "outsiders."

Ulama An Arabic word that means "learned ones" or "scholars"; used for those who devoted themselves to knowledge of Islamic sciences.

Umayyads A family who founded the first dynasty in Islam. They established family rule and dynastic succession to the role of caliph. The first Umayyad caliph established Damascus as his capital and was named Mu'awiya ibn Abi Sufyan.

Umma The Arabic word for "community"; used to refer to the "Islamic politu" or "Islamic community."

Universal Declaration of Human Rights (1948) United Nations declaration that laid out the rights to which all human beings are entitled.

Universitas Beginning at the end of the twelfth century, this term denoted scholars who came together, first in Paris. They formed a *universitas*, a term borrowed from the merchant communities, where it denoted the equivalent of the modern "union."

Untouchables Caste in the Indian system whose jobs, usually in the more unsanitary aspects of urban life, rendered them "ritually and spiritually" impure.

Upanishads Collected in the first half of the first millennium BCE, this Vedic wisdom literature took the form of dialogues between disciples and a sage.

Urban-rural divide One of history's most durable worldwide distinctions, the division between those living in cities and those living in rural areas eventually encompassed the globe. In areas where cities arose, communities adopted lifestyles based on the mass production of goods and on specialized labor. Those living in the countryside remained close to nature, cultivating the land or tending livestock. They diversified their labor and exchanged their grains and animal products for necessities available in urban centers.

Utopian socialism The most visionary of all Restoration-era movements; Utopian socialists, like Charles Fourier, dreamed of transforming states, workplaces, and human relations and proposed plans to do so.

Vaishyas Householders or lesser clan members in Vedic society who worked the land and tended livestock.

Vardhamana Mahavira Advocate of Jainism who lived from 540 to 468 BCE; he emphasized interpretation of the Upanishads to govern and guide daily life.

Varna Caste system established by the Vedas in 600 BCE.

Vedas Rhymes, hymns, and explanatory texts composed by Aryan priests; the Vedas became their most holy scripture and part of their religious rituals. They were initially passed down orally, in Sanskrit. Brahmans, priests of Vedic culture, incorporated the texts into ritual and society. The Vedas are considered the final authority of Hinduism.

Vedic people People who came from the steppes of Inner Asia around 1500 BCE and entered the fertile lowlands of the Indus River basin, gradually moving as far south as the Deccan plateau. They called themselves Aryan, which means "respected ones," and spoke Sanskrit, an Indo-European language.

Veiling Introduced by Assyrian authorities in the thirteenth century BCE, this practice of modest dress was required of respectable women in the empire.

Venus figures Representations of the goddess of fertility drawn on the Chauvet Cave in southeastern France. Discovered in 1994, they are probably about 35,000 years old.

Versailles Conference (1919) Peace conference between the victors of World War I; resulted in the Treaty of Versailles, which forced Germany to pay reparations and to give up its colonies to the victors.

Viet Cong Vietnamese Communist group committed to overthrowing the government of South Vietnam and reunifying North and South Vietnam.

Viet Minh Group founded in 1941 by Ho Chi Minh to oppose the Japanese occupation of Indochina; it later fought the French colonial forces for independence. Also known as the Vietnamese Independent League.

Vikings A people from Scandinavia who were literally "on the warpath." They wanted to replace the Franks as the dominant warrior class in northern Europe and set about doing so in the ninth century.

Vishnu The second of three Vedic deities, signifying existence. *See also* Brahma *and* Siva.

Viziers Bureaucrats of the Ottoman Empire.

Vodun Mixed religion of African and Christian customs practiced by slaves and free blacks in the colony of Saint Domingue.

Voting Rights Act (1965) Law that granted universal suffrage in the United States.

Wafd Nationalist party that came into existence during a rebellion in Egypt in 1919 and held power sporadically after Egypt was granted limited independence from Britain in 1922.

Wahhabi Movement Early-eighteenth-century reform movement organized by Muhammad Ibn abd al-Wahhab, who preached the absolute oneness of Allah and a return to the pure Islam of Muhammad.

Wang Mang Han minister who usurped the throne in 9 CE because he believed that the Han had lost the mandate of heaven. He ruled until 23 CE.

War of 1812 Conflict between Britain and the United States arising from U.S. grievances over oppressive British maritime practices in the Napoleonic Wars.

War on Poverty President Lyndon Johnson's push for an increased range of social programs and increased spending on social security, health, education, and assistance for the disabled.

Warring States period This period extended from the fifth century BCE to 221 BCE, when the regional warring states were unified by the Qin dynasty.

Warsaw Pact (1955–1991) Military alliance between the Soviet Union and other Communist states that was established in response to the creation of the NATO alliance.

Weimar Republic (1919–1933) Constitutional Republic of Germany that was subverted by Hitler soon after he became chancellor.

Western Front Military front that stretched from the English Channel through Belgium and France to the Alps during World War I.

White and Blue Niles Rising out of central Africa and Ethiopia, the two main branches of the Nile are called the *White and Blue Niles.* They come together at the present-day capital city of Sudan, Khartoum.

White Lotus Rebellion Series of uprisings in northern China (1790–1800s) inspired by mystical beliefs in folk Buddhism and, at times, the idea of restoring the Ming dynasty.

White Wolf Popular myth depicted this mysterious militia leader as a Chinese Robin Hood whose mission was to rid the country of the injustices of Yuan Shikai's government in the early years of the Chinese Republic (1910s).

Whites Refers to the "counterrevolutionaries" of the Bolshevik Revolution (1918–1921) who fought the Bolsheviks (the "Reds"); included former supporters of the tsar, Social Democrats, and large independent peasant armies.

Witnessing Dying for one's faith, or becoming a martyr.

Wokou Supposedly Japanese pirates, many of these thieves were actually Chinese subjects of the Ming dynasty.

Works Progress Administration (WPA) New Deal program instituted in 1935 that put nearly 3 million people to work building roads, bridges, airports, and post offices.

World Bank International agency established in 1944 to provide economic assistance to war-torn and poor countries. Its formal title is the International Bank for Reconstruction and Development.

Wu or Wudi Known as the "Martial Emperor" because of his many military campaigns during the Han dynasty. He reigned from 141 to 87 BCE.

Wu Zhao Chinese empress who lived from 626 to 706 CE. She began as a concubine in the court of Li Shimin and became the mother of his son's child. She eventually gained more and more power, equal to that of the emperor, and named herself regent when she finagled a place for one of her own sons after their father's death.

Xiongnu The most powerful and intrusive of the nomadic peoples; originally pastoralists from the eastern part of the Asian steppe in what is modern-day Mongolia. They appeared along the frontier with China in the late Zhou dynasty and by the third century BCE had become the most powerful of all the pastoral communities in that area.

Xunzi A Confucian moralist whose ideas were influential to Qin rulers. He lived from 310 to 237 BCE and believed that rational statecraft was more reliable than fickle human nature and that strict laws and severe punishments could create stability in society.

Yalta Accords Results of the meeting between President Roosevelt, Prime Minister Churchill, and Premier Stalin that occurred in the Crimea in 1945 to plan for the postwar order.

Yavana kings In Sanskrit culture, Greek rulers were known as Yavan kings, a name which derives from the Greek name for the area of western Asia Minor called Ionia, a term that then extended to anyone who spoke Greek or came from the Mediterranean.

Yellow press Newspapers that sought a mass circulation by featuring sensationalist reporting that appealed to the masses.

Yellow Turbans One of several local Chinese religious movements that emerged across the empire, especially under Wang Mang's officials, who considered him a usurper. The Yellow Turbans, so-called because of the yellow scarves they wore around their heads, were Daoist millenarians.

Yin City that became the capital of the Shang in 1350 BCE, ushering in a golden age.

Young Egypt Antiliberal, fascist group that gained a large following in Egypt during the 1930s.

Young Italy Nationalist organization made up of young students and intellectuals, devoted to the unification and renewal of the Italian state.

Yuan dynasty After the defeat of the Song, the Mongols established this dynasty, which was strong from 1280 to 1386 CE; its capital was at Dadu, or modern-day Beijing.

Yuan Mongols Mongol rulers of China who were overthrown by the Ming dynasty in 1368.

Yuezhi A Turkic nomadic people who roamed on pastoral lands to the west of the Xiongnu territory of central Mongolia. They had friendly relationships with the farming societies in China, but the Yuezhi detested the Xiongnu and had frequent armed clashes with them.

Zaibatsu Large-scale, family-owned corporations in Japan consisting of factories, import-export business, and banks that dominated the Japanese economy up until 1945.

Zamindars Archaic tax system of the Mughal empire where decentralized lords collected tribute for the emperor.

Zapatistas Group of indigenous rebels that rose up against the Mexican government in 1994 and drew inspiration from an earlier Mexican rebel, Emiliano Zapata.

Zheng King during the Qin era who defeated what was left of the Warring States between 230 and 221 BCE. He assumed the mandate of heaven from the Zhou and declared himself First August Emperor, to distinguish himself from other kings.

Zhong Shang The administrative central complex of the Shang.

Zhongguo Term originating in the ancient period and subsequently used to emphasize the central cultural and geographical location of China in the world. Meaning "Middle Kingdom."

Ziggurat By the end of the third millennium BCE, the elevated platform base of a Sumerian temple had transformed into a stepped platform called a *ziggurat*.

Zionism Political movement advocating the reestablishment of a Jewish homeland in Palestine.

Zoroaster Sometimes known as Zarathustra, he was thought to have been a teacher around 1000 BCE in eastern Iran and is credited with having solidified the region's religious beliefs into a unified system that moved away from animistic nomadic beliefs. The main source for his teachings is a compilation called the Avesta.

Zulus African tribe that, under Shaka, created a ruthless warrior state in southern Africa in the early 1800s.

Credits

World political map and world satellite map appear in the book courtesy of the National Geographic Society.

PRIMARY SOURCE DOCUMENTS

ROBERTUS AVESBURY: "Flagellants in England" from "The Black Death," *Manchester Medieval Sources*, Rosemary Horrox, trans./ed., pp. 153–54. Reprinted with permission of Manchester University Press.

MARGOT BADRAN AND MIRIAM COOKE, EDS.: "Industrialization and Women's Freedom in Egypt," from *Opening the Gates: An Anthology of Arab Feminist Writing*. Reprinted by permission of Indiana University Press.

SSU-MA CH'IEN: "Sima Qian on the Ruler's Mandate" from *The Grand Scribe's Records*, ed. William H. Nienhauser Jr. Copyright © 2002 by William H. Nienhauser Jr. Reprinted by permission of Indiana University Press.

STEPHANIE DALLEY: "The Epic of Gilgamesh" from *Myths from Mesopotamia: Creation, the Flood, Gilgamesh, and Others*, pp. 100–101, ed. Stephanie Dalley (1989). Reprinted with permission of Oxford University Press.

N. J. DAWOOD: Excerpt from *The Koran*, translated and with an introduction by N. J. Dawood. Copyright © N. J. Dawood, 1956, 1959, 1966, 1968, 1974, 1990, 1993, 1997, 1999, 2003. Reproduced by permission of Penguin Books Ltd.

DE BARY AND BLOOM: "A Qin Legal Document: Memorial on the Burning of the Books" from *Sources of Chinese Tradition*, Volume 1, eds. William Theodore de Bary and Irene Bloom, © 1999 Columbia University Press. Reprinted with the permission of the publisher.

PATRICIA BUCKLEY EBREY: "Proclamations of the HongWu Emperor" and "Qui Jin: An Address to Two Hundred Million Fellow Countrywomen." Reprinted with the permission of The Free Press, a division of Simon & Schuster Adult Publishing Group, from *Chinese Civilization: A Sourcebook*, Second Edition, Revised and Expanded by Patricia Buckley Ebrey. Copyright © 1993 by Patricia Buckley Ebrey. All rights reserved.

ROBERT FAGLES: "The Truce Erupts in War" from *The Iliad* by Homer, translated by Robert Fagles, copyright © 1990 by Robert Fagles. Used by permission of Viking Penguin, a division of Penguin Group (USA), Inc.

BETTY FRIEDAN: "The Problem That Has No Name" from *The Feminine Mystique* by Betty Friedan. Copyright © 1983, 1974, 1973, 1963 by Betty Friedan. Used by permission of W. W. Norton & Company, Inc., and Victor Gollancz, an imprint of The Orion Publishing Group Ltd.

J. GONZALEZ: "The Lex Irnitana: A New Copy of the Flavian Municipal Law," from *Journal of Roman Studies,* Vol. 76 (1986). Reprinted with permission of the Society for the Promotion of Roman Studies.

ROKEYA SAKHAWAT HOSSAIN: "Sultana's Dream" from *Sultana's Dream: A Feminist Utopia and Selections from the Secluded Ones,* edited and translated by Roushan Jahan. Copyright © 1988. Reprinted with the permission of The Feminist Press at the City University of New York, feministpress.org. All rights reserved.

SARAH BLAFFER HRDY: From *Mother Nature* by Sarah Blaffer Hrdy, copyright © 1999 by Sarah Blaffer Hrdy. Published by Chatto & Windus. Used by permission of Pantheon Books, a division of Random House, Inc., and The Random House Group Ltd.

ERNEST R. HUBER: "Führergewalt," from *Nazism 1919–1945: A Documentary Reader; Volume 2: State, Economy, and Society 1933–1939,* pp. 198–99, edited by J. Noakes and G. Pridham, new edition 2000. Copyright © 2000, 1984 University of Exeter Press. Reprinted with the permission of University of Exeter Press.

HUANG LIU-HUNG: "Elimination of Authorized Silversmiths" from *A Complete Book Concerning Happiness and Benevolence,* translated and edited by Djang Chu. Copyright © 1984 the Arizona Board of Regents. Reprinted by permission of the University of Arizona Press.

AHMET KARAMUSTAFA: "Dervish Groups in the Ottoman Empire, 1450–1550" from *God's Unruly Friends: Dervish Groups in the Islamic Later Middle Period,* pp. 6–7. Oneworld Publications, Oxford, 2006. Reprinted with the permission of Oneworld Publications.

JOMO KENYATTA: Excerpt from *Facing Mount Kenya: The Tribal Life of the Gikuyu* by Jomo Kenyatta, published by Vintage Books, a division of Random House, Inc. Used by permission of Alfred A. Knopf, a division of Random House, Inc. Published by William Heinemann Ltd. Reprinted by permission of The Random House Group Ltd.

RICHARD B. LEE AND IRVEN DEVORE: "Problems in the Study of Hunters and Gatherers" from *Man the Hunter*, pp. 3 and 5. Copyright © 1968 Transaction Publishers. Reprinted with permission.

BEVERLY B. MACK AND JEAN BOYD: "Gikku Bello" from *One Woman's Jihad* by Beverly B. Mack and Jean Boyd. Copyright © 2000 by Beverly B. Mack and Jean Boyd. Reprinted by permission of Indiana University Press.

NANAK: "Nanak's Teachings in India" from *Sources of Indian Tradition*, ed. William Theodore de Bary, © 1958 Columbia University Press. Reprinted with the permission of the publisher.

R. C. PADDEN, ED.: "Claudia the Witch," pp. 117–21, from *Tales of Potosí*. Copyright © 1975 by Brown University Press. Reprinted by permission of University Press of New England, Lebanon, NH.

JAMES PRITCHARD: "The Admonitions of Ipuwer" from *Ancient Near Eastern Texts Relating to the Old Testament*, Third Edition with Supplement. Copyright © 1950, 1955, 1969, renewed 1978 by Princeton University Press. Reprinted by permission of Princeton University Press.

SHEREEN RATNAGAR: "The Mystery of Harrapan Writing" from *Understanding Harappan Civilization in the Greater Indus Valley*, 2001, Tulika Publishers.

ADRIAN RECINOS: *Popol Vuh: The Sacred Book of the Ancient Quiché Maya*, trans. Delia Goetz and Sylvanus G. Morley, pp. 165–67. Reprinted with permission of University of Oklahoma Press.

ANN TUSA: "A Fatal Error" from *Media Studies Journal*, Fall 1999, pp. 26–29. Copyright © 1999. Reprinted by permission of *Media Studies Journal*.

FRANZISKA VON REVENTLOW: "Viragines oder Hetaere" in *Autobiographisches, Novellen, Schriften, Selbtzeugnisse*, edited by Else Reventlow, translated by Suzanne Marchand. Reprinted with the permission of Suzanne Marchand.

JIA YI: "Faults of the Qin" from *Sources of Chinese Tradition*, Volume 1, eds. William Theodore de Bary and Irene Bloom, © 1999 Columbia University Press. Reprinted with the permission of the publisher.

DONG ZHONGSHU: "Responsibilities of Han Rulership" from *Sources of Chinese Tradition*, Volume 1, eds. William Theodore de Bary and Irene Bloom, © 1999 Columbia University Press. Reprinted with the permission of the publisher.

ART AND PHOTOS

CHAPTER 1: pp. 2–3: Erich Lessing/Art Resource; p. 5: Granger Collection; p. 7: Robert Preston/Alamy; p. 11: Kenneth Garrett/National Geographic Image Collection; p. 12: (top): Des Bartlett/Photo Researchers; (bottom): John Reader/Photo Researchers; p. 13: Staffan Widstrand/Corbis; p. 14: JTB Photo Communications, Inc./Alamy; p. 15: Pascal Goetgheluck/Photo Researchers; p. 16: Lionel Bret/Photo Researchers; p. 17: John Reader/Photo Researchers; p. 20: Images of Africa Photobank/Alamy; p. 22: Archivo Iconografico, S.A./Corbis; p. 23 (both): French Ministry of Culture and Communication, Regional Direction for Cultural Affairs–Rhône-Alpes Region–Regional Department of Archaeology; p. 24: Archivo Iconografico, S.A./Corbis; p. 25: Ancient Art & Architecture/Danita Delimont; p. 34 (top): Copyright © Christie's Images Ltd. All rights reserved; (bottom): Lowell Georgia/Corbis; p. 36: Image courtesy of Professor Jeremy B. Rutter, Department of Classics, Dartmouth College; p. 37: Bruce Smith, *The Emergence of Agriculture* (New York: Diane Publishing Company, 1998), p. 104; p. 38: Boltin Picture Library/Bridgeman Art Library; p. 40: Interfoto/Pressebildagentur/Alamy; p. 42: Erich Lessing/Art Resource; p. 43: Catalhoyuk Research Project, Institute of Archaeology, University College London.

CHAPTER 2: pp. 50–51: © The Trustees of the British Museum/Bridgeman Art Library; p. 53: *Illustrated London News*; p. 59: Granger Collection; p. 60: Peter Bull Art Studio; p. 61: Dean Conger/Corbis; p. 62: © The Trustees of the British Museum; p. 63 (from left to right): HIP/Art Resource; Granger Collection; University of Pennsylvania Museum of Archaeology and Anthropology, B16693; p. 65: University of Pennsylvania Museum of Archaeology and Anthropology; p. 66: image copyright © The Metropolitan Museum of Art/Art Resource; p. 68: Scala/Art Resource; p. 71: Diego Lezama Orezzoli/Corbis; p. 72 (top): Réunion des Musées Nationaux/Art Resource; (bottom): Borromeo/Art Resource; p. 73: Roger Wood/Corbis; p. 76: Kenneth Garrett/National Geographic Image Collection; p. 77: © The Trustees of the British Museum; p. 78 (clockwise from top left): Gianni Dagli Orti/Corbis; Christine Osborne/Corbis; The Art Archive/Corbis; p. 79 (left): Scala/Art Resource; (right): Sandro Vannini/Corbis; p. 83: Asian Art & Archaeology, Inc./Corbis; p. 85: HIP/Art Resource; p. 86: The Museum of East Asian Art/Heritage Images/The Image Works; p. 89: Werner Foreman/Topham/The Image Works; p. 90: Adam Woolfitt/Corbis; p. 91: Ashmolean Museum, University of Oxford.

CHAPTER 3: pp. 96–97: JTB Photo Communications/Alamy; p. 102: Department of Archaeology and Museums, Karachi. A. H. Dani, "Recent Archaeological Discoveries in Pakistan," The Center for East Asian Cultural Studies. UNESCO Japan: 1988. p. 103 (clockwise from top left): Scala/Art Resource; JTB Photo Communications/Alamy; Art Resource; p. 107: Roger Wood/Corbis; p. 109: Sandro Vannini/Corbis; p. 111: Berlin Museum; p. 114: Erich Lessing/Art Resource; p. 115: Vanni/Art Resource; p. 116: National Museum of India, New Delhi; p. 117: A. H. Dani, "Recent Archaeological Discoveries in Pakistan," The Center for East Asian Cultural Studies. UNESCO Japan: 1988; p. 123 (left): Yale University Art Gallery/Art Resource; (right): HIP/Art Resource; p. 124: Louis Mazzatenta/National Geographic Image Collection; p. 125: Zhenyu Ji Luo, *Yin xu shu qi jing hua*. China: Shangyu Luo shi, Minguo 3: 1914; p. 128 (top): Albrecht G. Schaefer/Corbis; (bottom): Bob Krist/Corbis; p. 130 (clockwise from top left): Institute of Nautical Archaeology, Bodrum, Turkey (2); Gianni Dagli Orti/Corbis; p. 131 (left): Peter Clayton; (right): University of Cincinnati; p. 132: Erich Lessing/Art Resource; p. 133: The Art Archive/National Archaeological Museum, Athens/Dagli Orti.

CHAPTER 4: pp. 140–41: Dagli Orti/Louvre/Bridgeman Art Library; p. 146 (left): © A. Paul Jenkin/Animals Animals; (right): S. Muller/Peter Arnold, Inc.; p. 148: © The Trustees of the British Museum; p. 149 (left): Erich Lessing/Art Resource; (right): HIP/Art Resource; p. 151: British Museum/Bridgeman Art Library; p. 154 (top): SEF/Art Resource; (bottom): Alinari/Art Resource; p. 156 (top): Bibliotheque Nationale, Paris, France, Bridgeman Art Library; (bottom): Dagli Orti/Louvre/Bridgeman Art Library; p. 157 (top): EmmePi Iran/Alamy; (bottom): Lloyd Cluff/Corbis; p. 158: The Art Archive/Dagli Orti; p. 159: Erich Lessing/Art Resource; p. 160: Scala/Art Resource; p. 162: akg-images/Peter Connolly; p. 164: Dagli Orti/Art Archive; p. 165: Art Archive; p. 166: Louvre/Lauros/ Giraudon/Bridgeman Art Library; p. 173: Giraudon/ Art Resource; p. 175 (left): Asia Society, New York: Mr. and Mrs. John D. Rockefeller 3rd Collection 1979, 100a, b. Photograph by Lynton Gardiner; (right): HIP/Art Resource; p. 176: HIP/Art Resource; p. 177: Victoria & Albert Museum, London/Art Resource.

CHAPTER 5: pp. 182–83: (from left to right): National Library of China; Scala/Art Resource; Erich Lessing/Art Resource; p. 191 (top): Asian Art & Archaeology, Inc./Corbis; (bottom): Erich Lessing/Art Resource; p. 192: Smithsonian Freer Gallery of Art and Arthur M. Sackler Gallery; p. 193 (left): British Library; (right): The Art Archive/Private Collection, London; p. 197: Borromeo/Art Resource; p. 198 (top): Paul Almasy/Corbis; (bottom): Corbis; p. 199: courtesy joelcoins.com; p. 201: Erich Lessing/Art Resource; p. 206 (both): Gillett Griffin; p. 208: JTB Photo Communications, Inc./Alamy; pp. 209–10: Princeton University Art Museum; p. 211: The Art Archive/Xalapa Museum, Veracruz, Mexico/Gianni Dagli Orti; p. 212: Maunus; p. 214: Vanni/Art Resource; p. 215 (left): Erich Lessing/Art Resource; (right): Michael Freeman/Corbis; p. 218: Erich Lessing/Art

WORLD · POLITICAL

NATIONAL BOUNDARIES

While man's impact is quite evident, and even striking, on many remotely sensed scenes, sometimes, as in the case with most political boundaries, it is invisible. State, provincial, and national boundaries can follow natural features, such as mountain ridges, rivers, or coastlines. Artificial constructs that possess no physical reality—for example, lines of latitude and longitude—can also determine political borders. The world political map (right) represents man's imaginary lines as they slice and divide Earth.

The National Geographic Society recognizes 192 independent states in the world as represented here. Of those nations, 185 are members of the United Nations.

Winkel Tripel Projection